Videogame Law

Videogame Law

Cases, Statutes, Forms, Problems & Materials

SECOND EDITION

Ashley Saunders Lipson
UNIVERSITY OF LA VERNE COLLEGE OF LAW

Robert D. Brain
LOYOLA LAW SCHOOL, LOS ANGELES

CAROLINA ACADEMIC PRESS
Durham, North Carolina

Print ISBN: 978-1-61163-645-1
eBook ISBN: 978-1-5310-0138-4
LCCN: 2015939947

Carolina Academic Press, LLC
700 Kent Street
Durham, North Carolina 27701
Telephone (919) 489-7486
Fax (919) 493-5668
www.cap-press.com

Printed in the United States of America

I dedicate this Second Edition to the Gamers who make this book possible.

RDB

To indispensable Anna.

ASL

Summary of Contents

Contents

Table of Cases

Table of Authorities

Books

Douglas G. Baird, *The Story of INS v. AP: Property, Natural Monopoly, and the Uneasy Legacy of a Concocted Controversy*, in Intellectual Property Stories (Jane C. Ginsburg & Rochelle Cooper Dreyfuss, eds., 2006) § 9.10

Roger D. Blair & Thomas F. Cotter, Intellectual Property (2005) § 9

Neil Boorstyn, Copyright Laws (1981) § 5.31

Van Burnham, Supercade: A Visual History of the Video game Age, 1971–1984 (2001) §§ 1.10, 6.20, 8.30

Thomas M. Cooley, A Treatise on the Law of Torts or Wrongs which Arise Independently of Contract 193 (1878) § 14.10

Magy Seif El-Nasr et. al, Game Analytics: Maximizing the Value of Player Data (2013). § 14.10

Jerome Gilson, 1-2A Gilson on Trademarks § 2A.04 (2007) § 8.50

Paul Goldstein, Copyright's Highway 224 (Hill & Wang 1994) § 6.74

James Love Hopkins, Hopkins on Trademarks (2d ed. 1905) § 8.30

W. Page Keeton, Dan B. Dobbs, Robert E. Keeton & David G. Owen, Prosser and Keeton on Law of Torts (5th ed. 1984) § 6.40

Steven L. Kent, The Ultimate History of Video Games (2001) §§ 1.10, 3.22

Chris Koehler, Power Up: How Japanese Video Games Gave the World an Extra Life (2004) § 8.60

Al Kohn and Bob Kohn, Kohn on Music Licensing (2002)

David Kushner, Masters of Doom (2003) § 1.10

William M. & Richard A. Posner, The Economic Structure of Intellectual Property Law (2003) § 8.30

F. Gregory Lastowka and Dan Hunter, *Virtual Crimes*, in The State of Play: Law, Games, and Virtual Worlds (Jack M. Balkin & Beth Simone Noveck eds., 2006) § 10.30

Mark A. Lemley, Peter S. Menell, Robert P. Merges, & Pamela Samuelson, Software and Internet Law (2003) § 1.10

J. Thomas McCarthy, McCarthy on Trademarks and Unfair Competition (4th ed. 2007) §§ 8.30, 8.50, 16.30

Melville B. Nimmer & David Nimmer, Nimmer on Copyright (2007) §§ 5.30, 5.32, 6.40, 6.74, 6.75

John E. Nowak and Ronald D. Rotunda, Constitutional Law (4th Ed. 1991) § 12.10

The New IEEE Standard Dictionary of Electrical and Electronics Terms 964 (5th ed. 1993). § 7.60

James J. White & Robert S. Summers, Uniform Commercial Code, §1.1 (3d ed. 1988) §10.10

Mark P. Wolf, The Video Game Explosion (2008) §1.10

Journal Articles

Emily Adelman, *Trademark Parodies: When is it OK to Laugh?*, 6 J. Marshall Rev. Intell. Prop. L. 72 (2006) §8.50

Craig A. Anderson & Karen E. Dill, *Personality Processes and Individual Differences—Video Games and Aggressive Thoughts, Feelings, and Behavior in the Laboratory and in Life*, 78 J. Personality & Soc. Psych. 772 (2000) §12.22

Jack M. Balkin, *Law and Liberty in Virtual Worlds*, 49 N.Y. L. Sch. L. Rev. 19 (2004–2005) §10.30

Mark Bartholomew & John Tehranian, *The Secret Life of Legal Doctrine: The Divergent Evolution of Secondary Liability in Trademark and Copyright Law*, 21 Berkeley Tech. L.J. 1363 (2006) §6.40

Charles Biederman & Danny Andrews, *Applying Copyright Law to User-Generated Content*, L.A. Law. 12, 15–17 (May 2008) §10.30

Edward G. Black & Michael H. Page, *Add-On Infringements: When Computer Add-Ons and Peripherals Should (and Should Not) Be Considered Infringing Derivative Works Under* Lewis Galoob Toys, Inc. v. Nintendo of America, Inc., *and Other Recent Decisions*, 15 Hastings Comm. & Ent. L. J. 615 (1993) §6.30

Jerald J. Block, M.D., Issue for DSM-V: Internet Addiction, 165 Am. J. Psychiatry 306, 307 (2008) §13.30

Lorin Brennan, Why Article 2 Cannot Apply to Software Transactions, 38 Duq. L. Rev. 459 (2000) §10.10

Kristin Bryant, *Not Child's Play: Compliance with the Children's Online Privacy Protection Rule*, 1 Shidler J.L. Com. & Tech. 4 (2004) §14.30

Brian Camp, *The Play's the Thing: A Theory of Taxing Virtual Worlds*, 59 Hastings L.J. 1 (2007) §10.30

Michael Cerrati, *Video Game Music: Where it Came From, How it is Being Used Today, and Where it is Heading Tomorrow*, 8 Vand. J. Ent. & Tech. L. 293 (2006) §2.32

Chafee, *Reflections on the Law of Copyright*, 45 Colum. L. Rev. 503 (1945) §6.20

David Chim, *Gambling Addiction in Asia: Need for a Medical Perspective*, 2 Asian J. Gambling Issues and Public Health 68 (Oct. 2011) §15.40

Bettina M. Chin, Comment, *Regulating your Second Life: Defamation in Virtual Worlds*, 72 Brook. L. Rev. 1303 (2007) §10.30

Amy B. Cohen, *"Arising Under" Jurisdiction and the Copyright Laws*, 44 Hastings L.J. 337 (1993) §8.10

Krista Correa, *All Your Face Belong to Us: Prohibiting Celebrity Images in Hyper-Realistic Video Games*, 34 Hastings. Comm. & Ent. L.J. 93, 101 (2011) §4.10

Peter Dang, *Criminal Defenses To Anti-Circumvention Charges For Modifying Video Game Consoles*, 9 Wash. J. L. Tech. & Arts 105 (2013) §6.60

Graeme B. Dinwoodie & Mark D. Janis, *Confusion Over Use: Contextualism in Trademark Law*, 92 Iowa L. Rev. 1597 (2007) §8.50

Stacey L. Dogan & Mark A. Lemley, *Grounding Trademark Law Through Trademark Use*, 92 Iowa L. Rev. 1669 (2007) §8.50

George Dwight II, *Monopoly, Anti-Monopoly: The Loss of Trademark Monopolies*, 8 Colum.–VLA Art & the L. 95 (1983) §8.20

Periodical Articles

Internet Resources & Articles

Miscellaneous

Table of Statutes and Constitutional Provisions

California Business and Professions Code Sections
14210 § 6.20
14401 § 6.20
17200 § 6.20
17201 § 6.20
17202 § 6.20
17203 § 6.20
22757 — 22579 § 14.30

California Civil Code Sections
1750, et seq. (California Consumer Legal Remedies Act "CLRA") § 3.10
3344 § 8.12

Code of Federal Regulations
Children's Online Privacy Protection Act "COPPA"
16 CFR § 312.1 § 14.20
19 C.F.R. § 133.44(a) § 2.42
45 C.F.R. § 160.102 § 14.30
29 CFR § 541.400 et seq. §§ 2.43, 2.44

California Penal Code Sections
258 § 4.10

Federal Rules of Civil Procedure
Rule 26 § 16.30
Rule 65(c) § 6.30

General Statutes of North Carolina
N.C. Gen. Stat. § 66-154(a) § 9.10

Illinois Trade Secrets Act
765 ILCS 1065/2(d) § 9.20
765 ILCS 1065/8(a) § 9.20

Restatement Provisions
Restatement (First) of Property
512 § 11.20
Restatement (Second) of Torts
281 § 13.10
302B § 13.20
402A § 13.20
652A § 4.10
652C § 4.10
Restatement (Third) of Torts
1 § 13.10
2 § 13.10
19 § 13.20
Restatement (Third) of Unfair Competition
2 § 13.20
39 cmt. a § 9
46 § 4.10
47 cmt. c § 4.20

Uniform Commercial Code
UCC § 2-102 § 10.10
UCC § 2-105 § 10.10
UCC § 2-207 § 10.10

Uniform Trade Secrets Act
UTSA § 1 § 9.20

Table of Videogames and Consoles Cited

Preface

The goal of this second edition, much like the first, is to provide professors and students with a comprehensive view of the cases, statutes and transactional documents that pertain to the construction, protection, marketing and regulation of videogames and consoles. As the first casebook devoted to the subject of videogame law, the first edition of this book was among the initial sources to recognize that the videogame industry had grown large enough, and had reached a sufficient level of complexity, so as to warrant its own, specialized treatment. There is no doubt that the subject has clearly outgrown its initial status as a mere subset of intellectual property and cyberspace law. Indeed, even with the prior global recession, annual videogame and console sales are rapidly approaching $100 *billion*, far overshadowing worldwide movie, recording, publishing, and sports revenue.

The first edition is only a few years old, but in the videogame world, each calendar year since the first edition was published has seemed like a dog year (about seven years' worth of materials generated). As such, a new edition was sorely needed. This second edition keeps the same general structure of the first: starting with an overview and then following the basic process a developer would use in bringing forth a game, beginning with acquisition of rights, dealing with intellectual property issues and finally, once the game is ready to launch, wrestling with various regulatory and marketing issues.

However, there have been a number of changes in this edition as well. Many of the "early industry" disputes that we could only introduce in the first edition have now been resolved, either through case law, statutes or regulation; those matters are now covered in detail. Also, we have extensively reorganized chapters dealing with gambling, addiction, and antitrust issues, and have introduced new chapters dealing with rights of publicity and rights of privacy in videogames. Because copyright issues continue to grow, we have separated our treatment of that topic into two chapters. We were introduced to many of these new issues, cases, and organizational ideas upon our collaboration with Roxanne Christ, Esq. who practices videogame law as a Partner in the law firm Latham & Watkins, and we want to thank and acknowledge Roxanne for all her help.

We likewise want to highlight two attributes that continue in the second edition that we think make our casebook unique. First, transactional forms are included within chapters. Most law-related books tend to draw a sharp line between casebooks, which are essentially for law students and focus on appellate decisions, and form books which are used primarily by practitioners who need to churn out agreements for their clients. We believe that this traditional gulf between academic theory and practical information is less warranted for videogame law. On the one hand, students want to know the general content and structure of videogame agreements, and to be able to see how many litigation disputes originate from sloppy or ambiguous drafting of those agreements; and on the other hand, practitioners remain interested in the foundational cases giving rise to the body of videogame law.

Next, our cases tend to be longer than most casebooks. But that's because we believe the facts that give rise to the cases are very important. Indeed, in many of those cases, the facts trace the history of the videogame industry, and that history is noteworthy in explaining the cases. Besides, we get a kick out of sharing the industry's history with our readers. But more significantly, we think there is a general underappreciation in the academy of the manner in which factual details ultimately determine liability. As such, we have only lightly edited the factual portions of many cases.

We were fortunate in having some superb help in revising and assembling this edition. As such, we want to express our sincere and profound gratitude to David Michie, La Verne College of the Law, Class of 2015; Hannah Dunn, Britta Norwick, and Selina Swatek, all Loyola Law School, Los Angeles, Class of 2016; and Matthew Dobil, Jasmyn Troncoso, and Andrew Wyah, Loyola Law School Class of 2017, for their help.

Finally we are very interested in hearing from you—whether you are a student, professor, or practitioner who has stumbled across our book, and whether your comments are critical, complimentary, or capable of any other characterization. The easiest way to get us is by email: you can get Ashley at ashley@objection.com; and Bob at bob.brain@lls.edu.

ASL
RDB
Los Angeles, CA
March 2016

Part I

Product Development

Chapter One

Product Development

Fun and games are now serious business as evidenced by the exponential growth of the multi-billion dollar, global videogame industry. This expansion, which has been continuing from year to year without much deceleration,[1] is not merely vertical. Videogames are no longer limited to male audiences[2] or any single demographic. The games' multivariate nature has caused them to become entangled with other traditional entertainment and educational media. The legal issues have also continued to expand and intertwine themselves with this relatively recent phenomenon. For many, this was expected as the industry's developers changed almost overnight from teenagers on low or no budgets using inexpensive home computers[3] to publicly traded corporations willing to spend millions to develop a single title.

§ 1.10 Pre-Game

The terminology that we use to describe electronic games seems to reflect our respective ages and generations. Those of us born in the 1960s and earlier might first recall the ubiquitous "pinball" machine, once a common fixture in bowling alleys and bars. Arcade games arrived in the 1970s followed by "videogames," whose consoles invaded our living rooms. In the latter part of the 1980s the variations were scooped up and delivered to our personal computers ("computer games") and eventually to our watches, cell phones and virtually every other portable device with a screen. Since then, we often use the terms "computer games" and "videogames" interchangeably despite some material differences. Consistent with the developing case law, the term "videogames" will be used to cover a wide variety of industry products.

As might be expected for any newly-conceived business, many of the initial rules governing videogames were borrowed from older industries. Until recently, the laws that generically governed software and cyberspace adequately dealt with disputes involving

---

1. STATISTA, http://www.statista.com/statistics/268954/revenues-of-global-video-games-industry (last visited Jan. 18, 2015).

2. NY TIMES, http://www.nytimes.com/2014/09/11/arts/international/women-get-in-on-the-action-in-video-games.html (last visited Jan. 18, 2015).

3. *See* DAVID KUSHNER, MASTERS OF DOOM (2003).

videogames.[4] Currently, however, the nature of the disputes, like the industry, has grown dramatically to the point where there is no area of the law untouched by contemporary statutes, regulation and case law. In addition to matters involving property rights, contracts, trademarks, copyrights and trade secrets, videogames are also impacting the laws of censorship and products liability.

Today, as the cases and commentaries in this casebook will later demonstrate, videogames have developed to the point where they require their own separate academic treatment.

Products

To avoid confusion and better define the subject matter of this text, lines of distinction should be drawn among the following listed products, all of which are often indistinguishably referred to as *videogames*:

[a] **Arcade Videogames** — These dresser-sized coin operated machines are still available as novelties and in an ever-dwindling number of public arcades; they were most prevalent in the 1970s and 1980s. The arcades and establishments that house the games are public businesses and are therefore subject to state and municipal regulation. Their numbers, however, have decreased dramatically in recent years.

[b] **Console Games** — Sometimes referred to as "Home Games," the Sony PlayStation, Nintendo Wii, and Microsoft Xbox are all present manifestations of the videogame's journey from the public arcade to the private living room. These consoles, which utilize television sets for display purposes, accept software in the form of game cartridges and, more recently, digital streaming.

[c] **Computer Games** — The substitution of the computer screen for the television provides the key feature distinguishing computer games and console games. The increasing power, speed, and resolution of the two media are rapidly erasing the differences. The significant remaining distinction involves the manner in which each manufacturer's console limits the particular brand of games that can be used.

[d] **Dedicated Hand-Held Videogames** — The Nintendo Gameboy DS and Sony PSP are common examples of portable games. Not to be confused with games that are downloaded to our cell phones, smart phones, and watches, these devices are dedicated solely to game play.

[e] **Mobile Device Games and Apps** — These terms provide a catch-all for the many new gadgets such as smart phones, tablets, "wearables," and electronic organizers that are capable of downloading, storing and playing games.

[f] **Internet Games** — "Social Media Game" is the term that often labels multi-player games that capitalize on Internet interactivity. Often, for monthly fees, a website links players around the world to one another and sometimes to virtual worlds with digital businesses, real estate, and people (referred to as "avatars"). Some online companies, such as Blizzard (producer of *World of Warcraft*) and Linden Labs (creator of *Second Life*), continuously host virtual worlds known as

---

4. *See, e.g.,* Mark A. Lemley, Peter S. Menell, Robert P. Merges, and Pamela Samuelson, Software and Internet Law (2003).

MMORPG's (Massive Multi-Player Online Role Playing Games) wherein millions of players can direct their avatars to interact with other players simultaneously.

[g] **Immersion Games**—Not as popular as everyone initially predicted, these games initially required players to wear bulky helmets or sit in claustrophobic containers designed to physically place them in a virtual world. *Battle Tech*, for example, required players to sit in small, enclosed pods (that appeared on a screen as tanks) designed to blow up other players. Unfortunately, for those wishing to breathe freely and enjoy a comfortable experience, the bulk of products proved to be somewhat intolerable. Despite their disfavor with the public in general, however, military and other training organizations still find the games helpful.

[h] **Gambling Devices**—The segregation of gambling devices from simple videogames has become an important pastime for regulators. The difference between *videogaming* and *gaming* is not always clear.

The videogame is truly a most sophisticated art form capable of assimilating photographs, paintings, animations, film, musical compositions, sound recordings, and sound effects. But in addition, there is the added dimension of interactivity combined with elements of instantly measurable challenges.

There may be differences of opinion as to what constitutes a "good" videogame. The convictions of parents and educators would, for example, differ sharply from those of many developers. But if the traditional game players themselves have anything to say about the subject, the following list of elements would likely emerge:

[1] **Variety:** Not only should there be multiple paths and solutions, but the internal structure of the game should vary continuously to prevent boredom.

[2] **Randomness:** Skill is important, but unpredictability keeps the games interesting. A good mix makes a good game.

[3] **Levels:** Measurable levels of progress are important. No self-respecting arcade game or home videogame would ever neglect this element, although many virtual worlds consciously avoid levelling.

[4] **Measured Difficulty:** The perfect balance between *frustration* and *success* is the goal of every designer. If a game is too simple, the player will complete it too quickly; thereafter, the incentive to repeat the conquest would be minimal. On the other hand, if the game is too difficult, the player may not attempt to advance, and again the game's purpose would be frustrated. The designer's goal, therefore, is to provide just enough frustration to provoke some adrenaline, repetitive play and *addiction*. Most contemporary games continually monitor game play and adjust the software to make the difficulty level just right.

[5] **Balanced Scoring:** Scores are important; they lead to advanced levels, satisfaction, publishable records, and competition in general. Sub-goals and sub-scores provide additional and continuous incentives.

[6] **Recognition:** Scores and levels provide measures for success. Somewhere on the video screen the top scores should be posted for the world to see.

[7] **Surprises:** Early videogames were quite repetitive. But even they had their surprises and unexpected rewards, sometimes referred to as "Easter Eggs." Unanticipated messages or images would appear for no apparent reason or due to the successful attainment of some interim goal. These surprises are to be distinguished from

other congratulatory messages because they are purely random and most often unexpected.

[8] **New Experiences:** Classic pigeonholes no longer govern the landscape. Creative developers are constantly designing new uses, purposes and goals. *SimCity* and *Second Life*, for example, have departed from the traditional notion of the individual gamer as one constantly playing *against* another person or entity and instead provide concerts, political debates, book clubs, or other experiences to keep their "residents" returning.

[9] **Edutainment:** Buzzers and whistles have their proper places in all games. The best games, however, will manage to teach or train the player with respect to some skill. At the very least, a good game should accentuate a player's hand-eye coordination. But those that are particularly effective training devices are sometimes referred to as "serious games." And the Nintendo Wii has taken physical education to a new level.

The preceding list is by no means exhaustive. The videogame industry was built upon innovation and unpredictability. Based on the new products that continue to be announced and developed, there is little indication that this will change anytime soon.

§ 1.20 Industry History

The history of the videogame industry is no less colorful than the sprites that dash across the screens of videogame arcades and television sets throughout the world.[5] It is a young industry to be sure, taking less than half a century to grow from a tiny little "pong" blip on a cathode ray tube to a multi-billion dollar global business. Its exponential growth along with its invasion of other more established media, suggest that the videogame industry is here to stay.

Reading through the history that follows, you will encounter the names of those games, individuals, and companies who set the milestones for the industry. Expect to see their names and find out more about their exploits throughout the remainder of this book. As might be expected for any explosive enterprise, litigation has also played a significant role in shaping the history that follows.

Pre-History

In 1932, Raymond Maloney formed the Bally Manufacturing Company, a small Chicago enterprise with a unique wooden pinball machine titled *Ballyhoo*. The enterprise, now known simply as "Bally," would eventually evolve into a conglomerate consisting of slot

---

5. Among the numerous resources used for this historical analysis, the following were especially helpful: Steven L. Kent, The Ultimate History of Video Games, (2001); Mark P. Wolf, The Video Game Explosion (2008); Marc Prensky, Digital Game-Based Learning (2001); Van Burnham, Supercade: A Visual History of the Video Game Age, 1971–1984 (2001); Ron Fortune, *Bally: Name of the Game is Technologies*, Gambling Today, March 21–March 27, 2007, at 4; David Kushner, Masters of Doom (2003); Jeff Jensen, *Video Game Nation*, Entertainment Weekly, December 6, 2002; Leonard Herman, Jer Horitz, Steve Kent, and Skyler Miller, *The History of Video Games*, http://gamespot.com/gamespot/ features/video/hov/index.html (last visited Jul. 4, 2008); ESA, *The Entertainment Software Association*, www.theesa.com (last visited Jan. 18, 2015).

machines, health and fitness spas, lottery games, casinos and videogames. Compared to the innovative giants of the videogame industry, Bally was more of a follower than a leader; nevertheless, the electronically circuited pinball machines developed in the 1950s and 1960s, with their colorful flash and noise, were worthy of being labeled predecessors of the modern game.

It was not until approximately four years after the birth of Bally's pinball machine that Alan Turing, often credited as the inventor of the computer, would begin his groundbreaking work on software and hardware theory. In the meanwhile, and for the next several decades, pinball machines would improve technologically and artistically—but aside from faster balls, snappier flippers, and sexier looking score boards—the basic look and feel witnessed no dramatic changes. Bally's videogame interests, on the other hand, boomed as its Aladdin's Castle Division expanded from 20 arcade centers in 1974 to over 200 by the end of the 1970s.

Coincidentally, 1932 was also the year that The Connecticut Leather Company, now known as "Coleco," was formed. Coleco's cartridge based videogame system, Colecovision, would eventually prove to be a major competitor in the sales wars that would follow.

In 1948, a patent for the "Cathode Ray Tube Amusement Device" was issued to Thomas T. Goldsmith, Jr. and Estle Ray Mann. The rudimentary equipment used vacuum tubes to create an imitation missile capable of firing a projectile at a target. Even though knobs were used to align the curved trajectory and adjust the speed, its graphics could not yet be created electronically. The targets were, therefore, drawn on overlays that were placed on the viewing screen.

In 1951, Fusajiro Yamauchi changed the name of his 1889 Japanese playing card company to a single word, meaning "Leave luck to heaven" (Nintendo); a few years later, a young U.S. engineer named Ralph Baer was told by his employer, Loral, to build the "best television in the world." At the time, Baer suggested that an interactive gamer element should be added in order to distinguish the product from others in the marketplace; his suggestions were ignored.

In 1954, U.S. Korean War veteran David Rosen established "Service Games," an export business designed to capitalize on the popularity of coin operated games on American military bases located in Japan. Within the next two years, Rosen was shipping electromagnetic games to Japan, thereby jump starting that country's coin-op business. Later, upon deciding to manufacture his own games, Rosen would purchase a jukebox and slot machine company which he chose to name by taking four letters from his former company's title ("SE" from "Service" and "GA" from "Game"), resulting in SE-GA or SEGA.

The year 1958 earned particular historical respect because it marked an experiment conducted by William Higinbotham, a physicist employed at the Brookhaven National Laboratories in New York. Using an oscilloscope in conjunction with an analog computer, the scientist invented a game that strongly resembled table tennis. Labeled *Tennis For Two*, the interactive apparatus presented on-screen displays for simple movement. Unlike its famous successor (*Pong*), a gravity factor required that the ball be elevated over the net before it could be returned by an opponent. If not a videogame in the true sense, it was certainly a close father. Following several exhibitions, the gadget was dismantled in 1959.

The 1960s: The Formative Years

The 1960s were turbulent but productive. The integrated circuit moved computing in a critical, rapid direction toward miniature components. By the end of the decade, Data

General had shipped a total of 50,000 Nova computers at a purchase price of $8,000 each. The Nova, one of the first 16-bit minicomputers, was also the first computer to employ medium-scale integration (MSI) circuits from Fairchild Semiconductor; subsequent models used large-scale integrated (LSI) circuits. Also notable was the fact that the entire central processor was contained on a single 15-inch printed circuit board. This technology, which continued to advance exponentially, would later be responsible for significantly lowering the costs of videogame production while improving the speed and resolution of the games.

In an age of increasing college student led fads and fashions, the university mainframe computers of the early 1960s intended for homework assignments, were employed by student-hobbyists to create and conduct experiments with early computer games. In 1961, MIT student Steven Russell, along with a group of fellow students, created *Spacewar*, reputed by many to be the first ever videogame. Using teletype terminals with CRT (Cathode Ray Tube) monitors on a Digital Programmed Data Processor (PDP-1 Computer), *Spacewar* enabled two players to shoot missiles at one another from rudimentary spaceships. The early offering was the first game to gain a significant following.

In 1964, a final version of *Spacewar* would inspire Nolan Bushnell, who was then enrolled in engineering school at the University of Utah, to develop *Computer Space*, the first ever coin operated videogame. This would, in turn, evolve into one of the most popular coin operated videogames of all time, *Asteroids* (*See* Color Insert, Figure C.6).

Computers were extremely expensive at this point in history; so when Bushnell, as part of a 1965 summer job, was placed in charge of a Salt Lake City carnival arcade, he could only fantasize that one day it would be filled with more sophisticated microprocessor based games. It was a fantasy that he would realize.

In 1966, Sega released an electronic game, *Periscope*, which became a huge hit in Japan, so much so that the game was later exported to the United States and Europe. Perhaps its greatest historical significance rested in its $.25 per play charge. The relatively high price, which became the arcade standard for many years to come, reflected the high cost of overseas shipping and handling.

In the Fall of 1966, while the Vietnam War was heating up, another significant videogame pioneer, Ralph Baer, was provided with some creative encouragement by his then employer Sanders Associates, a defense contractor. With Sanders' permission, he began research on interactive television games. The following year, to help with his project, Baer gathered together and managed a group of co-workers, most notably William T. Rusch and William L. Harrison. The group completed the first television game in June of 1967, which later led to the noted United States patent titled "Television Gaming and Training Apparatus" which named Ralph Baer as the inventor. Rusch had previously joined the Sanders game group during the Spring of 1967 and began working on the project by the end of October 1967. Rusch's work resulted in a reissue patent, number RE 28,507. This "507" Patent and the Baer Patent are credited as the sparks that began the home videogame industry.

In January 1968, Rusch and the group successfully constructed a video display that would allow an object, now referred to as a "sprite," to randomly move across a screen until it collided with one of two simple short line segments that could be controlled by one or more players. The game, though called by different names and copied by many different entities, would later become most recognizable as *Pong*, with its simple moving ball that ricocheted back and forth between the line segments that represented two rudimentary paddles (*See* Color Insert, Figure C.1).

Starting in 1968 and continuing for the next few years, Sanders demonstrated the new television game equipment to a number of companies in order to capitalize on the successful efforts of its employees. These included: RCA Corporation, Zenith Radio Corporation, General Electric Company, Motorola, Inc., Warwick Electronics, Inc., and The Magnavox Company, to name a few. Magnavox would later negotiate a licensing agreement with Sanders, employing Baer and Rusch to create the first home console game system. During this period, Gulf + Western purchased Sega.

The 1970s: The Golden Age

For the public in general, the 1970s marked the beginning of the videogame revolution. No longer the exclusive province of engineering students and hobbyists, the colorful new machines would now move into malls, corner restaurants, and our living rooms. The new decade also indicated that it was time for the inventors of the industry (such as Baer and Rusch) to pass the baton to creative game developers and innovative entrepreneurs, such as the young Nolan Bushnell, who having graduated from college with a firm grasp of computer graphics, had accepted a job in California.

Early in the decade, Bushnell commenced and, with the help of Ted Dabney, completed the game *Computer Space,* which ushered in the coin operated videogame industry and gave us the "Arcade." In 1971, the game was licensed to Nutting Associates, Inc. of Mountainview, California, which, in turn, retained the services of the duo to assist in its manufacture. Nutting manufactured approximately 1,500 *Computer Space* machines for a November release. Unfortunately, due to its degree of manufacturing difficulty, the landmark product was commercially unsuccessful, though it is credited with having been the first mass produced videogame.

Also credited as the inventor of *Pong* (subject to the achievements of Ralph Baer and the assistance of one Al Alcorn), Bushnell is best known as the founder of videogame pioneer Atari. A brilliant innovator, Bushnell had previously gained some local recognition as a youth when he nearly burned down his family's garage by constructing a home-made liquid fuel rocket that had been mounted on a roller skate. As that incident might suggest to some, Bushnell was definitely a risk taker.

1971 was the year that the microprocessor finally arrived. That technological leap came in the form of a chip designed by Intel employee Marcian Hoff. Another four years would elapse before the chip would find its way into a videogame. Another notable arrival of that year was the first email message.

1972 was most significant. As a first connection between Ralph Baer (forerunner of the home game) and Nolan Bushnell (arcade developer), it was the year that Magnavox, as a licensee of Sanders, began demonstrating Baer's Odyssey home game system. On May 24 of that year, Bushnell specifically traveled to the show to witness the game firsthand. He not only watched the new device in use as it simulated ping pong, but actually played it too. Bushnell then left Nutting, teamed up with Ted Dabney, and began a company called "Syzygy," whose name had already been registered to a different owner, thereby causing the pair to instead adopt "Atari," a Japanese word that means "a hit." Atari, which was capitalized for only $500, hired Al Alcorn who then created the addictively simple *Pong.* Two paddles (simple line segments) appeared at each end of a black and white screen; a simple ball represented by nothing more than a single pixel (i.e., *dot*) would ricochet back and forth until one of the two players missed. The rudimentary game was an instant hit. Atari eventually sold more than 19,000 *Pong* machines, giving rise to many imitations.

Pong made its first appearance in 1972 at "Andy Capp's," a small bar in Sunnyvale, California, where the videogame was literally overplayed as eager customers tried to cram quarters into an already heavily overloaded coin slot. A complaint from the bar owner to come and take the "broken" machine away had Bushnell initially worried. He then discovered that the malfunction resulted solely from its popularity. A more substantive worry, however, was provided by Magnavox, which had released its Odyssey home system that same year. *Pong's* huge success prompted Magnavox to sue Atari claiming infringement; the two companies would eventually settle out of court.

It would be a mistake to leave 1972 without noting it as the year that Xerox developed the first Graphical User Interface (GUI) later labeled the Xerox Star. Nine years later, using GUI technology, the Xerox 8010 would provide the first set of "windows," icons, menus, and pointers, similar to those that we've long grown accustomed to seeing on both Apple and PC-based computers. Also in 1972, Bell Laboratories developed the ever popular *C* Programming Language, a longtime favorite for computer game developers because of its compiler speed, high level of control, and elegant simplicity.

By 1973, the entrepreneurial lantern was lit, signaling other companies to rush to get into the action. Midway, Chicago Coin, Taito, Allied Leisure, and Kee Games (a secret subsidiary of Atari) entered the arcade videogame business. A year later, *Tank* by Kee Games became the first videogame to store graphics on a ROM (Read Only Memory) chip. *TV Basketball* by Midway became the first arcade game to use human figures (avatars) instead of block figures.

In 1975, Bill Gates and Paul Allen generated an implementation of the BASIC programming language and founded Microsoft. During the year that followed, Apple Computers, founded by Steve Jobs, began marketing and selling the first Apple Computers.

1975 also witnessed the microprocessor's entry into the videogame arena as Midway's *Gunfight* (an import from Taito) was first to employ the revolutionary technology. At this time, even though it became short on cash, Atari nevertheless managed to chalk up some more firsts. The company's *Steeplechase* became the first 6-player arcade game, and if that didn't create a large enough crowd, Kee Games produced *Indy 800*, the first 8-player game. During this year, Bushnell made an agreement with Sears to sell a home version of *Pong*. Television sets were becoming truly interactive.

Back on campus, in 1975, Don Daglow, a graduate student at Claremont University, wrote the first computer role playing game on a PDP-10 mainframe computer, titled *Dungeon*. The program was based on the popular board game *Dungeons and Dragons* even though Daglow never received a license to create such a derivative work.

Meanwhile, John Landis released his over the top, second-rate film *Death Race 2000* in 1975 featuring David Carradine and Sylvester Stallone. The movie dealt with a futuristic society where the national sport involved homicidal auto races; points would be achieved by running over pedestrians. Exidy's 1976 videogame release, titled the same as the film, featured rudimentary automobiles designed to run down pedestrian stick figures. Despite the total lack of any sophisticated graphics, *Death Race 2000* assumed its place in history as the first videogame with controversial violence. It is notable that despite the theme and its target as a *60 Minutes* feature, the violence is considered extremely benign by today's standards.

In 1976, with the release of the AY-3-8500 chip by General Instruments, all of the circuitry required for a videogame could be placed on a single chip for the first time. This integrated circuit component meant that videogames could be manufactured with many fewer components and at a much lower cost.

On the heels of the revolutionary new chip, Magnavox commercially introduced the Odyssey 300, Odyssey 400, Odyssey 500, and Odyssey 3000 in a series of models, including the Model BG 4305, a television receiver with a built-in television game. Later in 1977, Magnavox would commercially introduce the Odyssey 2000 and Odyssey 4000 television games, the Models BH 7510 and BH 7511, respectively. The Magnavox Odyssey 300, Odyssey 2000, Odyssey 3000, and Odyssey 4000 television games all utilized the AY-3-8500 chip. The Fairchild Zircon Channel F became the first programmable cartridge-based home videogame console.

In 1976, Atari released *Night Driver*, one of the first of the first-person perspective games, and the classic *Breakout*, the subject of a number of see-saw battles between the courts and the U.S. Copyright Office, the latter of which had not yet learned how to handle the new media (*Breakout* was developed by Steve Jobs and Steve Wozniak of Apple fame). With videogame copyright limitations relatively new and undefined in 1976 Coleco released *Telstar*, its own tennis game. In the meantime, Atari continued to produce some of history's greatest videogames. Then, Bushnell decided to sell Atari to Time Warner Communications for $28 million.

In 1977, the year that Tandy announced its entry into the home computer market with the Radio Shack TRS-80, Mattel, a picture frame and doll house furniture business started in 1945 by Harold Matson and Elliot Handler (the letters of their names were used to form its name), began to develop its own "television game" product. Mattel had received a demonstration of the AY-3-8500 chip during the course of the Consumer Electronics Show in Chicago, Illinois.

During 1977, Nintendo, the century old manufacturer of trading cards, released its first videogame, which was basically a *Pong* spin-off. More significantly, the soon-to-become legendary game artist and designer Shigeru Miyamoto joined Nintendo. Meanwhile, Bally released a programmable videogame console called the Bally Professional Arcade. The system, however, failed due its $350 price tag.

In 1977, Atari opened the first Pizza Time Theater, a combination arcade-pizzeria that featured electronic games, robotic animals, food, drinks, and a newcomer rat named "Chuckie Cheese." It was an instant hit with children, particularly those having birthday parties.

Atari subsidiary Kee Games released *Super Bug*, the first arcade game with 4-directional scrolling. Near the year's end, as the infant industry was feeling threatened by a slump in sales, and just in time for the 1977 Christmas season, Atari released the first programmable console and its first home cartridge game system employing joysticks, the famous Video Computer System (VCS). It was later renamed the Atari 2600 to distinguish it from the company's subsequent release, the Atari 5200.

1978 was the year that a new copyright act took effect, granting better protection for authors and artists. It was also the year that Ray Kassar assumed the role of CEO of Atari as Nolan Bushnell left the company and purchased the Pizza Time Theater, which he later turned into a franchise. That year, Atari released *Football*, which utilized two-directional side scrolling and introduced the trackball controller.

1978 was also the year that Magnavox released the Odyssey 2, the first programmable console with a built in membrane keyboard, Nintendo released *Othello*, that company's first arcade game, and Cinematronics released *Space Wars*, an arcade spin-off of MIT's

Spacewars. But perhaps the most memorable event was Midway's release of the Taito videogame *Space Invaders*. (*See* Color Insert, Figure C.2). Because of its phenomenal popularity, *Space Invaders* inspired a number of vertical shooter games; it broke all relevant sales records and actually created a coin shortage in Japan.

Videogame developer Namco delivered *Galaxian* (See Color Insert, Figure C.3), which became the first game to have all of its graphics in a RGB (Red, Green, Blue) color format (a standard for color video). This was considered revolutionary. But the accomplishments of the iconic Namco didn't end there. For, if *Space Invaders* was the blockbuster for the year 1978, then the Japanese release of *Pac-Man* was certainly its counterpart for 1979. The iconic Namco game was another global record breaker. It was initially tagged *Puckman*; the "puck" in Japanese was suggestive of an eating sound, appropriate for *Pac Man's* dot-eating sprites. However, fear that puckish pranksters might erase the leading portion of the "P" prompted the change from "Puck" to "Pac." *Pac-Man* became the first videogame that appealed to a mass audience of both males and females. (*See* Color Insert, Figure C.4).

In 1979, Mattel released the Intellivision Game Console, while Milton Bradley released Microvision, the first portable handheld programmable videogame system, and a game producer known as "Capcom" was started in Japan. Also in that year, Vectorbeam released *Warrior*, one of the first one-on-one fighting games. Atari released *Lunar Lander*, its first vector-graphics game; as opposed to traditional bit map graphics, vector graphics draw and redraw faster and consume less microchip memory. Also released by Atari in vector graphics format was *Asteroids*, one of the most successful products in videogame history. Less successful, however, was Atari's adventure into the home computer market.

Atari's 1979 release of its 400 and 800 home computers could not compete with Apple, which was perceived as a computer manufacturer as opposed to a videogame maker. The Atari computers were capable of playing all of the 2600's game cartridges. Even though the 400 would serve as both a game console and a computer, chains such as K-mart sold the 400 for *less* than the 2600 stand-alone. To quote a K-Mart salesperson, "We want to get rid of them because there will never be a home market for computers."

As the decade neared its end, Atari's game designer Warren Robinett introduced us to the idea of the "Easter Egg" by hiding a room bearing his name in the Atari 2600 game titled *Adventure*. The concept suggests that the player should receive this "extra" reward for successful play. The otherwise pleasant concept behind this gratuitous surprise, however, became controversial in later decades, when some of the "prizes" turned into scenes involving rape and nudity in games like Grand Theft Auto.

The 1980s: Industry Turmoil

The 1980s provided a series of home based innovations as the arcades continued to flourish. The decade also witnessed the development of our present Internet protocol and the appearance of Apple's Lisa Computer, along with the debut of the Commodore 64, a machine whose success relied heavily upon computer videogame development. During this period, the videogame creators managed to intertwine themselves with the motion picture industry by their release of the first arcade games predicated upon film characters and themes. Included among the most notable were: *Star Wars, Tron, E.T.*, and, of course, *Indiana Jones and the Temple of Doom*.

In 1980, Atari released *Space Invader* cartridges for its 2600 console, a move that ushered in the practice of selling arcade hits that could be played on home consoles. It also released

Battlezone, the first of the real 3D environments. Other popular contemporaries included *Defender* and *Ultima,* the first home videogame with 4-directional scrolling. *Star Fire* became the first "sit in the cockpit" game. Namco continued its exceptional success by selling several hundred thousand home versions of *Pac-Man.* In the arcade scene, it became the most popular videogame of the time and one of the most popular of all time.

There were troubles in the industry in 1980. Atari suffered the loss of some of its best programmers; dissatisfied over the manner in which Atari refused to give credit to individual developers, the group left the company and started Activision, the first of the major third-party developers. Activision, unlike Atari, gave recognition to its programmers on its packaging and during the course of marketing. Meanwhile, Minoru Arakawa, son-in-law of Nintendo's CEO, opened Nintendo of America in New York City, then moved the company to Seattle, Washington. That venture unfortunately produced some mediocre games that resulted in poor sales.

1980 also witnessed the emergence of the ZX80, which its manufacturer, Sinclair, claimed to be the first home computer, despite the presence of the TRS-80. The IBM PC made its debut the following year.

In 1981, arcades were everywhere, collecting billions of dollars in revenue. United States arcade game revenues alone reached $5 billion. The MS-DOS operating system emerged, with its first virus soon to follow, which was spread by Apple II's floppy discs. "Electronic Games," founded by Arnie Katz, Bill Kunkel, and Joyce Worley, became the first magazine devoted entirely to videogames. Later, Coleco released Colecovision, its own cartridge based videogame console.

Special mention should be given to a low resolution Nintendo stick figure, named *Jumpman,* whose only purpose in life was to save his girlfriend, Pauline, from the arms of a crazy monkey. Later, Nintendo artist Shigeru Miyamoto dressed *Jumpman* up a bit, added some weight, changed his name to Mario (due to his resemblance to Mario Segale, landlord of the Nintendo staff), and created *Donkey Kong,* another mega hit.

1982 indicated that it was time to send in the clones. Magnavox heeded the call and released *K.C. Munchkin* for its Odyssey system, which so closely resembled *Pac-Man* that it prompted a successful infringement lawsuit by Atari, which led to *Munchkin's* demise. On the other hand, Atari did an extremely *poor* job of cloning its own version of *Pac-Man* for cartridge use on its 2600. Atari fans and *Pac-Man* fans alike were most disappointed in the quality of the offering. The beleaguered Atari released its advanced 5200 System to compete with the superior sound and graphics delivered by the Colecovision. Atari also released the videogame *Tempest,* a foreboding title that was to signal events to come as more programmers bailed out of Atari; along with several Intellivision defectors, they formed another third party videogame development company, "Imagic." Prior to the exodus, it was probably fair to state that while Atari had some of the best developers and innovators of its time, the quality of its management left much to be desired.

As if things weren't already bad enough for Atari and the videogame industry, which was now declining, the long anticipated *E.T.* game, programmed by Howard Scott Warshaw and rushed to market in just six weeks, just in time for Christmas, was nothing to phone home about. It was more than a significant failure with respect to both quality and sales. The hurried attempt to exploit Stephen Spielberg's hit film *E.T.—The Extraterrestrial* resulted in a game that was so defective and poor that to many once-loyal Atari players, its movements basically made no sense. Historically, the game is looked upon by some as the single worst videogame in history. Some even attribute Atari's demise to the game (a bit of an overstatement). More than 30 years later, in 2014, the game's failure was celebrated by a pilgrimage to the desert garbage dump where massive numbers of unsold *E.T.* game cartridges are rumored to have been buried by Atari.

There were some industry bright spots in 1982. Gottlieb released the very popular *Q*bert*. Sega released *Zaxxon*, the first arcade game to be the subject of a television advertisement. Midway's release of *Ms. Pac-Man* provided us with the most successful arcade game in history to date.

Despite the release of some of video gaming's greatest classics, the industry as a whole was heading for a crash. When Warner Communications announced that Atari's sales would be disappointing, on December 7, 1982, at 3:04 PM Eastern Standard Time, Warner's stock plunged 38%. A controversy later arose when it was learned that Atari's CEO, Ray Kassar, had dumped $200,000 worth of Warner stock on December 6th. He was later cleared by the SEC.

At the January 1983 Consumer Electronics Show, Coleco released its Adam Computer. Commodore later released the Commodore 64, a videogame console that, despite its modest price, was superior to its competitors. Using a laser disc, *Dragon's Lair* by Cinematronics, became the first popular arcade game to employ more colorful cartoon like characters. This was a dramatic move away from the rudimentary stick-like figures that arcade gamers had become accustomed to. Meanwhile, Nolan Bushnell began an arcade business labeled "Sente Games," and Sega released its first home videogame console in Japan, the SG 1000. As for Atari, James Morgan, a former tobacco company executive, replaced Ray Kassar as the CEO of Atari as the company released *I, Robot* and *Star Wars*.

In 1983, Bally's amusement game revenue plunged 60%; but because of its diversification (as the largest owner of fitness centers), it was spared the fate of other videogame enterprises that were also suffering. For the industry in general, by the end of 1983, inventories were overloaded and shelves were bloated with cheap videogames. The public was finally fed up with low quality, repetitive clones disguised by dazzling packages and charged up titles. Unsold videogames filled the shelves forcing many third party developers out of business.

By 1984, you could find stacks of videogame cartridges selling for a few dollars each at your local garage sale. The industry crash had arrived. Coleco had shifted a substantial portion of its corporate assets toward the manufacture of the Adam Computer; 60% of the machines were eventually returned due to defects. After very significant losses, Mattel, apparently finding that it was safer to stick with Barbie, sold Intellivision to one of its vice presidents. And then there was Atari; Warner dumped its consumer division to Jack Tramiel (who had started Commodore), but retained its arcade division, which was re-titled "Atari Games." Tramiel then announced that the new company would focus on computers and games but would not build consoles.

In 1984, David Rosen, Hayao Nakayama and Isao Okawa purchased Sega Enterprises from Gulf + Western. In Japan, Nintendo released the Famicom, its so-called Family Computer. The product became the best-selling game console in that country by the end of 1984, but even it couldn't escape the misfortunes of the year. It appears that a defective chip in the initial product caused the system to crash. Following a product recall, however, and a reissued motherboard, the Famicom's popularity later surged. Meanwhile, Bally's managed to survive the turmoil because it decided to shift focus to tamper-free electronic lottery machines, with 18 states on its customer list.

1985 marked the year that Nintendo would lead the industry's successful dig out of its cavern. Loaded with some good original titles and offers to buy back any unused inventory from its retailers, Nintendo brought the Famicom to the United States and called it the Nintendo Entertainment System, or simply the NES. But Nintendo had a new weapon in its arsenal, which later became known as the infamous "lock out chip." In order to avoid the disastrous consequences that befell the Atari 2600 from cheap third party games, Nintendo's little 16-pin "lock out" or "Key" chip would not permit *just anyone* to manufacture games for the NES. On the contrary, cartridges developed by unauthorized third parties simply wouldn't work on the NES. Therefore, the chip forced companies to pay the price of each cartridge (due to the fact that a bypass chip had to be added to the cartridge), and only companies deemed capable of producing quality games would be permitted to obtain the cartridges. Various methods were published for disabling the lockout chip, either by applying a high or negative voltage, or by cutting and grounding one of the pins. Lawsuits, of course, were certain to follow.

1985 produced some interesting new products. NBA basketball star "Dr. J" became the first athlete to license his name and image for use in a videogame. The company RDI released a laserdisc home videogame system, the Halcyon. Electronic Arts developed a product that eventually turned into one of the bestselling sports games in history, *John Madden Football*. And, while Madden was placing his endorsement on an American pastime, Russian Alexey Pajitnov was busy designing a game that would sweep the world (*Tetris*) and eventually embroil game producers Tengen, Atari, and Nintendo in vicious ownership litigation.

The 1985 was particularly significant because it signaled the beginning of fierce competition among the remaining major console producers, particularly Nintendo, Atari, and Sega. That year also witnessed the release of Windows (software that would allegedly and litigiously turn a PC into a Macintosh). The year included the invention of the CD-Rom, a combined effort by Phillips and Sony.

The Atari ST was released. The letters officially represented the numbers "Sixteen/Thirty-Two," which referred to Motorola 68000's 16-bit external bus and 32-bit internal processor. On a less technical note, competitor Nintendo released another success, *Super Mario Brothers*.

In 1986, Nintendo began selling its NES nationwide. The videogame *Defender of the Crown* helped launch the Amiga Home Computer. Sega released the Sega Master System (also known as the SMS). And, contrary to Tramiel's 1984 statement, Atari released the Atari 7800 game console. The successful *Legend of Zelda* was released for the Famicom; it would later give birth to a series of Zelda games. Taito's *Araknoid* and *Bubble Bobble* started to appear in arcades. By the year's end, Nintendo would outsell its competitors by a huge margin.

1987 was a year of increased computer power and technological growth for videogame hardware as manufacturers began to recognize that 8-bit systems were not strong enough for future sound, speed, graphics or resolution. NEC released an 8-bit/16-bit hybrid videogame console in Japan. Sega released its 16-bit Mega Drive game console. *Yokai Dochuki*, released in Japan by Namco, became the first 16-bit arcade game. *The Manhole*, by Cyan, became the first videogame to be released on a CD-Rom. Lucas Arts released *Maniac Mansion*, the first adventure game with a point-click interface. And Incentive Software released *Driller* with improved 3D graphics.

Also in 1987, VGA computer screens began to provide enhanced viewing quality. The new screens delivered 256 colors with a screen covered by 640 × 480 pixels, thereby improving two critical videogame factors, resolution *and* color. At this particular juncture it became apparent to the industry that the demand for better, faster, snappier games was fast becoming a motivating force for computer manufacturers.

During 1987, Atari continued its economic gasp for air by restyling its defunct Atari 800 Computer and calling it the Atari XE Game System (XEGS); critics were unimpressed. Journalists and consumers were more impressed with Nintendo as it continued its industry blitz by welcoming new developers (several of whom were prior Atari supporters), most notably Namco.

1988 continued to witness strong competition among the survivors of the early 1980s crash. Nintendo continued its success. Atari continued its struggle. "If you can't beat them …" must have been on Atari's mind when it created Tengen, a subsidiary designed to produce third party home videogames for its competitors. Its first target was the lucrative NES. The relationship between the two pioneers, Atari and Nintendo, began as that of *licensor/licensee* but wound up as *plaintiff/defendant*. Nintendo was less than pleased when Atari's Tengen decided to circumvent Nintendo's lock out chip, and it was even less pleased when Atari alleged that Nintendo established an illegal monopoly through price fixing and its use of the chip. Overall, the fiercely competitive environment of 1988 proved to be too difficult for some. Coleco filed for bankruptcy.

In 1989, Tim Berners Lee, the father of the Internet, developed the World Wide Web. That same year, a revolution in hand-held videogames was sparked by Nintendo's release of the ever-popular Game Boy, which, along with its several successors, remains ubiquitous today. Atari released its handheld, the Atari Lynx.

The Sega Genesis console was released in 1989. NEC brought the PC engine to the United States and called it the TurboGrafx.

The 1990s: Increased Competition

The 1990s witnessed some creative new enhancements and augmentations for videogames. New objectives appeared. Education became more of a factor. And amidst the classic videogame goals (destroy, shoot, kill, rescue, survive, dismember, duck, or solve) arose Will Wright's *SimCity*, a 1990 release, wherein the purpose was to build, create, and govern a fictional metropolitan area. Many derivative *Sim* games would follow. 1990 also witnessed the release of the Gamegear, Sega's handheld answer to the Gameboy. NEC released its handheld, Turbografx-16 and then released Turboexpress, a handheld version of Turbografx-16 that came with a separately sold TV tuner.

In 1990, Squaresoft released *Final Fantasy*, another set of classic successes. Nintendo released *Super Mario Brothers 3*, one of the most successful non-bundled cartridge videogames of all time. SNK, a third party developer of Nintendo games, released the 24-bit NeoGeo with superior sound and graphics, which unfortunately was also accompanied by a superior price tag of $399. Commodore released its Commodore CDTV (Commodore Dynamic Total Vision), a Commodore Computer with the keyboard missing. The system was designed to promote educational objectives and employed CD's as opposed to cartridges.

In 1991, the Sound Blaster provided another critical game component, enhanced sound. Sega debuted its new hero, a snappy sprite starring in *Sonic the Hedgehog*. Philips Electronics released its CD-i (Compact Disc Interactive) game console. Capcom released the immensely popular videogame, *Streetfighter*.

Galoob Toys released a game device that permitted NES game players to cheat. For gamers, this meant benefits such as extra lives and increased speed of user-controlled sprites that allowed them to better kill whatever happened to be chasing them at the moment. A lawsuit resulted from Nintendo's fear that the device would negatively impact the sales of NES units and cartridges.

In 1992, TransMedia's *Objection!* became the first educational computer game to receive professional certification when the California State Bar Association approved it for purposes of Mandatory Continuing Legal Education (MCLE). It has since been approved by nearly all states that permit lawyers to receive credits through home study. By way of contrast, Midway released *Mortal Kombat*, a blood splashing fighter game, where the ultimate victory was to reach into your opponent's chest and pull out his heart as it continued to beat and squirt blood.

In the same year, the home game *Wolfenstein 3D* by id Software, and *Virtual Racing* by Sega, made their respective big hits among consumers. The Sega game was timely named since it would help the Sega Genesis race to the sales lead for the U.S. console market. Also in 1992, Newcomer 3DO would launch its 32-bit home game console.

In 1993, advances in computer storage capabilities led to the creation of Jpeg (Joint Photographic Experts Group) and Mpeg (Motion Picture Experts Group), which provided the desktop computer with standards for storing photographic and moving images. Panasonic began to market the 3DO, Broderbund released the artistic *Myst* for Macintosh computers, and Sega released *Virtual Fighter*. Refusing to give up the ghost, Atari released the *Jaguar*, a 64-bit console.

Doom, a "first person" shooter game designed by some youngsters in Shreveport, Louisiana, made its bloody splash in 1993. During this period, Senators Joseph Lieberman (of Connecticut) and Herbert Kohl (of Wisconsin) scheduled Congressional hearings targeting videogame violence. In response, the Entertainment Software Rating Board (ESRB) created a rating system designed to label products so that purchasers and parents could be warned whenever games contained obscene materials or violence.

By 1994, Nintendo and Sega were neck in neck in the race for sales superiority. Nintendo released *Donkey Kong Country* with its beautiful jungle graphics to retake the lead. Sega released the arcade game *Daytona USA*, the first game with texture mapping. Blizzard released the real time strategy game *Warcraft*.

1994 also marks the beginning of the videogame industry's attempts at self-regulation. During that year, the Entertainment Software Rating Board (with its heightened specificity) became a creation of the Entertainment Software Association.

By mid-decade, the battle among the game console giants of the industry reached new levels when the industry witnessed what might be termed a "bit-bidding" war (which Atari seemed to have begun two years earlier). In 1994, Sega released the Saturn (32 bits) and Sony followed suit with the Sony Playstation; both releases occurred in Japan. The company SNK released the NeoGeo home system. Then Nintendo released a 64-bit system, Project Reality. A year later, the Saturn and Playstation were released in the United States. Nintendo demonstrated its new Nintendo 64 at its own trade show in 1995; the results were tumultuous. The popularity of the 64-bit system, it was said, nearly caused riots when retailers first offered them for sale. But the mania cooled when it became apparent that there were a limited number of titles available. Nintendo also released the 32-bit portable game console, Virtual Boy. After much negative press, the product failed in sales, but Nintendo's Gameboy remained strong.

In 1996, competition caused console prices to drop. The Sony Playstation fell to under $200. Also dropping was the popularity of arcades across the U.S., even though they were now being populated by a rash of new combination-ride games (more expensive to manufacture and maintain) that permitted players to simulate snowboarding, skiing, and jet skiing.

In 1996, Jack Tramiel sold Atari to disc drive manufacturer JTS. Meanwhile, Atari's founder Nolan Bushnell became the president of Aristo Games, a company that manufactured Internet stations for arcades. It might be mentioned at this juncture that to date, Bushnell has founded 18 companies and has worked in many fields, including personal computers and robotics; but he continues to develop videogames. In 1996, Sony killed its one-year-old Virtual Boy, thereby avoiding sibling rivalry with its winner Game Boy. The failure was blamed on Gumpei Yokoi who was ironically responsible for the Game Boy's success. Yokoi left Nintendo (sadly, the great game designer would later die in an automobile accident). Lastly, Digipen Institute of Technology became the first school to offer college degrees in videogame development.

As prices were dropping in the year 1996, attempts to regulate videogame sex and violence were heating up. It was the year that Congress took action to combat the growing "sexolence." [In truth, sex and violence are constitutionally separate issues, but since the media and, at times the courts, insist upon lumping them together, your authors have constructed the term "sexolence."] To combat sexolence, the 1996 Communications Decency Act (CDA) was passed as part of the Telecommunications act of 1996. It was later determined to be unconstitutional, as was COPA (The Child Online Protection Act). Both attempted to deprive minors of constitutionally protected materials.

In 1997, Voodoo's graphics introduced computer gamers to enhanced 3D technology. A year later, the recordable and re-writable CD's made their respective appearances. That was the year that Sega discontinued the Saturn. Nintendo released *Goldeneye 007* for the Nintendo 64. Squaresoft released *Final Fantasy VII* for the Sony Playstation. *Ultima Online*, the MMORPG (Massive Multi-player Online Role Playing Game), was released.

Due to a new series of restrictive licensing laws enacted by the European Economic Commission, Nintendo was prohibited from selling software companies the privilege of developing Nintendo games. Nor could Nintendo continue to monopolize the manufacture of its cartridges.

Continuing the trend of a closer relationship between the film and videogame industries, in 1997, Universal Studios, DreamWorks Pictures, and Sega join to form "Gameworks," a series of videogame super arcades. Their first opened in Seattle, Washington on March 15, 1997. Los Angeles and Las Vegas would follow suit before the end of the year, as would nearly 100 other venues.

In 1998, Nintendo's Game Boy moved from black-and-white to color. Meanwhile, a new craze over the *Pokemon* role-playing series for the Game Boy hit Japan and quickly spread to the United States. SNK released The NeoGeo Pocket handheld videogame system. Rockstar Games released the first of its series of controversially violent and sexual *Grand Theft Auto* games.

In 1999, JTS filed for bankruptcy and sold the remains of Atari to Hasbro Interactive. (Will Atari never rest in peace?) Sega released the Dreamcast game console. *Everquest* and *Asheron's Call* went online. Nintendo released *Donkey Kong 64*. The Game Developers Conference held its first Independent Games Festival.

The New Millennium

The Millennium Bug did not bring doom to the world despite predictions to the contrary. The new millennium did, however, reveal that the journey from a successful videogame to a $100 million motion picture can spell doom at the box office, as Sony's *Final Fantasy* proved when the film flopped in a big way. In 2000, the United States Post Office honored the industry by issuing a stamp that depicted videogames.

In 2001, Microsoft's Xbox and Nintendo's Gamecube entered the arena. Sega announced that it would be bailing out of the console manufacturing business. As part of the plan, it disconnected from Dreamcast. Sega's chairman Isao Okawa died.

Judge Posner's landmark decision in *Am. Amusement Mach. Ass'n v. Kendrick*, 244 F.3d 572, 574 (7th Cir. 2001), finding that videogames were entitled to First Amendment protection, warned about attempts to suppress this "kid's" popular culture. (*See* §§ 12.2, *et seq. infra* for a further discussion of *Kendrick*.)

In 2002, The University of La Verne College of Law in California became the first law school in the United States, if not the world, to provide a course in *Computer Game Law*. Prior to this time, the subject of videogame law had been combined with courses such as The *Law of Cyberspace*, *Software Law*, and *Computer Law*.

2002 was also the year that the United States District Court in Colorado handed down its landmark decision prohibiting attempts to blame anti-social conduct (such as school shootings) on videogame content; the case was *Sanders v. Acclaim Ent., Inc.*, 188 F. Supp. 2d 1264 (2202) (6th Cir.). (*See* § 13.20, *infra* for a further discussion of *Sanders*.)

In 2003, Nintendo halted production of the NES. Cell phone company Nokia released the N-Gage handheld videogame system, and Atari's *Enter the Matrix* was released.

In 2004, Sony released the Playstation Portable in Japan and the Playstation 2 in China. Nintendo released the dual screen follow up to its Gameboy, the Nintendo DS. In that year, according to the Entertainment Software Association, Americans spent $7.3 billion on videogames; other statistics indicated that the average American child spent nine hours per week playing videogames. In 2004, the violent videogame *Grand Theft Auto: San Andreas* sold more copies in America than any other videogame.

Also in 2004, the virtual world greatly expanded in popularity due to Sony's *EverQuest II* and Blizzard Entertainment's extremely popular *World of Warcraft*, the latter of which surpassed 1.5 million subscribers within six months of its November 2004 launch.

In 2005, Sony released the Playstation Portable in North America, while Nintendo released the Game Boy Micro. Microsoft released the Xbox 360. *The Sims* appeared on postage stamps in France. On July 25, 2005, amidst much media fanfare, Governor Blagojevich of Illinois signed into law the Violent Videogames Law and the Sexually Explicit Videogames Law; which provided that any person who sold or rented a violent or sexually explicit videogame to a minor committed a petty offense for which a fine of $1,000 could be imposed. In press releases, the Governor's office applauded its own "landmark" legislation, which was promptly struck down as an unconstitutional restraint on free expression before it could take effect on January 1, 2006. Other states, such as Michigan, Missouri, Washington, and California followed Illinois' lead, all with similar fates. For the year 2005, the gross revenues for videogames exceeded $38.2 billion.

In 2006, the Nintendo Wii and the Sony Playstation 3 were released. Microsoft released the Xbox 360 in Australia. The Wii introduced the concept of physical movement and exercise to a new generation of previously sedentary gamers.

By 2007, the *World of Warcraft* MMORPG was estimated to have more than 9 million players worldwide.

In 2008, social networking games and so-called "casual games" (lacking in great violence or complexity) began to appear. It must have come as quite a shock to macho fans of *Doom* and *Mortal Kombat* to encounter titles such as *Happy Farm, Sunshine Ranch,* and *Barn Buddy.* The introduction of simplicity, however, apparently did not hurt sales. *Farmville* has enjoyed a worldwide audience exceeding 70 million.

With cloud computing and storage on the horizon, 2009 witnessed some new game-related services. The cloud permitted the rendering of graphics away from the end user; this permitted the rendered graphics to be streamed to the game, then to the end user.

As the decade closed, the battle between the First Amendment and state legislative attempts to regulate videogame sex and violence continued, with the First Amendment holding all of the cards. Nevertheless, the FTC's December 2009 Report to Congress ("Marketing Violent Entertainment To Children") offered encouraging words as to the effectiveness of industry self-regulation.

In 2009, at the Electronic Entertainment Expo (E3), Microsoft introduced Project Natal (later branded as the Kinect), its new motion capture controller. At the same E3, Sony presented its own motion controllers labeled Playstation Move.

The Twenty-Teens

A good place to open our brief summary of the decade is with the U.S. Supreme Court's landmark decision directed at attempts to regulate videogame sexolence (sex and violence). The battle began in California in 2005 with the passage of legislation pressed by then Governor Schwarzenegger. The fight ran its course in the courts through the end of the prior decade. Finally, on June 27, 2011, the High Court issued its decision in *Brown v. Ent. Merchs. Ass'n,* 564 U.S. __ 131 S. Ct. 2729 (2011), wherein Justice Scalia, speaking on behalf of the majority, struck down the state's attempt to prohibit the sale or rental of offensive games to minors. The decision, predicated upon First Amendment and other grounds, put the final nail in a lengthy coffin containing a decade of unconstitutional attempts by both state and federal legislatures to regulate what minors may or may not experience while playing videogames.

On June 14, 2010, Microsoft uncovered its cloud-based Xbox 360 console during the E3 Conference. Initially termed the Xbox 360 S (For Slim), it delivered a smaller, quieter, smoother console with a 250 gigabyte hard drive. Later that same year, Microsoft released the Kinect as both a console and a peripheral for the Xbox 360. The Kinect, unlike the Wii, used a sensor and dual-camera device to obtain motion capture. With sales passing the 10 million unit mark in 2011, the product earned the distinction of being the "fastest selling consumer electronics device."

In 2011, in a long-running matter, it was reported that U.S. business entities incurred $29 billion in costs due to a rapidly growing, often-maligned set of patent assertion entities (PAE's), also known as Patent Trolls. These non-industry entities profit from the imprecise language inherent in patent claims. Software patents are particularly prone to abuse. The entities buy up patents, then start lawsuits against many companies hoping to shake licensing fees out defendants who would rather pay than litigate. The problem began many years prior, but has more recently exploded. Despite the problems, not all non-practicing entities (NPE's) are to be criticized; some serve useful purposes.

On September 16, 2011, portions of the American Invents Act (AIA) took effect, thereby spearheading the greatest changes in United States Patent laws in over 50 years; the changes are certain to impact future videogame intellectual property rights. As one of many changes, under the AIA, patent trolls can no longer sue hundreds of defendants in a single action; separate suits are required.

On June 7, 2011, following earlier announcements, Nintendo officially introduced its follow up to the Wii. Named the Wii U, the successor to the popular motion game console featured HD graphics and a 6.2 inch touchscreen in addition to other improvements.

November of 2011 deserves to be remembered as the 10th anniversary of the release of the first game of the *Halo* series on November 15, 2001. *Halo* was a military science fiction first-person shooter videogame franchise developed by game producer Bungie and later managed by a subsidiary of Microsoft. The series, with its outstanding graphics, involves nothing less than an interstellar war with humanity.

During November 2012, Activision Blizzard broke all prior videogame sales records when it released *Call of Duty: Black Ops II*. The game's sales crossed the billion dollar mark 15 days after its release.

In May of 2013, Microsoft announced that Xbox One would be the official successor to the Xbox 360.

In the Fall of 2013, as reported in Forbes and later confirmed by the Guinness Book of World Records, *Grand Theft Auto V* became the first videogame in history to cross the billion dollar sales mark in less than one week. The 15th title in the long running series published by Rockstar Games was released for the Xbox and Playstation. The series has been both critically acclaimed for its graphics and condemned for its violence. The open-action adventure game sold over 11 million units within the first 24 hours of its release.

November 15, 2013, was the official release date for Sony's PS4 (Playstation 4), following a February 2013 press conference announcing the new game. The PS4 delivered 8 Gigabytes of Ram and a faster Blu-ray.

In the Spring of 2014, Amazon released the Amazon Fire TV for $99, with a strangely priced controller ($40). The product is a general purpose music and video streamer with a high power processor.

In October of 2014, pursuant to the motion of Activision's attorney Rudy Giuliani, a California Superior Court judge dismissed a lawsuit by Panamanian dictator Manuel Noriega on First Amendment grounds. The convicted murderer and former drug king had alleged that the unauthorized use of his persona in *Call of Duty: Black Ops I,* damaged his reputation.

As of the spring of 2016, there are no less than 43 films in the works based on videogames, not to mention an uncountable number of games in development.

The Future

In terms of both popularity and artistic creativity, there is every indication that the industry will continue to expand and prosper. At least in the immediate term, with industry sales crossing the $100 billion mark in 2014, there is no sign that business is going to slow down any time soon.

Notes and Questions

1. Based on the history in the preceding section, who do you think deserves the title "Father of the videogame"?

2. From the preceding history, can you anticipate the types of legal disputes that transpired? Can you predict who the parties are going to be?

3. How would you compare the history and development of the videogame industry to other economic enterprises such as those pertaining to film, television, music, and even automobiles?

4. What unique videogame elements and characteristics might have been responsible for the up's and down's that the industry experienced in the 1980s?

5. Which company had the greatest influence and impact on the videogame industry in the 1970s? The 1990s? The 2000s?

6. Hackers and videogamers have long been associated with one another, either rightfully or wrongfully. In the midst of the videogame revolution, the classic 1983 John Badham film *War Games,* starring Matthew Broderick, depicted a videogame, *Thermonuclear War,* whose developer managed to confuse fantasy and reality; the defect was brought to light when a young videogamer/hacker was able to tap into the Pentagon's sensitive defense system computers and bring the superpowers to the brink of nuclear annihilation. Knowing that the military currently uses videogames as an excellent training device for its combat soldiers, is the premise of the film *War Games* that far-fetched?

7. In the mid-1990s, some of the major computer hardware manufacturers pooled their resources and threw a "Million Dollar Party" for a group of computer game programmers (at the time, commonly referred to as "Geeks") who attended the Computer Game Developers Conference in the Silicon Valley. Why do you suppose that the manufacturers would have an interest in hosting such a party?

§ 1.30 The Business of Videogames

Although there may be some legitimate difference of opinion as to whether Nolan Bushnell and Atari, or Ralph Bare and Magnavox, are properly credited with being the patriarch of the videogame industry, one fact not in dispute is that the industry they both helped found is HUGE. The 2014 revenue from just game-related hardware and software was about $46.5 billion,[6] and if other economic activity associated with the industry, such as mergers and acquisitions of videogame companies, is taken into account, the figure for videogames' contributions to the worldwide economy rises to $64 billion.[7] Others put the total even higher, with Statista.com reporting the 2015 worldwide revenue for videogames at $101.6 billion, including hardware and software. Domestic videogame

---

6. STATISTA, http://www.statista.com/statistics/237187/global-video-games-revenue/ (last visited Jan. 18, 2015).

7. POLYGON, http://www.polygon.com/2014/6/25/5840882/games-industry-revenue-hit-100-billion-by-2018-dfc-Intelligence (last visited Jan. 18, 2015).

software sales in 2014 were $17 billion.[8] Forbes predicts that the worldwide gross for the videogame software industry will grow to $82 billion in 2017.[9] By contrast,

- the 2014 worldwide gross revenues for movies were a little under $38 billion,[10] (with domestic distribution accounting for $9 billion of that figure[11]);

- the global revenues from book and journal sales were about $37 billion[12] (with domestic book and journal publishing revenues totaling $27 billion[13]);

- the latest figures for global revenues from the music industry were about $15 billion[14] (with domestic sales accounting for about $7 billion[15]); and

- the National Football League's revenues were about $9 billion.[16]

Over 47,000 public videogame tournaments were scheduled in the world in 2014,[17] with prizes of up to $11 million per tournament to be split among the winning teams.[18] Several players make their livings solely playing videogames, with a few of the top players earning nearly $1 million annually.[19] People are watching as well. Major League Gaming, the largest active videogame channel, has over a million registered users and the August 2014 MLG championships had over 2 million viewers watching two teams play *Call of Duty*. Further, in the aggregate, YouTube gaming channels bring in over 3.5 billion views per month. Big Fish Games has estimated that more than 71 million people have viewed some form of egames competition, an eightfold increase since 2010.

As many as several hundred people make their real world livings by working exclusively in the virtual world *Second Life*, and one person, Ailin Graef, has made over $1 million as a result of her real estate speculation within *Second Life*.[20] There are as many as 50,000

8. Wikia, http://vgsales.wikia.com/wiki/Video_game_industry (last visited Jan. 18, 2015).

9. Forbes, http://www.forbes.com/sites/johngaudiosi/2012/07/18/new-reports-forecasts-global-video-game-industry-will-reach-82-billion-by-2017/ (last visited Jan. 18, 2015).

10. Statista, http://www.statista.com/statistics/259987/global-box-office-revenue/ (last visited Jan. 18, 2015).

11. Box Office Mojo, http://www.boxofficemojo.com/yearly/chart/?page=7&view=releasedate &view2=domestic&yr=2014&p=.htm (last visited Jan. 18, 2015).

12. Publishers Weekly, http://www.publishersweekly.com/pw/by-topic/industry-news/bookselling/article/62720-pwc-predicts-slow-growth.html (last visited Jan. 18, 2015).

13. Book Industry Study Group, https://www.bisg.org/news/bookstats-volume-4-now-available-aap-press-release (last visited Jan. 18, 2015).

14. IFPI, http://www.ifpi.org/global-statistics.php (last visited Jan. 18, 2015).

15. LA Times, http://www.latimes.com/entertainment/music/posts/la-et-ms-music-industry-revenue-riaa-report-streaming-digital-20140318-story.html (last visited Jan. 18, 2015).

16. Forbes, http://www.forbes.com/sites/monteburke/2013/08/17/how-the-national-football-league-can-reach-25-billion-in-annual-revenues/ (last visited Jan. 18, 2015).

17. CNN, http://money.cnn.com/2014/10/09/technology/six-figures-to-play-video-games/ (last visited Jan. 18, 2015).

18. NY Times, http://www.nytimes.com/2014/08/31/technology/esports-explosion-brings-opportunity-riches-for-video-gamers.html?_r=0 (last visited Jan. 18, 2015).

19. NY Times, http://www.nytimes.com/2014/11/16/technology/esports-call-of-duty-nadeshot-celebrity-success.html?emc=eta1;http://money.cnn.com/2014/10/09/technology/six-figures-to-play-video-games/ (last visited Jan. 18, 2015).; The Economist, http://www.economist.com/blogs/economist-explains/2014/05/economist-explains-11?zid=319&ah=17af09b0281b01505c226b1e574f5cc1 (last visited Jan. 18, 2015).

20. CNN Money, http://money.cnn.com/ magazines/business2/business2_archive/2005/12/01/8364581/index.htm, (last visited Jan. 18, 2015); *see also, e.g.,* Business Week, http://www.businessweek.com/the_thread/techbeat/archives/2006/11/second_lifes_fi.html (last visited Jan. 18, 2015).

in-world business owners in *Second Life* as well.[21] Most large virtual worlds have their own currency and in-game currency exchanges, and according to *Second Life's* developer, Linden Labs, the *Second Life* in-world currency exchange, called Lindex, converts $100 million worth of U.S. currency annually to Linden dollars.[22]

Videogaming has certainly permeated different sectors of society, including academia. In 2009, over 250 universities offered courses in videogames,[23] a number which could only have increased by now, and colleges such as the University of Southern California, MIT, and the University of Utah offer various types of degrees in videogames.[24] Robert Morris University-Illinois has awarded a partial "athletic" scholarship to a competitive *League of Doom* team, which plays in a league against other universities, and other colleges are considering awarding scholarships for egaming as well.[25] Yahoo and ESPN even have channels dedicated to egaming.

Because of the size of this economic activity, an understanding of the business of videogames is necessary for any lawyer who wants to make his or her living in the industry, and is helpful to any student in a videogame law course to understand some of the legal/business issues in videogame cases.

Below we give you an idea of the business surrounding how a game is made, followed by a primer on the different business models used to market videogames.

§ 1.31 The Business of Creating a Videogame

Although all games are created uniquely, the process by which games are brought to the market has some common features. There are generally three indispensable roles in getting a videogame from concept to market: (1) the Game Developer; (2) the Producer; and (3) the Publisher or Distributor. (Many large games would also add a fourth "indispensable" individual, the "Quality Assurance" Manager). Of course, the roles can become blurred, and such blurring was especially true in the early days of the industry when it took only one or two people to turn out a game. As time went on, and games became increasingly complex with teams of more than a hundred working to produce a game, these functions became somewhat more defined, but still some individuals have responsibilities in more than one capacity.

For the most complex games out today, it is more likely that one of the large videogame companies assumes all the described roles under its corporate umbrella, assigning its employees to the various tasks. These are companies like Microsoft, Sony, Nintendo, Blizzard, EA, Sega, Take-Two Interactive (the parent of Rockstar), Unisoft and Capcom.

Indeed, Ailin Graef's story is an interesting one. Shortly after being featured on CNN and in *Business Week* for having accumulated her virtual fortune, she sold much of her in-game portfolio and used the proceeds to finance a real world start-up company, Anshe Chung Studios, which develops 3D environments for web sites, and in 2008 employed more than 80 people. *See,* http://acs.anshechung.com (last visited Jan. 18, 2015). Anshe Chung is the name of her avatar in *Second Life*.

21. Second Life Database, http://secondlife.com/whatis/economy_stats.php (last visited June 26, 2008).

22. Second Life Database, http://secondlife.com/whatis/economy.php (last visited May 17, 2008).

23. US News, http://www.usnews.com/science/articles/2009/10/16/colleges-offering-video-game-courses (last visited Jan. 18, 2015).

24. Game Design Schools, http://game-designschools.com/colleges-offering-degrees-in-video-game-design/ (last visited Jan. 18, 2015).

25. Inside Higher Ed, https://www.insidehighered.com/news/2014/06/23/illinois-university-makes-league-legends-varsity-sport (last visited Jan. 18, 2015).

Similarly, there are companies like Linden Labs, which is responsible for *Second Life*, that play a similar all-encompassing role in developing, producing, and maintaining the virtual world. To give truth to the old adage that what is old is new again, in the last few years, with the rise of mobile app gaming, there is a growing segment of the market where only one or two individuals can once again develop a game and get it to market in the Apple App Store, Google Play, or even directly to users via streaming.

A brief description of each of these roles follows.

Game Developer

The Game Developer is the individual who comes up with the idea for the game. Often he or she is also known as the "writer" or the "game designer." Generally this individual (or his or her team) is responsible for coming up with game concepts, general rules of gameplay, identifying the target audience, and the target platforms and languages for the game.

Producer

The Producer is the individual who is responsible for getting the game made. He or she takes over the project from the Game Developer and ensures the final game is on budget, on schedule, and has all legal entitlements. The Producer ensures that the game will work on all desired platforms and operating systems, and is properly translated in all desired languages. If it is an "independent" producer, i.e., one who is not employed by a Distributor, the Producer often initially funds the project. Such independent Producers typically end up with the intellectual property rights to the game.

Publisher/Distributor

The Publisher or Distributor is the one who takes the completed game from the Producer and gets it to the user, either indirectly through retailers like GameStop, Google Play, and amazon.com, or directly through digital downloads. The Publisher is also in charge of advertising the game. Further, the Publisher handles the post-release complaints from consumers and, with Internet based and networked games, the Publisher downloads software fixes. In games that are serialized, or in massive multiplayer online role playing games ("MMORPGs") that never close, the Publisher keeps a production team employed to send out new levels, characters, challenges, lands, and "chapters" every few weeks. Some Distributors advance funding to the Producer, or directly finance the games with promised payment to the Game Developer, and if it is the funding source, it is the Publisher that ends up with the intellectual property rights to the game. Typically the Publisher is also responsible for securing the appropriate industry ratings in each country in which the game is distributed, and the Publisher tracks down and litigates game piracy.

* * *

Just as there are common roles to fill in the production of videogames, there are common stages in the development and production of games. Again, the lines separating these phases are fluid, as some parts of two of the phases can be occurring at once, and there is game-to-game variance as well. But generally, getting a game from concept to market and beyond has four recognized stages: (1) Pre-Production; (2) Production; (3) Product Testing; and (4) Post-Production. Again, each is briefly summarized below, along with the role of lawyers in each phase.

Pre-Production

Pre-Production describes the process of getting a game from concept to the Producer. The Game Developer (or his or her team) is the primary driver of this phase, where the object and theme of the game is put on paper, and general rules for gameplay, core features, operating systems and platforms, costs, schedule for the finished project, necessary licenses, desired game engines, and proposed staffing to finish the game, are identified. Main characters are also identified and drawn during this period. These days, it is becoming more typical for an "alpha" version of the game to be created during pre-production, which is the first functional version of the game with major gameplay elements included. If the Game Developer is not an employee of a Distributor, the Pre-Production phase often ends in a "pitch" to the Producer and/or Distributor to get funding for the remainder of the project. Pre-Production takes somewhere between 10–20% of the total time for a project.

Lawyers are (or at least should be) involved in Pre-Production. If a game is based on an existing product, such as a movie, TV show, book, etc., licenses need to be obtained. Licenses are also necessary if another's patents are used in game creation. Lawyer involvement is also required for the acquisition of any publicity rights if the voices or features of particular individuals are to be used in the game, as well as for the acquisition of rights for any product to be used for in-game advertising. Further, employment contracts, work for hire agreements, and non-disclosure agreements for those who create and produce the games, are often negotiated and signed during this period, as are agreements with the platform manufacturers to which the game will be offered, like Sony for the PS4 or Microsoft for the Xbox. Finally, to the extent that the Pre-Production phase ends with a financing arrangement with a Producer or Distributor, that agreement will eventually divvy up the revenues from the game and set forth when the game is to be finished, and so lawyer involvement in its negotiation and documentation is prudent.

Production

Production is where the game comes together. Art, sound effects, musical score, programming, and languages, are all assimilated into the game. The Producer is the driving force during this phase, and his or her job is to make sure that everyone is on schedule and, more importantly, on budget, especially when the invariable technical difficulties are encountered as different parts of the game are joined together. This phase takes over 50% of the total time allocated for the project and ends when a workable beta version of the game is produced. A beta version is a feature and asset complete version of the game. The key to a beta version is that the Producer believes only those things identified as "bugs" will be changed, and no new characteristics will be added.

Lawyers are involved during this phase in documenting any employment or related contracts that were not settled during the Pre-Production phase, and in documenting any modifications to contracts promising delivery of the game on a certain date or promising funding on certain conditions. Further, End User Licensing Agreements ("EULAs"), and Terms of Use ("TOU") and Terms of Service ("TOS") Agreements, which regulate the rights of the gamer and the intellectual property holder of the game, are drafted toward the end of this phase.

Testing

During this phase, the beta version is distributed to willing users. In those games with a separate Quality Assurance manager, he or she is the driving force as the game is tested. Who gets beta versions has become very important to major games, as beta version Internet buzz can make or break a game. The Distributor must send out enough beta copies to ensure that the game is working on all desired operating systems, and that any language translations for dialogue or graphic images make sense. Further, the first beta versions are generally sent to the platform manufacturers for their approval during the testing phase. Finally, the Distributor submits the beta version of the game to industry ratings groups in each country of expected distribution, such as the Entertainment Software Ratings Board ("ESRB") for the United States and the Pan European Game Information ("PEGI") organization for the European Union. For a large game, beta testing can take as long as three months and ends when there is a final, "shippable" version of the game.

Lawyers polish the EULA and TOS/TOU Agreements during this phase. Once the game is in "final" shippable form, it is eligible for copyright protection and the holder of the intellectual property rights to the game will typically file the final product with the Copyright Office for copyright protection.

Post-Production

Once the game is in shippable form, the Publisher or Distributor takes over the process of marketing the game, distributing the game to retailers or directly to users, and handling questions, technical glitches, and complaints from game players. Here the Quality Assurance manager (for games where such an individual is attached) again assumes control. With the advent of Internet connectivity and constant updating of games, Distributors are now also responsible for keeping a production team of Game Developers, Producers, and Quality Assurance officers to continue to introduce new levels, characters, weapons, etc. In MMORPGs like *League of Legends*, *World of Warcraft*, or *Second Life*, Post-Production also includes maintaining order in the world, hosting chat rooms, conducting in-game auctions, issuing and regulating in-game currency, and selling in-game real estate and other items, etc.

Up until Post-Production, most lawyers involved in game creation are transactional lawyers. Once the game is released, however, litigators often become involved. They bring and defend the intellectual property and financial dispute lawsuits that can arise among Producers, Game Developers, and Distributors after games are distributed. Lawyers are also involved in warranty and class action consumer-related lawsuits, as well as suits like *Brown v. Ent. Merchs. Ass'n*, 564 U.S. __, 131 S. Ct. 2729 (2011) which challenged state regulation of videogames. Finally, as serialized games continue, lawyers continue to do the intellectual property and employment contract work mentioned earlier.

* * *

The development cost of early videogames like *Pong* and *Space Invaders* was relatively small, since the game could be developed by one or two people over a couple of months. During that time (the early 1970s), the more expensive proposition was the hardware to display the game—either the arcade game with its expensive large CRT screens or home consoles, such as the Magnavox Odyssey. With the current ability to distribute games in mobile applications, development costs for some casual games can again be, and often are, relatively small.

For large, complicated games like *Grand Theft Auto V*, and *Call of Duty: Ghosts*, development costs can exceed $250 million.[26] However, such investments were justified as *GTA V* had $800 million in direct sales to users *on its first day of release*,[27] and *Ghosts* sold over $1 billion to retailers on its release day.[28] These games are, of course, parts of franchises

---

26. GAME RANT, http://gamerant.com/grand-theft-auto-5-development-cost/ (last visited Jan. 18, 2015).

27. CINEMA BLEND, http://www.cinemablend.com/games/Call-Duty-Ghosts-Sales-Hit-1-Billion-Did-It-Outsell-GTA-5-60368.html (last visited Jan. 18, 2015).

28. *Id.*

which have a track record, making the expenditures a reasonable gamble, but they nonetheless required a well-funded videogame publisher to be able to make the investment. For the more common situation, the latest figures suggest that the average reasonably sophisticated videogame has a development budget of $10 million for a single platform game, and $25–$40 million for a multi-platform one.[29]

An emerging trend is to finance games through some sort of crowdfunding, such as kickstarter.com or gofundme.com, or even by direct funding from future users. The undisputed champion of this later method is Cloud Imperium's game entitled *Star Citizen*. In 2012, Cloud Imperium had a clever game description and a few workable features for the game, such as exploding space ships. It then went on various game sites to advertise the game. The pitch was that if a gamer pre-purchased the game, which was years away from being in "shippable" form, Cloud Imperium would send the customer a monthly update on the progress of the game's development, give the pre-purchasers a say in characteristics to be included in the final version of the game, send the customer free alpha iterations of the game as it was assembled, and give these early "investors" the opportunity to purchase additional features, such as space yachts, as they were developed. By October 2014, it had raised over $56 million in pre-orders and purchases of features from over 600,000 gamers, and was on schedule to deliver a final game in 2016.[30]

The idea of giving users a say in what is included in the final versions of a game during the game's development seems to be catching on. Some of the larger videogame companies, such as Sony Online Entertainment and Epic Games, are distributing interim pre-beta versions of games during creation and development to eager gamers, seeking feedback on desired features and the generation of a positive "buzz" about the game.[31]

§ 1.32 The Business Models Used to Generate Videogame Revenue

Those involved in videogame production and distribution do so to make money. This requires a business model to generate revenue. One way of looking at various revenue models over time is to split it into three phases: (1) the "ship-it-and-forget-it" model where the manufacturer expected a game to keep a user's interest for a only limited period of time, and were constantly working on new releases to replace the game in the hearts of the gaming community when interest in it waned; (2) the "subscription" model, where users would pay a monthly fee for the right to enter a MMORPG; and (3) the "freemium" model, whereby a user can download the program for free, but pays for upgraded versions of the game and for in-game amenities. (Note that the developers of many MMORPGs also sell such upgrades and in-game weapons, real estate, etc.) These days, many developers also have ancillary streams of revenue for their games, like in-game advertising or selling rights to their game to other intellectual property creators. All of these models are discussed below.

Before describing each model in greater detail, however, a couple of points can be made. One is that the various revenue models followed changes in technology. Indeed, some have chronicled the business history of the videogame industry according to the

---

29. Develop, http://www.develop-online.net/news/study-average-dev-costs-as-high-as-28m/0106030 (last visited Jan. 18, 2015).

30. LA Times, http://www.latimes.com/business/la-fi-1019-star-citizen-20141017-story.html#page=1 (last visited Jan. 18, 2015).

31. Fortune, http://fortune.com/2014/11/07/rob-pardo-blizzard/ (last visited Jan. 18, 2015).

computing power of the hardware involved and Internet and network connectivity.[32] However, the focus here is on the business revenue models recognized by the industry, and how those models (in conjunction with technology) shaped the history of the products made available to the public. The second, related point is that the industry has consistently tried to get on as many platforms as possible, within each revenue model. So if games were played on consoles, designers created handhelds like GameBoy and Game Genie, to increase the markets for their products. This is especially true today, where getting gamers to play on phones, tablets, consoles, as well as computers, has become a driving force in the industry.

The Ship-it-and-Forget-It Model

The ship-it-and-forget-it model itself has had roughly three phases. Phases overlapped and all still remain today, but in different times, each has had an ascendency. The phases are: (1) arcade play; (2) retail sales; and (3) digital distribution.

Arcade Sales

In the early days of the industry (the early 1970s) arcade gaming certainly trumped home gaming and drove the revenue streams of the industry—a quarter (or 100 yen coin) at a time. Arcade games were faster, brighter, and certainly more complex than anything that could be delivered at home—the only home console during that period was Magnavox's Odyssey—and arcade games found a world-wide audience, although most of the revenues were generated in North America and Asia. Starting with *Space Invaders* in 1978, and continuing with *Galaxian, Pac Man, Battlezone,* and the like in the next few years, the arcade side of the business accounted for over $8 billion in revenue in 1981 (which would translate to approximately $20 billion in 2014 dollars).[33] In North America, the games were first placed in bars, but it didn't take long for dedicated arcades, and restaurant/arcade combinations such as Chuck E. Cheese and Dave & Buster's, to populate the scene.

The late 1980s saw a steady decrease in the popularity of arcade gaming. By 1991, worldwide arcade revenue had fallen to $2.1 billion. But by then Distributors had begun to take more of a role in developing content. This meant more funding for better and more spectacular games. Games with true 3D graphics started appearing, first person fighter games like *Street Fighter* and *Mortal Kombat* became popular, and motion controller hydraulic games where, e.g., the gamer could "ride" a replica car or motorcycle, such as *Virtual Racing,* gave the player experiences that again could not be duplicated in home consoles and brought a resurgence in arcades. Revenue in 1994 was back up to $7 billion, but that turned out to be arcade games' last revenue blip. As the graphics and speed of home systems increased in the mid-1990s, followed by 3D-graphics cards and enhanced sound cards available for home computers and consoles, and finally with the advent of the Internet allowing for multiplayer interconnectivity, arcade gaming in the United States

---

32. Joost van Dreunen, *A Business History of Video Games: Revenue Models from 1980 to Today,* http://www.superdataresearch.com/content/uploads/2011/01/BusinessHistoryofVideoGames.pdf. (last visited Jan. 18, 2015).

33. The Philadelphia Enquirer, *Can Lasers Save Videogames?,* (1984), http://nl.newsbank.com/nlsearch/we/Archives?p_product=PI&s_site=philly&p_multi=PI&p_theme=realcities&p_action=search&p_maxdocs=200&p_topdoc=1&p_text_direct-0=0EB29715971BCAA2&p_field_direct-0=document_id&p_perpage=10&p_sort=YMD_date:D&s_trackval=GooglePM.

Table 1.1 Highest-Grossing Arcade Videogames

Game	Release Year	Hardware Units Sold	Gross Revenue (US$ Without Inflation)	Gross Revenue (US$ With 2014 Inflation)
Space Invaders	1978	360,000 (up to 1980)	$2.702 billion (up to 1982)	$9.77 billion
Pac-Man	1980	400,000 (up to 1982)	$2.5 billion (up to 1999)	$7.16 billion
Street Fighter II	1991	200,000 (up to 1992)	$2.312 billion (up to 1995)	$4 billion
Donkey Kong	1981	132,000 (up to 1982)	$280 million (up to 1982) (US hardware sales)	$726 million (US hardware sales)
Ms. Pac-Man	1981	125,000 (up to 1988)		
Asteroids	1979	100,000 (up to 2001)	$800 million (up to 1991)	$1.39 billion
Galaxian	1979	40,000 (in the US up to 1982)		
Donkey Kong Jr.	1982	30,000 (in the US up to 1982)		
NBA Jam	1993	20,000 (up to 2013)	$1 billion (up to 2010)	$1.08 billion
Mortal Kombat	1992	24,000 (up to 2002)	$570 million (up to 2002)	$747 million
Tron	1982	800 (in the US up to 1982)	$45 million (up to 1983)	$102 million
Pong	1972	8,500–19,000	$11 million (up to 1973)	$58.4 million

plummeted. The nadir for arcade gaming was in 2004, where it accounted for only $844 million in revenue.[34]

By the new millennia, players had figured out that paying a few dollars for thirty minutes of play in an arcade made no sense when, for the same few dollars, the player could rent the game for weeks worth of play, or for a few dollars more, the player could own it. As such, distributors stopped putting their new releases into arcade games, leaving arcade games now as a niche part of the industry in the United States, with such games appearing mostly at miniature golf courses, in resort hotels' "activity rooms," Dave & Buster's, and the like.

In some countries, however, videogame arcades have remained popular. In 2009, the arcade market in Japan generated $6 billion, beating out both the home console and the mobile phone game markets, which earned $3.5 billion and $2 billion, respectively.[35]

---

34. EAST VALLEY TRIBUNE, *Video Killed the Arcade Star*, (2006), http://www.eastvalleytribune.com/article_9b22d9ea-1810-5465-8bd9-a4e3204de569.html?mode=story.

35. Yukiharu Sambe, *Japan's Arcade Games and Their Technology*, (2009), http://link.springer.com/chapter/10.1007/978-3-642-04052-8_62.

Table 1.1 above is a recent chart published in Wikipedia, listing some of the more popular arcade games. The figures include the revenues garnered from game play and from sale of the machines.[36]

Retail Sales

As arcade sales waned in the 1980s, home consoles became the principal revenue driver for the industry. These units, and their cartridges, were initially largely sold in brick and mortar stores like Wal-Mart, Target, GameStop, and Best Buy, but over time were also sold online by retailers like amazon.com. The first consoles in this time period had only 8-bit processors, but they had many features that appealed to gamers, such as D-pad controllers, enhanced color palettes and sound channels, and 3D graphics capabilities. The Nintendo Entertainment System ("NES") clearly dominated the market in the 1980s; over 7 million NES consoles were sold in 1988 and by 1990, 30% of American households owned an NES.[37] There were two reasons NES dominated this era: (1) it was first console on the market; and (2) Nintendo had sufficient market power to lock up games exclusively on the NES for two years (a market power that no platform has today). Hence, for some period of time, if a gamer wanted to play *Super Mario Brothers* or *The Legend of Zelda* at home, an NES was a necessary product. By the beginning of the 1990s, other consoles had gained a foothold in the market, such as the Sega Master System and Atari's 7800 system.

Home computers were becoming more popular in the late 1980s and early 1990s, but the market penetration of computers was still much less than gaming consoles in the United States. For example, in 1990, when 30% of households owned an NES, only 23% of American households owned a computer,[38] and those with a computer usually did not use it for gaming. In 1989, for example, the U.S. market for cartridge games played on consoles was over $2 billion, whereas computer based gaming software generated less than $300 million in retail sales.[39]

The retail sector of the industry is still significant today, but it is on the wane. Its apex was in 2007, where it accounted for 81% of the industry's revenue, but market share has dropped about 5% a year since.[40] Retail sales are now mostly hardware driven, with most gamers downloading software directly.[41] The future for retailers will likely see more complex home controllers, with the *Kinect* and some 3D helmets from Oculus already on the market, and more immersive connected body suits to come.

Another reason retail sales are on the decline is that videogame manufacturers are now pushing to get their games on mobile platforms, like tablets and smart phones. With direct downloads and mobile hardware purchases from AT&T and Verizon, retailers are simply not participating in the videogame market as they used to. To give an idea of the expected

---

36. WIKIPEDIA, *The History of Video Games,* http://en.wikipedia.org/wiki/History_of_video_games (last visited Jan. 18, 2015).

37. COMPUTER GAMING WORLD, *Fusion, Transfusion or Confusion / Future Directions In Computer Entertainment,* 26 (Dec. 1990).

38. *Id.*

39. COMPUTER GAMING WORLD, *Soaring Into 1989,* 8 (Mar. 1989).

40. Joost van Dreunen, *A Business History of Video Games: Revenue Models from 1980 to Today,* 6 (2011), http://www.superdataresearch.com/content/uploads/2011/01/BusinessHistoryofVideoGames.pdf.

41. *Id.* at 5.

ramp up in mobile gaming, Digi-Capital foresees the markets as shown in Figure 1.1, and Big Fish Gaming estimated in 2014 that by 2016, mobile revenue will exceed console revenue for the first time and will total over $27 billion.

More non-mobile gameplay is taking place on computers, with specially fitted gaming computers like the Envy helping the trend, but still most gamers prefer the dedicated features of a console.[42] The total sales of the latest (128-bit) versions of consoles through the end of 2014 are as follows, but recently it appears the PS4 is the global choice for gamers.[43]

Figure 1.1 Global Videogames Sector Revenue ($B)

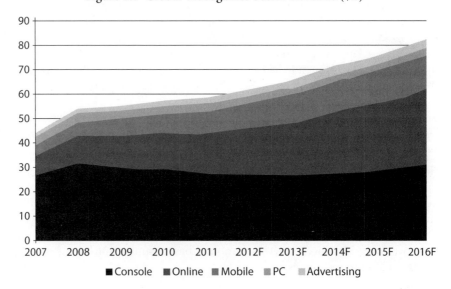

Figure 1.2 Global Hardware Totals

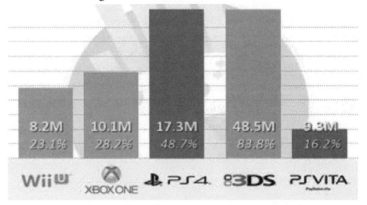

42. PERFORMANCE PSU, http://www.performancepsu.com/gaming/percentage-console-vs-pc-gamersinfographic/ (last visited Jan. 18, 2015).

43. VG CHARTZ, http://www.vgchartz.com/ (last visited Jan. 18, 2015).

Figure 1.3 Month-to-Month Sales for Packaged Entertainment Software

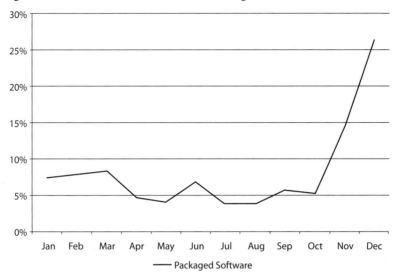

Another reason for the decline in the retail sector of the industry is related to the seasonal nature of retail software sales as shown in Figure 1.3.[44]

As a result, videogame advertising, production, etc. is crowded into a two month window in retail establishments, which requires manufacturers to increase advertising costs, cut prices, and add "free" features, in an attempt to stand above the crowd. To avoid this problem, Distributors much prefer direct digital distribution of games, which is the third, and most recent, phase of the ship-it-and-forget-it revenue model.

Digital Distribution

Most game software is now directly digitally downloaded to users.[45] While early generation consoles allowed for direct downloads, this distribution medium did not become very popular until the mid-1990s, and even then it was only used in fits and starts because of persistent technical problems in downloading and storing large files.[46] These problems have now largely been eliminated, and digital distribution has smoothed out the cyclical nature of software purchasing, and tends to be cheaper for users since brick and mortar and distribution center overhead is eliminated.[47]

As MMORPGs became more popular, the economic success of the ship-it-and-forget-it model has suffered. But a comeback for ship-it-and-forget it games has recently occurred with the popularity of "casual" games, i.e., inexpensive games which are intended for

---

44. Joost van Dreunen, *A Business History of Video Games: Revenue Models from 1980 to Today*, 5 (2011), http://www.superdataresearch.com/content/uploads/2011/01/BusinessHistoryofVideoGames.pdf.

45. Sociology of Video Games, http://sociologyofvideogames.com/2014/04/26/esa-2014-facts-and-stats-about-video-game-consumption/ (last visited Jan. 18, 2015).

46. Joost van Dreunen, *A Business History of Video Games: Revenue Models from 1980 to Today*, 6 (2011), http://www.superdataresearch.com/content/uploads/2011/01/BusinessHistoryofVideoGames.pdf.

47. *Id.*

limited play such as *Bejeweled,* re-issues of classics like *Tetris,* and various versions of *Solitaire* designed for mobile platforms.

The Subscription Model

The idea of paying a monthly fee for access to a game started relatively early in the videogame industry, with CompuServe charging $12/hour for modem access to its stable of games as early as 1964.[48] But what we think of subscriptions today—a $10–$15/month payment to a game distributor—really began in the late 1990s, as hard disc capacity grew and Internet and network connections became faster and more reliable. Many point to *Ultima Online* as the first really successful subscription game, as it had 100,000 subscribers at $10/month in 1997. The popularity of subscriptions has only increased since then. *World of Warcraft* currently has over 3 million subscribers in North America,[49] and about 7.5 million monthly subscribers worldwide.[50] Table 1.2 lists the most popular subscription websites in 2013, along with a list of the revenue they generated.[51]

One change that subscription games have ushered in vis-à-vis ship it and forget it models is long term contracts for writers and producers. Players now expect new scenes, characters and challenges every few weeks and so, as with a serialized TV show, writers are signed to five and seven year contracts and characters introduced in year one come back to be major players in year four.

Table 1.2 Top Subscription-Based MMO Titles, 2013—Worldwide

Rank	Title	Publisher	Worldwide Revenues ($Mil)	Market Share 2013
1	World of Warcraft (East & West)	Activision/Blizzard	$1,041	38%
2	Lineage 1	NCsoft	$253	9%
3	TERA: Online	NHN Corporation	$236	8%
4	Star Wars: The Old Republic	Electronic Arts	$165	6%
5	Lord of the Rings Online	Turbine, Inc.	$104	4%
6	EVE Online	CCP Games	$93	3%
7	Aion	NCsoft	$88	3%
8	Blade and Soul	NCsoft	$65	2%
9	Lineage 2	NCsoft	$45	2%
10	RIFT	Trion	$36	1%
Worldwide Market for Subscription-Based MMOs, 2013			$2,882	

---

48. *Id.* at 9.

49. *Id.*

50. Statista, http://www.statista.com/statistics/276601/number-of-world-of-warcraft-subscribers-by-quarter/ (last visited Jan. 18, 2015).

51. Game Spot, http://www.gamespot.com/articles/wow-was-the-top-subscription-mmo-in-2013-star-wars/1100-6421191/ (last visited Jan. 18, 2015).

While the numbers who are signing up for subscription games has begun to decline since 2010,[52] another segment of the subscription market is increasing. Companies like Big Fish and Pogo give access to a number of bundled, casual games for a relatively inexpensive payment of $5–$6/month. To show the success of that model, in 2010, Big Fish's revenues from such a model was over $130 million.[53]

The "Freemium" Model

The latest revenue model for the industry is the so-called "freemium" model, where a basic level of the game can be downloaded free of charge. This is also known as the "Free to Play" or "F2P" model within the industry. Developers make money by: (1) selling a premium version of the game; and (2) selling amenities within the game, e.g., a fence around the user's farm in *Farmville*, or extra gems in *Clash of Clans,* often for less than $3 (giving them the title of "microtransactions" in the industry). Giving away a game for free means there is no piracy problem for the Developer to worry about, and is an easy way to get users drawn in and "hooked" on the game. But progress in the free version of the game is often slow, and defeating puzzles and monsters can be difficult without the purchase of weapons and aids provided by the developer.

An example of an additional fee being required for a premium version of the game is *Second Life.* It is free to download the regular version and create an avatar to roam most of the world, but if the "resident" (Linden Labs' preferred term for a user) wants additional features, such as the right to "build" a home in a popular area, or access to certain areas of *Second Life* such as the "adult's only" section, then a premium monthly subscription (at $48/year or $10/month) has to be purchased.

Microtransactions can also add up quickly. GameSpot reports that in mid-2014, SuperCell, the Developer of *Clash of Titans,* was making over $650,000 per day on the sale of in-game amenities,[54] and *Candy Crush* made $240 million in microtransactions in 2013.[55] The theory behind microtransactions was explained by an industry insider:

> In [freemium] games, designers give players a special power for free at first, and then take it away and offer it back at a price.
>
> Zynga, the creator of *Farmville*, calls this fun pain, according to [Ramin] Shokrizade [a game designer]. "The idea is that, if you make the consumer uncomfortable enough, and then tell them that for money we'll make you less uncomfortable, then [they] will give us money."
>
> Kids, Shokrizade explains, are especially susceptible to this ...[56]

---

52. *See, e.g.,* Ars Technica, *http://arstechnica.com/gaming/2012/08/good-riddance-the-death-of-online-gamings-monthly-subscription-model/* (last visited Jan. 18, 2015).

53. Joost van Dreunen, *A Business History of Video Games: Revenue Models from 1980 to Today,* 10 (2011), http://www.superdataresearch.com/content/uploads/2011/01/BusinessHistoryofVideoGames.pdf.

54. Game Spot, http://www.gamespot.com/articles/report-clash-of-clans-generates-654-000-per-day/1100-6417656/ (last visited Jan. 18, 2015).

55. PR Web, http://www.prweb.com/releases/2013/7/prweb10970004.htm (last visited Jan. 18, 2015).

56. NPR, *Minecraft's Business Model: A Video Game That Leaves You Alone,* http://www.npr.org/blogs/money/2014/09/16/348770036/minecrafts-business-model-a-video-game-that-leaves-you-alone (last visited Jan. 18, 2015).

The ease of marketing microtransactions to children in games targeted to them has not gone unnoticed. In 2014, Google agreed to refund over $19 million in such transactions,[57] and Apple agreed to refund over $32 million,[58] to settle claims that it was too easy to unknowingly order the proprietary features, increased functionality, or virtual goods that are the staples of the freemium model's microtransactions. Primarily, but not exclusively, these claims were made about games that were targeted to children.

Note also that in Chapter 14, we explain in some detail how certain marketing firms have created an algorithm which attempts to categorize, in real time, how eager a player is to buy his or her way out of trouble by purchasing a "cheat," a weapon, etc. This, in turn, allows manufacturers to offer in-game amenities to different players at different prices, depending on how likely they are predicted to pay for help.

Many in the industry believe almost all but the most "casual" games will eventually be distributed on the freemium model:

> The future of all games is with free-to-play and microtransactions, according to the man behind *Candy Crush*.
>
> During an interview with IGN, King Games Guru (that's his real job title) Tommy Palm spoke about other, more traditional games publishers exploring the free-to-play models frequently adopted by King.
>
> "The micro-transaction is so strong and it's definitely a much better model. I think all companies have to transition over to that. If you talk to many hardcore gamers, they're not happy about it right now, but if you asked them about the long term, 'Do you want to continue playing your favorite game for years to come?' And the answer will be 'yes.'"
>
> Palm went on to stress the importance of sensible pricing and making games truly F2P. "I think for companies it is very important to find a good balance. Free-to-play games are difficult to do, and you really need to be good at making it feel balanced to the gamers. So it's not too greedy."[59]

One exception to contemporary games being distributed on a freemium model are "diary" games, in which a game recreates activities of a real person's life. One of these is *That Dragon, Cancer*, which the parents of Joel Green, a 5-year-old who died of cancer, created to memorialize the life of their son. The player plays until the "Joel" avatar dies. Others in this genre include *The Marriage, Gravitation* and *dys4ia*.

Ancillary Income

Any business looks for alternate streams of income other than its core enterprise. The two that have arisen in the videogame industry are: (1) in-game advertising; and (2) having videogames be the subjects of other intellectual property franchises, such as movies, TV shows, novels, and Internet serialization.

---

57. Game Spot, http://www.gamespot.com/articles/google-must-pay-19m-over-unfair-microtransactions/1100-6422122/ (last visited Jan. 18, 2015).

58. Game Spot, http://www.gamespot.com/articles/apple-to-pay-at-least-32-5-million-to-refund-kids-in-app-purchases/1100-6417149/ (last visited Jan. 18, 2015).

59. IGN, http://www.ign.com/articles/2014/04/14/the-future-of-games-is-free-to-play-says-candy-crush-developer (last visited Jan. 18, 2015).

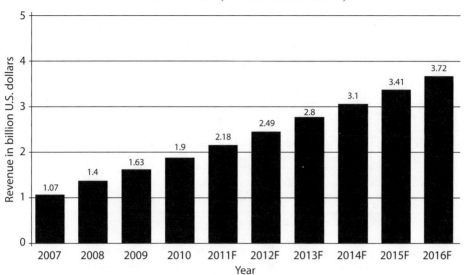

**Figure 1.5 Global Videogames Advertising Revenue
from 2007 to 2016 (in Billion U.S. Dollars)**

For developers who are good at it, adding in-game advertising can be very lucrative. For example, *Flappy Bird* was, at one point, making $50,000 per day from in-game advertising,[60] and Statista estimates the overall market for in-game advertising exceeds $3 billion.

Often, popular videogames are based on movies and TV shows, with *Star Wars* and *Star Trek* being examples. But a recent phenomenon flips this traditional scenario, and now videogames are licensing their rights to studios to become movies, TV shows, and the like. The prime example of a game becoming a movie is *World of Warcraft*. In late 2014, Legendary Pictures completed shooting for the movie *Warcraft*, which is based on the game and is wound around a conflict between humans and orcs; the movie is currently scheduled for release in 2016. Similarly, some videogames have served as the basis for TV shows, such as *The Adventures of Super Mario Brothers* and *Where in the World is Carmen Sandiego?* There are also Internet series, often available on special YouTube channels, which are based on games, such as *The Legend of Zelda*.[61] Finally, there are many novels, both graphic and otherwise, that are based on videogames, such as *Doom* and *Call of Duty*.

* * *

The videogame market is international, of course, and any large videogame developer would be foolish to ignore producing multilingual versions of its game. Table 1.3, taken from wikia.com gives an idea of the current distribution of revenue from different regions.[62]

The Gaming industry statistics for 2014 give us some interesting insights to gamer habits and demographics around the globe. The average age of a gamer falls in the 30–35 age range

---

60. Quora, https://www.quora.com/How-much-does-it-cost-to-develop-a-video-game (last visited Jan. 18, 2015).

61. For additional internet shows, *see* Prima Games, http://www.primagames.com/games/halo-4/news/best-video-game-related-web-shows-you-should-be-wa (last visited Jan. 18, 2015).

62. Wikia, http://vgsales.wikia.com/wiki/Video_game_industry (last visited Jan. 18, 2015).

Table 1.3 Regional Videogame Industry Revenues

Region/Country	2013	2012	2011	2010
Asia-Pacific	$49.623 billion	$44.063 billion	$42.358 billion	$38.77 billion
Japan	$22.29 billion	$22.29 billion	$23.04 billion	$21.13 billion
China	$14 billion	$9.8 billion	$7.3 billion	$6.9 billion
South Korea	$9.64 billion	$9.23 billion	$9.082 billion	$7.784 billion
Australia	$2 billion	$1.16 billion	$1.5 billion	$1.67 billion
Taiwan	$825 million	$773 million	$713 million	$660 million
Indonesia	$492 million	$463 million	$429 million	$396 million
India	$376 million	$347 million	$294 million	$230 million
Europe	$20 billion	$21.3 billion	$21.3 billion	$20.66 billion
United Kingdom	$3.67 billion	$2.6 billion	$5.4 billion	$3.812 billion
France	$6.9 billion	$4 billion	$3.352 billion	$3.416 billion
Germany	$3.7 billion	$3.36 billion	$2.757 billion	$2.659 billion
Italy	$1.961 billion	$1.85 billion	$1.428 billion	$1.371 billion
Russia	$1.5 billion	$1.3 billion	$1.4 billion	$1.207 billion
Netherlands	$807 million	$807 million	$809 million	$801 million
North America	$22.8 billion	$20.7 billion	$20.7 billion	$20.49 billion
United States	$17.39 billion	$17.1 billion	$16.6 billion	$18.58 billion
Canada	$2.3 billion	$2.773 billion	$2.171 billion	$1.682 billion
Latin America	$3.9 billion	$5.4 billion	$5.4 billion	$4.74 billion
Brazil	$1.4 billion	$2 billion	$2 billion	$391 million
Mexico	$1.56 billion	$1.2 billion	$636 million	$1.25 billion
Middle East	$2.6 billion	$2.6 billion	$1.983 billion	$1.2 billion
Arab World		$1.31 billion	$1.31 billion	
Turkey		$593 million	$593 million	$50 million
Israel	$89 million	$85 million	$80 million	$76 million

within the U.S. and over three-fourths of all gamers play for more than one hour each week. Examining the statistics of today against the State of Gaming in the not-so-distant past, it is easy to see how the generation of gamers that cut their teeth on *Mega Man 2* have graduated to making gaming a part of their daily lives. These facts truly speak to the passion gamers have had ever since gaming burst onto the scene just a few decades ago.

US:

59% of Americans play videogames

62% of all gamers are adults

48% of players are female (up from 42% in 2012) although videogame purchases are split 50/50 among men and women

Average of 2 gamers per household

51% of households own at least one console

Average age of a videogame purchaser: 35. Average age of a videogame player: 31

22% of the worldwide videogame workforce is female with 24% of the total developers being female.

77% of gamers play at least one hour a week

36% play games on their smart phone

Parents are involved in their kids' game purchases 89% of the time

79 percent of parents place time limits on videogame playing, compared with 78 percent who limit Internet usage and 72 percent who limit TV viewing

UK:

The average UK gamer is 35

Most are male

Plays for almost 3 hours a day

The average gamer fights with their partner over their gaming hobby twice a week, with some 15% of people saying they've broken up over the amount of time spent gaming.

The UK is just behind the U.S. in terms of iPad game purchases

Other Countries:

Japan and China lead the pack when it comes to iPhone/iPad games — Russia is also a major user, ranking #6 in the world

91% of all people on earth have a mobile phone

56% of people own a smart phone

50% of mobile phone users use mobile as their primary Internet source

80% of time on mobile is spent inside apps or games

Other Stats:

120,000 people [in the United States] are employed in the videogame industry across 34 states

43% of tablet owners spend more time with their tablets than their TVs or PCs, and 84% of tablet owners spend *most* of their time playing games on it.

Chapter Two

Asset Acquisition

The elements used to construct a modern videogame, commonly referred to as "assets," are often derived from many sources of creative endeavor. This asset diversity opens a veritable Pandora's box of infringement problems and potential causes of action with respect to: intellectual property interests, transgressions upon privacy, interference with rights of celebrity and publicity, and unique contract issues engendered by continuing technological advances. In addition, as we explain further in Chapter 5, the fact that most computer and videogames were published after the effective date of the 1976 Copyright Act means that there is a lessened opportunity for authored works to fall into the public domain,[1] where they might otherwise be freely utilized by anyone.

§ 2.10 Basic Game Elements

Videogames are living, functional, interactive works of art. Reflective of more conventional art forms, some are hideous and violent, while others are beautiful, even poetic. But while the videogame can display and present every medium and form of art, it also has capabilities that art alone cannot match. In particular, due to its interactivity, a videogame has the power to engage, teach and entertain well beyond our more traditional works of art or authorship.

The cases and rules governing videogames are bound to draw heavily from the areas of law pertaining to software in general. Nevertheless, as our *Table of Contents* indicates, the issues and problems involving the game industry and its products have spread into nearly every field of legal endeavor. Today's videogames have as many different components as motion pictures and more; they are, indeed, as complex.

Authors on the subject are quick to classify videogames according to their respective types or appearances (e.g., Maze, Racing, Shooting, Sports, etc.); at this juncture, however, it would be more productive to classify the components that comprise the game in order to better analyze the issues and potential disputes involving their acquisition. There are

---

1. For recent works, a copyright attaches automatically upon creation. More specifically, according to Title 17 U.S.C. § 102(a), an author's copyright becomes effective at the moment that his or her work becomes "fixed in any tangible medium of expression."

three basic groups of elements: Audio Elements, Video Elements, and Computer Code.[2] Each group might then consist of the following respective subgroups or components:

I. Audio Elements

1. Musical compositions[3]

2. Sound Recordings

3. Voice

4. Imported Sound Effects

5. Internal Sound Effects

II. Video Elements

1. Photographic Images (i.e., Giff, Tiff, Jpeg)[4]

2. Digitally Captured Moving Images (i.e., Mpeg)[5]

3. Live Motion Capture

4. Animation

5. Text

III. Computer Code (Source Code & Object Code)

1. Primary Game Engine or Engines

2. Ancillary Code

3. Plug-Ins (Third Party Subroutines)

4. Comments

Each of the above components can be further subdivided into an endless variety of pictures, shapes, images, and sounds, all of which may be subject to someone else's rights or proprietary interests. Keep the above categories in mind as we examine the related forms and cases presented throughout this chapter. Excepting fair use and an ever-diminishing public domain, some form of license or permission may be required for most of the items on the list.

For videogame developers and producers, acquisition concerns can begin at virtually any stage of the creative process. For a game that is to be produced pursuant to a work-for-hire arrangement, acquisition considerations and agreements could precede the beginning of the creation process. By contrast, a skilled programmer/developer might complete most of the project before ever requiring assets or assistance from others. There has been a gap in the days when a single programmer would typically create a game from "start to stop," but with new games being apps, single developer games are making a bit of a comeback.

For any creative endeavor, there are a limited number of methods whereby the creative elements or assets might be obtained without unlawful infringement; they are:

a. Create them yourself,

---

2. The key computer code elements that give the game its unique look and feel are often referred to as the "Game engine."

3. Musical compositions, such as those embodied in sheet music are copyrightable entities separate and apart from the sound recordings that may be derived from those compositions.

4. Giff (Graphic Image File Format), Tiff (Tagged Image File Format), Jpeg (Joint Photographic Expert's Group). These formats are among the most common, but they are by no means exclusive.

5. Mpeg (Motion Picture Expert's Group).

b. Take them from the public domain,

c. Take them from another while claiming fair use, or

d. Obtain a license, release or permission.

§ 2.20 Avoiding Liability

There is a common saying among amateur film and game producers: *It's always easier to obtain forgiveness than permission*. While this adage may work well for minor clearances, it can be very dangerous, particularly for large budget computer and videogame development where the stakes are high. Indeed, the list of remedies available for the potential victim of an intellectual property misappropriation runs the entire gamut, and does so in a liberal fashion. Whereas the *taking* of a tangible object is relatively easy to identify, the theft or misuse of intangible assets is often more difficult to establish; for that reason alone, more remedial leeway must be accorded to a potential plaintiff if an abstract asset is involved.

The creative pioneer game developers of the 1970s and early 1980s were not always concerned about, nor sophisticated with respect to legal formalities, particularly those that involved costly licenses or entailed attorney fees. Fortunately for those potential past-defendants, the video screen resolution of their days was too poor to permit images to resemble any live human or infringe upon the artistry of others. In particular, it would have been relatively difficult to claim that a person's trademark, copyright or right of publicity was infringed upon by a stick figure.

Things have, of course, changed dramatically. Today, screen resolutions are so high that it is becoming difficult to distinguish images of real people from artificially constructed cartoon figures. Similarities to living persons (or once-living celebrities), intended or otherwise, were bound to surface. Licensing became more prevalent. Unfortunately, however, obtaining licenses and waivers would not necessarily grant a developer total immunity from litigation, particularly where the consideration is weak or where there were ambiguities with respect to the language contained in the permission or license.

The cases provided in Chapter 4 set the stage for many disputes wherein performers, actors, artists, photographers, and creative persons from every imaginable industry sought to protect their respective images, movements, and unique traits. Not all deal with video and computer games, but the theories, issues, and reasoning of each certainly have important implications for the videogame industry, and will certainly be applicable when an appropriate computer or videogame case is filed. Thereafter, Chapters 5 through 9 address the entire remaining range of intellectual property problems as they pertain to the videogame industry.

A cautionary instruction is warranted for those game producers and developers who elect to use the works, images, or the celebrity rights of others without first obtaining permission. In addition to a wide variety of generic state causes of action for unfair competition and breach of various statutes, here are the more common remedies available to an aggrieved plaintiff:

1. Copyright Infringement

2. Patent Infringement

3. Trademark Infringement

4. Misappropriation of a Trade Secret

5. Misappropriation of Name, Likeness or Persona

6. Violation of Rights of Publicity and Celebrity[6]

7. Invasion of Privacy

8. Defamation

9. False Light

10. Unfair Competition

11. Violation of Specific State Statutes

In most cases, where any *one* of the above causes of action is pled, several others will be attached. Many of the remedies listed are two-edged swords. Copyright claims, for example, might create numerous barriers, both hidden and apparent, for the game developer during the asset-acquisition stage; on the other hand, after the game is completed, that same device will provide indispensable protection for that developer's finished product.

Cases throughout several of the remaining chapters will focus on infringement with respect to completed products.[7] This chapter, however, as the title indicates, directs itself more toward the raw assets that ultimately comprise a finished game. This is not to imply that there is some bright line between the rights considered in this chapter and those presented in Part II (Intellectual Property Protection); on the contrary, cases were selected for this chapter based primarily upon their relevance to the early stages of videogame production.

Videogames, with their vast variety of movement, sounds, visual images and interactivity, provide one of the liveliest art forms known to mankind. It should, therefore, come as no surprise that the lawsuits they engender should be no less varied. Raw assets for videogames can be particularly tricky to identify. Because the games draw upon every conceivable art form, when one becomes successful, infringement claims can spring from many unexpected sources. Consider a few: *Reece v. Marc Ecko, Unltd*, 2011 U.S. Dist. Lexis 102199 (S.D., N.Y., 2011) (revealing a New York graffiti artist's claims of copyright infringement against game developers); *EMI April Music, Inc. v. 4MM Games*, 2014 WL 1383468 (U.S. Dist., S.D., N.Y. 2014) (showing a music publisher alleging a lack of proper permission with respect to a game allowing players to perform popular rap songs); *Escobedo v. THQ, Inc.*, No.2:12-cv-02470-JAT (D. Az., 2012) (providing a claim where a tattoo artist sues for copyright infringement after the artist's tattoos allegedly appear on videogame fighters); and *Bouchat v. NFL Properties, LLC*, 910 F. Supp.2d 798 (D. Md. 2012) (containing an artist's claim over a professional football team logo appearing in videogame).

* * *

---

6. There is much overlap with respect to this and other items on the list. The difference between a *celebrity* (possessing *rights of publicity* worth value in the market) and a private citizen (having publicity rights, but which are not worth much), for example, is not always clear. In addition, torts relating to invasions of privacy are also closely aligned, as some of the cases suggest. These concepts are becoming increasingly important for the game producer because the graphics are becoming increasingly realistic. As the following cases indicate, rights in "one's own name and likeness" are evidently important enough to conflict with First Amendment principles and survive.

7. In particular, Chapters 5 through 8.

Carefully examine the following simplified authorization. Then compare it to the form that follows in Note 3. Under what circumstances should a more detailed writing be prepared?

FORM 2.1
Release
(Personal Image & Voice)

Full Name:

Address:

Videogame Title:

Producer:

Date:

To: Producer:

I have appeared as an image, voice or both in the above named Videogame (hereafter referred to only as the "Game"). In consideration of my appearance in the Game and without any further consideration, I hereby give my permission to the Producer for the use in perpetuity of my name, likeness, and voice in conjunction with the Game in any and all manner and media throughout the universe from the date hereof through the end of the world. As used herein, "Game" includes all of its derivative works and sequels.

I agree that my participation in the Game may be edited in your sole discretion and, if you deem necessary, deleted in its entirety. I consent to the use of my name, likeness, and voice in connection with the Game and all related publicity and promotional activities.

I expressly release you, your agents, employees, licensees, and assigns from and against any and all claims that I have or may have for invasion of privacy, interference with rights of celebrity or publicity, false light, defamation, or any other cause or causes of action arising out of the production, distribution, broadcast or exhibition of the Game.

AGREED: _____

Signed this _____ day of _____, 20____

* * * * *

Notes and Questions

1. Consider the following authorization. When is it advisable to combine several functions into a single one-page document?

FORM 2.2
Authorization, Release, and Assignment
(Personal Image, Voice, and Persona)

For consideration in the sum of $....., the receipt and adequacy of which is hereby acknowledged, I, the undersigned Contributor, do hereby give and grant to Gamebuilder, Inc., its affiliates, successors, and assigns ("GAMEBUILDER") the unqualified right, privilege, and permission to publish, circulate, reproduce, and sell every manner and form of videogame, compact disc, DVD, videotape, audiocassette or film of my voice, image, likeness, persona, including but not limited to my voice, image or character as it appears or may appear on a work of authorship titled:_____, which work of authorship I claim no proprietary interest in, and to the extent that a court may find otherwise, I do hereby grant, assign, convey and transfer any such interest to GAMEBUILDER.

I specifically authorize, permit and empower GAMEBUILDER to cause any such videogames, compact discs, videotapes, audiocassettes, films and recordings to be copyrighted and in any other manner to be legally registered in the name of GAMEBUILDER.

My contribution to this work shall be considered a work made for hire, and as such, I, my heirs, executors, administrators, and assigns, do hereby remise, release and discharge GAMEBUILDER from any and all claims of any kind whatsoever on account of the use of such material, including, but not limited to any and all claims for damages for libel, slander, and invasion of the right of privacy.

It is understood that all information obtained while providing service will remain confidential and that Contributor will not directly or indirectly disclose such information to any third party or use such information for that third party's own benefit or for any purpose other than the above mentioned project.

Contributor is of lawful age and sound mind, and has read and understand this Authorization, Release, and Assignment.

Signed this _____ day of _____, 20____

_____
DEVELOPER

_____
CONTRIBUTOR

* * * * *

§ 2.30 Concrete Media Assets

Having considered rights of publicity and celebrity likeness in the preceding sections, it would be a mistake to ignore the more prevalent, though less esoteric property rights that commonly populate today's videogames. It might even be worthwhile to draw a distinction between the more diffused "personal" assets discussed in the preceding portions of this chapter and what might otherwise be termed tangible or "hard" assets. Historically, it seems as if videogame developers more thoroughly appreciated and recognized the need to obtain written permission to use film clips, music samples and non-public domain photographs. Consider the examples in the subsections that follow.

§ 2.31 Music Licenses

In the world of intellectual property, technically, there is no such thing as a "song." There are *Musical Compositions* and there are *Sound Recordings*. Each is separately copyrightable. Musical compositions may further be subdivided into their *lyrics* and *music*, each of which may also be separately copyrightable. Therefore, anyone desiring to publicly display or perform a "song" or a part thereof directly from a record or CD must first obtain two licenses, one from the composer and another from the owner of the sound recording. For convenience, it is often the case that a "publisher" will own the copyrights for both or otherwise possess authority to issue licenses and permission.

For videogame developers, an additional license is required if the musical segment or piece is to become part of the game. In a manner analogous to the film industry, the developer must obtain a "sync" license whereby he or she obtains permission to digitize and synchronize the musical piece for use in the videogame.[8]

_____

Notes and Questions

1. Because of the increasing complexity and variety of today's media, licenses tend to be very specific and specialized. For example, instead of a general license granting a licensee permission to use a musical composition or recording use for "all video media," a modern license might be limited to use for a specific videogame, or even a specific few scenes within a game, as well as a specific type of downloadable device, such as a cell phone.

2. Consider the following "short cut" in the form of a simple, brief *Authorization & Release* as opposed to a more formalized document. Compare this form to the more detailed synchronization license that follows. Then compare both to the licensing agreement in the Notes for § 2.62.

FORM 2.3
Authorization & Release
(Music & Voice)

To: _____ (Developer)

For the sum of $........ .and other valuable consideration, the receipt and adequacy of which is hereby acknowledged, I the undersigned, do hereby give, grant and convey to Developer, its agents, affiliates, successors, and assigns the unqualified right, privilege, and permission to reproduce, publish and circulate in every manner or form, various videogames, computer games, compact discs, videotapes, audiocassettes and films containing recordings of my voice and my musical contribution to the production titled: .... , and I do further hereby grant, assign, transfer and convey all my rights and interest therein to Developer.

I specifically authorize and empower Developer to cause any such videogames, computer games, compact discs, videotapes, audiocassettes, films and recordings of my voice and/ or musical performance, to be copyrighted or in any other manner to be legally registered in the name of Developer

My contribution to this work shall be considered a work made for hire, and as such, I, my heirs, executors, administrators, and assigns, hereby remise, release and discharge Developer for and from any and all claims to any kind whatsoever on account of the use of such recordings, including, but not limited to, any and all claims for damages for copyright infringement, libel, slander, and invasion of the right of privacy or right of publicity.

It is understood by the below signed individual that all information obtained while providing service will remain confidential and that such individual shall not directly or

_____

8. While current federal copyright law covers virtually every tangible video game asset (See Chapter 5), it should be noted that original sound recordings fixed prior to February 15, 1972 were only protected by state common law. *See Capitol Records, Inc. v. Naxos of America, Inc.*, 262 F. Supp.2d 204 (S.D.N.Y. 2003). For a substantial authoritative work on the subject, see AL KOHN AND BOB KOHN, MUSIC LICENSING, Aspen Law & Business.

indirectly disclose the information to any third party or use it for any purpose other than the above mentioned project

I am of lawful age and sound mind, and have read and understand this Authorization of Release.

AGREED: _____

Signed this _____ day of _____, _____

* * * * *

3. Musical compositions are, of course, written. Sound recordings, however, may assume several forms in addition to vinyl records and audiotapes. For game developers the sounds must eventually be digitized.

FORM 2.4
Synchronization License For Musical Composition

Date of Issuance: _____

PURSUANT TO THIS AGREEMENT, which is entered into and effective as of the above Date of Issuance, by and between Licensor and Licensee, the Licensor does hereby grant to Licensee a limited, nonexclusive license in accordance with the following terms and conditions:

1. **Subject Matter:** The musical composition or compositions, which may be of a form commonly known as Musical Instrument Digital Interface (i.e., "MIDI"), for which this license is granted, are as follows (and shall hereafter be referred to as the "Composition"). The following is a basic description of the Game, which unlike the working title set forth herein, shall not change without the express written consent of the Licensor:

2. **Title:** This license is granted for the individual video/computer game currently titled (which title might change): _____ (hereafter "Game").

3. **Term:** The term of this license (hereafter referred to as "Term") shall commence on the date hereof and continue perpetually until the subject Game is no longer sold or marketed.

4. **Territory:** The territory for which this license is granted is the Universe.

5. **Consideration:** As sole consideration for the license granted herein, the Licensee shall, upon the execution of this Agreement, pay to the Licensor the sum of $_____ in United States currency.

6. **Grant of License:** In consideration of the fee specified in Paragraph 5, Licensor hereby grants to Licensee, its successors and assigns with respect to Licensor's interest in the Composition, the non-exclusive right and license to record in synchronism or in timed-relation with the Game, but not otherwise, and to make copies of such recordings and import said recordings and copies thereof into any country of the Territory all in accordance with the provisions of this Agreement.

7. **Limitations:** The license herein granted is only for recording the Composition for use in connection with the Game. This Agreement does not grant to Licensee, and Licensee shall have no rights hereunder to synchronize or reproduce the Composition in any audio-visual devices other than the Game. This Agreement does not authorize or permit any use of the Composition not expressly authorized and licensed in accordance with the provisions of this Agreement. Without limitation to the foregoing sentence, this Agreement does not include the right to perform the

Composition; to alter the fundamental character of the music or change the original lyrics of the Composition; to use the title, subtitle or any portion of the lyrics of the Composition as the title or subtitle of any program other than the Game; to dramatize or to use the play or story content of the lyrics of the Composition; to record the Composition on phonorecords or other sound recordings; or to use the Composition on any item of merchandise.

8.   **Warranty:** Licensor warrants only that it has the legal right to grant this license. If said warranty shall be breached in whole or in part, Licensor shall at Licensor's option either repay to Licensee the consideration theretofore paid to Licensor by Licensee under this Agreement or shall hold Licensee harmless to the extent of the consideration theretofore paid to Licensor by Licensee. In no event shall the total liability of the Licensor exceed the consideration actually paid and received by Licensee under this Agreement.

9.   **Reservation of Rights:** Licensor reserves all rights not expressly granted to Licencee hereunder. All rights granted herein are granted on a non-exclusive basis.

10. **Credits:** Licensee shall accord credit in the titles of each Copy of the Game to the writers of the Composition and to the Licensor as the publisher of the Composition. Credit accorded to Licensor and the said writers of the Composition in accordance with the provisions of this paragraph shall be no less favorable than any other credit accorded to the writers and/or publishers of any other musical compositions recorded in the soundtrack of the Game.

11. **Integration:** This Agreement constitutes the entire agreement between the Licensor and Licensee, and cannot be altered, modified, amended or waived, in whole or in part, except by a written instrument signed by the party sought to be bound. Should any provision of this Agreement be held to be void, invalid and unenforceable, no other provision of this Agreement shall be affected, and this Agreement shall be construed as if it never included such provision.

12. **Governing Laws and Venue:** This Agreement shall be governed by, and subject to, the laws of the State of _____ applicable to agreements made and to be wholly performed within such state. The venue for any action, suit or proceeding brought by either party against the other respecting this Agreement shall be the applicable court or courts located in the county of _____, state of _____. Both parties hereby consent to such jurisdiction and venue and agree that personal service may be effected by mailing a copy of the summons and complaint to either party at the address below, written by certified or registered mail, return receipt requested, which mailing shall have the same force and effect as actual personal service within such jurisdiction.

IN WITNESS WHEREOF, the parties hereto have executed this Agreement as of the date first set above.

LICENSOR:

By:_____

Address:_____

LICENSEE:

By:_____

Address:_____

* * * * *

§ 2.32 Cinematic Licenses

Increasingly, videogames are being based upon themes, stories and characters derived from the motion picture industry. In fact, the film industry is currently taking measures to see to it that its contracts are negotiated in such a manner as to encompass rights to produce videogames, including agreements from the actors and actresses themselves.[9]

Notes and Questions

1. The following form may appear to be somewhat *one-sided* in favor of the movie studio. That is to be expected, especially where the game developer seeks the license of a motion picture that has already demonstrated success at the box office. Review the Agreement and be prepared to discuss its terms and provisions; also be prepared to discuss the modification of those provisions that are skewed toward the film industry's benefit:

FORM 2.5
Motion Picture Studio Licensing Agreement for the Development and Marketing of Videogames and Computer Games

THIS LICENSE AGREEMENT, made and entered into as of the _____ day of _____, _____ is by and between _____ ("Licensor"), having its principal place of business located at _____ and _____ ("Licensee"), having its principal place of business located at _____.

WHEREAS, Licensor owns all of the rights, title and interest, including but not limited to the copyrights and trademarks, with respect to the motion picture, directed by _____, bearing the copyright date _____, and titled _____ (the "Film"); and,

WHEREAS, Licensee is a developer and publisher of interactive computer games and videogames, which Licensee desires to develop, produce, advertise, market and distribute a game, or a series of games predicated upon the Film, its characters and subject matter; and,

WHEREAS, Licensor is willing to grant Licensee a license for such development, production, marketing and distribution on the terms and conditions specified in this agreement;

NOW, THEREFORE, in consideration of the payment being made and the license being granted herewith, and of the mutual promises and agreements set forth herein, the parties hereto do hereby agree as follows:

1. Grant of License: (a) Subject to the terms and conditions set forth in this Agreement Licensor hereby grants to Licensee and Licensee hereby accepts for

---

9. For an excellent article, *see* Michael Cerrati, "*Video Game Music: Where it Came From, How it is Being Used Today, and Where it is Heading Tomorrow,*" 8 Vand. J. Ent. & Tech. L. 293 (2006).

the Term of this Agreement (as defined herein), a license to utilize certain specified Derived Film Assets solely upon, or in conjunction with the development, manufacture, use, distribution and sale of videogames and computer games (hereafter collectively referred to as "Games") for sale within the Territory as defined herein, provided that the Licensee shall obtain Licensor's written approval for the use of any actual material from the Film, such as footage (film, tape, disk, or other medium), outtakes, music, effects tracks, voice tracks or sound tracks.[10] As used herein, "Derived Film Assets" means the title of the Film including the Film's logos, related trademarks and copyrights in the literary, pictorial and audiovisual elements from the Film; these assets, however, do not include any rights or interests in trademarks or logos beyond the limited ones necessary to effectuate the intent of this Agreement.

(b) Names and Likeness. This license also entitles Licensee to use the personalities and likenesses of the performers whose names are set forth in Paragraph 1(a) of Schedule "A" attached, under the heading: "Names of Consenting Performers," but specifically does not include the right to use the names or likenesses of those whose names appear in Paragraph 1(b) of that Schedule, titled "Names of Non-Consenting Performers."

2. License Limitations: (a) No license is granted for the manufacture, distribution or sale of the Games for publicity purposes, for sale or gift in combination with other products or services, as giveaways, as premiums used for the purpose of publicizing, promoting or increasing the sales of any other products or services, or in connection with any similar method of merchandising. No television commercials may be utilized under this License without the specific prior approval of Licensor. No sublicenses may be granted hereunder except as specifically provided in Paragraph 11(b).[11]

(b) Territory. The License granted herein with respect to the Derived Film Assets shall be exclusive with respect to the Games in the Territory during the Term. For purposes of this Agreement, the Territory is limited to the following regions:

_____.

(c) Materials: Licensor shall use its reasonable commercial efforts to deliver to Licensee, for its use in creating, developing, marketing, and selling the Games, key artwork, film clips, and other property approved for use by Licensee in conjunction with the Games. Licensee and Licensor both acknowledge that Licensor's performance under this provision is subject to the consent of _____ for the release of specific property, and Licensor represents to Licensee that it shall use its best commercial efforts to obtain such consent on or before

_____.

3. Term: The term ("Term") of the Agreement with respect to Games referred to above shall commence on _____ and terminate on _____.

---

10. The game developer may wish to insert: "provided however, that such consent shall not be unreasonably withheld, particularly where the Licensor is able to secure the consents or releases necessary to obtain such actual material."

11. For the benefit of the programmer, it is not recommended that the Games be limited to any particular platform (i.e., such as PlayStation or Xbox), but if there is such a limitation, it might be inserted here.

4. Consideration: As full consideration for the rights, licenses and privileges granted herein to Licensee, Licensee shall pay to Licensor the following royalty payments:

(a) Guaranteed Consideration: Upon execution of this Agreement, Licensee shall pay to Licensor the sum of $_____.[12]

(b) Allocation: The Guaranteed Consideration shall be allocated to the following countries in the following amounts:

United States: $_____

Japan: $_____

_____: $_____

_____: $_____

All Others: $_____

(c) All Guaranteed Consideration paid by Licensee pursuant to Subparagraph (b) shall be applied against such royalties that become due to Licensor under this Subparagraph (c) on a country-by-country basis. There shall be no cross-collateralization. By way of example, and not by way of limitation, no credits from one country shall be applied to the payment of royalties due for another country. No part of the Guaranteed Consideration shall be repayable to Licensee.

(d) Royalty Payments: With respect to the Games, Licensee shall pay to Licensor a sum equal to $_____ per cartridge sold. With respect to the Games that do not utilize cartridge installation, Licensee shall pay to Licensor a sum equal to _____ percent (_____%) of all net sales (as such term "Net sales" is defined herein) by Licensee or any of its affiliated, associated or subsidiary companies. All royalties shall be paid in U.S. dollars at the address specified in Paragraph 17. The term "Net Sales" shall mean the gross invoice price billed customers, less quantity discounts, and returns, but no deduction shall be made for uncollectible accounts. In non-United States territories, the royalty rate shall be $_____. No cost incurred in the manufacture, sale, distribution or exploitation of the Games shall be deducted from any royalties payable by Licensee. Licensee shall have the right to distribute without charge, on a royalty-free basis, and not for resale, a reasonable number of review, promotional and demo copies of the Games. Royalties shall be payable concurrently with the periodic statements required in Paragraph 6 hereunder. It is a material term and condition of this Agreement that Licensee report net sales on a country-by-country basis. In the event Licensee fails to do so. Licensor shall have the right to terminate this Agreement, in accordance with the provisions of Paragraph 15 herein.

5. Reservation of Rights; Premiums: (a) Licensor retains all rights not expressly and exclusively conveyed to Licensee hereunder, and Licensor may grant licenses to others to use the Derived Film Assets in conjunction with other products. Notwithstanding anything to the contrary in the foregoing paragraph or elsewhere in this Agreement, Licensor specifically reserves the right without limitation (throughout the universe) to itself to use, or license to any third party of its choice with respect to the manufacture, distribution and sale of products similar

---

12. Installment provisions more favorable to the Game Developer are subject to negotiation and would be inserted here.

or identical to those licensed herein through any catalog produced or distributed by, or on behalf of, Licensor or for sale or distribution in any motion picture theaters or in any retail stores operated by, or on behalf of, Licensor. Further, licensor reserves the right to use, or license others to use and/or manufacture, identical items as premiums.

(b) Licensee agrees that it will not use, or knowingly permit the use of the Games as a premium, except with the prior written consent of Licensor, which consent Licensor may grant or withhold in its sole and unfettered discretion. In the event that Licensor consents to the use of the Games as a premium, the royalty rate applicable to such premium sales shall be subject to the mutual agreement of the parties. For purposes of this paragraph, the term "premium" shall be defined as including, but not necessarily limited to, combination sales, free or self-liquidating items offered to the public in conjunction with the sale or promotion of a product or service, including traffic building or continuity visits by the customer, or any similar scheme or device, the prime intent of which is to use the Games in such a way to promote, publicize or sell the products, services or business image of the user of such item.

6. **Accountings:** Promptly on the 30th (thirtieth) day of every calendar quarter following the initial commercial shipment of the Games, Licensee shall furnish to Licensor complete and accurate statements certified to be accurate by Licensee (or if a corporation, by a duly authorized officer of Licensee) showing the number, country of manufacture, country in which sold or shipped, description and gross sales price, itemized deductions from gross sales price, and net sales price of the Games distributed or sold by Licensee and any of its affiliated, associated or sub-sidiary companies during the preceding calendar quarter, together with any returns made during the preceding calendar quarter. Such statements shall be furnished to Licensor regardless of whether or not any of the Games have been sold during the calendar quarters to which such statements refer. The receipt or acceptance by Licensor of any such statement or of any sums paid hereunder shall not preclude Licensor from challenging the accuracy thereof at any time, and in the event that any inconsistencies or mistakes are discovered in such statements or payments, they shall immediately be rectified and the appropriate payments shall be made by Licensee. Licensee shall be entitled to withhold a reserve for returns, to be reconciled and liquidated quarterly, equal to fifteen percent (15%) of the sales for the quarter being reported.

7. **Books and Records:** (a) Licensee shall keep, maintain and preserve in Licensee's principal place of business for at least two years following termination or expiration of this Agreement or any renewal thereof, complete and accurate records of accounts including but not limited to invoices, correspondence, banking and fi-nancial, and other records pertaining to the various items required by Licensee. Such records and accounts shall be made available for inspection and audit, copying and the taking of extracts therefrom, at any time or times during or after the term of this Agreement or any renewal hereof, but not more frequently than once per calendar quarter, during reasonable business hours and upon rea-sonable notice. All materials shall be held in confidence and not used for any purpose other than enforcing the terms of this Agreement. Licensee agrees not to cause or permit any interference with Licensor or agents of Licensor in the performance of their duties of inspection or audit. Any such audits shall be con-ducted at Licensor's expense unless the audit establishes an underpayment of

five percent (5%) or more for the period subject to audit, in which case the expense of such audit shall be borne completely by Licensee.

(b) The exercise by Licensor at any time of the right to audit records or of any other right herein granted, the acceptance by Licensor of any statement or the receipt and deposit by Licensor of any payment tendered by or on behalf of the Licensee, shall be without prejudice to any rights or remedies of Licensor and shall not stop or prevent Licensor from thereafter disputing the accuracy of any such statement or payment.

8. Indemnification: (a) Licensor hereby indemnifies and agrees to hold Licensee and its agents, servants, employees, officers, and directors harmless from and against any loss, liability, damage, cost, or expense (including reasonable attorneys' fees) arising out of any claims or suits that may be brought or made against Licensee by reason of the breach by Licensor of the warranties or representations as set forth in this agreement.

(b) Licensee hereby indemnifies and agrees to hold Licensor and its agents, servants, employees, officers, and directors harmless from and against any loss, liability, damage, cost, or expense (including reasonable attorneys' fees) arising out of any claims or suits which may be made against Licensor by reason of, or alleging any unauthorized or infringing use by Licensee of any patent, process, trade secret, copyright, or other similar property. Licensee agrees to obtain at its own expense, product liability insurance providing adequate protection for Licensor and its agents, servants, employees, officers, and directors, and Licensee against any such claims or suits in amounts no less than one million dollars ($1,000,000.00) per claim or suit and within thirty (30) days from the date hereof, Licensee will submit to Licensor a fully paid policy or certificate of insurance naming Licensor as an additional insured party, providing that coverage shall extend to all claims or suits arising out of the use of the Games sold or manufactured pursuant to this Agreement, regardless of when such claim or suit may be asserted, and further providing that the insurer shall not terminate or materially modify such coverage without written notice to Licensor at least twenty (20) days in advance thereof, and that if it does so, Licensor will have the option to pay the premiums necessary to maintain or continue such insurance in effect.

(c) The indemnifications provided herein are conditioned upon the indemnified party's furnishing the indemnifying party with prompt written notice of any such claim or suit and upon the indemnified party's furnishing of reasonable cooperation and witnesses, if necessary, in defense of such claim. In such event, the indemnifying party shall have the option and right to undertake and conduct the defense of any such claim or suit.

9. Trademarks and Copyrights: (a) Trademarks: (i) Licensee agrees that it will cause to appear indelibly and legibly on each of the Games and all advertising materials, tags, labels, and devices bearing any trademarks or service marks included in the Derived Film Assets, the following notice: In the case of registered marks, "(mark) ® is a registered trademark of [Licensor]," or otherwise, "(mark) ® is a trademark of [Licensor]." (ii) Licensee further agrees that it will not apply for, nor seek to obtain any trademark registration for the Licensed Trademarks and that Licensor may, at its option, apply for and obtain in its own name trademark registrations for the Licensed Trademarks in conjunction with the Games. Upon request, Licensee will furnish necessary specimens or facsimiles to Licensor for such purposes, at no cost as well as evidence of the date of first shipment or sale of each Game in interstate or foreign or other federally regulated U.S. commerce and, if earlier, also in intrastate commerce. (iii) Licensee agrees that if it receives knowledge of the unauthorized use of the Licensed Trademarks or of any use confusingly similar thereto, Licensee will promptly call such fact to the attention of Licensor. Licensor shall then have the option to institute legal proceedings to prevent such use, and Licensee shall cooperate and assist, and, if requested by Licensor, join in the prosecution of any such action. Any such legal proceedings shall be the sole expense of Licensor.

(b) Copyrights: (i) The copyright for any Game (including object and source code) shall be owned as follows:

> (A) If a Game is created solely by Licensee or a sublicensee under the Licensee (or pursuant to the authority of the Licensee) without any contribution by Licensor to the creation of the Game in the form of programming efforts, then the copyright and all other proprietary rights in and to such Game shall be owned solely by Licensee.

> (B) If a Game is created jointly by Licensee and Licensor, then the copyright and all other proprietary rights in and to such Game shall be owned jointly by Licensor and Licensee.

(ii) Audio-Visual Displays: Notwithstanding the foregoing, the copyrights in and to the images displayed on the screen and the sounds produced during the course of the game play, including all possible combinations and sequences thereof, in both the "attract mode" and the "play mode" (hereinafter the Audio-Visual Display") shall be owned as follows:

> (A) The copyright and all other proprietary rights in and to all elements of the Audio-Visual Display constituting pre-existing material of Licensor from the Film, including without limitation, the characters portrayed in the Film or any reproductions thereof (hereinafter "Pre-Existing Material"), are acknowledged to be the sole and exclusive property of Licensor and shall remain the sole and exclusive property of Licensor, and

> (B) The copyright and all other proprietary rights in and to all elements of the Audio-Visual Display other than the Pre-Existing Material that constitutes original material created by Licensee shall be the sole and exclusive property of Licensee. Licensee retains sole and exclusive ownership of all of Licensee's inventions, whether patented or not, trade secrets and similar information and processes of a confidential nature, and works of authorship whether copyrighted or not, whether manifested in the Audio-Visual Display or not, and whether embodied in hardware or software used to create the Audio-Visual Display. Licensee shall be free to use and license others to use elements of the Audio-Visual Display owned by Licensee.

(iii) Packaging, Advertising and Promotional Materials: The copyright in and to any original material, other than the Games and the Audio-Visual Displays, that is created by or for Licensee for the purpose of packaging, advertising or promoting the Games, including but not limited to the enclosure for the Games, all cartons, containers, packing and wrapping material, tags, labels, imprints, or other devices, and all advertising and promotional materials (all such material hereinafter referred to as the "Other Materials"), shall be owned solely and exclusively by Licensee; provided, however, that the copyright in and to all elements of the

Other Materials that constitute Licensor's Pre-Existing Material is the sole and exclusive property of Licensor.

(iv) Copyright Notice: Licensee agrees that it will cause the following copyright notice to appear on Audio-Visual Displays and Other Materials that include Licensor's Pre-Existing Material: "(Licensor [Year of first publication of Pre-Existing Material]) and (Licensee [Year of first publication of Audio-Visual Display or other Material]). All Rights Reserved."

(v) Limitations on Ownership Rights: The parties agree and acknowledge that each shall have the same right as any person or party with regard to any material incorporated in the Games, Other Materials, Programs, or Audio-Visual Displays that is in the public domain (provided that it has not entered into the public domain as the result of an act or omission in breach of this Agreement or the breach of any other written agreement by or between the parties hereto).

10. Quality of Games: (a) Licensee agrees that the Games shall be of a high standard and of such style, appearance and quality as shall be adequate and suitable to their promotion, distribution and sale to the best advantage of Licensee and Licensor. To this end, Licensee shall, before selling or distributing any of the Games, furnish to Licensor free of cost for its written approval a sample of each such product together with its cartons and containers, including packaging and wrapping material. The quality and style of such product and its cartons and containers shall be subject to Licensor's approval.[13] In the event that any item submitted to Licensor shall not have been approved, disapproved or otherwise commented upon within fifteen (15) days after receipt thereof by Licensor, then Licensee shall have the right to so notify Licensor of such fact via notice by facsimile in accordance with Paragraph 17. In the event that Licensor fails to then approve, disapprove or otherwise comment upon the submitted items within three (3) business days after receipt by it of such notice, any items so submitted shall be deemed to have been approved. Licensee shall, in addition, thereafter furnish to Licensor, upon its request from time to time, free of cost, for its written approval, twenty (20) production samples of each set of Games together with their cartons and containers, including packaging and wrapping material. After samples of Games have been approved pursuant to this paragraph, Licensee shall not depart therefrom in any material respect without Licensor's prior written consent. Licensor shall have the right to withdraw its approval of samples if the quality of any Licensed Product ceases to be acceptable.

(b) Subject to the terms hereof, Licensee may utilize the Licensed Trademarks for such advertising, promotional and display materials for the Games as in its judgment will best promote the sale of said Games. Licensee agrees that it will not use the Games or any reproduction thereof in any advertising, promotional or display material or in any other manner without Licensor's prior written approval, which shall not be unreasonably withheld. In the event that any advertising, promotional or display material submitted to Licensor shall not have been approved, disapproved or otherwise commented upon within thirty (30) days after receipt thereof by Licensor, then Licensee shall have the right to so notify Licensor of such fact by notice by facsimile in accordance with Paragraph 17. In the event that Licensor fails to then approve, disapprove or otherwise

---

13. The game developer should insert: "provided however, that such approval shall not be unreasonably withheld."

comment upon the submitted items within three (3) business days after receipt by it of such notice, any items so submitted shall be deemed to have been approved. There shall be _____ number of production copies of all such advertising, promotional and display materials furnished to Licensor free of charge.

11. Distribution, Sublicense, and Manufacture: (a) The Licensee shall sell the Games either to jobbers, wholesalers, distributors, retailers, or by direct marketing for sale or resale and distribution directly to the public. If Licensee sells or distributes the Games at a special price, directly or indirectly, to itself including, without limitation, any subsidiary of any Licensee or to any other person, firm or corporation affiliated with the Licensee or its officers, directors or major stock-holders, for ultimate sale to unrelated third parties, the Licensee shall pay royalties with respect to such sales or distribution as set forth in Paragraph 4(b).

(b) Licensee shall not be entitled to sublicense any of its rights under this Agreement without the consent of Licensor, which approval shall not be unreasonably withheld. Further, in the event Licensee is not the manufacturer of the Games, Licensee shall be, subject to the prior written approval of Licensor (which approval shall not be unreasonably withheld), entitled to utilize a third party manufacturer in connection with the manufacture and production of the Games. Licensee shall remain primarily obligated under all of the provisions of this Agreement. In no event shall any such sublicense agreement include the right to grant any further sublicenses.

12. Goodwill: The Licensee recognizes the great value of the publicity and goodwill associated with the Licensed Trademarks and acknowledges that such goodwill exclusively belongs to Licensor, that Licensee's use of the Licensed Trademarks will inure to the benefit of Licensor, and that the Licensed Trademarks have acquired a secondary meaning in the mind of the purchasing public. Licensee further recognizes and acknowledges that a breach by Licensee of any of its covenants, agreement or undertakings hereunder will cause Licensor irreparable damage which cannot be readily remedied in damages in an action at law, and may, in addition thereto, constitute an infringement of Licensor's rights in the Licensed Trademarks, thereby entitling Licensor to equitable remedies, costs and reasonable attorneys' fees.

13. Licensor's Warranties and Representations: Licensor represents and warrants to Licensee that: (a) It has, and will have throughout the term of this Agreement, the right to License the subject Trademarks to Licensee in accordance with the terms and provisions of this Agreement. This warranty does not extend beyond the territorial limits of _____. (b) The execution of this Agreement by Licensor does not violate any agreements, rights or obligations existing between Licensor and any other person, firm or corporation.

14. Specific Undertaking of Licensee: During the term and any renewal period herein provided for, Licensee agrees that:

> (a) It will not harm, misuse or bring into disrepute the subject Trademarks or their reputation or that of their owners;

> (b) It will manufacture, sell and distribute the Games in an ethical manner and in accordance with the terms and intent of this Agreement;

> (c) It will not incur or create any expenses chargeable to Licensor without the prior written approval of Licensor;

(d) It will protect to the best of its ability its right to manufacture, sell and distribute the Games hereunder;

(e) It will comply with all laws and regulations pertaining to the manufacture, sale, advertising or use of the Games and shall maintain the highest quality and standards, and shall comply with any regulatory agencies which shall have jurisdiction over the Games; and

(f) It will provide Licensor with the dates of first use of the Games in interstate commerce; and

(g) (i) It will use its reasonable best efforts to manufacture, distribute and sell the Games throughout the Territory; specifically, it shall manufacture, distribute and sell the Games in such price and quality brackets as are required to meet competition by reputable manufacturers of similar articles (ii) Make and maintain adequate arrangements for the distribution of the Games throughout the Territory;

(iii) Supply retail outlets with the necessary sizes and types of the Games during the first and final thirds of each calendar year; and (iv) Depending on the quantities of Games available, shall not refuse to sell the Games to any retail outlet desiring to purchase the same whose credit rating, sales and merchandising policies warrant such sale.

15. Termination by Licensor: (a) Licensor shall have the right to terminate this Agreement without prejudice to any rights that it may have hereunder, whether in law, or in equity, or otherwise, upon the occurrence of any one or more of the following events (herein called "defaults"): (i) If Licensee defaults in the performance of any of its material obligations provided for in this Agreement; (ii) if Licensee shall have failed to deliver to Licensor or to maintain in full force and effect the insurance referred to in Subclause 8(b) hereof; (iii) if Licensee shall fail to make any payment due hereunder on the date due; (iv) if Licensee shall fail to deliver any of the statements or records referred to herein or to give access to the premises or its records to Licensor's authorized agents for the purposes permitted hereunder, and Licensee fails to cure such breach ten (10) days after its receipt of written notice by Licensor; (v) if any governmental agency finds that the Games are defective in any way; (vi) if Licensee shall become insolvent or unable to pay its debts when due, or shall make any assignment for the benefit of creditors, or shall file any petition under the bankruptcy or insolvency laws of any nation, jurisdiction, county or place, or shall have a receiver or trustee appointed for its business or property, or be adjudicated a bankrupt or an insolvent; (vii) in the event that Licensee does not commence in good faith to manufacture, distribute and sell the games throughout the Territory on or before the _____ day of _____.(Marketing Date), but such default and Licensor's right of termination shall only apply to the specific nation or nations wherein Licensee fails to meet said requirements);[14] (viii) if Licensee shall manufacture, sell or distribute, whichever first occurs, any of the Games without the prior written approval of Licensor as provided in Paragraph 10 hereof; or (ix) if a manufacturer approved pursuant to Subparagraph 11(b) engages in conduct that would constitute a material breach of this Agreement if engaged in by Licensee.

---

14. For developers, this is a very dangerous clause; software always takes longer to program, polish and debug than anticipated. Programmers are notoriously optimistic about their deadlines, and at the same time notoriously slow.

(b) In the event any of these defaults occur, Licensor shall give notice of termination in writing to Licensee by certified mail. The Licensee shall have thirty (30) days after receipt of such notice in which to correct any of these defaults (except subdivisions (vi), (vii), and (viii) above), and if such defaults remain uncured upon the expiration of the thirty (30) day period, this Agreement shall terminate, and any and all payments then or later due from Licensee hereunder (including Guaranteed Consideration) shall then be promptly due and payable and no portion of prior payments shall be refunded to Licensee.

16. Final Statement upon Termination: Licensee shall deliver, as soon as practicable, to Licensor, following expiration or termination of this Agreement, a statement indicating the number and description of Games on hand. Following the expiration or termination, Licensee may manufacture no more Games in association with the Licensed Trademarks but may continue to distribute and sell its remaining inventory for a period not to exceed _____ days following such termination or expiration, subject to the payment of any royalties that are applicable thereto. Thereafter, Licensee agrees to make no use of the Licensed Trademarks whatsoever, either in, or on, products or in advertising, publicity, promotional, or display materials. Licensor shall have the right to conduct a physical inventory in order to ascertain or verify such inventory and statement. In the event that Licensee refuses to permit Licensor to conduct such a physical inventory, the Licensee shall forfeit its right hereunder to dispose of such inventory. In addition to such forfeiture, Licensor shall also have recourse to all other legal remedies available to it. Notwithstanding the foregoing, in the event that Licensor terminates this Agreement pursuant to any of the provisions of Paragraph 15, Licensee shall have no right to dispose of its inventory beyond the effective date of such termination.

17. Payments and Notices: All notices hereunder (a) shall be in writing, (b) shall be forwarded by hand delivery, ordinary first-class or certified or registered U.S. mail (postage prepaid), by Federal Express, U.P.S. or other nationally recognized overnight courier service, or by fax (followed up by a mailed copy), (c) shall be addressed to the recipient at its address or fax number as specified below (or in the event of a change, as shall have been specified by the recipient in a notice given hereunder), provided that a party may specify that particular fax numbers shall be used only for specified types of notices, and (d) shall be effective on receipt. The applicable addresses and fax numbers with respect to such notices, and the addresses for accounting payments and statements, are as follows:

TO LICENSOR: [Attention]

TO LICENSEE: [Attention]

18. Confidentiality: Each party agrees that without the express consent of the other party, none of its employees or agents shall disclose to any other party, or use for any purpose other than the performance of this Agreement, any tangible or intangible information or material that the other party designates as confidential (including without limitation the terms and conditions of this Agreement, and the content of any source code, object code or technical documentation relating to the Games) unless such information or material, (a) is or becomes publicly known through no wrongful act of the receiving party; (b) is received from a third party without restriction and without breach of any confidentiality obligation to the other party; (c) is independently developed by the receiving party; or (d) is required by law to be disclosed (provided that the other party is given advance notice of and an opportunity to contest any such requirement).

19. No Partnership or Agency: Nothing contained in this agreement shall be construed as constituting a partnership, joint venture or agency relationship between Licensor and Licensee. Neither party shall have any right to obligate or bind the other party in any manner whatsoever, and nothing herein contained shall give, or is intended to give, any rights of any kind to any third persons.

20. Non-Assignability: This Agreement shall be binding upon, and inure to the benefit of, the parties hereto and their respective successors and assigns, provided that this agreement may not be assigned in whole or in part by the Licensee without the express prior written consent of Licensor, except to an affiliate of the Licensee (as defined in Rule 12b-2 as promulgated under the Securities and Exchange Act of 1934) or to any other entity that succeeds to the business of the Licensee associated with the Games other than by operation of law, such as by sale of assets.

21. Governing Law: This Agreement shall be interpreted and construed in accordance with the laws of the State of _____ of the United States of America, excluding any conflict of laws rules of said State which would have the affect of applying the laws of any other jurisdiction.

22. Integration: This agreement represents the entire agreement and understanding between the parties hereto pertaining to the subject matter and supersedes all prior oral and written negotiations and agreements. No waiver, modification or cancellation of any of the terms or conditions of this Agreement shall be effective unless executed in writing by the party to be charged therewith. No written waiver shall excuse the performance of any act other than those specifically referred to therein. Licensor makes no warranties to the Licensee except those specifically expressed herein.

23. No Endorsement: This Agreement does not carry with it any right to the name or likeness of any performer, except as may be expressly set forth above. Licensee shall not exercise the rights granted hereunder in any manner that will constitute an endorsement of a Licensed Product by, or an exploitation of, any performer without the specific consent of such performer.

24. Survival: The representations and warranties of the parties set forth herein and the provisions hereof regarding confidentiality, indemnification, accounting and payment of royalties, audit rights and the ownership of intellectual property shall survive any expiration or termination of this Agreement for any reason whatsoever, together with any monetary obligations accrued but as yet unpaid as of the time of such expiration or termination.

25. Acceptance by Licensor: This instrument, when signed by Licensee, shall be deemed an application for a license and not a binding agreement unless and until accepted by the Licensor by way of the signature of a duly authorized officer and the delivery of such a signed copy to Licensee. The receipt and/or deposit by Licensor of any check or other consideration given by Licensee or the delivery of any material by the Licensor to the Licensee shall not be deemed an acceptance by Licensor of this application. The foregoing shall apply to any documents relating to renewals or modifications hereof.

IN WITNESS WHEREOF, the parties hereto have signed this Agreement individually or by their duly authorized representatives as of the day and year first above written.

LICENSOR:

By:_____

LICENSEE:

By:_____

EXHIBIT "A"

This Exhibit "A" is attached to and made a part of the "Motion Picture Studio Licensing Agreement For Developing and Marketing Videogames and Computer Games," executed on the date hereof by the parties hereto:

The following lists relate to the license granted in Paragraph 1 of the subject Agreement:

(a) Names of Consenting Performers:

1. _____

2. _____

(b) Names of Non-Consenting Performers:

1. _____

2. _____

* * *

2. With respect to Paragraph 1(b), what if the Licensee uses the name of a performer whose name appears on *neither* list in Paragraph 1 of Attachment "A"?

3. If you were the Licensee, might you question and demand a clarification of Paragraph 2(c)? What might you demand as alternative language?

4. Whom does the anti-cross collateralization clause in Paragraph 4(c) benefit—the Licensor or the Licensee?

5. Because of the ever-increasing variety of media formats, this particular contract lumps all types and forms of videogames into a single category (i.e. "Games"). Which paragraph (and subparagraph) appears to draw a distinction between Computer Games and Console Videogames? Why the distinction?

6. Ongoing disputes between the videogame developers and film licensors reflect a fundamental disagreement over the amount of control that the film licensor should possess, particularly for non-joint projects. Does Paragraph 10 further fan this fire of discontent, or does it resolve the problem? How might Paragraph 10 be improved?

———————

§ 2.40 Product Ownership

Games consist of many components; some are as diverse and complex as a high budget, special effects-laden action film. As is the case with motion pictures, in order to assemble game-development components, an initial determination of the proprietary interests must be made. Smaller projects by independent game developers often proceed without adequate consideration of the problems that are certain to follow if their games are successful. A larger project, however (in keeping with the most common model established by the film industry) will normally be owned entirely by a single, specifically constructed entity.

Because of the multiplicity and diversity of assets, ideas and creative efforts that went into the construction of the classic videogames, proprietary disputes often arose. Today, developers take greater care in drafting agreements designed to avoid these confrontations; nevertheless, the increasing complexity and magnitude of the projects assure the continuation of proprietary disputes.

Before considering videogame ownership, a proprietary distinction must be drawn between the ownership of the game itself and its by-products. There are games, for example, that permit players (i.e., end users) to create their own characters or screens; the issue then shifts to the ownership of the user-created assets. On the other hand, there are those virtual world games, sometimes referred to as Massive Multiplayer On-line Games (MMOGs or MMORPGs) that permit the creation and ownership of virtual property and real estate that has actual real-world value. Both are discussed in § 10.30 *infra*.

§ 2.41 The Public Domain

Unlike the other methods of ownership discussed throughout the remainder of this chapter, the term "public domain" refers to properties that may be claimed by everyone, but exclusively by no one. There are two basic classes of public domain property. First, there are those items and subjects that have always been, and will always be available to the general public because they are, by their very nature, unable to be copyrighted; historical facts, laws of physics, and, closer to home, the rules of popular games are but a few examples. The second group of materials consists of items that were copyrighted but whose copyrights have expired. For modern videogames, it will be many years before this second class of materials falls into the public domain. Under the 1976 Copyright Act, copyright protection attaches automatically upon creation of the subject work and will not expire for at least 70 years thereafter.[15] The issues that are likely to arise in video and computer game litigation in this area are illustrated in the board and tabletop game cases that follow.

Chamberlin v. Uris Sales Corp.

United States Court of Appeals, Second Circuit, 1945
150 F.2d 512

FRANK, Circuit Judge.

The plaintiff brought this action in the district court to restrain an alleged infringement of his copyrighted game, 'Acy-Ducy,' and for damages resulting from the infringement. The facts as found by the district court and substantiated by the evidence are these: The copyright on the rules and layout of the game 'Acy-Ducy' was granted to Raymond Sabin on October 2, 1928, and was assigned by him to Emma L. Chamberlin, the plaintiff's mother, on October 29, 1930, and by her to the plaintiff, Coleman R. Chamberlin, on February 5, 1942. Sabin did not create the game nor did he write the rules for the game. The game is a variation of backgammon and the Maskee game, taught to the plaintiff by his grandmother when he was eight years old. The game was known as 'Acey-Ducy' as early as 1910, when the plaintiff and his acquaintances played it. The plaintiff wrote the rules in 1928 and the game was manufactured and distributed as early as 1928 by Sabin and Chamberlin. 'Acey-Ducy' was played by four people prior to 1928, and the practice

---

15. *See* § 5.23, *infra*.

of 'kicking,' which the plaintiff also claims to be original, was theretofore employed in and was part of backgammon and Acey-Ducy at all times. The defendant, the Uris Sales Corporation, did not manufacture any part of the game. It merely purchased the component parts, including the rules, and assembled them for sale. On these facts, the district judge dismissed the complaint on the merits and the plaintiff appealed.

1. The first question with which we must deal is that of the validity of the copyright. Our starting point must be the Constitution. For, as the constitutional power to enact the Copyright Act, 17 U.S.C.A. § 1 et seq., derives from Article 1, Sec. 8, that Act would be void if it went beyond granting monopolies (or exclusive franchises) to authorize whose works 'promote the progress of science and the useful arts.'[16] Obviously the Constitution does not authorize such a monopoly grant to one whose product lacks all creative originality. And we must, if possible, so construe the statute as to avoid holding it unconstitutional.[17] Plaintiff therefore must lose unless he has shown that his work contains some substantial, not merely trivial, originality and that the defendant sold copies embodying the original aspects of his work.

2. The defendant contends that the rules drafted by plaintiff are not copyrightable for lack of the requisite 'originality.' But the cases indicate that the 'originality' required refers to the form of expression and not to novelty in the subject matter. *Whist Club v. Foster*, 42 F.2d 782 (S.D.N.Y. 1929).[18]

3. Precisely, however, because it is the form of expression and not the idea that is copyrightable, we hold that the defendant did not infringe on the plaintiff's statement of the rules. The similarities of the two sets of rules derive from the fact that they were necessarily drawn from the same source. 'Defendant has not infringed, because he has not copied the literary composition of the plaintiff's publication, but, in language quite distinctly his own, has restated the same set of conventional precepts.' *Whist Club, supra*, at 782.

4. There remains one item to be considered. Plaintiff, as part of his registered rules, included a drawing of the board. Plaintiff copied this drawing from the traditional backgammon board. However, plaintiff's copy contains some inadvertent defects in shading, adding nothing to its worth in any conceivable way and so minute as to escape the attention of the ordinary observer.

If one made an unintentional error in copying which he perceived to add distinctiveness to the product, he might perhaps obtain a valid copyright on his copy, although the question would then arise whether originality is precluded by lack of intention.[19] That question we need not consider. For plaintiff's error yields nothing new of substance or distinction. Without originality, his drawing, if it stood lone, could not be the subject of a valid copyright.[20] We assume, arguendo, that that fact does not invalidate the entire

---

16. *Pennock v. Dialogue*, 2 Pet. 1, 16, 7 L.Ed. 327; *Burrow-Giles Lithographic Co. v. Sarony*, 111 U.S. 53, 59.

17. Perhaps Congress could grant monopolies for non-useful and non-original material if Congress based its authority to do so on the constitutional interstate commerce power. But we need not consider that question here, for Congress has not so acted.

18. *Cf.* 'The right secured by a copyright is ... the right to that arrangement of words which the author has selected to express his ideas (and not) ... the right to employ ideas expressed thereby.' *Dorsey v. Old Surety Life Ins. Co.*, 98 F.2d 872, 873 (10th Cir. 1938).

19. It is not easy to ascertain what is intended and what inadvertent in the work of genius: That a man is color-blind may make him a master of black and white art; a painter's unique distortions, hailed as a sign of his genius, may be due to defective muscles. Consider the great scientific discoveries—such as the X-ray and the galvanic circuit—which resulted from accidents.

20. *General Drafting Co. v. Andrews*, 37 F.2d 54 (2d Cir. 1930).

copyright. But since the only copying here was of that portion of the subject matter which, standing alone, could not validly be copyrighted, we hold there is no infringement.

Judgment AFFIRMED.

* * *

Affiliated Hosp. Prods., Inc. v. Merdel Game Mfg. Co.

United States Court of Appeals, Second Circuit, 1975
513 F.2d 1183

WATERMAN, Circuit Judge:

Affiliated Hospital Products, Inc. (Affiliated) filed an amended complaint on January 23, 1970 in the United States District Court for the Southern District of New York seeking damages for alleged unfair competition and breaches of contract, for rescission of a court-filed stipulation, for an accounting, for the delivery and destruction of the alleged offending materials, and for permanent injunctive relief. Affiliated alleged that the defendants had injured it in various ways: (1) by breach of contract governing the respective uses of the parties in the words Carom and Caroms and Carrom and Carroms; (2) by infringement of Affiliated's trademark Carrom; (3) by infringement of Affiliated's trademark Kik-it; (4) by infringement of Affiliated's copyright of a rulebook for Carroms and for other games played on its gameboard; and (5) for unfair competition. On January 23, 1970 Merdel Game Manufacturing Company (Merdel) filed an answer denying the allegations of Affiliated. In an amended answer, filed August 5, 1970, Merdel stated as an affirmative defense the res judicata effect of a consent judgment, entered March 2, 1967, upon a stipulation filed in the United States District Court for the Western District of Michigan and also the stipulated agreement, itself, between the parties as to the use Merdel could make of the word Carom.

After a bench trial, Judge Tyler, on April 30, 1973, dismissed the claims of Affiliated with the exception of damages for breach of contract by Merdel as to one use of the word Carom. Damages for this breach were to be determined at a later hearing. By letter of May 21, 1973, Affiliated stated that it "prefers an early appeal, and therefore chooses not to proceed at the present time on such a limited issue." Thereafter Judge Tyler entered a final order dismissing all of Affiliated's claims. Affiliated limits its appeal to three general issues: infringement of its trademarks Carroms and Kik-it; infringement of its copyrighted rulebook; and rescission of the 1967 agreement. Affiliated has not pursued its claim for money damages for breach of contract or its unfair competition claim.

We affirm the decision below.

The appellant, Affiliated Hospital Products, Inc. (Affiliated), through its Carrom Division and its predecessors in interest, has been manufacturing and marketing games for children for many years. Carroms, a tabletop pool game, has been marketed by Affiliated since the late 1800s. Involved in this suit is the alleged misuse of the trademark Carrom,[21] owned by Affiliated, and the alleged violation of appellant's copyright of its copyrighted rule book for Carroms. Affiliated also manufactures a tabletop soccer game called Kik-it, the subject of the other trademark involved in the present action. The appellee, Merdel Game Manufacturing Company (Merdel), whose motivating figures are

---

21. Trademark Registration No. 49,996. The registration was originally obtained for the mark Carroms in 1906, and the registration was subsequently amended to Carrom. The last renewal was on February 27, 1967.

former employees of Affiliated, has been marketing similar games, including the 100 Play Game Board and Kick'er, since 1961.[22] The 100 Play Game Board includes a carom board, as the game's carton makes clear, as well as a rulebook for caroms and related games. Kick'er is, like Kik-it, a tabletop soccer game.

In 1963, Affiliated sued Merdel for, among other things,[23] infringement of its registered trademark Carrom. Trial commenced in late February 1967. After two days of trial the parties negotiated an agreement, dated March 2, 1967, which led to the settlement of the action and its dismissal with prejudice. The agreement provides in relevant part:

The parties hereto, by their respective attorneys, hereby stipulate and agree as follows:

1. The defendants stipulate that plaintiff's trademark registration No. 49,996 is valid and agree not to use the words Carrom or Carroms as a trademark. If the words Carrom or Carroms cease to be trademarks, there shall be no restriction on the defendants' use thereof.

2. Plaintiff stipulates that it will not object to the use of the word Carom or Caroms by the defendant where such use is no more prominent than the use on the date of this stipulation. The defendants agree that they will not expand such use for the period of three years from this date. The defendants agree as part of the foregoing that they will not use the word Carom or Caroms during such three-year period to describe their game board. At the termination of such three-year period there shall be no restriction on the use of the words Carom or Caroms by the defendants.

It is clear from the record in the Michigan proceedings that the stimulus to settle was the possibility of a judicial decision invalidating Affiliated's trademark.[24] In exchange for Merdel's unrestricted right to use the word Carom after March 2, 1970, Affiliated received valuable present consideration: Merdel's recognition of the trademark's validity, dismissal with prejudice of Merdel's counterclaim, and the stipulated limitation on Merdel's use of the term Carom for a three-year period.

After the 1967 agreement Merdel continued to use the word Carom on its price lists, catalogues, invoices and cartons. In 1969 Merdel changed its carton so that the carton end flaps read "100 Play Game Board (Carom & Crokinole)" which made the word Carom visible when cartons were stacked in retail stores. And, of course, after March 1970 Merdel has, in reliance upon the terms of the stipulation, greatly expanded its use of the word Carom.

The 1967 agreement controls the rights of the respective parties in the use of the word Carom; and, preliminary to any claim of trademark infringement, Affiliated must demonstrate conduct by Merdel sufficiently grave to warrant rescission of that agreement. Absent grounds for rescission, Merdel has had since March 2, 1970, the right to use the word Carom, and Affiliated has only the right to compensatory damages for breach of the agreement. It is clear that not every breach of contract will justify rescission, but rather this remedy will be permitted only when, as one court has stated, "the complaining party has suffered breaches of so material and substantial a nature that they affect the very essence of the contract and serve to defeat the object of the parties." *Nolan v. Williams*

---

22. The other two defendants, Wm. Richman Associates, Ltd. and Bernard Cahn, who were responsible for marketing Merdel products in the metropolitan New York area, were named as defendants with Merdel in the unfair competition claim. They prevailed below and, on appeal, Affiliated has focused exclusively on its claims against the principal appellee, Merdel.

23. Affiliated sued Merdel not only alleging trademark infringement but also claiming misappropriation of trade secrets, breach of fiduciary duties, and unfair competition.

24. The trial judge in that action intimated strongly that he would hold the mark Carrom invalid.

Music Co., 300 F.Supp. 1311, 1317 (S.D.N.Y.1969), *aff'd sub nom. Nolan v. Sam Fox Publishing Company, Inc.*, 499 F.2d 1394 (2nd Cir. 1974).

Affiliated argues that Merdel had used the term Carom prior to 1967 in ways then unknown to Affiliated and that these pre-agreement uses, hidden to Affiliated, emerged after the 1967 agreement and lay outside the fair intendment of the agreement. It claims that this initial ignorance of actual usage misled Affiliated into entering into the stipulated agreement and thus provides grounds for rescission. Judge Tyler found, and we agree, that the parties intended to cover promotional activity centered on the word Carom. It is clear that Affiliated knew, or should have known, that Merdel's use of the word was not solely limited to the carton labeling, the use of which Affiliated now claims it was aware, but rather extended to other, standard, promotional devices.[25] Merdel's use of the word Carom in its catalogues, price lists, and other advertising was fairly within the scope of the agreement.

In the years prior to the agreement, Merdel variously described its 100 Play Game Board on its customer invoices. The legends "100 Play Game Board," "100 Play Game Board (Carom & Crokinole)," and "100 Play Carom Board" all appear typewritten on invoices during this period. Although not within the scope of promotional activity, and perhaps unknown to Affiliated at the time of entering into the agreement, this usage, which continued after the agreement, appears unexceptionable. The invoices were in response to the placement of orders by customers, who were in turn responding to Merdel's advertising. The invoices therefore were not a source of possible further confusion between the products. Although this use was a use hidden to Affiliated at the time of entering the agreement, the carom description on the invoices represents an insignificant intrusion by Merdel which is insufficient to warrant rescission of the contract on the basis of unilateral mistake in the formation of a contract. Williston on Contracts §§ 1573, 1578 (3rd ed. 1970). It was not necessary that Affiliated be aware of each specific item of Merdel's use of the word Carom: It was enough that Affiliated knew that Merdel was making considerable use of the word in many phases of its promotional and marketing activities. In this light, it is evident that the invoices provide no ground for rescission of the agreement.

Affiliated also urges that during the three-year period there was a substantial breach of the agreement by Merdel in its use of the word Carom which justifies rescission. During the restricted use period Merdel agreed to abide by three limitations: (1.) there would be no use "more prominent" than the use prior to the date of the agreement; (2.) there would be no expansion of such use; and (3.) "as part of the foregoing" the word Carom would not be used to describe the game board. Judge Tyler found that Merdel's introduction of a new carton whose end flaps stated "100 Play Game Board (Carom & Crokinole)" was an expanded use of the word Carom. Uncertain as to whatever possible harm this expanded use caused Affiliated, the trial judge postponed a determination of the damages for further proof of harm. Our examination of the record indicates Merdel did use the word Carom to describe its game board in some instances of catalogue advertising which, although paralleling earlier pre-agreement use, did violate the terms of the agreement. In view of the valuable considerations Affiliated obtained by the agreement, these advertising breaches are not, we believe, serious enough to warrant a rescission of the agreement. Affiliated was properly limited to a recovery for the damages it could prove it sustained from the breach of the agreement, a remedy which appellant failed to pursue below or on appeal. In another context, Judge Learned Hand, speaking for this court, stated that rescission, as an equitable remedy:

---

25. However, Affiliated did not engage in discovery in the Michigan action, which makes it difficult to discern precisely the extent of its knowledge of Merdel's actions.

… is a remedy dependent upon balancing the relative interests involved, and in a case where the injured party has another and a complete remedy and where rescission will deprive the wrongdoer of rights which are his in spite of his wrong, a court of equity will not grant rescission. *Dabney v. Chase Nat. Bank of City of New York*, 201 F.2d 635, 639 (2nd Cir. 1953).

Here we conclude that, despite the breaches by Merdel, the relative interests militate against rescission. Affiliated has received its consideration under the agreement which Merdel has in substantial part adhered to. Under the agreement Merdel has had the right, as of March 2, 1970, to the unrestricted use of the word Carom; in reliance of this it has changed its position. For any breaches of the agreement by Merdel from 1967 to 1970 Affiliated had the right to compensatory damages, a right abandoned below.[26]

Affiliated's Kik-it and Merdel's Kick'er are similar tabletop games in which wooden figures, manipulated by the players, play a soccer game. Judge Tyler in response to Affiliated's claim of trademark infringement found that the games' names employed the work "kick" in a manner merely descriptive of the games involved.

This is a close question, in one respect because of the similarity, not only of names, but also of the games themselves which compete for the same market. In addition, the word "kick" and its variations not only describe the nature of the game, but also, to a degree, the word is used as a "symbol to attract public attention." *Safeway Stores, Inc. v. Safeway Properties, Inc.*, 307 F.2d 495, 499 (2nd Cir. 1962). However, on balance, we agree with the trial judge that there was no trademark infringement by Merdel. Affiliated cannot claim exclusive rights over every variation of the word "kick." In the game field alone there is a profusion of games whose names, designed to catch the fancy of either children or parents, are derived from the work kick and which involve typically a football or soccer format.[27] Also buttressing our conclusion is the finding of the trial judge that there was substantial proof that there was no actual confusion between the products by the intermediate purchasers. Although the Lanham Act speaks of the "likelihood of confusion," 15 U.S.C. 1114(1), it is certainly proper for the trial judge to infer from the absence of actual confusion that there was also no likelihood of confusion.

Finally, the trial judge dismissed Affiliated's claim of infringement of its copyrighted rulebook for Carroms and related games. Since the introduction of its 100 Play Game Board in 1961, Merdel has published a similar rulebook, which contains the rules for 100 games. In the preparation of the rulebook, Merdel's employee testified that he had used Affiliated's rulebook and that the changes that had been made were made for clarification. Affiliated at trial presented a thorough textual analysis of the two books in an attempt to demonstrate the frequent instances of identical wording. It is clear, however, from an examination of the two rulebooks that Merdel's copying was not slavish, and that Merdel made a good faith attempt to improve upon, and to clarify, the presentation of the rules.

The issue that is squarely raised, therefore, is to what extent a copyright holder can prevent a competitor from publishing a similar rulebook to the copyrighted rulebook. No claim is of course made that appellant can protect the game of Carroms or its variations which are in the public domain. The rules of the game are perforce in the public domain as well as the game itself. Affiliated's copyright only protects Affiliated's arrangement of the rules and the manner of their presentation, and not their content. Here, however,

---

26. Our disposition of the rescission issue makes it unnecessary to consider the issue of the validity of the Carrom mark, or the issue of whether a valid mark was infringed.

27. For example, there are "Kick-In," "Kicker" and "Kick-It" which are soccer games; "Kick-Off" is a football game.

the simplicity of the games makes the subject matter extremely narrow, and the distinction between substance and arrangement blurs. On these facts we hold that Merdel, although admitting to access and use of Affiliated's work, did not infringe Affiliated's copyright. Merdel did not copy Affiliated's rules verbatim, and indeed its changes enhanced the clarity of the rules. This conclusion, based on the facts here present, in no way affects the general rule, applicable in other situations, that upon a showing of access to copyrighted material, an alleged infringer cannot escape liability for his appropriation through the introduction of slight changes.[28] *Orgel v. Clark Boardman Co.*, 301 F.2d 119 (2nd Cir.). We are encouraged in this conclusion through recognition of the fact that a contrary result would prevent publication of the rules of any simple game in the public domain unless the second entrant in the field developed his rules solely through watching the game being played; a result which would afford protection to the game itself.[29]

Notes and Questions

1. The case of *Whist Club v. Foster*, 42 F.2d 782 (S.D.N.Y. 1929) resulted from the defendant's publication titled "Foster's Simplified Auction Bridge (with the New Laws)," which plaintiff claimed to have infringed upon "The Laws for Auction Bridge." Finding for the defendant, the court held:

> In the conventional laws or rules of a game, as distinguished from the forms or modes of expression in which they may be stated, there can be no literary property susceptible of copyright. Defendant has not infringed, because he has not copied the literary composition of the plaintiff's publication, but, in language quite distinctly his own, has restated the same set of conventional precepts. This under all the authorities he was entitled to do, and neither the general acceptance of the rules as official, nor, if it were true, their rejection as officious, could have any bearing on this controversy.

Id. at 784.

2. Might other forms of protection be available for creators of game concepts? *See* chapters 5 and 6 (Copyrights), 7 (Patents) and 8 (Trademarks). The issue of copyrighting of game rules is also an issue under the "merger" doctrine, *see Allen v. Academic Games*, 89 F.3d 14 (9th. Cir. 1996).

3. While rules, concepts and ideas in general may fall into the public domain, the names and personal statistics of famous individuals are a bit more problematical. In *Uhlaender v. Henrickson*, 316 F. Supp. 1277 (D. Minn. 1970), for example, major league baseball players and their players' association were able to enjoin the unpermitted use of their names and statistics for use in a commercial table game. In response to the defendant's claims that the personal information was in the public domain, the court said:

> A celebrity must be considered to have invested his years of practice and competition in a public personality which eventually may reach marketable status. That identity, embodied in his name, likeness, statistics and other personal characteristics, is the fruit of his labors and is a type of property. Defendants' contention

---

28. For a similar result on the issue of copyrightability of contest rules, see *Morrissey v. Proctor & Gamble Co.*, 379 F.2d 675 (1st Cir. 1967).

29. Our disposition of the issue of infringement makes it unnecessary to discuss the alternative grounds appellee advances for dismissal of this claim, i.e., the Statute of Limitations and res judicata.

has no merit that by the publication in the news media and because of the ready availability to anyone of the names and statistical information concerning the players, such information is in the public domain and the players thus have waived their rights to relief in this case. Such argument may or may not have some weight against a right of privacy claim, but in an appropriation action such as in the case at bar the names and statistics are valuable only because of their past public disclosure, publicity and circulation.

A name is commercially valuable as an endorsement of a product or for use for financial gain only because the public recognizes it and attributes good will and feats of skill or accomplishments of one sort or another to that personality. To hold that such publicity destroys a right to sue for appropriation of a name or likeness would negate any and all causes of action, for only by disclosure and public acceptance does the name of a celebrity have any value at all to make its unauthorized use enjoinable. It seems clear to the court that a celebrity's property interest in his name and likeness is unique, and therefore there is no serious question as to the propriety of injunctive relief. Defendants have violated plaintiffs' rights by the unauthorized appropriation of their names and statistics for commercial use. The remedy at law, considering particularly the difficulty in determining and measuring damages, past or future, is inadequate. *Id.* at 1282–3.

Injunctive relief was granted in favor of the major league players and their association. With respect to celebrity rights, *See generally*, Chapter 4.

* * *

With respect to attempts to balance celebrity rights with the First Amendment, the scales may be tilting in favor of the latter. *See C.B.C. Dist. And Mktg., Inc. v. Major League Baseball Adv. Media*, 443 F. Supp. 2d 1077 (E.D. Mo. 2006).

4. In the case of *Avalon Hill Co. v. Gebhardt*, 166 A.2d 740 (Md. 1961), the manufacturer of a game involving the Battle of Gettysburg could not acquire any exclusive property rights with respect to the name of the battle or the colors "blue and gray," which are, of course, symbolic of the Civil War. The names and colors are also in the public domain.

5. All works published in the United States prior to 1923 are in the public domain, and therefore, unrestricted. Works that were published after 1922, but before 1978 are protected for 95 years from the date of publication. If the work was created, but not published, before 1978, the copyright lasts for the life of the author plus 70 years. However, even if the author died over 70 years ago, the copyright in an unpublished work lasted until December 31, 2002. And if such a work is published before December 31, 2002, the copyright will last until December 31, 2047. These matters are more thoroughly considered in Chapter 5.

6. There are those who advocate the extreme position that in order to maximize freedom and a creative atmosphere for new original endeavors, virtually every work of authorship should be considered as being in the public domain. With respect to videogames, what are the arguments pro and con?

---

§ 2.42 Individual Ownership

For films, corporations and limited liability companies (LLCs) serve as the most common ownership vehicle. These entities are created separate and apart from the large mega-corporations that own the studios or the conglomerates that own the companies that own the studios. Today, high budget videogames likewise employ corporations and LLCs; but historically, that was not always the case.

The use of a single entity that owns the finished product greatly simplifies the process by bringing together under a single roof the diverse talents and resources of many. Games created by individual developers, on the other hand, can present troublesome ownership disputes, particularly where significant rights are carelessly assigned. Bitter disputes can destroy the marketability of an otherwise very successful product, as the next case so vividly illustrates.

Blue Planet Software, Inc. v. Games Int'l, LLC

United States District Court, Southern District New York, 2004
334 F. Supp. 2d 425

STEIN, District Judge.

INTRODUCTION

In this action arising over the intellectual property rights to the popular video game Tetris, the parties have brought cross-motions for preliminary injunctions to enjoin the other from interfering in the movant's purported ownership rights to Tetris until the dispute over those rights is resolved. Specifically, all parties agree that the intellectual property associated with Tetris is suffering irreparable harm; yet each of the parties asserts that they are both likely to succeed on the merits or that they have raised serious questions as to the merits to make them fair ground for litigation and a balance of the hardships tips decidedly in their favor. For the reasons set forth below, including this Court's finding that the assignment of rights, and the documents supporting that assignment, are ambiguous, plaintiffs' motion for a preliminary injunction is denied and defendants' motion for a preliminary injunction is granted in part and denied in part.

Discussion

I. Factual Background: The Tetris Story

The Tetris story swells with contradictory tales that describe the scope of unrecorded grants of intellectual property rights, and conflicting writings that inconsistently memorialize those grants. Yet the ultimate question for this Court's resolution is straightforward: who now owns the intellectual property rights to Tetris?

While employed by the Computer Center of the Academy of Sciences of the U.S.S.R. ("CCAS"), plaintiff Alexey Pajitnov created, named, and developed Tetris in 1984 and 1985, now recognized as one of the most popular video games in the world "in which the goal is to manipulate seven geometric shapes and fit them together to form solid lines of blocks as they 'fall' from the top of the video screen." As Tetris gained in popularity globally, Pajitnov, as a citizen of the U.S.S.R., was unable to benefit commercially from his creation, but had the option to allow the Soviet government to exploit it. Pajitnov did just that in 1986 by making at least one grant of his rights to the Soviet government. The government agency to which Pajitnov assigned the rights to Tetris was the CCAS, his employer. The almost mysterious scope of that assignment is a central issue in this case to be discussed at length infra; still, the dispute may be succinctly described: plaintiffs assert that the grant was limited to ten years expiring at the end of 1995, while defendants argue that Pajitnov in fact granted his rights to Tetris in perpetuity.

Following that initial assignment of rights to CCAS, the same Computer Center then assigned its rights (whatever rights Pajitnov had in fact granted) to the then export agency of the Soviet Union, V/O Electronorg-technica ("Soviet Elorg"), to enable Soviet Elorg to act as CCAS's licensing agent for transactions abroad. Defendants assert that they are the successors-in-interest of Soviet Elorg; defendants also independently claim they are the assignees of the Tetris intellectual property rights of Soviet Elorg, irrespective of their status as successors-in-interest.

After the authorization to Soviet Elorg to handle international licenses, Soviet Elorg granted Nintendo Entertainment Systems ("Nintendo") in March 1989 an exclusive worldwide license for five years (plus a one-year extension option) to produce and distribute the Tetris program on Nintendo and other home video game systems. *See Tengen, Inc. v. Nintendo Co., Ltd.*, Civil Action No. C-89-1334 FMS (N.D.Cal.). As part of the agreement between Nintendo and Soviet Elorg, Nintendo was required to file U.S. trademark and copyright registrations for the Tetris game "in the name of Soviet Elorg."

The current dispute began to manifest itself toward the end of Nintendo's license term which approximately coincided with the expiration of the alleged overall ten-year limit on the original grant as claimed by Pajitnov. As the expiration of the Nintendo license and the underlying alleged ten-year limit drew near, both Pajitnov and Soviet Elorg prepared to retake control over the Tetris property rights in accordance with their respective views on the duration of the original grant by Pajitnov.

Pajitnov entered into an exclusive licensing agreement with Henk Rogers' Japanese Company, Bullet-Proof Software, to take effect after the expiration of the ten-year period at the end of 1995; meanwhile, Soviet Elorg continued to assert its prospective rights after the same time. In an apparent resolution of the conflicting claims, Rogers and Nikolai Belikov, an officer of Soviet Elorg, reached an agreement aimed at resolving the dispute. Rather than litigate, Pajitnov and Rogers agreed with Belikov to create a new company that would possess the respective ownership rights that each party contended they possessed. (Id.). That new company was called The Tetris Company, L.L.C. ("TTC"), governed by the Limited Liability Company Agreement of The Tetris Company, L.L.C. ("TTC Agreement"). The TTC Agreement provides, inter alia, that if any member elects to withdraw, the remaining member or members "shall have the option of either dissolving the Company or purchasing ... the withdrawing Member's Interest."

In order to form this new company, each side created new corporate entities through which it would control the shared company: Rogers created Blue Planet Software, Inc. ("BPS") and the rights that Pajitnov had granted to Rogers were further transferred to BPS, and Belikov formed defendant Elorg L.L.C. of Delaware ("Elorg USA") and Games International, Inc. ("Games"). In turn, Pajitnov—through BPS—joined with Elorg USA—through Games—to form TTC "as a mechanism to exploit Tetris and share the licensing revenues from Tetris." Each side maintained a 50% interest.

Though the parties agree upon the facts surrounding the formation of TTC, they maintain opposing views of what role each side played as part owners. Rogers contends that BPS "almost exclusively" performed all quality assurance, game design, and research and development. Yet defendants maintain that Elorg was "solely responsible for quality control of the products sold by Nintendo." Ultimately, the mutual arrangement failed; BPS withdrew from TTC pursuant to the TTC Agreement because of conditions "detrimental to BPS and Mr. Pajitnov and detrimental to the preservation of the Tetris name and mark...."

Subsequent to BPS's withdrawal, each side allegedly acted in a manner that its adversaries contend is now causing the Tetris mark irreparable harm. On the one hand, plaintiffs assert that "Games has recently contacted virtually all of the companies that have licensed rights to Tetris and wrongly asserted that Mr. Pajitnov has no right, title, and interest in the Tetris game or mark and that BPS has no rights to license the Tetris game or mark ..." and that such actions "are causing confusion among the Tetris licensees and damage to the Tetris intellectual property." Additionally, TTC sent a letter to one licensee stating that "you deal with Henk Rogers/Blue Planet Software at your own risk." Plaintiffs further assert that defendants' actions have "cast a substantial cloud on title to the property," alleging significant economic harm including threats to terminate and actual terminations of licensing deals for Tetris specifically "due to the dispute over the ownership of Tetris between Games and BPS ..." and the inability to negotiate new licensing deals for Tetris.

On the other hand, defendants claim that BPS interfered with their claimed rights. Defendants point out that BPS sent out letters to Tetris licensees informing them that TTC is being dissolved and that "[i]n the future you may license the Tetris trademark and copyright from Blue Planet Software, Inc" and that Pajitnov "is the rightful owner of all 'Tetris' copyrights and trademarks." After TTC responded to BPS' first letter to Tetris licensees, BPS sent out another letter to the licensees rebutting TTC's statements and affirming BPS's rights to Tetris. Moreover, defendants allege that plaintiffs have distributed copies of the Complaint in this action to the licensees, which defendants contend violates the confidentiality provision of the TTC Agreement.

The parties remain bitterly at odds as to who is the rightful owner of the Tetris intellectual property rights. Yet all agree that the Tetris rights are suffering irreparable harm and that a resolution is required.

II. Legal Standard

A party moving for a preliminary injunction must show (1) irreparable harm in the absence of the injunction (The parties agree that this prong is satisfied—that the Tetris rights are suffering irreparable harm—though each side believes it is the one that endures the harm.) and (2) either (a) a likelihood of success on the merits or (b) sufficiently serious questions going to the merits to make them a fair ground for litigation and a balance of hardships tipping decidedly in the movant's favor.

III. The Assignment and The Conflicting Document Trail

A. The Assignment of Rights:

In 1986, sometime after the creation of Tetris, Pajitnov assigned—perhaps through more than one grant—the intellectual property rights to Tetris to his employer CCAS for a certain time period, the length of which the parties contest. As noted above, the issue is whether that grant of rights was for only ten years—as plaintiffs contend—or were they granted in perpetuity—as defendants contend. Four categories of documents form the paper trail that postdates and refers to this illusive grant: (1) subsequent affirmations by parties to that grant confirming its substance, (2) contractual agreements between parties that either directly or collaterally reference the scope of the grant (3) subsequent letters from parties referring to the substance of the grant, and (4) subsequent copyright and trademark registrations to which the law attaches presumptions of ownership.

B. The Conflicting Affirmations, Agreements, and Letters:

The spate of affirmations, agreements, and letters—with their conflicting terms— are best analyzed only after the text of each is fully set forth for ease of comparison.

1. *The Documents*

The earliest document—Pajitnov's "Affirmation by the Creator and Author of the Game 'TETRIS'" signed by the same on March 17, 1989 ("the March 1989 Affirmation")—

offers the initial instance in which a party memorialized the assignment of rights at issue. (Games confirmed in 2003 that this Affirmation is "genuine.") The final paragraph of the March 1989 Affirmation states:

> I [Pajitnov] confirm that I granted the Computer Center of the USSR Academy of Sciences the exclusive rights in the Game Tetris including the trademark, all copyright and other rights (with the sole exclusion-the right to use the trademark Tetris for products not related to the game) in the beginning of 1986 for a period of 10 years. On the basis of this grant of rights, the Computer Center of the USSR Academy of Sciences, in conformity with the Soviet Legislation in force, legally is the owner of the right and license for selling the program product — the Game Tetris on the world market.

Besides the obvious limitation in time affirmed to have been placed upon the grant, at least two other features become relevant in this action that will later be discussed in depth. First, "merchandising rights" — as the parties refer to the right to use the Tetris trademark in connection with other "products not related to the game" — were affirmed to have been explicitly excluded from the grant. Second, this document presents the first piece of evidence illuminating the parties' intent as to the meaning of the term "owner" as used in their course of dealing. That meaning — from an internal analysis of this document alone — appears to be different than the most common meaning of an owner — someone in possession for perpetuity — because the document confirms the CCAS as "the owner" despite only confirming a grant of ten years. Every subsequent document need be viewed in light of this ten year time span that began in 1986.

Five days after that affirmation, Soviet Elorg entered into the contract with Nintendo ("the Nintendo License") to license to Nintendo for five years "the exclusive rights to manufacture, market, distribute, sell, and sub-license the Game all over the world for play on Home Video Game Systems." Signed on March 22, 1989 by representatives of Soviet Elorg, Nintendo, and the CCAS, as well as by Pajitnov, it set forth that Soviet Elorg as "Licensor" "has all exclusive rights to the game ... its program or software, its design script and its audiovisual work, including but not limited to copyrights, trademarks and other related rights in said Game."

Roughly one month later — on April 20, 1989 — Belikov, as an officer of Soviet Elorg, swore via an annexed declaration to the truth of a letter addressed to John J. Kirby, then counsel for Nintendo and counsel for plaintiffs on these motions for preliminary injunctions. In that letter, Belikov writes in relevant part:

> [Pajitnov] granted his employer, the [CCAS], the exclusive rights in the Tetris game, including all trademarks, copyrights and other rights, in early 1986 for a period of 10 years. The sole exception to this grant of rights was the right to use the Tetris trademark [merchandising]. In early 1987 the [CCAS] authorized Elorg to represent it in licensing Tetris on the world market. (emphasis added).

Belikov concluded the letter: "This letter is complitely [sic] truthful and absolutely correct." At some point probably in 1989 (Though no date is discernable from the document, it must have been signed before Belikov authored his letter on April 19, 1989, but after 1987, a year referenced in the letter to Belikov), the Director of CCAS wrote a letter to Belikov stating that the CCAS is "the owner of the exclusive rights and licenses" for Tetris and that Soviet Elorg is its agent. Comparing those two documents, it becomes evident that Belikov subsequently described the scope of the grant differently from what the CCAS Director has stated; i.e., Belikov in April of 1989 confined the grant to ten years even though the letter he received simply stated that CCAS was "the owner."

Some seven months after the ink on the March 1989 Affirmation had dried, Pajitnov and a representative of the CCAS co-signed an "Assignment Agreement" on October 16, 1989 ("the Merchandising Assignment") in which Pajitnov assigned to the CCAS the merchandising rights previously excluded from the March 1989 Affirmation. The Merchandising Assignment states in relevant part:

> [F]or sufficient, good and valuable consideration, the receipt of which is hereby acknowledged, the parties agree as follows: ... Assignor [Pajitnov] does hereby sell, assign, and transfer to Assignee [CCAS] all of his merchandising rights to the personal computer, hand-held, arcade and home video game versions of Tetris as well as the merchandising rights in associated programs and software, design scripts, visual and auditory representations, symbols, designs, copyrights, trademarks and art work ...

This latter document differs from the March 1989 Affirmation in two fundamental ways. First, unlike the March 1989 Affirmation, the October 1989 Assignment was constructed as an operative legal document—an assignment of rights—rather than an affirmation that a prior assignment took place. Second, only merchandising rights are addressed and no time limit is set forth.

Approximately one year after signing the March 1989 Affirmation, Pajitnov issued a second affirmation—titled "Affirmation of Game 'TETRIS'" signed on March 11, 1990 ("the March 1990 Affirmation")—in which he "confirm[ed]" CCAS's ownership in the rights to Tetris, albeit this time without an explicit time limitation of ten years or otherwise. In the March 1990 Affirmation, Pajitnov stated:

> I, [Pajitnov], the author and creator of Game "TETRIS" ("Game"), should like to confirm that the [CCAS], to which I belong, is the owner of the exclusive rights and licensees for the Game, including the trademark, copyrights and all other rights in said Game. I should like to further confirm that [Soviet Elorg] was granted all the exclusive rights to represent the interests of the [CCAS] regardind [sic] the Game on the international markets and any other Soviet organizations except Elorg do not had [sic] said rights in the USSR. (emphasis added).

Separately from the affirmations and agreement set forth above, the Director of the CCAS alone signed a separate affirmation in 1990 confirming CCAS's purported ownership rights in Tetris and setting forth Soviet Elorg's role as the agent for CCAS. That affirmation stated in relevant part:

> [T]he [CCAS] is the owner of the exclusive rights and licenses for the game "TETRIS", ("GAME"), including the trademark, copyright and all other rights in said Game. The Game was created in our Center by our staff member of the Computer Center, [Pajitnov] in 1985. In the beginning of 1987, the [CCAS] authorized [Soviet Elorg] to introduce the Game "TETRIS" in the world market, acting in our interest, and we have given them all necessary proxy.

Crucial to placing this document in context with the others is that this document was issued while the ten year period in the March 1989 Affirmation was still running.

Finally, defendants cite to an order by U.S. District Judge Fern M. Smith for the proposition that Pajitnov transferred all of his rights to Tetris without any time limit. *See Tengen, Inc. v. Nintendo of America, Inc.*, Order Granting Partial Summary Judgment, No. C-89-1334, 1989 WL 201201 (N.D.Cal.1989). Judge Smith wrote that Pajitnov "transferred all of his rights in the program to [Soviet Elorg] which became responsible for negotiating the sale of distribution rights to the program." Yet that order focused on an unrelated issue and made only a passing reference to the transfer of rights; accordingly, this Court finds that order to not control the issue at bar.

2. Analysis

What becomes clear from the documents set forth above is that the record of and references to the grant of rights is collectively anything but clear. Most obviously, the scope of the grant remains uncertain. Additionally, the mode by which the grant was made—orally or by writing—is as elusive as its intended scope. Moreover, the record fails to indicate whether only one grant was made, and was simply recorded or referenced inconsistently, or whether a differing superseding grant was made subsequent to the initial grant, and the parties failed to memorialize the fact that a latter grant replaced the former (Games apparently has taken the position that the October 1989 Assignment is a superceding assignment that includes "all rights, copyrights, trademark, and merchandising rights, without limitation to time.") Ultimately, the parties' intent is ambiguous and this Court turns to the fundamentals of contract law.

An assignee generally may not acquire more rights than were possessed by the assignor and simply stands in the shoes of the assignor. With that background in mind, well-recognized principles addressing ambiguous language in contracts provide the necessary legal framework within which to analyze this action.

It is well settled that "the primary objective in contract interpretation is to give effect to the intent of the contracting parties as revealed by the language they chose to use." Moreover, it is axiomatic that where the language of the contract is clear and unambiguous, the parties' intent is to be determined from the four corners of the document without consulting extrinsic evidence. However, where the agreement contains ambiguous language, evidence external to the contract may be offered by the parties in an effort to resolve the ambiguity in their favor.

Determining whether contractual language is ambiguous presents a question of law for the trial court. Contractual language is deemed ambiguous when it is capable of more than one meaning when viewed objectively by a reasonably intelligent person who has examined the context of the entire integrated agreement and who is cognizant of the customs, practices, usages, and terminology as generally understood in the particular trade or business.

a. Insofar As All Rights Are Concerned, Excluding Merchandising Rights, the Term "Owner" Is Ambiguous.

No singular document exists that evidences the grant or grants of rights. Rather, the rights to Tetris were assigned at some point in 1986 and other documents merely refer to that grant, some by explicit intent and some by indirect reference. An examination of these documents, set forth above, reveals that the term "owner" as used by the parties is ambiguous as to its intended meaning. "Owner" is defined as "one that owns" and "one that has the legal or rightful title whether the possessor or not." Webster's Third New International Dictionary 1613 (1993). This definition is silent as to the temporal aspect of ownership and it remains unclear whether the parties intended "owner" to incorporate an understanding as to time.

The March 1989 Affirmation by Pajitnov sets the ambiguous tone for all subsequent documents that refer to the grant. That affirmation is itself internally ambiguous. On the one hand, plaintiffs argue that "owner" connotes only a present ownership, rather than absolute possessory rights, because Pajitnov states in that document both that he grants

CCAS the exclusive rights simply "for a period of 10 years" and that CCAS is "legally ... the owner." Accordingly, "owner"—plaintiffs reasonably contend—could only connote present possession; otherwise, the document would be internally inconsistent and that is an unlikely scenario.

Moreover, plaintiffs posit that the other documents support their understanding of the grant. They contend that the Nintendo Agreement only refers to present rights, and in any event, does not convey any ownership rights because that agreement is not an operative document between Pajitnov and another party. Additionally, plaintiffs emphasize that Belikov's letter referring to the ten-year limit expressly corroborates Pajitnov's March 1989 Affirmation that confirms the limit on the grant. As for Pajitnov's March 1990 Affirmation, despite its lack of a time limitation, plaintiffs urge that the term "owner" must be read in the context of the earlier affirmation to connote only present ownership and that the holder of a ten year license was considered an "owner" under Soviet legal principles. (Pls' Mem. Supp. at 19–20). Plaintiffs maintain similar arguments as they address the other documents set forth above and broadly argue that "[d]efendants' motion, and this entire case, hinges on whether Defendants have proven that Mr. Pajitnov, sometime after September 1989, gave away all of his right in his creation, for no reason and without compensation."

On the other hand, while defendants would have a difficult task arguing that "owner" meant more than an ownership for some limited time period if just viewing the March 1989 Affirmation, defendants reasonably maintain that "owner" connotes perpetual ownership when analyzed in the context of the entire relationship of the parties. In particular, defendants argue that plaintiffs' case "hinge[s] on one thing: a single writing, made three-years after-the-fact, internally ambiguous, recalling an oral limitation, that is contradicted by each and every subsequent writing, at least three of which were signed by Mr. Pajitnov." Defendants claim that the grant may have changed at one point, that subsequent records reflect this change, and that those later documents should be controlling because they embody the most recent agreement between the parties. However, this last point cannot be determinative at this stage because it remains ambiguous whether there was in fact a later agreement—plaintiffs' interpretation of the evidence rejects that possibility.

Ultimately, each side finds some support for its reasonable and respective ownership claims. For this very reason, the scope of ownership rights (except for the merchandising rights) conveyed by the actual grant is ambiguous as a matter of law. Accordingly, it cannot be said at this point in the litigation that either side is likely to succeed on the merits based upon its respective ownership claim for the non-merchandising rights.

b. Merchandising Rights.

The Merchandising Agreement, and the corresponding merchandising rights for Tetris, present a situation quite different than the copyright and trademark rights for several reasons. First, whereas many of the prior documents only confirm or reference a transfer of non-merchandising rights, the Merchandising Agreement purports to actually "sell, assign, and transfer" the merchandising rights from Pajitnov to the CCAS. Its title—"Assignment Agreement"—reflects its nature. In fact, it appears to be the only operative document that actually conveys rights from Pajitnov to another party. Second, the term "owner," ambiguous in the context of these parties' dealings, does not appear in the Merchandising Agreement. Nor is any other ambiguity present. Because the merchandising rights were expressly excluded in the other documents set forth above, the parties apparently considered these rights separately from the transfer of all the other rights.

Accordingly, this Court will not look beyond the plain and unambiguous language of this agreement. Though plaintiffs stress that Pajitnov understood the transfer of rights to take place within the context of the ten year limit confirmed months earlier, that parol evidence would most likely be inadmissible at trial to refute the plain terms of the contract. As such, defendants have shown a likelihood of success as to their ownership claim for the merchandising rights and their preliminary injunction shall be granted insofar as those rights are concerned.

C. The Copyright and Trademark Registrations

1. Statutory Presumptions and Evidence of Ownership

In connection with its obligations pursuant to the Nintendo Agreement, Nintendo filed U.S. trademark and copyright registrations for the Tetris trademark and video game in the name of Soviet Elorg (By registering those rights in Soviet Elorg's name, one of the attorneys responsible for submitting the registration documents states that his firm did not "intend to represent that Soviet Elorg had any rights in the Tetris trademark or copyrights beyond those described [in two documents—one by Pajitnov and one by Belikov—that each limit Pajitnov's grant of rights to ten years]."). Defendants put forth substantial effort detailing and place heavy reliance upon the legal presumption of ownership afforded the registrant of copyright and trademark registrations. Defendants stress that their status as registrants for the Tetris copyrights and trademarks signifies that they are the presumed owner, and in the instance of one trademark the conclusive owner, arguing that these presumptions thereby entitle them to a preliminary injunction. However, the law sets forth merely a presumption of ownership, which is rebuttable even in the case of an "incontestable" registration. Rather, plaintiffs place at bar several arguments which require a more focused analysis than a simple reliance upon a statutory presumption to yield a dispositive answer.

In particular, defendants correctly assert that the fact that they have registered the Tetris trademarks and copyrights in their name provides prima facie evidence as to the ownership of those rights. A registration of a trademark shall be prima facie evidence of the validity of the registered mark and of the registration of the mark, of the registrant's ownership of the mark, and of the registrant's exclusive right to use the registered mark in commerce ... but shall not preclude another person from proving any legal or equitable defense or defect, including those set forth in subsection (b) of this section, which might have been asserted if such mark had not been registered. 15 U.S.C. § 1115(a). As set forth in section 1115(a), legal and equitable defenses are available to rebut a prima facie showing of ownership.

Moreover, the right of the registrant to use the trademark shall become "incontestable" when the mark "has been in continuous use for five consecutive years" after the date of registration and is still being used in commerce. 15 U.S.C. § 1065. An incontestable mark shall be "conclusive evidence: of its validity and the registrant's ownership." 15 U.S.C. § 1115(a). Despite what the name suggests, "incontestable" status is subject to several defenses as set forth in section 1115(a).

In addition, copyright law provides a similar presumption, though does not offer a parallel "incontestable" status. For copyrights, the certificate of a registration made before or within five years after first publication of the work shall constitute prima facie evidence of the validity of the copyright and of the facts stated in the certificate. The evidentiary weight to be accorded the certificate of a registration made thereafter shall be within the discretion of the court. 17 U.S.C. § 410(c). Though no defenses are set forth in section 410 to rebut the presumption of ownership for copyrights, the Second Circuit has made clear that the validity of the facts in the registration too may be rebutted "'where other evidence in the record casts doubt on the question....'" *Estate of Hogarth v. Edgar Rice Burroughs, Inc.*, 342 F.3d 149, 166–67 (2d Cir. 2003).

Despite the presumptions of ownership that attach to copyright and trademark registrations, plaintiffs successfully retort with several distinct points. (Building upon these statutory presumptions, defendants argue the additional point that insofar as the copyrights are concerned, only the author or the author's assignee may be identified on a registration, and never a licensee. Accordingly, defendants reason that the fact that they are listed on the registration is further evidence that they are the assignee of the copyrights and not just licensees. However, as plaintiffs correctly point out, a licensee being listed as a claimant or owner may be a technical error, but in any event, a party does not acquire ownership merely by virtue of having been listed as the claimant or owner. Plaintiffs' argument is further supported by the fact that the attorney responsible for those registrations has stated that he and his firm did not "intend[ ] to represent that Soviet Elorg had any rights: to Tetris beyond the ten-year limit.).

a. The Mere Registration Of A Trademark Or Copyright Does Not Create Property Rights.

First, while registrations may be prima facie evidence of ownership, the mere fact that a party registers its copyrights or trademark rights does not create substantive ownership rights in the registrant. Rather, substantive copyrights spring to life at the moment of the genesis of the creative work and attach to the creator or author immediately, and similarly, trademark rights attach based upon use of the mark in commerce and registration provides no additional substantive rights against infringement beyond acquired common law rights.

Accordingly, registrations merely offer evidence of ownership, and that showing need not be dispositive of the matter if contrary proof is available. For purposes of these motions, plaintiffs have made a sufficient showing to rebut defendants' prima facie case of ownership based upon defendants' status as registrants of the Tetris trademarks and copyrights.

b. Registrations Will Not Trump Contractually Agreed Upon Ownership Rights.

Second, as a separate challenge to the statutory presumptions afforded registrations, plaintiffs correctly point out that the law will not permit these presumptions to supercede a contractual arrangement between the parties. A licensee's right to use a licensor's intellectual property ceases when the license expires. Accordingly, an ultimate determination that plaintiffs in this action had reversionary property rights to Tetris pursuant to a contract with defendants would successfully rebut any evidence of ownership demonstrated by the registrations.

c. The "Incontestable" Trademark Is Subject to Challenge.

Third, defendants urge that one of their trademarks has obtained an "incontestable" status because they have used it in commerce for five continuous years subsequent to the date of registration. See 15 U.S.C. § 1065. While they do not contest that defendants have made this initial showing, plaintiffs contend that several affirmative defenses or exceptions defeat the purported incontestable status. ("The words 'incontestable' and 'exclusive' sound more impressive than the legal rights that the Lanham Act actually conveys, however." *Eco Mfg. LLC. v. Honeywell Intern., Inc.*, 357 F.3d 649, 651 (7th Cir. 2003)). In particular, plaintiffs contend: (1) that defendants' inequitable conduct defeats the mark's incontestable status, (2) equitable estoppel must prevent defendants from even raising an incontestability claim, and (3) defendants committed fraud in obtaining the registration they allege is now incontestable and that conduct is an absolute defense. Any of the affirmative defenses, if established, would strip defendants of the conclusive presumption of ownership linked to an incontestable trademark and thus the registration would be only prima facie evidence of ownership.

i. Plaintiffs May Be Able To Demonstrate Inequitable Conduct By Defendants And Thereby Defeat The Incontestable Status Of The Trademark.

Section 1115(b)(9) provides that the status of "conclusive evidence" afforded an "incontestable" mark may be defeated if "equitable principles, including laches, estoppel, acquiescence, are applicable." Plaintiffs proffer that defendants' filing of the '499 Registration—the document registering the purported incontestable trademark—was a blatant example of inequitable conduct. Specifically, they contend that defendants filed the '499 Registration after the parties had—as plaintiffs describe—"effectively reached an interim settlement agreement [embodied by the TTC Agreement] regarding the disputed rights … and without disclosing to Plaintiffs that [defendants were] doing so." Moreover, according to plaintiffs, defendants never informed them "that there was a clock running on their ownership claims and that the interim resolution of the parties' dispute by creating TTC would be used against Plaintiffs to argue that … Pajitnov's contractual rights purportedly expired because he had chosen not to litigate." Plaintiffs essentially claim that defendants sang two different tunes—on the one hand engaging in an apparent good faith resolution, while on the other hand solidifying their own claim by registering the trademark in their name out of plaintiffs' earshot.

Defendants vehemently dispute plaintiffs' position that the TTC Agreement was "effectively an interim settlement." Ultimately though, just what impression and expectations defendants conveyed to plaintiffs is a factual issue that cannot be resolved at this stage of the litigation. Accordingly, neither party has demonstrated a likelihood of success in this regard; therefore, an equitable defense to defendants' incontestable claim will be able to be raised at trial and defendants are not entitled to a preliminary injunction as to their alleged incontestable registration.

ii. Plaintiffs May Be Able to Prove the Elements of Equitable Estoppel, Thereby Barring Defendants From Raising The Alleged Incontestability Of The '499 Registration.

Equitable estoppel requires a showing of (1) a material misrepresentation, (2) reasonable reliance upon that representation, and (3) damage and is a defense to an alleged incontestable registration. See 15 U.S.C. § 1115(b)(9) Plaintiffs allege that Pajitnov was instructed by an attorney for CCAS to sign the confirmations and they were "merely a confirmation of the then-current status of the rights to Tetris" which Pajitnov understood to be that he had granted his rights for a ten-year period. Whether defendants indeed misrepresented the purpose of the confirmations, or whether they omitted to inform Pajitnov that they would seek incontestable status for the Tetris trademarks, and whether any reliance upon any misrepresentation was reasonable and caused plaintiffs damage are questions of fact that cannot be decided on these motions. Because neither side has demonstrated a likelihood of success on the merits as to equitable estoppel, an equitable defense to defendants' incontestable claim cannot be foreclosed to plaintiffs at this point and defendants' are not entitled to a preliminary injunction as to their alleged incontestable registration.

iii. Plaintiffs May Be Able To Show That Defendants Obtained The Alleged Incontestable Registration By Fraud, Thereby Defeating Its Incontestable Status.

Plaintiffs assert that defendants committed acts of fraud on the U.S.P.T.O. in obtaining the '499 Registration, thereby defeating its incontestable status. In particular, plaintiffs allege that at the time Soviet Elorg filed the '499 Registration, it knew that it was not the owner, but merely a licensee, all the while allowing Pajitnov to believe that neither that registration nor any other documents he signed would be used in any way to affect his rights after the ten-year limit. Belikov—plaintiffs claim—submitted false "assignments" of the trademark on behalf of entities which Belikov now states either no longer existed or had no rights to assign at the time of execution. Again, these allegations present factual issues that cannot be decided at this stage of the litigation. Those claims do preclude defendants now from demonstrating a likelihood of success on the merits as to the incontestable mark and accordingly, they are not entitled to a preliminary injunction as to their alleged incontestable registration.

D. Plaintiffs' Claims Are Not Barred As A Matter Of Law

Defendants assert that plaintiffs' challenges to their motion for preliminary relief are legally barred. First, defendants contend that plaintiffs are estopped from now challenging defendants' ownership claims by virtue of plaintiffs having acquiesced to defendants' asserted rights. Second, according to defendants, various statutes of limitations now bar plaintiffs from presenting certain of their challenges.

1. Plaintiffs Have Not As A Matter Of Law Acquiesced
To Defendants' Asserted Ownership Claims.

Defendants claim that plaintiffs have acquiesced to their asserted ownership rights because Pajitnov and Rogers both have stated that the dispute as to ownership arose as early as 1995 or 1996. At that time, all the trademark registrations were in Elorg's name, yet according to defendants, plaintiffs made no challenge to defendants' asserted ownership.

The U.S. Court of Appeals for the Second Circuit has "long held in the context of trademark actions that '[w]here a person entitled to exclusive use of a trademark is guilty of unreasonable delay in asserting his rights against an infringer..., or acquiesces in the latter's use, ... a court of equity has the discretionary power ... to deny injunctive relief.'" *ProFitness Physical Therapy Center v. Pro-Fit Orthopedic and Sports Physical Therapy P.C.*, 314 F.3d 62, 67 (2d Cir. 2002). The defense of acquiescence has three elements: (1) the senior user actively represented that it would not assert a right or a claim; (2) the delay between the active representation and assertion of the right or claim was not excusable; and (3) the delay caused the defendant undue prejudice. *Id.*

Plaintiffs contend that their failure to bring suit earlier was reasonable in light of their view of having reached an interim settlement. Because defendants have not demonstrated that plaintiffs' actions meet the standard as a matter of law, the defense of acquiescence will require as to each element findings of fact that are inappropriate for resolution at this stage of the litigation.

VI. Conclusion

For the reasons set forth above, the motions for preliminary injunctions are denied, except insofar as defendants' motion is granted as to the merchandising rights to Tetris. Accordingly, plaintiffs are hereby preliminarily enjoined from interfering with defendants' enjoyment of the Tetris merchandising rights in a manner inconsistent with this Opinion and Order.

Notes and Questions

1. As the court in *Blue Planet* indicated, the ownership battles inflicted irreparable harm to the game *Tetris* and its marketers. The dispute even extended to the United States

Customs Service which, pursuant to its authority, seized a shipment of hand held *Tetris* games. The proper procedure, whenever Customs finds an infringement, mandates that "the port director shall seize the imported article" 19 C.F.R. § 133.44(a) (1998). *See Luxury Int'l, Inc. v. United States*, 90 F. Supp. 2d 1294 (Ct. Int'l Trade 2000).

2. Other than the reasons discussed in *Blue Planet*, can you think of any logical rationale explaining why Pajitnov would grant exclusive rights in the Game *Tetris* "for a period of 10 years," and in the very same paragraph refer to the grantee as the legal "owner of the right and license for selling the Game Tetris" on the world market?

3. Is there a difference between an "affirmation of assignment" and an actual assignment? Should there be?

4. Extremely popular games are destined to spark infringement claims. See *Tetris Holding, LLC v. Xio Interactive, Inc.*, 863 F. Supp. 2d 394 (N.J., 2012), which we reproduce in § 6.75 *infra*.

§ 2.43 Employees and Works for Hire

One of the most familiar arrangements among developers and publishers of intellectual property involves the so-called "Work made for hire" agreement (more commonly referred to only as a 'Work for hire.')." The concept is relatively simple, provided that there is a clear meeting of the minds with respect to each specific component and item of intellectual creativity. In our context, a video game developer may hire or commission several people to work on, or contribute to the finished product. The developer will want to be assured that he or she owns the finished video game in its entirety. A properly drafted "Work for hire" agreement will accomplish that end.

The business models for videogame development have changed over the years as the industry's developers grew from individuals or a small team to large corporations. So too have their titles changed. Today a large "publisher," as opposed to a more personal "developer," is likely to own the finished product.

If *A* wishes to restore an old automobile retrieved from a junk yard, and he agrees to pay *B* to help paint and restore it, there is little doubt about who owns the finished product. Because the car is tangible and is accompanied by a title of ownership, it is clear that *A* retains ownership. Likewise, if *A* paid *B* to create a new automobile for *A*, there would be little doubt about the intention of the parties or the rightful ownership of the finished product. But unlike videogames and other forms of intellectual property, the value of the automobile lies in a single, identifiable, tangible asset *rather* than in the power to freely make and distribute copies. Unlike tangible property, a given item of intellectual property can be transferred to many separate purchasers without destroying the value of the original asset.

Section 201(a) of the Copyright Act (pertaining to "Ownership of Copyright") provides: "Initial Ownership. — Copyright in a work protected under this title vests initially in the author or authors of the work. The authors of a joint work are co-owners of copyright in the work."

Thus, having initially equated authorship and ownership, Section 201(b) pertaining to "Works made for hire," then states: "In the case of a work made for hire, the employer or other person for whom the work was prepared is considered the author for purposes of this title, and, unless the parties have expressly agreed otherwise in a written instrument signed by them, owns all of the rights comprised in the copyright."

Whenever another person's efforts or labors are utilized during the production of an intellectual product, any one of several relationships might occur, ranging from that of *employer-employee* to *independent contractor*, with some other added possibilities along the way, such as *principle-agent*, *joint venturers*, and even *partners*. It is not uncommon, however, for one member of the relationship to perceive himself or herself as something that is *not* intended by the other. As indicated above, a written agreement is the best way to avoid ownership disputes and the problems presented by the following landmark case.

Community for Creative Non-Violence v. Reid

Supreme Court of the United States, 1989
490 U.S. 730

MARSHALL, Associate Justice

In this case, an artist and the organization that hired him to produce a sculpture contest the ownership of the copyright in that work. To resolve this dispute, we must construe the "work made for hire" provisions of the Copyright Act of 1976 (Act or 1976 Act), 17 U.S.C. §§ 101 and 201(b), and in particular, the provision in § 101, which defines as a "work made for hire" a "work prepared by an employee within the scope of his or her employment" (hereinafter § 101(1)).

I.

Petitioners are the Community for Creative Non-Violence (CCNV), a nonprofit unincorporated association dedicated to eliminating homelessness in America, and Mitch Snyder, a member and trustee of CCNV. In the fall of 1985, CCNV decided to participate in the annual Christmastime Pageant of Peace in Washington, D.C., by sponsoring a display to dramatize the plight of the homeless. As the District Court recounted:

> Snyder and fellow CCNV members conceived the idea for the nature of the display: a sculpture of a modern Nativity scene in which, in lieu of the traditional Holy Family, the two adult figures and the infant would appear as contemporary homeless people huddled on a streetside steam grate. The family was to be black (most of the homeless in Washington being black); the figures were to be life-sized, and the steam grate would be positioned atop a platform 'pedestal,' or base, within which special-effects equipment would be enclosed to emit simulated 'steam' through the grid to swirl about the figures. They also settled upon a title for the work — 'Third World America' — and a legend for the pedestal: 'and still there is no room at the inn.' 652 F.Supp. 1453, 1454 (DC 1987).

Snyder made inquiries to locate an artist to produce the sculpture. He was referred to respondent James Earl Reid, a Baltimore, Maryland, sculptor. In the course of two telephone calls, Reid agreed to sculpt the three human figures. CCNV agreed to make the steam grate and pedestal for the statue. Reid proposed that the work be cast in bronze, at a total cost of approximately $100,000 and taking six to eight months to complete. Snyder rejected that proposal because CCNV did not have sufficient funds, and because the statue had to be completed by December 12 to be included in the pageant. Reid then suggested, and Snyder agreed, that the sculpture would be made of a material known as "Design Cast 62," a synthetic substance that could meet CCNV's monetary and time constraints, could be tinted to resemble bronze, and could withstand the elements. The parties agreed that the project would cost no more than $15,000, not including Reid's services, which he offered to donate. The parties did not sign a written agreement. Neither party mentioned copyright.

After Reid received an advance of $3,000, he made several sketches of figures in various poses. At Snyder's request, Reid sent CCNV a sketch of a proposed sculpture showing the family in a creche like setting: the mother seated, cradling a baby in her lap; the father standing behind her, bending over her shoulder to touch the baby's foot. Reid testified that Snyder asked for the sketch to use in raising funds for the sculpture. Snyder testified that it was also for his approval. Reid sought a black family to serve as a model for the sculpture. Upon Snyder's suggestion, Reid visited a family living at CCNV's Washington shelter but decided that only their newly born child was a suitable model. While Reid was in Washington, Snyder took him to see homeless people living on the streets. Snyder pointed out that they tended to recline on steam grates, rather than sit or stand, in order to warm their bodies. From that time on, Reid's sketches contained only reclining figures. Throughout November and the first two weeks of December 1985, Reid worked exclusively on the statue, assisted at various times by a dozen different people who were paid with funds provided in installments by CCNV. On a number of occasions, CCNV members visited Reid to check on his progress and to coordinate CCNV's construction of the base. CCNV rejected Reid's proposal to use suitcases or shopping bags to hold the family's personal belongings, insisting instead on a shopping cart. Reid and CCNV members did not discuss copyright ownership on any of these visits.

On December 24, 1985, 12 days after the agreed-upon date, Reid delivered the completed statue to Washington. There it was joined to the steam grate and pedestal prepared by CCNV and placed on display near the site of the pageant. Snyder paid Reid the final installment of the $15,000. The statue remained on display for a month. In late January 1986, CCNV members returned it to Reid's studio in Baltimore for minor repairs. Several weeks later, Snyder began making plans to take the statue on a tour of several cities to raise money for the homeless. Reid objected, contending that the Design Cast 62 material was not strong enough to withstand the ambitious itinerary. He urged CCNV to cast the statue in bronze at a cost of $35,000, or to create a master mold at a cost of $5,000. Snyder declined to spend more of CCNV's money on the project.

In March 1986, Snyder asked Reid to return the sculpture. Reid refused. He then filed a certificate of copyright registration for "Third World America" in his name and announced plans to take the sculpture on a more modest tour than the one CCNV had proposed. Snyder, acting in his capacity as CCNV's trustee, immediately filed a competing certificate of copyright registration. Snyder and CCNV then commenced this action against Reid and his photographer, Ronald Purtee, seeking return of the sculpture and a determination of copyright ownership. The District Court granted a preliminary injunction, ordering the sculpture's return. After a 2-day bench trial, the District Court declared that "Third World America" was a "work made for hire" under § 101 of the Copyright Act and that Snyder, as trustee for CCNV, was the exclusive owner of the copyright in the sculpture. 652 F.Supp., at 1457. The court reasoned that Reid had been an "employee" of CCNV within the meaning of § 101(1) because CCNV was the motivating force in the statue's production. Snyder and other CCNV members, the court explained, "conceived the idea of a contemporary Nativity scene to contrast with the national celebration of the season," and "directed enough of [Reid's] effort to assure that, in the end, he had produced what they, not he, wanted." *Id.* at 1456.

The Court of Appeals for the District of Columbia Circuit reversed and remanded, holding that Reid owned the copyright because "Third World America" was not a work for hire. 270 U.S.App.D.C. 26, 35, 846 F.2d 1485, 1494 (1988). Adopting what it termed the "literal interpretation" of the Act as articulated by the Fifth Circuit in *Easter Seal Society for Crippled Children & Adults of Louisiana, Inc. v. Playboy Enterprises*, 815 F.2d 323, 329

(1987), the court read § 101 as creating "a simple dichotomy in fact between employees and independent contractors." 270 U.S.App.D.C., at 33, 846 F.2d, at 1492. Because, under agency law, Reid was an independent contractor, the court concluded that the work was not "prepared by an employee" under § 101(1). Id., at 35, 846 F.2d, at 1494. Nor was the sculpture a "work made for hire" under the second subsection of § 101 (hereinafter § 101(2)): sculpture is not one of the nine categories of works enumerated in that subsection, and the parties had not agreed in writing that the sculpture would be a work for hire. Ibid. The court suggested that the sculpture nevertheless may have been jointly authored by CCNV and Reid, id., at 36, 846 F.2d, at 1495, and remanded for a determination whether the sculpture is indeed a joint work under the Act, id., at 39–40, 846 F.2d, at 1498–1499. We granted certiorari to resolve a conflict among the Courts of Appeals over the proper construction of the "work made for hire" provisions of the Act.[30] 488 U.S. 940, 109 S.Ct. 362, 102 L.Ed.2d 352 (1988).

We now affirm.

II.

A.

The Copyright Act of 1976 provides that copyright ownership "vests initially in the author or authors of the work." 17 U.S.C. § 201(a). As a general rule, the author is the party who actually creates the work, that is, the person who translates an idea into a fixed, tangible expression entitled to copyright protection. § 102. The Act carves out an important exception, however, for "works made for hire." [31] If the work is for hire, "the employer or other person for whom the work was prepared is considered the author" and owns the copyright, unless there is a written agreement to the contrary. § 201(b). Classifying a work as "made for hire" determines not only the initial ownership of its copyright, but also the copyright's duration, § 302(c), and the owners' renewal rights, § 304(a), termination rights, § 203(a), and right to import certain goods bearing the copyright, § 601(b)(1). See 1 M. Nimmer & D. Nimmer, Nimmer on Copyright § 5.03[A], pp. 5–10 (1988). The contours of the work for hire doctrine therefore carry profound significance for freelance creators—including artists, writers, photographers, designers, composers, and computer programmers—and for the publishing, advertising, music, and other industries which commission their works.[32] Section 101 of the 1976 Act provides that a work is "for hire" under two sets of circumstances:

> "(1) a work prepared by an employee within the scope of his or her employment; or
>
> (2) a work specially ordered or commissioned for use as a contribution to a collective work, as a part of a motion picture or other audiovisual work, as a translation, as a supplementary work, as a compilation, as an instructional text, as a test, as answer material for a test, or as an atlas, if the parties expressly agree

---

30. *Compare Easter Seal Soc'y for Crippled Children & Adults of Louisiana, Inc. v. Playboy Enters.,* 815 F.2d 323 (CA5 1987) (agency law determines who is an employee under § 101) *with Brunswick Beacon, Inc. v. Schock-Hopchas Publ'g Co.,* 810 F.2d 410 (CA4 1987) (supervision and control standard determines who is an employee under § 101).

31. We use the phrase "work for hire" interchangeably with the more cumbersome statutory phrase "work made for hire."

32. As of 1955, approximately 40 percent of all copyright registrations were for works for hire, according to a Copyright Office study.

in a written instrument signed by them that the work shall be considered a work made for hire."[33]

Petitioners do not claim that the statue satisfies the terms of § 101(2). Quite clearly, it does not. Sculpture does not fit within any of the nine categories of "specially ordered or commissioned" works enumerated in that subsection, and no written agreement between the parties establishes "Third World America" as a work for hire. The dispositive inquiry in this case therefore is whether "Third World America" is "a work prepared by an employee within the scope of his or her employment" under § 101(1). The Act does not define these terms. In the absence of such guidance, four interpretations have emerged. The first holds that a work is prepared by an employee whenever the hiring party[34] retains the right to control the product. *See Peregrine v. Lauren Corp.*, 601 F.Supp. 828, 829 (Colo.1985). Petitioners take this view. A second, and closely related, view is that a work is prepared by an employee under § 101(1) when the hiring party has actually wielded control with respect to the creation of a particular work. This approach was formulated by the Court of Appeals for the Second Circuit, *Aldon Accessories Ltd. v. Spiegel, Inc.*, 738 F.2d 548 (1984) and, at times, by petitioners. A third view is that the term "employee" within § 101(1) carries its common-law agency law meaning. This view was endorsed by the Fifth Circuit in *Easter Seal Society for Crippled Children & Adults of Louisiana, Inc. v. Playboy Enterprises*, 815 F.2d 323 (1987), and by the Court of Appeals below. Finally, respondent and numerous amici curiae contend that the term "employee" only refers to "formal, salaried" employees. The Court of Appeals for the Ninth Circuit recently adopted this view. *See Dumas v. Gommerman*, 865 F.2d 1093 (1989).

The starting point for our interpretation of a statute is always its language. The Act nowhere defines the terms "employee" or "scope of employment." It is, however, well established that where Congress uses terms that have accumulated settled meaning under ... the common law, a court must infer, unless the statute otherwise dictates, that Congress means to incorporate the established meaning of these terms.

In the past, when Congress has used the term "employee" without defining it, we have concluded that Congress intended to describe the conventional master-servant relationship as understood by common-law agency doctrine. Nothing in the text of the work for hire provisions indicates that Congress used the words, "employee" and "employment" to describe anything other than the conventional relation of employer and employee. On the contrary, Congress' intent to incorporate the agency law definition is suggested by § 101(1)'s use of the term, "scope of employment," a widely used term of art in agency law. See Restatement (Second) of Agency § 228 (1958) (hereinafter Restatement).

In past cases of statutory interpretation, when we have concluded that Congress intended terms such as "employee," "employer," and "scope of employment" to be understood in light of agency law, we have relied on the general common law of agency, rather than on the law of any particular State, to give meaning to these terms. This practice reflects the fact that federal statutes are generally intended to have uniform nationwide application. Establishment of a federal rule of agency, rather than reliance on state agency law, is particularly appropriate here given the Act's express objective of creating national, uniform

---

33. Section 101 of the Act defines each of the nine categories of "specially ordered or commissioned" works.

34. By "hiring party," we mean to refer to the party who claims ownership of the copyright by virtue of the work for hire doctrine.

copyright law by broadly pre-empting state statutory and common-law copyright regulation. See 17 U.S.C. § 301(a). We thus agree with the Court of Appeals that the term "employee" should be understood in light of the general common law of agency.

In contrast, neither test proposed by petitioners is consistent with the text of the Act. The exclusive focus of the right to control the product test on the relationship between the hiring party and the product clashes with the language of § 101(1), which focuses on the relationship between the hired and hiring parties. The right to control the product test also would distort the meaning of the ensuing subsection, § 101(2). Section 101 plainly creates two distinct ways in which a work can be deemed for hire: one for works prepared by employees, the other for those specially ordered or commissioned works which fall within one of the nine enumerated categories and are the subject of a written agreement. The right to control the product test ignores this dichotomy by transforming into a work for hire under § 101(1) any "specially ordered or commissioned" work that is subject to the supervision and control of the hiring party.

Because a party who hires a "specially ordered or commissioned" work by definition has a right to specify the characteristics of the product desired, at the time the commission is accepted, and frequently until it is completed, the right to control the product test would mean that many works that could satisfy § 101(2) would already have been deemed works for hire under § 101(1). Petitioners' interpretation is particularly hard to square with § 101(2)'s enumeration of the nine specific categories of specially ordered or com- missioned works eligible to be works for hire, e.g., "a contribution to a collective work," "a part of a motion picture," and "answer material for a test." The unifying feature of these works is that they are usually prepared at the instance, direction, and risk of a publisher or producer. By their very nature, therefore, these types of works would be works by an employee under petitioners' right to control the product test.

The actual control test, articulated by the Second Circuit in *Aldon Accessories*, fares only marginally better when measured against the language and structure of § 101. Under this test, independent contractors who are so controlled and supervised in the creation of a particular work are deemed "employees" under § 101(1). Thus work for hire status under § 101(1) depends on a hiring party's actual control of, rather than right to control, the product. *Aldon Accessories*, 738 F.2d, at 552. Under the actual control test, a work for hire could arise under § 101(2), but not under § 101(1), where a party commissions, but does not actually control, a product which falls into one of the nine enumerated categories. Nonetheless, we agree with the Court of Appeals for the Fifth Circuit that "[t]here is simply no way to milk the 'actual control' test of Aldon Accessories from the language of the statute." *Easter Seal Society*, 815 F.2d, at 334. Section 101 clearly delineates between works prepared by an employee and commissioned works. Sound though other distinctions might be as a matter of copyright policy, there is no statutory support for an additional dichotomy between commissioned works that are actually controlled and supervised by the hiring party and those that are not.

We therefore conclude that the language and structure of § 101 of the Act do not support either the right to control the product or the actual control approaches.[35] The structure of § 101 indicates that a work for hire can arise through one of two mutually exclusive means, one for employees and one for independent contractors, and ordinary canons of statutory interpretation indicate that the classification of a particular hired party should be made with reference to agency law.

---

35. We also reject the suggestion of respondent and amici that the § 101(1) term "employee" refers only to formal, salaried employees.

The Act, which almost completely revised existing copyright law, was the product of two decades of negotiation by representatives of creators and copyright-using industries, supervised by the Copyright Office and, to a lesser extent, by Congress. Despite the lengthy history of negotiation and compromise which ultimately produced the Act, two things remained constant. First, interested parties and Congress at all times viewed works by employees and commissioned works by independent contractors as separate entities. Second, in using the term "employee," the parties and Congress meant to refer to a hired party in a conventional employment relationship. These factors militate in favor of the reading we have found appropriate.

Because the 1909 Act did not define "employer" or "works made for hire," the task of shaping these terms fell to the courts. They concluded that the work for hire doctrine codified in §62 referred only to works made by employees in the regular course of their employment. As for commissioned works, the courts generally presumed that the commissioned party had impliedly agreed to convey the copyright, along with the work itself, to the hiring party. *See, e.g., Shapiro, Bernstein & Co. v. Jerry Vogel Music Co.*, 221 F.2d 569, 570 (CA2 1955).

In 1965, the competing interests reached a historic compromise, which was embodied in a joint memorandum submitted to Congress and the Copyright Office, incorporated into the 1965 revision bill, and ultimately enacted in the same form and nearly the same terms 11 years later, as §101 of the 1976 Act. The compromise retained as subsection (1) the language referring to "a work prepared by an employee within the scope of his employment." However, in exchange for concessions from publishers on provisions relating to the termination of transfer rights, the authors consented to a second subsection which classified four categories of commissioned works as works for hire if the parties expressly so agreed in writing: works for use "as a contribution to a collective work, as a part of a motion picture, as a translation, or as supplementary work." S. 1006, H.R. 4347, H.R. 5680, H.R. 6835, 89th Cong., 1st Sess., §101 (1965). The interested parties selected these categories because they concluded that these commissioned works, although not prepared by employees and thus not covered by the first subsection, nevertheless should be treated as works for hire because they were ordinarily prepared "at the instance, direction, and risk of a publisher or producer." Supplementary Report, at 67.

In 1966, the House Committee on the Judiciary endorsed this compromise in the first legislative Report on the revision bills. See H.R.Rep. No. 2237, 89th Cong., 2d Sess., 114, 116 (1966). Retaining the distinction between works by employees and commissioned works, the House Committee focused instead on "how to draw a statutory line between those works written on special order or commission that should be considered as works made for hire, and those that should not." *Id.* at 115.

The House Committee added four other enumerated categories of commissioned works that could be treated as works for hire: compilations, instructional texts, tests, and atlases. *Id.*, at 116. With the single addition of "answer material for a test," the 1976 Act, as enacted, contained the same definition of works made for hire as did the 1966 revision bill, and had the same structure and nearly the same terms as the 1966 bill.

Thus, the legislative history of the Act is significant for several reasons. First, the enactment of the 1965 compromise with only minor modifications demonstrates that Congress intended to provide two mutually exclusive ways for works to acquire work for hire status: one for employees and the other for independent contractors. Second, the legislative history underscores the clear import of the statutory language: only enumerated categories of commissioned works may be accorded work for hire status. The hiring party's right to control the product simply is not determinative. Indeed, importing a test based on a hiring party's right to control, or actual control of, a product would unravel the "'carefully worked out compromise aimed at balancing legitimate interests on both sides.'" H.R.Rep. No. 2237, *supra*, at 114.[36]

Finally, petitioners' construction of the work for hire provisions would impede Congress' paramount goal in revising the 1976 Act of enhancing predictability and certainty of copyright ownership. See H. R. Rep. No. 94-1476, *supra*, at 129. In a "copyright marketplace," the parties negotiate with an expectation that one of them will own the copyright in the completed work. Dumas, 865 F.2d, at 1104–1105, n. 18. With that expectation, the parties at the outset can settle on relevant contractual terms, such as the price for the work and the ownership of reproduction rights.

To the extent that petitioners endorse an actual control test,[37] CCNV's construction of the work for hire provisions prevents such planning. Because that test turns on whether the hiring party has closely monitored the production process, the parties would not know until late in the process, if not until the work is completed, whether a work will ultimately fall within § 101(1). Under petitioners' approach, therefore, parties would have to predict in advance whether the hiring party will sufficiently control a given work to make it the author. "If they guess incorrectly, their reliance on 'work for hire' or an assignment may give them a copyright interest that they did not bargain for." *Easter Seal Society*, 815 F.2d, at 333. This understanding of the work for hire provisions clearly thwarts Congress' goal of ensuring predictability through advance planning. Moreover, petitioners' interpretation leaves the door open for hiring parties, who have failed to get a full assignment of copyright rights from independent contractors falling outside the subdivision (2) guidelines, to unilaterally obtain work-made-for-hire rights years after the work has been completed as long as they directed or supervised the work, a standard that is hard not to meet when one is a hiring party.

In sum, we must reject petitioners' argument. Transforming a commissioned work into a work by an employee on the basis of the hiring party's right to control, or actual control of, the work is inconsistent with the language, structure, and legislative history of the work for hire provisions. To determine whether a work is for hire under the Act, a court first should ascertain, using principles of general common law of agency, whether the work was prepared by an employee or an independent contractor. After making this determination, the court can apply the appropriate subsection of § 101.

B.

We turn, finally, to an application of § 101 to Reid's production of "Third World America." In determining whether a hired party is an employee under the general common law of agency, we consider [Lettering of subparagraphs was added by ED] —

[a] the hiring party's right to control the manner and means by which the product is accomplished. Among the other factors relevant to this inquiry are:

[b] the skill required;

[c] the source of the instrumentalities and tools;

---

36. Strict adherence to the language and structure of the Act is particularly appropriate where, as here, a statute is the result of a series of carefully crafted compromises. *See Rodriguez v. Compass Shipping Co.*, 451 U.S. 596, 617 (U.S. 1981).

37. Petitioners concede that, as a practical matter, it is often difficult to demonstrate the existence of a right to control without evidence of the actual exercise of that right.

[d] the location of the work;

[e] the duration of the relationship between the parties;

[f] whether the hiring party has the right to assign additional projects to the hired party;

[g] the extent of the hired party's discretion over when and how long to work;

[h] the method of payment;

[i] the hired party's role in hiring and paying assistants; whether [j] the work is part of the regular business of the hiring party;

[k] whether the hiring party is in business;

[l] the provision of employee benefits;

[m] and the tax treatment of the hired party.

Examining the circumstances of this case in light of these factors, we agree with the Court of Appeals that Reid was not an employee of CCNV but an independent contractor. 270 U.S.App.D.C., at 35, n. 11, 846 F.2d, at 1494, n. 11. True, CCNV members directed enough of Reid's work to ensure that he produced a sculpture that met their specifications. 652 F.Supp., at 1456. But the extent of control the hiring party exercises over the details of the product is not dispositive. Indeed, all the other circumstances weigh heavily against finding an employment relationship. Reid is a sculptor, a skilled occupation. Reid supplied his own tools. He worked in his own studio in Baltimore, making daily supervision of his activities from Washington practically impossible. Reid was retained for less than two months, a relatively short period of time. During and after this time, CCNV had no right to assign additional projects to Reid.

Apart from the deadline for completing the sculpture, Reid had absolute freedom to decide when and how long to work. CCNV paid Reid $15,000, a sum dependent on "completion of a specific job, a method by which independent contractors are often compensated." *Holt v. Winpisinger*, 811 F.2d 1532, 1540 (D.C. 1987). Reid had total discretion in hiring and paying assistants. "Creating sculptures was hardly 'regular business' for CCNV." 270 U.S.App.D.C., at 35, n. 11, 846 F.2d, at 1494, n. 11. Indeed, CCNV is not a business at all. Finally, CCNV did not pay payroll or Social Security taxes, provide any employee benefits, or contribute to unemployment insurance or workers' compensation funds.

Because Reid was an independent contractor, whether "Third World America" is a work for hire depends on whether it satisfies the terms of § 101(2). This petitioners concede it cannot do. Thus, CCNV is not the author of "Third World America" by virtue of the work for hire provisions of the Act. However, as the Court of Appeals made clear, CCNV nevertheless may be a joint author of the sculpture if, on remand, the District Court determines that CCNV and Reid prepared the work "with the intention that their contributions be merged into inseparable or interdependent parts of a unitary whole." 17 U.S.C. § 101. In that case, CCNV and Reid would be co-owners of the copyright in the work. See § 201(a).

For the aforestated reasons, we AFFIRM the judgment of the Court of Appeals for the District of Columbia Circuit.

Notes and Questions

1. Do you agree with *Reid*? If someone pays for property, shouldn't there at least be a *presumption* that he owns it? There is such a "Work-for-hire presumption," when work is

produced at the instance and expense of another party, but this presumption can be overcome by evidence that parties did *not* intend to create work-for-hire. *See Twentieth Century Fox Film Corp. v. Entm't Distrib.*, 429 F.3d 869 (9th Cir. 2005).

2. What interest, if any, would the Internal Revenue Service have with respect to the common law test of agency, as explained in *Reid*?

3. Should a high level employee be permitted to escape the consequences of *Reid* by facilitating a transfer of intellectual property to a third party entity? *See First Games Publisher Network, Inc. v. Oleg Afonin*, 32 Misc. 3d 1245(A) (N.Y. Sup. Ct. 2011), suggesting that in New York, the answer is "no." That case involved the development of the massively multiplayer online role playing game *The Magic Key*.

Lewis v. Activision Blizzard, Inc.

United States District Court, Northern District of California, 2013
2013 U.S. Dist. LEXIS 149784

WILKEN, United States District Judge

Plaintiff Amanda Lewis brought this copyright infringement action against her former employer, Defendants Activision Blizzard, Inc., and Blizzard Entertainment, Inc. (collectively, Blizzard). Blizzard moves for summary judgment. Plaintiff opposes the motion. After considering the parties' submissions and oral argument, the Court grants the motion.

BACKGROUND

The following facts are undisputed. Blizzard is a videogame company that develops, markets, and distributes computer games. One of its most popular games is World of Warcraft, a "multiplayer role-playing game, in which thousands of people play simultaneously in a 'virtual world' created by Blizzard."

Plaintiff was employed at Blizzard as a "game master" for World of Warcraft from May 2005 through August 2006. In that role, she was responsible for answering customers' questions about the game, assisting them when they encountered difficulties with other players or game mechanics, and solving any problems with game functionality. According to the "Game Master Job Description" in Blizzard's training manual:

> Game Masters are customer service specialists with expert knowledge of the game who are present as characters within World of Warcraft's epic fantasy setting to provide assistance and guidance to players while also coordinating world functionality. In this capacity, GM's serve as the direct link between Blizzard and its customers. Additionally, GM's are responsible for in-game customer support, helping manage our online community, and assisting with the creation of content during the ever ongoing development of the game.

Plaintiff received a copy of this manual during an employee training session that she attended during her first week on the job. In July 2005, a Blizzard game writer sent an e-mail to all game masters inviting them to participate in "open auditions" for voiceover work related to World of Warcraft. Roughly one hundred and twenty game masters signed up to participate in the auditions, including Plaintiff. After Plaintiff auditioned in late July, she was invited to record a voice for a newly created game character called the "baby murloc." The character was conceived by Blizzard's design team as a "cuter, smaller version of the original murloc," a mythical creature featured in earlier versions of the game. Before the recording session, Blizzard's sound engineer told Plaintiff that the character would be unveiled at BlizzCon 2005, an annual fan convention, and used in videos to promote the game. He did not say whether Blizzard would ultimately use the recording for any other purpose—such as to voice any characters within the game itself—and Plaintiff never asked whether the recordings might be used outside of BlizzCon.

On September 7, 2005, Plaintiff participated in a recording session at Blizzard's offices. The session lasted about ten minutes and yielded roughly five minutes of raw audio recording. Blizzard's sound engineer subsequently edited the raw recording to produce a condensed set of sound files. Two weeks later, Plaintiff was invited to participate in another recording session to develop a short "dance" song for the baby murloc character using her voice. On September 22, Plaintiff attended a second recording session at Blizzard's offices. The session yielded roughly four minutes of raw audio recording, which Blizzard's sound engineer once again edited and condensed into smaller sound files. Plaintiff was compensated for her participation in both recording sessions at her usual hourly rate and never sought additional compensation for her work on either recording.

Sometime in 2006, shortly before she was terminated by Blizzard, Plaintiff discovered that her voice from the recordings had been used to create a baby murloc character that appeared in the game itself. Although Plaintiff was "surprised to find out that her voice had been used beyond the scope of what she had been told it would be used for," she did not convey her surprise to any of her friends, co-workers, or supervisors.

In November 2010, Plaintiff filed this lawsuit against Blizzard alleging that the company had infringed her copyright in the baby murloc recordings by using parts of the recordings in the game without her consent. Plaintiff also asserted various state claims against Blizzard in her complaint but those claims were dismissed in October 2012. Docket No. 26, Order on Motion to Dismiss Second and Third Claims for Relief, at 13. In August 2013, Blizzard filed the instant motion for summary judgment on Plaintiff's sole remaining claim for copyright infringement.

DISCUSSION

Blizzard argues that it is entitled to summary judgment on Plaintiff's copyright infringement claim for two reasons. First, it contends that Plaintiff does not own a copyright in the baby murloc recordings because the recordings constitute a "work made for hire" under the Copyright Act, 17 U.S.C. § 201(b). Second, and in the alternative, Blizzard argues that it is a joint author of the recordings and thus cannot be held liable for copyright infringement.

I. Work Made for Hire

The Copyright Act provides, "In the case of a work made for hire, the employer or other person for whom the work was prepared is considered the author ... and, unless the parties have expressly agreed otherwise in a written instrument signed by them, owns all of the rights comprised in the copyright." 17 U.S.C. § 201(b). The Act defines a "work made for hire" as "a work prepared by an employee within the scope of his or her employment." *Id.* § 101. "Although the Copyright Act does not define either 'employee' or 'scope of employment,' these terms must be 'understood in light of the general common law of agency.'" *U.S. Auto Parts Network, Inc. v. Parts Geek, LLC,* 692 F.3d 1009, 1015 (9th Cir.2012) (citing *Cmty. for Creative Non-Violence v. Reid,* 490 U.S. 730, 739–41 (1989)). Various circuits, including the Ninth Circuit, rely on the three-prong "scope of employment" test set forth in section 228 of the Restatement (Second) of Agency to determine whether a given work was "made for hire" under the Copyright Act. *Id.* Under that test, an employee's conduct falls "within the scope of employment if, but only if: (a) it is of the kind he is employed to perform; (b) it occurs substantially within the authorized time and space limits; [and] (c) it is actuated, at least in part, by a purpose to serve the [employer]." *Restatement (Second) of Agency* § 228. Here, the undisputed facts demonstrate that Plaintiff was an employee of Blizzard and that her contributions to the baby murloc recordings fell squarely within the scope of her employment.

A. "Employed To Perform"

Blizzard's training manual states that game masters are responsible for "assisting with the creation of content during the ever ongoing development of the game." Plaintiff admits that she read this job description in the training manual when she first began working at Blizzard in 2005. She argues, however, that because she was not required to produce original content for the game on a regular basis, her contributions to the baby murloc recordings do not qualify as the kind of work she was "employed to perform."

This argument fails for several reasons. First, as noted above, the training manual Plaintiff received specifically identified content-creation as one of her official responsibilities. Even if she only performed this responsibility on occasion, it was still expressly listed in her job description and therefore fell within the scope of her stated duties. What's more, producing content is very similar to the other duties that game masters were routinely expected to perform. Although Plaintiff seeks to cast game masters as customer service representatives who lacked any influence over game content, she acknowledged in her declaration that game masters frequently exercised direct control over elements of the game world. ("I would go into the game world about 3–5 times every shift to assist players who were experiencing issues such as becoming stuck, not receiving 'loot,' or to remove a monster in an improper location."). Thus, Plaintiff's own evidence suggests that game masters did not simply interact with Blizzard's customers but also engaged directly with game content.

Blizzard's evidence confirms that game masters sometimes produced original content for the game. The company's human resources manager asserted in her declaration that other game masters besides Plaintiff were asked to contribute—and did, in fact, contribute—original content to the game, including visual artwork and designs, while Plaintiff was employed there. The human resources manager also asserted that, in addition to their day-to-day responsibilities, game masters were "expected to assist with any other [game]-related tasks that they may be asked to do." Plaintiff does not dispute either of these assertions. Indeed, Plaintiff's own description of her experience recording the baby murloc voice suggests that this work fell within the scope of her ordinary job duties. Plaintiff testified at her deposition that she was paid her normal hourly wage for participating in each recording session and never sought any additional compensation for her voice work. In addition, she admitted that her supervisor praised her work on the recordings during a November 2005 review of her job performance. ("Amanda was thrilled to be chosen as the voice of the baby murloc."). Taken together, this evidence indicates that both Plaintiff and her co-workers understood that her contributions to the baby murloc recordings constituted the kind of work she was "employed to perform."

Plaintiff attempts to analogize this case to *TAP Worldwide, LLC v. Becker,* where a court found that an export manager for an auto-parts manufacturer was acting outside the scope of his employment when he designed a software program to expedite the processing of export shipments. 2010 WL 2757354 (C.D. Cal.). *TAP Worldwide* is inapposite, however, because in that case the export manager's job description did not include software development. In fact, the court specifically used this fact to distinguish *TAP Worldwide* from another case where "it was found that the employee's *job description* could be interpreted to include the development of the computer program that was at issue." The *TAP Worldwide* court also noted that the export manager had not received any "praise" or "guidance" from his supervisor regarding the software he developed, which further suggested that he was not "employed to perform" that kind of work. Here, in contrast, Plaintiff has acknowledged not only that her job description includes "the creation of game content" but also that her supervisor praised her contributions to the baby murloc recordings. Thus, *TAP Worldwide* is distinguishable from the present case.

B. "Substantially Within Authorized Time and Space Limits"

Both of Plaintiff's recording sessions were conducted at Blizzard's offices, using Blizzard's equipment, and under the supervision of Blizzard's sound engineer. Furthermore, both sessions occurred on weekdays during normal working hours while Plaintiff was employed at Blizzard. Although the sessions took place on her days off, Plaintiff received her normal hourly wage for all of the time she spent in the recording studio. Finally, Plaintiff never requested or received her own copies of the recordings from either session. In short, Plaintiff's participation in the recording sessions occurred substantially within the authorized time and space limits of her position at Blizzard.

Plaintiff's assertion that she developed the baby murloc voice "on her own time" and through her "own creative effort, does not change this outcome. The Copyright Act makes clear that, while "sound recordings" may be copyrighted, the Act's protections do not "extend to any idea, procedure, process, system, method of operation, concept, principle, or discovery, regardless of the form in which it is described, explained, illustrated, or embodied in such work." 17 U.S.C. § 102. Because the "voice" that Plaintiff allegedly created is merely an idea—and, thus, is not copyrightable—it does not matter when or where she conceived of it. She has not presented any evidence to suggest that the recordings themselves were made outside of the time and space limits of her job.

C. "Actuated, At Least In Part, By a Purpose To Serve the Employer"

At oral argument, Plaintiff conceded that she was motivated by a desire to serve Blizzard's interests when she participated in the baby murloc recording sessions. She also admitted in her declaration that, when she first agreed to work on the recordings, she understood that the recordings would be used principally to promote the game. Thus, it is undisputed that her work on the recordings was "actuated, at least in part, by a purpose to serve" her employer.

In sum, Plaintiff's contributions to the baby murloc recordings satisfy all three prongs of section 228's "scope of employment" test. The recordings therefore constitute a "work made for hire" under the Copyright Act.

II. Joint Authorship

Because the baby murloc recordings are a "work made for hire," as explained above, Blizzard is the sole copyright holder in the recordings. Accordingly, there is no need to address whether the recordings are a "joint work" under the Copyright Act.

———————

Notes and Questions

1. If Amanda Lewis (*Lewis v. Blizzard*) had not been an employee of Blizzard at the time that she performed the disputed voice-over work, could she have escaped the "work for hire" conclusion reached by the court?

2. Would your answer to the preceding question be different if Amanda Lewis had never received a Blizzard training manual?

3. The federal minimum wage law (i.e., *The Fair Labor Standards Act*) and similar state statutes provide that employers must pay a minimum wage to their employees in addition to time-and-a-half for hours worked in excess of a forty hour week. See 29 U.S.C. §§ 206–207. There are, however, some significant exemptions for employees classified as "white collar," managerial, executive, administrative or professional workers. Are computer programmers exempt? Should the exemptions include all workers who are proficient in the "theoretical and practical application" of computer programming? See 29 U.S.C. §§ 213(a)(17); 29 CFR § 541.400 et seq.

4. For any creative endeavor requiring the assistance of temporary or part time labor, the work for hire agreement is often a critical component. Its purpose is to define the compensation or consideration to be paid to the hired labor and to clarify ownership of the primary project and the individual assets that comprise it. It should be designed to avert the *CCNV v. Reid* types of disputes.

5. Form work-for-hire agreements are very common. It is interesting to note that even though the subject matter of the agreement may concern issues of federal copyright law, an agreement between an author and publisher will be construed according to state law principles of contract interpretation. *See Gary Friedrich Enters., LLC v. Marvel Characters, Inc.*, 716 F.3d 302 (2d Cir. 2013), involving a battle between the freelance author who developed the popular "Ghost Rider" comic book character and a lengthy list of videogame and toy producing defendants; the fight involved an assignment of copyright renewal rights through an ambiguous form work-for-hire agreement. Summary judgment in favor of the defendants was denied because of the ambiguity.

* * *

In the following short form, the "developer" is designated as the project owner. Due to the increasing magnitude of contemporary video game projects, the owner is more likely to be designated as the "Publisher."

FORM 2.6
General Work for Hire Agreement

THIS AGREEMENT, which is signed and effective as of this _____ day of _____, 20___ is by and between _____, ("Developer"), the author, creator and manufacturer of new and unique computer games and _____ ("Contributor"), an individual (or company) that possesses skills, talents and training in the field of computer _____.[38] The parties hereby agree as follows:

1.   **Commission:** Developer does hereby agree to commission the Contributor to perform various services and enhancements that will add to the Developer's creation of a computer game bearing the working title, which may change: _____ (referred to as "Game"). By the signatures hereunder, the Contributor accepts this commission and agrees that all contributions and enhancements performed by Contributor shall constitute a work made for hire as defined by Title 17 of the United States Code.

---

38. The most common works for hire for video games involve computer programmers, artists, photographers, cartoonists and musicians. It is not uncommon to have one person possess several talents; all such talents should be included and listed.

2. **Exclusive Ownership:** All parties agree that Developer is the sole owner of the Game along with all enhancements provided by Contributor; and, that Developer shall have all rights of ownership provided by law, including but not limited to, the right to copyright, patent, alter, sell and assign the Game and the enhancements of Contributor, and create derivative works from them. All parties agree that Developer is the author, creator, and originator of the Game, whereas the Contributor is involved only in a portion of the creation of the Game.

3. **Assignment of Rights.** As previously stated, all work product created by Contributor shall belong exclusively to the Developer. To the extent that the work product or any portion thereof is deemed to be owned by Contributor and not by the Developer as a work made for hire, the Contributor hereby assigns to the Developer all rights to such work products, including but not limited to all other property rights, patent rights, copyrights, and trade secret rights. Contributor agrees to execute all documents that are reasonably requested by the Developer in order to further evidence the foregoing assignment and to provide all reasonable assistance to the Developer in perfecting and protecting the Developer's rights in such work product.

4. **Consideration:** As sole consideration for this agreement, Contributor shall receive the sum of $_____ to be paid upon completion of the subject work.[39]

5. **Trade Secret:** All of the information relating to the Work is considered to be a valuable trade secret of the Developer. Contributor agrees to keep all information concerning the project confidential. Contributor shall not subcontract nor hire anyone else to assist without the prior written consent of Developer.

6. **Integration Clause:** This agreement represents the entire understanding between the parties and may only be modified by a writing signed by both parties.

7. **Brief Description of Work:** Programming & artistic contributions using various platforms, including but not limited to _____.

Signed this _____ day of _____, 2_____

_____
Developer

_____
Contributor

* * * * *

The following is a more specialized work for hire agreement directed toward one specific component of the game.

FORM 2.7
Sound Audio Work for Hire Agreement

This Work For Hire Agreement (the "Agreement") is effective as of _____, 2____ ("Effective Date") by and between Company X, Inc. (hereinafter referred to as the "Company"), a California corporation located at _____ and Composer Y (hereinafter referred to as "Contractor"), an individual residing at _____.

---

39. A lump sum payment is the simplest method, but it is not always practical. A more common practice suggests the attachment of an installment payment schedule, in which case, the paragraph would read as follows: "As sole consideration for this agreement, Contributor shall receive payment in the amounts and at the times set forth on Schedule 'A' attached."

In consideration of the mutual covenants herein contained, the parties hereby agree as follows:

1.   **Services.** (a) Contractor shall create audio content as determined by Company from time to time in a manner consistent with the outlines, explanations, and designs established by the Company (hereinafter "Services"). (b) The Contractor agrees that any work he submits to Company under this contract, when accepted and payment is honored, becomes the property of Company and Contractor further agrees and acknowledges he has no proprietary interest in any of these works. Ownership rights to any work not paid for shall be returned to the Contractor immediately.

2.   **Term and Termination.** This Agreement shall continue until terminated by either party upon 10 days' written notice, provided that termination by Contractor shall not be effective until completion of any work requested by the Company.

3.   **Payment For Services.** The Company shall pay Contractor in a manner mutually agreed upon by each party for each project contemplated.

4.   **Independent Contractor.** It is understood and agreed that Contractor shall perform the Services as an independent contractor. Contractor shall not be deemed to be an employee of the Company. Contractor shall not be entitled to any benefits provided by the Company to its employees, and the Company will make no deductions from any of the payments due to Contractor hereunder for state or federal tax purposes. Contractor agrees that he shall be personally responsible for any and all taxes and other payments due on payments received by him from the Company hereunder.

5.   **Warranties.** (a) Original Development. Contractor represents and warrants that all work performed by him for or on behalf of the Company, and all work products produced thereby, will not infringe upon or violate any patent, copyright, trade secret, or other property right of any former employer, client, or other third party.

(b) Warranty of Expertise. Contractor represents and warrants that he is highly skilled and experienced in providing the Services required. Contractor acknowledges that the Company is relying on his skill and expertise in the foregoing for the performance of this Agreement, and agrees to notify the Company whenever he does not have the necessary skill and experience to fully perform hereunder.

(c) Other Agreements. Contractor represents and warrants that his signing of this Agreement is not and will not be in violation of any other contract, agreement or understanding to which he is a party.

6.   **Indemnification.** Contractor shall indemnify the Company from all claims, losses and damages that may arise from the breach of any of his obligations under this Agreement.

7.   **Protection of Confidential Information.** (a) Confidential Information. For purposes of this Agreement, the term "Confidential Information" means all information that is not generally known and that: (i) is obtained by Contractor from the Company, or that is learned, discovered, developed, conceived, originated, or prepared by Contractor during the process of providing Services to the Company, and (ii) relates directly to the business or assets of the Company. The term "Confidential Information" shall include, but shall not be limited to: inventions, discoveries, trade secrets, and know-how; computer software code, designs, routines, algorithms, and structures; product information; research and development information; lists of clients and other information relating thereto; financial data and information; business plans and processes; and any other information of the Company that the Company informs

Contractor, or that Contractor should know by virtue of his position, is to be kept confidential.

(b) Obligation of Confidentiality. During the term of this Agreement with the Company, and at all times thereafter, Contractor agrees that he will not disclose to others, use for his own benefit or for the benefit of anyone other than the Company, or otherwise appropriate or copy, any Confidential Information, whether or not developed by Contractor, except as required in the lawful performance of his obligations to the Company hereunder. The obligations of Contractor under this paragraph shall not apply to any information that becomes public knowledge through no fault of Contractor.

8.   **Ownership and Assignment of Rights.** All Work Product created by Contractor shall belong exclusively to the Company and shall, to the extent possible, be considered a work made for hire for the Company within the meaning of Title 17 of the United States Code. To the extent the Company does not own such Work Product as a work made for hire, Contractor hereby assigns to the Company all rights to such Work Products, including but not limited to all other patent rights, copyrights, and trade secret rights. Contractor agrees to execute all documents reasonably requested by the Company to further evidence the foregoing assignment and to provide all reasonable assistance to the Company in perfecting or protecting the Company's rights in such Work Product.

9.   **Duty Upon Termination of Services.** Contractor shall immediately deliver to Company all Work Product created under the Agreement. Contractor shall not delete any Work Product for 6 months after expiration or earlier termination of the Agreement unless such deletion is requested by Company.

10. **Subcontracting and Assignment.** The Agreement and the rights and obligations of Contractor hereunder may not be subcontracted, assigned or transferred by Contractor, in whole or in part, without the written consent of the Company. The Company may at its sole discretion assign or transfer the rights of the Agreement.

11. **Governing Law.** This contract will be governed by and construed in accordance with the laws of the State of California.

12. **Consent to Breach.** No term or provision hereof shall be deemed waived and no breach excused, unless such waiver or consent be in writing and signed by the party claimed to have waived or consented. No consent by any party to, or waiver of, a breach by the other party shall constitute consent to, waiver of, or excuse of any other different or subsequent breach.

13. **Gender.** Whenever the content of this Agreement requires, the masculine gender shall be deemed to include the feminine.

14. **Right to Self-Promotion.** Contractor has the right to self promotion and is allowed to use, as creator of said works, any works created under this contract, to demonstrate the capabilities of contractor either in demo reel or computer file format at any time after acceptance of the work as final, without any further permissions required from Company.

15. **Sound Credits.** Credit for creation of any sounds produced under this contract will be included in the appropriate "credits" section of any software product and its corresponding print media in which the sounds appear, as created by Contractor.

16. **Entire Agreement.** This Agreement constitutes the complete and exclusive statement of the agreement between the parties with regard to the matters set forth

herein, and it supersedes all other agreements, proposals, and representations, oral or written, express or implied, with regard thereto.

IN WITNESS WHEREOF, the parties have executed this Agreement as of the Effective Date.

CONTRACTOR	COMPANY
By: _____	By: _____
Its: _____	Its: _____
Date: _____	Date: _____

* * * * *

§ 2.44 Joint Ownership

An author, for purposes of the Copyright Act, is the person who exercises artistic control over the subject. 17 U.S.C. §§ 102, 201(a). A "joint work" is defined by the Copyright Act as "a work prepared by two or more authors with the intention that their contributions be merged into inseparable or interdependent parts of a unitary whole." 17 U.S.C. § 101.

Joint authorship is akin to a joint venture. It involves a combination of talents and time to produce a tangible work of authorship. To be considered as "joint authors" for purposes of the Copyright Act, the parties must have intended to be joint authors at the time that the work was created, and each alleged author's contribution to the work must be independently copyrightable. A mere assistant is not a joint author. See 17 U.S.C.A. §§ 102, 201(a). *See also, e.g., J.C.W. Invs, Inc. v. Novelty, Inc.*, 289 F. Supp. 2d 1023 (N.D. Ill. 2003).

As is the case with joint ownership of real estate, both co-owners are said to own an undivided interest in the work. As co-owners, both have a right to exploit the finished product with or without the consent of the other. But with or without cooperation, each joint author must account to the other with respect to earnings and revenues. A court may find individuals are coauthors, for purposes of the Copyright Act, if they made objective expressions of a shared intent to be coauthors. 17 U.S.C.A. §§ 102, 201(a).

* * *

Ahn v. Midway Mfg. Co.

United States District Court, Northern District Illinois, 1997
965 F. Supp. 1134

GETTLEMAN, District Judge.

Plaintiffs Philip Ahn, Elizabeth Malecki, and Katalin Zamiar bring this seven count action against defendants Midway Corporation ("Midway"), Williams Electronics Games, Inc. ("Williams"), Acclaim Entertainment, Inc. ("Acclaim"), Nintendo of America, Inc. ("Nintendo"), and Sega of America, Inc. ("Sega"), alleging infringement of the common law right of publicity, and violations of: Section 43(a) of the Lanham Act; the Illinois Consumer Fraud and Deceptive Practices Act; the Illinois Uniform Deceptive Trade Practices Act; and, the Copyright Act of 1976, along with one count under common law quantum meruit. Plaintiffs seek a constructive trust on all moneys defendants received and continue to receive from the alleged breach of their duty to plaintiffs. Defendants have filed a motion for summary judgment on all counts. For the reasons set forth below, defendants' motion is granted.

FACTS

Plaintiff Philip Ahn is a fourth degree black belt in Tae Kwon Do and has practiced martial arts for approximately twenty years. Plaintiff Elizabeth Malecki holds a degree in ballet and modern dance and is a professional dancer, actress, and aerobics instructor. Plaintiff Katalin Zamiar is a first degree black belt in Karate and has twelve years of experience. Midway designs, manufactures, and sells coin-operated amusement games and licenses home video games, including Mortal Kombat and Mortal Kombat II, to which Midway owns the copyright to the computer program and related audiovisual materials. Williams acts in conjunction with Midway in designing, manufacturing, and selling coin-operated video games. Acclaim manufactures software for use in Nintendo and Sega hardware systems for home video games. Nintendo and Sega design, market and sell home video games.

Plaintiffs' versions of the events that lead to their association with Midway are essentially identical. All plaintiffs allege that on separate occasions between 1992 and 1993 they were approached by Midway's agents about the possibility of using their images, names and performances for various characters in the coin-operated arcade format of Mortal Kombat and Mortal Kombat II. Plaintiff Malecki modeled the character Sonja Blade for Mortal Kombat. Plaintiff Ahn modeled the character Shang Tsung in the coin-operated version of Mortal Kombat II, while plaintiff Zamiar modeled for three characters, Kitana, Mileena, and Jade, all of whom appeared in Mortal Kombat II. Plaintiffs' movements were videotaped by Midway and these images were eventually digitalized and incorporated into the coin-operated arcade games.

All plaintiffs signed a release form with Midway at the time of the videotaping. This agreement authorized Midway to film each plaintiff in a martial arts performance in order to use that plaintiff's name or likeness in connection with the manufacture, design, advertising, promotion, sale, and use of the coin-operated video games. The agreement also made Midway the sole and exclusive owner of all of plaintiffs' copyrightable expression, defining any such expression as "works for hire," and permitted Midway, at its sole discretion, to use plaintiffs' likeness in any copyright obtained in connection with the coin-operated arcade games.

Plaintiffs allege that they were required to sign the release in case of injury and that Midway lead them to believe that only a small number of arcade games were being contemplated. However, in the event the game proved successful, they were told they would receive bonuses, or if the coin-operated versions of the game developed into ancillary uses, plaintiffs would receive royalties, and would be considered for movie parts, personal appearances and television commercials. Plaintiffs allege that based on these representations they all signed the agreement, which the parties refer to as the General Release.

The arcade version of Mortal Kombat and its successor, Mortal Kombat II, proved to be successful. In September, 1993, Acclaim, Nintendo and Sega released the home video game version of Mortal Kombat, and in September, 1994, they released the home game version of Mortal Kombat II. In April of 1994, all plaintiffs attended a meeting with agents of Midway and Williams. At this meeting plaintiffs were promised what plaintiffs have termed "wonderful opportunities" if they signed an additional agreement, known as the Non-disclosure Agreement and Release. Plaintiffs allege that at this meeting they were informed that various companies were interested in utilizing plaintiffs' images in various products and commercial endorsements. All three plaintiffs refused to sign this second agreement.

Plaintiffs' seven count complaint against defendants is based on the alleged unauthorized use of their names, persona and likenesses in connection with the home video, home computer, and hand-held versions of Mortal Kombat and Mortal Kombat II. Plaintiffs' response to defendants' motion for summary judgment indicates that they do not contest defendants' motion on the counts dealing with the Lanham Act (Count II), the Illinois Consumer Fraud and Deceptive Practices Act (Count III) and the Illinois Uniform Deceptive Trade Practices Act (Count IV). Accordingly, the only counts remaining are Count I alleging infringement of the right of publicity, Count V alleging violation of the Copyright Act of 1976, and Count VII, the common law quantum meruit count.

DISCUSSION

The Right of Publicity

In Count I plaintiffs allege that defendants' unauthorized use of their names, personas, and likenesses violated their common law right of publicity. Defendants argue both that the right of publicity is preempted by the Copyright Act of 1976, 17 U.S.C. § 301(a), and that plaintiffs have not satisfied the requirements for a claim under the right of publicity.

A state claim is preempted by the Copyright Act if two elements are satisfied. First, the work in which the right is asserted must be fixed in a tangible form and fall within the subject matter of copyright under § 102 of the Act. Second, the right asserted must be equivalent to any of the rights specified in § 106 of the Act. Section 102 sets forth three conditions for copyrightability. First, the work must be fixed in a tangible form; second, the work must be the original work of authorship; and third, the work must come within the subject matter of copyright. Under § 106, the copyright owner has certain rights including reproduction, the preparation of derivative works, and distribution. A state claim is equivalent to one of the rights asserted under the Copyright Act if it is violated by the exercise of any of the rights set forth in § 106. In *Baltimore Orioles* [*v. Major League Baseball Players Ass'n*, 805 F.2d 663 (7th Cir. 1986)], the Major League Baseball Players Association asserted that the telecasts of Major League Baseball games were made without the players' consent, and that the telecasts misappropriated the players' property right in their performances. The plaintiffs, representing the Major League baseball clubs, brought an action seeking declaratory judgment that the clubs possessed the exclusive right to broadcast the games and the exclusive right to the telecasts. *Id.* at 665.

Applying the two-part test, the Seventh Circuit held that the baseball clubs' copyright in the telecasts preempted the players' right of publicity in their game time performances. The court held that the first condition for preemption, fixation in a tangible form, was satisfied because the telecasts of the baseball games were recorded simultaneously. *Id.* at 674. The court then examined whether the right of publicity was equivalent to one of the rights specified in § 106 of the Copyright Act. The court held that because the right to broadcast telecasts of the games infringes on the players' right of publicity in their performance, and because the right of publicity does not differ in kind from copyright, the players' right was equivalent to one of the rights encompassed in § 106 of the Copyright Act. Accordingly, because both elements of preemption were satisfied, the players' state claim under the right of publicity was preempted. *Id.* at 677.

In the instant case, plaintiffs' images were videotaped and, as a result, became fixed in a tangible form. To be fixed in a tangible form, the work must be recorded by or under the authority of the author. 17 U.S.C. § 101 (1994). Because plaintiffs' consented to the videotaping, the definition of 'fixed' is satisfied. Further, the choreographic works were all original works of authorship. Finally, choreographic works fall within the subject matter of copyright. See, Nimmer on Copyright, § 2.07(B). Thus, the first condition for preemption has been satisfied.[40] Applying the § 106 test, the right of publicity is equivalent to one of the rights in § 106 because it is infringed by the act of distributing, performing or preparing derivative works. Thus, plaintiffs' claim is preempted.

Copyright Act of 1976

In Count V of their complaint, plaintiffs allege that defendants, in filing and securing an exclusive copyright to the exclusion of plaintiffs, unlawfully appropriated plaintiffs' choreographic work. Plaintiffs further allege that defendants violated the copyright laws when they reproduced plaintiffs' protected expression, and ask this court to grant a permanent injunction pursuant to §§ 502–506 of the Copyright Act prohibiting all defendants from using plaintiffs' choreographic works, personas, names and/or likenesses. In the alternative, plaintiffs ask that this court find that the software for Mortal Kombat and Mortal Kombat II are joint works, as evidenced by their limited release.

Defendants correctly argue that Midway's certificates of registration from the Copyright Office constitute prima facie evidence of the validity of their copyright, and upon introduction of the certificates the burden shifts to the party challenging the invalidity of the copyright to overcome this presumption and affirmatively demonstrate invalidity. Defendants argue that because plaintiffs have failed to rebut this presumption, they are entitled to summary judgment. In addition, defendants argue that because defendants Midway and Williams alone developed the source code for the games—and it was that source code that was copyrighted—those defendants must, as a matter of law, be considered the sole authors of the work.

Under federal copyright law, if a work is considered "joint" the joint authors hold undivided interests in the work. 17 U.S.C. § 201 (1994). Each author, as a co-owner, has the right to use or to license the use of the work, subject to an accounting to the other co-owners for any profits. Thus, this court must determine whether plaintiffs and defendant Midway are to be considered joint authors in the computer program that incorporates plaintiffs' performances.

A joint work is defined as "a work prepared by two or more authors with the intention that their contribution be merged into inseparable or interdependent parts of the unitary whole." 17 U.S.C. § 101 (1994). In *Erickson v. Trinity Theatre, Inc.*, 13 F.3d 1061 (7th Cir.1994), a playwright successfully sought to enjoin a theater whose actors had contributed ideas to the plaintiff's copyrighted plays and videotapes from performing these plays without license from the plaintiff. The Seventh Circuit adopted Professor Goldstein's copyrightable subject matter test to determine the issue of joint authorship. Under this standard, "[a] collaborative contribution will not produce a joint work, and a contribution will not obtain a co-ownership interest, unless the contribution represents original expression that could stand on its own as the subject matter of copyright." *Id.* at 1070.

In addition, the Goldstein test requires that the parties must have intended to be joint authors at the time the work was created. The intent requirement is satisfied if the parties intended to merge their respective contributions into a single whole. The mere fact, however, of contemporaneous input into the copyrighted work does not satisfy the statutory requirement of intent. "To qualify as an author, one must supply more than

---

40. Even if plaintiffs argue that it is their performance in which they claim a right and not the videotape of the performance, the plaintiffs' claim must still fail. In *Baltimore Orioles*, plaintiffs' claimed a right in their performances, and not in the telecast. *Baltimore Orioles*, 805 F.2d at 674. The court, however, held that because the performances were embodied in a copy, the performances were fixed in a tangible form and thus satisfied the definition of 'fixed' under 17 U.S.C. § 101. *Id.* at 675.

mere direction or ideas. An author is the party who actually creates the work, that is, the person who translates an idea into a fixed, tangible expression entitled to copyright expression." *Erickson*, 13 F.3d at 1071. As to the requirement of fixation, § 101 states: "A work is 'fixed' in a tangible medium of expression when its embodiment in a copy or phonorecord, by or under the authority of the author, is sufficiently permanent or stable to permit it to be perceived, reproduced, or otherwise communicated for a period of more than transitory duration." *Id.* In *Erickson*, the Seventh Circuit held there was no intent between the playwright and the theater to be joint authors at the time the plays were written. The court relied on certain factors to determine the absence of joint authorship. First, the works were largely created before the actors offered their improvisations. Second, final contents of the plays, including which suggestions to be incorporated, were solely determined by the playwright. Third, neither the playwright nor the theater considered the actors to be joint authors. Based on these factors the court in Erickson ruled that the defendants could not overcome the presumption in favor of the plaintiff's copyright.

In the present case plaintiffs incorrectly assert that they are co-authors of the copyrighted work. First, plaintiffs offer no evidence to rebut Midway's affidavit that it never considered plaintiffs to be collaborators or joint authors of the games. More importantly (since plaintiffs correctly point out that it is difficult to come up with hard evidence to rebut a self-serving statement of intent),[41] Midway's agents had the final authority to decide on the selection of movements and poses that would be recorded during the videotaping session as well as the authority to decide which frames of the videotape and in what manner and order the frames would be incorporated into the computer program that drives the game.

Indeed, Midway alone decided which portions of plaintiffs' "performances" to digitalize and alone transformed the video images into the cartoon-like images in the game. It is apparent to the court, in viewing videotapes of the actual games, that the superhuman gyrations and leaps high into the air of the characters, including plaintiffs' characters, are fanciful products of the imaginations of the creators of the source codes—much like the playwright's penmanship in *Erickson*. To be sure, according to their testimony, plaintiffs contributed their images and movements to the creation of the games, but, like the actors in Erickson, that contribution was transitory. It was Midway alone that translated the ideas "into a fixed, tangible expression entitled to copyright protection." *Erickson*, 13 F.3d at 1071.

Finally, the general release signed by all plaintiffs made Midway the sole and exclusive owner of all plaintiffs' copyrightable expression in connection with the coin-operated arcade games and stipulated that plaintiffs' efforts were "works for hire." Plaintiffs have conceded that this agreement partially governed their relationship with respect to the production of the arcade games. It is also uncontested that the source codes (that are the subject of Midway's copyright) for the arcade games are the same source codes used in the hand-held and home video versions. It is hard to see how plaintiffs could have conveyed any and all their rights with respect to the original source codes, yet retain additional

---

41. Midway, however, has presented some hard evidence of its intent that plaintiffs not be considered joint authors. The Release Agreement specifically identified each plaintiff's contributions as a "work for hire." This document, prepared and signed contemporaneously with plaintiffs' performances, clearly indicates defendants' intent that plaintiffs not be considered joint authors. *Erickson*, 13 F.3d at 1072. In their complaint plaintiffs suggest that they were "induced" into signing the general releases. Plaintiffs have failed, however, to plead a separate claim for fraudulent inducement, and their attorney candidly admitted at oral argument that they could not prove such a claim.

rights when that same code is used in another application. Accordingly, this court concludes that the uncontested facts demonstrate that plaintiffs cannot prove that they are joint authors of the copyrighted source codes. Summary judgment will therefore be entered for defendants on Count V.

―――――――

Notes and Questions

1. In *JCW Invs., Inc. v. Novelty, Inc.*, 289 F. Supp. 2d 1023 (N.D. Ill. 2003), two developers (Wirt and Bevington) of a farting, talking toy doll hired a voice-over actor to speak phrases that would be recorded and used as a voice for the doll (such as "Silent, but deadly" and "Did somebody step on a duck?"). As part of its defense in this copyright infringement action, the defendant, a competitor, claimed that one of the plaintiffs, Bevington, should not be considered as a joint author of the doll because he was not involved in the production of the sound recording. Rejecting the argument, the court held that defendant correctly asserted that to be a joint author the parties must have intended to be joint authors at the time the work was created, and each alleged author's contribution must be "independently copyrightable." *See, e.g., Erickson v. Trinity Theatre, Inc.*, 13 F.3d 1061, 1070–1071 (7th Cir. 1994). However, according to the court, this did not mean that both Bevington and Wirt had to contribute jointly to both the sound recording and the 3-D sculpture of the doll. The relevant inquiry was whether either Wirt or Bevington was a co-author in the copyrighted work as a whole per 17 U.S.C. § 101.

2. As previously discussed, a joint author is free to exploit a jointly authored work without permission from the other (or others). If a joint owner (co-author) of a copyright in joint work uses or licenses use of the work, however, he or she must account to other co-authors for any profits. *See Team Play, Inc. v. Boyer*, 391 F. Supp. 2d 695 (N.D. Ill. 2003), involving a sequel for the video game *Police Trainer*.

3. Can you think of circumstances where a joint authorship arrangement would be preferable for creating a videogame? What entities would be better and why?

4. Filing a copyright registration claiming joint authorship for a work whose ownership is disputed should not be undertaken lightly. See § 506(e) of the Copyright Act, pertaining to criminal sanctions for "false representation."

Chapter Three

Construction

As we consider the development and construction process, it is important to distinguish the large videogame producers (such as Electronic Arts, Nintendo, Sony, etc.) from the much-smaller independent game-makers (often referred to as "*Indies*"). A similar distinction exists in the motion picture industry, but as compared to videogame budgets, film dollars seem to range across a smoother more continuous set of numbers. At the high end of the spectrum, the videogame business has been emulating the film industry, with its hundred million dollar budgets and massive technical/artistic labor pools. For the videogame industry, however, moving downward involves sharp drops instead of mild slopes. And, unlike film production costs, videogame development expenses can be extremely low, even when compared to modest budget films. A lone programmer, with a next-to-nothing budget could easily create the next billion dollar game in an app. The same might rarely, if ever, be said of a lone film maker; and producing a billion dollar movie on a close-to-zero-budget is unlikely.

For the high end producer of films *or* games, it is impossible to ignore the technological merger that has been occurring between the two industries. Overlapping action heroes and personalities were only the beginning. More significant is the migration from analog to digital technologies, which has created an inseparable marriage between the two industries with respect to every aspect of creation, display, marketing and distribution. Therefore, lawyers representing clients in *either* industry are well advised to become familiar with *both*. Our focus, at this juncture, however, is aimed toward the separable aspects of the videogame development.

§ 3.10 The Developer-Programmer Relationship

Analogous to the production of a motion picture, the construction of a videogame may entail the efforts of many, but in either case, there must be a director who, in a game context might appropriately be termed the "lead programmer" or "developer" and a producer (often referred to as the "publisher"). As the creator of the finished product, the developer is generally toward the top of the managerial chain, and is primarily responsible for the look, feel and operation of the final product. (We explain videogame development in some detail in § 1.20, *infra*.)

In Chapter 2, we considered a relatively simple, basic *Work Made For Hire* agreement. That particular contract works best for a one-time project, where the developer happens to be an experienced programmer or game designer in his own right. Where, however, the bulk of the work is going to be entrusted to a programmer on an ongoing basis, a more detailed agreement might be in order.

To gain a better understanding of the particular obligations and responsibilities that are demanded by the construction of a videogame as compared to other group projects, consider the following skeletal checklist. The items should be carefully considered prior to drafting a developer/programmer contract. Attention might best be directed toward those contractual concerns that are unique to the industry:

I. **PARTIES**
    A. Identify and carefully define the parties and their respective:
        1. Roles,
        2. Titles,
        3. Basic responsibilities.
    B. For limited entities (Corporations, LLCs, etc.) consider:
        1. Personal guarantees,
        2. Venue and jurisdictional problems.

II. **SUBJECT MATTER OF THE CONTRACT**
    A. Provide basic identification for the game including a:
        1. Working title,
        2. General description (*Maze, Serious*, etc.),
    B. Provide technical identification for the game, including the:
        1. Platform for construction (i.e., programming language),
        2. Device (PC, Mac, Mobile, Console, etc.) compatibility for the end user,
        3. Target audience.

III. **WORK TO BE PERFORMED BY DEVELOPER**
    A. Specify what the developer wishes to develop:
        1. The game's functional specifications,
        2. The game's design specifications,
        3. The user interface,
        4. Arrangements for alpha and beta testing.
    B. Set time tables:
        1. Define separate phases and benchmarks,
        2. Provide specifications for each milestone,
        3. Provide rules governing corrections and modifications.

IV. **WORK TO BE PERFORMED BY PROGRAMMER**
    A. Specify content and:
        1. Specific game elements to be included,
        2. The appearance of the interface,
        3. The capabilities of the interface.

   B. Specify documentation including:
1. User documentation,
2. Technical documentation,
3. Comments within code,
4. Identification of deliverables.

V. **DELIVERABLES**

   A. Specify deliverables due *from* the Developer, including:
1. Directives and specifications,
2. Content requirements,
3. Development software and hardware,
4. Documentation.

   B. Specify deliverables due *to* the Developer:
1. Executable code,
2. Supporting documentation,
3. The Golden Master.

   C. Provide for a final deadline by specifying:
1. The delivery date of completed game,
2. Provisions for extensions,
3. Legitimate excuses for delay,
4. Remedies for delay,
5. Changes warranting extension.

VI. **ACCEPTANCE OF GOLDEN MASTER**

   A. Specify with particularity rights of review and rejection:
1. The requirements that the game must meet,
2. Consequences of test failure,
3. Standards for determining whether test has been passed.

   B. Consider standards for acceptance to determine:
1. Subjective or objective satisfaction,
2. Compliance with written specifications and warranties,
3. Compliance with other predefined test criteria,
4. When the game is deemed to be officially accepted.

VII. **WARRANTIES, INDEMNITIES & INSURANCE**

   A. Specify express warranties and related information:
1. Warranty of original authorship,
2. Warranty that assets were properly licensed,
3. Warranty that game conforms to specifications,
4. Warranty of proper performance of game,
5. Warranty of adequacy of documentation.

  6. Warranty of non-infringement of:

   a. Copyrights,

   b. Patents,

   c. Trademarks,

   d. Trade Secrets, and

   e. Licensing agreements.

  7. Warranty of compatibility for listed operating systems,

  8. Warranty of compatibility with specified hardware,

  9. Warranty of freedom from defects in workmanship,

  10. Warranty of freedom from date bombs and viruses,

  11. Warranty of compliance with industry ratings,

  12. Duration of warranties,

  13. Remedies for breaches.

 B. Specify indemnity for breaches of warranty, such as:

  1. Payment of damages and expenses of litigation,

  2. Payment of attorney fees,

  3. Conditions for indemnification.

 C. Specify insurance requirements.

VIII. SUPPORT

 A. State what support, if any, will be provided to developer:

  1. Telephone assistance,

  2. Error corrections,

  3. Updates and enhancements.

 B. State the support, if any, that will be provided to end users.

IX. CONSIDERATION

 A. Specify payment terms:

  1. Fixed lump sum,

  2. Hourly rate plus out-of-pocket expenses,

  3. Periodic payment.

 B. Specify due dates for payments.

X. OWNERSHIP OF GAME

 A. Clearly determine the ownership of the finished game:

  1. The Developer or Publisher,

  2. The Programmer, or

  3. Both parties (joint ownership).

 B. Define the rights of the non-owner with respect to the:

  1. Right to copy,

  2. Right to modify game,

      3.   Right to distribute game,

      4.   Right to create derivative works.

XI. CONFIDENTIALITY

  A. Require confidentiality by both:

      1.   Developer and

      2.   Programmer.

  B. Define the duration of confidentiality.

  C. Consider Agreements not to compete.

XII. LIMITATIONS OF LIABILITY

  A. State the recovery limits against Developer.

  B. State the limits on remedies or types of damages.

XIII. DEFAULT

  A. Provide for potential remedies for default, such as:

      1.   Suspended performance,

      2.   Termination of contract,

      3.   Liquidated damages,

      4.   Injunctive relief.

  B. Spell out notice provisions for breach.

  C. Provide for opportunities to cure breaches.

  D. Consider clause specifically allowing for injunctive relief in the case of breach of certain terms, such as confidentiality or acting contrary to ownership rights set forth in the agreement.

XIV. TERMINATION

  A. Specify start dates.

  B. Specify completion dates.

  C. Consider unanticipated termination for:

      1.   The default of each party,

      2.   Pursuant a specified number of days notice,

      3.   At the terminating party's discretion,

      4.   On the bankruptcy or insolvency of a party.

  D. Determine what should occur upon termination, such as:

      1.   Discontinuing development,

      2.   Retaining the work to date of each party,

      3.   Payment of all past due or accrued sums.

  E. Provide that certain obligations survive termination, such as:

      1.   Ownership of work-to-date,

      2.   Confidentiality,

      3.   Indemnification, and

4.   Payments of sums due and owing.

XV. STANDARD "BOILERPLATE" PROVISIONS

A.   Consider inclusion of an integration clause,

B.   Consider inclusion of a prohibition against oral modifications,

C.   Consider inclusion of jurisdiction and venue provisions,

D.   Consider using Alternative Dispute Resolution provisions,

E.   Consider an attorneys' fees provision,

F.   Include a "Notices" provision.

Those studying entertainment law, and more particularly those problems relating to the motion picture industry, should notice more than a mild similarity with respect to high budget videogames. It is still possible for an individual computer programmer working alone to design, develop and construct a videogame from start to finish. In fact, many early games were designed in such a fashion. But more often than not, some additional assistance or skills will be required thereby necessitating a contractual relationship. As is the case with any relatively new industry, we can expect to find basic principles of commerce and contract law working side by side with some new terms, conventions, and usages.

* * *

Greenberg v. Sir-Tech Software, Inc.

Supreme Court, Appellate Division, New York, 1997
667 N.Y.S.2d 83, 245 A.D.2d 1004

MERCURE, Justice

Appeal from an order of the Supreme Court (Bradley, J.), entered May 1, 1997 in Sullivan County, which, inter alia, granted defendants' motions for summary judgment dismissing the complaint in action No. 2.

Andrew Greenberg Inc. (hereinafter AGI) is the creator of the computer game "Wizardry." In 1981, AGI granted Sir-Tech Software Inc. an exclusive license to manufacture and market Wizardry, related products and any subsequent Wizardry games and related products. As here relevant, the contract between AGI and Sir-Tech provided for graduated royalty payments to AGI and also that all Wizardry games and Wizardry-related products be copyrighted, with copyrighting notices recognizing AGI as a co-owner. Sir-Tech thereafter proceeded to market Wizardry, Wizardry-related products and, under the authorship of game designer David W. Bradley, subsequent Wizardry games.

In June 1991, at a time when Bradley was involved in developing the Wizardry game "Crusaders of the Dark Savant" (hereinafter Crusaders), AGI commenced an action against Sir-Tech and Bradley in U.S. District Court for the Northern District of New York, alleging causes of action for trademark and copyright infringement and seeking an accounting and for fraud. District Court dismissed AGI's second cause of action (trademark infringement and fraudulent trademark registration) with prejudice, dismissed AGI's third and fourth causes of action (accounting and fraud) without prejudice pursuant to 28 U.S.C. § 1367(c)(3) (declination of supplemental jurisdiction over State claims), and also denied Sir-Tech's motion for sanctions. In February 1992, the Federal action was dismissed against Bradley with prejudice by stipulation of the parties.

In April 1992, AGI pursued its claim for an accounting against Sir-Tech and a related entity in action No. 1. In August 1992, Sir-Tech responded with action No. 2, alleging that AGI, its principal, Andrew Greenberg, and their attorneys, the law firm of Orseck, Orseck, Greenberg & Gaiman (hereinafter collectively referred to as defendants), tortiously interfered with Sir-Tech's contract with Bradley for development of Crusaders. Specifically, the complaint in action No. 2 alleges that Bradley's contract with Sir-Tech required him to deliver the completed Crusaders game on or before September 1, 1991, that although Bradley was on schedule with his work at the time the Federal court action was commenced defendants' assertion of claims against Bradley caused him to stop working on Crusaders, and that as a result Sir-Tech missed the 1991 Christmas selling season, causing it to lose an investment in promotional materials and sales totaling $950,000. After considerable discovery and motion practice that need not be detailed here, Supreme Court granted defendants' motions for summary judgment and dismissed the complaint in action No. 2. Sir-Tech appeals. We affirm.

In order to defeat defendants' prima facie showing on the summary judgment motion, Sir-Tech was obligated to support its tortious interference cause of action with competent evidence tending to establish (1) its contract with Bradley, (2) defendants' knowledge of the existence of the contract, (3) that the contract was not carried out, (4) that defendants initiated the Federal court action with intent to induce Bradley's breach of the contract, (5) that the initiation of the Federal court action was a substantial factor in preventing Bradley from carrying out the contract, and (6) that Sir-Tech suffered damage as a result.

We agree with Supreme Court's conclusion that Sir-Tech failed to competently establish a number of the critical elements, including defendants' knowledge of the existence of the contract and their solely malicious intent in commencing the Federal court action. Sir-Tech argues, however, that it was prevented from completely establishing these elements because of defendants' refusal to respond to relevant deposition questions and interrogatories and that, in fact, a motion to compel those responses was pending before Supreme Court at the time of its ruling on the summary judgment motion.

Although there appears to be little merit to Sir-Tech's claims concerning the need for further discovery with regard to defendants' knowledge and motive, we need not address that issue because Sir-Tech's evidentiary showing was deficient concerning yet another element, causation. As correctly contended by defendants, Sir-Tech failed to come forth with any evidence in admissible form tending to establish that the commencement of the Federal court action actually interfered with Bradley's performance under his contract to produce Crusaders. Notably, Sir-Tech produced no affidavit, deposition testimony or any other form of first-hand evidence from Bradley indicating that his progress on Crusaders was actually impeded by the Federal court action. An August 20, 1992 letter from Sir-Tech's counsel to Bradley's counsel stating that "Sir-tech incurred substantial expense in paying [Bradley's] costs and fees in connection with the [Federal] litigation" is surely not probative on the issue.

Also lacking in probative value is Bradley's conclusory averment, made in connection with the Federal court action, as to his belief that AGI named him as a party in that litigation "solely to harass [him] and to interfere with [his] creative work and relationship with Sir-tech." Perhaps most telling is an extensive series of communications between Sir-Tech and Bradley spanning the period from August 1991 through the end of August 1992 and detailing Bradley's progress (or, more appropriately, lack of progress) on the Crusaders project. These contemporaneous memoranda do not indicate that Bradley was ever unable to work and, in fact, make absolutely no reference to the Federal court action. In sharp contrast to the position taken in Sir-Tech's complaint, these writings provide persuasive evidence that the sheer magnitude of the Crusaders project, programming and operating system problems and, quite possibly, Sir-Tech's own impatience and interference were the major causes for the delay, which extended for a full year beyond the September 1, 1991 deadline and, in fact, approximately six months beyond the dismissal of the Federal court action. Under the circumstances, we are permitted to find as a matter of law that defendants' institution of the Federal court action did not impede Bradley's performance under his contract with Sir-Tech.

The parties' remaining contentions have either been rendered academic or have been considered and found to lack merit.

––––––––––

Notes and Questions

1. Do you think that the federal lawsuit filed against Sir-Tech and Bradley was used as an excuse for Bradley's delay in completing his contract? If so, was it a justifiable excuse?

2. Where marketing efforts are designed to create public awareness and excitement for a new game or its sequel, development delays can be particularly frustrating; in some cases, they might even be actionable. Consider the class action in *Perrine v. Sega of America, Inc. and Gearbox Software, LLC*, 2013 Lexis 173311 (United States District Court, N.D. California, 2013). Plaintiff customer was excited about *Aliens: Colonial Marines*. In his complaint, Plaintiff claimed that the Defendants delayed the release date of the game in order to allocate resources to other projects. Under the gun due to bad publicity over the delays, the Defendants, it is alleged, decided to address the problem by developing a "non-retail" demonstration version in place of the retail version of the game. The Plaintiff pre-ordered the game and paid $60.00 based on the demonstration. When the retail version finally arrived, Plaintiff immediately noticed that it was quite inferior and that there were many differences with respect to the demonstration version. Among other problems, the effects were inferior and the artificial intelligence aspects were allegedly *less* intelligent. Plaintiff returned the game to the store where it was purchased and sold it for $17.00, thus prompting the class action, filed on April 29, 2013, alleging violations of the California Consumer Legal Remedies Act ("CLRA"), *California Civil Code* §§ 17500, *et seq.* and a claim for breach of express warranty. The District Court's Order denying Defendants' Motion to Dismiss as to all claims was entered on October 3, 2013.

3. For a case which describes what *not* to do in setting up a videogame company, *see Silicon Knights v. Crystal Dynamics, Inc.*, 983 F. Supp. 1303 (N.D. Cal. 1997), which we reproduce in § 16.40.

4. As opposed to a simple *work for hire* agreement, a more detailed contract may be warranted where the hired individual is to have a continuing relationship with the developer. This is especially true where the programmer is to assume a major role in the overall design of the game.

5. Independent programmers and developers should not be intimidated by the industry giants. In conjunction with the 2016 releases of its popular Unity game engines, Unity Technologies reminds us that it provides download-free, royalty-free versions of its state of the art 3D development tools. See https:/Unity3d.com/.

6. Consider pairing-off with your classmates into sets of two (or more) students in order to renegotiate some of the key terms of the following contract. Let half of each set represent the developer, while the other half handles negotiations on behalf of the pro-

grammer. As previously discussed, it is commonplace for the "Publisher" to occupy the position referred to as the "Developer" in the following sample.

* * *

FORM 3.1

Computer Programmer Contract

THIS AGREEMENT, made and entered into as of this _____ day of _____, 20_____ is by and between _____, whose address is _____ ("Developer") and _____ whose address is _____ ("Programmer").

WHEREAS the Developer is currently a manufacturer, producer and distributor of computerized videogames who requires assistance from skilled individuals, including computer programmers, and

WHEREAS the Programmer is a skilled computer programmer who possesses knowledge, talent and experience with respect to the _____ programming language, and

WHEREAS the Developer and Programmer desire to work with one another to develop computerized videogames,

NOW THEREFORE, in consideration of the mutual promises and agreements set forth herein, the Developer and Programmer do hereby agree as follows:

1. Scope of Services. The Programmer agrees to perform for the Developer the computer programming services and work ("Services") required to complete various Project Assignments from time to time as they are agreed upon by both Developer and Programmer.

2. Project Assignments Defined: Each Project Assignment shall be in substantially the same form that appears in Exhibit A and will be subject to the terms and conditions of this Agreement. Each Project Assignment will include a description of the Services to be completed by Programmer, together with a completion date by which Programmer shall complete such Services ("Completion Date"), and any interim or partial deadlines ("Milestones"), subject to agreement by both parties. Each Project Assignment may contain additional terms and conditions that apply only to that Project, which for purposes of such Project Assignment supersede any conflicting provisions herein, but do not modify the provisions of any other Project Assignments. The term "Project Assignment" includes any modification to a pre-existing Project agreed upon by the parties and memorialized by one or more executed Change Orders.

3. Deliverables: Each Project Assignment may include a description of Deliverables that Programmer is required to submit to Developer with respect to the Services covered by such Project Assignment. As used in this agreement, the term "Deliverables" means:

(a) All items described in a Project Assignment that Programmer agrees to deliver to Developer in performance of the Services governed by such Project Assignment, including, but not limited to source code and object code; and

(b) any written reports stating Programmer's assumptions, findings, results, notes, and recommendations with respect to such Services, whether or not described in a Project Assignment ("Reports"); and

(c) originals or copies of all other tangible materials prepared or developed by Programmer in the performance of the Services, whether or not described in a Project, including but not limited to listings, layouts, documents, templates, calculations, maps, sketches, notes, reports, algorithms, data, models, samples, regardless of the form of media (e.g., paper, diskettes, etc.) on which the same may exist ("Programmer Materials").

(d) No Services governed by an executed Project Assignment will be deemed complete until Programmer delivers all Deliverables to Developer and the Deliverables are satisfactory to Developer in its sole discretion.

4. Change Orders: If the parties agree upon changes in the scope of the Services, Completion Date, Milestones (if any), Deliverables or other matters provided for in an executed Project Assignment, they shall execute a Change Order in substantially the same form attached hereto as Exhibit B; a Project Assignment will be deemed to include all executed Change Orders that modify or refer to such Project Assignment.

5. Project Fee: As full consideration for the satisfactory and complete performance by Programmer of the Services described in a Project Assignment and the delivery of all Deliverables thereunder, Developer shall pay to Programmer the amount ("Project Fee") specified in such Project Assignment for the Programmer's services therein, subject to the other terms and conditions of this Agreement. Notwithstanding the foregoing, Developer will not be obligated to pay Programmer the Project Fee if any of the Services Performed or any Deliverable delivered thereunder fails to comply with any of the warranties set forth in Paragraph 12 below or fails to satisfy any separate acceptance test set forth in such Project Assignment or Change Order.

6. Responsibility for Costs:

(a) Developer shall reimburse Programmer for any Reimbursable Expenses specified in each Project Assignment up to the limit (the "Maximum Reimbursable Expenses"), if any, specified therein, but only to the extent that they are reasonably required for performing the Services and acquiring, making and delivering the Deliverables. Programmer will be responsible for all other expenses incurred by Programmer, and Programmer will bear all sales, excise, use and other taxes assessed against or associated with the Services and the Deliverables unless otherwise indicated in the Project Assignment.

(b) Programmer will be responsible, at no cost to Developer, for obtaining facilities and services, such as office space or support personnel that may be required to perform the Services under any Project Assignment.

(c) Programmer will be responsible for all transportation expenses required to perform the Services under any Project Assignment, except to the extent that such transportation expenses are included in any Reimbursable Expenses specified in the Project Assignment.

7. Maximum Total Cost: If a Project Assignment specifies a "Maximum Total Cost," then the sum of the Project Fee and the Maximum Reimbursable Expenses which Developer is required to pay Programmer with respect to that Project Assignment shall not exceed that amount. Nevertheless, Programmer will be required to perform all Services specified in such Project Assignment.

8. Invoices: Programmer may submit an invoice to Developer for the Project Fee any time after completion of the Services and delivery of all Deliverables under a Project Assignment. Notwithstanding the foregoing, if the Project Assignment provides for interim payments upon completion of Milestones, Programmer may submit invoices to Developer after each such interim payment date provided therein. Each such invoice submitted by Programmer will include a detailed statement of the Services performed, including the dates and total number of days and hours worked thereon, and the Reimbursable Costs related thereto, accompanied by the appropriate receipts.

9. Payment: Unless otherwise specified on the Project Assignment, within thirty (30) days after receipt of Programmer's invoice submitted in accordance with Paragraph 8, Developer will approve and pay the same or else notify Programmer that it disapproves and provide a statement of the reasons for such disapproval.

10. Deadlines and Delays: Time is of the essence in the performance of the Services and other obligations hereunder, and Programmer agrees to complete the Services by the Completion Date (or Milestones, if any) provided in the Project Assignment. If Programmer fails to complete the Services in a satisfactory manner by the Completion Date specified therefor, fails to complete any specified portion of the Services by the Milestone (if any), or fails to make reasonable progress toward satisfactorily completing the Services by the Completion Date specified therefor in a Project Assignment which does not specify Milestones, Developer may, at its option and in its sole discretion:

(a) defer all sums payable hereunder until Programmer is in compliance with all performance and delivery requirements related to those Services and, in the case of Services under a Project Assignment that does not specify Milestones, demonstrates to Developer' reasonable satisfaction that Programmer will complete the Services by the Completion Date, or

(b) notify Programmer that the Project Assignment will be terminated unless Programmer cures all breaches hereof and, if the Project Assignment does not specify Milestones, demonstrates to Developer's reasonable satisfaction that Programmer will complete the Services by the Completion Date. Unless Programmer timely complies with this requirement: (A) Programmer will discontinue performance under that Project Assignment, and Programmer will deliver to Developer all Deliverables under the Project Assignment, whether or not completed; (B) notwithstanding the provisions of Paragraph 20(b), Developer will have no obligation to make any further payments to Programmer under the Project Assignment for the Project Fee, Reimbursable Costs (if any) or otherwise, and Developer will not be required to pay Programmer the value (if any) of any Deliverables delivered to Developer under that Project Assignment; and (C) until terminated as provided herein, the remainder of this Agreement will remain in full force and effect.

11. Independent Contractor: In performing the Services under this Agreement, Programmer will occupy the status of an independent contractor and will not act as, or be, an agent or employee of Developer. All of Programmer's activities will be at Programmer's own risk, and Programmer will not be entitled to workers' compensation or similar benefits or any other insurance protection provided by Developer. As an independent contractor, Programmer will be solely responsible for (i) all taxes payable by Programmer arising out of payment made to him hereunder (including, without limitation, estimated quarterly income tax payments and any FICA obligations) and (ii) determining the means and methods of performing the Services described in the Project Assignments. Programmer will determine the time, the place and the manner in which to accomplish the Services within the Completion Date and Milestones (if any) agreed upon in such Project Assignments. Developer will receive only the resulting product of Programmer's efforts and work.

12. Warranties: Programmer agrees and warrants that:

(a) Programmer will perform the Services using that standard of care, skill and diligence normally provided by a professional person in the performance of similar services with respect to work similar to that specified by any Project Assignment;

(b) upon delivery of each Deliverable to Developer, Developer will have marketable title to that Deliverable, free and clear of all liens and encumbrances;

(c) the Deliverables will meet the standards customarily met by professional persons providing such Deliverables and also any specifications set forth therefor in the Project Assignment applicable thereto;

(d) the use, duplication and distribution of the Deliverables for the purposes contemplated under any Project Assignment will not infringe any patent, copyright or trademark owned or controlled by a third party or violate any other proprietary right of any third party; and

(e) in performing the Services under any Project Assignment, Programmer will not engage in any conduct or practice which violates any applicable law, order, rule or regulation.

13. Ownership: Developer will own and, to the extent permissible under applicable law, Programmer hereby assigns to Developer all proprietary rights in any and all inventions, works of authorship (including, without limitation, software, data, audiovisual works and artistic works), products or processes, whether or not patentable, conceived or reduced to practice or fixed in any tangible medium of expression by Programmer in the performance of the duties hereunder ("Innovations"). If requested by Developer, Programmer agrees to do all things necessary, at Developer's expense, to assist Developer in obtaining patents, copyrights or other proprietary rights for the Innovations. Programmer agrees to execute any documents as may be necessary to implement and carry out the provisions of this Paragraph. All Programmer Materials and Reports will become the property of Developer when prepared, whether delivered to Developer or not, and will, together with any materials furnished by Developer hereunder, be delivered to Developer upon request and, in any event, with Programmer's final invoice. If utilizing any creation or recommendation of Programmer or making, using, selling, copying or distributing any Deliverable or copies of any Deliverable would infringe upon any patent or copyright owned or controlled by Programmer, Developer shall have a universe-wide, permanent, assignable, nonexclusive, royalty-free license (with the right to sublicense) under all such patents and copyrights to do all things necessary to implement the recommendation and creations, to make, use, sell, copy and distribute all Deliverables and copies of all Deliverables, to create works of authorship derived from Deliverables, and to use, sell, copy and distribute any such derivative works.

14. Confidentiality:

(a) Without the written consent of Developer, Programmer shall not use any Confidential Information except in performing Services, and will not, by any act or failure to act, divulge to any third party any Confidential Information. For purposes of this Paragraph, the term "Confidential Information" means any information obtained from or through Developer or Developer's suppliers, or developed or obtained by Programmer in connection with the performance of this Agreement or any Project Assignment hereunder, including any information contained in any Deliverables; provided, however, "Confidential Information" does not include (a) any information that is known to Programmer prior to obtaining it from or through Developer, (b) any information that is, at the time of use or disclosure by Programmer, then in the public domain through no fault of Programmer, or (c) any information obtained by Programmer (other than for the performance of its obligations hereunder) without an obligation of confidentiality and from a third party who did not receive it directly or indirectly from Developer.

(b) Programmer will not refer to Developer in any publicity, press release, advertising, document or publication without Developer's prior written consent.

(c) The parties agree that Developer may disclose the terms and existence of this Agreement, including its compensation provisions, to whomever Developer determines in good faith as having a legitimate need to know such terms.

(d) Programmer acknowledges that any breach or threatened breach of the obligations of confidentiality contained in subparagraphs (a) and (b) of this Paragraph 14 will cause substantial harm to Developer. Accordingly, Programmer recognizes and consents to Developer's right to seek injunctive relief to force Programmer to abide by the terms of this Paragraph.

15. Indemnification:

(a) Developer, the officers, directors, employees, agents, representatives, contractors and subcontractors of Developer (collectively, the "Developer Parties") shall not be liable for any personal injury to or death of any employee of Programmer or Programmer's agents, representatives and subcontractors, if any (collectively, the "Programmer Parties"), howsoever caused (except to the extent caused by the willful misconduct or gross negligence of any of the Developer Parties), or any damage to or loss of the property of the Programmer Parties, and Programmer shall indemnify, defend and hold the Developer Parties harmless from any claim, loss or expense whatsoever in relation thereto.

(b) Programmer agrees to defend, indemnify, and hold the Developer Parties harmless from any and all damages, liabilities, costs and expenses (including without limitation attorneys' fees and costs) incurred by any of the Developer Parties as a result of any claim, judgment or proceeding against any of the Developer Parties or Developer's agents, customers, or other vendors arising out of or connected in any manner with the performance of Services hereunder. Developer may be represented by and actively participate through its own counsel in any claim, suit, or proceeding if it so desires. In case that any game, software or product developed pursuant to the Services is held to constitute an infringement and the use thereof is enjoined, Programmer will, at Developer's option and Programmer's expense, procure for Developer the right to continue using the product as contemplated under this Agreement, or modify the product so that it ceases to infringe.

(c) Should any claim for loss, damage or expense be raised against any of the Developer Parties for which indemnification may be claimed from Programmer under the provisions of this Agreement, Programmer shall be informed promptly in writing of such claim by any of the Developer Parties against whom the claim is made; provided, however, the failure of any of the Developer Parties to promptly inform Programmer of such claim shall not reduce the obligations of Programmer set forth in this Cause, except to the extent that Programmer has been prejudiced thereby. No such claim shall be settled without the approval of Programmer.

16. Assignment: Developer, without the consent of Programmer, may assign any or all rights and licenses granted herein or any interest therein to any parent corporation, subsidiary corporation or affiliate corporation of Developer as herein defined, or to any corporation with which Developer may merge or consolidate, or any corporation which may purchase Developer or a material part of its business or assets; provided, however, that (i) such corporation shall assume and agree in writing delivered to Programmer to perform the covenants of Developer contained in this Agreement, and (ii) Developer shall remain responsible for any breach of this Agreement by its assignee. The terms "parent corporation," "subsidiary corporation," and "affiliate corporation" refer to any parent, subsidiary, or affiliate corporation of Developer, provided that such parent, subsidiary or affiliate corporation controls or is controlled by Developer or by persons or entities controlling or controlled by Developer. The term "control" pertains to ownership of at least a majority of the voting stock of the corporation controlled.

17. Records: If a Project Assignment provides for a Project Fee that is based upon the time incurred by Programmer for the Services described therein, or provides for the payment of Reimbursable Expenses, then Programmer will keep true and particular accounts and records of all information necessary to substantiate the same, and will permit both Developer and representatives of Developer, at all reasonable times, to inspect and take copies of the accounts and records for the purpose of verifying the same.

18. Insurance: Programmer will comply with all laws relating to worker's compensation in all states wherein Services are performed during the term of this Agreement. With respect to each Project Assignment, Programmer will: (a) obtain prior to commencing, and maintain at all times while performing, the Services specified therein, all policies of insurance specified therein, with deductibles no greater than, and with coverage at least as great as, specified therein, and naming Developer as an additional named insured under such policies, and (b) prior to commencing such Services, submit to Developer a certificate of insurance evidencing such policies, with copies of all required endorsements attached thereto. Each policy of insurance obtained by Programmer pursuant to the preceding sentence will obligate the insurance carrier thereof to notify Developer no less than thirty (30) days prior to cancellation of such policy.

19. Notices: Any notice required or permitted to be given in writing by either party to this Agreement to the other party may be personally served, sent by telecopier, fax machine, or sent by express mail or deposited in the United States Mail as certified mail, return receipt requested, postage prepaid, addressed to the other party as designated on the signature page hereof. Any notice will be deemed effective on the date personally served or when actually received. Either party may, by written notice to the other party as provided in this paragraph, change its address or "Fax" telephone number for receipt of notices hereunder, or reasonably add, delete or modify third parties to whom duplicate copies of such notices will be provided.

20. Termination:

(a) This Agreement may be terminated by either party at any time upon sixty (60) days written notice to the other party; provided, however, any such termination will not excuse the nonperformance of either parties' obligations with respect to any unfinished Services (or payment therefor) under an open Project Assignment.

(b) Developer will have the right immediately to terminate Programmer's services with respect to any Services or specific Project Assignment at any time by giving written notice to Programmer, in which case (unless Programmer is in breach of this Agreement) Developer will reimburse Programmer for all reasonable expenses incurred by Programmer prior to receiving such notice of termination and all reasonable costs incurred by Programmer thereafter required to return or dispose of unused materials and equipment acquired by Programmer to perform the Services or deliver the Deliverables under such Project Assignment.

(c) Programmer agrees not to interfere with Developer's business in any manner, including, without limitation, by encouraging anyone to leave Developer's employ or by encouraging a consultant or independent contractor to sever that person's relationship with Developer.

21. Remedies: The remedies provided herein are not exclusive, and the party suffering from a breach or default of this Agreement may pursue all other remedies, both legal and equitable, alternatively or cumulatively. No express or implied waiver by a party to this Agreement of any default will be construed as a waiver of any future or subsequent default. The failure or delay of any party to this Agreement in exercising any rights granted it hereunder will not constitute a waiver of any such right, and any single or partial exercise of any particular right by any party to this Agreement will not exhaust the same or constitute a waiver of any other right provided herein.

22. Integration: This Agreement contains the entire agreement between the parties with respect to the transactions contemplated hereby, and supersedes all negotiations, agreements, and representations, whether written or oral, prior to the date hereof. This Agreement may not be modified or terminated orally; and no modification or waiver will be valid unless contained in a writing signed by both parties. In addition, no such modification or waiver will be effective for any purpose unless it is signed for Developer by the signatories of this Agreement or another person or persons whose authority is affirmed in writing by the President.

23. Governing Law: This Agreement will be governed by the laws of the State of _____ as applied to agreements entered into and to be performed entirely within that state.

24. Saving Provision: In the event any provision of this Agreement or the application of any such provision to any party is held by a court of competent jurisdiction to be contrary to law, such provision will be deemed amended to comply with such law, and the remaining provisions of this Agreement will remain in full force and effect. Paragraph headings will not be used in the interpretation of this Agreement.

IN WITNESS WHEREOF, the undersigned have executed this Agreement on the date first set forth above.

Signed this _____ day of _____, 20____

_____
Developer

_____
Programmer

[Schedules are not included in this model form]

* * * * *

7. Notice that Paragraph 13 of the *Computer Programmer Contract* (pertaining to "ownership") does not make mention of the term "work for hire." What distinguishes this contract from the work for hire agreements in § 2.43? Also, with respect to Paragraph 13, consider the circumstance that might warrant including the following language: "The term 'Proprietary Rights,' as used herein shall include all game engines together with all other reusable software, works, inventions and devices that, enhance, comprise or assist any part of the Deliverables."

8. Business relationships are always subject to unanticipated problems, particularly where the underlying industries are in the process of experiencing growing pains. The videogame industry is no exception. Your competence and value as a lawyer often depends upon your ability to foresee problems that your clients cannot. Severe disagreements and misunderstandings rarely arise from specific, well drafted provisions. Can you nevertheless anticipate any problems or disagreements that were not addressed by the preceding contract?

9. Why didn't the developer just hire the programmer and make him a full time or part time employee?

10. Carefully examine Paragraph 3(d). On behalf of the programmer, would you be concerned with the amount of discretion possessed by the developer? Under that language, what if the developer rejected a perfectly good product? What language might you propose on behalf of the Programmer in order to provide a more balanced agreement? Consider and discuss the following alternatives:

> [a] "No Services governed by an executed Project Assignment will be deemed complete until Programmer delivers all Deliverables to Developer and the Deliverables are satisfactory according to the Developer's **sole uncontrollable, unrestricted discretion.**"

> [b] "No Services governed by an executed Project Assignment will be deemed complete until Programmer delivers all Deliverables to Developer and the Deliverables are accepted as being satisfactory to Developer in its **sole discretion**; provided, however, that such acceptance shall **not be unreasonably withheld.**"

> [c] "No Services governed by an executed Project Assignment will be deemed complete until Programmer delivers all Deliverables to Developer and the Deliverables **reasonably comply** with the terms of the Project Assignment."

> [d] "The Services governed by an executed Project Assignment will be deemed complete when Programmer delivers all Deliverables to Developer where those Deliverables **reasonably comply** with the terms of the Project Assignment."

> [e] "The Services governed by an executed Project Assignment will be deemed complete when the Deliverables **are approved** in writing in accordance with the Videogame Development Process of videogame publisher _____ "

Is there a difference between Paragraphs [c] and [d] above?

11. Where, as in the *Outdoor Partners* case, acceptance is to be predicated upon the approval of a non-contracting third party entity (such as Nintendo, Microsoft or Sony), care must be taken to include provisions for correction-and-resubmission in the event of an initial rejection. There must, however, be limitations placed upon repetitious failure; but those limitations should best be time-based, as opposed to error-based. The best games are often complex and laden with correctable bugs.

§ 3.20 Development Concerns

Every industry has its unique problems and development issues. The videogame creation business is no exception.

§ 3.21 The Game Engine

Throughout this book, you will encounter many references to a so-called *"game engine."* This engine, as the name implies, lies at the heart of the game's operation. It is essentially the computer code that drives the game and makes it operate.

A given engine may be used to generate several versions of the same basic game, each with different graphics, characters and scenery. For example, compare Color Plate 1.2 (Atari's *Space Invaders*) with Color Plate 1.3 (Atari's *Galaxian*). The artwork for the two games appears to be different even though the configuration is similar. The engines would also appear similar to a professional programmer, even though the movement of the sprites is radically different.[7] Another popular product, *Doom*, commonly referred to as a "first person shooter game," has the player, as the shooter, looking down the barrel of a gun, aiming the sight, and seeing exactly what a shooter would see as he or she travels through a maze populated by monsters and evil targets. *Doom*, because of its initial simplicity and popularity, was the subject of many sequels. The subsequent versions of *Doom* could be created by changing the scenery in the mazes, but the basic engine could remain the same. Just as a single lathe in a factory may be used to generate many different metal parts for different products, so too might a game engine be used to generate different works.

A developer's engine may be copyrightable as software, and if it is new and "non-obvious" it may also be eligible for patent protection. As a protectable asset, the engine might be licensed to other game developers in exchange for a flat fee or a royalty.

———————

Notes and Questions

1. Examine Paragraph 13 of Form 3.1. Assume that the Programmer were to develop a new and unique game engine while constructing a videogame in accordance with a Project Assignment. Who would own the engine? What language would you suggest in order to resolve any ambiguities?

2. Identifying an "engine" and separating it from the other components of a newly created videogame may be difficult, but it is certainly not insurmountable since licensing of game engines occurs regularly.

3. Assume that *EngineMaker* is the owner of a unique motion capture engine comprised of both hardware and software. The hardware consists of specially designed and patented clothing with electrodes and wires connecting it to a computer. A human model would wear the clothing; then as he or she moves about, animated images of a corresponding avatar would be simultaneously generated and rendered by the software. This engine would thereby permit animated images to engage in more realistic human-like movement.

———————

7. In *Space Invaders*, the sprites (in the form of aliens) move in predictable, repetitive vertical and horizontal planes. For *Galaxian*, however, the killer bees fly in radical unpredictable curved patterns, thereby providing a greater challenge for the player.

A hypothetical videogame manufacturer, such as *GameCo*, might wish to license the engine in order to create lifelike games. In such a case, *EngineMaker* and *GameCo* might enter into a combination rental and licensing agreement for use of the engine. In the alternative, *GameCo* might, on a work for hire basis, contract with *EngineMaker* to conduct the motion capture and provide the finished images to *GameCo*.

4. A more complex drafting challenge might involve a situation wherein *EngineMaker* is hired to create and render the images upon the condition that after they are delivered to *GameCo*, *GameCo* would then have the ability to take the finished product from *EngineMaker* and modify it. Assume that *EngineMaker* requests you to draft a licensing agreement between *EngineMaker* and *GameCo* that would grant *GameCo* the power to make the alterations that it requires; but *EngineMaker* does not want to convey to *GameCo* any rights that extend beyond the narrow limits of the subject single game. How would you draft such a contract? How would you improve upon the following agreement?

* * *

DEVELOPER AGREEMENT

(a) *EngineMaker* shall design, develop and render for *GameCo* a set of animations referred to as "*GameAvatars*" which set shall be deemed a specially ordered and commissioned work made for hire by *GameCo* as that term is defined by the U.S. Copyright Act, subject, however, to the limitations hereunder; and, as between *EngineMaker* and *GameCo*, *GameCo* shall be deemed the sole author thereof. The term "*GameAvatars*" as used herein pertains to a set of finished real time animations to be used for the subject videogame ("*VidGame*"), the details and specifications of which are on the Delivery Schedule attached hereto; provided however, that under no circumstances does the product to be delivered to *GameCo* ("*Delivery Elements*") include any portions or elements of the "Technology" or "Digital Assets" as defined hereunder.

(b) "Technology," as used herein, includes all materials, engines, tools, technological developments, methods, and algorithms that *EngineMaker* has developed, used, or may in the future develop or use, to create, construct, or render the Characters, Virtual Sets, Digital Assets or any item set forth on the Delivery Schedule. The term "Technology" also includes, but is not limited to: computer source code, object code, databases, algorithms, programs, computer routines and subroutines, hardware, software, along with specialized clothing and accouterments—To the extent that *GameCo* may nevertheless acquire any rights in the "Technology," it hereby assigns, transfers and conveys all such rights to *EngineMaker*.

(c) The term "Digital Assets" refers to all software, digital images and digital components which are owned or controlled by *EngineMaker* and which are used in conjunction with this agreement. To the extent that any rendering of a Digital Asset is included in *VidGame*, although the game as a whole may be copyrighted by *GameCo*, the parties acknowledge and agree that *EngineMaker* expressly retains and reserves all rights, title and interests in the Digital Assets, and *EngineMaker* shall have the exclusive right, title and interest to exploit and use the Digital Assets in any fashion or media, in perpetuity, whether known or unknown.

(d) The parties acknowledge and agree that any and all results and proceeds created, developed or invented by *EngineMaker* with regard to the Technology and Digital Assets, during and in connection with the development and rendering of the Deliverables, shall be the sole and exclusive property of *EngineMaker* forever. The parties further agree on behalf of their respective agents, employees, personnel, and representatives, that the Technology and Digital Assets constitute a valuable trade secret, and that they shall treat any information that they may receive as confidential, and shall not disclose any such information to any person or entity without the prior written consent of *EngineMaker*.

(e) Subject to the foregoing, if, under any applicable law, the "work made for hire" status of Delivery Elements is not effective to place authorship and ownership of such materials in *GameCo*, or in the event that it is determined that the *EngineMaker* Delivery Elements and such other production elements do not constitute a "work made for hire" for *GameCo* within the meaning of the copyright laws of the United States, then to the fullest extent allowable and for the full term of protection otherwise accorded to *EngineMaker* under such applicable law, *EngineMaker* hereby assigns to *GameCo* irrevocably, exclusively and perpetually all rights of every kind in and to the *EngineMaker* Delivery Elements created by *EngineMaker* to the extent that such elements are necessary to enable their use for creation of the *VidGame*. The "Delivery Elements" do not include the "Digital Assets" or "Technology" as defined in Subparagraphs "(a)" through "(c)" above.

(f) *EngineMaker* waives all rights of "droit moral" and agrees not to institute or permit any action or lawsuit on the ground that the *VidGame* or any other production based upon the *EngineMaker* Delivery Elements constitutes an infringement of any of its droit moral or is in any way a defamation or mutilation of the *EngineMaker* Delivery Elements, or contains unauthorized variations, alterations, modifications, changes or translations. *EngineMaker* expressly acknowledges that many parties will contribute to *VidGame* and other games that may or will embody all or part of the *EngineMaker* Delivery Elements and/or other production elements. Accordingly, if under any applicable law the above waiver or assignment by *EngineMaker* of "droit moral" or "moral rights" is not effective, then *EngineMaker* agrees to exercise such rights in a manner which recognizes the contribution of, and does not have a material adverse effect upon, such other parties. Every provision of this clause notwithstanding, *EngineMaker* shall have the right to vigorously defend and protect its Technology and Digital Assets by any legal means available.

5. To guard against copying by competitors, programmers have a list of tricks that they employ to make matters more difficult for would-be infringers. *See* § 3.40, *infra*.

---

§ 3.22 Interoperability Concerns

One of the most significant problems involving videogames is the issue of compatibility and interoperability with respect to the systems and consoles of the markets that they are intended to serve. The best game in the world is useless if it will not work on the hardware for which it is intended.

Whereas a select group of programmers was responsible for the first videogames, by the mid-to-late 1980s, anyone with a computer and some relatively inexpensive software could create a computer game. Before then consumers had become accustomed to seeing only high quality games; so many of the early offerings became classics. During this time, players began to associate the games with their compatible consoles. In other words, if a cartridge were playable on the Atari 2600 or Atari's computers, gamers considered it to be an Atari-produced game regardless of the actual manufacturer. Soon, less than excellent developers began to exploit this consumer laden presumption. Redundant and repetitive games of poor quality, but sporting attractive packages and unique names, began to flood the scene. The industry suffered and sales began to drop. As an alleged response to this problem, Nintendo devised its own solution in the form of a lock-out chip. The chip would, in effect, cause Nintendo's hardware to *lock out* and deny access to any cartridges that did not possess the chip, which only Nintendo could provide. This chip would, theoretically, restrict access to those games that Nintendo considered to be less than the required quality.

The next several cases, which concern reverse engineering, provide an excellent introduction for the many intellectual property issues that pervade the videogame industry. Part II of this Book (Chapters 5–9) provides even more detail. Meanwhile, attention is directed toward reverse engineering, sometimes referred to as "deprocessing." Such a practice sounds complicated, but it simply involves taking a product apart to see "how it ticks" and learn how it is constructed.

* * *

Atari Games Corp. v. Nintendo of America, Inc.

United States Court of Appeals, Federal Circuit, 1992
975 F.2d 832

RADER, Circuit Judge

Nintendo of America Inc., and Nintendo Co., Ltd. sell the Nintendo Entertainment System (NES). Two of Nintendo's competitors, Atari Games Corporation and its wholly-owned subsidiary, Tengen, Inc., sued Nintendo for, among other things, unfair competition, Sherman Act violations, and patent infringement. Nintendo sued Atari for, among other things, unfair competition, patent infringement, copyright infringement, and trade secret violations. The United States District Court for the Northern District of California consolidated the two cases and preliminarily enjoined Atari from exploiting Nintendo's copyrighted computer program. Because Nintendo has shown a likelihood of success on its copyright infringement claims, this court affirms.

BACKGROUND

Nintendo's home video game system—the NES—includes a monitor, console, and controls. The console is a base unit into which a user inserts game cartridges. These cartridges contain the various game programs for the NES. As dictated by the program on the cartridge, the console controls an image on a video monitor, often a television set. In response to this video display, the user interacts with the system by manipulating the controls. Thus, by operating the controls in response to the video image, an individual plays the game on the cartridge in the NES console. For instance, the game program may control a maze or set of obstacles on the video display. The user then manipulates the controls to guide an object through the maze or set of obstacles. The game program then awards the user points for proficiently passing through the maze or obstacles.

Nintendo designed a program—the 10NES—to prevent the NES from accepting unauthorized game cartridges. Both the NES console and authorized game cartridges contain microprocessors or chips programmed with the 10NES. The console contains a "master chip" or "lock." Authorized game cartridges contain a "slave chip" or "key." When a user inserts an authorized cartridge into a console, the slave chip in effect unlocks the console; the console detects a coded message and accepts the game cartridge. When a user inserts an unauthorized cartridge, the console detects no unlocking message and refuses to operate the cartridge. Nintendo's 10NES program thus controls access to the NES.

Atari first attempted to analyze and replicate the NES security system in 1986. Atari could not break the 10NES program code by monitoring the communication between the master and slave chips. Atari next tried to break the code by analyzing the chips themselves. Atari analysts chemically peeled layers from the NES chips to allow microscopic examination of the object code.[8] Nonetheless, Atari still could not decipher the code sufficiently to replicate the NES security system.

In December 1987, Atari became a Nintendo licensee. Atari paid Nintendo to gain access to the NES for its video games. The license terms, however, strictly controlled Atari's access to Nintendo's technology, including the 10NES program. Under the license, Nintendo would take Atari's games, place them in cartridges containing the 10NES program, and resell them to Atari. Atari could then market the games to NES owners. Nintendo limited all licensees, including Atari, to five new NES games per year. The Nintendo license also prohibited Atari from licensing NES games to other home video game systems for two years from Atari's first sale of the game.

In early 1988, Atari's attorney applied to the Copyright Office for a reproduction of the 10NES program. The application stated that Atari was a defendant in an infringement action and needed a copy of the program for that litigation. Atari falsely alleged that it was a present defendant in a case in the Northern District of California. Atari assured the "Library of Congress that the requested copy [would] be used only in connection with the specified litigation." In fact, no suit existed between the parties until December 1988, when Atari sued Nintendo for antitrust violations and unfair competition. Nintendo filed no infringement action against Atari until November 1989.

After obtaining the 10NES source code from the Copyright Office, Atari again tried to read the object code from peeled chips. Through microscopic examination, Atari's analysts transcribed the 10NES object code into a handwritten representation of zeros and ones. Atari used the information from the Copyright Office to correct errors in this transcription. The Copyright Office copy facilitated Atari's replication of the 10NES object code.

After deciphering the 10NES program, Atari developed its own program—the Rabbit program—to unlock the NES. Atari's Rabbit program generates signals indistinguishable from the 10NES program. The Rabbit uses a different microprocessor. The Rabbit chip, for instance, operates faster. Thus, to generate signals recognizable by the 10NES master chip, the Rabbit program must include pauses. Atari also programmed the Rabbit in a different language. Because Atari chose a different microprocessor and programming language, the line-by-line instructions of the 10NES and Rabbit programs vary. Nonetheless, as the district court found, the Rabbit program generates signals functionally indistinguishable from the 10NES program. The Rabbit gave Atari access to NES owners without Nintendo's strict license conditions.

Nintendo asked the district court to enjoin Atari's alleged infringement of its 10NES copyright. Atari sought in a separate motion to enjoin Nintendo's alleged antitrust violations and alleged misuse of its property rights. Nintendo prevailed on both motions. Atari appealed both rulings but subsequently moved to dismiss its appeal from the denial of its motion for a preliminary injunction. This court granted that motion. Atari asserts copyright misuse as a defense to copyright infringement.

---

8. Object code is machine readable, binary code, represented on paper as a series of ones and zeroes. In actuality, those ones and zeroes represent "on" and "off" states of switches on a computer chip. In the 10NES chips, the object code, contained in chip memories, is implemented when the chips are operational. When operational, the chips generate a series of "ons" and "offs" in a particular sequence. That results in a pulsating signal which conveys messages to the computer.

Copyright Infringement

To prevail on its copyright infringement claim, Nintendo must show ownership of the 10NES program copyright and copying by Atari of protectable expression from the 10NES program. *Feist Publications v. Rural Tel. Serv. Co.*, 499 U.S. 340, 111 S.Ct. 1282, 1296, 113 L.Ed.2d 358 (1991). The parties do not dispute that Nintendo owns the 10NES copyright. Therefore, Nintendo need only prove that Atari copied protectable expression from the 10NES program.

Nintendo can show copying by proving that Atari made literal copies of the 10NES program. Alternatively, Nintendo can show copying by proving that Atari had access to the 10NES program and that Atari's work—the Rabbit program—is substantially similar to Nintendo's work in ideas and the expression of those ideas. The parties do not dispute that Atari had access to the 10NES program. Thus, to show non-literal copyright infringement, Nintendo must ultimately prove substantial similarity between the 10NES and the Rabbit in protectable expression. To determine whether Nintendo is likely to so prove, this court must first distinguish protectable expression from the unprotected elements of the 10NES program.

Copyright Overview

Article I, §8, cl. 8, of the Constitution gives Congress power "[T]o promote the Progress of Science and useful Arts, by securing for limited Times to Authors and Inventors the exclusive Right to their respective Writings and Discoveries." The Constitution thus gives Congress the authority to set the parameters of authors' exclusive rights. *Sony Corp. of Am. v. Universal City Studios*, 464 U.S. 417.[9] The Copyright Act of 1976, in general, protects "original works of authorship fixed in any tangible medium of expression." 17 U.S.C. §102(a) (1988). To explain the term "works of authorship," the Act sets forth a statutory list of categories within the term. The first category on this non-exclusive list is "literary works."

The statutory definition of "literary works" embraces computer programs: "Literary works" are works, other than audiovisual works, expressed in words, numbers, or other verbal or numerical symbols or indicia, regardless of the nature of the material objects, such as books, periodicals, manuscripts, phonorecords, film, tapes, disks, or cards, in which they are embodied. 17 U.S.C. §101 (1980). As works "expressed in words, numbers, or other verbal or numerical symbols or indicia," computer programs fall within the terms of the 1976 Act. The House Report for the 1976 Act explicitly includes computer programs within "literary works":

The term "literary works" does not connote any criterion of literary merit or qualitative value: it includes … computer data bases, and computer programs to the extent that they incorporate authorship in the programmer's expression of original ideas, as distinguished from the ideas themselves. H.R.Rep. No. 1476, 94th Cong., 2d Sess. 54 (1976), reprinted in 1976 U.S.C.C.A.N. 5659, 5667. As literary works, copyright protection extends to computer programs and to instructions encoded on silicon chips, *Apple Computer v. Formula International*, 725 F.2d 521 (9th Cir.1984). The 1976 Act, however, sets limits on the scope of copyright protection. In the words of the Supreme Court, "[t]he mere fact that a work is copyrighted does not mean that every element of the work may be protected." Feist, 499 U.S. at ___, 111 S.Ct. at 1289.

Section 102(b) of title 17 states:

---

9. For a thorough historical presentation of Congress's copyright enactments, *see Lotus Development v. Paperback Software International*, 740 F. Supp. 37, 47–51 (D.Mass.1990).

In no case does copyright protection for an original work of authorship extend to any idea, procedure, process, system, method of operation, concept, principle, or discovery, regardless of the form in which it is described, explained, illustrated, or embodied in such work.17 U.S.C. § 102(b).

The 1976 House Report on section 102(b) applies this limitation directly to computer programs. Some concern has been expressed lest copyright in computer programs should extend protection to the methodology or processes adopted by the programmer, rather than merely to the "writing" expressing his ideas. Section 102(b) is intended, among other things, to make clear that the expression adopted by the programmer is the copyrightable element in a computer program, and that the actual processes or methods embodied in the program are not within the scope of the copyright law.

Protectable Expression

This overview of copyright law explains the trial court's initial task is separating protectable expression in the 10NES program from unprotectable ideas, facts, processes, and methods of operation. The Copyright Act, however, contains no explicit standards for separating a computer program's expression from its idea. Rather this court must examine tests used for other literary works to distinguish expression from idea. Judge Learned Hand devised an abstraction test to separate the idea from expression in written or dramatic works: Upon any work ... a great number of patterns of increasing generality will fit equally well, as more and more of the incident is left out.... [T]here is a point in this series of abstractions where they are no longer protected, since otherwise the playwright could prevent the use of his "ideas," to which, apart from their expression, his property is never extended. *Nichols v. Universal Pictures Corp.*, 45 F.2d 119, 121 (2d Cir.1930). Judge Hand's abstraction analysis forces differentiation of the unprotectable idea and protectable expression. The abstraction method also properly recognizes that a computer program contains many distinct ideas. By separating the program into manageable components, this method eases the court's task of discerning the boundaries of protectable expression.

After separating the program into manageable components, the court must next filter the unprotectable components of the program from the protectable expression. The court must filter out as unprotectable the ideas, expression necessarily incident to the idea, expression already in the public domain, expression dictated by external factors (like the computer's mechanical specifications, compatibility with other programs, and demands of the industry served by the program), and expression not original to the programmer or author.

In addition, copyright protection does not "extend to any ... procedure, process, system [or] method of operation." 17 U.S.C. § 102(b). In conformance with the standards of patent law, title 35 provides protection for the process or method performed by a computer in accordance with a program. Thus, patent and copyright laws protect distinct aspects of a computer program. *See Baker v. Selden*, 101 U.S. 99 (1879). Title 35 protects the process or method performed by a computer program; title 17 protects the expression of that process or method. While title 35 protects any novel, nonobvious, and useful process, title 17 can protect a multitude of expressions that implement that process. If the patentable process is embodied inextricably in the line-by-line instructions of the computer program, however, then the process merges with the expression and precludes copyright protection.

This court must determine whether each component of the 10NES program qualifies as an expression of an idea, or an idea itself. This determination depends on "the particular facts of each case." Nintendo's 10NES program contains more than an idea or expression necessarily incident to an idea. Nintendo incorporated within the 10NES program creative organization and sequencing unnecessary to the lock and key function. Nintendo chose arbitrary programming instructions and arranged them in a unique sequence to create a purely arbitrary data stream. This data stream serves as the key to unlock the NES. Nintendo may protect this creative element of the 10NES under copyright.

External factors did not dictate the design of the 10NES program. Nintendo may have incorporated some minimal portions of the program to accommodate the microprocessor in the NES, but no external factor dictated the bulk of the program. Nor did Nintendo take this program from the public domain. By registering the 10NES with the Copyright Office, Nintendo obtained the benefit of a presumption of originality which Atari does not rebut on this record.

Finally, Nintendo seeks to protect the creative element of its program beyond the literal expression used to effect the unlocking process. The district court defined the unprotectable 10NES idea or process as the generation of a data stream to unlock a console. This court discerns no clear error in the district court's conclusion. The unique arrangement of computer program expression which generates that data stream does not merge with the process so long as alternate expressions are available. In this case, Nintendo has produced expert testimony showing a multitude of different ways to generate a data stream which unlocks the NES console.

At this stage in the proceedings of this case, Nintendo has made a sufficient showing that its 10NES program contains protectable expression. After filtering unprotectable elements out of the 10NES program, this court finds no error in the district court's conclusion that 10NES contains protectable expression. Nintendo independently created the 10NES program and exercised creativity in the selection and arrangement of its instruction lines. *See Bellsouth Advertising & Publishing v. Donnelly Info. Publishing*, 933 F.2d 952, 957 (11th Cir. 1991) (selection, coordination, or arrangement of information constitutes originality). The security function of the program necessitated an original signal combination to act as a lock and key for the NES console. To generate an original signal, Nintendo had to design an original program. In sum, the district court properly discerned that the 10NES program contains protectable expression. At a minimum, Nintendo may protect under copyright the unique and creative arrangement of instructions in the 10NES program.

Next, this court must determine whether the district court correctly determined that Nintendo has shown sufficient evidence that Atari either literally copied the 10NES or had access to the 10NES and produced a substantially similar copy. Nintendo argues that Atari's unauthorized acquisition of a copy from the Copyright Office literally infringed the 10NES program. Nintendo also argues that copies of the 10NES program made in the reverse engineering process literally infringe the 10NES copyright. Finally, Nintendo argues that Atari's Rabbit program is substantially similar to the 10NES and therefore infringes the 10NES copyright. A single copy is sufficient to support a claim of copyright infringement. Even for works warranting little copyright protection, verbatim copying is infringement.

Verbatim Copying

Atari acquired a copy of the 10NES program from the Copyright Office and used it to replicate the 10NES source code. The Copyright Act states:

> Copies or reproductions of deposited articles retained under the control of the Copyright Office shall be authorized or furnished only under the conditions specified by the Copyright Office regulations. 17 U.S.C. §706(b). In conformance

with protective regulations, this provision permits access to copyrighted works. Copies obtained from the Copyright Office in violation of the regulations, however, are unauthorized reproductions.

Section 201.2(d)(2) of the Regulations of the Copyright Office (as amended through July 1, 1986), permit reproduction only if: (1) the copyright owner grants permission, (2) a court orders reproduction, or (3) (ii) The Copyright Office receives a written request from an attorney on behalf of either the plaintiff or defendant in connection with litigation, actual or prospective, involving the copyrighted work. The following information must be included in such a request: (A) The names of all the parties involved and the nature of the controversy; (B) the name of the court in which the actual case is pending or, in the case of a prospective proceeding, a full statement of the facts of the controversy in which the copyrighted work is involved; and (C) satisfactory assurance that the requested reproduction will be used only in connection with the specified litigation. Under this regulation, Atari requested the 10NES program in 1988.[10]

Section 201.2(d)(2) refers to "litigation, actual or prospective." The term "prospective litigation," as used in the regulation, means more than a subjective expectation of litigation at some unspecified future time. Otherwise, anyone desiring a copy of a deposited work would only need to allege a speculative future dispute. Instead, the regulation repeatedly refers to and requests information about an actual controversy between parties. This language, in context, clarifies that the regulation requires an objective, reasonable apprehension of litigation.

In this case, Nintendo is likely to show that Atari had no reasonable apprehension of litigation in 1988. In fact, Atari was not in a position to infringe before acquiring the 10NES program from the Copyright Office. Atari was Nintendo's licensee in 1988. Atari had no product, allegedly infringing or not, to perform the function of the 10NES program. Without any allegedly infringing program at all in 1988, Atari had no reason to fear a copyright infringement suit from Nintendo. Therefore, no controversy at all existed when Atari acquired the 10NES program from the Copyright Office. Without an actual controversy, Atari's acquisition of the 10NES source code violated Copyright Office rules. Reproduction of an unauthorized copy from the Copyright Office violates 17 U.S.C. § 106(1).

On this record, the district court did not err in determining that Nintendo is likely to show successfully that Atari infringed the 10NES copyright by obtaining and copying the source code from the Copyright Office.

Reverse Engineering

Atari made copies of the 10NES program in its attempts to "reverse engineer" Nintendo's program. Atari made intermediate copies in two very different settings. Before obtaining the Copyright Office copy of 10NES, Atari tried to understand the program. Atari stripped some 10NES chips and copied portions of the 10NES object code from the chips.

After obtaining the copy of the code from the Copyright Office, Atari made other intermediate copies of the program. Atari made photocopies of the Copyright Office copy, deprocessed chips, and hand-copied the 10NES object code from the deprocessed chip.

---

10. In 1991, the Copyright Office circulated the following notice:
The Copyright Office has recently become aware that an attorney completing the previous Litigation Statement form provided by the Office could generally allege that a controversy existed when in fact no real controversy did exist. An attorney could thus receive reproductions of deposits not authorized by the regulations. The Litigation Statement form has been amended to require the applicant to give more specific information regarding prospective proceedings and to include supporting documentation. 56 Fed.Reg. 12,957 (1991).

Atari then entered this copied 10NES object code into a computer which aided in understanding the ideas in the program. The district court determined that this intermediate copying infringed Nintendo's copyright.

The Copyright Act encourages authors to share their creative works with society. The Constitution sets forth the purpose of copyright protection as the promotion of "the Progress of Science", not the rewarding of authors. U.S. Const. art. I, §8, cl. 8; *Feist*, 499 U.S. at __, 111 S.Ct. at 1290. The Copyright Act thus balances the interests of authors ... in the control and exploitation of their writings ... on the one hand, and society's competing interests in the free flow of ideas, [and] information ... on the other hand. Thus, while providing exclusive rights to expression, the Act "encourages others to build freely upon the ideas and information conveyed by a work."

The author does not acquire exclusive rights to a literary work in its entirety. Under the Act, society is free to exploit facts, ideas, processes, or methods of operation in a copyrighted work. To protect processes or methods of operation, a creator must look to patent laws. *See Bonito Boats v. Thunder Craft Boats*, 489 U.S. 141 (1989). An author cannot acquire patent-like protection by putting an idea, process, or method of operation in an unintelligible format and asserting copyright infringement against those who try to understand that idea, process, or method of operation. *See, e.g., Feist*, 499 U.S. at __, 111 S.Ct. at 1290; 17 U.S.C. §102(b). The Copyright Act permits an individual in rightful possession of a copy of a work to undertake necessary efforts to understand the work's ideas, processes, and methods of operation. This permission appears in the fair use exception to copyright exclusivity. Section 107 of the Copyright Act states that "fair use of a copyrighted work, including such use by reproduction in copies ... for purposes such as criticism, comment, news reporting, teaching ... scholarship or research" is not infringement. 17 U.S.C. §107. The legislative history of section 107 suggests that courts should adapt the fair use exception to accommodate new technological innovations. *See also Twentieth Century [Music v. Aiken]*, 422 U.S. at 156 ("When technological change has rendered its literal terms ambiguous, the Copyright Act must be construed in light of [its] basic purpose.").

Thus, the Act exempts from copyright protection reproductions for "criticism, comment ... or research." These activities permit public understanding and dissemination of the ideas, processes, and methods of operation in a work: The copyright holder has a property interest in preventing others from reaping the fruits of his labor, not in preventing the authors and thinkers of the future from making use of, or building upon, his advances. The process of creation is often an incremental one, and advances building on past developments are far more common than radical new concepts. Where the infringement is small in relation to the new work created, the fair user is profiting largely from his own creative efforts rather than free-riding on another's work. A prohibition on all copying whatsoever would stifle the free flow of ideas without serving any legitimate interest of the copyright holder.

When the nature of a work requires intermediate copying to understand the ideas and processes in a copyrighted work, that nature supports a fair use for intermediate copying. Thus, reverse engineering object code to discern the unprotectable ideas in a computer program is a fair use. *See Feist*, 499 U.S. at __, 111 S.Ct. at 1290, ("[C]opyright does not prevent subsequent users from copying from a prior author's work those constituent elements that are not original—for example ... facts, or materials in the public domain—as long as such use does not unfairly appropriate the author's original contributions.").

Fair use to discern a work's ideas, however, does not justify extensive efforts to profit from replicating protected expression. Any reproduction of protectable expression must be strictly necessary to ascertain the bounds of protected information within the work.

In this case, the source code obtained from the Copyright Office facilitated Atari's intermediate copying of the 10NES program. To invoke the fair use exception, an individual must possess an authorized copy of a literary work. Because Atari was not in authorized possession of the Copyright Office copy of 10NES, any copying or derivative copying of 10NES source code from the Copyright Office does not qualify as a fair use.

Reverse engineering, untainted by the purloined copy of the 10NES program and necessary to understand 10NES, is a fair use. An individual cannot even observe, let alone understand, the object code on Nintendo's chip without reverse engineering. Atari retrieved this object code from NES security chips in its efforts to reverse engineer the 10NES program. Atari chemically removed layers from Nintendo's chips to reveal the 10NES object code. Through microscopic examination of the "peeled" chip, Atari engineers transcribed the 10NES object code into a handwritten list of ones and zeros. While these ones and zeros represent the configuration of machine readable software, the ones and zeros convey little, if any, information to the normal unaided observer. Atari then keyed this handwritten copy into a computer. The computer then "disassembled"[11] the object code or otherwise aided the observer in understanding the program's method or functioning. This "reverse engineering" process, to the extent untainted by the 10NES copy purloined from the Copyright Office, qualified as a fair use.

The district court assumed that reverse engineering (intermediate copying) was copyright infringement. This court disagrees. Atari did not violate Nintendo's copyright by deprocessing computer chips in Atari's rightful possession. Atari could lawfully deprocess Nintendo's 10NES chips to learn their unprotected ideas and processes. This fair use did not give Atari more than the right to understand the 10NES program and to distinguish the protected from the unprotected elements of the 10NES program. Any copying beyond that necessary to understand the 10NES program was infringement. Atari could not use reverse engineering as an excuse to exploit commercially or otherwise misappropriate protected expression.

Substantial Similarity

Even in the absence of verbatim copying, a copyright owner may show infringement by showing that the infringer had access to the work and that the two works are substantially similar. This doctrine prevents a plagiarist from escaping infringement by making immaterial changes in the protected work.

The Ninth Circuit uses a two-step analysis to evaluate substantial similarity: First, an "extrinsic" test is used to determine whether two ideas are substantially similar. This is an objective test which rests upon specific criteria that can be listed and analyzed. Second, an "intrinsic" test is used to compare forms of expression. This is a subjective test which depends on the response of the ordinary reasonable person. In the context of computer programs, the "ordinary reasonable person" with the ability to intelligently respond to computer expression is a computer programmer. Thus, in addition to the lay response of a fact-finder, the Ninth Circuit permits expert testimony about the second prong of the substantial similarity test.

---

11. Computer programs are normally written in a high-level language such as C or FORTRAN. Once written, the program is translated from the high-level language to machine-readable object code. This translation process, called compiling, is performed by a computer as instructed by a compiling program. As mentioned previously, the idea or process expressed in a program is not easily discernible from object code. Object code is disassembled to facilitate understanding the idea or process expressed. Disassembly is basically the reverse of compilation. Object code is translated via a disassembly program to a higher, more intelligible language called assembly language.

In applying this test, the district court correctly considered expert testimony recounting striking similarities between the Rabbit and 10NES programs. Moreover, the trial court detected similarities between the programs beyond the similarities necessary to accommodate the programming environment, or similarities necessary to embody the unprotectable idea, process, or method of the 10NES program.

Specifically, the district court noted that the Rabbit program incorporates elements of the 10NES program unnecessary for the chip's performance. The 10NES slave chip performs some functions beyond unlocking the NES console. For example, the 10NES slave chip shuts down upon receipt of an erroneous message from a master chip. The Rabbit program too contains this feature. This disabling feature is unnecessary to achieve Atari's stated purpose—unlocking the NES console.

While Atari may freely reproduce the idea or process of Nintendo's 10NES code, copying of fully extraneous instructions unnecessary to the 10NES program's function strongly supports the district court's imposition of an injunction on the likelihood Nintendo will show infringement. The unnecessary instructions in the Rabbit program suggest copying, not independent creation.

In sum, Nintendo is likely to show that its 10NES program contains protectable expression. Atari's efforts to reverse engineer the 10NES chip to learn the ideas in the program will not alone support a copyright infringement claim. To the extent, however, Nintendo is likely to show misappropriation and copying of the unauthorized Copyright Office copy, it is likely to succeed on the merits of its infringement claim. Alternatively, Nintendo is likely to prove substantial similarity between the Rabbit and 10NES programs sufficient to support its infringement claims. This record thus justifies the trial court's imposition of a preliminary injunction.

Notes and Questions

1. Even though Atari had made false statements to cause the U.S. Copyright Office to release the records that permitted the duplication of the subject code, Atari won the copyright infringement portion of the lawsuit. Nintendo, on the other hand, had the foresight to also obtain patent protection on its 10NES software (U.S. Pat. No. 4,799,635). Nintendo prevailed on its charges of patent infringement. The parties eventually settled the case, and Nintendo, of course, has since become a dominant player in the U.S. console market, while Atari faded.

2. How is it possible that Atari prevailed on its copyright defense but for the very same conduct lost with respect to the patent issue? Hold that thought until you have reviewed Chapters 5–7.

* * *

Sega Enterprises Ltd. v. Accolade, Inc.

United States Court of Appeals, Ninth Circuit, 1993
977 F.2d 1510

REINHARDT, Circuit Judge

This case presents several difficult questions of first impression involving our copyright and trademark laws. We are asked to determine, first, whether the Copyright Act permits persons who are neither copyright holders nor licensees to disassemble a copyrighted computer program in order to gain an understanding of the unprotected functional elements of the program. In light of the public policies underlying the Act, we conclude that, when the person seeking the understanding has a legitimate reason for doing so and when no other means of access to the unprotected elements exists, such disassembly is as a matter of law a fair use of the copyrighted work.

Second, we must decide the legal consequences under the Lanham Trademark Act of a computer manufacturer's use of a security system that affords access to its computers to software cartridges that include an initialization code which triggers a screen display of the computer manufacturer's trademark. The computer manufacturer also manufactures software cartridges; those cartridges all contain the initialization code. The question is whether the computer manufacturer may enjoin competing cartridge manufacturers from gaining access to its computers through the use of the code on the ground that such use will result in the display of a "false" trademark. Again, our holding is based on the public policies underlying the statute.

We hold that when there is no other method of access to the computer that is known or readily available to rival cartridge manufacturers, the use of the initialization code by a rival does not violate the Act even though that use triggers a misleading trademark display. Accordingly, we reverse the district court's grant of a preliminary injunction in favor of plaintiff-appellee Sega Enterprises, Ltd. on its claims of copyright and trademark infringement. We decline, however, to order that an injunction pendente lite issue precluding Sega from continuing to use its security system, even though such use may result in a certain amount of false labeling. We prefer to leave the decision on that question to the district court initially.

I. Background

Plaintiff-appellee Sega Enterprises, Ltd. ("Sega"), a Japanese corporation, and its subsidiary, Sega of America, develop and market video entertainment systems, including the "Genesis" console (distributed in Asia under the name "Mega-Drive") and video game cartridges. Defendant-appellant Accolade, Inc., is an independent developer, manufacturer, and marketer of computer entertainment software, including game cartridges that are compatible with the Genesis console, as well as game cartridges that are compatible with other computer systems.

Sega licenses its copyrighted computer code and its "SEGA" trademark to a number of independent developers of computer game software. Those licensees develop and sell Genesis-compatible video games in competition with Sega. Accolade is not and never has been a licensee of Sega. Prior to rendering its own games compatible with the Genesis console, Accolade explored the possibility of entering into a licensing agreement with Sega, but abandoned the effort because the agreement would have required that Sega be the exclusive manufacturer of all games produced by Accolade.

Accolade used a two-step process to render its video games compatible with the Genesis console. First, it "reverse engineered" Sega's video game programs in order to discover the requirements for compatibility with the Genesis console. As part of the reverse engineering process, Accolade transformed the machine-readable object code contained in commercially available copies of Sega's game cartridges into human-readable source code using a process called "disassembly" or "decompilation."[12] Accolade purchased a

---

12. Computer programs are written in specialized alphanumeric languages, or "source code". In order to operate a computer, source code must be translated into computer readable form, or "object code." Object code uses only two symbols, 0 and 1, in combinations which represent the alphanumeric

Genesis console and three Sega game cartridges, wired a decompiler into the console circuitry, and generated printouts of the resulting source code. Accolade engineers studied and annotated the printouts in order to identify areas of commonality among the three game programs. They then loaded the disassembled code back into a computer, and experimented to discover the interface specifications for the Genesis console by modifying the programs and studying the results. At the end of the reverse engineering process, Accolade created a development manual that incorporated the information it had discovered about the requirements for a Genesis-compatible game. According to the Accolade employees who created the manual, the manual contained only functional descriptions of the interface requirements and did not include any of Sega's code.

In the second stage, Accolade created its own games for the Genesis. According to Accolade, at this stage it did not copy Sega's programs, but relied only on the information concerning interface specifications for the Genesis that was contained in its development manual. Accolade maintains that with the exception of the interface specifications, none of the code in its own games is derived in any way from its examination of Sega's code. In 1990, Accolade released "Ishido," a game which it had originally developed and released for use with the Macintosh and IBM personal computer systems, for use with the Genesis console.

Even before Accolade began to reverse engineer Sega's games, Sega had grown concerned about the rise of software and hardware piracy in Taiwan and other Southeast Asian countries to which it exported its products. Taiwan does allow prosecution of trademark counterfeiters. However, the counterfeiters had discovered how to modify Sega's game programs to blank out the screen display of Sega's trademark before repackaging and reselling the games as their own. Accordingly, Sega began to explore methods of protecting its trademark rights in the Genesis and Genesis-compatible games. While the development of its own trademark security system (TMSS) was pending, Sega licensed a patented TMSS for use with the Genesis home entertainment system. The most recent version of the Genesis console, the "Genesis III," incorporates the licensed TMSS. When a game cartridge is inserted, the microprocessor contained in the Genesis III searches the game program for four bytes of data consisting of the letters "S-E-G-A" (the "TMSS initialization code"). If the Genesis III finds the TMSS initialization code in the right location, the game is rendered compatible and will operate on the console. In such case, the TMSS initialization code then prompts a visual display for approximately three seconds which reads "PRODUCED BY OR UNDER LICENSE FROM SEGA ENTERPRISES LTD" (the "Sega Message"). All of Sega's game cartridges, including those disassembled by Accolade, contain the TMSS initialization code.

Accolade learned of the impending release of the Genesis III in the United States in January, 1991, when the Genesis III was displayed at a consumer electronics show. When a demonstration at the consumer electronics show revealed that Accolade's "Ishido" game cartridges would not operate on the Genesis III, Accolade returned to the drawing board. During the reverse engineering process, Accolade engineers had discovered a small segment of code—the TMSS initialization code—that was included in the "power-up" sequence

---

characters of the source code. A program written in source code is translated into object code using a computer program called an "assembler" or "compiler," and then imprinted onto a silicon chip for commercial distribution. Devices called "disassemblers" or "decompilers" can reverse this process by "reading" the electronic signals for "0" and "1" that are produced while the program is being run, storing the resulting object code in computer memory, and translating the object code into source code. Both assembly and disassembly devices are commercially available, and both types of devices are widely used within the software industry.

of every Sega game, but that had no identifiable function. The games would operate on the original Genesis console even if the code segment was removed. Mike Lorenzen, the Accolade engineer with primary responsibility for reverse engineering the interface procedures for the Genesis console, sent a memo regarding the code segment to Alan Miller, his supervisor and the current president of Accolade, in which he noted that "it is possible that some future Sega peripheral device might require it for proper initialization."

In the second round of reverse engineering, Accolade engineers focused on the code segment identified by Lorenzen. After further study, Accolade added the code to its development manual in the form of a standard header file to be used in all games. The file contains approximately twenty to twenty-five bytes of data. Each of Accolade's games contains a total of 500,000 to 1,500,000 bytes. According to Accolade employees, the header file is the only portion of Sega's code that Accolade copied into its own game programs.

In 1991, Accolade released five more games for use with the Genesis III, "Star Control", "Hardball!", "Onslaught", "Turrican", and "Mike Ditka Power Football." With the exception of "Mike Ditka Power Football", all of those games, like "Ishido", had originally been developed and marketed for use with other hardware systems. All contained the standard header file that included the TMSS initialization code. According to Accolade, it did not learn until after the Genesis III was released on the market in September, 1991, that in addition to enabling its software to operate on the Genesis III, the header file caused the display of the Sega Message. All of the games except "Onslaught" operate on the Genesis III console; apparently, the programmer who translated "Onslaught" for use with the Genesis system did not place the TMSS initialization code at the correct location in the program.

All of Accolade's Genesis-compatible games are packaged in a similar fashion. The front of the box displays Accolade's "Ballistic" trademark and states "for use with Sega Genesis and Mega Drive Systems." The back of the box contains the following statement: "Sega and Genesis are registered trademarks of Sega Enterprises, Ltd. Game 1991 Accolade, Inc. All rights reserved. Ballistic is a trademark of Accolade, Inc. Accolade, Inc. is not associated with Sega Enterprises, Ltd. All product and corporate names are trademarks and registered trademarks of their respective owners."

Sega filed suit against Accolade on October 31, 1991, alleging trademark infringement and false designation of origin in violation of sections 32(1) and 43(a) of the Lanham Act, 15 U.S.C. §§ 1114(1)(a), 1125(a). On November 29, 1991, Sega amended its complaint to include a claim for copyright infringement. Accolade filed a counterclaim against Sega for false designation of origin under section 43(a) of the Lanham Act, 15 U.S.C. § 1125(a). The parties filed cross-motions for preliminary injunctions on their respective claims.

After expedited discovery and a hearing, the district court granted Sega's motion. Prior to the hearing, Sega introduced the declaration of Takeshi Nagashima, an employee of Sega. Nagashima stated that it was possible either to create a game program which did not contain the TMSS code but would still operate on the Genesis III, or to modify a game program so that the Sega Message would not appear when the game cartridge was inserted. Nagashima stated that he had been able to make both modifications using standard components, at a total extra cost of approximately fifty cents. At the hearing, counsel for Sega produced two game cartridges which, he represented, contained the modifications made by Nagashima, and demonstrated to the district judge that the Sega Message did not appear when the cartridges were inserted into a Genesis III console. Sega offered to make the cartridges available for inspection by Accolade's counsel, but declined to let Accolade's software engineers examine the cartridges or to reveal the manner in which the cartridges had been modified. The district court concluded that the TMSS code was not functional and that Accolade could not assert a functionality defense to Sega's claim of trademark infringement.

With respect to Sega's copyright claim, the district court rejected Accolade's contention that intermediate copying of computer object code does not constitute infringement under the Copyright Act. It found that Accolade had disassembled Sega's code for a commercial purpose, and that Sega had likely lost sales of its games as a result of Accolade's copying. The court further found that there were alternatives to disassembly that Accolade could have used in order to study the functional requirements for Genesis compatibility. Accordingly, it also rejected Accolade's fair use defense to Sega's copyright infringement claim.

Based on its conclusion that Sega is likely to succeed on the merits of its claims for copyright and trademark infringement, on April 3, 1992, the district court enjoined Accolade from: (1) disassembling Sega's copyrighted code; (2) using or modifying Sega's copyrighted code; (3) developing, manufacturing, distributing, or selling Genesis-compatible games that were created in whole or in part by means that included disassembly; and (4) manufacturing, distributing, or selling any Genesis-compatible game that prompts the Sega Message. On April 9, 1992, in response to a request from Sega, the district court modified the preliminary injunction order to require the recall of Accolade's infringing games within ten business days.

III. Copyright Issues

Accolade raises four arguments in support of its position that disassembly of the object code in a copyrighted computer program does not constitute copyright infringement. First, it maintains that intermediate copying does not infringe the exclusive rights granted to copyright owners in section 106 of the Copyright Act unless the end product of the copying is substantially similar to the copyrighted work. Second, it argues that disassembly of object code in order to gain an understanding of the ideas and functional concepts embodied in the code is lawful under section 102(b) of the Act, which exempts ideas and functional concepts from copyright protection. Third, it suggests that disassembly is authorized by section 117 of the Act, which entitles the lawful owner of a copy of a computer program to load the program into a computer. Finally, Accolade contends that disassembly of object code in order to gain an understanding of the ideas and functional concepts embodied in the code is a fair use that is privileged by section 107 of the Act.

Neither the language of the Act nor the law of this circuit supports Accolade's first three arguments. Accolade's fourth argument, however, has merit. Although the question is fairly debatable, we conclude based on the policies underlying the Copyright Act that disassembly of copyrighted object code is, as a matter of law, a fair use of the copyrighted work if such disassembly provides the only means of access to those elements of the code that are not protected by copyright and the copier has a legitimate reason for seeking such access. Accordingly, we hold that Sega has failed to demonstrate a likelihood of success on the merits of its copyright claim. Because on the record before us the hardships do not tip sharply (or at all) in Sega's favor, the preliminary injunction issued in its favor must be dissolved, at least with respect to that claim.

A. Intermediate Copying

We have previously held that the Copyright Act does not distinguish between unauthorized copies of a copyrighted work on the basis of what stage of the alleged infringer's work the unauthorized copies represent. *Walker v. University Books*, 602 F.2d 859, 864 (9th Cir.1979) ("[T]he fact that an allegedly infringing copy of a protected work may itself be only an inchoate representation of some final product to be marketed commercially does not in itself negate the possibility of infringement."). Our holding in *Walker* was based on the plain language of the Act. Section 106 grants to the copyright owner the exclusive rights "to reproduce the work in copies", "to prepare derivative works based upon the copyrighted work", and to authorize the preparation of copies and derivative works. 17 U.S.C. § 106(1)-(2). Section 501 provides that "[a]nyone who violates any of the exclusive rights of the copyright owner as provided by sections 106 through 118 ... is an infringer of the copyright." *Id.* § 501(a). On its face, that language unambiguously encompasses and proscribes "intermediate copying". *Walker*, 602 F.2d at 863–64.

In order to constitute a "copy" for purposes of the Act, the allegedly infringing work must be fixed in some tangible form, "from which the work can be perceived, reproduced, or otherwise communicated, either directly or with the aid of a machine or device." 17 U.S.C. § 101. The computer file generated by the disassembly program, the printouts of the disassembled code, and the computer files containing Accolade's modifications of the code that were generated during the reverse engineering process all satisfy that requirement. The intermediate copying done by Accolade therefore falls squarely within the category of acts that are prohibited by the statute.

[T]he question whether intermediate copying of computer object code infringes the exclusive rights granted to the copyright owner in section 106 of the Copyright Act is a question of first impression. In light of the unambiguous language of the Act, we decline to depart from the rule set forth in *Walker* for copyrighted works generally. Accordingly, we hold that intermediate copying of computer object code may infringe the exclusive rights granted to the copyright owner in section 106 of the Copyright Act regardless of whether the end product of the copying also infringes those rights. If intermediate copying is permissible under the Act, authority for such copying must be found in one of the statutory provisions to which the rights granted in section 106 are subject.

B. The Idea/Expression Distinction

Accolade next contends that disassembly of computer object code does not violate the Copyright Act because it is necessary in order to gain access to the ideas and functional concepts embodied in the code, which are not protected by copyright. 17 U.S.C. § 102(b). Because humans cannot comprehend object code, it reasons, disassembly of a commercially available computer program into human-readable form should not be considered an infringement of the owner's copyright. Insofar as Accolade suggests that disassembly of object code is lawful per se, it seeks to overturn settled law.

Accolade's argument regarding access to ideas is, in essence, an argument that object code is not eligible for the full range of copyright protection. Although some scholarly authority supports that view, we have previously rejected it based on the language and legislative history of the Copyright Act. *Apple Computer, Inc. v. Formula Int'l Inc.*, 725 F.2d 521, 524–25 (9th Cir.1984).

As recommended by the National Commission on New Technological Uses of Copyrighted Works (CONTU), the 1980 amendments to the Copyright Act unambiguously extended copyright protection to computer programs. Pub. L. 96-517, sec. 10, 94 Stat. 3028 (1980) (codified at 17 U.S.C. §§ 101, 117); see National Commission on New Technological Uses of Copyrighted Works, Final Report 1 (1979) [CONTU Report].[13] "[T]he

---

13. Congress adopted all of the statutory changes recommended by CONTU verbatim. Subsequent Congresses, the courts, and commentators have regarded the CONTU Report as the authoritative guide to congressional intent.

Act makes no distinction between the copyrightability of those programs which directly interact with the computer user and those which simply manage the computer system." *Formula*, 725 F.2d at 525. Nor does the Act require that a work be directly accessible to humans in order to be eligible for copyright protection. Rather, it extends protection to all original works which ... can be perceived, reproduced, or otherwise communicated, either directly or with the aid of a machine or device." 17 U.S.C. § 102(a); *see Formula*, 725 F.2d at 525. The statutory language, read together with the CONTU report, leads inexorably to the conclusion that the copyright in a computer program extends to the object code version of the program. *Formula*, 725 F.2d at 525; CONTU Report at 21.

Nor does a refusal to recognize a per se right to disassemble object code lead to an absurd result. The ideas and functional concepts underlying many types of computer programs, including word processing programs, spreadsheets, and video game displays, are readily discernible without the need for disassembly, because the operation of such programs is visible on the computer screen. The need to disassemble object code arises, if at all, only in connection with operations systems, system interface procedures, and other programs that are not visible to the user when operating—and then only when no alternative means of gaining an understanding of those ideas and functional concepts exists. In our view, consideration of the unique nature of computer object code thus is more appropriate as part of the case-by-case, equitable "fair use" analysis authorized by section 107 of the Act. *See infra* Part III(D). Accordingly, we reject Accolade's second argument.

C. Section 117

Section 117 of the Copyright Act allows the lawful owner of a copy of a computer program to copy or adapt the program if the new copy or adaptation "is created as an essential step in the utilization of the computer program in conjunction with a machine and ... is used in no other manner." 17 U.S.C. § 117(1). Accolade contends that section 117 authorizes disassembly of the object code in a copyrighted computer program. Section 117 was enacted on the recommendation of CONTU, which noted that "[b]ecause the placement of any copyrighted work into a computer is the preparation of a copy [since the program is loaded into the computer's memory], the law should provide that persons in rightful possession of copies of programs be able to use them freely without fear of exposure to copyright liability." CONTU Report at 13. We think it is clear that Accolade's use went far beyond that contemplated by CONTU and authorized by section 117. Section 117 does not purport to protect a user who disassembles object code, converts it from assembly into source code, and makes printouts and photocopies of the refined source code version.[14]

D. Fair Use

Accolade contends, finally, that its disassembly of copyrighted object code as a necessary step in its examination of the unprotected ideas and functional concepts embodied in the code is a fair use that is privileged by section 107 of the Act. Because, in the case before us, disassembly is the only means of gaining access to those unprotected aspects of the program, and because Accolade has a legitimate interest in gaining such access (in order to determine how to make its cartridges compatible with the Genesis console), we agree with Accolade. Where there is good reason for studying or examining the unprotected aspects of a copyrighted computer program, disassembly for purposes of such study or examination constitutes a fair use.

---

14. We need not decide whether section 117 protects only the use intended by the copyright owner, as Sega argues. *See Vault Corp. v. Quaid Software Ltd.*, 847 F.2d 255, 261 (5th Cir.1988) (authorization of section 117(1) not limited to use intended by copyright owner).

1.

As a preliminary matter, we reject Sega's contention that the assertion of a fair use defense in connection with the disassembly of object code is precluded by statute. First, Sega argues that not only does section 117 of the Act not authorize disassembly of object code, but it also constitutes a legislative determination that any copying of a computer program other than that authorized by section 117 cannot be considered a fair use of that program under section 107. That argument verges on the frivolous. Each of the exclusive rights created by section 106 of the Copyright Act is expressly made subject to all of the limitations contained in sections 107 through 120. 17 U.S.C. § 106. Nothing in the language or the legislative history of section 117, or in the CONTU Report, suggests that section 117 was intended to preclude the assertion of a fair use defense with respect to uses of computer programs that are not covered by section 117, nor has section 107 been amended to exclude computer programs from its ambit.

Moreover, sections 107 and 117 serve entirely different functions. Section 117 defines a narrow category of copying that is lawful per se. 17 U.S.C. § 117. Section 107, by contrast, establishes a defense to an otherwise valid claim of copyright infringement. It provides that particular instances of copying that otherwise would be actionable are lawful, and sets forth the factors to be considered in determining whether the defense applies. Id. § 107. The fact that Congress has not chosen to provide a per se exemption to section 106 for disassembly does not mean that particular instances of disassembly may not constitute fair use.

Second, Sega maintains that the language and legislative history of section 906 of the Semiconductor Chip Protection Act of 1984 (SCPA) establish that Congress did not intend that disassembly of object code be considered a fair use. Section 906 of the SCPA authorizes the copying of the "mask work" on a silicon chip in the course of reverse engineering the chip. 17 U.S.C. § 906. The mask work in a standard ROM chip, such as those used in the Genesis console and in Genesis-compatible cartridges, is a physical representation of the computer program that is embedded in the chip. The zeros and ones of binary object code are represented in the circuitry of the mask work by open and closed switches. Sega contends that Congress's express authorization of copying in the particular circumstances set forth in section 906 constitutes a determination that other forms of copying of computer programs are prohibited.

The legislative history of the SCPA reveals, however, that Congress passed a separate statute to protect semiconductor chip products because it believed that semiconductor chips were intrinsically utilitarian articles that were not protected under the Copyright Act. H.R.Rep. No. 781, 98th Cong., 2d Sess. 8–10, reprinted in 1984 U.S.C.C.A.N. 5750, 5757–59. Here we are dealing not with an alleged violation of the SCPA, but with the copying of a computer program, which is governed by the Copyright Act. Accordingly, Sega's second statutory argument also fails. We proceed to consider Accolade's fair use defense.

2.

Section 107 lists the factors to be considered in determining whether a particular use is a fair one. Those factors include: (1) the purpose and character of the use, including whether such use is of a commercial nature or is for nonprofit educational purposes; (2) the nature of the copyrighted work; (3) the amount and substantiality of the portion used in relation to the copyrighted work as a whole; and (4) the effect of the use upon the potential market for or value of the copyrighted work. 17 U.S.C. § 107.

The statutory factors are not exclusive. In determining that Accolade's disassembly of Sega's object code did not constitute a fair use, the district court treated the first and fourth statutory factors as dispositive, and ignored the second factor entirely. Given the nature and characteristics of Accolade's direct use of the copied works, the ultimate use to which Accolade put the functional information it obtained, and the nature of the market for home video entertainment systems, we conclude that neither the first nor the fourth factor weighs in Sega's favor. In fact, we conclude that both factors support Accolade's fair use defense, as does the second factor, a factor which is important to the resolution of cases such as the one before us.

(a)

With respect to the first statutory factor, we observe initially that the fact that copying is for a commercial purpose weighs against a finding of fair use. However, the presumption of unfairness that arises in such cases can be rebutted by the characteristics of a particular commercial use.

Sega argues that because Accolade copied its object code in order to produce a competing product, the presumption applies and precludes a finding of fair use. That analysis is far too simple and ignores a number of important considerations. We must consider other aspects of "the purpose and character of the use" as well. As we have noted, the use at issue was an intermediate one only and thus any commercial "exploitation" was indirect or derivative.

The declarations of Accolade's employees indicate, and the district court found, that Accolade copied Sega's software solely in order to discover the functional requirements for compatibility with the Genesis console—aspects of Sega's programs that are not protected by copyright. 17 U.S.C. §102(b). With respect to the video game programs contained in Accolade's game cartridges, there is no evidence in the record that Accolade sought to avoid performing its own creative work. Indeed, most of the games that Accolade released for use with the Genesis console were originally developed for other hardware systems. Moreover, with respect to the interface procedures for the Genesis console, Accolade did not seek to avoid paying a customarily charged fee for use of those procedures, nor did it simply copy Sega's code; rather, it wrote its own procedures based on what it had learned through disassembly. Taken together, these facts indicate that although Accolade's ultimate purpose was the release of Genesis-compatible games for sale, its direct purpose in copying Sega's code, and thus its direct use of the copyrighted material, was simply to study the functional requirements for Genesis compatibility so that it could modify existing games and make them usable with the Genesis console. Moreover, as we discuss below, no other method of studying those requirements was available to Accolade. On these facts, we conclude that Accolade copied Sega's code for a legitimate, essentially non-exploitative purpose, and that the commercial aspect of its use can best be described as of minimal significance.

We further note that we are free to consider the public benefit resulting from a particular use notwithstanding the fact that the alleged infringer may gain commercially. Public benefit need not be direct or tangible, but may arise because the challenged use serves a public interest. *Id.* In the case before us, Accolade's identification of the functional requirements for Genesis compatibility has led to an increase in the number of independently designed video game programs offered for use with the Genesis console. We conclude that given the purpose and character of Accolade's use of Sega's video game programs, the presumption of unfairness has been overcome and the first statutory factor weighs in favor of Accolade.

(b)

As applied, the fourth statutory factor, effect on the potential market for the copyrighted work, bears a close relationship to the "purpose and character" inquiry in that it, too, accommodates the distinction between the copying of works in order to make independent creative expression possible and the simple exploitation of another's creative efforts. We must, of course, inquire whether, "if [the challenged use] should become widespread, it would adversely affect the potential market for the copyrighted work," *Sony Corp. v. Universal City Studios,* 464 U.S. 417, 451 (1984), by diminishing potential sales, interfering with marketability, or usurping the market. If the copying resulted in the latter effect, all other considerations might be irrelevant.

Unlike the defendant in *Harper & Row* [*Publishers v. Nation Enterprises,* 471 U.S. 539 (1985)], which printed excerpts from President Ford's memoirs verbatim with the stated purpose of "scooping" a Time magazine review of the book, 471 U.S. at 562, Accolade did not attempt to "scoop" Sega's release of any particular game or games, but sought only to become a legitimate competitor in the field of Genesis-compatible video games. Within that market, it is the characteristics of the game program as experienced by the user that determine the program's commercial success. As we have noted, there is nothing in the record that suggests that Accolade copied any of those elements.

By facilitating the entry of a new competitor, the first lawful one that is not a Sega licensee, Accolade's disassembly of Sega's software undoubtedly "affected" the market for Genesis-compatible games in an indirect fashion. We note, however, that while no consumer except the most avid devotee of President Ford's regime might be expected to buy more than one version of the President's memoirs, video game users typically purchase more than one game. There is no basis for assuming that Accolade's "Ishido" has significantly affected the market for Sega's "Altered Beast," since a consumer might easily purchase both. In any event, an attempt to monopolize the market by making it impossible for others to compete runs counter to the statutory purpose of promoting creative expression and cannot constitute a strong equitable basis for resisting the invocation of the fair use doctrine. Thus, we conclude that the fourth statutory factor weighs in Accolade's, not Sega's, favor, notwithstanding the minor economic loss Sega may suffer.

(c)

The second statutory factor, the nature of the copyrighted work, reflects the fact that not all copyrighted works are entitled to the same level of protection. The protection established by the Copyright Act for original works of authorship does not extend to the ideas underlying a work or to the functional or factual aspects of the work. 17 U.S.C. § 102(b). To the extent that a work is functional or factual, it may be copied, *Baker v. Selden,* 101 U.S. (11 Otto) 99, 102–04 (1879), as may those expressive elements of the work that "must necessarily be used as incident to" expression of the underlying ideas, functional concepts, or facts, id. at 104. Works of fiction receive greater protection than works that have strong factual elements, such as historical or biographical works, or works that have strong functional elements, such as accounting textbooks, *Baker,* 101 U.S. at 104. Works that are merely compilations of fact are copyrightable, but the copyright in such a work is thin.

Computer programs pose unique problems for the application of the "idea/expression distinction" that determines the extent of copyright protection. To the extent that there are many possible ways of accomplishing a given task or fulfilling a particular market demand, the programmer's choice of program structure and design may be highly creative and idiosyncratic. However, computer programs are, in essence, utilitarian articles— articles that accomplish tasks. As such, they contain many logical, structural, and visual display elements that are dictated by the function to be performed, by considerations of efficiency, or by external factors such as compatibility requirements and industry demands.

Computer Assoc. Int'l, Inc. v. Altai, Inc., 1992 WL 372273, 23 U.S.P.Q.2d (BNA) 1241, 1253–56 (2d Cir.1992) ("*CAI*"). In some circumstances, even the exact set of commands used by the programmer is deemed functional rather than creative for purposes of copyright. "[W]hen specific instructions, even though previously copyrighted, are the only and essential means of accomplishing a given task, their later use by another will not amount to infringement. CONTU Report at 20; *see CAI*, 23 U.S.P.Q.2d at 1254.[15]

Because of the hybrid nature of computer programs, there is no settled standard for identifying what is protected expression and what is unprotected idea in a case involving the alleged infringement of a copyright in computer software. Sega argues that even if many elements of its video game programs are properly characterized as functional and therefore not protected by copyright, Accolade copied protected expression. Sega is correct. The record makes clear that disassembly is wholesale copying. Because computer programs are also unique among copyrighted works in the form in which they are distributed for public use, however, Sega's observation does not bring us much closer to a resolution of the dispute.

The unprotected aspects of most functional works are readily accessible to the human eye. The systems described in accounting textbooks or the basic structural concepts embodied in architectural plans, to give two examples, can be easily copied without also copying any of the protected, expressive aspects of the original works. Computer programs, however, are typically distributed for public use in object code form, embedded in a silicon chip or on a floppy disk. For that reason, humans often cannot gain access to the unprotected ideas and functional concepts contained in object code without disassembling that code—i.e., making copies.

Sega argues that the record does not establish that disassembly of its object code is the only available method for gaining access to the interface specifications for the Genesis console, and the district court agreed. An independent examination of the record reveals that Sega misstates its contents, and demonstrates that the district court committed clear error in this respect.

First, the record clearly establishes that humans cannot read object code. The relevant fact for purposes of Sega's copyright infringement claim and Accolade's fair use defense is that translation of a program from object code into source code cannot be accomplished without making copies of the code.

Second, the record provides no support for a conclusion that a viable alternative to disassembly exists. The district court found that Accolade could have avoided a copyright infringement claim by "peeling" the chips contained in Sega's games or in the Genesis console, as authorized by section 906 of the SCPA, 17 U.S.C. § 906. Even Sega's amici agree that this finding was clear error. The declaration of Dr. Harry Tredennick, an expert

---

15. We therefore reject Sega's belated suggestion that Accolade's incorporation of the code which "unlocks" the Genesis III console is not a fair use. Our decision on this point is entirely consistent with *Atari v. Nintendo*, 975 F.2d 832 (Fed.Cir.1992). Although Nintendo extended copyright protection to Nintendo's 10NES security system, that system consisted of an original program which generates an arbitrary data stream "key" which unlocks the NES console. Creativity and originality went into the design of that program. *See id.* at 840. Moreover, the federal circuit concluded that there is a "multitude of different ways to generate a data stream which unlocks the NES console." *Atari*, 975 F.2d at 839. The circumstances are clearly different here. Sega's key appears to be functional. It consists merely of 20 bytes of initialization code plus the letters S-E-G-A. There is no showing that there is a multitude of different ways to unlock the Genesis III console.

witness for Accolade, establishes that chip peeling yields only a physical diagram of the object code embedded in a ROM chip. It does not obviate the need to translate object code into source code.

In summary, the record clearly establishes that disassembly of the object code in Sega's video game cartridges was necessary in order to understand the functional requirements for Genesis compatibility. The interface procedures for the Genesis console are distributed for public use only in object code form, and are not visible to the user during operation of the video game program. Because object code cannot be read by humans, it must be disassembled, either by hand or by machine. Disassembly of object code necessarily entails copying. Those facts dictate our analysis of the second statutory fair use factor. If disassembly of copyrighted object code is per se an unfair use, the owner of the copyright gains a de facto monopoly over the functional aspects of his work—aspects that were expressly denied copyright protection by Congress. 17 U.S.C. § 102(b). In order to enjoy a lawful monopoly over the idea or functional principle underlying a work, the creator of the work must satisfy the more stringent standards imposed by the patent laws. *Bonito Boats, Inc. v. Thunder Craft Boats, Inc.*, 489 U.S. 141, 159–64 (1989). Sega does not hold a patent on the Genesis console.

Because Sega's video game programs contain unprotected aspects that cannot be examined without copying, we afford them a lower degree of protection than more traditional literary works. In light of all the considerations discussed above, we conclude that the second statutory factor also weighs in favor of Accolade.

(d)

As to the third statutory factor, Accolade disassembled entire programs written by Sega. Accordingly, the third factor weighs against Accolade. The fact that an entire work was copied does not, however, preclude a finding a fair use. In fact, where the ultimate (as opposed to direct) use is as limited as it was here, the factor is of very little weight.

(e)

In summary, careful analysis of the purpose and characteristics of Accolade's use of Sega's video game programs, the nature of the computer programs involved, and the nature of the market for video game cartridges yields the conclusion that the first, second, and fourth statutory fair use factors weigh in favor of Accolade, while only the third weighs in favor of Sega, and even then only slightly. Accordingly, Accolade clearly has by far the better case on the fair use issue.

We are not unaware of the fact that to those used to considering copyright issues in more traditional contexts, our result may seem incongruous at first blush. To oversimplify, the record establishes that Accolade, a commercial competitor of Sega, engaged in wholesale copying of Sega's copyrighted code as a preliminary step in the development of a competing product. However, the key to this case is that we are dealing with computer software, a relatively unexplored area in the world of copyright law.

In determining whether a challenged use of copyrighted material is fair, a court must keep in mind the public policy underlying the Copyright Act. As discussed above, the fact that computer programs are distributed for public use in object code form often precludes public access to the ideas and functional concepts contained in those programs, and thus confers on the copyright owner a de facto monopoly over those ideas and functional concepts. That result defeats the fundamental purpose of the Copyright Act— to encourage the production of original works by protecting the expressive elements of those works while leaving the ideas, facts, and functional concepts in the public domain for others to build on.

Sega argues that the considerable time, effort, and money that went into development of the Genesis and Genesis-compatible video games militate against a finding of fair use. Borrowing from antitrust principles, Sega attempts to label Accolade a "free rider" on its product development efforts. In *Feist Publications*, however, the Court unequivocally rejected the "sweat of the brow" rationale for copyright protection. 499 U.S. at __, 111 S.Ct. at 1290–95. Under the Copyright Act, if a work is largely functional, it receives only weak protection. "This result is neither unfair nor unfortunate. It is the means by which copyright advances the progress of science and art." *Id.* 499 U.S. at __, 111 S.Ct. at 1290; see also id. 499 U.S. at __, 111 S.Ct. at 1292. Here, while the work may not be largely functional, it incorporates functional elements which do not merit protection. The equitable considerations involved weigh on the side of public access. Accordingly, we reject Sega's argument.

(f)

We conclude that where disassembly is the only way to gain access to the ideas and functional elements embodied in a copyrighted computer program and where there is a legitimate reason for seeking such access, disassembly is a fair use of the copyrighted work, as a matter of law. Our conclusion does not, of course, insulate Accolade from a claim of copyright infringement with respect to its finished products. Sega has reserved the right to raise such a claim, and it may do so on remand.

IV. Trademark Issues

Ordinarily in a trademark case, a trademark holder contends that another party is misusing the holder's mark or is attempting to pass off goods or services as those of the trademark holder. The other party usually protests that the mark is not being misused, that there is no actual confusion, or that for some other reason no violation has occurred. This case is different. Here, both parties agree that there is a misuse of a trademark, both agree that there is unlawful mislabeling, and both agree that confusion may result. The issue, here, is — which party is primarily responsible? Which is the wrongdoer — the violator? Is it Sega, which has adopted a security system governing access to its Genesis III console that displays its trademark and message whenever the initialization code for the security system is utilized, even when the video game program was manufactured by a Sega competitor? Or is it Accolade, which, having discovered how to gain access to the Genesis III through the initialization code, uses that code even though doing so triggers the display of Sega's trademark and message in a manner that leads observers to believe that Sega manufactured the Accolade game cartridge? In other words, is Sega the injured party because its mark is wrongfully attached to an Accolade video game by Accolade? Or is Accolade wronged because its game is mislabeled as a Sega product by Sega? The facts are relatively straightforward and we have little difficulty answering the question.

Sega's trademark security system (TMSS) initialization code not only enables video game programs to operate on the Genesis III console, but also prompts a screen display of the SEGA trademark and message. As a result, Accolade's inclusion of the TMSS initialization code in its video game programs has an effect ultimately beneficial neither to Sega nor to Accolade. A Genesis III owner who purchases a video game made by Accolade sees Sega's trademark associated with Accolade's product each time he inserts the game cartridge into the console. Sega claims that Accolade's inclusion of the TMSS initialization code in its games constitutes trademark infringement and false designation of origin in violation of sections 32(1)(a) and 43(a) of the Lanham Trademark Act, 15 U.S.C.

§§ 1114(1)(a), 1125(a), respectively. Accolade counterclaims that Sega's use of the TMSS to prompt a screen display of its trademark constitutes false designation of origin under Lanham Act section 43(a), 15 U.S.C. § 1125(a).

Because the TMSS has the effect of regulating access to the Genesis III console, and because there is no indication in the record of any public or industry awareness of any feasible alternate method of gaining access to the Genesis III, we hold that Sega is primarily responsible for any resultant confusion. Thus, it has not demonstrated a likelihood of success on the merits of its Lanham Act claims. Accordingly, the preliminary injunction it obtained must be dissolved with respect to the trademark claim also.

Sega argues that even if the legal analysis we have enunciated is correct, the facts do not support its application to this case. Specifically, Sega contends that the TMSS does not prevent legitimate unlicensed competitors from developing and marketing Genesis III-compatible cartridges that do not trigger a display of the Sega trademark and message. In other words, Sega claims that Accolade could have "engineered around" the TMSS. Accolade strongly disagrees with Sega's factual assertions. It contends that the TMSS initialization sequence is a functional feature that must be included in a video game program by a manufacturer in order for the game to operate on the Genesis III. Sega's factual argument stands or falls on the Nagashima declaration and the accompanying modified game cartridges that Sega introduced at the hearing. Having carefully reviewed the declaration, we conclude that Sega has not met its burden of establishing nonfunctionality.

Viewed in the correct light, the record before us supports only one conclusion: The TMSS initialization code is a functional feature of a Genesis-compatible game and Accolade may not be barred from using it. Functional features of a product are features which constitute the actual benefit that the consumer wishes to purchase, as distinguished from an assurance that a particular entity made, sponsored, or endorsed a product. A product feature thus is functional if it is essential to the use or purpose of the article or if it affects the cost or quality of the article. The Lanham Act does not protect essentially functional or utilitarian product features because such protection would constitute a grant of a perpetual monopoly over features that could not be patented. Even when the allegedly functional product feature is a trademark, the trademark owner may not enjoy a monopoly over the functional use of the mark.

In determining whether a product feature is functional, a court may consider a number of factors, including — but not limited to the availability of alternative designs; and whether a particular design results from a comparatively simple or cheap method of manufacture. The availability of alternative methods of manufacture must be more than merely theoretical or speculative, however. The court must find that commercially feasible alternative configurations exist. Moreover, some cases have even suggested that in order to establish nonfunctionality the party with the burden must demonstrate that the product feature serves no purpose other than identification. With these principles in mind, we turn to the question whether the TMSS initialization code is a functional feature of a Genesis-compatible game.

It is indisputable that, in the case before us, part of "the actual benefit that the consumer wishes to purchase" is compatibility with the Genesis III console. The TMSS initialization code provides that compatibility. Sega argues that the modified cartridges that were introduced in the district court establish the actual existence of technically and commercially feasible alternative methods of gaining access to the Genesis III. The cartridges were prepared by Nagashima, an employee in Sega's Hardware Research and Development Department who was "familiar with the TMSS system". At most, the Nagashima affidavit establishes that an individual familiar with the operation of the TMSS can discover a way to engineer around it. It does not establish that a competitor with no knowledge of the workings of the TMSS could do so. Nor is there any evidence that there was any public or industry awareness of any alternate method for gaining access to the Genesis III. Because the TMSS serves the function of regulating access to the Genesis III, and because a means of access to the Genesis III console without using the TMSS initialization code is not known to manufacturers of competing video game cartridges, there is an insufficient basis for a finding of nonfunctionality.

Sega argues that it is not required to share with Accolade or with any other competitor the secrets of how the TMSS works, and how to engineer around it. Sega is correct—the law does not require that it disclose its trade secrets to Accolade in connection with its effort to prevail on its Lanham Act claim, nor in connection with its effort to defend itself against Accolade's counterclaim. Nevertheless, a Lanham Act plaintiff is not entitled to prevail in litigation solely on the basis of unsupported assertions. Rather, it has a choice. It can take its chances and proceed to trial without the sensitive evidence. Alternatively, if it believes the evidence important to the resolution of the dispute, it may seek a protective order from the court pursuant to Federal Rule of Civil Procedure 26(c)(7) governing discovery.

In summary, because Sega did not produce sufficient evidence regarding the existence of a feasible alternative to the use of the TMSS initialization code, it did not carry its burden and its claim of nonfunctionality fails. Sega was not entitled to preliminary injunctive relief under the Lanham Act.[16]

C. Accolade's Request for Preliminary Injunctive Relief

Finally, we decline to order the district court to grant Accolade preliminary injunctive relief on its Lanham Act claim. If requested, the district court may reconsider that issue in light of the legal principles we have set forth.

Notes and Questions

1. Even though Accolade prevailed in its appeal before the Ninth Circuit, the consequences of its initial loss in the district court were significant. On April 3, 1992, District Court Judge Caulfield enjoined Accolade from developing or distributing any Genesis games. On April 9th, she issued an additional order requiring Accolade to recall all of its Genesis games that were already on the market. While it is true that the Ninth Circuit stayed its April 9th order, the April 3rd injunction remained in effect until the Ninth Circuit dissolved it on August 28, 1992. According to Alan Miller, the co-founder of Accolade (and a co-founder of Activision), "Just to fight the injunction, we had to pay at least a half million dollars in legal fees, and the commercial damage associated with the injunction ultimately proved to be somewhere around $15 to $25 million to our

---

16. Sega contends that even if the TMSS code is functional, Accolade, as the copier, was obligated to take the most effective measures reasonably available to eliminate the consumer confusion that has arisen as a result of the association of Sega's trademark with Accolade's product. Assuming arguendo that the rules applicable to copiers apply here, the measures adopted by Accolade satisfy a reasonableness standard. Accolade placed disclaimers on its packaging materials which stated that "Accolade, Inc. is not associated with Sega Enterprises, Ltd." While Accolade could have worded its disclaimer more strongly, the version that it chose would appear to be sufficient.

company." *See* STEVEN L. KENT, THE ULTIMATE HISTORY OF VIDEO GAMES 381, 386 (2001). It is interesting to note that following the litigation, Accolade became a licensee of Sega.

2. From a developer's perspective, is the Ninth Circuit's ruling in *Sega v. Accolade* still significant today? The ability of unlicensed individuals to create compatible console games has diminished significantly since the early 1990s. The most popular consoles (i.e., The Xbox One, Playstation 4, and Nintendo Wii U) are all enabled for online use and are subject to regular firmware updates; presumably, the console manufacturers could quickly overcome any successful attempts to circumvent their security features by making unlicensed software unusable. In any event, there is greater cooperation today between third party vendors and console manufacturers.

* * *

Sony Computer Ent., Inc. v. Connectix Corp.

United States Court of Appeals, Ninth Circuit, 2000
203 F.3d 596

CANBY, Circuit Judge

In this case we are called upon once again to apply the principles of copyright law to computers and their software, to determine what must be protected as expression and what must be made accessible to the public as function. Sony Computer Entertainment, Inc., which brought this copyright infringement action, produces and markets the Sony PlayStation console, a small computer with hand controls that connects to a television console and plays games that are inserted into the PlayStation on compact discs (CDs). Sony owns the copyright on the basic input-output system or BIOS, which is the software program that operates its PlayStation. Sony has asserted no patent rights in this proceeding.

The defendant is the Connectix Corporation, which makes and sells a software program called "Virtual Game Station." The purpose of the Virtual Game Station is to emulate on a regular computer the functioning of the Sony PlayStation console, so that computer owners who buy the Virtual Game Station software can play Sony PlayStation games on their computers. The Virtual Game Station does not contain any of Sony's copyrighted material. In the process of producing the Virtual Game Station, however, Connectix repeatedly copied Sony's copyrighted BIOS during a process of "reverse engineering" that Connectix conducted in order to find out how the Sony PlayStation worked. Sony claimed infringement and sought a preliminary injunction. The district court concluded that Sony was likely to succeed on its infringement claim because Connectix's "intermediate copying" was not a protected "fair use" under 17 U.S.C. § 107. The district court enjoined Connectix from selling the Virtual Game Station or from copying or using the Sony BIOS code in the development of other Virtual Game Station products.

Connectix now appeals. We reverse and remand with instructions to dissolve the injunction.

The intermediate copies made and used by Connectix during the course of its reverse engineering of the Sony BIOS were protected fair use, necessary to permit Connectix to make its non-infringing Virtual Game Station function with PlayStation games. Any other intermediate copies made by Connectix do not support injunctive relief, even if those copies were infringing. The district court also found that Sony is likely to prevail on its claim that Connectix's sale of the Virtual Game Station program tarnishes the Sony PlayStation mark under 15 U.S.C. § 1125. We reverse that ruling as well.

The products

Sony is the developer, manufacturer and distributor of both the Sony PlayStation and Sony PlayStation games. Sony also licenses other companies to make games that can play on the PlayStation. The PlayStation system consists of a console (essentially a mini-computer), controllers, and software that produce a three-dimensional game for play on a television set. The PlayStation games are CDs that load into the top of the console. The PlayStation console contains both (1) hardware components and (2) software known as firmware that is written onto a read-only memory (ROM) chip. The firmware is the Sony BIOS. Sony has a copyright on the BIOS. It has claimed no patent relevant to this proceeding on any component of the PlayStation. PlayStation is a registered trademark of Sony.

Connectix's Virtual Game Station is software that "emulates" the functioning of the PlayStation console. That is, a consumer can load the Virtual Game Station software onto a computer, load a PlayStation game into the computer's CD-ROM drive, and play the PlayStation game. The Virtual Game Station software thus emulates both the hardware and firmware components of the Sony console. The Virtual Game Station does not play PlayStation games as well as Sony's PlayStation does. At the time of the injunction, Connectix had marketed its Virtual Game Station for Macintosh computer systems but had not yet completed Virtual Game Station software for Windows.

Reverse engineering

Copyrighted software ordinarily contains both copyrighted and unprotected or functional elements. *Sega Enters. Ltd. v. Accolade, Inc.*, 977 F.2d 1510, 1520 (9th Cir.1992) (amended opinion); see 17 U.S.C. §102(b). Software engineers designing a product that must be compatible with a copyrighted product frequently must "reverse engineer" the copyrighted product to gain access to the functional elements of the copyrighted product.

Reverse engineering encompasses several methods of gaining access to the functional elements of a software program. They include: (1) reading about the program; (2) observing the program in operation by using it on a computer; (3) performing a static examination of the individual computer instructions contained within the program; and (4) performing a dynamic examination of the individual computer instructions as the program is being run on a computer. Method (1) is the least effective, because individual software manuals often misdescribe the real product. See id. It would be particularly ineffective in this case because Sony does not make such information available about its PlayStation. Methods (2), (3), and (4) require that the person seeking access load the target program on to a computer, an operation that necessarily involves copying the copyrighted program into the computer's random access memory or RAM.[17]

Method (2), observation of a program, can take several forms. The functional elements of some software programs, for example word processing programs, spreadsheets, and video game displays may be discernible by observation of the computer screen. Of course, the reverse engineer in such a situation is not observing the object code itself,[18] only the

---

17. Any purchaser of a copyrighted software program must copy the program into the memory of a computer in order to make any use at all of the program. For that reason, 17 U.S.C. §117(a)(1) provides that it shall not be an infringement for one who owns a software copy to make another copy "created as an essential step in the utilization of the computer program in conjunction with a machine and that it is used in no other manner." Connectix contends that its copying is within the protection of section 117, but our disposition of the fair use issue makes it unnecessary for us to address that contention.

18. Object code is binary code, consisting of a series of the numerals zero and one, readable only by computers.

external visual expression of this code's operation on the computer. Here, the software program is copied each time the engineer boots up the computer, and the computer copies the program into RAM. Other forms of observation are more intrusive. One method of "observing" the operation of these programs is to run the program in an emulated environment. In the case of the Sony BIOS, this meant operating the BIOS on a computer with software that simulated the operation of the PlayStation hardware; operation of the program, in conjunction with another program known as a "debugger," permitted the engineers to observe the signals sent between the BIOS and other programs on the computer. This latter method required copying the Sony BIOS from a chip in the PlayStation onto the computer. The Sony BIOS was copied again each time the engineers booted up their computer and the computer copied the program into RAM. All of this copying was intermediate; that is, none of the Sony copyrighted material was copied into, or appeared in, Connectix's final product, the Virtual Game Station.

Methods (3) and (4) constitute "disassembly" of object code into source code.[19] In each case, engineers use a program known as a "disassemble" to translate the ones and zeros of binary machine-readable object code into the words and mathematical symbols of source code. This translated source code is similar to the source code used originally to create the object code,[20] but lacks the annotations drafted by the authors of the program that help explain the functioning of the source code. In a static examination of the computer instructions, method (3), the engineer disassembles the object code of all or part of the program. The program must generally be copied one or more times to perform disassembly. In a dynamic examination of the computer instructions, method (4), the engineer uses the disassembler program to disassemble parts of the program, one instruction at a time, while the program is running. This method also requires copying the program and, depending on the number of times this operation is performed, may require additional copying of the program into RAM every time the computer is booted up.

Connectix's reverse engineering of the Sony BIOS

Connectix began developing the Virtual Game Station for Macintosh on about July 1, 1998. In order to develop a PlayStation emulator, Connectix needed to emulate both the PlayStation hardware and the firmware (the Sony BIOS).

Connectix first decided to emulate the PlayStation's hardware. In order to do so, Connectix engineers purchased a Sony PlayStation console and extracted the Sony BIOS from a chip inside the console. Connectix engineers then copied the Sony BIOS into the RAM of their computers and observed the functioning of the Sony BIOS in conjunction with the Virtual Game Station hardware emulation software as that hardware emulation software was being developed by Connectix. The engineers observed the operation of the Sony BIOS through use of a debugging program that permitted the engineers to observe the signals sent between the BIOS and the hardware emulation software. During this process, Connectix engineers made additional copies of the Sony BIOS every time they booted up their computer and the Sony BIOS was loaded into RAM. Once they had developed the hardware emulation software, Connectix engineers also used the Sony BIOS to "debug" the emulation software. In doing so, they repeatedly copied and disassembled discrete portions of the Sony BIOS.

Connectix announced its new product at the MacWorld Expo on January 5, 1999. At MacWorld, Connectix marketed the Virtual Game Station as a "PlayStation emulator." The

---

19. Source code is readable by software engineers, but not by computers.

20. Software is generally written by programmers in source code (and in other more conceptual formats) and then assembled into object code.

materials stated that the Virtual Game Station permits users to play "their favorite PlayStation games" on a computer "even if you don't yet have a Sony PlayStation console."

Fair use

Central to our decision today is the rule set forth in *Sega*:

> [W]here disassembly is the only way to gain access to the ideas and functional elements embodied in a copyrighted computer program and where there is a legitimate reason for seeking such access, disassembly is a fair use of the copyrighted work, as a matter of law.

In *Sega*, we recognized that intermediate copying could constitute copyright infringement even when the end product did not itself contain copyrighted material. But this copying nonetheless could be protected as a fair use if it was "necessary" to gain access to the functional elements of the software itself. This approach is consistent with the " 'ultimate aim [of the Copyright Act], to stimulate artistic creativity for the general public good.' " *Sony Corp. of Am. v. Universal City Studios, Inc.*, 464 U.S. 417, 432 (1975)). We turn then to the statutory fair use factors, as informed by our precedent in Sega.

Nature of the copyrighted work

Under our analysis of the second statutory factor, nature of the copyrighted work, we recognize that "some works are closer to the core of intended copyright protection than others." *Campbell v. Acuff-Rose Music, Inc.*, 510 U.S. 569, 586 (1994). Sony's BIOS lies at a distance from the core because it contains unprotected aspects that cannot be examined without copying. We consequently accord it a lower degree of protection than more traditional literary works. As we have applied this standard, Connectix's copying of the Sony BIOS must have been "necessary" to have been fair use. We conclude that it was. There is no question that the Sony BIOS contains unprotected functional elements. Nor is it disputed that Connectix could not gain access to these unprotected functional elements without copying the Sony BIOS.

The question then becomes whether the methods by which Connectix reverse-engineered the Sony BIOS were necessary to gain access to the unprotected functional elements within the program. We conclude that they were. Connectix employed several methods of reverse engineering (observation and observation with partial disassembly) each of which required Connectix to make intermediate copies of copyrighted material. Neither of these methods renders fair use protection inapplicable. *Sega* expressly sanctioned disassembly. We see no reason to distinguish observation of copyrighted software in an emulated computer environment. Both methods require the reverse engineer to copy protected as well as unprotected elements of the computer program. Because this intermediate copying is the gravamen of the intermediate infringement claim, see 17 U.S.C. § 106(1); and both methods of reverse engineering require it, we find no reason inherent in these methods to prefer one to another as a matter of copyright law.

We decline to follow the approach taken by the district court. The district court did not focus on whether Connectix's copying of the Sony BIOS was necessary for access to functional elements. Instead, it found that Connectix's copying and use of the Sony BIOS to develop its own software exceeded the scope of *Sega*. See Order at 17 ("[T]hey disassembled Sony's code not just to study the concepts. They actually used that code in the development of [their] product."). This rationale is unpersuasive. It is true that Sega referred to "studying or examining the unprotected aspects of a copyrighted computer program." 977 F.2d at 1520 (emphasis added). But in *Sega*, Accolade's copying, observation and disassembly of Sega's game cartridges was held to be fair use, even though Accolade "loaded the disassembled code back into a computer, and experimented to discover the interface specifications for the Genesis console by modifying the programs and studying the results." Id. at 1515. Thus, the distinction between "studying" and "use" is unsupported in *Sega*. Moreover, reverse engineering is a technically complex, frequently iterative process. Within the limited context of a claim of intermediate infringement, we find the semantic distinction between "studying" and "use" to be artificial, and decline to adopt it for purposes of determining fair use.

Sony contends that Connectix's reverse engineering of the Sony BIOS should be considered unnecessary on the rationale that Connectix's decision to observe the Sony BIOS in an emulated environment required Connectix to make more intermediate copies of the Sony BIOS than if Connectix had performed a complete disassembly of the program. Under this logic, at least some of the intermediate copies were not necessary within the meaning of *Sega*. This construction stretches *Sega* too far. The "necessity" we addressed in *Sega* was the necessity of the method, i.e., disassembly, not the necessity of the number of times that method was applied. *See* 977 F.2d at 1524–26. In any event, the interpretation advanced by Sony would be a poor criterion for fair use. Most of the intermediate copies of the Sony BIOS were made by Connectix engineers when they booted up their computers and the Sony BIOS was copied into RAM. But if Connectix engineers had left their computers turned on throughout the period during which they were observing the Sony BIOS in an emulated environment, they would have made far fewer intermediate copies of the Sony BIOS (perhaps as few as one per computer). Even if we were inclined to supervise the engineering solutions of software companies in minute detail, and we are not, our application of the copyright law would not turn on such a distinction. Such a rule could be easily manipulated. More important, the rule urged by Sony would require that a software engineer, faced with two engineering solutions that each require intermediate copying of protected and unprotected material, often follow the least efficient solution. (In cases in which the solution that required the fewest number of intermediate copies was also the most efficient, an engineer would pursue it, presumably, without our urging.) This is precisely the kind of "wasted effort that the proscription against the copyright of ideas and facts ... [is] designed to prevent." *Feist Publications, Inc. v. Rural Tel. Serv. Co.*, 499 U.S. 340 (1991). Such an approach would erect an artificial hurdle in the way of the public's access to the ideas contained within copyrighted software programs. These are "aspects that were expressly denied copyright protection by Congress." *Sega*, 977 F.2d at 1526 (citing 17 U.S.C. § 102(b)). We decline to erect such a barrier in this case. If Sony wishes to obtain a lawful monopoly on the functional concepts in its software, it must satisfy the more stringent standards of the patent laws. This Sony has not done. The second statutory factor strongly favors Connectix.

Amount and substantiality of the portion used

With respect to the third statutory factor, amount and substantiality of the portion used in relation to the copyrighted work as a whole, Connectix disassembled parts of the Sony BIOS and copied the entire Sony BIOS multiple times. This factor therefore weighs against Connectix. But as we concluded in *Sega*, in a case of intermediate infringement when the final product does not itself contain infringing material, this factor is of very little weight.

Purpose and character of the use

Under the first factor, purpose and character of the use, we inquire into whether Connectix's Virtual Game Station merely supersedes the objects of the original creation, or instead adds something new, with a further purpose or different character, altering the first with new expression, meaning, or message; it asks, in other words, whether and to what extent the new work is "transformative." *Campbell v. Acuff-Rose Music, Inc.*, 510 U.S. 569, 579 (1994). We find that Connectix's Virtual Game Station is modestly transformative. The product creates a new platform, the personal computer, on which consumers can play games designed for the Sony PlayStation. This innovation affords opportunities for game play in new environments, specifically anywhere a Sony PlayStation console and television are not available, but a computer with a CD-ROM drive is.

Finally, we must weigh the extent of any transformation in Connectix's Virtual Game Station against the significance of other factors, including commercialism, that militate against fair use. See *Acuff-Rose*, 510 U.S. at 579. Connectix's commercial use of the copyrighted material was an intermediate one, and thus was only "indirect or derivative." *Sega*, 977 F.2d at 1522. Moreover, Connectix reverse-engineered the Sony BIOS to produce a product that would be compatible with games designed for the Sony PlayStation. We have recognized this purpose as a legitimate one under the first factor of the fair use analysis. Upon weighing these factors, we find that the first factor favors Connectix.

Effect of the use upon the potential market

We also find that the fourth factor, effect of the use upon the potential market, favors Connectix. Under this factor, we consider not only the extent of market harm caused by the particular actions of the alleged infringer, but also "whether unrestricted and widespread conduct of the sort engaged in by the defendant ... would result in a substantially adverse impact on the potential market" for the original. *Acuff-Rose*, 510 U.S. at 590. Whereas a work that merely supplants or supersedes another is likely to cause a substantially adverse impact on the potential market of the original, a transformative work is less likely to do so. The district court found that "[t]o the extent that such a substitution [of Connectix's Virtual Game Station for Sony PlayStation console] occurs, Sony will lose console sales and profits." Order at 19. We recognize that this may be so. But because the Virtual Game Station is transformative, and does not merely supplant the PlayStation console, the Virtual Game Station is a legitimate competitor in the market for platforms on which Sony and Sony-licensed games can be played. For this reason, some economic loss by Sony as a result of this competition does not compel a finding of no fair use. This factor favors Connectix.

The four statutory fair use factors must be weighed together, in light of the purposes of copyright. Here, three of the factors favor Connectix; one favors Sony, and it is of little weight. We reverse the grant of preliminary injunction on the ground of copyright infringement.

Tarnishment

Sony has not shown a likelihood of success on each element of the tarnishment claim. To prevail on its tarnishment claim, Sony must show that (1) the PlayStation "mark is famous;" (2) Connectix is "making a commercial use of the mark;" (3) Connectix's "use began after the mark became famous;" and (4) Connectix's "use of the mark dilutes the quality of the mark by diminishing the capacity of the mark to identify and distinguish goods and services." *Films of Distinction, Inc. v. Allegro Film Prods., Inc.*, 12 F.Supp.2d 1068, 1078 (C.D.Cal.1998); 15 U.S.C. §§ 1125(c)(1), 1127 (definition of "dilution"). Connectix does not dispute the first and third of these elements. We address only the fourth element. Because Sony proceeds under a tarnishment theory of dilution, it must show under this fourth element that its PlayStation mark will suffer negative associations through Connectix's use. The district court found the Virtual Game Station does not play

PlayStation games as well as the PlayStation console, and that although the Virtual Game Station's packaging contains a disclaimer to this effect, "game players do not comprehend this distinction." Order at 24–25. The Sony PlayStation mark therefore suffers negative associations because of this confusion on the part of consumers who play Sony games on the Virtual Game Station software.

The evidence on the record does not support such a finding of misattribution. The district court relied primarily on a series of semi-anonymous reviews posted on the Internet and submitted by Connectix. As the district court acknowledged, these reviews were neither authenticated nor identified. More important, the print-out of the comments does not reveal the context in which the comments were made; this omission makes the extent of any confusion by game players difficult to assess reliably. The district court also referred to two focus group studies conducted by market research firms at Sony's bequest. These studies address the difference of quality between the Virtual Game Station and PlayStation, but shed no light on the question of misattribution. Thus, we reject as clearly erroneous the district court's finding that the Virtual Game Station tarnishes the Sony PlayStation mark on a misattribution theory of tarnishment.

Notes and Questions

1. In the early 1980s a wide array of proprietary, incompatible formats constituted a source of continuing frustration and aggravation for videogamers. Fortunately, the courts began to recognize the value of compatibility and interoperability to consumers, and accordingly fashioned rules and protections designed to encourage same. Perhaps the most notable methods for achieving interoperability concerned "reverse engineering," whereby a potential infringer would disassemble copyrighted computer code in order to manufacture and fashion compatible products. The notable case of *Vault Corp. v. Quaid Software Ltd.*, 847 F.2d 255, 261 (5th Cir. 1988) answered in the *affirmative* the question as to whether or not a person could properly reverse engineer copyrighted software, and copy code from the software for the purpose of unlocking its copy protection features. Since, the very purpose of "seeking compatibility" (which is thought of as ultimately benefitting the consumer) has formed a defense to copyright infringement claims. *See* § 5.30, *supra*.

2. In *Atari Games Corp. v. Nintendo of Am., Inc.*, the United States Court of Appeals, Federal Circuit, 975 F.2d 832 (Fed. Cir. 1992), declared that when the nature of a work requires intermediate copying in order to understand the ideas and processes in a copyrighted work, that nature supports a finding of fair use for such copying; thus, the reverse engineering of object code to discern unprotectable ideas in a computer program is fair use. 17 U.S.C.A. § 107(2). However, copying beyond that which is necessary to understand the program constitutes an infringement; a competitor cannot, therefore, use reverse engineering as an excuse to commercially exploit a program.

3. In *Sega Enterprises Ltd. v. Accolade, Inc.*, 977 F.2d 1510 (9th Cir., 1993) the quest for interoperability spared the defendant liability for what would otherwise have clearly constituted copyright and trademark infringement. *See also* The Digital Millennium Copyright Act of 1998, Title 17, § 1200(f).

4. In 1998 Congress amended the Copyright Act by adding Chapter 12, The Digital Millennium Copyright Act (DMCA) to Title 17 of the United States Code. § 1201(a)(1)(A) of the Act specifically prohibits the circumvention of copy protection devices. But § 1201(f) provides this exemption:

(1) Notwithstanding the provisions of subsection (a)(1)(A), a person who has lawfully obtained the right to use a copy of a computer program may circumvent a technological measure that effectively controls access to a particular portion of that program for the sole purpose of identifying and analyzing those elements of the program that are necessary to achieve interoperability of an independently created computer program with other programs, and that have not previously been readily available to the person engaging in the circumvention, to the extent any such acts of identification and analysis do not constitute infringement under this title.

(2) Notwithstanding the provisions of subsections (a)(2) and (b), a person may develop and employ technological means to circumvent a technological measure, or to circumvent protection afforded by a technological measure, in order to enable the identification and analysis under paragraph (1), or for the purpose of enabling interoperability of an independently created computer program with other programs, if such means are necessary to achieve such interoperability, to the extent that doing so does not constitute infringement under this title.

(3) The information acquired through the acts permitted under paragraph (1), and the means permitted under paragraph (2), may be made available to others if the person referred to in paragraph (1) or (2), as the case may be, provides such information or means solely for the purpose of enabling interoperability of an independently created computer program with other programs, and to the extent that doing so does not constitute infringement under this title or violate applicable law other than this section. (4) For purposes of this subsection, the term "interoperability" means the ability of computer programs to exchange information, and of such programs mutually to use the information which has been exchanged.

5. Do you think that reverse engineering is generally proper or improper? Under what circumstances would you favor the right of a developer to engage in reverse engineering?

6. For more information concerning the Digital Millennium Copyright Act, *see infra*, §6.50.

---

§ 3.23 Defensive Construction

Protecting an original idea or videogame can often be challenging. The protections and sanctions of the Copyright Act notwithstanding, software piracy and counterfeiting are rampant. And since ideas alone are not protectable, it is often difficult for a game developer or programmer to protect against competitors who are willing to copy another's work and then, with minor modifications, disguise the illegal activity. There are, however, some countermeasures that astute attorneys can advise their programming clients to take:

A. Delete all comments from the code. Recall that comments are nothing more than non-functioning personal notes that enable others to read and better understand the code.

B. Sprinkle copyright notices throughout the code. There is no better evidence that your code has been copied than to have your own "*signature*" (or copyright notice) appear in the code of a would-be infringer.

C. Include some useless, non-functioning code. Suggestion "B" will only catch blatant literal infringement. To expose the more subtle infringers, include some useless code that does nothing whatsoever. (During depositions, the infringing programmer might then be asked to explain the reason for the code, which of course, he will be unable to do.)

D. Place hidden markers. In hidden portions of non-functioning code, include significant birthdays, wedding engagement dates, or even the names of pets to prove a link to the rightful author.

E. Misspell some non-functioning words. Such errors could be used to prove "striking similarity" in conjunction with an infringement action, particularly if the mis-spellings are uncommon.

* * *

In *Williams Elecs., Inc. v. Arctic Int'l, Inc.*, 685 F.2d 870 (3d Cir. 1982) a copyright infringement case (*see infra*, § 5.31), raised a factual issue as to whether or not Arctic's "*Defense Command*" copied "*Defender*," the plaintiff's popular hit game of the early 1980s. Finding in favor of the plaintiff, the court observed:

> There is overwhelming evidence in the present case that the Williams computer program has been copied in some form. The following facts, among others, manifest the similarities between the Williams program and that stored in the Arctic memory devices: (1) The game created by the Arctic circuit boards contains an error which was present in early versions of the Williams computer program— it displays the wrong score value for destroying a particular alien symbol; (2) The attract mode of both games displays a listing of high scores achieved by previous players alongside their initials, and Arctic's game contains the initials of Williams employees, including its president, who initially achieved the highest scores on the DEFENDER game; (3) Using a laboratory developmental device, Williams' employees printed out a listing in code of the contents of the memory devices of both games. In excess of 85% of the listings are identical; (4) The Williams program provided that the words "Copyright 1980-Williams Electronics" in code were to be stored in its memory devices, but were not to be displayed on the CRT at any time, thus providing a "buried" or hidden copyright notice. When the contents of Arctic's memory devices were printed out by Williams' employees, the listings contained the "buried" Williams copyright notice in code.

Id. at 866.

---

§ 3.30 The Publisher-Developer Relationship

As the videogame industry grows, so too does the personnel layering for the creation, programming, development, licensing and distribution of the games. Even though it is still possible for a lone programmer to write, develop and sell a game on the Internet, when that game becomes successful, entire companies may spring up around it. The production process becomes akin to that of a major motion picture.

The publisher is generally viewed as the top of the food chain, similar to a motion picture producer. But as long as there are still a few industry giants (such as Sony and Nintendo), even the publishers may be playing second fiddle.

Outdoor Partners LLC v. Rabbit Hole Interactive Corp.

United States District Court, Southern District New York, 2013
2013 WL 6503525, No. 13 Civ. 1797 (KBF)

FORREST, District Judge

On March 18, 2013, following the failed settlement of a prior lawsuit dating back to 2011 asserting alleged breaches of a developer agreement for two software applications to comply with specifications for Nintendo of America, Outdoor Partners LLC ("OPL") again filed suit against Rabbit Hole Interactive ("RHI"). The second lawsuit, currently pending before this Court, asserts the same causes of action based on the same facts as the first. On September 30, 2013, RHI answered and counterclaimed for breaches of both the settlement and developer agreements.

Now pending before the Court is RHI's motion for summary judgment as to each of its counterclaims and to dismiss the affirmative claims brought by OPL. For the reasons set forth below, RHI's motion is DENIED as to each of its counterclaims and OPL's claim for breach of contract; its motion is GRANTED solely with respect to OPL's two tort claims.

I. BACKGROUND

On February 18, 2011, OPL and RHI entered into the Bass Pro Video Game Developer Agreement ("the Developer Agreement"), pursuant to which RHI would develop video games for OPL, and OPL would pay royalties to RHI, conditioned on approval of the games by Nintendo of America. RHI developed a game that failed Nintendo's approval process four times. OPL suffered several hundred thousand dollars in harm from this failure. On September 30, 2011, Chris Pauwels, a principal of RHI, proposed to OPL that RHI and OPL "agree to share the increased costs due to changes in scope of $184,000.00 equally, therefore $92,000.00 to each party."

On November 14, 2011, OPL's principal terminated the Developer Agreement pursuant to paragraph 11.2 of the Agreement, which provided that it could be terminated for cause. The parties disputed whether OPL owed RHI a Termination Fee. On November 18, 2011, Pauwels wrote in an email to Chip Pedersen of OPL, "The bugs have been fixed and tested."

On December 13, 2011, OPL sued RHI and its principals in this Court for, inter alia, breach of contract. On September 14, 2012, the parties entered into a Stipulation of Settlement and Order ("the Settlement Agreement") that dismissed the action without prejudice.

In sum, the Settlement Agreement provided for: (1) a series of advance payments to RHI ("Royalty Advance payments"); (2) a deposit in trust with Pryor Cashman for the benefit of RHI of the sum of $106,901.75, at which time Pryor Cashman would issue a "Deposit Confirmation Notice"; and (3) a process by which RHI could deliver to a third party, War Drum Studios LLC ("War Drum") a personal computer on which versions of two games ("the Hunt" and "the Strike" games, together "the Games") reside. War Drum would then report on whether the Games compiled (passed certain technical tests). If the results of the initial testing were negative, OPL would issue to RHI an Initial Game Rejection Notice; RHI would then have the opportunity, in its sole discretion, to correct any bugs. If the results of the initial testing were positive, OPL would issue a Game Acceptance Notice, and Pryor Cashman would release the $106,901.75 to RHI. If the initial testing resulted in a Game Rejection Notice and RHI chose to try to fix any bugs, the Games would then be sent to War Drum for testing a second time. If the Games failed a second round of testing, then OPL could issue a Final Rejection Notice and would be entitled to have the funds deposited with Pryor Cashman returned to it.

In short, the Settlement Agreement provides that RHI's obligation to provide the Games to War Drum for testing occurs after OPL deposits the $106,901.75 in trust with Pryor Cashman, not before. The process for acceptance and rejection of the Games, and either final payment of the funds to RHI or their return to OPL, occurs thereafter. The terms relating to payment, release, and termination are set forth as specified below.

The Settlement Agreement required OPL to pay "Royalty Amounts," which were defined as "the royalty amounts payable to RHI for the period from October 1, 2011 to March 31, 2012, pursuant to the agreement between OPL and RHI, dated February 18, 2011 (the 'Developer Agreement'), which totals U.S. $121,901.75." The Settlement Agreement sets forth OPL's payment obligations as follows:

> a. OPL shall make three advance payments of $5,000 each (each, a "Royalty Advance") to RHI, as follows:
>
> > i. OPL agrees that within ten (10) business days of the Settlement Date, OPL will make the first Royalty Advance and shall pay the amount of $5,000 to RHI; and
> >
> > ii. OPL agrees that within thirty (30) business days of the Settlement Date, OPL will make the second Royalty Advance and shall pay to RHI the amount of $5,000; and
> >
> > iii. OPL agrees that within sixty (60) business days of the Settlement Date, OPL will make the final Royalty Advance payment to RHI in the amount of $5,000.
>
> b. OPL agrees that on or before January 15, 2013, OPL will deposit the sum of $106,901.75 ... in trust for the benefit of RHI and to be released pursuant to the terms of this Settlement Agreement.

The Settlement Agreement provides for releases that only go into effect once RHI has received the Royalty Amounts. There is no provision for releases in the event that RHI does not receive the Royalty Amounts for any reason. Both paragraphs 16 and 17 start with the phrase, "Upon receipt by RHI of the Royalty Amounts, [OPL/RHI] ... hereby releases and forever discharges" the other party to the Agreement.

The Settlement Agreement does not contain a separate provision for termination (or non-termination) prior to completion of the acceptance or rejection process of the Games. However, the clear language of the Agreement contemplates that either party may terminate before that testing ever commences as follows:

> If this Settlement Agreement is breached or terminated by either party before the receipt of the Royalty Amounts by RHI, each of the parties shall be entitled to proceed with the Litigation with all of their rights preserved and this Settlement Agreement shall be of no force or effect other than those requiring the return of the PC and Games to RHI.

Since termination following testing requires prior payment of the Royalty Amounts, and paragraph 18 contemplates termination that may occur prior to that event, it follows that the Settlement Agreement contemplates a right of termination by either party.

Finally, the Agreement provides as follows:

> OPL hereby unconditionally and irrevocably agrees that if it fails to make any payment due and payable under this Settlement Agreement within five (5) business days of OPL's receipt of a Notice of Default, the entire Royalty Amount less any

amounts paid under this Settlement Agreement (the "Remaining Balance") shall be due and payable immediately. . . .

On January 10, 2013, RHI's counsel emailed OPL's counsel a Notice of Default concerning OPL's failure to pay the Royalty Advances. According to paragraph 18 of the Settlement Agreement, OPL therefore had until January 17, which was five business days later, within which to make the required payment, or the unconditional agreement to pay the "Remaining Balance" (pursuant to paragraph 28) would be triggered. On January 14, 2013, OPL's counsel responded that OPL would cure its default by paying the Royalty Advances, but also stated that OPL was exercising its right to terminate the Settlement Agreement.

On January 15, 2013, RHI sent OPL a second and separate Notice of Default regarding its failure to pay the $106,901.75 balance, which, pursuant to the Settlement Agreement, was due on or before January 15. On January 17, 2013, OPL timely paid RHI the $15,000 Royalty Advances. RHI remains in sole possession of the Games.

On March 18, 2013, OPL filed the instant complaint, which alleges breach of the Developer Agreement against RHI as well as conversion and replevin against RHI and three of its principals. On September 30, 2013, RHI filed an answer and counterclaims in which it alleged that OPL had breached both the Settlement Agreement and the Developer Agreement. (ECF No. 12.) On December 9, 2013, the Court granted RHI's motion to dismiss the complaint against the three individual defendants.

II. STANDARD OF REVIEW

Summary judgment may not be granted unless a movant shows, based on admissible evidence in the record, "that there is no genuine dispute as to any material fact and the movant is entitled to judgment as a matter of law."

III. DISCUSSION

RHI has moved for summary judgment as to each of its counterclaims as well as with respect to OPL's three affirmative claims. Except as to two tort claims that may not stand in light of OPL's primary claim for breach of contract, all of RHI's requests for summary judgment fail.

A. RHI's First Counterclaim

RHI's first counterclaim asserts that OPL has breached the Settlement Agreement by failing to deposit the sum of $106,901.75 with Pryor Cashman, as provided for in paragraph 2(b) of that agreement.

This counterclaim is based on an erroneous premise: that OPL did not have the right to terminate the Settlement Agreement when it did. As the provisions set forth above make clear, OPL acted within the four corners of the contract when it terminated the Settlement Agreement, and its payment obligation as to the remaining Royalty Amount ceased at that time.

The Settlement Agreement contemplates payment by OPL of certain amounts either directly or into escrow preceding RHI's obligation to provide the Games for testing. It is certainly possible that the parties could have negotiated for an agreement that neither party could terminate, or that rendered the total Royalty Amounts non-contingent. They did not. First, paragraph 1 defines "Royalty Amounts" as the aggregate of the Royalty Advances plus the "remaining sum." Thus, partial payment of only the Royalty Advances does not equate with payment of the Royalty Amounts. Next, paragraph 18 contemplates that there could be some circumstance under which termination could occur prior to the payment of the Royalty Amounts. On January 14, 2013, OPL did exactly that.

Finally, the Settlement Agreement also provides that, if termination occurs prior to the Royalty Amounts being paid and in the absence of paragraph 28 being triggered, the parties are returned to their respective litigation positions status quo ante. In this regard, the Settlement Agreement states explicitly that, if terminated, it "shall be of no force or effect other than those requiring the return of the PC and Games to RHI." Paragraph 28, which does impose an unconditional obligation to pay remaining amounts due, was not triggered here, since OPL cured the first Notice of Default within five business days — that is, by January 17. OPL had cancelled the Settlement Agreement on January 14, the day before it received the second Notice of Default. Its obligation to cure that default terminated when it terminated the agreement. "It is a well established principle of law that when a contract affords a party the unqualified right to limit its life by notice of termination that right is absolute and will be upheld in accordance with its clear and unambiguous terms." Red Apple Dev. Ctr. v. Cmty. Sch. Dists. Two, 303 A.D.2d 156, 157, 756 N.Y.S.2d 527 (N.Y. App. Div. 1st Dep't 2003) (citations omitted).

RHI argues that the cancellation provision of the Agreement only applied if OPL failed to pay any of the Royalty Amounts. That argument is contrary to the plain language of the Settlement Agreement, which enables either party to terminate the Agreement "before the receipt of the Royalty Amounts by RHI," and defines the Royalty Amounts as the total $121,901.75 due to RHI. (emphasis added).) Because OPL had not yet paid that full amount, but merely the Royalty Advances, OPL retained the right to terminate the Agreement in compliance with its terms. Where parties agree on a termination procedure, the clause must be enforced as written if it is not ambiguous.").

B. RHI's Second and Third Counterclaims

RHI's arguments in support of summary judgment on its second and third counterclaims, which allege breaches of the Developer Agreement due to OPL's failure to pay $106,901.75 in royalties to RHI and to pay a $263,600 Termination Fee, also fail.

OPL proffers several facts that raise triable issues and therefore preclude summary judgment. For instance, OPL asserts, with supporting facts, that RHI itself breached the Developer Agreement by failing to develop a video game that complied with Nintendo's specification, as required by the Agreement. OPL also proffers evidence that RHI acknowledged the flaws in its software: on September 30, 2011, Chris Pauwels, a principal of RHI, proposed that RHI share in OPL's increased costs due to required changes, and on November 18, 2011, Pauwels acknowledged bugs in the game to OPL.

The factual issues regarding whether RHI was in fact the breaching party with respect to the Developer Agreement preclude summary judgment. See, e.g., Kasper Global Collection & Brokers, Inc. v. Global Cabinets & Furniture Mfrs. Inc., 952 F.Supp.2d 542, 576 (S.D.N.Y.2013) (finding that factual disputes over the quality of goods that the defendant received gave "rise to triable issues of fact as to whether Plaintiff complied with its own obligations under any contracts governing the parties' transactions").

This Court also denies RHI's motion for summary judgment on its third counterclaim for payment of the Termination Fee. The Developer Agreement allowed for termination for cause in the event of a material breach, and separately allowed OPL to terminate the Agreement without cause so long as it paid a "Termination Fee." Contrary to RHI's argument, the Developer Agreement clearly contemplates that OPL would pay a Termination Fee (a requirement that appears only in the provision regarding termination without cause) only in the event of a termination without cause. Here, OPL has proffered evidence that it terminated the Agreement for cause, because RHI breached the Developer Agreement by developing a game that failed Nintendo's approval process. A triable issue therefore exists as to whether RHI is in fact entitled to a Termination Fee.

C. RHI's Motion as to OPL's Claims

1. The Release

RHI has moved for summary judgment with respect to OPL's cause of action for breach of the Developer Agreement on the basis that OPL's release in the Settlement Agreement precludes such claim. This argument is without merit.

The releases in the Settlement Agreement never went into effect. The Agreement plainly states, "Upon receipt by RHI of the Royalty Amounts, OPL ... hereby releases and forever discharges each of the Defendants." (emphasis added).) As set forth above, the Royalty Amounts included not only the Royalty Advances but also the balance, for a total of $121,901.75. OPL did not pay the $106,901.75 balance, and OPL terminated the Settlement Agreement before its obligation to do so arose. Accordingly, OPL did not release its claims against RHI.

2. OPL's Tort Claims

Finally, RHI argues that OPL's breach-of-contract claim precludes its tort claims for conversion and replevin. The Court agrees. Here, OPL's tort claims are duplicative of its breach-of-contract claim. OPL alleges that RHI wrongly exercised control over the software in question while OPL had legal ownership over it, and demands return of the software. However, the Developer Agreement governs the delivery and ownership of the software. The Agreement thus precludes OPL's tort claims. OPL shall include its argument that it is entitled to return of the software within its request for a remedy on its breach-of-contract claim.

IV. CONCLUSION

For these reasons, RHI's motion for summary judgment is DENIED IN PART as to RHI's counterclaims and OPL's breach-of-contract claim, and GRANTED IN PART as to OPL's tort claims. The Clerk of Court is directed to close the motion at ECF No. 22.

SO ORDERED.

————————

Notes and Questions

1. With respect to contract compliance in general, issues pertaining to delays, failures to meet deadlines and problems such as those presented in *Greenberg v. Sir-tech Software, Inc.* and *Outdoor Partners*, are prevalent in every creative industry. That is why such matters are normally addressed at length in contracts. But unlike many endeavors, problems encountered during software development are exacerbated by constantly changing technologies. Try to imagine the construction of a simple brick house in a city where the building and zoning codes change several times before the project has been completed. And, instead of bricks (which haven't significantly changed in 200 years), imagine building materials that are modified monthly. It is no wonder that programmers are notoriously delinquent.

2. In a growing dynamic industry, employment mobility can be a two-edged sword. In 2002, videogame giant Activision acquired Infinity Ward Studios, a company created

by Jason West and Vincent Zampella, the team that was credited with two of Xbox 360's greatest hits—*Modern Warfare* and *Call of Duty*. West and Zampella entered into employment agreements with Activision granting the two creative control over the development of games by Infinity Ward Studios. Pursuant to the agreements, royalty payments were scheduled to begin on March 31, 2010. However, on March 1, 2010, Activision decided to terminate the agreement, claiming that the two were guilty of insubordination. West and Zampella commenced suit against Activision claiming that the latter fired them as a pretext to avoid paying royalties. Activision counter-claimed alleging that West and Zampella were engaging in collusive conduct will rival giant Electronic Arts (EA). Activision eventually added EA as a party defendant to the suit, claiming contractual interference. Following a denial of Activision's motion for summary judgment, the case was settled. *West v. Activision Publishing, Inc.*, No. SC107041 (Cal. Super. Ct. L.A., 2010).

3. Compare the length and complexity of Form 3.1, *supra* (Computer Programmer Contract) to the following agreement:

FORM 3.2
Videogame Development Contract

THIS AGREEMENT, made and entered into as of this _____ day of _____, 20__ is by and between _____ whose address is _____ ("Publisher") and _____ whose address is _____ ("Developer").

WHEREAS the Publisher is currently the business of selling, licensing, advertising, marketing and distributing videogames to the general public, and

WHEREAS the Developer is currently the business of creating, designing programming and developing videogames, and

WHEREAS the Publisher and Developer wish to enter into a Publishing Agreement whereby Developer shall create and develop a videogame, generally described as _____ with a working title _____ (the "Product") and Publisher shall publish the Product on the terms and conditions set forth herein.

NOW, THEREFORE, for and in consideration of the mutual promises and the agreements stated herein, the Publisher and the Developer hereby agree as follows:

1. Ownership and Licensing. At all times relevant hereto, Developer shall retain all copyrights and all other intellectual property rights in and to the Product, including all original elements of design and game software, and all rights in all source code, tools, technology, and other development aids embodied in and used in connection with the development of the Product. Any rights not explicitly granted to Publisher hereunder are reserved by Developer. Developer hereby grants to Publisher the exclusive right during the Term (as hereinafter defined), throughout the world and universe (the "Territory") to produce, reproduce, perform, promote, advertise, export, import, rent, license, sublicense, translate, localize, package, market, merchandise, distribute (through any channels, including electronic distribution by download), display, sell, lease and otherwise exploit the Product, including products without original narrative or interactive elements designed to support or promote the Product using the names, renderings, dialog, sound effects or screen shots from the Product (including, without limitation, clothing, posters, novelties and strategy guides of every kind and nature whatsoever) (hereinafter referred to as "Ancillary Products") on the Platform (as hereinafter defined). Developer also hereby grants to Publisher the non-exclusive right throughout the Territory to use and reproduce the object code and an exclusive right to use the name of the Product (and any trademarks which may be applied for by Developer at Developer's sole cost and expense) in accordance with the provisions of this Agreement. Developer shall not exercise the exclusive rights granted to Publisher during the Term anywhere in the Territory.

2. Marketing. Publisher shall determine, in its sole discretion, the manner and method of marketing and distribution of the Product, including, but not limited to, marketing expenditures, advertising and promotion, packaging, channels of distribution and the price of the Product, provided however, that Publisher shall use commercially reasonable efforts to cause the Product to be released within nine _____ months of the date the Product is approved by major console manufacturer and distributor _____ ("Corporation") and shall spend at least $_____ on advertising. Neither party makes any guarantee of success with respect to revenue to be achieved or royalties to be earned from the Product.

3. Competing Products. Developer shall not, directly or indirectly, develop, manufacture or distribute a product of the same genre (i.e., third-person urban conflict simulation similar in theme, look and feel) as the Product for any party other than Publisher until the date two (2) years following the initial release of the Product. The parties acknowledge and agree that the foregoing restriction is of the essence of this Agreement and is necessary for the protection of Publisher's ongoing business. During the Term and following the commercial release of the Product, Publisher shall have a right of first and last refusal for the exclusive, worldwide publishing rights to sequels, add-ons, mission packs and other platform versions of the Product. Any refusal right must be exercised in writing within fifteen (15) days of receipt of written notice by Developer of a bona fide third-party offer.

4. Development. The parties agree to the following benchmarks and milestones with respect to the creation of the Product:

(a) Within thirty (30) days following the date hereof, Developer shall submit to Publisher for Publisher's acceptance the design specifications ("Design Specifications") for the Product. Publisher shall, within fifteen (15) business days of submission of the Design Specifications, review the Design Specifications and shall notify Developer, in writing, indicating either acceptance or rejection of the Design Specifications, and, if rejection, the specific reasons therefore. Upon rejection of the Design Specifications, Developer shall have fifteen (15) business days from Publisher's notice to revise the Design Specifications and resubmit the Design Specifications for acceptance. Should Developer fail, to the reasonable satisfaction of Publisher, to deliver satisfactory Design Specifications, Publisher may terminate this Agreement by written notice to Developer and all amounts paid by the Publisher in connection with the Product shall be fully refundable.

(b) Developer shall develop the Product for the Corporation's console currently known, advertised and marketed as _____ (the "Platform") in accordance with the approved Design Specifications, the development schedule annexed hereto as Exhibit A (the "Development Schedule) and the terms and conditions of this Agreement. Material changes to the Design Specifications shall be mutually agreed to in good faith by the parties.

(c) Publisher shall have the right to request translations or localization of the Product by providing written notice to Developer. Publisher shall pay to Developer the reasonable costs incurred by Developer set forth in an approved budget for each localization, such costs to be deemed an advance hereunder and shall be payable 50% upon commencement of development of additional language(s), and 50% upon Publisher's acceptance of the gold master of the localized version.

(d) Approval. After delivery to Publisher by Developer of each deliverable pursuant to the milestones identified in the Development Schedule (collectively, "Unapproved Deliverables"), Publisher will have thirty (30) calendar days to examine and test such Unapproved Deliverable to determine whether it conforms in all material respects to the approved design specifications and whether it is complete and free from material error (the "Acceptance Criteria"). On or before the thirtieth day after delivery, Publisher will notify Developer in writing of Publisher's acceptance or rejection of the Unapproved Deliverable based upon the Acceptance Criteria and, in case of any rejection, will provide Developer with a reasonably detailed list of deficiencies in the Unapproved Deliverable. In the event that Publisher fails to provide Developer with such written notification within thirty days of the date of delivery of an Unapproved Deliverable, Publisher shall be deemed to have accepted such Unapproved Deliverable. In the event of a rejection, Developer will use its good faith, best efforts to correct the deficiencies (including, without limitation, any material bugs and deficiencies that affect game play and/or compatibility) and will resubmit such Unapproved Deliverable, as corrected, as soon as reasonably practicable following Publisher's rejection. Publisher will either accept or reject the corrected Unapproved Deliverables based upon the Acceptance Criteria. This procedure will continue until Publisher either (i) accepts the Unapproved Deliverable or (ii) elects to terminate this Agreement for material breach after the Cure Period (as defined herein) pursuant to Section 14(b)(ii).

5. Delivery. Developer shall deliver to Publisher four (4) copies of the fully functional gold master for the Product (in executable object code form), on the Platform in electronic format, Bug (as hereinafter defined) free, and from which Publisher can create copies of the Product. Timely delivery in accordance with the Development Schedule is of the essence of this Agreement. In the event Developer fails to deliver the gold master for the Product by _____, 20 ___ (the "Gold Master Delivery Date") unless such delivery date is extended by mutual agreement of Publisher and Developer, Developer shall be deemed to be in material breach of this Agreement. For the avoidance of doubt, the Cure Period (as hereinafter defined) shall not apply to any termination by Publisher pursuant to this Section. If Publisher terminates this Agreement pursuant to this section, all amounts paid by Publisher in connection with the Product shall be fully refundable in accordance with Section 14(b)(ii). "Bug" means any deviation from the commonly accepted standards for normal operation of games or any material error including, without limitation, an abnormal cessation of functioning of the Product.

6. Credits. Developer shall submit on-screen credits for the Product to Publisher for Publisher's approval, which approval shall not be unreasonably withheld. Publisher shall accord credit to Developer as developer with reasonable prominence on all printed materials related to the product, including without limitation, on front of the package, in the manual and advertising materials which shall contain Developer's logo. Developer's website address shall be displayed on the back of the package. The Product, user manual and Ancillary Products shall contain the following legal designation: (c) _____ , 20_____ or such other legal as may be provided by Developer.

7. Developer Support. During the three months following the initial release of the Product, at Publisher's request, Developer shall provide reasonable telephone support to Publisher's designated employees in connection with the technical support of users of the Product. Publisher shall reimburse Developer its reasonable pre-approved out-of-pocket expenses (as documented) in connection with rendering telephone support and training services.

8. Advance. Provided Developer has performed in accordance with the terms hereof, Publisher shall pay to Developer a fully recoupable advance in the aggregate amount of $ _____ (of which $ _____ has been paid, the receipt of which is hereby acknowledged by Developer), payable (i) $ _____ delivery of the gold master by the Gold Master Delivery Date (as defined in the Development Schedule); and (ii) $ _____ upon approval by Corporation. All advances paid to Developer or on Developer's behalf in respect of the Product shall be recoupable by Publisher at any time from any and all royalties accruing hereunder with regard to the Product.

9. Royalties. Publisher shall accrue to Developer's account royalties at a rate of fifty percent (50%) of the net receipts derived worldwide by Publisher and its affiliates from the commercial exploitation (including without limitation sales of, rental of, and time charged services derived from) of the Product and Ancillary Products. Net receipts means amounts actually received by Publisher, less returns, credits, freight, taxes and similar charges and manufacturing expenses and royalties.

10. Royalty Payments. The parties agree to the following provisions shall govern the manner in which royalties are to accrue:

(a) Royalties earned hereunder will be accrued quarterly and paid in United States dollars, less all advances and other permitted charges, within seventy-five (75) days following the last day of January, April, July, and October, in accordance with Publisher's regular accounting practices. Royalties statements shall be sent to _____ . Publisher shall have the right to establish reserves for returns and defective products in accordance with Publisher's business practices (not to exceed 15% of royalties owed to Developer). Unused reserves shall be liquidated during the second quarter following the quarter the reserve was taken.

(b) Each royalty payment hereunder shall be accompanied by a statement in United States dollars, in accordance with Publisher's regular accounting practices. Each royalty statement shall contain information relating to the life to date activity of the Product including period of statement, units sold, cost of goods, gross royalty, reserves, earned royalties, territories, sublicensed and repackaged sales and Ancillary Product sales. Each statement shall become binding on both parties and Developer shall neither have nor make any claim against Publisher with respect to such statement, unless Developer objects in writing to the statement of the specific basis of such claim within one (1) year after the date Publisher renders such statement.

(c) Royalty payments shall be less whatever taxes the laws of the applicable jurisdiction require be withheld in connection with such royalties and subject to applicable local currency remittance laws or foreign exchange remittance regulations.

(d) Publisher agrees that Developer may, not more than once during any calendar year, but only once with respect to any statement rendered hereunder, audit its books and records for the purpose of determining the accuracy of Publisher's statements to Developer. If Developer wishes to perform any such audit, Developer will be required to notify Publisher in writing at least thirty (30) days before the date when Developer plans to begin it. All audits shall be made during regular business hours, and shall be conducted on Developer's behalf by a certified independent public accountant. Each examination shall be made at Developer's own expense at Publisher's regular place of business in _____, where the books and records will be made available to Developer's accountant. In the event that Developer establishes as a result of an audit conducted by Developer, that there is a discrepancy in the royalty payments due to Developer of ten percent (10%) or more for the period covered by the audit, then Publisher shall pay to Developer, upon settlement of the audit, Developer's reasonable third-party legal and auditor's fees and disbursements actually incurred in connection with such audit and interest at the rate of 2% per annum on underpaid accountings.

(e) If Developer claims that additional monies are payable to Developer, Publisher shall not be deemed to be in material breach of this Agreement unless (i) Publisher fails to produce appropriate books and records of manufacture and sales for audit, or (ii) such claim shall have been reduced to a final judgment by a court of competent jurisdiction and Publisher shall have failed to pay Developer the amount thereof within thirty (30) days after Publisher shall have received written notice of the entry of such judgment or (iii) Publisher agrees that there are royalties owing and does not pay the amount thereof within thirty (30) days.

11. Confidential Information. (a) Publisher and Developer recognize that, in connection with the performance of this Agreement, each of them may disclose to the other information about the disclosing party's business or activities, which such party considers proprietary and confidential. All of such proprietary and confidential information of each party (which shall include, without limitation, all business, financial and technical information of a party, identities of customers, clients or licensees, proprietary software code and any other information whether oral or written which is not generally known or available to the public) is hereinafter referred to as "Confidential Information." (b) The party who receives any Confidential Information agrees to maintain the confidential status for such Confidential Information, not to use any such Confidential information for any purpose other than the purpose for which it was originally disclosed to the receiving party, and not to disclose any of such Confidential Information to any third party unless required by law or court order.

12. Representations And Warranties. The parties hereby agree to the following representations and warranties:

(a) Ownership and Non-infringement. Developer represents and warrants to Publisher that it has obtained all rights, licenses and authorizations necessary to enter into this agreement and grant the rights granted herein; each of Developer and Publisher represent and warrant that the execution and performance of this Agreement does not and will not violate or interfere with any other agreement to which it is a party, Developer represents and warrants that the source code and development tools for the Product is or will be original to Developer and/ or exclusively owned by Developer and/or validly licensed by Developer at Developer's expense for all uses to be made of them pursuant to this Agreement and that the source code and development tools are not nor will they be a violation of the rights of any other person or organization; and Developer represents and warrants that no part of the Product or the exercise of the rights granted hereunder violates or infringes upon any rights of any person or entity, including, but not limited to, copyrights, trademark rights, patent rights, trade secrets rights, or contractual, common law or statutory rights. Publisher represents and warrants that it will not reverse-engineer the Product.

(b) Authority. Each of Publisher and Developer represents and warrants that it is duly organized and in good standing under the laws of the jurisdiction of its incorporation or existence; that it has (and shall at all times remain possessed of) the full right, power and authority to enter into and perform this Agreement; that it is not presently the subject of a voluntary or involuntary petition in bankruptcy, does not presently contemplate filing any such voluntary petition, and is not aware of any intention on the part of any other person to file such an involuntary petition against it; and the person(s) executing this Agreement on its behalf has the actual authority to bind Developer to this Agreement.

(c) Performance. Each of Publisher and Developer represents and warrants that it is under no disability, restriction or prohibition, whether contractual or otherwise with respect to its rights to execute and perform this Agreement; that the agreement of any person who is not a party to this Agreement is not necessary or required for it to carry out its obligations hereunder, or for it to enjoy the benefits contemplated by this Agreement; that during the Term of this Agreement, it will not enter into any agreement or make any commitments which would interfere with the grant of rights hereunder or its performance of any of the terms and provisions hereto; and that it will not, nor will it, sell, assign, lease, license or in any other way dispose of or encumber the rights granted to Publisher hereunder.

(d) Operation. Developer represents and warrants to Publisher that the gold master for the Product will operate in accordance with the applicable design specifications and with commonly accepted standards for operation of such product, will be free from any Bugs, significant programming errors or anomalies, and will operate and run in a reasonable and efficient business manner as described in the user and system configuration documentation which fully explains the operation and design of the Product.

13. Indemnity. The parties do hereby agree that the following indemnity provisions apply to this agreement:

(a) Developer does hereby indemnify, save and hold harmless Publisher and Publisher's subsidiaries, affiliates, licensees, assigns, officers and employees from any and all loss and damage (including, without limitation, fees and disbursements of counsel incurred by Publisher in any action or proceeding between Developer and Publisher or between Publisher and any third party or otherwise) arising out of or in connection with any claim by any third party based on facts or alleged facts inconsistent with any of the warranties, representations or agreements made by Developer under this Agreement or any breach of, or act by Developer which is inconsistent with, any of the warranties, representations or agreements made by Developer under this Agreement, and agrees to reimburse Publisher on demand for any payment made or loss suffered with respect to any claim or act to which the foregoing indemnity applies. In the case of a claim by a third party, Publisher shall give Developer prompt written notice of any such claim and shall be entitled to conduct the defense or settlement thereof. Publisher shall give Developer reasonable progress reports and Developer shall give Publisher reasonable assistance in defending or settling any such claim.

(b) In the event that, through the breach of any of Developer's representations and warranties or the failure of Developer to perform any of its obligations herein, distribution of the Product is, or is reasonably likely, to be adjudged infringing or otherwise unlawful or violate of any right of any third party ("Infringing Product"), Developer shall, at its sole cost and expense, either (i) promptly modify the Product so that Publisher's distribution as permitted hereunder ceases to be infringing or wrongful, or (ii) promptly procure for Publisher the right to continue distributing the Product. In the case of an Infringing Product (a) Developer shall promptly reimburse Publisher for all costs incurred in replacing copies of the Product or for all refunds given, as well as all reasonable costs of removing all infringing copies of the Product from the channels of distribution; (b) Publisher shall be entitled to offset any royalty or other payments due to Developer under this Agreement (or any other agreement) against any sums owed by Developer to Publisher under clause (a); and (c) following the commencement of any litigation covered by this Section in which Publisher is named as a defendant, Publisher shall be entitled to withhold royalty payments and all other sums payable to Developer hereunder pending the outcome of such litigation.

(c) Publisher does hereby indemnify, save and hold harmless Developer and Developer's subsidiaries, affiliates, licensees, assigns, officers and employees from any and all loss and damage (including, without limitation, fees and disbursements of counsel incurred by Developer in any action or proceeding between Publisher and Developer or between Developer and any third party or otherwise) arising out of or in connection with any claim by any third party or any breach of, or act by Publisher which is inconsistent with, any of the warranties, representations or agreements made by Publisher in this Agreement, and agrees to reimburse Developer on demand for any payment made or loss suffered with respect to any claim or act to which the foregoing indemnity applies.

14. Term And Termination. The parties hereby agree to the following provisions shall govern the duration of this agreement:

(a) Term. This Agreement shall become effective on the date set forth above and shall continue until the seventh anniversary of the date of this agreement or the date terminated as set forth in this Agreement.

(b) Breach. The following provisions shall apply with respect to breaches of this agreement:

(i) In the event of a material breach of this Agreement by Developer, Publisher shall have the right to suspend Publisher's obligations to make payments to Developer and/or offset any royalties or other payments due to Developer under this Agreement against any sums owed by Developer to Publisher under this Agreement until Developer has cured such breach. If such breach is not cured within thirty (30) days of written notice (the "Cure Period") Publisher shall have the right to terminate this Agreement. Nothing contained herein shall in any way limit Publisher's other rights and remedies under this Agreement at law or equity.

(ii) In the event of termination by Publisher prior to the release of the Product for a material breach by Developer, Publisher shall have the right to obtain a refund of all unrecouped advances and other reimbursable sums paid by Publisher to Developer hereunder. All rights granted hereunder in and to the Product shall remain with Publisher until the full repayment of the unrecouped advances by Developer to Publisher. Thereafter, the license granted pursuant to Section 1 hereof shall revert to Developer and neither Publisher nor Developer shall have any further obligation to the other hereunder.

(iii) In the event of termination of this Agreement for a material breach by Publisher, all of Publisher's rights to market and distribute the Product shall cease and all rights granted to Publisher shall revert to Developer.

(c) Delivery. In the event that Developer fails to deliver the Product by the Gold Master Delivery Date, Publisher may make other arrangements, including but not limited to engaging third party consultants, to develop the Product. All costs associated therewith shall be fully recoupable at any time from any and all royalties and other sums accruing to Developer under this Agreement. Upon notice by Publisher of its intention to develop the Product in the manner aforesaid, Developer shall deliver to Publisher all materials reasonably requested or required by Publisher to do so, including, but not limited to, the source code and the development tools to be used solely in connection with exploiting the Product, subject to Publisher's continuing obligation to account for royalties.

(d) Events on Termination. After the Product has been released by Publisher and the advance has been paid, notwithstanding termination of this Agreement for any reason whatsoever, Publisher shall have the exclusive continuing right to market and distribute the Product for a period of six (6) months following termination, subject to Publisher's obligation to account for royalties.

15. General Provisions. The parties hereby agree to the following general provisions of this agreement:

(a) **Agency:** Publisher acknowledges that Developer has appointed _____ ("Publisher's Agent"), as its true and lawful agent and attorney-in-fact for purposes of this Agreement. Developer agrees that payments made hereunder to Publisher's Agent, if any, will be automatically deemed payments made directly to Developer in discharge of Publisher's obligations hereunder, and Developer hereby indemnifies Publisher to the same extent as set forth above in connection with any claim arising out to any payment made to Publisher's Agent. Publisher shall make all payments that become due to Developer to Publisher's Agent in accordance with written instructions from Publisher's Agent.

(b) **Assignment.** Neither party shall have the right to assign this Agreement or any of its rights or obligations hereunder without the prior written consent of the other party which consent shall not be unreasonably withheld.

(c) **Notices.** All notices and other items from one party to the other hereunder will, unless herein indicated to the contrary, be sent by email with a copy by mail addressed as follows:

To Developer: _____

To Publisher: _____

(Notices sent by email, to the email address of the party to be served and shall be deemed complete at the time of receipt.)

(d) **Governing Law.** This Agreement shall be construed under the internal laws of the State of _____ applicable to agreements to be performed wholly therein, and both parties agree that _____ courts and the American Arbitration Association in _____ shall have jurisdiction over this Agreement and any controversies arising out of this Agreement shall be brought by the parties to the Supreme Court of the State of _____ or to the United States District Court for _____ or to the appropriate arbitration tribunal in _____ and they hereby grant exclusive jurisdiction to such court(s) and to any appellate courts having jurisdiction over appeals from such court(s).

(e) **Survival.** The representations, warranties, indemnification, termination and confidentiality obligations set forth in this Agreement shall survive the termination of this Agreement by either party for any reason.

(f) **Amendments.** No supplement, modification, amendment, waiver, termination or discharge of this Agreement shall be binding, unless executed in writing by a duly authorized representative of each party to this Agreement.

(g) **Entire Agreement.** This Agreement constitutes the complete and entire agreement of the parties and supersedes all previous communications, oral or written, and all other communications between them relating to the subject matter hereof.

(h) **Force Majeure.** No party shall be responsible for delays or failure of performance resulting from acts beyond the reasonable control of such party, including, acts of God, war, power failures, floods, earthquakes and other natural disasters.

(i) **Counterparts.** This Agreement may be executed in one or more counterparts, each of which when taken together, shall be deemed to constitute one and the same instrument

(j) **Electronic Signatures.** Electronic signatures on this Agreement shall be deemed originals for all purposes.

(k) **Severability.** If any provision of this Agreement shall be adjudicated to be invalid or unenforceable, it shall be construed by limiting and reducing it so as to be enforceable or eliminating it, without invalidating the remaining provisions of this Agreement.

IN WITNESS WHEREOF, the parties have executed this Agreement on the date specified below.

_____

Publisher

_____

Developer

Date: _____

Part II

Intellectual Property Protection

Chapter Four

Rights of Publicity

Stars sell products. Your gut reaction may be that any time a star's image is used without his or her permission—in a videogame or otherwise—the star should be paid. After all, the star has invested time, and perhaps money, in cultivating a valuable property right in his or her image, right? But it's not that simple.

Let's run a gauntlet of possibilities regarding golfer Tiger Woods (assume in each case below Tiger has not given his permission for the use of his likeness):

- Let's start with a producer of a golf videogame who uses Tiger's image on the box, dressed in his famous "Sunday" red shirt and black pants with the Augusta National clubhouse (where the Masters is played) in the background, next to a quote, "This is the most realistic video golf game I have ever used." Let's say the Producer also distributes ancillary merchandise about the game, like Tiger bobbleheads clutching a miniaturized version of the game.

- Next let's imagine that Sony produces a "Professional" video golf game for the PS4 with many avatars with capabilities based on the statistics and characteristics of assorted professional golfers, allowing the player to match the golfers head to head on different programmed courses. One of the avatars is "built" with all the statistical attributes of Tiger's game, and is dressed in a red shirt and black pants, but is unnamed and only generically looks like him.

- Assume John Grisham decides that a plot point in his next book of fiction is an encounter between his lead character and Tiger Woods the same day that Tiger wins the Masters. Mr. Grisham describes Tiger dressed in red and black and his character meets with Tiger outside the Augusta National clubhouse.

- Now let's say that *Sports Illustrated* publishes an article about the current state of Tiger's golf game and puts a picture of him, dressed in red shirt and black pants taken at the 1997 Masters (which he won by 12 strokes), on the cover. Suppose also that *SI* takes out an ad in *USA Today*, with that same picture of Tiger over text that says, "Buy this week's SI and find out about the *real* Tiger Woods today."

- Next, suppose someone publishes an unauthorized biography of Tiger, using the 1997 Masters picture of Tiger on the cover.

- Now let's assume that a portrait artist produces a painting based on the 1997 Masters picture, with the Augusta National clubhouse in the background, along with images of other past Master's champions such as Jack Nicklaus and Arnold Palmer. The painter sells lithographs, T-shirts, and computer "wallpaper" with that image.

- Finally, assume that another artist takes the same picture and paints it in different colors and contrasts, similar to the famous Andy Warhol pictures of Marilyn Monroe and Campbell's soup cans.

In each case, someone else is trying to make money off of Tiger's image without his permission. But the law looks at these situations differently, and lets Tiger successfully sue to enforce his publicity rights in some circumstances, but not in others. Figuring out the tests, policies, and claims involved is the challenge of this Chapter.

§ 4.10 Rights of Publicity: A Primer

The traditional view is the right of publicity derives from the right of privacy that was the focus of what is perhaps the most famous law review article of all time, Samuel D. Warren & Louis D. Brandeis, *The Right to Privacy*, 4 Harv. L. Rev 193 (1890). The gist of the article was its defense of what the authors characterized as the constitutional and common law right "to be left alone," *id.* at 193.[1] After joining the United States Supreme Court, Justice Brandeis characterized the right to be left alone as "the most comprehensive of rights and the right most valued by civilized men." *Olmstead v. United States,* 277 U.S. 438, 478 (1928) (Brandeis, J. dissenting). However, the article was not all about the right to be free from a gossiping press or otherwise to be left alone. Warren and Brandeis presciently addressed two limitations to that right which have framed privacy arguments ever since: (1) "The right of privacy does not prohibit any publication of matter which is of public or general interest,"[2] and (2) "The right to privacy ceases upon the publication of the facts by the individual, or with his consent."[3]

While the latter quote is suggestive of a substantive right to control one's image, it was left to others to conjure a protectable and monetized right of *publicity* from the general right of *privacy*. That is, to recognize that some appropriation of likeness is not so much a dignitary harm resulting from a disturbance to an individual's privacy, but rather an economic harm to the property interest of that individual in his or her own image. In other words, he or she may choose *not* to be left alone in order to take advantage of his or her image or likeness for public or commercial use.

The first to conjure such a right of publicity was probably the New York legislature in 1903,[4] when it enacted Section 51 of the N.Y.S., providing:

> Any person whose name, portrait, picture or voice is used within this state for advertising purposes or for the purposes of trade without the written consent first obtained as above provided may maintain an equitable action in the supreme court of this state against the person, firm or corporation so using his name, portrait, picture or voice, to prevent and restrain the use thereof; and may also sue and recover damages for any injuries sustained by reason of such use and if

---

1. Judge Thomas Cooley, then of the Michigan Supreme Court, was probably the first to use the phrase, and the first champion of "the right to be left alone" in Thomas M. Cooley, A Treatise on the Law of Torts or Wrongs which Arise Independently of Contract 193 (1878).

2. Warren & Brandeis at 195–96.

3. *Id.* at 218.

4. Some say that the California legislature was first, when it enacted Cal. Penal Code § 258 in 1899 which placed criminal restrictions on the publication of portraits or caricatures of individuals. However, this provision was repealed in 1915 and generally the New York statute is looked to as the first to codify a right of publicity.

the defendant shall have knowingly used such person's name, portrait, picture or voice in such manner as is forbidden or declared to be unlawful ...

While the *concept* of a right to publicity may have been encapsulated in the statute, it was left to the case law to coin the *phrase* "right of publicity" in connection with the economic protection of a celebrity's identity. This was accomplished by Judge Jerome Frank in *Haelan Labs v. Topps Chewing Gum, Inc.*, 202 F.2d 866 (2d Cir. 1953). There, professional baseball players had granted Haelan Labs the exclusive rights to use their images on baseball cards, then packaged with, and used as inducements to buy, the company's bubble gum. The defendant, Topps, also sold bubble gum with baseball cards with the players' images on them, but had not secured the rights from the players. Haelan sued to protect its exclusive image rights granted via contracts with the players. In holding for Haelan, the court stated there was a right to control one's image and:

> This right might be called a "right of publicity." For it is common knowledge that many prominent persons (especially actors and ball-players), far from having their feelings bruised through public exposure of their likenesses, would feel sorely deprived if they no longer received money for authorizing advertisements, popularizing their countenances, displayed in newspapers, magazines, busses, trains and subways. This right of publicity would usually yield them no money unless it could be made the subject of an exclusive grant which barred any other advertiser from using their pictures. We think the New York decisions [and statutes] recognize such a right.

Id. at 868. As can be seen, the decision was largely based on the fact that the players received money in return for using their likenesses in Haelan's "advertising" and merchandizing a product, a point which will be recurring throughout the Chapter.

The next major step in recognizing a right of publicity was Dean Prosser's famous article, *Privacy*, published in 1960,[5] in which he broke the right of privacy into four separate torts, one of which was, "appropriation, for the defendant's advantage of the plaintiff's name and likeness."[6] The "misappropriation" tort was incorporated into the Restatement (Second) of Torts §§ 652A and 652C (1977),[7] again in the Restatement (Third) of Unfair Competition § 46 (1977)[8] and eventually in state common law and statutes.[9]

An accurate summary of the now generally recognized differences between privacy claims and publicity claims was provided by Krista Correa as follows:

> The privacy-based action is designed for individuals who have not placed themselves in the public eye. It shields such people from the embarrassment of having their faces plastered on billboards and cereal boxes without their permission. The interests protected are dignity and peace of mind, and damages are measured in terms of emotional distress. By contrast, a right of publicity action is designed

---

5. William L. Prosser, *Privacy*, 48 Calif. L. Rev. 383 (1960).

6. *Id.* at 401.

7. Section 652A provides, "(1) One who invades the right of privacy of another is subject to liability for the resulting harm to the interests of the other. (2) The right of privacy is invaded by ... (b) appropriation of the other's name or likeness, as stated in § 652C ..."
Section 652C provides, "One who appropriates to his own use or benefit the name or likeness of another is subject to liability to the other for invasion of his privacy."

8. Section 46 provides, "One who appropriates the commercial value of a person's identity by using without consent the person's name, likeness, or other indicia of identity for purposes of trade is subject to liability ..."

9. The other three torts identified by Dean Prosser were: (1) Intrusion; (2) Public disclosure of private facts; and (3) False Light. *Prosser, supra*, 48 Calif. L. Rev. at 389.

for individuals who have placed themselves in the public eye. It secured for them the exclusive right to exploit the commercial value that attaches to their identities by virtue of their celebrity. The right to publicity protects that value as property, and infringement is a commercial rather than a personal tort. Damages stem not from embarrassment but from the unauthorized use of the plaintiff's property.[10]

Today the right of publicity is alive and well, but perhaps not even yet universally recognized in the United States. According to a leading author in the field, as of 2012 only thirty-one states have explicitly recognized a right of publicity, some by statute only, some by case law, and some by both.[11] Moreover, its enforcement is uneven throughout the country. This is, in part, because its enforcement is largely state-based, as opposed to federally-enforced, and the states have different common law or statutory tests as to when the right is violated.

In addition to a "right of publicity" action, the other major source for protection of publicity rights[12] asserted by some plaintiffs is Section 43(a) of the Lanham Act, 11 U.S.C. § 1125 (2011), which grants a private right of action against the unauthorized use of an individual's name, "on or in connection with any goods or services" when it is likely to cause confusion as to the, "affiliation connection, or association" between the parties as to the "sponsorship" or "approval" of the individual whose named is used. We deal with Lanham Act claims in more detail in the *White* and *Brown* cases and accompanying notes in § 4.20 *infra.*, and in Chapter 8.

Before jumping into the cases, a huge limitation on the ability of even someone who is quite famous to limit the appropriation of his or her likeness must be addressed. This limitation is based on freedom of expression principles derived from the first amendment of the federal constitution, like provisions in state constitutions, and the common law. The cases articulate this limitation by stating that there is a First Amendment "defense" or "privilege" that trumps tort claims based on the right of publicity. This is one aspect of the "public or general interest" limitation of Warren and Brandeis. The freedom of expression encompassed by this principle can be split into three different parts. One part provides that no privacy claim can be successfully asserted when the celebrity's image or identity is related to the communication of ideas in the normal course of business of a constitutionally protected medium of expression. The drafters of the Restatement (Third) of Unfair Competition explain the concept as follows:

> The right of publicity as recognized by statute and common law is fundamentally constrained by the public and constitutional interest in freedom of expression. The use of a person's identity primarily for the purpose of communicating information or expressing ideas is not generally actionable as a violation of the person's right of publicity. The scope of the activities embraced within this

---

10. Krista Correa, *All Your Face Belong to Us: Prohibiting Celebrity Images in Hyper-Realistic Video Games*, 34 HASTINGS. COMM. & ENT. L.J. 93, 101 (2011), citing *Jim Henson Prods., Inc. v. John T. Brady & Assocs., Inc.*, 867 F. Supp. 175, 188 (S.D.N.Y. 1994). *See also* the definition of publicity rights provided by Professor McCarthy who described the right as, "[T[he inherent right of every human to control the commercial use of his or her identity." 1 J. Thomas McCarthy, THE RIGHTS OF PUBLICITY AND PRIVACY § 1-3 (2d ed. 2012).

11. *Id.* at § 6-3. Probably the best source for state variances on the rights of publicity is Professor Jennifer Rothman's blog, *Rothman's Roadmap to the Right of Publicity*, www.rightofpublicityroadmap.com

12. Occasionally plaintiffs sue to enforce under state unfair competition laws or, in unusual factual situations, even copyright, *see, e.g., Zacchini v. Scripps-Howard Broad. Co.*, 433 U.S. 562 (1977). However, the major claims made by plaintiffs are based on state statutory and common law bases, and the Lanham Act.

limitation on the right of publicity has been broadly construed. Thus, the use of a person's name or likeness in news reporting, whether in newspapers, magazines, or broadcast news, does not infringe the right of publicity. The interest in freedom of expression also extends to use in entertainment and other creative works, including both fiction and nonfiction. The use of a celebrity's name or photograph as part of an article published in a fan magazine or in a feature story broadcast on an entertainment program, for example, will not infringe the celebrity's right of publicity. Similarly, the right of publicity is not infringed by the dissemination of an unauthorized print or broadcast biography. *Use of another's identity in a novel, play, or motion picture is also not ordinarily an infringement.* The fact that the publisher or other user seeks or is successful in obtaining a commercial advantage from an otherwise permitted use of another's identity does not render the appropriation actionable.[13]

The second part of the freedom of expression limitations on privacy actions is related to the first, but is based on parody. That is, if the expression of the celebrity's identity is made in the course of a protected parody, then no right of misappropriation of identity can be successfully alleged. The most famous example of this First Amendment defense is found in *Hustler Magazine v. Falwell*, 485 U.S. 46 (1988). There, the famous minister Jerry Falwell was the subject of a parody in Hustler Magazine, which insinuated that Mr. Falwell's first sexual encounter was with his mother in an outhouse. In ruling that parody is protected from tort claims, the Court stated:

> But in the world of debate about public affairs, many things done with motives that are less than admirable are protected by the First Amendment. In *Garrison v. Louisiana*, 379 U.S. 64 (1964), we held that even when a speaker or writer is motivated by hatred or ill will his expression was protected by the First Amendment. Thus while such a bad motive may be deemed controlling for purposes of tort liability in other areas of the law, we think the First Amendment prohibits such a result in the area of public debate about public figures.

> Were we to hold otherwise, there can be little doubt that political cartoonists and satirists would be subjected to damages awards without any showing that their work falsely defamed its subject. Webster's defines a caricature as "the deliberately distorted picturing or imitating of a person, literary style, etc. by exaggerating features or mannerisms for satirical effect." Webster's New Unabridged Twentieth Century Dictionary of the English Language 275 (2d ed. 1979). The appeal of the political cartoon or caricature is often based on exploitation of unfortunate physical traits or politically embarrassing events—an exploitation often calculated to injure the feelings of the subject of the portrayal.

Id. at 53–54.

The third limitation on privacy claims traces back to Warren and Brandeis, and holds that the use of a celebrity's image that is a matter of "public concern" is immune from a privacy claim from the individual. *See, e.g.,* Restatement (Third) Unfair Competition §§ 47–49 (1995).

The current state of the law suggests that a right of publicity claim ends up falling somewhere along a continuum that can be divided into three parts: (1) at one end is the use of a celebrity's image as part of the advertising or merchandising of a product, like putting Tiger's image on the box of a golf-related game indicating that he endorses it or

---

13. Restatement (Third) Unfair Competition § 47, Cmt. c (1995).

making a bobblehead of Tiger without his permission; (2) at the other end is use of the individual's image in a traditionally protected medium, such as in an article about, and picture of, Tiger mentioned in *Sports Illustrated* article about him; and (3) in the middle is the use of celebrity identity in a game, where the use is relevant to the game, but is neither used as an endorsement or advertisement of the game nor is part of a traditionally constitutionally protected medium such as a newspaper article or biography. The first scenario is actionable; the second is not. The cases in this chapter largely fall within the third category, where the tensions posed by the antagonistic pulls of privacy and protected expression lead different courts to form different opinions as to the viability of a celebrity's publicity claim.

§ 4.20 Rights of Publicity: Use of a Celebrity's Image Without the Celebrity's Permission

Our first case deals with the assertion of a right of publicity based on an appropriation for a non-videogame advertisement by a videogame-like avatar. It is a good example of all the elements of privacy claims as discussed above.

White v. Samsung Electronics America, Inc.

United States Court of Appeals, Ninth Circuit, 1992
971 F.2d 1395

GOODWIN, Senior Circuit Judge:

This case involves a promotional "fame and fortune" dispute. In running a particular advertisement without Vanna White's permission, defendants Samsung Electronics America, Inc. (Samsung) and David Deutsch Associates, Inc. (Deutsch) attempted to capitalize on White's fame to enhance their fortune. White sued, alleging infringement of various intellectual property rights, but the district court granted summary judgment in favor of the defendants. We affirm in part, reverse in part, and remand.

Plaintiff Vanna White is the hostess of "Wheel of Fortune," one of the most popular game shows in television history. An estimated forty million people watch the program daily. Capitalizing on the fame which her participation in the show has bestowed on her, White markets her identity to various advertisers. The dispute in this case arose out of a series of advertisements prepared for Samsung by Deutsch. The series ran in at least half a dozen publications with widespread, and in some cases national, circulation. Each of the advertisements in the series followed the same theme. Each depicted a current item from popular culture and a Samsung electronic product. Each was set in the twenty-first century and conveyed the message that the Samsung product would still be in use by that time. By hypothesizing outrageous future outcomes for the cultural items, the ads created humorous effects.

The advertisement which prompted the current dispute was for Samsung video-cassette recorders (VCRs). The ad depicted a robot, dressed in a wig, gown, and jewelry which Deutsch consciously selected to resemble White's hair and dress. The robot was posed next to a game board which is instantly recognizable as the Wheel of Fortune game show set, in a stance for which White is famous. The caption of the ad read: "Longest-running game show. 2012 A.D." Defendants referred to the ad as the "Vanna White" ad. Unlike the other celebrities used in the campaign, White neither consented to the ads nor was she paid.

Following the circulation of the robot ad, White sued Samsung and Deutsch in federal district court under: (1) California Civil Code § 3344; (2) the California common law right of publicity; and (3) § 43(a) of the Lanham Act, 15 U.S.C. § 1125(a). The district court granted summary judgment against White on each of her claims. White now appeals.

I. Section 3344

White first argues that the district court erred in rejecting her claim under Section 3344. Section 3344(a) provides, in pertinent part, that "[a]ny person who knowingly uses another's name, voice, signature, photograph, or likeness, in any manner, ... for purposes of advertising or selling, ... without such person's prior consent ... shall be liable for any damages sustained by the person or persons injured as a result thereof."

White argues that the Samsung advertisement used her "likeness" in contravention of section 3344. In this case, Samsung and Deutsch used a robot with mechanical features, and not, for example, a manikin molded to White's precise features. Without deciding for all purposes when a caricature or impressionistic resemblance might become a "likeness," we agree with the district court that the robot at issue here was not White's "likeness" within the meaning of section 3344. Accordingly, we affirm the court's dismissal of White's section 3344 claim.

II. Right of Publicity

White next argues that the district court erred in granting summary judgment to defendants on White's common law right of publicity claim. In *Eastwood v. Superior Court*, 149 Cal. App. 3d 409 (1983), the California court of appeal stated that the common law right of publicity cause of action "may be pleaded by alleging (1) the defendant's use of the plaintiff's identity; (2) the appropriation of plaintiff's name or likeness to defendant's advantage, commercially or otherwise; (3) lack of consent; and (4) resulting injury." *Id.* at 417. The district court dismissed White's claim for failure to satisfy Eastwood's second prong, reasoning that defendants had not appropriated White's "name or likeness" with their robot ad. We agree that the robot ad did not make use of White's name or likeness. However, the common law right of publicity is not so confined.

The *Eastwood* court did not hold that the right of publicity cause of action could be pleaded only by alleging an appropriation of name or likeness. *Eastwood* involved an unauthorized use of photographs of Clint Eastwood and of his name. Accordingly, the *Eastwood* court had no occasion to consider the extent beyond the use of name or likeness to which the right of publicity reaches. That court held only that the right of publicity cause of action "may be" pleaded by alleging, *inter alia*, appropriation of name or likeness, not that the action may be pleaded only in those terms.

The "name or likeness" formulation referred to in *Eastwood* originated not as an element of the right of publicity cause of action, but as a description of the types of cases in which the cause of action had been recognized. The source of this formulation is Prosser, *Privacy*, 48 Cal. L. Rev. 383, 401–07 (1960), one of the earliest and most enduring articulations of the common law right of publicity cause of action. In looking at the case law to that point, Prosser recognized that right of publicity cases involved one of two basic factual scenarios: name appropriation, and picture or other likeness appropriation.

Even though Prosser focused on appropriations of name or likeness in discussing the right of publicity, he noted that "[i]t is not impossible that there might be appropriation of the plaintiff's identity, as by impersonation, without the use of either his name or his likeness, and that this would be an invasion of his right of privacy." At the time Prosser wrote, he noted however, that "[n]o such case appears to have arisen."

Since Prosser's early formulation, the case law has borne out his insight that the right of publicity is not limited to the appropriation of name or likeness. In *Motschenbacher v. R.J. Reynolds Tobacco Co.*, 498 F.2d 821 (9th Cir. 1974), the defendant had used a photograph of the plaintiff's racecar in a television commercial. Although the plaintiff appeared driving the car in the photograph, his features were not visible. Even though the defendant had not appropriated the plaintiff's name or likeness, this court held that plaintiff's California right of publicity claim should reach the jury.

In *Midler* [*v. Ford Motor Co.*, 849 F.2d 460 (9th Cir. 1988)], this court held that, even though the defendants had not used [singer Bette] Midler's name or likeness, Midler had stated a claim for violation of her California common law right of publicity because "the defendants … for their own profit in selling their product did appropriate part of her identity" by using a Midler sound-alike.

In *Carson v. Here's Johnny Portable Toilets, Inc.*, 698 F.2d 831 (6th Cir. 1983), the defendant had marketed portable toilets under the brand name "Here's Johnny" — Johnny Carson's signature "Tonight Show" introduction — without Carson's permission. The district court had dismissed Carson's Michigan common law right of publicity claim because the defendants had not used Carson's "name or likeness." In reversing the district court, the sixth circuit found "the district court's conception of the right of publicity … too narrow" and held that the right was implicated because the defendant had appropriated Carson's identity by using, inter alia, the phrase "Here's Johnny."

These cases teach not only that the common law right of publicity reaches means of appropriation other than name or likeness, but that the specific means of appropriation are relevant only for determining whether the defendant has in fact appropriated the plaintiff's identity. The right of publicity does not require that appropriations of identity be accomplished through particular means to be actionable. It is noteworthy that the *Midler* and *Carson* defendants not only avoided using the plaintiff's name or likeness, but they also avoided appropriating the celebrity's voice, signature, and photograph. The photograph in *Motschenbacher* did include the plaintiff, but because the plaintiff was not visible the driver could have been an actor or dummy and the analysis in the case would have been the same.

Although the defendants in these cases avoided the most obvious means of appropriating the plaintiffs' identities, each of their actions directly implicated the commercial interests which the right of publicity is designed to protect. As the *Carson* court explained: [t]he right of publicity has developed to protect the commercial interest of celebrities in their identities. The theory of the right is that a celebrity's identity can be valuable in the promotion of products, and the celebrity has an interest that may be protected from the unauthorized commercial exploitation of that identity.… If the celebrity's identity is commercially exploited, there has been an invasion of his right whether or not his "name or likeness" is used. *Carson*, 698 F.2d at 835. It is not important how the defendant has appropriated the plaintiff's identity, but whether the defendant has done so. *Motschenbacher*, *Midler*, and *Carson* teach the impossibility of treating the right of publicity as guarding only against a laundry list of specific means of appropriating identity. A rule which says that the right of publicity can be infringed only through the use of nine different methods of appropriating identity merely challenges the clever advertising strategist to come up with the tenth.

Viewed separately, the individual aspects of the advertisement in the present case say little. Viewed together, they leave little doubt about the celebrity the ad is meant to depict.

The female-shaped robot is wearing a long gown, blond wig, and large jewelry. Vanna White dresses exactly like this at times, but so do many other women. The robot is in the process of turning a block letter on a game-board. Vanna White dresses like this while turning letters on a game-board but perhaps similarly attired Scrabble-playing women do this as well. The robot is standing on what looks to be the Wheel of Fortune game show set. Vanna White dresses like this, turns letters, and does this on the Wheel of Fortune game show. She is the only one. Indeed, defendants themselves referred to their ad as the "Vanna White" ad. We are not surprised.

Television and other media create marketable celebrity identity value. Considerable energy and ingenuity are expended by those who have achieved celebrity value to exploit it for profit. The law protects the celebrity's sole right to exploit this value whether the celebrity has achieved her fame out of rare ability, dumb luck, or a combination thereof. We decline Samsung and Deutch's invitation to permit the evisceration of the common law right of publicity through means as facile as those in this case. Because White has alleged facts showing that Samsung and Deutsch had appropriated her identity, the district court erred by rejecting, on summary judgment, White's common law right of publicity claim.

III. The Lanham Act

White's final argument is that the district court erred in denying her claim under § 43(a) of the Lanham Act, 15 U.S.C. § 1125(a). The version of section 43(a) applicable to this case provides, in pertinent part, that "[a]ny person who shall ... use, in connection with any goods or services ... any false description or representation ... shall be liable to a civil action ... by any person who believes that he is or is likely to be damaged by the use of any such false description or designation." 15 U.S.C. § 1125(a).

To prevail on her Lanham Act claim, White is required to show that in running the robot ad, Samsung and Deutsch created a likelihood of confusion over whether White was endorsing Samsung's VCRs, *Allen v. National Video, Inc.*, 610 F. Supp. 612 (D.C.N.Y. 1985).

[W]e will look for guidance to the 8-factor test enunciated in *AMF, Inc. v. Sleekcraft Boats*, 599 F.2d 341 (9th Cir. 1979). According to *AMF*, factors relevant to a likelihood of confusion include: (1) strength of the plaintiff's mark; (2) relatedness of the goods; (3) similarity of the marks; (4) evidence of actual confusion; (5) marketing channels used; (6) likely degree of purchaser care; (7) defendant's intent in selecting the mark; and (8) likelihood of expansion of the product lines.

We turn now to consider White's claim in light of each factor. In cases involving confusion over endorsement by a celebrity plaintiff, "mark" means the celebrity's persona. The "strength" of the mark refers to the level of recognition the celebrity enjoys among members of society. If Vanna White is unknown to the segment of the public at whom Samsung's robot ad was directed, then that segment could not be confused as to whether she was endorsing Samsung VCRs. Conversely, if White is well-known, this would allow the possibility of a likelihood of confusion. For the purposes of the *Sleekcraft* test, White's "mark," or celebrity identity, is strong.

In cases concerning confusion over celebrity endorsement, the plaintiff's "goods" concern the reasons for or source of the plaintiff's fame. Because White's fame is based on her televised performances, her "goods" are closely related to Samsung's VCRs. Indeed, the ad itself reinforced the relationship by informing its readers that they would be taping the "longest-running game show" on Samsung's VCRs well into the future.

The third factor, "similarity of the marks," both supports and contradicts a finding of likelihood of confusion. On the one hand, all of the aspects of the robot ad identify White;

on the other, the figure is quite clearly a robot, not a human. This ambiguity means that we must look to the other factors for resolution.

The fourth factor does not favor White's claim because she has presented no evidence of actual confusion. Fifth, however, White has appeared in the same stance as the robot from the ad in numerous magazines, including the covers of some. Magazines were used as the marketing channels for the robot ad. This factor cuts toward a likelihood of confusion.

Sixth, consumers are not likely to be particularly careful in determining who endorses VCRs, making confusion as to their endorsement more likely.

Concerning the seventh factor, "defendant's intent," the district court found that, in running the robot ad, the defendants had intended a spoof of the "Wheel of Fortune." The relevant question is whether the defendants "intended to profit by confusing consumers" concerning the endorsement of Samsung. We do not disagree that defendants intended to spoof Vanna White and "Wheel of Fortune." That does not preclude, however, the possibility that defendants also intended to confuse consumers regarding endorsement. The robot ad was one of a series of ads run by defendants which followed the same theme.

Finally, the eighth factor, "likelihood of expansion of the product lines," does not appear apposite to a celebrity endorsement case such as this. Application of the *Sleekcraft* factors to this case indicates that the district court erred in rejecting White's Lanham Act claim at the summary judgment stage. White has raised a genuine issue of material fact concerning a likelihood of confusion as to her endorsement. Whether White's Lanham Act claim should succeed is a matter for the jury.

IV. The Parody Defense

In defense, defendants cite a number of cases for the proposition that their robot ad constituted protected speech. *Falwell*, involved [a] parody of [an] advertisement run for the purpose of poking fun at Jerry Falwell. This case involves a true advertisement run for the purpose of selling Samsung VCRs. The ad's spoof of Vanna White and Wheel of Fortune is subservient and only tangentially related to the ad's primary message: "buy Samsung VCRs." Defendants' parody arguments are better addressed to non-commercial parodies. The difference between a "parody" and a "knock-off" is the difference between fun and profit.

[E]ven if some forms of expressive activity, such as parody, do rely on identity evocation, the first amendment hurdle will bar most right of publicity actions against those activities. *Cf. Falwell*, In the case of commercial advertising, however, the First Amendment hurdle is not so high. *Central Hudson Gas & Electric Corp. v. Public Service Comm'n of New York*, 447 U.S. 557, 566 (1980). Realizing this, Samsung attempts to elevate its ad above the status of garden-variety commercial speech by pointing to the ad's parody of Vanna White. Samsung's argument is unavailing. Unless the first amendment bars all right of publicity actions—and it does not, *see Zacchini v. Scripps-Howard Broadcasting Co.*, 433 U.S. 562 (1977)—then it does not bar this case.

ALARCON, Circuit Judge, concurring in part, DISSENTING in part:

I must dissent from the majority's holding on Vanna White's right to publicity claim. The district court found that, since the commercial advertisement did not show a "likeness" of Vanna White, Samsung did not improperly use the plaintiff's identity. The majority asserts that the use of a likeness is not required under California common law. According to the majority, recovery is authorized if there is an appropriation of one's "identity." I cannot find any holding of a California court that supports this conclusion. Furthermore, the record does not support the majority's finding that Vanna White's "identity" was appropriated.

All of the California cases that my research has disclosed hold that a cause of action for appropriation of the right to publicity requires proof of the appropriation of a name or likeness. *See, e.g., Lugosi v. Universal Pictures*, 25 Cal.3d 813 (1979) ("The so-called right of publicity means in essence that the reaction of the public to name and likeness ... endows the name and likeness of the person involved with commercially exploitable opportunities.")

Notwithstanding the fact that California case law clearly limits the test of the right to publicity to name and likeness, the majority concludes that "the common law right of publicity is not so confined." The interest of the California Legislature as expressed in California Civil Code section 3344 appears to preclude the result reached by the majority. The original section 3344 protected only name or likeness. In 1984, ten years after our decision in *Motschenbacher v. R.J. Reynolds Tobacco Company*, 498 F.2d 821 (9th Cir. 1974) and 24 years after Prosser speculated about the future development of the law of the right of publicity, the California legislature amended the statute. California law now makes the use of someone's voice or signature, as well as name or likeness, actionable. Cal. Civ. Code sec. 2233(a) (Deering 1991 Supp.). Thus, California, after our decision in *Motschenbacher* specifically contemplated protection for interests other than name or likeness, but did not include a cause of action for appropriation of another person's identity.

In each of the federal cases relied upon by the majority, the advertisement affirmatively represented that the person depicted therein was the plaintiff. In this case, it is clear that a metal robot and not the plaintiff, Vanna White, is depicted in the commercial advertisement. The record does not show an appropriation of Vanna White's identity.

In *Motschenbacher*, a picture of a well-known race driver's car, including its unique markings, was used in an advertisement. *Id.* at 822. Although the driver could be seen in the car, his features were not visible. *Id.* The distinctive markings on the car were the only information shown in the ad regarding the identity of the driver. These distinctive markings compelled the inference that Motschenbacher was the person sitting in the racing car.

In *Midler v. Ford Motor Co.*, 849 F.2d 460 (9th Cir. 1988), a singer who had been instructed to sound as much like Bette Midler as possible, sang a song in a radio commercial made famous by Bette Midler. *Id.* at 461. A number of persons told Bette Midler that they thought that she had made the commercial. *Id.* at 462. Aside from the voice, there was no information in the commercial from which the singer could be identified. We noted that "[t]he human voice is one of the most palpable ways identity is manifested." *Id.* at 463. We held that, "[t]o impersonate her voice is to pirate her identity," *id.*, and concluded that Midler had raised a question of fact as to the misappropriation of her identity.

In *Carson v. Here's Johnny Portable Toilets, Inc.*, 698 F.2d 831 (6th Cir. 1983), the Sixth Circuit was called upon to interpret Michigan's common-law right to publicity. The case involved a manufacturer who used the words, "Here's Johnny," on portable toilets. *Id.* at 832–33. These same words were used to introduce the star of a popular late-night television program. There was nothing to indicate that this use of the phrase on the portable toilets was not associated with Johnny Carson's television program. The common theme in these federal cases is that identifying characteristics unique to the plaintiffs were used in a context in which they were the only information as to the identity of the individual. The commercial advertisements in each case showed attributes of the plaintiff's identities which made it appear that the plaintiff was the person identified in the commercial. No effort was made to dispel the impression that the plaintiffs were the source of the personal attributes at issue. The proper interpretation of *Motschenbacher*, *Midler*, and *Carson* is that where identifying characteristics unique to a plaintiff are the only information as to the identity of the person appearing in an ad, a triable issue of fact has been raised as to whether his or her identity as been appropriated.

The case before this court is distinguishable from the factual showing made in *Motschenbacher*, *Midler*, and *Carson*. It is patently clear to anyone viewing the commercial advertisement that Vanna White was not being depicted. No reasonable juror could confuse a metal robot with Vanna White.

The majority contends that "the individual aspects of the advertisement ... [v]iewed together leave little doubt about the celebrity the ad is meant to depict." It derives this conclusion from the fact that Vanna White is "the only one" who "dresses like this, turns letters, and does this on the Wheel of Fortune game show." In reaching this conclusion, the majority confuses Vanna White, the person, with the role she has assumed as the current hostess on the "Wheel of Fortune" television game show. A recognition of the distinction between a performer and the part he or she plays is essential for a proper analysis of the facts of this case. As is discussed below, those things which Vanna White claims identify her are not unique to her. They are, instead, attributes of the role she plays. The representation of those attributes, therefore, does not constitute a representation of Vanna White.

Vanna White is a one-role celebrity. She is famous solely for appearing as the hostess on the "Wheel of Fortune" television show. There is nothing unique about Vanna White or the attributes which she claims identify her. Although she appears to be an attractive woman, her face and figure are no more distinctive than that of other equally comely women. She performs her role as hostess on "Wheel of Fortune" in a simple and straightforward manner. Her work does not require her to display whatever artistic talent she may possess.

The majority appears to argue that because Samsung created a robot with the physical proportions of an attractive woman, posed it gracefully, dressed it in a blond wig, an evening gown, and jewelry, and placed it on a set that resembles the Wheel of Fortune layout, it thereby appropriated Vanna White's identity. But an attractive appearance, a graceful pose, blond hair, an evening gown, and jewelry are attributes shared by many women, especially in Southern California. These common attributes are particularly evident among game-show hostesses, models, actresses, singers, and other women in the entertainment field. They are not unique attributes of Vanna White's identity.

The only characteristic in the commercial advertisement that is not common to many female performers or celebrities is the imitation of the "Wheel of Fortune" set. This set is the only thing which might possibly lead a viewer to think of Vanna White. The Wheel of Fortune set, however, is not an attribute of Vanna White's identity. It is an identifying characteristic of a television game show. To say that Vanna White may bring an action when another blond female performer or robot appears on such a set as a hostess will, I am sure, be a surprise to the owners of the show.

The record shows that Samsung recognized the market value of Vanna White's identity. No doubt the advertisement would have been more effective if Vanna White had appeared in it. But the fact that Samsung recognized Vanna White's value as a celebrity does not necessarily mean that it appropriated her identity. The advertisement was intended to depict a robot, playing the role Vanna White currently plays on the Wheel of Fortune. I quite agree that anyone seeing the commercial advertisement would be reminded of Vanna White. Any performance by another female celebrity as a game-show hostess, however, will also remind the viewer of Vanna White because Vanna White's celebrity is so closely associated with the role. But the fact that an actor or actress became famous for playing a particular role has, until now, never been sufficient to give the performer a proprietary interest in it.

The Lanham Act

Vanna White's Lanham Act claim is easily resolved by applying the proper legal standard. Vanna White seeks damages for violation of section 43(a) of the Lanham Act. To succeed, Vanna White must prove actual deception of the consuming public. Vanna White offered no evidence that any portion of the consuming public was deceived. The district court was correct in granting summary judgment on Vanna White's Lanham Act claim.

The majority finds that because a majority of factors set forth in *AMF, Inc. v. Sleekcraft Boats* favor Vanna White, the district court erred in granting summary judgment. The *AMF* test is designed to aid in determining whether two marks are so sufficiently similar that it is likely that a consumer would confuse them. Where the marks are so obviously different that no confusion could possibly occur, the test is unnecessary. That is the situation in this matter.

Samsung's First Amendment Defense

The majority gives Samsung's First Amendment defense short shrift because "[t]his case involves a true advertisement run for the purpose of selling Samsung VCRs." I respectfully disagree with the majority's analysis of this issue as well.

The majority's attempt to distinguish this case from *Hustler Magazine v. Falwell*, 485 U.S. 46 is unpersuasive. The majority notes that the parodies were made for the purpose of poking fun at the Reverend Jerry Falwell. But the majority fails to consider that the defendant [was] making fun of the Reverend Jerry Falwell for the purely commercial purpose of selling soft-core pornographic magazines.

Generally, a parody does not constitute an infringement on the original work if it takes no more than is necessary to "conjure up" the original. The majority has failed to consider these factors properly in deciding that Vanna White may bring an action for damages solely because the popularity of the fame show, Wheel of Fortune.

The majority's reading of the Lanham Act would provide a basis for "commercial" enterprises to maintain an action for section 43(a) violations even in the absence of confusion or deception.

Samsung clearly used the idea of a glamorous female game show hostess. Just as clearly, it avoided appropriating Vanna White's expression of that role. Samsung did not use a likeness of her. The performer depicted in the commercial advertisement is unmistakably a lifeless robot. Vanna White has presented no evidence that any consumer confused the robot with her identity. Indeed, no reasonable consumer could confuse the robot with Vanna White or believe that, because the robot appeared in the advertisement, Vanna White endorsed Samsung's product. I would affirm the district court's judgment in all respects.

———————

Notes and Questions

1. Do you agree with the majority's distinction between "likeness" and "identity" as a distinction between the statutory and common law publicity rights? What is the test for

when an "identity" is misappropriated? Is "identity" used in a legal or a colloquial sense by the court? That is, do you think that Ms. White believes her "identity" is a person who turns letters on a game show stage?

2. Was Judge Alarcon correct in the dissent in suggesting that any appropriation was that of a role and not of Ms. White's identity? In a part of the dissent that was edited out of the opinion above, Judge Alarcon noted:

> The majority's position seems to allow any famous person or entity to bring suit based on any commercial advertisement that depicts a character or role performed by the plaintiff. Sylvester Stallone could sue actors who play blue-collar boxers. Chuck Norris could sue all karate experts who display their skills in motion pictures. Arnold Schwarzenegger could sue body builders who are compensated for appearing in public. To say that Vanna White may bring an action when another blond female performer or robot appears on such a set as a hostess will, I am sure, be a surprise to the owners of the show.

White, 971 F.2d at 1405, 1407 (Alarcon, dissenting). Is that a fair characterization of the majority's position?

The concept of protecting "character," as opposed to identity, is a complicated one. Typically the issue is one of copyright protection of a fictional character described in words (e.g., Sherlock Holmes or Sam Spade as described by Dashiell Hammett), animation (e.g., Mickey Mouse or Iron Man), or video image (e.g., Rocky or James Bond on the movie screen). There is still no universally accepted test for when such characters deserve intellectual property protection, *compare, e.g., Nichols v. Universal Pictures Corp.*, 45 F.2d 119 (2d Cir. 1930) (articulating the test that a character is protected when "sufficiently delineated") *with Warner Bros. v. CBS*, 215 F.2d 945 (9th Cir. 1945) (holding that character protection occurs when the character is an integral part of "the story to be told") *and Walt Disney Prods. v. Air Pirates*, 581 F.2d 751 (9th Cir. 1978) (holding that protection for an animated character is easier to attain than for one described only in words).

The protection for a living person who plays, or is made into, a character, as in *White*, more directly implicates the right of privacy. For a well-written argument that a role/ character and the actor playing it can become synonymous and thus may create a right of privacy claim in the actor, *see* Chief Justice Bird's opinion in *Lugosi v. Universal Pictures*, 25 Cal. 3d 813, 828 (1979) (Bird, C.J. dissenting) (arguing that Bella Lugosi's character was so identifiable in his role in *Dracula* that he had a right of publicity claim when Universal Studios licensed the use of the Dracula character developed by the studio). *See also Wendt v. Host Int'l, Inc.*, 125 F.3d 806, 812 (9th Cir. 1997) holding that, "[a] false endorsement claim based on the unauthorized use of a celebrity's identity ... alleges the misuse of a trademark, i.e., a symbol or device such as a visual likeness, vocal imitation, or other uniquely distinguishing characteristic, which is likely to confuse consumers as to the plaintiff's sponsorship or approval of the product"; and *Winter v. DC Comics*, 30 Cal. 4th 881 (2003), discussed below, in which the facial image of blues guitarist Edgar Winter was placed on a half-man/half-worm character in a graphic novel.

3. The last line in the majority's decision in *White* mentions *Zacchini v. Scripps-Howard Broadcasting Co.*, 433 U.S. 562 (1977), one of the first cases to address the tension between the First Amendment privilege and commercial misappropriation. There, Mr. Zacchini was a human cannonball and performed his acts at carnivals, state fairs and the like. A local news station filmed his act (which was about 15 seconds long) and played it on a broadcast about the activities at a local fair. The case was on appeal from the Ohio Supreme Court, which interpreted a number of United States Supreme Court precedents and

reached the conclusion that traditionally protected media had absolute immunity to report on newsworthy events, which included acts at the local carnival. In examining these cases itself, the U.S. Supreme Court in *Zacchini* stated:

> [I]n none of them was there an attempt to broadcast or publish an entire act for which the performer ordinarily gets paid. It is evident, and there is no claim here to the contrary, that petitioner's state-law right of publicity would not serve to prevent respondent from reporting the newsworthy facts about petitioner's act. Wherever the line in particular situations is to be drawn between media reports that are protected and those that are not, we are quite sure that the First and Fourteenth Amendments do not immunize the media when they broadcast a performer's entire act without his consent.
>
> The Constitution no more prevents a State from requiring respondent to compensate petitioner for broadcasting his act on television than it would privilege respondent to film and broadcast a copyrighted dramatic work, or a baseball game, without liability to the copyright owner, where the promoters or the participants had other plans for publicizing the event.

Id. at 574. What are the similarities and differences between *White* and *Zacchini*?

4. Many have described *White* as a case which has gone the furthest in the protection of celebrity likeness, suggesting that most courts would have followed the dissent. What sorts of damages do you think Ms. White would have been entitled to if she prevailed on remand?

5. As we explain in greater detail in Chapter 8, in broad strokes the Lanham Act claim deals with creating confusion in the mind of consumer that the celebrity is endorsing the product. It thus protects a narrow part of a celebrity's publicity rights. Many plaintiffs allege it, however, to get into federal court for whatever procedural or other forum shopping benefits they believe a federal court would bestow. Our next case shows a potential pitfall arising from such a strategy.

Brown v. Electronic Arts, Inc.

United States Court of Appeals, Ninth Circuit, 2013
724 F.3d 1235

BYBEE, Circuit Judge:

Plaintiff — Appellant James "Jim" Brown alleges that Defendant — Appellee Electronic Arts, Inc. ("EA") has violated § 43(a) of the Lanham Act through the use of Brown's likeness in EA's *Madden NFL* series of football video games. Although claims under § 43(a) generally relate to the use of trademarks or trade dress to cause consumer confusion over affiliation or endorsement, we have held that claims can also be brought under § 43(a) relating to the use of a public figure's persona, likeness, or other uniquely distinguishing characteristic to cause such confusion.

Section 43(a) protects the public's interest in being free from consumer confusion about affiliations and endorsements, but this protection is limited by the First Amendment, particularly if the product involved is an expressive work. Recognizing the need to balance the public's First Amendment interest in free expression against the public's interest in being free from consumer confusion about affiliation and endorsement, the Second Circuit created the "*Rogers* test" in *Rogers v. Grimaldi*, 875 F.2d 994 (2d Cir. 1989). Under the *Rogers* test, § 43(a) will not be applied to expressive works "unless the [use of the trademark or other identifying material] has no artistic relevance to the underlying work whatsoever, or, if it has some artistic relevance, unless the [use of trademark or other identifying material] explicitly misleads as to the source or the content of the work."

Applying the *Rogers* test, the district court in this case granted EA's motion to dismiss Brown's Lanham Act claim, finding that Brown had not alleged facts that satisfied either condition that allow a § 43(a) claim to succeed. We affirm the district court's decision.

I

Jim Brown is widely regarded as one of the best professional football players of all time. He starred for the Cleveland Browns from 1957 to 1965 and was inducted into the National Football League ("NFL") Hall of Fame after his retirement. After his NFL career, Brown also achieved success as an entertainer and public servant. There is no question that he is a public figure whose persona can be deployed for economic benefit.

EA is a manufacturer, distributor and seller of video games and has produced the *Madden NFL* series of football video games since 1989. The *Madden NFL* series allows users of the games to control avatars representing professional football players as those avatars participate in simulated NFL games. Each version of *Madden NFL* includes the current year's NFL teams with the teams' current rosters. Each avatar on a current team is designed to mirror a real current NFL player, including the player's name, jersey number, physical attributes, and physical skills. Some versions of the game also include historical and all-time teams. Unlike for players on the current NFL teams, no names are used for the players on the historical and all-time teams, but these players are recognizable due to the accuracy of their team affiliations, playing positions, ages, heights, weights, ability levels, and other attributes. Although EA enters into licensing agreements with the NFL and NFL Players Association ("NFLPA") for its use of the names and likenesses of current NFL players, Brown, as a former player, is not covered by those agreements and has never entered into any other agreement allowing EA to use his likeness in *Madden NFL*. Brown asserts that EA has used his likeness in several versions of the game dating back at least to 2001 but that he has never been compensated.

II

The legal issues raised by this case are not novel, but their lack of novelty should not be mistaken for lack of difficulty. Significant judicial resources, including the resources of this court, have been expended trying to find the appropriate balance between trademark and similar rights, on the one hand, and First Amendment rights, on the other. Brown suggests that the case law has produced a lack of clarity as to the appropriate legal framework to apply in this case and urges us to consider the "likelihood of confusion" test and the "alternative means" test in addition to the *Rogers* test. We are convinced that the *Rogers* test remains the appropriate framework.

A decade ago, in *Mattel, Inc. v. MCA Records, Inc.,* we adopted the *Rogers* test as our method for balancing the trademark and similar rights protected by § 43(a) of the Lanham Act against First Amendment rights in cases involving expressive works. *MCA*, 296 F.3d at 902. [W]e clarified in *E.S.S. Entertainment 2000, Inc. v. Rock Star Videos, Inc.* that application of the *Rogers* test was not dependent on the identifying material appearing in the title but "also appl[ies] to the use of a trademark in the body of the work." 547 F.3d 1095, 1099 (9th Cir. 2008).

The *Rogers* test is reserved for expressive works. Even if *Madden NFL* is not the expressive equal of *Anna Karenina* or *Citizen Kane,* the Supreme Court has answered with an emphatic "yes" when faced with the question of whether video games deserve the same protection as more traditional forms of expression. In *Brown v. Entertainment Merchants Ass'n,* the Court said that "[l]ike the protected books, plays, and movies that preceded them, video games communicate ideas—and even social messages—through many familiar literary devices (such as characters, dialogue, plot, and music) and through features distinctive to the medium (such as the player's interaction with the virtual world)" and that these similarities to other expressive mediums "suffice[ ] to confer First Amendment protection." Although there may be some work referred to as a "video game" (or referred to as a "book," "play," or "movie" for that matter) that does not contain enough of the elements contemplated by the Supreme Court to warrant First Amendment protection as an expressive work, no version of *Madden NFL* is such a work. Every version of the game features characters (players), dialogue (between announcers), plot (both within a particular simulated game and more broadly), and music. Even if there is a line to be drawn between expressive video games and non-expressive video games, and even if courts should at some point be drawing that line, we have no need to draw that line here. Each version of *Madden NFL* is an expressive work, and our precedents dictate that we apply the *Rogers* test in §43(a) cases involving expressive works. Brown acknowledges that *Rogers* may apply here, but he argues that the "likelihood of confusion" test, or the "alternative means" test, are also relevant. We disagree. We have previously rejected the "likelihood of confusion" test as "fail[ing] to account for the full weight of the public's interest in free expression" when expressive works are involved. The "alternative means" test was rejected for the same reason in *Rogers* itself. The only relevant legal framework for balancing the public's right to be free from consumer confusion about Brown's affiliation with *Madden NFL* and EA's First Amendment rights in the context of Brown's §43(a) claim is the *Rogers* test.

III

Rogers involved a suit brought by the famous performer Ginger Rogers against the producers and distributors of *Ginger and Fred,* a movie about two fictional Italian cabaret performers who imitated Rogers and her frequent performing partner Fred Astaire. Among Rogers' claims was that the use of her name in the title of the movie violated §43(a) by creating the false impression that she was involved with the film. Recognizing that enforcing §43(a) in this context might constrain free expression in violation of the First Amendment, the Second Circuit asserted that the Lanham Act should be "appl[ied] to artistic works only where the public interest in avoiding consumer confusion outweighs the public interest in free expression." The *Rogers* court introduced a two-pronged test, under which the Lanham Act should not be applied to expressive works "unless the [use of the trademark or other identifying material] has no artistic relevance to the underlying work whatsoever, or, if it has some artistic relevance, unless the [trademark or other identifying material] explicitly misleads as to the source or the content of the work." *Id.*

A

As we explained in *E.S.S [Entertainment 2000, Inc. v. Rock Star Videos, Inc.,* 547 F.3d 1095 (9th Cir. 2008)] a case with similar facts to Brown's case in which we applied the *Rogers* test to a §43(a) claim related to the use of the likeness of a Los Angeles strip club in the video game *Grand Theft Auto: San Andreas,* "the level of [artistic] relevance [of the trademark or other identifying material to the work] merely must be above zero" for the trademark or other identifying material to be deemed artistically relevant. This black-and-white rule has the benefit of limiting our need to engage in artistic analysis in this context.

We agree with the district court that the use of Brown's likeness is artistically relevant to the *Madden NFL* games. As Brown points out in trying to undermine the status of the games as expressive works, EA prides itself on the extreme realism of the games. As Brown emphasizes in arguing that it is in fact his likeness in the games: "[I]t is axiomatic the '65 Cleveland Browns simply, by definition, cannot be the '65 Cleveland Browns without the players who played for the '65 Cleveland Browns. This fundamental truth applies especially to that team's most famous player, Jim Brown." Given the acknowledged centrality of realism to EA's expressive goal, and the importance of including Brown's likeness to realistically recreate one of the teams in the game, it is obvious that Brown's likeness has at least some artistic relevance to EA's work. The fact that any given version of *Madden NFL* includes likenesses of thousands of different current and former NFL players does not impact this analysis. In *E.S.S.*, the virtual strip club in question was just one of many virtual structures included by the designers of *Grand Theft Auto: San Andreas* in an attempt to simulate the feel of East Los Angeles, but we nonetheless concluded that the strip club was artistically relevant to the work. There is no significant distinction to be made here.

In letters to Brown's attorneys, EA officials have claimed that "Brown has not appeared in any *Madden NFL* game since 1998," and that "Brown's name and likeness does not appear in *Madden NFL 08* or any packaging or marketing materials associated with the product." EA has not denied that Brown's likeness is relevant to *Madden NFL;* rather, it has denied that Brown has appeared in the *Madden NFL* games released since 1998. If the denials are true — that is, if Brown's likeness does not in fact appear in the games — Brown has no claim at all under the Lanham Act. In order to have a valid § 43(a) claim based on artistic irrelevance, Brown needs to show both that his likeness was used and that his likeness was artistically irrelevant to the *Madden NFL* games. If artistic irrelevance can only be proven by accepting the truth of EA's denial of the use of Brown's likeness, Brown cannot possibly satisfy both of these burdens. Moreover, in the context of a motion to dismiss, we accept Brown's factual allegations as true, and Brown alleges that his likeness was used. We must thus assume that EA's denials are false, meaning they provide no support for artistic irrelevance.

EA did not produce a game called *Jim Brown Presents Pinball* with no relation to Jim Brown or football beyond the title; it produced a football game featuring likenesses of thousands of current and former NFL players, including Brown.

Brown asserts that our interpretation of the *Rogers* test in *E.S.S.* more or less automatically protects expressive works regardless of the deception involved. The language in *Rogers* is clear. "[T]hat balance will normally not support application of the [Lanham] Act unless the [use of the trademark or other identifying material] has *no artistic relevance to the underlying work whatsoever....*" (emphasis added). The *Rogers* test is applicable when First Amendment rights are at their height — when expressive works are involved — so it is no surprise that the test puts such emphasis on even the slightest artistic relevance. Our interpretation of the "artistic relevance" prong of the *Rogers* test in *E.S.S.* is correct, and Brown fails to allege facts that satisfy that prong in this case.

B

Even if the use of a trademark or other identifying material is artistically relevant to the expressive work, the creator of the expressive work can be subject to a Lanham Act claim if the creator uses the mark or material to "explicitly mislead[ ] [consumers] as to the source or the content of the work." It is key here that the creator must *explicitly* mislead consumers. "[T]he slight risk that ... use of a celebrity's name might implicitly suggest endorsement or sponsorship to some people is outweighed by the danger of restricting artistic expression, and [in cases where there is no explicit misleading] the Lanham Act is not applicable." This second prong of the *Rogers* test "points directly at the purpose of trademark law, namely to avoid confusion in the marketplace by allowing a trademark owner to prevent others from duping consumers into buying a product they mistakenly believe is sponsored by the trademark owner." We must ask "whether the [use of Brown's likeness] would confuse [*Madden NFL*] players into thinking that [Brown] is somehow behind [the games] or that [he] sponsors [EA's] product," and whether there was an "explicit indication," "overt claim," or "explicit misstatement" that caused such consumer confusion.

Brown argues that the use of his likeness in the game coupled with a consumer survey demonstrating that a majority of the public believes that identifying marks cannot be included in products without permission at least raises a triable issue of fact as to the second prong of the *Rogers* test. It is well established that the use of a mark alone is not enough to satisfy this prong of the *Rogers* test. In *MCA,* we noted that if the use of a mark alone were sufficient "it would render *Rogers* a nullity." We reiterated this point in *E.S.S.,* asserting that, "the mere use of a trademark alone cannot suffice to make such use explicitly misleading." Adding survey evidence changes nothing. The test requires that the use be *explicitly* misleading to consumers. To be relevant, evidence must relate to the nature of the behavior of the identifying material's user, not the impact of the use. Even if Brown could offer a survey demonstrating that consumers of the *Madden NFL* series believed that Brown endorsed the game, that would not support the claim that the use was explicitly misleading to consumers.

Brown argues that certain written materials that accompanied versions of the game demonstrate EA's attempts to explicitly mislead consumers about his endorsement or involvement with the game's production. Brown points to materials that say that one of the game's features was the inclusion of "[f]ifty of the NFL's greatest players and every All–Madden team." Since Brown is one of the fifty greatest NFL players of all time and has been named to the "All Madden, All Millennium" team, Brown argues that the statement "explicitly represents that Brown was in EA's game." But Brown needs to prove that EA explicitly misled consumers about Brown's endorsement of the game, not that EA used Brown's likeness in the game; nothing in EA's promotion suggests that the fifty NFL players who are members of the All Madden, All Millennium team endorse EA's game. EA's statement is true and not misleading.

V

As expressive works, the *Madden NFL* video games are entitled to the same First Amendment protection as great literature, plays, or books. Brown's Lanham Act claim is thus subject to the *Rogers* test, and we agree with the district court that Brown has failed to allege sufficient facts to make out a plausible claim that survives that test. Brown's likeness is artistically relevant to the games and there are no alleged facts to support the claim that EA explicitly misled consumers as to Brown's involvement with the games. The *Rogers* test tells us that, in this case, the public interest in free expression outweighs the public interest in avoiding consumer confusion. The district court's judgment is thus **AFFIRMED.**

Notes and Questions

1. Note 5 following the *White* case indicated that there were pitfalls in asserting a Lanham Act claim to invoke federal jurisdiction. In the preceding case, Mr. Brown also brought common law and state claims of privacy. In a part of the case that was edited out, both the District Court and the Court of Appeals declined to take supplemental jurisdiction over the state-based claims, so when the Lanham Act claim was dismissed, the case was over. However, if Brown sued under common law rights of publicity, and not trademark

law, it is likely he would have prevailed. Such a result occurred in *Davis v. Elec. Arts*, where former professional football players sued Electronic Arts for the unauthorized use of their likenesses in EA's *Madden NFL* series of videogames.[14] There the court held that EA's use of the former players' likenesses was not "incidental" to First Amendment protection because it was central to the company's commercial purpose of creating realistic virtual football games involving current and former NFL teams. Why do you think these claims yield different results?

2. One of EA's arguments was that there was no misappropriation of Mr. Brown's identity because the game did not identify any retired player by name, and thus there was no confusion as to whether those players endorsed the game. Given the nature of the opinion and the *Rogers* test, would it make any difference if EA had put Mr. Brown's name and the number he used when he played (32) on the back of the avatar playing running back for the 1965 Cleveland Browns? Note than after the lawsuit was filed, EA used the number "37" for the running back for the 1965 Browns. Is there any significance to that?

3. What is the significance of EA paying the NFL Players Association for the rights to current NFL players, but not Mr. Brown or any of the retired players appearing in the game?

4. Do you believe EA when it said, "Brown has not appeared in any *Madden NFL* game since 1998," and that "Brown's name and likeness does not appear in *Madden NFL 08* or any packaging or marketing materials associated with the product"?

5. What do you think of the *Rogers* test? If the standard is really "no artistic relevance to the underlying work whatsoever," will there ever be a case, other than something farfetched, like a *Jim Brown Presents Pinball* game posited by the majority, where the test is met by the plaintiff-celebrity? In examining the *Rogers* test's focus on explicit acts indicating endorsement of the product, Professor J. Michael Monahan of the Chicago-Kent College of the Law School has opined that *Rogers* asks whether the celebrity's likeness is *on* the box (indicating endorsement) or only *in* the box (i.e., found as an avatar in the game). Is that apt? Does the *Rogers* test appropriately give deference to protected modes of expression?

6. *Brown* was decided by the same court, the United States Circuit Court of Appeals for the Ninth Circuit, that decided *White*. Obviously its test for a Lanham Act violation had changed from the multi-factored test based on *Sleekcraft* (used in *White*) to the *Rogers* test. If Ms. White's case had been decided under the *Rogers* test, would there have been a different result?

7. The case references other Lanham Act tests adopted by different courts. One is the "likelihood of confusion" test. Under that test, it is possible that the survey results indicating that a majority of consumers believed Mr. Brown had agreed to, and been compensated for, his likeness being used in the game would have been relevant and thus admissible. In rejecting the "likelihood of confusion" test in favor of keeping the *Rogers* test, the court explained:

> The Sixth Circuit's decision in *ETW Corp. v. Jireh Publishing, Inc.*, 332 F.3d 915 (6th Cir. 2003), demonstrates this point. In that case, Tiger Woods' licensing agent, ETW Corporation, brought a Lanham Act claim against the publisher of artwork commemorating Woods' 1997 victory at The Masters. A survey was produced in which participants were shown the artwork and asked if they thought Tiger Woods was affiliated or connected with the work or had approved or sponsored it. Over sixty percent of the participants answered affirmatively, but

---

14. *Davis v. Elec. Arts, Inc.*, 2015 U.S. App. LEXIS 154 (9th Cir. Cal. Jan. 6, 2015).

the Sixth Circuit asserted: "[P]laintiff's survey evidence, even if its validity is assumed, indicates at most that some members of the public would draw the incorrect inference that Woods had some connection with [the work]. The risk of misunderstanding, not engendered by any explicit indication on the face of the [work], is so outweighed by the interest in artistic expression as to preclude application of the [Lanham] Act." In *Rogers* itself, the Second Circuit rejected similar survey data for the same reasons. The use of Brown's likeness together with the cited survey do not provide a valid argument to allow Brown's case to go forward based on this prong of the *Rogers* test.

Brown, 724 F.3d at 1246 [brackets in original]. If the Lanham Act is principally concerned with mistaken endorsement, is the "likelihood of confusion" test the better test, or does it not take into sufficient account freedom of expression concerns in constitutionally protected works?

8. The *Rogers* test has become one of the accepted tests regarding whether a celebrity has a publicity claim when his or her likeness is used in a videogame without permission. The other major test is discussed in the next case, once again decided by the Ninth Circuit Court of Appeals, and by the same judge who decided *Brown*, Judge Bybee.

In re NCAA Student-Athlete Name & Likeness Licensing Litigation (Keller v. Electronic Arts, Inc.)

United States Court of Appeals, Ninth Circuit, 2013
724 F.3d 1268

BYBEE, Circuit Judge

Video games are entitled to the full protections of the First Amendment, because "[l]ike the protected books, plays, and movies that preceded them, video games communicate ideas—and even social messages—through many familiar literary devices (such as characters, dialogue, plot, and music) and through features distinctive to the medium (such as the player's interaction with the virtual world)." *Brown v. Entm't Merchs. Ass'n*, —— U.S. ——, 131 S. Ct. 2729, 2733 (2011). Such rights are not absolute, and states may recognize the right of publicity to a degree consistent with the First Amendment. *Zacchini v. Scripps–Howard Broad. Co.*, 433 U.S. 562, 574–75 (1977). In this case, we must balance the right of publicity of a former college football player against the asserted First Amendment right of a video game developer to use his likeness in its expressive works.

The district court concluded that the game developer, Electronic Arts ("EA"), had no First Amendment defense against the right-of-publicity claims of the football player, Samuel Keller. We affirm. Under the "transformative use" test developed by the California Supreme Court, EA's use does not qualify for First Amendment protection as a matter of law because it literally recreates Keller in the very setting in which he has achieved renown. The other First Amendment defenses asserted by EA do not defeat Keller's claims either.

I

Samuel Keller was the starting quarterback for Arizona State University in 2005 before he transferred to the University of Nebraska, where he played during the 2007 season. EA is the producer of the *NCAA Football* series of video games, which allow users to control avatars representing college football players as those avatars participate in simulated games. In *NCAA Football*, EA seeks to replicate each school's entire team as accurately as possible. Every real football player on each team included in the game has a corresponding avatar in the game with the player's actual jersey number and virtually identical height, weight, build, skin tone, hair color, and home state. EA attempts to match any unique, highly identifiable playing behaviors by sending detailed questionnaires to team equipment managers. Additionally, EA creates realistic virtual versions of actual stadiums; populates them with the virtual athletes, coaches, cheerleaders, and fans realistically rendered by EA's graphic artists; and incorporates realistic sounds such as the crunch of the players' pads and the roar of the crowd.

EA's game differs from reality in that EA omits the players' names on their jerseys and assigns each player a home town that is different from the actual player's home town. However, users of the video game may upload rosters of names obtained from third parties so that the names do appear on the jerseys. In such cases, EA allows images from the game containing athletes' real names to be posted on its website by users. Users can further alter reality by entering "Dynasty" mode, where the user assumes a head coach's responsibilities for a college program for up to thirty seasons, including recruiting players from a randomly generated pool of high school athletes, or "Campus Legend" mode, where the user controls a virtual player from high school through college, making choices relating to practices, academics, and social life.

In the 2005 edition of the game, the virtual starting quarterback for Arizona State wears number 9, as did Keller, and has the same height, weight, skin tone, hair color, hair style, handedness, home state, play style (pocket passer), visor preference, facial features, and school year as Keller. In the 2008 edition, the virtual quarterback for Nebraska has these same characteristics, though the jersey number does not match, presumably because Keller changed his number right before the season started.

Objecting to this use of his likeness, Keller filed a putative class-action complaint in the Northern District of California asserting, as relevant on appeal, that EA violated his right of publicity under California Civil Code § 3344 and California common law.

II

EA did not contest before the district court and does not contest here that Keller has stated a right-of-publicity claim under California common and statutory law. Instead, EA raises four affirmative defenses derived from the First Amendment: the "transformative use" test, the *Rogers* test, the "public interest" test, and the "public affairs" exemption.

A

The California Supreme Court formulated the transformative use defense in *Comedy III Productions, Inc. v. Gary Saderup, Inc.*, 25 Cal. 4th 387 (2001). The defense is "a balancing test between the First Amendment and the right of publicity based on whether the work in question adds significant creative elements so as to be transformed into something more than a mere celebrity likeness or imitation." The California Supreme Court explained that "when a work contains significant transformative elements, it is not only especially worthy of First Amendment protection, but it is also less likely to interfere with the economic interest protected by the right of publicity."

Comedy III gives us five factors to consider in determining whether a work is sufficiently transformative to obtain First Amendment protection. First, if "the celebrity likeness is one of the 'raw materials' from which an original work is synthesized," it is more likely to be transformative than if "the depiction or imitation of the celebrity is the very sum and substance of the work in question." Second, the work is protected if it is "primarily the defendant's own expression"—as long as that expression is "something other than the likeness of the celebrity." This factor requires an examination of whether a likely purchaser's primary motivation is to buy a reproduction of the celebrity, or to buy the expressive work of that artist. Third, to avoid making judgments concerning "the quality of the artistic contribution," a court should conduct an inquiry "more quantitative than qualitative" and ask "whether the literal and imitative or the creative elements predominate in the work." Fourth, the California Supreme Court indicated that "a subsidiary inquiry" would be useful in close cases: whether "the marketability and economic value of the challenged work derive primarily from the fame of the celebrity depicted." Lastly, the court indicated that "when an artist's skill and talent is manifestly subordinated to the overall goal of creating a conventional portrait of a celebrity so as to commercially exploit his or her fame," the work is not transformative.

California courts have applied the transformative use test in relevant situations. First, in *Comedy III* itself, the California Supreme Court applied the test to T-shirts and lithographs bearing a likeness of The Three Stooges and concluded that it could "discern no significant transformative or creative contribution." The court reasoned that the artist's "undeniable skill is manifestly subordinated to the overall goal of creating literal, conventional depictions of The Three Stooges so as to exploit their fame." "[W]ere we to decide that [the artist's] depictions were protected by the First Amendment," the court continued, "we cannot perceive how the right of publicity would remain a viable right other than in cases of falsified celebrity endorsements."

Second, in *Winter v. DC Comics,* the California Supreme Court applied the test to comic books containing characters Johnny and Edgar Autumn, "depicted as villainous half-worm, half-human offspring" but evoking two famous brothers, rockers Johnny and Edgar Winter. 30 Cal. 4th 881 (2003). The court held that "the comic books are transformative and entitled to First Amendment protection." It reasoned that the comic books "are not just conventional depictions of plaintiffs but contain significant expressive content other than plaintiffs' mere likenesses." "To the extent the drawings of the Autumn brothers resemble plaintiffs at all, they are distorted for purposes of lampoon, parody, or caricature." Importantly, the court relied on the fact that the brothers "are but cartoon characters ... in a larger story, which is itself quite expressive."

Third, in *Kirby v. Sega of America, Inc.,* the California Court of Appeal applied the transformative use test to a video game in which the user controls the dancing of "Ulala," a reporter from outer space allegedly based on singer Kierin Kirby, whose " 'signature' lyrical expression ... is 'ooh la la.' " 144 Cal. App. 4th (2006). The court held that "Ulala is more than a mere likeness or literal depiction of Kirby," pointing to Ulala's "extremely tall, slender computer-generated physique," her "hairstyle and primary costume," her dance moves, and her role as "a space-age reporter in the 25th century," all of which were "unlike any public depiction of Kirby." "As in *Winter,* Ulala is a 'fanciful, creative character' who exists in the context of a unique and expressive video game."

We have also had occasion to apply the transformative use test. In *Hilton v. Hallmark Cards,* we applied the test to a birthday card depicting Paris Hilton in a manner reminiscent of an episode of Hilton's reality show *The Simple Life.* 599 F.3d at 899. We observed some differences between the episode and the card, but noted that "the basic setting is the same: we see Paris Hilton, born to privilege, working as a waitress." We reasoned that "[w]hen we compare Hallmark's card to the video game in *Kirby,* which transported a 1990s singer (catchphrases and all) into the 25th century and transmogrified her into a space-age reporter, ... the card falls far short of the level of new expression added in the video game." As a result, we concluded that "there is enough doubt as to whether Hallmark's card is transformative under our case law that we cannot say Hallmark is entitled to the defense as a matter of law."

With these cases in mind as guidance, we conclude that EA's use of Keller's likeness does not contain significant transformative elements such that EA is entitled to the defense as a matter of law. Here, users manipulate the characters in the performance of the same activity for which they are known in real life—playing football. The context in which the activity occurs is realistic—depictions of actual football stadiums As the district court found, Keller is represented as "what he was: the starting quarterback for Arizona State" and Nebraska, and "the game's setting is identical to where the public found [Keller] during his collegiate career: on the football field."

EA argues that the district court erred in focusing primarily on Keller's likeness and ignoring the transformative elements of the game as a whole. EA suggests that the fact that *NCAA Football* users can alter the characteristics of the avatars in the game is significant.

[W]e do not read the California Court's decision as turning on the inability of users to alter the avatars. The key contrast with *Winter* and *Kirby* was that in those games the public figures were transformed into "fanciful, creative characters" or "portrayed as … entirely new character[s]."

The Third Circuit came to the same conclusion in *Hart v. Electronic Arts, Inc.*, 717 F.3d 141 (3d Cir. 2013). In *Hart*, EA faced a materially identical challenge under New Jersey right-of-publicity law, brought by former Rutgers quarterback Ryan Hart. Though the Third Circuit was tasked with interpreting New Jersey law, the court looked to the transformative use test developed in California (noting that the right-of-publicity laws are "strikingly similar … and protect similar interests" in New Jersey and California, and that "consequently [there is] no issue in applying balancing tests developed in California to New Jersey") [and] (holding that "the Transformative Use Test is the proper analytical framework to apply to cases such as the one at bar"). Applying the test, the court held that "the *NCAA Football* … games at issue … do not sufficiently transform [Hart]'s identity to escape the right of publicity claim," reversing the district court's grant of summary judgment to EA.

As we have, the Third Circuit considered the potentially transformative nature of the game as a whole, and the user's ability to alter avatar characteristics Asserting that "the ability to modify the avatar counts for little where the appeal of the game lies in users' ability to play as, or alongside [,] their preferred players or team," the Third Circuit agreed with us that these changes do not render the *NCAA Football* games sufficiently transformative to defeat a right-of-publicity claim.

B

EA urges us to adopt for right-of-publicity claims the broader First Amendment defense that we have previously adopted in the context of false endorsement claims under the Lanham Act: the *Rogers* test. *See Brown v. Elec. Arts*, 724 F.3d at 1239–41 (applying the *Rogers* test to a Lanham Act claim brought by former NFL player Jim Brown relating to the use of his likeness in EA's *Madden NFL* video games).

In this case, EA argues that we should extend this test, created to evaluate Lanham Act claims, to apply to right-of-publicity claims because it is "less prone to misinterpretation" and "more protective of free expression" than the transformative use defense. Although we acknowledge that there is some overlap between the transformative use test formulated by the California Supreme Court and the *Rogers* test, we disagree that the *Rogers* test should be imported wholesale for right-of-publicity claims. Our conclusion on this point is consistent with the Third Circuit's rejection of EA's identical argument in *Hart*. As the history and development of the *Rogers* test makes clear, it was designed to protect consumers from the risk of consumer confusion—the hallmark element of a Lanham Act claim. The right of publicity, on the other hand, does not primarily seek to prevent consumer confusion. Rather, it primarily "protects a form of intellectual property [in one's person] that society deems to have some social utility." As the California Supreme Court has explained:

> Often considerable money, time and energy are needed to develop one's prominence in a particular field. Years of labor may be required before one's skill, reputation, notoriety or virtues are sufficiently developed to permit an economic return through some medium of commercial promotion. For some, the investment may eventually create considerable commercial value in one's identity.

The right of publicity protects the *celebrity*, not the *consumer*. Keller's publicity claim is not founded on an allegation that consumers are being illegally misled into believing that he is endorsing EA or its products. Indeed, he would be hard-pressed to support such an allegation absent evidence that EA explicitly misled consumers into holding such a belief. *See Brown* (holding under the *Rogers* test that, since "Brown's likeness is artistically relevant to the [*Madden NFL*] games and there are no alleged facts to support the claim that EA explicitly misled consumers as to Brown's involvement with the games," "the public interest in free expression outweighs the public interest in avoiding consumer confusion"). Instead, Keller's claim is that EA has appropriated, without permission and without providing compensation, his talent and years of hard work on the football field. The reasoning of the *Rogers*—that artistic and literary works should be protected unless they explicitly mislead consumers—is simply not responsive to Keller's asserted interests here. *Cf. Hart*, 717 F.3d at 157 ("Effectively, [EA] argues that [Hart] should be unable to assert a claim for appropriating his likeness as a football player precisely because his likeness was used for a game about football. Adopting this line of reasoning threatens to turn the right of publicity on its head.").

Lastly, we note that the only circuit court to import the *Rogers* test into the publicity arena, the Sixth Circuit, has done so inconsistently. In *Parks v. LaFace Records,* the Sixth Circuit indicated that the *Rogers* test was appropriate for right-of-publicity claims, noting that the Restatement (Third) of Unfair Competition had endorsed use of the test in that context. 329 F.3d 437, 461 (6th Cir. 2003) (citing *Restatement (Third) of Unfair Competition* § 47 Cmt. c). Subsequently, in *ETW Corp. v. Jireh Publishing, Inc.,* the court acknowledged the *Parks* decision but did not apply the *Rogers* test to the Ohio right-of-publicity claim in question. 332 F.3d at 915, 936 & n. 17 (6th Cir. 2003). Instead, the court applied a balancing test from comment d in the *Restatement* (analyzing "the substantiality and market effect of the use of the celebrity's image ... in light of the informational and creative content"), as well as the transformative use test from *Comedy III. see Hart,* 717 F.3d at 157 ("We find *Parks* to be less than persuasive [as to the applicability of the *Rogers* test to right-of-publicity cases] given that just over a month later another panel of the Sixth Circuit decided [*ETW*], a right of publicity case where the Circuit applied the Transformative Use Test."). Similarly, the Tenth Circuit in *Cardtoons, L.C. v. Major League Baseball Players Ass'n,* 95 F.3d 959 (10th Cir. 1996), and the Eighth Circuit in *C.B.C. Distribution and Marketing, Inc. v. Major League Baseball Advanced Media, L.P.,* 505 F.3d 818 (8th Cir. 2007), rejected the *Rogers* test in favor of a flexible case-by-case approach that takes into account the celebrity's interest in retaining his or her publicity and the public's interest in free expression. Therefore, we decline EA's invitation to extend the *Rogers* test to right-of-publicity claims.

C

California has developed two additional defenses aimed at protecting the reporting of factual information under state law. One of these defenses only applies to common law right-of-publicity claims while the other only applies to statutory right-of-publicity claims. Liability will not lie for common law right-of-publicity claims for the "publication of matters in the public interest." Similarly, liability will not lie for statutory right-of-publicity claims for the "use of a name, voice, signature, photograph, or likeness in connection with any news, public affairs, or sports broadcast or account, or any political campaign."

EA argues that these defenses give it the right to "incorporate athletes' names, statistics, and other biographical information" into its expressive works, as the defenses were "designed to create 'extra breathing space' for the use of a person's name in connection with matters of public interest." Keller responds that the right of publicity yields to free use of a public figure's likeness only to the extent reasonably required to report information to the public or publish factual data, and that the defenses apply only to broadcasts or accounts of public affairs, not to EA's *NCAA Football* games, which do not contain or constitute such reporting about Keller.

California courts have generally analyzed the common law defense and the statutory defense separately, but it is clear that both defenses protect only the act of publishing or reporting. By its terms [the statutory defense] is limited to a "broadcast or account," and we have confirmed that the common law defense is about a publication or reporting of newsworthy items. However, most of the discussion by California courts pertains to whether the subject matter of the communication is of "public interest" or related to "news" or "public affairs," leaving little guidance as to when the communication constitutes a publication or reporting.

For instance, in *Dora v. Frontline Video, Inc.,* a well-known surfer sued the producer of a documentary on surfing entitled "The Legends of Malibu," claiming misappropriation of his name and likeness. 15 Cal. App. 4th 536, (1993). The court held that the documentary was protected because it was "a fair comment on real life events which have caught the popular imagination." The court explained that surfing "has created a lifestyle that influences speech, behavior, dress, and entertainment," has had "an economic impact," and "has also had a significant influence on the popular culture," such that "[i]t would be difficult to conclude that a surfing documentary does not fall within the category of public affairs." Similarly, in *Gionfriddo v. Major League Baseball,* retired professional baseball players alleged that Major League Baseball violated their right of publicity by displaying "factual data concerning the players, their performance statistics, and verbal descriptions and video depictions of their play" in game programs and on its website. 94 Cal. App. 4th 400 (2001). The court reasoned that "[t]he recitation and discussion of factual data concerning the athletic performance of these plaintiffs command a substantial public interest, and, therefore, is a form of expression due substantial constitutional protection." And in *Montana v. San Jose Mercury News, Inc.,* former NFL quarterback Joe Montana brought a right-of-publicity action against a newspaper for selling posters containing previously published pages from the newspaper depicting the many Super Bowl victories by Montana and the San Francisco 49ers. The court found that "[p]osters portraying the 49'ers' [sic] victories are ... a form of public interest presentation to which protection must be extended." *Id.* at 641 (internal quotation marks omitted).

We think that, unlike in *Gionfriddo, Montana,* and *Dora,* EA is not publishing or reporting factual data. EA's video game is a means by which users can play their own virtual football games, not a means for obtaining information about real-world football games. Although EA has incorporated certain actual player information into the game (height, weight, etc.), its case is considerably weakened by its decision not to include the athletes' names along with their likenesses and statistical data. EA can hardly be considered to be "reporting" on Keller's career at Arizona State and Nebraska when it is not even using Keller's name in connection with his avatar in the game. Put simply, EA's interactive game is not a publication of facts about college football; it is a game, not a reference source. These state law defenses, therefore, do not apply.

III

Under California's transformative use defense, EA's use of the likenesses of college athletes like Samuel Keller in its video games is not, as a matter of law, protected by the First Amendment. We reject EA's suggestion to import the *Rogers* test into the right-of-publicity arena, and conclude that state law defenses for the reporting of information do not protect EA's use.

THOMAS, Circuit Judge, dissenting:

I

As expressive works, video games are entitled to First Amendment protection. The First Amendment affords additional protection to *NCAA Football* because it involves a subject of substantial public interest: collegiate football. Because football is a matter of public interest, the use of the images of athletes is entitled to constitutional protection, even if profits are involved.

Where it is recognized, the tort of appropriation is a creature of common law or statute, depending on the jurisdiction. However, the right to compensation for the misappropriation for commercial use of one's image or celebrity is far from absolute. In every jurisdiction, any right of publicity must be balanced against the constitutional protection afforded by the First Amendment. Courts have employed a variety of methods in balancing the rights. The California Supreme Court applies a "transformative use" test it formulated in *Comedy III Productions, Inc. v. Gary Saderup, Inc.*

As the majority properly notes, the transformative use defense is "a balancing test between the First Amendment and the right of publicity based on whether the work in question adds significant creative elements so as to be transformed into something more than a mere celebrity likeness or imitation." The rationale for the test, as the majority notes, is that "when a work contains significant transformative elements, it is not only especially worthy of First Amendment protection, but it is also less likely to interfere with the economic interest protected by the right of publicity."

The five considerations articulated in *Comedy III* are often distilled as analytical factors, Justice Mosk was careful in *Comedy III* not to label them as such. Indeed, the focus of *Comedy III* is a more holistic examination of whether the transformative and creative elements of a particular work predominate over commercially based literal or imitative depictions. The distinction is critical, because excessive deconstruction of *Comedy III* can lead to misapplication of the test. And it is at this juncture that I must respectfully part ways with my colleagues in the majority.

The majority confines its inquiry to how a single athlete's likeness is represented in the video game, rather than examining the transformative and creative elements in the video game as a whole. In my view, this approach contradicts the holistic analysis required by the transformative use test The salient question is whether the entire work is transformative, and whether the transformative elements predominate, rather than whether an individual persona or image has been altered.

When EA's *NCAA Football* video game series is examined carefully, and put in proper context, I conclude that the creative and transformative elements of the games predominate over the commercial use of the likenesses of the athletes within the games.

A

The first step in conducting a balancing is to examine the creative work at issue. At its essence, EA's *NCAA Football* is a work of interactive historical fiction. The college teams that are supplied in the game do replicate the actual college teams for that season, including virtual athletes who bear the statistical and physical dimensions of the actual college athletes. But, unlike their professional football counterparts in the *Madden NFL* series, the NCAA football players in these games are not identified.

The gamers can also change their abilities, appearances, and physical characteristics at will. Keller's impressive physical likeness can be morphed by the gamer into an overweight and slow virtual athlete, with anemic passing ability. And the gamer can create new virtual players out of whole cloth. Players can change teams. The gamer could pit Sam Keller against himself, or a stronger or weaker version of himself, on a different team. Or the gamer could play the game endlessly without ever encountering Keller's avatar. In the simulated games, the gamer controls not only the conduct of the game, but the weather, crowd noise, mascots, and other environmental factors. Of course, one may play the game leaving the players unaltered, pitting team against team. But, in this context as well, the work is one of historic fiction. The gamer controls the teams, players, and games.

Applying the *Comedy III* considerations to *NCAA Football* in proper holistic context, the considerations favor First Amendment protection. The athletic likenesses are but one of the raw materials from which the broader game is constructed. The work, considered as a whole, is primarily one of EA's own expression. The creative and transformative elements predominate over the commercial use of likenesses. The marketability and economic value of the game comes from the creative elements within, not from the pure commercial exploitation of a celebrity image. The game is not a conventional portrait of a celebrity, but a work consisting of many creative and transformative elements.

The video game at issue is much akin to the creations the California Supreme Court found protected in *Winter*, where the two fabled guitarists Johnny and Edgar Winter were easily identifiable, but depicted as chimeras. It is also consistent with the California Court of Appeal's decision in *Kirby*, where a character easily identified as singer Kierin Kirby, more popularly known as Lady Miss Kier, was transformed into a " 'fanciful, creative character' who exists in the context of a unique and expressive video game." So, too, are the virtual players who populate the world of the *NCAA Football* series.

Unlike the majority, I would not punish EA for the realism of its games and for the skill of the artists who created realistic settings for the football games. That the lifelike roar of the crowd and the crunch of pads contribute to the gamer's experience demonstrates how little of *NCAA Football* is driven by the particular likeness of Sam Keller, or any of the other plaintiffs, rather than by the game's artistic elements.

In short, considering the creative elements alone in this case satisfies the transformative use test in favor of First Amendment protection.

B

Although one could leave the analysis with an examination of the transformative and creative aspects of the game, a true balancing requires an inquiry as to the other side of the scales: the publicity right at stake. Here, as well, the *NCAA Football* video game series can be distinguished from the traditional right of publicity cases, both from a quantitative and a qualitative perspective.

As a quantitative matter, *NCAA Football* is different from other right of publicity cases in the sheer number of virtual actors involved. Most right of publicity cases involve either one celebrity, or a finite and defined group of celebrities. *Comedy III* involved literal likenesses of the Three Stooges. *Hilton v. Hallmark Cards*, involved the literal likeness of Paris Hilton. *Winter* involved the images of the rock star brother duo. *Kirby* involved the likeness of one singer.

In contrast, *NCAA Football* includes not just Sam Keller, but thousands of virtual actors. This consideration is of particular significance when we examine, as instructed by *Comedy III*, whether the source of the product marketability comes from creative elements or from pure exploitation of a celebrity image. There is not, at this stage of the litigation, any evidence as to the personal marketing power of Sam Keller, as distinguished from the appeal of the creative aspects of the product. Regardless, the sheer number of athletes involved inevitably diminish the significance of the publicity right at issue. *Comedy III* involved literal depictions of the Three Stooges on lithographs and T-shirts. *Winter* involved characters depicted in a comic strip. *Kirby* involved pivotal characters in a video game. The commercial image of the celebrities in each case was central to the production, and its contact with the consumer was immediate and unavoidable. In contrast, one could play *NCAA Football* thousands of times without ever encountering a particular avatar. In context of the collective, an individual's publicity right is relatively insignificant. Put another way, if an anonymous virtual player is tackled in an imaginary video game and no one notices, is there any right of publicity infringed at all?

The sheer quantity of the virtual players in the game underscores the inappropriateness of analyzing the right of publicity through the lens of one likeness only. Only when the creative work is considered in complete context can a proper analysis be conducted.

As a qualitative matter, the essence of *NCAA Football* is founded on publicly available data, which is not protected by any individual publicity rights. It is true that EA solicits and receives information directly from colleges and universities. But the information is hardly proprietary. Personal vital statistics for players are found in college programs and media guides. Likewise, playing statistics are easily available. In this respect, the information used by EA is indistinguishable from the information used in fantasy athletic leagues, for which the First Amendment provides protection, or much beloved statistical board games, such as Strat–O–Matic. An athlete's right of publicity simply does not encompass publicly available statistical data.

Further, the structure of the game is not founded on exploitation of an individual's publicity rights. The players are unidentified and anonymous. It is true that third-party software is available to quickly identify the players, but that is not part of the EA package. And the fact that the players can be identified by the knowledgeable user by their position, team, and statistics is somewhat beside the point. The issue is whether the marketability of the product is driven by an individual celebrity, or by the game itself. Player anonymity, while certainly not a complete defense, bears on the question of how we balance the right of publicity against the First Amendment.

Finally, as a qualitative matter, the publicity rights of college athletes are remarkably restricted. This consideration is critical because the "right to exploit commercially one's celebrity is primarily an economic right." NCAA rules prohibit athletes from benefitting economically from any success on the field. NCAA Bylaw 12.5 specifically prohibits commercial licensing of an NCAA athlete's name or picture. NCAA, *2012–13 NCAA Division I Manual* § 12.5.2.1 (2012). Before being allowed to compete each year, all Division I NCAA athletes must sign a contract stating that they understand the prohibition on licensing and affirming that they have not violated any amateurism rules. In short, even if an athlete wished to license his image to EA, the athlete could not do so without destroying amateur status. Thus, an individual college athlete's right of publicity is extraordinarily circumscribed and, in practical reality, nonexistent.

In sum, even apart from consideration of transformative elements, examination of the right of publicity in question also resolves the balance in favor of the First Amendment. The quantity of players involved dilutes the commercial impact of any particular player and the scope of the publicity right is significantly reduced by the fact that: (1) a player cannot own the individual, publicly available statistics on which the game is based; (2) the players are not identified in the game; and (3) NCAA college athletes do not have the right to license their names and likenesses, even if they chose to do so.

II

Given the proper application of the transformative use test, [t]he balance of interests falls squarely on the side of the First Amendment. The stakes are not small. The logical consequence of the majority view is that all realistic depictions of actual persons, no matter how incidental, are protected by a state law right of publicity regardless of the creative context. This logic jeopardizes the creative use of historic figures in motion pictures, books, and sound recordings. Absent the use of actual footage, the motion picture *Forrest Gump* might as well be just a box of chocolates. Without its historical characters, *Midnight in Paris* would be reduced to a pedestrian domestic squabble. The majority's holding that creative use of realistic images and personas does not satisfy the transformative use test cannot be reconciled with the many cases affording such works First Amendment protection. I respectfully disagree with this potentially dangerous and out-of-context interpretation of the transformative use test.

_____

Notes and Questions

1. On March 21, 2016, the United States Supreme Court punted on the *Keller* case by refusing to hear the appeal to the 9th Circuit decision filed by Electronic Arts, Inc.

2. A claim similar to *Keller* was brought by retired professional football players in *Davis v. Elec. Arts* with similar results, *Davis v. Elec. Arts, Inc.*, 2015 U.S. App. LEXIS 154 (9th Cir. Cal. Jan. 6, 2015). Why might there be more difficulties in cases involving retired professional athletes as opposed to current professional athletes?

3. The history of celebrities appearing in games starts with board games and goes back centuries. The first appears to be an English game called *Royal Genealogical Pastime*, first published in 1791, where pictures of various monarchs were used in a race to become King. In the United States, the first game was *The Great Wall Street Game*, introduced in 1883, which included caricatures of three "robber baron" railroad tycoons, William Vanderbilt, Jay Gould, and Cyrus Field. Various games with Mark Twain (*Autograph Authors*, 1886), Charles Zimmer (*Zimmer's Baseball Game*, 1894), Teddy Roosevelt (*Roosevelt at San Juan*, 1889), Eddie Cantor (*Eddie Cantor's Tell it to the Judge*, 1920) and many more followed. A few of such celebrities, but by no means all, were compensated for the use of their likenesses, especially when their names appeared in the title of the games.[15]

The modern litigation history of athletes appearing in sports-related games probably starts with *Palmer v. Schonhorn Enterprises, Inc.*, 232 A.2d 458 (N.J. Super. Ct. 1967).

_____

15. William K. Ford & Raziel Liebler, *Games Are Not Coffee Mugs: Games and the Right of Publicity*, 29 SANTA CLARA COMPUTER & HIGH TECH L.J. 1, 20 (2012).

There, the defendant produced *Pro-Am Golf*, a game in which the profiles and statistics of over twenty professional golfers, including plaintiff Arnold Palmer, were incorporated via cards and stat sheets into the game. No golfer gave his permission for his statistics to be used in the game. No mention of the players was made on the box or in the limited advertising for the game. The New Jersey trial court, without specifically mentioning privacy or publicity rights, granted an injunction against the defendant. *Id.* at 459. In the late 1960s, the Major League Baseball Player's Association (MLBPA) made a deal with Strat-O-Matic Baseball to license the use of their members' statistics. Shortly thereafter, a center fielder for the Minnesota Twins, Ted Uhlaender, and the MLBPA brought suit against the manufacturer of a competing game to Strat-O-Matic, called *Major League Baseball*, which used the statistics for real major league ballplayers as part of the game, but where its developers had not paid for a license for the right to do so. Rejecting the manufacturer's argument that the game transformed the statistics, i.e., that the enjoyment from playing the game was in how the game was put together and how it used and incorporated the publicly available statistics, the court granted an injunction against further production of the competing game. *Uhlaender v. Hendrickson*, 316 F. Supp. 1277 (D. Minn. 1970).[16]

If the litigation had stopped with *Uhlaender*, EA certainly would have had shaky precedent on which to rely in *Keller* and similar cases. However, two cases in the 2000s changed the landscape. In the first, *C.B.C. Distrib. and Mktg., Inc. v. Major League Baseball Advanced Media, LP*, 505 F.3d 818 (8th Cir. 2007), plaintiff C.B.C., which operated a fantasy baseball game using actual players' statistics, prevailed in a declaratory judgment action. In a complicated opinion, the Eighth Circuit found that the players' rights of publicity may have been violated by the unauthorized use of their statistics, but that the protected communicative aspect of the game provided a complete defense. The gist of the opinion is that the statistics used were available publicly, and so the game manufacturers were only reporting on events that a newspaper could publish without liability and there was no reason to treat the game manufacturer differently from the paper viz-a-viz the players' right of publicity. *Id.* at 823. A few years later, a similar decision was reached concerning the use of statistics in a fantasy football game in *CBS Interactive, Inc. v. NFL Players Ass'n, Inc.*, 259 F.R.D. 398, 419 (D. Minn. 2009).

The question was thus whether EA was using the statistics of the players such as Keller in a twenty-first century form of game by making an avatar exhibiting those characteristics (rather than just having them on paper sheets as was true in *C.B.C.* and *CBS Interactive*), or whether it was misappropriating Keller's identity in doing so? The second issue is whether the placing of those attributes in a game with different stadia, fan noises, etc., coupled with the ability to change the characteristics of the Keller avatar made any difference?

4. Returning to *Keller* itself, one question you may be asking is what a court is looking for in determining whether the work is impermissibly infringing or not. In *Saderup* (the case discussed in *Keller* with the Three Stooges in which the transformative use test was first used), the court explained it as follows:

> [H]ow may courts distinguish between protected and unprotected expression? Some commentators have proposed importing the fair use defense from copyright law which has the advantage of employing an established doctrine developed

---

16. Ford & Liebler, *supra*, at 27–32.

from a related area of the law. Others disagree, pointing to the murkiness of the fair use doctrine.

We conclude that a wholesale importation of the fair use doctrine into right of publicity law would not be advisable. Nonetheless, the first fair use factor— "the purpose and character of the use" (17 U.S.C. § 107(1))—does seem particularly pertinent to the task of reconciling the rights of free expression and publicity. As the Supreme Court has stated, the central purpose of the inquiry into this fair use factor "is to see, in Justice Story's words, whether the new work merely 'supersede[s] the objects' of the original creation, [citations], or instead adds something new, with a further purpose or different character, altering the first with new expression, meaning, or message; it asks, in other words, whether and to what extent the new work is 'transformative.' Although such transformative use is not absolutely necessary for a finding of fair use, the goal of copyright, to promote science and the arts, is generally furthered by the creation of transformative works." (*Campbell v. Acuff-Rose Music, Inc.* (1994) 510 U.S. 569, 579.)

Comedy III Prods., Inc. v. Gary Saderup, Inc, 25 Cal. 4th 387, 403–04 (2001).

5. As can be seen in both *Brown* and *Keller*, the *Rogers* test was imported from Lanham Act law. On the other hand, the transformative use test, as indicated in the above note, came from a couple of the factors used in assessing the "fair use" defense found in copyright law.[17] Should there be a separate test that applies just to this issue which is not taken from other bodies of law? If so, what should the test be?

Expressing a dissatisfaction with both the *Rogers* and the transformative use tests, at least one court has come up with a third test. *Doe v. TCI Cablevision,* 110 S.W.3d 363 (Mo. 2003) was a case that considered a hockey player's right of publicity claim against a comic book publishing company. Anthony "Tony" Twist, a hockey player, brought suit against a number of individuals and entities involved in producing and publishing the *Spawn* comic book series after the introduction of a villainous character named Anthony "Tony Twist" Twistelli. In evaluating the claim, the Missouri Supreme Court adopted the "predominant use" test, which it explained as follows:

If a product is being sold that predominantly exploits the commercial value of an individual's identity, that product should be held to violate the right of publicity and not be protected by the First Amendment, even if there is some 'expressive' content in it that might qualify as 'speech' in other circumstances. If, on the other hand, the predominant purpose of the product is to make an expressive comment on or about a celebrity, the expressive values could be given greater weight.

Id. at 374 (quoting Mark S. Lee, *Agents of Chaos: Judicial Confusion in Defining the Right of Publicity-Free Speech Interface,* 23 Loy. L.A. Ent..L. Rev. 471, 500 (2003)). The test has not proven popular, with one court complaining that it "is subjective at best, arbitrary at worst, and in either case calls upon judges to act as both impartial jurists and discerning art critics. These two roles cannot co-exist." *Hart v. Electronic Arts, Inc,* 717 F.3d 141, 154 (3d Cir. 2013). What do you think of the predominant use test?

6. Would adoption of the transformative use test resulted in a different result in *Brown*? In *White*? Do you like it better than the *Rogers* test? Better than the "predominant use" test?

---

17. We discuss all copyright defenses, including fair use, in some detail in Chapter 6.

7. In a jurisdiction where the proper test has not yet been decided, lawyers for the videogame industry pretty much uniformly argue for adoption of the *Rogers* test, arguing it gives the proper weight to the use of a celebrity's identity in a constitutionally protected medium. That is, these lawyers argue that if an unauthorized biography, a fictional work, or a newspaper article, etc., can freely use a celebrity likeness and describe the celebrity in just the arena where the celebrity's status is earned (e.g., by describing Keller's best game at ASU in Sun Devil Stadium),[18] then denying a videogame developer's right to depict Keller in the Sun Devil Stadium with the team from which he derives his publicity is both unfair and illogical. On the other side, lawyers bringing rights to publicity claims argue that *Rogers* is too defense friendly. Who has the better argument?

8. Is the transformative use test merely stating that when the image of the depicted celebrity is so transformed so that no longer looks like the depicted celebrity, then there is no misappropriation? For example, in the *Winter* case mentioned in *Keller* (*Winter v. DC Comics*, 30 Cal. 4th 881 (2003)) is it that there is no claim for Edgar Winter because a half-human/half-worm creature is simply not a depiction of the guitarist, and thus not an infringement of his publicity rights? If that is the case, is the transformative test really an application of a First Amendment defense or is it a test for determining whether there has been misappropriation in the first place?

9. Do you find it interesting that EA maintained in *Brown* that Mr. Brown had not appeared in the game, but chose here not to contest that Keller established a prima facie case under both California statutory and common law?

10. Some have stated that the most significant part of the *Keller* litigation was whether the case was granted class action status. Why do you think that is?

11. One argument often made by plaintiffs in these cases is that there should be only a limited form of First Amendment protection at best because the videogame manufacturers charge for the game. However, as the Court in *Saderup* noted, "[t]he First Amendment is not limited to those who publish without charge.... [An expressive activity] does not lose its constitutional protection because it is undertaken for profit." 25 Cal. 4th at 396. This concept goes back at least as far as *New York Times v. Sullivan*, 376 U.S. 254 (1964) (holding that a potentially defamatory advertisement run in the New York Times was entitled to full first amendment protection).

12. What do you think of the dissent's idea that the proper focus should be whether the game as a whole is transformative, and not on whether an individual player's identity is used?

13. On the dissent's questioning as to whether any particular player's image is important to the game, in light of the vast number of players in the game and the fact that the game can be played endlessly without, e.g., Keller's image, ever coming up, the majority stated:

---

18. *See, e.g., Ann-Margaret v. High Society Magazine, Inc.*, 498 F. Supp. 401 (S.D.N.Y. 1980) (holding a celebrity had no right to object to her appearance in a news story); *Frosch v. Grosset & Dunlap, Inc.*, 427 N.Y.S. 2d 828 (1980) (holding a celebrity had no right to object to his appearance in an unauthorized biography); *and Lerman v. Flynt Distrib. Co.*, 745 F.2d 123 (2d Cir. 1984) (holding that a celebrity had no right to object when a magazine sought to solicit subscriptions by referencing a prior story). *See gen.* Restatement (Third) Unfair Competition, §47, Cmt. c (1995), and cases cited therein. *But see Spahn v. Julian Messner, Inc.*, 233 N.E.2d 840 (N.Y. 1967) (holding that an unauthorized biography of a public figure with "material and substantial falsification(s)," including made up dialogue between characters and imputing thoughts and motivations of the pitcher Warren Spahn and those in his circle without justification was not protected by the first amendment.).

Judge Thomas argues that the "sheer number of virtual actors," the absence of "any evidence as to the personal marketing power of Sam Keller," and the relative anonymity of each individual player in *NCAA Football* as compared to the public figures in other California right-of-publicity cases all mitigate in favor of finding that the EA's First Amendment rights outweigh Keller's right of publicity. These facts are not irrelevant to the analysis — they all can be considered in the framework of the five considerations from *Comedy III* laid out above — but the fact is that EA elected to use avatars that mimic real college football players for a reason. If EA did not think there was value in having an avatar designed to mimic each individual player, it would not go to the lengths it does to achieve realism in this regard. Having chosen to use the players' likenesses, EA cannot now hide behind the numerosity of its potential offenses or the alleged unimportance of any one individual player.

Keller, 724 F.3d at 1276, n. 7.

14. From reading the case, you might think that EA did not pay anyone for the rights to use the players' identities. That's not true. EA had exclusive dealing contracts with the NCAA for both its football and basketball games.[19]

The dissent quotes the NCAA by-laws for the proposition that athlete's individually may have assigned away their publicity rights in return for getting a scholarship. The NCAA bylaws provide that amateur status is lost if the student athlete uses his or her athletic skill for pay (which is broadly defined).[20] If the right to publicity is assignable, could the NCAA require the prospective student athlete to assign his or her publicity rights to the NCAA, or an individual's conference, without pay, while playing under NCAA guidelines? If so couldn't EA make a deal for those rights with the appropriate body?

Assuming that the Supreme Court had yet to rule on *Keller*, can EA continue to produce the game? ESPN has reported, "After a 14-year run publishing *NCAA March Madness*, EA Sports discontinued its college basketball title in 2009. Its only competition, 2K Sports' NCAA series, stopped publishing new college hoops titles in 2008."[21] Sean O'Brien, EA Sports executive, refused to say "no" when he was asked whether there could one day be another college basketball video game. SB Nation has reported that "EA Sports announced in September that it would no longer make the NCAA Football video game franchise," but that and they may return to the market if EA can pay players for the use of their likenesses.[22]

15. *Keller* was not the only suit in which a college player has asserted a right of privacy based on his use in a videogame. A decision by the Third Circuit Court of Appeals came to a similar conclusion on almost identical reasoning as that used in *Keller* in a case involving a former Rutgers quarterback in *Hart v. Elec. Arts, Inc.*, 717 F.3d 141 (3d Cir.2013).

---

19. Anastasios Kaubrakis, *et al.*, *NCAA Student-Athletes' Rights of Publicity, EA Sports and the Video Game Industry*, 27 Ent. & Sports Lawyer 5, (Vol. 2, Summer 2009).

20. Nat'l Collegiate Athletic Ass'n, 2013–2014 NCAA Division I Manual, Operating Bylaws art. 12.1.2 (2014), *available at* http://grfx.cstv.com/photos/schools/usc/genrel/auto_pdf/2013-14/misc_non_event/ncaa-manual.pdf

21. Eamonn Brennan, *The College Basketball Video Game is Dead*, ESPN (July 18, 2014, 2:41 PM), http://espn.go.com/blog/collegebasketballnation/post/_/id/86183/the-college-basketball-video-game-is-dead

22. Kevin Trahan, *EA Sports Might Bring Back College Football Game, If It Can Play Players*, SB Nation (July 18, 2014 2:37 PM), http://www.sbnation.com/college-football/2014/6/18/5822084/ea-sports-ncaa-football-video-game-return

Similar, but legally distinct, claims were adjudicated in *O'Bannon v. NCAA*. Whereas the focus of *Keller* is on the constitutional privilege to use an athlete's name, image, and likeness (known as a "NIL") without compensation in videogames, the focus of *O'Bannon* is on antitrust law. There, it was claimed that the NCAA attempts to gain the exclusive right to use the player's image while the athlete is in college through its Form 08-3a, which all NCAA athletes must sign[23] illegally fixes the price of an athlete's NIL at $0, and restrains trade by denying the players the right to collectivize and market their NILs in videogames, as well as other media pursuits. The rights to market their NILs is also an issue in the case decided by the NLRB rejecting the athletes' at Northwestern University attempts to unionize.[24] We have included the opinion in *O'Bannon* in Chapter 16.

16. Imagine you were general counsel of a videogame company that wanted to produce a golf game with Tiger Woods in it. What would you advise if you were in a jurisdiction that followed the transformative use test? The *Rogers* test?

17. To give you even a better sense of how the transformative test is applied, we now have three cases in which a sketch is on issue, *Saderup* in which the sketch of the Three Stooges was not considered transformative (*Comedy III Productions, Inc. v. Gary Saderup, Inc.*, 25 Cal. 4th 387 (2001)), *ETW* in which a painting of Tiger Woods was considered transformative (*ETW Corp. v. Jireh Pub., Inc.*, 332 F.3d 915 (6th Cir. 2003)) because it was, as one court put it, "worthy of First Amendment protection because it was a 'panorama' of Woods' historic 1997 victory at the world-famous Masters Tournament and conveyed a message about the significance of Woods' achievement through images suggesting that Woods would eventually join the ranks of the world's best golfers," and *Winter*, in which a caricature of the musician Edgar Winter was considered transformative, *Winter v. DC Comics*, 30 Cal. 4th 881 (2003).

The pictures from the first two cases appear below.

---

23. Form 08-3a is a release which provides, in part, that the athlete "authorize(s) the NCAA (or a third party acting on behalf of the NCAA) to use your name or picture to generally promote NCAA championships or other NCAA events, activities, or programs." *See gen*, Lester Munson, "*NCAA Athletes Get Their Day in Court*" ESPN (June 8, 2014), http://espn.go.com/espn/print?id-11045682&type-story.

24. *See, e.g.,* Southall, R.M. & Weiler, J.D., *NCAA Division-I Athletic Departments: 21st Century Athletic Company Towns* 7 J. of Issues in Intercollegiate Athletics 161 (2014); and Jensen, Erik M., *Taking the Student Out of Student Athlete: College Sports and the Unrelated Business Income Tax* (July 2014). *Journal Taxation of Investments, Forthcoming;* Case Legal Studies Research Paper No. 2014-20. *Available at* SSRN: http://ssrn.com/abstract=2469946. For an explanation of the NLRB's rejection of the athletes' attempt to unionize, *see* espn.go.com/college-football/story/_id13455477/nlrb-says-north-western-players-cannot-unionize.

Figure 4.1

Figure 4.2

18. In early 2016, yet another faction of plantiffs suing sports-related videogames was heard from. A company called Solid Oak Sketches sued Take-Two Interactive Software (the developer of *NBA 2K16*), claiming: (1) that it owned the copyright on various tattoos featured on NBA stars like LeBron James, Kobe Bryant, and Kenyon Martin, among others, and (2) that these players were depicted in *NBA 2K16* with their tattoos and without Solid Oak's permission. Apparently no one is contesting that Solid Oak put the

tattoos on the players. An earlier case that we cited in § 2.20, *Escabedo v. THQ, Inc.*, No. 212-CV-02470-JAT (D. Az. 2012) did not settle the issue. What result do you foresee?

§ 4.30 Rights of Publicity: Use of a Celebrity's Image With the Celebrity's Permission

It might seem obvious that when the maker of a videogame decided to err on the side of caution and get permission for the right to use a celebrity's or other person's image, there would be no subsequent right of publicity or privacy litigation. Once again, as the following cases show, it is not that simple.

No Doubt v. Activision Publishing, Inc.

California Court of Appeals, 2011
192 Cal.App.4th 1018

WILLHITE, J.

INTRODUCTION

The rock band No Doubt brought suit against the videogame publisher Activision Publishing, Inc. (Activision) based on Activision's release of the *Band Hero* videogame featuring computer-generated images of the members of No Doubt. No Doubt licensed the likenesses of its members for use in *Band Hero*, but contends that Activision used them in objectionable ways outside the scope of the parties' licensing agreement. Applying the transformative use test first adopted in *Comedy III Productions, Inc. v. Gary Saderup, Inc.*, 25 Cal. 4th 387 (2001), we conclude that the creative elements of the *Band Hero* videogame do not transform the images of No Doubt's band members into anything more than literal, fungible reproductions of their likenesses. Therefore, we reject Activision's contention that No Doubt's right of publicity claim is barred by the First Amendment.

FACTUAL AND PROCEDURAL BACKGROUND

Band Hero Dispute

Defendant Activision is a leading international videogame distributor and the creator and owner of the interactive *Band Hero* videogame. *Band Hero* is a version of Activision's *Guitar Hero* franchise that has sold over 40 million units. The game allows players to simulate performing in a rock band in time with popular songs. By choosing from a number of playable characters, known as "avatars," players can "be" a guitarist, a singer, or a drummer. Some of the available avatars are fictional characters created and designed by Activision while others are digital representations of real-life rock stars. Players can also design their own unique fictional avatars. Represented by the avatars of their choosing, players "perform" in various settings, such as venues in Paris and Madrid, a rock show at a shopping mall, and even outer space.

In addition to allowing players to perform over 60 popular songs, *Band Hero* permits players to create their own music and then play their compositions using an avatar. As with all the *Guitar Hero* videogames, as players advance in the *Band Hero* game, they can "unlock" characters and use them to play songs of the players' choosing, including songs the players have composed as well as songs made famous by other artists.

Plaintiff No Doubt is an internationally-recognized rock band featuring Gwen Stefani as its lead singer. No Doubt entered into a Professional Services and Character Licensing Agreement (Agreement) with Activision permitting Activision to include No Doubt as one of the rock bands featured in *Band Hero*.

The pertinent language of the Agreement is as follows: "This Agreement sets out the terms upon which Artist [No Doubt] has agreed to grant to Activision certain rights to utilize Artist's name(s), likeness(es), logo(s), and associated trademark(s) and other related intellectual property rights (the 'Licensed Property') and to provide Activision certain production and marketing services in connection with Activision's 'Band Hero' video game (the 'Game')." The Agreement specifically provides that "Artists grant to Activision the non-exclusive, worldwide right and license to use the Licensed Property (including Artist's likeness as provided by or approved by Artist) solely in the one (1) Game for all gaming platforms and formats, on the packaging for the Game, and in advertising, marketing, promotional and PR materials for the Game."

In a section entitled "Approval Rights," the Agreement states that "Artist's likeness as implemented in the Game (the 'Character Likeness'), any use of Artist's name and/or likeness other than in a 'billing block' fashion on the back of the packaging for the Game, and the b-roll and photography or other representation of the Services or of Artist, shall be subject to Artist's prior written approval. [¶] Activision shall submit each of the above (i.e., the Character Likeness, name uses, and b-roll and photography or other representation) to Artist for review and Artist shall have ten (10) business days to either approve or disapprove.... [¶] Activision shall not be required to submit for approval uses of previously approved assets, provided such uses fall within the rights granted herein (e.g., using a previously approved Character Likeness depiction in multiple advertising materials)."

As part of the Agreement, Activision agreed to license no more than three No Doubt songs for use in "Band Hero," subject to No Doubt's approval over the song choice. (Ultimately, the game included two No Doubt songs.) No Doubt agreed to participate in one day of game production services "for the purposes of photographing and scanning Artist's likeness, and capturing Artist's motion-capture data."

Pursuant to the Agreement, the members of No Doubt participated in a full-day motion capture photography session at Activision's studios so that the band members' *Band Hero* avatars would accurately reflect their appearances, movements, and sounds. No Doubt then closely reviewed the motion capture photography and the details related to the appearance and features of their avatars to ensure the representations would meet their approval. The end results are avatars that closely match the appearance of each of the No Doubt band members.

Approximately two weeks prior to the release of *Band Hero,* No Doubt became aware of the "unlocking" feature of the game that would permit players to use No Doubt's avatars to perform any of the songs included in the game, including songs that No Doubt maintains it never would have performed. Two of No Doubt's members could be unlocked at the seventh level of the game, and the remaining members could be unlocked at level nine. The band also learned that female lead singer Gwen Stefani's avatar could be made to sing in a male voice, and the male band members' avatars could be manipulated to sing songs in female voices. The individual band member avatars could be made to perform solo, without their band members, as well as with members of other groups. No Doubt contends that in the numerous communications with No Doubt, Activision never communicated its intention to permit such manipulations of the No Doubt avatars. Rather, No Doubt insists, Activision represented that No Doubt's likenesses within *Band Hero* would be used only in conjunction with the selected No Doubt songs.

When No Doubt complained about the additional exploitation of their likenesses, Activision admitted that it hired actors to impersonate No Doubt in order to create the representations of the band members' performances of the additional musical works other than the No Doubt songs licensed for the game. No Doubt demanded that Activision remove the "unlocking" feature for No Doubt's avatars, but Activision refused.

DISCUSSION

No Doubt's Probability of Success on the Merits of the Claims

Right of Publicity Claim

No Doubt has alleged a claim for violation of the right of publicity. Because one of the elements of both the statutory and common law claim for violation of the right of publicity is a lack of prior consent on No Doubt's part, No Doubt's claim would fail if Activision were found to hold a valid license to use No Doubt's likenesses in the manner in which they are used in *Band Hero*. However, Activision argued below that for purposes of ruling on the [current] motion, the trial court did not need to resolve the issue whether the challenged use of the No Doubt avatars was outside the parties' license agreement. Rather than contesting No Doubt's ability to support the "lack of consent" element or any other substantive element of its right of publicity claim, Activision asserted below, and contends here, only that the First Amendment provides a complete defense to the claim. Thus, we limit our analysis to the strength of that First Amendment defense.

Videogames generally are considered "expressive works" subject to First Amendment protections. *Schwarzenegger v. Ent. Merchants Ass'n* ——U.S. ——, 130 S. Ct. 2398 (2010). *See also Romantics v. Activision Pub., Inc.* 574 F. Supp.2d 758, 765–766 (E.D. Mich. 2008) [finding that Activision's *Guitar Hero* videogame is "an expressive artistic work that is entitled to First Amendment protection"].) Further, Activision's use of No Doubt's likenesses in *Band Hero* is a matter of public interest because of the widespread fame No Doubt has achieved: "there is a public interest which attaches to people who, by their accomplishments, mode of living, professional standing or calling, create a legitimate and widespread attention to their activities…." (*Stewart v. Rolling Stone LLC* (2010) 181 Cal. App. 4th 664, 677–678 (2010) [magazine's publication of "indie rock" bands' names was matter of public interest].) However, Activision's First Amendment right of free expression is in tension with the rights of No Doubt to control the commercial exploitation of its members' likenesses.

[The court explained *Comedy III* (*Saderup*) and related cases and held the "transformative use" test would apply.] With these cases as a backdrop, we now turn to Activision's use of No Doubt's likenesses in *Band Hero*.

Activision does not dispute that the avatars of No Doubt are computer-generated recreations of the real band members, painstakingly designed to mimic their likenesses. Indeed, as part of the licensing agreement between Activision and No Doubt, No Doubt posed for motion-capture photography to enable Activision to reproduce their likenesses, movements, and sounds with precision. Activision intentionally used these literal reproductions so that players could choose to "be" the No Doubt rock stars. The game does not permit players to alter the No Doubt avatars in any respect; they remain at all times immutable images of the real celebrity musicians, in stark contrast to the "fanciful, creative characters" in *Winter* and *Kirby*.

No Doubt asserts that such realistic depictions categorically disqualify their *Band Hero* avatars from First Amendment protection. However, as *Comedy III* held, even literal reproductions of celebrities can be "transformed" into expressive works based on the context into which the celebrity image is placed. Thus, when the context into which a literal celebrity depiction is placed creates "something new, with a further purpose or different character, altering the first [likeness] with new expression, meaning, or message," the depiction is protected by the First Amendment.

Nonetheless, although context may create protected expression in the use of a celebrity's literal likeness, the context in which Activision uses the literal likenesses of No Doubt's members does not qualify the use of the likenesses for First Amendment protection. Activision contends that as in *Kirby,* where Sega used Kirby's likeness in a unique and expressive videogame, Activision's use of No Doubt's likenesses in *Band Hero* is transformative because the videogame shows the No Doubt avatars "surrounded by unique, creative elements, including in fanciful venues such as outer space ... and performing songs that No Doubt avowedly would never perform in real life." Indeed, according to Activision, No Doubt's objection that the band can be made to perform songs it would never perform demonstrates that the use of the No Doubt avatars is transformative.

However, that the members of No Doubt object to being shown performing certain songs is irrelevant to whether that element of *Band Hero* combined with others transforms the literal depictions of No Doubt's members into expression that is more Activision's than pure mimicry. In that inquiry, it is the differences between *Kirby* and the instant case, not the similarities, which are determinative. In *Kirby,* the pop singer was portrayed as an entirely new character — the space-age news reporter Ulala. In *Band Hero,* by contrast, no matter what else occurs in the game during the depiction of the No Doubt avatars, the avatars perform rock songs, the same activity by which the band achieved and maintains its fame. Moreover, the avatars perform those songs as literal recreations of the band members. That the avatars can be manipulated to perform at fanciful venues including outer space or to sing songs the real band would object to singing, or that the avatars appear in the context of a videogame that contains many other creative elements, does not transform the avatars into anything other than exact depictions of No Doubt's members doing exactly what they do as celebrities.

Moreover, Activision's use of life-like depictions of No Doubt performing songs is motivated by the commercial interest in using the band's fame to market *Band Hero,* because it encourages the band's sizeable fan base to purchase the game so as to perform as, or alongside, the members of No Doubt. Thus, insofar as the depiction of No Doubt is concerned, the graphics and other background content of the game are secondary, and the expressive elements of the game remain "manifestly subordinated to the overall goal of creating a conventional portrait of [No Doubt] so as to commercially exploit [its] fame." In other words, nothing in the creative elements of the *Band Hero* elevates the depictions of No Doubt to something more than "conventional, more or less fungible, images" of its members that No Doubt should have the right to control and exploit.

DISPOSITION

The judgment is affirmed. No Doubt shall recover its costs and attorneys fees on appeal.

———————

Notes and Questions

1. Are you surprised that Activision did not argue that its release covered the unlocked characters? Given the contract language as set forth in the case, do you believe Activision

would have prevailed in that argument? Is this case really no more than a breach of contract case as opposed to a right of publicity case?

2. Does Activision have a point when it states that what No Doubt objects to (e.g., giving Gwen Stefani a male voice, having the band members sing solo or in different bands, and having the band sing songs it would never otherwise sing), shows that the characters are "transformed" within the meaning of the transformative test?

3. Does the fact that the court in *No Doubt* put some emphasis on the fact that the characters couldn't be altered shed some light on why Electronic Arts made the argument in *Keller* that the avatars could take on different characteristics?

4. Go back and look at different scenarios involving Tiger Woods at beginning of the Chapter. Which would give Tiger a valid right of publicity claim and which would not?

––––––––––

Special Note on Best Practices: Releases

Assume in *No Doubt* that the release was as clear as it could be that the band was, individually and collectively, allowing its images to be used for the No Doubt songs *and* for the unlocked portions of the game. But also assume that No Doubt claims that the Activision representatives it met during the negotiation of the deal told the group that the avatars would only be available in the game for the No Doubt songs, and could not be accessed for the unlocked portions of the game. Could (or should) the alleged oral representations of the party seeking the release trump the written contract?

For many years, in California and elsewhere, the answer was "no." That is, if a written release said "X", a party could not allege in a lawsuit that the other contracting party had said "not X" during the negotiation of the agreement. *Bank of America Ass'n v. Pendergrass*, 4 Cal. 2d 258 (1935). The rationale was that "not X" was a "contradictory term" and thus its admissibility at trial was barred by the parol evidence rule. And if the plaintiff could not introduce the "not X" statement into trial, then the written release would control and the case would have to be decided in the defendant's favor, assuming it was not subject to ambiguity.

But over time a couple things changed. First, at least some courts stated that the written word in a contract was not "gospel" in breach of contract cases, and that the salient task for the court was discovering what the parties actually intended when they entered into the contract, not what they actually wrote, since the words in the written agreement might or might not reflect that intent. *See, e.g., Pacific Gas & Electric Co. v. G.W. Thomas Drayage & Rigging Co.*, 69 Cal.2d 33 (1968). Second, the common law developed "exceptions" to the parol evidence rule, one of which was fraud. That is, the courts were not going to allow a party who fraudulently misrepresented a material fact to another who relied on that misrepresentation in deciding to enter into the contract, to prevail in a law suit by using the parol evidence rule as a technical defense to enforcement. *Riversland Cold Storage v. Madera Prod'n Credit Ass'n*, 55 Cal. 4th 1169 (2013).

Accordingly, the law of releases is now changed. In *Doe v. Gangland, Productions* 730 F.3d 946 (9th Cir. 2013) the producers of the television show *Gangland* secured a written and signed release from a "snitch" which provided that his face, voice, and name could appear on the show and that such use might put "Doe" in danger. However, Doe claimed that when he was signing the release, he was assured that his face would be "pixilated," his voice modulated and his name withheld. When Doe appeared on the show without any shielding of his identity, he brought suit alleging fraud, breach of contract, undue influence, etc. The Ninth Circuit held the *Gangland* producers could not rely on the language of the release in light of Doe's allegations that he was misled during the bargaining process. The defendants were not helped by the fact that Doe claimed he was illiterate and dyslexic, that the producers knew those facts when they had him sign the release, and that he claimed the producers told him that the release he signed was just a receipt for the $300 appearance fee he received. However, it is reasonably clear that even without such allegations, the case would have gone forward as the literal language of the release is no longer controlling.

Perhaps the result would be different for a group such as No Doubt, which has lawyers and managers actually reading and negotiating the release/rights agreement, but if the group alleges the videogame producers misled the band's members during their time together, it is not clear that the result would be any different.

Assume you are the General Counsel to a videogame producer and you want to make sure that your acquisition of rights agreement is not challengeable later. What "best practices" would you advise your client to take?

Chapter Five

Copyright Protection

In order to encourage creative incentives and "promote the progress of science and useful arts," Article I, Section 8 of the United States Constitution has granted Congress the power to convey "for limited times to authors and inventors the exclusive right to their respective writings and discoveries." Due in part to its simplicity and very low cost, copyright registration has been the overwhelming favorite protection device for authors, artists, musicians, and videogame programmers alike. It does not grant the extraordinary monopoly-like exclusivity enjoyed by patent holders. But patents are more expensive, often difficult to obtain, and far more time consuming to enforce.

§ 5.10 The Copyright Act

While there will always be those programmers and hobbyists who create games for the sheer joy of doing so, the majority of today's successful videogames involve a profit motive; this in turn implies substantial investments of both time and money, which would not be feasible in the absence of intellectual property protection. It is doubtful, for example, that Microsoft would have invested resources exceeding a reported $60 million in the development and marketing of the videogame *Halo 3*[1] if, once created, anyone could copy the software. Incentive is the purpose behind intellectual property protection.[2] Without copyright laws designed to protect its property ownership, Microsoft would not have had the financial incentive to develop any of its software.

Generally, a copyright secures works of authorship, while a patent protects inventions. Those nice distinctions, however, have gone by the wayside in this digital age where software can embody both an invention and a work of authorship.[3] A videogame engine might, for example, be patentable while, at the same time, it may generate copyrightable audio and video; the game, therefore, would be eligible for copyright protection. To answer the question "What is copyrightable?" we look to the Copyright Act, in particular, Title 17 U.S.C. § 102: Any "original works of authorship fixed in any tangible medium of expression …"[4]

---

1. Alex Pham and Josh Friedman, *Halo Guns $150 Million*, L.A. Times, Sep. 25, 2007, at C1.

2. *See* Jane C. Ginsberg, *A Tale of Two Copyrights: Literary Property in Revolutionary France and America*, Tul. L. Rev. 991 (1990).

3. David A. Einhorn, *Copyright and Patent Protection for Computer Software: Are They Mutually Exclusive?*, Law and Technology Press, Vol. VII, No. 12 (May 1990); *See also, infra* § 6.20.

4. The key elements of the definition are: (1) Originality, (2) Authorship and (3) Fixation.

This definition is broad, and it should be. Flexibility is important in today's era of rapidly changing media of expression. To provide further substance to the otherwise general definition, the Act then provides a list of categories that are subject to copyright protection in § 102(a):

(1) Literary works;

(2) Musical works, including any accompanying words;

(3) Dramatic works, including any accompanying music;

(4) Pantomimes and choreographic works;

(5) Pictorial, graphic, and sculptural works;

(6) Motion pictures and other audiovisual works;

(7) Sound recordings; and

(8) Architectural works.

While "videogames" are not specifically mentioned, it is clear that the elements comprising them are. In fact, it is conceivable that most, if not all, of the listed items might appear in a videogame. Nevertheless, the term "audiovisual" best describes the content of most videogames. But what about the computer code itself?

In the early days, incomprehensible sets of zeros and ones would generate (create) the audio and video images that appeared on the viewing screen. In general, computer code, comprehensible or not, can be considered as a literary work. *Vault Corp. v. Quaid Software, Ltd.*, 847 F.2d 255, 259 (5th Cir. 1988). Even though this designation might seem oversimplistic to a computer programmer, it does simplify the registration process. A knowledgeable programmer is likely to suggest that the output from the code should be the determining factor, not the repetitive zeros and ones; after all, we distinguish the dramatic work from a pictorial piece of art by its output, not by the texture of the ink or paint used to create it. These particular registration issues are more particularly addressed in § 5.21, *infra*.

Unlike a patent, a copyright does not grant a monopoly. Theoretically, two individuals could coincidentally author the same identical work, with each maintaining a valid copyright in his or her respective creation. Only the *copying* of another's work is prohibited. To establish copyright infringement, the plaintiff must prove: (1) Access to the protected work plus (2) Substantial similarity between the infringed and infringing works. Neither requirement is taken for granted. If direct access is not demonstrated, the plaintiff must show striking similarity. To apply the concept to videogames, consider *Roginski v. Time Warner Interactive*, 967 F. Supp. 821 (M.D. Pa. 1997), where the plaintiff filed a copyright infringement action against defendants Time Warner Interactive, Atari Games Corp. and Sega of America, alleging that the defendants copied his unpublished manuscript entitled *Awesome Possum* and then created a related videogame and comic book. Defendants filed a motion for summary judgment claiming that their products were independently created and, in addition, that there was no evidence that they had access to Roginski's manuscript. The court agreed with the defendants, agreeing that the concept of an "awesome possum" was independently created and Roginski failed to show that defendants had reasonable access to his work or, in the alternative, that there were striking similarities between the two works.

Because videogames came of age in the 1970s, it is to be expected that the 1976 Copyright Act (Title 17) would play a vital role in the development of the industry. Attention should be directed to the structure of the Act. The definition of "audiovisual works" in § 101, for example, is intended to encompass several of the items listed in the "protection section" of § 102(a), including, for our purposes, items 1, 2, 5, 6, and 7. The "exclusive rights" Section (§ 106), which encompasses all works of authorship, should then be compared and contrasted with the additional rights granted to works of "visual art" in § 106A. We set forth those rights in § 6.10, *infra*.

Of critical importance are the "fair use" provisions which are spelled out in § 107 (discussed briefly in § 4.30, *supra*, and thoroughly addressed later in this chapter) and which constitute important exceptions to the otherwise "exclusive" rights granted in both of the preceding sections. The "ownership" provisions of § 201 et seq. play a critical role in determining disputes that typically follow the construction and publication of the authored works. Particular attention should also be directed toward the "work made for hire" provisions of both § 102(b) and § 101, which target those situations where authors are paid to create, or add to, works that are to be owned by others. Finally, we discuss the "first sale" doctrine protections of 106(3) in § 11.10, *infra*.

Special Word About the DMCA

At this juncture, a word or two should be said about the Digital Millennium Copyright Act ("DMCA"), whose title is far more intimidating than its content. Though it is often thought of and treated as an independent piece of legislation, the DMCA could better be described as a 1998 amendment to the 1976 Copyright Act. It was designed to address the rapidly growing problems caused by copyright infringement over the Internet. As relevant to the issues in this book, it has three major provisions. First, it allows copyright holders victimized via the net to enjoin infringers of its works for acts like circumventing anti-copying safeguards built into programs by developers. Second, the DMCA imposes various obligations on internet service providers (ISPs) who host infringing works, but then, third, it provides "safe harbors," i.e., immunity from suit, for conscientious ISPs that follow certain, spelled out steps once they are informed by the copyright holder of an alleged infringement on their sites. 17 U.S.C. § 512.

The DMCA is divided into 5 titles. Title I concerns the implementation of the World Intellectual Property Treaty, commonly known as "WIPO." Title II, which will surface throughout this book, is descriptively labeled, "The Online Copyright Infringement Liability Limitation Act." Title III, the "Maintenance Competition Assurance Act," creates certain exemptions pertaining to computer maintenance and repair. Title IV grants certain limited rights to webcasters and distance learning centers such libraries and educators. The last title deals with vessel hulls and is unrelated to the issues in this book.

We have a more detailed discussion of the DCMA in § 6.50, *infra*.

―――――――――

§ 5.20 The Registration Process

The videogame industry witnessed its greatest expansion and development *after* passage of the Copyright Act of 1976. The Act constituted a significant change as compared to earlier copyright statutes dating back to 1909; the early laws required notice and registration as a prerequisite to owning a valid copyright. A goal of the 1976 Act, along with its subsequent amendments and related legislation, has been to reduce the formalities required to obtain copyright protection. *See* Christopher Sprigman, *Reformalizing Copyright*, 57 STAN. L. REV. 485 (2004), and Richard A. Epstein, *The Dubious Constitutionality of the Copyright Term Extension Act*, 36 LOY. L.A. L. REV. 123, 124 (2002). Today, a copyright attaches when the author creates an original work and fixes it in a tangible medium of expression, even if no paperwork ever gets filed in the Copyright Office.

While it is not necessary to register or provide notice for a copyright to attach, it is certainly advisable to do both. Registration is required as a prerequisite to filing a lawsuit for infringement. 17 U.S.C.A. § 411(a); *Jefferson Airplane v. Berkeley Sys., Inc.*, 886 F. Supp. 713 (N.D. Cal. 1994). And subject to certain exceptions, registration may be required in order to recover attorneys' fees and statutory damages. 17 U.S.C. § 412; *Troll Co. v. Uneeda Doll Co.*, 483 F.3d 150, 158–59 (2d Cir. 2007). In addition, registration notice is still required for works published prior to March 1, 1989.

Registration is simple, inexpensive, and relatively expedient.[5] When a person obtains a certificate of copyright registration within five years of publication, there is a presumption that the copyright is valid and that the registering author is the proper holder of that copyright. 17 U.S.C. § 410(c); *Apple Computer, Inc. v. Formula Int'l Inc.*, 725 F.2d 521, 523 (9th Cir. 1984).

---

§ 5.21 Copyright Registration Forms

There are a variety of copyright registration forms available depending upon the nature of the subject work.[6] In *Williams Elec., Inc. v. Artic Int'l, Inc.*, 685 F.2d 870 (3d Cir. N.J. 1982), plaintiff filed *three* separate copyright registration forms for the game *Defender*, one Form TX covering the computer code along with two Form PAs covering the audiovisual effects. This was done out of an abundance of caution, but it raises a fair question. How many forms should a videogame developer file to be totally protected?

For software, in general, the Copyright Office favors a single filing regardless of the different expressions in multimedia software such as in videogames. Its official position states: "[A]ll copyrightable expression owned by the same claimant and embodied in a computer program, including computer screen displays, is considered a single work and should be registered on a single application form." Library of Congress, Copyright Office, *Registration of Computer Screen Displays*, Docket No. 87-4, 53 Fed. Reg. 21,817 (1988). More recently, the Copyright Office issued the following bulletin:

> Copyright protection for computer screen displays, including video games, has been an issue in the courts for some time. Courts have differed in their opinions

---

5. Forms may be obtained from the Library of Congress, Copyright Office in Washington D.C. or alternatively may be downloaded from the official government site: www.copyright.gov.

6. The following are basic copyright forms used for an original registration (excluding short forms, specialized forms and renewal forms):

Form PA: For published and unpublished works of the performing arts (musical and dramatic works, pantomimes and choreographic works, motion pictures and other audiovisual works).

Form SE: For serials, works issued or intended to be issued in successive parts bearing numerical or chronological designations and intended to be continued indefinitely (periodicals, newspapers, magazines, newsletters, annuals, journals, etc.).

Form SR: For published and unpublished sound recordings.

Form TX: For published and unpublished nondramatic literary works.

Form VA: For published and unpublished works of the visual arts (pictorial, graphic, and sculptural works, including architectural works).

regarding whether screen displays may be registered separately. The Copyright Office has consistently believed that a single registration is sufficient to protect the copyright in a computer program and related screen displays, including video games, without a separate registration for the screen displays or a specific reference to them on the application for the computer program. An application may give a general description in the "nature of authorship" space, such as "entire work" or "computer program." This description will cover any copyrightable authorship contained in the computer program and screen displays, regardless of whether identifying material for the screen is deposited. A specific claim in the screen displays may be asserted on the application. In such a case, identifying materials for the screens must be deposited.

Copyright Registration for Computer Programs, U.S. Copyright Office Circular 61 (Dec. 2004).

Therefore, filing either a single Form TX (Literary Works) *or* a single Form PA (audiovisual works) should suffice to protect the entire videogame. Circular 61 further states that: "Because the computer program is a literary work, literary authorship will predominate in most works, including many in which there are screen graphics. Therefore, registration will usually be appropriate on Form TX. If pictorial or graphic authorship predominates, registration may be made on Form PA as an audiovisual work." *Id.*

Notes and Questions

1. The "one form only" policy seems practical and is certainly favored. *Mfrs. Techs., Inc. v. Cams, Inc.*, 706 F. Supp. 984, 993 (D. Conn. 1989) held that the single registration of a computer program accomplished two interrelated yet distinct registrations; one of the program itself and one of the screen displays or user interface of that program, to the extent that each contained copyrightable subject matter. "This approach creates the legal fiction of two separate registrations," while also "recognizing that a computer program and its screen displays are, for copyright purposes, fundamentally distinct." *Id.*

2. More recently *Clarity Software, LLC v. Allianz Life Ins. Co. of N. Am.*, 2006 U.S. Dist. LEXIS 56219 (W.D. Pa. Aug. 11, 2006) endorsed the single filing rule of the Copyright Office. Earlier, however, the courts were by no means unanimous with respect to the single filing rule. *Digital Commc'n Assocs., Inc. v. Softklone Distrib. Corp.*, 659 F. Supp. 449, 455 (N.D. Ga. 1987), for example, held that copyright protection of a computer program did *not* extend to screen displays generated by the copyrighted program. The *Softklone* court relied, in part, upon earlier cases finding that the audiovisual screen displays of a videogame were separately copyrightable:

> After careful review of the relevant case law and of the thorough arguments made by counsel, this court concludes that copyright protection of a computer program does not extend to screen displays generated by the program. The court recognizes that there are strong arguments on both sides, but concludes, consistent with those cases finding the audiovisual screen displays of a video game to be separately copyrightable, that screen displays generated by computer programs are not direct "copies" or "reproductions" of the literary or substantive content of the computer programs. This distinction results from the fact that the same screen can be created by a variety of separate and independent computer programs. It is somewhat illogical to conclude that a screen can be a "copy" of many different

programs. Therefore, it is this court's opinion that a computer program's copyright protection does not extend to the program's screen displays and that copying of a program's screen displays, without evidence of copying of the program's source code, object code, sequence, organization or structure, does not state a claim of infringement.

Id. See also Jefferson Airplane v. Berkeley Sys., Inc., 886 F. Supp. 713 (N.D. Cal. 1994)(accord).

3. With respect to videogames, in particular, does the registration option (TX or PA) provided by the Copyright Office serve any purpose? In light of the fact that nearly every video or computer game since its inception has presented an inextricable mixture of computer code, video, and audio, would it not make more sense for the Copyright Office to merely pick and announce one form or develop a new one for videogames, or for Congress to recognize a new category subject to copyright protection?

4. Have you ever written a computer program? Low level programming languages (such as "Assembler" or "Machine Language") would permit the programmer to generate audiovisual effects through source code alone. Today's higher level (i.e., easier to learn and use) languages, such as Java, Visual Basic or C++ often access or "run" separate audio or video files that were created and generated independently. Do you suspect that the courts in the preceding discussions did not appreciate the distinction? Would such knowledge have influenced their decisions? Should it have?

5. Is there a good reason why computer software should or should not have its own independent registration form?

6. It is not uncommon for defendants to attempt to engage the court in a registration "shell game." Because of the multifaceted nature of videogames, regardless of the method of registration selected, an astute defendant in a copyright infringement action will invariably claim that the plaintiff should have chosen a different one.

7. Assume that an applicant creates a videogame similar to *Asteroids* (*See* Color Plate 1.6) and is not certain how to register his copyright. As a result, he or she decides to file a videotape as part of his registration showing the display screen, which represented only one of an infinite number of possible game sequences. When the applicant later sues for copyright infringement, the defendant argues that the computer program as embodied in the printed circuit board should have been the subject of the registration, claiming that the "game" was embodied in the circuit board, not the videotape. How would you decide the dispute? *See Atari, Inc. v. Amusement World, Inc.*, 547 F. Supp. 222 (D.C. Md. 1981); *see also* § 6.20, *infra*.

---

§ 5.22 Content of Submission

For a typical literary submission, copies of the subject work, in their entirety, are provided to the Copyright Office in accordance with requirements of the applicable form. Videogame and software developers face an interesting dilemma in this regard. The more information that is provided, the greater the exposure to the public, and therefore competitors. As a partial solution (regarding Form TX), *supra*, 37 CFR § 202.20(c)(2)(vii), titled "Computer programs and databases embodied in machine-readable copies other than CD-ROM format," states, in pertinent part:

> In cases where a computer program, database, compilation, statistical compendium, or the like, if unpublished is fixed, or if published is published only in the form of machine-readable copies (such as magnetic tape or disks, punched

cards, semiconductor chip products, or the like) other than a CD-ROM format, from which the work cannot ordinarily be perceived except with the aid of a machine or device, the deposit shall consist of:

(A) For published or unpublished computer programs, one copy of identifying portions of the program, reproduced in a form visually perceptible without the aid of a machine or device, either on paper or in microform. For these purposes "identifying portions" shall mean one of the following:

(1) The first and last 25 pages or equivalent units of the source code if reproduced on paper, or at least the first and last 25 pages or equivalent units of the source code if reproduced in microform, together with the page or equivalent unit containing the copyright notice, if any. If the program is 50 pages or less, the required deposit will be the entire source code. In the case of revised versions of computer programs, if the revisions occur throughout the entire program, the deposit of the page containing the copyright notice and the first and last 25 pages of source code will suffice; if the revisions do not occur in the first and last 25 pages, the deposit should consist of the page containing the copyright notice and any 50 pages of source code representative of the revised material; or

(2) Where the program contains trade secret material, the page or equivalent unit containing the copyright notice, if any, plus one of the following: the first and last 25 pages or equivalent units of source code with portions of the source code containing trade secrets blocked-out, provided that the blocked-out portions are proportionately less than the material remaining, and the deposit reveals an appreciable amount of original computer code; or the first and last 10 pages or equivalent units of source code alone with no blocked-out portions; or the first and last 25 pages of object code, together with any 10 or more consecutive pages of source code with no blocked-out portions; or for programs consisting of, or less than, 50 pages or equivalent units, entire source code with the trade secret portions blocked-out, provided that the blocked-out portions are proportionately less than the material remaining, and the remaining portion reveals an appreciable amount of original computer code. If the copyright claim is in a revision not contained in the first and last 25 pages, the deposit shall consist of either 20 pages of source code representative of the revised material with no blocked-out portions, or any 50 pages of source code representative of the revised material with portions of the source code containing trade secrets blocked-out, provided that the blocked-out portions are proportionately less than the material remaining and the deposit reveals an appreciable amount of original computer code. Whatever method is used to block out trade secret material, at least an appreciable amount of original computer code must remain visible.

(B) Where registration of a program containing trade secrets is made on the basis of an object code deposit the Copyright Office will make registration under its rule of doubt and warn that no determination has been made concerning the existence of copyrightable authorship.

(C) Where the application to claim copyright in a computer program includes a specific claim in related computer screen displays, the deposit, in addition to the identifying portions specified in paragraph (c)(2)(vii)(A) of this section, shall consist of:

(1) Visual reproductions of the copyrightable expression in the form of printouts, photographs, or drawings no smaller than 3 × 3 inches and no larger than 9 × 12 inches; or

(2) If the authorship in the work is predominantly audiovisual, a one-half inch VHS format videotape reproducing the copyrightable expression, except that printouts, photographs, or drawings no smaller than 3 × 3 inches and no larger than 9 × 12 inches must be deposited in lieu of videotape where the computer screen material simply constitutes a demonstration of the functioning of the computer program.

* * *

Still undecided about which copyright forms to file? Here is a shortened version of § 202.20(c)(2)(vii) from the Copyright Office (*See* http://www.copyright.gov/fls/fl108.html):

Copyright does not protect the idea for a game, its name or title, or the method or methods for playing it. Nor does copyright protect any idea, system, method, device, or trademark material involved in developing, merchandising, or playing a game. Once a game has been made public, nothing in the copyright law prevents others from developing another game based on similar principles. Copyright protects only the particular manner of an author's expression in literary, artistic, or musical form.

Material prepared in connection with a game may be subject to copyright if it contains a sufficient amount of literary or pictorial expression. For example, the text matter describing the rules of the game or the pictorial matter appearing on the gameboard or container may be registrable.

If your game includes any written element, such as instructions or directions, the Copyright Office recommends that you apply to register it as a literary work. Doing so will allow you to register all copyrightable parts of the game, including any pictorial elements. When the copyrightable elements of the game consist predominantly of pictorial matter, you should apply to register it as a work of the visual arts.

The deposit requirements for copyright registration will vary, depending on whether the work has been published at the time of registration. If the game is published, the proper deposit is one complete copy of the work. If, however, the game is published in a box larger than 12" × 24" × 6" (or a total of 1,728 cubic inches) then identifying material must be submitted in lieu of the entire game. (See "identifying material" below.) If the game is published and contains fewer than three three-dimensional elements, then identifying material for those parts must be submitted in lieu of those parts. If the game is unpublished, either one copy of the game or identifying material should be deposited.

Identifying material deposited to represent the game or its three-dimensional parts usually consists of photographs, photostats, slides, drawings, or other two-dimensional representations of the work. The identifying material should include as many pieces as necessary to show the entire copyrightable content of the work, including the copyright notice if it appears on the work. All pieces of identifying material other than transparencies must be no less than 3" × 3" in size, and not more than 9" × 12", but preferably 8" × 10". At least one piece of identifying material must, on its front, back, or mount, indicate the title of the work and an exact measurement of one or more dimensions of the work.

Notes and Questions

1. Do the Copyright Office's suggestions really solve the problem that it intended to correct? More particularly, as a programmer, how can you claim protection for those portions of computer code that you never registered?

2. There are certain simple tricks and rules that astute, litigation-wise videogame developers (and computer programmers in general) use while writing computer code. *See Williams Elec., Inc. v. Artic Int'l, Inc.*, 685 F.2d 870 (3d Cir. N.J. 1982); *see also* §§ 5.21, 5.22, 5.31, *supra*.

3. For more information concerning computer code registration, see the Compendium of Copyright Office Practices, Section 321 at: http://www.copyrightcompendium.com/.

§ 5.23 Copyright Duration

With respect to copyright duration, following the extensions added by the "Sonny Bono" Amendment to the Copyright Act for works published after midnight, December 31, 1977, a copyright lasts for the life of the author plus 70 years. If the copyright holder is a corporation or other entity, the duration is 95 years.[7] However, if the work is a work for hire or is published anonymously or under a pseudonym, then the copyright lasts between 95 and 120 years, depending upon the date that the work is first published.

All works published in the United States before 1923 are in the public domain, and therefore, unrestricted. Works published prior to 1977 without a copyright notice are also in the public domain. Works published after 1922, but before 1978, with a copyright notice, are protected for 95 years from the date of publication. If the work was created, but not published, before 1978, the copyright lasts for the life of the author plus 70 years. However, even if the author died over 70 years ago, the copyright in an unpublished work lasts until December 31, 2002. And if such a work is published before December 31, 2002, the copyright will last until December 31, 2047.

Most of the landmark-creating videogames were created and published after December 1977 and will, therefore, fall within the scope of the new Act. But awareness of the earlier copyright statutes is nevertheless significant for those creating games that embody music or literary content that pre-dates the latest Act.

According to the Copyright Office's Circular 61, pertaining to the "Effective Date of Registration":

---

7. For works published between January 1, 1978 and March 1, 1989 (Enactment date of the Berne Convention), complications can arise if the copyright notice was omitted from a published work. *See, e.g., Neimark v. Ronai & Ronai, LLP*, 500 F. Supp. 2d 338, 341–44 (S.D.N.Y. 2007). Such a failure can cause the work to be injected into the public domain, unless the author takes steps to cure the lack of notice. *See Bridge Publications, Inc. v. F.A.C.T. Net, Inc.*, 183 F.R.D. 254, 262 (D. Colo. 1998). In addition, a great resource is Peter Hirtle, the Intellectual Property Officer for the Cornell University Library, which itself maintains a comprehensive chart on copyright duration. *See also* Peter B. Hirtle, *Copyright Term and the Public Domain in the United States*, published on January 1, 2008, which can be found at http://www.copyright.cornell.edu/public_domain/.

A copyright registration is effective on the date the Copyright Office receives all the required elements in acceptable form, regardless of how long it then takes to process the application and mail the certificate of registration. The time the Copyright Office requires to process an application varies, depending on the amount of material the Office is receiving. It may take several days for mailed material to reach the Copyright Office and for the certificate of registration to reach the recipient. If you apply for copyright registration, you will not receive an acknowledgment that your application has been received (the Office receives more than 600,000 applications annually), but you can expect: a letter or a telephone call from a Copyright Office staff member if further information is needed, or a certificate of registration indicating that the work has been registered, or if the application cannot be accepted, a letter explaining why it has been rejected.

---

§ 5.24 Cancellation of Copyright Assignments

Those who have assigned their copyright interests, pursuant to an exclusive or non-exclusive grant, should be aware of a not-so-widely publicized right to cancel that assignment after 35 years. According to 17 U.S.C. § 203, in the case of any work other than a work made for hire, the transfer or license of a copyright, or of any right under a copyright, executed by the author on or after January 1, 1978 (other than by will), is subject to cancellation. If the conditions of the statute are met, even licenses designated as "irrevocable" or "perpetual" can be terminated after the 35 year period. The statutory provisions of § 203 are bit wordy. Perhaps it is the lack of clarity that has contributed to its obscurity. In any event, an official statement from the Copyright Office has attempted to provide some simplification:[8]

Termination of Transfers and Licenses Under 17 U.S.C. § 203

Section 203 of the Copyright Act permits authors (or, if the authors are not alive, their surviving spouses, children or grandchildren, or executors, administrators, personal representatives or trustees) to terminate grants of copyright assignments and licenses that were made on or after January 1, 1978 when certain conditions have been met. Notices of termination may be served no earlier than 25 years after the execution of the grant or, if the grant covers the right of publication, no earlier than 30 years after the execution of the grant or 25 years after publication under the grant (whichever comes first). However, termination of a grant cannot be effective until 35 years after the execution of the grant or, if the grant covers the right of publication, no earlier than 40 years after the execution of the grant or 35 years after publication under the grant (whichever comes first). Because notices of termination under section 203 may be served, at their earliest, 25 years after the execution of a post-1977 grant, the first date on which any section 203 notices of termination could be served was January 1, 2003. Notices of termination must comply in form, content, and manner with requirements in a regulation issued by the Register of Copyrights. The Register of Copyrights proposed a regulation governing notices of termination under section 203, and sought comments

---

8. See http://www.copyright.gov/docs/203.html. *See also* Sean F. Kane, *Copyright Assignment Termination After 35 Years: The Video Game Industry Comes of Age*, 26 No.1 INTELL. PROP. & TECH. L.J. 15 (2014). Kane's article provides suggestions for both obtaining and avoiding the 35 year cancellation provisions.

on the regulation. The proposed regulation was based on the existing regulation governing notices of termination under section 304 of the Copyright Act. Section 304 permits termination of grants of copyright assignments and licenses during the extended renewal term for pre-1978 works, and authors and other qualified successors have been serving notices of termination under section 304 since 1978.

The § 203 cancellation provisions have particular significance for the videogame industry which moved into the mainstream with the release of Atari's *Pong* in 1972. From this birth point, many classic games followed as the industry crossed the billion dollar mark. Some of the earliest programmers were youngsters or even children who gladly assigned away their rights for the price of a new set of rollerblades. They had next to nothing in terms of negotiating power. A standard contract would normally involve the assignment of all intellectual property rights and copyrights. No doubt, a disparity in bargaining power, in the arts in general, provided a key factor behind § 203.

With a trigger date of January 1, 1978, it is evident that many classic videogame licenses and assignments are fast becoming vulnerable. Older videogame programmers and creators may be able to give their negotiating stance a second life.

§ 5.30 Copyrightability of Videogames

In the 1960s and 1970s there was uncertainty as to whether or not a computer program could be provided with any copyright protection. In fact, it wasn't until 1980 that a definition for a "computer program" was provided for the Copyright Act (17 U.S.C. § 101). Before then, the Copyright Office agreed to accept computer programs under its so-called "rule of doubt" procedure whereby doubts were resolved in favor of the copyright applicant. Of course, if software in general was in doubt, so too were videogames. Today, there is no doubt; videogames are clearly copyrightable, even though the road to that status has been rocky.[9]

Analysis best begins with the requirements of § 102(a) of the Copyright Act:

> Copyright protection subsists, in accordance with this title, in original works of authorship fixed in any tangible medium of expression, now known or later developed, from which they can be perceived, reproduced, or otherwise communicated, either directly or with the aid of a machine or device.

Whether or not holes punched in cards or groups of zeros and ones are capable of being copyrighted has apparently been resolved by the latter part of the above sentence, which permits a "machine or device" to make sense out of otherwise unintelligible computer code. This leaves the elements of originality and fixation open for discussion. But first it is important to consider those items which the Act considers as being *outside* the scope of copyright protection; according to § 102(b):

> In no case does copyright protection for an original work of authorship extend to any idea, procedure, process, system, method of operation, concept, principle, or discovery, regardless of the form in which it is described, explained, illustrated, or embodied in such work.

---

9. *See* Pamela Samuelson, *CONTU Revisited: The Case Against Copyright Protection for Computer Programs in Machine-Readable Form*, 1984 Duke L.J. 663, 692–94 (1984). *See also* William Patry, *Can Our Current Conception of Copyright Law Survive the Internet Age?*, 46 N.Y.L. Sch. L. Rev. 201, 201–02 (2002–2003).

At first reading, the above language would seem to fly in the face of everyone's ability to copyright a computer program of any nature. Fortunately, however, in practice the language is not so restrictive. § 102(b) does, however, influence the dividing line between an original copyrightable game and a "system or manner of playing a game or engaging in any other sporting or like activity." The latter, according to conventional wisdom, may not be subject to copyright protection.[10]

Cases that follow will tend to demonstrate that there may be difficulty distinguishing between a game whose elements may be subject to copyright protection and a "system or manner of playing a game," which are not.

The "fixation" and "originality" requirements of § 102 of the Act have presented their own problems as the videogame traveled the road from a rudimentary novelty to a status of artistic expression worthy of first amendment protection. Chronologically, the courts were first confronted with the videogame's fleeting sprites, most of which never seemed to stay "fixed" for more than a moment.

---

§ 5.31 Fixation

When we speak of a novel, a film, or a sculptured product, there is little difficulty visualizing such works of authorship as being "fixed" in their respective tangible media. The fixation is solid regardless of whether the medium is ink on paper, paint on canvas, or chiseled stone. Videogames, however, depending upon one's perspective, do not provide such stable manifestations. The source code used to generate the game play of a typical videogame may be fixed into the memory of a computer chip or hard disk drive, but the resulting object code along with the resulting images, sound, and movement are only temporary. And then there is the issue of who, indeed, is creating the images and sounds that are the subject of the videogame, the author or the player?

According to 17 U.S.C. § 101, "[A] work is 'fixed' in a tangible medium of expression when its embodiment in a copy or phonorecord, by or under the authority of the author, is sufficiently permanent or stable to permit it to be perceived, reproduced, or otherwise communicated for a period of more than transitory duration. A work consisting of sounds, images, or both, that are being transmitted, is fixed for purposes of this title if a fixation of the work is being made simultaneously with its transmission."

* * *

Stern Elec., Inc. v. Kaufman

United States Court of Appeals, Second Circuit, 1982
669 F.2d 852

Newman, Circuit Judge.

This appeal from the grant of a preliminary injunction concerns primarily the availability of copyright protection for the visual images electronically displayed by a coin-operated

---

10. *See* 1 Melville Nimmer & David Nimmer, *Nimmer on Copyright* § 2.18[H][3][a] (2007). *Morrissey v. Procter & Gamble Co.*, 379 F.2d 675, 678 (1st Cir. 1967); *See also* Thomas M. S. Hemnes, *The Adaptation of Copyright Law to Video Games*, 131 U. Pa. L. Rev. 171, 174–75 (1982). See generally, William Patry, *Electronic Audiovisual Games: Navigating the Maze of Copyright*, 31 J. Copr. Soc'y 1 (1983).

videogame of the sort currently enjoying widespread popularity throughout the country. Omni Video Games, Inc., its distributor, and two of its officers appeal from an order entered May 22, 1981 in the District Court for the Eastern District of New York (Eugene H. Nickerson, Judge), preliminarily enjoining them from infringing the copyright of Stern Electronics, Inc. in the audiovisual work entitled "Scramble" and from making further use of the trademark "SCRAMBLE" in connection with electronic video games. 523 F. Supp. 635. Appellants contend that the visual images and accompanying sounds of the video game fail to satisfy the fixation and originality requirements of the Copyright Act, 17 U.S.C. App. § 102(a) (1976), and that they, rather than appellees, have superior rights to the mark "SCRAMBLE." We reject these contentions and affirm the preliminary injunction.

Video games like "Scramble" can roughly be described as computers programmed to create on a television screen cartoons in which some of the action is controlled by the player. In Stern's "Scramble," for example, the video screen displays a spaceship moving horizontally through six different scenes in which obstacles are encountered. With each scene the player faces increasing difficulty in traversing the course and scoring points. The first scene depicts mountainous terrain, missile bases, and fuel depots. The player controls the altitude and speed of the spaceship, decides when to release the ship's supply of bombs, and fires lasers that can destroy attacking missiles and aircraft. He attempts to bomb the missile bases (scoring points for success), bomb the fuel depots (increasing his own diminishing fuel supply with each hit), avoid the missiles being fired from the ground, and avoid crashing his ship into the mountains. And that is only scene one. In subsequent scenes the hazards include missile-firing enemy aircraft and tunnel-like airspaces. The scenes are in color, and the action is accompanied by battlefield sounds.

The game is built into a cabinet containing a cathode ray tube, a number of electronic circuit boards, a loudspeaker, and hand controls for the player. The electronic circuitry includes memory storage devices called PROMs, an acronym for "programmable read only memory."[11] The PROM stores the instructions and data from a computer program in such a way that when electric current passes through the circuitry, the interaction of the program stored in the PROM with the other components of the game produces the sights and sounds of the audiovisual display that the player sees and hears. The memory devices determine not only the appearance and movement of the images but also the variations in movement in response to the player's operation of the hand controls.

Stern manufactures amusement equipment, including video games, for distribution worldwide. In January 1981 at a London trade exhibit Stern became aware of "Scramble," an electronic video game developed in late 1980 by a Japanese corporation, Konami Industry Co., Ltd. The audiovisual display constituting what Stern alleges is the copyrightable work was first published in Japan on January 8, 1981. Stern secured an exclusive sub-license to distribute the "Scramble" game in North and South America from Konami's exclusive licensee, and began selling the game in the United States on March 17, 1981. Even in the fast-paced world of video games, "Scramble" quickly became a big

---

11. Memory devices of computers are generally either RAM (random access memory) or ROM (read only memory). RAM, used in most sophisticated computers, is a memory device in which stored information can be changed simply by writing in new information that replaces old information. The stored information in a ROM cannot be changed; it is imprinted into the ROM when the device is manufactured. A PROM is a ROM into which information can be imprinted (programmed) after manufacture; once the information is programmed in a PROM, it cannot be changed simply by writing in a new program.

success. Approximately 10,000 units were sold at about $2,000 each in the first two months for an initial sales volume of about $20 million.

On April 14, 1981, a Certificate of Copyright Registration for the audiovisual work "Scramble" was issued to Konami by the United States Copyright Office, and shortly thereafter documents were filed with the Copyright Office reflecting the license and sub-license to Stern. To satisfy the statutory requirement for deposit of copies of a work to be copyrighted, 17 U.S.C.App. s 408(b) (1976), Konami submitted video tape recordings of the "Scramble" game, both in its "attract mode" and in its "play mode."[12]

Omni alleges that, concurrently with Stern's sales of the "Scramble" game and even earlier, it was endeavoring to sell a line of video game products so constructed that each unit could be equipped for playing different games by substituting a PROM containing the program for a particular game. Omni contends that it planned to market this line of interchangeable games with the label "Scramble" affixed to the headboard of each unit; the name of the particular game was also to be prominently displayed. On December 1, 1980, Omni's president ordered ten silk screen name plates bearing the name "Scramble." Between that date and March 17, 1981, the date of Stern's first sale of its "Scramble" game, Omni sold five units of video games bearing the name "Scramble" on the headboard. In April 1981 Omni began to sell a video game called "Scramble" that not only bears the same name as the "Scramble" game Stern was then marketing, but also is virtually identical in both sight and sound. It sold this copy of Stern's "Scramble" game, known in the trade as a "knock-off," for several hundred dollars less than Stern's game.

1. Copyright Issues

In challenging the preliminary injunction that bars distribution of its "Scramble" game, Omni does not dispute that Konami and its sub-licensee Stern are entitled to secure some copyright protection for their "Scramble" game. Omni contends that Konami was entitled to copyright only the written computer program that determines the sights and sounds of the game's audiovisual display.[13] While that approach would have afforded some degree of protection, it would not have prevented a determined competitor from manufacturing a "knock-off" of "Scramble" that replicates precisely the sights and sounds of the game's audiovisual display. This could be done by writing a new computer program that would interact with the hardware components of a video game to produce on the screen the same images seen in "Scramble," accompanied by the same sounds. Such replication is possible because many different computer programs can produce the same "results," whether those results are an analysis of financial records or a sequence of images and sounds. A program is simply "a set of statements (i.e., data) or instructions to be used directly or indirectly in a computer in order to bring about a certain result," Pub.L.No. 96-517, s 10(a), 94 Stat. 3015, 3028 (1980) (amending 17 U.S.C.App. s 101 (1976)). To take an elementary example, the result of displaying a "4" can be achieved by an instruction to add 2 and 2, subtract 3 from 7, or in a variety of other ways. Obviously, writing a new program to replicate the play of "Scramble" requires a sophisticated effort, but it is a manageable task.

To secure protection against the risk of a "knock-off" of "Scramble" based upon an original program, Konami eschewed registration of its program as a literary work and

---

12. "Attract mode" refers to the audiovisual display seen and heard by a prospective customer contemplating playing the game; the video screen displays some of the essential visual and sound characteristics of the game. "Play mode" refers to the audiovisual display seen and heard by a person playing the game.

13. Written computer programs are copyrightable as literary works. See 1 M. Nimmer, Nimmer on Copyright s 2.04(C) (1981).

chose instead to register the sights and sounds of "Scramble" as an audiovisual work. *See* 17 U.S.C.App. s 102(a)(6) (1976). The Act defines "audiovisual works" as "works that consist of a series of related images which are intrinsically intended to be shown by the use of machines, or devices such as projectors, viewers, or electronic equipment, together with accompanying sounds, if any, regardless of the nature of the material objects, such as films or tapes, in which the works are embodied." 17 U.S.C.App. § 101 (1976). Omni contends that Konami is not entitled to secure a copyright in the sights and sounds of its "Scramble" game because the audiovisual work is neither "fixed in any tangible medium of expression" nor "original" within the meaning of s 102(a). Both contentions arise from the fact that the sequence of some of the images appearing on the screen during each play of the game will vary depending upon the actions taken by the player. For example, if he fails to avoid enemy fire, his spaceship will be destroyed; if he fails to destroy enough fuel depots, his own fuel supply will run out, and his spaceship will crash; if he succeeds in destroying missile sites and enemy planes, those images will disappear from the screen; and the precise course traveled by his spaceship will depend upon his adjustment of the craft's altitude and velocity.

If the content of the audiovisual display were not affected by the participation of the player, there would be no doubt that the display itself, and not merely the written computer program, would be eligible for copyright. The display satisfies the statutory definition of an original "audiovisual work," and the memory devices of the game satisfy the statutory requirement of a "copy" in which the work is "fixed."[14] The Act defines "copies" as "material objects ... in which a work is fixed by any method now known or later developed, and from which the work can be perceived, reproduced, or otherwise communicated, either directly or with the aid of a machine or device" and specifies that a work is "fixed" when "its embodiment in a copy ... is sufficiently permanent or stable to permit it to be perceived, reproduced, or otherwise communicated for a period of more than transitory duration." 17 U.S.C.App. § 101 (1976). The audiovisual work is permanently embodied in a material object, the memory devices, from which it can be perceived with the aid of the other components of the game.

We agree with the District Court that the player's participation does not withdraw the audiovisual work from copyright eligibility. No doubt the entire sequence of all the sights and sounds of the game are different each time the game is played, depending upon the route and speed the player selects for his spaceship and the timing and accuracy of his release of his craft's bombs and lasers. Nevertheless, many aspects of the sights and the sequence of their appearance remain constant during each play of the game. These include the appearance (shape, color, and size) of the player's spaceship, the enemy craft, the ground missile bases and fuel depots, and the terrain over which (and beneath which) the player's ship flies, as well as the sequence in which the missile bases, fuel depots, and terrain appears. Also constant are the sounds heard whenever the player successfully destroys an enemy craft or installation or fails to avoid an enemy missile or laser. It is true, as appellants contend, that some of these sights and sounds will not be seen and

---

14. In arguing that the permanent "imprinting" of the computer program in the game's memory devices satisfies the requirement of fixation in a tangible medium, appellees direct our attention to the PROM, which contains, in electronically usable form, the computer program for the game. While the PROM device contains the program specifically written for the "Scramble" game, there are undoubtedly some items of program stored in memory devices located in other components of the game. Whether located in the PROM prepared for this particular game or elsewhere in the total assembly, all portions of the program, once stored in memory devices anywhere in the game, are fixed in a tangible medium within the meaning of the Act.

heard during each play of the game in the event that the'player's spaceship is destroyed before the entire course is traversed. But the images remain fixed, capable of being seen and heard each time a player succeeds in keeping his spaceship aloft long enough to permit the appearances of all the images and sounds of a complete play of the game. The repetitive sequence of a substantial portion of the sights and sounds of the game qualifies for copyright protection as an audiovisual work.

Appellants' claim that the work lacks originality proceeds along two lines. Repeating their attack on fixation, they assert that each play of the game is an original work because of the player's participation. The videotape of a particular play of the game, they assert, secured protection only for that one "original" display. However, the repeated appearance of the same sequence of numerous sights and sounds in each play of the game defeats this branch of the argument. Attacking from the opposite flank, appellants contend that the audiovisual display contains no originality because all of its reappearing features are determined by the previously created computer program. This argument is also without merit. The visual and aural features of the audiovisual display are plainly original variations sufficient to render the display copyrightable even though the underlying written program has an independent existence and is itself eligible for copyright. Nor is copyright defeated because the audiovisual work and the computer program are both embodied in the same components of the game. The same thing occurs when an audio tape embodies both a musical composition and a sound recording. Moreover, the argument overlooks the sequence of the creative process. Someone first conceived what the audiovisual display would look like and sound like. Originality occurred at that point. Then the program was written. Finally, the program was imprinted into the memory devices so that, in operation with the components of the game, the sights and sounds could be seen and heard. The resulting display satisfies the requirement of an original work.

We need not decide at what point the repeating sequence of images would form too insubstantial a portion of an entire display to warrant a copyright, nor the somewhat related issue of whether a sequence of images (e.g., a spaceship shooting down an attacking plane) might contain so little in the way of particularized form of expression as to be only an abstract idea portrayed in noncopyrightable form, *see Nichols v. Universal Pictures Corp.*, 45 F.2d 119, 121 (2d Cir. 1930). Assessing the entire effect of the game as it appears and sounds, we conclude that its repetitive sequence of images is copyrightable as an audiovisual display. *See Atari, Inc. v. Amusement World, Inc.*, No. 81-803 (D.Md. Nov. 27, 1981); *Midway Manufacturing Co. v. Drikschneider*, No. 81-0-243 (D.Neb. July 15, 1981)

The preliminary injunction is AFFIRMED.

* * *

Williams Elec., Inc. v. Artic Int'l, Inc.

United States Court of Appeals, Third Circuit, 1982
685 F.2d 870

SLOVITER, Circuit Judge.

Defendant Artic International, Inc. appeals from the district court's entry of a final injunction order permanently restraining and enjoining it from infringing plaintiff's copyrights on audiovisual works and a computer program relating to the electronic video game DEFENDER.

Plaintiff-appellee Williams Electronics, Inc. manufactures and sells coin-operated electronic video games. A video game machine consists of a cabinet containing, inter alia, a cathode ray tube (CRT), a sound system, hand controls for the player, and electronic circuit boards. The electronic circuitry includes a microprocessor and memory devices, called ROMs (Read Only Memory), which are tiny computer "chips" containing thousands of data locations which store the instructions and data of a computer program. The microprocessor executes the computer program to cause the game to operate. Judge Newman of the Second Circuit described a similar type of memory device as follows: "The (ROM) stores the instructions and data from a computer program in such a way that when electric current passes through the circuitry, the interaction of the program stored in the (ROM) with the other components of the game produces the sights and sounds of the audiovisual display that the player sees and hears. The memory devices determine not only the appearance and movement of the (game) images but also the variations in movement in response to the player's operation of the hand controls." *Stern Electronics, Inc. v. Kaufman*, 669 F.2d 852, 854 (2d Cir. 1982).

In approximately October 1979 Williams began to design a new video game, ultimately called DEFENDER, which incorporated various original and unique audiovisual features. The DEFENDER game was introduced to the industry at a trade show in 1980 and has since achieved great success in the marketplace. One of the attractions of video games contributing to their phenomenal popularity is apparently their use of unrealistic fantasy creatures, a fad also observed in the popularity of certain current films. In the DEFENDER game, there are symbols of a spaceship and aliens who do battle with symbols of human figures. The player operates the flight of and weapons on the spaceship, and has the mission of preventing invading aliens from kidnapping the humans from a ground plane.

Williams obtained three copyright registrations relating to its DEFENDER game: one covering the computer program, Registration No. TX 654-755, effective date December 11, 1980; the second covering the audiovisual effects displayed during the game's "attract mode,"[15] Registration No. PA 97-373, effective date March 3, 1981; and the third covering the audiovisual effects displayed during the game's "play mode,"[16] Registration No. PA 94-718, effective date March 11, 1981. Readily visible copyright notices for the DEFENDER game were placed on the game cabinet, appeared on the CRT screen during the attract mode and at the beginning of the play mode, and were placed on labels which were attached to the outer case of each memory device (ROM). In addition, the Williams program provided that the words "Copyright 1980-Williams Electronics" in code were to be stored in the memory devices, but were not to be displayed on the CRT at any time.

Defendant-appellant Artic International, Inc. is a seller of electronic components for video games in competition with Williams. The district court made the following relevant findings which are not disputed on this appeal. Artic has sold circuit boards, manufactured by others, which contain electronic circuits including a microprocessor and memory devices (ROMs). These memory devices incorporate a computer program which is virtually identical to Williams' program for its DEFENDER game. The result is a circuit board "kit" which is sold by Artic to others and which, when connected to a cathode ray tube, produces audiovisual effects and a game almost identical to the Williams DEFENDER game including both the attract mode and the play mode. The play mode and actual play of Artic's game, entitled "DEFENSE COMMAND," is virtually identical to that of the Williams game, i.e.,

---

15. The "attract mode" refers to the audiovisual effects displayed before a coin is inserted into the game. It repeatedly shows the name of the game, the game symbols in typical motion and interaction patterns, and the initials of previous players who have achieved high scores.

16. The "play mode" refers to the audiovisual effects displayed during the actual play of the game, when the game symbols move and interact on the screen, and the player controls the movement of one of the symbols (e.g., a spaceship).

the characters displayed on the cathode ray tube including the player's spaceship are identical in shape, size, color, manner of movement and interaction with other symbols. Also, the attract mode of the Artic game is substantially identical to that of Williams' game, with minor exceptions such as the absence of the Williams name and the substitution of the terms "DEFENSE" and/or "DEFENSE COMMAND" for the term "DEFENDER" in its display. App. at 204a–206a. Based on the evidence before it, the district court found that the defendant Artic had infringed the plaintiff's computer program copyright for the DEFENDER game by selling kits which contain a computer program which is a copy of plaintiff's computer program, and that the defendant had infringed both of the plaintiff's audiovisual copyrights for the DEFENDER game by selling copies of those audiovisual works. App. at 207a–209a.

In the appeal before us, defendant does not dispute the findings with respect to copying but instead challenges the conclusions of the district court with respect to copyright infringement and the validity and scope of plaintiff's copyrights. The recent market interest in electronic audiovisual games has created an active market for original work, and as frequently happens, has also spawned copies.

In the case before us, the parties agreed at the district court level that the only issues to be decided on the injunction were legal ones. Essentially, defendant Artic attacks the validity and the scope of the copyrights which it has been found by the district court to have infringed. Plaintiff possesses certificates of registration issued by the Copyright Office. Under the Copyright Act, these certificates constitute prima facie evidence of the validity of plaintiff's copyright. 17 U.S.C. s 410(c). Defendant, therefore, has the burden of overcoming this presumption of validity.

With respect to the plaintiff's two audiovisual copyrights, defendant contends that there can be no copyright protection for the DEFENDER game's attract mode and play mode because these works fail to meet the statutory requirement of "fixation." Section 101 of the 1976 Copyright Act, 17 U.S.C. s 102, provides in part:

> (a) Copyright protection subsists … in original works of authorship *fixed in any tangible medium of expression*, now known or later developed, from which they can be perceived, reproduced, or otherwise communicated, either directly or with the aid of a machine or device. Works of authorship include the following categories:
>
>> (1) literary works;
>>
>> ….
>>
>> (6) motion pictures and other audiovisual works;
>>
>> ….

(emphasis added). The fixation requirement is defined in section 101 in relevant part as follows:

> A work is "fixed" in a tangible medium of expression when its embodiment in a copy or phonorecord, by or under the authority of the author, is sufficiently permanent or stable to permit it to be perceived, reproduced, or otherwise communicated for a period of more than transitory duration.

Defendant claims that the images in the plaintiff's audiovisual game are transient, and cannot be "fixed." Specifically, it contends that there is a lack of "fixation" because the video game generates or creates "new" images each time the attract mode or play mode is displayed, notwithstanding the fact that the new images are identical or substantially identical to the earlier ones.

We reject this contention. The fixation requirement is met whenever the work is "sufficiently permanent or stable to permit it to be ... reproduced, or otherwise communicated" for more than a transitory period. Here the original audiovisual features of the DEFENDER game repeat themselves over and over. The identical contention was previously made by this defendant and rejected by the court. Moreover, the rejection of a similar contention by the Second Circuit is also applicable here. The court stated:

> The [video game's] display satisfies the statutory definition of an original "audiovisual work," and the memory devices of the game satisfy the statutory requirement of a "copy" in which the work is "fixed." The Act defines "copies" as "material objects ... in which a work is fixed by any method now known or later developed, and from which the work can be perceived, reproduced, or otherwise communicated, either directly or with the aid of a machine or device" and specifies that a work is "fixed" when "its embodiment in a copy ... is sufficiently permanent or stable to permit it to be perceived, reproduced, or otherwise communicated for a period of more than transitory duration." 17 U.S.C. App. § 101 (1976). The audiovisual work is permanently embodied in a material object, the memory devices, from which it can be perceived with the aid of the other components of the game.

Stern Electronics, Inc. v. Kaufman, 669 F.2d at 855–56 (footnote omitted; emphasis added).

Defendant also apparently contends that the player's participation withdraws the game's audiovisual work from copyright eligibility because there is no set or fixed performance and the player becomes a co-author of what appears on the screen. Although there is player interaction with the machine during the play mode which causes the audiovisual presentation to change in some respects from one game to the next in response to the player's varying participation, there is always a repetitive sequence of a substantial portion of the sights and sounds of the game, and many aspects of the display remain constant from game to game regardless of how the player operates the controls. *See Stern Electronics, Inc. v. Kaufman*, 669 F.2d at 855–56. Furthermore, there is no player participation in the attract mode which is displayed repetitively without change.

Defendant argues that there can be no copyright protection for the ROMs because they are utilitarian objects or machine parts. Defendant's argument in this regard is misdirected. The issue in this case is not whether plaintiff, if it sought, could protect the ROM itself under the copyright laws. Rather, before us is only the plaintiff's effort to protect its artistic expression in original works which have met the statutory fixation requirement through their embodiment in the ROM devices. Defendant Artic's challenge to the validity of a copyright based upon this "utilitarian object" argument was recently raised by Artic and rejected by the district court in *Midway Manufacturing Co. v. Artic International, Inc.,* *supra*, slip op. at 19–20. In granting a preliminary injunction against Artic's infringement of audiovisual copyrights on similar electronic video games, Judge Decker stated:

> Artic initially claims that Midway's attempt to copyright the audiovisual aspects of its games was, in reality, an attempt to copyright the ROMs in the games. Because the ROMs are utilitarian objects, they may not be copyrighted.... While the court agrees that utilitarian objects may not be copyrighted, it appears that Artic has misconstrued the copyrights at issue in this case. As noted above, Midway has sought and obtained protection for the audiovisual aspects of its games that appear on the screen. Midway no more restricts the use of ROMs than an author with a valid copyright restricts the use of books.

Id. at 19 (citation omitted).

Defendant also claims that plaintiff failed to comply with the statutory deposit requirement that copies of the works as published be filed with the Copyright Office, 17 U.S.C.§ 408, because plaintiff apparently deposited videotapes of the DEFENDER game's attract and play modes instead of depositing the ROM circuit board or the video game machine itself. However, section 408(c)(1) of the statute provides that the Register of Copyrights is authorized "to specify by regulation … the nature of the copies or phonorecords to be deposited" and also "may require or permit, for particular classes, the deposit of identifying material instead of copies." The plaintiff Williams has substantially complied with these regulations. *See* 37 C.F.R. § 202.20(c) (2) (1981). The deposit of videotapes as a satisfactory method of complying with the statutory deposit requirement has been universally accepted in cases considering copyrights for the audiovisual works displayed in these video games.

In the cases previously decided dealing with video games, the courts considered only the copyrights secured in audiovisual works; counsel have represented that this is the first case dealing with copyrighted computer programs in the video game context. Defendant has conceded both in the district court and before us that a computer program can be the subject of a copyright as a literary text. *See* 1 *Nimmer on Copyright* § 2.04(C) (1981), cited with approval in *Stern Electronics, Inc. v. Kaufman*, 669 F.2d at 855 n.3. The parties have differed over whether such copyright protection was first extended by the 1980 amendments to the 1976 Copyright Act, Act of Dec. 12, 1980, Pub.L.No. 96-517, § 10, 94 Stat. 3028, which explicitly refers to computer programs in revised sections 101 and 117, or whether computer programs had already been covered under the 1976 Copyright Act as suggested by the legislative history[17] and the 1978 report of the congressionally created National Commission on New Technological Uses of Copyrighted Works (CONTU).[18] Since the copyrightability of computer programs is firmly established after the 1980 amendment to the Copyright Act, and the infringement in this case took place after the effective date of that Act, we need not consider the scope of prior Acts for purposes of affirming the injunction order.

Defendant contends that the computer program would be infringed only if an unauthorized copy of the program text was made. Since Artic does not make the boards but buys them from others, it argues Artic cannot be an infringer. Brief for Appellant at 19. We believe defendant is not free to make that argument at this phase of the litigation. The district court made a finding that "The kits sold by defendant Artic International, Inc. contain a computer program which is a copy of plaintiff's computer program for its video game DEFENDER and which is the subject of copyright registration TX 654-755." App. at 209a (emphasis added). Indeed the extent of the copying could reasonably lead

---

17. The House Report on the 1976 Act contains the following statement:

> The term "literary works" does not connote any criterion of literary merit or qualitative value: it includes catalogs, directories, and similar factual, reference, or instructional works and compilations of data. It also includes computer data bases and computer programs to the extent that they incorporate authorship in the programmer's expression of original ideas, as distinguished from the ideas themselves.

H.R.Rep.No. 94-1476, 94th Cong., 2d Sess. 54 (1976) (emphasis added). *See also* S.Rep.No. 94-473, 94th Cong., 1st Sess. 50–51 (1975), U.S.Code Cong. & Admin.News 1976, 5659, 5667.

18. The CONTU Report states that "it was clearly the intent of Congress to include computer programs within the scope of copyrightable subject matter in the Act of 1976." National Commission on New Technological Uses of Copyrighted Works, Final Report 16 (1978). *See also* Boorstyn, Copyright Law s 2.21 (1981).

to no other conclusion.[19] The parties stipulated and agreed "that there was no dispute of fact concerning the plaintiff's copyright claim and that the matters in dispute were solely issues of law." App. at 199a. Whether and by whom an unauthorized copy of the computer program text was made or whether the copying was effected by copying the ROM are issues of fact which, by agreement, are not before us now. Since defendant has stated at oral argument that there is no dispute that the printed circuit board which it sold contained programs which have been copied from the plaintiff, we must sustain the district court's order unless it can be challenged on some basis other than who is responsible for the copying or how the copying was effected.

Defendant argues that the basic question presented is whether the ROMs, which it views as part of a machine, can be considered a "copy" of a copyrighted work within the meaning of the Copyright Act. Defendant argues that a copyright for a computer program is not infringed when the program is loaded into electronic memory devices (ROMs) and used to control the activity of machines. That use, it claims, is a utilitarian one not within the scope of the Copyright Act. We have already rejected defendant's similar argument in the context of the copyrights for the audiovisual works. Defendant makes the further point that when the issue is the copyright on a computer program, a distinction must be drawn between the "source code" version of a computer program, which it would hold can be afforded copyright protection, and the "object code" stage, which it contends cannot be so protected.[20] Its theory is that a "copy" must be intelligible to human beings and must be intended as a medium of communication to human beings.

---

19. There is overwhelming evidence in the present case that the Williams computer program has been copied in some form. The following facts, among others, manifest the similarities between the Williams program and that stored in the Artic memory devices: (1) The game created by the Artic circuit boards contains an error which was present in early versions of the Williams computer program—it displays the wrong score value for destroying a particular alien symbol; (2) The attract mode of both games displays a listing of high scores achieved by previous players alongside their initials, and Artic's game contains the initials of Williams employees, including its president, who initially achieved the highest scores on the DEFENDER game; (3) Using a laboratory developmental device, Williams' employees printed out a listing in code of the contents of the memory devices of both games. In excess of 85% of the listings are identical; (4) The Williams program provided that the words "Copyright 1980-Williams Electronics" in code were to be stored in its memory devices, but were not to be displayed on the CRT at any time, thus providing a "buried" or hidden copyright notice. When the contents of Artic's memory devices were printed out by Williams' employees, the listings contained the "buried" Williams copyright notice in code.

20. According to the Final Report of the National Commission on New Technological Uses of Copyrighted Works:

> A source code is a computer program written in any of several programming languages employed by computer programmers. An object code is the version of a program in which the source code language is converted or translated into the machine language of the computer with which it is to be used.

Id. at 21 n.109 (majority report).

A somewhat different explanation of these terms is provided in Commissioner Hersey's dissent to the CONTU Report:

> All computer programs go through various stages of development....
>
> The stages of development of a program usually are: a definition, in eye-legible form, of the program's task or function; a description; a listing of the program's steps and/or their expression in flow charts; the translation of these steps into a "source code," often written in a high-level programming language, such as FORTRAN or COBOL; the transformation of this source code within the computer, through intervention of a so-called compiler or assembler program, into an "object code." This last is most often physically embodied, in

The answer to defendant's contention is in the words of the statute itself. A "copy" is defined to include a material object in which a work is fixed "by any method now known or later developed, and from which the work can be perceived, reproduced, or otherwise communicated, either directly or with the aid of a machine or device." 17 U.S.C. § 101 (emphasis added). By this broad language, Congress opted for an expansive interpretation of the terms "fixation" and "copy" which encompass technological advances such as those represented by the electronic devices in this case.[21] We reject any contention that this broad language should nonetheless be interpreted in a manner which would severely limit the copyrightability of computer programs which Congress clearly intended to protect. We cannot accept defendant's suggestion that would afford an unlimited loophole by which infringement of a computer program is limited to copying of the computer program text but not to duplication of a computer program fixed on a silicon chip. This was also the conclusion reached in *Tandy Corp. v. Personal Micro Computers, Inc.*, 524 F.Supp. 171, 175 (N.D.Cal.1981) (Peckham, C. J.), albeit in the context of computers rather than video games.

The only authority upon which defendant relies for its claim that plaintiff is entitled to no copyright protection is the district court's opinion in *Data Cash Systems, Inc. v. JS &A Group, Inc.*, 480 F.Supp. 1063 (N.D.Ill.1979). Significantly, the statements of the district court in that case that the copying of ROMs was not actionable under the copyright laws was not the basis of the affirmance by the Court of Appeals which expressly stated that it did not reach the merits of this issue. 628 F.2d at 1041. It has been suggested that the Court of Appeals implicitly reversed the district court on that issue. *See* 2 Nimmer on Copyright, s 8.08 at 8-106.3 n.18 (1981); *Tandy Corp. v. Personal Micro Computers, Inc.*, 524 F.Supp. at 175. The district court's analysis in Data Cash has been expressly rejected in both the video game audiovisual copyright context, *Midway Manufacturing Co. v. Artic International, Inc., supra*, slip op. at 27–29, and the computer program copyright context, *Tandy Corp. v. Personal Micro Computers, Inc.*, 524 F.Supp. at 175. Accordingly, we find that defendant has failed to provide any persuasive reason which would overcome the statutory presumption of validity of the copyright registration and we will affirm the district court's grant of an injunction.

Defendant contends that the district court erred in finding that defendant's copyright infringement was "willful and deliberate" without a hearing to determine this issue. The district court issued the injunction based only upon the verified complaint, affidavits, and exhibits, after finding that the parties had stipulated and agreed that there was no factual dispute concerning the plaintiff's copyright claim and that the matters in dispute

---

the present state of technology, in punched cards, magnetic disks, magnetic tape, or silicon chips — its mechanical phase.

Id. at 28.

21. The legislative history of the 1976 Copyright Act supports this interpretation. It emphasizes the expanded scope of the fixation requirement:

This broad language is intended to avoid the artificial and largely unjustifiable distinctions, derived from cases such as *White-Smith Publishing Co. v. Apollo Co.*, 209 U.S. 1, (1908), under which statutory copyrightability in certain cases has been made to depend upon the form or medium in which the work is fixed. Under the bill it makes no difference what the form, manner, or medium of fixation may be — whether it is in words, numbers, notes, sounds, pictures, or any other graphic or symbolic indicia, whether embodied in a physical object in written, printed, photographic, sculptural, punched, magnetic, or any other stable form, and whether it is capable of perception directly or by means of any machine or device "now known or later developed."

H.R.Rep.No. 94-1476, at 52; S.Rep.No. 94-473, at 51, U.S. Code Cong. & Admin. News 1976, at 5665.

were solely issues of law. App. at 196a, 199a. As a result, defendant has not had the opportunity to rebut plaintiff's charge that its infringement was "willful and deliberate." A finding of willfulness was not necessary in order for the district court to enter the injunction in the present case. It is settled that innocent intent is generally not a defense to copyright infringement, and injunctions may be issued without a showing of willful or deliberate infringement.

On the other hand, the issue of the defendant's intent may affect the amount of damages available to the plaintiff. *See Universal City Studios, Inc. v. Sony Corp. of America*, 659 F.2d 963, 975 (9th Cir. 1981); 3 *Nimmer on Copyright* § 13.08 (1981). For example, section 504(c)(2) of the 1976 Copyright Act provides in part:

> In a case where the copyright owner sustains the burden of proving, and the court finds, that infringement was committed willfully, the court in its discretion may increase the award of statutory damages to a sum of not more than $50,000. In a case where the infringer sustains the burden of proving, and the court finds, that such infringer was not aware and had no reason to believe that his or her acts constituted an infringement of copyright, the court in its discretion may reduce the award of statutory damages to a sum of not less than $100.

See also 17 U.S.C. § 405(b). If the district court's finding of willfulness stands, it might bind defendant in the damage phase of the litigation, which we believe was not the intent of the stipulation below. Certainly, no such finding is appropriate without giving the defendant the opportunity to present evidence rebutting the charge of willful and deliberate infringement.

For the above reasons, the district court's order granting the injunction will be affirmed except for Conclusion of Law No. 8 finding that the infringement was willful and deliberate. The case will be remanded for further proceedings consistent with this opinion.

Notes and Questions

1. There is no doubt that the early videogames of the 1970s and 1980s were extremely repetitive. If repetition of graphic images and screen sequences is truly relevant, how would the fixation requirement apply to today's videogames? In *Midway Mfg. v. Artic Int'l*, 704 F.2d 1009, 1012 (7th Cir. 1983), the court drew the following distinction:

> Playing a video game is more like changing channels on a television than it is like writing a novel or painting a picture. The player of a video game does not have control over the sequence of images that appears on the video game screen. He cannot create any sequence he wants out of the images stored on the game's circuit boards. The most he can do is choose one of the limited number of sequences the game allows him to choose. He is unlike a writer or a painter because the video game in effect writes the sentences and paints the painting for him; he merely chooses one of the sentences stored in its memory, one of the paintings stored in its collection.

Do you consider this explanation acceptable even though, unlike changing channels on a television set, the player is responsible for generating the details of appearance and movement with respect to the images that appear on the screen?

2. What if some developer devised a computer game wherein virtually all of the graphical images were constructed by the player during the course of the game? Under such cir-

cumstances, could anything be considered "fixed" by the developer? Would this have an impact on the ability to copyright the game?

---

§ 5.32 Originality

Measures of originality, creativity, and quality often overlap one another when a work of authorship is being critiqued for its literary or dramatic value. As used in § 101 of the Copyright Act, however, the originality requirement has a very definite and separate meaning. It is a minimal requirement, to be sure, but one that nevertheless managed to raise some significant hurdles for Atari, Inc., when it tried to copyright its *Breakout* videogame. Atari Inc. released its classic *Breakout* (*see* Color Insert) in 1976, a relatively elementary game with a simple goal; eliminate the bricks of an overhead wall by striking them with a pong-like ball. Most gamers would agree that, although the addictive game was simple, it was by no means non-original. Nevertheless, when Atari, Inc. sought to register the videogame, the Copyright Office refused the registration on the basis of a lack of originality. A lawsuit was commenced by Atari, Inc. against the Copyright Office; the United States District Court for the District of Columbia ruled in favor of the Copyright Office, thereby prompting two separate appeals to the Washington D.C. Circuit. The proceedings resulted in a series of up's and down's that more resembled a game of Pong than a judicial proceeding.

As you read the two decisions, keep in mind that after the first appeal was decided, the United States Supreme Court weighed in on the quantum of originality required to satisfy § 101. In *Feist Publ'ns, In.c v. Rural Tel. Serv. Co.*, 499 U.S. 340, 345 (1991), the Supreme Court ruled that the "the requisite level of creativity for copyrightability is extremely low." According to *Feist*, a work that is original to the author qualifies for copyright protection if that work is "independently created by the author and possesses some minimal degree of creativity." *Id.* Stated yet another way: "In order for a work to meet the originality requirement for copyright protection … the work satisfies that requirement as long as it possesses some creative spark, no matter how crude, humble or obvious it might be; originality does not signify novelty." *Id.*

Atari Games Corp. v. Oman

United States Court of Appeals, District of Columbia Circuit, 1989
888 F.2d 878

GINSBURG, Circuit Judge.

By letter dated December 7, 1987, the Copyright Office reported its final action refusing to register a claim to copyright in the video game BREAKOUT, an audiovisual work created in 1975 by Atari, Inc., the predecessor of plaintiff-appellant Atari Games Corporation (Atari). The December 1987 letter, written on behalf of the United States Register of Copyrights (Register), stated that the video game in question "does not contain sufficient original visual or musical authorship to warrant registration." Invoking the judicial review prescriptions of the Administrative Procedure Act, 5 U.S.C. §§ 701–706, Atari unsuccessfully challenged the agency's determination in the district court as "arbitrary, capricious, an abuse of discretion, or otherwise not in accordance with law." 5 U.S.C. § 706(2)(A).

In this appeal from the district court's entry of summary judgment for the Register, we hold that the Copyright Office did not intelligibly account for its ruling. Because we are unable to determine on the current record whether the Register's action comports with the demand of reasoned decision making, we vacate the district court's judgment and remand the case to that court with instructions to return the matter to the Copyright Office for further consideration consistent with this opinion.

I. Background and Prior Proceedings

BREAKOUT, the audiovisual work that is the subject of this dispute, is a coin-operated, ball and paddle video game created in 1975 and successfully marketed by Atari in the following years. BREAKOUT's audiovisual display features a wall formed by red, amber, green, and blue layers of rectangles representing bricks. A player maneuvers a control knob that causes a rectangular-shaped representation of a paddle to hit a square-shaped representation of a ball against the brick wall. When the ball hits a brick, that brick disappears from its row, the player scores points, and a brick on a higher row becomes exposed. A "breakout" occurs when the ball penetrates through all rows of bricks and moves into the space between the wall and the top of the screen; the ball then ricochets in a zig-zag pattern off the sides of the screen and the top layer of the wall, removing bricks upon contact and adding more points to the player's score. Various tones sound as the ball touches different objects or places on the screen. The size of the paddle diminishes and the motion of the ball accelerates as the game is played.

By letter dated February 5, 1987, Atari sought expedited registration of a copyright claim in the audiovisual work embodied in BREAKOUT. Atari asserted an "urgent need for special handling because of prospective litigation in which [Atari] would be acting as plaintiff." *See infra* note 3. The Copyright Office responded promptly, but unfavorably. By letter dated February 13, 1987, Copyright Examiner Carmen Martorana declared the work not copyrightable. She reasoned that "to be considered an audiovisual work for registration purposes, the work must contain related pictorial or graphic images, and at least one of those images must be copyrightable." BREAKOUT did not qualify, she wrote, because neither the "common geometric shapes ... contained in th[e] work" nor "the coloring of those shapes" constituted copyrightable subject matter. Similarly, she stated, "there is not enough original authorship to register a claim in the sounds." She further said that the "images ... created by playing the video game ... are also not registrable since they are created randomly by the player and not by the author of the video game."

By letter dated May 22, 1987, Shirley B. Wendell of the Examining Division denied reconsideration. She repeated that the common geometric shapes contained in BREAKOUT are not copyrightable, that adding color did not render the work copyrightable, and that "the individual tones or sounds are not copyrightable."

By letter dated December 7, 1987, Harriet L. Oler, Chief of the Examining Division, denied further reconsideration and announced the agency's final action on the claim. She initially stated that the Register views the work "as a whole" to determine whether registration is warranted. However, to explain her conclusion that BREAKOUT "does not contain sufficient original visual or musical authorship to warrant registration," she separately treated the work's several parts:

[T]he use of a symbol for a wall drawn in a familiar tile type design is not copyrightable. The same is true of the image of a rectangle used in place of a paddle, a circle [sic] for a ball, and a common four colored stripe embellishing the wall.

The game's sounds, she added, "the three tones used before the ball, and the string of double tones used after it," do not "constitute any copyrightable audio authorship." She further stated that the arrangement of the "stationary screen display" contains no copyrightable authorship because "so few items" appear on the screen and "the arrangement is basically dictated by the functional requirements of this or similar backboard type games." Finally, she noted, Atari was not precluded "from registering a claim in the computer program."

Atari sought court review of the agency's final action. On cross-motions for summary judgment, the district court concluded that the Register reasonably applied controlling law to the facts before him. Describing the three letters from the Copyright Office as "thoughtful and well-orchestrated" expositions of the "pertinent considerations," the court held that the Register did not abuse his discretion in treating BREAKOUT as one of the "rare" instances of expressive value so slight as to be insufficient for copyright purposes. *Atari Games Corp. v. Oman*, 693 F. Supp. 1204, 1206, 1207 (D.D.C. 1988).

II. The Significance of Registration in this Controversy

Section 410 of the Copyright Act, 17 U.S.C. §410, provides in part:

> (a) When, after examination, the Register of Copyrights determines that, in accordance with the provisions of this title, the material deposited constitutes copyrightable subject matter and that the other legal and formal requirements of this title have been met, the Register shall register the claim and issue to the applicant a certificate of registration under the seal of the Copyright Office....

> (b) In any case in which the Register of Copyrights determines that, in accordance with the provisions of this title, the material deposited does not constitute copyrightable subject matter or that the claim is invalid for any other reason, the Register shall refuse registration and shall notify the applicant in writing of the reasons for such refusal.

If registration is refused, the applicant may seek immediate judicial review, as Atari did here, in an action under the Administrative Procedure Act, 5 U.S.C. §§701–706. Alternatively, as noted in the Register's final decision, determination of the copyrightability of the work may be sought in the context of an infringement suit.

Section 411(a) of the Copyright Act, 17 U.S.C. §411(a), permits an infringement suit, despite the Register's refusal to register a copyright claim, if registration submissions to the Copyright Office were in proper form and the Register is notified so that he may exercise a right to intervene. Registration carries evidentiary weight in an infringement suit. Registration before or within five years after first publication of the work constitutes prima facie evidence of the validity of the copyright; registration after the five-year period may be accorded weight "within the discretion of the court." 17 U.S.C. §410(c). For Atari, then, registration of a copyright in BREAKOUT might have evidentiary force in an action against an alleged infringer and would assure against the Register's appearance in the infringement action as a party adverse to Atari on the issue of registrability.

III. Appellate Measurement of the Register's Action

We accord due respect to decisions made by the Copyright Office pursuant to authority vested in the Register by Congress. Accordingly, we review the Register's decision under an "abuse of discretion" standard.

We initially summarize our concerns; then, to facilitate the Register's further consideration, and guard against rudderless administrative pronouncements, we develop those concerns more fully. First, we note the Copyright Act's definition of "audiovisual works" as "a series of related images ... intrinsically intended to be shown by the use of ... devices such as ... electronic equipment, together with accompanying sounds, if any, regardless of the nature of the material objects ... in which the works are embodied." 17

U.S.C. § 101 (definitions). Although the Act uses the phrase "a series of related images," the Copyright Office, even in its final action, emphasized the non-copyrightability of the work's several parts—the wall, paddle, ball, and tones—and also treated "the stationary screen display." * * * We are at a loss to understand why the Register did not more solidly link the final decision to the Act's apparent recognition that the whole—the "series of related images"—may be greater than the sum of its several or stationary parts.

Second, we do not grasp the standard of creativity the Copyright Office employed in determining whether to register BREAKOUT as an audiovisual work. Was it the normal standard under which a very modest degree of intellectual labor will suffice? Or did the Office test BREAKOUT against a higher standard, one resembling the "substantial creativity" measuring rod sometimes used to judge derivative works? And if an elevated creativity requirement was employed, what justified use of a heightened standard?

Third, the cryptic character of the final agency decision leaves us uncertain whether the action regarding BREAKOUT is consistent with earlier and later pronouncements of the Copyright Office and courts. Put more particularly, we are concerned that the Register may have confused or blended in this case the analytically and operationally separate questions: (1) is a work registrable as one constituting "copyrightable subject matter," *see* 17 U.S.C. § 410(a), (b); and (2) what is the extent of copyright protection—solid or thin—due a given "original work of authorship." The first question relates to the *existence* of copyright, the second, to the *scope* of protection.

V. Copyrightable Subject Matter

"Copyright protection subsists … in original works of authorship" including, among several categories of copy-rightable subject matter, "audiovisual works." 17 U.S.C. § 102(a)(6). Video games, case law confirms, rank as "audiovisual works" that may qualify for copyright protection.

This court and others have defined the word "original" in the Copyright Act's term "original works of authorship," 17 U.S.C. § 102(a), to mean "only that the work 'owes its origin to the author'—i.e., that the work is independently created, rather than copied from other works." As the district court stated, "there is no dispute in this case, and the Register expressly recognized, that BREAKOUT originated with or was independently created by Atari." *Atari Games Corp.*, 693 F. Supp. at 1205.

While the Register concedes that BREAKOUT is an independent creation, he concluded that the game is not a "work of authorship" within the meaning of the statute. To constitute a "work of authorship," the material deposited with the Register must pass a "creativity" threshold, i.e., it must embody "some modest amount of intellectual labor."

A. The focus of inquiry

The Register subjected BREAKOUT to a component-by-component analysis, and considered in the aggregate "the stationary screen display" (arguing that BREAKOUT "does not qualify for copyright because the *components* of the audiovisual display are not original works of authorship") (emphasis added). The Act, however, uses the definitional term "series of related images," 17 U.S.C. § 101, and the case law correspondingly indicates that the Register's focus, even if initially concentrated on discrete parts, *ultimately* should be on the audiovisual work as a whole, i.e., the total sequence of images displayed as the game is played. *Stern Elecs.*, 669 F.2d at 857 ("Assessing the entire effect of the [video] game [SCRAMBLE] as it appears and sounds, we conclude that its repetitive sequence of images is copyrightable as an audiovisual display."); *see also* 113 CONG. REC. 8587–88 (1967) (Congressman Poff) ("A series of related images includes any group of two or more images having some type of relationship in their subject matter which gives unity to the group as a whole. However, the fact that some or all of the individual images in the group would also constitute separate works does not prevent the group of images from being an audiovisual work.").

In the clarification forthcoming on reconsideration by the Copyright Office, we anticipate that the Register will take careful account of our recent opinion in *Reader's Digest*, 821 F.2d at 806, in which we observed:

> None of the individual elements of the Reader's Digest cover—ordinary lines, typefaces, and colors—qualifies for copyright protection. But the distinctive arrangement and layout of those elements is entitled to protection as a graphic work.... Reader's Digest has combined and arranged common forms to create a unique graphic design and layout. This design is entitled to protection under the Copyright Act as a graphic work.

See also Apple Barrel Prods., Inc. v. Beard, 730 F.2d 384, 388 (5th Cir. 1984) (component parts "neither original to the plaintiff nor copyrightable" may, in combination, create a "separate entity [that] is both original and copyrightable"); *Roth Greeting Cards v. United Card Co.*, 429 F.2d 1106, 1109 (9th Cir. 1970) (greeting cards held to be copyrightable although textual matter standing alone was not copyrightable; "all elements of each card including text, art work, and association between art work and text, [must] be considered as a whole").

B. The creativity threshold

The level of creativity necessary and sufficient for copyrightability has been described as "very slight," "minimal," "modest." In defense of the judgment that BREAKOUT does not pass the "modest" creativity threshold, appellate counsel for the Register pointed to the Copyright Office regulation providing that "familiar symbols or designs" and "mere variations of typographic ornamentation, lettering or coloring" are not subject to copyright. 37 C.F.R. § 202.1. Again, we are concerned that the Register's attention may have trained dominantly on components, not on the work as a whole—the full "series of related images." 17 U.S.C. § 101 (defining "audiovisual works").

Furthermore, we note that simple shapes, when selected or combined in a distinctive manner indicating some ingenuity, have been accorded copyright protection both by the Register and in court. *See, e.g., Soptra Fabrics Corp. v. Stafford Knitting Mills, Inc.*, 490 F.2d 1092, 1094 (2d Cir. 1974) (concluding that fabric design consisting of strip of crescents with scalloping or ribbons and rows of semicircles "constitutes modest but sufficient originality so as to support the copyright"). We are thus uncertain whether or how the Register's decision on BREAKOUT harmonizes with prior Copyright Office actions and court rulings on the creativity threshold.[22]

---

22. After oral argument, in response to the court's inquiry, the Copyright Office identified three instances, in addition to BREAKOUT, in which registration as an audiovisual work was denied to a video game: TIC TAC TOE (registration rejected Aug. 30, 1989), OCTASY (registration rejected Oct. 21, 1988), and DRAW POWER DOUBLE DOWN (registration originally rejected Aug. 26, 1983, final rejection after appeal, Aug. 12, 1989). Notice to the Court of Other Video game Rejections by the United States Copyright Office (Sept. 27, 1989). Before this post-argument submission, the Copyright Office had not drawn the court's attention to any instance, other than BREAKOUT, of the Register's refusal to register a video game as an audiovisual work. The court cannot discern from the Notice whether the three audiovisual works now specified by the Copyright Office are comparable to BREAKOUT. Nor do we know why the screen displays in these cases were found to lack sufficient authorship. For example, we are not informed whether any of these submissions were derivative works based on prior models.

In its brief on appeal, the Copyright Office compared Atari's claim for protection of its work "as a whole," to the protection copyright law affords to compilations and other derivative works. Derivative works, several decisions state, to be copyrightable, must meet a test of "substantial," not merely "minimal," creativity. *See, e.g., Past Pluto Prods. Corp. v. Dana*, 627 F. Supp. 1435, 1441 (S.D.N.Y. 1986). To our knowledge, however, neither the Copyright Office nor any court has ranked as "derivative" a video game that, like the BREAKOUT game Atari produced in 1975, is not based on prior models.

We recall here the suggestion initially made by the Copyright Office that BREAKOUT's images are created "by the player and not by the author of the video game." We are mindful, however, of the cogent exposition of our sister circuit regarding another video game:

> Although there is player interaction with the machine during the play mode which causes the audiovisual presentation to change in some respects from one game to the next in response to the player's varying participation, there is always a repetitive sequence of a substantial portion of the sights and sounds of the game, and many aspects of the display remain constant from game to game regardless of how the player operates the controls.

Williams Elecs., Inc. v. Artic Int'l, Inc., 685 F.2d 870, 874 (3d Cir. 1982); *accord Midway Mfg. Co.*, 704 F.2d at 1012 ("The player of a video game does not have control over the sequence of images that appears on the video game screen.... The most he can do is choose one of the limited number of sequences the game allows him to choose.").[23]

C. "Idea" or "expression," scenes a faire, and the distinction between registrability and scope of copyright protection

Copyright protection extends only to "expression," not to "ideas." 17 U.S.C. § 102(b); *Mazer v. Stein*, 347 U.S. 201 (1954). The Register sees the two as merged in the BREAKOUT game. BREAKOUT contains no expression, he maintains, separable from the game itself, and therefore does not qualify as copyrightable subject matter. Eleven months prior to the final agency action in this case, the Fourth Circuit declared "untenable" lump categorization of video games as "idea" rather than "expression." *M. Kramer Mfg. Co.*, 783 F.2d at 436–37.

The Fourth Circuit, in *M. Kramer Mfg. Co.*, acknowledged and distinguished precedent holding that when the subject matter allows for only a very limited manner of expression, the idea and its expression remain a unit, so that there is no copyrightable material. *Morrissey v. Procter & Gamble*, 379 F.2d 675, 678–79 (1st Cir. 1967) (copyright does not extend to rules for "sweepstakes" type sales promotion contest). But works in the computer's domain generally have not fit that bill, the *M. Kramer Mfg. Co.* panel observed. Instead, the variety of ways to perform the same function sustains the classification of such works as "expression." *M. Kramer Mfg. Co.*, 783 F.2d at 436. *Compare Herbert Rosenthal Jewelry Corp. v. Kalpakian*, 446 F.2d 738, 742 (9th Cir. 1971) (rejecting infringement of registered copyright claim brought by manufacturer of jeweled pin in the shape of a bee; court held that idea of pin and its expression were inseparable, defendants were therefore free to copy the idea and, consequently, to produce a jeweled bee pin that looked like plaintiff's) *with Atari, Inc. v. Amusement World, Inc.*, 547 F. Supp. 222, 227 (D. Md. 1981) (observing that "the idea of a video game involving asteroids is a much more general idea than the rather specific concept of a jewelled pin in the shape of a bee, and the former is capable of many forms of expression," i.e., differently designed and combined symbols, movements,

---

23. It now appears settled that video games can qualify as works "fixed in [a] tangible medium of expression." 17 U.S.C. § 102(a); *see M. Kramer Mfg. Co. v. Andrews*, 783 F.2d 421, 440–42 (4th Cir. 1986).

and sounds). *But cf. Stern Elecs.*, 669 F.2d at 857 (leaving open the issue whether "a sequence of images ... might contain so little in the way of particularized form of expression as to be only an abstract idea portrayed in noncopyrightable form").

In this light, we do not follow the Register's thought in describing BREAKOUT's arrangement as dictated by "functional requirements." * * * Atari demonstrated that a large variety of "arrangements" or designs might have been devised in lieu of those featured in BREAKOUT, i.e., in place of the objects represented (multi-colored brick wall, square ball, and shrinkable rectangular paddle), the sounds employed (their tones and duration), and the speed and artificial direction of the ball's movement. *See* Addendum to Reply Brief for Appellant; *Williams Elecs., Inc. v. Bally Mfg. Corp.*, 568 F. Supp. 1274, 1281 (N.D.Ill. 1983) (observing that, unlike an arcade pinball game, the audiovisual aspects of a video game "are conceptually separable from its utilitarian aspects").

Nor can it convincingly be maintained that audiovisual display and computer program are so linked that it is necessary or sufficient for Atari to register a claim in the computer program. Registering a claim in the program would not securely protect "the series of related images," 17 U.S.C. § 101, for which Atari seeks an "original work of authorship" copyright seal. "Many different computer programs can produce the same 'results,' whether those results are an analysis of financial records or a sequence of images and sounds." *Stern Elecs.*, 669 F.2d at 855. "Writing a new program to replicate the play of [a video game] requires a sophisticated effort, but it is a manageable task." *Id.*; *see* Patry, 31 J. COPR. SOC'Y at 5 ("A knock-off manufacturer could ... write a computer program which would exactly replicate the audiovisual display but which would not replicate the underlying computer program. In such an event, the registration of the computer program ... would be ineffective since it is the audiovisual display which is sought to be protected.").

Even if BREAKOUT contains "expression," the Register additionally suggests, the symbols displayed are so ordinary and commonplace as to fail under scenes a faire analysis. The term scenes a faire refers to stereotyped expressions, incidents, characters or settings which are as a practical matter indispensable, or at least standard, in the treatment of a given topic.

We are unable to detect from the final decision before us the standard the Register is using to differentiate material that cannot constitute copyrightable subject matter and therefore should not be registered, from material that may be copyrightable, although perhaps meriting only "thin" protection when the character of its "expression" is tested in an infringement suit. Because neither the idea/expression dichotomy nor the scenes a faire doctrine, under the prevailing case law, reveals to us why BREAKOUT should rank as a work in which no copyright can exist, we are currently unable to approve the Register's decision under those rubrics.

We remand this case to that court with instructions to return the matter of Atari's application to the Register for renewed consideration consistent with this opinion.

SILBERMAN, Circuit Judge, concurring in the judgment.

We are asked in this case to review the decision of the Register of Copyrights denying Atari's application for a registration in the audio-visual display accompanying its game BREAKOUT. The copyrightability of the display is an issue currently before the District Court for the Northern District of Illinois where Atari has brought an action against a putative infringer. Because a registration would afford something of an evidentiary advantage in that suit, *see infra* at 2, Atari has chosen to pursue this petition for review simultaneously with the infringement suit.

I join the judgment of the court—remanding the case to the Register of Copyrights for adequate explanation—because I cannot determine confidently from the Register's

December 7, 1987 letter, the final agency action, what standard the Office used to deny registration. I write separately because I think the majority opinion could be misinterpreted so as to confine improperly the Register's discretion on remand.

We must bear in mind that when we review the Register's determination to accept or reject an application for registration, we do not make a final decision on the copyrightability of the item. In fact, as the majority opinion recognizes, the Copyright Office's imprimatur is worth only a rebuttable presumption as to copyrightability in an infringement action. And as the government points out, the Copyright Office receives over a 100,000 applications every year. Every time the Register denies registration for too little creativity it cannot be expected to issue an opinion that compares with the learned offerings of my colleagues. I think that is why the courts have generally thought abuse of discretion to be the appropriate standard to review the Office's denial of a registration. Since the applicant can gain full judicial review of copyrightability in an infringement action, the costs of forcing too fine an analysis and too extensive an explanation of a denial of registration[24] are not worth the benefits—particularly when reviewing a question which has unavoidably subjective aspects such as how much creativity is sufficient to force the Copyright Office to register a proffered work.

If, however, the Register wishes to make a *categorical* distinction between classes of works such as video games as compared to other offerings such as works of art, and that distinction is to be based on the Register's interpretation of the Copyright Act—which distinguishes between "idea" and "expression"—his determination might even be subject to a somewhat stricter scope of review than abuse of discretion—but it would still be quite deferential.

The Copyright Act is quite explicit as to the weight a registration decision is to be given in that kind of judicial proceeding. The Register's decision to grant a copyright merely constitutes *prima facie evidence* of the copyright's validity in any infringement action brought within five years of the works first publication (and only whatever weight the court deems appropriate for actions brought after that time), *see* 17 U.S.C. §410(c); judicial review of questions of law, including the question of copyrightability, is otherwise entirely *de novo*.

I agree with the majority that we properly remand here because, in my view, the Register has not explained if or why it is employing a categorical distinction between the registrability thresholds for video game displays and other works. But we must be careful when we choose this procedural option not to make it a device to induce an agency to provide the explanation and the result we think correct. If improperly read, the majority opinion might have the effect of causing the Copyright Office to register virtually any offering.

* * *

Atari Games Corp. v. Oman

United States Court of Appeals, District of Columbia Circuit, 1992
979 F.2d 242

GINSBURG, Circuit Judge.

This is the replay of the match refereed by this court in *Atari Games Corp. v. Oman*, 888 F.2d 878 (D.C. Cir. 1989) (*Atari I*), reversing 693 F. Supp. 1204 (D.D.C. 1988)

---

24. The Register typically gives no explanation when the Office registers an offering; the Act requires an explanation if the Office denies registration. *See* 17 U.S.C. §410(c). [This provision is now in 17 U.S.C. §410(b).—ED.]

(summary judgment that Register of Copyright's refusal to register video game BREAKOUT as an audiovisual work was not an abuse of discretion). In *Atari I*, this court remanded the matter because we were unable to determine what standard the Copyright Office in fact used to deny registration to the audiovisual work before it, i.e., the video game BREAKOUT. *See Atari I*, 888 F.2d at 879 (court's opinion); *id*. at 887 (Silberman, J., concurring in the judgment). The court found the Register's letter refusing registration opaque in four key areas: the standard of creativity; the consideration of the work as a complex whole; the use of the idea/expression dichotomy; and the relevance of the scenes a faire doctrine to the issue of copyrightability.

After remand, the Register again refused registration. Reconsideration of "Breakout," Letter Ruling, April 30, 1990 (Letter). The district court again granted summary judgment to the Register. Memorandum Opinion and Order Testing the Register's disposition only for "abuse of discretion," we hold that the rejection of BREAKOUT was unreasonable when measured against the Supreme Court's instruction that "the requisite level of creativity [for copyrightability] is extremely low.: *Feist Publications v. Rural Tel. Serv. Co.*, [499] U.S. [340] (1991).

I.

In his second refusal to register BREAKOUT, the Register characterized the representations of the wall, ball, and paddle as "simple geometric shapes and coloring" which "per se are not copyrightable." Letter at 3 (citing 37 C.F.R. § 202.1 (1988)).[25] Viewing BREAKOUT "as a whole," the Register found "no original authorship in either the selection or arrangement of the images or their components." He therefore refused registration, stating in conclusion that "the display screens both individually and as a whole simply lack sufficient creativity to make them registrable as audiovisual works."

II.

To be copyrightable, a work must be fixed, original (i.e., not copied), and a "work of authorship." 17 U.S.C. § 102; *see Feist*, 111 S. Ct. 1287 at 1287–88 (requirements for copyrightability). The only dispute now presented concerns BREAKOUT's qualification as a "work of authorship," which on statutory and constitutional grounds necessitates a modicum of creativity. See Feist, 111 S. Ct. 1287 at 1287–88, 1296–97.[26]

BREAKOUT was presented to the Register as an audiovisual work:

> "Audiovisual works" are works that consist of a series of related Images which are intrinsically intended to be shown by the use of machines or devices such as projectors, viewers, or electronic equipment, together with accompanying sounds, if any, regardless of the nature of the material objects, such as films or tapes, in which the works are embodied.

---

25. The Letter further observed that the "flat, unadorned geometric shapes" in BREAKOUT "do not evince authorship in the nature of perspective, shading, depth or brushstroke." Letter at 3; *see also id*. at 2 ("If the Copyright Office were to examine a painting consisting entirely of rectangles and find it copyrightable, it is important to understand that this decision would be based on creative elements such as depth, perspective, shading, texture of brushstroke, etc. and not on the geometric shapes per se."). Recalling the creativity of the work of Mondrian and Malevich, for example, we note that arrangement itself may be indicative of authorship. *Cf. OddzOn Products, Inc. v. Oman*, 924 F.2d 346, 348 n.1 (D.C. Cir. 1991) (district court judge asked counsel for the Register, "If Picasso had painted a round object on a canvas, would you say because it depicts a familiar subject—namely, something that's round—it can't be copyrighted?").

26. The Register's second refusal does not rest on the *scenes a faire* doctrine or idea/expression dichotomy addressed in *Atari I*, 888 F.2d 884 at 884–86.

17 U.S.C. § 101. In *Atari I*, we inquired whether the Register considered video games, although fitting within the "audiovisual works" category, to require a different level of creativity than other works. *See Atari I*, 888 F.2d at 888 (Silberman, J., concurring). The Register has disclaimed any such approach. He stated that the Copyright Office is applying the same creativity standard to the video game "Breakout" as it would to any other type of work, be it a pictorial, graphic, dramatic, musical, or literary work, etc. Letter at 2; *see also id.*, at 1 ("We have applied the generally accepted modest degree of creativity standard[.]").

In *Feist*, decided eleven months after the Register reconsidered BREAKOUT, the Supreme Court extensively discussed and elucidated the creativity standard; the Court left no doubt that the requirement is indeed modest:

> [T]he requisite level of creativity is extremely low; even a slight amount will suffice. The vast majority of works make the grade quite easily, as they possess some creative spark, "no matter how crude, humble or obvious" it might be.

Id. at 1287 (quoting M. Nimmer & D. Nimmer (Nimmer), COPYRIGHT § 1.08[C][1]. While enunciating the copyright creativity standard for all works, *Feist* deals with a compilation of facts:

> A "compilation" is a work formed by the collection and assembling of preexisting materials or of data that are selected, coordinated, or arranged in such a way that the resulting work as a whole constitutes an original work of authorship.

17 U.S.C. § 101.

An audiovisual work is, among other requirements, "a series of related images." *Id.* Therefore, as this court pointed out in *Atari I*, 888 F.2d at 883, the interrelationship of the successive BREAKOUT screens is crucial. We can accept the Register's assertion that the individual graphic elements of each screen are not copyrightable. Even so, BREAKOUT would be copyrightable if the requisite level of creativity is met by either the individual screens or the relationship of each screen to the others and/or the accompanying sound effects. *See Stillman v. Leo Burnett Co.*, 720 F. Supp. 1353, 1361 (N.D. Ill. 1989)("synergy of ... nonprotectable elements in [television] commercial creates a whole that is greater than the sum of its parts"); *cf. Roth Greeting Card v. United Card Co.*, 429 F.2d 1106, 1109 (9th Cir. 1970) (greeting cards held copyrightable though text standing alone was not; "all elements of each card, including text, arrangement of text, art work, and association between art work and text, [must] be considered as a whole"). An audiovisual work is analogous to the compilation of facts discussed in *Feist* in this critical respect: both involve a choice and ordering of elements that, in themselves, may not qualify for copyright protection; the author's *selection* and *arrangement*, however, may "entail [the] minimal degree of creativity" needed to bring the work within the protection of the copyright laws. *See Feist*, 111 S. Ct. at 1289.

Feist concerned a white-page telephone directory. The publisher of the directory had taken the names, telephone numbers, and addresses of all persons using its telephone service and arranged the material alphabetically by subscriber's name. This manner of selecting and presenting facts was held not to involve "the modicum of creativity" necessary for copyright protection because the choices and arrangement were "mechanical," "garden-variety," "typical," and "obvious"; the alphabetized list followed "an age-old practice, firmly rooted in tradition," one "so commonplace that it has come to be expected as a matter of course," or as "practically inevitable." *Id.* at 1296–97.

When this case was remanded to the Register pre-*Feist* the circuit's leading decision on authorship based on the arrangement of uncopyrightable elements was *Reader's Digest*

Ass'n v. Conservative Digest, Inc., 261 U.S. App. D.C. 312, 821 F.2d 800, 806 (D.C. Cir. 1987) (holding magazine cover copyrightable). We anticipated that the Register would "take careful account of" that decision. *Atari I*, 888 F.2d at 883. The *Reader's Digest* panel held that:

> [n]one of the individual elements of the Reader's Digest cover — ordinary lines, typefaces, and colors — qualifies for copyright protection. But the distinctive arrangement and layout of those elements is entitled to protection as a graphic work.... Reader's Digest has combined and arranged common forms to create a unique graphic design and layout.

Reader's Digest, 821 F.2d at 806.

III.

Our first problem with the Register's Letter rejecting BREAKOUT for a second time is its apparent focus on the individual screens, rather than the flow of the game as a whole. The hallmark of a video game is the expression found in the entire effect of the game as it appears and sounds, its sequence of images.

The Register states that he considered BREAKOUT "as a whole" and as a "series of related images." However, the sounds were mentioned only in the quoted statutory definition. The purported discussion of the "movement of the pieces" through the "series of related images" centered invariably on the "images or their components." We are left with the impression that the Register may have so trained his observation on the details of the individual screens that he neglected genuinely to consider the sequential aspect of the work.

IV.

On remand, the Register stated that BREAKOUT was too trivial for protection; he also repeated the words "distinctive" and "unique" as if they were talismanic. * * * ("The Copyright Office finds no 'distinctive arrangement' or 'unique graphic design' in 'Breakout.'"). The *Reader's Digest* panel, however, did not state that "distinctive" or "unique" qualities were requirements for protection. The opposite is implied by Reader's Digest's long quotation from a case finding protectable a "distinguishable variation in the arrangement and manner of presentation" of public domain elements. *Reader's Digest*, 821 F.2d at 806.

The Register reported that he reconsidered BREAKOUT under the "generally accepted modest degree of creativity standard." On brief he contended that "*Feist* confirms the Copyright Office's understanding of the statutory standard of original work of authorship." We do not comprehend, however, how one reconciles *Feist's* elucidation with the Register's analysis in this case.

Undisputedly, the ball's path in BREAKOUT varies depending on which of four sections of the paddle it hits. Its trajectory does not follow from the laws of physics. Atari created this motion by selecting and arranging the graphic elements in individual screens and then selecting and arranging the sequence of these screens. The Register does not mention this aspect of the work. The choice of "motion" made for BREAKOUT (and the selection and arrangement of art work subsumed therein) is not understandably characterized as "mechanical," "garden-variety," "typical" or "obvious," or as projecting "age-old practice[s], firmly rooted in tradition and so commonplace that [the combination of elements] has come to be expected as a matter of course," or as "practically inevitable." *See Feist*, 111 S. Ct. 1296 at 1296–97. The assemblage of elements in BREAKOUT does not appear to follow "a convention" that is "purely functional," allowing "no opportunity for variation."

In tension with *Feist*, counsel for the Register suggested at oral argument that BREAKOUT's resort to nonrepresentational images shows a lack of creativity. Counsel stated, specifically:

> [T]he idea ... could have been expressed in expressive ways. They could have added graphics to it. They could have had a brick wall that looked like a brick wall. They could have added ivy that was expressive.

Shortly later the Court asked:

> You have a ball that doesn't operate in any standard way, a wall that doesn't look like a wall. Those are fanciful elements. Are they not?

To which counsel replied:

> I certainly would not agree that the brick wall is a fanciful element because it is not a brick wall. It is simply common symbols that had been run together.

Abstract representation, however, is neither an "obvious: nor an "inevitable" choice. Nor is the coordination of a *square* "ball" and a rectangular *shrinking* paddle a "time-honored" or "conventional" combination. The same may be said of the choice of colors (not the solid red, brown, or white of most brick walls), the placement and design of the scores, the changes in speed, the use of sounds, and the synchronized graphics and sounds which accompany the ball's bounces behind the wall.[27]

We do not in any way question the Register's position that "simple geometric shapes and coloring alone are per se not copyrightable." Nor do we hold that all video games are *per se* copyrightable. We are mindful, however, of the teaching of *Feist* that "the vast majority of works make the [copyright] grade quite easily." *Feist*, 111 S. Ct. at 1287. It is not the Register's task to shape the protection threshold or ratchet it up beyond the "minimal creative spark required by the Copyright Act and the Constitution."

Conclusion

The rational basis for finding the elements as combined and arranged in BREAKOUT "so commonplace that [they have] come to be expected as a matter of course," *Feist*, 111 S. Ct. at 1297, eludes us. Therefore, we remand the case to the district court with instructions to again return the matter of Atari's application to the Register for renewed consideration consistent with this court's opinion.

———————

Notes and Questions

1. Is it the proper business of the Register of Copyrights to evaluate the quality or complexity of an audiovisual work as a material factor in its decision whether or not to issue a copyright?

2. If, instead of 1987, the videogame *Breakout* had been submitted for registration today, do you think that the ruling of the Copyright Office would have been the same? Which registration form would you prefer if you were to seek registration today?

3. Assume that the requirements of "fixation" and "originality" are both satisfied. There is still a potential hurdle with respect to § 102(b) of the Copyright Act which declares:

———————

27. We list these features as examples, not as a complete catalog of aspects of BREAKOUT in which one might see "some creative spark."

In no case does copyright protection for an original work of authorship extend to any idea, procedure, process, system, method of operation, concept, principle, or discovery, regardless of the form in which it is described, explained, illustrated, or embodied in such work.

To further restrict the ability to obtain a copyright, a leading treatise suggests that: "[N]o copyright may be obtained in the system or manner of playing a game or engaging in any other sporting or like activity." Melville Nimmer & David Nimmer, *Nimmer on Copyright* § 2.18[H][3][a] (2007). *See also Baker v. Selden*, 101 U.S. 99 (1880). Shouldn't an accumulation of the preceding restrictions imply that no copyright should ever be granted for a "manner" of playing a videogame, nor should it be granted for the process, system, or operation of the videogame? Indeed, what is left to protect?

4. The arrangement, shape, and color of the *Breakout* bricks (*See* Color Insert C.7) should artistically comply with the minimum requirements of *Feist*. But who really cares about protecting a mere configuration of static bricks? Isn't the essence of *Breakout* precisely embodied in its process, system, concept, method of operation, and manner of playing, all of the things that are specifically deemed unprotected?

5. One of the best arguments toward resolution of the "Section 102(b) dilemma" can be found in *Sheehan v. MTV Networks*, 1992 U.S. Dist. LEXIS 3028 (S.D.N.Y. Mar. 12, 1992). In *Sheehan*, the plaintiffs claimed that the MTV game show "Remote Control" infringed upon their copyright with respect to a game show proposal titled *Laser Blitz*. The plaintiffs lost because the court determined that there was a lack of basic substantial similarity between the two works. More significantly, the court found that the plaintiffs' method of playing the game was in fact copyrightable. District Court Judge Louis Freeh (who later became Director of the F.B.I.) wrote:

> Plaintiffs are not claiming that MTV copied their game rules. Nor are plaintiffs claiming that MTV copied the mere idea of a game show involving music videos. Rather, plaintiffs seek to protect "the concrete structure, sequence and organization" of "Laser Blitz," as well as the combination of "the props, the set, the nature of the contestants and audience, the character and style of the host, and the atmosphere of the show."

> Although plaintiffs' proposal is, to some extent, a mere combination of standard ideas for a game show, the proposal does have unique elements, such as its distinctive arrangement and its primary "hook," *the use of the laser gun to shoot at music videos displayed on nine video screens.* This particular feature requires manual and visual skills somewhat akin to operating a "Nintendo" game, rather than the completely unskilled operation of a television remote control device. In combination, those unique elements transform the proposal into a copyrightable work.

Id. at 6.

Did employment of the terms "unique elements" and "original selection" solve the problems posed by § 102(b) or merely skirt them? Today, no one would seriously doubt the fact that a videogame should comply with § 102(a). Yet the *Sheehan* Court seemed to focus on the originality issues and use them in an attempt to solve the unrelated matters posed by § 102(b). Do you agree? Or are the problems posed by § 102(b) in some manner intertwined with uniqueness and originality?

Chapter Six

Copyright Litigation

§ 6.10 Jurisdiction

Copyright infringement is basically a matter of exclusive federal concern. In accordance with 28 U.S.C. § 1338(a): "The district courts shall have original jurisdiction of any civil action arising under any Act of Congress relating to patents, plant variety protection, copyrights and trademarks. Such jurisdiction shall be exclusive of the courts of the states in patent, plant variety protection and copyright cases." To further drive home the federal nature of the action, § 501(a) of the Copyright Act provides in part that: "Anyone who violates any of the exclusive rights of the copyright owner as provided by sections 106 U.S.C. through 122 U.S.C. [17 §§ 106–122] or of the author as provided in section 106A(a) [17 106A(a)] ... is an infringer of the copyright or right of the author, as the case may be." The sections following § 501 provide a variety of remedies for copyright infringement, including: injunctive relief (§ 502), impounding the infringing works (§ 503 and § 509), damages for lost profits (§ 504), costs and attorney fees (§ 505), and criminal sanctions (§ 506).

There are a few exceptions to the basic rule that disputes involving copyright infringement are subject to exclusive federal jurisdiction. Contract disputes, for example, involving arguments over the ownership of a copyright or the terms of a licensing agreement may often be resolved in a state setting as would other contractual issues. And where copyright law is presented as a defense or counterclaim in a state based action, federal jurisdiction may be avoided. *See Holmes Group, Inc. v. Tornado Air Circulation Sys.*, 535 U.S. 826 (2002); *Louisville & N. R. Co. v. Motley*, 211 U.S. 149 (1908); *Green v. Hendrickson Pubs.*, 770 N.E.2d 784, 786–77 (Ind. 2002). In addition, despite the sweeping nature of that 1976 Copyright Act, there still exists some remnants of "common law copyright" that can be initiated in a state court. *See Capitol Records, Inc. v. Naxos of Am., Inc.*, 372 F.3d 471 (2d Cir. 2004); *Capitol Records, Inc. v. Naxos of Am., Inc.*, 4 N.Y.3d 540 (N.Y. 2005).

When we speak of an infringement, we might best refer to those rights and actions that are exclusively enjoyed by the copyright holder. They are spelled out in § 106 of the Act:

Exclusive rights in copyrighted works: Subject to sections 107 through 122, the owner of copyright under this title has the exclusive rights to do and to authorize any of the following:

(1) to reproduce the copyrighted work in copies or phonorecord;

(2) to prepare derivative works based upon the copyrighted work;

(3) to distribute copies or phonorecord of the copyrighted work to the public by sale or other transfer of ownership, or by rental, lease, or lending;

(4) in the case of literary, musical, dramatic, and choreographic works, pantomimes, and motion pictures and other audiovisual works, to perform the copyrighted work publicly;

(5) in the case of literary, musical, dramatic, and choreographic works, pantomimes, and pictorial, graphic, or sculptural works, including the individual images of a motion picture or other audiovisual work, to display the copyrighted work publicly; and

(6) in the case of sound recordings, to perform the copyrighted work publicly by means of a digital audio transmission.

With respect to videogames, the following § 106A, which was added after passage of the 1976 Copyright Act, is of particular importance and interest. Notice that it grants additional rights to creators of visual arts:

§ 106A. Rights of certain authors to attribution and integrity:

Rights of attribution and integrity. Subject to section 107 and independent of the exclusive rights provided in section 106, the author of a work of visual art:

(1) shall have the right (A) to claim authorship of that work, and (B) to prevent the use of his or her name as the author of any work of visual art which he or she did not create;

(2) shall have the right to prevent the use of his or her name as the author of the work of visual art in the event of a distortion, mutilation, or other modification of the work which would be prejudicial to his or her honor or reputation; and

(3) subject to the limitations set forth in section 113(d), shall have the right (A) to prevent any intentional distortion, mutilation, or other modification of that work which would be prejudicial to his or her honor or reputation, and any intentional distortion, mutilation, or modification of that work is a violation of that right, and (B) to prevent any destruction of a work of recognized stature, and any intentional or grossly negligent destruction of that work is a violation of that right.

Because the copyright owner is the only person entitled to the benefits listed in the preceding sections, he or she may maintain an action for infringement against anyone who might usurp them by establishing the following elements (For the first two, *see Feist Pub's, Inc. v. Rural Tel. Serv. Co.*, 499 U.S. 340, 361 (1991)):

[1] The Plaintiff is the copyright owner,

[2] The Defendant has copied the copyrighted work, and

[3] The Plaintiff has registered or attempted to register the work.

Registration is a prerequisite for filing an infringement lawsuit. 17 U.S.C. § 411(a) states:

Except for an action brought for a violation of the rights of the author under section 106A(a) and subject to the provisions of subsection (b), no action for infringement of the copyright in any United States work shall be instituted until preregistration or registration of the copyright claim has been made in accordance with this title. In any case, however, where the deposit, application, and fee required for registration have been delivered to the Copyright Office in proper form and registration has been refused, the applicant is entitled to institute an action for infringement if notice thereof, with a copy of the complaint, is served on the Register of Copyrights. The Register may, at his or her option, become a party to the action with respect to the issue of registrability of the copyright claim by entering an appearance within sixty days after such service, but the Register's failure to become a party shall not deprive the court of jurisdiction to determine that issue.

It is clear from the above language that federal courts would have subject matter jurisdiction over an infringement action where a copyright registration was properly filed and refused by the Copyright Office; there is, however, a split of authority as to whether such courts have jurisdiction *after* an application has been filed but before the Copyright Office grants or denies it. *Compare La Resolana Architects, PA v. Clay Realtors Angel Fire*, 416 F.3d 1195, 1200–1205 (10th Cir. 2005), (holding against federal jurisdiction) with *Positive Black Talk Inc. v. Cash Money Records Inc.*, 394 F.3d 357, 365 (5th Cir. 2004) (requiring only the filing of the application).

---

§ 6.20 Direct Copyright Infringement

There are several ways to infringe upon a copyright. Direct, literal infringement is the most obvious if not the most common. A literal infringement implies direct, verbatim copying; whereas, a more common form of direct, but non-literal infringement involves copies that are *substantially similar* to the protected work. There are also several other *indirect* methods of engaging in unlawful infringing conduct that must also be considered, such as vicarious, contributory and induced infringement (more thoroughly considered in § 6.40, *infra*).

As we shall soon see, there are many different tests, mechanisms and standards for determining whether or not there has been a direct infringement of a copyright; as used herein, the term "direct" includes both literal and non-literal infringement. While the former is *clearly* actionable, it is also accepted practice that non-literal copying must also be subject to recourse. If copyright protection were limited to the exact work and nothing more, a "plagiarist would escape by immaterial variations." *Nichols v. Universal Pictures Co.*, 45 F.2d 119, 121 (2d Cir. 1930).

Where the offensive copying is literal and obvious, the plaintiff's job is relatively simple, but that rarely occurs in real life. From an evidentiary stance, it is far more common for the plaintiff to discharge his or her burden of proof by showing: [a] Access to the copyrighted work by the defendant and [b] and a substantial similarity between the copyrighted work and the offending work. *Novelty Textile Mills, Inc. v. Joan Fabrics Corp.*, 558 F.2d 1090, 1091 (2d Cir. 1977). In place of "substantial similarity," some courts use the term: "probative similarity." *Positive Black Talk, Inc. v. Cash Money Records, Inc.*, 394 F.3d 357, 368 n. 7 (5th Cir. 2004), indicating that the First, Second, Third, Tenth, and Eleventh Circuits use "probative similarity."

The distinction was created to suggest that not all copying should be actionable and that there should be additional requirements pertaining to the "illicit" nature of the copying.

* * *

Atari, Inc. v. Amusement World, Inc.

United States District Court, District Maryland, 1982
547 F. Supp. 222

YOUNG, District Judge

Atari, Inc., holder of a copyright on the electronic video game "Asteroids," seeks to enjoin defendants Amusement World, Inc. and its president Stephen Holniker, from manufacturing or distributing any product in violation of plaintiff's copyright.

In October, 1979, plaintiff Atari, introduced "Asteroids," a video game in which the player commands a spaceship through a barrage of space rocks and enemy spaceships. Plaintiff has sold 70,000 copyrighted "Asteroids" games for a total of $125,000,000, making "Asteroids" the largest-selling video game ever (not counting sales in Japan).

Defendant Amusement World, Inc., is a small closely-held corporation employing a total of five people. Its business has consisted largely of repair work on coin-operated games, but recently it has attempted to enter the lucrative video business by producing and distributing a video game called "Meteors."

On March 13, 1981, plaintiff first became aware that defendants were selling "Meteors," which plaintiff alleges is substantially similar to "Asteroids." On March 18, 1981, plaintiff sent defendants a cease and desist letter, which defendants have ignored. Plaintiff then filed suit and now seeks injunctive relief.

THE GAMES

Each of the two video games is contained in a cabinet with a display screen and a control panel for the player. The course of the game is controlled by a computer program, which has been chemically implanted in printed circuit boards inside the cabinet. When no one is playing the game, the machine is in the so-called "attract mode," in which there appears on the display screen an explanation of the game and/or a short simulated game sequence, which is intended to attract customers. Placing a coin in the machine causes it to go into "play mode," in which the computer program generates scenes of dangerous situations, to which the player responds by pressing various buttons on the control panel.

The principle of the two games is basically the same. The player commands a spaceship, represented by a small symbol that appears in the center of the screen. During the course of the game, symbols representing various sized rocks drift across the screen, and, at certain intervals, symbols representing enemy spaceships enter and move around the screen and attempt to shoot the player's spaceship. Four control buttons allow the player to rotate his ship clockwise or counterclockwise, to move the ship forward, and to fire a weapon. A variety of appropriate sounds accompany the firing of weapons and the destruction of rocks and spaceships. Many of the design features of the two games are similar or identical. *In both games:*

1. There are three sizes of rocks.
2. The rocks appear in waves, each wave being composed initially of larger rocks.
3. Larger rocks move more slowly than smaller ones.
4. When hit, a large rock splits into two medium rocks, a medium rock splits into two small ones, and a small rock disappears.
5. When a rock hits the player's spaceship, the ship is destroyed.
6. There are two sizes of enemy spaceships.

7. The larger enemy spaceship is an easier target than the smaller one.

8. The player's ship and enemy ships shoot projectiles.

9. When a spaceship's projectiles hit a rock or another ship, the latter is destroyed immediately.

10. The destruction of any rock or spaceship is accompanied by a symbol of an explosion.

11. When an enemy spaceship is on the screen, the player hears a beeping tone.

12. There is a two-tone beeping noise in the background throughout the game, and the tempo of this noise increases as the game progresses.

13. The player gets several spaceships for his quarter. The number of ships remaining is displayed with the player's score.

14. The score is displayed in the upper left corner for one player and the upper right and left corners for two players.

15. The control panels are painted in red, white, and blue.

16. Four control buttons from left to right, rotate the player's spaceship counter-clockwise, rotate it clockwise, move it forward, and fire the weapon.

17. When a player presses the "thrust" button, his spaceship moves forward and when he releases the button the ship begins to slow down gradually (although it stops more quickly in "Meteors").

18. The player gets an extra spaceship if he scores 10,000 points.

19. Points are awarded on an increasing scale for shooting (a) large rock, (b) medium rock, (c) small rock, (d) large alien craft, (e) small alien craft.

20. When all rocks are destroyed a new wave of large rocks appears.

21. Each new wave of rocks has progressively more large rocks than the previous waves to increase the challenge of the game.

22. A general overhead view of the battle field is presented.

There are also a number of differences between the games:

1. "Meteors" is in color, while "Asteroids" is in black and white.

2. The symbols for rocks and spaceships in "Meteors" are shaded to appear three-dimensional, unlike the flat, schematic figures in "Asteroids."

3. The rocks in "Meteors" appear to tumble as they move across the screen.

4. "Meteors" has a background that looks like distant stars.

5. At the beginning of "Meteors," the player's spaceship is shown blasting off the earth, whereas "Asteroids" begins with the player's spaceship in outer space.

6. The player's spaceship in "Meteors" rotates faster.

7. The player's spaceship in "Meteors" fires faster and can fire continuously, unlike the player's spaceship in "Asteroids," which can fire only bursts of projectiles.

8. The pace of the "Meteors" game is faster at all stages.

9. In "Meteors," after the player's spaceship is destroyed, when the new spaceship appears on the screen, the game resumes at the same pace as immediately before the last ship was destroyed; in "Asteroids" the game resumes at a slower pace.

The necessary elements for copyright infringement have been stated succinctly in 3 Nimmer, *The Law of Copyright*, § 13.01:

> Reduced to most fundamental terms, there are only two elements necessary to the plaintiff's case in an infringement action: ownership of the copyright by the plaintiff, and copying by the defendant.

OWNERSHIP OF THE COPYRIGHT

As stated by Nimmer, *supra*, § 13.01(A):

> Plaintiff's ownership in turn breaks down into the following constituent parts: (1) Originality in the author, (2) copyrightability of the subject matter, (3) citizenship status of the author such as to permit a claim of copyright, (4) compliance with applicable statutory formalities, and (5) (if the plaintiff is not the author) a transfer of rights or other relationship between the author and the plaintiff so as to constitute the plaintiff the valid copyright claimant.

The copyright registration certificate provides prima facie evidence of the above elements of the claim of ownership:

> In any judicial proceedings, the certificate of a registration made before or within five years after first publication of the work shall constitute prima facie evidence of the validity of the copyright and of the facts stated in the certificate....

17 U.S.C. § 410(c). Plaintiff entered into evidence its certificate of copyright registration, and defendants challenge only the second and fourth elements of copyright ownership. Therefore, the Court finds for the plaintiff on the remaining elements and addresses only the two challenged elements.

Defendants challenge the copyrightability of plaintiff's video game. However, the "Asteroids" game clearly fits the Act's definitions of copyrightable material. The Act includes among the types of works of authorship that may be copyrighted "motion pictures and other audiovisual works." 17 U.S.C. § 102(a)(6). The Act, 17 U.S.C. § 101, defines "audiovisual works" as:

> works that consist of a series of related images which are intrinsically intended to be shown by the use of machines or devices such as projectors, viewers, or electronic equipment, together with accompanying sounds, if any, regardless of the nature of the material objects, such as films or tapes, in which the works are embodied.

"Motion pictures" are defined as:

> audiovisual works consisting of a series of related images which, when shown in succession, impart an impression of motion, together with any accompanying sounds, if any.

Id.

Defendant contends that plaintiff has not properly copyrighted the "Asteroids" game, arguing that the original work of authorship is the computer program, as embodied in the printed circuit board.[1] Plaintiff filed a video-tape of what appeared on the display screen during one of an infinite number of possible game sequences with the copyright

---

1. Defendant uses the term "read-only memory" (ROM), which is the electronic circuit that consists of the thousands of tiny "switches" that have been chemically imprinted on the printed circuit board.

office, rather than the printed circuit board. Defendant argues that this registration affords no protection for the underlying computer program/printed circuit board.

Defendants' analysis is faulty, because it fails to distinguish between the work and the medium in which it is fixed. In order to receive a copyright, a work must be both copyrightable (that is, it must fit one of the definitions of a copyrightable work) and fixed in a tangible medium of expression. 17 U.S.C. § 102(a). Plaintiff's "work," the thing that plaintiff has created and desires to protect, is the visual presentation of the "Asteroids" game. That work is copyrightable as an audiovisual work and as a motion picture. 17 U.S.C. s 101. Plaintiff's work also happens to be fixed in the medium of circuitry on a printed circuit board. This follows from the definition in 17 U.S.C. § 102 of a tangible medium of expression as a medium "from which (the work) can be perceived, reproduced, or otherwise communicated, either directly or with the aid of a machine." A video game's printed circuit board is clearly such a medium of expression, since the "work," the audiovisual presentation, can be communicated from the printed circuit board with the aid of the video game's display screen. Thus, plaintiff's work meets both the requirements of copyrightability and fixation and is entitled to copyright protection. The specific medium in which the work is fixed is irrelevant-as long as a copyrightable work is fixed in some tangible medium, the work is entitled to copyright protection. 17 U.S.C. § 101. The owner of a copyrightable work need not, and indeed, cannot copyright the medium in which the work is fixed.

Defendants also argue that plaintiff is attempting to copyright an idea, rather than the expression of an idea. The Copyright Act adopted the longstanding common law doctrine that this is impermissible. 17 U.S.C. § 102(b). Apparently defendants are claiming that plaintiff is attempting to monopolize the use of the idea of a video game in which the player fights his way through asteroids and spaceships. Defendants cite the case of *Herbert Rosenthall v. Kalpakian*, 446 F.2d 738 (9th Cir. 1971), in which the court held that plaintiff could not copyright his jewelled pin in the shape of a bee because such a copyright would amount to a copyright of the idea of a jewelled bee pin. The court based this holding on the finding that the idea of a jewelled bee pin is capable of only one expression, and, therefore, when defendant used plaintiff's idea of a jewelled bee pin, as defendant was entitled to do, it was inevitable that defendant's pin would look like plaintiff's pin. The critical difference in this case is that the idea of a video game involving asteroids is a much more general idea than the rather specific concept of a jewelled pin in the shape of a bee, and the former is capable of many forms of expression. Thus, when plaintiff copyrighted his particular expression of the game, he did not prevent others from using the idea of a game with asteroids. He prevented only the copying of the arbitrary design features that makes plaintiff's expression of this idea unique. These design features consist of the symbols that appear on the display screen, the ways in which those symbols move around the screen, and the sounds emanating from the game cabinet. Defendants are entitled to use the idea of a video game involving asteroids, so long as they adopt a different expression of the idea—i.e., a version of such a game that uses symbols, movements, and sounds that are different from those used in plaintiff's game.

Defendants' second challenge concerns plaintiff's compliance with the applicable statutory procedures for registering a copyright. The Copyright Act requires the registrant to deposit two "complete copies" of the work, 17 U.S.C. s 408. Plaintiff submitted a videotape of one game sequence, and defendants contend that this is not a complete copy of the "Asteroids" game. However, the Copyright Office Regulation, 37 C.F.R. 202.20(d), allow the Register of Copyrights to permit the deposit of only one copy or "alternative identifying material." Given the bulkiness and cost of the actual video game, a video tape of the audiovisual presentation in the game is a reasonable "alternative identifying material."

INFRINGEMENT BY DEFENDANTS

Since direct evidence of copying is seldom available, plaintiff may prove copying by showing that defendants had access to plaintiff's work and that the two works are substantially similar. *Novelty Textile Mills, Inc. v. Joan Fabrics Corp.*, 558 F.2d 1090, 1092 (2d Cir. 1977). Access was shown indirectly by evidence that plaintiff's work had been widely disseminated.

Therefore, the crucial issue is whether defendants' game, "Meteors," is substantially similar to plaintiff's game, "Asteroids." Substantial similarity is determined by a general comparison of the two works:

> 'Substantial similarity' is to be determined by the 'ordinary observer' test. Judge Learned Hand in defining this test stated there is substantial similarity where 'the ordinary observer, unless he set out to detect the disparities, would be disposed to overlook them, and regard their aesthetic appeal as the same.' *Peter Pan Fabrics, Inc. v. Martin Weiner Corp.*, 274 F.2d 487, 489 (2d Cir. 1960). More recently this court formulated the test as 'whether an average lay observer would recognize the alleged copy as having been appropriated from the copyright work.' *Ideal Toy Corp. v. Fab-Lu Ltd.*, 360 F.2d 1021, 1022 (2d Cir. 1966). And, of course, by definition, '(t)he copying need not be of every detail so long as the copy is substantially similar to the copyrighted work.' *Comptone Co. v. Rayex Corp.*, 251 F.2d 487, 488 (2d Cir. 1958).

Novelty Textile Mills, supra, at 1093. Another court has held that a work is substantially similar to a preceding work when it captures the "total concept and feel" of the first work. *Roth Greeting Cards v. United Card Co.*, 429 F.2d 1106, 1110 (9th Cir. 1970).

However, in applying the "ordinary observer" test, a court must also apply the principles of the law of copyright. One of the most basic of these is the concept that, while one's expression of an idea is copyrightable, the underlying idea one uses is not. *Mazer v. Stein*, 347 U.S. 201, 217 (1954); 17 U.S.C. s 102(b). A corollary to this principle is that when an idea is such that any use of that idea necessarily involves certain forms of expression, one may not copyright those forms of expression, because to do so would be in effect to copyright the underlying idea. The classic case illustrating this concept is Kalpakian, *supra*. In that case, the court held that plaintiff could not copyright his version of a jewelled bee pin, because the idea of such a pin was capable of only one expression, and a copyright on his expression would amount to a copyright on the basic idea.

This principle must also apply in less extreme cases in which a creator's expression of an idea includes some forms of expression that are essential to the idea (i.e., forms of expression which cannot be varied without altering the idea) and some forms of expression that are not essential to the idea. In such a case, the latter forms of expression are copyrightable, but the former are not, because if the creator could copyright the essential forms of expression, then others would effectively be barred from using the underlying idea.

This doctrine has been recognized by courts in a variety of situations. In *Rehyer v. Children's Television Workshop*, 533 F.2d 87, 91 (2d Cir. 1976) the court stated that:

> Another helpful analytic concept is that of scenes a' faire, sequences of events which necessarily follow from a common theme. "(S)imilarity of expression ... which necessarily results from the fact that the common idea is only capable of expression in more or less stereotyped form will preclude a finding of actionable similarity." 1 Nimmer s 143.11 at 626.2; see Yankwich, Originality in the Law of Intellectual Property, 11 F.R.D. 457, 462 (1951). Copyrights, then, do not protect

thematic concepts or scenes which necessarily must follow from certain similar plot situations.

In *Franklin Mint Corp. v. Nat. Wildlife Art Exchange*, 575 F.2d 62 (3d Cir. 1978), the court considered two paintings of a pair of cardinals. The court noted that:

> There are indeed obvious similarities. Both versions depict two cardinals in profile, a male and a female perched one above the other on apple tree branches in blossom. But there are also readily apparent dissimilarities in the paintings in color, body attitude, position of the birds and linear effect. In one, the male cardinal is perched on a branch in the upper part of the picture and the female is below. In the other, the positions are reversed. In one, the attitude of the male is calm; in the other, he is agitated with his beak open. There is a large yellow butterfly in "Cardinals on Apple Blossom," and none in "The Cardinal." Other variances are found in the plumage of the birds, the foliage, and the general composition of the works.

The court also observed that the nature of the idea, namely a painting of cardinals, necessarily limits the forms of expression that can be utilized in articulating the idea:

> Expert testimony described conventions in ornithological art which tend to limit novelty in depictions of the birds.

Given this, the court said that "(a) pattern of differences is sufficient to establish a diversity of expression rather than only an echo," and the court affirmed the lower court holding of no copyright infringement.

This Court has held that plaintiff is entitled to a copyright on "Asteroids," because the idea of a video game in which the player shoots his way through a barrage of space rocks is an idea that is sufficiently general so as to permit more than one form of expression. However, under the doctrine set forth above, the Court must be careful not to interpret plaintiff's copyright as granting plaintiff a monopoly over those forms of expression that are inextricably associated with the idea of such a video game. Therefore, it is not enough to observe that there are a great number of similarities in expression between the two games. It is necessary to determine whether the similar forms of expression are forms of expression what simply cannot be avoided in any version of the basic idea of a video game involving space rocks.

There are, as noted *supra*, a number of similarities in the design features of the two games. However, the Court finds that most of these similarities are inevitable, given the requirements of the idea of a game involving a spaceship combatting space rocks and given the technical demands of the medium of a video game. There are certain forms of expression that one must necessarily use in designing a video game in which a player fights his way through space rocks and enemy spaceships. The player must be able to rotate and move his craft. All the spaceships must be able to fire weapons which can destroy targets. The game must be easy at first and gradually get harder, so that bad players are not frustrated and good ones are challenged. Therefore, the rocks must move faster as the game progresses. In order for the game to look at all realistic, there must be more than one size of rock. Rocks cannot split into very many pieces, or else the screen would quickly become filled with rocks and the player would lose too quickly. All video games have characteristic sounds and symbols designed to increase the sensation of action. The player must be awarded points for destroying objects, based on the degree of difficulty involved.

All these requirements of a video game in which the player combats space rocks and spaceships combine to dictate certain forms of expression that must appear in any version of such a game. In fact, these requirements account for most of the similarities between

"Meteors" and "Asteroids." Similarities so accounted for do not constitute copyright infringement, because they are part of plaintiff's idea and are not protected by plaintiff's copyright.

In light of this conclusion that the similarities in the forms of expression are inevitable, given the idea and the medium, the large number of dissimilarities becomes particularly significant. Given the unavoidable similarities in expression, the Court finds that the ordinary player would regard the aesthetic appeal of these two games as quite different. The overall "feel" of the way the games play is different. In "Meteors" the symbols are more realistic, the game begins with the player's spaceship blasting off from earth, and the player's spaceship handles differently and fires differently. "Meteors" is faster-paced at all stages and is considerably more difficult than "Asteroids."

It seems clear that defendants based their game on plaintiff's copyrighted game; to put it bluntly, defendants took plaintiff's idea. However, the copyright laws do not prohibit this. Copyright protection is available only for expression of ideas, not for ideas themselves. Defendants used plaintiff's idea and those portions of plaintiff's expression that were inextricably linked to that idea. The remainder of defendants' expression is different from plaintiff's expression. Therefore, the Court finds that defendants' "Meteors" game is not substantially similar to and is not an infringing copy of plaintiff's "Asteroids" game.

* * *

Atari Inc. v. No. Am. Philips Consumer Elec. Corp.

United States Court of Appeals, Seventh Circuit, 1982
672 F.2d 607

WOOD JR., Circuit Judge

Plaintiffs-appellants Midway Manufacturing Co. ("Midway") and Atari, Inc. ("Atari") instituted this action against defendants-appellees North American Philips Consumer Electronics Corp. ("North American") and Park Magnavox Home Entertainment Center ("Park") for copyright infringement of and unfair competition against their audiovisual game "PAC-MAN." The district court denied plaintiffs' motion for a preliminary injunction, and this appeal followed, 28 U.S.C. § 1292(a)(1).

I. FACTS

Atari and Midway own the exclusive United States rights in PAC-MAN under the registered copyright for the "PAC-MAN audiovisual work." Midway sells the popular coin-operated arcade version, and Atari recently began to market the home video version. As part of its Odyssey line of home video games, North American developed a game called "K. C. Munchkin" which Park sells at the retail level. Plaintiffs filed this suit alleging that K. C. Munchkin infringes their copyright in PAC-MAN in violation of 17 U.S.C. §§ 106, 501 (Supp. I 1977), and that North American's conduct in marketing K. C. Munchkin constitutes unfair competition in violation of the Illinois Uniform Deceptive Trade Practices Act, Ill.Rev.Stat. Ch. 1211/2, §§ 311–17 (1980), and the common law. The district court denied plaintiffs' motion for a preliminary injunction, ruling that plaintiffs failed to show likelihood of success on the merits of either claim. Because this appeal requires us to make an ocular comparison of the two works, we describe both games in some detail.

A. The Copyrighted Work

The copyrighted version of PAC-MAN is an electronic arcade maze-chase game. Very basically, the game "board," which appears on a television-like screen, consists of a fixed maze, a central character (expressed as a "gobbler"), four pursuit characters (expressed as "ghost monsters"), several hundred evenly spaced pink dots which line the pathways of the maze, four enlarged pink dots ("power capsules") approximately located in each of the maze's four corners, and various colored fruit symbols which appear near the middle of the maze during the play of the game.

Using a "joy stick," the player guides the gobbler through the maze, consuming pink dots along the way. The monsters, which roam independently within the maze, chase the gobbler. Each play ends when a monster catches the gobbler, and after three plays, the game is over. If the gobbler consumes a power capsule, the roles reverse temporarily: the gobbler turns into the hunter, and the monsters become vulnerable. The object of the game is to score as many points as possible by gobbling dots, power capsules, fruit symbols, and monsters.

The PAC-MAN maze has a slightly vertical rectangular shape, and its geometric configuration is drawn in bright blue double lines. Centrally located on the left and right sides of the maze is a tunnel opening. To evade capture by a pursuing monster, the player can cause the central character to exit through one opening and re-enter through the other on the opposite side. In video game parlance this concept is called a "wraparound." In the middle is a rectangular box ("corral") which has a small opening on the upper side. A scoring table, located across the top of the maze, displays in white the first player's score on the left, the high score to date in the middle, and the second player's score on the right. If a player successfully consumes all of the dots, the entire maze flashes alternately blue and white in victory, and a new maze, replenished with dots, appears on the screen. When the game ends a bright red "game over" sign appears below the corral.

At the start of the game, the gobbler character is located centrally near the bottom of the maze. That figure is expressed as a simple yellow dot, somewhat larger than the power capsules, with a V-shaped aperture which opens and closes in mechanical fashion like a mouth as it travels the maze. Distinctive "gobbling" noises accompany this action. If fate (or a slight miscalculation) causes the gobbler to fall prey to one of the monsters, the action freezes, and the gobbler is deflated, folding back on itself, making a sympathetic whining sound, and disappearing with a star-burst.

The four monster characters are identical except that one is red, one blue, one turquoise, and one orange. They are about equal in size to the gobbler, but are shaped like bell jars. The bottom of each figure is contoured to stimulate three short appendages which move as the monster travels about the maze. Their most distinctive feature is their highly animated eyes, which appear as large white circles with blue irises and which "look" in the direction the monster is moving. At the start of each play, the monsters are located side-by-side in the corral, bouncing back and forth until each leaves through the opening. Unlike the gobbler, they do not consume the dots, but move in a prearranged pattern about the maze at a speed approximately equal to that of the gobbler. When the gobbler consumes a power capsule and the roles reverse, the monsters panic: a siren-like alarm sounds, they turn blue, their eyes contract into small pink dots, a wrinkled "mouth" appears, and they immediately reverse direction (moving at a reduced speed). When this period of vulnerability is about to end, the monsters warn the player by flashing alternately blue and white before returning to their original colors. But if a monster is caught during this time, its body disappears, and its original eyes reappear and race back to the corral. Once in the corral, the monster quickly regenerates and reenters the maze to resume its pursuit of the gobbler.

Throughout the play of PAC-MAN, a variety of distinctive musical sounds comprise the audio component of the game. Those sounds coincide with the various character movements and events occurring during the game and add to the excitement of the play.

B. The Accused Work

North American's K. C. Munchkin is also a maze-chase game that employs a player-controlled central character (also expressed as a "gobbler"), pursuit characters (also expressed as "ghost monsters"), dots, and power capsules. The basic play of K. C. Munchkin parallels that of PAC-MAN: the player directs the gobbler through the maze consuming dots and avoiding capture by the monsters; by gobbling a power capsule, the player can reverse the roles; and the ultimate goal is to accumulate the most points by gobbling dots and monsters.

K. C. Munchkin's maze also is rectangular, has two tunnel exits and a centrally located corral, and flashes different colors after the gobbler consumes all of the dots. But the maze, drawn in single, subdued purple lines, is more simple in overall appearance. Because it appears on a home television screen, the maze looks broader than it is tall. Unlike that in PAC-MAN, the maze has one dead-end passageway, which adds an element of risk and strategy.[2] The corral is square rather than rectangular and rotates ninety degrees every two or three seconds, but serves the same purpose as the corral in PAC-MAN. The scoring table is located below the maze and, as in PAC-MAN, has places on the left and right for scores for two players. But instead of simply registering the high score in the middle, the K. C. Munchkin game displays in flashing pink and orange a row of question marks where the high scorer can register his or her name.

The gobbler in K. C. Munchkin initially faces the viewer and appears as a round blue-green figure with horns and eyes. The gobbler normally has an impish smile, but when a monster attacks it, its smile appropriately turns to a frown. As it moves about the maze, the gobbler shows a somewhat diamond-shaped profile with a V-shaped mouth which rapidly opens and closes in a manner similar to PAC-MAN's gobbler. A distinctive "gobbling" noise also accompanies this movement. When the gobbler stops, it turns around to face the viewer with another grin. If captured by a monster, the gobbler also folds back and disappears in a star-burst. At the start of each play, this character is located immediately above the corral. If successful in consuming the last dot, the munchkin turns to the viewer and chuckles.[3]

K. C. Munchkin's three ghost monsters appear similar in shape and movement to their PAC-MAN counterparts.[4] They have round bodies (approximately equal in size to the gobbler) with two short horns or antennae, eyes, and three appendages on the bottom. The eyes are not as detailed as those of the PAC-MAN monsters, but they are uniquely similar in that they also "look" in the direction in which the monster is moving. Although slightly longer, the "legs" also move in a centipede-like manner as the monster roams about the maze. The similarity becomes even more pronounced when the monsters move vertically because their antennae disappear and their bodies assume the more bell jar-like shape of the PAC-MAN monsters. Moreover, the monsters are initially stationed inside the corral (albeit in a piggyback rather than a side-by-side arrangement) and exit into the maze as soon as play commences.

---

2. The K. C. Munchkin home video game has several modes with an almost indefinite variety of mazes. One mode, for example, employs a constantly changing configuration, in another, the player can build his or her own maze, and in yet another, the maze disappears when the gobbler moves.

3. The district court stated that "the central character is made to have a personality which the central character in 'PAC-MAN' does not have."

4. The district court, however, characterized the K. C. Munchkin monsters as much "spookier."

K. C. Munchkin's expression of the role reversal also parallels that in PAC-MAN. When the gobbler consumes one of the power capsules, the vulnerable monsters turn purple and reverse direction, moving at a slightly slower speed. If caught by the gobbler, a monster "vanishes": its body disappears and only white "eyes" and "feet" remain to indicate its presence. Instead of returning directly to the corral to regenerate, the ghost-like figure continues to wander about the maze, but does not affect the play.[5] Only if the rotating corral happens to open up toward the monster as it travels one of the adjacent passageways will the monster re-enter the corral to be regenerated. This delay in regeneration allows the gobbler more time to clear the maze of dots. When the period of vulnerability is about to end, each monster flashes its original color as a warning.

There are only twelve dots in K. C. Munchkin as opposed to over two hundred dots in PAC-MAN. Eight of those dots are white; the other four are power capsules, distinguished by their constantly changing color and the manner in which they blink. In K. C. Munchkin, the dots are randomly spaced, whereas in PAC-MAN, the dots are uniformly spaced. Furthermore, in K. C. Munchkin, the dots are rectangular and are always moving. As the gobbler munches more dots, the speed of the remaining dots progressively increases, and the last dot moves at the same speed as the gobbler. In the words of the district court, "the last dot … cannot be caught by overtaking it; it must be munched by strategy." At least initially, one power capsule is located in each of the maze's four corners, as in PAC-MAN.

Finally, K. C. Munchkin has a set of sounds accompanying it which are distinctive to the whole line of Odyssey home video games. Many of these sounds are dissimilar to the sounds which are played in the arcade form of PAC-MAN.

C. The Creation and Promotion of the Accused Work

Ed Averett, an independent contractor, created K. C. Munchkin for North American. He had previously developed approximately twenty-one video games, including other maze-chase games. He and Mr. Staup, who is in charge of North American's home video game development, first viewed PAC-MAN in an airport arcade. Later, after discussing the strengths and weaknesses of the PAC-MAN game and its increasing popularity, they decided to commence development of a modified version to add to North American's Odyssey line of home video games. Mr. Averett also played PAC-MAN at least once before beginning work on K. C. Munchkin.

Mr. Staup and Mr. Averett agreed, however, that the PAC-MAN game, as is, could become popular as a home video game, but only if marketed under the "PAC-MAN" name. Thus, as Mr. Averett worked on K. C. Munchkin, North American sought to obtain from Midway a license under the PAC-MAN copyright and trademark. Mr. Staup later learned that the license was not available and so informed Mr. Averett. At that time, Mr. Averett had not yet completed K. C. Munchkin.

When Mr. Averett finished the project, North American examined the game and concluded that it was "totally different" from PAC-MAN. To avoid any potential claim of confusion, however, Mr. Averett was told to make further changes in the game characters. As a result, the color of the gobbler was changed from yellow to its present bluish color. North American also adopted the dissimilar name "K. C. Munchkin" and issued internal instructions not to refer to PAC-MAN in promoting K. C. Munchkin.

---

5. During this time, the white eyes disappear and reappear in alternating sequence with the reappearance and disappearance of the monster's body silhouetted in white.

An independent retailer in the Chicago area nonetheless ran advertisements in the *Chicago Sun-Times* and the *Chicago Tribune*, describing K. C. Munchkin as "a Pac-Man type game" and "as challenging as Pac-Man." Another printed advertisement referred to K. C. Munchkin as "a PAC-MAN game." Plaintiffs also sent investigators to various stores to purchase a K. C. Munchkin game. In response to specific inquiries, sales persons in two stores, one being the aforementioned independent retailer, described the Odyssey game as "like PAC-MAN" and as "Odyssey's PAC-MAN."

III. COPYRIGHT INFRINGEMENT

To establish infringement a plaintiff must prove ownership of a valid copyright and "copying" by the defendant. *See* 3 M. Nimmer, Nimmer On Copyright s 13.01, at 13-3 (1981) ("Nimmer"). Because direct evidence of copying often is unavailable, copying may be inferred where the defendant had access to the copyrighted work and the accused work is substantially similar to the copyrighted work. *Warner Brothers, Inc. v. American Broadcasting Cos., Inc.*, 654 F.2d 204, 207 (2d Cir. 1981). The parties stipulated to the validity of plaintiffs' copyright and to access; the district court's ruling turned solely on the question of substantial similarity.

Some courts have expressed the test of substantial similarity in two parts: (1) whether the defendant copied from the plaintiff's work and (2) whether the copying, if proven, went so far as to constitute an improper appropriation. Our analysis focuses on the second part of that test and the response of the "ordinary observer." Specifically, the test is whether the accused work is so similar to the plaintiff's work that an ordinary reasonable person would conclude that the defendant unlawfully appropriated the plaintiff's protectable expression by taking material of substance and value. Judge Learned Hand, in finding infringement, once stated that "the ordinary observer, unless he set out to detect the disparities, would be disposed to overlook them, and regard their aesthetic appeal as the same." *Peter Pan Fabrics, Inc. v. Martin Weiner Corp.*, 274 F.2d 487, 489 (2d Cir. 1960). It has been said that this test does not involve "analytic dissection and expert testimony," *Arnstein*, 154 F.2d at 468, but depends on whether the accused work has captured the "total concept and feel" of the copyrighted work,

While dissection is generally disfavored, the ordinary observer test, in application, must take into account that the copyright laws preclude appropriation of only those elements of the work that are protected by the copyright. It is an axiom of copyright law that the protection granted to a copyrightable work extends only to the particular expression of an idea and never to the idea itself. The Copyright Act of 1976 codifies this idea-expression dichotomy. 17 U.S.C. § 102(b). Thus, if the only similarity between plaintiff's and defendant's works is that of the abstract idea, there is an absence of substantial similarity and hence no infringement results.

It follows that copyright protection does not extend to games as such. As Professor Nimmer notes, however, "some limited copyright protection is nevertheless available in connection with games.... (A) relatively minimal artistic expression, if original, would render copyrightable ... the pattern or design of game boards and playing cards as pictorial or graphic works." 1 Nimmer § 2.18(H)(3), at 2–212. Recognizing this principle, the Second Circuit has held copyrightable as an audiovisual work, *see* 17 U.S.C. § 102(a)(6), the "repetitive sequence of a substantial portion of the sights and sounds" of a video game called "SCRAMBLE." This appeal requires us to address the related question of the scope of copyright protection to be afforded audiovisual games such as PAC-MAN. To do so, we must first attempt to distill the protectable forms of expression in PAC-MAN from the game itself.

There is no litmus paper test by which to apply the idea-expression distinction; the determination is necessarily subjective. As Judge Learned Hand said, "Obviously, no principle can be stated as to when an imitator has gone beyond copying the 'idea,' and has borrowed its 'expression.' Decisions must therefore inevitably be ad hoc." *Peter Pan Fabrics*, 274 F.2d at 489. Courts and commentators nevertheless have developed a few helpful approaches. In *Nichols v. Universal Pictures Corp.*, 45 F.2d 119, 121 (2d Cir. 1930), Judge Hand articulated what is now known as the "abstractions test":

> Upon any work ... a great number of patterns of increasing generality will fit equally well, as more and more of the incident is left out.... (T)here is a point in this series of abstractions where they are no longer protected, since otherwise the playwright could prevent the use of his "ideas," to which, apart from their expression, his property is never extended. Nobody has ever been able to fix that boundary, and nobody ever can.... As respects plays, the controversy chiefly centers upon the characters and sequence of incident, these being the substance.

(citations omitted). This "test" has proven useful in analyzing dramatic works, literary works, and motion pictures, where the recurring patterns can readily be abstracted into very general themes.[6]

A related concept is that of idea-expression unity: where idea and expression are indistinguishable, the copyright will protect against only identical copying. *Herbert Rosenthal Jewelry Corp. v. Kalpakian*, 446 F.2d 738 (9th Cir. 1971), presents a good example and discussion of this limitation. Plaintiff charged defendants with copyright infringement of a pin in the shape of a bee encrusted with jewels. The court assumed the validity of plaintiff's copyright, but refused to find substantial similarity:

> What is basically at stake is the extent of the copyright owner's monopoly-from how large an area of activity did Congress intend to allow the copyright owner to exclude others? We think the production of jeweled bee pins is a larger private preserve than Congress intended to be set aside in the public market without a patent. A jeweled bee pin is therefore an "idea" that defendants were free to copy. Plaintiff seems to agree, for it disavows any claim that defendants cannot manufacture and sell jeweled bee pins and concedes that only plaintiff's particular design or "expression" of the jeweled bee pin "idea" is protected under its copyright. The difficulty, as we have noted, is that on this record the "idea" and its "expression" appear to be indistinguishable. There is no greater similarity between the pins of plaintiff and defendants than is inevitable from the use of jewel-encrusted bee forms in both.

> When the "idea" and its "expression" are thus inseparable, copying the "expression" will not be barred, since protecting the "expression" in such circumstances would confer a monopoly of the "idea" upon the copyright owner free of the conditions and limitations imposed by the patent law.

Id. at 742.

---

6. One commentator offered a further refinement of this test:
   No doubt the line does lie somewhere between the author's idea and the precise form in which he wrote it down.... Protection covers the 'pattern' of the work ... the sequence of events, and the development of the interplay of characters.
Chafee, *Reflections on the Law of Copyright*, 45 COLUM. L. REV. 503, 513 (1945).

In the context of literary works, some courts have adopted a similar *scenes a faire* approach. *Scenes a faire* refers to incidents, characters or settings which are as a practical matter indispensable, or at least standard, in the treatment of a given topic. Such stock literary devices are not protectable by copyright. Thus, similarity of expression, whether literal or nonliteral, which necessarily results from the fact that the common idea is only capable of expression in more or less stereotyped form will preclude a finding of actionable similarity. Courts have applied this concept to written game rules and to the pictorial display of game boards.

[T]hat a work is copyrighted says very little about the scope of its protection. As a work embodies more in the way of particularized expression, it moves farther away from the bee pin in *Kalpakian*, and receives broader copyright protection. At the opposite end of the spectrum lie the "strongest" works in which fairly complex or fanciful artistic expressions predominate over relatively simplistic themes and which are almost entirely products of the author's creativity rather than concomitants of those themes.

Plaintiffs' audiovisual work is primarily an unprotectable game, but unlike the bee pin, to at least a limited extent the particular form in which it is expressed (shapes, sizes, colors, sequences, arrangements, and sounds) provides something "new or additional over the idea." In applying the abstractions test, we find that plaintiffs' game can be described accurately in fairly abstract terms, much in the same way as one would articulate the rules to such a game. PAC-MAN is a maze-chase game in which the player scores points by guiding a central figure through various passageways of a maze and at the same time avoiding collision with certain opponents or pursuit figures which move independently about the maze. Under certain conditions, the central figure may temporarily become empowered to chase and overtake the opponents, thereby scoring bonus points. The audio component and the concrete details of the visual presentation constitute the copyrightable expression of that game "idea."

Certain expressive matter in the PAC-MAN work, however, should be treated as *scenes a faire* and receive protection only from virtually identical copying. The maze and scoring table are standard game devices, and the tunnel exits are nothing more than the commonly used "wrap around" concept adapted to a maze-chase game. Similarly, the use of dots provides a means by which a player's performance can be gauged and rewarded with the appropriate number of points, and by which to inform the player of his or her progress. Given their close connection with the underlying game, K. C. Munchkin's maze design, scoring table, and "dots" are sufficiently different to preclude a finding of infringement on that basis alone.

Rather, it is the substantial appropriation of the PAC-MAN characters that requires reversal of the district court. The expression of the central figure as a "gobbler" and the pursuit figures as "ghost monsters" distinguishes PAC-MAN from conceptually similar video games. Other games, such as "Rally-X"[7] and North American's own "Take the Money and Run,"[8] illustrate different ways in which a basic maze-chase game can be expressed. PAC-MAN's particular artistic interpretation of the game was designed to create a certain

---

7. In Rally-X, the object is to guide a car through a maze clearing various check-points (represented by flags) to score points and avoiding collision with a number of pursuit cars.

8. In Take the Money and Run, the player-controlled figure and the pursuit figures are presented as humanoid forms.

impression which would appeal to a nonviolent player personality. The game as such, however, does not dictate the use of a "gobbler" and "ghost monsters." Those characters are wholly fanciful creations, without reference to the real world.

North American not only adopted the same basic characters but also portrayed them in a manner which made K. C. Munchkin appear substantially similar to PAC-MAN. The K. C. Munchkin gobbler has several blatantly similar features, including the relative size and shape of the "body," the V-shaped "mouth," its distinctive gobbling action (with appropriate sounds), and especially the way in which it disappears upon being captured. An examination of the K. C. Munchkin ghost monsters reveals even more significant visual similarities. In size, shape, and manner of movement, they are virtually identical to their PAC-MAN counterparts. K. C. Munchkin's monsters, for example, exhibit the same peculiar "eye" and "leg" movement. Both games, moreover, express the role reversal and "regeneration" process with such great similarity that an ordinary observer could conclude only that North American copied plaintiffs' PAC-MAN.

Defendants point to a laundry list of specific differences—particularly the concept of moving dots, the variations in mazes, and certain changes in facial features and colors of the characters—which they contend, and the district court apparently agreed, shows lack of substantial similarity. Although numerous differences may influence the impressions of the ordinary observer slight differences between a protected work and an accused work will not preclude a finding of infringement where the works are substantially similar in other respects. Exact reproduction or near identity is not necessary to establish infringement. In comparing the two works, the district court focused on certain differences in detail and seemingly ignored (or at least failed to articulate) the more obvious similarities. The *sine qua non* of the ordinary observer test, however, is the overall similarities rather than the minute differences between the two works. When analyzing two works to determine whether they are substantially similar, courts should be careful not to lose sight of the forest for the trees.[9]

To assess the impact of certain differences, one factor to consider is the nature of the protected material and the setting in which it appears. Video games, unlike an artist's painting or even other audiovisual works, appeal to an audience that is fairly undiscriminating insofar as their concern about more subtle differences in artistic expression. The main attraction of a game such as PAC-MAN lies in the stimulation provided by the intensity of the competition. A person who is entranced by the play of the game "would be disposed to overlook" many of the minor differences in detail and "regard their aesthetic appeal as the same." *Cf. Krofft*, 562 F.2d at 1166–67 (children would view accused characters as substantially similar to the protected characters despite differences in detail).

---

9. Many of the differences, such as North American's inability to duplicate some of the more distinctive features of PAC-MAN's monsters, may be due to the lesser capacity of the home video medium. That a work is transferred into a different medium is not itself a bar to recovery. *Universal Pictures*, 162 F.2d at 360; 2 Nimmer § 8.01(B), at 8–13. An author has the exclusive right to produce derivative works based on the original work, 17 U.S.C. § 106(2), and that right often can be more valuable than the right to the original work itself. Although dissection and expert testimony is not favored, the judicially created ordinary observer test should not deprive authors of this significant statutory grant merely because the technical requirements of a different medium dictate certain differences in expression. Without deciding the question, we note that in some cases it may be important to educate the trier of fact as to such considerations in order to preserve the author's rights under the Copyright Act. *See* 3 Nimmer § 13.03(E), at 13–45. We do not, however, propose that wholly voluntary changes in expression be given any less weight by the trier of fact.

The defendants and the district court order stress that K. C. Munchkin plays differently because of the moving dots and the variety of maze configurations from which the player can choose. The focus in a copyright infringement action, however, is on the similarities in protectable expression. Even to the extent that those differences alter the visual impression of K. C. Munchkin, they are insufficient to preclude a finding of infringement. It is enough that substantial parts were lifted; no plagiarist can excuse the wrong by showing how much of his work he did not pirate. It is irrelevant that K. C. Munchkin has other game modes which employ various maze configurations. The only mode that concerns this court is the one that uses a display most similar to the one in PAC-MAN.

While not necessarily conclusive, other extrinsic evidence additionally suggests that plaintiffs are likely to succeed on their copyright claim. In promoting K. C. Munchkin, several retailers and sales clerks described that game by referring to PAC-MAN. Comments that K. C. Munchkin is "Odyssey's PAC-MAN" or "a PAC-MAN game" especially reflect that at least some lay observers view the games as similar.

Based on an ocular comparison of the two works, we conclude that plaintiffs clearly showed likelihood of success. Although not "virtually identical" to PAC-MAN, K. C. Munchkin captures the "total concept and feel" of and is substantially similar to PAC-MAN.

The district court's conclusion that the two works are not substantially similar is clearly erroneous, and its refusal to issue a preliminary injunction constitutes an abuse of discretion.

Notes and Questions

1. Compare and distinguish *Atari v. Amusement World* and *Atari v. North American Philips*. In the process of your analysis, examine C.4 and C.6 (in the Color Insert). Compare C.6 to the Court's description of the game "*Meteors*" in the *Amusement World* case; likewise, compare C.4 to the description of "*Munchkin*" in the *Philips* case. Do you think that the court's assessment is correct in each of the two cases?

2. Asteroids, the first coin operated videogame to permit high scorers to enter their initials, became one of the most popular coin operated videogames of all time. (*See* Figure 1.6). *See also* Tom Vanderbilt, "Asteroids," *in* Van Burnham, Supercade: A Visual History of the Video game Age 197 (MIT Press 2001).

3. The Seventh Circuit in the *North American Philips* case provides the following distinction and supporting citations: "Unlike a patent, a copyright gives no exclusive right to the art disclosed; protection is given only to the expression of the idea—not the idea itself." How is the term "*art*" being used? Does the term "art disclosed" actually refer to a tangible work of art or is the term being used to refer to a more abstract concept?

4. In the *North American Philips* case, the Seventh Circuit found that "The impact of North American's infringement therefore extends even beyond the PAC-MAN game to the whole Atari system." Was this a valid observation or an exaggerated justification for issuing the injunction?

5. Would the holdings of *Atari v. Amusement World* and *Atari v. North American Philips* be any different today?

6. *Atari v. Amusement World* considered the "scènes à faire" concept. This term of art applies to necessary or common elements that normally flow from less tangible ideas. See § 6.75, *infra*. Explain what the court (in *Atari v. Amusement World*) meant when it said:

"It seems clear that defendants based their game on plaintiff's copyrighted game; to put it bluntly, defendants took plaintiff's idea. However, the copyright laws do not prohibit this."

7. The two preceding cases mentioned several "extrinsic" tests to determine substantial similarity: The "Ordinary Observer" Test (quoting Judge Learned Hand in *Peter Pan Fabrics, Inc.*), a "Total Concept and Feel" test (*Roth Greeting Cards*), and an "Ocular Comparison Test" (from *North American Philips*). Is there any significant difference among these three tests? Does common sense not suggest that unlike other copyrightable works, any test involving videogames should incorporate an element of *feel*? Does the Ordinary Observer Test suggest that the trial judge be compelled to play the subject videogames in much the same fashion that he or she might view a film to determine whether or not it was pornographic?

8. In *Computer Assocs. Int'l, Inc. v. Altai, Inc.*, 982 F.2d 693 (2d Cir. 1992), the Second Circuit developed a rather elaborate test to determine whether or not the "substantial similarity" requirement had been met. Rejecting the notion that one could effectively resolve the issue by merely separating ideas from expressions or otherwise utilizing a simple "observation," the *Altai* test proposed a three-step process:

> In ascertaining substantial similarity under this approach, a court would first break down the allegedly infringed program into its constituent structural parts. Then, by examining each of these parts for such things as incorporated ideas, expression that is necessarily incidental to those ideas, and elements that are taken from the public domain, a court would then be able to sift out all non-protectable material. Left with a kernel, or possibly kernels, of creative expression after following this process of elimination, the court's last step would be to compare this material with the structure of an allegedly infringing program. The result of this comparison will determine whether the protectable elements of the programs at issue are substantially similar so as to warrant a finding of infringement. It will be helpful to elaborate a bit further.

The three steps are commonly referred to as: *Abstraction, Filtration* and *Comparison*.

9. In the *North American Philips* case, the Seventh Circuit considered the statements made by independent retailers in Chicago to the effect that the offending product resembled "a Pac-Man type game." In truth, those statements were mild compared to some salespersons who simply stated that offending game *was*, in fact Pac-Man; the name "Munchkin" was not mentioned. Should the hearsay statements of unsworn sales associate be relevant to whether there was copyright infringement?

10. According to the *North American Philips* decision: "Video games, unlike an artist's painting or even other audiovisual works, appeal to an audience that is fairly undiscriminating insofar as their concern about more subtle differences in artistic expression." *Atari*, 672 F.2d at 619. Do you consider this statement true? False? Arrogant? Or uninformed? [Suggestion: Before volunteering your opinion, first ascertain whether or not your professor was a gamer, next ascertain whether or not your exams are anonymously graded.]

11. Compare Color Insert C.4 and Figure 6.1, then decide the *North American Philips* dispute for yourself.

Figure 6.1

12. Many complaints alleging copyright infringement include other claims; additional counts for trademark infringement are among the most common (*See* Chapter 8). For example, the video games discussed in *Midway Mfg. Co. v. Bandai-America, Inc.*, 546 F. Supp. 125 (D.N.J. 1982), such as *Galaxian*, may also be entitled to broad trademark protection because they have distinctive marks. (*See* §7.30, *infra*). *Frybarger v. IBM Corp.*, 812 F.2d 525 (9th Cir. 1987) is a typical case in which the plaintiff argued claims of copyright infringement, trademark infringement, unfair competition, in addition to state law claims for misappropriation of trade secrets, unfair competition, conversion and unjust enrichment. For operating an online videogame bulletin board providing unauthorized downloads, the defendants in *Sega Enterprises Ltd. v. Maphia*, 948 F. Supp. 923 (N.D. Cal. 1996) were found to have engaged in a variety of copyright and trademark related offenses including federal trademark infringement under 15 U.S.C. §§ 1051 et seq., federal unfair competition for false designation of origin under 15 U.S.C. § 1125(a), California trade name infringement under California Business and Professions Code §§ 14401 et seq. and California unfair competition under California Business and Professions Code §§ 14210, 17200–17203.

13. Perhaps the most fascinating overlap issues (copyright infringement and trademark infringement) resulted from attempts by videogame producer Accolade to make its games operable on the Sega Genesis game console, which required Accolade to copy and *take* a portion of Sega's computer code. *Sega Enterprises Ltd v. Accolade, Inc.*, 977 F.2d 1510 (9th Cir. 1993).

14. A surefire method for being charged with direct infringement involves the use of a copyrighted work in reliance upon a license or use permission that does not exist. See *Firesabre Consulting, LLC v. Sheehy, et. al*, 2013 Copr. L. Dec. ¶ 30,497 (S.D.N.Y., 2013), an infringement action that resulted from a dispute over payment for computer programming and digital design services that were rendered in conjunction with the virtual world commonly known as *Second Life*.

15. *Midway Mfg. Co. v. Bandai-Am., Inc*, 351 F. Supp. 2d 546 (D.N.J. 1983), which is set forth in §8.30, *infra*, provides an another example of a "direct infringement" case.

16. Cases and treatises commonly echo the accepted rule: While ideas are not copyrightable, the expressions of those ideas are. See Christopher Lunsford, *Drawing a Line Between Idea and Expression in Videogame Copyright: The Evolution of Substantial Similarity for Videogame Clone,"* 18 INTELL. PROP. L. BULL. 87 (2013). What issues does that raise with regard to videogames?

17. In *Amusement World*, the court lists a series of dissimilarities between the two games. Won't there always be several dissimilarities, absent exact copying? Isn't the better approach to examine the alleged similarities?

———————

§ 6.30 Derivative Works Infringement

A derivative work is one that is based upon one or more preexisting works. The case that follows provides a more precise definition, citing § 101 of the Copyright Act. In the context of a copyright infringement action, a court's use of the term "derivative work" generally signals bad news for the defendant. Since the copyright owner is the only one allowed to license or create a derivative work, a determination by the court that the defendant has created such a work is tantamount to a ruling that the defendant has infringed.

For any successful entertainment-related product, there will always be those manufacturers who recognize a legitimate opportunity to create and market embellishments and enhancements. At what point, however, do these augmentations become derivative works and, thereby infringe upon the subject matter of the enhancement? These are the issues that follow.

* * *

Midway Mfg. Co. v. Artic Int'l, Inc.
United States Court of Appeals, Seventh Circuit, 1983
704 F.2d 1009

CUMMINGS, Chief Judge

This appeal involves questions regarding the scope of protection video games enjoy under the 1976 Copyright Act, 90 Stat. 2541, 17 U.S.C. § 101 *et seq*.

Plaintiff manufactures video game machines. Inside these machines are printed circuit boards capable of causing images to appear on a television picture screen and sounds to emanate from a speaker when an electric current is passed through them. On the outside of each machine are a picture screen, sound speaker, and a lever or button that allows a person using the machine to alter the images appearing on the machine's picture screen and the sounds emanating from its speaker. Each machine can produce a large number of related images and sounds. These sounds and images are stored on the machine's circuit boards — how the circuits are arranged and connected determines the set of sounds and images the machine is capable of making. When a person touches the control lever or button on the outside of the machine he sends a signal to the circuit boards inside the machine which causes them to retrieve and display one of the sounds and images stored in them. Playing a video game involves manipulating the controls on the machine so that some of the images stored in the machine's circuitry appear on its picture screen and some of its sounds emanate from its speaker.

Defendant sells printed circuit boards for use inside video game machines. One of the circuit boards defendant sells speeds up the rate of play—how fast the sounds and images change—of "Galaxian," one of plaintiff's video games, when inserted in place of one of the "Galaxian" machine's circuit boards. Another of defendant's circuit boards stores a set of images and sounds almost identical to that stored in the circuit boards of plaintiff's "Pac-Man" video game machine[10] so that the video game people play on machines containing defendant's circuit board looks and sounds virtually the same as plaintiff's "Pac-Man" game.

Plaintiff sued defendant alleging that defendant's sale of these two circuit boards infringes its copyrights in its "Galaxian" and "Pac-Man" video games. In a memorandum opinion and order reported at 547 F. Supp. 999 (N.D.Ill.1982), the district court granted plaintiff's motion for a preliminary injunction and denied defendant's motion for summary judgment. The district court's order enjoins defendant from manufacturing or distributing circuit boards that can be used to play video games substantially similar to those protected by plaintiff's copyrights. Defendant appeals from that order on the ground that plaintiff has not shown a likelihood of succeeding on the merits of its claim of copyright infringement. We affirm for the reasons that follow.

[The court first considered whether video games qualify for copyright protection. Its conclusion: "We thus conclude that video games are copyrightable as audiovisual works under the 1976 Copyright Act and we note that every other federal court (including our own) that has confronted this issue has reached the same conclusion." — ED.]

Defendant next argues that plaintiff's copyrights are invalid because the 1976 Copyright Act does not apply to plaintiff's video games. Section 117 of the 1976 Copyright Act was amended in 1980 to define the exclusive rights of owners of copyrights in computer programs. As originally enacted, Section 117 provided that the 1909 Copyright Act and common law were to govern the rights of a copyright owner "with respect to the use of the [copyrighted] work in conjunction with" computers. Defendant argues that the 1980 amendment does not apply to copyrights, like those of plaintiff, in existence before the amendment took effect and that the original Section 117 requires that we look to the 1909 Act and common law to determine whether the circuit boards defendant manufactures are copies of plaintiff's audiovisual works.

We disagree. Even if the 1980 amendment applies only to copyrights issued after its effective date—an issue we do not decide—the district court properly applied the 1976 Act. The language and legislative history of the 1980 amendment are convincing that original Section 117 was intended only to leave unaltered the existing law governing the exclusive rights of owners of copyrights in computer programs. It was not intended to permit pirating of audiovisual works stored in computers.

The final argument of defendants that we address is that selling plaintiff's licensees circuit boards that speed up the rate of play of plaintiff's video games is not an infringement of plaintiff's copyrights. Speeding up the rate of play of a video game is a little like playing at 45 or 78 revolutions per minute ("RPMs") a phonograph record recorded at 33 RPMs. If a discotheque licensee did that, it would probably not be an infringement of the record company's copyright in the record. One might argue by analogy that it is not a copyright infringement for video game licensees to speed up the rate of play of video games, and

---

10. We described the "Pac-Man" video game in some detail in *Atari, Inc. v. North American Philips Consumer Elec. Corp.*, 672 F.2d 607, 610, 611 (7th Cir.1982).

that it is not a contributory infringement for the defendant to sell licensees circuit boards that enable them to do that.

There is this critical difference between playing records at a faster than recorded speed and playing video games at a faster than manufactured rate: there is an enormous demand for speeded-up video games but there is little if any demand for speeded-up records. Not many people want to hear 33 RPM records played at 45 and 78 RPMs so that record licensors would not care if their licensees play them at that speed. But there is a big demand for speeded-up video games. Speeding up a video game's action makes the game more challenging and exciting and increases the licensee's revenue per game. Speeded-up games end sooner than normal games and consequently if players are willing to pay an additional price-per-minute in exchange for the challenge and excitement of a faster game, licensees will take in greater total revenues. Video game copyright owners would undoubtedly like to lay their hands on some of that extra revenue and therefore it cannot be assumed that licensees are implicitly authorized to use speeded-up circuit boards in the machines plaintiff supplies.

Among a copyright owner's exclusive rights is the right "to prepare derivative works based upon the copyrighted work." 17 U.S.C. § 106(2). If, as we hold, the speeded-up "Galaxian" game that a licensee creates with a circuit board supplied by the defendant is a derivative work based upon "Galaxian," a licensee who lacks the plaintiff's authorization to create a derivative work is a direct infringer and the defendant is a contributory infringer through its sale of the speeded-up circuit board.

Section 101 of the 1976 Copyright Act defines a derivative work as "a work based upon one or more preexisting works, such as a translation, musical arrangement, dramatization, fictionalization, motion picture version, sound recording, art reproduction, abridgment, condensation, or any other form in which a work may be recast, transformed, or adapted." It is not obvious from this language whether a speeded-up video game is a derivative work. A speeded-up phonograph record probably is not. But that is because the additional value to the copyright owner of having the right to market separately the speeded-up version of the recorded performance is too trivial to warrant legal protection for that right. A speeded-up video game is a substantially different product from the original game. For that reason, the owner of the copyright on the game should be entitled to monopolize it on the same theory that he is entitled to monopolize the derivative works specifically listed in Section 101. The current rage for video games was not anticipated in 1976, and like any new technology the video game does not fit with complete ease the definition of derivative work in Section 101 of the 1976 Act. But the amount by which the language of Section 101 must be stretched to accommodate speeded-up video games is, we believe, within the limits within which Congress wanted the new Act to operate.

AFFIRMED.

* * *

Lewis Galoob Toys, Inc. v. Nintendo of Am., Inc.

United States Court of Appeals, Ninth Circuit, 1992
964 F.2d 965

FARRIS, Circuit Judge

Nintendo of America appeals the district court's judgment following a bench trial (1) declaring that Lewis Galoob Toys' Game Genie does not violate any Nintendo copyrights and dissolving a temporary injunction and (2) denying Nintendo's request for a permanent injunction enjoining Galoob from marketing the Game Genie. *Lewis Galoob Toys, Inc. v.*

Nintendo of America, Inc., 780 F. Supp. 1283 (N.D.Cal.1991). We have appellate jurisdiction pursuant to 15 U.S.C. § 1121 and 28 U.S.C. §§ 1291 and 1292(a)(1). We affirm.

FACTS

The Nintendo Entertainment System is a home video game system marketed by Nintendo. To use the system, the player inserts a cartridge containing a video game that Nintendo produces or licenses others to produce. By pressing buttons and manipulating a control pad, the player controls one of the game's characters and progresses through the game. The games are protected as audiovisual works under 17 U.S.C. § 102(a)(6).

The Game Genie is a device manufactured by Galoob that allows the player to alter up to three features of a Nintendo game. For example, the Game Genie can increase the number of lives of the player's character, increase the speed at which the character moves, and allow the character to float above obstacles. The player controls the changes made by the Game Genie by entering codes provided by the Game Genie Programming Manual and Code Book. The player also can experiment with variations of these codes.

The Game Genie functions by blocking the value for a single data byte sent by the game cartridge to the central processing unit in the Nintendo Entertainment System and replacing it with a new value. If that value controls the character's strength, for example, then the character can be made invincible by increasing the value sufficiently. The Game Genie is inserted between a game cartridge and the Nintendo Entertainment System. The Game Genie does not alter the data that is stored in the game cartridge. Its effects are temporary.

DISCUSSION

1. Derivative Work

The Copyright Act of 1976 confers upon copyright holders the exclusive right to prepare and authorize others to prepare derivative works based on their copyrighted works. *See* 17 U.S.C. § 106(2). Nintendo argues that the district court erred in concluding that the audiovisual displays created by the Game Genie are not derivative works. A derivative work must incorporate a protected work in some concrete or permanent "form." The Copyright Act defines a derivative work as follows:

> A "derivative work" is a work based upon one or more preexisting works, such as a translation, musical arrangement, dramatization, fictionalization, motion picture version, sound recording, art reproduction, abridgment, condensation, *or any other form in which a work may be recast, transformed, or adapted.* A work consisting of editorial revisions, annotations, elaborations, or other modifications which, as a whole, represent an original work of authorship, is a "derivative work."

17 U.S.C. § 101 (emphasis added). The examples of derivative works provided by the Act all physically incorporate the underlying work or works. The Act's legislative history similarly indicates that the infringing work must incorporate a portion of the copyrighted work in some form.

Our analysis is not controlled by the Copyright Act's definition of "fixed." The Act defines copies as "material objects, other than phonorecord, in which a work is *fixed* by any method." 17 U.S.C. § 101 (emphasis added). The Act's definition of "derivative work," in contrast, lacks any such reference to fixation. *See id.* Further, we have held in a copyright infringement action that "[i]t makes no difference that the derivation may not satisfy certain requirements for statutory copyright registration itself." *Lone Ranger Television v. Program Radio Corp.,*

740 F.2d 718, 722 (9th Cir.1984). *Cf. Kalem Co. v. Harper Bros.*, 222 U.S. 55, 61 (1911) (finding the movie "Ben Hur" infringed copyright in the book *Ben Hur* even though Copyright Act did not yet include movies as protectable works). A derivative work must be fixed to be *protected* under the Act, see 17 U.S.C. § 102(a), but not to *infringe*.

The argument that a derivative work must be fixed because "[a] 'derivative work' is a work," 17 U.S.C. § 101, and "[a] work is 'created' when it is fixed in a copy or phonorecord for the first time," *id.*, relies on a misapplication of the Copyright Act's definition of "created":

> A work is 'created' when it is fixed in a copy or phonorecord for the first time; where a work is prepared over a period of time, the portion of it that has been fixed at any particular time constitutes the work as of that time, and where the work has been prepared in different versions, each version constitutes a separate work.

Id. The definition clarifies the *time* at which a work is *created*. If the provision were a definition of "work," it would not use that term in such a casual manner. The Act does not contain a definition of "work." Rather, it contains specific definitions: "audiovisual works," "literary works," and "pictorial, graphic and sculptural works," for example. The definition of "derivative work" does not require fixation.

The district court's finding that no independent work is created, *see Galoob*, 780 F.Supp. at 1291, is supported by the record. The Game Genie merely enhances the audiovisual displays (or underlying data bytes) that originate in Nintendo game cartridges. The altered displays do not incorporate a portion of a copyrighted work in some concrete or permanent *form*. Nintendo argues that the Game Genie's displays are as fixed in the hardware and software used to create them as Nintendo's original displays. Nintendo's argument ignores the fact that the Game Genie cannot produce an audiovisual display; the underlying display must be produced by a Nintendo Entertainment System and game cartridge. Even if we were to rely on the Copyright Act's definition of "fixed," we would similarly conclude that the resulting display is not "embodied," see 17 U.S.C. § 101, in the Game Genie. It cannot be a derivative work.

Nintendo asserted at oral argument that the existence of a $150 million market for the Game Genie indicates that its audiovisual display must be fixed. We understand Nintendo's argument; consumers clearly would not purchase the Game Genie if its display was not "sufficiently permanent or stable to permit it to be perceived ... for a period of more than transitory duration." 17 U.S.C. § 101. But, Nintendo's reliance on the Act's definition of "fixed" is misplaced. Nintendo's argument also proves too much; the existence of a market does not, and cannot, determine conclusively whether a work is an infringing derivative work. For example, although there is a market for kaleidoscopes, it does not necessarily follow that kaleidoscopes create unlawful derivative works when pointed at protected artwork. The same can be said of countless other products that enhance, but do not replace, copyrighted works.

Nintendo also argues that our analysis should focus exclusively on the audiovisual displays created by the Game Genie, i.e., that we should compare the altered displays to Nintendo's original displays. Nintendo emphasizes that "'[a]udiovisual works' are works that consist of a series of related images ... *regardless of the nature of the material objects ... in which the works are embodied.*" 17 U.S.C. § 101 (emphasis added). The Copyright Act's definition of "audiovisual works" is inapposite; the *only* question before us is whether the audiovisual displays created by the Game Genie are "derivative works." The Act does not similarly provide that a work can be a derivative work regardless of the nature of the material objects in which the work is embodied. A derivative work must incorporate a protected work in some concrete or permanent form. We cannot ignore the actual source of the Game Genie's display.

Nintendo relies heavily on *Midway Mfg. Co. v. Artic Int'l, Inc.*, 704 F.2d 1009 (7th Cir. 1983). *Midway* can be distinguished. The defendant in *Midway,* Artic International, marketed a computer chip that could be inserted in Galaxian video games to speed up the rate of play. The Seventh Circuit held that the speeded-up version of Galaxian was a derivative work. *Id.* at 1013–14. Artic's chip substantially copied and *replaced* the chip that was originally distributed by Midway. Purchasers of Artic's chip also benefited economically by offering the altered game for use by the general public. The Game Genie does not physically incorporate a portion of a copyrighted work, nor does it supplant demand for a component of that work. The court in *Midway* acknowledged that the Copyright Act's definition of "derivative work" "must be stretched to accommodate speeded-up video games." *Id.* at 1014. Stretching that definition further would chill innovation and fail to protect "society's competing interest in the free flow of ideas, information, and commerce." *Sony Corp. of America v. Universal Studios, Inc.*, 464 U.S. 417, 429 (1984).

In holding that the audiovisual displays created by the Game Genie are not derivative works, we recognize that technology often advances by improvement rather than replacement. Some time ago, for example, computer companies began marketing spell-checkers that operate within existing word processors by signaling the writer when a word is misspelled. These applications, as well as countless others, could not be produced and marketed if courts were to conclude that the word processor and spell-checker combination is a derivative work based on the word processor alone. The Game Genie is useless by itself, it can only enhance, and cannot duplicate or recast, a Nintendo game's output. It does not contain or produce a Nintendo game's output in some concrete or permanent form, nor does it supplant demand for Nintendo game cartridges. Such innovations rarely will constitute infringing derivative works under the Copyright Act.

2. Fair Use

The doctrine of fair use allows a holder of the privilege to use copyrighted material in a reasonable manner without the consent of the copyright owner. The district court concluded that, even if the audiovisual displays created by the Game Genie are derivative works, Galoob is not liable under 17 U.S.C. § 107 because the displays are a fair use of Nintendo's copyrighted displays.

Section 107 codifies the fair use defense:

In determining whether the use made of a work in any particular case is a fair use the factors to be considered shall include—

(1) the purpose and character of the use, including whether such use is of a commercial nature or is for nonprofit educational purposes;

(2) the nature of the copyrighted work;

(3) the amount and substantiality of the portion used in relation to the copyrighted work as a whole;

(4) the effect of the use upon the potential market for or value of the copyrighted work.

The factors are nonexclusive and section 107 does not indicate how much weight should be ascribed to each.

Much of the parties' dispute regarding the fair use defense concerns the proper focus of the court's inquiry: (1) Galoob or (2) consumers who purchase and use the Game

Genie. Nintendo's complaint does not allege direct infringement, nor did it try the case on that theory. The complaint, for example, alleges only that "Galoob's marketing advertising [sic], promoting and selling of Game Genie has and will *contribute* to the creation of infringing derivatives of Nintendo's copyrighted ... games." (emphasis added). Contributory infringement is a form of third party liability. The district court properly focused on whether consumers who purchase and use the Game Genie would be infringing Nintendo's copyrights by creating (what are now assumed to be) derivative works.

Nintendo emphasizes that the district court ultimately addressed its direct infringement by authorization argument. The court concluded that, "[b]ecause the Game Genie does not create a derivative work when used in conjunction with a copyrighted video game, Galoob does not 'authorize the use of a copyrighted work without the actual authority from the copyright owner.'" *Galoob*, 780 F.Supp. at 1298 (quoting *Sony*, 464 U.S. at 435 n. 17). Although infringement by authorization is a form of direct infringement, this does not change the proper focus of our inquiry; a party cannot authorize another party to infringe a copyright unless the authorized conduct would itself be unlawful.

Nintendo disputes this conclusion. According to Nintendo, a party can unlawfully authorize another party to use a copyrighted work even if that party's use of the work would not violate the Copyright Act. Nintendo's argument is unpersuasive. In *Sony*, 464 U.S. at 449, for example, the Court considered whether *consumers* were using the Betamax for a commercial or noncommercial purpose even though Sony itself obviously was acting in its own commercial self-interest. Professor Nimmer similarly concludes that, "to the extent that an activity does not violate one of those five enumerated rights [*see* 17 U.S.C. § 106], authorizing such activity does not constitute copyright infringement." 3 *Nimmer on Copyright* § 12.04[A][3] [a], at 12–80 n.82.

The district court concluded that "a family's use of a Game Genie for private home enjoyment must be characterized as a non-commercial, nonprofit activity." *Galoob*, 780 F.Supp. at 1293. Nintendo argues that Game Genie users are supplanting its commercially valuable right to make and sell derivative works. Nintendo's reliance on *Harper & Row Publishers, Inc. v. Nation Enters.*, 471 U.S. 539, 562 (1985), is misplaced. The commercially valuable right at issue in *Harper & Row* was the right of first publication; Nation Enterprises intended to publish the copyrighted materials *for profit*. *See id.* at 562–63. *See also Sony*, 464 U.S. at 449 ("If the Betamax were used to make copies for a commercial or profit-making purpose, such use would presumptively be unfair."). Game Genie users are engaged in a non-profit activity. Their use of the Game Genie to create derivative works therefore is presumptively fair.

The district court also concluded that "[t]he [Nintendo] works' published nature supports the fairness of the use." *Galoob*, 780 F. Supp. at 1293. Nintendo argues that it has not published the derivative works created by the Game Genie. This argument ignores the plain language of section 107: "the factors to be considered shall include ... the nature of the copyrighted work." The argument also would make the fair use defense unavailable in all cases of derivative works, including "criticism, comment, news reporting, teaching..., scholarship, or research." 17 U.S.C. § 107. A commentary that incorporated large portions of *For Whom the Bell Tolls*, for example, would be undeserving of fair use protection because the incorporated portions would constitute an unpublished derivative work. This cannot be the law.

The district court further concluded that the amount of the portion used in relation to the copyrighted work as a whole "cannot assist Nintendo in overcoming the presumption of fair use." *Galoob*, 780 F. Supp. at 1293. The video tape recorders at issue in *Sony* allowed consumers to tape copyrighted works in their entirety. The Supreme Court nevertheless held that, "when one considers ... that [video tape recording] merely enables a viewer to see such a work which he had been invited to witness in its entirety free of charge, the fact that the entire work is reproduced does not have its ordinary effect of militating against a finding of fair use." 464 U.S. at 449–50. Consumers are not invited to witness Nintendo's audiovisual displays free of charge, but, once they have paid to do so, the fact that the derivative works created by the Game Genie are comprised almost entirely of Nintendo's copyrighted displays does not militate against a finding of fair use.

Nintendo would distinguish *Sony* because it involved copying copyrighted works rather than creating derivative works based on those works. In other words, the consumers in *Sony* could lawfully copy the copyrighted works because they were invited to view those works free of charge. Game Genie users, in contrast, are not invited to view derivative works based on Nintendo's copyrighted works without first paying for that privilege. *Sony* cannot be read so narrowly. It is difficult to imagine that the Court would have reached a different conclusion if Betamax purchasers were skipping portions of copyrighted works or viewing denouements before climaxes. *Sony* recognizes that a party who distributes a copyrighted work cannot dictate how that work is to be enjoyed. Consumers may use a Betamax to view copyrighted works at a more convenient time. They similarly may use a Game Genie to enhance a Nintendo Game cartridge's audiovisual display in such a way as to make the experience more enjoyable.

The fourth factor is the most important, and indeed, central fair use factor. The district court concluded that "Nintendo has failed to show any harm to the present market for its copyrighted games and has failed to establish the reasonable likelihood of a potential market for slightly altered versions of the games at suit." *Galoob*, 780 F.Supp. at 1295. Nintendo's main argument on appeal is that the test for market harm encompasses the potential market for derivative works. Because the Game Genie is used for a non-commercial purpose, the likelihood of future harm may not be presumed. Nintendo must show by a preponderance of the evidence that *some* meaningful likelihood of future harm exists.

Nintendo's argument is supported by case law. Although the Copyright Act requires a court to consider "the effect of the use upon the potential market for or value of the *copyrighted work*" 17 U.S.C. § 107(4) (emphasis added), we held in *Abend* that "[a]lthough the motion picture will have no adverse effect on bookstore sales of the [underlying] novel—and may in fact have a beneficial effect—it is 'clear that [the film's producer] may not invoke the defense of fair use.'" 863 F.2d at 1482. We explained: "'If the defendant's work adversely affects the value of any of the rights in the copyrighted work ... the use is not fair even if the rights thus affected have not as yet been exercised by the plaintiff.'" *Id*. The Supreme Court specifically affirmed our finding that the motion picture adaptation "impinged on the ability to market new versions of the story." *Stewart* [*v. Abend*], 495 U.S. [207] at 238 [(1990)].

Still, Nintendo's argument is undermined by the facts. The district court considered the potential market for derivative works based on Nintendo game cartridges and found that: (1) "Nintendo has not, to date, issued or considered issuing altered versions of existing games," *Galoob*, 780 F.Supp. at 1295, and (2) Nintendo "has failed to show the reasonable likelihood of such a market." *Id*. The record supports the court's findings. According to Stephen Beck, Galoob's expert witness, junior or expert versions of existing Nintendo games would enjoy very little market interest because the original version of each game already has been designed to appeal to the largest number of consumers. Howard Lincoln, Senior Vice President of Nintendo of America, acknowledged that Nintendo has no present plans to market such games.

The district court also noted that Nintendo's assertion that it may wish to re-release altered versions of its game cartridges is contradicted by its position in various other lawsuits:

> In those actions, Nintendo opposes antitrust claims by using the vagaries of the video game industry to rebut the impact and permanence of its market control, if any. Having indoctrinated this Court as to the fast pace and instability of the video game industry, Nintendo may not now, without any data, redefine that market in its request for the extraordinary remedy sought herein.... While board games may never die, good video games are mortal.

Galoob, 780 F.Supp. at 1295. The existence of this potential market cannot be presumed. The fourth and most important fair use factor also favors Galoob.

Nintendo's most persuasive argument is that the creative nature of its audiovisual displays weighs against a finding of fair use. The Supreme Court has acknowledged that "fair use is more likely to be found in factual works than fictional works." *Stewart*, 495 U.S. at 237. This consideration weighs against a finding of fair use, but it is not dispositive. *See Sony*, 464 U.S. at 448 (fair use defense is an "equitable rule of reason"). The district court could properly conclude that Game Genie users are making a fair use of Nintendo's displays.

Notes and Questions

1. How did the *Galoob* court reconcile its holding with *Midway Mfg. Co. v. Artic Int'l, Inc.*? Both cases involved videogame enhancements.

2. There was an interesting follow up action to the *Galoob* case set forth above. In *Nintendo of Am., Inc. v. Lewis Galoob Toys, Inc.*, 16 F.3d 1032 (9th Cir. 1994), the Ninth Circuit determined that: "Galoob was wrongfully enjoined from selling the Game Genie. Consequently, the company sought damages against Nintendo as result of the wrongly issued injunction. Rule 65(c) of the Federal Rules of Civil Procedure provides: 'The court may issue a preliminary injunction or a temporary restraining order only if the movant gives security in an amount that the court considers proper to pay the costs and damages sustained by any party found to have been wrongfully enjoined or restrained.'"

In conjunction with that rule, the District Court required Nintendo to post a $15 million dollar bond in return for the injunction. By prevailing in the action, Galoob was able collect its damages against the bond, rather than have to wait for Nintendo to pay up. Galoob established to the district court's satisfaction that its lost profits damages exceeded $15 million, and so authorized Galoob to recover the entire amount of the bond. Nintendo appealed, claiming that the District Court erred in three ways: first, by not weighing equitable considerations before deciding to execute the bond; second, by improperly finding the injunction harmed Galoob; and third, by improperly calculating the amount of Galoob's damages. The Ninth Circuit rejected all three claims and affirmed, allowing Galoob to collect the $15 million

3. According to Judge Posner, a Rule 65(c) bond "discourages the seeking of preliminary injunctions on flimsy (though not necessarily frivolous) grounds." *Coyne-Delany Co. v. Capital Dev. Bd.*, 717 F.2d 385, 392 (7th Cir. 1983). But might the Rule also discourage legitimately aggrieved smaller companies from seeking just relief in the form of a preliminary injunction?

4. As a defense used by Galoob during its motion for a preliminary injunction and as an issue in *Midway v. Artic,* 17 U.S.C. § 117 was raised. § 117(a) provides as follows:

a) **MAKING OF ADDITIONAL COPY OR ADAPTATION BY OWNER OF COPY.** — Notwithstanding the provisions of Section 106 it is not an infringement for the owner of a copy of a computer program to make or authorize the making of another copy or adaptation of that computer program provided:

(1) that such a new copy or adaptation is created as an essential step in the utilization of the computer program in conjunction with a machine and that it is used in no other manner, or

(2) that such new copy or adaptation is for archival purposes only and that all archival copies are destroyed in the event that continued possession of the computer program should cease to be rightful.

Though ambiguously worded, it would seem that the intention behind § 117(a) is clear. It may be necessary to create a copy of software in order to have it function. Nevertheless, arguments based on that section have been made in attempts to defeat protection against unlawful derivative works. See Edward G. Black & Michael H. Page, *Add-On Infringements: When Computer Add-Ons and Peripherals Should (and Should Not) Be Considered Infringing Derivative Works Under* Lewis Galoob Toys, Inc. v. Nintendo of America, Inc., *and Other Recent Decisions,* 15 HASTINGS COMM. & ENT. L. J. 615, 647 (1993). *See also Krause v. Titleserv, Inc.,* 402 F.3d 119 (2d Cir. 2005), where the Second Circuit considered the scope of § 117(a)(1). In *Krause,* the plaintiff (Krause) wrote several computer programs for Titleserv. Titleserv modified Krause's computer programs by correcting malfunctions (bugs) and adding new capabilities. The court found that fixing bugs was clearly within the scope of § 117(a)(1), since these modifications were "essential" to making the programs function properly. *Id.* at 125. A more difficult problem was posed by the additional capabilities. The Second Circuit looked to the legislative history for guidance. The court focused on one passage in the Final Report of the National Commission on New Technological Uses of Copyrighted Works (1979), referred to as the CONTU Report: "Thus, a right to make those changes necessary to enable the use for which it was both sold and purchased should be provided. The conversion of a program from one higher-level language to another to facilitate use would fall within this right, *as would the right to add features to the program that were not present at the time of rightful acquisition.*" *Id.* at 128 (quoting CONTU Report at 13). The Second Circuit then concluded,

We can see no reason why the modest alterations to Titleserv's copies of the programs should not qualify. We need not address whether other types of improvements might be too radical, or might fail to qualify because they somehow harm the interests of the copyright owner. The sentence of the CONTU Report after the one speaking of the right to add features states that the rights granted by § 117(a) could "only be exercised so long as they did not harm the interests of the copyright proprietor." A different scenario would be presented if Titleserv's alteration somehow interfered with Krause's access to, or ability to exploit, the copyrighted work that he authored, or if the altered copy of Krause's work were to be marketed by the owner of the copy. But on our facts, we see no harm whatsoever to Krause's enjoyment of his copyright. The changes made by Titleserv were made only to its copies of Krause's programs. Krause enjoyed no less opportunity after Titleserv's changes, than before, to use, market, or otherwise reap the fruits of the copyrighted programs he created.

Id. at 128–29.

§ 6.40 Secondary Liability

With the foregoing "direct infringement" cases in mind, we should next be concerned about those persons and companies who, while not directly infringing, nevertheless enable others to do so, and thereby profit from the resulting unlawful copyright infringements.

The concept of "vicarious" liability is a fundamental mainstay in the law of torts and contracts; it is, therefore, no surprise that the concept also applies to the law of copyright infringement. At its most basic level, *respondeat superior* imposes liability and responsibility upon employers and those who "control" the actions of a wrongdoer. As simply stated in *Ellison v. Robertson*, 357 F.3d 1072, 1078 (9th Cir. 2004), and amplified by *A & M Records, Inc. v. Napster, Inc.*, 239 F.3d 1004 (9th Cir. 2001), in order to establish a claim for vicarious copyright infringement, a plaintiff must allege that:

(1) There has been a direct infringement by a primary party,

(2) the defendant has the right and ability to control the infringing activity, and

(3) there is a direct financial benefit from the infringing activity.

In any relationship whereby a controlling entity or person has the right to direct or control an infringer, vicarious liability may be imposed upon the controlling party. An employer — employee relationship is typical but not mandatory. Any person or entity with the power to control a corporate infringer, for example, might be a vicarious infringer. *Fonovisa, Inc. v. Cherry Auction, Inc.*, 76 F.2d 259 (9th Cir. 1996). With respect to the "corporate receipt doctrine," *see JCW Investments, Inc. v. Novelty, Inc.*, 289 F. Supp. 2d 1023 (N.D. Ill. 2003).

In *Marvel Enterprises, Inc. v. NCSoft Corp.*, No. CV04-9253RGKPLAx, 2005 WL 878090 (C.D. Cal. March 9, 2005), the plaintiffs, Marvel Enterprises, Inc. and Marvel Characters, Inc. brought an action against NCSoft Corp. and other named defendants claiming: direct, contributory, and vicarious copyright infringement under 17 U.S.C. §§ 101, et seq., in addition to several trademark related actions, contending that the defendants created, marketed, distributed and hosted a computer game that allowed customers to play online and create characters that were virtually identical in name, appearance, and characteristics to characters owned by Plaintiffs (such as Captain America, Wolverine, and The Incredible Hulk).

With respect to vicarious copyright infringement, the court found that the plaintiffs had clearly pled a direct primary infringement by a third party. The plaintiffs alleged that they held valid copyrights to the characters. The complaint further stated: "It is reasonable to assume there are literally thousands of infringing Heroes roaming the streets of Paragon City at any given moment," and that the defendants' "game induces, causes and materially contributes to" the direct infringement. Plaintiffs were not required to plead details of the infringements with particularity. Therefore, said the court, the plaintiffs have sufficiently alleged primary direct infringement by the game users.

In addition, the defendants financially benefitted from the primary infringement "where the availability of infringing material acts as a *draw* for customers," citing *Ellison v. Robertson*, 357 F.3d 1072, 1078 (9th Cir. 2004). The court further held that "there was no requirement that the draw be substantial." The determining factor was whether "there is a causal relationship between the infringing activity and any financial benefit a defendant reaps, regardless of how substantial the benefit."

The court also noted that the plaintiffs alleged that the defendants "reap a significant financial benefit by virtue of their increased revenues and increased user base, directly as a result of the ongoing infringements, as players and prospective players become aware that they can unlawfully copy Marvel Characters." Plaintiffs had thus clearly pled a causal connection between the alleged infringement by game users, and a financial benefit to the defendants. Therefore, concluded the court, the plaintiffs sufficiently stated a claim for vicarious copyright infringement. *See* § 8.60, *infra* for a further discussion of the *NCSoft* case.

* * *

From the cases that follow it would appear that the concept of *vicarious* infringement is closely aligned with the notion of a *contributory* infringement. But there is a definite distinction. To prevail on a claim for contributory infringement, a plaintiff must show that:

(1) Defendants had knowledge of the infringing activity; and

(2) induced, caused, or materially contributed to that infringing activity.

In addition to the foregoing secondary forms of liability, there is the concept of *induced* infringement which is very similar to contributory infringement. The added concept is perceived to be necessary where the defending party has been guilty of encouraging the infringement and profiting from it, while at the same time has not caused, or materially contributed to it. *MGM Studios v. Grokster, Ltd.*, 545 U.S. 913 (2005).

* * *

Sega Enter. Ltd v. Maphia

United States District Court, Northern District, California, 1996
948 F. Supp. 923

WILKEN, District Judge.

STATEMENT OF FACTS

Sega[11] is a major manufacturer and distributor of computer video game systems and computer video game programs which are sold under the SEGA logo, its registered trademark. (Federal Registration No. 1,566,116, issued November 14, 1989). As part of its development process, Sega takes care to ensure the quality and reliability of the video game programs and products sold under SEGA trademarks.

Sega also owns the copyright for the game programs that Sega develops, and has federal copyright registrations for several video games, including Jurassic Park and Sonic Spinball.

The Sega game system consists of two components, the base unit game console, and software stored on video game cartridges which are inserted into the base unit. The base unit contains a microcomputer which, when connected to a cartridge and a television, permits an individual to play a video game stored on the inserted cartridge. The cartridge format is not susceptible to breakdown or erasure. Defective Sega cartridges are replaced by Sega.

---

11. Sega Enterprises, Ltd. is a corporation organized and existing under the laws of Japan. Sega of America, Inc. is a California corporation.

Sega's game system is designed to permit the user only to play video game programs contained in Sega cartridges. The system does not permit the copying of video game programs. Sega does not authorize the copying or distribution of its video game programs on other storage media such as floppy disks or hard disks.

Sega takes steps to keep its methods of developing video game programs, its works-in-progress, and the codes of its released products confidential, and the employees and contractors who work with Sega sign non-disclosure agreements regarding their work. Video game programs which are in development are referred to as "pre-release" programs. During the development period, pre-release software may be stored on cartridges, floppy disks or hard disks for internal use by Sega. Upon completion of the program, however, the program is distributed only on cartridges.

Sherman is the system operator for MAPHIA, an electronic bulletin board. An electronic bulletin board ("BBS") consists of electronic storage media, such as computer memories or hard disks, which are connected to telephone lines by modem devices, and are controlled by a computer. Users of BBSs can transfer information from their own computers to the storage media on the BBS by a process known as "uploading." Users can also retrieve information from the BBS to their own computer memories by a process known as "downloading." Video game programs, such as Sega's video game programs, are among the kinds of information that can be transferred in these ways.

The software and computer hardware Sherman used to run MAPHIA is owned by him and located at his residence in San Francisco, California. The MAPHIA bulletin board is open to the public and has approximately 400 users who routinely download and upload files from and to the MAPHIA BBS. The users of this BBS are identified by a handle and a password. A handle is a pseudonym by which individuals are known to other users of the system. The password is not displayed to other users and is known only to the system operator and the authorized user.

The evidence shows that "Brujjo Digital" is the alias used by Sherman as the system operator of the MAPHIA BBS, and in communicating with others. For example, Sherman admitted that he was the system operator of the MAPHIA BBS, and the MAPHIA BBS indicates that Brujjo Digital is its operator.

This action was initiated after Sega allegedly received an anonymous tip that Sherman was an operating computer BBS which contained and distributed pirated and unauthorized versions of Sega's video game software. Sega collected evidence of these activities by having a Sega employee gain access to the MAPHIA BBS under a pseudonym, using information supplied by an authorized user who was an informant.

Pursuant to the *ex parte* Temporary Restraining Order and Seizure Order issued by Judge Fern M. Smith of this Court on December 9, 1993, a search of Sherman's premises was conducted. Pursuant to the Order, Sherman's computer and memory devices were seized, the memory was copied, and the computers and other seized hardware were returned to Sherman, with the Sega games deleted.

Data from the MAPHIA BBS indicates that it is linked to another BBS called PSYCHOSIS, whose system operator is called Caffeine. This data also indicates that Sherman and the MAPHIA BBS are part of or linked to a network of BBSs, called PARSAC (also spelled "PARSEC" by Sherman), for business purposes. A newsletter displayed on the MAPHIA BBS refers to MAPHIA as the "WorldHeadquarters" for a group called "PARSEC" of which PSYCHOSIS is the "USHQ." Sherman is the "acting world leader" of PARSAC. A message file located on Sherman's computer, authored by Brujjo Digital, states:

NOTES WORTHY OF MENTION:

... You probably noticed that I am taking over the World Leader Position and that's because I felt like I pulled a lot of this together with A LOT A LOT of help from Caffeine ...

PARSEC VOICE MAIL BOXES:

I'm setting up a VMB system at my house for PARSEC ONLY! ... the kewl thing about it is that the VMB can page myself and Caffeine when an original game is ready for release or anything important comes up.

ADVERTISING CAMPAIGN:

As you know we have PARSEC TRADING CO. as our business that sells everything from Copiers to ... I'll have some Advertisements ready by the time I install Caffeine's REXX DOOR to handle Customer's Orders online at the !MAPHIA! like the system Caffeine runs on Psychosis ...

NEW MEMBERS:

... we are selling ... Super Magic Drives ... but me and Caffeine will handle all the business side of that ...

At the time it was seized, the MAPHIA BBS contained unauthorized copies of 12 Sega games developed by Sega, ten Sega-licensed games, and six Sega pre-release or "beta" version games, developed in-house by Sega. The copies of Sega's programs uploaded to and downloaded from the MAPHIA BBS are substantially similar to Sega's video game programs as stored in the cartridges sold by Sega. Prior to the seizure, each of the Sega-developed and beta version games on the MAPHIA BBS was available for downloading by MAPHIA users who access the board through their own computers by modem telephone connections. Sega had U.S. copyright registration in at least two of the games found on the MAPHIA BBS, namely Jurassic Park and Sonic Spinball.

Sega games are generally listed on the MAPHIA BBS in a file area entitled "<<< !MAPHIA! > SEGA CONSOLES <<<." The games are identified by a "file descriptor" which includes the title of the game, the manufacturer, and either the word "SEGA" or "Sega," the same word that is in the SEGA registered trademark. Additionally, the SEGA trademark appears on the screen whenever a Sega game which has been downloaded from the MAPHIA BBS is subsequently played. Sherman acknowledged that the SEGA trademark is displayed when the downloaded games are played.

The directory of video game programs available on MAPHIA also contains numerous references to video game programs containing "patches" or "fixes." These words refer to user-introduced changes to problems which may have been introduced in the copying process or which existed in beta version games.

Printouts of the data on Sherman's BBS seized pursuant to this Court's Order and on-line data captured from Sherman's BBS show that the uploading and downloading of unauthorized copies of Sega's copyrighted video games was known to Sherman. Sherman acknowledges that users of the MAPHIA bulletin board were allowed to upload and download Sega games with the authorized password. A screen printout of user uploading and downloading statistics from his MAPHIA BBS shows that Sherman tracked, or at least had the ability to track, user uploads and downloads. Additionally, another message authored by Brujjo Digital and located on Sherman's BBS states:

Please UPLOAD *ALL* the missing CONSOLE Files NOT HERE from the time I closed the !MAPHIA! Oct 17th until up to now!! Time to get some free credits for someone if you get them all in here and get me caught up.

Sherman also sold video game copiers, referred to as "Super Magic Drives" ("copiers"), through the MAPHIA BBS in collaboration with the PSYCHOSIS BBS, collectively known as PARSAC. Sherman's business plan as described by his alias "Brujjo Digital," states:

> As you know we have PARSEC TRADING CO. as our business that sells everything from Copiers to Modems to Hard Drives to Calling Cards (off the record, hehe), and even Pentium Chips now. So, the next step is a MEDIA BLITZ! ... I'll have some Advertisements ready ...

> Also, we are selling Super Wild Cards, Pro Fighter Q's and Super Magic Drives for AKIRA and that part of PARSEC will be dedicated for him but me and CAFFEINE will handle all the business side of that and paying him the money and dealing with the customers, etc.

According to a data file found on Howard Silberg's computer, Parsec Trading has the following policy:

> As you know, if you read the policies of PARSEC TRADING, each customer receives free-downloads up to ten (10) megabytes. This is so you can use your back-up unit and enjoy it! After your ten megabytes has been used up, you can donate $35 per month for a month of free-downloads, $200 for a year of free-downloads, or $500 for unlimited free-downloads.

A copier is necessary to play games which have been downloaded from the BBSs. The Super Magic Drive copier consists of a connector which plugs into the video game console, a receptacle which accepts video game cartridges, a main unit which contains a random access memory (RAM) to store games, and a floppy disk drive. A MAPHIA BBS user can download video programs through his or her computer onto a floppy disk and make copies with his or her computer or play those game programs through the adaptor drive. To play a downloaded game, the user places the floppy disk into the video game copier. The user can choose the "run program" option and run the video game program from the floppy disk without a video game cartridge.

The adaptor drive also allows the user to copy the contents of a game cartridge onto a floppy disk. The user plugs the video game copier into the game console and places a video game cartridge into the receptacle of the video game copier. The user then turns on the adaptor drive. Through a menu screen, the user can select the "dump" option which will permit the user to copy the contents of the cartridge to a floppy disk.

Sega has attempted to obtain additional information from Sherman through deposition and discovery. Sherman was deposed on March 1, 1994, at which time he refused to answer substantive questions by invoking his Fifth Amendment privilege.

DISCUSSION

I. Copyright Infringement

Sega contends that Sherman is liable for copyright infringement under direct, contributory, and vicarious liability theories. Sherman admits that users of the MAPHIA BBS were allowed to upload and download Sega games with the authorized password, but maintains that this copying fits under the fair use defense because it was nothing more that the use of the games at people's homes, and that any copyright violation was *de minimis*.

A. Direct Infringement

To establish a prima facie case of direct copyright infringement, Sega must prove (1) ownership of a valid copyright in the infringed work, and (2) "copying" by the defendant.

See Religious Technology Center v. Netcom On-Line Communication Services, Inc., 907 F.Supp. 1361, 1366–67 (N.D.Cal.1995).

A certificate of copyright registration establishes a presumption that the copyright is valid. 17 U.S.C. §410(c). Sega has submitted several certificates of copyright registration for its video games, including certificates for Jurassic Park and Sonic Spinball. These certificates establish a presumption that Sega owns a valid copyright in those video game programs.

"[C]opying," for the purposes of copyright law, occurs when a computer program is transferred from a permanent storage device to a computer's random access memory. In this case, copies were made when the Sega game files were uploaded to or downloaded from Sherman's BBS. Thus, copying by someone is established.

This does not end the inquiry, however, because it does not establish whether Sherman, as the BBS operator, is directly liable for the copying. In *Netcom*, the court found that the Internet provider was not directly liable for copyright infringement of a copyrighted work posted and distributed through its system. *Netcom*, 907 F.Supp. at 1368–70. The *Netcom* court held that "[a]lthough copyright is a strict liability statute, there should be some element of volition or causation which is lacking where a defendant's system is merely used to create a copy by a third party." *Id.* at 1370. "Where the infringing subscriber is clearly directly liable for the same act, it does not make sense to adopt a rule that could lead to the liability of countless parties whose role in the infringement is nothing more that setting up and operating a system that is necessary for functioning of the Internet," even where the Internet provider has knowledge of potential copyright infringement by its subscribers. *Id.* at 1372–73.

While Sherman's actions in this case are more participatory than those of the defendants in *Netcom*, the Court finds Netcom persuasive. Sega has not shown that Sherman himself uploaded or downloaded the files, or directly caused such uploading or downloading to occur. The most Sega has shown is that Sherman operated his BBS, that he knew infringing activity was occurring, and that he solicited others to upload games. However, whether Sherman knew his BBS users were infringing on Sega's copyright, or encouraged them to do so, has no bearing on whether Sherman directly caused the copying to occur. *Id.* at 1372. Furthermore, Sherman's actions as a BBS operator and copier seller are more appropriately analyzed under contributory or vicarious liability theories. Therefore, because Sega has not shown that Sherman directly caused the copying, Sherman cannot be liable for direct infringement.

B. Contributory Infringement

Just because Sherman is not liable for direct infringement, however, does not mean that he is free from liability. Although the Copyright Act does not expressly impose liability on anyone other than direct infringers, courts have long recognized that in certain circumstances, liability for contributory infringement will be imposed. Contributory copyright infringement stems from the notion that one who directly contributes to another's infringement should be held liable. Such liability is established where the defendant with knowledge of the infringing activity, induces, causes or materially contributes to the infringing conduct of another.

To impose liability on Sherman for contributory infringement, Sega must first establish that the users of Sherman's MAPHIA BBS directly infringed Sega's copyright. Second, Sega must establish that (i) with knowledge of the users' infringing activity, (ii) Sherman induced, caused, or materially contributed to their infringing activity.

1. Direct infringement by MAPHIA BBS users:

As discussed above, Sega has established that copies were made when unauthorized copies of Sega game files were downloaded from, or uploaded to, Sherman's BBS by Sherman's BBS users. Therefore, Sega has established direct copyright infringement by Sherman's BBS users.

2. Sherman's knowledge of his users' activities:

The standard for the knowledge requirement is objective, and is satisfied where the defendant knows or has reason to know of the infringing activity. Here, it is undisputed that Sherman had knowledge that his users were copying the games. Sherman admits that users were allowed to upload and download Sega games from his MAPHIA BBS. Moreover, evidence of a screen printout of user uploading and downloading statistics from the MAPHIA BBS shows that Sherman tracked, or at least had the ability to track, user uploads and downloads. Thus, Sega has established that Sherman knew of the infringing conduct by MAPHIA BBS users.

3. Sherman's participation in his users' activities:

[P]roviding the site and facilities for known infringing activity is sufficient to establish contributory liability. In this case, Sherman provided the BBS as a central depository site for the unauthorized copies of games, and allowed subsequent distribution of the games by user downloads. He provided the facilities for copying the games by providing, monitoring, and operating the BBS software, hardware, and phone lines necessary for the users to upload and download games.

However, even under an alternative and higher standard of "substantial participation," Sherman is liable. Under this standard, Sherman is only liable if he knew of the users' infringing actions, and yet substantially participated by inducing, causing or materially contributing to the users' infringing conduct. *Netcom*, 907 F.Supp. at 1382. In this case, Sherman did more than provide the site and facilities for the known infringing conduct. He actively solicited users to upload unauthorized games, and provided a road map on his BBS for easy identification of Sega games available for downloading. Additionally, through the same MAPHIA BBS medium, he offered copiers for sale to facilitate playing the downloaded games. Moreover, Sherman's business, Parsec Trading, had a policy of providing limited free downloading of games and thereafter selling downloading privileges to customers who had purchased copiers. Thus, Sherman's role in the copying, including providing facilities, direction, knowledge, encouragement, and seeking profit, amounts to a prima facie case of contributory copyright infringement.

Because the Court finds that Sega has established a *prima facie* case of contributory copyright infringement liability, it need not address whether Sherman is also liable under the theory of vicarious liability.

C. Fair Use Defense

Sherman argues that the copying done by the MAPHIA BBS users was fair because there is no evidence that the users went beyond simply playing the games in their own homes, nor any evidence that the users further distributed the games.

Under the fair use defense, there is no infringement, even where a person violates one of the copyright holder's exclusive rights, if that person's use is a fair one. 17 U.S.C. § 107. In determining whether a use is fair, the following four, non-exclusive factors are considered: the purpose and character of the use; the nature of the copy-righted work; the amount and substantiality of the copy-righted work used; and the effect of the use upon the potential market for the copyrighted work. Title 17 U.S.C. § 107; *Campbell v. Acuff-Rose Music, Inc.*, 510 U.S. 569 (1994). Because fair use is an affirmative defense, Sherman carries the burden of demonstrating it.

In considering this defense, the Court will consider whether Sherman has shown that either his actions or the users' actions constitute fair use. If the users' actions constitute fair use, they will not be considered direct infringers. Then, Sherman cannot be contributorily liable because contributory infringement requires direct infringement by someone. If the users' actions do not constitute fair use, Sherman may still avoid liability if his contributing actions qualify as fair use.

1. Purpose and character of use

With respect to Sherman's activities, the evidence shows that Sherman encouraged up-loading and downloading of Sega's games in order to induce sales of copiers. Such a use is clearly commercial. Sherman intended to profit directly from the content of the information made available on his BBS because his copier customers could use the game files to play the games rather than purchase Sega game cartridges. This distinguishes Sherman from the Internet provider in [*Religious Technology Center v*]. *Netcom* [*On-Line Comm. Serv.*, 907 F. Supp. 1361 (N.D. Cal. 1995)] who did not gain anything from the content of the information available to subscribers. *Id.* at 1379 (fact that the Internet provider did not directly gain anything from the content of the information available to its subscribers on the Internet helps weigh this factor in its favor despite commercial character of Internet provider's use). This factor weighs against a finding of fair use with respect to Sherman's activities.

The BBS users were encouraged to download games from the BBS in order to avoid having to buy video game cartridges from Sega. Such a purpose weighs against the fair use defense. *See American Geophysical Union v. Texaco, Inc.*, 802 F. Supp. 1, 14–16 (S.D.N.Y. 1992), aff'd 60 F.3d 913 (2nd Cir. 1994), *cert. dismissed* 116 S. Ct. 592 (1995) (no fair use where scientists photo-copied publication to avoid cost of purchasing additional copies from publisher).

Furthermore, this case is distinguishable from *Sega Enter., Ltd. v. Accolade, Inc.*, 977 F.2d 1510 (9th Cir. 1992), where the court found reverse engineering to be a fair use, in part because the reverse engineering promoted a growth in creative expression. *Id.* at 1523. In contrast, in this case, there is no evidence of any actual reverse engineering or any intent on the part of the users to do so. Thus, the absence of evidence that the copying was creative weighs against a finding of fair use.

2. Nature of the copyrighted work

This factor provides that the closer the copyrighted work is to the core of intended copyright protection, the more difficult it is to establish the fair use defense. In assessing this factor, one consideration is whether the copyrighted work is informational or creative. *Netcom*, 907 F. Supp. at 1379. Because the Sega video games are for entertainment uses and involve fiction and fantasy, which are more creative than informational, consideration of the nature of the copyrighted work weighs against a finding of fair use.

3. Extent of the work copied

The third factor concerns both the percentage of the original work that was copied, and whether what was copied constitutes the "heart" of the copyrighted work. Although not a per se rule, the copying of an entire work will ordinarily militate against a finding of fair use.

Here, Sega has shown that the BBS users copied virtually entire copyrighted works by way of their uploads and downloads of Sega games, and that Sherman made these games available through his BBS. While this does not per se preclude a finding of fair use, Sherman has not shown any public benefit nor explanation for the complete copying. Therefore, this factor weighs against a finding of fair use.

4. Effect of the use upon the market

The fourth and final statutory factor concerns whether unrestricted and widespread conduct of the sort engaged in by the defendant would result in a substantially adverse impact on the potential market for the copyrighted work. While all factors must be weighed together, the fourth factor is the most important consideration.

By utilizing the MAPHIA BBS, users are able to download and distribute one or more copies of Sega video game programs from a single copy of a Sega video game program on the MAPHIA BBS, and thereby obtain unauthorized copies of Sega's copyrighted video game programs.

This unauthorized copying of Sega video game programs works to decrease Sega's sales of video game cartridges. The Super Magic Drives could be used for copying Sega's video game programs onto disks. Sherman admits users were allowed to upload and download Sega games through the MAPHIA BBS onto magnetic media like floppy disks, and that users who had Sega games on disks could play them directly using the copiers. The copiers sold and advertised by Sherman through his business Parsec Trading came with downloading privileges to the purchaser, giving the purchaser the ability to copy Sega copyrighted video game programs from the MAPHIA BBS. The copiers in conjunction with the MAPHIA BBS supplanted the need to purchase the genuine Sega video games.

While Sherman contends that the copiers have other non-infringing uses, the Court is unpersuaded by this argument. It is unlikely that customers would pay $350 to back up the Sega game cartridges, which are not susceptible to breakdown and which sell for between $ 30 and $ 70. The Court finds that the only substantial use of the copiers is to avoid having to buy video game cartridges from Sega by copying the video game program and playing such unauthorized, copied games.

Sherman also argues that, because there are only a limited number of BBS users that have copiers, and these users would likely play the games only in their own homes, their use should be considered *de minimis*. He contends that because there is no evidence that these users are further distributing the games, these users' actions cannot be considered to have a tendency to dilute Sega's sales.

The Court finds this argument unpersuasive. Even if the users are only playing the games in their own homes and even if there are currently only a limited number of users that have copiers, unrestricted and widespread conduct of this sort would result in a substantial adverse impact on the market for the Sega games. By downloading the games from the BBS, users avoid paying for the games. Sherman's conduct in providing the BBS for up-loading and downloading games, and offering for sale the copiers on which to play these unauthorized games, facilitated the users' conduct. This conduct, if widespread, would adversely impact the market for Sega games.

5. Analysis

All of the factors discussed above weigh against the application of the fair use defense. Because the fair use defense does not apply, and Sega has met its burden to show contributory copyright infringement by Sherman, the Court GRANTS Sega's motion with respect to its copyright claim.

D. Willfulness

Sega contends that Sherman's actions show that he willfully infringed upon their copyrights, which would entitle it to greater damages under 17 U.S.C. § 504(c)(2). Infringement is willful if the responsible party acts with knowledge that he or she is infringing a copyright. Willfulness may also be found where the defendant's infringing actions are undertaken with reckless disregard for the copyright holder's rights. Such knowledge may be inferred from the defendant's conduct. Generally, a determination as to willfulness requires an assessment of a party's state of mind, a factual issue that is not usually susceptible to summary judgment.

Here, however, the evidence shows that Sherman willfully infringed upon Sega's copyright. He used, or knowingly allowed others to use, the Sega mark to identify Sega games on the Maphia BBS. He knowingly allowed others to upload and download the Sega games, and expressly solicited others to upload games to his BBS. He offered for sale copiers that play and copy Sega downloaded games from disks. His business, Parsec Trading, sold or planned to sell copiers. Parsec Trading had a policy of giving customers limited free downloads after they had purchased a copier. This evidence shows that Sherman intentionally contributed to the users' infringement of Sega's copyright, and that he intended to profit in sales of copiers. Sherman has offered nothing to rebut this evidence. Therefore, the Court finds that Sherman's contributory copyright infringement was willful.

Notes and Questions

1. In *Sega Enters. Ltd. v. Sabella*, No. C 93-04260 CW, 1996 WL 780560 (N.D. Cal., Dec. 18, 1996), the court found that the system operator of an electronic bulletin board system ("BBS") for videogames called The Sewer Line was liable for contributory infringement. A BBS, such as The Sewer Line, consists of information stored on electronic storage media, such as hard disks, which were connected to third party "users" over telephone lines by modems, and controlled by a computer. Users could transfer information over the telephone lines from their own computers to the storage media on the BBS by uploading. Uploaded information was thereby recorded or copied onto the storage media of the host bulletin board, in this case on The Sewer Line BBS owned by Sabella. Third party users could also download information from the BBS to their own computer memories. Programs, such as Sega's videogame programs, were one type of information which could be transferred by means of a BBS. In this way, video games could be distributed by a BBS.

Sabella only provided the facilities for copying the games by providing, monitoring, and operating the BBS software, hardware, and phone lines necessary for the users to upload and download games. "However," found the court, "even under an alternative and higher standard of "substantial participation," Sabella is liable. Under this standard, a defendant is only liable if he or she knew of the users' infringing actions, and substantially participated by inducing, causing or materially contributing to the users' infringing conduct. In this case, Sabella did more than provide the site and facilities for the known infringing conduct. She provided a road map on the BBS for easy identification of Sega games available for downloading. Through the same The Sewer Line BBS medium, she offered copiers for sale to facilitate playing the downloaded games. The court thus concluded that, "Sabella engaged in contributory copyright infringement by providing facilities, direction, and encouragement for the unauthorized copying of Sega games." [Sabella was also known by the pseudonym or handle: "Dirty Scum." — ED.]

2. *Ellison v. Robertson*, 357 F.3d 1072, 1076 (9th Cir. 2004), mentioned at the beginning of this section, suggests that to engage in contributory copyright infringement, it is not sufficient for the defendants to merely contribute to the general business of the infringer. Rather, they must materially contribute to copyright infringement, and "the ... assistance must bear some direct relationship to the infringing acts." *See also* MELVILLE NIMMER & DAVID NIMMER, NIMMER ON COPYRIGHT § 12.04[A][2][a] (2004); *Fonovisa, Inc. v. Cherry Auction, Inc.*, 76 F.3d 259, 264 (9th Cir. 1996). The contributing conduct must also be substantial. *Religious Tech. Ctr. v. Netcom On-line Comm. Servs.*, 907 F. Supp. 1361, 1375 (N.D. Cal. 1995).

3. The courts do not go to any great lengths to distinguish *contributory infringement* and *induced infringement*. In fact, it would appear that the concept of "inducement" is an element of contributory infringement and should not be viewed as a separate basis for infringement. On the other hand, where it is not clear that the alleged infringer has actually caused, or materially contributed to that infringing activity, the "inducement" element becomes significant. Consider the following dicta from *MGM Studios v. Grokster, Ltd.*, 545 U.S. 913, 915–16 (2005), reversing the Ninth Circuit's exoneration of Grokster's free music downloading service:

> The rule on inducement of infringement as developed in the early cases is no different today. Evidence of active steps ... taken to encourage direct infringement, such as advertising an infringing use or instructing how to engage in an infringing use, show an affirmative intent that the product be used to infringe, and a showing that infringement was encouraged overcomes the law's reluctance to find liability when a defendant merely sells a commercial product suitable for some lawful use, *see, e.g., Water Technologies Corp. v. Calco, Ltd.*, 850 F.2d 660, 668 (C.A.Fed.1988) (liability for inducement where one "actively and knowingly aids and abet[s] another's direct infringement" (emphasis omitted)); *Fromberg, Inc. v. Thornhill*, 315 F.2d 407, 412–413 (C.A.5 1963) (demonstrations by sales staff of infringing uses supported liability for inducement); *Cf.* W. Keeton, D. Dobbs, R. Keeton, & D. Owen, *Prosser and Keeton on Law of Torts* 37 (5th ed. 1984) ("There is a definite tendency to impose greater responsibility upon a defendant whose conduct was intended to do harm, or was morally wrong:)....

> We adopt it [the inducement rule] here, holding that one who distributes a device with the object of promoting its use to infringe copyright, as shown by clear expression or other affirmative steps taken to foster infringement, is liable for the resulting acts of infringement by third parties. We are, of course, mindful of the need to keep from trenching on regular commerce or discouraging the development of technologies with lawful and unlawful potential. Accordingly, just as Sony did not find intentional inducement despite the knowledge of the VCR manufacturer that its device could be used to infringe, 464 U.S., at 439, n. 19, mere knowledge of infringing potential or of actual infringing uses would not be enough here to subject a distributor to liability. Nor would ordinary acts incident to product distribution, such as offering customers technical support or product updates, support liability in themselves. The inducement rule, instead ... does nothing to compromise legitimate commerce or discourage innovation having a lawful promise.

4. It has been often stated and repeated that most of the great inventions of the past few decades have been devices that promoted or assisted infringement. How many examples

of this can you recall? The home videotape recorder was once considered a major threat to the revenues of the film industry; the opposite turned out to be the case. Nevertheless, there were moments when our ability to purchase these now-common household products were in doubt. *See Sony Corp. of Am. v. Universal City Studios, Inc.*, 464 U.S. 417 (1984), where the Supreme Court found that copyright holders who licensed their works for broadcast over "free" television would not object to having their broadcasts time-shifted by private viewers; therefore, the home videotape recorder was capable of substantial noninfringing uses. Therefore, the manufacturers' sale of the recorders to the general public did not constitute contributory infringement of respondents' copyrights.

5. Is there a way to strike a balance between the interests of copyright holders and the innovators of new technologies designed to make information more portable and easy to transmit and use?

6. For additional related discussions, *see* Mark Bartholomew & John Tehranian, *The Secret Life of Legal Doctrine: The Divergent Evolution of Secondary Liability in Trademark and Copyright Law*, 21 Berkeley Tech. L.J. 1363 (2006); *See also* Alfred C. Yen, *Third-Party Liability After* Grokster, 91 Minn. L. Rev. 184, 225–226 (2006).

---

§ 6.50 The Digital Millennium Copyright Act

The Digital Millennium Copyright Act of 1998 ("DMCA") represents an attempt by law to keep pace with technology. Whereas the 1976 Act protects copyrighted material, the DMCA, among other functions, takes aim at those who would hack or circumvent devices that copyright owners use to control and protect their materials from unauthorized copying. For videogame developers, owners, and users, the DMCA can be looked at as a multi-edged sword, but one that is primarily designed to benefit industry as opposed to consumers. The scattering of the Act's multi-faceted subject matter tends to cause confusion with regard to what the Act does and does not cover; therefore, it might help to single out and list those provisions that directly impact the videogame industry:

1. Anti-circumvention penalties designed to control access to games or consoles.

2. Permitted circumvention of copy protection for interoperability.

3. Safe harbor (Take-Down) provisions for Internet Service Providers.

The DMCA added its substantial anti-circumvention provisions to the 1976 Act in the form of a new Chapter 12.[12] On the one hand, the DMCA declared as contraband devices

---

12. The Digital Millennium Copyright Act of 1998, Pub. L. No. 105-304, 112 Stat. 2860 was signed into law on October 28, 1998. The Act is divided into five Titles: (I) The "WIPO Copyright and Performances and Phonograms Treaties Implementation Act of 1998" implements the treaties of the World Intellectual Property Organization (WIPO); (II) the "Online Copyright Infringement Liability Limitation Act," places limitations on the liability of online service providers with respect to potential claims of copyright infringement; (III) the "Computer Maintenance Competition Assurance Act," creates an exemption for making back-up copies of computer software with respect to the maintenance or repair of computer hardware; (IV) contains some miscellaneous provisions relating to the Copyright Office, distance education, the exceptions in the Copyright Act for libraries and for ephemeral recordings, "webcasting" of sound recordings on the Internet, and the applicability of collective bargaining agreement obligations with respect to transfers of rights in motion pictures; and (V) the "Vessel Hull Design Protection Act," relates to watercraft and is of no concern to our subject matter.

designed to circumvent copy protection devices, while at the same time providing a safe haven for those who would circumvent copy protection if the purpose was to create interoperability for a new product.

Anti-Circumvention:

Directing attention to the heart of the DMCA's anti-circumvention provisions, 17 U.S. Code § 1201(a) titled "Violations Regarding Circumvention of Technological Measures," provides in part:

(1) (A) No person shall circumvent a technological measure that effectively controls access to a work protected under this title.

(2) No person shall manufacture, import, offer to the public, provide, or otherwise traffic in any technology, product, service, device, component, or part thereof, that—

(A) is primarily designed or produced for the purpose of circumventing a technological measure that effectively controls access to a work protected under this title;

(B) has only limited commercially significant purpose or use other than to circumvent a technological measure that effectively controls access to a work protected under this title; or

(C) is marketed by that person or another acting in concert with that person with that person's knowledge for use in circumventing a technological measure that effectively controls access to a work protected under this title.

§ 1201(a)(2) addresses trafficking: "No person shall manufacture, import, offer to the public, provide, or otherwise traffic in any technology, product, service, device, component, or part thereof, that ... [The subparts mirror (A), (B) and (C) above]."

§ 1201(b)(1) adds: No person shall manufacture, import, offer to the public, provide, or otherwise traffic in any technology, product, service, device, component, or part thereof, that—

(A) is primarily designed or produced for the purpose of circumventing protection afforded by a technological measure that effectively protects a right of a copyright owner under this title in a work or a portion thereof;

(B) has only limited commercially significant purpose or use other than to circumvent protection afforded by a technological measure that effectively protects a right of a copyright owner under this title in a work or a portion thereof; or

(C) is marketed by that person or another acting in concert with that person with that person's knowledge for use in circumventing protection afforded by a technological measure that effectively protects a right of a copyright owner under this title in a work or a portion thereof.

For purposes of the DMCA, copy protection devices can take many shapes and forms. In *Realnetworks, Inc. v. Streambox, Inc*, No. 2:99CV02070 2000 WL 127311 (W.D. Wash. Jan. 18, 2000), a "secret handshake" in the form of the Plaintiff's *RealPlayer* (which supplies required information to the Plaintiff's *RealServer* in a proprietary authentication sequence) permits paying users to gain access to otherwise protected audio visual works of the Plaintiff. Copyright owners also use Real Networks' technology so that end-users can listen to, but not record, music that is on sale, either at a Web site or in retail stores. Still other copyright owners can enable users to listen to content on a "pay-per-play: basis that requires a payment for each time the end-user wants to hear the content. The Defendant sold and distributed products designed to bypass the *secret handshake* to gain access to the file. The products circumvented the "Copy Switch," enabling users to make copies of a file that the copyright owner had sought to protect. In its decision granting the Plaintiff an injunction, the court cited the three alternative conditions set forth above as §§ 1201(a)(2)(A), (B), and (C).

Permitted Circumvention:

The DMCA's blessings for compatibility are embodied in 17 U.S. Code § 1201(f) titled "Reverse Engineering," which provides an important interoperability permission for video game developers in particular. § 1201(f) provides this exemption: "Notwithstanding the provisions of subsection (a)(1)(A), a person who has lawfully obtained the right to use a copy of a computer program may circumvent a technological measure that effectively controls access to a particular portion of that program for the sole purpose of identifying and analyzing those elements of the program that are necessary to achieve interoperability of an independently created computer program with other programs, and that have not previously been readily available to the person engaging in the circumvention, to the extent any such acts of identification and analysis do not constitute infringement under this title." See *supra*, § 3.30.

Safe Harbor:

Where copyrighted material is improperly posted on the Internet, a rather elaborate procedure is spelled out in § 512 whereby an Internet Service Provider can be immunized from secondary copyright infringement liability. See *infra*, § 6.78.

* * *

One might rationally, though incorrectly, assume that in order to violate the Digital Millennium Copyright Act, a person or entity would have to engage in some form of copyright infringement. At least up until the ruling in the following case, this assumption was true. After all, experience has taught that the only way to infringe upon a copyright is to copy something or encourage, facilitate, or assist such copying. For the next case, therefore, a distinction must be drawn between a violation of the DMCA and a copyright infringement. The two actions are not synonymous.

MDY Indus., LLC v. Blizzard Entm't, Inc.

United States Court of Appeal, Ninth Circuit, 2011
629 F.3d 928

CALLAHAN, Circuit Judge

Blizzard Entertainment, Inc. ("Blizzard") is the creator of World of Warcraft ("WoW"), a popular multiplayer online role-playing game in which players interact in a virtual world while advancing through the game's 70 levels. MDY Industries, LLC and its sole member Michael Donnelly ("Donnelly") (sometimes referred to collectively as "MDY") developed and sold Glider, a software program that automatically plays the early levels of WoW for players.

MDY brought this action for a declaratory judgment to establish that its Glider sales do not infringe Blizzard's copyright or other rights, and Blizzard asserted counterclaims under the Digital Millennium Copyright Act ("DMCA"), 17 U.S.C. § 1201 *et seq.*, and for tortious interference with contract under Arizona law.

The district court found MDY and Donnelly liable for secondary copyright infringement, violations of DMCA § 1201(a)(2) and (b)(1), and tortious interference with contract. We reverse the district court except as to MDY's liability for violation of DMCA § 1201(a)(2) and remand for trial on Blizzard's claim for tortious interference with contract.

I.

A. World of Warcraft

In November 2004, Blizzard created WoW, a "massively multiplayer online role-playing game" in which players interact in a virtual world. WoW has ten million subscribers, of which two and a half million are in North America. The WoW software has two components: (1) the game client software that a player installs on the computer; and (2) the game server software, which the player accesses on a subscription basis by connecting to WoW's online servers. WoW does not have single-player or offline modes.

WoW players roleplay different characters, such as humans, elves, and dwarves. A player's central objective is to advance the character through the game's 70 levels by participating in quests and engaging in battles with monsters. As a player advances, the character collects rewards such as in-game currency, weapons, and armor. WoW's virtual world has its own economy, in which characters use their virtual currency to buy and sell items directly from each other, through vendors, or using auction houses. Some players also utilize WoW's chat capabilities to interact with others.

B. Blizzard's Use Agreements

Each WoW player must read and accept Blizzard's End User License Agreement ("EULA") and Terms of Use ("ToU") on multiple occasions. The EULA pertains to the game client, so a player agrees to it both before installing the game client and upon first running it. The ToU pertains to the online service, so a player agrees to it both when creating an account and upon first connecting to the online service. Players who do not accept both the EULA and the ToU may return the game client for a refund.

C. Development of Glider and Warden

Donnelly is a WoW player and software programmer. In March 2005, he developed Glider, a software "bot" (short for robot) that automates play of WoW's early levels, for his personal use. A user need not be at the computer while Glider is running. As explained in the Frequently Asked Questions ("FAQ") on MDY's website for Glider:

> Glider ... moves the mouse around and pushes keys on the keyboard. You tell it about your character, where you want to kill things, and when you want to kill. Then it kills for you, automatically. You can do something else, like eat dinner or go to a movie, and when you return, you'll have a lot more experience and loot.

Glider does not alter or copy WoW's game client software, does not allow a player to avoid paying monthly subscription dues to Blizzard, and has no commercial use independent of WoW. Glider was not initially designed to avoid detection by Blizzard.

The parties dispute Glider's impact on the WoW experience. Blizzard contends that Glider disrupts WoW's environment for non-Glider players by enabling Glider users to advance quickly and unfairly through the game and to amass additional game assets. MDY contends that Glider has a minimal effect on non-Glider players, enhances the WoW experience for Glider users, and facilitates disabled players' access to WoW by auto-playing the game for them.

In summer 2005, Donnelly began selling Glider through MDY's website for fifteen to twenty-five dollars per license. Prior to marketing Glider, Donnelly reviewed Blizzard's

EULA and client-server manipulation policy. He reached the conclusion that Blizzard had not prohibited bots in those documents.

In September 2005, Blizzard launched Warden, a technology that it developed to prevent its players who use unauthorized third-party software, including bots, from connecting to WoW's servers. Warden was able to detect Glider, and Blizzard immediately used Warden to ban most Glider users. MDY responded by modifying Glider to avoid detection and promoting its new anti-detection features on its website's FAQ. It added a subscription service, Glider Elite, which offered "additional protection from game detection software" for five dollars a month. Thus, by late 2005, MDY was aware that Blizzard was prohibiting bots. MDY modified its website to indicate that using Glider violated Blizzard's ToU. In November 2005, Donnelly wrote in an email interview, "Avoiding detection is rather exciting, to be sure. Since Blizzard does not want bots running at all, it's a violation to use them." Following MDY's anti-detection modifications, Warden only occasionally detected Glider. As of September 2008, MDY had gross revenues of $3.5 million based on 120,000 Glider license sales.

D. Financial and Practical Impact of Glider

Blizzard claims that from December 2004 to March 2008, it received 465,000 complaints about WoW bots, several thousand of which named Glider. Blizzard spends $940,000 annually to respond to these complaints, and the parties have stipulated that Glider is the principal bot used by WoW players. Blizzard introduced evidence that it may have lost monthly subscription fees from Glider users, who were able to reach WoW's highest levels in fewer weeks than players playing manually. Donnelly acknowledged in a November 2005 email that MDY's business strategy was to make Blizzard's anti-bot detection attempts financially prohibitive:

> The trick here is that Blizzard has a finite amount of development and test resources, so we want to make it bad business to spend that much time altering their detection code to find Glider, since Glider's negative effect on the game is debatable.... We attack this weakness and try to make it a bad idea or make their changes very risky, since they don't want to risk banning or crashing innocent customers.

E. Pre-Litigation Contact Between MDY and Blizzard

In August 2006, Blizzard sent MDY a cease-and-desist letter alleging that MDY's website hosted WoW screenshots and a Glider install file, all of which infringed Blizzard's copyrights. Donnelly removed the screenshots and requested Blizzard to clarify why the install file was infringing, but Blizzard did not respond. In October 2006, Blizzard's counsel visited Donnelly's home, threatening suit unless MDY immediately ceased selling Glider and remitted all profits to Blizzard. MDY immediately commenced this action.

II.

On December 1, 2006, MDY filed an amended complaint seeking a declaration that Glider does not infringe Blizzard's copyright or other rights. In February 2007, Blizzard filed counterclaims and third-party claims against MDY and Donnelly for, *inter alia*, contributory and vicarious copyright infringement, violation of DMCA § 1201(a)(2) and (b)(1), and tortious interference with contract.

In July 2008, the district court granted Blizzard partial summary judgment, finding that MDY's Glider sales contributorily and vicariously infringed Blizzard's copyrights and tortiously interfered with Blizzard's contracts. The district court also granted MDY partial summary judgment, finding that MDY did not violate DMCA § 1201(a)(2) with respect to accessing the game software's source code.

In September 2008, the parties stipulated to entry of a $6 million judgment against MDY for the copyright infringement and tortious interference with contract claims. They further stipulated that Donnelly would be personally liable for the same amount if found personally liable at trial. After a January 2009 bench trial, the district court held MDY liable under DMCA § 1201(a)(2) and (b)(1). It also held Donnelly personally liable for MDY's copyright infringement, DMCA violations, and tortious interference with contract.

On April 1, 2009, the district court entered judgment against MDY and Donnelly for $6.5 million, an adjusted figure to which the parties stipulated based on MDY's DMCA liability and post-summary judgment Glider sales. The district court permanently enjoined MDY from distributing Glider. MDY's efforts to stay injunctive relief pending appeal were unsuccessful. On April 29, 2009, MDY timely filed this appeal. On May 12, 2009, Blizzard timely cross-appealed the district court's holding that MDY did not violate DMCA § 1201(a)(2) and (b)(1) as to the game software's source code.

III.

We review de novo the district court's (1) orders granting or denying summary judgment; (2) conclusions of law after a bench trial; and (3) interpretations of state law. *Padfield v. AIG Life Ins.*, 290 F.3d 1121, 1124 (9th Cir.2002); *Twentieth Century Fox Film Corp. v. Entm't Distrib.*, 429 F.3d 869, 879 (9th Cir.2005); *Laws v. Sony Music Entm't, Inc.*, 448 F.3d 1134, 1137 (9th Cir.2006). We review the district court's findings of fact for clear error. *Twentieth Century Fox*, 429 F.3d at 879.

IV.

We first consider whether MDY committed contributory or vicarious infringement (collectively, "secondary infringement") of Blizzard's copyright by selling Glider to WoW players.1 *See ProCD, Inc. v. Zeidenberg*, 86 F.3d 1447, 1454 (7th Cir.1996) ("A copyright is a right against the world. Contracts, by contrast, generally affect only their parties."). To establish secondary infringement, Blizzard must first demonstrate direct infringement. *See A & M Records, Inc. v. Napster, Inc.*, 239 F.3d 1004, 1019, 1022 (9th Cir.2001). To establish direct infringement, Blizzard must demonstrate copyright ownership and violation of one of its exclusive rights by Glider users. *Id.* at 1013. MDY is liable for contributory infringement if it has "intentionally induc[ed] or encourag[ed] direct infringement" by Glider users. *MGM Studios Inc. v. Grokster, Ltd.*, 545 U.S. 913, 930, 125 S.Ct. 2764, 162 L.Ed.2d 781 (2005). MDY is liable for vicarious infringement if it (1) has the right and ability to control Glider users' putatively infringing activity and (2) derives a direct financial benefit from their activity. *Id.* If Glider users directly infringe, MDY does not dispute that it satisfies the other elements of contributory and vicarious infringement.

As a copyright owner, Blizzard possesses the exclusive right to reproduce its work. 17 U.S.C. § 106(1). The parties agree that when playing WoW, a player's computer creates a copy of the game's software in the computer's random access memory ("RAM"), a form of temporary memory used by computers to run software programs. This copy potentially infringes unless the player (1) is a licensee whose use of the software is within the scope of the license or (2) owns the copy of the software. *See Sun Microsystems, Inc. v. Microsoft Corp.*, 188 F.3d 1115, 1121 (9th Cir.1999) ("*Sun I*"); 17 U.S.C. § 117(a). As to the scope of the license, ToU § 4(B), "Limitations on Your Use of the Service," provides:

> You agree that you will not ... (ii) create or use cheats, bots, "mods," and/or hacks, or any other third-party software designed to modify the World of Warcraft

experience; or (iii) use any third-party software that intercepts, "mines," or otherwise collects information from or through the Program or Service.

By contrast, if the player owns the copy of the software, the "essential step" defense provides that the player does not infringe by making a copy of the computer program where the copy is created and used solely "as an essential step in the utilization of the computer program in conjunction with a machine." 17 U.S.C. § 117(a)(1).

A. Essential Step Defense

We consider whether WoW players, including Glider users, are owners or licensees of their copies of WoW software. If WoW players own their copies, as MDY contends, then Glider users do not infringe by reproducing WoW software in RAM while playing, and MDY is not secondarily liable for copyright infringement. In *Vernor v. Autodesk, Inc.*, we recently distinguished between "owners" and "licensees" of copies for purposes of the essential step defense. *Vernor v. Autodesk, Inc.*, 621 F.3d 1102, 1108–09 (9th Cir.2010); *see also MAI Sys. Corp. v. Peak Computer, Inc.*, 991 F.2d 511, 519 n. 5 (9th Cir.1993); *Triad Sys. Corp. v. Se. Express Co.*, 64 F.3d 1330, 1333, 1335–36 (9th Cir.1995); *Wall Data, Inc. v. Los Angeles County Sheriff's Dep't*, 447 F.3d 769, 784–85 (9th Cir.2006). In *Vernor*, we held "that a software user is a licensee rather than an owner of a copy where the copyright owner (1) specifies that the user is granted a license; (2) significantly restricts the user's ability to transfer the software; and (3) imposes notable use" restrictions. 621 F.3d at 1111 (internal footnote omitted). Applying *Vernor*, we hold that WoW players are licensees of WoW's game client software. Blizzard reserves title in the software and grants players a non-exclusive, limited license. Blizzard also imposes transfer restrictions if a player seeks to transfer the license: the player must (1) transfer all original packaging and documentation; (2) permanently delete all of the copies and installation of the game client; and (3) transfer only to a recipient who accepts the EULA. A player may not sell or give away the account.

Blizzard also imposes a variety of use restrictions. The game must be used only for non-commercial entertainment purposes and may not be used in cyber cafes and computer gaming centers without Blizzard's permission. Players may not concurrently use unauthorized third-party programs. Also, Blizzard may alter the game client itself remotely without a player's knowledge or permission, and may terminate the EULA and ToU if players violate their terms. Termination ends a player's license to access and play WoW. Following termination, players must immediately destroy their copies of the game and uninstall the game client from their computers, but need not return the software to Blizzard.

Since WoW players, including Glider users, do not own their copies of the software, Glider users may not claim the essential step defense. 17 U.S.C. § 117(a)(1). Thus, when their computers copy WoW software into RAM, the players may infringe unless their usage is within the scope of Blizzard's limited license.

B. Contractual Covenants vs. License Conditions

"A copyright owner who grants a nonexclusive, limited license ordinarily waives the right to sue licensees for copyright infringement, and it may sue only for breach of contract." *Sun I*, 188 F.3d at 1121 (internal quotations omitted). However, if the licensee acts outside the scope of the license, the licensor may sue for copyright infringement. *Id.* (citing *S.O.S., Inc. v. Payday, Inc.*, 886 F.2d 1081, 1087 (9th Cir.1989)). Enforcing a copyright license "raises issues that lie at the intersection of copyright and contract law." *Id.* at 1122.

[The Court discussed the consequences of treating the EULA and ToU as covenants (requiring contractual enforcement) as opposed to conditions, the violation of which could result license cancellations, thereby subjecting the user to copyright infringement claims. The Court ruled that they were covenants as opposed to conditions. — ED]

We thus reverse the district court's grant of summary judgment to Blizzard on its secondary copyright infringement claims. Accordingly, we must also vacate the portion of the district court's permanent injunction that barred MDY and Donnelly from "infringing, or contributing to the infringement of, Blizzard's copyrights in WoW software."

V.

After MDY began selling Glider, Blizzard launched Warden, its technology designed to prevent players who used bots from connecting to the WoW servers. Blizzard used Warden to ban most Glider users in September 2005. Blizzard claims that MDY is liable under DMCA § 1201(a)(2) and (b)(1) because it thereafter programmed Glider to avoid detection by Warden.

A. The Warden technology

Warden has two components. The first is a software module called "scan.dll," which scans a computer's RAM prior to allowing the player to connect to WoW's servers. If scan.dll detects that a bot is running, such as Glider, it will not allow the player to connect and play. After Blizzard launched Warden, MDY reconfigured Glider to circumvent scan.dll by not loading itself until after scan.dll completed its check. Warden's second component is a "resident" component that runs periodically in the background on a player's computer when it is connected to WoW's servers. It asks the computer to report portions of the WoW code running in RAM, and it looks for patterns of code associated with known bots or cheats. If it detects a bot or cheat, it boots the player from the game, which halts the computer's copying of copyrighted code into RAM.

B. The Digital Millennium Copyright Act

Congress enacted the DMCA in 1998 to conform United States copyright law to its obligations under two World Intellectual Property Organization ("WIPO") treaties, which require contracting parties to provide effective legal remedies against the circumvention of protective technological measures used by copyright owners. *See Universal City Studios, Inc. v. Corley*, 273 F.3d 429, 440 (2d Cir.2001). In enacting the DMCA, Congress sought to mitigate the problems presented by copyright enforcement in the digital age. *Id.* The DMCA contains three provisions directed at the circumvention of copyright owners' technological measures. The Supreme Court has yet to construe these provisions, and they raise questions of first impression in this circuit.

The first provision, 17 U.S.C. § 1201(a)(1)(A), is a general prohibition against "circumventing a technological measure that effectively controls access to a work protected under [the Copyright Act]." The second prohibits trafficking in technology that circumvents a technological measure that "effectively controls access" to a copyrighted work. 17 U.S.C. § 1201(a)(2). The third prohibits trafficking in technology that circumvents a technological measure that "effectively protects" a copyright owner's right. 17 U.S.C. § 1201(b)(1).

C. The District Court's Decision

The district court assessed whether MDY violated DMCA § 1201(a)(2) and (b)(1) with respect to three WoW components. First, the district court considered the game client software's **literal elements**: the source code stored on players' hard drives. Second, the district court considered the game client software's **individual non-literal elements**: the 400,000+ discrete visual and audible components of the game, such as a visual image of a monster or its audible roar. Finally, it considered the game's **dynamic non-literal elements**:

that is, the "real-time experience of traveling through different worlds, hearing their sounds, viewing their structures, encountering their inhabitants and monsters, and encountering other players." The district court granted MDY partial summary judgment as to Blizzard's § 1201(a)(2) claim with respect to WoW's literal elements. The district court reasoned that Warden does not effectively control access to the literal elements because WoW players can access the literal elements without connecting to a game server and encountering Warden; they need only install the game client software on their computers. The district court also ruled for MDY following trial as to Blizzard's § 1201(a)(2) claim with respect to WoW's individual non-literal elements, reasoning that these elements could also be accessed on a player's hard drive without encountering Warden.

The district court, however, ruled for Blizzard following trial as to its § 1201(a)(2) and (b)(1) claims with respect to WoW's dynamic non-literal elements, or the "real-time experience" of playing WoW. It reasoned that Warden effectively controlled access to these elements, which could not be accessed without connecting to Blizzard's servers. It also found that Glider allowed its users to circumvent Warden by avoiding or bypassing its detection features, and that MDY marketed Glider for use in circumventing Warden.

We turn to consider whether Glider violates DMCA § 1201(a)(2) and (b)(1) by allowing users to circumvent Warden to access WoW's various elements. MDY contends that Warden's scan.dll and resident components are separate, and only scan.dll should be considered as a potential access control measure under § 1201(a)(2). However, in our view, an access control measure can both (1) attempt to block initial access and (2) revoke access if a secondary check determines that access was unauthorized. Our analysis considers Warden's scan.dll and resident components together because the two components have the same purpose: to prevent players using detectable bots from continuing to access WoW software.

D. Construction of § 1201

One of the issues raised by this appeal is whether certain provisions of § 1201 prohibit circumvention of access controls when access does not constitute copyright infringement. To answer this question and others presented by this appeal, we address the nature and interrelationship of the various provisions of § 1201 in the overall context of the Copyright Act. 2627 We begin by considering the scope of DMCA § 1201's three operative provisions, §§ 1201(a)(1), 1201(a)(2), and 1201(b)(1). We consider them side-by-side, because "we do not ... construe statutory phrases in isolation; we read statutes as a whole. Thus, the [term to be construed] must be read in light of the immediately following phrase...." *United States v. Morton*, 467 U.S. 822, 828, 104 S.Ct. 2769, 81 L.Ed.2d 680 (1984); *see also Padash v. I.N.S.*, 358 F.3d 1161, 1170 (9th Cir.2004) (we analyze the statutory provision to be construed "in the context of the governing statute as a whole, presuming congressional intent to create a coherent regulatory scheme").

In sum, we conclude that a fair reading of the statute (supported by legislative history) indicates that Congress created a distinct anti-circumvention right under § 1201(a) without an infringement nexus requirement. Thus, even accepting the validity of the concerns expressed in *Chamberlain*, 381 F.3d 1178 (Fed.Cir.2004), those concerns do not authorize us to override congressional intent and add a non-textual element to the statute. *See In Re Dumont*, 581 F.3d 1104, 1111 (9th Cir.2009) ("[W]here the language of an enactment is clear or, in modern parlance, plain, and construction according to its terms does not lead to absurd or impracticable consequences, the words employed are to be taken as the final expression of the meaning intended."). Accordingly, we reject the imposition of an infringement nexus requirement. We now consider whether MDY has violated § 1201(a)(2) and (b)(1).

E. Blizzard's § 1201(a)(2) Claim

1. WoW's literal elements and individual non-literal elements

We agree with the district court that MDY's Glider does not violate DMCA § 1201(a)(2) with respect to WoW's literal elements and individual non-literal elements, because Warden does not effectively control access to these WoW elements. First, Warden does not control access to WoW's literal elements because these elements—the game client's software code—are available on a player's hard drive once the game client software is installed. Second, as the district court found:

> WoW's individual nonliteral components may be accessed by a user without signing on to the server. As was demonstrated during trial, an owner of the game client software may use independently purchased computer programs to call up the visual images or the recorded sounds within the game client software. For instance, a user may call up and listen to the roar a particular monster makes within the game. Or the user may call up a virtual image of that monster.

Since a player need not encounter Warden to access WoW's individual non-literal elements, Warden does not effectively control access to those elements. Our conclusion is in accord with the Sixth Circuit's decision in *Lexmark International v. Static Control Components*, 387 F.3d 522 (6th Cir.2004). In *Lexmark*, the plaintiff sold laser printers equipped with an authentication sequence, verified by the printer's copyrighted software, that ensured that only plaintiff's own toner cartridges could be inserted into the printers. *Id.* at 530. The defendant sold microchips capable of generating an authentication sequence that rendered other manufacturers' cartridges compatible with plaintiff's printers. *Id.*

The Sixth Circuit held that plaintiff's § 1201(a)(2) claim failed because its authentication sequence did not effectively control access to its copyrighted computer program. *Id.* at 546. Rather, the mere purchase of one of plaintiff's printers allowed "access" to the copyrighted program. Any purchaser could read the program code directly from the printer memory without encountering the authentication sequence. *Id.* The authentication sequence thus blocked only one form of access: the ability to make use of the printer. However, it left intact another form of access: the review and use of the computer program's literal code. *Id.* The Sixth Circuit explained:

> Just as one would not say that a lock on the back door of a house "controls access" to a house whose front door does not contain a lock and just as one would not say that a lock on any door of a house "controls access" to the house after its purchaser receives the key to the lock, it does not make sense to say that this provision of the DMCA applies to otherwise-readily-accessible copyrighted works. Add to this the fact that the DMCA not only requires the technological measure to "control access" but requires the measure to control that access "effectively," 17 U.S.C. § 1201(a)(2), and it seems clear that this provision does not naturally extend to a technological measure that restricts one form of access but leaves another route wide open.

Id. at 547.

Here, a player's purchase of the WoW game client allows access to the game's literal elements and individual non-literal elements. Warden blocks one form of access to these elements: the ability to access them while connected to a WoW server. However, analogously to the situation in *Lexmark*, Warden leaves open the ability to access these elements directly via the user's computer. We conclude that Warden is not an effective access control measure with respect to WoW's literal elements and individual non-literal elements, and therefore, that MDY does not violate § 1201(a)(2) with respect to these elements.

2. WoW's dynamic non-literal elements

We conclude that MDY meets each of the six textual elements for violating § 1201(a)(2) with respect to WoW's dynamic non-literal elements. That is, MDY (1) traffics in (2) a technology or part thereof (3) that is primarily designed, produced, or marketed for, or has limited commercially significant use other than (4) circumventing a technological measure (5) that effectively controls access (6) to a copyrighted work. *See* 17 U.S.C. § 1201(a)(2).

The first two elements are met because MDY "traffics in a technology or part thereof"— that is, it sells Glider. The third and fourth elements are met because Blizzard has established that MDY *markets* Glider for use in circumventing Warden, thus satisfying the requirement of § 1201(a)(2)(C). Indeed, Glider has no function other than to facilitate the playing of WoW. The sixth element is met because, as the district court held, WoW's dynamic non-literal elements constitute a copyrighted work. *See, e.g., Atari Games Corp. v. Oman,* 888 F.2d 878, 884–85 (D.C.Cir.1989) (the audiovisual display of a computer game is copyrightable independently from the software program code, even though the audiovisual display generated is partially dependent on user input).

The fifth element is met because Warden is an effective access control measure. To "effectively control access to a work," a technological measure must "in the ordinary course of its operation, require[ ] the application of information, or a process or a treatment, with the authority of the copyright owner, to gain access to the work." 17 U.S.C. § 1201(a)(3)(B). Both of Warden's two components "require[ ] the application of information, or a process or a treatment ... to gain access to the work." For a player to connect to Blizzard's servers which provide access to WoW's dynamic non-literal elements, scan.dll must scan the player's computer RAM and confirm the absence of any bots or cheats. The resident component also requires a "process" in order for the user to continue accessing the work: the user's computer must report portions of WoW code running in RAM to the server. Moreover, Warden's provisions were put into place by Blizzard, and thus, function "with the authority of the copyright owner." Accordingly, Warden effectively controls access to WoW's dynamic non-literal elements. We hold that MDY is liable under § 1201(a)(2) with respect to WoW's dynamic non-literal elements. Accordingly, we affirm the district court's entry of a permanent injunction against MDY to prevent future § 1201(a)(2) violations.

F. Blizzard's § 1201(b)(1) Claim

Blizzard may prevail under § 1201(b)(1) only if Warden "effectively protect[s] a right" of Blizzard under the Copyright Act. Blizzard contends that Warden protects its reproduction right against unauthorized copying. We disagree.

First, although WoW players copy the software code into RAM while playing the game, Blizzard's EULA and ToU authorize all licensed WoW players to do so. We have explained that ToU § 4(B)'s bot prohibition is a license covenant rather than a condition. Thus, a Glider user who violates this covenant does not infringe by continuing to copy code into RAM. Accordingly, MDY does not violate § 1201(b)(1) by enabling Glider users to avoid Warden's interruption of their *authorized* copying into RAM.

Second, although WoW players can theoretically record game play by taking screen shots, there is no evidence that Warden detects or prevents such allegedly infringing copying.[20] This is logical, because Warden was designed to reduce the presence of cheats and bots, not to protect WoW's dynamic non-literal elements against copying. We conclude that Warden does not effectively protect any of Blizzard's rights under the Copyright Act, and MDY is not liable under § 1201(b)(1) for Glider's circumvention of Warden.

VI.

The district court granted Blizzard summary judgment on its claim against MDY for tortious interference with contract ("tortious interference") under Arizona law and held that Donnelly was personally liable for MDY's tortious interference. We review the district court's grant of summary judgment de novo. *See Canyon Ferry Rd. Baptist Church of East Helena, Inc. v. Unsworth*, 556 F.3d 1021, 1027 (9th Cir.2009). We view the evidence in the light most favorable to non-movant MDY in determining whether there are any genuine issues of material fact. *Id.* Because we conclude that there are triable issues of material fact, we vacate and remand for trial.

A. Elements of Blizzard's Tortious Interference Claim

To recover for tortious interference under Arizona law, Blizzard must prove: (1) the existence of a valid contractual relationship; (2) MDY's knowledge of the relationship; (3) MDY's intentional interference in inducing or causing the breach; (4) the impropriety of MDY's interference; and (5) resulting damages. *See Safeway Ins. Co. v. Guerrero*, 106 P.3d 1020, 1025 (Ariz.2005); *see also Antwerp Diamond Exch. of Am., Inc. v. Better Bus. Bur. of Maricopa County, Inc.*, 130 Ariz. 523, 637 P.2d 733, 740 (1981).

Blizzard satisfies four of these five elements based on undisputed facts. First, a valid contractual relationship exists between Blizzard and its customers based on the operative EULA and ToU. Second, MDY was aware of this relationship: it does not contend that it was unaware of the operative EULA and ToU, or unaware that using Glider breached their terms. In fact, after Blizzard first attempted to ban Glider users, MDY modified its website to notify customers that using Glider violated the ToU. Third, MDY intentionally interfered with Blizzard's contracts. After Blizzard used Warden to ban a majority of Glider users in September 2005, MDY programmed Glider to be undetectable by Warden. Finally, Blizzard has proffered evidence that it was damaged by MDY's conduct.

Thus, Blizzard is entitled to summary judgment if there are no triable issues of material fact as to the fourth element of its tortious interference claim: whether MDY's actions were improper. To determine whether a defendant's conduct was improper, Arizona employs the seven-factor test of Restatement (Second) of Torts § 767. *See Safeway*, 106 P.3d at 1027; *see also Wagenseller v. Scottsdale Mem'l Hosp.*, 147 Ariz. 370, 710 P.2d 1025, 1042–43 (1985), *superseded in other respects* by A.R.S. § 23–1501. The seven factors are (1) the nature of MDY's conduct, (2) MDY's motive, (3) Blizzard's interests with which MDY interfered, (4) the interests MDY sought to advance, (5) the social interests in protecting MDY's freedom of action and Blizzard's contractual interests, (6) the proximity or remoteness of MDY's conduct to the interference, and (7) the relations between MDY and Blizzard. *Id.* A court should give greatest weight to the first two factors. *Id.* We conclude that summary judgment was inappropriate here, because on the current record, taking the facts in the light most favorable to MDY, the first five factors do not clearly weigh in either side's favor, thus creating a genuine issue of material fact.

B. Copyright Act Preemption

MDY contends that Blizzard's tortious interference claim is preempted by the Copyright Act. The Copyright Act preempts state laws that confer rights equivalent to the exclusive rights of copyright under 17 U.S.C. § 106 (i.e., reproduction, distribution, public display, public performance, and creation of derivative works). 17 U.S.C. § 301(a). However, the Copyright Act does not preempt state law remedies with respect to "activities violating legal or equitable rights that are not equivalent to any of the exclusive rights [of copyright]." 17 U.S.C. § 301(b)(3).

Whether, in these circumstances, tortious interference with contract is preempted by the Copyright Act is a question of first impression in this circuit. However, we have previously addressed a similar tortious interference cause of action under California law and found it not preempted. *See Altera Corp. v. Clear Logic, Inc.*, 424 F.3d 1079, 1089–90 (9th Cir.2005). In so holding, we relied on the Seventh Circuit's analysis in *ProCD*, 86 F.3d 1447, which explained that because contractual rights are not equivalent to the exclusive rights of copyright, the Copyright Act's preemption clause usually does not affect private contracts. *Altera*, 424 F.3d at 1089; *see ProCD*, 86 F.3d at 1454 ("A copyright is a right against the world. Contracts, by contrast, generally affect only their parties; strangers may do as they please, so contracts do not create 'exclusive rights.'"). The Fourth, Fifth, and Eighth Circuits have also held that the Copyright Act does not preempt a party's enforcement of its contractual rights. *See Nat'l Car Rental Sys., Inc. v. Comp. Assoc. Int'l, Inc.*, 991 F.2d 426, 433 (8th Cir.1993); *Taquino v. Teledyne Monarch Rubber*, 893 F.2d 1488, 1501 (5th Cir.1990); *Acorn Structures, Inc. v. Swantz*, 846 F.2d 923, 926 (4th Cir.1988).

This action concerns the anti-bot provisions of ToU § 4(b)(ii) and (iii), which we have held are contract-enforceable covenants rather than copyright-enforceable conditions. We conclude that since Blizzard seeks to enforce contractual rights that are not equivalent to any of its exclusive rights of copyright, the Copyright Act does not preempt its tortious interference claim. *Cf. Altera*, 424 F.3d at 1089–90. Accordingly, we hold that Blizzard's tortious interference claim under Arizona law is not preempted by the Copyright Act, but we vacate the grant of summary judgment because there are outstanding issues of material fact.

VII.

The district court found that Donnelly was personally liable for MDY's tortious interference with contract, secondary copyright infringement, and DMCA violations. We vacate the district court's decision because we determine that MDY is not liable for secondary copyright infringement and is liable under the DMCA only for violation of § 1201(a)(2) with respect to WoW's dynamic non-literal elements. In addition, we conclude that summary judgment is inappropriate as to Blizzard's claim for tortious interference with contract under Arizona law. Accordingly, on remand, the district court shall reconsider the issue of Donnelly's personal liability. The district court's decision is VACATED and the case is REMANDED to the district court for further proceedings consistent with this opinion.

Each side shall bear its own costs.

Notes and Questions

1. Do you agree with the *MDY* decision?

2. Consider the fairness of the *MDY* ruling while comparing it to the outcome in *Lewis Galoob Toys, Inc. v. Nintendo of Am., Inc.*, 964 F.2d 965 (1992), § 6.30 *supra*. Didn't the *Game Genie* in the Galoob case perform a function that was similar to the *Glider* in the *MDY* case? In particular, both the *Game Genie* and the *Glider* were designed to provide a player advantage, contrary to the wishes of the copyright holder. How would you distinguish or reconcile the opposite holdings?

3. The *MDY* case has attracted its share of controversy. Some critics agree with the decision; others disagree. For someone who does both simultaneously, see James Harrell,

"*Permissible Error: Why the Ninth Circuit's Incorrect Application of the DMCA in MDY Industries, LLC v. Blizzard Entertainment, Inc. Reaches the Correct Result,*" 14 WAKE FOREST J. BUS. & INTEL. PROP. L. 211 (Fall, 2013). See also Ross Shikowitz, "*License to Kill: MDY v. Blizzard and the Battle over Copyright in World of Warcraft,*" 75 BROOK. L. REV. 1015 (Spring, 2010).

———

§ 6.60 Criminal Responsibility

In addition to criminal liability for willful copyright infringement, both statutory and common law damages are available to an aggrieved plaintiff. Also, as suggested from the preceding cases in this chapter, a full range of equitable and legal remedies are available. Criminal sanctions are normally reserved for repetitious or voluminous violations of the Copyright Act or the related Digital Millennium Copyright Act. But isolated incidents may also draw prosecutorial attention, resulting in monetary damages and incarceration.

* * *

United States v. Kah Choon Chay

United States Court of Appeals, Seventh Circuit, 2002
281 F.3d 682

RIPPLE, Circuit Judge

After his indictment for participating in an international computer-program piracy ring, Kah Choon Chay pleaded guilty to one count of trafficking in counterfeit documents and packaging for computer programs in interstate commerce. See 18 U.S.C. § 2318(a). The district court sentenced him to eight months of incarceration, three years of supervised release and $49,941.02 in restitution to the owners of the copyrighted programs that Mr. Chay had pirated. This restitution figure is based on Mr. Chay's gross income from sales of the illegal programs and counterfeit packaging in the United States. In this appeal, Mr. Chay raises three arguments regarding the restitution portion of his sentence. For the reasons set forth in the following opinion, we affirm the judgment of the district court.

BACKGROUND

After meeting a "Ms. Lee" in a Kuala Lumpur, Malaysia computer store in December 1996, Mr. Chay, a Malaysian citizen residing in the United States, embarked on a scheme of international computer-software piracy. For the next several years, Mr. Chay bought newly released computer games in the United States and then sent them to Ms. Lee in Malaysia for copying. In return, he would receive 20 to 30 copies of the games with counterfeit packaging and instructions. These counterfeit items were so realistic that some of his subsequent customers could not distinguish them from the real products. Mr. Chay, using a variety of aliases on eBay and other electronic bulletin boards and auction sites, advertised and sold these pirated copies over the internet.

The scheme came to an end after one of Mr. Chay's former roommates, suspicious of Mr. Chay's activities, retrieved from a dumpster a box of Mr. Chay's business records and turned them over to the FBI. The records were enough to prompt an investigation during which an undercover agent bought counterfeit computer games from Mr. Chay via the internet. After confirming the former roommate's allegations, the FBI searched Mr. Chay's apartment and seized his computer, records of his illegal sales of copyrighted programs, and numerous illegally copied computer games, some still in packages bearing a Malaysian postmark.

Mr. Chay then confessed to his crimes and pleaded guilty to one count of violating 18 U.S.C. § 2318(a). The plea agreement, which reserved Mr. Chay's right to appeal, acknowledged his willingness to pay restitution for all the victims' losses caused by his activities: "The defendant agrees to pay restitution for all losses relating to the offense of conviction, all losses covered by the same course of conduct or common scheme or plan as the offense of conviction.... The exact restitution figure will be agreed upon by the parties prior to sentencing or, if the parties are unable to agree upon a specific figure, restitution will be determined by the Court at sentencing."

Notably, the plea agreement did not specify how the "losses" caused by Mr. Chay's activities would be calculated. Mr. Chay and the Government could not agree on the proper restitution figure before sentencing; accordingly, the court determined the amount of restitution and ordered that Mr. Chay pay $49,941.02 in restitution to the 52 victim companies holding copyrights that Mr. Chay had infringed. The court set the restitution amount according to charts, generated by the Government and incorporated into the Presentence Investigation Report (PSR) through an addendum. This analysis showed that Mr. Chay had grossed $49,941.02 from the sale of pirated computer games. The charts also set forth the precise amount that Mr. Chay owed each of the 52 victim copyright holders of the pirated games. The Government had computed losses for each company by multiplying the number of that company's pirated programs that Mr. Chay sold by the actual price he received for them. The charts were based on evidence obtained from eBay, Mr. Chay's computer, and the box of Mr. Chay's discarded records turned over to the FBI by Mr. Chay's former roommate; this evidence revealed how many programs Mr. Chay had sold and the price at which he had sold them.

At sentencing, Mr. Chay raised two objections to the Government's calculation of the losses caused by his piracy. The first was to the Government's determination of the number of games that had copyrights, but the court overruled the objection because Mr. Chay had presented no evidence undermining the Government's figure. The other objection concerned the restitution amount. Through counsel, Mr. Chay argued that the court should reduce the amount of restitution by his costs in producing and distributing the pirated games and programs. Mr. Chay argued that the court should use his net profit rather than his gross sales as the restitution amount. Mr. Chay did not, however, present any evidence of his costs. The court rejected his argument, stating that:

> [H]e owes the legal owner the full amount of what he sold because that was a gain he never should have realized, just as I would owe you the full $50 for [a stolen watch] because it wasn't my watch to sell. Not just the difference between what the watch cost you and what I received for it, but the full amount of my gain.... [I]f he had costs, those are his to absorb. Those aren't chargeable to the defendant [sic] whose copyright he stole. The copyright owners, the people that were defrauded of the opportunity to sell those games don't have to pay Mr. Chay's costs.

DISCUSSION

On appeal, Mr. Chay raises three arguments concerning the court's order of restitution.[13]

---

13. First, he argues that, under U.S.S.G. § 5E1.1, the restitution guideline, the PSR should have included a victim impact statement. Second, he asserts that the district court should have considered

A. Victim Impact Statement

Citing only commentary to sec. 5E1.1 of the 1995 sentencing guidelines, Mr. Chay first argues that a "victim impact statement" regarding the crime's financial impact on the victim should have been included in the PSR and that the Government's failure to do so mandates a remand. Mr. Chay was, however, sentenced under the 1998 guidelines, not the 1995 guidelines. The commentary to sec. 5E1.1 of the 1998 guidelines, which was amended to conform with the Antiterrorism and Effective Death Penalty Act of 1996, see U.S.S.G. Appendix C, amendment 571, lacks the provision from the 1995 sentencing guidelines cited by Mr. Chay, and nothing else in the section requires that a victim impact statement be included in the PSR.

Federal Rule of Criminal Procedure 32(b)(4)(D) does, however, require that a PSR contain "verified information ... containing an assessment of the financial ... impact on any individual against whom the offense has been committed." Rule 32(b)(4)(F) also provides that "in appropriate cases, information sufficient for the court to enter an order of restitution" should be included in the PSR. These requirements were both met in this case by the Second Addendum to the PSR, which listed the individual victim companies along with the amount of loss each sustained (calculated according to the number of each company's copyrighted games that Mr. Chay sold multiplied by the price at which he sold them). This list was based on eBay records, computer logs and Mr. Chay's discarded records. Mr. Chay never specifies what additional information should have been included or how the absence of that information affected his substantial rights.

B. Consideration of Mr. Chay's Finances

Mr. Chay claims that the district court should have considered his modest financial condition, revealed in the PSR, before imposing the restitution order. Mr. Chay's crime is, however, a crime against property covered by the Mandatory Victim Restitution Act (MVRA), 18 U.S.C. §3663A, which prohibits the court from examining the defendant's ability to pay restitution. See 18 U.S.C. §3664(f)(1)(A).

C. Calculation of Victims' Losses

Mr. Chay also renews his contention that his restitution amount should have been reduced by the costs of his piracy because his "gain" consisted of only his profits, not gross sales. We review a district court's order of restitution for an abuse of discretion, and we will disturb that order only if the sentencing court exercised its discretion using inappropriate factors or by failing to use any discretion at all. Given this very deferential standard of review, Mr. Chay's argument is unpersuasive.

Restitution is designed to compensate the victim for the harm suffered because of the defendant's criminal conduct. In determining the amount of the victims' losses, the district court relied upon Mr. Chay's gross sales to measure the victims' losses resulting from Mr. Chay's conduct. Mr. Chay submits that his costs in manufacturing and distributing the pirated programs should offset the amount of restitution due the victims. By focusing on his personal "gain" rather than the calculation of the victims' loss, Mr. Chay fails to address the real issue posed by the statutory scheme: whether the district court's calculation of the amount of loss Mr. Chay caused the victims was within the bounds of its discretion. Mr. Chay's position is somewhat analogous to a bank robber asking that the amount of money he returns to a bank be offset by the cost of robbing it. We do not think the holder

---

his ability to pay restitution before setting the amount. Third, he renews his argument that the court should have reduced the restitution amount by his costs.

of the copyright ought to be required to subsidize the cost of Mr. Chay's illegal activity. Although the record in this case is sparse, we note that any other approach might well require a victim to incur double costs if, in addition to absorbing the costs of the malefactor, it had to absorb the costs associated with the failure to sell its own product in the regular course of doing business.

Notes and Questions

1. Counterfeiting computer games is a continuing world-wide problem; those who engage in such activities are subject to both criminal and civil sanctions. 18 U.S.C. § 2320 (trafficking in counterfeit goods). For matters involving both, *see Nintendo of Am., Inc. v. Ntdec*, 51 F.3d 281 (Table), No. 93-16858 1995 WL 135996 (9th Cir., March 28, 1995), 1995 Corp. L. Dec. ¶ 27,402.

2. The penalties for counterfeiting can be severe. 17 U.S.C. § 506(a) makes reference to 18 U.S.C. § 2319 (Criminal Infringement of a Copyright) which provides that persons engaged in counterfeiting "shall be imprisoned not more than 5 years," fined, or both.

3. The blatant copying of video games can give rise to several different civil causes of action, state and federal, each with its own set of remedies. What happens when remedies overlap or are otherwise inconsistent? Could a successful plaintiff in a copyright infringement action collect treble damages if state law provided for such relief? *See Nintendo of Am., Inc. v. Aeropower Co.*, 34 F.3d 246 (4th Cir. 1995), where Nintendo sued an alleged infringer for violations of federal copyright and trademark laws, in addition to North Carolina's unfair business practices law. The United States District Court granted Nintendo's request for monetary and injunctive relief. The Circuit Court of Appeals held that the Copyright Act's remedial scheme provides exclusive federal remedies for copyright infringement, and contains no provision for trebling statutory damages, either as an integral feature of the federal remedial scheme or by invoking any trebling provisions of state law. Thus, the state's Unfair and Deceptive Practices Act could not be used as a basis for awarding damages over and above those permitted by federal copyright law.

4. A preliminary injunction is issued during circumstances where there is no adequate remedy at law and upon a showing that the plaintiff may suffer irreparable harm if he or she is required to await trial before obtaining relief. Where such an injunction is going to interfere with a defendant's business enterprise, the plaintiff should be required to show a high likelihood of eventual success on the merits. Should a preliminary injunction be issued in favor a video game manufacturer against the distributor of a game back-up device allegedly designed only for purposes of protection and archiving as opposed to copying video games? *See Nintendo of Am. Inc., v. Comp. & Ent., Inc.*, Civil No. C96-0187 1996 WL 511619 (W.D. Wash. May 31, 1996). In that case, the defendant stated to customers that the device could be used to back up game cartridges. He also stated it would be illegal to copy game cartridges owned by others, but "laughingly" added that what the user did with the device was not under his control.

* * *

Section 1201(a)(1)(A) of The Circumvention of Copyright Protection Systems provision of the Digital Millennium Copyright Act provides in part that: "No person shall circumvent a technological measure that effectively controls access to a work protected under this title." The term "protected under this title," essentially equates to "copyrighted." Section 1201(a)(2) of that then Act states:

No person shall manufacture, import, offer to the public, provide, or otherwise traffic in any technology, product, service, device, component, or part thereof, that—

(A) is primarily designed or produced for the purpose of circumventing a technological measure that effectively controls access to a work protected under this title;

(B) has only limited commercially significant purpose or use other than to circumvent a technological measure that effectively controls access to a work protected under this title; or

(C) is marketed by that person or another acting in concert with that person with that person's knowledge for use in circumventing a technological measure that effectively controls access to a work protected under this title.

Criminal sanctions attach to prohibited conduct. It is interesting to note that those sanctions can be increased if the defendant happens to be a skilled computer technician. United States Sentencing Guideline 3B1.3 ("Abuse of Position of Trust or Use of Special Skill") provides in part: "If the defendant abused a position of public or private trust, or used a special skill, in a manner that significantly facilitated the commission or concealment of the offense, increase by 2 levels. This adjustment may not be employed if an abuse of trust or skill is included in the base offense level or specific offense characteristic."

* * *

United States v. Reichert

United States Court of Appeals, Sixth Circuit, 2014
110 U.S.P.Q.2d 1169

GRIFFIN, Circuit Judge.

Jeffrey J. Reichert appeals his criminal conviction and sentence under the Digital Millennium Copyright Act (the "DMCA") asserting three grounds: (1) that the jury received an inaccurate "deliberate ignorance" instruction that had the effect of negating the requirement that Reichert's conduct be a "willful" violation of the DMCA; (2) that the exclusion of a defense witness' testimony violated Reichert's constitutional right to present a defense; and (3) that he was improperly assessed a "special skills" sentencing enhancement under U.S.S.G. § 3B1.3. We hold that the jury instructions as a whole properly stated the law, the excluded testimony was not so vital to Reichert's defense that its exclusion caused him constitutional injury, and Reichert's self-taught technical expertise merited a § 3B1.3 enhancement. We therefore affirm.

I.

"Congress enacted the DMCA in 1998 to comply with international copyright treaties and to update domestic copyright law for the online world." *Ellison v. Robertson*, 357 F.3d 1072, 1076 (9th Cir.2004). In large part, the DMCA was intended to give copyright owners additional means to protect copyrighted materials in the digital age. Although copyright owners often attempted to protect digitized materials behind digital passwords or encryption codes, "prior to the DMCA, a copyright owner would have had no cause of action against anyone who circumvented any sort of technological control, but did not infringe the copyright." *Chamberlain Group, Inc. v. Skylink Technologies, Inc.*, 381 F.3d 1178, 1195–96 (Fed.Cir.2004). Due to the ease of digital piracy, copyright owners feared that the ability to pursue only infringers, rather than those who "picked the lock" and enabled the infringement to occur in the first place, was inadequate to protect their copyrighted material. *See Universal City Studios, Inc. v. Corley*, 273 F.3d 429, 435 (2d Cir.2001).

In response to this problem, the DMCA gave copyright owners a remedy against those who did not themselves infringe a copyright but instead circumvented technological controls and thereby enabled others to infringe. It did so by creating both "circumvention liability for digital trespass under [17 U.S.C.] § 1201(a)(1)," and "trafficking liability under [17 U.S.C.] § 1201(a)(2) for facilitating such circumvention." *Chamberlain Group,* 381 F.3d at 1196. Thus, the DMCA "targets the *circumvention* of digital walls guarding copyrighted material (and trafficking in circumvention tools)," even though it "does not concern itself with the *use* of those materials after circumvention has occurred." *Corley,* 273 F.3d at 443; *see also MGE UPS Sys., Inc. v. GE Consumer & Indus., Inc.,* 622 F.3d 361, 366 (5th Cir.2010). Circumventing or trafficking in circumvention tools in violation of § 1201 is a criminal offense if it is committed "willfully" and for commercial or private financial gain. 17 U.S.C. § 1204(a).

Reichert was prosecuted under the DMCA for trafficking in circumvention technology. Federal agents had begun investigating Xbox-scene.com, a website that hosted online forums dedicated to the discussion of modifying video game consoles by installing "modification chips" (or "mod chips") in them so that they could run software for which the consoles were not originally designed. Reichert was one of the moderators of the discussion forums hosted on Xbox-scene.com, and an undercover agent contacted him in 2007, requesting a modified Nintendo Wii. Reichert responded to the agent's requests, purchased a Wii, installed a modification chip, and sold the modified Wii to the agent for a $50 profit. When the Wii was tested, it was able to play both legitimate video games and pirated ones. Agents subsequently obtained a search warrant and seized modification chips, a soldering iron, computers, and business cards advertising Reichert's services from Reichert's residence, as well as from the garage of one of his friends, Kevin Belcik. Reichert ultimately was charged in a one-count indictment under 17 U.S.C. § 1201(a)(2)(A), which prohibits, in relevant part, the trafficking of any technology that "is primarily designed or produced for the purpose of circumventing a technological measure that effectively controls access to a work protected [by copyright]." *Id.*

At trial, the government put on evidence that modification chips are used to fool or bypass a game console's security measures and enable users to run software for which the console was not originally intended. One of the government's expert witnesses testified that the "primary purpose" of modification chips is to enable a user to play pirated video games. Although each particular hardware version of a console requires its own specialized modification chip, the government's witness detailed in general terms how a modification chip would typically be installed: the console would be opened, and wires from the modification chip would be soldered to the appropriate locations on a console's circuit board. According to the witness, it is a "pretty complicated process," given that the modifier needs to identify the proper locations to which to attach the wires and because holding a soldering iron on the circuit board for too long could damage the board. As an example, the witness referenced one modification that required soldering twenty-nine individual wires to the circuit board.

Several online postings were also admitted against Reichert at trial. In one, Reichert informed an inquirer that a specific type of modification chip "is the best chip for sure, but it's not for people, normal people. You can screw stuff up if you are not careful." In another, an Xbox-scene.com user lauded Reichert as "the only person ... on any forum that knew there was another way beside the 29 wire mod" to modify a certain type of console. Some of Reichert's other online postings directed forum users to sites and chat rooms where they could obtain pirated games and thwart console manufacturers' ability to detect that their consoles were modified.

One government agent noted that in March 2007, Reichert posted on an online forum discussion board, "ha ha, I meant that no one cares if people are doing installs. We aren't technically supposed to do it." Another agent, who had interviewed Reichert during the search of his residence, testified that, while Reichert "never stated to me that it was illegal to sell and install modification chips, ... he did state that he knew the mod chips were in a gray area." Finally, although one agent testified that Reichert did not knowingly order his modified chips from an international source, another witness testified that "it is pretty well known among the community that in the United States mod chips without licenses are illegal."

After the conclusion of the prosecution's case, Reichert's friend Belcik testified as the lone witness on Reichert's behalf. Belcik testified that he and Reichert learned in a "vocational program in high school" how to build computers, and that Reichert modified his first Xbox in about 2003, while in eleventh or twelfth grade. Belcik testified that Reichert believed that some people were using modified consoles to play illegal software. Belcik began to state that Reichert "indicated that what he was doing was basically a hardware modification, not dissimilar from any work that we would do on a normal PC," but the government objected. The district court sustained the objection and refused to allow Belcik to testify about whether Reichert had ever stated whether he thought his conduct was illegal. Defense counsel proffered that, if the objection had been overruled, Belcik would have testified that Reichert "indicated that he believed that modifying the hardware was legal but selling the copyrighted games was illegal."

Before the jury was instructed, Reichert objected to the proposed instruction on deliberate ignorance, contending that "deliberate actions" must be proven in order to prove deliberate ignorance. The district court overruled Reichert's objection and declined to give the alternative deliberate ignorance instruction proposed by Reichert. Before instructing the jury on deliberate ignorance, the district court gave the following instruction on "willfulness":

> As used in these instructions, an act is done willfully if it is done voluntarily and intentionally with the intent to do something unlawful, that is, with the intent either to disobey or disregard the law. While a person must have acted with the intent to do something the law forbids, the person need not be aware of the specific law or the rule his conduct is violating. Willfulness requires the Government to prove that the law imposed a duty on the Defendant, that the Defendant knew of this duty, and that he voluntarily and intentionally violated that duty.

The court then gave the following deliberate ignorance instruction:

> Next, I want to explain a little something about proving a Defendant's knowledge. No one can avoid responsibility for a crime by deliberately ignoring the obvious. If you are convinced that the Defendant deliberately ignored a high probability that he was trafficking in technology primarily designed to circumvent technological measures designed to effectively control access to a work copyrighted under federal law, then you may find that he knew he was violating the Digital Millennium Copyright Act. But to find this, you must be convinced beyond a reasonable doubt that the Defendant was aware of a high probability that he was violating the
>
> Digital Millennium Copyright Act, and that the Defendant deliberately closed his eyes to what was obvious. Carelessness or negligence or foolishness on his part is not the same as knowledge and is not enough to convict.

The jury convicted Reichert on the indictment's lone charge. The presentence report ("PSR") prepared in Reichert's case assigned him an offense level of 12 under U.S.S.G.

§ 2B5.3(b)(3)(B) and added a two-point "special skills" enhancement under U.S.S.G. § 3B1.3, concluding that Reichert's crime was facilitated by his possession of technical computer skills "not ... possessed by members of the general public." Reichert's total offense level of fourteen and criminal history category of I subjected him to an advisory Guidelines range of fifteen to twenty-one months.

Reichert objected to the special skills enhancement, but the district court overruled his objection, expressing its opinion that the enhancement was proper. Nevertheless, the court observed that Reichert was "getting a tough deal" and varied downward "two levels" from the Guidelines, ultimately sentencing Reichert to twelve months and one day of imprisonment. Reichert now appeals his conviction and sentence.

II.

A. Jury instructions.

Reichert's first line of argument, which implicates the jury's finding that his conduct was "willful," is notably narrow. Reichert does not argue that the pertinent portions of the DMCA are so vague or of such uncertain application that no defendant could know that his conduct was actually illegal. Nor does Reichert challenge any of the jury's findings — including its willfulness finding — as supported by insufficient evidence. Instead, Reichert claims that the jury was given a deliberate ignorance instruction that was erroneous in at least two respects. First, Reichert argues that the instruction failed to properly reflect that a defendant is willfully blind only if he took "deliberate action" to avoid actual knowledge. But Reichert is incorrect. The deliberate ignorance instruction given in this case tracks the language of Sixth Circuit Pattern Criminal Jury Instruction § 2.09. The pattern instruction explicitly incorporates the requirement that a defendant act "deliberately" to avoid full knowledge, and we have "repeatedly" held the instruction to be an accurate statement of the law. *United States v. Mitchell,* 681 F.3d 867, 876 n. 51 (6th Cir.2012).

Second, Reichert asserts that the deliberate ignorance instruction incorrectly implemented the pattern jury instruction and consequently eviscerated the DMCA's willfulness requirement by allowing the jury to convict him upon finding only that he knew that he was trafficking in circumvention technology, rather than after finding that he knew that he was violating the law by trafficking in such technology.

Despite Reichert's assertions, we cannot agree with Reichert that the jury instructions, viewed as a whole, improperly negated the DMCA's willfulness requirement. No court has yet discussed the reach of 17 U.S.C. § 1204(a)'s willfulness requirement, and on this appeal we do not decide its scope. For this appeal, the parties agree that it requires the government to prove that Reichert voluntarily and intentionally violated a known legal duty. This is consistent with our typical approach, as "generally..., in criminal cases, in order to establish a 'willful' violation of a statute, the Government must prove that the defendant acted with knowledge that his conduct was unlawful." *Roth,* 628 F.3d at 834. It is also ordinarily the case that a defendant need not be aware of the specific provision of law that his conduct violates, as long as he is aware that his act is illegal. *Id.; see Bryan v. United States,* 524 U.S. 184, 196, 118 S.Ct. 1939, 141 L.Ed.2d 197 (1998) (willful violation of 18 U.S.C. § 924(a)(1)(D) requires only "knowledge that the conduct is unlawful," not knowledge of the specific legal provisions prohibiting the defendant's conduct); *see also United States v. Cross,* 816 F.2d 297, 300 (7th Cir.1987). Reichert also concedes that the DMCA's willfulness requirement may be satisfied by a showing of willful blindness; that is, a defendant's conscious decision to remain ignorant of the illegality of his conduct even when the defendant is aware of a high probability that his conduct is in fact illegal. *See Mitchell,* 681 F.3d at 876–77.

Reichert's argument rests primarily in the first portion of the deliberate ignorance instruction. It advised the jury, "If you are convinced that the Defendant deliberately ignored a high probability that he was trafficking in technology primarily designed to circumvent technological measures designed to effectively control access to a work copyrighted under federal law, then you may find that he knew he was violating the Digital Millennium Copyright Act." Given that this language hinges the requisite *mens rea* finding on Reichert's knowledge that the technology in which he trafficked was primarily purposed to facilitate illegal conduct, Reichert's claim that it eviscerated the DMCA's willfulness requirement is tenuous. *See Roth,* 628 F.3d at 834–35 (indicating that awareness of broad criminal regulations obviously applicable to defendant's conduct may suffice for willfulness). Still, devoid of context, this part of the instruction lends some support to Reichert's position, as it seems to inform the jury that if Reichert deliberately ignored a high probability that he merely engaged in the conduct at issue, then the jury could find that Reichert knew that his conduct violated the DMCA.

But Reichert's focus is too myopic. Even to the extent that the challenged portion of the instruction could have been more precise, it was not given in a vacuum. Instead, it was sandwiched between two instructions that stated the stricter requirement and clarified the challenged language. Immediately before giving the challenged instruction, the district court gave an instruction on "willfulness," explaining that an act is willful if done "with the intent either to disobey or disregard the law," that the defendant "must have acted with the intent to do something the law forbids," and that the government must prove "that the law imposed a duty on the Defendant, that the Defendant knew of this duty, and that he voluntarily and intentionally violated that duty." And immediately after giving the portion of the deliberate ignorance instruction to which Reichert objects, the district court cautioned the jury that, to find that Reichert knew that he was violating the DMCA, "you must be convinced beyond a reasonable doubt that the Defendant was aware of a high probability that he was violating the Digital Millennium Copyright Act, and that the Defendant deliberately closed his eyes to what was obvious."

In context, therefore, the language relied upon by Reichert did not detract from the jury instructions' overall import: when viewed "as a whole," the jury instructions given in this case properly instructed the jury on the issue of willfulness. *Ross,* 502 F.3d at 527. Reichert has never objected to the district court's willfulness instruction, and it informed the jury that, for a defendant's conduct to be willful, he "need not be aware of the specific law or the rule his conduct is violating." Even in Reichert's formulation, then, the jury was not required to find that Reichert knew that his conduct violated any specific statute; all that was required to convict Reichert was a finding that he knew that his conduct was illegal. *Roth,* 628 F.3d at 834–35. This is exactly what the district court's "willfulness" instruction told the jury, and the mildly imprecise deliberate ignorance instruction did not fatally undermine it.

Having been properly instructed, the jury found that Reichert constructively knew that his conduct was against the law, given his admissions that he was operating in a "gray" area of the law and was "technically" not supposed to be engaging in his conduct. Reichert does not directly challenge the jury's factual finding in this regard, claiming that he is due a reversal based purely on instructional error. Because the jury instructions accurately stated the law, however, Reichert's position is without merit.

B. Constitutional right to present a defense.

Reichert next claims that he was denied his constitutional right to present a defense when the district court excluded Belcik's testimony indicating that Reichert had previously expressed a belief that modifying consoles was not illegal. We readily conclude that the exclusion of Belcik's testimony did not cause Reichert a constitutional injury. To be sure, the statements may have been admissible under Federal Rule of Evidence 803(3) as a statement of Reichert's then-existing state of mind. However, the government correctly observes that Belcik admitted that he was in the Navy between 2004 and 2008 and that he was "away" in 2007 at the time of Reichert's sale of the modified console and the search of his residence. Belcik never indicated that Reichert's statements about the legality of his conduct were made at any time contemporaneous to 2007. Belcik's proffered testimony, therefore, had only marginal relevance to whether Reichert believed in 2007 that his conduct was legal.

C. Special skills enhancement.

Finally, Reichert challenges the district court's decision to enhance his sentence pursuant to U.S.S.G. § 3B1.3. Section 3B1.3 provides for a two-point enhancement if a defendant "abused a position of public or private trust, or used a special skill, in a manner that significantly facilitated the commission or concealment of the offense." *Id.* While a district court's factual findings underlying its application of the enhancement are reviewed for clear error, *see United States v. Wilson,* 345 F.3d 447, 449 (6th Cir.2003), "[t]he district court's conclusion that skills possessed by a defendant are 'special' within the meaning of the Guideline ... is a mixed finding of law and fact that this court reviews de novo." *United States v. Godman,* 223 F.3d 320, 322 (6th Cir.2000); *see United States v. Tatum,* 518 F.3d 369, 372 (6th Cir.2008).

Reichert contends that his skills are not "special" within the meaning of § 3B1.3. Emphasizing that he is a truck driver with only a high school diploma, Reichert points to § 3B1.3, cmt. n. 4, which explains, "'Special skill' refers to a skill not possessed by members of the general public and usually requiring substantial education, training or licensing. Examples would include pilots, lawyers, doctors, accountants, chemists, and demolition experts." *Id.* Claiming that he "learned how to modify game consoles through trial and error, using how-to books and information from the internet," Reichert argues that his ability to modify game consoles is not reasonably comparable to the skills listed.

We cannot agree. In *Godman,* we observed that requisitely "special" skills may be acquired "through months (or years) of training, *or the equivalent in self-tutelage.*" *Godman,* 223 F.3d at 323 (emphasis added). Nevertheless, we underscored that, to qualify for the enhancement, a defendant's self-taught skills must be "particularly sophisticated." *Id.* In this respect, emphasis is best placed "on the difficulty with which a particular skill is acquired." *Id.* at 322. In *Godman,* for instance, we observed that the defendant's familiarity with a computer scanner and experience in desktop publishing—which the defendant used to manufacture "fairly good quality" counterfeit bills, *id.*—could be replicated in fairly short order by "[m]ost persons of average ability" with "a minimum of difficulty." *Id.* at 323. We therefore concluded that the defendant's skills were not similar to those listed in Application Note 4 and were thus not special for purposes of the enhancement. *Id.*

Reichert's skills, by contrast, are much more sophisticated than those at issue in *Godman.* Building on skills learned in a high school vocational program that taught him how to build his own computer systems from components, Reichert continued to modify consoles for almost half of a decade. As one of the prosecution's expert witnesses testified at trial, modification of a game system can be a "pretty complicated process," requiring both familiarity with consoles' specialized circuitry and the technical deftness to install the modification chip without damaging the delicate circuit board. Over time, Reichert became exceptionally skilled at making these modifications, eventually serving as a moderator of a specialized internet discussion forum that was largely dedicated to console modification. In fact, Reichert was lauded within the gaming community as one of a very few individuals who knew a work-around for one of the most complicated modifications, and his expert assistance was actively sought out and paid for by gamers who had attempted to modify consoles on their own but were unable to do so or who were trying to prevent console manufacturers from detecting that their consoles had been modified. At one point, Reichert even cautioned that certain types of modifications were "not for ... normal people" because a modifier could "screw stuff up" if he was "not careful."

This evidence suggests what we did not find in *Godman:* that Reichert's specialized abilities could not be duplicated by "most persons of average ability" with "a minimum of difficulty." *Godman,* 223 F.3d at 323. Although we agree with Reichert that his skills were not as sophisticated as those at issue in *United States v. Petersen,* 98 F.3d 502, 504– 07 (9th Cir.1996), where the defendant's self-taught computer skills enabled him to hack into the secure computer systems of major financial institutions, the record here demonstrates that Reichert's skill with computer hardware and specialized game console components was substantially more difficult to acquire than the mere familiarity with desktop publishing that was present in *Godman. See United States v. Berry,* 717 F.3d 823, 835 (10th Cir., 2013) (ability to drive an eighteen-wheeler truck was sufficiently "special" where the driver possessed almost five years of truck-driving experience in addition to the basic "small potatoes" training initially required). The district court's findings with respect to Reichert's self-training, ability, and sophistication support the determination that his console-modification skills are "special." Accordingly, the district court did not err in applying § 3B1.3's special skills enhancement to Reichert.

III.

Having discerned no reversible error, we affirm Reichert's conviction and sentence.

BERNICE BOUIE DONALD, Circuit Judge, dissenting

This appeal concerns the criminal enforcement of the Digital Millennium Copyright Act ("DMCA"). A violation of the DMCA may rise to the level of a criminal offense if it is committed "willfully" and for "commercial advantage or private financial gain." 17 U.S.C. § 1204(a).

As the majority explains, Jeffrey Reichert operated a small business of sorts, providing modification services for video game consoles. He did so openly and advertised his services on the Internet. For a fee of approximately $50, Reichert would install a "mod chip" into a video game console that could enhance its functionality in a number of legitimate ways, but that also enabled the console to play unauthorized pirated copies of video games. In 2007, Reichert sold one of these modified consoles—a Nintendo Wii—to an undercover agent of the U.S. Immigration and Customs Enforcement's ("ICE") anti-piracy enforcement group during an investigation known as Operation Tangled Web. As a result, Reichert was charged under the DMCA's criminal provision, § 1204(a), for trafficking in "service[s], device[s] ... or part[s] thereof" designed to circumvent technological protection measures that prevent copyright infringement, in violation of the DMCA's anti-circumvention provision. 17 U.S.C. §§ 1201(a)(2)(A).

To establish that Reichert "willfully" violated the DMCA, as is required for criminal liability to attach under § 1204(a), the Government had to prove that Reichert acted "with knowledge that his conduct was unlawful." *United States v. Roth,* 628 F.3d 827, 834 (6th Cir.2011) (quoting *Bryan v. United States,* 524 U.S. 184, 191, 118 S.Ct. 1939, 141 L.Ed.2d 197 (1998)). Reichert claims that he could not have "willfully" violated the DMCA, because he was unaware that installing mod chips into video game consoles was against the law.

On appeal, Reichert argues, *inter alia,* that the jury instruction provided at trial misstated the DMCA's willfulness requirement and thus precluded the jury from properly considering his defense. The majority concedes that the district court misstated the law in its jury instruction, but concludes that the error was harmless.

If the statute of conviction in this case were itself less ambiguous, I might be more inclined to agree with the majority. Here, however, an otherwise excusable fault in the jury instruction compounded the already heightened risk for error in a case where the charging statute was arguably subject to various interpretations as to the exact legal status of the defendant's conduct. Under these circumstances, I cannot agree with the majority that the additional confusion resulting from the instruction was harmless.

Therefore, I respectfully dissent from Part II of the majority opinion.

I.

This case requires a sophisticated understanding of the technologies at issue and their legal status under the DMCA.

A. Technological Protection Measures and Technological Circumvention

The term "technological protection measure" ("TPM") refers to a wide variety of technologies that are used to control or restrict access to digital content or electronic devices. TPMs "range from the basic to the sophisticated" and include "password protection, copy protection, encryption, digital watermarking and, increasingly, rights management systems incorporating one or more of the foregoing." June M. Besek, *Anti–Circumvention Laws and Copyright: A Report from the Kernochan Center for Law, Media and the Arts,* 27 Columb. J.L. & Arts 385, 391–392 (2004) [hereinafter *Kernochan Study*] (internal quotation marks omitted).

Technology manufacturers use TPMs to limit the functionality of a device or program to a particular use, to implement security measures, to strengthen privacy controls, and of course, to protect intellectual property by preventing unauthorized duplication and/or access. *Id.* at 446–466. Today, the vast majority of commercially available software and hardware devices are embedded with TPMs designed to achieve the manufacturer's interests in maintaining control of the technology after it has been purchased by a consumer. *Id.* at 446–466. TPMs are useful and often necessary tools for businesses that operate in the digital realm. This is particularly true in the context of intellectual property, where TPMs can provide varying degrees of protection against the general ease with which the Internet and digital technology "have made it possible to reproduce copyrighted works and disseminate them around the world with ever greater speed and efficiency." *Id.* at 391.

On the other hand, overly restrictive or impractical TPMs can also interfere with a consumer's ability to use technology in legitimate, but perhaps unintended or unforeseen ways. *See id.* at 393–394; *see also Universal City Studios, Inc. v. Reimerdes,* 111 F.Supp.2d 294, 322 n. 159 (S.D.N.Y.2000), *aff'd sub nom. Universal City Studios, Inc. v. Corley,* 273 F.3d 429 (2d Cir.2001). As a result, various circumvention technologies designed to bypass TPMs have proliferated to meet the consumer demand for interoperability and unrestricted access to various technologies. *Id.* at 392 ("TPMs can be broken quickly by the technologically able; these individuals can then create and distribute tools to those with less technological sophistication, allowing them to circumvent protection measures.").

Generally speaking, circumvention technology is computer code that overrides or bypasses a TPM and can be accessed by downloading a program, running an application, or, as in this case, inserting a computer chip embedded with such a code into a hardware device. The DMCA describes circumvention technology as any mechanism that "descramble[s]" or "decrypt[s]" or otherwise "avoid[s], bypass[es], remove[s], deactivate[s], or impair[s]" a technological protection measure. 17 U.S.C. § 1201(a)(3)(A).

Although circumvention technologies can serve a number of legitimate, non-infringing purposes, some can also be used to access or reproduce copyrighted works without authorization. The DMCA was designed in part to remedy this problem.

B. The DMCA's "Anti–Circumvention" Provision, 17 U.S.C. § 1201(a)(2)

Congress enacted the DMCA to address "the ease with which pirates could [use web-based services to] copy and distribute ... copyrightable work[s] in digital form." *Microsoft Corp. v. AT & T Corp.*, 550 U.S. 437, 458, 127 S.Ct. 1746, 167 L.Ed.2d 737 (2007) (quoting *Universal City Studios, Inc. v. Corley*, 273 F.3d 429, 435 (2d Cir.2001)) (internal quotation marks omitted). Specifically, the DMCA's anti-circumvention provision was designed to support "the efforts of copyright owners to protect their works from piracy behind digital walls such as encryption codes or password protections" by banning the use, manufacture, or sale of technologies that circumvent digital copyright controls. *Id.*

The DMCA's anti-circumvention provision prohibits the act of circumvention itself, 17 U.S.C. § 1201(a)(1), and also targets the availability of circumvention technologies by making it unlawful to traffic in technologies designed to circumvent TPMs that control access to copyrighted works, § 1201(a)(2).

In order to prevent the DMCA from adversely affecting otherwise lawful uses of circumvention technologies, Congress built several exceptions into the anti-circumvention provision. *See* 17 U.S.C. § 1201(d)-(j). Congress also charged the Librarian of Congress, in conjunction with the U.S. Copyright Office and the National Telecommunications and Information Administration ("NTIA") of the U.S. Department of Commerce, with the task of creating additional regulatory exemptions in the future, to ensure that the anti-circumvention provision would continue serving its intended purpose in a rapidly evolving technology industry. As directed in § 1201(a)(1)(C), the Librarian of Congress carves out exceptions to § 1201 in rulemaking proceedings every three years. *See* Bill D. Herman, *Oscar H. Gandy, Jr., Catch 1201: A Legislative History and Content Analysis of the DMCA Exemption Proceedings*, 24 Cardozo Arts & Ent. L.J. 121, 128 (2006) (providing a comprehensive overview of the rulemaking process).

The legislative history of the DMCA makes clear that the anti-circumvention provision is not intended to function as a comprehensive ban on all circumvention technologies; rather, its purpose is to prevent those technologies from being used as a tool for copyright infringement and to provide remedies for copyright holders against individuals and entities who facilitate the widespread unauthorized reproduction of copyrighted works by making such technologies available to the public. *See Kernochan Study*, 404–406 (providing a detailed legislative history of the DMCA's anti-circumvention provision); *Lexmark Int'l, Inc. v. Static Control Components, Inc.*, 387 F.3d 522, 551–52 (6th Cir.2004) ("Such a reading would ignore the precise language—'for the purpose of'—as well as the main point of the DMCA—to prohibit the pirating of copyright-protected works such as movies, music, and computer programs."), *aff'd on other grounds*, 572 U.S. ——, 134 S.Ct. 1377, ——L.Ed.2d ——, 2014 WL 1168967 (2014).

Accordingly, several courts, including ours, have held that circumvention technologies designed primarily for purposes other than to bypass copyright restrictions are not within the ambit of the DMCA's anti-circumvention provision. *See Lexmark*, 387 F.3d 522 (holding that a modification chip designed to make third party ink cartridges compatible with Lexmark printers was not primarily designed to circumvent copyright and thus did not violate the DMCA); *Chamberlain Group, Inc. v. Skylink Techs., Inc.*, 381 F.3d 1178, 1203–

1204 (Fed.Cir.2004) (stating that circumvention alone does not establish a violation of the DMCA unless it can also be demonstrated that there is a nexus between the use of a particular circumvention technology and actual copyright infringement); *see also Storage Tech. Corp. v. Custom Hardware Eng'g & Consulting, Inc.*, 421 F.3d 1307, 1318 (Fed.Cir.2005) ("[C]ourts generally have found a violation of the DMCA only when the alleged access was intertwined with a right protected by the Copyright Act.") (*citing Universal City Studios v. Corley*, 273 F.3d 429, 435 (2d Cir.2001); *RealNetworks, Inc. v. Streambox, Inc.*, 2000 WL 127311 (W.D. Wash. Jan. 18, 2000)).

The Ninth Circuit, however, disagrees and construes the DMCA's anti-circumvention more broadly. *See MDY Indus., LLC v. Blizzard Entm't, Inc.*, 629 F.3d 928, 948 (9th Cir.2010) (rejecting the "infringement nexus" requirement). As the Ninth Circuit's recent opinion demonstrates, competing interpretations of the anti-circumvention provision give § 1201 the potential to function as a broader prohibition against circumvention technologies with only an incidental relation to copyrighted works. *Id.* Indeed, the circuit split is representative of an ongoing debate over the statutory construction and scope of the DMCA's anti-circumvention provision among scholars and other commentators who question whether certain applications of § 1201 have undermined the delicate balance that Congress sought to achieve between strengthening copyright law and preserving consumer rights, promoting technological innovation, and protecting First Amendment speech in our increasingly digitized culture. *See Kernochan Study*, at 411–15 (compiling sources).

C. Legal Status of "Mod Chips" and Video Game Console Modifications

A modification chip, or "mod chip," is a computer chip with software that — once installed into a video game system's motherboard — can enhance its capabilities or add to its functionality. Like other circumvention technologies, mod chips can serve both lawful and unlawful purposes. Although some modifications are designed to "allow users to play unauthorized and illegal copies" of video games, *Sony Computer Entm't Am., Inc. v. Filipiak*, 406 F.Supp.2d 1068, 1070 (N.D.Cal.2005) ("A unmodified PlayStation console ... but if a mod chip is installed in a PlayStation console, the counterfeit, unlicensed 'burnt' game disc will play."); many legitimate, non-infringing, uses exist for mod chips that do not involve or facilitate copyright infringement.

The fact that modified video game consoles can be used for both legitimate, non-infringing purposes as well as to facilitate copyright infringement makes it all the more difficult to determine the precise legal status of mod chips. In a vacuum, the plain language of § 1201(a), certainly lends itself to a reading under which mod chips would be considered unlawful. *See* 17 U.S.C. § 1201(a)(2)(A). When read in conjunction with the provision's statutory exceptions and subsequent exemptions added through regulatory rulemaking, however, the actual legal status of mod chips and video game console modifications is not entirely clear.

Perhaps the most important of these exceptions is the "reverse engineering" provision, which permits circumvention of TPMs through reverse engineering for the purpose of "achiev[ing] interoperability of an independently created computer program with other programs," that are not otherwise readily available. 17 U.S.C. § 1201(f); *see Lexmark,* 387 F.3d at 549 ("[T]he interoperability provision [was designed to] ensure that the DMCA would not diminish the benefit to consumers of interoperable devices in the consumer electronics environment."). Because video games are essentially computer programs, the reverse engineering exception has often been relied upon for the proposition that video game modifications are not *per se* unlawful under the anti-circumvention provision. Indeed, in the very first rulemaking proceeding to consider exemptions to the DMCA's anti-circumvention provision, the Librarian of Congress considered, but ultimately declined to create an exemption for mod chips designed achieve the interoperability of video games across multiple platforms, based on its reasoning that § 1201(f) was sufficient to safeguard legitimate users of mod chips and modified consoles from adverse action. *See Exemption to Prohibition on Circumvention of Copyright Protection Systems for Access Control Technologies,* 65 Fed.Reg. 64556, 64570 (Oct. 27, 2000) (codified at 37 C.F.R. 201).

In 2003, however, the Librarian of Congress reversed course and carved out several exemptions for circumvention technologies which had previously been thought to fall within the statutory exception for reverse engineering at § 1201(f). *See generally,* 68 Fed.Reg. 62011 (Oct. 31, 2003). One of those exemptions permitted the circumvention of TPMs on video games and video game consoles for the purpose of accessing "video games distributed in formats that have become obsolete and which require original media or hardware as a condition of access." 68 Fed.Reg. 62011 (Oct. 31, 2003). Although the intent of the 2003 rulemaking was to clarify the DMCA's application to mod chips and other circumvention technologies, the addition of this new regulatory exemption, which covered a particular use for mod chips that had previously been thought to fall under an existing statutory exception, seems to have caused even greater uncertainty. *See generally* Joe Linhoff, *Video Games and Reverse Engineering: Before and After the Digital Millennium Copyright Act,* 3 J. on Telecomm. & High Tech. L. 209, 229 (2004). Subsequent rulemakings renewed this exemption and introduced several others, but did little to clarify the legal status of mod chips and other circumvention technologies under the DMCA. 71 Fed.Reg. 68472, 68476 (Nov. 27, 2006).

II.

Having established a basic understanding of the DMCA's anti-circumvention provision and the technologies it governs, it is now possible to delve into the more specific argument raised by Reichert's appeal. Reichert argues that the jury instruction provided at trial misstated applicable law and so confused the jury on the willfulness element of the DMCA's criminal provision that the jury was precluded from properly considering his defense. Because I find that the jury instruction fundamentally undercut his defense, which in turn, was particularly susceptible to confusion due to conflicting interpretations of the DMCA, I dissent from the majority's opinion.

A. The Jury Instruction

A violation of § 1201 is only a criminal offense under § 1204(a) if it is committed "willfully" and for commercial or private financial gain. In order to establish a willful violation of a statute, "the Government must prove that the defendant acted with knowledge that his conduct was unlawful." *Id.* at 192, 118 S.Ct. 1939 (quoting *Ratzlaf v. United States,* 510 U.S. 135, 137, 114 S.Ct. 655, 126 L.Ed.2d 615 (1994)); *accord Dixon v. United States,* 548 U.S. 1, 5, 126 S.Ct. 2437, 165 L.Ed.2d 299 (2006) ("[T]he term willfully ... requires a defendant to have acted with knowledge that his conduct was unlawful."); *United States v. Roth,* 628 F.3d 827, 834 (6th Cir.2011) ("[I]n criminal cases, in order to establish a willful violation of a statute, the Government must prove that the defendant acted with knowledge that his conduct was unlawful."). Therefore, at trial, the Government was required to prove that Reichert knew that it was unlawful for him to sell modified video game consoles.

The district court should have instructed the jury to deliver a guilty verdict if it was convinced that Reichert:

> [D]eliberately ignored a high probability that *he was breaking the law* designed to effectively control access to a work copyrighted under federal law.

Instead, the district court instructed the jury to deliver a guilty verdict if Reichert:

> [D]eliberately ignored a high probability that *he was trafficking in technology primarily designed to circumvent technological measures* designed to effectively control access to a work copyrighted under federal law ...

It is undisputed that, standing alone, this portion of the jury instruction did not properly reflect the DMCA's mandate that, in order for criminal liability to attach, the Government had to prove that Reichert *knew* his conduct to be unlawful. 17 U.S.C. § 1204(a); *Roth,* 628 F.3d at 834 ("[I]n order to establish a 'willful' violation of a statute, the Government must prove that the defendant acted with knowledge that his conduct was unlawful."). Moreover, the district court's error was not a minor misstatement of law—it directly undermined Reichert's only defense at trial.

The only remaining question is whether other portions of the instruction, when combined with the district court's misstatement of law and viewed in its entirety, salvaged the jury instruction such that Reichert was not deprived of a fair trial. In my view, it did not. Accordingly, the judgment should be reversed because the instruction, viewed as a whole, permitted the jury to deliver a guilty verdict upon a lesser finding than the statute's willfulness requirement. See 17 U.S.C. § 1204.

The majority concludes that the misstated part of the instruction was harmless because it was accompanied by and "sandwiched between" two proper statements of law, but the fact that other portions of the jury instruction provided a more accurate statement of law did nothing to restore the incorrectly stated part of the instruction. If the district court had acknowledged its mistake and explicitly corrected itself, then perhaps it could be said that the jury instruction, viewed as a whole, was proper. Here, however, there is simply no way of knowing whether the jurors relied on the district court's incorrect misstatement of law or its accompanying, yet contradictory, correct statements of the law. Although other parts of the instruction may have provided the necessary clarity for *some* jurors to understand what the district court meant, there was no indication that the court was correcting its earlier statement or that the jury should apply the correct statement of the law instead of relying on the district court's incorrect statement. While it is certainly possible that the jury relied on the correct portion of the instruction, the likelihood that it relied on the incorrect portion seems equally probable. Since we simply cannot know, to conclude otherwise would require impermissible speculation. *See Davis v. Georgia,* 451 U.S. 921, 922, 101 S.Ct. 2000, 68 L.Ed.2d 312 (1981) (explaining that reversal is necessary when "[a]n appellate court can do no more than guess at what a jury might have done ... [if] properly instructed").

I would be more inclined to agree with the majority if the DMCA's anti-circumvention provision were itself less ambiguous. In this case, however, the charging statute was arguably open to various interpretations. Under these circumstances, I cannot agree with the majority that the additional confusion generated by a jury instruction that muddled the mens rea element of the charge was harmless. *See United States v. Salisbury,* 983 F.2d 1369, 1377 (6th Cir.1993).

The emphasis upon mens rea in the vast majority of criminal statutes is "in keeping with our longstanding recognition of the principle that ambiguity concerning the ambit of criminal statutes should be resolved in favor of lenity."

In cases such as this one, where the charging statute is subject to various interpretations, the relationship between adequacy of notice and a statute's scienter requirement may, under certain circumstances, resolve potential ambiguities. *See Vill. of Hoffman Estates v. Flipside, Hoffman Estates, Inc.,* 455 U.S. 489, 499, 102 S.Ct. 1186, 71 L.Ed.2d 362 (1982) (finding that "a scienter requirement may mitigate a law's vagueness, especially with respect to the adequacy of notice to the complainant that his conduct is proscribed"). Therefore, latent ambiguities in the DMCA's anti-circumvention provision could have been less of a concern in this case if the jury instruction had properly ensured that the Government met its obligation to prove the willfulness element of Reichert's alleged crime. Here, however, the opposite is true — the jury instructions convoluted the scienter element of the charge and aggravated the already heightened risk of error stemming from a statute that was itself subject to various interpretations concerning the exact legal status of the defendant's conduct.

Finally, although the issue on appeal is neither the weight nor sufficiency of the evidence, I mention it here because it leads to the conclusion that an error must have been present for the jury to deliver a guilty verdict despite overwhelming the evidence in support of Reichert's defense. If the evidence at trial had done more to establish the Government's contention that Reichert knew he was breaking the law, then I might be more inclined to agree with the majority. Here, however, Reichert put forth overwhelming evidence to establish his defense. It is undisputed that Reichert operated his console modification business openly; he advertised his services and even opened a separate bank account for the business because he planned to file tax returns on the income it generated. Moreover, at trial, an agent who had engaged in online conversations with Reichert during the investigation testified that Reichert seemed to believe that video game modifications and mod chips occupied a legal "gray area." Given the ongoing debate over the scope of the DMCA's anti-circumvention provision, Reichert's point of view was not unsupported. *See e.g., Chamberlain,* 381 F.3d at 1203–04; *Lexmark,* 387 F.3d at 547–48; *cf. MDY Indus.,* 629 F.3d at 948. In fact, several law review articles published around the time of Reichert's arrest suggest that his understanding of mod chips' legal status was no different from the views expressed by individuals who had a much more sophisticated understanding of the law. *See, e.g.,* Vijay G. Brijbasi, *Game Console Modification Chips: The Effect of Fair Use and the Digital Millennium Copyright Act on the Circumvention of Game Console Security Measures,* 28 Nova L. Rev. 411, 426 (2004); Phillip A. Harris Jr., *Mod Chips and Homebrew: A Recipe for Their Continued Use in the Wake of Sony v. Divineo,* 9 N.C. J.L. & Tech. 113, 115–118 (2007); Zvi Rosen, *Mod, Man, and Law: A Reexamination of the Law of Computer Game Modifications,* 4 Chi.-Kent J. Intell. Prop. 196 (2005); Lewis Stevenson, *Fair Circumvention: A Judicial Analysis for the Digital Millennium Copyright Act Using the Playstation 3 as a Case Study,* 21 S. Cal. Interdisc. L.J. 681 (2012). Nevertheless, the jury delivered a guilty verdict.

If the jury had received a proper instruction on the law, which imposed the highest possible burden upon the Government to demonstrate that Reichert "willfully" violated the DMCA, it seems highly improbable that it would have convicted Reichert on the evidence presented at trial.

III.

For the foregoing reasons, I respectfully dissent from Part II of the majority opinion. While I agree with the majority as to the other issues presented by this appeal, I would reverse on the basis of the erroneous jury instruction.

———————

Notes and Questions

1. Do you agree with the *Reichert* holding or the dissent? Was Reichert's prosecution designed to put a serious criminal behind bars or to "send a message"? Is it fair that the

Digital Millennium Copyright Act should protect reverse engineering (which tends to benefit development companies), but, at the same time, proscribes modifications that tend to enhance benefits to consumers in the form of an expanded use of their products?

2. Judge Donald's dissent in *Reichert* raises several valid points, not the least of which involves ambiguity: "I would be more inclined to agree with the majority if the DMCA's anti-circumvention provision were itself less ambiguous." In fact, a charge of constitutional vagueness was leveled against the technological circumvention provisions of the DMCA in *United States v. Sylvius*, 2014 WL1057009 (United States Court of Appeals, 6th Circuit, 2014). Sylvius argued that modification chips and swap discs were not specifically mentioned in the statute, and that there were legitimate uses for these particular items which would permit their fair use by consumers; unfortunately, his plea agreement included an admission that he offered consumers illegal modification chips and swap discs that were specifically designed to circumvent the copyright protection features of various video game systems. In any event, the court determined that the statute was not unconstitutionally vague under Fourteenth Amendment standards.

3. Were there some defenses that the defense overlooked? *See* Peter Dang, *Criminal Defenses To Anti-Circumvention Charges For Modifying Video Game Consoles*, 9 Wash. J. L. Tech. & Arts 105 (2013).

---

§ 6.70 Copyright Infringement Defenses

Copyrights are double-edged swords. On the one hand, they are intended to protect creativity and originality; on the other hand, they stand as a potential impediment to those very ideals; in truth most creative works draw upon, or are inspired by *other* creative works. For game developers and producers, the problems are multiplied by the very nature of the *multiple*-media assets involved.

Knowing full well that issuance of copyrights might otherwise tend to chill creative endeavors for other artists and developers, statutes and case law have presented some effective defenses to avoid certain of these impediments. The most common defenses are:

[1] There was a lack of *access* or *substantial (or probative) similarity.*

[2] The claimant has an *invalid (or unregistered) copyright.*

[3] The allegedly infringed materials were in the *public domain.*

[4] The allegedly infringed materials were subject to *fair use.*

[5] The allegedly infringed materials were *scènes à faire.*

[6] There was a *misuse* of the subject copyright.

[7] The claim is federally *preempted.*

[8] The claim is within scope of statutory *safe harbor* provisions.

---

§ 6.71 Non-Infringement

A lack of access by the alleged infringer or a lack of substantial similarity between the copyrighted work and accused material will defeat a claim of copyright infringement.

These are not matters involving affirmative defenses. Rather, they are negations of the plaintiff's obligation to establish a prima facie case. Defense attorneys, nevertheless, often list the items among their affirmative defenses even though the burdens of proof for such issues remain with the plaintiff.

---

§ 6.72 Copyright Invalidity

There are several reasons why an individual plaintiff might be unable to successfully pursue a copyright infringement claim. First, of course, in order to maintain such a claim the plaintiff must be the copyright owner. See § 501(b) of the *Copyright Act*. (*See* Appendix A). Second, even a valid copyright owner cannot sue for infringement unless he or she first files a copyright registration with the Copyright office. And, even though the receipt of a registration may be prima facie evidence of a valid copyright, it is by no means conclusive. 17 U.S.C.A. § 411(a). *See Jefferson Airplane v. Berkeley Syss., Inc.*, 886 F.Supp. 713 (N.D. Cal. 1995). Also, there may be notice requirements, depending upon the year that the work was first published. See § 401 of the *Act*. The issue as to whether or not video games are, in general, entitled to copyright protection has been put to rest. (*See* § 5.2, *supra*).

---

§ 6.73 The Public Domain

The "public domain" is a broad residuary that covers a wide range of literary, artistic and creative products. The laws of mathematics, physics, science in general, and the "law" as embodied in judicial decisions are all in the public domain. So too are historical facts. Items or works within the public domain may be used by everyone, and exclusively claimed by no one. In essence, all literary works that are not otherwise protected by copyright might be considered as being *in the public domain*. They are, therefore, available for free use by videogame developers.

Recognizing the *public domain* concept, in any copyright infringement action there are certain "unprotectable elements" which the court must filter out as it compares a copyrighted work and an allegedly infringing work. These include: ideas (as distinguished from the expression of those ideas), facts, historical events, or other information over which no individual is entitled to claim a monopoly. *Idema v. Dreamworks, Inc.*, 162 F. Supp. 2d 1129 (C.D. Cal. 2001).

Under earlier copyright acts it was not uncommon for once-protected copyrighted works to *fall into* the public domain. A defect in a copyright notice or a failure to follow the strict renewal requirements could cause a work to fall into the public domain. For example, in *Religious Tech. Center v. Netcom On-line Comm. Serv., Inc.*, 923 F. Supp. 1231 (N.D. Cal. 1995), it was held that a copyright for works that were registered under the Copyright Act of 1909 that was not renewed 28 years after the initial publication fell into the public domain and could not be the subject of an infringement action, even though the works were registered within the required 28 year period as part of the collection. *See also* 17 U.S.C.A. §§ 101 et seq. Thus, prior to the more recent copyright statutes (i.e., pre-1976), published works could fall into the public domain through mere general neglect. With the more liberal statutory provisions of the 1976 Act, the public domain defense has diminished.

Recall that under the 1976 Copyright Act, an author's copyright attaches automatically to an authored work as it is created. Unless early music or video is employed, video game developers are, therefore, not likely to encounter the problems raised by the earlier copyright statutes. In fact, games and authored works, in general, created after March 1, 1989, do not even require a copyright notice to be enforceable. 17 U.S.C.A. §§ 401 et seq. Coupled with the extended durations granted by 17 U.S.C.A. §§ 301 et seq., it is highly unlikely that any video games will slip into the public domain in the near future. Though rare, it is, however, still possible for a video game concept to be so general or generic that the product itself may be considered as public domain *ab initio*. *See Atari Games Corp. v. Oman*, 693 F. Supp. 1204 (D.D.C. 1988); *but see Feist Pubs. v. Rural Tel. Serv. Co.*, 499 U.S. 340 (1991), which lowered the bar considerably.

---

§ 6.74 Fair Use

Fair use can be thought of as an *anti-copyright* provision. It is a complete defense to a copyright infringement action. Once a vague, unpredictable concept, it covered a variety of uses and suspected uses; in many cases, one could not be certain whether or not it applied to a given situation. A few matters have always been relatively certain. First, fair use does not require permission. In fact, where fair use applies, the rightful author and copyright holder of the work cannot prevent its limited copying nor its dissemination by the "fair user." Secondly, fair use has always been limited in its scope. There were no uses that are completely unrestricted. Next, common sense and some spotted precedents suggest that certain uses fell within the scope of "fair use" protection, including: Use for educational purposes, historical purposes, and for purposes of criticism or parody.

Because of its diverse nature, the videogame industry must be particularly sensitive about fair use. The application of the doctrine must be fair to both the authors of existing creative works and to those who wish become authors of future works. Perhaps Judge Blackmun said it best in his dissenting opinion in *Sony Corp. of Am. v. Universal City Studios, Inc.*, 464 U.S. 417, 479 (1984):

> The fair use doctrine must strike a balance between the dual risks created by the copyright system: on the one hand, that depriving authors of their monopoly will reduce their incentive to create, and, on the other, that granting authors a complete monopoly will reduce the creative ability of others.

Historically, "*Public Domain*" and "*Fair Use*" were among the most widely asserted common law defenses to copyright infringement claims. Since the public domain issues have diminished, *Fair use* has now taken center stage. Once considered a vague ad hoc topic, it has now been codified as part of Title 17, which sets forth a four element test:

§ 107. **Limitations on exclusive rights: Fair use.**

Notwithstanding the provisions of sections 106 and 106A,[14] the fair use of a copyrighted work, including such use by reproduction in copies or phonorecords or by any other means specified by that section, for purposes such as criticism, comment, news reporting, teaching (including multiple copies for classroom use), scholarship, or research, is not an infringement of copyright. In determining whether the use made of a work in any particular case is a fair use the factors to be considered shall include—

---

14. Section 106 and 106A list the basic proprietary rights to which copyright owners are entitled. *See* Appendix A.

(1) the purpose and character of the use, including whether such use is of a commercial nature or is for nonprofit educational purposes;

(2) the nature of the copyrighted work;

(3) the amount and substantiality of the portion used in relation to the copyrighted work as a whole; and

(4) the effect of the use upon the potential market for or value of the copyrighted work.

The debates and uncertainties over which of the fair use test elements predominated, were put to rest by the landmark *Campbell v. Acuff-Rose Music, Inc.*, 510 U.S. 569 (1994), where the Court determined that they were essentially equal. Prior to the ruling, there was a split among the circuits as to whether or not a commercial motive should automatically weight heavily against fair use. According to the High Court, it was error for the Court of Appeals to conclude that the commercial nature of a parody rendered it "presumptively unfair."

It is important to note that fair use is a rather ubiquitous defense and one that might be expected whenever the defendant admits copying or is otherwise caught red-handed; the defense continues to be important even though in this digital age of increased piracy, there is increasing pressure to reduce or diminish its efficacy. PAUL GOLDSTEIN, COPYRIGHT'S HIGHWAY 224 (Hill & Wang 1994).

Other than the *Bleem* case that follows, can you identify other cases in this chapter or other chapters where the defense was asserted?

* * *

Sony Computer Entm't of Am. v. Bleem

United States Court of Appeals, Ninth Circuit, 2000
214 F.3d 1022

O'SCANNLAIN, Circuit Judge

We must decide whether the unauthorized use of a "screen shot," a frozen image from a personal video game, falls within the fair use exception to the law of copyright.

I.

Personal video games come in two basic varieties: console games and PC games. Console games are played by loading a game disk into a console, which is connected to the user's television. PC games are played by loading a game disk into the CD drive of a personal computer. Sony Computer Entertainment America, Inc., ("Sony") manufactures both consoles—the highly popular Sony PlayStation—and their game disks. Sony PlayStation game disks are engineered such that they cannot be played on a PC.

Bleem, LLC ("Bleem"), has developed a product, called a "software emulator," that allows one to cross the divide between console games and PC games. By using Bleem's software, one can now play a Sony PlayStation game on a personal computer. This development has two consequences: first, one need not buy a PlayStation console in order to enjoy Sony PlayStation games; second, the quality of the games' graphics may be greater because a computer screen is capable of greater resolution than a television screen. Bleem's product therefore allows it to tap into the two segments of video game players. For those enthusiastic video game players who do not want to pay for a PlayStation console, they can avoid having to do so by paying a smaller sum for the Bleem software. For those afficionados who have already purchased a Sony PlayStation console, the new Bleem software allows them to enjoy their games even more by playing them on a computer.

The video game market is enormous and lucrative, and Sony, with its PlayStation console and games, is a market leader, having sold more than 60 million consoles and 460 million video game disks worldwide. Emulators, such as that produced by Bleem, may not adversely affect the sales of Sony game *disks*—in fact, they may help them—but emulators very likely will reduce the sales of *consoles*.

The Bleem emulator was developed by Randy Linden who, together with David Herpolsheimer, comprise the entire staff of Bleem. Linden developed PC software that effectively emulates the function performed by Sony's hardware console through a process of reverse-engineering the components in the console. He devised a computer program to perform these same functions on a personal computer. The legality of the emulator is not at issue in this lawsuit.

The issue in this appeal is the validity of the method by which Bleem is advertising its product. In various advertising media, Bleem has included comparative "screen shots" of Sony PlayStation games. The shots show what the game looks like when played with a Sony console on a television screen, what it looks like when played with Bleem's emulator on a computer screen, and also at times what it looks like when played with Bleem's emulator and speed-enhancing hardware (called a graphics card) on a computer screen.

Screen shots are ubiquitous in the packaging of video games because they convey to the purchaser exactly what the game will look like on a screen when it is played. This slice of verisimilitude is important because the majority of the packaging of most typical video games is ornate artwork that evokes the spirit of the game, if not necessarily the visual truth of it. For instance, a video game such as *Gran Turismo*—Sony's best-selling, racing car game—might come packaged in a box featuring an almost photographic reproduction of a racing car in action. Since graphics in video games are good, but not that good, however, Sony also places a few screen shots on the packaging to show what the game actually does look like.

The veracity of the screen shots is not at issue in this appeal. Sony has not alleged that Bleem's depictions of the games played in different ways are inaccurate or misleading; it simply contends that Bleem may not use those screen shots because they are Sony's copyrighted material.

As one might imagine, screen shots for console games are regularly generated by freezing a game in mid-action and "grabbing" the image as it is displayed on the television. Screen shots can also be generated by grabbing the image as the game is played on a computer, but then adjusting the resolution downward to approximate the inferior resolution of a television screen. The first method involves a greater degree of verisimilitude to the claim that the screen shot represents what the game in fact looks like when played with a PlayStation console. The second method, however, is technologically easier.

The only issue on appeal is whether Bleem's unauthorized use of Sony PlayStation game screen shots in its advertising was a violation of Sony's copyright. The district court ruled in favor of Sony, entering a preliminary injunction against Bleem. Bleem filed a timely appeal.

II.

Bleem admits that it copied Sony's copyrighted games to create screen shots for its advertising but contends that doing so was protected as a fair use under 17 U.S.C. § 107.

III.

Justice Story introduced the concept of an exception to the law of copyright for fair uses in 1841. *See Folsom v. Marsh*, 9 F. Cas. 342 (C.C.D.Mass.1841). Distilling the common law from earlier cases, he provided that courts should:

> look to the nature and objects of the selections made, the quantity and value of the materials used, and the degree in which the use may prejudice the sale, or diminish the profits, or supersede the objects, of the original work.

Id. at 348. Expressed as such, fair use continued as exclusively a judge-made doctrine until the enactment of the 1976 Copyright Act, in which Justice Story's words were codified:

> Notwithstanding the provisions of section 106, the fair use of a copyrighted work, including such use by reproduction in copies or phonorecords or by any other means specified by that section, for purposes such as criticism, comment, news reporting, teaching (including multiple copies for classroom use), scholarship, or research, is not an infringement of copyright. In determining whether the use made of a work in any particular case is a fair use the factors to be considered shall include (17 U.S.C. § 107) : (a) the purpose and character of the use, including whether such use is of a commercial nature or is for nonprofit educational purposes; (b) the nature of the copyrighted work; (c) the amount and substantiality of the portion used in relation to the copyrighted work as a whole; and (d) the effect of the use upon the potential market for or value of the copyrighted work.

The fair use doctrine thus "permits [and requires] courts to avoid rigid application of the copyright statute when, on occasion, it would stifle the very creativity which that law is designed to foster." *Campbell v. Acuff-Rose Music, Inc.*, 510 U.S. 569, 577 (1994). The process of applying these fair use factors to the facts of any particular scenario calls for case-by-case analysis, and the "task is not to be simplified with bright-line rules." The four factors are to be considered together in light of the purposes of copyright, not in isolation.

In this analysis, the commercial use of copyrighted material is not presumptively unfair; rather, commercial use is but one of four factors that we must weigh. The Supreme Court expressly rejected the irrebutability of the presumption against fair use in commercial contexts in *Campbell* when the Court flatly reversed the Sixth Circuit for making just such a presumption. 510 U.S. at 590–91, 114 S.Ct. 1164. The Court emphasized that, although the fourth factor may be the most important, all factors must be considered, and the commercial nature of the copies is just one element in the broader calculus. We must therefore examine each of the § 107 factors to evaluate Bleem's fair use defense.

A.

The fact that Bleem copied Sony's copyrighted material for commercial purposes is an element of both the first § 107 factor and the fourth. Bleem used screen shots for Sony games on its advertising to provide a comparison between what the games look like when played with a Sony PlayStation console and what they look like when played with Bleem's emulator on a personal computer. We conclude that Bleem's use of the screen shots constitutes comparative advertising.

This question of whether the two companies compete is an important consideration because, with respect to the first factor, interpreting the copying as comparative advertising is *more* likely to lead to a conclusion of fair use; but, with respect to the fourth factor, determining that the copying will have a detrimental impact on the copyright holder's profits is *less* likely to lead to a conclusion of fair use. These issues thus cut against one another, which forces advocates into awkward argumentative corners. Bleem, for instance, insists that the two companies do not compete with respect to any impact on profits but that they can be comparatively advertised. Similarly, Sony argues that of course Bleem's product will harm its sales, but that it is not a competitor, so it should not therefore be allowed the benefit of comparative advertising.

What is manifestly clear, however, is that the Bleem emulator does compete directly with the Sony PlayStation console. In order to play a Sony video game, one can choose to purchase either a PlayStation console (assuming one has a television) or the Bleem emulator (assuming one has a personal computer). Thus, the greater Bleem's sales, the less likely people will buy Sony's consoles. Of course, people can buy both. Of course, to the extent Bleem's software affects sales of Sony *games*, it will only do so beneficially, since a greater universe of people will now be able to play them. Nevertheless, Bleem's software competes with Sony's *consoles* with respect to both comparative advertising under the first factor and profits under the fourth.

We have not decided, apparently, any cases on the issue of comparative advertising after the codification of the fair use doctrine, but the Fifth Circuit has. The leading case involved a television commercial in which the *Miami Herald* displayed a cover of the copyrighted magazine, *TV Guide*, for the purposes of comparing it to its own analogous publication. *See Triangle Publications, Inc. v. Knight-Ridder Newspapers, Inc.*, 626 F.2d 1171 (5th Cir.1980). The Fifth Circuit noted that the cover of *TV Guide* was clearly copyrighted and the *Herald* had just as clearly reproduced it for a commercial purpose: to sell its own product. The court nevertheless found, after a § 107 analysis, that the reproduction was a fair use. With respect to the first factor, the Fifth Circuit noted the public benefit of comparative advertising as a means of providing more information to the public and concluded that this factor weighed in the defendant's favor.

Sony does not contend that Bleem's screen shots are untruthful or deceptive. [B]y seeing how the games' graphics look on a television when played on a console as compared to how they look on a computer screen when played with Bleem's emulator, consumers will be most able to make "rational purchase decisions." Sony argues that Bleem can advertise without the screen shots, which is certainly true, but no other way will allow for the clearest consumer decisionmaking. Indeed, Bleem's advertising in this fashion will almost certainly lead to product improvements as Sony responds to this competitive threat and as other emulator producers strive for even better performance.

The first factor, considered in light of the animating principles of the copyright regime, weighs in Bleem's favor. [C]omparative advertising redounds greatly to the purchasing public's benefit with very little corresponding loss to the integrity of Sony's copyrighted material.

B.

The second factor under § 107 is the nature of the copyrighted work. This factor is of most relevance to the fair use analysis when the original material and the copy are of a different nature. For instance, if the copyrighted work is out of print and cannot be purchased, a user may be more likely to prevail on a fair use defense. On the other hand, if the copyrighted material is unpublished and creative while the copy is a commercial publication, courts would be less receptive to the defense of fair use. In this case, the copyrighted work and the copies are both commercial video game products; although the copyrighted work is creative in nature generally, a screen shot is not necessarily. A screen shot is merely an inanimate sliver of the game.

The Supreme Court has passed over this factor without giving it much attention, stating that it is often "not much help." *Campbell*, 510 U.S. at 586. [I]n this appeal this factor "neither supports nor hurts [defendant's] claim that a fair use defense is appropriate here."

C.

Clearly, the greater the degree of copying involved and the closer those copies are to the essence of the copyrighted work, the less likely the copying is a fair use. To evaluate this factor with respect to screen shots, some more technical detail may be helpful. Video games, much like motion pictures, create the illusion of movement by displaying in rapid succession a series of still pictures with incremental differences. Film is projected at 24 frames per second; video is projected at 30 frames per second. A screen shot is therefore 1/30th of a second's worth of the video game. Temporally, therefore, there can be no doubt that a screen shot is a small amount of a video game. Inasmuch as these games involve plots that can be controlled interactively by the player and may elapse over several hours, it also seems true that a screen shot is of little substance to the overall copyrighted work. [T]he third factor will almost always weigh against the video game manufacturer since a screen shot is such an insignificant portion of the complex copyrighted work as a whole. Here, too, it seems clear that the third factor supports a finding of fair use.

D.

In addressing this fourth and most important factor, the Supreme Court considered not only the extent of market harm caused by the particular actions of the alleged infringer, but also "whether unrestricted and widespread conduct of the sort engaged in by the defendant ... would result in a substantially adverse impact on the potential market." *Campbell*, 510 U.S. at 590, 114 S.Ct. 1164 (quoting 3 M. Nimmer & D. Nimmer, *Nimmer on Copyright*, § 13.05[A][4], at 13-102.61 (1993)). The first question in this appeal is what precisely the market is. The market cannot be the video games themselves because it is the emulator that competes in that niche, not the screen shots that adorn the emulator's advertising. We have already ruled that the emulator is not a violation of the copyright laws. Sony argues that the market is in the screen shots themselves: Bleem's use of the screen shots impinges upon Sony's ability to use the screen shots for promotional purposes in the market. Bleem responds by contending that there is no *market* in screen shots. Certainly screen shots are a standard device used in the industry to demonstrate video game graphics, but there is not a market for them, or at least not one in which Bleem may participate given Sony's refusal to license to it.

Assuming there is a market for screen shots, however, this factor still weighs in Bleem's favor, not because Bleem does not compete with Sony, as it contends, but because almost all precedent indicates that this sort of use does not sufficiently impair Sony. First, the Supreme Court has noted that commercial use is not a controlling factor in this question and that a use of the copyrighted work to critique the work may harm its market without producing cognizable harm under the Copyright Act. *Campbell*, 510 U.S. at 591–92 (providing the example of a "scathing theater review" that "kills demand for the original" while still being a fair use). Second, the Fifth Circuit's comparative advertising decision similarly plays down such a "de minimis" effect on the copyrighted material's market:

> If the plaintiff loses a significant share of its present market, that would result not from the display of plaintiff's cover in defendant's advertising but from commercial competition with a work that does not in any way make use of plaintiff's copyrighted material.

Triangle Publications, 626 F.2d at 1177. We made a similar observation in our recent decision, also involving Sony, stating that

> some economic loss by Sony as a result of this competition does not compel a finding of no fair use. Sony understandably seeks control over the market for devices that play games Sony produces or licenses. The copyright law, however, does not confer such a monopoly.

Connectix, 203 F.3d at 607.

Bleem's use of a handful of screen shots in its advertising will have no noticeable effect on Sony's ability to do with its screen shots what it chooses. If sales of Sony consoles drop, it will be due to the Bleem emulator's technical superiority over the PlayStation console, not because Bleem used screen shots to illustrate that comparison. This fourth factor, like all the others, appears to weigh in Bleem's favor.

V.

We must qualify our holding with one caveat. Our conclusions with respect to Bleem's use of screen shots apply only to those screen shots that Bleem has generated by taking the actual images of Sony's games from a television screen. The entire premise of comparative advertising is that the consumer is being made aware of the true choices. To the extent Bleem merely approximates what the PlayStation games look like, by generating screen shots through a process of degrading a computer image, it is simply creating a simulation. If Bleem insists on generating simulated approximations of Sony's games, there is no need for Bleem to use Sony's copyrighted material whatsoever.

We conclude that it is a fair use for Bleem to advertise comparatively only between what PlayStation games *actually* look like on a television and what they *actually* look like on a computer when played with the emulator. It is in this context alone that the comparison is necessarily Sony-specific. We are persuaded by the need for Bleem to impose minimally upon Sony's copyright with respect to these screen shots because there is no other way to create a truly accurate comparison for the user. The way of simulations is a slippery one for Bleem and if it chooses to embark upon it, it must do so without the support of Sony's copyright. With that limitation in mind, we conclude that Bleem's use of Sony's copyrighted material was fair.

Notes and Questions

1. Do you think that there was any validity whatsoever to Sony's claim that Bleem was *not* a competitor? How did the court handle the apparent inconsistency in Sony's argument with respect to the fourth Fair Use Factor (i.e., If Bleem wasn't a competitor, then there would no loss of business resulting from an adverse effect on the Sony's market)? When considering the fourth factor, the Court said: "Bleem's uses of a handful of screen shots in its advertising will have no noticeable effect on Sony's ability to do with its screen shots what it chooses." Did this statement by the Ninth Circuit truly address the fourth Factor, or did it merely restate Sony's rights under Section 106 of the Copyright Act?

2. Did *Bleem* present an issue regarding substantial similarity? Could Sony ever demonstrate substantial similarity between a video game and a single screen shot? The Ninth Circuit suggested there was no substantial similarity when it said, "a screen shot is such an insignificant portion of the complex copyrighted work as a whole." Is this a non-issue? Remember that where there is literal copying, a showing of substantial similarity would be superfluous.

3. How does the "substantial similarity" requirement interact with the third Fair Use factor? ("The amount and substantiality of the portion used in relation to the copyrighted work as a whole." 17 U.S.C. § 107). Should it? With respect to the potential confusion caused by these related concepts, *see* MELVILLE B. NIMMER & DAVID NIMMER, 4–13 NIMMER ON COPYRIGHT § 13.03[A][2][a], concerning cases "that purport to turn on the doctrine of fair use, but actually simply determine whether, in the given instance, there is substantial similarity between the two works." *See also Castle Rock Entertainment v. Carol Publ'g Group*, 150 F.3d 132, 144 (2d Cir. 1998), and *M. Kramer Mfg. Co. v. Andrews*, 783 F.2d 421 (4th Cir. 1986).

4. For most, our earliest encounters with the Fair Use Doctrine came in grade school as our teachers freely photocopied and distributed a variety of copyrighted works without giving a second thought about potential copyright violations. In order to keep everyone on the "straight and narrow" with respect to potential piracy and attempts to place some restraints on the Fair Use Doctrine, The Entertainment Software Association has taken upon itself to produce a series of articles and activities for elementary school children. In its materials, teachers are taught to complete one activity as follows:

> Conclude this discussion by reminding students that the special rules for respecting intellectual property in school *don't* apply outside the classroom. Students are allowed to copy short passages of copyrighted text, individual copyrighted images, and excerpts from other copyrighted material in their school work, as long as they credit their sources. This is called "fair use." But *no one* is allowed to copy copyrighted material outside the classroom for any reason without permission.

See *Join the ©Team!: An Educational Program Encouraging Creativity and Respect for Intellectual Property Law*, Grades 4–5 at 9 (ESA 2005). How does the above agenda connect with the ESA's interests?

5. In *Sony Computer Ent. Am., Inc. v. GameMasters, Inc.*, 87 F. Supp. 2d 976 (N.D. Cal. 1999), the district court considered a fair use problem involving photocopies of video game covers. GameMasters was a retail store that sold used video games. Instead of placing actual games or the original packaging for the games on the sales floor, GameMasters instead displayed color-photocopies of the video game covers, claiming that this prevented shoplifting. *Id.* at 989. Sony requested that the court enjoin GameMasters from "using color photo-copies of SCEA video-game covers to display second hand games for sale from defendant's inventory." *Id.* It is notable that GameMasters was also accused of selling counterfeit video games. The District Court denied fair use, relying on the Supreme Court's statement that "every commercial use of copyrighted material is presumptively an unfair exploitation of the monopoly privilege that belongs to the owner of the copyright." *Id.* (quoting *Sony Corp. of Am. v. Universal City Studios, Inc.*, 464 U.S. 417, 451 (1984)). Was this ruling by the District Court defensible in light of *Campbell v. Acuff-Rose Music*, 510 U.S. 569 (1994), that had been decided several years earlier? Consider this dicta from *Campbell*:

> The Court of Appeals, however, immediately cut short the enquiry into 2 Live Crew's fair use claim by confining its treatment of the first factor essentially to one relevant fact, the commercial nature of the use. The court then inflated the significance of this fact by applying a presumption ostensibly culled from *Sony*, that "every commercial use of copyrighted material is presumptively ... unfair...." *Sony*, 464 U.S. at 451. In giving virtually dispositive weight to the commercial nature of the parody, the Court of Appeals erred.
>
> The language of the statute makes clear that the commercial or nonprofit educational purpose of a work is only one element of the first factor enquiry

into its purpose and character. Section 107(1) uses the term "including" to begin the dependent clause referring to commercial use, and the main clause speaks of a broader investigation into "purpose and character." As we explained in *Harper & Row* [471 U.S. 539 (1985)], Congress resisted attempts to narrow the ambit of this traditional enquiry by adopting categories of presumptively fair use, and it urged courts to preserve the breadth of their traditionally ample view of the universe of relevant evidence. 471 U.S. at 561; House Report, p. 66. Accordingly, the mere fact that a use is educational and not for profit does not insulate it from a finding of infringement, any more than the commercial character of a use bars a finding of fairness. If, indeed, commerciality carried presumptive force against a finding of fairness, the presumption would swallow nearly all of the illustrative uses listed in the preamble paragraph of § 107, including news reporting, comment, criticism, teaching, scholarship, and research, since these activities "are generally conducted for profit in this country." *Harper & Row, supra,* at 592 (Brennan, J., dissenting). Congress could not have intended such a rule, which certainly is not inferable from the common-law cases, arising as they did from the world of letters in which Samuel Johnson could pronounce that "no man but a blockhead ever wrote, except for money." 3 Boswell's Life of Johnson 19 (G. Hill ed. 1934).

Id. at 583–84.

6. In *Bleem,* the plaintiff contended that the Game Enhancer permitted users to play counterfeit copies of original PlayStation software. Defendants denied the claim. The user instructions for the Game Enhancer referred to "Play Imports" but did not in any way refer to "backups" or "bootlegs" or "copies." Sony submitted advertising from a website suggesting that the Game Enhancer did in fact enable users to play counterfeit games, but no evidence suggested that GameMasters sold or possessed any such game. Should the manner in which the subject product is advertised be relevant? *See MGM Studios v. Grokster, Ltd.,* 545 U.S. 913 (2005).

7. For videogames in particular, the Fair Use doctrine assumes importance due to the multitude of artistic endeavors from which the media borrows. Sound effects, music, songs, photographic images, animation, plots, stories, game elements and computer code are but a few. Can you think of any others?

8. During the widely publicized murder and wrongful death trials of O.J. Simpson in the 1990s, a videogame company considered creating a law-related game titled: "*Circus O.J.*" The content involved a rancorous parody of the defendant, along with the attorneys and prosecutors in the case. Photographic images of the actual parties would be used along with copyrighted newsreel footage. What problems, if any would you foresee?

---

§ 6.75 Merger and *Scènes à Faire*

Because videogames are often perceived as possessing a finite, limited number of themes, the *scènes à faire* concept is particularly significant. It pertains to standard elements with respect to a given topic, theme or subject. Those elements are not protected. The closely related doctrine of "merger" is derived from the basic premise that ideas, like *scènes à faire,* cannot be protected by copyright. Thus, where a non-protectable idea "merges" with an authored work, that work will not be protectable. These concepts are best clarified by the cases and discussions that follow.

Scènes à faire refers to "incidents, characters or settings which are as a practical matter indispensable, or at least standard, in the treatment of a given topic." *Alexander v. Haley*, 460 F. Supp. 40, 45 (S.D.N.Y. 1978); *see also Hoehling v. Universal City Studios, Inc.*, 618 F.2d 972, 979 (2d Cir. 1980). Stated yet another way, "similarity of expression, whether literal or nonliteral, which necessarily results from the fact that the common idea is only capable of expression in more or less stereotyped form will preclude a finding of actionable similarity." 3 Melville B. Nimmer & David Nimmer, Nimmer on Copyright § 13.03(A)(1), at 13–28. *See also Morrissey v. Procter & Gamble Co.*, 379 F.2d 675, 678 (1st Cir. 1967); *Affiliated Hosp. Prods., Inc. v. Merdel Game Mfg. Co.*, 513 F.2d 1183, 1188–89 (2d Cir. 1975). For example, it would be difficult to imagine a "zombie" game that did not have "dead" avatars who walk with a stiff gait and their arms held out in front of them. No company could copyright such a character.

An idea or generic concept, which cannot be protected by copyright, often implies and entails more specific elements which *can* be fixed in a tangible medium of expression. The popular videogame *Flight Simulator* by Microsoft, for example, was predicated upon an "idea" for a game that placed a player in the make-believe cockpit of an airplane. The game screen provided a steering wheel, altimeter, gas gage, and all of the other instruments that one would normally expect to see in real aircraft. Copyright holder Microsoft would never claim that it held a monopoly that prohibited everyone else from making a similar game. And, while Microsoft could, in fact, protect its particular art work and game engine, it *could not* prevent others from displaying a steering wheel, altimeter, gas gage, and all of the other commonly used instruments. These elements, sometimes referred to as "*scènes à faire*," follow directly from the "*idea*" of an aircraft simulator and are, therefore, no more protectable than the idea of the aircraft simulator itself. In other words, copyright protection cannot be granted to elements of expression that necessarily follow from an idea, or to *scènes à faire*, expressions that are "as a practical matter, indispensable or at least standard in the treatment of a given idea." *Atari, Inc. v. North Am. Phillips Consumer Electronics Corp.*, 672 F.2d 607, 616 (7th Cir. 1982).

Atari v. Amusement World, Inc., 547 F. Supp. 222, 215 U.S.P.Q. 929 (D. Md. 1981) provided a classic *scènes à faire* showdown between *Asteroids* (See *Figure* 1.6) and the alleged infringer "*Meteors.*" The court provided an element comparison of the two games and found: "It seems clear that defendants based their game on plaintiff's copyrighted game; to put it bluntly, defendants took plaintiff's idea. However, the copyright laws do not prohibit this. Copyright protection is available only for expression of ideas, not for ideas themselves. Defendants used plaintiff's idea and those portions of plaintiff's expression that were inextricably linked to that idea. The remainder of defendants' expression is different from plaintiff's expression. Therefore, the Court finds that defendants' *Meteors* game is not substantially similar to and is not an infringing copy of plaintiff's *Asteroids* game."

Notes and Questions

1. How far could the *scènes à faire* argument be expanded and applied to some of the classic videogames? More particularly, might it be said that all maze games or first-person shooter games share certain indispensable elements?

2. *Team Play, Inc. v. Boyer*, 391 F. Supp. 2d 695 (N.D. Ill., 2003) involved infringement battles over videogames *Police Trainer, Police Trainer 2*, and *Sharpshooter*. The controverted game elements featured a shooting gallery scenario wherein targets floated out of a

cylindrical opening in the floor. The targets were randomly arranged so that the player was required to remember them and keep the targets in order. These elements along with other embellishments relating to silver iconic objects that appeared next to each completed challenge (to indicate progress) were, according to the court, embodiments of an un-copyrightable idea, *scènes à faire*, or both.

3. In *JCW Investments, Inc., Novelty, Inc.*, 289 F. Supp. 2d 1023, (N.D. Ill. 2003), a doll manufacturer sued a competitor for copyright infringement. On cross-motions for summary judgment, the District Court held that features shared by the subject competing dolls were not "*scènes à faire*" so as to preclude an infringement claim. The copyrighted work consisted of a doll that talked and farted. The court determined that the Defendant's argument that those features (which were shared by the two dolls) as "*scènes à faire*" was unpersuasive. "*Scènes à faire*," according to the court, refers to "incidents, characters or settings which are as a practical matter indispensable, or at least standard, in the treatment of a given topic." The court indicated that defendant's assertion that it is "standard" to stereotype a character that finds humor in farting and joking about it as having low socioeconomic status is mere conjecture, unsupported by any evidence (empirical or otherwise) in the record. This court also found defendant's argument more than "a bit insulting and condescending." Defendant directed the court's attention to excerpts from Jim Dawson's Who Cut the Cheese? A Cultural History of the Fart, Ten Speed Press (1999), as evidence that "'fart jokes' have long been popular 'among the lower classes' and 'poor people.'" Assuming arguendo that this proposition is true, however, did not dictate that it was "standard" to depict a farting character as having low socioeconomic status.

4. For evidentiary purposes, is *scènes à faire* to be treated as an affirmative defense with the burden of proof resting upon the defendant or is it a potential hurdle with respect to copyrightability? Should it matter? *See Satava v. Lowry*, 323 F.3d 805, 810, n.3 (9th Cir. 2003), and *Ets-Hokin v. Sky Spirits*, 225 F.3d 1068, 1082 (9th Cir. 2000) (indicating that it is the former).

* * *

Data East USA v. Epyx, Inc.

United States Court of Appeals, Ninth Circuit, 1988
862 F.2d 204

TROTT, Circuit Judge

Plaintiff-appellee Data East USA, Inc., brought this action against defendant-appellant Epyx, Inc. for copyright, trademark, and trade dress infringement. The district court found a copyright infringement and issued a permanent injunction and impoundment. Epyx appeals the grant of the permanent injunction. Epyx contends (1) the district court erred in granting the injunction because Epyx never had access to Data East's copyrighted work, (2) the district court erred in finding substantial similarity, and (3) the district court's injunction was impermissibly vague and overbroad. We reverse.

I. FACTS

Data East is a California corporation engaged in the design, manufacture, and sale of audio-visual works embodied in video games for coin-operated and home computer use. In July 1984, Data East commenced distribution in Japan of an arcade game entitled "Karate Champ" ("Arcade # 1"). In September 1984, Data East commenced distribution in Japan and later in the United States and Europe of an updated version of "Karate Champ" ("Arcade # 2" or more generally as "arcade game"). Finally, on October 12, 1985,

Data East commenced distribution in the United States of a home computer game version of "Karate Champ" ("home game"). Data East applied for and received audio-visual copyright certificates for each game.

In November of 1985, System III Software, Ltd., an English company, commenced distribution in England of a home computer game entitled "International Karate." Epyx, a California corporation engaged in the development and distribution of audio-visual works for use on home computers, obtained a license agreement with System III and commenced distribution in the United States on April 30, 1986 of a Commodore-compatible version of "International Karate" under the name "World Karate Championship."

Each competing product, "Karate Champ" and "World Karate Championship," consists of the audio-visual depiction of a karate match or matches conducted by two combatants, one clad in a typical white outfit and the other in red. Successive phases of combat are conducted against varying stationary background images depicting localities or geographic scenes. The match is supervised by a referee who directs the beginning and end of each phase of combat and announces the winning combatant of each phase by means of a cartoon-style speech balloon. Each game has a bonus round where the karate combatant breaks bricks and dodges objects. Similarities also exist in the moves used by the combatants and the scoring method.

Data East alleged that the overall appearance, compilation, and sequence of the audio-visual display of the video game "World Karate Championship" infringed its copyright for "Karate Champ" as embodied in the arcade and home versions of the video game. Data East also charged Epyx with trademark and trade dress infringement.

The district court found that except for the graphic quality of Epyx's expressions, part of the scoreboard, the referee's physical appearance, and minor particulars in the "bonus phases," Data East's and Epyx's games are qualitatively identical. The district court then held that Epyx's game infringes the copyright Data East has in "Karate Champ." The district court, however, found no trademark or trade dress infringement. Based upon its decision, the district court permanently restrained and enjoined Epyx from copying, preparing derivative works, distributing, performing, or displaying the copyrighted work in the "Karate Champ" video game, the "World Karate Championship" game, or the "International Karate" game. A recall of all Commodore computer games of "World Karate Championship" and "International Karate" was ordered. This appeal followed.

II. DISCUSSION

To establish copyright infringement, Data East must prove both ownership of a valid copyright and "copying" by Epyx of the copyrighted work. *Sid & Marty Krofft Television Products, Inc. v. McDonald's Corp.*, 562 F.2d 1157, 1162 (9th Cir.1977). It is undisputed that Data East is the registered copyright owner of the audio-visual work for each version of "Karate Champ." Thus we need only determine whether Epyx[15] copied "Karate Champ." This sounds simple and straightforward. It is not.

As in most infringement cases of this kind, no direct evidence was developed that System III Software or anybody else copied any version of Data East's product. There seldom is any direct evidence of copying in these matters. Therefore, copying may be established instead by circumstantial evidence of (1) the defendant's access to the copyrighted work prior to defendant's creation of its work, and (2) the substantial similarity of both

---

15. In actuality, Data East contends that Mr. Cale, the creator of "International Karate," copied "Karate Champ." We refer generally, however, to Epyx, the defendant, as the "copier."

the general ideas and expression between the copyrighted work and defendant's work. *Id.* In essence, the question of copying becomes a matter of reasonable inferences. Because we find no substantial similarity, we decline to address the issue of access.

To show that two works are substantially similar, plaintiff must demonstrate that the works are substantially similar in both ideas and expression. Although plaintiff must first show that the ideas are substantially similar, the ideas themselves are not protected by copyright and therefore, cannot be infringed. It is an axiom of copyright law that copyright protects only an author's expression of an idea, not the idea itself.[16] There is a strong public policy corollary to this axiom permitting all to use freely ideas contained in a copyrightable work, so long as the protected expression itself is not appropriated. Thus, to the extent the similarities between plaintiff's and defendant's works are confined to ideas and general concepts, these similarities are noninfringing.

The Ninth Circuit has developed a two-step test for the purposes of determining substantial similarity. First, an "extrinsic" test is used to determine whether two ideas are substantially similar. This is an objective test which rests upon specific criteria that can be listed and analyzed. *Krofft, id.* Second, an "intrinsic" test is used to compare forms of expression. This is a subjective test which depends on the response of the ordinary reasonable person. *Id.*

In applying the extrinsic test, the district court found that the idea expressed in plaintiff's game and in defendant's game is identical. The idea of the games was described by the court as follows:

> ... a martial arts karate combat game conducted between two combatants, and presided over by a referee, all of which are represented by visual images, and providing a method of scoring accomplished by full and half point scores for each player, and utilizing dots to depict full point scores and half point scores.

The district court further found that:

> In each of the games, the phases of martial arts combat are conducted against still background images purporting to depict geographic or locality situses and located at the top of the screen as the game is viewed. The action of the combatants in each of the games takes place in the lower portion of the screen as the game is viewed, and is against a one color background in that portion of the screen as the game is viewed.

Once an idea is found to be similar or identical, as in this case, the second or intrinsic step is applied to determine whether similarity of the expression of the idea occurs. This exists when the "total concept and feel of the works" is substantially similar. Analytic dissection of the dissimilarities as opposed to the similarities is not appropriate under this test because it distracts a reasonable observer from a comparison of the total concept and feel of the works.

The rule in the Ninth Circuit, however, is that "[n]o substantial similarity of expression will be found when 'the idea and its expression are ... inseparable,' given that 'protecting the expression in such circumstances would confer a monopoly of the idea upon the copyright owner.'" *Id.* (quoting *Herbert Rosenthal Jewelry Corp. v. Kalpakian*, 446 F.2d 738, 742 (9th Cir. 1971)).

---

16. This axiom is expressly codified in 17 U.S.C. § 102(b) (1982): "In no case does copyright protection for an original work of authorship extend to any idea ... [or] ... concept ... regardless of the form in which it is described, explained, illustrated, or embodied in such work."

Nor can copyright protection be afforded to elements of expression that necessarily follow from an idea, or to "scènes à faire," i.e., expressions that are as a practical matter, indispensable or at least standard in the treatment of a given [idea].

To determine whether similarities result from unprotectable expression, analytic dissection of *similarities* may be performed. If this demonstrates that all similarities in expression arise from use of common ideas, then no substantial similarity can be found. *Id.*

The district court performed what can be described as an analytic dissection of similarities in its findings of fact and stated:

Plaintiff's and defendant's games each encompass the idea of depicting the performance of karate martial arts combat in each of the following respects:

A. Each game has fourteen moves.

B. Each game has a two-player option.

C. Each game has a one-player option.

D. Each game has forward and backward somersault moves and about-face moves.

E. Each game has a squatting reverse punch wherein the heel is not on the ground.

F. Each game has an upper-lunge punch.

G. Each game has a back-foot sweep.

H. Each game has a jumping sidekick.

I. Each game has low kick.

J. Each game has a walk-backwards position.

K. Each game has changing background scenes.

L. Each game has 30-second countdown rounds.

M. Each game uses one referee.

N. In each game the referee says "begin," "stop," "white," "red," which is depicted by a cartoon-style speech balloon.

O. Each game has a provision for 100 bonus points per remaining second.

The district court found that the visual depiction of karate matches is subject to the constraints inherent in the sport of karate itself. The number of combatants, the stance employed by the combatants, established and recognized moves and motions regularly employed in the sport of karate, the regulation of the match by at least one referee or judge, and the manner of scoring by points and half points are among the constraints inherent in the sport of karate. Because of these constraints, karate is not susceptible of a wholly fanciful presentation. Furthermore, the use of the Commodore computer for a karate game intended for home consumption is subject to various constraints inherent in the use of that computer. Among the constraints are the use of sprites,[17] and a somewhat limited access to color, together with limitations upon the use of multiple colors in one visual image.

The fifteen features listed by the court "encompass the idea of karate." These features, which consist of the game procedure, common karate moves, the idea of background

---

17. A "sprite" involves the use of a special technique for creating mobile graphic images on a computer screen that is appropriate for animation. An increase in sophistication of sprite techniques used in the computer program will increase the graphic quality of the game's animation.

scenes, a time element, a referee, computer graphics, and bonus points, result from either constraints inherent in the sport of karate or computer restraints. After careful consideration and viewing of these features, we find that they necessarily follow from the *idea* of a martial arts karate combat game, or are inseparable from, indispensable to, or even standard treatment of the *idea* of the karate sport. As such, they are not protectable. "When idea and expression coincide, there will be protection against nothing other than identical copying." *Krofft*, 562 F.2d at 1168. A comparison of the works in this case demonstrates that identical copying is not an issue.

Accordingly, we hold that the court did not give the appropriate weight and import to its findings which support Epyx's argument that the similarities result from unprotectable expression. Consequently, it was clear error for the district court to determine that protectable substantial similarity existed based upon these facts.

The lower court erred by not limiting the scope of Data East's copyright protection to the author's contribution—the scoreboard and background scenes. In actuality, however, the backgrounds are quite dissimilar and the method of scorekeeping, though similar, is inconsequential. Based upon these two features, a discerning 17 year-old boy[18] could not regard the works as substantially similar. Accordingly, Data East's copyright was not infringed on this basis either.

* * *

Tetris Holding, LLC v. Xio Interactive, Inc.

United States District Court, District of New Jersey, 2012
863 F.Supp.2d 394

WOLFSON, District Judge

Presently before the Court are cross-motions for summary judgment. Plaintiffs Tetris Holding, LLC and the Tetris Company, LLC (collectively "Tetris Holding" or "Plaintiffs") claim that Defendant Xio Interactive, Inc. ("Xio" or "Defendant") has infringed the copyright and trade-dress of Plaintiffs' video game *Tetris*. Xio does not raise any issue of fact in response, but makes a purely legal argument that because it meticulously copied only non-protected elements, in particular the rules and functionality of the game, and not its expressive elements, that judgment should be entered in its favor. The motions stem from Tetris Holding's First Amended Complaint that alleges the Xio infringed Tetris Holding's copyright under 17 U.S.C. §§ 101 et seq. (Count One) [Discussions pertaining to other counts are omitted]

For the reasons that follow, Plaintiffs' motion is granted and Defendant's motion is denied.

I. BACKGROUND

The Court only recounts the facts necessary to resolve the parties' motions. The following facts are undisputed by the parties. The game of *Tetris* gained fame in the United States

---

18. The district court found that the average age of individuals purchasing "Karate Champ" is 17.5 years, that the purchasers are predominantly male, and comprise a knowledgeable, critical, and discerning group.

during the late 1980s and early 1990s as an electronic video game initially played on Nintendo's portable platform, the Gameboy, and on its console systems. Since that time, Tetris Holding has developed many versions for modern platforms.

Tetris is a facially simple puzzle game in which the player is tasked with creating complete horizontal lines along the bottom of the playing field by fitting several types of geometric block pieces (called tetrominos) together. The game becomes more complex and more difficult as you progress and are left with fewer options to arrange the pieces and less area of the playing field is available. Originally developed in Russia during the mid-1980s by Russian computer programmer Alexy Pajitnov, *Tetris* was exported to the United States and has since been adapted for the myriad electronic video game platforms available to consumers, including Apple Inc.'s iPhone. Pajitnov formed Tetris Holding, LLC, along with game designer, Henk Rogers. Tetris Holding, LLC owns the copyrights to the visual expression of the numerous *Tetris* iterations and licenses those rights to Tetris Company, LLC, which then sublicenses its rights. Companies have licensed Tetris Holding's intellectual property rights for a number of reasons. For example, Tetris Holding licensed the visual look of *Tetris:* (1) to Hallmark so it could design a *Tetris*-themed greeting card, (2) to states, such as New Jersey and Idaho, to create *Tetris*-themed lottery cards; and (3) to various television shows to use and reference *Tetris* in episodes. In the years since its development, *Tetris* has won numerous awards and accolades, and has been ranked high on several lists as one of the greatest video games of all time. It has sold over 200 million units worldwide. And *Tetris* continues to enjoy success through smart phones and social networking, with billions of games of *Tetris* being downloaded and played online.

Tetris Holding's success has also bred many unauthorized attempts at imitation. In response, *Tetris* has vigorously made a concerted effort to protect its intellectual property by pursuing such infringers through the legal process and removing hundreds of imitation games from the market. Tetris Holding alleges that Xio is one such company that has infringed its intellectual property, namely its copyrights and its trade dress, trading off the creative aspects of its work without authority.

Xio was formed by Desiree Golden, a recent college graduate, who decided to create a multiplayer puzzle game for the iPhone called "*Mino*" and admittedly used *Tetris* as inspiration. Indeed, Xio was more than inspired by *Tetris* as Xio readily admits that its game was copied from *Tetris* and was intended to be its version of *Tetris*. Plaintiffs point to Ms. Golden's statements that she was "trying to get a company started to make a MultiPlayer game similar to Tetris for the iPhone;" that some iPhone games "made by private developers have made 250K each in 2 months!;" and that Xio's game would "absolutely succeed" because "The concept is popular—everyone knows about it." Plaintiffs also point to admissions by Xio's principals that Xio downloaded Tetris's iPhone application for the purpose of developing its own version and used it in the development of *Mino*. Xio does not dispute any of these facts. Yet, Xio says, it copied *Tetris* in such a way so as to not copy any protected elements after diligently researching intellectual property law, and that it also tried to obtain a license from Tetris Holding, but was refused. Xio released *Mino* version 1.0 in May 2009, *Mino* version 1.1 in July 2009, and *Mino Lite* shortly thereafter. Tetris Holding became aware of *Mino* and *Mino Lite* and in August 2009, sent take-down notices pursuant to the Digital Millennium Copyright Act to Apple, Inc., which removed *Mino* and *Mino Lite* from its online apps marketplace. Xio's counsel sent two counter-notifications soon after and Apple, Inc. informed Tetris Holding that the games would be reinstated unless Tetris Holding filed a lawsuit. This litigation was then commenced in December 2009.

Tetris Holding argues that *Mino* infringed the following copyrightable elements:

1. Seven Tetrimino playing pieces made up of four equally-sized square joined at their sides;

2. The visual delineation of individual blocks that comprise each Tetrimino piece and the display of their borders;

3. The bright, distinct colors used for each of the Tetrimino pieces;

4. A tall, rectangular playfield (or matrix), 10 blocks wide and 20 blocks tall;

5. The appearance of Tetriminos moving from the top of the playfield to its bottom;

6. The way the Tetrimino pieces appear to move and rotate in the playfield;

7. The small display near the playfield that shows the next playing piece to appear in the playfield;

8. The particular starting orientation of the Tetriminos, both at the top of the screen and as shown in the "next piece" display;

9. The display of a "shadow" piece beneath the Tetriminos as they fall;

10. The color change when the Tetriminos enter lock-down mode;

11. When a horizontal line fills across the playfield with blocks, the line disappears, and the remaining pieces appear to consolidate downward;

12. The appearance of individual blocks automatically filling in the playfield from the bottom to the top when the game is over;

13. The display of "garbage lines" with at least one missing block in random order; and

14. The screen layout in multiplayer versions with the player's matrix appearing most prominently on the screen and the opponents' matrixes appearing smaller than the player's matrix and to the side of the player's matrix.

II. LEGAL STANDARD

"Summary judgment is proper if there is no genuine issue of material fact and if, viewing the facts in the light most favorable to the non-moving party, the moving party is entitled to judgment as a matter of law." *Pearson v. Component Tech. Corp.,* 247 F.3d 471, 482 n. 1 (3d Cir.2001) (*citing Celotex Corp. v. Catrett,* 477 U.S. 317, 322, 106 S.Ct. 2548, 91 L.Ed.2d 265 (1986)); *accord* Fed.R.Civ.P. 56(c).

III. DISCUSSION

Copyright Infringement

"To establish a claim of copyright infringement, a plaintiff must establish: (1) ownership of a valid copyright; and (2) unauthorized copying of original elements of the plaintiff's work." The parties agree that there are no genuine issues of fact in connection with their motions on either the copyright or federal trade dress claim. The question before the Court then is not whether summary judgment is appropriate, but rather, which party is entitled to summary judgment. There are no issues of material facts, in part, because Xio concedes much. Xio acknowledges that Tetris Holding owns the registered copyrights to the various iterations of *Tetris* and further admits that Xio copied *Tetris,* purposefully and deliberately, in designing *Mino.* Xio does not dispute that it downloaded Tetris Holding's iPhone application and used it to develop its own iPhone *Tetris*-like application for profit. What Xio does not concede is that it copied any protected elements. Instead, it argues the elements it copied were not original expression, because they were part of the game itself—the rules, function, and expression essential to the game play—which is not protected. Before releasing its product, Xio researched copyright law, both through its own independent studying and based on advice of counsel, before designing its game. Based on this research, Xio believed it could freely copy any part of *Tetris* that was based on a "rule of the game" or that Xio viewed as being functional to the game. There is no question that Xio thought of its game as essentially a version of *Tetris*. Xio's principals referred to their game as "*Tetris*" multiple times during its development and admitted that their intention was to market and profit from making a *Tetris*-type product for the iPhone, using as much of the look and feel of *Tetris* that it thought it could copy based on its view of copyright law. According to Defendant:

> There is no question that *Mino* and *Tetris* look alike. But the only similarities between the games are elements not protected by copyright. This is no coincidence. Before developing its games, Xio analyzed the intellectual property laws to determine what parts of *Tetris* they could use and what parts they couldn't. Xio discovered that no one had a patent to the rules and other functional elements of *Tetris*. Xio carefully, intentionally, and purposefully crafted its game to exclude all protected, expressive elements.

Implied, but not stated, in this admission is that Xio's careful, intentional, and purposeful attempt to exclude all protected elements was based on its opinion of what it believed was protected; the validity of that opinion, or lack thereof, underlies this litigation.

i. *Idea–Expression Dichotomy*

To resolve the claim of copyright infringement, I must first determine which elements of Plaintiffs' *Tetris* game are protected and which are not. I begin with the relevant language from 17 U.S.C. § 102. Subsection (a) outlines what a copyright protects, and reads in part:

> Copyright protection subsists, in accordance with this title, in original works of authorship fixed in any tangible medium of expression, now known or later developed, from which they can be perceived, reproduced, or otherwise communicated, either directly or with the aid of a machine or device.

17 U.S.C. § 102(a). Courts in this Circuit and others have long held that elements of computer programs may be protected by copyright law. This includes both the code for the program as well as the graphical elements for programs such as video games. Apple ("Thus a computer program, whether in object code or source code, is a 'literary work' and is protected from unauthorized copying, whether from its object or source code version."); *Midway Mfg. Co. v. Bandai–America, Inc.*, 546 F.Supp. 125, 139 (D.N.J.1982) ("It is also unquestionable that video games in general are entitled to copyright protections as audiovisual works."); *Hart v. Elec. Arts, Inc.*, 808 F.Supp.2d 757, 778 (D.N.J.2011) (discussing copyrightability of video games in the context of First Amendment issues); *see also Midway Mfg. Co. v. Artic Intern. Inc.*, 704 F.2d 1009, 1012 (7th Cir.1983) ("We thus conclude that video games are copyrightable as audiovisual works under the 1976 Copyright Act and we note that every other federal court (including our own) that has confronted this issue has reached the same conclusion."). Conversely, subsection (b) outlines what copyright law will not protect:

> In no case does copyright protection for an original work of authorship extend to any idea, procedure, process, system, method of operation, concept, principle, or discovery, regardless of the form in which it is described, explained, illustrated, or embodied in such work.

17 U.S.C. § 102(b). Together § 102(a) and § 102(b) codify what courts have come to call the "idea-expression dichotomy." *Whelan Assocs., Inc. v. Jaslow Dental Laboratory, Inc.*, 797 F.2d 1222, 1234 (3d Cir.1986); H.R.Rep. No. 1476, 94th Cong., 2d Sess. 57 (1976), reprinted

in 1976 U.S.C.C.A.N. 5659, 5670 ("Section 102(b) in no way enlarges or contracts the scope of copyright protection under the present law. Its purpose is to restate, in the context of the new single Federal system of copyright, that the basic dichotomy between expression and idea remains unchanged."); *see also Mazer v. Stein,* 347 U.S. 201, 217, 74 S.Ct. 460, 98 L.Ed. 630 (1954) ("Unlike a patent, a copyright gives no exclusive right to the art disclosed; protection is given only to the expression of the idea—not the idea itself").

The doctrine is simple to state—copyright will not protect an idea, only its expression—but difficult to apply, especially in the context of computer programs. As Judge Stahl of the First Circuit aptly wrote: "Applying copyright law to computer programs is like assembling a jigsaw puzzle whose pieces do not quite fit." *Lotus Dev. Corp. v. Borland Int'l,* 49 F.3d 807, 820 (1st Cir.1995); *see also* Melville Nimmer, et al., NIMMER ON COPYRIGHT § 2.18[H] ("Accordingly, analyzing the substantial similarity of computer programs is especially challenging") (hereinafter "Nimmer").5 Different circuits have developed different tests for how to separate unprotectible ideas from protectible expression pertaining to computer software.

The Third Circuit was perhaps the first to weigh in on this issue in *Whelan,* although this decision has been criticized outside this Circuit.6 *Computer Assocs. Int'l v. Altai,* 982 F.2d 693, 705 (2d Cir.1992) ("We think that *Whelan's* approach to separating idea from expression in computer programs relies too heavily on metaphysical distinctions and does not place enough emphasis on practical considerations.") (collecting cases and academic articles criticizing *Whelan*); *Plains Cotton Coop. Ass'n v. Goodpasture Computer Serv., Inc.,* 807 F.2d 1256, 1262 (5th Cir.1987) (criticizing and declining to adopt *Whelan*); *Sega Enters. v. Accolade, Inc.,* 977 F.2d 1510, 1525 (9th Cir.1992) ("The *Whelan* rule, however, has been widely—and soundly—criticized as simplistic and overbroad.");*Gates Rubber Co. v. Bando Chem. Indus.,* 9 F.3d 823, 840, n. 17 (10th Cir.1993). Yet even in the face of such criticism, the Third Circuit, sitting *en banc,* has declined to abandon its holding. In *Southco, Inc. v. Kanebridge Corp.,* 390 F.3d 276 (3d Cir.2004), the Circuit briefly discussed the holding in *Whelan,* but left it untouched, denying there was any tension between the holding there and in Whelan *Id.* at 285 n. 4

Shortly thereafter, the Second Circuit developed the abstraction-filtration-comparison that purported to depart from *Whelan. Altai,*982 F.2d at 706 ("[W]e think that district courts would be well-advised to undertake a three-step procedure, based on the abstractions test utilized by the district court, in order to determine whether the non-literal elements of two or more computer programs are substantially similar."). Unlike *Whelan,* this test has been widely accepted by other courts. *See Atari Games Corp. v. Nintendo of Am. Inc.,* 975 F.2d 832, 839 (Fed.Cir.1992) (employing *Altai's* abstraction-filtration-comparison method); *Sega Enters. Ltd. v. Accolade, Inc.,* 977 F.2d 1510, 1525 (9th Cir.1992) ("the Second Circuit's approach is an appropriate one"); *Gates Rubber Co. v. Bando Chem. Indus., Ltd.,* 9 F.3d 823, 834 (10th Cir.1993); *Engineering Dynamics, Inc. v. Structural Software, Inc.,* 26 F.3d 1335, 1342, 1343 (5th Cir.1994); *Bateman v. Mnemonics, Inc.,* 79 F.3d 1532, 1543 n. 24, 1544 (11th Cir.1996); *Comprehensive Technologies Int'l, Inc. v. Software Artisans, Inc.,* 3 F.3d 730, 734–735 (4th Cir.1993) (also citing Third Circuit opinion in Whelan, discussed below).

I do not find, however, that these approaches require widely differing analyses, at least based on the facts before me today; both rest on similar premises and applications. In *Whelan,* the court held "*the purpose or function of a utilitarian work would be the work's idea, and everything that is not necessary to that purpose or function would be part of the expression of the idea.* Where there are various means of achieving the desired purpose, then the particular means chosen is not necessary to the purpose; hence, there is expression, not idea." *Id.* at 1236 (emphasis in original). The computer program at issue was aimed at helping business operations for dental laboratories. *Id.* at 1238. The court addressed other doctrines, such as scènes à faire and fact intensive works, in conjunction with its analysis and then applied these concepts to address whether there was substantial similarity between the original and allegedly copied programs. *Id.*

In *Altai*, the Second Circuit suggested district courts undertake much the same analysis, albeit in three distinct steps. First, a court should "abstract" the program at issue, then filter out the unprotected material, and finally compare whatever remains (the protected expression) to the copied work. The last two steps are mostly identical to what the Third Circuit did in *Whelan*. It is the first step of the analysis, the abstraction, where differences purportedly lie. To abstract a computer program, the Second Circuit suggested that: "a court would first break down the allegedly infringed program into its constituent structural parts." *Altai*, 982 F.2d at 706. This is an overly complicated way of saying a court should first try to understand the principles or ideas driving the program and the essential processes and functions by which it achieves those purposes. *See id.* ("Upon any work a great number of patterns of increasing generality will fit equally well, as more and more of the incident is left out. The last may perhaps be no more than the most general statement of what the work is about, and at times might consist only of its title; but there is a point in this series of abstractions where they are no longer protected, since otherwise the author could prevent the use of his 'ideas,' to which, apart from their expression, his property is never extended.") (internal quotation and alterations omitted). This is similar, at least in principle, to what the Third Circuit expressed: "[t]he line between idea and expression may be drawn with reference to the end sought to be achieved by the work in question." *Whelan*, 797 F.2d at 1236. In any event, what needs to be "abstracted" or considered and how one achieves this will depend greatly on the type of program at issue and what precisely is being accused of copyright infringement. For example, analyzing whether source code was misappropriated would likely entail a different inquiry—or different abstraction—than analyzing whether the graphical interface or display of a program was copied. The *Whelan* Court was careful to note that its analysis would vary depending on the underlying facts. *Id.* at 1238, n. 34. ("We do not mean to imply that the idea or purpose behind every utilitarian or functional work will be precisely what it accomplishes, and that structure and organization will therefore always be part of the expression of such works.").

Indeed, criticism of *Whelan* seems aimed more at its application than the general principles underlying the holding inasmuch as the court found only one unprotectible idea at issue. Nimmer, § 13.03[F][1] ("The crucial flaw in this reasoning it that it assumes that only one 'idea,' in copyright law terms, underlies any computer program, and that once a separable idea can be identified, everything else must be expression."); *Gates Rubber Co.*, 9 F.3d at 840, n. 17 ("The criticisms of the *Whelan* analysis primarily concern the high level of abstraction at which the court chose to separate idea from expression. The criticisms of the *Whelan* decision are valid when the opinion is read to imply that a computer program can have only one idea."). But the *Whelan* Court never explicitly said or suggested a program can have only one idea behind it. Perhaps in 1983 when the case was decided such a result was more conceivable, but three decades and exponential increases in the power, range, and scope of computer programs make it less likely today.

At the end of the day, no matter how one expresses the test, the task is clear: because copyright only protects original expression, I must delineate between the copyrightable expression in *Tetris* and the unprotected elements of the program, then evaluate whether there is substantial similarity between such expression and Defendant's *Mino* game. The starting point in this analysis must be to understand the ideas and concepts of *Tetris* itself.

ii. *Doctrines of Merger and Scènes à Faire*

In determining what elements are not protected, two related doctrines must be considered: merger and scènes à faire. Merger exists when an idea and its particular expression become inseparable. *Kay Berry, Inc. v. Taylor Gifts, Inc.,* 421 F.3d 199, 209 (3d Cir.2005) ("In some instances, there may come a point when an author's expression becomes indistinguishable from the idea he seeks to convey, such that the two merge."). If the law were to protect expression in such instances, then the copyright holder would have an unacceptable monopoly over that idea. In striking the balance between the two unenviable positions of either allowing an infringer to unlawfully copy another's expression or preventing the use of ideas rightly in the public domain, it is better to allow such copying rather than suffer the loss of future works that would have been developed based on those ideas. *See Educ. Testing Services v. Katzman,* 793 F.2d 533, 539 (3d Cir.1986) ("When the idea and the expression of the idea coincide, then the expression will not be protected in order to prevent creation of a monopoly on the underlying art.") (citation omitted). Merger is appropriate when "there are no or few other ways of expressing a particular idea." *Id.* (quotation omitted). But "if the same idea can be expressed in a plurality of totally different manners, a plurality of copyrights may result" and merger will not prevent protection of one's expression. ID (quotation omitted) ("If other methods of expressing that idea are not foreclosed as a practical matter, then there is no merger."). Indeed, the Third Circuit has explained that merger "is rare." *Kay Berry,* 421 F.3d at 209.6

The second, related doctrine, known as "scènes à faire" (literally meaning a scene that must be done), applies to expression that is so associated with a particular genre, motif, or idea that one is compelled to use such expression. *Jackson v. Booker,* 465 Fed. Appx. 163, 168 (3d Cir.2012) (describing scènes à faire as the "incidents, characters or settings which are as a practical matter standard in the treatment of" a particular subject); *Hoehling v. Universal City Studios, Inc.,* 618 F.2d 972, 979 (2d Cir.1980)("Because it is virtually impossible to write about a particular historical era or fictional theme without employing certain 'stock' or standard literary devices, we have held that scènes à faire are not copyrightable as a matter of law."). For much the same reason as merger, such scenes are unprotectible by copyright law. *Whelan,* 797 F.2d at 1236 ("It is well-settled doctrine that scènes à faire are afforded no copyright protection."); *Mortg. Mkt. Guide,* 2008 WL 2991570, at 2008 U.S. Dist. LEXIS 56871 ("[W]hen similar features in a videogame are as a practical matter indispensable, or at least standard, in the treatment of a given idea, they are treated like ideas and are therefore not protected by copyright.") (quotation omitted).

iii. *Copyright Law As Applied to Games*

With these principles and doctrines in mind, I now turn to the law as it has developed with regard to games and videogames in order to parse out the unprotected elements of *Tetris* from Plaintiffs' protectible expression. Neither party disputes that a game is deserving of some copyright protection. The game mechanics and the rules are not entitled to protection, but courts have found expressive elements copyrightable, including game labels, design of game boards, playing cards and graphical works. *Affiliated Hosp. Prods., Inc. v. Merdel Game Mfg. Co.,* 513 F.2d 1183, 1188–89 (2d Cir.1975) ("The rules of the game are perforce in the public domain as well as the game itself. Affiliated's copyright only protects Affiliated's arrangement of the rules and the manner of their presentation, and not their content"); *Anti-Monopoly, Inc. v. General Mills Fun Group, Inc.,* 611 F.2d 296, 300, n. 1 (9th Cir.1979)("The copyright laws are not involved in this case because business ideas, such as a game concept, cannot be copyrighted...."); *Hoopla Sports & Entertainment v. Nike, Inc.,* 947 F.Supp. 347, 354 (N.D.Ill.1996) ("Courts have also held that 'games' themselves (as opposed to the cards, boards, instruction books, etc. with which games may be played) are not copyrightable."); Nimmer, § 2.18[H]. In particular, courts have found the audiovisual display of a video game to be expression. *Atari Games Corp. v. Oman*, 979 F.2d 242, 245 (D.C.Cir.1992) ("The hallmark of a video game is the expression found in 'the entire effect of the game as it appears and sounds,' its 'sequence of images.'") (per then-Judge Ginsburg); *Atari, Inc. v. North American Philips Consumer Electronics Corp.*, 672 F.2d 607, 617 (7th Cir.1982) (finding copyright protection extends "to at least a limited extent the particular form in which [a game] is expressed (shapes, sizes, colors, sequences, arrangements, and sounds)" and holding that defendant's use of similar video game characters infringed plaintiff's copyright); *Midway*, 546 F.Supp. at 139 (finding graphical characters of video game were protectible expression). This distinction then between a game's rules and its appearance is merely the application of the familiar idea-expression dichotomy as applied to the particular field of games. *See, e.g., Durham Industries, Inc. v. Tomy Corp.*, 630 F.2d 905, 913 (2d Cir.1980) (discussing copyright as applied to games and stating that "[j]ust as copyright protection extends to expression but not ideas, copyright protection extends only to the artistic aspects, but not the mechanical or utilitarian features, of a protected work.").

Rather than following this analysis, Defendant's primary argument takes a somewhat different path. Xio repeatedly emphasizes that Tetris Holding cannot protect by copyright what is only protectible by patent and therefore not only are the ideas of *Tetris* (or the rules of the game) not protectible, but neither are the "functional aspects" of the game or expressive elements related to the game's function or play. Def. Motion, at 6. As part of this argument, Xio conflates the doctrines of merger and scènes à faire to say that Tetris Holding cannot protect expression inseparable from either game rules or game function.

Xio's brief devotes many pages to explain how patents protect particular aspects of intellectual property while copyright protects other, distinct aspects, but I find that Defendant extracts much from this distinction—too much. Xio is correct that one cannot protect some functional aspect of a work by copyright as one would with a patent. But this principle does not mean, and cannot mean, that *any and all expression* related to a game rule or game function is unprotectible. Such an exception to copyright would likely swallow any protection one could possibly have; almost all expressive elements of a game are related in some way to the rules and functions of game play. Tetris Holding is as entitled to copyright protection for the way in which it chooses to express game rules or game play as one would be to the way in which one chooses to express an idea.

The cases Xio cites in support of its argument do not stand for expanding the law so that any expression related to functionality is *a fortiori* outside the ambit of copyright law. Rather, expression is not protected only when it is integral or inseparable from the idea or the function under the doctrines of merger or scènes à faire. Defendant relies on the seminal case, *Baker v. Selden*, as the starting point for its analysis. There the Supreme Court held that plaintiff could not copyright certain forms used in his new system of bookkeeping ostensibly as a means to protect the idea underlying that system. *Baker v. Selden*, 101 U.S. 99, 103, 25 L.Ed. 841 (1879). The defendant in *Baker* developed similar charts, although arranged differently, and plaintiff sued him for copyright infringement arguing defendant's work embodied the system that plaintiff originally described. But the plaintiff did not have rights to his new bookkeeping idea, nor to those elements that were a necessary accompaniment to the idea. *Id.* The Court explained its holding this way:

> The copyright of a work on mathematical science cannot give to the author an exclusive right to the methods of operation which he propounds, or to the diagrams which he employs to explain them, so as to prevent an engineer from

using them whenever occasion requires. The very object of publishing a book on science or the useful arts is to communicate to the world the useful knowledge which it contains. But this object would be frustrated if the knowledge could not be used without incurring the guilt of piracy of the book. And where the art it teaches cannot be used without employing the methods and diagrams used to illustrate the book, or such as are similar to them, such methods and diagrams are *to be considered as necessary incidents to the art*, and given therewith to the public; not given for the purpose of publication in other works explanatory of the art, but for the purpose of practical application.

Id. (emphasis added). That the charts (i.e. the expression of the idea) were "necessary incidents" is key in applying this case here; the art was unusable without that expression. The Court, holding plaintiff's expression unprotectible, in essence applied the merger doctrine to prevent the plaintiff from precluding the use of his idea, which he had already donated to the public domain. But the Court did not hold that any expression, even if related to a use or method of operation, was beyond the boundary of copyright. Indeed, it said the opposite: "But as embodied and taught in a literary composition or book, their essence consists only in their statement. This alone is what is secured by the copyright. The use by another of the same methods of statement, whether in words or illustrations, in a book published for teaching the art, would undoubtedly be an infringement of the copyright." *Id.* at 104.

Many of the other cases cited by Xio reach the same result based on the same reasoning. In *Taylor Instrument,* the court found that plaintiff's chart was an integral part of its recording thermometer and therefore an object of use not entitled to copyright protection. Taylor ("The description of the art in a book, though entitled to the benefit of copyright, lays no foundation for *an exclusive claim* to the art itself. The object of the one is explanation; the object of the other is use.") (emphasis added); *see also Brown Instrument Co. v. Warner,* 161 F.2d 910, 911 (D.C.Cir.1947) ("Since the machines which cooperate with the charts in suit *are useless without them,* to copyright the charts would in effect continue appellant's monopoly of its machines beyond the time authorized by the patent law.").

The case that appears to come closest to Defendant's point is *Lotus Development Corp. v. Borland International, Inc.,* 49 F.3d 807 (1st Cir.1995). The First Circuit held that a nearly identical menu hierarchy in a computer program could not be protected by copyright because it was a method of use. In particular, Xio cites to the following language: "Accepting the district court's finding that the Lotus developers made some expressive choices in choosing and arranging the Lotus command terms, we nonetheless hold that that expression is not copyrightable because it is part of Lotus 1–2–3's 'method of operation.'" *Id.* at 816. I am not convinced, however, that this means that *no expression* is copyrightable if it is part of a method of operation. There the court was reviewing a simple menu hierarchy that has commands such as "Save," "Exit," or "Quit." It analogized such a system to the buttons on a VCR remote control and explained: "That the buttons are arranged and labeled does not make them a 'literary work,' nor does it make them an 'expression' of the abstract 'method of operating' a VCR via a set of labeled buttons. Instead, the buttons are themselves the 'method of operating' the VCR." *Id.* at 817. Under this premise, there was no expression—there was only the method of operation because the menu titles were themselves the useful tool. *Id.* ("Just as one could not operate a buttonless VCR, it would be impossible to operate Lotus 1–2–3 without employing its menu command hierarchy. Thus the Lotus command terms are not equivalent to the labels on the VCR's buttons, but are instead equivalent to the buttons themselves."). Moreover, the court's holding implicates the merger doctrine because there are few ways of expressing such commands.

Xio, in quoting from the opinion, omits the following crucial language and replaces it with an ellipse: "If specific words are essential to operating something, then they are part of a 'method of operation' and, as such, are unprotectible." *Id.* at 816; *see also id.* ("Concluding, as we do, that users operate Lotus 1–2–3 by using the Lotus menu command hierarchy, and that the entire Lotus menu command hierarchy is essential to operating Lotus 1–2–3, we do not inquire further whether that method of operation could have been designed differently."); *id.* at 818 ("When there are a limited number of ways to express an idea, however, the expression 'merges' with the idea and becomes uncopyrightable."). I do not find that this opinion stands for a proposition as broad as Xio suggests.8 Of course, Tetris Holding cannot copyright a method of operation, but may copyright an expression of a method of operation if it is distinguished from the method itself and is not essential to its operation.

Xio also relies on a number of opinions discussing video games. In no case, however, did a court find that expression was unprotectible merely because it was related to a game rule or game function. Xio cites to *Atari, Inc. v. North American Philips Consumer Elecs. Corp.*, 672 F.2d 607, 616 (7th Cir.1982) to argue that infringement cannot be found based on "functional commonalities." Def. Motion, at 17. But the Seventh Circuit found that certain elements of Atari's *Pac–Man* game, (the maze design, scoring table, and "dots") were unprotected not because of functional commonalities but because "[c]ertain expressive matter ... should be treated as scènes à faire and receive protection only from virtually identical copying." *Atari*, 672 F.2d at 617. Nevertheless, the court went on to find that "the substantial appropriation of the *Pac–Man* characters" qualified as copyright infringement. *Id.* The characters "functioned" in the same manner in both games. This District also analyzed *Pac–Man* and found the following to be protected by copyright: the characters, the sequences and arrangements of the graphics, the characters' motions and actions, the musical theme, and the introductory cartoon sequence. *Midway Mfg. Co. v. Bandai–America, Inc.*, 546 F.Supp. 125, 152 (D.N.J.1982). The court did not suggest whether there were functional similarities or whether these expressive elements were related to the "game rules."

The *Midway* decision also involved the copyright of the video game *Galaxian*. There the defendant argued that *Galaxian* had no copyright in its game because the game *Space Invaders* was a pre-existing work. The court disagreed because it was only the basic structure or concept of the game that was copied: "Nonetheless, the most cursory perusal of the two works indicates that the only similarity between them is in the idea of the underlying games, i.e., outer space games wherein a defendant base or rocket ship, controlled by the player, attempts to fend off attacking hordes of aliens ... When the expressions of the *Galaxian* and *Space Invaders* works are compared, it is clear there is no similarity beyond that of idea." *Id.* at 144–45. Again the court included under the umbrella of expression the look and feel of the characters and how they move and act. Midway took the unprotectible idea and found a new, novel way to express it.

In *Data East USA, Inc. v. Epyx, Inc.*, 862 F.2d 204 (9th Cir.1988), the Ninth Circuit followed a similar approach to that of the Seventh Circuit in *Atari*. The game at issue involved a karate fighting simulation and the court found that "karate is not susceptible of a wholly fanciful presentation" and the characters, their actions, the scenery, and the like, were not subject to copyright because they were scènes à faire. *Id.* at 209. This did not foreclose the possibility of protection for other expressive content that was not "indispensable or at least standard in the treatment of a given idea." *Id.* Tellingly, the court noted that its holding was in part mandated by the limited abilities of computers in 1988: "Furthermore, the use of the Commodore computer for a karate game intended for home consumption is subject to various constraints inherent in the use of that computer. Among the constraints are the use of sprites, and a somewhat limited access to color, together with limitations upon the use of multiple colors in one visual image." *Id.*

Finally, in another Seventh Circuit decision, the court analyzed arcade golf games and found no infringement because the expressive elements were not protected under the scènes à faire doctrine.

In contrast, we see no error of law in Judge Kennelly's finding that the Global VR video display is subject to the scènes à faire doctrine. Like karate, golf is not a game subject to totally "fanciful presentation." In presenting a realistic video golf game, one would, by definition, need golf courses, clubs, a selection menu, a golfer, a wind meter, etc. Sand traps and water hazards are a fact of life for golfers, real and virtual. The menu screens are standard to the video arcade game format, as are prompts showing the distance remaining to the hole. As such, the video display is afforded protection only from virtually identical copying. *Incredible Techs., Inc. v. Virtual Techs., Inc.,* 400 F.3d 1007 (7th Cir.2005).9 Also, the two games each employed a track ball, which the user would roll back to simulate a back stroke and then roll forward to simulate the swing itself. The court found the use of the trackball itself to be functional and not subject to copyright. While Xio relies heavily on this analysis, it is inapposite to the facts here. There is no equivalent functional, structural element at issue here. Tetris Holding is not arguing that some particular controller or mechanism is infringed, only its visual expression.

Nonetheless, from the foregoing cases, Xio draws the following conclusion: "where a feature of a videogame is dictated by functional considerations, regardless of whether there may be a number of different ways to implement that feature's functionality, copyright does not protect that feature." This is incorrect as a matter of law and fails as a matter of logic. If an expressive feature is dictated by functional considerations then there cannot be a number of ways to implement it. Rather, one's original expression is protected by copyright—even if that expression concerns an idea, rule, function, or something similar—unless it is so inseparable from the underlying idea that there are no or very few other ways of expressing it. "If other methods of expressing that idea are not foreclosed as a practical matter, then there is no merger." *Educational Testing Services,* 793 F.2d at 539. Moreover, Xio does not dispute that *Tetris* is a purely fanciful game, meaning it has no grounding in the real world, unlike a video game simulating a karate match or a golf game. Therefore, the analyses in *Data East* and *Incredible Technologies* are largely inapplicable; the scènes à faire doctrine has little weight in instances such as this because there are no expressive elements "standard, stock, or common" to a unique puzzle game that is divorced from any real world representation.

iv. *Substantial Similarity of Tetris and Mino*

With this framework, I can compare the audio-visual aspects of the two games at issue: *Tetris* and *Mino.* To separate ideas from expression, the parties offer competing definitions of game rules, but I do not need to articulate a rigid, specific definition. While the unenviable task of dissecting a game's ideas from its expression is difficult, I am guided by case law and common sense, and find that the ideas underlying *Tetris* can be delineated by understanding the game at an abstract level and the concepts that drive the game. *See, e.g., Atari,* 672 F.2d at 617 ("In applying the abstractions test, we find that plaintiffs' game can be described accurately in fairly abstract terms, much in the same way as one would articulate the rules to such a game."); *Midway,* 546 F.Supp. at 144 (describing the "idea" of a Space Invader type game as an "outer space game[ ] wherein a defendant base or rocket ship, controlled by the player, attempts to fend off attacking hordes of aliens");

id. at 153 (adopting the Seventh Circuit's description of the PAC-MAN game idea: "PAC-MAN is a maze-chase game in which the player scores points by guiding a central figure through various passageways of a maze and at the same time avoiding collision with certain opponents or pursuit figures which move independently about the maze."). These decisions further make clear that the idea of a game is expressed, in part, through its rules. *Tetris* is a puzzle game where a user manipulates pieces composed of square blocks, each made into a different geometric shape, that fall from the top of the game board to the bottom where the pieces accumulate. The user is given a new piece after the current one reaches the bottom of the available game space. While a piece is falling, the user rotates it in order to fit it in with the accumulated pieces. The object of the puzzle is to fill all spaces along a horizontal line. If that is accomplished, the line is erased, points are earned, and more of the game board is available for play. But if the pieces accumulate and reach the top of the screen, then the game is over. These then are the general, abstract ideas underlying *Tetris* and cannot be protected by copyright nor can expressive elements that are inseparable from them.

The parties argue over a number of particular features of both games, which I will address in turn. Before that, however, I note that it is appropriate to compare the two works "as they would appear to a layman" concentrating "upon the gross features rather than an examination of minutiae." *Universal Athletic Sales Co. v. Salkeld,* 511 F.2d 904, 908 (3d Cir.1975); *Atari,* 672 F.2d at 614 ("It has been said that this test does not involve 'analytic dissection and expert testimony,' but depends on whether the accused work has captured the 'total concept and feel' of the copyrighted work."); *Oman,* 979 F.2d at 245 (criticizing an administrative opinion for "its apparent focus on the individual screens, rather than the flow of the game as a whole").

Xio has provided the court with links to uploaded videos at www.youtube.com showing the game play of both *Tetris* and *Mino*; Tetris Holding has provided similar video evidence. The Court has reviewed these videos as well as screen shots of the individual game screens, the declarations and attached exhibits, and the parties' respective statements of fact. Screenshots of both games are shown here side by side:

Figure 6.2

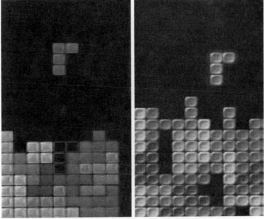

The first is *Tetris* and the second is *Mino.* Without being told which is which, a common user could not decipher between the two games. Any differences between the two are slight and insignificant. If one has to squint to find distinctions only at a granular level, then the works are likely to be substantially similar. Reviewing the videos of the game play bolsters this conclusion as it is apparent that the overall look and feel of the two games is identical. There is such similarity between the visual expression of *Tetris* and *Mino* that it is akin to literal copying. While there might not have actually been "literal copying" inasmuch as Xio did not copy the source code and exact images from *Tetris*, Xio does not dispute that it copied almost all of visual look of *Tetris*. This leaves one to wonder what Xio believed was protectible expression. After the purportedly careful analysis it undertook to understand copyright law, apparently Xio believed it could engage in wholesale copying of the *Tetris* look and relate almost every visual element to a "rule," finding none of *Tetris's* visual expression copyrightable. In particular, the style of the pieces is nearly indistinguishable, both in their look and in the manner they move, rotate, fall, and behave. Similar bright colors are used in each program, the pieces are composed of individually delineated bricks, each brick is given an interior border to suggest texture, and shading and gradation of color are used in substantially similar ways to suggest light is being cast onto the pieces. Showing the pieces in more detail highlights these similarities: the first piece of each pair is from *Tetris* and the second is from *Mino*.

Figure 6.3

Xio was also free to design a puzzle game using pieces of different shapes instead of using the same seven pieces used in *Tetris*. The pieces in *Tetris* are based on combining four equally sized squares in different patterns, but the idea of *Tetris*—fitting different shaped pieces together to form complete lines—can be achieved with nearly limitless shaped pieces and geometric shapes. Xio's expert, Jason Begy, agreed at his deposition that a "a game designer could design the playing pieces for a video game in an almost unlimited number of ways" and that the specific *Tetris* pieces were "not necessary ... to design a puzzle video game." The video evidence also shows how the pieces move in precisely the same manner. Again, there are almost unlimited options for expressing the pieces' movement and rotation and one can play the same game even if different styles are used or the game has a different look and feel to it, which was also admitted by Xio's expert during his deposition. The style, design, shape, and movement of the pieces are expression; they are not part of the ideas, rules, or functions of the game nor are they essential or inseparable from the ideas, rules, or functions of the game.

Without even considering the other allegedly infringing aspects, courts have found copyright infringement based on the fact that video game characters or pieces are nearly identical. In both *Atari* and *Midway,* the Seventh Circuit found infringement entirely on the substantial similarities between the style, color, and movement of the game characters. *Atari,* 672 F.2d at 617; *Midway,* 546 F.Supp. at 144 (finding infringement on the same elements as well as copied music and introduction animation). As described above, Xio's argument that the *Tetris* pieces are unprotectible because they are related to a rule or function of the game is without merit. The idea of *Tetris* does not necessitate the particular characteristics of the audio-visual display. And *Tetris's* copyright is not protecting the style and movement of the pieces as methods of operation, but instead the expression associated with those elements. There are many ways Xio could have expressed these same concepts. To accept Xio's reasoning would give a copyright defendant free reign to copy another's expression, to pilfer another's creativity, merely by describing that expression in sufficient detail related to a rule or a function. Tetris Holding has given the rules of its game to the public domain, but has kept the rights to its expression. Tetris Holding made specific and deliberate design choices and its product has enjoyed great success; to allow Xio to profit off that expression, and that success, by blatant copying, without offering any originality or ingenuity of its own, defies the very purpose of copyright law. Any game expression can always be defined as relating to a game rule and be defined in such detail that the description of the expression would add nothing to the idea. There was no necessity for *Mino* to mimic *Tetris's* expression other than to avoid the difficult task of developing its own take on a known idea.

I am not convinced that either the doctrine of merger or scènes à faire applies here. The latter, as discussed earlier, is inapposite because *Tetris* is a wholly fanciful presentation; it is a unique puzzle game and does not have stock or common imagery that must be included. Nor does merger apply because there are many novel ways Xio could have chosen to express the rules of *Tetris*. Xio's own expert admitted there are "almost unlimited number" of ways to design the pieces and the board and the game would still "function perfectly well." Xio itself points to an example from the early 1990s. Dr. Mario was a video game, published by Nintendo Co. Ltd., that used the rules of *Tetris* expressed in a unique way. Nintendo obtained a patent in the game mechanics and in the specification described itself as a variation on the rules of *Tetris*, but with a more exciting theme and expression. That expression was shown by the patentees in the patent drawings, for example:

Figure 6.4 U.S. Patent No. 5,265,888, Figures 10(c), 10(f).

Instead of using bricks to form complete rows, the user aligns pills and viruses of different colors to form patterns and eliminate the viruses as part of the pattern based on the color of the objects. Considering the exponential increase in computer processing and graphical capabilities since that unique variation on *Tetris's* rules, the Court cannot accept that Xio was unable to find any other method of expressing the *Tetris* rules other than a wholesale copy of its expression.

v. *Other Discrete Copyrightable Elements of Tetris*

[The court detailed several other similarities between *Tetris* that Xio such as the use of bright colors, individually delineated squares, movement, shadow pieces, etc. — ED]

Xio's defenses fail as a matter of law and there are no issues of fact regarding Tetris Holding's claim of copyright infringement. Accordingly, summary judgment is granted on Count One in favor of Plaintiffs.

In light of the above and there being no issues of fact raised by either party, summary judgment is granted on Count Two, Plaintiffs' claim of trade dress infringement, in favor of Plaintiffs.

IV. CONCLUSION

Plaintiffs' motion for summary judgment on Counts One and Two is granted. Defendant's motion for summary judgment is denied. An order will be entered consistent with this Opinion.

Plaintiffs have subsequently withdrawn their unjust enrichment claim.

————————

Notes and Questions

1. Distinguish the holdings of *Data East* and *Tetris*.

2. A final disposition for *Tetris Holding, LLC v. Xio Interactive, Inc.* in the form of a Consent Order and Permanent Injunction was entered on January 31, 2013. As you read through the facts of the case and examine the "concessions," do you think that the Plaintiff consented to too much?

3. *Capcom U.S.A., Inc. v. Data East,* No. 93-3259, 1994 U.D. Dist. LEXIS 5306 (N.D. Cal. March 16, 1994), provided another battle among the "kick and punch" game developers. Capcom's *Street Fighter II*, released in 1991, was among the most successful videogames of its time. Capcom sold over two million home versions of the *Street Fighter II* series in the United States alone. Data East, a successful competing video game developer subsequently released *Fighter's History.* Capcom alleged that Data East's game copied the distinctive fighting styles, appearances, special moves and combination attacks, as well as the control sequences used to execute their moves. As the court stated "Copying alone, however, is not sufficient to state a claim in copyright if the elements copied are not protectable." Denying Capcom's request for an injunction, the court further found that: "The vast majority of the moves—over 650 of them—are unprotectable, commonplace punches and kicks. In addition, the Court finds that even a majority of the moves that are allegedly special and fanciful are ultimately unprotectable either because they are unoriginal scenes-a-faire or have not actually been copied by Data East. As a result, the virtual identity standard is the appropriate standard for the Court to apply in assessing the subjective similarity between the two games."

The District Court in *Capcom* first ascertained that the plaintiff's characters were ostensibly protectable, and then applied the stricter standards described above, *id.* at **36–38:

> Ordinarily the standard of similarity to be applied to adjudicate infringement is a standard of "substantial similarity." Where the alleged similarities in a plaintiff's work consists primarily of elements that are unprotectable, or are capable of only a narrow range of expression, then a court must apply a "virtual identity standard" when comparing the plaintiff's work with the challenged one.

> It is indisputable that Street Fighter II is largely comprised of unprotectable elements. The vast majority of the moves—over 650 of them—are unprotectable, commonplace punches and kicks. In addition, the Court finds that even a majority of the moves that are allegedly special and fanciful are ultimately unprotectable either because they are unoriginal scenes-a-faire or have not actually been copied by Data East. As a result, the virtual identity standard is the appropriate standard for the Court to apply in assessing the subjective similarity between the two games.

> The subjective determination involved in the intrinsic test employs a reasonable person standard and examines the works for similarity in "total concept and feel."

The perspective is that of the relevant audience which in the case of video games is a discerning teenager, approximately seventeen years old.

Applying the virtual identity standard, the Court finds that Data East has not copied the core, protectable expression in Street Fighter II. Although the Court has concluded that three Fighter's History characters—Matlok, Feilin and Ray, are similar to Guile, Chun Li and Ken in Street Fighter II, the characters are not virtually identical and Data East certainly has not bodily appropriated them for use in its game.

4. In *Sheehan v. MTV Networks*, No. 89-Civ-6244 (LJF) 1992 WL 58876 (S.D.N.Y. 1992), 22 U.S.P.Q.2d 1394 (1992), the allegations were that during March of 1987, the plaintiffs developed an idea for a game show involving music video trivia ("Laser Blitz" or "Video Blitz") which they pitched to Defendant MTV. The plaintiffs prepared written rules, a format for the show, artwork and a schematic drawing detailing some of the audiovisual features of the program. The court described the plaintiff's game and background of the claim as follows:

> As indicated in the rules and format prepared by plaintiffs, "Laser Blitz" involves "two players competing in a two round front game and 'Video Blitz' bonus." In each of the two "front rounds," players are asked four music/music video questions, earning two "shots" for each correct answer. At the end of each question and answer, players take their "laser guns" and go to the 'Video Blitz' gameboard, "a nine monitor wall controlled by a computer which randomly selects and projects videos, prizes, cash, free shots and blow outs [forfeits of all cash and prizes to date]. When a player aims and shoots his lazer gun at a video, the board rotation stops, and whatever is showing on the gameboard dictates what happens to the player." Although not set forth in the written rules, the artwork submitted with those rules indicates that, during part of the game, players are seated in large, comfortable chairs, and are able to snack during the game. The successful operation of the laser gun requires a certain degree of manual and visual skill. The gun itself is an operating device as opposed to a non-functional prop.

> Thereafter, the plaintiffs met with Jock McLean, MTV's vice-president in charge of acquisitions. At that time, MTV had not yet produced a game show for broadcast on its channel. Plaintiffs provided McLean with a copy of the written proposal. Several months later, Sheehan met in London with Liz Nealon, MTV's executive producer for MTV Europe, and also gave Nealon a copy of plaintiffs' written proposal for the game. Meanwhile, other MTV employees obtained copies of plaintiffs' written proposal. Finally, the plaintiffs met with Doug Herzog, MTV's senior vice president in charge of programming and development, and gave him copies of their written proposal. At the end of that meeting, Herzog informed the plaintiffs that MTV was already developing its own game show and in December 1987, MTV broadcast "Remote Control" for the first time, which the court described as follows:

> "Remote Control" is set in the basement of the host, Ken Ober, a character who supposedly always dreamed of having his own game show. The focus of the game is a Zenith television set. During the game, three players are strapped to large easy chairs and given a non-functional prop resembling the hand-held remote control device for a television. The players then select among various categories of questions by calling out the appropriate television "channel" number and by pretending to use the remote control prop. The

questions during the early portion of the game are primarily about television shows, although the "prize round" involves identification of music videos within a time limit. A variety of "comedy gimmicks" are also used on the show, such as having food fall on contestants' heads during "snack breaks."

Id. at *1. The plaintiffs established that they held a valid copyright on their game and that the defendant had access, but as to the determinative issue of substantial similarity, the court found:

In order to establish that MTV infringed their copyright, plaintiffs must demonstrate a substantial similarity between their copyrighted work and the alleged copy, or that an average lay observer would recognize the alleged copy as having been appropriated from the copyrighted work. MTV argues that it is entitled to summary judgment on plaintiffs' infringement claim because plaintiffs have not shown sufficient similarity between their proposal and 'Remote Control.' Plaintiffs disagree and argue that, in any event, 'substantial similarity' is a question of fact, that must be resolved by the jury. Because the Court concludes that no reasonable jury could find that 'Laser Blitz' and 'Remote Control' are substantially similar, MTV's motion for summary judgment is granted. Plaintiffs claim that 'Laser Blitz' and 'Remote Control' are 'virtually identical' in their sequence and structure, rules, and style. While both shows do involve three players, multiple rounds of play in order to eliminate contestants, a 'host' posing questions to contestants, and the some kind of 'hand-held device,' these features are simply 'stock devices' common to game shows generally. The essential aspects of the games have substantial differences—an operable laser gun requiring skilled use as opposed to a non-functional prop resembling a television remote control, a multi-panel wall unit as opposed to a large television, questions limited to music videos as opposed to questions involving television trivia as well as music. As discussed above, 'Laser Blitz' is an original work of authorship because it has a number of unique attributes. However, those same attributes render it sufficiently different from 'Remote Control' to preclude a claim of infringement. *Id.* at 4.

---

§ 6.76 Federal Preemption

A variety of lawsuits, claims, and counterclaims for matters relating to state causes of action, such as unfair competition, breach of contract and unfair business practices are nothing more than veiled infringement actions that are subject to exclusive federal court jurisdiction. *See Capcom, Ltd. v. MKR Group, Inc.*, No. C 08-0904 RS 2008 WL 4661479(N.D. Cal. Oct. 20, 2008). Nevertheless, in order for one to establish the defense that the plaintiff's "state" claims are preempted by the Copyright Act, 17 U.S.C. § 301, two conditions must be satisfied:

(1) The content of the protected right must fall within the subject matter of copyright as described in 17 U.S.C. §§ 102 and 103, and

(2) The right asserted under state law must be equivalent to the exclusive rights contained in section 106 of the Copyright Act.

Summarily, the two conditions only require only that the rights the plaintiff seeks to protect are subject to copyright protection and further that those rights are equivalent to the rights provided by the Copyright Act. *See Amanda Lewis v. Activision Blizzard, Inc.*, 212 WL 5199501 (United States District Court, N.D., California, 2012). Amanda's name may sound familiar since her case was considered *supra*, §2.43. Amanda, recall, had performed voice over services for the virtual game *World of Warcraft* pursuant to a work for hire agreement. Prior to the eventual dismissal of her case, the Defendant Activision Blizzard raised the defense of preemption. In face of the court's decision to find in favor of preemption, Amanda was granted permission to amend her complaint. Amanda Lewis conceded the first leg of the test (i.e., her claim was protected by the Copyright Act); as to the second leg, the court stated: "As currently plead, Lewis's claims for commercial misuse of voice and quantum meruit are based wholly on Blizzard's use of her voice recordings and are therefore dismissed as preempted by federal copyright law. Because amendment does not appear to be futile, Lewis is granted leave to amend her state law claims only to the extent that she can allege, subject to Rule 11, commercial misuse of her name, voice, signature, photograph, or likeness that is not fixed in a recording."

---

§ 6.77 Copyright Misuse by Copyright Holder

The defense of "copyright misuse" may be available in situations wherein the copyright holder seeks to use its copyright to exert authoritative, monopolistic control to such an extent that equitable relief for an infringing defendant may be warranted. How much control by the copyright holder is too much is a diffuse concept, and the doctrine may be better explained by example. In *Practice Mgmt. Info. Corp. v. Am. Medical Assoc.*, 121 F.3d 516, 520–21 (9th Cir.1997) the American Medical Association copyrighted something called "the Physician's Current Medical Terminology," which is a detailed list of some 6,000 different medical procedures with a 5 digit code identifying each. Congress passed a law requiring the Health Care Financing Administration ("HCFA") to establish a uniform coding system nationwide for physicians to use when they seek Medicare and Medicaid reimbursement. Rather than develop its own codes, the HCFA entered into a licensing agreement with the AMA whereby the HCFA agreed "not to use any other system of procedure nomenclature ... for reporting physicians' services." This essentially gave the AMA a monopoly on the coding information physicians had to use in order to get Medicare and Medicaid reimbursement. The Ninth Circuit held this was "copyright abuse," and precluded the AMA from enforcing its copyright until the license was changed. *See also, e.g., Lasercomb Am., Inc. v. Reynolds*, 911 F.2d 970 (4th Cir. 1990).

Copyright misuse is not statutory, but the United States Supreme Court has given at least tacit approval of the defense. *United States v. Loew's, Inc.*, 371 U.S. 38 (1962). There is, however, a split of authority, with several circuits rejecting the defense. *See* Jaclyn M. Morgese, *Proper Misuse: How Courts Should Develop Copyright Misuse To Protect Copyright Holders' Brand Image And Market Reputation*, 64 SYRACUSE L. REV. 197 (2014).

---

§ 6.78 Safe Harbors

Statutory provisions granting a form of immunity from liability in exchange for following certain specified procedures are often referred to as "Safe harbors." The Digital Millennium Copyright Act of 1998 (DMCA), discussed *supra* §6.50, provides such a protection for Internet service providers (ISP's). The concept is relatively simple, even though the Act's so-called *take-down* procedures are not. An entity that merely accumulates and transmits material provided by others (*i.e.*, electronic bulletin boards) should not be subject to liability because those "others" happen to post material that infringes upon someone's copyright. In more euphemistic terms, *"Don't shoot the messenger because the message happens to infringe."* After all, we wouldn't think of suing the telephone company if someone used it for defamatory speech. It is argued that ISP's should enjoy similar immunity—in the name of free speech. But there is a difference between innocent, passive Internet service providers and not-so-innocent active purveyors of unlawful materials. Recall *Sega Enterprises Ltd. v. Mathai*, 948 F. Supp. 923 (N.D. Cal. 1996) and In *Sega Enterprises Ltd. v. Sabella*, No. C 93-04260 CW, 1996 WL 780560 (N.D. Cal., Dec. 18, 1996), which ran bulletin boards devoted to downloading copyrighted video games.

The statutory challenge, therefore, was to create a set of rules that would protect the innocent ISP's but not the guilty secondarily liable web sites. § 512(a) of the DMCA (titled: "Transitory Digital Network Communications.") provides only the basic ingredients:

> A service provider shall not be liable for monetary relief ... for injunctive or other equitable relief, for infringement of copyright by reason of the provider's transmitting, routing, or providing connections for, material through a system or network controlled or operated by or for the service provider, or by reason of the intermediate and transient storage of that material in the course of such transmitting, routing, or providing connections, if—
>
> > (1) the transmission of the material was initiated by or at the direction of a person other than the service provider;
> >
> > (2) the transmission, routing, provision of connections, or storage is carried out through an automatic technical process without selection of the material by the service provider;
> >
> > (3) the service provider does not select the recipients of the material except as an automatic response to the request of another person;
> >
> > (4) no copy of the material made by the service provider in the course of such intermediate or transient storage is maintained on the system or network in a manner ordinarily accessible to anyone other than anticipated recipients, and no such copy is maintained on the system or network in a manner ordinarily accessible to such anticipated recipients for a longer period than is reasonably necessary for the transmission, routing, or provision of connections; and
> >
> > (5) the material is transmitted through the system or network without modification of its content.

The remaining subparts for § 512 spell out additional conditions and procedures for the ISP seeking safe harbor immunity. Assuming that those requirements are adhered to, the ISP would not be liable for innocently posting a pirated video game or any protected materials.

Notes and Questions

1. Try to draft a take-down notice procedure for a videogame company. To find out how you did, go onto the website of a popular game that permits comments to be posted, such as *Second Life*, and see how the safe harbor provisions are articulated. See also § 10.20, *infra*.

Chapter 7

Patent Protection

Article I, Section 8, Clause 8 of the U.S. Constitution grants Congress the power to: "Promote the progress of science and useful arts, by securing for limited times to authors and inventors the exclusive right to their respective writings and discoveries." Patents are, therefore, created, regulated and enforced pursuant to federal law, which underwent substantial statutory alterations during 2011 through 2013. But despite these significant changes, imposed by the America Invents Act (AIA) and the Patent Law Treaties Implementation Act (PLTIA), the basic patent prerequisite of the Consolidated Patent Laws of the United States has not changed; according to § 101, U.S.C, Title 35, a patent has been, and still is, available under this condition:

> Whoever invents or discovers any new and useful process, machine, manufacture, or composition of matter, or any new and useful improvement thereof, may obtain a patent therefor, subject to the conditions and requirements of this title.

From this (and § 103), the courts have derived three requirements for obtaining a utility patent; the invention must be: [1] New, [2] Useful and [3] Non-obvious. For design patents, the design must be [1] New, [2] Ornamental and [3] Non-obvious.

In exchange for the rights granted under the patent, the patentee is required to disclose the invention in his or her application in sufficient detail so as to enable persons of ordinary skill in the art to make and use the invention. Section 112(a) of the Act requires the patent application to specify that which the patentee is claiming:

> The specification shall contain a written description of the invention, and of the manner and process of making and using it, in such full, clear, concise, and exact terms as to enable any person skilled in the art to which it pertains, or with which it is most nearly connected, to make and use the same, and shall set forth the best mode contemplated by the inventor or joint inventor of carrying out the invention.

The wrong choice of words can be a very tricky deal breaker in determining both the validity and scope of a patent. Terminology is, therefore, more than a matter of mere semantics. Words must carefully be selected and defined. This may not be an easy task, particularly where a new concept is involved. Otherwise simple words such as "attached" and "embedded," for example, may assume special meaning. Such was the case in *Thorner v. Sony Computer Ent. of Am., LLC,* 699 F.3d 1362 (Fed. Cir. 2012), a dispute over a tactile feedback controller for game systems; the devices provided the controller with touch-related sensations (such as vibrations) during the play of the game. The Court noted: "To act as its own lexicographer, a patentee must clearly set forth a definition of the disputed claim term, other than its plain and ordinary meaning. It is not enough for a patentee to simply disclose a single embodiment or use a word in the same manner in all embodiments; the patentee must clearly express an intent to redefine the term." This *disclosure element* inherent in the patent prosecution process generally conflicts with notions of trade secrecy (Chapter 8).

Upon expiration of the patent, the patentee loses all exclusive rights in the invention thereby permitting anyone to freely manufacture, duplicate or use it. Patents may be reissued, but not in the same sense that copyrights are renewed. A "reissue" patent may be granted where there is a mistake or defect in the original patent in accordance with § 251 of the Act. The reissued patent could either broaden or narrow the scope of the original patent depending upon the error. History's most notorious videogame claim involved a reissue patent (*Magnavox Co. v. Mattel, Inc.*, 216 U.S.P.Q. 28 (1982)), discussed in § 7.40 *infra*.

It should also be noted that patent rights are territorial in nature, limited in geographical scope by the boundaries of the countries that issue them. Subject to conventions and treaties, foreign patents must therefore be obtained to protect an invention outside of the United States. For this reason, a key purpose of the AIA was to bring the United States into greater conformity with the industrialized international community.

Reading the cases that follow requires a bit of caution for those unfamiliar with the patent process and its terminology. The field has a language of its own that tends to borrow familiar words and then change their meaning, which can cause confusion. For example, in patent parlance, a "claim" refers to the patentee's description of his or her invention, not a cause of action brought against an infringer. Likewise, the word "prosecution" refers to the processing of a patent application and has nothing to do with the penal system or attempts to incarcerate people. In that vein, the term "prosecution history" refers to the application process and the various communications between the Patent and Trademark Office and the applicant. The word "accused" most often refers to an infringing device or technology as opposed to a person.

Other important patent terms include: "Prior Art" (Technology or material that is publicly available prior to filing an application, which may "anticipate" the applicant's subject matter and thereby prevent the grant of a patent); "Read on" (If a patentee's claim *reads on* a technology, then that technology would infringe upon the patentee's patent; on the other hand, a patent claim that *reads on* prior art can be subject to invalidation); and, "Priority date" (The initial date of the filing of a patent application).

§ 7.10 Patents v. Copyrights: A Brief Comparison

In the United States a patent grant is formalized by an official document issued by the United States Government. The rights conveyed in that grant arise under the same Article I, Section 8 of the Constitution that empowers Congress to grant and regulate copyrights. For practical purposes, however, many of the similarities between copyrights and patents end there.

A patent holder, unlike a copyright owner, possesses a monopoly. In particular, the grant of a patent conveys to the patentee the right to exclude all others from making, using or selling the invention as defined in the "claims" portion of the patent. The copyright, by comparison, only prohibits unlawful copying; it carries no prohibition against others who may wish to create similar works on their own accord. Whereas two different individuals are both capable of owning copyrights for strikingly similar works, such is not the case for patent holders. Theoretically, a patent holder can prohibit another from manufacturing the patented product even though the potential infringer's actions occurred without any knowledge of the patent holder's right or interest. The patent is indeed a stronger bundle of rights than the copyright, but its duration is significantly less.

There once was a time when inventions were very distinguishable from works of authorship. No one ever confused a fiction novel with a cotton gin or a light bulb. As a general rule, if a creative work happens to be new, useful and non-obvious, it might qualify for a patent. But if, on the other hand, the original work happened to be artistic or literary, as *opposed* to useful, it would qualify for a copyright. There was also a time when the creative endeavors fell into one pigeonhole or the other, but not both. Technology, however, has changed that. For this reason, the road to copyrighting computer games, and software in general, has not always been a smooth or obvious path.

We know that videogame consoles along with an ever-increasing variety of mechanical and tangible electronic components are subject to patent protection. Moreover, the potential ability to patent any type of digital hardware is relatively uncontroversial. *See e.g., Honeywell v. Sperry Rand,* No. 4-67 Civ. 138, 1973 WL 903 (D. Minn., Oct. 19, 1973), 180 U.S.P.Q. 673 (1973). Software is also eligible for patent protection, *Diamond v. Diehr,* 450 U.S. 175 (1981), though its acceptability into this realm has not been quite as obvious. *See Gottschalk v. Benson,* 409 U.S. 63 (1972), and Pamela Samuelson, *Benson Revisited: The Case Against Patent Protection for Algorithms and Other Computer Related Inventions,* 39 Emory L.J. 1025 (1990). Despite this, videogames, as we shall soon see have encountered a rockier road to patent protection, even though the Patent and Trademark Office has generally become increasingly generous with respect to the types of patents that it normally grants. *See State St. Bank & Trust v. Signature Fin. Grp.,* 149 F.3d 1368 (Fed. Cir. 1988).

With respect to the games themselves, whether console-based or otherwise, it is of particular significance that software can simultaneously embody both an invention and a work of authorship. In the event of an overlap or potential conflict with respect to the benefits of registration, an issue may be raised as to which process should prevail. In that regard, it has been properly stated that patent law protects the *process or method* performed by a computer program while copyright law protects the *expression* of that process or method. But there are conflicting views.

One view tends to disfavor the granting of extensive copyright protection. It has, therefore, been stated that an author cannot acquire patent-like protection by placing an idea, process, or method in an unintelligible format and asserting copyright infringement against those who try to understand that idea, process, or method of operation. 17 U.S.C.A. § 102(b). *See Atari Games Corp. v. Nintendo of Am. Inc,* 975 F.2d 832, 839 (Fed. Cir. 1992). *See also Apple Computer, Inc. v. Formula Int'l, Inc.* 725 F.2d 521, 525 (9th Cir. 1984); *Apple Computer, Inc. v. Franklin Computer Corp.,* 714 F.2d 1240, 1253 (3d Cir. 1983). This view supports the notion that if a patentable process is embodied inextricably in the line-by-line instructions of a computer program, then the process merges with its expression and thereby precludes copyright protection. 17 U.S.C.A. § 101 et seq., *and* 35 U.S.C.A. § 1 et seq. To protect the processes or methods of operation, the creator must, therefore, look to the patent laws.

A better and more pragmatic view suggests that computer software is capable of both copyright protection and patent protection:[1]

---

1. David A. Einhorn, *Copyright and Patent Protection for Computer Software: Are They Mutually Exclusive?,* 30 IDEA 265 (1990).

There is no justification whatsoever in the Constitution, the federal statutes, or the case law to justify a denial of joint patent and copyright protection to computer software. While the Copyright Office regulations may create an obstacle to obtaining copyright protection for previously design-patented icons in computer screen displays, the Patent and Trademark Office regulations expressly permit items which are previously copyrighted to later be the subject of design patents. While the case law and federal regulations do not directly address the availability of joint copyright and utility patent protection for computer software, the same considerations apply as in the design patent context. Joint copyright and patent protection for software, regardless of whether the patent is a design or utility patent, does not constitute an illegal extension of the patent grant because copyrights and patents are very different types of protection—each protecting computer programming at differing levels of generality and to differing extents [Citations omitted].

* * *

Consider an example. The antagonistic prelude to *Atari Games Corp. v. Nintendo of Am. Inc.*, 975 F.2d 832 (Fed. Cir. 1992) involved Nintendo's attempt to lock-out unauthorized third party game developers. Basically, Nintendo's lock-and-key sent synchronized encoded data streams which unlocked the console when an authorized game was inserted. When, however, an unauthorized game was inserted, the same console remained locked thereby discouraging videogame manufacturers from designing games of the popular NES without first receiving the "keys" from Nintendo. Developers were upset that Nintendo was forcing them to pay for the privilege of developing games for the NES console. Atari was so upset that it refused and simply copied the NES software from records filed in the U.S. Copyright Office. Atari was exonerated with respect to Nintendo's claims of copyright infringement even though Atari had made misrepresentations to the Copyright Office to obtain the required information. In addition to copyrighting its software, Nintendo also obtained a patent for its software, U.S. Pat. No. 4,799,635. The patent was deemed valid and it was determined that Atari had in fact infringed. Thus, the patent protection prevailed while, simultaneously, the copyright shield failed. The matter was thereafter settled.

In summary, despite the increasing number of do-it-yourself books, obtaining a patent is a specialized and complex process, requiring expertise. Unlike registering a copyright, a function which can easily be performed by the most unsophisticated author, obtaining a patent is more complicated, time consuming and often expensive. Both copyrights and patents play important roles in protecting the products of videogame industry. Up until 10–15 years ago, a large videogame company like Nintendo had hundreds of copyrights, but only a few patents. However, patent protection has become more prevalent in the past decade.

§ 7.20 United States
Consolidated Patent Laws

The Patent Act of 1790, titled "An Act to Promote the Progress of Useful Arts," was the first federal patent statute of the United States. Prior to that time, patent matters were left to the states; recall that the U.S. Constitution (including Article I, Section 8) didn't take effect until 1787. The 1790 Act was replaced by the Patent Act of 1793. This was then followed by the Patent Act of 1836 which created the Patent Office. Patent Number 1 was issued in 1836 for the wheel (i.e., the "traction" wheel). The first modern revision of the patent system occured in 1952 when Congress passed legislation which laid out the basic scheme that we are familiar with today, requiring the often cited three requirements, newness, usefulness and non-obviousness.

In 1947 Thomas T. Goldsmith Jr. and Settle Ray Mann developed an electronic gizmo and called it "The Cathode Ray Tube Amusement Device," which in reality became the first missile simulation game; and, it might even be considered as the first patented videogame. It was inspired by radar displays shown on early cathode ray tubes during World War II. A patent for this game device was applied for in January 1947, and granted as U.S. Patent #2,455,992 in 1948.

Presently, the patent laws of the United States are complex, consisting of several separate acts promulgated at different times and subjected to periodical amendments; they are collectively referenced as "United States Code, Title 35 — Patents." Since 2011 those laws have been witnessing a major overhaul, perhaps the most significant and substantial changes since the Patent Act of 1952, in an effort to create some consistency with the other developed countries of the world.

Some very dramatic changes arrived in the form of the Leahy-Smith America Invents Act ("AIA"). As of March 16, 2013, a key date to remember, patent applications move from a "first inventor to *invent*" to a "first inventor to *file*" system. This changes the important *who's first* measurement scheme for the patent applicant's race to the goal line. It provides a more readily determinable measurement date and tends to harmonize the U.S. patent system with those of other industrialized countries. The post-AIA measurement date (a matter of simple documentary evidence) should prove to be more ascertainable than an invention date; even more ascertainable than the now-obsolete and quite questionable "Flash of Genius" Doctrine.[2]

With the *First to Invent* standard comes a limited one-year grace period within which an invention can be disclosed publicly by an inventor, or another person or entity who obtained it from the inventor, before filing a patent application claiming the invention. Many countries do not permit prior disclosures, even by an inventor. Under the AIA, U.S. patents that originate in foreign jurisdictions may also be counted as prior art based on when they were originally filed in those foreign jurisdictions, rather than when ultimately filed in the United States.

The AIA also expands the scope of prior art under 35 U.S.C. § 102 to include foreign offers for sale, sales, and public uses. The *prior art* concept bears heavily of the newness or "novelty" requirement set forth in § 101. Novelty is identified by post-AIA 35 U.S.C § 102(a), which states, in relevant part, that a person shall be entitled to a patent *unless*: (1) the claimed invention was patented, described in a printed publication, or in public use, on sale, or otherwise available to the public before the effective filing date of the claimed invention; or (2) the claimed invention was described in a patent or in an application for patent published or deemed published, in which the patent or application, as the case may be, names another inventor and was effectively filed before the effective filing date of the claimed invention.

---

2. Rejected by Congress in the 1952 Patent Act, the so-called "*Flash of Genius*" Test or Doctrine was enunciated by Justice William O. Douglas in *Cuno Eng'g v. Automatic Devices*, 314 U.S. 84 (1941).

§ 7.30 Infringement

The patent's true test, it is said, comes with litigation. This common theme among the patent industry suggests, though erroneously, that a patent is not valid until it has been court-tested.

§ 7.31 The Prima Facie Case

Unlike infringing a copyright, which involves a conscious effort to copy the specific works of another, a person may be deemed guilty of infringing upon a patent without such a showing. According to 35 U.S.C. § 271(a), the lack of knowledge of a preexisting patent is irrelevant: "Whoever without authority makes, uses, offers to sell, or sells any patented invention, within the United States or imports into the United States any patented invention during the term of the patent therefor, infringes the patent." In conjunction with § 271(b), anyone who "actively induces infringement of a patent" is also guilty of infringement.

Where there has been a direct duplication of a mechanical apparatus, infringement may be relatively simple to establish. The plaintiff, as owner of the patent, will have previously filed a "claim" to accompany the application. It will provide a specific description of what the applicant is claiming as his, her or its patent. The plaintiff will allege that the owner or manufacturer of the infringing apparatus (the "accused device") had violated plaintiff's rights by constructing or owning an item that is described in plaintiff's patent "claim." Grammatically, the plaintiff asserts that the claim "reads on the accused device." Where the patent claim reads "directly" on the accused device, literal infringement is established. *Hanson v. Alpine Valley Ski Area, Inc.*, 611 F.2d 156, 161 (6th Cir. 1979). More common by far, however, are disputes over the differences, subtle or otherwise, between a patented product and that of a potential competitor. When determining an infringement based upon such "real identity," an examination and comparison of each apparatus with respect to *means, operation* and *result* must be undertaken.

As is the case with copyright infringement, in order to breach a patent, literal duplication is not required. Infringement can also be established under the theory known as the "*Doctrine of Equivalents.*" If a device conforms to the following three-element test, then infringement may (but not necessarily) be found. *Pennwalt Corp. v. Durand-Wayland, Inc.*, 833 F.2d 931, 934 (Fed. Cir. 1987) (en banc). This test is satisfied if the complained of device, as compared to the patented invention: (1) performs substantially the same overall function or work, (2) in substantially the same way, (3) to obtain substantially the same overall result.

A court will not permit an "unscrupulous copyist to make unimportant and insubstantial changes and substitutions in the patent which, though adding nothing, would be enough to take the copied matter outside the claim." *Graver Tank & Mfg. Co. v. Linde Air Prods. Co.*, 339 U.S. 605, 607 (1950). However, the doctrine does *not* automatically apply to every patent infringement action. In fact, application of the *Doctrine of Equivalents* is the exception, not the rule. *London v. Carson Pirie Scott & Co.*, 946 F.2d 1534, 1538 (Fed. Cir. 1991).

* * *

This next case is presented as a demonstration of the manner in which a district court analyses and decides a patent infringement action.

Fitness Gaming Corp. v. Icon Health & Fitness

United States District Court, Eastern District of Virginia, 2011
2011 U.S. Dist. Lexis 90605

HILTON, United States District Judge.

MEMORANDUM OPINION

This case is before the Court on Defendant ICON Health & Fitness, Inc.'s ("ICON") Motion For Summary Judgment. This is a patent infringement action brought by Plaintiff Fitness Gaming Corporation ("FGC") against Defendant. It involves FGC's patent directed to the combination of (1) a piece of exercise equipment and (2) a gambling device, which device the patent refers to as an "electronic game of chance device." This motion for summary judgment of non-infringement turns on the interpretation of that term.

Pursuant to 35 U.S.C. §271(a), "whoever without authority makes, uses, offers to sell, or sells any patented invention, within the United States or imports into the United States any patented invention during the term of the patent therefor, infringes the patent." The "patented invention" is defined by "one or more claims particularly pointing out and distinctly claiming the subject matter which the applicant regards as his invention." 35 U.S.C. §112. In general, a claim defines the subject matter that it covers by setting forth a list of requirements that must be met in order to qualify as "the patented invention." The more requirements, the narrower the scope of the claim. The requirements of a claim are generally referred to as "claim elements" or "claim limitations."

To determine whether a particular device or method is covered by a claim, a two-step analysis is performed. First, the patented invention, as set forth in the words of the patent claims, must be clearly understood. This is a question of claim construction, or claim interpretation, and it is determined by a court as a matter of law. *Markman v. Westview Instruments, Inc.*, 517 U.S. 370 (1996). Under the second step of the analysis, the accused device or process is compared to the claims to determine whether there is infringement. *Hormone Research Foundation v. Genentech, Inc.*, 904 F.2d 1558, 1562 (Fed. Cir. 1990).

Infringement can occur in two ways: there can either be literal infringement or infringement under the doctrine of equivalents. "Literal infringement exists if each of the limitations of the asserted claim(s) read on, that is, are found in, the accused device." *Baxter Healthcare Corp. v. Spectramed, Inc.*, 49 F.3d 1575, 1583 (Fed. Cir. 1995). "The absence of even a single limitation … precludes a finding of literal infringement." *Kahn v. General Motors Corp.*, 135 F.3d 1472, 1477 (Fed. Cir. 1998). Even if there is no literal infringement, there still may be infringement under the doctrine of equivalents, but only if, for each limitation not present literally, the accused product nevertheless contains a permissible "equivalent." *Warner-Jenkinson Co. v. Hilton Davis Chemical Co.*, 520 U.S. 17 (1997). Each and every requirement of a claim must be met, either literally or by a permissible equivalent, in order to find infringement. *Id.* at 29.

The purpose of "claim interpretation" or "claim construction" is to make an objective assessment about what a person of ordinary skill in the art at the time the patent was filed would have understood to be the meaning employed by the patentee for the words in the claims. *Phillips v. AWH Corp.*, 415 F.3d 1303, 1313, 1316–17, 1321–23 (Fed. Cir. 2005) (en banc). The focus is on "how the patentee used the claim term in the claims, specification, and prosecution history." *Id.* at 1321. "Ultimately, the interpretation to be given a term can only be determined and confirmed with a full understanding of what the inventors actually invented and intended to envelop with the claim. That construction that stays true to the claim language and most naturally aligns with the patent's description of the invention will be, in the end, the correct construction." *Renishaw PLC v. Marposs Societá per Azioni,* 158 F.3d 1243, 1250 (Fed. Cir. 1998).

The prosecution history of the patent is also important evidence in determining the meaning of the claims. *Phillips,* 415 F.3d at 1317. The administrative procedure conducted in the PTO before the patent was granted is called "prosecution," and the written record of prosecution is called the "prosecution history" of the application. The prosecution history contains the complete record of all the proceedings before the PTO, including any representations made by the applicant regarding the scope of the claims.

The prosecution history limits the interpretation of claims so as to exclude any interpretation that may have been disclaimed or disavowed during prosecution in order to obtain claim allowance. *Phillips, 415 F.3d at 1317; Vitronics,* 90 F.3d at 1583. "Claims may not be construed one way in order to obtain their allowance and in a different way against accused infringers." *Southwall Techs. Inc. v. Cardinal IG Co.,* 54 F.3d 1570, 1576 (Fed. Cir. 1995); *see also Spectrum Int'l, Inc. v. Sterilite Corp.,* 164 F.3d 1372, 1378 (Fed. Cir. 1998). Arguments made during the prosecution history may not only limit the interpretation of claim terms, but may also "estop an applicant from recapturing that surrendered matter under the doctrine of equivalents." *Augustine Medical, Inc. v. Gaymar Indus., Inc.,* 181 F.3d 1291, 1299 (Fed. Cir. 1999) (internal quotation marks omitted). This is so, whether or not such assertions were truly required to secure allowance of the claim. *Texas Instruments Inc. v. United States Int'l Trade Comm'n,* 988 F.2d 1165, 1174–75 (Fed. Cir. 1993).

The specification and prosecution history are together referred to as the "intrinsic evidence." *Vitronics,* 90 F.3d at 1582. Evidence other than the specification and prosecution history ("extrinsic evidence"), such as dictionaries, can be used to help interpret claim terms, but cannot be used to contradict the intrinsic evidence. *Id.* at 1584. In the end, the proper interpretation is one that is "consistent with a patent's internal logic," "comports with the instrument as a whole," and "preserve[s] the patent's internal coherence." *Markman,* 517 U.S. at 389–90.

Summary judgment is appropriate where a party cannot "make a showing sufficient to establish the existence of an element essential to that party's case, and on which that party will bear the burden of proof at trial." *Celotex Corp. v. Catrett,* 477 U.S. 317, 322, (1986). Here, the burden of proving infringement is on the patent owner. *Mannesmann Demag Corp. v. Engineered Metal Prods. Co.,* 793 F.2d 1279, 1282 (Fed. Cir. 1986). Thus, the burden of the moving party (here, ICON) may be discharged by simply pointing out "that there is an absence of evidence to support the nonmoving party's case." *Id.* at 325.

Here, the specification and prosecution history make clear what the claims require as a matter of law, and FGC has no evidence that the accused devices have what the claims require.

Therefore, summary judgment of non-infringement should be granted.

---

§ 7.32 Defenses To Infringement

The defenses to a patent infringement lawsuit are many. The most common defenses are either contained in or derived from the Patent Act and its amendments and revisions. Let's begin:

[A] Independent Invention

The infrequently asserted defense of "Independent Invention" arises when the defendant argues that he, she or it coincidentally invented the same product as the patented item and did so innocently without any knowledge of the existing patent. This brand of "innocence" might prevail in a copyright infringement lawsuit, but not with respect to patent infringement. As might be expected, § 271(a) says nothing about knowledge of the patent needed for a valid claim. *See also* Samson Vermont, *Independent Invention as a Defense to Patent Infringement*, 105 MICH L. REV. 475 (2006).

[B] Non-Infringement

Of the valid defenses, claiming "non-infringement" is obvious. If the plaintiff's patent claim does not read on the accused device, the defense of non-infringement may be quite viable. Even though showing infringement would seem to be incumbent upon the plaintiff, § 282(b)(1) of the Patent Act seems to suggest otherwise: "The following shall be defenses in any action involving the validity or infringement of a patent and *shall be pleaded*: (1) Noninfringement, absence of liability for infringement or unenforceability ..." (Emphasis supplied).

[C] Patent Invalidity (General)

Patent invalidity is certainly a defense to an infringement suit, per § 282(b)(2) of the Patent Act, but § 282(a) makes it clear where the burden is placed: "A patent shall be presumed valid. Each claim of a patent (whether in independent, dependent, or multiple dependent form) shall be presumed valid independently of the validity of other claims; dependent or multiple dependent claims shall be presumed valid even though dependent upon an invalid claim. The burden of establishing invalidity of a patent or any claim thereof shall rest on the party asserting such invalidity." Invalidity may occur for any one of a number of reasons stated in § 282, including failure to comply with the strict requirements of the application procedure as set forth in § 112 and its several subparts.

[D] Prior Art

It may be argued that a patent that results from prior art fails to satisfy the newness requirement. This can be a very tricky defense since all improvement patents are, at least theoretically predicated upon some form of prior art. Were this not so, a "better mousetrap" could never be patented. Nevertheless, no patent infringement defense is complete without allegations of prior art. It seems that AIA § 102(a), titled "Novelty; Prior Art" provides six novelty-destroying categories of defenses is a single sentence. It essentially states that a person shall be entitled to a patent unless the claimed invention was:

[i]   Patented,

[ii] described in a printed publication,

[iii] in public use,

[iv] on sale,

[v]   otherwise available to the public before the effective filing date; or

[vi] claimed and described in an application naming another inventor per § 102(a)(2).

The public disclosures listed above are effective if they occur *anywhere* in the world. This is a substantial change made by the AIA, since during pre-AIA, the disclosures were not effective unless they happened in the United States.

Several related defenses spring from the requirement that the invention be novel or new. The *prior printed publication* defense, for example, suggests that a defendant can achieve victory by locating a prior printed reference that describes the plaintiff's invention, with a date that precedes the date of the claimed invention. 35 U.S.C. 35 § 102(a). Or a defendant can successfully defend by showing that the plaintiff's claimed invention was in existence prior to plaintiff's claim. 35 U.S.C. § 102(g). It is also a defense to show that the claimed invention was sold or in prior use in this country 1 year prior to the application date. 35 U.S.C. 35 § 102(b).

[E] Obviousness

Closely related to the prior defense, the *obviousness* concept is designed to attack the patent limitation set forth in § 103 of the AIA:

> A patent for a claimed invention may not be obtained, notwithstanding that the claimed invention is not identically disclosed as set forth in section 102, if the differences between the claimed invention and the prior art are such that the claimed invention as a whole would have been obvious before the effective filing date of the claimed invention to a person having ordinary skill in the art to which the claimed invention pertains. Patentability shall not be negated by the manner in which the invention was made.

In order to fall within this pigeonhole, the AIA added language indicating that the differences between prior art and the claimed invention as a whole must have been obvious "before the effective filing date of the claimed invention."

[F] Estoppel

Patent prosecution often involves negotiation between the applicant and the Patent and Trademark Office. During the give-and-take process, the applicant may relinquish certain claims in order to obtain others. Thus, the defense of "prosecution history estoppel" may be available to defendants in the event that the patentee attempts to enforce relinquished rights.

[G] Misconduct

Misconduct is a broad concept that comes in a variety of forms. One of several methods for establishing that a patent and claim are invalid involves a showing that there was a fraudulent or inadequate disclosure to the Patent and Trademark Office by the patentee during the application process. The defense of "Inadequate Disclosure" can be complex but has in the past been quite successful because the disclosure process has been quite rigorous. During that process, the patentee must provide a written description of the invention that is detailed and definite enough to "enable" someone skilled in the relevant art to make it.

Other defenses include "*patent misuse*," which typically results from anti-competitive conduct, such as "bundling," where consumers wishing to purchase the invented item are forced to buy another product or products that the consumers do not want. Monopolistic deployment of patent infringement litigation and charges of antitrust often go hand in hand.

Inequitable conduct with respect to the use of a patent or the application process may also constitute a defense and it may provide independent grounds for invalidating an existing patent. *See, Nintendo of Am. Inc. v. The Magnavox Co.,* § 7.40 *infra.* It should be noted that this particular line of defenses has been somewhat curtailed by the AIA.

For certain patents that control broad-based technological standards, sometimes referred to as "SEP's" (Standard Essential Patents), there exist special international organizations, called "Standard Setting Organizations," (SSO's) to ensure that required patented technology is available at a reasonable price. For a battle over the technological standards of WiFi. *See Microsoft Corp. v. Motorola, Inc.*, 963 F.Supp.2d 1176 (W.D. Wash., 2013).

[H] Expiration

Last but not least, unlike copyrights, the life of a patent is relatively short. For a utility patent, the life is 20 years; it is 14 years for a design patent.

---

§ 7.40 The *'507* Pioneer Patent

If a patent for the invention of a better mousetrap is a typical *improvement* patent, a *pioneer* patent would best represent the mousetrap itself. Unlike a mere modification or betterment, a pioneer patent exists when it introduces "a wholly new device, or one of such novelty and importance as to mark a distinct step in the progress of the art." *Ziegler v. Phillips Petroleum Co.*, 483 F.2d 858, 870 (5th Cir. 1973). The following case, which takes us back to 1972 then historically forward, deals with such a patent. It involves disputes among some of the key companies and pioneers that helped trigger the videogame industry as outlined in our preceding history (§ 1.30). It tells of the invention of an apparatus capable of simply generating and moving a dot on a screen. By today's standards, the ability to control that small blip on a television-like screen might not seem like much, but as reflected in our preceding history, it was enough to trigger a multi-billion industry.

For introductory purposes, the significance of the *Magnavox* case at this juncture relates more to Judge Leighton's factual analysis and findings than from the intricacies of the applicable patent law principles. It may, nevertheless, be helpful to preface the case with a brief description of the term "means plus function," which is referenced in *Magnavox*. Classically, a patent application required rigorous structural specifications for an invention. By statute, however, in order to simplify the patent process, Congress has provided requirements for construing certain types of patent claims known as "means plus function." *See* 35 U.S.C. § 112. A "means-plus-function" patent claim defines a "means" for performing some function without specifying a definite structure. *See Cole v. Kimberly-Clark Corp.*, 102 F.3d 524, 531 (Fed. Cir. 1996). The Court of Appeals for the Federal Circuit has developed a series of rules for invoking a means plus function analysis. Therefore, as you examine the next case, the term "means" should signal such an analysis.

With the preceding in mind, *Magnavox* provides numerous patent-related issues of significance. As previously indicated, it also presents a rich identification and description of the founding fathers of videogames and the pioneer companies who made early contributions to the videogame revolution.

It is particularly interesting to observe the manner in which the validity of a pioneer parent isn't necessarily settled by a single action, judgment or ruling. On the contrary, as the following three cases indicate, the battle for such a prize may have to be fought against several challengers in separate cases.

Magnavox Co. v. Mattel, Inc.

United States District Court, Northern District of Illinois, 1982
216 U.S.P.Q. 28

Leighton, United States District Judge.

This cause having been heard without a jury, witnesses having testified, excerpts from depositions having been admitted, and exhibits offered having been received in evidence, the court, in accordance with Rule 52(a) Fed. R. Civ. P., 28 U.S.C., makes its findings of fact and reaches the following conclusions of law.

I. Findings of Fact

[Plaintiff Sanders & Associates owned the "507" patent, which, as noted above in § 1.30, *supra*, provided for the display of a lighted dot across a screen and allowed a user to manipulate a symbol to intercept and manipulate that dot. Plaintiff Magnavox was a licensee of the 507 patent.

Defendant Mattel manufactured and distributed a control box console, which the court refers to as the "Master Component," which is hooked up to a television. It also manufactured a number of cartridges that could be inserted into the Master Component to play various games on the connected television, including: tennis, baseball, football, hockey, soccer, and basketball games on a television. Together, the Master Component and the cartridges were known as the Mattel Intellivision. The defendants were Mattel and a number of retailers and marketers of the Mattel Master Component and the cartridges, including Sears, Roebuck & Co. The court refers to them collectively as "Mattel."

Plaintiffs asserted that all the games were based on the patented process by which a lighted dot (be it a tennis ball, a baseball, a football, a hockey puck, etc.) is interfered with by the manipulation of the user.

There were slight differences in the arguments made for each of the games, but the gist of each were identical, so the decision below is edited to focus only on the alleged infringement of the tennis game.

Note that the decision was rendered by a district court and so is in a style favored by some district courts, i.e., split into findings of facts and conclusions of law — ED.]

A. Pretrial procedural background, the parties, and the claims of infringement

This is a patent infringement suit in which the plaintiffs charge defendants Mattel, Inc. and others, with infringement of U.S. Reissue Patent No. Re. 28,507 (hereinafter referred to as the "507 patent" or the "patent-in-suit") by the manufacture, use, or sale of certain Intellivision video games. Evidence now of record reveals the phenomenon of a patent that heralded the beginning of an industry, the home video game.

The issues of validity and infringement of the '507 patent were heard by the Honorable Judge John F. Grady of this court in a trial of [various] prior cases which commenced on November 4, 1976 and terminated on January 10, 1977. Prior to commencement of that trial, certain parties had settled out of the litigation.

The prior trial before Judge [Grady] was in Magnavox Co. v. Chicago Dynamic Industries, 1977 U.S. Dist. LEXIS 17996 (N.D. Ill. 1977), where the '507 patent-in-suit was held to be valid and infringed. None of the accused products at the Chicago Dynamics trial was a computer-based video game or was a video game having a microprocessor. This is the first trial involving an accused computer-based video game or a video game embodying a microprocessor. Mattel does not challenge validity in the present action, but has alleged and does contend that the '507 patent is not infringed and is unenforceable.

B. Work that led to the '507 patent

The '507 patent resulted from experimental work done by William T. Rusch while he was an employee of the plaintiff Sanders in the period beginning 1967. He did this while a member of a group of Sanders' employees working on television games. That group included primarily, besides Rusch, Ralph H. Baer and William L. Harrison.

This group of Sanders' employees was started by Baer in early 1967. He did this as a result of early ideas he had concerning television games in September 1966. By June 1967, the first television game by the group had been completed. That work led to United States patent 3,728,480 entitled "Television Gaming and Training Apparatus" showing Baer as the inventor.

Rusch joined the Sanders television game group in April or May 1967; he commenced work on the project by the end of October 1967. His work resulted in the patent-in-suit.

By January 1968, an apparatus had been constructed and successfully operated embodying some of Rusch's work. The apparatus generated a display on the screen comprising a television picture including a symbol on the right side of the screen representing a first player, a symbol on the left side of the screen representing a second player, and a symbol which moved across the screen representing a ball. Player controls were provided so that each human player could move his corresponding player symbol on the face of the television screen. Each human player manipulated his corresponding player symbol to intercept the path of the ball as it moved across the screen. When the player symbol intercepted the ball symbol, i.e., two symbols appeared to be coincident on the screen, the motion of the ball was changed.

In the television game apparatus operated in January 1968 and embodying some of Rusch's work, the horizontal motion of the ball was reversed so that it traveled back toward the other player. Each player had an "English" control which permitted him to alter the vertical motion of the ball after he had intercepted it.

The apparatus is described in the '507 patent.

From 1968 through 1971, Sanders demonstrated television game apparatus using various pieces of equipment and playing various games to parties it thought might be interested in entering into some type of arrangement to commercialize the work it had done through its employees. Demonstrations of that work were made to representatives of Teleprompter Corporation, RCA Corporation, Zenith Radio Corporation, General Electric Company, Motorola, Inc., Warwick Electronics, Inc., The Magnavox Company, and others.

C. The evolution of the television game industry

In March 1971, Sanders and Magnavox entered into an agreement under which Magnavox received an option for an exclusive license under the pending United States patent application which eventually resulted in the '507 patent, other Sanders' United States patent applications relating to television games, and corresponding applications in foreign countries. Then, by an agreement effective January 27, 1972, Magnavox exercised its option and became the exclusive licensee of Sanders under the patent application which eventually resulted in the '507 patent, other Sanders' United States patent applications relating to television games, corresponding applications in foreign countries, and the patents to issue therefrom.

Magnavox made a limited number of television games and market tested them at a few locations around the country following the March 1971 agreement. After these market tests, Magnavox commercially introduced the product.

Since entering into this exclusive license agreement, Magnavox has manufactured and sold television games in the United States under the trademark "Odyssey." The Odyssey television games are intended for use by consumers with their home television receivers.

The first model Odyssey television game commercially introduced by Magnavox was the Model 1TL 200; the Model 1TL 200 Odyssey television game was first placed on sale by Magnavox in 1972.

In the 1972 Magnavox Odyssey television game, the display shown on the television picture tube screen included a white rectangular symbol on the right side of the screen representing a first player, a white rectangular symbol on the left side of the screen representing a second player, and a symbol which moved across the screen representing a ball or similar playing piece. Player controls were provided so that each human player could move his corresponding player symbol on the face of the television screen both horizontally and vertically. Each human player manipulated his corresponding player symbol to intercept the path of the ball as it moved across the screen. When the player symbol intercepted the ball symbol, i.e., two symbols appeared to be coincident on the screen, the motion of the ball was changed and, in particular, the horizontal motion of the ball was reversed so that it traveled back toward the other player. Each player had an "English" control which permitted him to alter the vertical motion of the ball after he had intercepted it.

This television game could be made to play different games by inserting different game cards into the game unit. Thus, it was a programmable game.

The Magnavox Odyssey television game Model 1TL 200 was nationally demonstrated to Magnavox dealers, distributors, sales personnel, and other persons at shows around the country during May 1972.

The first television game manufactured by any party other than Magnavox, and alleged by it to infringe the '507 patent-in-suit, was the game known as "Pong," which was manufactured and sold by Atari, Inc. (hereinafter "Atari").

Pong was designed and built by Nolan K. Bushnell and Allen Alcorn of Atari.

Prior to August 21, 1969, Bushnell had had extensive experience in the field of coin-operated amusement games, had been employed as a television technician, and had had experience in the programming of general purpose, stored program, digital computers and had had experience in the programming of general purpose, stored program, digital computers operated in conjunction with cathode ray tube displays. Prior to this date, he had not invented, designed, built, or constructed any apparatus for playing games using a television type, raster scan display; and he had no knowledge of the existence of any apparatus for playing games using a television type, raster scan display:

Prior to August 21, 1969, Bushnell had no knowledge of the existence of any apparatus using a cathode ray tube display for simulating the playing of the game table tennis or ping pong.

On May 24, 1972, and while employed by Nutting Associates, Inc., Mountain View, California, Bushnell attended the demonstration of the Magnavox Odyssey television game in Burlingame, California and saw the game played; he had gone to that show for the specific purpose of seeing the Magnavox Odyssey television game. He saw the Odyssey television game in use to play a game simulating ping pong and actually played that game.

Some time after June 26, 1972, Allen Alcorn became an employee of Atari and Bushnell assigned Alcorn the task of developing a video game which would simulate a tennis game. His work resulted in an arcade video game named "Pong," first manufactured and sold by Atari in 1973.

The display of this game, shown on a picture tube screen, included a white rectangular symbol on the right side of the screen representing a first player, a white rectangular symbol on the left side of the screen representing a second player, and a symbol which moved across the screen representing a ball. Player controls were provided so that each human player could move his corresponding player symbol on the face of the screen. Each human player manipulated his corresponding symbol to intercept the path of the ball as it moved across the screen. When the player symbol intercepted the ball symbol, i.e., two symbols appeared to be coincident on the screen, the motion of the ball was changed and, in particular, the horizontal motion of the ball was reversed so that it traveled back toward the other player.

Following the commercial introduction of the Atari arcade Pong game, many other manufacturers commercially introduced similar arcade games having a display substantially the same as Pong. Those games included the games TV Ping Pong, TV Tennis, Olympic TV Hockey, and TV Goalee by Chicago Dynamic Industries, Inc., the games Paddle Ball, Pro Hockey, Pro Tennis, and Olympic Tennis by Seeburg Industries, Inc., Paddle Battle and Tennis Tourney by Allied Leisure Industries, Inc., and Winner and Playtime by Midway Mfg. Co.

The Atari arcade Pong game was the first arcade television game to be sold in large quantities. It, and games substantially identical to it, were responsible for the creation of the arcade television game industry.

Then, in 1975, Atari commercially introduced a Pong game for use by consumers in the home which was intended to be attached to a broadcast receiver.

[The display shown on the television screen, according to this allegation, is identical to the display described above, i.e., a white symbol on both sides of the screen indicating each player with another symbol moving across the screen representing a ball—Ed.]

In 1975, Magnavox commercially introduced the Odyssey 100 and Odyssey 200 home television games, the Models YF7010 and 7015, respectively.

[The displays in these home television games, according to the allegations, is identical to the displays described above—ED.]

In 1976 General Instrument Corporation, New York, New York (hereinafter "General Instrument") commercially introduced an electronic integrated circuit component which included in a single integrated circuit device the great majority of electrical components previously needed to manufacture a television game. That integrated circuit component was designated by General Instrument as the AY-3-8500 component.

The basic design of this component was done by Gilbert Duncan Harrower of General Instrument.

The presence on the market of the General Instrument's AY-3-8500 integrated circuit component permitted the manufacture of television games with many fewer components, and thus at a much lower cost, than was previously possible.

The General Instrument AY-3-8500 integrated circuit component included within it a read only memory or ROM which was used in part to define the size and shape of the symbols which were displayed on the television screen.

[The displays in the television games which could be constructed using the General Instrument AY-3-8500 integrated circuit component, according to this allegation, are identical to the displays described above—ED.]

In 1976, Magnavox commercially introduced the Odyssey 300, Odyssey 400, Odyssey 500, and Odyssey 3000 television games, the Models BG 7500, BG 7516, BG 7520, BH

7514, respectively, and the Model BG 4305, a television receiver having a built-in television game.

[The displays in these television games, and the Model BG 4305 television receiver, are identical to the displays described above—ED.]

In 1977, Magnavox commercially introduced the Odyssey 2000 and Odyssey 4000 television games, the Models BG 7510 and BH 7511, respectively.

[The displays in these television games, according to this allegation, are identical to the displays described above—ED.]

Magnavox's Odyssey 300, Odyssey 2000, Odyssey 3000, and Odyssey 4000 television games, utilized the General Instrument AY-3-8500 component. The Magnavox Odyssey 300 is a typical one of the games using that component.

Prior to the commercial introduction of television games using microprocessors, most of the television games sold for use in the home were of the type known as "ball and paddle" games. The 1972 Odyssey, Odyssey 100, Odyssey 200, Odyssey 300, Odyssey 400, Odyssey 500, Odyssey 2000, Odyssey 3000, Odyssey 4000, and Atari's consumer Pong television games are examples of such games.

The ball and paddle television games formed the basis for the establishment of the home television game industry prior to the commercial introduction of home television games using microprocessors.

Commencing in 1977, various manufacturers commercially introduced television games which included microprocessors. These manufacturers included Atari, Fairchild, and Bally.

The use of a microprocessor in a television game permitted construction of a television game console which could be readily made to play a variety of television games. Cartridges are provided which can be plugged into the television game console and thereby connected to the circuitry within the console. Different cartridges are provided for different games. Each cartridge contains the read only memory also known as ROM.

This feature includes information used by the circuitry of the television game console to define the game to be played when that cartridge is plugged into the console. The cartridge manufacturer defines the game to be played with a particular cartridge by the information placed into the read only memory used in that cartridge when the read only memory is manufactured.

The consumer user of a television game console is unable to alter the information stored in the read only memory of the game cartridge, and thus is unable to alter the definition of the game which may be played using that cartridge.

[Atari, Bally and Fairchild made licensing deals with the plaintiffs to use technology covered by the '507 patent in their games—ED.]

D. Development of the Accused Mattel Television Games

In early 1977, Mattel commenced development of a television game product; Mattel approached a number of suppliers of integrated circuit components concerning the possibility of developing such a product.

In June, it became aware that General Instrument had commenced development of the integrated circuit components including a microprocessor which could be used for the manufacture of television games.

In about that time, representatives of Mattel received a demonstration of the General Instrument development during the course of the Consumer Electronics Show in Chicago,

Illinois. Josh Denham was one of those representatives; he was then Senior Vice-President of Operations of the Toy Division of Mattel.

After a number of meetings between Mattel and General Instrument, they agreed to jointly develop a television game making use of a microprocessor.

David Chandler participated in the meetings with General Instrument on behalf of Mattel; he was then Senior Design Engineer of the Toy Division of Mattel.

It was Chandler at Mattel who was primarily responsible for the technical design of the Mattel Intellivision television game.

He had no specific knowledge of the circuitry within the components developed by General Instrument.

Four employees of Mattel had primary management responsibility for the decision to use the components developed by General Instrument in the Mattel Intellivision television game. They were Ray Wagner, President of the Toy Division, Josh Denham, Senior Vice-President of Operation of the Toy Division, Ed Hamway, Senior Vice-President of Marketing of the Toy Division, and Ed Krakauer, Vice-President of Marketing for New Business of the Toy Division. Chandler and Jeff Rochlis, a director of marketing of the Toy Division of Mattel, were also involved in making the decision.

The Mattel Intellivision television game was first manufactured in commercial quantities in the latter half of 1979.

When the Mattel Intellivision game was first introduced, only three cartridges were available for it. Two of those cartridges were Baseball and Basketball.

The principal component developed as a result of the joint development agreement of Mattel and General Instrument is a component referred to as a Standard Television Integrated Circuit Chip or STIC chip. The Mattel Master Components sold in the United States include a STIC chip manufactured by General Instrument under the part number AY-3-8900-1.

The basic design of the General Instrument AY-3-8900-1 STIC chip was done by Gilbert Duncan Harrower of General Instrument.

The STIC chip is principally responsible for the display of symbols on the television screen at positions determined by the microprocessor which is also included within the Master Component.

It also generates the timing information needed for the generation of horizontal and vertical synchronization and blanking signals.

E. The accused Mattel television games; the elements of the '507 patent

In the television game formed by the combination of the Mattel Master Component and the Tennis cartridge:

(a) The display shown on the television screen includes a symbol on the right side of the screen representing a first player with a tennis racquet, a symbol on the left side of the screen representing a second player with a tennis racquet, and a symbol which moves across the screen representing a ball.

(b) Player controls are provided so that each human player can move his corresponding player symbol on the face of the screen and cause that player symbol to appear to swing its racquet.

(c) Each human player manipulates his corresponding symbol to intercept the path of the ball as it moves across the screen and, at the same time, cause the player symbol to appear to swing its racquet.

(d) When the player successfully intercepts the ball symbol, i.e., the player and racquet symbol appears to hit the ball symbol on the screen, the motion of the ball is changed and, in particular, the horizontal motion of the ball is reversed so that it travels back toward the other player.

The principal argument advanced by Mattel that the claims of the '507 patent do not read on the television game formed by the combination of the Mattel Master Component and the Tennis cartridge is that the game does not include any "means for ascertaining coincidence" between the hitting symbols as recited in Claims 25 and 51 or "means for determining ... coincidence" as recited in Claim 60.

(a) Mattel argues that only the presence of proximity is determined and that because the ball symbol can appear to be hit and change direction without any actual overlap of the ball and player or racquet symbols occurring on the screen, actual coincidence of the ball and player or racquet symbols is neither ascertained or determined. As explained at trial, this possibility exists because of the manner in which the program for the Tennis cartridge was written. However, it is clear from the very nature of the game of tennis that the intent of the Mattel game is to have the player symbol appear to hit the ball symbol when the two symbols are coincident. The mere fact that a peculiarity of the tennis program departs from that intent is not sufficient to avoid infringement of the '507 patent. Moreover, the fact that any computation must be made after the occurrence of coincidence to determine the subsequent path of the ball is not sufficient to avoid the claim language.

(b) Mattel points to a statement made in the prosecution of the '507 patent. In a citation of references to the Patent and Trademark Office, the applicant in a discussion of a reference patent stated that it did "not detect true coincidence" of two symbols since the apparatus of the reference determined only whether the two symbols were at the same vertical location and not whether they were at the same horizontal location. Any such statements in the prosecution of the '507 patent were not made as a result of any rejection of the claims by the Patent and Trademark Office over the reference being discussed. Moreover, even if the claim language were to be restricted by that statement, it would not prevent the claims from reading on the Mattel Tennis game since the apparatus for ascertaining coincidence in that game is responsive to both the horizontal and vertical locations of the two symbols.

(c) Mattel points to the specification of the '507 patent and the work done in television games at Sanders and concludes that there are shown there only "true coincidence" circuits. It also points to a statement made in the prosecution of the original '284 patent of which the '507 patent is a reissue. In a discussion of Claim 21 of the then pending application, a claim which did not become one of the claims asserted by plaintiffs here, it was stated, "[t]he hit symbols represent a device which goes in a particular direction at a particular speed, etc., determined by 'contact' (actually electrical coincidence) with the hitting symbol." The word "contact" was placed in quotes in that statement, clearly indicating that coincidence was to be more expansive than inclusion of just a contact of two images. Further, because it is electrical circuitry that generates the images on the screen, it is apparent that coincidence between two symbols will be determined electrically rather than, say, optically. Thus, there is nothing in the '507 specification or the prosecution of the '507 patent which requires that the language of the '507 patent be restricted to the circuitry for determining coincidence shown in the '507 patent specification.

In the television game formed by the combination of the Mattel Master Component and the Tennis Cartridge:

(a) Either player/racquet symbol is a hitting symbol.

(b) The ball symbol is a hit symbol.

(c) The player/racquet symbol and the ball symbol are in coincidence when the player/racquet symbol appears to hit the ball symbol.

(d) A distinct motion is imparted to the ball symbol upon the occurrence of such coincidence.

(e) There is a symbol for generating a hitting symbol.

(f) There is means for generating a hit symbol.

(g) The means for generating a hit symbol includes means for ascertaining coincidence between the hitting symbol and the hit symbol.

(h) The means for generating a hit symbol includes means for imparting a distinct motion to said hit symbol upon coincidence.

(i) There is means for generating vertical and horizontal synchronization signals.

(j) When connected in combination with a television receiver, there is means responsive to the vertical and horizontal synchronization signals for deflecting the beam of the cathode ray picture tube in the television receiver to generate raster on the screen of that picture tube.

(k) When connected in combination with a television receiver, there is means coupled to the synchronization signal generating means and the cathode ray picture tube in the television receiver for generating a first symbol on the screen of that picture tube at a position which is directly controlled by a player.

(l) When connected in combination with a television receiver, there is means coupled to the synchronization signal generating means and the cathode ray picture tube for generating a second symbol on the screen of that picture tube which is movable.

(m) There is means coupled to the first symbol generating means and the second symbol generating means for determining coincidence between the first symbol and the second symbol.

(n) There is means coupled to the coincidence determining means and the second symbol generating means for imparting a distinct motion to the second symbol in response to said coincidence.

[The claims, defenses and arguments with respect to the Football, Hockey, Soccer, Basketball and Baseball components are similar to those of the Tennis components—ED.]

Mattel contends that its Master Component and game cartridges are so different from the television game circuits disclosed in the '507 patent in means, operation, and result that there can be no infringement of that patent even if the patent claims are bound to literally apply to its games. The asserted claims, however, are not directed to specific circuitry; and even Mattel does not contend that they should be limited to only the circuits disclosed in the '507 patent specification.

The apparatus disclosed in the '507 patent are basically analog circuits for producing the electrical signals necessary to play television games having hit and hitting symbols of the type described in Claims 25, 51, and 60 of the patent.

Mattel contends that its Master Component includes a game play processor and a display processor, that the game play processor includes a microprocessor, an executive program located in a read only memory, a random access memory, a game program located in a read only memory in the game cartridge, and hand controllers for the Master

Component, that the display processor includes the STIC, a graphic read only memory, a graphic random access memory, and a color circuit and radio frequency modulator for converting the output of the STIC into a form suitable for application to the antenna terminals of a standard television receiver, that a control or system random access memory is used to interconnect the two processors, and that its game play processor is a digital computer.

The result of the apparatus disclosed in the '507 patent is to permit the playing on a television receiver or monitor of games such as hockey, ping pong, tennis, or baseball having hit and hitting symbols and of the type described in that patent, and, in particular, of such games in which play is achieved by a human player manipulating a player controlled or hitting symbol on the face of the television screen so as to intercept, catch, hit, or come into coincidence with a hit symbol which is under control of the game. The result of the '507 patent is the playing of games like tennis, soccer, and hockey in which two player controlled symbols move about under human control to try to make something happen to another symbol, a hit symbol, and change its motion.

The result of the Mattel Master Component in combination with each of the Tennis, Baseball, Football, Hockey, Soccer, and Basketball cartridges is to permit the playing on a television receiver of such games having hit and hitting symbols of the type described in the '507 patent. In particular, the combination of the Mattel Master Component with each of those six cartridges permits the playing on a television receiver of a game in which a human player manipulates a player controlled or hitting symbol on the face of the television screen so as to intercept, catch, hit, or come into coincidence with a symbol representing a ball or puck which is under control of the game.

Because of the advances in technology which have occurred since Rusch invented the subject matter of the '507 patent in 1967 and filed his original patent application in 1969, Mattel is able to achieve at relatively low cost games of much greater complexity and variety than those achieved by the apparatus disclosed in the '507 patent. The technology available today for the manufacture of television games was simply not available in the 1967 time frame. However, the use of currently available technology to implement its television games does not alter the basic nature of those games or avoid the Rusch '507 patent.

The result achieved by the Mattel Master Component in combination with each of the Tennis, Baseball, Football, Hockey, Soccer, and Baseball cartridges is essentially the same result as is achieved with the apparatus disclosed in the '507 patent.

The function of the apparatus described in the '507 patent is to generate the electrical signals necessary for application to a television monitor or television receiver to permit the playing on the television receiver or monitor of games such as hockey, ping pong, tennis, or baseball having hit or hitting symbols and of the type described in the patent and, in particular, of such games in which play is achieved by a human player manipulating a player controlled hitting symbol on the face of the television screen so as to intercept, catch, hit, or come into coincidence with a hit symbol which is under control of the game.

The function of the Mattel Master Component in combination with each of the Tennis, Baseball, Football, Hockey, Soccer, and Basketball cartridges is to generate the electrical signals necessary for application to a television receiver to permit the playing on the television receiver of such games having hit and hitting symbols of the type described in the '507 patent. In particular, the combination of the Mattel Master Component with each of those six cartridges generates the electrical signals necessary for application to a television receiver to permit the playing on a television receiver of a game in which a human player manipulates a player controlled or hitting symbol on the face of the television screen so as to intercept, catch, hit, or come into coincidence with a symbol representing a ball or puck which is under control of the game.

The function of the Mattel Master Component in combination with each of the Tennis, Baseball, Football, Hockey, Soccer, and Baseball is essentially the same function as apparatus described in the '507 patent.

There are many differences between details of the electrical circuits disclosed in the '507 patent, and the electrical circuitry of the Mattel Master Component in combination with each of the Tennis, Baseball, Football, Hockey, Soccer, and Basketball cartridges. The most evident difference is referred to above, that the circuitry described in the '507 patent was basically analog circuitry while the Mattel television game uses basically digital circuitry using a microprocessor. However, these means are fully equivalent to each other in the context of the '507 patent. This is in full accord with the decision of Judge Grady and the testimony of Drs. Ribbens, Chandler, and Slotnick.

The accused Mattel television games use digital circuitry. I reach the same conclusion as that reached by Judge Grady, that the mere substitution of digital circuitry for analog circuitry is not sufficient to avoid infringement of the '507 patent.

Judge Grady of this court reached a similar conclusion in the prior infringement action on the '507 patent. The accused games in the case before him used digital circuitry. Judge Grady extensively considered the difference between analog and digital circuitry and concluded as follows:

> First, the use of digital instead of analog circuitry, it seems to me, is a difference which is not material. I regard analog and digital circuitry as two means which are interchangeable largely, which are equivalent, and which are, therefore, essentially the same means for achieving substantially the same results in substantially the same way.
>
> Both of these methods involve measurement of time, it seems to me, because time is what is involved in these games. It is expressed variously as spatial and as counting, but in each instance what the user of the circuit is really attempting to do is to put an image on the screen in a particular time relationship to some other image or to some other component of the video signal.
>
> One of the defendants' witnesses—I forget which one—conceded, as I recall, that the purpose for which one programs the computer to have it count in a particular way—or rather, the purpose for which one presets the count—is that one wishes the count to arrive at a particular point at a particular time. If one were to say that a mere change from analog circuitry to digital circuitry were to be a sufficient change to deprive an analog patent of protection, then it seems to me that every electronic invention would be fair game for anyone who simply used the reverse method of circuitry to achieve the same result. Had the plaintiffs, for instance, chosen to use the digital method, the defendants could as easily have used the analog method and claimed immunity by reason of having done that.
>
> I listened with great attention and with, I hope, some modicum of understanding to the testimony on both sides as to the differences and similarities between analog and digital circuitry, and I am convinced, on the basis of my understanding of it, that these are substantially the same thing. They simply are different choices open to the designer of the particular device, and that choice is dictated by such things as economy and items of that kind.

Mattel argues that the circuitry of its television game is more than just a digital circuit, but that it includes the basic components of a digital computer in that it is based upon using a microprocessor as a game play processor and a display processor, and that the '507 patent includes no mention of any microprocessor or many of the items which are associated with a microprocessor such as a random access memory, a read only memory, an addressable multiple-bit memory device, graphic random access memory, graphics read only memory, content addressable memory, X and Y position registers, character start address registers, no interaction matrix, no software program, no dispatch table, no binary data, no arithmetic and logic unit, no central processing unit, no game play processor, and no display processor.

However, and as was particularly pointed out during the cross examination of Mattel's own witnesses, the circuitry of the Mattel Master Component is in many ways directly analogous to the circuitry of the Rusch patent. The various components listed are merely the circuit components that one would use once the choice is made to use that particular approach to the design using hardware currently available.

The circuitry of the '507 patent can be divided into game play portions and display portions just as can the circuitry of the MC. This was made clear in the testimony of Drs. Ribbens, Chandler, and Slotnick, but most clearly in the Slotnick testimony. An expanded version of PX 174 showing the division of the circuitry of the '507 patent into game play circuits and display circuits can be seen in the attached Figure A. [See original.]

The game play processor in the Mattel Master Component provides digital data information to the display processor, i.e., to the X and Y position registers in the STIC, which specifies the horizontal and vertical position on the television screen of the various symbols to be displayed. The circuitry of the '507 patent similarly includes portions which provide voltage data signals which specify the horizontal and vertical positions of the symbols to be displayed. For example, in Figure 12A of the Rusch patent, the player control knobs 131 and 132 are coupled to potentiometers 129 and 130 which provide at their outputs voltage data signals proportional to the vertical positions on the television screen of the left and right hitting symbols, and the flip flop 120 and the circuitry connected to it provides at the outputs 119 and 118 voltage data signals proportional to the vertical and horizontal positions of the hit symbol. Figure 11A of the '507 patent likewise shows game play circuitry for generating at its output voltage data signals proportional to the vertical and horizontal positions of the hit symbol.

The display processor in the Mattel Master Component receives the digital data information specifying the horizontal and vertical position of the various symbols to be displayed and converts that data into the electrical signals timed with relation to horizontal and vertical synchronization signals necessary for connection to the antenna terminals of a broadcast television receiver to result in the display of the desired symbols. The circuitry of the '507 patent similarly includes portions which receive voltage data signals specifying the horizontal and vertical positions of the symbols to be displayed and converts them into the electrical signals timed with relation to the horizontal and vertical synchronization signals to result in the display of the desired symbols. Such circuitry is shown in Figure 8 of the '507 patent, for example. Although the display processor in the Mattel game uses in the STIC a counting scheme which compares binary numbers stored in the X and Y position registers with binary numbers stored in registers representing the current X and Y locations of the electron beam of the television cathode ray tube, and the circuitry disclosed in the '507 patent uses a diode slicer technique in which voltage data signals representing horizontal and vertical signals are compared to sawtooth or ramp voltages representing the current horizontal and vertical locations of the electron beams of the television cathode ray tube, Mattel's own witnesses admitted that the digital counting technique of the Mattel game was the equivalent of the ramp technique disclosed in the '507 patent. A refined version of PX 175 used to demonstrate that equivalency can be seen in the attached Figure B. [See original.]

The Rusch display circuit such as Figure 8 and the Mattel display processor are two techniques, the analog and digital approaches, for producing symbol displays on a television screen in response to object data, and they are doing essentially the same thing.

While it is true that the '507 patent includes no disclosure of a microprocessor or any of its associated components or even of any type of general purpose digital computer, this is hardly surprising. All the trial witnesses agreed that microprocessors were simply not available until the 1970s, particularly around 1972. That is more than three years after the filing date of the '507 patent. Moreover, both of Mattel's witnesses at trial agreed that the general purpose digital computers available during the 1960s were so expensive that they would be completely impractical for use in a television game intended for use in the home. Thus, the lack of disclosure of a microprocessor or associated components in the '507 patent forms no support for any argument that the inventor or Sanders made any conscious decision that the claims of the '507 were not intended to include games based on a microprocessor.

The game play processor in the Mattel Master Component receives inputs from the hand controller operated by the human players, interprets those inputs to provide data signals representing the positions and locations of the player controlled hitting symbols to be displayed, and combines those inputs according to predetermined game rules to provide data signals representing the position and location of the game controlled or hit symbols to be displayed. Likewise, the '507 patent includes circuitry which receives inputs from the hand controls operated by the human player, interprets those inputs to provide data signals representing the position and location of the player controlled hitting symbols to be displayed, and combines those inputs according to predetermined game rules to provide data signals representing the position and location of the game controlled or hit symbols to be displayed.

The electronics industry of this country, and indeed the world, in general has gone through great changes between the mid-1960s and the present as integrated circuit technology was developed and improved to permit greater and greater amounts of electronic circuitry having more and more complex functions to be included within a single integrated circuit component. These rapid advances in technology have been applied to the television game field, as well as many other fields. The commercial availability of the microprocessor in the early 1970s is one example of such development. Mattel followed others including Magnavox in using microprocessors in the development of television games. Nevertheless, the foundation for the television games accused in this action is the invention of the '507 patent and its commercialization by Mattel and others. In this context, the substitution of a microprocessor and related components in the accused television games for the analog circuitry disclosed in the '507 patent is not sufficient to avoid infringement and I find them to be, in the context of the invention of that patent, substantially the same means.

Mattel contends that it does not infringe the '507 patent because its accused games follow the teachings of the prior art rather than the '507 patent. In this connection, Mattel relies on the following items of prior art:

(a) U. S. Patent 3,135,815 to Spiegel entitled "Method for the Representation of the Movement of Two Bodies by Means of Electron Beams and Apparatus for Carrying Out this Method" which issued on June 2, 1964. This patent purports to disclose a simulator apparatus for training the military in the operation of missiles and displaying on a television receiver at least two symbols, one representing a target and one representing a missile. At least the movement of the missile on the screen is controlled by the student. The patent does make some reference to an event occurring if coincidence of the missile and target is achieved, but no circuitry is shown or suggested for achieving this. No circuitry is shown for controlling the target.

(b) U. S. Patent 3,396,377 to F. D. Strout entitled "Display Data Processor" which issued on August 6, 1968 from an application filed on June 29, 1964. This patent purports to disclose a display processor for a device such as a digital computer using a rotating magnetic drum memory and displaying its output in the form of characters or symbols on a raster scanned cathode ray tube.

(c) U.S. Patent 3,528,068 to J. D. Johnson entitled "Device for Converting Binary Coded Digital Information to Symbol Form for Video Display" which issued on September 8, 1970 from an application filed on February 24, 1967. This patent resulted from work done on the CC-30 display system. It, like Strout, purports to disclose a display device for a digital computer using a raster scan cathode ray tube. The Johnson patent makes reference to use of an ordinary television receiver.

(d) A computer terminal system known as the CC-30 Communications system constructed and sold in the United States by Computer Communications, Inc. in 1967. That system was a display system for a general purpose digital computer. The display device actually used was a modified television receiver. It was necessary to connect a further interface device between the CC-30 system and the digital computer with which it was to be used. The display system alone cost about $6,000 in 1967.

(e) A computer game known as Space War which was run on the PDP-1 general purpose digital computer manufactured by Digital Equipment Company and which was used and known at the Massachusetts Institute of Technology and Stanford University prior to 1967. In the Space War game, two players were operative to control symbols representing spaceships on the face of a Digital Equipment Company Type 30 display. The object of the game was for each player to fire torpedoes from his spaceship and hit the other player's spaceship. Each player had four switches or buttons by which he could cause his spaceship to rotate clockwise, cause his spaceship to rotate counterclockwise, apply thrust to his spaceship causing it to accelerate in the direction it is pointed, and fire torpedoes from the front of his spaceship in the direction his spaceship is pointing. Simultaneous activation of the clockwise and counterclockwise rotation switches or buttons by the same player would cause his spaceship to go into "hyperspace," i.e., to temporarily disappear from the screen and reappear shortly thereafter at a random location on the screen but with some probability that the act of going into hyperspace would cause his spaceship to be destroyed. When the symbol representing a missile appeared to hit a symbol representing a spaceship, the spaceship and missile appeared to explode on the screen and disappear shortly thereafter. That was the end of that game and the players would start over. The display used with the Space War game was an X-Y or point plotting display, not a raster scan display of the type used in television. The PDP-1 computer cost approximately $120,000 when it was sold, and occupied an area of about 88 X 26 inches and was 69 inches high.

(f) A computer demonstration of a pool game shown at an Open House held from September 28 to October 1, 1967 in conjunction with a 25th anniversary celebration of the RCA Laboratories at the David Sarnoff Research Center in Princeton, New Jersey. In the pool demonstration, there was displayed on the face of a cathode ray tube the outline of a pool table with pockets, a cue ball, and 15 object balls; no symbol representing a cue stick was displayed. A single shot was initiated by the player placing a light pen on the face of the cathode ray tube on the side of the cue ball opposite the direction the cue ball was to move. The pool demonstration utilized a display manufactured by IDI. It was an X-Y or point plotting display, not a raster scan display of the type used in television. The computer used on RCA Spectra 70/25, which alone cost about $90,000, and a custom interface between the Spectra 70/25 and the IDI display was necessary and was constructed by RCA. At the demonstration, the Spectra 70/25 was not fast enough to make all the required calculations when there were many object balls on the table close together, such as on the break, so the motion of the balls was noticeably slower than at other times. Demonstrations of the well known work of RCA in the field of television also occurred at the same open house. Work in the television field and the work which resulted in the pool demonstration both occurred at the RCA David Sarnoff Research Center in Princeton, New Jersey. RCA failed to see any product potential in its pool demonstration or in creating a television game.

(g) Noyce, "Making Integrated Electronics Technology Work", IEEE Spectrum (May 1968), pp. 63–68. This paper contains a general discussion of the integrated circuit filed in 1968. It specifically states that integrated circuits have been successfully used in digital circuits, but specifically recognizes that integrated circuits had not yet found wide acceptance in the consumer electronics market.

(h) Hobbs, "Present and Future State-of-the-Art in Computer Memories," IEEE Transaction on Electronic Computers (August 1966), pp. 534–550. This paper contains a general discussion of computer memories as of the time it was written.

Mattel does not here contend that the '507 patent or any of its claims is invalid over the prior art upon which it relies. Nevertheless, at trial, it did compare Claim 25 of the '507 patent with the prior art. Such a comparison is, of course, irrelevant to Mattel's contention that it is practicing the prior art. To support such a contention, the comparison that must be made is between Mattel's accused television games and the prior art. However, since Mattel did elect to make the comparison between Claim 25 of the '507 patent and the prior art, the court concludes that none of the prior art anticipates or shows all the elements of Claim 25 of the '507 patent or any of the other claims asserted by plaintiffs against Mattel in this case for the same reasons as articulated by Judge Grady based on much the same prior art including Space War, the RCA Pool demonstration, and the Baer '480 patent. The Baer '480 patent, of all the prior art, best shows the importance of the Rusch invention in the development of the television game industry.

None of the prior art relief by Mattel shows, discloses, or even suggests a television game having a hitting symbol or a television game having a hit symbol. In the absence of such a teaching in the prior art, the prior art, of course, cannot and does not teach any television game including any means for ascertaining or determining coincidence between a hit and hitting symbol or means for imparting distinct motion to the hit symbol upon or in response to such coincidence.

(a) The meaning of the terms "hit symbol" and "hitting symbol" are made clear from the specification of the '507 patent. At Column 10, Lines 39–42, the following appears: For playing games, two functionally different types of spots are often generated, a hit spot and a hitting spot. The hit spot simulates a ball, a hockey puck, etc. A hitting spot simulates a paddle, a hockey stick, a golf club, a hand, etc.

(b) Moreover, during the prosecution of the application which matured into the original '284 patent which was reissued as the '507 patent, the applicant in responding to an Office Action issued by the Patent Examiner including a rejection of the claim which ultimately matured into Claim 25 of the reissue patent as being indefinite, first stated the following in describing the general subject matter of the application:

> Principally, in this application Applicant teaches how to generate two functionally different spots which he calls a 'hitting' spot and 'hit' spot. The 'hitting' spot is controlled by, for example, a pair of knobs on potentiometers and allows this spot to be moved over the screen of the television receiver by direct manipulation of the knobs. That is, the viewer directly controls the position of this spot. This spot may be used to simulate a hand, a paddle, a bat, a hockey stick, or other implementation directly controlled by a player in a game.
>
> The second functional spot is referred to as a 'hit' spot, and this spot is not directly controlled by the viewer but its position, movement, etc., is determined in part by other electronic signal generating means in the unit, including signal generating means responsive to the position, direction, etc. of the so-called 'hitting' spot. This type of spot represents, for example, a ball, a hockey puck, etc. In the games described in the body of the application, various different control signals are set forth to cause this 'hit' spot to move in different patterns, as, for example, one control causes it to automatically go from an off-screen left position to an off-screen right position and vice versa continually unless coincidence is made with a 'hitting' spot, whereby it would reverse direction, or, alternatively, the 'hit' spot will remain in a steady position until 'hit' by a 'hitting' spot whereupon it will travel in a direction and with a velocity proportional to the direction and velocity of the 'hitting' spot, causing it to move toward an off-screen right position and vice versa continually unless coincidence is made with a 'hitting' spot, whereby it would reverse direction, or, alternatively, the 'hit' spot will remain in a steady position until 'hit' by a 'hitting' spot whereupon it will travel in a direction and with a velocity proportional to the direction and velocity of the 'hitting' spot, causing it to move toward an off-screen position, whereupon it will bounce away from the screen in the same fashion as a ball would.

Further, and more specifically with reference to the rejection for indefiniteness, the applicant stated:

> After a reading of the specification including all the various games set forth therein, no one should have any doubt as to the meaning of 'hit' and 'hitting' spots. A 'hitting' spot is one under the control of the viewer and represents things generally directly controlled by a user in a game such as a racket, a bat, a stick, etc. A 'hit' spot is one that operates in conjunction with a 'hitting' spot and not under direct control of the viewer and represents things not generally directly controlled by a user in a game such as a ball, a puck, etc. Certainly the law is well established that the applicant may be his own lexicographer and in this particular application the words selected most aptly describe the invention.

(c) The Space War, RCA Pool, and Spiegel references include no hit or hitting symbols as those terms are used in the '507 patent. They further include no means for ascertaining or determining coincidence between any hit and hitting symbols and no means for imparting a distinct motion to a hit symbol upon or in response to such a coincidence. Additionally, the work of Baer in 1966 and 1967 which resulted in U.S. Patent 3,728,480 does also not include any teaching of hit or hitting symbols. Judge Grady had each of the Space War, RCA Pool, and Baer references before him and he did not conclude that any of them showed a hit or hitting symbol. This court agrees.

(d) There is no proof of record that either the CC-30 Communications System or the display systems shown in the Strout or Johnson patents were ever used to play any games involving moving symbols on the face of the display screen. Likewise, there is no proof of record that either of the CC-30 Communications System, or the display systems shown in the Strout or Johnson patents were ever connected to a PDP-1 computer for the purpose of displaying Space War thereon or to an RCA Spectra 70/25 computer for the purpose of displaying the RCA Pool demonstration thereon. While there is some testimony to the effect that one or more of the computers to which CC-30 display systems theoretically could have been connected theoretically could possibly have been programmed to play games such as the ping pong game of the '507 patent, there is no evidence whatever that this was actually done at a date early enough to constitute prior art to the '507 patent.

The Mattel Master Component in combination with each of the Tennis, Baseball, Football, Hockey, Soccer, and Basketball cartridges does not follow the teachings of the prior art.

(a) First, it is apparent from a viewing of videotapes and movies of the Space War game and the RCA Pool demonstration that the accused Mattel games simply are not found in these items of prior art. Even if those items of prior art were combined with the other items of prior art showing a raster scan display, the combination would not result in the accused Mattel games.

(b) Second, as has been stated above, each of the accused television games includes hit and hitting symbols, means for ascertaining for determining coincidence between those symbols, and means or imparting a distinct motion to the hit symbol upon the occurrence of such coincidence. None of the prior art references, taken singly or in combination, includes any of these elements.

(c) Third, although Mattel points to some similarities between various separate items in the prior art and the circuitry of its Mattel Master Component, it is clear from the evidence presented at trial that the Mattel Master Component takes advantage of late 1970s technology, not 1960s hardware, and also that it includes many elements not shown in the prior art. Mattel's own expert did not even contend that all the important elements of the Mattel games which he identified during his direct testimony were found in any single item of prior art. Moreover, Mattel has pointed to no prior art which shows certain features of its Mattel Master Component. None of the prior art cited by Mattel shows a separate central processor and display processor which use a common clock signal to operate both, which clock signal is generated in the display processor. None of the prior art cited by Mattel shows circuitry in which a signal generated by the display processor at a predetermined time with reference to the vertical retrace interval is used to interrupt the central processor unit at the end of every vertical field. None of the prior art cited by Mattel shows circuitry in which a signal or signals generated in timed relation to the display on a raster scan display device is used to halt the operation of the central processor unit for a period of time during which the display circuitry requires access to an area of memory it shares with the central processing unit. None of the prior art cited by Mattel shows circuitry in a display processor such as the interaction matrix in the STIC for determining when two displayed symbols are coincident on the screen.

(d) The extensive efforts to which Mattel went to keep the trial proceedings concerning the construction and operation of its Master Component and the individual components thereof under seal is an admission by Mattel that it considers its accused games to be much more than simply a practicing of the prior art.

(e) Finally, it is clear from the evidence that Mattel did not in fact follow the prior art but, instead, followed developments in the television game industry, an industry which was created because of the work done at Sanders in developing the first television games and an industry which expanded and developed and become economically viable largely because of television games which followed the teachings of the '507 patent.

Mattel has not pointed to any position taken by plaintiffs in the prior cases on the '507 patent which are inconsistent with their position taken in this action. Mattel points to two related statements made by plaintiffs' counsel occurring at four pages of a trial record which included in excess of 2,000 pages. Those statements do not justify Mattel's argument that plaintiffs are estopped from taking the position that the Mattel television games infringe the '507 patent.

(a) The statements relied upon relate to a distinction drawn between the '507 patent and the Space War game and RCA Pool demonstration. But, as found above, those two items of prior art simply do not disclose the elements of the claims here in suit, and Mattel is not merely practicing those items of prior art. Thus, plaintiffs are not here attempting to include material within their patent claims which they argued fell outside of those same patent claims in the prior case.

(b) The Space War and RCA Pool games both use X-Y or point plotting displays rather than a raster scan display used in television. Thus, they clearly did not use or have any need for the use of television vertical and horizontal synchronization signals for use in either generating or displaying any type of symbols. Plaintiffs argued that this distinction existed in the prior case and in this case. Moreover, Mattel does make use of and requires such synchronization signal information in its accused games.

(c) The portions of the prior transcript Mattel makes reference to include statements of plaintiffs' counsel that the RCA Pool demonstration used the "conventional memory technique of a large computer." But other portions of the same record make it clear that the "conventional memory technique" being referred by is the technique of using an X-Y or point plotting display. Thus, plaintiffs' counsel, in explaining to Judge Grady the significance of the use of horizontal and vertical synchronization signals, stated:

> I believe that [defendant's counsel] is going to tell the court that in 1950 or 1954 or 1960 somebody played a simulated pool game, for example, not interactively with the player hitting the ball, but nevertheless a ball moved on a screen, and it wasn't done with horizontal and vertical sync at all, that they

used what is called a point plotter that used a totally different principle, a principle of actually storing of addresses, not using time, as the basis for creating the game.

In a computer there is a location where you store an address or information about a particular point. You break down the TV—excuse me. Not the TV screen. What he is going to say is a cathode ray tube. You break that down to display a point on the screen, but it is not done with a raster scan. In a computer, in a very complex, expensive piece of equipment, you say at point 20 down and 30 to the left a ball is located, and it is stored in memory, and every once in a while the memory is called out and puts a spot right there. Then it blanks out, no sweeping, no synchronization, no timing involved, and then in the computer they have an equation of motion, a physical equation, in terms of X and Y and they process the data in the computer. It is a way of demonstrating computers.

They then decide a few seconds later, a fraction of a second later, where the ball is, and they assign the ball a new address, and this is now still a pool ball, not an interactive game, but I think that is another weakness in the position. They now call out that new address, and they say that the ball has now moved, it is no longer at X20 Y15, that it is now moved to X21 Y16, and they put the spot there with a cathode ray tube, not with a TV screen display. It costs several hundreds of thousands of dollars to build a piece of equipment like that. It certainly did in the 1950s and 1960s when they were trying to do it. It was not practical. It didn't simulate real time games, and we say it was totally different.

Certainly the games accused in this action do not use any X-Y or point plotting display like that used in the RCA Pool demonstration. Plaintiffs are not estopped from arguing that the accused Mattel games, which games use a raster scan or television type display just like the games accused in the prior cases, are covered by the claims of the '507 patent.

F. Magnavox's licensing practices under the '507 patent

[The court rejected Mattel's claims that Magnavox committed acts of misuse of its patent by failing to negotiate its license and sub-license agreements in good faith—ED.]

G. Findings as to infringement of the '507 patent

The manufacture, use, and/or sale of the combination of the Mattel Master Component and the Tennis, Football, Baseball, Hockey, Soccer, and Basketball cartridges constitute acts of infringement of the '507 patent.

The sales by Mattel of the Tennis, Football, Baseball, Hockey, Soccer, and Basketball cartridges constitute acts of contributory infringement of the '507 patent.

II. Conclusions of Law

A. The presumption of patent validity.

Under the provisions of 35 U.S.C. § 282, a patent shall be presumed valid; each claim of a patent shall be presumed valid, independent of other claims; and the burden of establishing a patent or claim as invalid shall rest on the party asserting it. The burden of proving invalidity is not to be taken lightly; it is a heavy burden and must be shown by at least clear and convincing evidence. *Laser Alignment, Inc. v. Woodruff & Sons, Inc.*, 491 F.2d 866, 871 (7th Cir. 1974).

The court of appeals for this circuit held in *American Photocopy Equip. Co. v. Rovico*, 384 F.2d 813 (7th Cir. 1967), that a prior judicial determination of patent validity creates a presumption that should only be disturbed when in the second action persuasive new evidence is presented or when there is a material distinction between the cases. Defendants here do not challenge the validity of the patent-in-suit; therefore, validity of the '507 patent is not in issue.

B. The claims determine the scope of the patent

A patentee can choose his own terms and use them as he wishes so long as he remains consistent in their use and makes their meaning reasonably clear.

Once the best mode contemplated by the inventor is presented, he is entitled to claim every form in which the invention may be used and to obtain all benefits therefrom regardless of whether those forms are mentioned in the patent or whether the inventor was aware of them. *King-Seeley Thermos Co. v. Tastee Freez Industries, Inc.*, 357 F.2d 875, 880 (7th Cir. 1966).

C. Infringement

In determining whether an accused device infringes a patent, courts look to see if literal infringement exists. When literal infringement is clearly found, that is the end of it. When a literal infringement is not found, courts look to the doctrine of equivalents to determine infringement. *Graver Tank & Mfg. Co. v. Linde Air Products Co.*, 339 U.S. 605, 607–609, (1950).

Literal infringement exists when accused matter falls clearly within the claims. In such a case, infringement is made out and that is the end of it. *Graver Tank & Mfg. Co v. Linde Air Products Co., supra,* 339 U.S. at 605, 607 (1950). Infringement depends upon the factual situation of a specific case, but when literal infringement is found, there is no occasion to resort to the doctrine of equivalents. *Paper Converting Machine Co. v. FMC Corp.*, 409 F.2d 344, 354, (7th Cir. 1969).

In determining whether there is literal infringement, the words in the claim of the patent must be compared with the accused device. Where the claim reads directly on the accused device, literal infringement is established.

In determining infringement of the claim based upon real identity of means, operation and result, "it is necessary to note that it is the claim and not the preferred embodiment which is to be used for comparison."

D. The doctrine of equivalents

The court concludes that in this case there is literal infringement, but even where a literal infringement does not exist, a patent can still be infringed and an infringer cannot defraud a patent. *Machine Co. v. Murphy*, 97 U.S. 120 (1878). In particular, the doctrine of equivalents may be invoked when an accused device performs substantially the same function, in substantially the same way, to obtain substantially the same result. *Graver Tank & Mfg. Co. v. Linde Air Products Co., supra; Paper Converting Machine Company v. Magna-Graphics Corp., supra.*

The doctrine of equivalents is not to be applied with a specific formula, rather the scope of an invention determines the range of equivalents on which the patentee is entitled to protection. *Graver Tank & Mfg. Co. v. Linde Air Products Co., supra,* 339 U.S. at 609. Thus, an invention which is broad and primary in its character should be given a liberal construction. *Continental Paper Bag Co. v. Eastern Paper Bag*, 210 U.S. 405, 414 (1908).

Except where form is of the essence of the invention, one device is an infringement of another if it performs substantially the same function in substantially the same way to obtain the same result, so that if two devices do the same work, in substantially the same way, and accomplish substantially the same result, they are the same, even though they differ in name, form or shape, and when one has achieved something new involving invention, it is infringed when someone does the same thing in substantially the same way and thereby produces the same result.

E. Broad scope for a patent that helps create an industry

The patent laws and the courts will give the broadest protection to "pioneer" patents. *Studiengesellschaft Kohle mbH v. Eastman Kodak Co.*, 616 F.2d 1315, 1324, (5th Cir. 1980). Pioneer patents, unlike improvements or perfections, exist when they introduce a wholly new device or one of such novelty and importance as to mark a distinct step in the progress of the art. *Ziegler v. Phillips Petroleum Co.*, 483 F.2d 858, 870 (5th Cir. 1973). The doctrine of equivalents also operates in favor of the patentee of a secondary invention consisting of a combination of old ingredients which produce new and useful results. *Graver Tank & Mfg. Co. v. Linde Air Products Co., supra.*

F. Improvement of patented invention does not avoid infringement

One who appropriates and manufactures or uses a patented invention or the substance thereof without consent of the patentee does not escape or avoid infringement by improving upon the invention, or using an improvement made by another. *Temco Electric Motor Co. v. Apco Mfg. Co.*, 275 U.S. 319 (1928).

An addition to a patented apparatus does not enable him who makes, uses, or sells the patented thing with the addition to avoid a charge of infringement. *Western Electric Co. v. LaRue*, 139 U.S. 601 (1891). This is true even where the added device facilitates the working of one of the parts of the patented combination, and thus makes the latter perform its function with more excellence and greater speed. *Cochrane v. Deener*, 94 U.S. 780 (1877).

If an infringing device performs the same function as a patented device, it is immaterial that it also performs some other function. It is, nonetheless, an equivalent of the patented device and an appropriation of the patented invention.

G. Defendant's assertion of non-infringement based upon prior art, and its burden of proof

Where the defendant attempts to establish non-infringement by reliance upon prior art after the patentee has pointed out that the patent claims read directly upon the alleged infringing device, the defendant is charged with the burden of demonstrating clearly that its device is based upon the prior art rather than the teachings of the patent in suit.

The prior art must fully anticipate the invention. An accused infringer who cannot or does not challenge validity of patent claims which read on his device but seeks to rely upon prior art to avoid a finding of infringement must successfully demonstrate that he has built his device solely according to the teachings of the prior art.

In other words if everything in defendant's construction was taught by the prior art and nothing included therein other than the application of such art, plus ordinary mechanical skill, then the mere fact that the device constructed reads upon the claims of patents, the validity of which it is estopped to deny, does not spell infringement. Our conception of our obligation, therefore, is that we must examine the prior art not only to determine the scope of plaintiff's invention but also to determine whether what is built by defendant springs entirely therefrom.

It has long been well settled that there is no defense to a claim of infringement that one or more elements of a patented combination, or one or more parts of a patented improvement, may be found in one old patent or publication, and others in another, and still others in a third. It is indispensable to the defense that all of them, or their mechanical equivalents, be found in the same description or machine, where they do the same work by substantially the same means.

If there is a significant feature or combination common to the patent claim and to the accused device, which feature or combination is not in the prior art, non-infringement is not made out by the prior art. Thus, where there is a significant difference between the prior art and the accused device, or merely "similarity" between them, the "prior art" defense to a conclusion of infringement must fail.

Where, as here, the prior art does not include any teaching of all of the elements of the invention cooperating in the same way, the combinations made by the patentee were not such as to be obvious to one having ordinary skill in the art at the time they were made and the prior art does not teach the accused device, the attempt to negative infringement on the assertion that the accused devices were built on the teachings of the prior art plus ordinary mechanical skill must fail.

H. The Magnavox License and alleged misuse, a patentee's right to license its patent

Under the United States patent statutes, a patent owner has the right to enforce his patent rights against direct infringers, against those who induce infringement and against contributory infringers. 35 U.S.C. §271.

The patentee has the right to file suit to protect his monopoly, to exact royalties "as high as he can negotiate with the leverage" of his monopoly, to select the licensees who will be authorized to practice the teaching of the patent, and to consider relevant factors affecting the patentee's own business in determining to who a license will be offered and conditions upon which a license will be granted.

I. The patentee is entitled to license the patented combination or a unique part of the combination

The combination of all of the elements required by a combination claim constitute the direct infringement of such a claim. *Deepsouth Packing Co. v. Laitram Corp.*, 406 U.S. 518 (1972).

One who sells all of the component parts for a patented combination or system with knowledge or instructions that those components are to be assembled in the patented combination in the United States is both a direct and a contributory infringer.

The statute defines the contributory infringer and prescribes his liability as follows:

> Whoever sells a component of a patented machine, manufactured, combination or composition, … constituting a material part of the invention, knowing the same to be especially made or especially adapted for use in an infringement of such patent, and not a staple article or commodity of commerce suitable for substantial noninfringing use, shall be liable as a contributory infringer. 35 U.S.C. §271(c).

The purpose of Section 271(c) is "'to provide for the protection of patent rights where enforcement against direct infringers is impracticable,' H.R. 5988, 80th Cong., 2d Sess.; H.R. 3866, 81st Cong., 1st Sess.," *Aro Manufacturing Co., Inc., et al. v. Convertible Top Replacement Co., Inc.*, 377 U.S. 476, 511 (1964), or to protect patent rights from subversion by another who does not directly infringe but facilitates or encourages infringement by another. *Dawson Chemical Co. v. Rohm and Haas Co.*, 448 U.S. 176 (1980).

Activity by a patentee to derive revenue from or to license others to perform acts which would constitute contributory infringement, or to enforce his patent against an infringer or contributory infringer is not patent misuse. 35 U.S.C. §271(d); *Dawson Chemical Co. v. Rohm and Haas Co., supra; Sola Electric Co. v. General Electric Co.*, 146 F. Supp. 625, 648 (N.D. Ill. 1956).

A patentee may recover from a contributory infringer damages based upon the entire infringing structure, even though such damages were primarily caused not by the contributory infringement but by the complete infringing combination, where those damages could not be recovered from the ultimate infringer. *Aro Manufacturing Co. Inc., et al. v. Convertible Top Replacement Co., Inc.*, 377 U.S. at 508.

Plaintiffs have not committed any acts of misuse of the '507 patent-in-suit.

The evidence, findings of fact, and conclusions of law require that judgment be entered in favor of plaintiffs and against defendants, each of them. Accordingly, an appropriate judgment will be entered. Counsel for the plaintiffs may propose one, as may counsel for defendants. The court will review the submissions and will direct the Clerk, in accordance with Rule 58, Fed. R. Civ. P., 28 U.S.C. to enter judgment. SO ORDERED

Notes and Questions

1. If, as Judge Leighton indicated in Part I(A) of the opinion, the material issues pertaining to patent validity and patent infringement had already been litigated and decided in favor of Magnavox during multiple prior hearings, why didn't Magnavox merely plead collateral estoppel in the instant action in order to seek an immediate summary judgment? Judge Leighton, nevertheless, treated the prior cases as "precedent." Did that have the same effect as collateral estoppel? *See Humphreys v. Tann*, 487 F.2d 666 (6th Cir. 1973).

2. The court described a division of the circuitry of the '507 patent into "game play" portions and "display" portions. How does this compare to the distinction between the "Attract mode" and "Play mode" in the context of an arcade video game?

3. As Judge Leighton's factual findings in *Magnavox* suggest, the court ultimately determined that Magnavox's '507 patent had been infringed. The ruling made reference to the distinctions that once existed between computer games and console games. Today, are there any significant differences between the two? If so, what are they?

4. The court refers to a "broad" scope of protection that should apply to "pioneer" patents, such as the '507 Patent. Pioneer patents, unlike improvements or perfections, exist when they introduce a wholly new device or one of such novelty and importance as to mark a distinct step in the progress of the art. *Ziegler v. Phillips Petroleum Co.*, 483 F. 2d 858, 870 (5th Cir. 1973).

The distinction between pioneer patents and improvement patents seems to make sense. But wouldn't granting such broad protection actually run the risk of chilling or preventing improvements?

5. Normally, where there has been a direct (literal), blatant copying of a mechanical apparatus, infringement may be relatively simple to establish; obviously, that is *not* what occurred in *Magnavox*. Rather, infringement was established under the "Doctrine of Equivalents." As we explained above, if a device conforms to the following three-element test, then infringement may (but not necessarily) be found under the Doctrine of Equivalents. *Pennwalt Corp. v. Durand-Wayland, Inc.*, cited in the *Magnavox* case provided

the test to determine whether the accused device (as compared to the patented invention, i.e. the device):

> [a] Performs substantially the same overall function or work,
>
> [b] in substantially the same way,
>
> [c] to obtain substantially the same overall result.

What is the purpose behind the Doctrine.

6. *Magnavox* mentions different methods by which a patent holder might establish a prima facie case of infringement. It might be helpful at this particular juncture to generalize the discussion by listing some variations that commonly apply, not only to patents, but to copyrights (Chapter 6) and trademarks (Chapter 8) as well:

> [a] Literal Infringement
>
> [b] Direct Infringement
>
> [c] Vicarious Infringement
>
> [d] Contributory Infringement
>
> [e] Induced Infringement

7. The *Magnavox* findings discuss the principal components of the videogame consoles that utilized television screens during the 1980s. How do those configurations compare to modern videogame consoles such as the Xbox and Sony PlayStation? To mobile devices?

8. For the latest information on a rapidly expanding industry, many web sites are available to provide late-breaking news. While the author does not endorse or oppose any particular blogs or their respective points of view, the following web sites are listed because they pertain to the subject matter of this casebook:

> a. The Entertainment Software Association: www.theesa.com.
>
> b. The Entertainment Software Rating Board: www.esrb.com.
>
> c. The Entertainment & Leisure Software Pub. Assoc. www.elspa.com.
>
> d. The International Game Developers Association: www.igda.org.
>
> e. Gamespot.com.
>
> f. Gamepolitics.com.

9. *Magnavox v. Mattel* was by no means the only challenge to the '507 Patent. *See Nintendo of Am. Inc. v. Magnavox Co.,* 659 F. Supp. 894 (S.D.N.Y. 1987) and *infra,* in addition to *Magnavox Co. v. Activision, Inc.,* 848 F.2d 1244 (Fed. Cir. 1988).

10. The court brushed aside the distinction between digital and analog circuitry as being not "sufficient" to avoid infringement. Do you agree?

* * *

In the preceding case we witnessed how Patent Number 28,507 (The '507 Patent) sparked the modern home videogame industry by providing player-controllable movements on a simple television screen. The *Mattel* case was an early battle involving the combination of game play and the microprocessor. The Magnavox '507 Patent was predicated upon electronic circuitry, similar to that found in commercial television sets of that era.

Using '507 technology, in 1972, Magnavox released the cartridge-based Odyssey, thereby launching the home videogame industry. As *Mattel* indicated, in 1977 Mattel, Inc. developed a television game product; and with the help of New York based General Instrument Corporation it was able to incorporate a microprocessor into its game console, thereby significantly reducing the number of required components. In its defense to Magnavox's infringement action, Mattel, Inc. claimed that its own cartridge-based game console, *Intellivision,* was too different (with respect to means, operation and result) and at the same time, argued that *Intellivision* was merely an extension of prior art resulting from computer game technology. Mattel, Inc. of course, lost on both counts. Judge Leighton determined that Mattel had infringed upon the '507 Patent, and in doing so, determined that the television videogame was indeed a significant departure from the console computer game. But the challenges to the '507 Patent did not end there. Major game-maker, Activision attempted to defend its Magnavox-compatible game cartridges. Having already lost at the district court level (*Magnavox Co. v. Activision, Inc.*, No. C-82-52790-CAL, 1985 WL 9496 (N.D. Cal. March 13, 1986)), Activision appealed.

Magnavox Co. v. Activision, Inc.

United States Court of Appeals, Ninth Circuit, 1988
848 F.2d 1244

NIES, Circuit Judge.

Activision, Inc. appeals from the judgment of the United States District Court for the Northern District of California, No. C-82-5270-CAL (March 13, 1986), holding that Activision failed to sustain its burden of proving invalid the asserted claims of U.S. Patent No. Re. 28,507 ('507 patent), owned by Sanders Associates, Inc. and exclusively licensed to Magnavox Co. (collectively Magnavox), and finding that the use of an Activision cartridge in conjunction with a coacting console directly infringed the asserted claims and that Activision contributed to, and induced infringement of, the asserted claims by manufacturing and selling within the United States eleven unlicensed video game cartridges. Magnavox cross-appeals from the district court's judgment finding that Activision did not willfully infringe the '507 patent and refusing to award increased damages and attorney fees or to grant an injunction against future infringement. We affirm the district court's judgment in all respects.

DIRECT INFRINGEMENT

The district court properly rejected Activision's attempt to narrowly construe the claim elements recited in means-plus-function format to cover only the analog circuitry described in the '507 specification.

Activision does not dispute that the words of the means elements read literally on the eleven accused Activision cartridge/console combinations. Its attack focuses on the court's finding that the means to perform the required function in each instance is equivalent to the means of the invention disclosed in the specification. Having considered all of Activision's arguments, we are unpersuaded that the district court's findings are clearly erroneous. In the context of this invention and its prosecution history, a change from analog circuitry to digital circuitry does not effect such a change in the principle of operation of the claimed invention that the accused devices should be found to fall outside the reasonable scope of the claims. Here, we conclude that the patent provided the "road map" for the substitutions. As the district court held, infringement is not avoided here by substituting later-developed technology.

CONTRIBUTORY INFRINGEMENT

Regarding the district court's finding of contributory infringement, Activision asserts that the issue comes down to the legal question of whether use of Activision cartridges constitutes a permissible repair or adaptation, or an impermissible reconstruction of the patented invention and further asserts that interchanging game cartridges is the former. Thus, even if a console using an Activision cartridge falls under the claims, per Activision, there is no direct infringement and, therefore, can be no contributory infringement.

Software Publishers Association, as amicus curiae, also argues that the court found contributory infringement where no direct infringement occurred. Per amicus curiae, the software is not a material part of the invention and, thus, no direct infringement occurs when consumers place any unpatented software into a patented console that consumers purchased from a licensed source.

The problem with amicus curiae's position is its faulty premise that the Atari 2600 console alone is a patented and licensed product. The Rusch patent does not cover the Atari console alone. The console is a staple article of commerce having substantial non-infringing uses. The district court correctly found that the particular game programmed on a cartridge is critical to determining whether the resulting cartridge/console combination is or is not within the scope of the '507 patent claims. Activision is free to sell game cartridges which in conjunction with the console do not infringe. Therefore, we conclude, as did the district court, that the purchase of a console carries with it no implied license to use the console in an infringing manner, i.e., with particular game cartridges that in combination with the console result in an infringement.

Contrary to Activision's assertions the district court correctly determined that use of Activision cartridges constitutes a reconstruction of Rusch's patented device. Activision's attempt to draw a parallel between the instant case and the Aro decisions is unconvincing. *See Aro Mfg. Co. v. Convertible Top Replacement Co.*, 377 U.S. 476 (1964); *Aro Mfg. Co. v. Convertible Top Replacement Co.*, 365 U.S. 336 (1961). Activision's supplying of nonstaple game cartridges for playing entirely new games goes well beyond permissible replacement of "worn" parts to "repair" a patented device. Rather, we view this case as being more in line with *Dawson Chemical Co. v. Rohm & Haas Co.*, 448 U.S. 176 (1980), and falling within the express language of section 35 U.S.C. § 271(c) (1982). The use of Activision's accused cartridges, like the use of nonstaple propanil in Dawson Chemical, is a recreation of the patented combination constituting an infringement. Activision's variation of this argument, namely that the substitute cartridge is an "accessory" to the patented device, is also rejected. The so-called "accessory" is not merely an addition to the patented invention. The Activision cartridge can be used only by destroying the licensed combination (i.e., the patented invention) and creating a wholly new one.

Consequently, the court's determination that Activision was guilty of contributory infringement through manufacture and sale of its eleven accused cartridges must be upheld. (The parties have not separately argued the issue of inducement of infringement, and, accordingly, it is unnecessary to address it in this case.)

REMEDIES

A. Permanent Injunction

In its cross-appeal Magnavox argues that the district court abused its discretion by denying Magnavox a permanent injunction. In this case the court found no evidence of a substantial threat of future infringement or irreparable harm. Having failed to convince this court that those facts are clearly erroneous, we cannot say that the court abused its discretion in denying Magnavox's request to enjoin Activision.

B. Increased Damages

Magnavox argues that the district court clearly erred in not finding that Activision willfully infringed the '507 patent and, therefore, should have awarded Magnavox increased damages under 35 U.S.C. § 284 (1982). Per Magnavox, Activision willfully infringed the '507 patent in view of its failure to obtain an opinion of counsel regarding the issues of validity and infringement after Magnavox notified Activision of infringement and brought the '507 patent to its attention.

Under the totality of the circumstances we are satisfied that the district court's finding of no willful infringement was not clearly erroneous. Because the court found no willful infringement, it properly refrained from exercising its discretion and declined to award Magnavox increased damages.

C. Attorney Fees

Magnavox maintains that Activision's willful infringement was sufficient to support a finding that this case is exceptional under 35 U.S.C. § 285 (1982) and, therefore, the district court should have awarded Magnavox attorney fees. It also asserts that Activision's dispute of validity without presenting new prior art is evidence of bad faith litigation which makes this case exceptional.

This case is not exceptional because, as discussed above, the district court did not clearly err in finding no willful infringement. Furthermore, the mere fact that another defendant raised invalidity once before without success does not necessarily imply bad faith.

Notes and Questions

1. Perhaps the most fascinating aspect of the *Magnavox* ruling was the manner in which a videogame *cartridge* was deemed capable of infringing upon a videogame *console*. How is this possible? Could one who manufactures only videotapes infringe upon the patent holder of a videotape recorder?

2. Why should Magnavox care whether or not another company makes games for its console? Shouldn't the availability of a wider variety of game cartridges increase sales and profits with respect to the *Odyssey*? Do you believe that *anyone* should be allowed to manufacture games for a Nintendo Gameboy, Sony PlayStation or Microsoft Xbox, *without* the manufacturer's permission?

3. *Compatibility* has been a heated issue, particularly in the 1980s when Nintendo introduced its infamous "lock out" chip designed to prevent third party manufacturers from making games that would operate on Nintendo's consoles. For those who insisted on reverse engineering and other methods to obtain compatibility, The Copyright Act was far more forgiving than the Patent Act.

4. In *Atari Games Corp. v. Nintendo of Am., Inc.*, No. C-88-4805 FMS, 1993 WL 214886 (N.D. Cal. Apr. 15, 1993), involving cross-motions for summary judgment, the District Court considered Nintendo's claims of patent infringement after Atari had produced compatible game cartridges. The court determined that a final judgment of infringement was likely.

5. Magnavox sought injunctive relief, not an uncommon practice in patent infringement suits. *Atari Corp. v. Sega of Am.*, 161 F.R.D. 417 (N.D. Cal. 1994) involved Atari's Patent Number 4,445,114, sometimes referred to as the '114 patent for scrolling a video display, a function that is all but indispensable to today's maze, shooter and racing games. Atari alleged infringement against Sega with respect to its Sega Genesis and Gamegear games. The court determined that even though Atari was likely to succeed at trial, it was not entitled to injunctive relief, finding that its damages would prove speculative. With respect

to equitable or injunctive relief, should lawsuits involving intellectual property claims in the videogame industry be subjected to the same standards that apply to other industries? *See gen.*, *Atari, Inc. v. North Am. Philips Consumer Elec. Corp.* (Discussion Part II) 672 F.2d 607 (7th Cir. 1982).

* * *

Not content to allow Magnavox, Activision and Mattel to duel it out alone, Nintendo removed itself from the sidelines and launched a two-pronged attack against Magnavox in the form of an action seeking a declaratory judgment that the '507 Patent was invalid notwithstanding the prior decisions. Nintendo argued that the Magnavox attorneys who prosecuted the patent claims obtained their issuance by deliberately concealing an important "prior art" (i.e. earlier computer game) from the United States Patent and Trademark Office. The first prong failed in *Nintendo of Am. Inc. v. Magnavox Co.*, 659 F. Supp. 894 (S.D.N.Y. 1987). Here is the second act (Pay particular attention to the distinctions between the hardware and the game itself).

* * *

Nintendo of Am., Inc. v. Magnavox Co.

United States District Court, Southern District New York, 1989
707 F. Supp. 717

SAND, District Judge.

This is a declaratory judgment action brought by plaintiff Nintendo of America Inc. ("Nintendo") seeking, inter alia, a declaration of invalidity and non-infringement of U.S. Patent No. Re 28,507 ("the '507 patent") and U.S. Patent No. Re 32,305 ("the '305 patent"). Both patents are owned by defendant Sanders Associates, Inc. ("Sanders"), which granted an exclusive license with a right to sublicense to defendant Magnavox Company ("Magnavox").[3] In its counterclaims, Magnavox alleges that several of the video games manufactured by Nintendo infringe its patents.

The action was bifurcated for purposes of trial, with the Court having held a hearing on the threshold issue of whether the '507 and '305 patents are unenforceable because of alleged inequitable conduct by Magnavox during the patent application process.

The inequitable conduct claimed by Nintendo relating to the '507 patent, which was issued by the Patent and Trademark Office ("PTO") on August 5, 1975, includes the following allegations:

> The deliberate failure to disclose to the Patent Examiner known relevant prior art, including the computer/video game Space War;

> The applicants' failure to investigate their knowledge of the Space War game;

> An improper off-the-record meeting with the Patent Examiner prior to filing the '507 patent application; and

> The deliberate failure to inform the Patent Examiner that U.S. Patent No. 3,728,480 had issued and the submission of misleading information to cover up that fact.

The inequitable conduct claimed by Nintendo relating to U.S. Patent No. 3,829,095, which issued on August 13, 1974, and its corresponding '305 reissue patent, which issued on December 16, 1986, includes the following allegations:

---

3. For the sake of simplicity, this opinion will refer to the defendants collectively as Magnavox.

The failure to disclose Space War in connection with the '095 patent application despite its materiality;

The concealment of the fact that, during the prosecution of the reissue of the '095 patent the German Patent Office rejected a corresponding German patent application based, in part, on the Glaser patent.

Nintendo also alleges that Magnavox's conduct with respect to a number of other patents—particularly U.S. Patent No. 4,395,045, which previously in this litigation Magnavox alleged to be infringed by Nintendo—is further evidence of Magnavox's inequitable conduct with respect to its video game patents. Magnavox denies all allegations of wrongdoing in the prosecution of the patents and claims that the patent examiner had before him all material prior art references.

This action calls upon us to revisit the early days of the video game industry, when a simple ping-pong game captured the imagination of America. Children nowadays—weaned on sophisticated video games that replicate laser wars and magical kingdoms and boxing matches—would scoff at the idea of playing such a primitive game. But without the pioneering work that is at issue in this litigation, television sets today would do no more than receive broadcast signals.

In brief, this action presents the issue of whether the patents received on those first video games were procured by inequitable conduct. The principal Nintendo claim is that one of Magnavox's patent attorneys had seen an experimental computer/video game called Space War while an undergraduate at Stanford University in the early 1960s and intentionally hid the existence of that game from the PTO during the prosecution of the '507 and '095 patent applications (SN '256 and SN '691 respectively) in the mid-1970s.

THE APPLICABLE LAW

Inequitable conduct vitiates a patent when a patent applicant fails to disclose material information, or submits false material information, with an intent to deceive the PTO. The party challenging the patent must prove the elements of materiality and intent by clear and convincing evidence. Nintendo and Magnavox agree that the test stated in *FMC Corp. v. Manitowoc Co.*, 835 F.2d 1411 (Fed. Cir. 1987), is controlling: One who alleges a "failure to disclose" form of inequitable conduct must offer clear and convincing proof of:

(1) prior art or information that is material;

(2) knowledge chargeable to applicant [or applicant's attorneys] of that prior art or information and of its materiality; and

(3) failure of the applicant to disclose the art or information resulting from an intent to mislead the PTO.

That proof may be rebutted by a showing that:

(a) the prior art or information was not material (e.g., because it is less pertinent than or merely cumulative with prior art or information cited to or by the PTO);

(b) if the prior art or information was material, a showing that applicant did not know of that art or information;

(c) if applicant did know of that art or information, a showing that applicant did not know of its materiality;

(d) a showing that applicant's failure to disclose art or information did not result from an intent to mislead the PTO. 835 F.2d at 1415 (footnote omitted and paragraphing added).

In other words, inequitable conduct is not established upon a mere showing that art or information having some degree of materiality was not disclosed. To be guilty of inequitable conduct one must have intended to act inequitably. The requirement that a patent applicant disclose material information primarily refers to information that would be covered under the standard applied by the PTO, which is codified at 37 C.F.R. § 1.56(a): "[I]nformation is material where there is a substantial likelihood that a reasonable examiner would consider it important in deciding whether to allow the application to issue as a patent."

An applicant cannot avoid the requirement that he disclose material prior art by ignoring clear indications that such prior art exists. The Federal Circuit has stated: "As a general rule, there is no duty to conduct a prior art search, and thus there is no duty to disclose art of which an applicant could have been aware. However, one should not be able to cultivate ignorance, or disregard numerous warnings that material information or prior art may exist, merely to avoid actual knowledge of that information or prior art. When one does that, the 'should have known' factor becomes operative." *FMC Corp. v. Hennessy Industries, Inc.*, 836 F.2d 521, 526 n. 6 (Fed. Cir. 1987).

Since the parties briefed the issue, the Federal Circuit, sitting en banc, clarified the intent requirement for a showing of inequitable conduct: We adopt the view that a finding that particular conduct amounts to 'gross negligence' does not of itself justify an inference of intent to deceive; the involved conduct, viewed in light of all the evidence, including evidence indicative of good faith, must indicate sufficient culpability to require a finding of intent to deceive. *Kingsdown Medical Consultants, Ltd.*, 863 F.2d at 876 (en banc in part). Previous opinions of the Federal Circuit have held that inferences of intent may be drawn from considerations touching on materiality and an applicant's knowledge thereof.

No single factor or combination of factors can be said always to require an inference of intent to mislead; yet a patentee facing a high level of materiality and clear proof that it knew or should have known of that materiality, can expect to find it difficult to establish "subjective good faith" sufficient to prevent the drawing of an inference of intent to mislead. *FMC Corp. v. Manitowoc Co.*, 835 F.2d at 1416. Thus, the presence or absence of inequitable conduct is determined by balancing overlapping considerations of materiality, knowledge and intent.

DISCUSSION

In the Pre-Trial Order the parties stipulated to many of the relevant facts surrounding this dispute ... Pursuant to Federal Rule of Civil Procedure 52(a), the Court makes the following supplemental findings of fact and conclusions of law.

I. Allegations Concerning the '507 Patent

The '507 reissue patent describes an apparatus and method for playing games on the screen of television receivers. A major purpose of the '507 reissue patent and the '284 original patent was to make video games accessible to people in their homes. Prior to the invention, video games required hookups to large computers.

Although a wide variety of games are described in the '507 patent (including bowling and baseball), the focus of the invention was on "ball and paddle"-type games like ping-pong and hockey. In ball and paddle games an object such as a ping-pong ball or a hockey puck (described in the patent as "hit spot") shuttles back and forth between objects representing ping-pong paddles or hockey sticks (described in the patent as "hitting spots"). Upon coincidence between the hit spot and a hitting spot, the hit spot changes direction. If there is no coincidence between a hit spot and a hitting spot, the hit spot either disappears off the edge of the screen (representing, for example, the end of the table in the ping-pong game or the goal in the hockey game) or rebounds off of a wall (representing, for example, the boards in the hockey game).

A. Failure to Disclose or Investigate Space War

The parties agree that the '284 patent was reissued as the '507 patent on August 5, 1975, without Space War ever having been brought to the attention of the PTO. Nintendo alleges that Space War would have been material to the PTO's consideration of claims 25, 45, 51 and 60 of the '507 patent and that Magnavox intended to deceive the PTO by failing to disclose the game. The relevant claims of the '507 patent state:

25. In combination with a standard television receiver, apparatus for generating symbols upon the screen of the receiver to be manipulated by at least one participant, comprising:

> means for generating a hitting symbol, and

> means for generating a hit symbol including means for ascertaining coincidence between said hitting symbol and said hit symbol and means for imparting a distinct motion to said hit symbol upon coincidence.

45. Apparatus for playing a hockey type game upon the screen of a cathode ray tube, comprising:

> means for displaying a first hitting spot;

> means for displaying a second hitting spot;

> means for displaying a hit spot;

> means for controlling the position of said first and second hitting spots;

> means for controlling the position of said hit spot including means for ascertaining coincidence between either of said hitting spots and said hit spot and means for imparting a distinct motion to said hit spot upon coincidence.

51. Apparatus for generating symbols upon the screen of a television receiver to be manipulated by at least one participant, comprising:

> means for generating a hitting symbol; and

> means for generating a hit symbol including means for ascertaining coincidence between said hitting symbol and said hit symbol and means for imparting a distinct motion to said hit symbol upon coincidence.

60. Apparatus for playing games by displaying and manipulating symbols on the screen of a cathode ray tube comprising:

> means for generating vertical and horizontal synchronization signals;

> means responsive to said synchronization signals for deflecting the beam of said cathode ray tube to generate a raster on said screen;

> means coupled to said synchronization signal generating means and said cathode ray tube for generating a first symbol on said screen at a position which is directly controlled by a player; means coupled to said synchronization signal generating means and said cathode ray tube for generating a second symbol on said screen which is movable; means coupled to said first symbol generating means and said second symbol generating means for determining a first coincidence between said first symbol and said second symbol; and

> means coupled to said coincidence determining means and said second symbol generating means for imparting a distinct motion to said second symbol in response to said coincidence.

In order to find inequitable conduct in the failure to disclose or investigate Space War during the prosecution of the '507 patent, it is necessary to find by clear and convincing evidence that Space War was material to any of the four cited claims of the '507 patent; that the applicant knew of Space War and its materiality; and that the applicant's failure to disclose Space War resulted from an intent to mislead the PTO. The game was developed in 1961–62 at the Massachusetts Institute of Technology for play on a PDP-1 computer manufactured by Digital Equipment Company ("DEC"). A copy of the game was brought to Stanford University in 1963, where it was played on a PDP-1 in Stanford's computer center. While an undergraduate at Stanford in the spring of 1963, James T. Williams observed the game being played. As of 1974, Williams was a member of the Chicago law firm of Neuman, Williams, Anderson & Olson, which was retained as outside patent counsel to Magnavox early that year. At the heart of Nintendo's inequitable conduct claim are contentions relating to Williams' recollection of that game and his failure to disclose it at the time the SN '256 reissue application was being considered by the PTO in 1974–75. Materiality: Nintendo contends that Space War is material to the four claims of the '507 patent because both the game and the patent involv[ed] the operation of symbols on the screen of a cathode ray tube one of which was controllable by a player and another of which was controlled by the game electronics, the detection of coincidence between these two symbols and the imparting of a "distinct motion" to one of the symbols upon coincidence.

Magnavox argues that their knowledge of Space War was incomplete and, in any event, that Space War is not material to the claims of the '507 patent. In addition, Magnavox argues that Space War is less material than other prior art that had been disclosed, in particular the '480 patent. Although the Court finds that Space War would have been material to the claims of the '507 patent, we discuss the issue briefly because we also find that Nintendo has failed to establish that the applicant either knew of that materiality at the time of the reissue application or intended to deceive the PTO. The Court's finding of the materiality of Space War is based primarily on the close study of the language of the patent and the viewing of a videotape of Space War made last year during a demonstration of the game on a PDP-1 computer at the Computer Museum in Boston.

A mere recitation of the important elements of the claims of the '507 patent illustrates the reasons for our finding of materiality. The elements of hit and hitting symbols are represented in Space War by the spaceship and torpedoes respectively. The object for one player is to aim his spaceship so as to achieve coincidence between the torpedo he fires and the other spaceship. The other player tries to avoid coincidence between the torpedo, the position of which is controlled by the computer, and his own spaceship, which moves under his own control. The element of "imparting a distinct motion" is represented in Space War by the explosion displayed when a torpedo strikes a spaceship. In that explosion, as observed on the videotape, the spaceship and torpedo disintegrate into an expanding ball of tiny dots of light, representing pieces of debris, which then disappears. As in the traditional ball and paddle games, a distinct motion is imparted to the hit object, to wit, the explosion that is imparted to the spaceship.

The arguments Magnavox makes to avoid the logical similarity between the '507 patent and Space War restrict "imparting a distinct motion" to ball and paddle games where a hit object (e.g., a ping-pong ball) retains its form and moves in a different direction once it achieves coincidence with a hitting object (e.g., a ping-pong paddle). In support of its limited interpretation of the phrase, Magnavox relies on a narrow reading of the patent specifications. But there is no such limitation in the language of the claims, and we see no reason to read one into the patent. Instead, we believe that the claim language "imparting a distinct motion" should be given its traditional English language meaning, which clearly encompasses the explosion in Space War.[4]

In that the computer-generated explosion following coincidence between a spaceship and a torpedo represents an explicit change in the position of the spaceship, we have no doubt that the explosion falls within the literal meaning of the term "imparting a distinct motion."

At the time of the patent application, the patent examiner would have considered the broadest reasonable interpretation of the actual claim language (which forms the basis of the invention that is being granted protection) and not the applicant's subjective interpretation of the claim language. It is well-established patent law that language from the specification is not to be used to limit the scope of the claims during the prosecution of a patent application. This is addressed by MPEP § 904.01, which provided:

> The breadth of the claims in the application should always be carefully noted; that is, the examiner should be fully aware of what the claims do not call for, as well as what they do require.

Even if we look beyond the claims, we find that Magnavox's limited reading of the claim language is unsupported by the specification. Among the many examples of games cited in the specifications is bowling, where the motion imparted ("If pin (pins) are hit, they disappear") is more like the explosion in Space War than the ball and paddle action of ping-pong and hockey. Thus, although a patent applicant can be his own lexicographer, we do not find that the language in the SN '256 reissue application should be given anything other than its everyday meaning.

Magnavox also claims that Space War was not material because the cited prior art included more material references, including the '480 patent. In the first place, we reject the explanation about the '480 patent because, as explained below, the applicants never directly cited that patent to the PTO as prior art. More importantly, we reject it because Williams testified that he cannot recall whether he considered the '480 patent to be a sufficient reason for not citing Space War. Magnavox cannot now claim that the '480 patent was more material than Space War when that apparently had nothing to do with its decision not to cite it at the time of the application. To allow such a post hoc justification would defeat the purpose of an inequitable conduct claim, which focuses on an applicant's conduct before the PTO.

We also reject the other explanations offered by Magnavox, including the fact that Space War was played on a point plot display and the '507 patent specified a raster scan. The technology at the time allowed an inventor to go back and forth between the two types of displays, and Williams acknowledged at trial that the absence of a raster scan was not a sufficient basis for not disclosing Space War to the PTO. Space War, after all, could have been disclosed in combination with other prior art references that taught raster scans. In addition, claim 45 of the '507 patent specifies "on the screen of a cathode ray tube" and

---

4. Impart: "1. To grant a share of; bestow. 2. To make known; disclose." The American Heritage Dictionary of the English Language 659 (1976). Distinct: "1. Not identical; individual; discrete. 2. Not similar; different; unlike. 3. Easily perceived by the senses or intellect; clear. 4. Well-defined; explicit; unquestionable." *Id.* at 383. Motion: "1. The action or process of change of position. 2. A meaningful or expressive change in the position of the body or a part of the body; a gesture or movement...." *Id.* at 856.

does not require a raster scan. Thus, we find that the Space War that existed in 1963 would have been material to the PTO's consideration of the SN '256 reissue application.

Knowledge of Materiality: The fact that Space War was material to the claims of the '507 patent does not end our inquiry. There must also be clear and convincing evidence that Williams or others involved in the prosecution of the SN '256 patent application had knowledge of that materiality and that he withheld it in an attempt to deceive the PTO. The knowledge element is critical in this action, for much of Nintendo's claim is based on Williams' eleven-year-old memory of a computer game he briefly saw on one occasion at Stanford's computer center.

There are several phases during which the applicants' knowledge can be measured. From the beginning of Williams' involvement with the reissue application in early 1974 until July 1975, the only information that was known about Space War was that which Williams recalled based on his having seen the game played at Stanford in 1963. Williams' recollection at that time was, understandably, very sketchy.

> Q.: [W]ill you tell us what you recall having seen at Stanford.

> A.: What I recall was a PDP-1 computer with a point [plotter] display on it and there was a game which involved two players, each player could manipulate a space ship on the face of the cathode ray tube. I believe that there were four switches. One switch—each player had four switches, one to cause his spaceship to rotate counterclockwise; one to cause it to rotate clockwise; one to cause thrust to be applied to the ship in the direction in which it was pointed and one to fire missiles or torpedoes at—in the direction in which the spaceship was pointed.

> Q.: ... [W]as your recollection distinct enough to know that you did not know about certain elements of the game?

> A.: There were things that I didn't recall, that's right.

> Q.: [D]id you ... recall what happened when a torpedo hit a spaceship?

> A.: No, sir, I didn't. Transcript at 240–41, 250–52.

Williams further testified that he had a five-minute conversation with Anderson about the relevance of Space War after the filing of the '284 and '285 reissue applications (SN '256 and SN '023 respectively).

> Q.: [I]s it fair to say that you and Mr. Anderson considered together whether you should cite your recollection to the Patent Office?

> A.: I think it was fair that—to say that we considered whether we should do anything about it at all, whether it was a matter of concern to us. And I think we decided that it was not a matter of concern and inherent in that was it didn't have to be cited.

> Q.: You mean a matter of concern in complying with your duty of candor to the Patent Office, is that what you're referring to?

> A.: Yes. In my view, that recollection could not have had anything—any real bearing on that application. The kinds of games we were talking about at that time were, as I said, these games where you could have a hit symbol and a hitting symbol. You maneuver the hitting symbol to cause coincidence with the hit symbol and then the hit symbol bounces off, like the ping-pong game that was talked about this morning. And those are the kind of symbols that we had in mind and those are the kinds of symbols we were thinking about and we certainly

had no reason to think that ... this game that I recalled had any kinds of symbols like that. We certainly had no reason to think that once the spaceship and the torpedo came into contact with each other that there was any distinct change in motion of the torpedo.

Transcript at 247–48, 256, 262–64. Based on this analysis, Williams and Anderson made a deliberate decision not to disclose Space War to the PTO. We find Williams' explanation credible. There is no doubt that his memory some eleven years after seeing Space War at Stanford was incomplete. His recollection of the game showed that he lacked specific knowledge of many elements that would correspond to the patent claims, including the specific representations of hit and hitting symbols and of imparting a distinct motion on coincidence. He also knew the game was not played on a raster scan.

Although Nintendo tries to cast doubt on the extent of Williams' recollection, we find no reason to believe that after eleven years he would have remembered more specific information, such as the response of a spaceship after it was hit by a torpedo.

Accepting Williams' testimony about the extent of his recollection, we find that it was insufficient to warrant disclosure to the PTO both because he failed to appreciate the association between the elements of Space War and the '507 patent and because his recollection was missing certain key elements. In particular, we find Williams' claim that he did not know of the materiality of Space War to be convincing because of the conceptual difficulty of reading the hit and hitting symbols of the patent onto Space War.

At the time the applicants sought reissue, their attention was focused on other aspects of the SN '256 patent application, such as the specific types of display used in playing the games. That, after all, was the purpose of seeking reissue in the first place. Magnavox sought to expand the scope of the '284 patent to insure that it covered video arcade games. Williams testified:

A.: The reason [for the reissue applications] was that in ... licensing discussions with Mr. Briody [Magnavox's corporate patent counsel], a number of the television game manufacturers had taken the position that the claims were not infringed because those coin operated games used television monitors or television receivers with the portions which enabled them to receive broadcast signals disabled. We had reviewed the 284 and the 285 patent and thought that the claim should not be that narrowly construed and that they did cover such devices, but in order to make it clear, we thought we would go to the Patent Office and present new claims which would eliminate that type of argument.

Q.: Is it fair to say, sir, that the focus of the reissue application was on the display of the games?

A.: The focus was on whether a television monitor was used or a television receiver was used.

Q.: So the focus of the reissue was on displays?

A.: Yes, the reason it was filed was because of this television monitor/television receiver distinction.

Transcript at 191–93. We accept this explanation and believe it further supports Williams' contention that he did not think of Space War as being material to the patent application.

On July 23, 1975, Magnavox was informed by Midway Manufacturing Company, a defendant in its pending patent infringement action, that Midway would rely on Space

War as prior art to invalidate the '284 and '285 patents. Midway's interrogatory response informing Magnavox of that fact read as follows:

> The development, construction and operation of the video game of Spacewar by various persons, not yet identified, at the Massachusetts Institute of Technology in 1961 and 1962, and the wide knowledge and use by others at other places, of Spacewar and other video games yet to be determined.

> Defendants Midway has not yet determined the exact dates of the acts referred to [above], but they are believed to have occurred between 1961 and May 27, 1969, the filing date of Patent No. 3,659,284.

Magnavox learned no additional information about the materiality of Space War from this vague interrogatory response.

Nintendo also alleges that employees of Sanders knew of the materiality of Space War and withheld it from the PTO. The evidence shows that John Sauter brought a copy of Space War with him from Stanford when he started working at Sanders in 1969. However, Sauter's familiarity with the game is not relevant to our inquiry; Nintendo must prove inequitable conduct by someone involved in the patent application process. Nintendo's claims about Louis Etlinger, the head of Sanders' patent department, also fail. Etlinger was not involved in the patent applications at issue here and had no knowledge of the existence of Space War at Sanders until September 1975, which was over a month after the '507 patent had issued. Nintendo has failed to produce evidence that any of the relevant Sanders employees had information about Space War at the time that they were required to disclose to the PTO.

The Court is aware of the difficulties Nintendo faces in proving Magnavox's intentional failure to disclose a material fact some fifteen years after the patent application was filed and twenty-six years after Williams actually saw the Space War game. However, Nintendo has failed to meet its burden. Although Nintendo argues persuasively that the undisclosed information known to Magnavox was material, there has been an insufficient showing of the applicants' knowledge of that materiality. Patent applicants have a duty of reasonable inquiry and cannot cultivate ignorance. We do not believe Magnavox's conduct violated that precept.

Intent to Deceive: We have found that the applicants did not have sufficient information about the materiality of Space War to require its disclosure to the PTO or to create a duty to investigate. Accordingly, we believe that the nondisclosure of Space War was made in good faith and not with an intent to deceive the PTO. In conclusion, we find that there was not inequitable conduct during the prosecution of the '507 reissue patent in the applicants' failure to disclose or investigate Space War.

B. Meeting with Examiner

On April 15, 1974, Magnavox filed suit against video arcade game manufacturers alleging infringement of the '284 and '285 patents. As noted above, Magnavox at that time sought to broaden the scope of its claims to insure that they covered non-television receiver displays such as video arcade games played on monitors. On April 23, 1974, Williams and Seligman conducted an off-the-record interview with Patent Examiner Trafton to discuss the filing of reissue applications for the '284 and '285 patents. Time was of the essence, for Magnavox's right to file for reissue was to expire two days later (two years after the issuance of the patents). Given the time pressure, Williams and Seligman sought the Examiner's reaction to the filing of the reissue applications.

The MPEP provides that an interview prior to filing is improper unless it is for the limited purpose of indicating the field of search to an attorney. See MPEP § 713.02 ("Prior to filing, no interview is permitted. However, in the examiner's discretion, a limited amount of time may be spent in indicating the field of search to an attorney, searcher or inventor."). Because Williams and Seligman already knew the relevant field of search for the patent applications, it is clear that the scope of the interview went beyond that. A letter from Etlinger to Briody dated April 23, 1974 confirms this, as does Williams' trial testimony.

Although the Examiner did not actually look at the application, it was described to him in sufficient detail that he was able to offer his opinion that he would be "favorably inclined" toward the refiling and that the claims, as stated in the existing patents, already cover the video arcade games against which Magnavox sought to protect itself. Furthermore, although Etlinger brought signed copies of the reissue applications with him to the meeting with the Examiner, they were not filed until two days later. In the interim, Williams broadened one claim and added another to the '285 patent reissue application. We find that there is only one rational explanation for this: the meeting with the Examiner went beyond a discussion of the field of search and provided Williams with sufficient information to make those amendments.

Nintendo's claim that this pre-filing meeting was improper is further supported by the applicants' failure to make a record of the meeting. The rules require that an applicant make of record in an application a "complete written statement as to the substance of any face-to-face … interview with regard to an application …" MPEP § 713.04. Insofar as the reissue application was the subject of the meeting, the lack of any such notice in the reissue application file was improper. Magnavox's attempts to justify its actions are unavailing. Neither the fact that the patent application later submitted to the PTO contained the substance of the material discussed in the interview nor the fact that the Examiner himself might have violated his own obligation to file a report about the meeting once it became clear the applicants had not done so, relieved applicants of the obligation to file the statement.

The prefiling meeting thus violated three separate provisions of the MPEP: § 713.02 (interviews prior to first official action not permitted unless for limited purpose of discovering field of search); § 713.03 (interview for "sounding out" Examiner not permitted); and § 713.04 (substance of interview must be made of record). Nevertheless, we believe these violations in and of themselves do not amount to inequitable conduct sufficient to render the patent invalid. There was no intent to deceive the PTO, just a flouting of the procedural requirements.

C. Failure to Inform Examiner That the '480 Patent Had Issued

Defendants have acknowledged that they made no reference to the '480 patent in the SN '256 reissue application. In the application filed April 25, 1974, Magnavox referred to the '480 patent by the patent application's serial number in spite of the fact that the '480 patent had issued on April 17, 1973. The consequence of this action is clear. An Examiner cannot rely on a pending application as prior art. See MPEP § 901.03 ("pending U.S. applications are preserved in secrecy … and are not available as references"). Not only was the mistake made in the initial application, but it was compounded by a later action. When the applicants filed Amendment A to the SN '256 application on February 13, 1975, they deleted the outdated reference to the SN '798 application and, instead of replacing it with the number of the '480 patent that had issued nearly two years earlier, replaced it with SN '966, the serial number of the continuation application to SN '798 that was filed in 1971. The updating of the application's serial number created the appearance that the '480 patent had not issued and was therefore not to be considered as prior art under 35 U.S.C. § 102(e).

Magnavox claims that the failure to inform the PTO of the issuance of the '480 patent was inadvertent and that the change to the SN '966 continuation application number was made to conform the SN '256 reissue application to the original patent as amended by a Certificate of Correction. Magnavox also claims that the patent examiner was not deceived by the omission of the '480 patent number in that he would have been aware that the application was granted once he did research into the original '284 patent application (SN '154) during the prosecution of the reissue application.

We accept the first explanation and reject the second. The updating of the application's serial number was a ministerial-type act that was performed without any intent to mislead the PTO. The applicant simply changed the serial number to conform the application to the amended original patent. While the applicant should have updated the serial number with the number of the issued patent, we believe this was an inadvertent mistake rather than an indication of an attempt to deceive the PTO.

As for Magnavox's second explanation, the focus in an inequitable conduct claim is on the actions of the patent applicant and not on the knowledge that might have been independently obtained by the PTO. The fact that the PTO had the means the discover that the '480 patent had issued does not absolve the applicants of their duty.

We find, however, that because the applicants knew that a competent patent examiner would have discovered the '480 patent in the course of a search of the prior art, their actions are more appropriately classified as negligent and not as illustrative of an intent to deceive the PTO. Accordingly, we find that there was no inequitable conduct in the failure to inform the PTO that the '480 patent had issued.

II. Allegations Concerning the '305 Patent

A. Failure to Disclose Space War During '095 Prosecution

The '095 patent issued on August 13, 1974 without Space War ever having been brought to the attention of the PTO. Because Williams had no role in the prosecution of the SN '691 patent application, Nintendo has to prove that Etlinger, who was responsible for the prosecution of the application, withheld material information with an intent to mislead the PTO. *See FMC Corp. v. Hennessy Industries, Inc.*, 836 F.2d at 525 n. 5 ("One attempting to prove inequitable conduct must prove by clear and convincing evidence that the conduct of the person charged was inequitable."). Nintendo admits that Etlinger's only source of knowledge about Space War was a discussion he had with Williams during an early 1974 meeting about the reissue applications for the '284 and '285 patents. Because we have found that Williams' recollection was so incomplete that he had no obligation to disclose Space War, it follows that no such obligation could flow to Etlinger.

B. Rejection of the German Patent

Nintendo contends that the applicants concealed the fact that in 1985, while the SN '542 application was still pending, the German Patent Office rejected a corresponding patent application based, in part, on the Glaser patent. Although the applicants, in a departure from Sanders' normal practice, did not inform the PTO of the rejection, we find that this did not amount to inequitable conduct. In the first place, notice of the German Patent Office's rejection would not have been material to the SN '542 application because the rejection itself would have added little to the information already before the Examiner. As noted above, the Examiner should have already considered the Glaser reference during the reissue process. In addition, it would have been immaterial for the Examiner to have been informed of the German rejection because the German Patent Office acts pursuant to German patent law and not United States patent law. Furthermore, there is no indication that Sanders' failure to inform the PTO was based on an intent to deceive nor was it under any affirmative obligation to disclose that information to the PTO.

CONCLUSION

The Court finds that Nintendo has failed to meet its burden of proving by clear and convincing evidence inequitable conduct during the prosecution of the '507 and '305 patents.

Notes and Questions

1. Were the differences between MIT's *Space War* and Magnavox's *Pong*-like game significant enough to warrant Magnavox's failure to mention it during its application for the '507 re-issue patent? If not, then why did the court specifically determine that *Space War* was in fact material to the '507 application and that it should have been mentioned in that application?

2. According to the key claim in the application for the '507 re-issue patent, a hitter would act upon the hit object by, "imparting a distinct motion" to the object. That would account for the ricochet motion of the ball after it was struck by a paddle. According to the argument advanced by Magnavox to negate similarity, the claim language should not cover the situation in *Space War* whereby the hit object would explode and break into pieces instead of moving or bouncing. Was that a valid argument? Did the court find merit in the argument?

3. The screen of a cathode ray tube does not require a raster scan as does a television receiver. According to the testimony, there was concern about whether or not the original '284 patent would cover arcade videogames. That, according to the court and the supporting testimony, was the reason for the re-issue patent applications. Because an arcade monitor is not the same as a television receiver, Magnavox sought the re-issue patent. In the process, it ignored the similarity of the game elements with respect to *Space War* and its own *Pong*-like game. Notwithstanding the court's determination, do you think that this *ignorance* was excusable?

4. Much of the discussion in the preceding case centered around the issue of whether or not the '507 patent was predicated upon "prior art." The concept is based on the notion that a patent should not be issued if someone other than the patentee is responsible for the invention; to allow otherwise would be to grant a monopoly to someone who did invent the subject matter of the patent. This would permit that person to prohibit all others from manufacturing or using the product, *even* the actual inventor. As the *Nintendo of America v. Magnavox* case suggests, the patent applicant has a duty to provide prior art information at the time of application. Section 301 of the Patent Act provides: "Any person at any time may cite to the Office in writing prior art consisting of patents or printed publications which that person believes to have a bearing on the patentability of any claim of a particular patent. If the person explains in writing the pertinence and manner of applying such prior art to at least one claim of the patent, the citation of such prior art and the explanation thereof will become a part of the official file of the patent. At the written request of the person citing the prior art, his or her identity will be excluded from the patent file and kept confidential." *See also* AIA § 102(a).

Section 302 places in jeopardy those patents that might be predicated upon applications that failed to mention applicable prior art; the section provides a reexamination process wherein an otherwise valid patent might be extinguished. The section states that: "Any person at any time may file a request for reexamination by the Office of any claim of a patent on the basis of any prior art cited under the provisions of section 301 of this title. The request must be in writing and must be accompanied by payment of a reexamination fee established by the Director pursuant to the provisions of section 41 of this title. The request must set forth the pertinence and manner of applying cited prior art to every claim for which reexamination is requested. Unless the requesting person is the owner of the patent, the Director promptly will send a copy of the request to the owner of record of the patent."

5. Matters involving prior art may be inextricably intertwined with the non-obviousness requirement. Inventions are normally the product of earlier advances and "prior art." According to the Supreme Court, a patent that claims a combination of elements of prior art is obvious if the improvement is no more than the predictable use of the prior art elements according to their established functions. *KSR Int'l Co. v. Teleflex Inc.*, 550 U.S. 398 (2007). *KSR* also held that in determining whether such a patent was obvious, the question was not whether the combination was obvious to the patentee but whether it was obvious to a person with ordinary skill in the art. If you knew how to construct *Space War*, would you also have been able to figure out how to make *Pong*?

6. Apparently the integrity of the patentee influenced the outcome of the *Nintendo* case. Was this correct? The validity or invalidity of a pioneer patent affects the entire industry and the public, not just the parties; does it make sense to predicate such an important result upon the conduct of one person or party as opposed to other more consequential factors? What other factors would you consider?

7. In order to oppose a patent consisting of a combination of prior art elements, it must be demonstrated that the prior art's documents teach, suggest or motivate the combination of those prior art elements. Under that standard, would you say that *Space War* taught, suggested or motivated Rausch or Baer?

8. Can you think of any new inventions of the past several years that reached the level of warranting a pioneer patent?

---

§ 7.50 Improvements and Peripherals

A pioneer patent's success is measured by the size of the industry (and related products) that it creates. Once a "pioneer" *mousetrap* is invented, we should expect an endless flow of peripherals, embellishments, accessories and, of course some better mousetraps. The videogame industry has been living up to this model with its own stream of physical, visual and acoustical improvements; they have spectacularly transformed what was once nothing more than a tiny dot bouncing off of small lines. The videogame improvements by their very nature were bound to overlap the patent claims and specifications of the consoles that they sought to modify.

Among the most significant additions, as we have seen, were the game cartridge systems; they not only permitted a variety of games for play on a single console, they also opened the door for third party game developers, who may or may not have been welcome by the console manufacturer. And, despite the successful attacks on early developers, as witnessed by the preceding cases, eventually the Patent and Trademark Office, in addition to the courts, would find it necessary to open the door for improvements by newcomers, who would, in turn, seek to restrict even later newcomers.

Fairchild Semiconductor Corp. v. Nintendo Co., Ltd.

United States District Court, Western District Washington, Feb. 14, 1994
No. C-92-1971 C, 1994 WL 560607

COUGHENOUR, District Judge.

I. Introduction

This case involves claims by Fairchild Semiconductor Corporation, producer of home video entertainment systems, against Nintendo Company, Ltd. and Nintendo of America, Inc., another home video entertainment company, for patent infringement. Fairchild alleges that Nintendo's "Super Nintendo Entertainment System" ("SNES") infringes U.S. Patent No. 4,095,791 ("the '791 patent").

II. Motion for Summary Judgment Regarding Nintendo's Noninfringement

A. Facts

In 1978, the U.S. Patent and Trademark Office issued the '791 patent naming Ronald Smith and Nicholas Talesfore as co-inventors, and Fairchild Camera and Instrument Corporation as assignee. The '791 patent, entitled "Cartridge Programmable Video Game Apparatus," was the result of Fairchild's efforts to commercialize the home video game. The Fairchild home video game provided structural improvements that allowed anyone, including small children, to easily program a computer chip to play games chosen by the consumer rather than play those built into the machine by the manufacturer.

The claims of the '791 patent are directed to a "video game apparatus" for use in connection with a television set. Claim 1 covers a console which includes a chute for receiving a cartridge. In the chute, there is a connector mechanism which provides an electrical connection to a data storage area, and a locking mechanism to hold the cartridge in place. The console also houses a plurality of parameter selection switches which control the play parameter signals.

In 1991, Nintendo introduced its home video game, the Super Nintendo Entertainment System. Nintendo's '082 patent describes the mechanical features of the SNES. In light of advances in the technology of circuit board connectors, the inventors no longer were concerned with repeated frictional insertion and removal of the connectors. Consequently, the connector in the SNES console does not rotate or use springs. The SNES cartridge is held in place by the friction of the card edge connector. A locking device connected to the power switch also holds the cartridge in place. The locking mechanism is moved into place by turning the power switch on. With certain circuit improvements, Nintendo later modified the SNES to remove the locking mechanism. The SNES has three parameter selection switches on its console: a power switch, a reset switch, and a channel 3/4 selection switch. Other switches which control game play are located on the hand controllers.

B. Analysis

Fairchild alleges that the Nintendo SNES console's locking mechanism, connector structure, and parameter switches on the console infringe its '791 patent. Nintendo seeks summary judgment determining that claims 1–3 of the '791 patent are not infringed by Nintendo's SNES machine.

Patent infringement analysis is a two-fold inquiry: a threshold question of claim interpretation followed by a determination of whether the properly construed claims encompass the structure or process. The patentee bears the burden of proving infringement.

1. Interpretation of the Claims:

The first step in a patent infringement analysis is claim interpretation. The parties in this case dispute what limitations are imposed on the invention by the claim elements "locking means," "connector means," and "parameter selection switches."

The claims of the patent provide the concise formal definition of the invention. They are numbered paragraphs which particularly [point] out and distinctly [claim] the subject matter which the applicant regards as his invention. 35 U.S.C. § 112. It is to these wordings that one must look to determine whether there has been infringement.

Before the elements of the claims can be applied to the accused device, the court must establish their meaning. This is known as "claim construction" or "claim interpretation." Claim interpretation is the process of elaborating terse language in order to understand and explain, but not to change, the scope of the claims. The words of a claim are generally given their ordinary and accustomed meaning, unless it appears from the specification or the file history that they were used differently by the inventor. In claim construction, the words of the claims are construed independent of the accused product, in light of the specification, the prosecution history, and the prior art. Additionally, when the meaning of key terms, or elements, of claims is disputed, the court may consider the testimony of witnesses.

Claim 1 of the '791 patent, includes the following elements in dispute:

> A plurality of parameter selection switches for developing play parameter signals.
>
> Chute means for receiving said cartridge means and having connector means for providing electrical connection to said data storage means, and chute means including a locking means having a detent for engaging said locking recess of said cartridge means to hold said cartridge means in a received position.

Fairchild alleges that Nintendo's SNES machine infringes on the elements "connector means," the "locking means" and the "parameter selection switches" within Claim 1 of the '791 patent. Before making a determination of infringement, however, the parties dispute the meaning of the elements or terms listed in the '791 patent.

a. Locking Means:

Claim 1 describes a "locking means having a detent for engaging said locking recess of said cartridge means to hold said cartridge means in a received position." The words of the claim refer to a "chute means" (i.e., passage for the cartridge containing a connector to move through) which includes the "locking means." The locking means is thus part of the claimed connector assembly mechanism where the video cartridge makes electrical contact with the console. This interpretation is important because Nintendo's accused device's locking mechanism is not part of the connector assembly structure.

Claim language can be written as a "means plus function" element or a "structural" element. A means plus function element is written to describe what an element of the invention does. A structural element refers to what the element is. The parties dispute the characterization of the claim language because the different types of elements are subject to different patent infringement tests discussed below.

The court does not need to look beyond the unambiguous language of the claim to determine that the "locking means" is written as a "means plus function" element. A "locking means" is a way for a device to lock. Fairchild contends that "locking means" should be interpreted as a structural description that uses non-means language. Yet the very language of the claim includes "means."

b. Connector means:

Claim 1 describes "a connector means for providing electrical connection to said data storage means." A "connector means" denotes electrical contact. Such an open-ended term in claim interpretation requires more than its structural meaning. Fairchild again contends that "connector means" is described in non-means language. Yet the structure is not known without understanding its function. The "Summary of the Present Invention" to the '791 patent states,

> [a] further object of the present invention is to provide a video game apparatus having an improved electrical connector assembly which reduces the force required to mate a cartridge-contained printed circuit board with console-contained electrical contacts. '791 patent, col 1, 50.

In light of the prior art and the specification, the connector means should be interpreted as being able to reduce the force required to mate a cartridge-contained printed circuit board with console-contained electrical contacts. The "locking means" and "connector means" elements of the '791 patent therefore are construed as means plus function elements for the purposes of claim interpretation.

c. Parameter Selection Switches:

Claim 1 describes "a console means including a plurality of parameter selection switches for developing play parameter signals." In incorporating these definitions, "play parameter switches" denotes keys or buttons on the console which allow the player to choose the variables of, or define the scope of, the game. The specification indicates that part of the "play parameter selection switch" is a reset switch. The reset switch is in fact the starting point for other selections the player must make in order to play a game. Therefore "parameter selection switches" includes a reset button to the extent that such a switch initializes the game.

The parties agree that "play parameter switches" is a structural description, and a person of ordinary skill in the art would find that the functional language does not add anything to the structural description.

2. Patent Infringement:

The second step is to determine whether the accused product infringes on the claims. Infringement is a question of fact. There are two ways to establish infringement: literal infringement and infringement under the doctrine of equivalents. Literal infringement of a patent requires every limitation set forth in a claim be found in the accused product. Under the doctrine of equivalents, infringement may be found if the accused device performs substantially the same overall function in substantially the same way to obtain substantially the same result.

a. Literal Infringement:

A patent claim with a means-plus-function element can be literally infringed only if the exact function is performed in the accused method or device. When an element of a claim is expressed as a "means" or step for performing a specified function, the element "shall be construed to cover the corresponding structure, material or acts described in the specification and equivalents thereof." 35 U.S.C. § 112(6). Thus, in order to "read" a means-plus-function limitation on an accused device, the accused device must employ means identical to or the equivalent of the structures, or acts described in the patent specification. The accused device must also perform the identical function as specified in the claim.

i. Locking means: In this case, the locking device in the SNES performs an identical function to Fairchild's claimed locking means. The function of Fairchild's "locking means" is "to hold the cartridge in a received position." The locking means employed by the SNES power interlock similarly works to hold the cartridge in place. Thus the SNES mechanism provides the same function as the locking means described in the '791 patent.

To prove literal infringement of a means plus function element, however, the patentee must also prove that the means in the accused device is structurally equivalent to the means described in the specification. 35 U.S.C. § 112(6). Stated another way, the accused devise must use the same structure listed in the patent specifications to perform the same function disclosed in the claim. Fairchild fails to provide any evidence that the structure of the SNES power interlock mechanism is identical or equivalent to Fairchild's specified "locking means" structure.

In fact, a simple comparison reveals the differences immediately. The '791 patent specification describes the locking mechanism as follows: When the cartridge is fully inserted, a rib at the bottom of the door automatically snaps into a recess on the bottom of the cartridge. The detent holds the cartridge in place against the pressure of the spring-loaded rotating connector.

In contrast, the insertion of a cartridge in the Nintendo SNES does not automatically activate the locking mechanism. The power interlock of the SNES consists of a lever which is linked to the power switch. There is no catch that slides across a surface of the cartridge and automatically snaps into a recess in the cartridge when it is inserted. Thus, the SNES locking device is not structurally equivalent to the Fairchild locking means as described in '791 patent specification. Therefore the SNES locking device does not literally infringe upon the claimed locking mechanism.

ii. Connector means: To prove literal infringement of the claimed connector, the court must again apply Section 112(6). The SNES connector and the connector described in the '791 patent provide the same function, i.e., electrical contact. Thus the structure of the accused product must be compared to the corresponding patent's structure described in the specification. Fairchild presents no evidence that the structure of the SNES connector mechanism is identical or equivalent to the connector assembly described in the '791 patent. The connector means described in the '791 patent is not structurally equivalent to the card edge connector used in the SNES.

iii. Parameter Selection Switches: The parties agree that the claim limitation of "a plurality of parameter selection switches" is a structural description, not a means plus function element, and is not subject to an analysis under Section 112(6). Therefore the court must compare the limitations set forth in a claim with the accused device. Claim 1 of the '791 patent discloses a "console means including a plurality of parameter selection switches for developing play parameter signals." The SNES, in contrast, has three switches on its console, a power switch, a reset switch, and a channel 3/4 switch.

Fairchild does not attempt to argue that the power switch and the channel 3/4 switch which is located at the back of the console are play parameter selection switches. The reset switch on Nintendo's SNES, however, is a play parameter switch since the same reset switch is identified in the '792 patent specification as a play parameter selection switch. One switch is clearly not a "plurality" of switches as defined in Claim 1 of the '791 patent.

Fairchild contends that SNES's parameter selection switches on the hand controller, which is connected to the console by wires, is equivalent to having the switches on the console. Claim 1 expressly states, however, that parameter selection switches are part of the "console means." Another claim element in the '791 patent describes hand controllers, and these do not include parameter selection switches. Because there is only one play parameter selection switch on Nintendo's console, and the SNES hand controllers are not part of the SNES console, there is no literal infringement.

b. Doctrine of Equivalents:

Infringement can also be established under the theory known as the "doctrine of equivalents." If a device performs substantially the same overall function or work, in substantially the same way, to obtain substantially the same overall result as the claims invention, then infringement may (but not necessarily) be found. The law will not allow an "unscrupulous copyist to make unimportant and insubstantial changes and substitutions in the patent which, though adding nothing, would be enough to take the copied matter outside the claim." *Graver Tank & Mfg. Co. v. Linde Air Prods. Co.*, 339 U.S. 605, 607 (1950). However, the doctrine of equivalents does not automatically apply to every patent infringement action:

> Application of the doctrine of equivalents is the exception however, not the rule, for if the public comes to believe (or fear) that the language of patent claims cannot be relied on, and the doctrine of equivalents is simply the second prong of every infringement charge, regularly available to extend protection beyond the scope of the claims, then claims will cease to serve their intended purpose. Competitors will never know whether their actions infringe a granted patent.

Inherent in our claim-based patent system is also the principle that the protected invention is what the claims say that it is, and thus that infringement can be avoided by avoiding the language of the claims. It is only when the changes are so insubstantial as to result in "a fraud on the patent" that application of the equitable doctrine of equivalents becomes desirable.

Thus the first question which must be asked is "has a substantial change been made?" Only if the answer to that question is "no" should the accused infringer be liable for improperly trying to appropriate the claimed invention.

In order to prove infringement under the doctrine of equivalents, the patentee must show the presence of every element or its substantial equivalent in the accused device.

i. Locking means: In this case, the SNES power interlock does not operate in the same way as the locking means in Claim 1. The SNES power interlock operates wholly separate from the connector assembly; the SNES power interlock is activated from the power switch. The two locking devices thus do not operate in the same way, and the SNES power interlock is not a substantial equivalent to Fairchild's locking device which is part of the claimed "chute" passageway.

ii. Connector means: The connector means also operates differently. As Fairchild's own expert witness testifies, the connector means has a "different implementation" in the SNES than the idea embodied in Claim 1. Fairchild's patented connector requires a zero or low friction cartridge assembly that locks into place using a spring device. By contrast, the accused connector uses a high friction edge card connector that is not locked into place by the connector assembly. Nintendo's high friction card edge connector would substantially change the way the low friction connector assembly is operated in Fairchild's patented device. Thus, Nintendo's connector device is not the substantial equivalent to Fairchild's claimed connector means.

The doctrine of prosecution history estoppel also applies with respect to the connector means. The extent to which prosecution history estoppel precludes a finding of infringement under the doctrine of equivalents is a question of law. Fairchild contends that it never surrendered card edge connectors in the prosecution history of its patent. Rather, it amended its claim to distinguish its connector from tape recording heads used to detect recorded signals on audio tape. It is undisputed, however, that card edge connectors at that time fatigued with use. Fairchild amended its patent application to explain that its claimed "connector means" includes a means for "rotating the contact elements into engagement" in order to make low friction contact. The amended claim provided an improvement over other connectors that required high friction electrical contact. Thus, the claimed connector, as amended, is an improvement over the card edge connector as it existed at that time. In light of the amendment, Nintendo's card edge connector, even with its technological improvements for sustained use, is outside the scope of Fairchild's claimed connector. Thus, the prosecution history precludes Fairchild from contending that Nintendo's card edge connector is substantially equivalent to its claimed connector means.

iii. Parameter Selection Switches: Finally, the parameter selection switches do not function in the same way or for the same result in Nintendo's SNES machine. Nintendo's parameter selection switches are on its hand controllers, not on the console as in the '791 patent claim. The hand controllers disclosed in Fairchild's patent are a separate claim element, and do not include parameter selection switches. In order to prove infringement under the doctrine of equivalents, the patentee must show the presence of every element or its substantial equivalent in the accused device. Nintendo's play selection switches on its hand controllers are not the substantial equivalent of the '791 patent parameter selection switches on the console.

The court concludes that no reasonable jury could find that the locking device, connector mechanism, or parameter selection switches meet the substantially similar test required under the doctrine of equivalents.

III. Nintendo's Motion on Patent Invalidity

Nintendo also seeks summary judgment determining that the '791 patent is invalid because of its failure to disclose the best mode in the patent claim as required by 35 U.S.C. § 112. Patent invalidity constitutes a defense available to an accused infringer. Validity of a patent should be addressed only after the court finds that the defendant infringes. Because the court grants Nintendo's motion for noninfringement, it must not address whether the '791 patent is valid.

Notes and Questions

1. As a review, what is the difference between a literal infringement and infringement involving the Doctrine of Equivalents? Can you draw an analogy with respect to copyright infringements? *See* § 7.32, *supra.*

2. The issue of "Patent prosecution history estoppel," raised in *Fairchild,* sounds more complicated than it truly is. The concept, which will appear again before we leave this chapter, is sometimes termed "file wrapper estoppel." It stands as a potential defense to a claim of infringement under the doctrine of equivalents. We have set forth the basics in § 7.32, *supra.*

During the course of the patent application process (patent prosecution) which may be lengthy, the applicant often has occasion to modify, change or amend his or her claims or specifications. Such modifications may be required as a matter of accommodation for the examiner at the Patent and Trademark Office, who might otherwise reject the patentee's application. It might be correct to think of the process as one of negotiation. Assume, for example, that when Samuel Morse sought to obtain a patent on his invention of the telegraph (and Morse Code), he also sought to *claim* the concept of electromagnetism as part of his patented invention. While electromagnetism happens to be a fundamental component of the telegraph, it is also necessary for the operation of the electric motor and many other subsequent inventions unrelated to the telegraph that nevertheless depended upon electrical current. In other words, the claim for "electromagnetism" by Morse would be deemed "too broad" (and also considered as a claim for a "law of nature" which is not patentable); granting such a patent would thus potentially stifle and prevent other inventions. The patent examiner would therefore, require Morse to amend his claim so as to exclude electromagnetism. This exclusion would become part of the patentee's prosecution history. Thereafter, should Morse sue another inventor for making an electromagnetic device other than the telegraph, the defending inventor could claim "prosecution history estoppel" as a defense. The authority for this defense is embodied in *Festo Corp. v. Shoketsu Kinzoku Kogyo Kabushiki Co.*, 535 U.S. 722 (2002), (holding that in order to accommodate the requirements of patent law, the patentee cannot claim indirect infringement of an element that was narrowed by a change or amendment during the course of patent prosecution.)

* * *

Alpex Computer Corp. v. Nintendo Co. Ltd.

United States Court of Appeals, Federal Circuit, 1996
102 F.3d 1214

Archer, Chief Judge.

Nintendo Company, Ltd. and Nintendo of America, Inc. (collectively Nintendo) appeal the January 6, 1995, judgment of the United States District Court for the Southern District of New York, *Alpex Computer Corp. v. Nintendo Co.*, 34 USPQ2d 1167 (S.D.N.Y.1994), holding U.S. Patent No. 4,026,555 (the '555 patent), owned by Alpex Computer Corporation (Alpex), not invalid, willfully infringed, and awarding $253,641,445 in damages and interest. We affirm the judgment as to validity and reverse the judgment of infringement.

I.

This case deals with an invention within the art of video games. The video game industry began in the early 1970s and includes two branches, arcade video games and home video games. Arcade video games are large, expensive, coin-operated machines that are placed in high traffic areas such as amusement arcades. These machines are generally referred to as "dedicated" because they can play only one game. Home video games, in contrast, are small, relatively inexpensive devices that are easily connected to the antennae terminals of a standard television. The Magnavox Odyssey was the first home video game. It too was a dedicated system playing only one game which was referred to as the "ball and paddle" because a dot of light bounced between two player-controlled vertical lines.

In early 1974, the inventors of the patent in suit conceived of a new microprocessor-based home video game system that used modular plug-in units — replaceable, read-only memory, or ROM, cartridges — to permit home video systems to play multiple games, including games with rotating images. The '555 patent on this invention issued to Alpex on May 31, 1977. The patented invention was commercialized in systems by Atari, Mattel, and Coleco.

In the early 1980s, Nintendo entered the home video game market with the Nintendo Entertainment System (NES). After the NES was featured at the 1985 Consumer Electronics

Show, Alpex notified Nintendo of possible infringement of the '555 patent. Soon thereafter, in February 1986, Alpex filed suit against Nintendo for patent infringement.

Following a four-week liability trial, the jury returned a verdict for Alpex. After this liability verdict, Nintendo filed a motion for judgment as a matter of law (JMOL) as to infringement and validity or, in the alternative, for a new trial. The damages trial followed before the same jury. The jury awarded Alpex a royalty of 6% which, when computed on the stipulated $3.4 billion of allegedly infringing products sold by Nintendo, resulted in a damage award of $253,641,445. Nintendo again filed motions for JMOL or a new trial and for a remittitur on damages. Alpex moved for entry of judgment and an award of prejudgment interest. The district court denied all of Nintendo's post-trial motions and entered judgment for Alpex with prejudgment interest. Nintendo now appeals the judgment as to validity, infringement, and damages, and Alpex cross-appeals the amount of damages.

II.

The '555 patent claims a keyboard-controlled apparatus for producing video signals by means of random access memory (RAM) with storage positions corresponding to each discrete position of the raster for a standard television receiver.

The television raster comprises numerous discrete dots or bars, approximately 32,000, which the cathode ray beam illuminates on a standard cycle, which in turn creates the image on the television screen. The patented invention requires sufficient RAM to accommodate each of the approximately 32,000 memory positions needed to represent the raster image. Thus, the RAM holds at least one "bit" of data for each position in the memory "map" of the raster. Accordingly, this video display system is called "bit-mapping." The advantage of this system, as disclosed in the patent, is that it provides for the representation of every image within the raster RAM, or display RAM, and thereby provides greater control of the display for the manipulation of complex images and symbols. To achieve this flexibility, however, bit-mapping requires the construction of each image within the display RAM before display, a process that requires the microprocessor to erase and rewrite each image. Because the microprocessor must refresh the display RAM for each frame to show the movement of images, the operation of the system is slowed down.

The accused NES with its game cartridges is also an apparatus for producing video signals by means of storage positions corresponding to discrete positions of the raster for a standard television receiver. The video display system for the NES does not include RAM with storage positions corresponding to each discrete position of the raster. Instead, the NES utilizes a patented picture processing unit, or PPU, to perform the generation of images on the screen. The PPU receives pre-formed, horizontal slices of data and places each slice in one of eight shift registers, each of which can store a maximum of 8 pixels. These slices of data are then processed directly to the screen. The PPU repeats this process to assemble the initial image on the screen. Thereafter it repeats the process as necessary to form changes in images throughout the progression of the game. Nintendo refers to the PPU as an "on-the-fly" system. It is undisputed that the NES video display system, using shift registers to process slices of images (as opposed to entire screens), is a faster means of displaying movement of images on the video screen than the bit-mapping of the RAM-based system of the '555 patent.

The claims at issue are 12 and 13 of the '555 patent:

> 12. Apparatus for playing games by displaying and manipulating player and ball image devices on the screen of a display tube, comprising first means for generating a video signal representing a linear player image device aligned in a first direction, second means for generating a video signal representing a ball image device,

manually operable game control means, and means responsive to said manually operable game control means for causing said first means to generate a video signal representing the player image device rotated so that it is aligned in a second direction different from said first direction.

13. Apparatus according to claim 12, wherein said means for causing includes programmed microprocessor means and a replaceable memory having program game instructions stored therein for controlling said microprocessor means, whereby different games may be played with said apparatus by replacing said replaceable memory.

The parties dispute the proper claim construction of independent claim 12 (and thus dependent claim 13) and specifically the meaning and scope of "means for generating a video signal."

III.

After the jury returned a verdict of infringement, Nintendo challenged on motion for JMOL the interpretation that the jury appeared to give the claim in reaching its verdict, but the district court denied Nintendo's motion. Nintendo argues that, by denying its JMOL, the district court approved an erroneous claim construction, allowing claims for a RAM-based, bit-map video display system to read on a device that used a shift register-based, on-the-fly video display system.

Nintendo argues that the '555 patent requires the use of a RAM memory map for all of the 32,000 pixels in the raster, whereas the NES uses shift registers that only provide for a maximum of 64 pixels. Because of this difference in structure, Nintendo contends that there can be neither literal infringement nor infringement under the doctrine of equivalents. Nintendo further contends that Alpex is barred from claiming that the NES infringes the '555 patent because during prosecution Alpex distinguished the invention of the '555 patent from a relevant prior art patent using shift registers.

In prosecuting its patent application before the Patent and Trademark Office (PTO), Alpex specifically distinguished the RAM-based, bit-map video display structure of the '555 patent from a prior art patent, Okuda, which claimed a shift register-based video display structure. Alpex explained to the PTO that, unlike Alpex's bit-map system, the Okuda video display system comprised an entirely different structure than the Alpex system.

Okuda contemplates modification of one line of data at a time and there is no provision for modifying a single "dot." The random access techniques of applicants' invention enables any single point on the TV screen to be altered at will (under control of the microprocessor). Alpex says nothing about the Okuda patent with regard to claim construction. It only argues that Nintendo waived any argument pertaining to Okuda for purposes of prosecution history estoppel.

IV.

Prosecution history is relevant not only for purposes of prosecution history estoppel but also for construing the meaning and scope of the claims. Indeed, prosecution history is a proper claim construction tool.

In this case, the Okuda patent is directly relevant to claim construction. The prosecution history of the '555 patent shows that the examiner rejected claim 1 of the application as being anticipated by Okuda. Claim 1 specified a series of limitations in means-plus-function format to a display control apparatus utilizing a RAM-based, bit-map system. Alpex distinguished Okuda before the PTO based on the structural difference of a RAM-based versus a shift register-based video display system: "Claim 1, as amended, now clearly distinguishes over Okuda. The claim requires a random access memory which, as indicated previously, is not disclosed in Okuda." [W]e discern no reason why prosecution history relating to the structure of the video display in the means-plus-function limitations of claim 1 is not pertinent to the same structure of the same display system in the means-plus-function limitations of claims 12 and 13. Statements made during the prosecution relating to structures disclosed in the specification are certainly relevant to determining the meaning of the means-plus-function limitations of the claims at issue.

The statements made by Alpex during prosecution with regard to the Okuda prior art patent emphasize that Alpex claimed a video display system based on the use of RAM capable of modifying a single bit, or pixel, on the television receiver. These statements distinguish any video display system based on shift registers, as shift registers do not allow the selective modification of a single bit in memory, that is, a single pixel. It is undisputed that the NES utilized this type of video display system. Indeed, Alpex's own technical expert, Mr. Milner, testified that the NES utilized shift registers, not RAM. Further, Mr. Milner explained that the NES could not directly modify a single pixel. Thus, Mr. Milner's testimony confirms that random access capability is not possible by use of shift registers. In short, the structure and operation of the NES paralleled the structure and operation of the Okuda video display system.

Therefore, because Alpex admitted during prosecution that its claims do not cover a video display system based on shift registers as in Okuda, i.e., it argued that a system based on shift registers is not structurally or functionally equivalent to a RAM based system that can randomly access a single bit, Alpex's claims cannot now be construed to cover the NES, which possesses the same structural and functional traits as Okuda.

V.

Because Alpex defined its claims during the prosecution of the '555 patent as not covering a system using shift registers we conclude the court erred in sustaining the jury verdict of literal infringement.

VI.

The district court also denied Nintendo's motion for JMOL on the issue of infringement under the doctrine of equivalents primarily based on its conclusion that the jury could reasonably have found infringement under § 112, ¶ 6. The court reasoned that equivalence under the doctrine of equivalents is a slightly broader concept than equivalence under § 112, ¶ 6, and that, as a result, its discussion of equivalence for literal infringement applied equally to infringement under the doctrine of equivalents.

While equivalency under the doctrine of equivalents and equivalency under § 112, ¶ 6, both relate to insubstantial changes, each has a separate origin, purpose and application. Under § 112, the concern is whether the accused device, which performs the claimed function, has the same or an equivalent structure as the structure described in the specification corresponding to the claim's means. Under the doctrine of equivalents, on the other hand, the question is whether the accused device is only insubstantially different than the claimed device. The latter question often turns on whether the accused device performs substantially the same function in substantially the same way to achieve substantially the same result.

In this case, the court concluded, based on the testimony of Alpex's expert, Mr. Milner, that the jury's finding of infringement under the doctrine of equivalents was supported by substantial evidence. However, Mr. Milner's testimony that the claimed and accused devices were substantially the same in terms of function/way/result was merely conclusory as acknowledged by the district court. However, the court said that Mr. Milner's conclusory statements on function/way/result, when considered with his testimony in relation to infringement under the § 112, ¶ 6, were sufficient to establish infringement under the doctrine of equivalents.

As discussed earlier, however, Mr. Milner's testimony concerning § 112, ¶ 6, only related to equivalence of the functional result. Neither he nor the court considered whether the accused device and the claimed device operated in substantially the same way. Indeed, in describing equivalency for § 112, ¶ 6, purposes, Mr. Milner acknowledged that the accused and claimed devices do not operate in the same way. This testimony does not support a conclusion that the claimed system and the NES operate in substantially the same way.

The evidence in this case, therefore, does not support a finding of infringement under the doctrine of equivalents. The evidence fails to establish that the claimed and accused devices operate in the same way or that the differences between them are insubstantial. As discussed above, Alpex described its claims during the prosecution of the '555 patent as covering random access systems capable of changing a single bit. It did not and could not claim image generation by shift registers. As the Supreme Court has explained, the purpose of the doctrine of equivalents is to prevent others from avoiding the patent by merely making "unimportant and insubstantial changes and substitutions in the patent." *Graver Tank*, 339 U.S. at 607. It is not meant to cover systems that are clearly defined as outside the bounds of the claims. In this case, using shift registers, instead of RAM, to process data for video display, is not merely an unimportant and insubstantial change.

Accordingly, because there is a lack of substantial evidence to support a finding of infringement either literally or under the doctrine of equivalents, the district court's judgment as to infringement and damages is reversed. Alpex's cross-motion on damages is, therefore, moot.

VII.

Nintendo also challenges the jury's finding that the '555 patent is not invalid. On JMOL, the district court made an exhaustive thirty-two page review of Nintendo's arguments relating to invalidity. We have carefully considered Nintendo's arguments and the district court's opinion on this issue and discern no error. Accordingly we affirm the judgment as to validity.

———————

Notes and Questions

1. Prosecution history played a dual role in the *Alpex* case. What were the two concepts at issue? How significant was the distinction between the use of the RAM memory map for all 32,000 pixels (as claimed in the '555 patent) and Nintendo's use of shift registers, which used only 64 pixels at a time? Do you know why the latter was a faster superior system?

2. In another action with a similar outcome, *Wiener v. NEC Electronics, Inc.*, 41 U.S.P.Q.2d 1023 (Fed. Cir. 1996), the Federal Circuit Court of Appeals rejected the opinion of the patentee's expert witness who claimed that the defendant's system was identical. The plaintiff patentee's system would "call" on or retrieve data from inside its data matrix, one byte at a time, whereas the defendant's system stored its data outside of the data matrix. In view of these victories by the defendants which seem to hinge upon very technical distinctions, can you reconcile these more recent cases with *Magnavox v. Mattel*?

3. For patent infringement actions in general, subject matter jurisdiction is rarely an issue, since the federal courts possess exclusive jurisdiction over such lawsuits. Territorial jurisdiction and venue issues are another matter. Where should a potential patent infringer be sued? *See North Am. Philips Corp. v. Am. Vending Sales, Inc.*, 35 F.3d 1576 (Fed. Cir. 1994) which held that the owner of a patent for an arcade videogame could exercise personal jurisdiction in Illinois over corporations that were domiciled in Texas and California. Because the infringing articles were shipped to an Illinois buyer, the corporations were deemed to have voluntarily placed them into the stream of commerce, knowing that they were destined for Illinois and, therefore, could have reasonably foreseen that the articles would be resold in Illinois. *See also Gray v. Am. Radiator & Std. Sanitary Corp.*, 176 N.E.2d 761 (Ill. 1961) (holding that a manufacturer placing an item in the stream of commerce might be subject to *in personam* jurisdiction in any state where that item causes injury). (See also Frank Deale, J. McIntyre and the Global Stream of Commerce, 16 CUNY L. Rev. 269 (2014).)

---

§ 7.60 Concepts, Game Play and Virtual Worlds

Historically, the term "patent" had been associated with tangible inventions bearing physical, machine-like characteristics. Without those mechanical utilitarian characteristics, creative works were once likely to fall into the "work of authorship" pigeonhole which aimed them toward the Bureau of Copyrights. But that has changed. Today, patent protection for videogame advances and related technological inventions have extended well beyond the physically tangible devices. How far? As you will soon see, the point in that line is a difficult one to determine. At one end of the spectrum rests those inventions and improvements pertaining to the console, peripherals and the physical construction of the cartridges, all of which are considered as hardware and well within the scope of patent protection. As we move toward the center we pass by the game engines and graphical user interfaces, all of which *might* qualify for patent protection. At the other extreme are the artistic elements of the games themselves including "game play."

As you read the cases that follow, notice the ever-diminishing line between hardware and software. In a videogame context, it is difficult to envision one without the other. To make matters more difficult, in this age of miniaturization, chips and circuitry are rapidly replacing our once-distinguishable mechanical inventions. As long as the so-called game play methods and elements are inextricably linked to the mechanical or electrical functions of the videogame there will always be a potential basis for patent protection.

Gussin v. Nintendo of Am., Inc.

United States Court of Appeals, Federal Circuit, Aug. 3, 1995
No. 95-1051, 1995 WL 460566

LOURIE, Circuit Judge.

Edward L. Gussin appeals from an order of the United States District Court for the Central District of California granting summary judgment that claims 1 and 2 of United States Patent 4,782,335 were not infringed by Nintendo of America, Inc. *Gussin v. Nintendo of Am., Inc.,* 33 USPQ2d 1418 (C.D.Cal.1994). Because we agree that prosecution history estoppel prevents a finding of infringement under the doctrine of equivalents, we affirm.

DISCUSSION

Gussin was granted U.S. Patent 4,782,335 (the '335 patent) entitled "Video Art Electronic System" on November 1, 1988. The invention is directed to an electronic system for drawing and coloring pictures on a conventional television monitor. A user operates the system using three controls. The first moves a drawing cursor on the screen; the second turns the drawing function on and off; and the third determines the color of the drawing when the drawing function is turned on.

Nintendo sells the "Super Nintendo Entertainment System" (SNES), a home video game system that allows a user of the system to play an assortment of video game cartridges on an ordinary television monitor. One such game cartridge that Nintendo developed is "Mario Paint." Like Gussin's invention, the Mario Paint cartridge and the SNES allow a user to draw and color pictures on a television monitor. In addition, the Mario Paint cartridge allows the user to compose music and animate pictures.

On July 21, 1993, Gussin sued Nintendo for infringement of claims 1 and 2 of the '335 patent. Claims 1 and 2 are independent claims, which read, in relevant part:

1. A video art electronic system for drawing and coloring on a conventional color television video monitor including a television screen having predetermined pixels, comprising: a draw switch ... ; means including a first joystick to produce first digital signals representing the "X" and "Y" coordinates of a pixel position of a cursor on the video monitors; means including a second joystick to produce second digital signals representing the color of the cursor on the video monitor; a pixel memory comprising a random access memory (RAM) having digital memory addresses corresponding to the pixels and adapted to be read in correspondence with the conventional horizontal and vertical scanning of the video monitor; first connecting means operative when the draw switch is in its first position to connect said first and second digital signals to said pixel memory so that the color and position of the cursor on the video monitor are written into said pixel memory; means to convert output signals from said pixel memory to conventional color television signals; and means to convert said first and second digital signals to conventional color television signals.

2. A video art electronics system for drawing and coloring on a conventional color television video monitor including a television screen having predetermined pixels, said system comprising a first and second member positionably movable by an operator ... said system further comprising:

> a draw switch having a first position for invoking said first mode of drawing and coloring on the video monitor and a second position for invoking said second mode of not drawing and coloring on the video monitor; a pixel memory comprising a random access memory, and means operative in said first mode to store the commanded color of the cursor in said pixel memory.

1. Literal Infringement

A literal infringement analysis requires two separate steps. First, the claims asserted to be infringed must be construed to determine their meaning and scope. Second, the claims as construed are compared to the allegedly infringing device. To infringe, the accused device must contain every limitation of the asserted claim.

On appeal, Gussin argues that the court improperly construed the "pixel memory" limitation of claims 1 and 2. We disagree. The court properly construed the claims, based on the specification and prosecution history, to require a pixel memory that stores actual color data, instead of one that stores "pointers"[5] to a memory separate from the pixel memory.

Both claims 1 and 2 state that the "color data" to be stored in the pixel memory should be the "color of the cursor." Specifically, claim 1 requires a "pixel memory comprising a random access memory (RAM)" into which "the color and position of the cursor on the video monitor are written." Claim 2, as amended after reexamination, requires "a pixel memory comprising a random access memory, and means operative in said first mode to store the commanded color of the cursor in said pixel memory." Thus, both claims require storage of the color of the cursor in the pixel memory rather than permitting the pixel memory to store pointers to color data stored in a separate color memory.

The specification and the prosecution history further make clear that the claims, as properly construed, only read on devices that store actual color data in the pixel memory. [The court recounted Gussin's long prosecution history before the PTO with regard to the '335 patent. One such instance was when Gussin testified in opposition to allowing a Mr. Hill to obtain a patent (the '867 patent) on similar technology. During those proceedings, Gussin argued the following — ED]:

> The PTO also fails to understand important differences between the function of the pixel memory in claim 1 of the '335 patent and the pixel memory in Mr. Hill's color palette systems. In Gussin's claim 1, the pixel memory receives and stores digital signals representing the actual color of the cursor. In Mr. Hill's color palette systems, the pixel memory does not receive or store a signal representing the actual color of the cursor. Instead, Mr. Hill's pixel memory receives, and stores a color pointer, namely a signal representing the address of a color in the separate color memory of Hill's color palette systems.

Gussin also submitted a declaration in which he argued that claims 1 and 2 were patentable over the '867 patent because "the products described in my '335 patent do not include color memory or color mixing means as described in the '867 patent...." Gussin asserts that these arguments were limited to distinguishing Gussin's claims from the '867 patent based on the use of a separate memory that stores "user-mixed" colors. Gussin therefore argues that the pixel memory limitation should be broadly construed to cover any pixel memory system that stores "pre-mixed" colors. We disagree that Gussin's arguments during reexamination were so limited.

While it is true that Gussin distinguished the claimed invention from Hill during prosecution based on the storage of "user-mixed" colors instead of "pre-mixed" colors, Gussin also distinguished the claims from the '867 patent based on the way the pixel memory operates. He consistently argued before the PTO that his invention was distinguishable from the '867 patent because he did not claim a pixel memory that stores a color pointer instead of actual color data. In fact, the examiner specifically noted this distinction when he allowed claim 1.

The examiner, accepting Gussin's argument, merely emphasized the difference between how the pixel memory in each system interacts with the rest of its respective system — the key distinction being that "the '867 patent does not store color cursor data in it's [sic] pixel memory." Based on the foregoing, we conclude that claims 1 and 2, as properly

---

5. A "pointer" is "[a] data item that specifies the location of another item." THE NEW IEEE STANDARD DICTIONARY OF ELECTRICAL AND ELECTRONICS TERMS 964, Christopher J. Booth, ed. (5th ed. 1993).

construed, require that the pixel memory store actual color data, not merely pointers to color data stored in a separate memory.

Finally, Gussin argues that even if the claims require that the pixel memory store actual color data, genuine issues of material fact exist as to whether Nintendo's SNES device meets this limitation. In support, Gussin claims that Nintendo's expert witnesses admitted in their declarations and during depositions that the SNES stores actual color data. However, the declarations indicate instead that the pixel memory in the SNES device stores pointers rather than actual color data, and the deposition testimony relied upon by Gussin is not inconsistent with these declarations. Thus, Gussin has failed to establish the existence of any genuine issue of material fact regarding the operation of the pixel memory of the SNES device.

Our determination that Nintendo's SNES device does not meet the pixel memory limitation as properly construed is sufficient to cause us to affirm the trial court's grant of summary judgment that Nintendo's device does not literally infringe.

2. Doctrine of Equivalents

An accused product that does not literally infringe may still infringe under the doctrine of equivalents. However, the doctrine of prosecution history estoppel limits the application of the doctrine of equivalents by preventing a patentee from using the doctrine to recapture subject matter previously surrendered in order to procure issuance of the patent. As discussed above, Gussin expressly distinguished his invention from the '867 patent during prosecution of the '335 patent based on two arguments: 1) his invention uses pre-mixed colors, not user-mixed colors; and 2) his invention stores actual color data in its pixel memory, not pointers. As indicated in his reasons for allowance, the examiner allowed the claims based on these distinctions. Therefore, prosecution history estoppel prevents a finding of infringement under the doctrine of equivalents against any device, including Nintendo's SNES device, that uses a pixel memory which stores pointers instead of actual color data.

The court's grant of summary judgment of noninfringement under the doctrine of equivalents was proper.

Notes and Questions

1. Once again prosecution history estoppel was used to defend against allegations of infringement under the Doctrine of Equivalents. Other procedural and pleading defects also played a role in the defeat of the claim. Were those just "excuses" to serve as a predicate to once again deny a monopoly to a single developer? Or was there real substance to the decision on the merits?

2. As the court indicated, in Gussin's claim, "the pixel memory receives and stores digital signals representing the actual color of the cursor," whereas in the defending system, the "pixel memory receives, and stores a color pointer ..." It might help to explain the distinction by understanding that a computer's internal processor spends much of its time moving data in and out of registers. There is a wide variety of such registers performing distinct, important functions (data registers, user-accessible registers, special purpose registers, etc.). Each register possesses an address (in much the same fashion that a house has a street address). Gussin's patent covered a method whereby the digital signals representing the color of the pixels that were to appear on the screen would be moved

and stored in a given register. The defending processor, on the other hand would instead store a pointer that would indirectly point to the information concerning the color. The end result might very well be the same. That being the case, if the offending system performed the same function with the same result, could it nevertheless be said that the use of a pointer (instead of a movement of data into a register) was a significant enough distinction to warrant dismissal of the infringement action?

3. In what might be referred to as the *Festo Fiasco*, the Court of Appeals for the Federal Circuit in 2000 held that any amendment narrowing the scope of a claim during the prosecution process (where the applicant failed to provide reasons for the amendment) would constitute a complete bar to a later use of the doctrine of equivalents by the applicant. Referring to the decision as "disruptive," the Supreme Court reversed. *Festo Corp. v. Shoketsu Kinzoku Kogyo Kabushiki Co.*, 535 U. S. 722 (2002).

* * *

Fantasy Sports Properties, Inc. v. Sportsline.com, Inc.

United States Court of Appeals, Federal Circuit, 2002
287 F.3d 1108

LOURIE, Circuit Judge.

Fantasy Sports Properties, Inc. appeals from the decisions of the United States District Court for the Eastern District of Virginia granting SportsLine.com, Inc.'s, Yahoo! Inc.'s, and ESPN/Starwave Partners' (collectively, "the defendants'") motions for summary judgment of noninfringement of Fantasy's U.S. Patent 4,918,603. *Fantasy Sports Props., Inc. v. Sportsline.com, Inc.*, 103 F.Supp.2d 886 (E.D.Va.2000) (granting summary judgment in favor of Yahoo!) ("*Fantasy I*"); *Fantasy Sports Props., Inc. v. SportsLine.com, Inc.*, No. 2:99cv2131 (E.D.Va. Jan. 25, 2001) (granting summary judgment in favor of SportsLine and ESPN) ("*Fantasy II*").

BACKGROUND

Fantasy is the assignee of the '603 patent, which relates to a method of and apparatus for playing a "fantasy" football game on a computer. '603 patent, col. 1, II. 6–11. The game is played by a number of "owners" or "managers" who operate fantasy "teams" or "franchises" based on actual football players. Points are awarded to each team based upon the performance of its players in actual professional football games for categories such as touchdowns, field goals, and points after touchdowns ("PATs"). The total points for each team are tabulated utilizing a database containing the relevant statistics for each player, which is automatically updated after the actual football games are played each week. The specification teaches that in addition to the standard points given for a particular play in an actual game, "bonus points" may be awarded based upon, inter alia, "the difficulty of the play." Claim 1 of the '603 patent is the only independent claim at issue, and it reads as follows:

> 1. A computer for playing football based upon actual football games, comprising: means for setting up individual football franchises; means for drafting actual football players into said franchises; means for selecting starting player rosters from said actual football players; means for trading said actual football players; means for scoring performances of said actual football players based upon actual game scores such that franchises automatically calculate a composite win or loss score from a total of said individual actual football players' scores; said players' scores are for quarterbacks, running backs and pass receivers in a first group and

kickers in a second group; and wherein said players in said first and second groups receive bonus points. The claim interpretation dispute in this appeal centers around the "bonus points" limitation.

Fantasy filed suit against the defendants alleging that the defendants' computerized fantasy football games infringed the '603 patent.[6] *Fantasy I*, 103 F.Supp.2d at 887. Yahoo! filed a motion for summary judgment of noninfringement, arguing that its Yahoo! Sports Fantasy Football game does not satisfy the "bonus points" limitation. The district court interpreted the "bonus points" limitation to mean points that are awarded "in addition to the normal points for a scoring play," and determined that Fantasy disclaimed any game that awards additional points for distance scoring and total yardage by amending claim 1 to add the "bonus points" limitation in order to overcome a rejection based upon a prior art publication entitled "All-Pro Yearbook—1987" ("the 1987 article"). Based on that construction, the court granted summary judgment that Yahoo!'s product does not infringe the patent as a matter of law because, except for the additional points awarded based on yardage, it only awards points equal to the points given in an actual professional football game.

ESPN and SportsLine thereafter filed separate motions for summary judgment of non-infringement based on the claim construction set forth in *Fantasy I*. The court clarified its previous construction of the term "bonus points" to mean "additional points, above and beyond standard scoring, that are based upon the difficulty of the play," i.e., "for scoring plays not typically associated with the position of the scoring player." Fantasy II, slip op. at 4–5. The court then determined that ESPN's Fantasy Football game did not infringe as a matter of law because that product does not award additional points for "out-of-position" scoring (e.g., a running back throwing a touchdown pass). The court also granted summary judgment of noninfringement with respect to SportsLine's Fantasy Football and Football Challenge games because it determined that those products awarded additional points based only upon yardage. Finally, the court determined that SportsLine's Commissioner.com product could not directly infringe because it found that the Commissioner.com is not a fantasy football game, but rather is a "software tool by which [subscribers] operate their own fantasy football leagues on customized internet Web pages." The court also rejected Fantasy's contributory infringement argument because it determined that Fantasy failed to prove that any subscriber actually operated the Commissioner.com in an infringing manner.

DISCUSSION

A determination of infringement requires a two-step analysis. First, the court determines the scope and meaning of the patent claims asserted and then the properly construed claims are compared to the allegedly infringing device. Claim construction is an issue of law, that we review de novo. Determination of infringement, whether literal or under the doctrine of equivalents, is a question of fact.

A. Claim Construction

Fantasy argues that the "bonus points" limitation should be broadly construed to cover any points awarded in addition to those given in an actual football game. Fantasy contends that the plain meaning of the term "bonus" is "anything given in addition to the customary or required amount," and that nothing in claim 1 limits that term to any specific type of

---

6. The games at issue on appeal include Yahoo! Sports Fantasy Football, ESPN Fantasy Football, and three SportsLine games: Fantasy Football, Football Challenge, and Commissioner.com.

additional points. Fantasy also argues that it did not disclaim coverage of all the bonus points discussed in the 1987 article because it distinguished that reference during prosecution on the grounds that it did not utilize a computer and did not disclose the combination of awarding bonus points and using two separate groups of players for scoring purposes. Fantasy further contends that the specification makes clear that the term "bonus points" includes non-scoring plays, such as total yardage, because it states that "[b]onus points are ... awarded based upon the difficulty of the play," not the scoring play. Finally, Fantasy argues that the doctrine of claim differentiation dictates that a broader construction must be given to claim 1 because claim 2 limits the definition of the term "bonus points" to "complex or difficult plays," and claim 3 defines that limitation in terms of specific examples, e.g., "extra points for a quarterback who receives or runs for [a] touchdown."

The defendants respond that the term "bonus points" means additional points awarded beyond those given in an actual football game for scoring plays in which a player scores out of position. The defendants argue that the prosecution history clearly shows that the examiner interpreted the "bonus points" limitation to exclude the scoring methods disclosed in the 1987 article, and that Fantasy acquiesced in that interpretation, thus surrendering a broader meaning for that term. The defendants also contend that, reading the specification as a whole, it is apparent that the "plays" that qualify for bonus points are scoring plays, and that therefore the "bonus points" limitation does not include points awarded for total yardage or any other non-scoring statistic. Finally, the defendants argue that the doctrine of claim differentiation must yield where, as here, the specification and prosecution history clearly define the scope of the invention.

We conclude that the term "bonus points" is limited to additional points awarded beyond those given in an actual football game for unusual scoring plays, such as when a player scores in a manner not typically associated with his position. The words of a claim are generally given their ordinary and accustomed meaning, unless it appears from the specification or the file history that they were used differently by the inventor. The specification states that "[c]omputerized football points are awarded for touchdowns, field goals, and points after touchdowns. Bonus points are also awarded based upon the difficulty of the play." '603 patent, col. 13, ll.20–23. The term "bonus points" therefore must be construed to mean points that are awarded for a scoring play in addition to the points given for that scoring play in an actual football game.

Furthermore, the prosecution history in this case clearly demonstrates that Fantasy surrendered any interpretation of the term "bonus points" that encompasses the methodologies taught in the 1987 article for awarding additional points beyond those given in an actual football game. In the application that eventually led to the '603 patent, Fantasy set forth a number of claims that did not include the "bonus points" limitation and cited the 1987 article as prior art in an Information Disclosure Statement. The 1987 article discloses the concept of "fantasy football" and teaches how to organize a fantasy football game played on paper. That article also details a number of scoring methods that may be utilized in tabulating the total points for each fantasy franchise, including but not limited to assigning points for distance scoring and total yardage. The examiner rejected all but three of the claims in Fantasy's application over, inter alia, the 1987 article, and in doing so made a number of comments relevant to this appeal. First, the examiner noted that the "[u]se of a computer to store data previously maintained on paper files is well known." Paper No. 7 at 6. The examiner also stated that "grouping players ... is obvious since running backs and pass receivers form the offensive line, special teams line backers and defensive backs form the defensive line; and kickers perform kickoffs and field goals, functions which differ from that of both offensive and defensive teams."

Finally, and most significant to the present appeal, the examiner rejected application claim 10, which incorporated the "computer" and "grouping" limitations by reference and added the further limitation that additional points are awarded "based upon the number of yards that were involved in the play that received a touchdown," because the 1987 article "discusses [the] use of a distance scoring method in which player scores are a function of the length of the play." *Id.* at 9. The examiner, however, also stated that claims 13–15, the only claims that contained the "bonus points" limitation at issue, "are found allowable over [the 1987 article] since the examiner fails to find reference to [the] award of bonus points for players of first and second groups in the prior art." *Id.* at 11. Fantasy, without comment, rewrote application claims 13–15 in independent form as suggested by the examiner, and those claims subsequently issued as claims 1–3 of the '603 patent.

Contrary to Fantasy's argument on appeal, the examiner found that the use of a computer to play fantasy football games and the organization of players in a first and second group were either known in the art or obvious therefrom. The examiner's rejection of claim 10 also demonstrates that he found the combination of one or more of those limitations with Fantasy's broad interpretation of the term "bonus points" to be unpatentable. Fantasy acquiesced in those rejections by canceling all claims that did not contain the "bonus points" limitation at issue on appeal, and thus cannot now be heard to argue post hoc that it was the combination of the aforementioned limitations that rendered its invention patentable over the prior art. Fantasy therefore disclaimed any interpretation of the term "bonus points" that encompasses scoring methods described in the 1987 article, including distance scoring and total yardage.

Fantasy's argument that the specification broadly defines the term "bonus points" to include non-scoring plays, such as total yardage, is not persuasive. Aside from the fact that the prosecution history defines the contours of the "bonus points" limitation, the portion of the specification cited by Fantasy must be read in context. The sentence "[b]onus points also are awarded based upon the difficulty of the *play*," *id.* at ll. 22–23 (emphasis added), uses the word "play" in the context of the preceding sentence. That sentence states that "points are awarded for touchdowns, field goals, and points after touchdowns," *id.* at ll. 20–22, all of which are scoring plays. Moreover, the specification makes clear elsewhere that only certain types of unusual plays are encompassed within the "bonus points" limitation, including, e.g.,: (1) when a quarterback "receives a pass or runs for [a] touchdown," '603 patent, col. 13, ll. 44–45; (2) when a running back "throw[s] or receive[s a] touchdown pass," *id.* at ll. 45–46; (3) when a wide receiver "pass[es] the ball or run[s] for [a] touchdown," *id.* at ll. 47–49; (4) when a "fumble ... result[s] in [a] touchdown[ ]," *id.* at ll. 44–45; or (5) when a "lateral recover[y is made] in the end zone," *id.* Accordingly, in light of the specification and the prosecution history, we interpret the "bonus points" limitation to mean additional points awarded beyond those given in an actual football game for unusual scoring plays, such as when a player scores in a manner not typically associated with his position.

Finally, Fantasy's claim differentiation argument is without merit. The doctrine of claim differentiation creates only a presumption that each claim in a patent has a different scope that cannot broaden claims beyond their correct scope. Although claims 2 and 3 attempt to further define the term "bonus points," that presumption is overcome by Fantasy's disclaimer of subject matter in the prosecution history. *See id.* at 1368–69, 53 USPQ2d at 1818–19 (determining that any presumption arising from the doctrine of claim differentiation was overcome by the written description and prosecution history). Consequently, the "bonus points" limitation must be given the same scope in all of the claims of the '603 patent.

We therefore conclude that the "bonus points" limitation must be construed to mean additional points awarded beyond those given in an actual football game for unusual scoring plays, such as when a player scores in a manner not typically associated with his position.

B. Infringement

Although most of Fantasy's infringement argument on appeal depends upon its proposed construction of the "bonus points" limitation, Fantasy argues that genuine issues of material fact exist that preclude entry of summary judgment of noninfringement as to each of the defendants' products even under the district court's claim construction. Because our interpretation of the term "bonus points" differs slightly from that of the district court, we will analyze whether summary judgment was properly granted as to each of the defendants' products under our construction of that term.

1. Yahoo!

Fantasy argues that the Yahoo! Sports Fantasy Football game infringes the '603 patent because it awards "miscellaneous points" when a kicker scores a touchdown, which constitutes an out-of-position score. Yahoo! responds that the claimed "bonus points" are not present in its product because a kicker receives no more than the normal six points for scoring a touchdown, and the term "miscellaneous points" merely describes an asterisk that is placed next to those six points in order to explain the unusual circumstance of awarding six points to a kicker for scoring a touchdown. We agree with Yahoo! that Fantasy has not raised any genuine issue of material fact that Yahoo!'s product infringes under the proper interpretation of the "bonus points" limitation. As explained by Yahoo!, the term "miscellaneous points" is used merely to indicate when an unusual play has taken place, and no additional points are awarded beyond those given for that play in an actual football game as a result of that label. The district court therefore properly granted summary judgment that Yahoo! does not infringe as a matter of law.

2. ESPN

Fantasy argues that ESPN's product infringes the '603 patent because it awards bonus points to players who score out of position. Fantasy argues that in ESPN's game, for example, a quarterback receives four points for a passing touchdown and six points for a rushing or receiving touchdown, and thus quarterbacks receive bonus points depending upon the type of scoring play. ESPN responds that ESPN's game does not infringe as a matter of law because it awards the same number of points for a particular type of touchdown regardless of a player's position.

We agree with ESPN that its product does not infringe the '603 patent as a matter of law. ESPN's game does not award additional points beyond those given in an actual football game, as a player can receive no more than the standard six points for scoring a touchdown. Furthermore, although ESPN's fantasy football game awards a different number of points depending upon the type of scoring play, that game does not distinguish between the positions of the players who performed those plays. For example, although quarterbacks receive six points for a receiving touchdown, wide receivers and running backs also receive the same number of points for that type of scoring play. The district court therefore properly granted summary judgment of noninfringement because no reasonable juror could conclude that ESPN's game infringes as a matter of law.

3. SportsLine

Fantasy concedes that SportsLine's Fantasy Football and Football Challenge games do not infringe the '603 patent under the district court's interpretation of the "bonus points" limitation. Fantasy argues, however, that the district court erred by granting summary judgment with respect to the Commissioner.com product even under the court's construction of that limitation. Fantasy contends that the district court erroneously analyzed that product under a contributory infringement framework, arguing that under *Intel Corp. v. ITC*, 946 F.2d 821 (Fed.Cir.1991), the Commissioner.com product directly infringes because it is capable of being configured to award bonus points when a player scores out of position. In support of that argument, Fantasy cites the declaration of Shanen Elliott, one of Fantasy's Product Specialists, who stated that he "was able to customize the 'Commissioner.com' football game to include essentially the same scoring system that is described in the ['603] patent," i.e., a system that awards bonus points for unusual plays such as out-of-position scoring. SportsLine responds that the Commissioner.com product does not directly infringe because it is not a computerized fantasy football game operated by SportsLine, but rather is a modifiable software tool that enables subscribers to operate their own fantasy football leagues on customized internet web pages. SportsLine also argues that Fantasy failed to prove any underlying direct infringement that could serve as the basis for a determination that it contributorily infringes the '603 patent.

We conclude that the district court erred in granting summary judgment with respect to the Commissioner.com product because genuine issues of material fact exist as to whether that product infringes under the proper infringement analysis. Although we disagree with Fantasy's characterization of Intel as requiring a finding of infringement when a device is capable of being altered in an infringing manner, we nevertheless agree with Fantasy that the Commissioner.com product must be analyzed under a direct infringement framework.

[C]laim 1 is directed to "[a] computer for playing football," and thus the claims of the '603 patent read on a computer executing fantasy football game software. Claim 1 also sets forth a number of functionally defined means that that software must contain, including a "means for scoring ... bonus points" for unusual scoring plays. Software is a set of instructions, known as code, that directs a computer to perform specified functions or operations. Thus, the software underlying a computer program that presents a user with the ability to select among a number of different options must be written in such a way as to enable the computer to carry out the functions defined by those options when they are selected by the user. Therefore, although a user must activate the functions programmed into a piece of software by selecting those options, the user is only activating means that are already present in the underlying software. Otherwise, the user would be required to alter the code to enable the computer to carry out those functions. Accordingly, in order to infringe the '603 patent, the code underlying an accused fantasy football game must be written in such a way as to enable a user of that software to utilize the function of awarding bonus points for unusual plays such as out-of-position scoring, without having to modify that code. In other words, an infringing software must include the "means for scoring ... bonus points" regardless whether that means is activated or utilized in any way.

SportsLine argues that the Commissioner.com product cannot directly infringe because it is not a "computer for playing football," as required by the claims. SportsLine contends that the district court properly found that the Commissioner.com product is a "modifiable software tool" that is "not a fantasy football game operated by SportsLine." *Fantasy II* at 11. We disagree. The record clearly demonstrates that the Commissioner.com product is software installed on a computer that enables a user to play fantasy football games over the Internet. Indeed, the web pages advertising the Commissioner.com product promote it as "a utility designed to run a head-to-head Fantasy Football League," and that "getting started is easy" in that a user may immediately begin playing fantasy football after performing a few simple steps. That material goes on to explain that "[a]fter you create your league web-site a simple Scoring Wizard will allow you to configure the many powerful options briefly described below." One of those options is the ability to have "*position-specific scoring*" by creating "different scoring configurations for *each position*." (Emphases added.) Consequently, a user need only utilize the Scoring Wizard program, as demonstrated by Mr. Elliott's declaration, to play a fantasy football game that provides for the awarding of bonus points for out-of-position scoring, and thus that means is necessarily present in the software that operates the Commissioner.com product. We therefore conclude that no reasonable juror could find that the Commissioner.com product is not software installed on a "computer for playing football" that may directly infringe the '603 patent.

We also reject SportsLine's argument that it cannot infringe the '603 patent because the Commissioner.com product is not a game operated and controlled by SportsLine, but rather is operated by the users of that product on their own computers. First, there is no "user participation" or "control" limitation in the claims of the '603 patent requiring that an accused fantasy football game be operated by any specific entity. The claims only require that the software utilized to play fantasy football provide the ability to award "bonus points," as that term has been construed. In any event, the web pages advertising the Commissioner.com product make clear that users "decide the scoring system, the schedule, the draft format, and all other league rules *while still receiving all the benefits of having your league on-line*." (Emphasis added.) Those pages also boast that the Commissioner.com product enables users to play fantasy football with "[n]o downloading of updates. No re-installing software. No losing the entire season's data because your computer crashed." The users of the Commissioner.com product therefore access the necessary software to play fantasy football at SportsLine's server on the Internet, and thus that software is maintained and controlled by SportsLine.

SportsLine's final argument, however, raises an issue that requires further factfinding. Specifically, SportsLine argues that kickers cannot be awarded points for out-of-position scoring (i.e., touchdowns, as distinct from field goals and PATs) in any fantasy football game created by the Commissioner.com product, and thus players in the "second group" cannot receive the "bonus points" required by the claims of the '603 patent. Peter Pezaris, Vice President of SportsLine, indicated in a declaration that the only way to vary the scoring for kickers is to award additional points based on the length of a field goal. Mr. Elliott, however, stated that he was able to configure the scoring system in the fantasy football league he created to award additional points to kickers for scoring a touchdown, but did not specifically describe how he was able to do so. It is unclear from the record on appeal whether the Commissioner.com product supports the awarding of "bonus points" to "kickers in a second group." That factual dispute therefore precludes us from concluding whether the Commissioner.com product infringes as a matter of law, and thus the district court must resolve that issue on remand.

We therefore vacate the district court's grant of summary judgment of noninfringement and remand the case for it to determine, using a direct infringement analysis, whether the software underlying that product supports the awarding of "bonus points" when kickers score touchdowns.

Notes and Questions

1. Do you agree with the *Fantasy Football* decision? Regardless of the arguments related to the scoring methodology, the "points" were derived from copyrighted performances

C.1 Atari's *Pong*

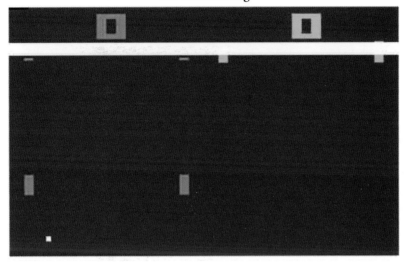

C.2 Atari's *Space Invaders*

C.3 Atari's *Galaxian*

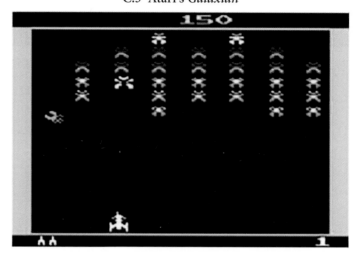

C.4 Atari's *Pac Man*

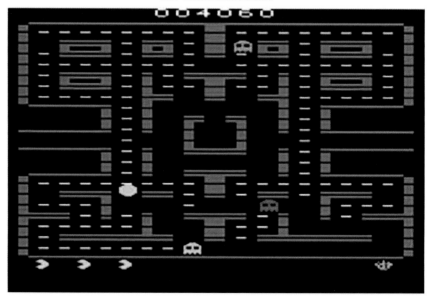

C.5 Atari's *Junior Pac Man*

C.6 Atari's *Asteroids*

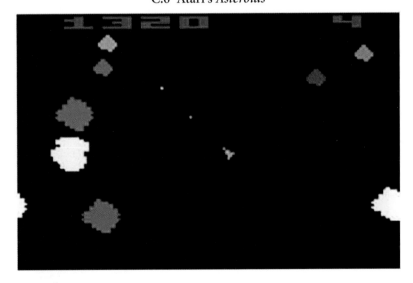

C.7 Atari's *Breakout*

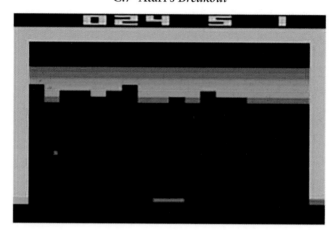

C.8 Atari's *Donkey Kong*

C.9 Atari's *Centipede*

C.10 *Chuck Norris Superkicks*

C.11 *Pete Rose Baseball*

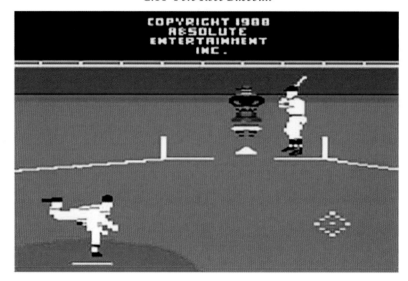

C.12 Atari's *Missile Command*

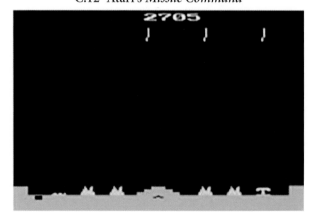

C.13 Atari's *Frogger*

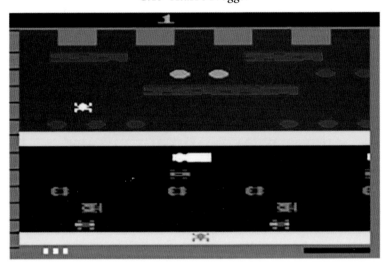

C.14 Atari's *Q*bert*

C.15 *Tetris* on the Nintendo GameBoy

C.16 Rockstar Games' *Grand Theft Auto: San Andreas*

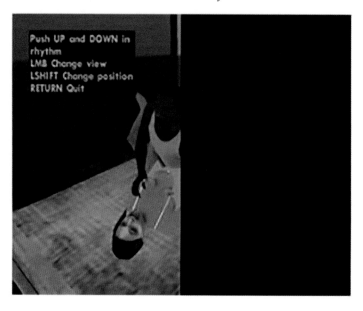

for which none of the litigants possessed rights. In particular, the points were generated by the performances owned by the National Football League. Should that make any difference? Before you answer consider the following proposition: Even if one were permitted to sell and distribute a for-profit product capitalizing from the labor and energy of the NFL and its membership, should that individual *also* have the right to exclude others from doing the same?

2. Gamasutra, a widely recognized videogame web site, posted the following as its list of "The Ten Most Important Video Game Patents" (*See* http://www.gamasutra.com):

1. RE28,507: "The One that birthed the Industry—Pong Patent"

2. 6,850,221: Motion sensing technology for the Wii

3. "General notion of patenting concepts"

4. 6,729,954: Method of attack for Koei's "Dynasty Warriors"

5. 6,200,138: Game concept in which player drives a car

6. "The one that never was": Sega's Genesis (Copyrighted codes)

7. 6,280, 327: Wireless game controller

8. 6,424,333: Controls vibration feedback in video controllers

9. 4,026,555: Early television display for bitmap graphics

10. 4,799,635: Nintendo's NES

The above list was posted as of January 19, 2007. Keeping in mind that the earliest pioneer patents for every industry are normally the most dramatic, based your reading of the newer cases in this chapter, what changes or additions, if any would you make?

3. Patent specifications, even for a relatively simple videogame, can appear to be quite complex. Here is an example of a patent abstract and claim for a videogame concept involving a "simple" car driving around a track:

Abstract:

A driving game, wherein players having various driving skills from beginners to those advanced may enjoy both aspects of amusement and simulation in consistency. The game device of the present invention has an element for providing to a player a plurality of different movement modes upon moving the vehicle along a traveling line. Upon selection of a desired movement mode, a vehicle-driving game relating to the driving mode selected by the player is executed. Included in this plurality of driving modes are an assist mode in which auto-brake control is performed and a training mode in which various indications, such as the timing of the braking point, are given.

Patent number: 6652376

Filing date: Feb 15, 2000

Issue date: Nov 25, 2003

Inventors: Shigeru Yoshida, Takuji Masuda, Takanori Kobayashi

Assignee: Kabushiki Kaisha Sega Enterprises

Primary Examiner: Derris H. Banks

Secondary Examiner: Corbett B Coburn

Attorneys: Finnegan, Henderson, Farabow, Garrett & Dunner, L.L.P.

Application number: 9/504,387

U.S. Classification

463/6; 463/7; 463/23; 434/62; 434/65

1. A game device for moving a vehicle along a traveling line in a virtual three-dimensional space pursuant to operations from a player and generating images of a driving state of such vehicle, comprising:

mode provision means for providing to the player a plurality of driving modes being selectably applicable to said vehicle and having mutually different driving characteristics of said vehicle upon moving said vehicle; selection means for enabling said player to select a desired driving mode from said plurality of driving modes; and game execution means for executing a game relating to a movement of said vehicle in the desired driving mode selected by said player, wherein said plurality of driving modes includes a training mode having an indication function for indicating the driving state upon said player virtually driving said vehicle, wherein said indication function indicates to the player a brake timing by altering a display mode of said traveling line, and wherein said game execution means exhibits said indication function by including: means for comparing successive blocks of speed data of reference data with a speed of said vehicle driven by said player and, when a comparative result shows that said speed data at a block of said reference data is greater than said speed of said vehicle, altering brake data of the block to zero as an alteration result so that said brake data is not applied when said vehicle reaches the block, and when the comparative result is not greater than said speed of said vehicle, not altering said brake data of the block as the alteration result, and means for altering the display mode of said traveling line pursuant to the alteration result.

2. A game device for moving a vehicle along a traveling line in a virtual three-dimensional space pursuant to operations from a player and generating images of a moving state of such vehicle.

3. A game processing method for moving a vehicle along a traveling line in a virtual three-dimensional space pursuant to operations from a player and generating images of a driving state of such vehicle.

4. A game processing method according to claim 3, wherein said plurality of driving modes includes an assist mode having an auto-brake function for automatically assisting the braking power of said vehicle.

5. A game processing method according to claim 3, wherein said indication function indicates to the player said driving state with, at least, either an image or a sound.

6. A game processing method according to claim 3, wherein said indication function is composed of at least one among:

a first indication function for indicating to the player a reference travel line by displaying this on said traveling line; a second indication function for indicating to the player the existence of a curve on said traveling line; and a third indication function for indicating to the player a gearshift position at the curve on said traveling line.

7. A game processing method according to claim 3, wherein said game execution step executes said game by exhibiting said indication function by referring to an ideal reference data including speed data and brake data per block along said traveling line obtained from the driving of an experienced player.

8. A game processing method for moving a vehicle along a traveling line in a virtual three-dimensional space pursuant to operations from a player and generating images of a moving state of such vehicle, comprising: [material not included—ED.]

9. A game processing method according to claim 8, further comprising:

a trace operation step for performing modeling conversion to traces pursuant to movement of said vehicle from a camera viewpoint and operating a conversion matrix thereof; a storage step for storing said conversion matrix; a trace judgment step for judging whether a display of said traces is necessary based on whether the trace is located within a field of view; and a display step for reading said conversion matrix stored by the storage step and displaying said conversion matrix when said judgment step judges that the display of said traces is necessary.

10. A game processing method according to claim 3, wherein said indication function includes:

a judgment step for judging whether or not brake application is necessary based on a speed and position of said vehicle operated by said player; a calculation step for calculating a brake application timing based on the speed and position of said vehicle operated by said player when said judgment step judges that brake application is necessary; and a notification step for notifying said player of said brake application timing based on the brake timing calculated by said calculation step.

11. A game processing method according to claim 10, wherein said judgment step and calculation step respectively perform judgment and calculation based on the speed and position of said vehicle operated by said player, and the reference data corresponding to such position.

12. A game processing method according to claim 10, wherein said notification step notifies, earlier than usual, said brake application timing when the speed of said vehicle is fast in comparison to when the speed of said vehicle is slow.

13. A computer program product for moving a vehicle in a virtual three-dimensional space pursuant to operations from a player and generating images of a driving state of such vehicle, the computer program product comprising the following computer-readable program code for effecting actions in a computing platform:

14. A computer program product according to claim 13, wherein said plurality of driving modes includes an assist mode having an auto-brake function for automatically assisting the braking power of said vehicle.

15. A computer program product according to claim 13, wherein said indication function indicates to the player said driving state with, at least, either an image or a sound.

16. A computer program product according to claim 13, wherein said indication function is composed of at least one among:

a first indication function for indicating to the player a reference travel line by displaying this on said traveling line; a second indication function for indicating to the player the existence of a curve on said traveling line; and a third indication function for indicating to the player a gearshift position at the curve on said traveling line.

17. A computer program product according to claim 13, wherein said program code for executing a game executes said game by exhibiting said indication function by referring to an ideal reference data including speed data and brake data per block along said traveling line obtained from the driving of an experienced player.

18. A computer program product according to claim 13, wherein said indication function includes: [material not included—ED.]

19. A computer program product according to claim 18, wherein said program code for judging and said program code for calculating respectively perform judgment and calculation based on the speed and position of said vehicle operated by said player, and the reference data corresponding to such position.

20. A computer program product according to claim 18, wherein said program code for notifying notifies, earlier than usual, said brake application timing when the speed of said vehicle is fast in comparison to when the speed of said vehicle is slow.

21. A computer program product for moving an object in a virtual three-dimensional space pursuant to operations from a player and generating images of a moving state of such object, the computer program product comprising the following computer-readable program code for effecting actions in a computing platform: [material not included—ED.]

22. A computer program product according to claim 21, further comprising:

program code for performing modeling conversion to traces pursuant to movement of said object from a camera viewpoint and operating a conversion matrix thereof; program code for storing said conversion matrix; program code for judging whether a display of said traces is necessary based on whether the trace is located within a field of view; and program code for reading said conversion matrix stored by the storage step and displaying said conversion matrix when said judgment step judges that the display of said traces is necessary.

4. The following patent contains a simpler abstract. The specifications are, as in the prior note, lengthier and more complex. (There is a growing camp of opposition to all such patents among a growing number of videogame creators. The so-called gameplay method patents constitute a perceived threat. Do you know why?)

A game display method displays a driving game which permits characters to be present in a city and can prevent cruel images of collisions with characters. Characters in a dangerous area are intentionally moved away from a motorbike B. Those H1, H2 of the characters behind the motorbike B as viewed in a moving direction of the motorbike B are intentionally moved away from a current position 01 of the motorbike B, a position of the center of the motorbike B. Those H3, H4, H5 of the characters in front of the motorbike B as viewed in the moving direction of the motorbike B are intentionally moved toward the back of the motorbike B, i.e., directions normal to a straight line interconnecting the position 01 of the center of the motorbike B and the characters H3, H4, H5. The characters H3, H4, who are forward left of the motorbike B, are moved left, and the character Hr, who is forward right, is moved right.

Patent number: 6200138

Filing date: Oct 30, 1998

Issue date: Mar 13, 2001

Inventors: Takeshi Ando, Kazunari Tsukamoto, Toshiya Yamaguchi, Tomoya Takasugi, Masaaki Ito, Toshikazu Goi

Assignees: Sega Enterprises, Ltd.

Primary Examiner: Chanda Harris

U.S. Classification

434/61; 434/307R; 434/69; 434/29; 273/148B; 273/442; 463/31; 463/23

International Classification

G09B 1916

5. With respect to videogame developments in general, if you were to compare the number of successful patent infringement actions with those that failed, you would discern a trend toward interpreting patent claims narrowly; stated another way, absent an outright literal infringement, the defendant seems to have the edge. Is this trend desirable? If so, for whom?

* * *

When belated patent claims threaten to disassemble or rattle an entire industry (not to mention millions of users and subscribers), the courts can turn a highly rationalized, thoroughly explained blind eye (as in the *Mattel* case when some very significant prior art was curiously un-scrutinized), or if required, can become extremely picky, as in the case that follows. With millions of users throughout the world, the frenetically popular games known as MMORPG's (Massive Multiplayer Online Role Playing Games) such as *World of Warcraft* utilize complex interactive technologies that produce three-dimensional virtual worlds; players stretched across the globe are able to simultaneously interact with one another. As the popular games (launched in 1994) neared their tenth anniversary, Worlds, Inc., founded in 1994, claiming to hold the patents for the virtual worlds technology, faced a showdown in a Massachusetts federal court with owners of some of the most popular MMORPG's.

* * *

Worlds, Inc. v. Activision Blizzard, Inc.
United States District Court, District Massachusetts, March 13, 2014
Civil Action No. 12-10576, 2014 WL 972135

CASPER, District Judge.

I. Introduction

In this patent dispute, Plaintiff Worlds, Inc., ("Worlds") alleges that Activision Blizzard, Inc., Blizzard Entertainment, Inc. and Activision Publishing, Inc. (collectively, "Defendants") infringe United States Patents Nos. 7,181,690 ("'690"), 7,493,558 ("'558"), 7,945,856 ("'856"), 8,082,501 ("'501") and 8,145,998 ("'998") (collectively, the "Patents-In-Suit"). The Defendants have filed a motion for summary judgment seeking a ruling that all of the asserted claims in the Patents-In-Suit are invalid. For the following reasons, the Court ALLOWS the Defendants' motion.

II. Factual Background

A. Patents-in-Suit

This lawsuit involves patents that teach an invention enabling large numbers of computer users to interact over a client-server network in a "virtual world" displayed on a computer screen. Plaintiff Worlds alleges that the Defendants infringe the following patent claims: '690 claims 1–20; '558 claims 4–9; '856 claim 1; '501 claims 1–8, 10, 12, 14–16; '998 claims 1–3, 7, 8, 11–20.1. Worlds asserts that the Patents-In-Suit are entitled to an effective filing date of November 13, 1995, which is the filing date of U.S. Provisional Application No. 60/020,296 ("the Provisional Application"). All of the Patents-in-Suit reference U.S. Patent No. 6,219,045 ("the '045 patent"). The '045 patent was filed on November 12, 1996 and issued on April 17, 2001. The '045 patent does not claim priority to any earlier filed application and does not contain any reference to the Provisional Application. The '045 patent is not asserted in this action. The '690 patent was filed on August 3, 2000 and issued on February 20, 2007. The '690 patent does not contain any reference to the Provisional Application. The '690 patent states that it is a "continuation of application No. 08/747,420, filed on Nov. 12, 1996, now Pat. No. 6,219,045," i.e., the '045 patent not asserted in this action.

The '558 patent was filed on November 2, 2006 and issued on February 17, 2009. The '558 patent states that it is a "continuation of application No. 09/632,154, filed on Aug. 3, 2000, now Pat. No. 7,181,690, which is a continuation of application No. 08/747,420, filed on Nov. 12, 1996, now Pat. No. 6,219,045." Unlike the '045 or '690 patents, the first sentence of the specification of the '558 patent states: "This application ... claims priority from provisional application No. 60/020,296, filed Nov. 13, 1995."

The '856 patent was filed on January 13, 2009 and issued on May 17, 2011. The '856 patent states that it is a "continuation of application No. 11/591,878, filed on Nov. 2, 2006, now Pat. No. 7,493,558, which is a continuation of application No. 09/632,154, filed on Aug. 3, 2000, now Pat. No. 7,181,690, which is a continuation of application No. 08/747,420, filed on Nov. 12, 1996, now Pat. No. 6,219,045." The first sentence of the specification of the '856 patent states: "This application ... claims priority from U.S. provisional patent application No. 60/020,296, filed Nov. 13, 1995."

The '501 patent was filed on March 19, 2009 and issued on December 20, 2011. The 501 patent states that it is a "continuation of application No. 12/353,218, filed on Jan. 13, 2009, now Pat. No. 7,945,856, which is a continuation of application No. 11/591,878, filed on Nov. 2, 2006, now Pat. No. 7,493,558, which is a continuation of application No. 09/632,154, filed on Aug. 3, 2000, now Pat. No. 7,181,690, which is a continuation of application No. 08/747,420, filed on Nov. 12, 1996, now Pat. No. 6,219,045." The first sentence of the specification of the '501 patent states: "This application ... claims priority from U.S. Provisional patent application Ser. No. 60/020,296, filed Nov. 13, 1995."

The '998 patent was filed on March 19, 2009 and issued on March 27, 2012. The 998 patent states that it is a "continuation of application No. 12/353,218, filed on Jan. 13, 2009, which is a continuation of application No. 11/591,878, filed on Nov. 2, 2006, now Pat. No. 7,493,558, which is a continuation of application No. 09/632,154, filed on Aug. 3, 2000, now Pat. No. 7,181,690, which is a continuation of application No. 08/747,420, filed on Nov. 12, 1996, now Pat. No. 6,219,045." The first sentence of the specification of the '998 patent states: "This application ... claims priority from U.S. Provisional Patent Application Ser. No. 60/020,296, filed Nov. 13, 1995."

To illustrate the relation of these patents, the Court reproduces here a graphic found in the Defendants' memorandum supporting summary judgment:

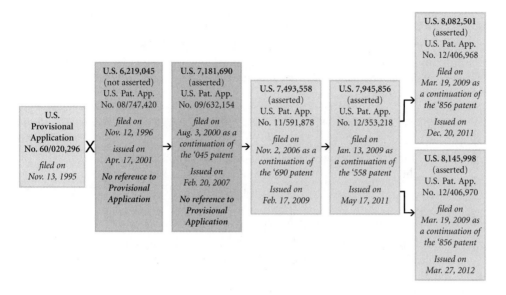

Although Worlds does not dispute these facts, Worlds cites three examples where the Provisional Application is mentioned in documents that are part of the 045 patent's prosecution history: (1) an application transmittal letter, (2) the inventors' declarations, and (3) a request for corrected filing receipt. The application transmittal letter and the inventors' declarations were filed in 1996 and cite the correct Provisional Application serial number but incorrectly list the Provisional Application's filing date as June 24, 1996. The request for a corrected filing receipt was filed on August 18, 2000 and identifies the correct serial number and filing date for the Provisional Application.

Worlds further submits a screen-shot of a public website operated by the United States Patent and Trademark Office ("USPTO") indicating that according to the website the '045 patent claims priority to the Provisional Application. Worlds also states that on July 5, 2013, it requested that the USPTO issue certificates of correction "to include references to the 1995 provisional application on the front pages of the '045 and '690 patents and at the beginning of their specifications." The USPTO granted these requests on September 24, 2013.

B. Invention Reduced to Practice

In 1995, Worlds created two software products called Worlds Chat and AlphaWorld. Worlds Chat was first demonstrated and publically released in April 1995. Worlds Chat embodied all of the asserted claims of the Patents-in-Suit at least as early as April 1995. AlphaWorld was first demonstrated in June 1995 and was released on approximately June 29, 1995. At least as of September 1995, AlphaWorld practiced all of the asserted claims of the Patents-In-Suit and subsequent versions of AlphaWorld also practiced the asserted claims. Thus, AlphaWorld and Worlds Chat practiced all of the asserted claims of the Patents-In-Suit and were in public use more than one year before November 12, 1996, which is the filing date of the '045 patent.

III. Standard of Review

The Court will grant a moving party's motion for summary judgment when there is no genuine dispute of material fact and the moving party is entitled to judgment as a matter of law. Fed.R.Civ.P. 56(a).

IV. Analysis

A. Statutory and Regulatory Background

Patents are entitled to a presumption of validity. 35 U.S.C. § 282(a). To overcome that presumption, a party must demonstrate by clear and convincing evidence that the patent is invalid. *State Contracting & Eng'g Corp. v. Condotte Am., Inc.*, 346 F.3d 1057, 1067 (Fed.Cir.2003). With certain exceptions (namely for disclosures made one year or less before the effective filing date of the claimed invention under 35 U.S.C. §§ 102(b)), "[a] person shall be entitled to a patent unless — (1) the claimed invention was patented, described in a printed publication, or in public use, on sale or otherwise available to the public before the effective filing date of the claimed invention;...." 35 U.S.C. §§ 102(a) (1). That is, the filing date of the patent normally becomes the "priority date" and the date twelve months prior is the invention's "critical date." *Eakin Enters., Inc. v. Specialty Sales LLC*, No. 1:11-cv-02008-LJO-SKO, 2012 WL 2445154 (E.D.Cal. June 26, 2012). Accordingly, [i]f any "public use or ... sale" occurred before the critical date, the patent is invalid." *Id.*

A patent's effective filing date, the "priority date," is usually the date on which the patent application is filed with the USPTO, unless the patentee claims the benefit of an earlier-filed application. *See, e.g., Cordis Corp. v. Boston Scientific Corp.*, 561 F.3d 1319, 1331–32 (Fed.Cir.2009). "Determination of a priority date is purely a question of law if the facts underlying that determination are undisputed." *Bradford Co. v. Conteyor N. Am., Inc.*, 603 F.3d 1262, 1268 (Fed.Cir.2010). 35 U.S.C. § 119 describes when a patent application may benefit from the earlier filing date of a provisional application. For patent claims filed prior to November 29, 2000 including the '045 patent, the statute provides that:

> An application for patent ... for an invention disclosed ... in a provisional application ... shall have the same effect, as to such invention, as though filed on the date of the provisional application ... if the application for patent ... is filed not later than 12 months after the date on which the provisional application was filed and ... contains or is amended to contain a specific reference to the provisional application. *See* 35 U.S.C. § 119(e)(1) (1994).

B. The '045 Patent May Not Claim Priority to the Provisional Application

The Code of Federal Regulations defines more precisely how this "specific reference" must be made. 37 C.F.R. § 1.78(a). The parties dispute which version of 37 C.F.R. § 1.78 should govern here to determine if Worlds may claim an earlier priority date by reference to a provisional application. See Defendant's Memorandum (stating that the regulation effective in 1996 should apply); and see Plaintiff's Opposition (arguing that the November 29, 2000 version of the statute should apply).

The Federal Register indicates, however, that "the changes to ... Rule 1.78 ... apply to any patent application filed on or after November 29, 2000." 65 F.R. 57024. It is undisputed that the applications for both of the patents-in-suit were filed before this date ('690 patent filed on Aug. 3, 2000 and '045 patent filed on Nov. 12, 1996). The 1996 version of the regulation requires reference to a "prior provisional application" "in the first sentence of the specification following the title." 37 C.F.R. § 1.78(a)(4) (1996). There is no dispute that neither the '690 patent nor the '045 patent reference the provisional application in the first sentence following the title. Accordingly, neither patent can claim priority to the provisional application.

Even if the 2000 version of the regulation did apply, the Patents-In-Suit could not claim priority to the provisional application. The November 29, 2000 version of the regulation states that:

Any nonprovisional application claiming the benefit of one or more prior filed copending provisional applications must contain a reference to each such prior provisional application, identifying it as a provisional application, and including the provisional application number (consisting of series code and serial number). Unless the reference required by this paragraph is included in an application data sheet (§ 1.76), the specification must contain or be amended to contain such reference in the first sentence following any title. 37 C.F.R. § 1.78(a) (2000).

Thus, according to that regulation, any reference to the Provisional Application must be either in "the specification … in the first sentence following any title" or in an "application data sheet." *See E.I. du Pont de Nemours & Co. v. MacDermid Printing Solutions, LLC*, 525 F.3d 1353, 1360–61 (Fed.Cir.2008) (stating that "35 U.S.C. § 119(e)(1) requires, for a claim of priority, that the non-provisional application contain 'a specific reference to the provisional application.' Under MPEP [the Manual of Patent Examining Procedure] § 201.11, the specific reference can be either in the first sentence of the specification or in the application data sheet"). An "application data sheet" ("ADS") is a specific document that was defined for the first time by 37 C.F.R. § 1.76 on September 8, 2000. See 65 F.R. 54604-01 (September 8, 2000) (describing the creation of "[a] new [section] 1.76 … added to provide for the voluntary inclusion of an application data sheet in provisional and non-provisional applications" and describing the ADS as a sheet "containing bibliographic data, which is arranged in a format specified by the [USPTO]"). The PTO's specifications for an ADS require that "[t]he top of a Patent Application Data Sheet should begin with the heading: 'Application Data Sheet.' "PTO Patent Application Data Sheet Format. Accordingly, an ADS must be "clearly labeled" as such.

As discussed above, the '045 patent contains no reference to the Provisional Application in "the specification … in the first sentence following any title." See 37 C.F.R. § 1.78(a). Defendants contend that no application data sheet exists in the prosecution history of the '045 patent. As noted above, the "ADS" regulation had not been promulgated when the application for what became the '045 patent was filed on November 12, 1996.4 Cf. 65 F.R. 54604-01 (describing the "new § 1.76" effective as of September 8, 2000). Defendants argue that Worlds did not later add an ADS to the application before the patent issued on April 17, 2001.

Worlds asserts that it referenced the Provisional Application in "data sheets" filed during prosecution of the '045 patent and that Worlds is entitled to the November 13, 1995 priority date. Although Worlds in its brief and again at oral argument referred to documents in the prosecution history as "data sheets," this characterization appears to be descriptive of a variety of documents, including application transmittals, inventor declarations, requests for corrected filing receipts, bib data sheets, amendments and petitions to make special. To that end, Worlds identifies references to the Provisional Application in an application transmittal letter, the inventors' declarations and in a request for a correct filing receipt dated almost four years after the '045 patent's application had been filed. The references in the application transmittal form and inventors' declarations do not list the correct filing date of the Provisional Application. However, none of the documents that Worlds identifies are "clearly labeled" "Application Data Sheet." See Defendant's Exhibit referencing Provisional Application, but not clearly labeled "Application Data Sheet." Furthermore, the PTO requires that an ADS "may not contain any other application data (i.e., abstract, amendments, transmittal letter, etc.)." Indeed, some of the documents that Worlds identifies do not comply with this requirement either.

Because the '045 patent application does not reference the Provisional Application in either of the two locations specified by the regulation, the Defendants argue that Worlds has not satisfied the regulation and is therefore is not entitled to claim an earlier priority date as to the '045 patent (and by the priority chain of continuation applications, as to the other Patents — In Suit).

Worlds counters that these errors are "harmless scriveners' errors." However, other courts confronted with similar facts have held that stray mentions of a provisional application within documents that are part of a patent's prosecution history do not overcome non-compliance with federal statute and regulation. For example, in *Carotek, Inc. v. Kobayashi Ventures, LLC*, 875 F.Supp.2d 313, 334 (S.D.N.Y.2012), the plaintiff's patent application included inventors' declarations that referenced an earlier application. The Court held that "these declarations, however, do not satisfy the "specific reference" requirement.... The language of the regulation is unequivocal: to claim the benefit of an earlier patent, "the specification must contain or be amended to contain such reference in the first sentence(s) following the title," *id.* (citing 37 C.F.R. § 1.78), or, as is true under the 2000 version of the regulation, be referenced in the ADS. *In Eakin Enters., Inc.*, 2012 WL 2445154, the plaintiff's patent application referenced an earlier provisional application and listed the correct provisional patent date but made a typographical error in the serial number of the provisional application. The patent "issued without reference to the provisional application." The Court found that "because of this error, the ... Patent does not permit [the Plaintiff] to take advantage of the provisional application's priority date." These cases are in line with the public policy requiring a patentee's reasonable compliance with patent regulations.

A patent grants the powerful "right to exclude others from making, using, offering for sale, or selling the invention throughout the United States." *Edwards Lifesciences AG v. CoreValue, Inc.*, 699 F.3d 1305, 1314 (Fed.Cir.2012) (quoting 35 U.S.C. § 154). Determining whether one is actually excluded from making an invention is supposed to be a relatively straightforward process; the public should not be obliged to hunt through hundreds of documents in a lengthy prosecution history to find a patent's priority date. *See* Kelly C. McKinney, *The Patent Reform Act of 2007 and International Patent Law Harmonization*, 31 Hous. J. Int'l L. 125, 141 (2008) (advocating for priority rule that will enhance legal certainty in the patent system). "The purpose of the 'specific reference' requirement is clearly to ensure that someone examining a patent claiming the benefit of one earlier filed is readily able to assess the patent's priority date." *Carotek, Inc.*, 875 F.Supp.2d at 335. This requirement is more than a mere technicality:

Although the "specific reference" requirement might appear to be a technical provision, it embodies an important public policy. The information required to be disclosed is information that would enable a person searching the records of the Patent Office to determine with a minimum of effort the exact filing date upon which a patent applicant is relying to support the validity of his application or the validity of a patent issued on the basis of one of a series of applications. In cases such as this, in which two or more applications have been filed and the validity of a patent rests upon the filing date of an application other than that upon which the patent was issued, a person, even if he had conducted a search of the Patent Office records, could unwittingly subject himself to exactly this type of infringement suit unless the later application adequately put him on notice that the applicant was relying upon a filing date different from that stated in the later application. As the court said in *Sticker Industrial Supply Corp. v. Blaw-Knox Co.*, 405 F.2d 90, 93 (7th Cir.1968):

"Congress may well have thought that [this requirement] was necessary to eliminate the burden on the public to engage in long and expensive search of previous applications in order to determine the filing date of a later patent.... The inventor is the person best suited to understand the relation of his applications, and it is no hardship to require him to disclose this information." *Sampson v. Ampex Corp.*, 463 F.2d 1042, 1045 (2d Cir.1972) (internal citation omitted). This is not a case falling into one of the potential equitable exceptions that some Courts have applied when considering defects in disclosure of a patent's priority date. Cf. *Carotek, Inc.*, 875 F.Supp.2d at 335 (finding that a correct reference to a prior application on a published patent's cover page provided sufficient notice); *Broadcast Innovation, L.L.C.*, 420 F.3d at 1368 (finding that a later patent's correct reference to a prior U.S. patent entitled the later patent to claim priority to the prior patent's international application filing date in accordance with federal statute). The references here (i.e., an application transmittal form, inventors' declarations and a request for a corrected filing receipt) are not the types of references that other courts, in some limited instances, have relied upon to allow claim to an earlier priority date.

C. The '690, '558, '856, '501 and '998 Patents, as Continuations in a Chain from the '045 Patent, Cannot Claim a Priority Date Earlier Than the '045 Patent's Filing Date

In this case, Worlds attempts to assert claims defined in the '690 patent, which is a continuation of the '045 patent and makes no reference to the Provisional Application. Worlds also attempts to assert claims defined in the '558 patent (a continuation of the '690 patent), the '856 patent (a continuation of the '558 patent) and the '501 and '998 patents (both continuations of the '856 patent). All of the '558, '856, '501 and '998 patents purport to claim benefit from the Provisional Application. None of these patents were filed "within 12 months after the date on which the provisional application was filed" and thus cannot claim the Provisional Application's priority date under 35 U.S.C. §119(e). Instead, any entitlement to priority would arise from a "priority chain" of applications pursuant to 35 U.S.C. §120. *Encyclopaedia Britannica, Inc. v. Alpine Elec. of America, Inc.*, 609 F.3d 1345, 1351 (Fed.Cir.2010) (quoting 35 U.S.C. §120). That statute allows an application for a patent "to have the same effect, as to such invention, as though filed on the date of the prior application." 35 U.S.C. §120. As the Federal Circuit has ruled, "35 U.S.C. §120 requires an intermediate application in a priority chain to 'contain a specific reference to the earlier filed application.'" *Encyclopaedia Britannica, Inc.*, 609 F.3d at 1349 (affirming that "each application in a series of continuing applications must contain a specific reference to the original application").

Here, because neither the '045 nor the '690 patents reference the Provisional Application, none of the asserted Patents-in-Suit, i .e., the '690, '558, '856, '501 and '998 patents, are entitled to claim the November 13, 1995 filing date of the Provisional Application. See *id.* at 1350–51 (stating that "[t]here is nothing in the language or legislative history of §120 to suggest that an application is entitled to an earlier priority date even if it fails to make a specific reference to an earlier application.... Later applications cannot amend [an earlier] application and restore its entitlement to priority.... Britannica's claim that a later application can cure this defect and restore the priority chain cannot be correct").

D. The Court Cannot "Correct" the Issued Patents

Worlds argues that this Court should use its power to "correct" the '045 and '690 patents. "Absent evidence of culpability or intent to deceive by delaying formal correction, a patent should not be invalidated based on an obvious administrative error." *Hoffer v. Microsoft Corp.*, 405 F.3d 1326, 1331 (Fed.Cir.2005). "When a harmless error in a patent is not subject to reasonable debate, it can be corrected by the court...." *Id.* (directing the district court to correct a typographic error made by the USPTO that was "apparent from the face of the patent"). Cf. *Group One, Ltd. v. Hallmark Cards, Inc.*, 407 F.3d 1297, 1303 (Fed.Cir.2005) (contrasting Hoffer with a scenario where "[t]he error ... is not evident on the face of the patent [and] one cannot discern what language is missing simply by reading the patent. The district court does not have authority to correct the patent in such circumstances"); *TracBeam, L.L.C. v. AT & T, Inc.*, No. 6:11-cv-96, 2013 WL 250532 (E.D.Tex. Jan.23, 2013) (noting that "district courts and the Patent Office have the authority to correct errors in patents, but the authority of district courts is more limited ... because a district court's correction applies retroactively in the action before it, while a Patent Office correction only applies prospectively" (citing *Novo Industries, L.P. v. Micro Molds Corp.*, 350 F.3d 1348, 1356 (Fed.Cir.2003)). This is a high bar for Worlds to meet, as an inadvertent addition to a claim can sometimes prove uncorrectable. *See Arlington Indus., Inc. v. Bridgeport Fittings, Inc.*, 345 F.3d 1318, 1331 n. 1 (Fed.Cir.2003) (finding claim uncorrectable where PTO erroneously added "and" to a claim and error was not obvious); *CA, Inc. v. Simple.com, Inc.*, 780 F.Supp.2d 196, 277 (E.D.N.Y.2009) (noting that correctable errors "usually involve little more than typographical errors").

Worlds cites several cases where district courts have corrected typographical errors. In these cases, the courts ruled that the errors were "apparent" or "obvious" on the face of a published patent. *See, e.g., CBT Flint Partners, LLC v. Return Path, Inc.*, 654 F.3d 1353, 1358 (Fed.Cir.2011) (adding the word "and" in a published claim to "correct[ ] an obvious error"); *TracBeam, L.L.C.*, 2013 WL 250532 (correcting printing error); *DR Sys, Inc. v. Fujifilm Med. Sys. USA, Inc.*, No. 06-cv-417-JLS, 2007 WL 4259164 (S.D.Cal. Dec.3, 2007) (correcting an "obvious" error that "apparent on the face of the printed patent"); *Fiber Systems Int'l, Inc. v. Applied Optical Sys., Inc.*, No. 2:06-cv-473, 2009 WL 3571350 (E.D.Tex. Oct.26, 2009) (finding that a published patent's single-digit typographical error referencing a prior provisional application was "apparent" and harmless error); *Lemelson v. Gen. Mills, Inc.*, 968 F.2d 1202 (Fed.Cir.1992) (finding inadvertent omission of a single word correctable). These cases are all distinguishable where, as is the case here, there is no reference in either the '045 and '690 patents to the Provisional Application. See Group One, 407 F.3d at 1303. Moreover, those patents' prosecution histories contained erroneous information, i.e., documents citing the Provisional Application but with an incorrect filing date. Here there is a "reasonable debate" as to whether the errors in the '045 and '690 patents are "harmless." *Hoffer*, 405 F.3d at 1331. Unlike Hoffer, it is not clear that what has occurred here is an "obvious administrative error" and as discussed below, the USPTO has refused to issue certificates of correction for lesser errors. Finally, Worlds has cited no case in which a court corrected a patent that inadvertently excluded a missing reference. Accordingly, the Court finds that a missing reference to the Provisional Application is not apparent from the face of the patent.

Finding otherwise would be inconsistent with the policy concerns discussed above. Were the Court to find that the inadvertent omission of a reference to a Provisional Application was correctable, by extension, this could support an argument that the inadvertent omission of reference to prior art should also be correctable. As a practical matter, this would increase the quantum of proof for all defendants in patent litigation seeking to assert an invalidity defense, because findings of invalidity against references disclosed to the PTO are inherently more difficult to demonstrate. *See Microsoft Corp. v. i4i Ltd. P'ship*, — U.S. —, —, 131 S.Ct. 2238, 2251, 180 L.Ed.2d 131 (2011) (discussing the "commonsense principle" that "new evidence supporting an invalidity defense may carry more weight in an infringement action than evidence previously considered by the PTO" and collecting cases observing that "the presumption of validity is weakened or dissipated" where evidence was "never considered by the PTO") (citation and internal quotation marks omitted).

E. The Resolution of Worlds' Petitions to the USPTO for "Certificates of Correction" Does Not Moot the Defendants' Invalidity Argument

On July 5, 2013, four days before filings its opposition to the Defendants' motion for summary judgment, Worlds filed with the USPTO petitions for "Certificates of Correction" for the '045 and '690 patents to reference the Provisional Application. D. 89 at 7. Worlds argues that the Defendants' motion for summary judgment "will become moot when the PTO issues Certificates of Correction for the '045 and '690 patents." *Id.* Indeed, the PTO issued the certificate of correction on September 24, 2013.

However, a certificate of correction applies only prospectively to future acts of infringement. *DuPont*, 525 F.3d at 1362 (citing *Southwest Software, Inc. v. Harlequin Inc.*, 226 F.3d 1280, 1295 (Fed.Cir.2000)); *see also TracBeam, L.L.C.*, 2013 WL 250532 (citing *Novo Industries, L.P.*, 350 F.3d at 1356). That is, given the USPTO has allowed Worlds' petitions for correction, Worlds could recover for any future infringement. Worlds cannot, however recover any damages for alleged infringement occurring prior to the date of the certificate of correction. *Worlds cites Pfizer, Inc. v. Teva Pharm.*, 882 F.Supp.2d 643 (D.Del.2012), which is a case where a certificate of correction was issued in the midst of litigation. The court there held that "generally speaking, a certificate of correction applies only to actions filed after that certificate issued" but in the unique circumstances of an Abbreviated New Drug Application ("ANDA") case, i.e., where infringement is generally "hypothetical … prior to the filing of a complaint," that "a certificate of correction can be applied where the defendants' ANDA products will prospectively infringe the patents-in-suit." *Id.* at 699. Such unique circumstances are not present here. Accordingly, Pfizer supports Activision's position that "a certificate of correction applies only to actions filed after that certificate issued."

F. The Asserted Claims of the Patents-in-Suit Are Invalid

For all of the above reasons, the Patents-in-Suit are not entitled to claim priority to November 13, 1995, the filing date of the Provisional Application. Instead, the Patents-in-Suit may claim priority to November 12, 1996, the filing date of the '045 patent. As discussed above, AlphaWorld and Worlds Chat embodied all of the asserted claims of the Patents-in-Suit and were in public use at least a year before November 12, 1996. A patent is invalid as a matter of law if the invention claimed was in public use or available to the public more than one year before the effective filing date of the claimed invention. 35 U.S.C. §§ 102(a) & (b). Because that is true here, the asserted claims of the Patents-in-Suit are invalid as a matter of law.

G. Conclusion

For all of the above reasons the Court ALLOWS the Defendants' motion for summary judgment,

So Ordered.

––––––––––

Notes and Questions

1. Consider and discuss the consequences if the court in *Worlds v. Activision* had determined that the subject patents-in-suit had been violated.

2. Would the outcome of *Worlds v. Activision* have been any different under the America Invents Act?

3. Virtual worlds, as we explain in further detail in § 10.30, *infra*, are no longer limited to abstract, non-existent unidentifiable properties. It is true that they may not be tangible in the real world sense, but the property, avatars and machinery are certainly identifiable and definable within the world. And, they are capable of enjoying several forms of intellectual property protection, including patents. Regardless of whether a patent application is sought for the real or the virtual world, the specifications had better be concrete. *Gametek LLC v. Zynga, Inc.*, 2014 WL 1665090 (N.D. Cal. 2014) was described by the court as a "rare case" where, despite the presumption that an issued patent is valid, the defendants established by clear and convincing evidence from their pleadings alone that Gametek's patent was too abstract and should, therefore, not be enforced. The patent's claim and specification used many words and terms, but they all seemed to boil down to nothing more than a "method" whereby game operators can offer items for sale to players without interrupting game play. The Court stated: "Gametek repeatedly emphasizes the twelve specific steps articulated in Claim One, to suggest either that the underlying abstract idea is not preempted or that the limitations imposed thereon are not overly-generalized, an argument discussed below. However, these twelve steps are nothing more than a teased-out version of the basic steps of any commercial transaction: a seller offers an item for sale to an interested and able buyer, the buyer accepts that offer, and the seller then provides the item in exchange for valuable consideration. While a seller could, of course, offer goods to a potential buyer without prequalifying the buyer or otherwise knowing anything about him or her, to preclude such a common-sense first step would effect a disproportionate burden on a third-party's ability to practice the abstract idea."

---

§ 7.70 Claims by Non-Game Industry Patentees

Not every patent owner with an invention capable of being used for games is interested in making, designing or improving them. On the contrary, some of the most important electronic and digital inventions of the past several decades may have had a substantial impact on videogames, but they also had other uses.

The fact that videogame development is quick to embrace the latest technologies makes the game developers tempting targets for patent infringement lawsuits. With individual videogame sales in the billions, suing game publishers and developers can be quite profitable. Once a game developer is found to have infringed upon a patent, a lucrative licensing agreement is often worked out; after all, there is no benefit to enjoining the manufacture of a profitable game regardless of the number of patents that might have been infringed.

The discussions and cases that follow are divided into two groups: Entities that use or "practice" the inventions or technologies for which they have been issued patents ("Practicing Entities"), and those who do not. The latter group of non-practicing entities (NPE's) acquires patents solely for the purpose of earning money through licensing fees and patent infringement lawsuits.

* * *

§ 7.71 Practicing Entities

Televisions, oscilloscopes and digital technologies were around long before the videogame industry ever caught on. Recall (from Chapter 1) that the videogame industry began as an amusing side show during the development of other ubiquitous visual media.

General Electric Co. v. Nintendo Co., Ltd.

United States Court of Appeals, Federal Circuit, 1999
179 F.3d 1350

MICHEL, Circuit Judge.

Plaintiff-Appellant General Electric Company ("GE"), the patent owner, appeals from the United States District Court for the District of New Jersey's grants of summary judgment to Defendants-Appellees, Nintendo Company, Ltd. and Nintendo of America, Inc. (collectively "Nintendo"), the accused infringers, terminating GE's infringement action. GE is the assignee of three patents: United States Patent No. 4,097,899 ("the '899 patent"), United States Patent No. 4,169,659 ("the '659 patent"), and United States Patent No. 4,279,125 ("the '125 patent"). All three of these patents are directed to television control circuitry. GE brought the instant action before the district court, claiming infringement of all three patents by three systems manufactured and sold by Nintendo.

BACKGROUND

GE filed this patent infringement action in the district court on March 17, 1995 alleging infringement of the '899 patent, the '659 patent and the '125 patent by Nintendo's video game systems (specifically the Nintendo Entertainment System ("NES"), the Super Nintendo Entertainment System ("SNES"), and the Gameboy). The '899, '659 and '125 patents pertain generally to electronic control circuitry used in connection with television systems. The '899 patent describes a switch to allow users of a television to switch between a signal from a television antenna, and a signal from a video record player, a video cassette recorder ("VCR"), or the like. The '659 patent is directed to a synchronization signal generator for use in video source equipment such as television cameras and video record players. The '125 patent is directed to devices for retrieving stored picture information from the memory of a computer and displaying that information on a standard television screen or other display device, e.g., a monitor. The NES and SNES systems are video game systems that display their games on television monitors. The Gameboy is a hand-held video game system with a built-in screen display.

DISCUSSION

I. United States Patent No. 4,097,899

A. Infringement Background

The '899 patent is directed towards a switch which allows the user of a television monitor to switch between video information received from an antenna and other sources of video information, for example, a video record player, when the user turns on or off the power to the alternative source. GE alleges that one or another of Nintendo's video game systems infringes each of Claims 12, 13 and 14 of the '899 patent. Claims 13 and 14 are dependent on Claim 12. Claim 12 provides:

Video record player apparatus comprising: a player RF signal input terminal; a player RF signal output terminal; a player power supply developing supply potentials when selectively enabled; means, rendered operative in response to supply potential development by said power supply, for forming a player output signal inclusive of picture carrier frequency oscillations and sound carrier frequency oscillations.

Claim 12 is directed to a switch that directs RF signals (signals in the radio frequency range) from the video record player to the television receiver, while disrupting the flow of broadcast signals from the antenna to the television receiver, when the video record player is on. The patent claim recites a system with two signal paths, one between an "RF signal output terminal" (television) and an "output signal forming means" (video record player), and one between an "RF signal output terminal" (television) and a "signal input terminal" (television antenna). Each of these signal paths has a switch on it. If the switch is closed, then the signal can flow freely along the signal path. If the switch is open, then the signal path is disrupted and there is no path for the signal to travel. This allows the television to display whatever the viewer wants to see — the signal from the antenna when the video record player is off, or the signal from the video record player if the video record player is on.

The dispute relates to the switch between the antenna and the television. As described in the '899 written description, the path between the antenna and the television contains an electromagnetic relay in series, and between the antenna and relay is a diode, which is shunted to ground. When the video record player is turned off, the relay is closed, the diode is nonconductive, and the signal flows from the antenna to the television. When the video record player is turned on, the relay is open, the diode is conductive, and the signal path from the antenna to the television is bypassed and disrupted.

The alleged infringing products, the Nintendo systems, do not disrupt the signal path. The accused systems control the signal flow through three transistors. When the Nintendo systems are turned on, the transistors enter saturation, passing the signal from the antenna to ground. When the Nintendo systems are turned off, the transistors leave saturation, and the signal passes from the antenna, past the transistors, to the television.

B. Infringement Discussion

Claim 12 of the '899 patent contains several limitations written in means-plus-function language. It can only be literally infringed if every such means limitation of that claim is found in Nintendo's accused devices. Furthermore, to find literal infringement of a section 112, ¶ 6 limitation, the fact-finder must determine whether the accused device performs an identical function to the one recited in the means-plus-function clause.... If the identical function is performed, the fact-finder must then determine whether the accused device utilizes the same structure or materials as described in the specification, or their equivalents. At issue in the instant appeal is whether the accused Nintendo devices perform the identical function as the one recited in the last limitation of Claim 12: means, responsive to the absence of supply potential development by said player power supply, for establishing a second signal path between said player RF signal input terminal and said player RF signal output terminal; said second signal path being disrupted in the presence of supply potential development by said player power supply.

Nintendo argues that its systems do not disrupt the signal path, while the switch disclosed in the written description of the '899 patent does. Nintendo points to language in the written description that differentiates between the functions of disrupting (i.e., establishing a high series impedance), and bypassing (i.e., by creating a path of lower resistance). We agree with Nintendo the written description of the '899 patent clearly distinguishes between the functions of disrupting and bypassing. We thus agree with the district court's acceptance of Nintendo's argument that a reasonable jury could only find that the Nintendo systems do not disrupt the signal path between the antenna and the television. Therefore, because the Nintendo systems bypass the signal path between the antenna and the television, establishing an alternative path of lower resistance allowing the antenna signal to flow to ground rather than to the television, the Nintendo systems do not perform the identical function recited in means-plus-function language in the last limitation of Claim 12. In short, they do not disrupt the signal path. Since the accused devices do not perform the identical function to that of Claim 12 of the '899 patent, the accused devices cannot literally infringe independent Claim 12, or dependent Claims 13 and 14 of the '899 patent.

The accused systems can, however, infringe the '899 patent, under the doctrine of equivalents, if, *inter alia*, they perform an equivalent function to the disruption function claimed in the last means-plus-function limitation in Claim 12. However, disrupting the signal path results in an alteration of the signal path, whereas bypassing the signal path does not. We, therefore, agree with the district court, that no reasonable jury could find that an equivalent function (substantially similar or substantially the same function) is performed in the accused systems.

C. Invalidity Background

Nintendo raised the issue of invalidity in its answer to GE's original complaint, in which Nintendo counterclaimed for a declaratory judgment that the '899 patent was invalid for failing to meet one or more of the conditions for patentability specified in 35 U.S.C. §§ 102 and 103. It then moved for summary judgment of invalidity, which was granted by the district court, but only as to anticipation. The court did not rule on obviousness.

Even though we conclude that the '899 patent is not infringed, however, we nevertheless must still review the holding of invalidity for anticipation of the '899 patent. *See Cardinal Chemical Co. v. Morton International, Inc.*, 508 U.S. 83 (1993). *Cardinal* held that "[t]hough the decision of non-infringement disposes of the bill and answer, it does not dispose of the counterclaim which raises the question of validity." *Id.* at 94. Therefore, our affirmance of a district court's judgment of noninfringement does not, by itself, moot the declaratory judgment claim of invalidity. *Id.* at 102–03. Accordingly, if we do not address the ruling on validity, we deprive the "patentee of the appellate review that is a component of the one full and fair opportunity to have the validity issue adjudicated correctly." *Id.* at 102.

D. Invalidity Discussion

A judgment of invalidity for anticipation requires that a single prior art reference disclose every limitation in a patent claim. The '899 patent claims a switch that allows a television to receive audio and video signals from the antenna, and then to switch automatically to receive a signal from the video record player when the video record player is turned on by the user. The switch taught in the Sharp II application does not specifically disclose sending audio and video signals to the television when the video record player is turned on, much less doing so automatically. Nintendo does not argue that this element is expressly recited in, or even taught by, the Sharp II application, but rather states that "a skilled artisan reading the Sharp II reference would immediately understand that the RF converter generates carrier signals as soon as it is turned on." It is undisputed that this limitation of the '899 patent claims is not disclosed by the Sharp II application. It was incorrect, therefore, to hold the '899 patent invalid for anticipation based on the Sharp II application, unless this element was proven to be inherent in the recitation of Sharp II. But it was not. Accordingly we reverse this part of the judgment.

II. United States Patent No. 4,169,659

A. Infringement Background

The '659 patent describes a technology for generating timing information for use by video source equipment such as television cameras and video tape recorders. Televisions display pictures as a series of frames, which consist of a fixed number of lines, which in turn consist of a number of pixels (or picture elements). The pixels are transmitted to the television receiver along with timing information which, in effect, associates a position on the television screen with each pixel. The timing information tells the television receiver when to end each line and begin painting a new line and when to end each frame and return to the top of the screen to begin a new frame. The '659 patent relates to the horizontal and vertical counters, which determine the location of each pixel on the television screen.

There are two independent claims at issue—Claims 1 and 4. The parties agree that the same phrases are at issue in both claims, and agree that the terms should be interpreted the same way in each claim. We, therefore, address the terms, rather than the individual claims, in our discussion below. It is undisputed that the two key phrases are: "drive signals" and "clocked by a signal which is advanced in phase."

B. Infringement Discussion

In order to infringe the '659 patent literally, the accused Nintendo systems must meet all of the limitations of the asserted claims. The parties only dispute two issues: whether the accused systems produce drive signals as defined in the '659 patent; and whether they contain vertical counters "clocked by a signal which is advanced in phase." Nintendo argues the accused systems do neither.

[The court ultimately agreed with Nintendo, concluding that while its systems produced "drive signals," the signals were not "clocked by a signal which is advanced in phase," and therefore there could be no direct infringement. It also held that because GE did not put on sufficient evidence in the trial court that would establish equivalent infringement of the '659 patent, summary judgment against it was appropriate on the equivalence issue and would not be overturned on appeal.—ED.]

III. United States Patent No. 4, 279,125

A. Infringement Background

The '125 patent is directed towards a method for displaying computer generated information on a display screen, such as a television or other device. A standard computer uses a Central Processing Unit ("CPU") to transfer data. The '125 patent discloses direct memory access ("DMA") capability, which allows the computer to transfer data without the intervention of the CPU. The '125 patent describes a method of transferring images from the computer's memory to the screen without using the CPU. GE alleges that Nintendo's systems infringe Claim 1 of the '125 patent.

B. Infringement Discussion

Nintendo argues that the accused systems do not infringe the '125 patent. First, Nintendo argues that its systems do not use the conventional DMA[7] circuit taught by the '125 patent

---

7. A DMA circuit is hardware dedicated to transferring data (in this case from the memory to the display) without use of the CPU.

and positively recited in Claim 1.[8] GE counters that the Nintendo systems use hardware, and not the CPU, to transfer data, and that this is a DMA circuit.

Nintendo's response is that the dedicated hardware is completely separate from the CPU and, thus, is not the conventional DMA circuit disclosed by the '125 patent. The DMA circuit, we conclude, is not part of the structure in the written description that corresponds to the "first decoder means" or any other means recited in the claim. '125 pat., col. 8, l. 10. The "first decoder means" supplies the DMA requests, but does not make the requests itself. '125 pat., col. 8, l. 10. Because the DMA circuit is not part of a means-plus-function limitation, GE's infringement claims are not limited to the DMA circuit structures described in the written description and their equivalents. Nintendo admits that the accused systems use dedicated hardware, completely separate from the CPU, to transfer the data, i.e., make DMA requests. A reasonable jury could find that the Nintendo systems operate in this manner, and therefore make DMA requests, as recited in Claim 1.

Nintendo's final argument in support of the finding as a matter of law of no infringement of the '125 patent is that Claim 1 requires a bit map display device, and the Nintendo systems do not meet this limitation. The threshold question here is whether a bit map display device is a limitation on Claim 1.

The claim recites a bit-map display device, and so we must determine whether the Nintendo systems display images by mapping bits. The Nintendo systems, as do any raster scan devices, create pictures on the screen by making pixels either light or dark, depending on the memory of the computer. The Nintendo systems, however, generate characters (e.g., the letter "V"), which are fixed compilations of bits, while the system described in the '125 patent creates pictures bit by bit (e.g., a dot in the middle of the letter "V"). A character generating system is thus limited in its display capability to the characters stored in its memory, while a bit mapping system is limited only by the number of bits displayable on the screen at any one time.

The memory mapped approach [bit mapping] requires relatively simple hardware but extensive memory and software processing, whereas in the block or object approach [character generation], memory is saved by using more complex hardware. In the object oriented display, the objects are moved by simply changing the display addresses. In the memory mapped approach, however, moving one pattern from one location to another involves considerable software processing on the refresh memory.

---

8. Claim 1 reads: A system for displaying a pattern on a raster scanned display device by mapping bits from a display location in a memory associated with a computer onto the raster as contrasting spots depending on the value of each bit, wherein said computer is responsive to a direct memory access request to produce on a data bus, data signals retrieved from said memory at a location specified by a pointer address register, comprising the combination of: clock means for producing timing signals; output means for coupling signals to said display device; means, including interval timing means, responsive to said timing signals, for producing horizontal synchronizing signals and applying them to said output means; line counter means responsive to said horizontal synchronizing signals for producing output signals identifying individual horizontal lines; first decoder means responsive to said interval timing means and to said line counter means for supplying direct memory access requests to said computer; second decoder means responsive to said line counter means for supplying vertical synchronization signals to said output means; means for storing data signals from said data bus in response to a signal derived from said timing signals when said computer responds to a direct memory access request and for shifting said data serially to said output means in response to said timing signals; and a plurality of gating means, responsive to a command signal, for coupling the output signals from the line counter means to the data bus means. '125 pat., col. 7–8,ll. 51–24 (emphasis added). Image 1 (1.5" × 5.25") Available for Offline Print.

During the prosecution of the '125 patent, the prosecuting attorney distinguished the '125 patent from a prior art reference that used a character generation display system. In doing so, the attorney stated the following: [The '125 patent] synchronizes the operation of a computer's direct memory access with the display device and displays the data as taken from the memory onto the display. On the other hand, the system of Reference A reads a character from memory in the form of binary bits, decodes the character into a matrix of dot elements, and then displays the dot matrix to provide the configuration of the character. The circuit of Reference A is thereby restricted only to characters which are coded into stored binary values and capable of being generated by the character generator, whereas the system of the ['125 patent] can display any desired configuration of dots.

Based on the above, we agree with Nintendo that the character generating system used in the Nintendo systems is significantly different from the bit-map display device claimed in the '125 patent. The Nintendo systems are, in fact, missing the bit-map display device required by the '125 patent, having no ability to display anything smaller than a character, or grouping of bits, on their display devices, and therefore the accused systems cannot literally infringe.

Interpreting claims in view of the prosecution history applies as a preliminary step in determining literal infringement. Prosecution history estoppel applies as a limitation to the doctrine of equivalents after the claims have been properly interpreted and no literal infringement is found. As can be seen in the above discussion of the prosecution history of the '125 patent, prosecution history estoppel here prevents the accused product from being deemed to contain any element identical or equivalent to the bit map limitation in the '125 patent claims. The patentee waived coverage of character generating systems by the '125 patent during prosecution. Without this element, there can be no equivalent infringement.

CONCLUSION

We, therefore, affirm the grants of summary judgment of no infringement as to all asserted claims of each of the three patents at issue in the instant case.

Notes and Questions

1. Would you think that it would be more or less difficult for the plaintiff patentee to prevail against a defendant in the same industry or a different industry? Why?

2. Seijiro Tomita, a former Sony engineer, successfully developed the technology for stereoscopic 3-D. For this invention, he obtained Patent No. 7,417,664 titled "Stereoscopic Image Picking Up and Display System Based Upon Optical Axes Cross-Point Information." Now known as the '664 patent, it deals with "technology relating to displaying stereoscopic images on-screen for viewing with the naked eye, i.e., without utilizing glasses or other devices." Tomita claimed that his company offered the product to Nintendo, which declined. Thereafter Nintendo released its 3DS system, which allows for gameplay featuring real 3-D graphics, with no need for special glasses. See *Tomita Technologies USA, LLC v. Nintendo Co.*, Case Number 11-cv-04256 (U.S.D.C., Southern District of New York, 2011). A jury awarded Tomita's company $30.2 million.

3. In the *General Electric* and *Fairchild* (*supra*, §7.50) lawsuits, not to mention many other cases throughout this book, the term "bitmap" has appeared. The concept was

somewhat indispensable with respect to early computer and videogame graphics. To better understand the matter, it might help to recall that computers can only communicate with the outside world through the use of 0s and 1s; in fact, the two digits are at the heart of all external and internal computer operations. Sequences of the two digits are conducive to an underlying binary system of arithmetic (hexadecimals also work well because of an evenly divisible structure). It might help to think of each element in a sequence as a "bit." Since there are by definition, 8 bits in a byte, a typical byte might be represented as follows: *0 0 0 0 0 1 1 0*. Early computers and videogame consoles utilized precious few of these strings of numbers due to limited storage capacity.

The combinations of 0s and 1s produce all of the sounds and images that we experience from our computers. They provide the representation of movements and color that are likewise indispensable for our videogames.

The early Atari 400 Computer (one of the earliest home computer systems), capable of playing game cartridges that were used for the Atari 2600 Console contained only 4 Kilobytes of ram; there was no other disc storage. *See* § 1.20, *supra*. If we were to string together several bytes, we might arrive at the following:

```
0 0 0 1 1 1 0 0
0 0 0 1 1 1 0 0
0 0 0 0 1 0 0 0
0 1 1 1 1 1 1 1
0 0 0 0 1 0 0 0
0 0 0 0 1 0 0 0
0 0 0 0 1 0 0 0
0 0 0 1 0 1 0 0
0 0 0 1 0 1 0 0
0 0 1 0 0 0 1 0
0 0 1 0 0 0 1 0
0 0 1 0 0 0 1 0
0 0 1 0 0 0 1 0
```

It is no coincidence that if you look very carefully, you may see a very rudimentary stick figure in the pattern of 0s and 1s. By "mapping" a combination of the 0s and 1s, early computer game developers would create what was known as "bit map" image of the sprites and obstacles that would appear in the historic games. The original "ball" in Pong may have only required a single bit. The stick figure represented by the above bit map is similar in structure to Jumpman, who later, with an exponentially expanded chip evolved into Mario, our rescue-the-girl-from-the-ape hero of *Donkey Kong* and beyond.

---

§ 7.72 Non-Practicing Entities

Non-practicing entities, often referred to as NPE's, and derogatorily referred to as "Patent Trolls," are not particularly interested in developing products, advancing technologies or actually "using" the patented inventions. Critics will quickly argue that they are only interested in owning patents to collect licensing fees and settlements by threatening to maintain expensive, time consuming litigation for their target defendants, which could number in the hundreds. Defending themselves, the trolls, who prefer to be called "Patent Assertion Entities (PAE's)" or "Patent Holding Companies (PHC's)," remind us that patents were meant to be enforced. The value of the patents, they say, rests with the patent's enforceability.

In 2011 alone, it was reported that U.S. business entities incurred nearly 30 billion dollars in costs associated with defending patent infringement lawsuits, often baseless. As might be expected, many of the defending targets were videogame developers and publishers. Patent trolling is less a problem in Europe and in other countries which, unlike the United States, have "*loser pays costs and fees*" judicial systems. Here in United States, with a few exceptions, the so-called American Rule provides that each party pays his or her own legal costs and fees, subject to certain specific rules and fee taxing statutes.

Examples of patent trolling are many. Uniloc, USA, Inc., for example, has filed more than 50 patent infringement lawsuits in the Eastern District of Texas, alone, against multiple defendants in both related and unrelated technologies. Many videogame developers were targeted including but not limited to: Electronic Arts, Square Enix, Mojang and Halfbrick, Gameloft and Madfinger. The extensive litigation arose from Uniloc's ownership of patents relating to software registration and programs preventing the unauthorized access to electronic data.

Perhaps the taste of a single large victory encourages such litigation. Consider the case of *Uniloc, USA, Inc. v. Microsoft, Inc.*, 447 F. Supp. 2d 177 (D.R.I., 2006), which preceded the multitude of lawsuits. The lengthy, protracted litigation ensued because both Uniloc and Microsoft used a certain product registration program that was intended to reduce unauthorized software copying. Uniloc claimed that Microsoft infringed its patent with respect to the program. The District Court granted a summary judgment of non-infringement for Microsoft. But the court's ruling was appealed to the U.S. Court of Appeals for the Federal Circuit, which reversed and remanded the action. Upon remand, the jury returned a verdict of willful infringement and awarded Uniloc $388 million in damages. The court, however, granted a new trial. In response, Uniloc appealed once again. The Federal Circuit reversed the *new trial* ruling regarding infringement, but affirmed the finding that Uniloc lacked evidence to prove willfulness, and granted a new trial on damage costs. In March 2012, Uniloc and Microsoft reached an undisclosed settlement.

The Eastern District of Texas is particularly appealing to the NPE's due its favorable attitude toward patent holding plaintiffs and, in particular, its very liberal attitude regarding the joinder provisions of Rule 20 of the Federal Rules of Civil Procedure.[9] In an effort to curtail the NPE issue, §299 of the AIA provides its own special joinder provisions for patent infringement actions, which includes this:

> (b) ALLEGATIONS INSUFFICIENT FOR JOINDER. For purposes of this sub-
> section, accused infringers may not be joined in one action as defendants or
> counterclaim defendants, or have their actions consolidated for trial, based solely
> on allegations that they each have infringed the patent or patents in suit.

The videogame industry is hopeful that forcing the plaintiffs to litigate one-on-one with the defendants will have a discouraging effect on those who promulgate volumes of litigation against "the many" in hopes of shaking some cash from a few. The industry is also encouraged by the Supreme Court's decision in *Alice Corporation PTY, LTD. v. CLS Bank Int'l*, 134 S. Ct. 2347 (2014), holding that claims based on abstract ideas are not

---

9. Rule 20(a)(2) of the Federal Rules permits the joinder of multiple defendants where "(A) any right to relief is asserted against them jointly, severally, or in the alternative with respect to or arising out of the same transaction, occurrence, or series of transactions or occurrences; and (B) any question of law or fact common to all defendants will arise in the action."

patentable. It is anticipated that this ruling will close the door on many patent trolls who rely upon abstract, broad based claims.

A somewhat egregious strategy involves an attack on a game publisher's retailers and wholesalers. Consider *UltimatePointer, LLC v. Nintendo Co., LTD., Nintendo of Am., Inc., Bestbuy Purchasing, LLC, Bestbuy Stores, L.P., Bestbuy.com. LLC, B.J.'s Wholesale Club, Inc., Compusa.com , Inc., Gamestop Corp., KMART Corp., PC Connection, Inc., QVC, Inc., Radioshack Corp., Sears, Roebuck and Co., Target Corp/, Tigerdirect, Inc., Toys "R" US— Delaware, Inc., and Trans world Entertainment Corp/*, 544 Fed. Appx. 934 (Fed. Cir. 2013). Ruling on a Petition for a Writ of Mandamus to the Federal Circuit, it was determined that the District Court improperly failed to exercise its discretion when it refused to sever the patent infringement claims of Nintendo from the claims against its numerous retailers and refused to stay the proceedings with respect to the latter. It appears that UltimatePointer's first complaint was filed before September 16, 2011, and later amended after September 16, 2011. As the district court noted, effective September 16, 2011, joinder in patent cases are governed by the America Invents Act ("AIA"). The Federal Circuit held that the AIA's joinder requirements are more "stringent" than those of the Federal Rules. In a footnote, however, that Court also found that under both Rule 20 and the AIA's joinder rules, severance should have been allowed. [Mandamus was clearly proper; there was no valid practical reason for continuing the joinder of virtually every major game retailer in an infringement suit involving Nintendo—ED.]

Another Nintendo method of combating a mass attack on its on retailers presented itself in *Secure Access v. Nintendo of America, Inc.*, 2:13-cv-289-JRG (E.D. Tex. 2014). In that case, the District Court specifically conditioned severing the many retailer defendants upon their stipulation to be bound by whatever rulings result from the claims against Nintendo. In its analysis, the Court stated: "The purpose of permitting severance by applying the customer suit exception, where joinder is otherwise proper, is premised on traditional notions of fundamental fairness and judicial efficiency. (Severance is also appropriate where a defendant is peripherally connected to the action with the consequence, whether intentional or not, that the burdens of trial are increased on other defendants.) Ultimately, the infringement claim against the manufacturer and central distributor is more likely to restore contested property rights nationwide than will enjoining one merchant from selling infringing products from existing inventory." The Court then cited *Codex Corp. v. Milgo Electric Corp.*, 553 F. 2d 735, 737–38 (1st Cir. 1977):

> At the root of the preference for a manufacturer's declaratory judgment action is the recognition that, in reality, the manufacturer is the true defendant in the customer suit.... it is a simple fact of life that a manufacturer must protect its customers, either as a matter of contract, or good business, or in order to avoid the damaging impact of an adverse ruling against its products.

* * *

Motiva, LLC v. Int'l Trade Commission and
Nintendo Company, Ltd. and Nintendo of Am., Inc., Intervenors

United States Court of Appeal, Federal Circuit, 2013
716 F.3d 596

PROST, Circuit Judge.

Motiva, LLC ("Motiva") appeals the decision of the International Trade Commission ("Commission") that Nintendo Co., Ltd. and Nintendo of America, Inc. (collectively

"Nintendo") did not violate § 337 of the Tariff Act of 1930 by importing, selling for importation, or selling certain video game systems and controllers. Because the Commission properly determined that a domestic industry does not exist nor is in the process of being established for U.S. Patent Nos. 7,292,151 ("'151 patent") and 7,492,268 ("'268 patent"), we affirm.

I. BACKGROUND

Motiva owns the '151 and '268 patents. The '151 patent issued in November 2007 and is titled "Human Movement Measurement System." It generally relates to a "system for ... testing and training a user to manipulate the position of ... transponders while being guided by interactive and sensory feedback ... for the purpose of functional movement assessment for exercise and physical rehabilitation." '151 patent abstract. The '268 patent issued in February 2009 and was a continuation of the application for the '151. It generally relates to the same subject matter as the '151 patent.

In 2008, Motiva filed suit against Nintendo in the United States District Court for the Eastern District of Texas accusing Nintendo's Wii video game system ("Wii") of infringing the '151 patent. The case was later transferred to the United States District Court for the Western District of Washington. In June 2010, that district court stayed the case pending completion of reexamination of the '151 patent by the U.S. Patent and Trademark Office.

Subsequent to the stay order, in September 2010, Motiva filed its complaint with the Commission that gave rise to this appeal. Motiva asserted that the Wii infringed the '151 and '268 patents and, therefore, that Nintendo's importation into, selling for importation into, and selling of the Wii in the United States violated Section 337 of the Tariff Act of 1930. Based on Motiva's complaint, the Commission initiated an investigation into whether Nintendo had violated Section 337.

Shortly after the Commission began its investigation, Nintendo moved for summary determination that the domestic industry requirement of Section 337 was not satisfied at the time Motiva filed its complaint with the Commission. Under Section 337, it is unlawful to import articles that infringe a valid and enforceable United States patent if "an industry in the United States, relating to the articles protected by the patent ... exists or is in the process of being established." 19 U.S.C. § 1337(a)(2). Section 337 details how that domestic industry requirement can be satisfied.

An industry in the United States shall be considered to exist if there is in the United States, with respect to the articles protected by the patent, copyright, trademark, mask work, or design concerned: (A) significant investment in plant and equipment; (B) significant employment of labor or capital; or (C) substantial investment in its exploitation, including engineering, research and development, or licensing. 19 U.S.C. § 1337(a)(3).

Nintendo argued that Motiva's domestic activities failed to satisfy any of those requirements. According to Nintendo, there were no commercialized products incorporating Motiva's patented technology, and Motiva's activity aimed at developing a domestic industry for articles protected by the asserted patents consisted solely of the district court litigation against Nintendo. Nintendo asserted that litigation was not a significant or substantial investment that could satisfy the domestic industry requirement.

In February 2011, the administrative law judge ("ALJ") granted Nintendo's motion. The ALJ agreed that the patent litigation suit against Nintendo was Motiva's only activity that could be related to commercializing the technology covered by the '151 and '268 patents at the time the complaint was filed. That activity, as the ALJ saw it, was insufficient to satisfy the domestic industry requirement because it was not adequately directed toward licensing activities related to the practical application of the patents' claimed inventions. The ALJ also found that Motiva was not engaged in any licensing activities: Motiva never offered to license, never received a request to license, and never in fact licensed either the '151 patent or the '268 patent.

On appeal, the Commission vacated the ALJ's summary determination and remanded for additional fact finding regarding Motiva's activities related to developing a domestic industry for the technology covered by the patents. It found that a genuine issue of material fact existed regarding whether Motiva's litigation efforts were—as Motiva claimed— adequate "to facilitate and hasten the practical application of the inventions of the patents at issue."

According to the Commission, litigation could be relevant in a licensing effort directed at "encouraging adoption and development of the patented technology by bringing a product to market" and protecting the ability of a patentee to derive revenues from patented technology by engaging "potential manufacturers, investors, and licensees who were not already involved in existing production." The Commission directed the ALJ to further explore the relationship of the Wii to Motiva's licensing efforts, determine how production-ready Motiva's technology was, and examine how Motiva's litigation related to its commercialization of the patented technology.

In November 2011, after briefing and a five-day evidentiary hearing, the ALJ once again ruled that Motiva had not shown that the economic prong of the domestic industry requirement of Section 337 was satisfied. The ALJ concluded that Motiva likely made substantial investments from 2003 to 2007 to commercialize the patented technology but ended those activities by January 2007 before a final product was ever produced or ever "close to being produced." Motiva's old development activities were "far too remote to be considered for purposes of demonstrating that a domestic industry exists." Thus, the ALJ found that Motiva had to rely on the district court litigation against Nintendo as its only evidence of an investment that would satisfy the domestic industry requirement.

According to Motiva, that litigation against Nintendo was "a necessary step to preserve and hasten its licensing opportunities, which would otherwise remain completely curtailed by the Wii's infringing presence on the market." As Motiva saw it, once Nintendo was forced to license its patents or leave the market for video-game-based motion tracking systems, potential partners would be willing to invest in and license Motiva's patented technology. It believed that the costs of litigation against Nintendo were, therefore, a substantial investment adequate to satisfy the economic prong of the domestic industry requirement. However, based on the testimony of witnesses and documentary evidence, the ALJ disagreed.

The ALJ found that the litigation costs related to the district court proceedings were not relevant to the domestic industry analysis because the litigation itself was not "in any way related to the exploitation of the patents." The ALJ concluded that the Wii had no effect on Motiva's attempt to create a market for the patented technology. Regardless of the Wii, Motiva's patented technology, according to the ALJ, was not even close to being "production-ready" at any point. Motiva's only remaining prototype of its patented technology had "exposed circuit boards, wiring, and sensors." And in its discovery responses, Motiva stated that, before the patented technology could be commercialized, contracts had to be obtained, the product had to go through final product and packaging design, and the product had to undergo beta, safety, and compliance testing.

The ALJ further found that testimony of investors and potential investors demonstrated that there was no interest in Motiva's technology prior to the release of the Wii: Motiva's last partner withdrew in 2004 and no others since that point ever showed enough interest to even examine Motiva's prototypes or patent applications. The only potential interest that the ALJ found to exist was directed at "excluding Nintendo from the market, not utilizing Motiva's patent technology" in a product.

Moreover, according to the ALJ, the Wii would not even compete with Motiva's potential products because they were in different markets. Motiva's product was an "expensive tool" designed for "exercise, athletic performance training, and physical therapy and research." The Wii, though, was a "relatively inexpensive video game system for home consumers" that had games for exercising but would not "compete with the expensive and sophisticated fitness product envisioned by Motiva."

Thus, the ALJ reasoned that the presence of the Wii—and the possibility of its removal from the market by successful litigation—did not and would not affect Motiva's attempts to commercialize its patented technology. The ALJ concluded that Motiva was not "concerned with taking swift actions to remove Nintendo from the market" through litigation; it was only interested in "extracting a monetary award either through damages or a financial settlement." The ALJ found support for this conclusion from emails between the inventors of the '151 patent discussing financial gains from litigation, Motiva's decision not to seek immediate injunctive relief from the district court, and Motiva's decision to delay filing a complaint with the Commission for more than three years after the allegedly devastating launch of the Wii. The ALJ therefore found that Motiva failed to prove that an industry for its patented technology existed or was in the process of being established: there is "no reason to believe that manufacturers of fitness and rehabilitation equipment will suddenly become interested in the [patented] technology because Nintendo is excluded from the market."

On appeal, the Commission adopted the ALJ's decision as its final determination on the investigation. It did not address the domestic industry holding in detail but did comment that the reliance on the filing date of the complaint to determine whether a domestic industry existed under Section 337 was not erroneous "in the context of this investigation."

Motiva filed a timely appeal of the Commission's decision.

II. DISCUSSION

Although the question of whether the domestic industry requirement is satisfied presents issues of both law and fact, this appeal presents only factual issues which we review for substantial evidence. *See John Mezzalingua Assocs. v. Int'l Trade Comm'n,* 660 F.3d 1322, 1327 (Fed.Cir.2011).

The Commission found—and Motiva does not dispute—that Motiva's investments in developing a domestic industry for the '151 and '268 patents were limited after 2007 to the litigation against Nintendo. Indeed, Motiva argues on appeal that its investment in that litigation satisfies the economic prong of the domestic industry requirement of Section 337. It asserts that removing the Wii from the market through litigation was essential to developing a successful "product-driven licensing business" that would encourage partners to develop and adopt its patented technology, which was "ready for a manufacturer to pick it up and incorporate it into a successful product."

Motiva's investment in the litigation against Nintendo could indeed satisfy the economic prong of the domestic industry requirement if it was substantial and directed toward a licensing program that would encourage adoption and development of articles that incorporated Motiva's patented technology. *InterDigital Commc'ns, LLC v. Int'l Trade Comm'n,*

707 F.3d 1295, 1299 (Fed.Cir.2013) (clarifying that efforts directed toward licensing a patent can satisfy the domestic industry requirement where they would result in the production of "goods practicing the patents"); *cf. John Mezzalingua*, 660 F.3d at 1328—29 (discussing how the "Commission is fundamentally a trade forum, not an intellectual property forum" and holding that litigation expenses directed at preventing instead of encouraging manufacture of articles incorporating patented technology does not satisfy the domestic industry requirement of Section 337).

However, the ALJ found that Motiva's litigation against Nintendo was not directed at developing such a licensing program. Relying on extensive documentary evidence and witness testimony, the ALJ concluded that the presence of the Wii in the market had no impact on Motiva's commercialization efforts or ability to encourage partners to invest in and adopt its patented technology. And Motiva was never close to launching a product incorporating the patented technology—nor did any partners show any interest in doing so, for years before or any time after the launch of the Wii. Motiva's only remaining prototype was a product far from completion, and a multitude of development and testing steps remained prior to finalizing a product for production. Moreover, the evidence demonstrated that Motiva's litigation was targeted at financial gains, not at encouraging adoption of Motiva's patented technology. The inventors looked forward to financial gains through Motiva's litigation, not hopes of stimulating investment or partnerships with manufacturers. Motiva also never asked for a preliminary injunction from the district court, and it waited three years before seeking relief from the Commission—even though the importation of the Wii was allegedly the only obstacle to adoption of its patented technology in the market.

Thus, on the record here, substantial evidence supports the Commission's finding that Motiva's litigation against Nintendo was not an investment in commercializing Motiva's patented technology that would develop a licensing program to encourage adoption and development of articles that incorporated Motiva's patented technology. *See John Mezzalingua*, 660 F.3d at 1328 (discussing how litigation expenses should not automatically be considered a substantial investment in licensing, even where litigation leads to a license). There is simply no reasonable likelihood that, after successful litigation against Nintendo, Motiva's patented technology would have been licensed by partners who would have incorporated it into "goods practicing the patents." *See InterDigital*, 707 F.3d at 1299.

III. CONCLUSION

The ALJ thoroughly reviewed the evidence in this case, and the Commission adopted the ALJ's conclusion that Motiva's litigation activities did not satisfy the economic prong of the domestic industry requirement of Section 337. Because that determination is supported by substantial evidence, we affirm the Commission's finding of no Section 337 violation.

AFFIRMED.

Notes and Questions

1. Do you agree with the *Motiva* decision? When reading the case, did you detect any bias against non-practicing entities?

2. The Administrative Law Judge (ALJ) found that the size of Motiva's investments in the litigation was not substantial. Because of a contingency fee arrangement, Motiva had

yet to pay any attorneys' fees or expenses related to Motiva's litigation against Nintendo, and never had to pay any of those costs unless Motiva obtained a recovery as a result of the litigation. Because Motiva might never actually pay any fees for the litigation, it was reasoned, by the ALJ, that Motiva's investment was too "speculative."

3. Would you argue that Motiva's action was particularly mean spirited since no one would benefit in the event that the Wii had been barred from importation into this country?

4. Patent holding companies often complain that they are being unfairly and negatively painted with an undeserving broad brush because of a few bad apples; some PHC's arguably serve important functions by providing some stability to the licensing quagmire caused by an exploding videogame industry. In deciding what brand of "*apple*" Motiva was, recall the Administrative Law Judge's finding that: "Motiva never offered to license, never received a request to license, and never in fact licensed either the '151 patent or the '268 patent." The ALJ further concluded that Motiva was "only interested in extracting a monetary award either through damages or a financial settlement." Semantically speaking, how close does the term "extraction" come to extortion?

5. As for the extremely popular Nintendo motion games (which we all know to be alive and well), the ALJ held that the Wii did not infringe either of the asserted patents, a determination that Motiva challenged on appeal. A decision by the ALJ in that matter, however, was not binding precedent; the Commission hearing was not tantamount to a patent infringement action.

6. McRo, Inc., a Delaware corporation based in California, describes itself as a company "actively involved in the advertising industry as a computer graphic, visual effects, and animation service company." Claiming to hold patents that "Cover a method and system for automating the lip synchronization process for three-dimensional animated characters as used in computer and/or videogames," McRo has filed thirteen lawsuits against a wide range of videogame developers, including Activision Blizzard, Inc., Lucasarts Entertainment Company LLC, Warner Bros. Interactive Entertainment, Inc., Rockstar Games, Inc., Namco Bandai Games America, Inc., Naughty Dog, Inc. and Take-Two Interactive Software, Inc. to name a few. There have been 20 lawsuits filed by McRo in the Central District of California alone. It is difficult to estimate the total cost to the industry that the litigation will eventually entail, once the numerous motions and procedural matters have been resolved. *See, e.g., McRo, Inc. v. Rockstar Games, Inc.,* 2014 WL 1051527 (D. Del. 2014).

Chapter 8

Trademark Protection

A trademark identifies the manufacturer of a product or service. More specifically, a trademark is a distinctive name, device, logo, image or symbol affixed to a manufacturer's product or associated with its service for the purpose of identifying that product or service and distinguishing it from other manufacturers, vendors, and service providers. The term *trademark* is often used in conjunction with other closely related concepts such as *trade name* and *trade dress*. It is common, though not always correct, to use the term "*trademark*" or just "*mark*" to denote any or all three concepts. In addition, a mark that identifies a service as opposed to a product is sometimes referred to as a *service mark*.

"Coca-Cola," or just "Coke," is often called the world's most valuable trade name. We might refer to the flared red lettering on the ubiquitous two-liter bottle as a trademark, or the older, classically curved bottle as trade dress. All three identify the Coca-Cola Bottling Company as the manufacturer of the product, in addition to identifying the product itself. Marks can come in many shapes and forms. Even the red angry bird face from the hit videogame *Angry Birds* is a registered trademark; see *Rovio Ent., LTD. v. Royal Plush Toys, Inc.*, 2014 WL 1153780, United State District Court (N.D. Cal., 2014).

We have seen similar multi-faceted trademarks with Microsoft's *Xbox*, Nintendo's *Wii*, and Sony's *Playstation*, to mention a few. As is the case with other areas of law, the expansion of videogame technology carries with it a demand for expanded rules and concepts for dealing with the so called "look and feel" of today's games. Every experienced videogamer knows that there are certain games that have their own special movements that transcend mere sounds and images, thereby adding a new dimension to the concept of trademarks and trade dress.

With respect to registration, trademarks are a bit more complex than filing for copyrights. Unlike copyrights and patents (both of which are entirely federal matters) there is no one-stop-shop for trademark filing. While it is highly recommended that trademarks be filed with the U.S. Patent and Trademark Office, it is also possible to register the marks among the individual states. Even then, it is important to remember that filing alone will not protect a trademark; it must be used in commerce and protected or it may be deemed abandoned. The Patent and Trademark Office provides excellent registration information on its web site: www.uspto.gov/trademarks/.

---

§ 8.10 A Multiplicity of Remedies

The remedies available to the producers and publishers of videogames upon an interference with their intellectual property rights are numerous. In earlier chapters, we considered copyright and patent protections, and pointed out that there was a great deal of overlap that included yet other causes of action, including trademark infringement. Unlike copyright and patent claims, causes of action for trademark-related claims are not quite so crisp, particularly because multiple state and federal remedies are available. For studying trademarks, federal protection is a good place to start.

---

§ 8.11 Federal Remedies [The Lanham Act]

The Federal Lanham Act, which is contained within Title 15, Chapter 22 of the United States Code, provides the focal point that targets federal remedies for trademark infringement. As is the case with the Copyright and Patent Acts, the Lanham Act contains rules and provisions for registrations and remedies for infringements, but the similarity ends there. According to 15 U.S.C. § 1127, "The term 'trademark' includes any word, name, symbol, or device, or any combination thereof, (1) used by a person, or (2) which a person has a bona fide intention to use in commerce and applies to register on the principal register established by this chapter, to identify and distinguish his or her goods, including a unique product, from those manufactured or sold by others and to indicate the source of the goods, even if that source is unknown." The same section 1127 defines the term "service mark" in similar fashion, except the word "services" is used in place of "goods" and "products." Section 1127 also defines the terms "trade name" and "commercial name" to mean "any name used by a person to identify his or her business or vocation."

The Act is designed to protect marks and provide or otherwise permit remedies for a plaintiff whose mark has been *confused, diluted, blurred, tarnished* or subjected to *unfair competition.* While "confusion" may form the most common basis for an infringement action, the others are significant as well. Section 1125 of the Lanham Act provides remedies for infringing activity that does not necessarily cause ambiguities in the mind of the public. If a mark is famous it can, for example, be protected against *dilution* by those who might use the mark for non-competing products.[1] In addition, the concept "*blurring*" (a close ancestor of "confusion") normally results when the connection between the mark and the consumer is weakened; or "*tarnishment*," whereby the defendant's use of the mark is negative, unsavory or unwholesome, or is used in conjunction with an inferior product.

The Act derives its jurisdictional authority from 28 U.S.C. § 1338(a), which states: "The district courts shall have original jurisdiction of any civil action arising under any Act of Congress relating to patents, plant variety protection, copyrights and trademarks. Such jurisdiction shall be exclusive of the courts of the states in patent, plant variety protection and copyright cases."

Federal courts may also exercise jurisdiction over a variety of state unfair competition complaints and other claims in conjunction with 28 U.S.C. § 1338(b) or the general sup-

---

1. Note, however, that certain trademark usages are protected. Fair use such as comparative advertising, noncommercial use (i.e., a noncommercial web page), and many forms of news reporting and commentary would not constitute dilution under the Act.

plemental jurisdiction provisions contained in 28 U.S.C. § 1367. Due to § 1367, the necessity and effect of § 1338(b) seems to be less than clear. *See* John B. Oakley, *Prospectus for the American Law Institute's Federal Judicial Code Revision Project*, 31 U.C. DAVIS L. REV. 855, 895–99 (1998); Arthur D. Wolf, *Comment on the Supplemental-Jurisdiction Statute: 28 U.S.C. § 1367*, 74 IND. L.J. 223, 233–34 (1998); Amy B. Cohen, *"Arising Under" Jurisdiction and the Copyright Laws*, 44 HASTINGS L.J. 337, 388 n.224 (1993).

To encounter overlap problems for trademarks with respect to other forms of intellectual property protection, it is not necessary to consider the potential numerous and varied state claims. There are enough such issues in the federal realm alone. The case that follows is illustrative and is designed to provide some insight with respect to the overlapping nature of some remedies, both civil and criminal. It tells tales of copyright and trademark infringement in addition to counterfeiting.

* * *

Nintendo of Am., Inc. v. Dragon Pacific Int'l

United States Court of Appeals, Ninth Circuit 1994
40 F.3d 1007

O'SCANNLAIN, Circuit Judge.

We decide whether an award of both statutory copyright infringement damages and trademark infringement damages for the sale of video game cartridges constitutes an inappropriate "double recovery."

I

George Sheng, the sole proprietor of Dragon Pacific International, imports electronic products from China. Nintendo of America, Inc.'s ("Nintendo") principal business is the marketing of hardware and software cartridges for its home video game system. In 1990, Sheng began importing and selling video cartridges that were compatible with Nintendo's system.

The cartridges sold by Nintendo usually contain one game. The cartridges sold by Sheng contained numerous games per cartridge, and came in three varieties: thirty-one games in one cartridge (which contained ten Nintendo copyrighted games), forty-two games in one cartridge (which contained eleven Nintendo copyrighted games), and fifty-two games in one cartridge (which contained twelve Nintendo copyrighted games). Sheng infringed a total of thirteen separate Nintendo copyrights. The district court found that Sheng acted "intentionally, willfully, and with actual knowledge that the multiple-game cartridges infringed Nintendo's copyrights." Sheng also represented that the cartridges were Nintendo products and marketed them as such, in violation of Nintendo's trademark rights.

On October 22, 1990, Nintendo filed suit to enjoin Sheng from importing the cartridges and to recover damages for copyright and trademark infringement. On November 15, 1990, the district court entered a preliminary injunction enjoining Sheng from selling, marketing or distributing cartridges using Nintendo's trademark or copyrights. On November 8, 1991, summary judgment on the issue of liability was granted for Nintendo. Sheng does not challenge these rulings.

In the interim, Sheng was also indicted for criminal infringement of copyright and trafficking in counterfeit goods. On November 15, 1991, Sheng filed a motion to continue his civil trial in order to allow the criminal trial to proceed first; the court granted it, but enjoined Sheng from seeking any continuances of the criminal trial. On December 20, 1991, Sheng moved for a second continuance; the court again granted it, even though Sheng had requested that the criminal trial be continued in violation of the court's order. On May 21, 1992, five days before the civil trial was scheduled to begin, Sheng sought a third continuance. In response, Nintendo requested that the court enjoin Sheng from transferring or encumbering any real property as a condition of the continuance. The court gave Sheng the choice of going to trial as scheduled or granting the continuance with the condition that a lis pendens be filed. Sheng agreed to this condition, and Nintendo filed a lis pendens on May 26, 1992, in accord with the court's order. On June 4, 1992, the court also enjoined Sheng from transferring or encumbering any real property, with the exception of a possible loan to obtain funds to pay his attorneys.

A bench trial on the issue of damages finally took place on December 29 and 30, 1992. At its conclusion, the court awarded Nintendo statutory damages under the Copyright Act of $65,000, representing $5,000 for each of the thirteen copyright infringements. The court also awarded $62,000 in actual damages under the Lanham Act. This sum represented the profits made by Sheng on the sale of the cartridges—3100 cartridges at a profit of $20 per cartridge, for a total of $62,000. Because Sheng's violations were found willful, this amount was trebled to $186,000.

II

Sheng claims that the award of both statutory copyright infringement damages and trademark infringement damages constitutes a "double recovery."

We examine each award separately.

The damage award for copyright infringement, standing alone, was appropriate. The damages provision of the Copyright Act states:

> [A]n infringer of copyright is liable for either—(1) the copyright owner's actual damages and any additional profits of the infringer … ; or (2) statutory damages….
> 17 U.S.C. § 504(a). Under section 504(c)(1), the copyright owner may elect which measure of damages to recover.

If statutory damages are elected, the court can award a minimum of $500 and a maximum of $20,000 per infringement. If the court finds the violation was willful, the maximum is raised to $100,000 per infringement. 17 U.S.C. § 504(c)(2). The district court has wide discretion in setting the amount of statutory damages under the Copyright Act. Nintendo opted for statutory damages. The district court specifically found that Sheng willfully infringed Nintendo's copyrights. The court awarded $5000 for each of the thirteen copyrighted works infringed by Sheng, for a total of $65,000. Given the wide range of damages permissible under the statute, and the willfulness of Sheng's infringements, it cannot be said that the court's award was an abuse of discretion.

The damage award for trademark infringement, standing alone, was also appropriate. The damages provision of the Lanham Act states:

> When a violation of any right of the registrant of a mark … shall have been established in any civil action arising under this chapter, the plaintiff shall be entitled … to recover (1) defendant's profits, (2) any damages sustained by the plaintiff, and (3) the costs of the action. 15 U.S.C. § 1117(a).

If the violation consists of "intentionally using a mark or designation, knowing such mark or designation is a counterfeit mark," section 1117(b) instructs that the court "shall" treble the damages. The district court's award of damages under the Lanham Act is reviewed for abuse of discretion.

The district court accepted Sheng's calculation of profits of $20 per cartridge, and multiplied this by 3100 cartridges, for a total of $62,000. Because the court specifically found that Sheng willfully infringed Nintendo's trademarks, trebling the damages was appropriate.

Again, given the willfulness of Sheng's violations, and the conservative estimate of actual damages, the court's award was not an abuse of discretion. Sheng correctly points out that, once a copyright owner elects to recover statutory damages, he may not recover actual damages as well under the Copyright Act. 17 U.S.C. § 504. Similarly, the recovery of both plaintiff's lost profits and disgorgement of defendant's profits is generally considered a double recovery under the Lanham Act. 15 U.S.C. § 1117. Sheng claims that when Nintendo was awarded damages under each act individually, it received a double recovery. However, one plus one does not necessarily equal two in this case.

First, Nintendo's claims were not, as Sheng suggests, based on the same wrongful act. If Sheng had sold the cartridges without representing that they were Nintendo products, he would have committed the wrong of copyright infringement. Or, if Sheng had represented that the cartridges were Nintendo products, even though they contained no Nintendo games, he would have committed the wrong of trademark infringement. Put together, selling the cartridges may have been one act, but it was two wrongs. *Cf. Dive N' Surf, Inc. v. Anselowitz*, 834 F.Supp. 379, 383–84 (M.D.Fla.1993) (awarding statutory copyright damages and trademark damages of lost profits for defendant's T-shirts, which simultaneously infringed plaintiff's copyright and its trademark). Congress created two separate statutory schemes to govern copyrights and trademarks; in order to effectuate the purposes of both statutes, damages may be awarded under both.

Second, Nintendo did not recover the same type of damages under both acts. A copyright owner may elect either actual damages or statutory damages under the Copyright Act. Actual damages consist of elements such as the profits lost by the copyright holder, the profits made by the infringer or the diminution in value of the copyright. Such damages are designed to compensate the plaintiff and to prevent the defendant's unjust enrichment. The same is true of actual damages under the Lanham Act, which states: "[The award] ... shall constitute compensation and not a penalty." 15 U.S.C. § 1117.

Statutory damages, on the other hand, may have different purposes. For instance, statutory damages may be appropriate when lost profits would be an inadequate measure. In addition, when infringement is willful, the statutory damages award may be designed to penalize the infringer and to deter future violations. The punitive and deterrent purposes explain the heightened maximum award of $100,000 per infringement under section 504(c)(2). Thus, statutory damages may serve completely different purposes than actual damages.

The line between statutory and actual damages is not always perfectly clear. *See, e.g., Roulo v. Russ Berrie & Co.*, 886 F.2d 931, 941 (7th Cir.1989) ("Profits are awarded [under the Lanham Act] under different rationales including unjust enrichment, deterrence, and compensation."). However, it is clear enough that, when a defendant violates both the Copyright Act and the Lanham Act, an award of both types of damages is appropriate. *See Nintendo of America, Inc. v. Ketchum*, 830 F.Supp. 1443, 1446 (M.D.Fla.1993) (awarding Nintendo both statutory damages under the Copyright Act and lost profits damages under the Lanham Act against a video game counterfeiter).[2]

---

2. In *Manufacturers Tech., Inc. v. Cams, Inc.*, 728 F.Supp. 75 (D.Conn.1989), which Sheng relies upon, the plaintiff sought both actual damages under the Copyright Act and lost profits under the Lanham Act. The court refused to award the latter on the grounds that it would be allowing a "double recovery." *Id.* at 85. This case is distinguishable on the grounds that the plaintiff sought the same type

Because Sheng committed two separate violations, we affirm the damages award.

III

Sheng contends that the district court erred in refusing to apportion damages based on the infringing and noninfringing elements of his cartridges.

If a plaintiff elects to recover actual damages under the Copyright Act, the court must determine what portion of defendant's profits are "attributable to factors other than the copyrighted work." 17 U.S.C. § 504(b). However, apportionment is simply not an option when statutory damages are elected. Section 504(c), the provision governing statutory damages, makes no mention of apportionment. Moreover, by assessing statutory damages for only the thirteen Nintendo copyrights that were infringed, the district court did not award Nintendo damages for any of the non-Nintendo games on Sheng's cartridges.

Under the Lanham Act, if the district court finds the amount of the award based on profits to be too high, it may "in its discretion" enter judgment for a lower sum. 15 U.S.C. § 1117(a). The district court's decision not to apportion damages in this case was not an abuse of discretion. First, although Sheng suggested a method of apportionment, it was inappropriate for apportioning trademark damages. Because the Nintendo copyrighted games made up an average of one-third of every cartridge, Sheng argues, any award should be cut to one-third. This method might be adequate to apportion actual damages under the Copyright Act. However, the trademark damages reflect the fact that Sheng advertised the cartridges as Nintendo products. The district court, in its findings of fact, found that Sheng "advertised and sold the multiple-game cartridges as 'Nintendo' games." If Sheng had advertised each cartridge as being only one-third a Nintendo product (and the remainder his own product), he might be entitled to some form of apportionment; but that is not the case here—the entire cartridge was advertised as a Nintendo product.

Second, where infringing and noninfringing elements of a work cannot be readily separated, all of a defendant's profits should be awarded to a plaintiff. Sheng contends that the multiple-game format and Nintendo-compatibility were the cartridges' selling point, not the use of the Nintendo trademark. However, it is difficult to see a workable distinction between Sheng's representations that his cartridges were Nintendo products and his representations that they were Nintendo-compatible Nintendo products. Even if Sheng's assertion was plausible, Sheng did not meet his burden of presenting any evidence at trial on how to apportion damages on this basis.

Notes and Questions

1. *Midway v. Dirkschneider*, 571 F. Supp. 282 (D. Neb. 1984) involved several separate causes of action, all of which were sparked by the defendants' copying of three popular arcade videogames. In the 1980s, Plaintiff Midway manufactured and sold many very popular coin-operated videogames, including *Pac-Man*, *Galaxian* and *Rally-X*. Midway registered the three games with the Copyright Office after acquiring the rights from Japanese game developer Namco, Ltd. The defendants thereafter purchased and distributed fully-assembled videogames and printed circuit boards that copied both the Midway games and trademarks; the purchase included at least ten "copy games" and three conversion kits from their distributor. The game names on the headboards of the video cabinets

---

of damages under both acts. By contrast, here Nintendo recovered statutory damages under the Copyright Act.

displayed variations of Midway's trademarks: *Pac Man* was replaced by *Mighty Mouth*, *Galaxian* was replaced by *Galactic Invader,* and the *Rally-X* name was appropriated completely onto the defendants' version of the game. None of the defendants' games had "Midway" imprinted on their respective cabinets. The movement, design, and sound effects of these games strongly resembled their Midway counterparts. The defendants resold these games or kits, or placed them in various locations for public use; they then divided the proceeds with the owners of the premises where the games were played. During the motions for summary judgment that followed, the court determined that at least three prima facie cases had been established:

[a] **Copyright infringement:** After the court considered the requirements for establishing copyright infringement in general, it was determined that the defendants' three games were virtually identical to those of the plaintiff Midway.

[b] **Lanham Act Violation:** "Under Lanham Act 43(a), 15 U.S.C. §1125(a), defendants are liable for infringement of the unregistered trademarks Pac-Man, Galaxian and Rally-X. Liability lies under section 43(a) when it is determined that materials used by the defendants created a likelihood of confusion among the consuming public. The evidence shows that on at least one occasion, a customer called Defendants and asked to purchase a Pac-Man game. The defendant Dirkschneider offered to sell the customer a Mighty Mouth game, explaining that it was very similar to the Pac-Man game. In the defendants' opinion, one of the selling points of the Mighty Mouth game was its similarity to the Pac-Man game. The fact that the Midway and counterfeit goods were sold side-by-side by the defendants within the same channels of commerce offends the Lanham Act."

[c] **State Deceptive Trade Practices:** "The facts supporting defendants' liability for trademark infringement also support a cause of action under the Nebraska Deceptive Trade Practices Act, Neb.Rev.Stat. §87-302 (1980 Supp.). The Act prohibits a broad panoply of deceptive trade practices, including passing off goods and services of another as your own id. at 87-302(1), and causing confusion in the minds of consumers as to the origin of goods id. at 87-302(2). Plaintiff correctly contends that defendants' misuse of Midway's trademark constitutes a violation of the Nebraska Deceptive Trade Practices Act."

2. In an earlier case involving the same parties as those referred to in Note 1 above, *Midway v. Dirkschneider*, 543 F.Supp. 466, 214 U.S.P.Q. 417 (D. Neb. 1982), the court issued a preliminary injunction after dealing with the threshold issue of videogame copyrightability. With respect to the trademark infringement issues, the court engaged in a lengthy analysis of the facts and the existence of "secondary meaning" for the games' characters (resulting from the broad popularity of the games); it then found that: "The record contains overwhelming evidence of the likelihood of confusion caused by the defendants' products. This confusion is evidence of the substantial injury which both the plaintiff and public will suffer if a preliminary injunction is not issued ... The Court therefore finds that the plaintiff is entitled to a preliminary injunction prohibiting the defendants from further violations of the Lanham Act."

3. In addition to the three causes of action mentioned in Notes 1 and 2 above, Plaintiff Midway also claimed that under Nebraska Law, trademark infringement constituted "unfair competition." *Kirsch Fabric Corp. v. Brookstein Ent., Inc.*, 209 Neb. 666, 309 N.W.2d 328 (1981). Thus, a fourth set of potential remedies was considered.

4. Would it make sense for congress to pass a comprehensive reform of the nation's trademark laws and provide for federal preemption of commonly used, related state claims?

§ 8.12 State Remedies

Unlike the singular remedies for copyright and patent infringements, there are many available for trademark protection, both state and federal. Congress never granted exclusive jurisdiction to the federal courts for trademark infringement. *Tafflin v. Levitt*, 493 U.S. 455, 459–60 (1990); *Claflin v. Houseman*, 93 U.S. 130 (1876). Because of their inherent multimedia nature, videogames present unique problems and challenges with respect to intellectual property protection. Not only is it possible for a single game to qualify for both patent and copyright protection, as demonstrated in our prior chapters, but a game may also find a variety of protective statutes within the law of trademarks alone.

The overlapping nature of all of these protections tend to add to the challenge; it is tantamount to a shopping list of causes of action, state and federal that may essentially be used for a single incidence of infringement. In addition to basic infringement, here are some favorite accompaniments:

Fraud

Unfair Competition

Disparagement of Title

Breach of Duty of Fair Dealing

Breach of Confidentiality

False and Misleading Advertising

Interference with a Prospective Economic Advantage

Violations of Specific State Statutes

Throughout the preceding chapters we observed the manner in which several intellectual property devices come together under a single fact pattern. In *White v. Samsung*, 971 F.2d 1395 (9th Cir. 1992) (the Vanna White case covered in Chapter 4, *supra*), for example, a simple female robot that suggested characteristics of a television personality gave rise to claims of trademark infringement, violations of California Civil Code § 3344, and breaches of California's common law right of publicity. (*See* § 2.30, *supra*.) *See also* § 16.40 *infra* for a discussion of state law claims arising from videogame dealings.

§ 8.20 Trademark Strength

Measurement for trademark strength consists of two components: *Conceptual Strength*, which relates to its distinctiveness and *Commercial Strength*, which is measured by its recognition in the marketplace. Strength, in turn, will determine how that mark will fare against other similar marks in the ensuing infringement battles.

Addressing conceptual strength first, it is fair to say that the value of a trademark is directly proportional to one's ability to protect it from confusion or use by others. And that ability, in turn, is proportional to the uniqueness of the trademark. Judge Friendly said it best in *Abercrombie & Fitch Co. v. Hunting World, Inc.*, 537 F.2d 4, 9 (2d Cir. 1976), as he created a categorical grouping (notably termed "The *Abercrombie Spectrum*") taking us from the least to the most protectable types of marks:

> The cases, and in some instances the Lanham Act, identify four different categories of terms with respect to trademark protection. Arrayed in an ascending order which roughly reflects their eligibility to trademark status and the degree of protection accorded, these classes, starting with the weakest (generic) to the strongest, are:
>
> (1) **Generic**,[3]
>
> (2) **Descriptive**,[4]
>
> (3) **Suggestive**[5], and
>
> (4) **Arbitrary or Fanciful**.[6]

The lines of demarcation, however, are not always bright. Moreover, the difficulties are compounded because a term that is in one category for a particular product may be in quite a different one for another. A term may shift from one category to another in light of differences in usage through time, and a term may have one meaning to one group of users and a different one to others.

The Lanham Act referred to by Judge Friendly, as previously discussed, provides a federal scheme for trademark protection, which is by no means exclusive. The four-tier array, however, generally applies to both federal and state trademarks. As the hierarchy

---

3. Examples of **generic** marks: *All News Channel* Broadcasting Services; *Bag Rack* Golf Bag Support Device, *Blinded Veterans* An Organization for Blinded Veterans, *Clipper* Sailing Ship Cruises, *Consumer Electronics Monthly* Magazine On Consumer Electronics, *Discount Mufflers* Car Muffler Repair and Replacement Services, *DOS* Computer Operating System, *Email* Messaging, *Ice Pak* Ice Substitute, *Imported Auto Parts* Business (that sells imported auto parts), *Multistate Bar Examination* (No explanation required), *Primal Therapy* Psychotherapy, *PROM* Computer Programmable Read Only Memory, *Shredded Wheat* Breakfast Cereal, *Super Glue* Adhesive, *Yellow Pages* Business Telephone Directory.

4. Examples of **descriptive** marks: *After Tan* Sun-Bathing Lotion, *Arthriticare* Treatment Substance for Arthritis, *America's Best Popcorn!* Popcorn, *Beef & Brew* Restaurant, *Bufferin* Buffered Aspirin, *Car Freshener* Air Deodorizer for Cars; *Cozy Warm Energy Savers* Pajamas, *Digital* Computers, *Easyload* Tape Recorders, *Fashionknit* Sweaters, *Food Fair* Supermarket, *Heritage* Life Insurance Plans, *Home Savings* Banking Services, *Intelligent Modem* Modems, *International* Maps and Globes, *Lasergage* Laser Measurement Device, *Nature's Medicine* Food Supplements, *Personal Finance* Financial Investment Publication, *Rich 'N Chips* Chocolate Chip Cookies, *Security Center* Storage Facility, *Sharp* Televisions, *Spex* Optician Services, *Sudsy* Ammonia, *Tender Vittles* Cat Food, *World Book* Encyclopedias.

5. Examples of **suggestive** marks: *At A Glance* Calendars, *Brim* Coffee, *Chicken Of The Sea* Tuna Fish, *Citibank* Urban-Based Bank, *Compugraphic* Typesetting Machinery, *Cyclone* Wire Fence, *Esprit* Casual Clothing, Florida Tan Suntan Lotion, *Glacier Ice*, *Heartwise* Low Cholesterol Foods, *Hulahoop* Plastic Toy Hoops, *Lektronic* Electric Shavers, *Liquid Paper* Correcting Fluid, *Loc-Top* Bottle Closure Caps, *Microsoft* Computer Software, *Netscape* Internet Browser, *Phoenix* Ventures, *Playboy* Magazine, *Rapid-Shave* Shaving Cream, *Roach Motel* Insect Trap, *Silicon Graphics* Computer Software, *Spray'n Vac* Aerosol Rug Cleaner, *Suave* Shampoo, *Sweetarts* Candy, *Verbatim* Computer Diskettes, *Wearever* Cookware, *WordPerfect* Word-Processing Computer Software, *Wrangler* Western Style Jeans And Boots.

6. Examples of **arbitrary** or **fanciful** marks: *Ajax* Cleanser, *Apple* Computers, *Arrow* Shirts, *Banana Republic* Clothes, *Atari* Computers, *Beefeater* Gin, *Blizzard* Computer Games, *Blue Diamond* Nuts, *Camel* Cigarettes, *Domino* Sugar, *Dutch Boy* Paints, *Exxon* Gasoline, *Guess?* Jeans, *Hang Ten* Clothes, *Hard Rock* Café, *Horizon* Banking Services, *Ice Cream* Chewing Gum, *Ivory* Soap, *Jellibeans* Skating Rink, *Kodak* Cameras, *Lotus* Software, *Nova* TV Series, *Penguin* Books, *Reebok* Shoes, *Shell* Gasoline and *Tea Rose* Flour, *Sun* Computers, *Xerox* Copy Machines.

suggests, "Generic" names are generally not entitled to any protection, state or federal; a laundry business that called itself the "*The Dry Cleaner*" could not, for example, prevent other businesses from using the same exact name. Descriptive marks (Such as *Chocolate Candy Bar*), are also extremely weak, but may, nevertheless, be entitled to trademark protection if they become "distinctive of the applicant's goods in commerce," i.e., have acquired secondary meaning. *See* 15 U.S.C. § 1152(f) and *KP Permanent Make-Up, Inc. v. Lasting Impression I, Inc.*, 543 U.S. 111, 122 (2004). Suggestive trademarks (such as *Coppertone*) receive greater protection. And, finally, marks that are "Arbitrary or Fanciful" (such as *Google*) are entitled to the greatest protection. As common sense would suggest, in order to best distinguish, identify and single out a specific merchant or manufacturer, a trademark should be unique.

Once the trademark has been placed into one of the four pigeonholes, the next step is to examine its *Commercial Strength*. Here, commercial impact and recognition by the public are the key factors, as opposed to the appearance of the mark. In particular, according to *Freedom Card, Inc. v. J.P. Morgan Chase & Co.*, 432 F.3d 463 (3rd Cir., 2005), in evaluating strength, in addition to the conceptual distinctiveness, the courts look to "the factual evidence of the mark's marketplace recognition or commercial strength."

While both factors are important for determining overall strength, they are not necessarily related. The suggestive mark "*Windows*," for example, may be far from fanciful or even descriptive, but its commercial strength with respect to computer software is undeniable.

The *Frosty Treats* case that follows purports to consider trademark dilution under both state and federal law, but more significantly the case explores the lines of demarcation among the four categories laid out by Judge Friendly in *Hunting World*.

* * *

Frosty Treats v. Sony Comp. Ent., Am., Inc.

United States Court of Appeals, Eighth Circuit, 2005
426 F.3d 1001

ARNOLD, Circuit Judge.

A group of affiliated companies, Frosty Treats, Inc., Frosty Treats of Louisville, Inc., Frosty Treats Whole-sale, Inc., and Frosty Treats of Atlanta, Inc., collectively known as "Frosty Treats," sued Sony Computer Entertainment America, Inc., (SCEA) asserting, inter alia, claims under state and federal law for trademark infringement and dilution, and for unfair competition. Frosty Treats premised these claims upon SCEA's depiction of an ice cream truck and clown character in SCEA's Twisted Metal video game series. Frosty Treats contends that because the ice cream truck in those games bears a clown graphic that it alleges is similar to the one on its ice cream trucks, and, in the final game, is labeled with its brand identifier, "Frosty Treats," the games create a likelihood of confusion as to Frosty Treats's sponsorship of or affiliation with the games. See 15 U.S.C. § 1125(a). The district court 1 granted SCEA's motion for summary judgment on all of Frosty Treats's claims, and Frosty Treats appeals. We affirm.

I

Frosty Treats argues first that the district court erred by holding that its "Frosty Treats" mark is not entitled to trademark protection because it is generic, or, in the alternative, descriptive without secondary meaning. Frosty Treats asserts that the mark is suggestive, or, at worst, descriptive with an acquired secondary meaning, and therefore protectible.

We disagree. At best, the "Frosty Treats" mark is descriptive, and there is no basis for concluding that it has acquired secondary meaning.

The stylized words "Frosty Treats" appear toward the rear of the passenger's side of plaintiffs' ice cream vans as pink capital letters with frost on the upper portion of each letter. The decal on which these words appear is approximately nine inches wide by four inches high and is surrounded by decals of the frozen products that the Frosty Treats vans sell.

To determine whether this mark is protectible, we must first categorize it. A term for which trademark protection is claimed will fall in one of four categories: (1) generic, (2) descriptive, (3) suggestive, or (4) arbitrary or fanciful. A generic mark refers to the common name or nature of an article, and is therefore not entitled to trademark protection. A term is descriptive if it conveys an immediate idea of the ingredients, qualities or characteristics of the goods, and is protectable only if shown to have acquired a secondary meaning. Suggestive marks, which require imagination, thought, and perception to reach a conclusion as to the nature of the goods, and arbitrary or fanciful marks, are entitled to protection regardless of whether they have acquired secondary meaning.

If it is not generic, the phrase "Frosty Treats" is, at best, descriptive. Frosty Treats is in the business of selling frozen desserts out of ice cream trucks. "Frosty Treats" conveys an immediate idea of the qualities and characteristics of the goods that it sells. No imagination, thought, or perception is required to reach a conclusion as to the nature of its goods. To prevail, therefore, Frosty Treats must demonstrate that the mark has acquired a secondary meaning. "Secondary meaning is an association formed in the minds of consumers between the mark and the source or origin of the product." To establish secondary meaning, Frosty Treats must show that "Frosty Treats" serves to identify its goods and distinguish them from those of others. Secondary meaning does not require the consumer to identify a source by name but does require that the public recognize the mark and associate it with a single source.

The record, when viewed in favor of Frosty Treats, demonstrates that SCEA is entitled to judgment as a matter of law on this issue. Frosty Treats has failed to put forth more than a scintilla of evidence that the public recognizes its "Frosty Treats" mark and associates it with a single source. Frosty Treats claims that its survey evidence demonstrates that the term "Frosty Treats" has acquired secondary meaning, but, if anything, it indicates the opposite. In the survey, respondents were shown images of the Frosty Treats ice cream van and asked, "Are you familiar with or have you ever seen or heard of this before?" Forty-seven percent responded affirmatively. They were then asked what they knew about the van. The respondents most frequently mentioned that it sold ice cream. Only one percent of the respondents in the survey mentioned Frosty Treats by name.

Although direct evidence such as consumer testimony or surveys are most probative of secondary meaning, it can also be proven by circumstantial evidence. Circumstantial evidence such as the exclusivity, length and manner of use of the mark; the amount and manner of advertising; the amount of sales and number of customers; the plaintiff's established place in the market; and the existence of intentional copying could also establish secondary meaning. But the circumstantial evidence that Frosty Treats offered to establish secondary meaning also fails to raise a genuine issue of material fact.

SCEA submitted indirect evidence that the term "Frosty Treats" has not acquired secondary meaning. SCEA's expert conducted a survey of 204 children and 200 adults who had purchased ice cream from an ice cream truck in Frosty Treats's largest markets. When asked to volunteer the names of any ice cream trucks that they had purchased ice cream from, not one recalled the name "Frosty Treats." The evidence as a whole simply does not provide a sufficient basis for concluding that the phrase "Frosty Treats" has acquired a secondary meaning. Accordingly, it is not protectible under trademark law.

II

Frosty Treats also maintains that the district court erred in holding that its Safety Clown graphic is functional and therefore not eligible for protection under the trademark laws. The Safety Clown graphic appears on the passenger's side door of plaintiffs' vans as well as the rear panel. It consists of a clown with black eyebrows, blue eyes with a black pupil, a bulbous red nose, white forehead, yellow cheeks and chin, and a mouth with a black center, outlined by a series of concentric red, white, and orange lips. The clown wears a blue ruffled collar and a yellow pointed hat with red polka-dots that is topped with a red pom-pom. A tuft of orange hair appears under the hat on each side of the clown's head. The clown's hand points to the rear of the van with the thumb and index finger extended. Below the clown appear the words "watch for cars — cross at rear." *See* Figure 8.1 (depicting the Safety Clown graphic). The clown's purpose is to promote safety by directing children to cross at the rear of the vehicle.

Figure 8.1

The district court held that because the clown serves a purpose, namely to enhance safety by directing children to cross at the rear, the graphic is functional and therefore not protectible. We respectfully disagree. We believe that the district court evaluated the issue using the colloquial meaning of "functional" rather than the specialized meaning that it has in trademark law. In trademark law, " 'a product feature is functional, and cannot serve as a trademark, if it is essential to the use or purpose of the article or if it affects the cost or quality of the article.'" *TrafFix Devices, Inc. v. Marketing Displays, Inc.*, 532 U.S. 23, 32, (2001).

The functionality doctrine serves as a buffer between patent law and trademark law by preventing a competitor from monopolizing a useful product feature in the guise of identifying itself as the source of the product. Furthermore, to be functional in the trade dress sense, the feature must be necessary to afford a competitor the means to compete effectively. There is no evidence that the exclusive use of the Safety Clown graphic would deny Frosty Treats's competitors the ability to compete effectively or place competitors at any non-reputational disadvantage. At the very least, whether the Safety Clown graphic is functional presents a factual issue not appropriate for resolution upon a motion for summary judgment. We therefore conclude that the district court erred in granting summary judgment on the ground that the clown was functional.

Notes and Questions

1. The *Frosty Treats* lawsuit presented claims under state and federal law for trademark infringement and dilution, and for unfair competition, yet there was little discussion about the role, if any, that state laws and statutes played in the ultimate outcome. Is there is a subtle hint of preemption? Or were the state claims deemed moot once the appellate court determined that the mark could not sustain federal muster?

2. The plaintiff in *Frosty Treats* never registered its mark. Unlike copyright infringement lawsuits which require registration prior to commencement of the litigation, an unregistered trademark may serve as a basis for an infringement lawsuit under the Lanham Act. In conjunction with 15 U.S.C. §1125 and §43(a) of the Lanham Act, the marks are entitled to protection under the so called "general principles" that qualify for a trademark under the Act. *See Two Pesos v. Taco Cabana*, 505 U.S. 763, 768 (1992).

* * *

Anti-Monopoly Inc. v. General Mills Fun Group, Inc.

United States Court of Appeals, Ninth Circuit, 1981

684 F.2d 1316

DUNIWAY, Circuit Judge.

This is the second appeal in this case. Our first opinion is reported in *Anti-Monopoly, Inc. v. General Mills Fun Group*, 9 Cir., 1979, 611 F.2d 296 (*Anti-Monopoly I*). On remand the district court again found that the "Monopoly" trademark was valid and had been infringed by Anti-Monopoly, Inc. *Anti-Monopoly, Inc. v. General Mills Fun Group, Inc.*, N.D.Cal., 1981, 515 F.Supp. 448 (*Anti-Monopoly II*). We reverse and remand for further proceedings.

Prior Proceedings

General Mills is the successor to Parker Brothers, Inc., which had produced and sold a game it called Monopoly since 1935. Parker Brothers registered "Monopoly" as a trademark in that year. In 1973 Anti-Monopoly, Inc. was established to produce and sell a game it called Anti-Monopoly. General Mills claimed that this infringed its trademark. This action was then brought by Anti-Monopoly, seeking a declaratory judgment that the registered trademark "Monopoly" was invalid, and cancelling its registration. In a counterclaim, General Mills sought declaratory and injunctive relief upholding its trademark, and the dismissal of the action. The case was tried without a jury in 1976. The court entered a judgment for General Mills. We reversed and remanded for further consideration of (i) the validity of the trademark, (ii) infringement of the trademark, if it is valid, by Anti-Monopoly, and (iii) state law claims concerning unfair competition and dilution. We also chose to defer consideration of (iv) Anti-Monopoly's defense that General Mills had unclean hands. On remand, after hearing further evidence, the district court again entered a judgment for General Mills.

The Burden of Proof

There is a presumption in favor of a registered trademark, and the burden of proof is upon one who attacks the mark as generic, but the presumption can be overcome by a showing by a preponderance of the evidence that the term was or has become generic.

Generic Terms—The Law

Our opinion in *Anti-Monopoly I* binds both this court and the district court. There, we set out the law about generic terms and explained how it was to be applied to the particular facts of this case. *Anti-Monopoly I*, 611 F.2d at 300–306. In this opinion, we assume that the reader will be familiar with that opinion. Here, we emphasize what we consider to be its essence. A word used as a trademark is not generic if "the primary significance of the term in the minds of the consuming public is not the product but the producer." *Id.* at 302. "(W)hen a trademark primarily denotes a product, not the product's producer, the trademark is lost." *Id.* at 301. A registered mark is to be cancelled if it has become "the common descriptive name of an article," 15 U.S.C. § 1064(c), and no incontestable right can be acquired in such a mark. 15 U.S.C. s 1065(4). We said "Even if only one producer—Parker Brothers—has ever made the MONOPOLY game, so that the public necessarily associates the product with that particular producer, the trademark is invalid unless source indication is its primary significance." *Anti-Monopoly I*, 611 F.2d at 302. "It is the source-denoting function which trademark laws protect, and nothing more." *Id.* at 301. "(O)ne competitor will not be permitted to impoverish the language of commerce by preventing his fellows from fairly describing their own goods." *Id.* "(W)hen members of the consuming public use a game name to denote the game itself, and not its producer, the trademark is generic and, therefore, invalid." *Id.* at 304.

Was "MONOPOLY" Generic at Time of Registration?

Anti-Monopoly, Inc. claims that the term "Monopoly" was generic at the time when Parker Brothers registered it. On this question, the trial judge made the following findings: Plaintiff (Anti-Monopoly) attempted to show at trial that at the time of Parker Brothers' trademark registration, MONOPOLY was already a widely played game known by that name. The evidence introduced to support this contention consists chiefly of isolated and sporadic examples of individuals playing old oilcloth games referred to in some instances as "Monopoly," the "Landlord's Game," or some other variation thereof.

In order to be "generic," the name MONOPOLY, in the minds of the consuming public, must primarily denote product rather than source. It remains unclear how widely played the precursors to modern MONOPOLY were in the 1920s and early '30s. Plaintiff has simply made no showing as to what the public conception of the term was at that juncture or indeed how widely played it actually was. As Clarence (sic) Darrow, and later his successor, Parker Brothers, popularized a specific game they called MONOPOLY, this court cannot find that the trademark when registered denoted "a game" rather than the "game's producer." Because Anti-Monopoly has the burden of showing genericness by convincing evidence, this finding must be for defendant. The district court found also that Darrow was the inventor of the game and that the game was "created" by Darrow.

[T]he court's reference to Darrow as the inventor or creator of the game is clearly erroneous. The record shows, as we stated in *Anti-Monopoly I*, that "The game of 'Monopoly' was first played from 1920 to 1932 on various college campuses by a small group of individuals, many of whom were related by blood or marriage. In late 1932 or early 1933 one of these players introduced Charles Darrow to the game, and gave him a handmade game board, rules, and associated equipment. Immediately thereafter Darrow commenced commercially producing and selling 'Monopoly' game equipment." 611 F.2d at 299.

We have re-examined the entire record on appeal. Here is what it shows. At some time between 1904 and 1934, the game of monopoly developed. Early equipment was handmade and copied from earlier handmade equipment. All the witnesses presented by Anti-Monopoly insisted that the game was known as "Monopoly" by all who played it, although in most cases the name did not appear on the board itself. The game was played in Reading, Pennsylvania, sometime between 1911 and 1917, but this date may be a little early. In the early 1920s the game was played at Princeton University, Massachusetts Institute of Technology, Smith College, the University of Pennsylvania, and Haverford College. On occasion the rules were privately printed. The game was offered to, but rejected by, Milton-Bradley, a leading competitor of Parker Brothers. It was played in and around Reading, Pennsylvania from the early 1920s to the early 1930s. It may have been brought there from the University of Pennsylvania. Players in Reading made up and sold some half dozen sets of equipment at Williams College and the University of Michigan. The game next appeared in Indianapolis, where some players marketed it under the name "Finance." (Players in Reading sold some of those games too.) The game of monopoly was brought to Atlantic City, New Jersey in 1931 or thereabouts. The street names used in the game were then changed to Atlantic City street names. The game was taught to Darrow. He sold it to Parker Brothers in 1935, claiming that it was his own invention. Parker Brothers also bought the Finance game from its owners.

It is true that Darrow, in his correspondence with Parker Brothers, claimed to have invented the game and offered to sign an affidavit stating his story. However, Robert B. M. Barton, the former President of Parker Brothers, who negotiated with Darrow in 1935, testified that he did not believe Darrow's claim. A precursor of monopoly, the Landlord's Game, was patented by Mrs. Maggie Elizabeth Phillips of Washington, D.C. in 1904 and again in 1924. Parker Brothers purchased this game from her in 1934 or thereabouts.

In 1957, Barton, the President of Parker Brothers, in a letter to an inquirer, wrote: "So far as we know The Landlord's Game, invented by Mrs. Elizabeth Maggie Phillips of Washington, D.C., was the basic game for both FINANCE and MONOPOLY. Mrs. Phillips patented her game and we purchased her patent. Mr. Charles Darrow later made many improvements in The Landlord's Game and called his game MONOPOLY. He, too, secured a patent which he assigned to us. Because of the fact that we purchased all three games, it does not make very much difference to us who invented either one of the games...."

The evidence clearly shows that the game of monopoly was played by a small number of people before Darrow learned of it, and that these people called the game "monopoly." It is unclear just how many people played. General Mills offered testimony that it was not widespread throughout the United States. The burden of proof was on Anti-Monopoly to show that the term was generic. We cannot presume that the evidence offered by Anti-Monopoly is the tip of the iceberg. Thus, we are faced with the following legal question: if a game is known about by a small number of people and they all call it by a particular term, may one member of the group appropriate that name by registering it as a trademark?

When a small number of people use a particular thing and call it by a particular name, one which is not a common descriptive term for the thing, a person may appropriate the name and register it as a trademark. The purpose of the doctrine that generic terms cannot be made trademarks is to prevent the appropriation of a term that is already in wide use among those who are potential purchasers of the thing that the term describes. If those who might purchase the thing know it by a particular name, then to forbid the use of that name by potential producers will erect unwarranted barriers to competition. As we said in Anti-Monopoly I, "Trademarks ... are not properly used as patent substitutes to further or perpetuate product monopolies," 611 F.2d at 300. On the other hand, where, as here, the potential market is nationwide, and where the name is used only by a small number of scattered consumers, appropriation of the name as the trademark of one who produces for that potential market does not restrain competition to a significant degree.

We agree with the trial judge's conclusion that "Monopoly" had not become generic before Parker Brothers registered it as a trademark.

Has "Monopoly" Become Generic Since It Was Registered?

This question is discussed, and the trial court's findings of fact appear in *Monopoly II*, 515 F.Supp. at 452–455. Under the heading "FINDINGS OF FACT," the following appears:

1. The court again finds as fact each fact found in this Opinion as set forth in the foregoing.

2. As a game trademark, MONOPOLY primarily denotes its producer, Parker Brothers, and primarily denoted its producer when registered. *Id.* at 455.

We now consider whether finding 2 of the district court is clearly erroneous. We conclude that it is. As we have seen, the district court relied in part upon the fact that General Mills and its predecessor have spent time, energy, and money in promoting and policing use of the term "Monopoly." That fact, however, is not of itself sufficient to create legally protectable rights. It is not, of itself, enough that over 55% of the public has come to associate the product, and as a consequence the name by which the product is generally known, with Parker Brothers. *Anti-Monopoly I*, 611 F.2d at 302. Even if one third of the members of the public who purchased the game did so because they liked Parker Brothers' products, that fact does not show that "Monopoly" is primarily source indicating. The very survey on which the district court placed emphasis by italicizing its result shows that two thirds of the members of the public who purchased the game wanted "Monopoly" and did not care who made it.

The real question is what did Parker Brothers and General Mills get for their money and efforts? To us, the evidence overwhelmingly shows that they very successfully promoted the game of Monopoly, but that in doing it they so successfully promoted "Monopoly" as "the name of the game," that it became generic in the sense in which we use that term in trademark law.

The principal evidence in the case was in the form of consumer surveys, and to these we now turn.

A. The Brand-name Survey

General Mills conducted a survey based upon a survey approved by a district court in the "Teflon" case, *E. I. Du Pont de Nemours & Co. v. Yoshida International, Inc.*, E.D.N.Y., 1975, 393 F.Supp. 502. In the survey conducted by General Mills, people were asked whether "Monopoly" is a "brand-name," and were told: "By brand name, I mean a name like Chevrolet, which is made by one company; by common name, I mean 'automobile,' which is made by a number of different companies." The results of this survey had no relevance to the question in this case. Under the survey definition, "Monopoly" would have to be a "brand name" because it is made by only one company. This tells us nothing at all about the primary meaning of "Monopoly" in the minds of consumers.

It is true that the witness through whom the survey was introduced testified on direct examination that as a result of it his opinion was that "Monopoly" primarily denotes source or producer. However, on cross-examination and redirect examination it became clear that this witness had done no more than reduplicate the "Teflon" survey (with appropriate substitutions and slight additions) and had no opinion on the relevance of this survey to any issue in the present case. The brand-name survey is not even some evidence to support finding 2; it is no evidence to support it.

B. The "Thermos" Survey

Anti-Monopoly's first survey was based upon that used in the "Thermos" case, *King-Seeley Thermos Co. v. Aladdin Industries, Inc.*, D.Conn., 1962, 207 F.Supp. 9, 20–21, aff'd, 2 Cir., 1963, 321 F.2d 577. In Anti-Monopoly's survey people were asked the question: "Are you familiar with business board games of the kind in which players buy, sell, mortgage and trade city streets, utilities and railroads, build houses, collect rents and win by bankrupting all other players, or not"? About 53% said they were. Those people were then asked: "If you were going to buy this kind of game, what would you ask for, that is, what would you tell the sales clerk you wanted"? About 80% said: "Monopoly." The witness through whom this survey was introduced testified that Anti-Monopoly gave his firm the questions used in the "Thermos" survey and asked it to conduct a similar one. Anti-Monopoly provided the wording of the questions in the present survey as well. The research firm was responsible for deciding how to reach a sample that would adequately represent the population of the United States. The witness gave no testimony as to the relevance of the results of the survey to the issues in the case.

[W]e think that the results of this survey are compelling evidence of a proposition that is also dictated by common sense: an overwhelming proportion of those who are familiar with the game would ask for it by the name "Monopoly."

C. The Motivation Survey

After the remand to the district court, Anti-Monopoly commissioned a further survey. This survey was based upon the following language from our opinion in *Anti-Monopoly I*: It may be that when a customer enters a game store and asks for MONOPOLY, he means: "I would like Parker Brothers' version of a real estate trading game, because I like Parker Brothers' products. Thus, I am not interested in board games made by Anti-Monopoly, or anyone other than Parker Brothers." On the other hand, the consumer may mean: "I want a 'Monopoly' game. Don't bother showing me Anti-Monopoly, or EASY MONEY, or backgammon. I am interested in playing the game of Monopoly. I don't much care who makes it."

In the first example, the consumer differentiates between MONOPOLY and other games according to source-particular criteria. In the second example, source is not a consideration. The relevant genus, or product category, varies accordingly. At the urging of Parker Brothers, the district court erred by first defining the genus, and then asking the "primary significance" question about the wrong genus-species dichotomy. The proper mode of analysis is to decide but one question: whether the primary significance of a term is to denote product, or source. In making this determination, the correct genus-species distinction, that is, the correct genericness finding, follows automatically. 611 F.2d at 305–306. The wording of the questions was provided by Dr. Anspach, Anti-Monopoly's president, and by the expert who testified at trial.

The people who said that they had purchased the [Monopoly] game within the last couple of years or would purchase it in the near future were then given a choice of two statements and were asked which best expressed their reasons. Sixty-five percent chose: "I want a 'Monopoly' game primarily because I am interested in playing 'Monopoly,' I don't much care who makes it." Thirty-two percent chose: "I would like Parker Brothers' 'Monopoly' game primarily because I like Parker Brothers' products."

We conclude that the survey does support the conclusion that the primary significance of "Monopoly" is product rather than source.

VII. Conclusion

We hold that Finding 2 is clearly erroneous because, although there is some evidence to support it, our examination of the evidence leaves us with the definite and firm conviction that a mistake has been committed. We hold that, as applied to a board game, the word "Monopoly" has become "generic," and the registration of it as a trademark is no longer valid.

Notes and Questions

1. The so-called "purchaser motivation test" used in the *Anti-Monopoly* case suggested that 65% of the tested consumers cared about the product not the manufacturer, Parker Brothers, stating: "I want a '*Monopoly*' game primarily because I am interested in playing '*Monopoly*,' I don't much care who makes it." The primary purpose of a trademark is to identify the source of the product, not the product itself. Is this a useful distinction?

2. Following the decision in the *Anti-Monopoly* case, Congress amended the Lanham Act. The Senate's report on the amendment describing the Ninth Circuit's "purchaser motivation test" was unkind to say the least; the report called it: "unprecedented, irrelevant, and contrary to established law and principles for determining whether a valid trademark exists." Senate Report No. 98-62, at 5 (1984), as reprinted in 1984 U.S.C.C.A.N. 5718, 5722 (98th Cong. 1984). Commentators basically agreed with the report's harsh characterization. *See, e.g.*, George Dwight II, *Monopoly, Anti-Monopoly: The Loss of Trademark Monopolies*, 8 Colum.–VLA Art & the L. 95 (1983); Lester L. Hewitt & Paul E. Krieger, *Anti-Monopoly — An Autopsy for Trademarks*, 11 APLA Q.J. 151 (1983). The Senate report explained that "the Ninth Circuit failed to recognize that a trademark does not automatically become a generic designation simply because the product on which it is used is a unique product." A trademark can identify both product and source at the same time. "The salient question," said the report, "is the primary significance of the term to the consumer. If the term indicates a product of a single producer to the consumer, it is a valid trademark."

3. As suggested by the *Anti-Monopoly* case, there is always danger in selecting a simple, correctly spelled noun (that is not a proper noun or name) for a product. Notice however, that even with respect to common terms such as "Monopoly," the words are not merely thrown into the public domain for all to use. On the contrary, the courts, in conjunction with the Lanham Act, will always be concerned about confusion in minds of the public, and as suggested by *Anti-Monopoly*, injunctions remain available to prevent such confusion.

4. Use is a critical factor in maintaining a trademark. "Use it or lose it," is a common industry statement. In *Stern Elec., Inc. v. Kaufman*, 669 F.2d 852 (2d Cir. 1982) (described in § 5.31, *supra*), an appeal from the grant of a preliminary injunction (enjoining defendants from infringing the copyright of the work entitled "Scramble" and from using the trademark "SCRAMBLE" in connection with electronic videogames) was rejected. The court found in favor of Stern, denying the appeal by the defendant (Omni), stating: "Stern has a substantial investment in the mark, having achieved success in the marketplace with its sales of a large number of units bearing the mark. By contrast, Omni has placed the mark on the headboard of five units of games that are not 'Scramble' and has used the mark for a 'Scramble' game that is a pirated 'knock-off' of Stern's game."

5. Based on the preceding notes, how would you reconcile *Anti-Monopoly* with *Stern*?

6. A Pandora's box full of game developers and trademark infringement claims was opened over attempts to capitalize on the popularity of the board game "*Civilization*." *See*

Micropose, Inc. v. Activision, Inc., 97-CV-08302-ER (C.D. Cal 1997) and *Micropose, Inc. v. Activision, Inc.*, 98-CV-00493-ER (C.D. Cal. 1998). The problems began back in the early 1990s when Micropose released "*Sid Meier's Civilization*," a strategy videogame based in part on the popular *Civilization* board game. In 1995, Avalon Hill Game Company released its own *Civilization* based videogame. In 1997 Avalon issued a license to Activision, resulting in the manufacture and release (two years later) of "*Civilization — Call To Power.*" In November, 1997, the first suit mentioned above was filed claiming causes of action for trademark infringement, trademark dilution, false designation of origin, false advertising, unfair competition, and deceptive trade practices. Next, Micropose purchased the company that owned the board game *Civilization*. Then, Micropose commenced the second lawsuit against Avalon. Both lawsuits were thereafter settled. Interestingly, Hasbro Toy Company ended up purchasing both Avalon and Micropose.

7. In *Kinbook, LLC v. Microsoft Corporation*, 866 F. Supp. 2d 453 (E.D. Pa., 2012), the court examined and analyzed the strength (both conceptual and commercial) of the trademarks "Kinbox" and "Munchkinbox," owned and used by the plaintiff on software applications designed for the online sharing of photographs. Plaintiff had filed an infringement suit against Microsoft, the owner of the trademark "Kinect," used on videogaming sensor products, and "KIN," a trademark used in mobile telephones, alleging unfair competition and reverse trademark infringement. (Reverse trademark infringement occurs when a large company infringes upon the mark of a small entity that used its mark first.) In granting Microsoft's motion for summary judgment, the court noted: "Kinbook has failed to provide any evidence that its Kinbox and Munchkinbox marks have any sort of marketplace recognition. Kinbook admits that its mark is not well-known by consumers. Indeed, Kinbox has, at most, only 16,752 active monthly users out of over 750 million regular Facebook users. Additionally, Kinbook acknowledges that it has not dedicated any significant time, money, or effort to advertise, promote, or market its marks or services. In fact, Kinbook admits that it affirmatively scaled down its advertising and marketing activities from aspirations of $250,000 to just a few thousand dollars following Microsoft's release of Kinect."

8. Theoretically, determining a mark's conceptual strength is relatively simple as compared to establishing its commercial muscle. Secondary meaning can likewise be problematical since, like commercial strength, it also depends upon what happens to be transpiring in the minds of the consumers. To read those minds, courts have held that consumer surveys were the most direct and persuasive evidence. In addition, consider *Gamermodz, LLC v. Mikhail Golubev*, 2011 U.S. Dist. Lexis 116608 (M.D., Fla., 2011). Plaintiff, owner of service mark "GAMERMODZ," used in conjunction with videogame controllers, claimed that defendants' similar use of "GamingModz" and "RapidModz" infringed. In determining that GAMERMODZ was descriptive, but had nevertheless achieved secondary meaning, the court noted that: "In the absence of consumer survey evidence, four other factors are considered in determining whether a particular mark has acquired a secondary meaning: (1) the length and manner of its use; (2) the nature and extent of advertising and promotion; (3) the efforts made by the plaintiff to promote a conscious connection in the public's mind between the name and the plaintiff's business: and (4) the extent to which the public actually identifies the name with the plaintiff. Additionally, instances of customer confusion, and intentional copying of the mark by the defendant, are relevant to a determination of secondary."

A more widely recognized authority for determining secondary meaning was presented by the Second Circuit in *Centaur Comms., LTD. v. ASM Communications, Inc.*, 830 F.2d 1217 (2nd Cir., 1989) and more recently cited in *Gameologist Group, LLC v. Scientific Games Corp., Inc.*, 2011 U.S. Dist. Lexis 123150, (S.D. N.Y., 2011). *Centaur* said to consider these factors:

(1) Advertising and promotional expenses;

(2) Consumer studies linking the mark to the source;

(3) Unsolicited media coverage of the product;

(4) Sales success;

(5) Attempts to plagiarize the mark; and

(6) Length and exclusivity of the mark's use.

---

§ 8.30 Game Elements

The most common underlying predicate for a lawsuit alleging trademark infringement is "likelihood of confusion" in the so-called *minds of the consumer or the public*. This "likelihood" is the "keystone of infringement," under both state and federal law. 4 J. Thomas McCarthy, McCarthy on Trademarks and Unfair Competition § 23:1 (4th ed. 2007). *See also* James Love Hopkins, Hopkins on Trademarks 262–63 (2d ed. 1905).

Confusion about the source of a product or service compromises the ability of the merchant to communicate information about his or her product, which in turn raises the costs to consumers with respect to the identification of that product or service. *See* William M. Landes & Richard A. Posner, The Economic Structure of Intellectual Property Law 167–68 (2003). A Nintendo, Accolade, or Atari trademark on a game, for example, conveys instant information about that product and the company that manufactured it. It is more or less presumed that such information will be considered by consumers prior to purchase.

With respect to the prevention of consumer confusion, the Lanham Act covers both registered and unregistered marks. See 15 U.S.C. §§ 1114, 1125(a)(1). Traditionally, there are several methods for testing "*a likelihood of confusion.*" One such method involves the application of an eight-factor test as enunciated in *AMF, Inc. v. Sleekcraft Boats*, 599 F.2d 341, 348–49 (9th Cir. 1979), and noted in *Bally Total Fitness Holding Corp. v. Faber*, 29 F. Supp. 2d 1161 (C.D. Cal.1998): [1] Strength of the allegedly infringed mark, [2] proximity of the goods, [3] similarity of the marks, [4] evidence of actual confusion, [5] marketing channels used, [6] type of goods and degree of care likely to be exercised by purchasers, [7] the intent of the alleged infringer in selecting the mark, and [8] the likelihood of the expansion of the product lines of both parties.

The Third Circuit prefers its own ten factor test (which is explained in the *Midway* case that follows) established in *Interpace Corp. v. Lapp, Inc.*, 721 F.2d 460, 463 (3d Cir. 1983). Other circuits likewise have their own methods for determining confusion. Unfortunately, the variety of methods for determining "confusion" can themselves be confusing. *See, e.g., Squirt Co. v. Seven-Up Co.*, 628 F.2d 1086, 1091 (8th Cir. 1990); and *Polaroid Corp. v. Polarad Elec. Corp.*, 287 F.2d 492, 495 (2d Cir. 1961). Courts generally consider the likelihood of confusion to be a question of fact. 4 J. Thomas McCarthy, McCarthy on Trademarks and Unfair Competition § 23:73 (4th ed. 2007) (federal courts), § 23:75 (state courts). According to Judge Easterbrook of the Court of Appeals for the Seventh Circuit: "the question of likelihood of confusion is all fact and no law." *Scandia Down Corp. v. Euroquilt, Inc.* 772 F.2d 1423 (7th Cir. 1985). The Federal Circuit, however, considers "confusion" to be a question of law. *China Healthways Inst., Inc. v. Wang*, 491 F.3d 1337, 1339 (Fed. Cir. 2007). Confused?

While the precise standards and tests are different in different courts. the general process and kinds of elements examined for determining confusion are pretty much the same everywhere, as the following cases demonstrate.

* * *

Midway Mfg. Co. v. Bandai-Inc.
United States District Court, District New Jersey, 1982
546 F. Supp. 125

MEANOR, District Judge.

Technological advances and the incessant quest for new forms of leisure time amusement converge in the instant case to thrust this Court into the center of the current video game mania gripping the United States. Specifically, this case involves two of the most popular video games of all time, Pac-Man and Galaxian. Plaintiffs, Midway Manufacturing (Midway) and Coleco Industries (Coleco), manufacture and sell, respectively, the full-size arcade and two of the authorized handheld miniaturized versions of these games. They are suing Bandai Industries (Bandai), a New Jersey corporation importing two other handheld games named Galaxian and Packri Monster. These games are manufactured and exported from Japan respectively by defendants Bandai Company, Ltd. (BL) and Bandai Overseas Corp., (BO). Both of these Japanese corporations are related to Bandai.[1] Plaintiffs allege that the Bandai handheld games violate the copyright and trademark laws of the United States, as well as the unfair competition laws of New Jersey and California. Midway in particular charges that the audiovisual displays of the Bandai games infringe its copyright in the audiovisual works of its own arcade games while the names of the Bandai games infringe Midway's trademarks in the names of its arcade machines. Coleco as a licensee of these copyrights and trademarks joins in Midway's allegations of infringements of same. Presently before the court are Midway's motions for summary judgment that:

Bandai's Galaxian game infringes Midway's trademark "Galaxian";

Bandai's Packri Monster game infringes Midway's trademark "Pac-Man."

In the alternative, Midway requests preliminary injunctive relief on these claims.[2]

I. Background

Midway is a well-known American producer of video arcade games. Its Galaxian and Pac-Man games were created by Namco, Ltd. (Namco), a Japanese corporation. Both games were first published in Japan by Namco, Galaxian on September 17, 1979 and Pac-Man on May 22, 1980. Midway learned of both games at showings in Japan and determined that they had commercial potential in the United States. Namco and Midway accordingly entered into an agreement whereby Midway would receive all copyright and trademark rights in the two games in both the United States and the rest of the Western Hemisphere. Assignments of the copyright rights in Galaxian and Pac-Man were recorded with the

---

1. The three Bandai defendants will be referred to collectively as "Bandai" except where discussion focuses solely on one of them.

2. By order of this court entered February 1, 1982, Bandai has been preliminarily enjoined from selling its Galaxian game under the name "Galaxian" and from selling Packri Monster in packaging highlighting "Pack" and "Mon."

Copyright Office on March 6, 1980 and November 13, 1980, respectively. On the strength of these assignments, Midway was issued copyright registrations in its name for both games as audiovisual works, effective the same dates as the assignments were filed.[3]

Midway began marketing Galaxian in the beginning of 1980 and Pac-Man in early 1981. It has promoted these games at considerable expense and they have proved to be two of the most successful video games ever. Although Midway ceased marketing its Galaxian in July 1981, it apparently continues to sell Pac-Man.[4] Midway has actively licensed rights to its two games. As part of a consent judgment, Midway granted Entex Ltd. a limited license, since expired, to produce handheld Pac-Man and Galaxian games. A similar license as to a Galaxian-type game was granted Epoch, originally a defendant here but since dismissed. Tomy Corporation also has a license to produce its own handheld Pac-Man electronic game. This license expires on December 1, 1983 and was part of a quit claim assignment by Tomy to Midway of any rights it might have claimed in the mark Pac-Man as well as in Tomy's mechanical game of the same name. Midway also licensed back Namco, its original assignor of the copyright rights, the rights to the home video versions of the games. Namco has since sublicensed Atari to manufacture such units. Finally, Midway has licensed its co-plaintiff in this suit, Coleco, to produce handheld versions of both Galaxian and Pac-Man bearing those marks. This "semi-exclusive" license is of an indefinite duration and commenced on February 1, 1982. Coleco has been soliciting orders for its games at least since January 1982. Its Pac-Man game was available for retail sale then and its Galaxian game apparently was so available the following month; in any event, both are now being sold to the public. Coleco has expended large sums in advertising and marketing its handheld games.

Bandai's Packri Monster Game was designed for it by another Japanese company named Kaken. Work on the game apparently began in October 1980; it was first produced for distribution in April or May 1981. BL created its Galaxian game in Japan apparently during early 1980. BL sells these games to BO; BO sells them, in Japan, to Bandai which, in turn, actually imports them into the United States. Bandai has been selling Galaxian units in the United States since late 1980 and Packri Monster Games since July 1981.

Midway's Arcade games cost several thousand dollars and are sold primarily to arcades, bars, and similar establishments. Bandai's games sell for approximately $30–$50 and are retailed to the general public mainly through toy stores.

Trademark Claims

A. Galaxian: Midway seeks summary judgment on its trademark infringement claim under 15 U.S.C. § 1125(a) (1982). In support of this motion, plaintiff relies essentially upon the distinctiveness of its mark, the identical nature of the two marks, and the evidence it has adduced of defendants' intent to benefit from the good will and popularity of Midway's Galaxian. Plaintiff contends that these elements are sufficient to demonstrate likelihood of confusion and thus warrant summary judgment. Defendants oppose summary judgment primarily by adverting to the ten factors going to likelihood of confusion set forth in *Scott Paper Co. v. Scott's Liquid Gold, Inc.*, 589 F.2d 1225, 1229 (3d Cir. 1978) and

---

3. Midway has not registered either Pac-Man or Galaxian as its trademark. It claims ownership of both marks by virtue of its prior and continuous use of them in the United States.

4. Indeed, it has recently introduced a new version called Ms. Pac-Man, whose success is reportedly outstripping even that of the original Pac-Man.

alleging that Midway has not satisfied each. They also note that in adapting the mark "Galaxian," they did not copy the exact design of plaintiff's mark.

Plaintiff is entitled to summary judgment on this trademark issue. "Galaxian" is clearly a distinctive mark as it is an arbitrary or fanciful name not descriptive of the product. It is therefore entitled to broad protection. 3 Callmann, Unfair Competition, Trademarks, and Monopolies, s 70.1 (1969). As such, no proof of secondary meaning is required. Plaintiff need only show that defendants' mark is likely to cause confusion in order to prevail. *Scott*, 589 F.2d at 1228. The factors in the Third Circuit going to the likelihood of confusion are:

> (1) the degree of similarity between the owner's mark and the alleged infringing mark; (2) the strength of owner's mark; (3) the price of the goods and other factors indicative of the care and attention expected of consumers when making a purchase; (4) the length of time the defendant has used the mark without evidence of actual confusion arising; (5) the intent of the defendant in adopting the mark; (6) the evidence of actual confusion; (7) whether the goods, though not competing, are marketed through the same channels of trade and advertised through the same media; (8) the extent to which the targets of the parties' sales efforts are the same; (9) the relationship of the goods in the minds of the public because of the similarity of function; (10) other facts suggesting that the consuming public might expect the prior owner to manufacture a product in the defendant's market.

Scott, 589 F.2d at 1229.

An examination of these factors in turn compels the conclusion that plaintiff has shown likelihood of confusion as a matter of law.

(1) similarity of marks:

The names involved are identical. The Third Circuit has noted that use of the exact trademark gives rise to a great likelihood of confusion.

(2) strength of owner's mark:

An arbitrary or fanciful mark, such as "Galaxian," is inherently a strong mark.

(3) price of goods/other factors showing consumer care in purchasing:

There is no dispute that plaintiff's machines cost about $2,000 while defendants' cost $30 to $50. There can also be no dispute that no one will buy defendants' goods thinking they are buying an arcade machine. This, however, is not relevant as will be discussed below (see (7) and (8)). On the other hand, the fact that defendants' goods are games or toys directed largely at children supports plaintiff's position by indicating that the ultimate purchasers of defendants' games are not likely to exercise a great deal of attention or care in acquiring these goods and will be more likely misled by an identity in trademark.

(4) length of time defendant has used mark without evidence of actual confusion:

It appears that defendants had ceased marketing Galaxian by early 1982 after only a year or so of sales. Thus, the absence of evidence of actual confusion is of little probative value here given the short period of availability of the goods in question.

(5) intent of the defendant in adopting the mark:

Plaintiff has introduced overwhelming evidence that defendants intended to benefit from the good will and popularity of plaintiff's Galaxian game. The evidence includes admissions by Bandai's vice-president, Gatto, that the mark was chosen to capitalize on the popularity of the Midway game. In addition, the packaging of the game itself refers to it as a portable arcade game and a replica of the most popular arcade games. Bandai has conceded in argument that it hopes its games will be bought by people "who have favorable association with the game concepts of the Galaxian … arcade game." Defendants' brief in opposition to motion for summary judgment at p. 20. There can be no reasonable doubt as to defendants' intention in adopting the mark.

(6) evidence of actual confusion:

None has been presented as to Galaxian but such evidence is not required.

(7) whether non-competing goods are sold in same channels of trade through same media:

and

(8) extent to which the targets of the parties' sales efforts are the same:

In the particular circumstances of this case, these two considerations may profitably be discussed together, as they are intimately related.

It is clear that these two products do not directly compete in the sense that sales of one will displace sales of the other. A mark may, however, be protected in a non-competing market. While true, as defendants contend, that it is ridiculous to suggest someone desiring to buy an arcade machine will be misled into buying one of defendants' products, that is not the issue here. Rather, the concern in the instant case is that purchasers of defendants' games may be confused as to the source of their origin, i.e., may believe that they are made by the same entity which manufactures the arcade game. In this connection, the purchaser of the arcade game (i.e., the arcade operator) is not the relevant party. Rather it is the user of the arcade machine—the person playing the game—whose confusion as to the source of origin of the handheld games is at issue. It is the user of the arcade machines to whom Bandai is clearly attempting to sell its Galaxian. Midway is attempting to sell its product to the arcade owners, but it hopes that it will be accepted by arcade users. Indeed, acceptance by arcade users is the single most important factor in an arcade owner's choice of a game. This fact is attested to by detailed information regarding the earning power of the most popular games which appears in trade journals. Thus, the fact that different channels of trade and advertising are employed is irrelevant since, although the purchasers of the games are different, the users are not. In this case, it is the user of the arcade machines who "leases" them in one context and "purchases" them in another—upon whom inquiry must focus. Indeed, if anything, the arcade machines provide de facto advertising for the handheld units. The different modes of video game use on the part of the same user population account for the lack of similarity in channels of trade and advertising while simultaneously rendering it irrelevant.

(9) relationship of goods in public's mind because of similarity of function:

There can be no contention that the two Galaxian games do not provide a similar leisure function and evince a similar mode of operation. Indeed, through packaging and advertising, each of the handheld units vies with the others to establish in the buyer's mind that it is the most like an arcade game. Defendants' game is no exception, proclaiming that it is a replica of the most popular arcade games.

(10) other facts suggesting that public might expect prior owner to manufacture a product in defendants' market:

In general, there has been a tremendous boom in the non-arcade video market over the past few years with various popular arcade games being translated into handheld or home video units. This constant feverish production of non-arcade embodiments of video games provides some support for an expectation on the part of the public that the producer of such a popular arcade game as Galaxian would come out with a handheld unit.

The facts underlying the discussion above are simple and before the court in the form of the games themselves and a rudimentary knowledge of the video game industry's workings, acquired from this case itself. Defendants have not and cannot challenge the factual basis of the foregoing discussion. Examination of the above considerations, and in particular the identity of the marks and Bandai's intent in adopting its mark, makes clear that on these facts, a likelihood of confusion has overwhelmingly been established as a matter of law.

B. Packri Monster: Unlike the "Galaxian" trademark, the Packri Monster mark is not identical to the Pac-Man mark. Thus, there is absent in this claim the "great likelihood of confusion" the Third Circuit attributes to use of an identical mark. In addition, defendants have raised the factual issue of abandonment of the mark on the part of Midway. Material fact issues thus preclude the grant of summary judgment for plaintiff. This denial is without prejudice to plaintiff's right to renew its motion at trial.

* * *

Morrison Ent. Group Inc. v. Nintendo of Am., Inc.

United States Court of Appeals, Ninth Circuit, 2002
56 Fed. App'x. 782

PER CURIAM.

Morrison Entertainment Group ("Morrison") appeals from the district court's grant of summary judgment to the defendants ("Nintendo"). Nintendo appeals from the district court's decision that it lacked standing to seek cancellation of the Monster in My Pocket mark. Because the facts are familiar to the parties, we recount them only as necessary to explain our decision.

I

Morrison contends that the Pokemon trademark is likely to cause "reverse confusion" with its mark, Monster in My Pocket. In other words, a consumer who sees a Monster in My Pocket product might think that the product was made by the same people who make Pokemon.

In reverse confusion cases, like forward confusion cases, in order to prevail on a trademark infringement action, a plaintiff must demonstrate a likelihood of confusion. To prevent summary judgment, a plaintiff must produce evidence sufficient to permit a reasonable trier of fact to find such a likelihood. The test for demonstrating likelihood of confusion traditionally turns on "whether a 'reasonably prudent consumer' in the marketplace is likely to be confused as to the origin of the good ... bearing one of the marks" or confused as to endorsement or approval of the product. *See Dreamwerks Prod. Group, Inc. v. SKG Studio*, 142 F.3d 1127, 1129 (9th Cir.1998); see also 15 U.S.C. § 1114 (Lanham Act § 32). In evaluating whether a consumer is likely to be confused we consider the eight non-exclusive *Sleekcraft* factors. *Dreamwerks*, 142 F.3d at 1129 (citing *AMF, Inc. v. Sleekcraft Boats*, 599 F.2d 341, 348–49 (9th Cir.1979)). Because no single factor is dispositive, we focus here only on the factors that are particularly instructive as to possible confusion between the two marks at issue.

The marks are significantly different in sight and sound. The two marks look very different when written out as text. Pokemon is a single word with seven letters and an accented "e." In contrast, Monster in My Pocket contains four separate words, two of which begin with "m."

When they appear in their logo form, as they do on all products, it is even more clear that these marks are dissimilar. Pokemon appears in yellow typeface with a blue border and bubbly cartoon-like lettering. The Monster in My Pocket logo, in contrast, is predominantly green. The lettering uses a gothic-style font with jagged edges suggestive of ghouls and goblins. The "in My Pocket" portion of the logo is on a second line and surrounded by a box.

Pokemon and Monsters in My Pocket also sound very different. Pokemon is a three syllable single word beginning with a "p." Monster in My Pocket sounds nothing like this—it has four words and six syllables total. The mark also begins with a "Ma" sound rather than a "Po" sound.

The meanings of the two marks are somewhat similar. The congruence in meanings, although not immediately apparent, stems from the fact that Pokemon is derived from the nickname for the Japanese version of the game, which is sold under the trademark Pocket Monster. In Japan, Pocket Monster is commonly shortened to "po-kay-mon." "Pocket monster" is undeniably similar, although not identical, in meaning to "monster in my pocket." (Because we decide that Pokemon does have a similar meaning to Monster in My Pocket, we do not further address the Plaintiff's argument that Pokemon is the foreign language equivalent of "Pocket Monster." *See* McCarthy on Trademarks § 23:37 (the foreign equivalents doctrine is pertinent only to the meaning aspect of the similarity of marks factor).) The similarity in meaning has less force than it might otherwise, however, as that similarity is not apparent to the casual observer, who will not know that Pokemon is short for "pocket monster." Instead, most observers are likely to simply view Pokemon as a fanciful word with no inherent meaning at all.

Further, any similarity in meaning between the two marks is not sufficient to overcome the very significant differences in the sight and sound of the mark. When the sight, sound, and meaning of the two marks are evaluated in combination, it is clear that the marks overall, and as encountered in the marketplace, are not similar.

Morrison has presented no evidence of actual confusion as to the source, affiliation, or endorsement of either its product or Nintendo's. The declarations upon which Morrison relies do not recount any specific instance of this type of actual confusion. Instead, they simply speculate that there may be some instances of future confusion. Morrison's best argument is that people who encounter Monster in My Pocket may think it is a "knock-off" of Pokemon. To the extent that such a showing would constitute trademark infringement, a question we need not decide, Morrison has failed to provide sufficient evidence of this type of confusion.

Morrison first relies on an eBay auction site for evidence that consumers think Monster in My Pocket is a knock-off of Pokemon. That site instead suggests the opposite conclusion—that Pokemon was "inspired" by the Monster in My Pocket video.

Second, Morrison points to one declaration that suggests confusion regarding whether Monster in My Pocket is a knock-off of Pokemon. This declaration of Gerry Hurst, by a promoter of Monster in My Pocket, states that he has been asked by consumers whether Morrison's product is a "knock-off." Nowhere in the declaration does Hurst suggest that consumers think Monster in My Pocket is a knock-off because of the trademarks themselves. Instead, the single specific example he points to demonstrates that one industry insider thought that Monster in My Pocket was a copy of Pokemon because of similarities between the products, not because of anything related to the trademarks. Thus, this so-called confusion evidence does not support a § 32 Lanham Act claim.

Although Morrison is not required to conduct a survey in order to demonstrate actual confusion, such surveys are often used by plaintiffs to bolster their cases. The absence of such a survey is somewhat telling here, where there is an actual confusion survey in the record conducted by Nintendo showing that children in the target age-group are unlikely to confuse the two trademarks. Morrison has the burden to establish actual confusion and has failed to do so.

Nor are any of the other *Sleekcraft* factors sufficient to support Morrison's trademark infringement claim on the current record. Evidence that the marks are used on similar or even identical product lines and in the same marketing channels and are sold to careless purchasers cannot support a finding of likelihood of confusion where the marks are objectively not similar and there is no persuasive evidence of actual confusion. *See, e.g., Miss World (UK) Ltd. v. Mrs. America Pageants*, Inc., 856 F.2d 1445, 1446–47, 1450–52 (9th Cir.1988) (deciding that there is no likelihood of confusion between Mrs. America and Miss World as names for beauty pageants, given the different appearance, sound, and meaning of the marks and the unconvincing evidence of actual confusion). We conclude that no rational trier of fact could find a likelihood of confusion on the evidence presented. We therefore affirm the district court's grant of summary judgment to Nintendo on the trademark infringement claim.

III

The final issue before us is the district court's dismissal of Nintendo's counterclaim cause of action to cancel Morrison's trademark. "A petition to cancel a registration of a mark [may] be filed by any person who believes that he is or will be damaged ... by the registration of [the] mark...." 15 U.S.C. § 1064.

In its pleadings, Nintendo's only stated basis for believing that it had been or would be damaged by Morrison's trademark was Morrison's "civil action alleging infringement of its registered trademark"—that is, this case. In other words, the cancellation counterclaim was essentially an affirmative defense to Morrison's infringement cause of action. Nintendo no longer has this interest in cancelling the trademark, because the infringement action by Morrison has failed on other grounds. Thus, Nintendo's cause of action for cancellation is moot because it no longer presents a live controversy.

Notes and Questions

1. Does it matter whether confusion is characterized as "reverse" or "forward" for purposes of determining a potential trademark violation? Perhaps before you answer the first question you will want to determine what those terms mean.

2. In addition to Bandai, *Galaxian*'s enormous popularity motivated several other companies to produce and market games with a similar name or title. In 1981, The International Trade Commission determined that as many as eight different defendants used the terms "*Galaxian*," "*Galaxy*," or "*Galaxip*" thereby infringing Midway's trademark. VAN BURNHAM, SUPERCADE: A VISUAL HISTORY OF THE VIDEO GAME AGE, 1971–1984 24 (2001).

3. Is imitation (often referred to as the most sincere form of flattery) necessarily unlawful or commercially detrimental? All great innovative products seem to draw imitations. It

is difficult to think of a great videogame that hasn't sparked other similar products. Imitators by their very nature seek to profit from the work of others, which has an inherent negative connotation. But by the same token, imitation creates competition. In *Midway*, the plaintiff "introduced overwhelming evidence that defendants intended to benefit from the good will and popularity of plaintiff's Galaxian game." Is that necessarily unlawful or actionable? According to the Seventh Circuit, imitation for purposes of competition is not a problem unless there is an intention to confuse. *See Libman Co. v. Vining Indus.*, 69 F.3d 1360, 1363 (7th Cir. 1995). *See also* Glynn S. Lunney, Jr., *Trademark Monopolies*, 48 Emory L.J. 367, 481 (1999).

4. Mythic Entertainment released an online game titled, *Dark Age of Camelot* predicated upon Norse mythology. On the heels of its popularity, Microsoft issued an announcement that it intended to produce and launch a game with similar mythological themes and would call the game *Mythica*. Assuming correctly that no one has a monopoly on games involving Norse mythology, do you nevertheless find it actionable that of all the names available to Microsoft, it selected *Mythica*? *See Mythic Ent. v. Microsoft Corp.*, 03-cv-1425 (E.D. Va. 2003).

5. Is it possible for a fictional animal to become so popular that virtually every characterization of that animal causes confusion? *See Universal City Studios, Inc. v. Nintendo, Inc.*, § 8.60, *infra*.

6. What if a videogame producer, without permission, copied into its games the source code of a console manufacturer which generated a misleading trademark logo whenever the game was booted? The result would be a trademark infringement lawsuit wherein both parties concede the element of confusion. See *Sega Enterprises Ltd. v. Accolade, Inc.*, § 6.20, *supra*.

---

§ 8.40 Game Affiliation or Access

The Lanham Act per 15 U.S.C. § 1125(a) provides in part that: "Any person who, on or in connection with any goods or services, uses in commerce any word, term, name, symbol," or "any combination thereof, or any false designation of origin," which is likely to cause confusion, or to cause mistake, or to deceive as to the affiliation, connection, or association of such person, as to the origin, sponsorship, or approval of his or her goods, "shall be liable in a civil action by any person who believes that he or she is or is likely to be damaged by such an act."

* * *

Sega Ents., Ltd. v. Sabella

United States District Court, Northern District of California, Dec. 18, 1996
No. C 93-04260 CW, 1996 WL 780560.

Wilken, District Judge.

Plaintiffs Sega Enterprises, Ltd. and Sega of America, Inc., (collectively "Sega") move for summary judgment for copyright infringement (under 17 U.S.C. §§ 101 et seq.), federal trademark infringement (under 15 U.S.C. §§ 1051 et seq.), federal unfair competition and false designation of origin (under 15 U.S.C. § 1125(a)), California trade name infringement (under California Business and Professions Code §§ 14401 et seq.) and California unfair competition (under California Business and Professions Code §§ 14210, 17200–17203) against Defendant Sharon Sabella individually and d/b/a Sharon's Data Systems, and THE SEWER LINE.

STATEMENT OF FACTS

I. Sega's Business

Sega is a major manufacturer and distributor of computer video game systems and computer video game programs which are sold under the SEGA logo, its registered trademark. (Federal Registration No. 1,566,116, issued November 14, 1989). As part of its development process, Sega takes care to ensure the quality and reliability of the video game programs and products sold under SEGA trademarks.

Sega also owns the copyright for the game programs that Sega develops, and has federal copyright registrations for several video games, including Sonic Spinball and Jurassic Park. The Sega game system consists of two major components sold by Sega, the Genesis game console base unit and software programs stored on video game cartridges which are inserted into the base unit. Each cartridge contains a single game program, and sells for between $30 and $70. The base unit contains a microcomputer which, when the unit is connected to a television, permits individuals to play the video game stored on the inserted cartridge. The cartridge format is not susceptible to breakdown or erasure. Defective Sega cartridges are replaced by Sega.

Sega's game system is designed to permit the user only to play video games contained in Sega cartridges. The system does not permit the copying of video game programs. Sega does not authorize the commercial copying or distribution of its video game programs on magnetic storage media such as floppy disks or hard disks.

II. Sabella's business

Sabella was the system operator ("sysop") of an electronic bulletin board system ("BBS") called THE SEWER LINE, and was known on THE SEWER LINE BBS by the pseudonym or handle "Dirty Scum."

A BBS, such as Sabella's THE SEWER LINE, consists of information stored on electronic storage media, such as computer memories or hard disks, which are connected to third party "users" over telephone lines by modem devices, and controlled by a computer. Users of BBSs can transfer information over the telephone lines from their own computers to the storage media on the BBS by a process known as "uploading." Uploaded information is thereby recorded or copied onto the storage media of the host bulletin board, in this case on THE SEWER LINE BBS owned by Sabella. Third party users can also retrieve or copy information from the BBS to their own computer memories by a process known as "downloading." Video game programs, such as Sega's video game programs, are one type of information which can be transferred by means of BBSs. In this way, video game programs can be distributed by a BBS.

Sabella was aware that her BBS contained a directory called "Genesis," a term Sabella knew to be associated with video games. The names of approximately 20 Sega games were present in this BBS directory as "file descriptors." A file descriptor is the text associated with a file to identify or describe the file. The word "SEGA," the exact word that is the SEGA trademark, was used in some of these file descriptors. For example, some file descriptors were:

Jurassic Park (Beta) [SEGA/16M/MGH] This works 100% on MGH

Released ver. of Jurassic Park Genesis

Sonic Spinball BETA ver.

US Final Release SonicSpin (or whatever the name was)

Dashing Desperados [SEGA/SMD/8MEG]

These files were available for download, and the BBS listed the number of times each file had been downloaded. However, Sabella has declared that she had no knowledge that games had been copied onto her BBS and that she herself had never copied nor authorized others to copy such games. She has also declared that she never used the word Sega in any of her BBS operations.

In some circumstances, Sabella charged users for having downloading privileges from her BBS. A SEWER LINE BBS message stated that the BBS had four access levels, which allowed users to download files under certain conditions. For example, an Elite+ user had no limits on the number of files downloaded per day but was requested to pay a monthly fee, while an Elite user was to maintain a five downloads to one upload ratio. Sabella admitted that she authored the information concerning user access levels.

THE SEWER LINE BBS also posted two main user rules. The first rule concerned console files, and stated:

> Now we will take files released from different groups. As some may work on one system and the other on another. We will take BETAs and DEMOs. If a [sic] OLD console file is REQUESTED and the REQUEST IS POSTED on the message base we will love to see that request U/Led or if the request is for a working console file. ANY POSTED REQUES[T] is OK for a U/L. Its ok if the file is not in English *HOWEVER POST it in the description!* OR you will not get credit for the file. (users DO NOT like paying for files they can not understand or play SO POST if it is PLAYABLE.)

The second rule stated:

> READ the message bases.... I and the co-sysop read the user log several times a day and we DO check to be sure each user reads the bases.... TAKE PART and support the BBS you call. You are giving very little to have HUNDRED's of $$$$$$$$ worth of games! I do my share won't you [sic] If not then maybe you don't need to be here? And if enough users fee[l] that way..HAY I'LL get the files ONLY for me and take the BBS down! loss to me! BUT I will save money on my phone bill so think it over ... SysOp and Staff

Jack Yang downloaded at least one of these files from Sabella's BBS on November 6, 1993, and was able to play a version of Sega's "Sonic Spinball" video game from one of the files downloaded. The disk file version of the game began with a screen showing the SEGA trademark and SEGA logo, and appeared to be substantially similar to a genuine Sega game. Sega's Sonic Spinball video game was not scheduled for release to the public until November 23, 1993. Several other game programs maintained on THE SEWER LINE BBS included "pre-release" versions of games. Sega did not authorize the copies of Sega's copyrighted video games which were on THE SEWER LINE BBS.

Sabella also owned a business named Sharon's Data Systems, which sold Multi-Game Hunter copiers ("copiers") priced from $350 to $525. The copiers can copy the video game programs from a Sega game cartridge onto other magnetic media such as hard or floppy disks.

DISCUSSION

[The court granted Sega's motion for summary judgment on the question of copyright infringement. *See* § 5.42, *supra.* — ED.]

II. Federal Trademark Infringement

Sega maintains that Sabella is liable for federal trademark infringement because her use of the Sega mark on her BBS caused a likelihood of consumer confusion. Sabella contends that she is not liable because she herself never used the mark, nor was she aware that the mark was being used on her BBS.

Under the Lanham Act, 15 U.S.C. § 1114, any person is liable for trademark infringement if that person, without the consent of the trademark registrant: (a) use[s] in commerce any reproduction, counterfeit, copy, or colorable imitation of a registered mark in connection with the sale, offering for sale, distribution, or advertising of any goods or services on or in connection with which use is likely to cause confusion, or to cause mistake, or to deceive. 15 U.S.C. § 1114.

A prima facie case for trademark infringement under the Lanham Act is established by a showing that (1) the mark is owned by or associated with a particular plaintiff, and (2) the defendant's use of the mark is likely to cause confusion or mistake among the public as to the origin of the goods. The latter element can be broken down into two requirements: (a) that use of the mark is likely to cause confusion, and (b) that the defendant used the mark.

A. Ownership

Sega owns the SEGA trademark which is the subject of Federal Trademark Registration No. 1,566,116. Sega's federal trademark registration is conclusive evidence of Sega's exclusive right to use the registered mark in commerce. 15 U.S.C. § 1115(a).

B. Likelihood of Confusion

In *AMF Inc. v. Sleekcraft Boats*, the Ninth Circuit found the following factors to be relevant to the determination of a likelihood of confusion: (1) strength of the mark; (2) proximity of the goods; (3) similarity of the marks; (4) evidence of actual confusion; (5) marketing channels used; (6) type of goods and the degree of care likely to be exercised by the purchaser; (7) the defendant's intent in selecting the mark; and (8) likelihood of expansion of product lines. *AMF Inc. v. Sleekcraft*, 599 F.2d 341, 348 (9th Cir.1979). Because each of these factors is not necessarily relevant to every case, the list of factors functions as a guide and is neither exhaustive nor conclusive.

1. Proximity of the Goods

The danger is that the public will mistakenly assume there is an association between the producers of related goods, although no such association exists. *Sleekcraft*, 599 F.2d at 350. The greater the similarity between the two products, the greater the likelihood of confusion. The games downloaded from THE SEWER LINE BBS are substantially identical to genuine Sega games. BBS users or third parties who may receive copies of Sega games from BBS users are likely to confuse the unauthorized copies downloaded and transferred from THE SEWER LINE BBS with genuine Sega video game programs.

2. Similarity of Marks

Here, there is no issue as to the similarity of the mark. The mark displayed when the games are played is identical to Sega's actual trademark. Moreover, the same word, "Sega," the only word used in the SEGA trademark, appears as part of the file descriptors for the game files appearing on Sabella's BBS.

3. Intention in adopting the mark

While a knowing adoption of a mark raises a presumption of confusion, an innocent state of mind is irrelevant on the issue of likelihood of confusion because the lack of intent to deceive does nothing to alleviate the confusion created.

Evidence suggests that Sabella intentionally adopted or allowed others to use the mark on her BBS. Sabella had the ability to police her BBS, and nonetheless allowed users to identify Sega game files with the word Sega on her BBS. She solicited users to upload playable files onto her BBS, and advertised her copiers through her BBS as well. However, Sabella has also declared that she did not know that Sega games bearing the Sega trademark were being uploaded to or downloaded from her BBS. Because there is a dispute of material fact as to this factor, the Court will not consider it in its determination of likelihood of consumer confusion.

4. Actual Confusion

While Sega has not shown any evidence of actual confusion, the Ninth Circuit has held that neither actual confusion nor intent are necessary to finding a likelihood of confusion under the Lanham Act. Similarly, Sega need not show that users of the BBS are likely to be confused. Once a product is put into commerce, the likelihood of confusion, mistake, or deception occurring at some future time is sufficient to establish liability for trademark infringement.

5. Analysis

From an examination of the factors mentioned above, the Court concludes that the use of the Sega mark on Sabella's BBS is likely to confuse customers. The word Sega, which is the only word used in the Sega mark, is displayed on Sabella's BBS to identify files containing video games that are virtually identical to Sega's games. When the game files downloaded from Sabella's BBS were played using copiers, such as those sold by Sabella, the Sega trademark appeared. Any member of the public who logged onto Sabella's BBS was likely to think that the trademark indicated that the games were sponsored by or affiliated with Sega. Additionally, any member of the public that played such a game using a copier sold by Sabella was also likely to be confused as to whether the game played with the copier was sponsored by, or affiliated with Sega.

C. Use of the Mark

Sega has not established as a matter of law that Sabella adopted, used, or even authorized the use of the Sega mark on her BBS. Sabella stated in her declaration that she did not know that Sega games were being uploaded and downloaded from her BBS, and that she never used the mark herself in any of her BBS operations.

Sega contends that Sabella's declaration is a sham, and should be disregarded. Sega points to the rules posted on her BBS, which solicit others to upload files that are "playable." However, Sega has not shown as a matter of law that Sabella authored all of these postings, nor has it shown that her declaration directly contradicts statements made at her deposition. Because of this, the Court cannot say at this time that her declaration is a sham and should be disregarded. Therefore, her denial that she used the mark or knew that users did so raises a material issue as to whether Sabella actually used, adopted, or authorized others to use the mark on her BBS.

D. Conclusion

Because a material issue of fact exists as to whether Sabella herself adopted, used, or authorized the use of the mark, Sega's motion for summary judgment with respect to direct trademark infringement is DENIED.

III. Federal Claim for False Designation of Origin

Sega claims that Sabella violated the Lanham Act, 15 U.S.C. § 1125 by using the Sega trademark and trade name to establish a false connection between the games available on Sabella's BBS and Sega. 15 U.S.C. § 1125(a) provides:

> Any person who, on or in connection with any goods or services, uses in commerce any word, term, name, symbol ... or any combination thereof, or any false designation of origin..which..is likely to cause confusion, or to cause mistake, or to deceive as to the affiliation, connection, or association of such person ... as to the origin, sponsorship, or approval of his or her goods ... shall be liable in a civil action by any person who believes that he or she is or is likely to be damaged by such an act.

To prevail on its false designation claim under the Lanham Act, Sega must establish that Sabella's use of the mark will cause a likelihood of consumer confusion. Like that used in trademark infringement, the test is whether the public is likely to be deceived or confused by the similarity of the marks. Id. For the same reasons set forth regarding Sega's trademark infringement claim, the Court finds that the use of the Sega trademark on Sabella's BBS with respect to the Sega game files is likely to be confusing and to cause damage to Sega. However, because a material issue of fact exists as to whether Sabella used or adopted the mark, summary judgment with respect to this claim is DENIED.

REMEDIES

[The court permanently enjoined Sabella from using the Sega mark and trade name on her BBS—ED.]

Notes and Questions

1. Assuming that a trademark or trade name is meant to convey information about the provider of a product or service, how might you advise Sabella about her choice of names such as "The Sewer Line" or "Dirty Scum," knowing that in our particularly litigious society, a jury might one day be inclined to take the selector of such terms at its word?

2. Notwithstanding Judge Wilken's determination that "the use of the Sega mark on Sabella's BBS is likely to confuse customers," how *likely* was it in the 1990s that any videogame purchaser would believe that Sabella a/k/a The Sewer Line a/k/a Dirty Scum was affiliated with any legitimate company?

3. The case of *Sega Ents. Ltd. v. Maphia*, 948 F. Supp. 923 (N.D. Cal. 1996), raised issues similar to *Sega Ents. Ltd. v. Sabella*. The defendant was the operator of *Maphia*, another electronic bulletin board ("BBS") consisting of electronic storage media, such as computer memories or hard disks, which were connected to telephone lines by modem devices, and are controlled by a computer. The BBS users were encouraged to download games from the BBS in order to avoid having to buy videogame cartridges from Sega. The court held:

> [T]he Court finds that there is a likelihood of consumer confusion regarding the sponsorship and origin of the game files available on the MAPHIA BBS. The exact

mark registered to Sega appears when games files downloaded from Sherman's BBS are played. These games files are identified in their file descriptor with the word Sega, the only word that is used in the Sega trademark, and are virtually identical to Sega's games.... Any member of the public that logged onto Sherman's [i.e., Defendant's] BBS was likely to think that the trademark indicated that the games were sponsored by or affiliated with Sega. Additionally, any member of the public who played such a game using a copier, such as those sold by Sherman, was also likely to be confused as to whether the game played with the copier was sponsored by, or affiliated with Sega.

Maphia, 948 F. Supp. at 938.

4. Review *Sega Ents. Ltd. v. Accolade, Inc.,* §6.20, *supra.* Recall in that case, Accolade intentionally and without permission copied a portion of Sega's code to enable its games to operate on Sega's console. Even though this use of the code caused Accolade's games to display a Sega trademark when booted, Accolade was exonerated. How can you reconcile *Sabella* and *Maphia* with *Accolade*? According to the district court in *Sega:* "Even if it were not possible to engineer around the TMSS [Sega's Trademark Security System] and prevent the false Sega Message, Accolade could have taken other steps to avoid confusion.... For example, Accolade could have followed the false Sega Message with a full disclaimer or placed a disclaimer on the game cartridges themselves." *Sega Ents. Ltd. v. Accolade, Inc.,* 785 F. Supp. 1392, 1400 (N.D. Cal. 1992). The Ninth Circuit responded to this argument in part: "When a product feature is both functional and source-identifying, the copier need only take reasonable measures to avoid consumer confusion." *Sega Ents. Ltd. v. Accolade, Inc.,* 977 F.2d 1510 (9th Cir. 1992).

How difficult would it have been for Accolade to place additional disclaimers on the screen after the Sega message or on the cartridges? How much weight would you give to the following argument: "The consumer would have no knowledge of the functionality of the TMSS and therefore, would only be further confused by a message from Accolade that appeared to contradict a simultaneous message from the same message-giver."?

5. In *Sony Comp Ent., Inc. v. Connectix Corp.,* 203 F.3d 596 (9th Cir. 2000), Sony commenced a copyright and trademark infringement action against the manufacturer of emulator software that permitted its games to be played on computers in addition to the manufacturer's console. The U.S. District Court for the Northern District of California entered a preliminary injunction enjoining the defendant from selling the emulator and from copying the game manufacturer's basic input-output system (BIOS) firmware for the development of other emulator products. Defendant appealed. The Court of Appeals reversed, holding that: (1) intermediate copying of BIOS that was necessary to access unprotected functional elements constituted fair use, and (2) the manufacturer's trademark was not tarnished by the sale of emulator. To prevail on a trademark tarnishment claim, the trademark owner must show that:

(1) its mark is famous;

(2) the defendant is making a commercial use of the mark;

(3) defendant's use began after the mark became famous; and

(4) it will suffer negative associations through defendant's use of the mark.

The court determined that the emulator ("Virtual Game Station") did not tarnish Sony's "PlayStation" trademark. The evidence did not support any finding of misattribution nor was the evidence sufficient to establish tarnishment; in fact, a review in a nationally recognized magazine stated that some games "rocked" when played on the emulator.

§ 8.50 Trade Dress

We have all come to recognize many products by their appearance and the appearance of their packaging. These features alone may be as significant as the trademark itself with respect to the identification of the product and its manufacturer. Trademark protection, therefore, is not limited to traditional word marks or symbols. As defined earlier in this chapter, a trademark includes "any word, name, symbol, or device, or any combination thereof." 15 U.S.C. § 1125.

Although trade dress is often defined broadly to include the "total image and overall appearance" of a product, *Two Pesos, Inc. v. Taco Cabana, Inc.*, 505 U.S. 763, 765 n.1 (1992), in general there are two primary categories: product packaging and product design. If a product's packaging is inherently distinctive, it may be protectable without a showing of secondary meaning. *Id.* at 776. And if a product's design is non-functional, it too might likewise be protectable as trade dress.

Because most products are meant to do something other than merely provide something to look at, product designs can never be inherently distinctive. Therefore, product designs are protectable only upon a showing of secondary meaning, such as Coca-Cola's classic curved bottle. *See, e.g., Wal-Mart Stores v. Samara Bros.*, 529 U.S. 205 (2000). Parties seeking trademark protection should be prepared to define the relevant trade dress with specificity. *Landscape Forms, Inc. v. Columbia Cascade Co.*, 113 F.3d 373, 381 (2d Cir. 1997); *see also* 1 J. Thomas McCarty, McCarthy on Trademarks and Unfair Competition § 8:3 (4th ed. 2007).

* * *

M. Kramer Mfg. Co. v. Andrews
United States Court of Appeals, Fourth Circuit, 1986
783 F.2d 421

Russell, Circuit Judge.

[Plaintiff produced a video card game called "Hi-Lo Double Up Joker Poker." The defendant copied the circuit board from one of plaintiff's machines, had an electronic engineer make minor changes, and then released a competing game. Not only were the rules, the play, etc. of defendant's game almost identical to plaintiff's Hi-Lo game, the defendant also housed it in a console that was virtually identical to the one housing plaintiff's game. The artwork was the same, the dimensions of the two consoles were identical, and defendant even included the name of the game, "Hi-Lo Double Up Joker Poker" in the exact same position as plaintiff did in the console housing plaintiff's game.

Plaintiff brought suit based on a number of theories, but only the court's discussion of the trade dress cause of action is set forth below.—ED.]

Trade Dress Infringement

We now turn to the plaintiff's trade dress infringement claim. The plaintiff claims that the defendants, by copying the console in which the game is housed, the artwork on the glass panel upon which the video graphics are displayed, and the name "Hi-Lo Double

Up Joker Poker," violated section 43(a) of the Lanham Act, 15 U.S.C. § 1125(a) (1983).[22] The district court held that because "the plaintiff ... failed to prove that the public has come to recognize its console design as indicating the games housed therein originate from or are connected with a single source[,] no 'secondary meaning,' which is a prerequisite to proof of alleged proprietary rights, has been attached to plaintiff's console." The court similarly found that Kramer Manufacturing did not prove that any secondary meaning had attached to either the name or the glasswork of the game.

Kramer Manufacturing insists that the requirement of secondary meaning is satisfied by proof of the defendant's intentional copying of the trade dress of the plaintiff's product. The defendants contend that the trial court was right on both the law and the facts: evidence of copying is not sufficient to establish secondary meaning and no facts regarding the public's identification of the game's trade dress with any particular producer were presented. We hold that evidence of intentional, direct copying establishes a prima facie case of secondary meaning sufficient to shift the burden of persuasion to the defendant on that issue, and, since the defendants have offered no credible evidence rebutting this presumption, the infringement is established.[24] Section 43(a), although enacted as part of the trademark protection act, does not apply exclusively to infringement of registered trademarks. Rather, the statute protects against certain deceptive practices whether or not a trademark is involved. To enjoin a competitor's use of a particular trade dress,[25] a plaintiff must show two things: that his own trade dress has acquired a secondary meaning and that there is a likelihood that the defendant's use of that trade dress will confuse the public. If a particular product's trade dress has acquired a secondary meaning, then the consuming public associates that product with a certain producer, and, most importantly, is likely to make that same association when the trade dress is used on another producer's

---

22. That section provides as follows:

> Any person who shall affix, apply, or annex, or use in connection with any goods or services, or any container or containers for goods, a false designation of origin, or any false description or representation, including words or other symbols tending falsely to describe or represent the same, and shall cause such goods or services to enter into commerce, and any persons who shall with knowledge of the falsity of such designation of origin or description or representation cause or procure the same to be transported or used in commerce ... shall be liable to a civil action ... by any person who believes that he is or is likely to be damaged by the use of any such false description or representation.

24. Kramer Manufacturing also would have us hold that intentional copying establishes the second prong under section 43(a), likelihood of confusion. Because the district court did not address whether a likelihood of confusion between the defendants' and the plaintiff's games existed due to their similarity, and because the parties have not fully briefed or argued the issue, we do not decide such issue. We note, however, that the leading commentator on the subject states that the courts almost unanimously presume a likelihood of confusion based upon a showing that the defendant intentionally copied the plaintiff's trademark or trade dress. 2 J. McCarthy, *Trademarks and Unfair Competition* §§ 23:34–:35 (2d ed. 1984). *See also Warner Bros., Inc. v. Am. Broadcasting Cos.*, 720 F.2d 231, 246–47 (2d Cir. 1983) (evidence of intentional copying raises a presumption of likelihood of confusion, but may not in all cases survive a directed verdict); *Brooks Shoe Mfg. Co. v. Suave Shoe Corp.*, 716 F.2d 854, 859 n.13 (11th Cir. 1983) (intentional copying is "evidence, but not conclusive" on issue of likelihood of confusion); *Processed Plastic Co. v. Warner Commc'n, Inc.*, 675 F.2d 852, 857 (7th Cir. 1982) (intentional copying establishes presumption of intent "to create a confusing similarity of appearance and to have succeeded at doing so").

25. Unlike trademark infringement, which focuses on one aspect of a product's "image," i.e., the trademark, trade dress infringement focuses on "the total image of plaintiff's product, package and advertising and compare[s] this with the defendant's image." The underlying purpose of section 43(a) is to protect both consumers and competitors from a wide variety of misrepresentations of products and service, implicating "a broad spectrum of marks, symbols, design elements and characters." *Warner Bros. v. Gay Toys, Inc.*, 658 F.2d 76, 78 (2d Cir. 1981).

product. The public need not be able to identify the name of the manufacturer that produces the product; it is enough if the public perceives that the product emanates from a single source.

The issue with which we are faced is the effect of a showing that the defendant deliberately copied the plaintiff's trade dress. The district court found that the glass frontpiece for the Kramer Manufacturing game was sent to a silk-screener by Andrews or someone at Drews Distributing and was used to create the glass frontpiece for their game. Andrews testified that when he first saw the design for the frontpiece even he was concerned about their similarity. The only difference between the two games is a change in the color of the lettering "Hi-Lo Double Up Joker Poker." The bottom half of the letters on the [defendant's] model are silkscreened blue while the letters on the Kramer game are silkscreened either red or a combination of red and blue. Other than slight differences in color and shadings, which result from slight changes in the silkscreening process, the two glass frontpieces are identical. It is clear beyond doubt that Drews Distributing copied Kramer's frontpiece. There is testimony, too, that the Kramer console was sent by someone at Drews Distributing to a cabinetmaker who duplicated it for Drews Distributing's use.

Some courts have held that evidence of "palming off," or an intentional effort to induce retailers to substitute his product for other products requested by consumers, is presumptive proof of secondary meaning. For trademark infringement, the courts have held that evidence of deliberate copying establishes a prima facie case of secondary meaning, subject to rebuttal by the defendant, with the defendant bearing the ultimate burden of proof once deliberate copying is proven. The rationale for this presumption is that when a defendant copies the trademark of a competitor, it is likely that he intended to appropriate some commercial advantage or benefit that his competitor derived from the use of the mark.

The Second Circuit has held that, under New York law, proof of secondary meaning is not required if the defendant deliberately copied the plaintiff's trade dress. *Harlequin Enterprises Ltd. v. Gulf & Western Corp.*, 644 F.2d 946, 950 (2d Cir. 1981). The rationale for this rule for trade dress is, in addition to the above rationale, that because the possible packaging and trade dress alternatives available are many, monopolization is not a concern in this area. As the secondary meaning rule was designed to limit the extent a producer could monopolize a particular mark, it is therefore inapplicable. *Perfect Fit Industries, Inc. v. Acme Quilting Co.*, 618 F.2d 950, 953 (2d Cir. 1980). If the plaintiff shows that the defendant intentionally copied the plaintiff's trade dress, then the burden is upon the defendant to prove a lack of secondary meaning. This burden the defendants have not borne. Judgment must issue in favor of the plaintiff on this issue.

Notes and Questions

1. The Fourth Circuit classified the title of the game, "*Hi-Lo Double Up Joker Poker*," as part of the game's trade dress rather than as a trademark. What was the significance of this classification? Would Kramer's trademark rights in the name of the game alone have been sufficient to establish the defendant's game as infringing?

2. At the time that *Kramer* was decided, the Supreme Court had yet to make its ruling in *Two Pesos Two Pesos, Inc. v. Taco Cabana Inc.*, 505 U.S. 763 (1992). Apparently, the Fourth Circuit, at the time of *Kramer*, viewed all trade dress as protectable only upon a showing of secondary meaning; the court was, however, willing to presume the existence of secondary meaning because the defendants intentionally copied Kramer's trade dress.

Does this rationale make any sense? According to the Fifth Circuit, "Although copyists undoubtedly incur the enmity of the product's creator, they serve the public interest by promoting competition and price reductions." *Roho, Inc. v. Marquis*, 902 F.2d 356, 360 (5th Cir. 1990). Does that logic make sense? Copying the functionality of a product clearly promotes competition; basically, imitation is the hallmark of a successful product. But can the same be said about trade dress?

3. The Sixth Circuit employs a seven-factor test to determine whether or not secondary meaning exists in a trade dress: "(1) Direct consumer testimony, (2) Consumer surveys, (3) Exclusivity, length, and manner of use, (4) Amount and manner of advertising, (5) Amount of sales and number of customers, (6) Established place in the market, and (7) Proof of intentional copying." *GMC v. Lanard Toys, Inc.*, 468 F.3d 405, 418 (6th Cir. 2007). *See also Echo Travel, Inc. v. Travel Assoc., Inc.*, 870 F.2d 1264 (7th Cir. 1989) (describing the same test). For the Eleventh Circuit's four factor test, *see Conagra, Inc. v. Singleton*, 743 F.2d 1508, 1513 (11th Cir. 1984).

4. Should courts place great weight on consumer surveys in order to establish secondary meaning? The surveys are often very expensive. *See* Robert H. Thornburg, *Trademark Surveys: Development of Computer-Based Survey Methods*, 4 J. MARSHALL REV. INTELL. PROP. L. 91, 91 (2004) ("Many different types of environments exist for conducting trademark surveys, including the traditional Mall-Intercept Survey, the Telephone Survey, and perhaps the lesser-known Central Location Survey. All of these survey forms require a huge amount of manpower, with prices ranging in the hundreds of thousands of dollars."). Having a product with secondary meaning implies spending power. Is it fair to require a defendant of modest means to rebut costly survey evidence?

* * *

Incredible Technols, Inc. v. Virtual Technols, Inc.

United States Court of Appeals, Seventh Circuit, 2005
400 F.3d 1007

EVANS, Circuit Judge.

As anyone who plays it knows, golf can be a very addicting game. And when real golfers want to tee-it-up, they head for their favorite course, which might be a gem like Brown Deer in Milwaukee, a public course that nevertheless plays host to an annual PGA Tour event every July. What most golfers do not do when they want to play 18 is head for a tavern. Also, most people are quite familiar with Tiger Woods. But who knows Jeff Harlow of Florissant, Missouri? This case is about "golfers" who prefer taverns to fairways and aspire to be more like Harlow than Tiger. Our case concerns video golf.

Golden Tee,[1] made by Incredible Technologies, Inc. (IT), is an incredibly successful video golf game, one of the most successful coin-operated games of all time, beating all kinds of classic games like PAC-MAN and Space Invaders. Forty thousand Golden Tee games (in a dedicated cabinet) were sold between 1995 and August 2003. The game can be found in taverns all over America and in other countries as well. IT spends millions on advertising, and the game generates huge profits in return.

Golden Tee is played by thousands, and the Harlow chap we mentioned, according to a November article in the St. Louis Post-Dispatch, just won the 3rd Annual Golden Tee

---

1. The version we will be discussing is Golden Tee Fore!, which IT started selling in February 2000.

World Championship in Orlando, Florida. Harlow pocketed $ 15,000 for the effort (not enough though, the paper reports, for him to give up his day job as a baker at a bagel factory). With money galore tied into the Golden Tee game, the people at IT, understandably, were not happy when PGA Tour® Golf, made by Virtual Technologies, Inc. (d/b/a Global VR), appeared on the tavern scene with a competing game. That's why we have before us IT's appeal from the denial of a preliminary injunction in its copyright/ trade dress case against Global VR.

IT has been manufacturing the Golden Tee game since 1989 and has several copyrights on various versions of the game. Involved in this appeal are copyrights on the video game imagery presented on the video display screen and the instructional guide presented on the control panel. In addition, there is a claim that the PGA game's control panel infringes the Golden Tee's trade dress.

Golden Tee employs a software program which projects images and sounds through a video screen and speakers in a kiosk-like display cabinet. The images are of players and golf courses. In front of the screen is a control panel with a "trackball" in the center, which operates the game. The "trackball" is a plastic white ball embedded on the gameboard. Approximately ¼ of the ball is visible to the player. The rest of the ball is underneath the game board.

To play the game the trackball is rolled back for the golfer-player's back swing and pushed forward to complete the swing. As in real golf, the virtual golfer must choose the club to be used and, for an accurate shot, consider things like wind and hazards (indicated on the display screen) on the course.

Aware of Golden Tee's popularity, Global VR determined to create a game that was similar enough to Golden Tee so that players of that game could switch to its new game with little difficulty. It obtained a Golden Tee game and delivered it to NuvoStudios (Nuvo), the firm hired to develop the new game. NuvoStudios was instructed to design a game that dropped into a Golden Tee box to work with its controls, which should correspond as closely as possible to Golden Tee, so that a Golden Tee player could play the new game with no appreciable learning curve.

Nuvo worked from the existing software of a computer golf game—Tiger Woods Golf— and made modifications to convert from a game, played on personal computers and operated with a mouse, to an arcade game, operated as is Golden Tee, with a trackball and buttons. Nuvo essentially copied, with some stylistic changes, the layout of buttons and instructions found on the Golden Tee control panel. Global VR terminated Nuvo's services before the work on the new game was completed, but it hired key Nuvo personnel to finish the job. The goal of making it easy for Golden Tee players to play the new game remained.

The completed new game, PGA Tour Golf, is very similar to the Golden Tee game. The size and shape of PGA Tour Golf's control panel, and the placement of its trackball and buttons, are nearly identical to those of Golden Tee. The "shot shaping" choices are depicted in a similar way and in the same sequence. Although the software on the two games is dissimilar, both allow a player to simulate a straight shot, a fade, a slice, a draw, a hook, etc. by the direction in which the trackball is rolled back and pushed forward. Although other games, such as Birdie King and Sega's Virtual Golf have used trackballs, Golden Tee claims to be the first to use both a backward and forward movement.

There are also significant differences between the two games. Golden Tee is played on make-believe courses and the player is given a generic title, like "Golfer 1." The PGA game, on the other hand, uses depictions of real courses, such as Pebble Beach and TPC at Sawgrass, and it permits a player to adopt the identity of certain professional golfers—

Colin Montgomerie and Vijay Singh, to name a few. The cabinets are somewhat different, within the realm of what is possible in arcade game cabinets, and the games use different color schemes.

IT filed this lawsuit in February 2003. Its request for a temporary restraining order was denied, and after expedited discovery, a 6-day hearing was held on its re-quest for a preliminary injunction. In denying the injunction, the district court found that Global VR had access to and copied IT's original instruction guide and the video display expressions from Golden Tee. But the court said that IT had not shown a likelihood of success on the merits of this lawsuit, in part because (1) IT's expressions on its control panel are not dictated by creativity, but rather are simple explanations of the trackball system; at best, they are entitled to protection only from virtually identical copying; (2) the video displays contain many common aspects of the game of golf; and (3) IT's trade dress is functional because something similar is essential to the use and play of the video game.

To a large degree, the layout of the controls seems to have been dictated by functional considerations. The trackball almost necessarily must be in the center of the control panel so that right- and left-handed players can use it equally well. It must not be so close to the upright video display that a player would smash her hand into the screen too forcefully after making a shot. Global VR claims that the buttons must be aligned across the center of the control panel for ease of manufacturing. We do not find an abuse of discretion in the district court's conclusions that the buttons appear to have been placed where they are for purposes of convenience and cannot be said to be expressive. We also note that on Golden Tee, the white button to the right of the trackball is labeled "backspin" and provides for just that; on the Global VR game, the corresponding button is labeled "shot type" and provides for backspin and topspin.

The trade dress claim requires little discussion. The term trade dress refers to the "appearance of a product when that appearance is used to identify the producer." *Publications Int'l, Ltd. v. Landoll, Inc.*, 164 F.3d 337, 338 (7th Cir. 1998). To prevail on a trade dress claim, IT must establish that its trade dress is nonfunctional, that it has acquired secondary meaning, and that a likelihood of confusion exists between the trade dress of the two games. *Computer Care v. Service Sys. Enters., Inc.*, 982 F.2d 1063 (7th Cir. 1992). Although IT frames the issue as involving only the control panel, both parties veer into a discussion of their cabinets. Of the cabinets, we will say only that they are somewhat similar in shape, but so are most arcade game cabinets. The shapes of the sides of the cabinets are different; the coloring is different. The sides of the Golden Tee cabinet are white, while the much less subdued PGA Tour cabinet is an intense blue. The only words or logos on the sides of the Golden Tee cabinet, set off in yellow, are "IT Incredible Technologies" in an upper corner and a circle with "G Fore T" printed inside. On the other hand, the Pro Tour cabinet has a good deal more going on. It starts with "Global VR Presents." Then there is a circle containing the words "EA Sports PGA Tour Golf." Below the circle are the words:

Real Courses

Real Golfers

Real Golf

all with the PGA Tour logo between the words. The PGA Tour logo, by the way, appears five times on each side of the cabinet.

As to the control panel, we see no error in the district court's conclusion that IT had no likelihood of success on this claim. The control panel and the trackball system are functional.

The Global VR game is emblazoned with the name EA Sports™; and PGA Tour® Golf logos. Its coloring is different and considerably bolder than that of the Golden Tee game. Golden Tee provides arrows to demonstrate its descriptions of the trackball system; Global VR does not. Global VR names the shots in its shot-shaping diagrams; Golden Tee does not.

IT argues, however, that the district court did not take into account what happens in the marketplace. IT says, "Bar and tavern patrons, often in dimly lit spaces, typically approach and play these video games while consuming alcohol; they are not consumers using high degrees of care in selecting, identifying, or differentiating the Golden Tee and PGA Tour games"! One wonders how different the control panels would have to be to avoid confusing such users. The decision of the district court denying IT's request for preliminary injunction relief is AFFIRMED.

Notes and Questions

1. Generally, trade dress protection is not available for functional features. *Traffix Devices v. Mktg. Displays*, 532 U.S. 23, 29 (2001). A party claiming infringement of unregistered trade dress has the burden of demonstrating that it is non-functional. See 15 U.S.C. §1125(a)(3). The logic behind this limitation is due to the fact that trademark protection, which does not expire after a fixed period, could then be used to acquire permanent monopolies over utilitarian product features. Protecting such features is within the province of patent law and its accompanying time limits. *See, e.g., Qualitex Co. v. Jacobson Prods. Co.*, 514 U.S. 159, 164–65 (1995). How then do we determine whether a feature is functional for trademark purposes? According to McCarthy, "It seems that there are as many definitions of what is 'functional' as there are courts." 1 J. THOMAS MCCARTHY, MCCARTHY ON TRADEMARKS AND UNFAIR COMPETITION §7:69 (4th ed. 2007). Gilson adds that functionality "has meant many things to many courts." JEROME GILSON, 1-2A GILSON ON TRADEMARKS §2A.04 (2007). In *Traffix*, the Supreme Court said:

> Discussing trademarks, we have said "'in general terms, a product feature is functional,' and cannot serve as a trademark, 'if it is essential to the use or purpose of the article or if it affects the cost or quality of the article.'" *Qualitex*, 514 U.S. at 165 (quoting *Inwood Laboratories, Inc. v. Ives Laboratories, Inc.*, 456 U.S. 844, 850, n. 10 (1982)). "Expanding upon the meaning of this phrase, we have observed that a functional feature is one the exclusive use of [which] would put competitors at a significant non-reputation-related disadvantage." The Court of Appeals in the instant case seemed to interpret this language to mean that a necessary test for functionality is "whether the particular product configuration is a competitive necessity." This was incorrect as a comprehensive definition. As explained in *Qualitex, supra*, and *Inwood, supra*, a feature is also functional when it is essential to the use or purpose of the device or when it affects the cost or quality of the device.

Traffix, 532 U.S. at 32–33 (some internal citations omitted).

Does the Court's description of functionality in the *Traffix* case help determine whether the trade dress in *Incredible Technologies* is functional?

2. In *Incredible Technologies*, should the court have given any more credence to the manner in which typical customers commonly encounter Golden Tee and PGA Tour Golf? The court seemed to lightly dismiss the issue as to how difficult it would be to avoid

confusion by referring to the "intoxicated" players of these videogames. In its reply brief, Incredible Technologies offered the following control panel comparison:

Figure 8.2 Golden Tee Control Panel

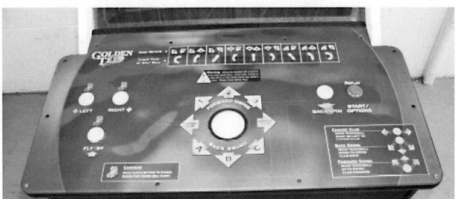

Figure 8.3 PGA Tour Control Panel

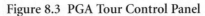

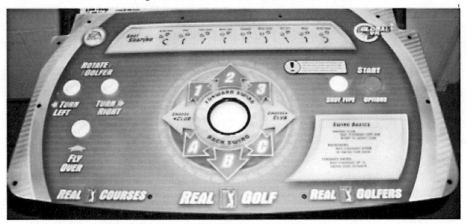

Would a view of these control panels have affected your decision?

3. In *Avalon Hill Co., v. Gebhardt*, 166 A.2d 740 (Md. 1961), the manufacturer of a game involving the Battle of Gettysburg could not acquire any exclusive property rights with respect to the name of the battle or the colors "blue and gray," which are, of course, symbolic of the Civil War. The names and colors are in the public domain. The court stated:

> We may note at the outset that the appellant does not claim here and did not claim below that it acquired or could acquire any exclusive property rights in the name of the famous Battle or in the colors blue and gray, which because of the battle uniforms of the respective sides are symbolic of the historic struggle. These are matters in the public domain. Manifestly, any game utilizing the subject matter of the Battle would be in competition with a similar game first in the field and create at least a possibility of confusion. It does not follow that the competition could be enjoined for that reason alone.

Id. at 742.

* * *

The next case, which involves one of the more controversial videogame manufacturers, presents some interesting questions about the use of a trademark as an *element* of the game itself (as trade dress) as opposed to its being used to identify the vendor of the subject game. Pay particular attention to the First Amendment issues raised by the defendant.

E.S.S. Ent. 2000 v. Rock Star Videos, Inc.

United States District Court, Central District California, 2006
444 F. Supp. 2d 1012

Morrow, District Judge.

On April 22, 2005, plaintiff E.S.S. Entertainment 2000, Inc. filed this action against defendants Rockstar Games, Inc. and Take-Two Interactive Software, Inc. Plaintiff, which does business as the Play Pen Gentlemen's Club (the "Play Pen"), operates a club in Los Angeles that provides adult-oriented entertainment. Rockstar Games, which is a wholly-owned subsidiary of Take-Two Interactive, manufactures and distributes a video game known as "Grand Theft Auto: San Andreas." Plaintiff alleges that defendants have used the Play Pen's distinctive logo and trade dress in Grand Theft Auto: San Andreas without its authorization, and created a likelihood of confusion among consumers as to whether plaintiff has endorsed, or is associated with, the video game. Plaintiff asserts four claims: (1) trade dress infringement and unfair competition under section 43(a) of the Lanham Act, 15 U.S.C. § 1125(a); (2) trademark infringement under California Business and Professions Code § 14320; (3) unfair competition under Business and Professions Code §§ 17200 et. seq.; and (4) unfair competition under California common law. Defendants have moved for summary judgment on all claims.

Background

The Play Pen is a strip club located on the eastern edge of downtown Los Angeles at 1109 S. Santa Fe Avenue. The Play Pen's "logo" consists of the words "the Play Pen" (and the lower- and upper-case letters forming those words) and the words "Totally Nude" displayed in publicly available font, with a silhouette of a nude female dancer inside the stem of the first "P."

Rockstar Games is the publisher of the Grand Theft Auto series of video games (the "Series"), including Grand Theft Auto: San Andreas ("San Andreas" or the "Game"). The Series is known for its signature brand of humor,[7] and consumers expect new games in the Series to contain the same type of irreverent humor as earlier games.

Each game in the Series is typically set in a cartoon-style city modeled after a real-world urban center such as New York and Miami. To play San Andreas, or one of the other games in the Series, players manipulate the story's protagonist and attempt to have him accomplish a series of "missions." Players must complete the missions to advance the plot and ultimately win the game. While plaintiff does not dispute that a player must complete set missions to "win," it contends that games in the Series can be played without undertaking the missions. San Andreas is similar to the rest of the Series in style, game play, and tone. By playing San Andreas, a player can experience the Game's version of

---

7. The parties dispute whether the Series' references are "parodic." (*Id.*) Whether the Series or the San Andreas game constitutes a "parody" within the meaning of *Mattel, Inc. v. Walking Mountain Productions*, 353 F.3d 792 (9th Cir.2003), and similar cases, is a legal question. Therefore, this dispute does not raise a genuine issue of material *fact*.

West Coast "gangster" culture.[14] The Game features three virtual cities, "Los Santos," "San Fierro," and "Las Venturas." These locations are based on Los Angeles, San Francisco, and Las Vegas. The "Los Santos" section of San Andreas is the Game's version of Los Angeles. Gangs control the Los Santos streets, random gunfire frequently erupts, and drug dealers and prostitutes are common. Los Santos police officers are corrupt.

San Andreas was released to the public in the PlayStation 2 format in October 2004, and in the Xbox and PC formats in June 2005. San Andreas was released to the public prior to the date of plaintiff's March 2005 California service mark registration. Millions of copies of San Andreas have been sold.

B. Los Santos

Los Santos mimics the look and feel of actual Los Angeles locations. Like Los Angeles, Los Santos is a hodgepodge of distinct areas, each with its own unique characteristics. Instead of "Hollywood," "Santa Monica," "Venice Beach," and "Compton," Los Santos contains "Vinewood," "Santa Maria," "Verona Beach," and "Ganton." The neighborhoods are populated with cartoon-style liquor stores, ammunition dealers, casinos, pawn shops, tattoo parlors, bars, and strip clubs, among other things. The brand names, business names, and other aspects of the locations have been changed to fit the overall "Los Santos" theme and the Series' irreverent tone.

The neighborhood of "East Los Santos" is the Game's version of East Los Angeles, or more specifically, the eastern edge of downtown Los Angeles. Strip clubs, taco stands, and warehouse-type architecture are found in this area of downtown Los Angeles. East Los Santos mimics the look and feel of actual Los Angeles locations. One of the businesses located in East Los Santos is a virtual, cartoon-style strip club known as the "Pig Pen."

C. Creation Of Los Santos And The Pig Pen

Cartoon-style, animated graphics give San Andreas its particular look. Thousands of virtual, cartoon-style locations are depicted in the game, and it includes a disclaimer stating that the locations depicted are fictional.

A team of artists in Scotland animated San Andreas. Some of the artists who drew Los Santos visited Los Angeles to take reference photographs for use as inspiration in creating the Game's animated neighborhoods. The artists took photographs of various Los Angeles businesses, streets, and other locations that appeared to fit the San Andreas theme. The artists who drew the Pig Pen took photographs of the Play Pen. The artists used the photographs of the Pig Pen and various other East Los Angeles locations to design aspects of the Pig Pen.

When drawing Los Santos, the artists changed the names, building designs, and overall look and feel of the locations and businesses they referenced to make them fit the virtual, cartoon-style world of San Andreas and the Series' irreverent tone.

According to Nikolas Taylor, the Lead Map Artist for the Los Santos section of San Andreas, he and other artists purposely made these alterations because they did not seek to "re-creat[e] a realistic depiction of Los Angeles; rather, [they] were creating 'Los Santos,' a fictional city that lampooned the seedy underbelly of Los Angeles and the people, businesses and places [that] comprise it."

---

14. Defendants argue that the Game "parodies" West Coast gangster culture. Plaintiff counters that the Game makes no parodic comment on "gangster" culture, but allows the user to experience it vicariously. As noted, whether the Game constitutes a "parody" is a legal question. Thus, the parties' disagreement does not create a genuine dispute of material fact.

D. Comparison Between The Pig Pen And The Play Pen

The Pig Pen building is a totally different size, color, shape, and structure than the Play Pen building. Furthermore, unlike the Play Pen, the Pig Pen does not have a stone facade, a valet stand, large plants and gold columns around the entrance, or a six foot black iron fence surrounding the parking lot. Although the Pig Pen and the Play Pen both have pole signs, the signs have different color schemes. Moreover, unlike the Play Pen's pole sign, the Pig Pen's sign has no trio of nude silhouettes above the logo, and no separate "totally nude" sign below. Pointing to these differences, defendants contend that the Pig Pen building was not modeled after the Play Pen building, but rather after another structure in the same neighborhood as the Play Pen. While plaintiff does not dispute that the Pig Pen building differs from that of the Play Pen in certain respects, it contends that the two clubs have similar awnings and logos.

The logo on the pole sign in a corner of the Play Pen parking lot is different from the logo that appears on the awning above the Play Pen door in certain respects. This is because there is no physical master or precise template for the Play Pen logo. How to draw the silhouette of the nude female dancer in the Play Pen logo is left to each artist who draws it, although the final drawing must be acceptable to the Play Pen's owners. There are several different versions of the silhouette used in the Play Pen logo. In fact, some advertisements and signs for the Play Pen do not contain the silhouettes of the nude females.

The Play Pen logo is written in a publicly available font. Defendants contend that some of the letters of the Pig Pen logo are in a different font than they are in the Play Pen logo. Plaintiff disputes this, and contends that the two logos use the same font.

E. Features Of Strip Clubs In General

Strip clubs other than the Play Pen have round awnings because awnings provide shelter from the weather. Many strip clubs also have parking lots. Many businesses are located on the southwest corner of an intersection, and placing a pole sign in the corner of a strip club parking lot closest to the intersection is not unique.

Many strip clubs display silhouettes of nude female dancers on the exterior of the building or in their logo. Displaying silhouettes of nude female dancers outside a strip club lets customers know what to expect inside the club. Many strip clubs also use the phrase "totally nude" outside the club or in their logo to tell customers that their dancers are totally nude.

Defendants' expert conducted an Internet search and found websites for at least six other strip clubs and sex-themed establishments in the United States that use the term "Play Pen" or "Playpen." The Internet also contains information about "Playpen" suites in a high-end Las Vegas hotel; each suite contains an in-room "stripper's pole." In addition, there is information on the Internet regarding a theme night at a Hollywood nightclub known as the "Playpen," which featured performances by adult film stars.

1. The Play Pen

The Play Pen has roughly 30,000 "admissions" per year; on any given day, up to 35 percent of Play Pen admissions come from repeat customers. Plaintiff markets its services in local print advertising (particularly, Spanish-language newspapers) and some small out-of-state publications, on the radio, and on a few billboards in and around the Los Angeles area, most of which do not feature the version of the logo with the nude, female silhouette.

2. The Pig Pen And The San Andreas Game

Rockstar Games has advertised San Andreas via television commercials on national networks and print advertisements in national magazines. The Pig Pen does not appear in any of San Andreas's advertising or promotional materials. Nor does it appear on the Game's exterior packaging. The Pig Pen is not visible to consumers until after they purchase the Game, insert it into a computer or other player, and actually play the Game.

The Pig Pen is just one of hundreds of locations in Los Santos section of San Andreas. A player who wishes to visit the Pig Pen may do so; there is a weapon available on the roof of the building. None of San Andreas's missions specifically directs the player to the Pig Pen, however. It is possible to play San Andreas for many hours and even to win the game without ever seeing the Pig Pen.

3. Relevant Consumer Markets

Strip club patrons exercise some degree of care in selecting which club to attend. Video game players are knowledgeable consumers.

Strip clubs and video games are not related products. The Play Pen is a public establishment, where food and refreshments are served and live nude dancers perform. Video games such as San Andreas are generally played at home, sitting in front of a screen. Although there may be an overlap in terms of customers, the Play Pen and San Andreas do not directly compete for purchasers. Plaintiff is not now and has never been in the video game business, and has no plans to enter that business. Defendants have never been in the strip club business and have no plans to enter that business.

4. Dr. Carol Scott's Survey

Defendants' expert, Dr. Carol Scott, conducted a survey of 503 San Andreas players. The players were shown a screen shot of the Pig Pen and asked what, if anything, the image called to mind. Of the 503 players surveyed, sixteen mentioned "the Play Pen," while twenty-seven said the Pig Pen was a generic strip club. Five thought that the Pig Pen was endorsed by, sponsored by, or affiliated with the Play Pen. Dr. Scott asked survey respondents whether they had been in a strip club or planned to go to a strip club. Of the consumers who answered yes, 4.4 percent thought that the Pig Pen was endorsed by, sponsored by, or affiliated with the Play Pen.

DISCUSSION

Plaintiff's First Cause Of Action For Trade Dress
Infringement And Unfair Competition

Plaintiff's first cause of action asserts a claim for trade dress infringement and unfair competition[95] under § 43(a) of the Lanham Act. Section 43(a) prohibits use of a "word, term, symbol, or device," or a "false designation of origin, false or misleading description of fact, or false or misleading representation of fact, which is likely to cause confusion, or to cause mistake, or to deceive as to the affiliation, connection, or association of such person with another person, or as to the origin, sponsorship, or approval of his or her goods, services, or commercial activities by another person." 15 U.S.C. § 1125(a).

---

95. Although the complaint is somewhat unclear, plaintiff's claim for unfair competition appears to be premised both on infringement of its trade dress and infringement of its unregistered trademark, i.e., its allegedly distinctive logo. Because the Lanham Act does not distinguish between trade dress and trademark, the court analyzes the two claims together.

"For a number of years after [Section 43(a)] was enacted, courts construed it narrowly to include only two kinds of wrongs: false advertising and the common-law tort of 'passing off' one's goods as those of another." *Kendall-Jackson Winery, Ltd. v. E. & J. Gallo Winery*, 150 F.3d 1042, 1046 (9th Cir.1998). Over time, however, "the section has been widely interpreted to create, in essence, a federal law of unfair competition." *Two Pesos*, 505 U.S. at 780 (Stevens, J. concurring); see *Kendall-Jackson*, 150 F.3d at 1046.

There are two bases for liability under section 43(a): (1) false representations concerning the origin, association, or endorsement of goods or services through the wrongful use of another's distinctive mark, name, trade dress, or other device ('false association'), and (2) false representations in advertising concerning the qualities of goods or services ('false advertising'). A trademark is a word, phrase or symbol that is used to identify a manufacturer or sponsor of a good or the provider of a service. In contrast, trade dress involves the total image of a product and 'may include features such as size, shape, color, color combinations, texture, or graphics. Infringement of an unregistered trademark constitutes unfair competition under the Lanham Act as does trade dress infringement.

1. Whether Defendants' Use Of Plaintiff's Trade Dress And Trademark Is A Nominative Fair Use

Defendants argue that they are entitled to summary judgment because their use of plaintiff's trade dress and trademark qualifies as a nominative fair use. Plaintiff contends the nominative fair use defense does not apply because San Andreas does not use the Play Pen mark or trade dress as a descriptive substitute.

a. Fair Use Defenses

There are two fair use defenses available in trade dress or trademark infringement cases—classic and nominative. A defendant's use is classic fair use where [he] has used the plaintiff's mark only to describe his own product, and not at all to describe the plaintiff's product. Stated differently, the classic fair use defense applies only to marks that possess both a primary meaning and a secondary meaning—and only when the mark is used in its primary descriptive sense rather than its secondary trademark sense.

To prevail on a classic fair use defense, a defendant must show: (1) that it has not utilized the term in dispute as a trademark or service mark; (2) that it has used the term fairly and in good faith; and (3) that it has used the term only to describe its own goods or services. [T]he classic fair use defense is not available if there is a likelihood of customer confusion as to the origin of the product. Thus, the classic fair use defense complements the eight factor likelihood of confusion test set forth in *AMF, Inc. v. Sleekcraft Boats*, 599 F.2d 341 (9th Cir.1979).

The nominative fair use defense, by contrast, applies where the defendant has used the plaintiff's mark to describe the plaintiff's product, even if the defendant's ultimate goal is to describe his own product. In other words, the goal of a nominative use is generally for the purposes of comparison, criticism [or] point of reference.

To prove nominative fair use, a defendant must satisfy three requirements: (1) the plaintiff's product or service in question must be one not readily identifiable without use of the trademark; (2) only so much of the mark or marks may be used as is reasonably necessary to identify the plaintiff's product or service; and (3) the user must do nothing that would, in conjunction with the mark, suggest sponsorship or endorsement by the trademark holder.

The nominative fair use test replaces the likelihood of customer confusion analysis set forth in *Sleekcraft*. See *Walking Mountain*, 353 F.3d at 810 n. 19 ("The nominative fair use test replaces the traditional [*Sleekcraft*] analysis"). As the Ninth Circuit explained in *Brother Records*, however, "the third requirement of the nominative fair use defense — the lack of anything that suggests sponsorship or endorsement — is merely the other side of the likelihood-of-confusion coin." *Brother Records*, 318 F.3d at 909 n. 5. "Therefore, whereas [the] plaintiff carries the burden of persuasion in a trademark infringement claim to show likelihood of confusion, the nominative fair use defense shifts to the defendant the burden of proving no likelihood of confusion." *Id.* (internal citation omitted).

b. Applicability Of The Nominative Fair Use Analysis In This Case

Defendants do not assert a classic fair use defense. They argue rather that, to the extent they used plaintiff's trade dress or trademark, it was a nominative fair use. Plaintiff disputes that the defense applies to this case.

New Kids on the Block, cited by the parties, offers helpful guidance as to when the nominative fair use defense applies. There, the Ninth Circuit explained the defense as follows:

> [I]t is often virtually impossible to refer to a particular product for purposes of comparison, criticism, point of reference, or any other such purpose without using the mark. For example, reference to a large automobile manufacturer based in Michigan would not differentiate among the Big Three; reference to a large Japanese manufacturer of home electronics would narrow the field to a dozen or more companies. Much useful social and commercial discourse would be all but impossible if speakers were under threat of an infringement lawsuit every time they made reference to a person, company or product by using its trademark....

> [W]e may generalize a class of cases where the use of the trademark does not attempt to capitalize on consumer confusion or to appropriate the cachet of one product for a different one. Such nominative use of a mark — where the only word reasonably available to describe a particular thing is pressed into service — lies outside the strictures of trademark law: Because it does not implicate the source-identification function that is the purpose of trademark, it does not constitute unfair competition; such use is fair because it does not imply sponsorship or endorsement by the trademark holder. *New Kids on the Block*, 971 F.2d at 306–08 (emphasis in original).

In *New Kids on the Block*, two national newspapers used photographs of members of the musical group New Kids on the Block, along with the group's name, to advertise reader polls regarding the group's popularity. *Id.* at 304. The Ninth Circuit held that defendants' use of the mark was nominative in nature, since the newspapers had used the New Kids trademark to refer to the New Kids themselves, albeit to advertise the newspapers' survey. *Id.* at 308. The court employed a three-pronged test to determine whether defendants were entitled to assert a nominative fair use defense. First, it determined that it was impossible to conduct a survey about the New Kids, or even to talk about the group, without using its trademarked name. See *id.* ("It is no more reasonably possible, however, to refer to the New Kids as an entity than it is to refer to the Chicago Bulls, Volkswagens, or the Boston Marathon without using the trademark. Indeed, how could someone not conversant with the proper names of the individual New Kids talk about the group at all? While plaintiff's trademark certainly deserves protection against copycats and those who falsely claim that the New Kids have endorsed or sponsored them, such protection does not extend to rendering newspaper articles, conversations, polls, and comparative advertising impossible").

Second, the court concluded that the newspapers had referenced the New Kids "only to the extent necessary to identify them as the subject of the polls; they [did] not use the

New Kids' distinctive logo or anything else that [was not] needed to make the announcements intelligible to readers." *Id.* Finally, the court held that nothing in the survey suggested sponsorship or endorsement by the New Kids. *Id.*

New Kids on the Block involved a trademark infringement claim. In *Walking Mountain*, the Ninth Circuit extended the nominative fair use defense to trade dress infringement claims. See *Walking Mountain*, 353 F.3d at 809–10 ("a defendant's use is nominative where he or she used the plaintiff's dress to describe or identify the plaintiff's product, even if the defendant's ultimate goal is to describe or identify his or her own product"). In *Walking Mountain*, the defendant, Thomas Forsythe, produced photographs of Barbie in various absurd and sexualized poses, often juxtaposed with vintage kitchen appliances; Forsythe contended that he was attempting in this manner to critique the objectification of women associated with Barbie. *See id.* at 796. The Ninth Circuit held Forsythe's use was nominative, in that his "use of the trade dress or mark [was] grounded in [his] desire to refer to the plaintiff's product as a point of reference for defendant's own work." *Id.* at 810. Stated differently, the Ninth Circuit concluded that "Forsythe used Mattel's Barbie figure and head in his works to conjure up associations of Mattel, while at the same time to identify his own work, which is a criticism and parody of Barbie." *Id.* (citation omitted).

The court also held that Forsythe's use of Barbie's trade dress satisfied each element of the nominative fair use test. First, his use of the Barbie figure and head was "reasonably necessary in order to conjure up the Barbie product in a photographic medium." *Id.* at 810 (explaining that "[i]t would have been extremely difficult for Forsythe to create a photographic parody of Barbie without actually using the doll"). Second, given the photographic medium and Forsythe's goal of depicting Barbie's social implications, his use of the Barbie torso and head was both reasonable and necessary. *Id.* at 811 (noting that "[i]t would be very difficult for him to represent and describe his photographic parodies of Barbie without using the Barbie likeness"). Finally, the court concluded that the third element was satisfied because, although Forsythe advised some galleries that one of his photographs hung in the office of Mattel's President of Production, "[t]he rest of the materials in the[ ] promotional packets sent to galleries reduce[d] the likelihood of any consumer confusion as to Mattel's endorsement of Forsythe's work." *Id.*

The evidence presented by defendants establishes that the artist(s) responsible for creating the Pig Pen did not design the virtual strip club to identify or refer specifically to the Play Pen. In his declaration, Nikolas Taylor, the Lead Map Artist for the Los Santos section of San Andreas, states that while he and other artists modeled parts of Los Santos on real places, they "purposely changed the names, building designs, and overall look and feel of the real-world places" to make the places fit the Game's cartoon-style world. Although Taylor drew inspiration for the Pig Pen from reference photographs he had taken of Los Angeles and of the Play Pen, he asserts that he "purposely twisted, altered, and distorted the look of the Playpen logo until it became a suitable logo for the Pig Pen, a cartoon-style strip club that fit with the rest of 'East Los Santos', and was consistent with San Andreas' style [and] irreverent tone." Taylor states, for instance, that he designed the exterior of the Pig Pen so that it would look different from the exterior of the Play Pen in several respects; indeed, he states he modeled the Pig Pen building on another location in the neighborhood. Taylor also changed the color of building "to fit the Pig Pen within the overall 'Los Santos' look and feel."

"Most obviously, [Taylor] used a different name" for the strip club; Taylor contends he chose the name "Pig Pen" not to make fun of the Play Pen, but so "it would be obvious to players of the Game that this was not a real East Los Angeles strip club, but rather, a parody of an East Los Angeles strip club."

In sum, defendants' own evidence demonstrates that they did not use the plaintiff's [trade dress and] mark to describe the plaintiff's product. Defendants' purpose in using plaintiff's trade dress and mark was not specifically to identify, criticize, or refer to the Play Pen, but rather to create a strip club that fit the virtual world of Los Santos, and was consistent with the theme and tone of San Andreas. Because the Pig Pen's name and appearance are not identical to the Play Pen's mark and trade dress, the general "likelihood of confusion" test can be applied, and there is no need to look to the alternative, three-part test articulated in *New Kids on the Block*.

Defendants argue that the fact ... the reference here is used to conjure the image of something broader than Plaintiff's mark does not affect the analysis because the nominative fair use defense is available "even if the defendant's ultimate goal is to describe his own product." In support, they cite *Walking Mountain*, where the Ninth Circuit held that the use of images of the torso and head of a "Barbie" doll was a nominative fair use, even though the work was intended to comment upon the social implications of Barbie, including issues of sexuality and body image.

Defendants are correct that the nominative fair use defense covers use of another's trademark or trade dress even if the goal is ultimately to describe or promote defendant's product. See *Walking Mountain*, 353 F.3d at 809 (stating that "a defendant's use of a plaintiff's mark is nominative when he or she used the plaintiff's mark to describe the plaintiff's product, even if the defendant's ultimate goal is to describe his own product"). In *Walking Mountain* and all other cases cited by defendants, however, the alleged infringer's work clearly identified or referenced plaintiff's product or service, even though defendant's ultimate goal in using the trademark or trade dress was to describe or promote his or her product.

Here, the evidence presented demonstrates that defendants' intention in creating the Play Pen was not to identify plaintiff's service, but only to describe their own product. The Game clearly reflects this intention. Based on the evidence in the record, the court concludes that defendants are not entitled to assert a nominative fair use defense. Their motion for summary judgment on this basis is therefore denied.

2. Whether Defendants' Use Of Plaintiff's Trade Dress And Trademark Is Protected Under The First Amendment

Citing *MCA Records*, 296 F.3d 894, defendants next argue that they are entitled to summary judgment because the First Amendment protects their use of plaintiff's trade dress and trademark. While plaintiff does not dispute that a First Amendment balancing test applies to this case, it argues that defendants have failed to satisfy the requirements of that test.

a. Applicability Of The First Amendment Defense In This Case

In *MCA Records*, the Ninth Circuit held that music companies' use of the "Barbie" trademark in a song parodying the doll was entitled to First Amendment protection, and thus not actionable under the Lanham Act. See *MCA Records*, 296 F.3d at 900 ("The First Amendment may offer little protection for a competitor who labels its commercial good with a confusingly similar mark, but trademark rights do not entitle the owner to quash an unauthorized use of the mark by another who is communicating ideas or expressing points of view") In so holding, the Ninth Circuit adopted the balancing test established by the Second Circuit in *Rogers v. Grimaldi*, 875 F.2d 994 (2d Cir.1989) for assessing use of a trademark in a literary title. The *Rogers* balancing test requires that courts construe the Lanham Act "to apply to artistic works only where the public interest in avoiding consumer confusion outweighs the public interest in free expression." *Walking Mountain*, 353 F.3d at 807 (quoting *Rogers*). A literary title falls outside the reach of the Lanham Act if it (1) has some artistic relevance and (2) does not explicitly mislead as to the source or content of the work. The Ninth Circuit in *MCA Records* found that the Barbie Girl song easily satisfied both requirements, and therefore did not infringe Mattel's trademark. See *id*.

Despite the fact that the alleged infringement and unfair competition do not involve the title of their work, defendants argue that the *Rogers* balancing test applies. Other courts that have considered the issue have extended the *Rogers* First Amendment balancing test to all expressive uses of a trademark or trade dress in artistic works, whether titular or not. See *Cliffs Notes, Inc. v. Bantam Doubleday Dell Publ'g Group*, 886 F.2d 490, 495 (2d Cir.1989) ("We believe that the overall balancing approach of *Rogers* and its emphasis on construing the Lanham Act 'narrowly' when First Amendment values are involved are both relevant in this case [assessing whether the appearance of a book's cover is confusing similar to the trademark elements of the cover of another work]." That is to say, in deciding the reach of the Lanham Act in any case where an expressive work is alleged to infringe a trademark, it is appropriate to weigh the public interest in free expression against the public interest in avoiding consumer confusion. And just as in *Rogers*, where we said that the expressive element of titles requires more protection than the labeling of ordinary commercial products, so here the expressive element of parodies requires more protection than the labeling of ordinary commercial products. Indeed, we have said, in the context of alleged copyright infringement, that a parody is entitled 'at least' to conjure up the original and can do more. Thus, we hold that "the *Rogers* balancing approach is generally applicable to Lanham Act claims against works of artistic expression, a category that includes parody"). *See, e.g., ETW Corp. v. Jireh Publ'g, Inc.*, 332 F.3d 915, 920, 937 (6th Cir.2003) (applying the *Rogers* test in a case where an artist used the registered mark, "Tiger Woods," in marketing materials that accompanied prints of a painting of the Masters of Augusta golf tournament, although the trademarked words did not appear on the face of the prints or in the title of painting).

Defendants' work is a highly complex video game. It features three virtual cities, each of which contains hundreds of interactive locations created by animated graphics. The Game also incorporates a narrative, and offers an array of musical soundtracks. San Andreas clearly qualifies as an "artistic work" entitled to First Amendment protection. See *Video Software Dealers Ass'n v. Schwarzenegger*, 401 F.Supp.2d 1034, 1044 (N.D.Cal.2005). See also *Interactive Digital Software Ass'n v. St. Louis County*, 329 F.3d 954, 957 (8th Cir.2003) ("The record in this case includes scripts and story boards showing the storyline, character development, and dialogue of representative video games, as well as excerpts from four video games submitted by the County. If the first amendment is versatile enough to 'shield [the] painting of Jackson Pollock, music of Arnold Schoenberg, or Jabberwocky verse of Lewis Carroll,' we see no reason why the pictures, graphic design, concept art, sounds, music, stories, and narrative present in video games are not entitled to a similar protection. The mere fact that they appear in a novel medium is of no legal consequence. Our review of the record convinces us that these 'violent' video games contain stories, imagery, 'age-old themes of literature,' and messages, 'even an "ideology," just as books and movies do.' Indeed, we find it telling that the County seeks to restrict access to these video games precisely because their content purportedly affects the thought or behavior of those who play them.") The court therefore turns to the individual elements of the *Rogers* test.

b. Whether The Pig Pen Has Artistic Relevance To The Game

To prevail on a First Amendment defense, defendants must first show that the use of plaintiff's trade dress and trademark "surpasses the minimum threshold of artistic relevance to the [work's] content." *Rogers*, 875 F.2d at 999. Plaintiff argues that defendants have not met this requirement. Specifically, plaintiff contends that while defendants may be entitled, under the First Amendment, to depict "such landmark structures as the Watts Towers and the Los Angeles Convention Center for Los Santos, and the Golden Gate Bridge and the Transmerica Pyramid for San Fiero (their virtual version of San Francisco)," defendants' use of the Play Pen trade dress and mark does not qualify for protection because the Play Pen logo and other features of its business premises have not "achieved that sort of iconic stature." Plaintiff also assert that "while the copying of the *architectural style* of the Play Pen building might be relevant to defendants' claimed purpose of achieving a realistic portrayal of the area, their copying of plaintiff's work mark, logo, and trade is not."

The content of San Andreas is undisputed. San Andreas is a video game that allows players to step into the shoes of Carl Johnson or "CJ," a former gang member, and experience the Game's version of West Coast "gangster" culture.

When creating Los Santos, defendants' artists sought to mimic the look and feel of real-life locations and businesses. They altered aspects of the actual locations, however, to fit their vision of Los Santos and the Series' signature brand of humor. For example, the Game features an ammunition store called "Ammu-Nation," located in downtown Los Santos. The advertisement for the store in the San Andreas City Guides states: "AMMU-NATION FOR ALL YOUR DAILY FIREARM NEEDS. NO RECORD NO WORRIES." The advertisement is endorsed by SAGA, the San Andreas Gun Association, whose slogan is "Say Yes to Guns."

The "ritzy Rodeo district" of Los Santos contains a retail clothing store called 'Victim.'" The store's advertisement has the word, "VICTIM," with what appears to be a pool of blood on the letters "I" and "C," and the slogan "TO DIE FOR" underneath. During one of the early missions, CJ and his brother Sweet visit the "Cluckin' Bell" drive-thru restaurant just before they become involved in a drive-by shooting and must, as the Signature Series Guide puts it, "Pursue Gang Car Before They Cap Your Homies!"

The Pig Pen has artistic relevance to defendants' twisted, irreverent image of urban Los Angeles. The undisputed evidence shows that in designing the Pig Pen, Nikolas Taylor used reference photographs of the Play Pen and other East Los Angeles locations for inspiration. Taylor made several modifications to the strip club, most obviously changing the name of the business to the "Pig Pen." In making these changes, Taylor did not specifically intend to parody the patrons of gentlemen's clubs or convey a humorous message about pigs. Rather, as his deposition and declaration demonstrate, however, Taylor sought to make the strip club fit the virtual environment of Los Santos and the irreverent tone of the Series in general. Rather than being arbitrary, defendants' decision to borrow the Play Pen trade dress and mark was closely connected to the artistic design of Los Santos and the overall theme of the Game.[142]

---

142. A "parody," in the legal sense, is a "'literary or artistic work that imitates the characteristic style of an author or a work for comic effect or ridicule.'" *Walking Mountain*, 353 F.3d at 801 (quoting Campbell, 510 U.S. at 580, 114 S.Ct. 1164). Under copyright law, "a parodist may claim fair use where he or she uses some of the 'elements of a prior author's composition to create a new one that, at least in part, comments on that author's works.'" *Id.* (same). As explained in *Walking Mountain*:

> The original work need not be the sole subject of the parody; the parody 'may loosely target an original' as long as the parody 'reasonably could be perceived as commenting on the original or criticizing it, to some degree.' That a parody is in bad taste is not relevant to whether it constitutes fair use; 'it would be a dangerous undertaking for persons trained only to the law to constitute themselves final judges of the worth of [a work].'" *Id.* (quoting *Campbell*, 510 U.S. at 580–83, 114 S.Ct. 1164 (internal citations omitted)).

Courts have applied the concept of parody to the trademark and trade dress contexts as well. See, e.g., *Cliffs Notes*, 886 F.2d at 494 ("[T]he keystone of parody is imitation. It is hard to imagine, for example, a successful parody of Time magazine that did not reproduce Time's trademarked red border. A parody must convey two simultaneous—and contradictory—messages: that it is the original, but

Plaintiff asserts that defendants cannot satisfy the first requirement of the *Rogers* test because the Play Pen is not as recognizable a landmark as the Los Angeles Convention Center or the Golden Gate Bridge, and also because defendants did not copy everything about the Play Pen, most notably, the architectural style of its building. Plaintiff cites no authority supporting its argument that these distinctions are material to the *Rogers* inquiry. If such authority exists, it would contradict *Rogers*, which makes it clear that the court's inquiry is limited to determining whether the title has some artistic relevance to the underlying work; it does not extend to assessing whether use of the trade dress or mark is absolutely necessary to the goals of the artist. See *Rogers*, 875 F.2d at 999 (literary titles do not violate the Lanham Act "unless the title has no artistic relevance to the underlying work whatsoever, or, if it has some artistic relevance, unless the title explicitly misleads as to the source or the content of the work"); *MCA Records*, 296 F.3d at 902 (same).

The court concludes that defendants' use of the Play Pen trade dress and mark satisfies this standard. Defendants' aim in creating East Los Santos was to evoke an image of East Los Angeles, but to tweak that image to fit the overall "look and feel" of San Andreas, as well as the narrative of a city overrun by gangs, drug dealers, and prostitutes.

Any visual work that seeks to offer an artistic commentary on a particular subject must use identifiable features of that subject so that the commentary will be understood and appreciated by the consumer. Furthermore, it would have been contrary to defendants' aesthetic theme to put a landmark like the Los Angeles Convention Center or the Golden Gate Bridge in the middle of East Los Santos. While it might have been possible for defendants to mimic a more famous strip club in East Los Angeles, if one exists, the Rogers test is not an "absolute necessity" or an "alternative means" test. Rogers simply requires that defendants' use of the trademark or trade dress bear some artistic relevance to the work. San Andreas satisfies this test.

c. Whether Defendants' Use Explicitly Misleads As To The Source Or Content Of The Game

The second prerequisite to assertion of a successful First Amendment defense is that the use of the mark not explicitly mislead as to the source or content of the work. *MCA Records*, 296 F.3d at 902; see also *Rogers*, 875 F.2d at 999. It is clear that defendants' use of plaintiff's trade dress and mark does not explicitly mislead consumers as to the content of the Game. Although Rockstar Games has advertised San Andreas nationally, both in print and on television, none of these advertisements features an image of the Pig Pen. The Pig Pen does not appear in any promotional literature for San Andreas, nor does it appear on the exterior packaging of the Game. Consequently, consumers are not exposed to the Pig Pen until after they purchase and play the Game. Even then, there is no guarantee that a consumer will actually see the Pig Pen. Although a player is free to visit any location in Los Santos, none of San Andreas's missions requires a player to go to the Pig Pen. It is possible to play the Game for many hours and accomplish all the set missions without ever entering or passing the Pig Pen.

As these facts show, defendants' use of the Play Pen trade dress and mark presents little, if any, chance that consumers will be misled about the content of the Game. The court also finds that the Pig Pen does not explicitly mislead consumers as to the *source* of

---

also that it is not the original and is instead a parody. To the extent that it does only the former but not the latter, it is not only a poor parody but also vulnerable under trademark law, since the customer will be confused").

The parties dispute whether the Pig Pen is a "parody" of the Play Pen, or part of a larger "parody" of Los Angeles. The court need not decide this question.

defendants' work. Although the Pig Pen incorporates certain elements of the Play Pen's logo, neither the Game nor any promotional materials for San Andreas "contain[ ][any] explicit indication that [the Play Pen's owners] endorsed the [work] or had a role in producing it." *Rogers*, 875 F.2d at 1001. While the similar font and common use of nude silhouettes might suggest an association between the Play Pen and the Game to some consumers, this is not enough to defeat First Amendment protection under Rogers. *Id.*; see also *MCA Records*, 296 F.3d at 902 ("The only indication that Mattel might be associated with the song is the use of Barbie in the title; if this were enough to satisfy this prong of the *Rogers* test, it would render *Rogers* a nullity").

Plaintiff disputes this, asserting that defendants' use of its trade dress and trademark explicitly misleads consumers about who might have endorsed the Game. It provides no evidence or argument explicating this contention, however. Rather, it relies on arguments regarding the likelihood of confusion, and in particular, on the results of Dr. Carol Scott's consumer survey. As *MCA Records* makes clear, however, when First Amendment interests are implicated, the Rogers "explicitly misleading" standard applies, not the traditional "likelihood of confusion" test.

Dr. Scott surveyed 503 San Andreas players. Each was shown a screen shot of the Pig Pen and asked what the image called to mind. Only sixteen of the 503 survey participants mentioned the Play Pen, and only five said they believed the Pig Pen was endorsed by, sponsored by, or affiliated with the Play Pen. Of the respondents who stated that they had been in a strip club or planned to go to one, only 4.4 percent thought the Pig Pen was endorsed by, sponsored by, or affiliated with the Play Pen. Dr. Scott's survey demonstrates that the Pig Pen presents a low likelihood of confusion regarding the Play Pen's sponsorship or endorsement of the Game—much lower, in fact, than the survey in *Rogers*. Rather than undercutting defendants' position, therefore, Dr. Scott's survey results support their contention that the Pig Pen does not explicitly mislead consumers into believing that Play Pen approved, or participated in making, San Andreas.

This conclusion is further supported by the fact that video games and strip clubs are not related products, and the Play Pen and San Andreas do not directly compete for purchasers. E.S.S. does not contend that it has ever been in the video game business or that it has plans to enter that business. Rockstar Games and Take-Two Interactive, on the other hand, have never been in the strip club business and have no plans to enter that business. The difference between the parties' businesses and product lines makes it improbable that a player who sees the Pig Pen, and recognizes that it was modeled after the Play Pen, will believe that the owners of the Play Pen endorsed or sponsored the Game. See *MCA Records*, 296 F.3d at 902 ("If we see a painting titled 'Campbell's Chicken Noodle Soup,' we're unlikely to believe that Campbell's has branched into the art business. Nor, upon hearing Janis Joplin croon 'Oh Lord, won't you buy me a Mercedes-Benz?,' would we suspect that she and the carmaker had entered into a joint venture.")[156]

---

156. Plaintiff also raised a slightly different argument: It asserted that defendants had misled consumers by using more of the mark and the trade dress than necessary to achieve their stated artistic purpose. Plaintiff cited no authority in support of this position, and the court is aware of none. It appears that plaintiff may have confused the First Amendment balancing test with the nominative fair use test. To prove nominative fair use, a defendant must show, *inter alia*, that it used "only so much of the mark or marks ... as was reasonably necessary to identify the plaintiff's product or service," and that it did "nothing that would, in conjunction with the mark, suggest sponsorship or endorsement by the trademark holder." *Walking Mountain*, 353 F.3d at 808 (citation omitted). The *Rogers* test, by contrast, has no requirement that the defendant use "only so much of the mark or

In sum, the court finds that defendants' use of the Play Pen trade dress and trademark (1) bears some artistic relevance to the Game, and (2) does not explicitly mislead consumers as to the source or content of the Game. Because defendants have met both requirements of the *Rogers* balancing test, they are entitled, as a matter of law, to a First Amendment defense to plaintiff's Lanham Act claims. The court therefore grants defendants' motion for summary judgment on plaintiff's first cause of action.

C. Plaintiff's Causes Of Action For State Law Trademark Infringement And Unfair Competition Claims

Plaintiff's remaining causes of action allege claims for state law trademark infringement under Business & Professions Code § 14330, and unfair competition under Business & Professions Code § 17200 and California common law. The legal framework used to analyze these claims is substantially the same as the framework used to evaluate Lanham Act claims under federal law. As the court has found, plaintiff's first cause of action fails because defendants' use of the Play Pen logo is protected under the First Amendment and falls outside the proscriptions of the Lanham Act. Plaintiff's related state law claims fail for the same reason. The court therefore grants defendants' motion for summary judgment on plaintiff's remaining causes of action as well.

* * *

Elec. Arts, Inc. v. Textron, Inc.

United States District Court, Northern District of California, 2012
103 U.S.P.Q.2d 1984

ALSUP, District Judge.

INTRODUCTION

In this declaratory relief action for non-infringement of trademarks and trade dress, plaintiff moves to dismiss defendants' Lanham Act and California state-law counterclaims

---

marks ... as is reasonably necessary" to convey an artistic idea or message. Thus, plaintiff's argument in this regard fails.

Another requirement of the nominative fair use test is that the user of the trademark or trade dress do "nothing that would, in conjunction with the mark, suggest sponsorship or endorsement by the trademark holder." *Walking Mountain*, 353 F.3d at 808 (citation omitted) Rogers, by contrast, states that an artistically relevant use of a mark falls outside the Lanham Act "unless the title explicitly misleads as to the source or the content of the work." *Rogers*, 875 F.2d at 999 (emphasis added). This standard appears to be less demanding than the comparable aspect of nominative fair use test. Compare *Walking Mountain*, 353 F.3d at 808 (the defendant must have done "nothing that would, in conjunction with the mark, suggest sponsorship or endorsement by the trademark holder" (emphasis added)). Defendants could satisfy the third requirement for nominative fair use, since no reasonable player who passed the Pig Pen and recognized that it was modeled after the Play Pen would believe that the Play Pen's owners had endorsed the virtual club. See *Walking Mountain*, 353 F.3d at 811 (stating that, in applying the nominative fair use test, "critical works are much less likely to have a perceived affiliation with the original work," citing *New Kids on the Block*, 971 F.2d at 309 (finding no suggested sponsorship in part because a poll in a magazine regarding the popularity of the New Kids asked if the New Kids had become a 'turn off')); see *id.* at 811–12 n. 21 (noting that the Ninth Circuit has "also found for the defendant on this factor even in situations where there was some amount of ambiguity," citing *Cairns*, 292 F.3d at 1154–56 (concluding that there was no suggestion of sponsorship despite an assertion by Franklin Mint in its advertisements that all proceeds would go to Diana's charities and that a Diana porcelain doll was the only authentic replica of Diana's famous gown)). Consequently, defendants clearly satisfy *Rogers'* requirement that their use of the trademark and trade dress not explicitly mislead as to source or content.

pursuant to FRCP 12(b)(6) and the First Amendment. For the following reasons, plaintiff's motion is Denied. The hearing scheduled for September 6 is Vacated.

STATEMENT

Counterclaim-defendant Electronic Arts Inc. is a developer and publisher of computer and video games. Counterclaim-plaintiffs are Textron Innovations Inc. and Bell Helicopter Textron Inc. Textron Innovations is the intellectual property holding company of Bell Helicopter, which is the designer and manufacturer of the helicopters to which counterclaim-plaintiffs claim intellectual property rights.

The instant action arises out of EA's depiction of these helicopters in its Battlefield 3 video game. Battlefield 3 "is a realistic first-person military combat simulation that depicts weapons and vehicles used by the United States military, including the Bell-manufactured AH–1Z, UH–1Y, and V–22 helicopters." Players can control weapons and vehicles, and can play in single-player and online multiplayer modes.

The parties were involved in a prior dispute over use of Bell-manufactured vehicles in the "Battlefield Vietnam, Battlefield Vietnam: Redux, and Battlefield 2" video games, which resulted in a confidential settlement agreement in February 2008. In October 2010, EA paid Textron Innovations a lump sum for a license to use certain vehicles in a "booster pack for the 'Battlefield: Bad Company 2' game, called 'Vietnam.'" Textron alleges that EA has entered into licensing arrangements with third parties in relation to other games, showing that EA's infringement of Textron's intellectual property in the instant dispute was willful.

In Fall 2011, the parties communicated regarding EA's planned use of the helicopters in Battlefield 3, but were unable to reach agreement. EA contended that the use was expressive and entitled to First Amendment protection, thus no license would be necessary. Textron believed the use—in the game, packaging, and marketing materials—infringed intellectual property rights and demanded EA cease and desist.

EA filed a complaint for declaratory relief for non-infringement in January 2012. In May 2012, Textron filed its answer and the counter-complaint, which alleges six counterclaims: (1) trademark infringement under 15 U.S.C. 1114, (2) trademark and trade dress infringement under 15 U.S.C. 1125(a), (3) false designation of origin under 15 U.S.C. 1125(a), (4) violation of California Business and Professions Code Section 17200, (5) California common law trademark infringement, and (6) California common law misappropriation.

Textron alleges infringement in the Battlefield 3 game, Back to Karkand expansion pack, advertising and marketing materials, and other Battlefield 3-related products. The alleged trademarks include federally-registered trademarks: "AH–1Z," "UH–1Y," and "V–22," and common-law trademarked product names: "VIPER," "VENOM," and "OSPREY." The alleged trade dress includes:

> (a) the design and shape of the fuselage and chin bubble on the UH–1Y; (b) the design and shape of the tandem-seat cockpit, fuselage, and wing pylons on the AH–1Z; (c) the design and shape of the fuselage, chin bubble, wings, rotatable engines, and empennage on the V–22. EA now moves to dismiss the counterclaims as barred by the First Amendment and doctrine of nominative fair use.

ANALYSIS

1. Request for Judicial Notice.

EA requests this Court take judicial notice of: (1) the content and packaging of the PC edition of Battlefield 3, (2) the content of the "Battlefield 3 Gulf of Oman Gameplay Trailer" and the "Wake Island" trailer, and (3) paragraphs 4–9 of the declaration of Patrick

Bach, summarizing the content of Battlefield 3. EA's request notes that the Bach declaration is intended as a FRE 1006 summary of voluminous evidence, and may be disregarded if the Court reviews the video game itself. Textron objects to this request on grounds that it "asks this Court to decide the ultimate factual issues in this case outside the adversarial process" and because "the full scope of the content and features of Battlefield 3 cannot be 'accurately and readily determined' by a quick review of the game."

As an initial matter, this order does not take notice of the Bach declaration to the extent it asserts conclusions and disputed facts such as: "Battlefield 3 combines computer software engineering and creative audiovisual elements" (Textron's answer denies that EA's use is "creative"); that the game "is constructed from an array of original graphics, music, soundtrack, dialogue and information;" and that the maps, weapons, accessories, and vehicles " are designed and rendered by EA artists and developers" (a fact not readily determinable by playing the game) (emphasis added). EA may ultimately be able to prove these facts and conclusions, but such questions are inappropriate to decide on a motion to dismiss. See United States v. Corinthian Colleges, 655 F.3d 984, 999 (9th Cir.2011) ("We may not, on the basis of evidence outside of the Complaint, take judicial notice of facts favorable to Defendants that could reasonably be disputed."). Moreover, this order recognizes the distinction between taking judicial notice of facts, and drawing conclusions as to the significance of those facts—which seems to be Textron's primary objection. As Textron points out, the trailers are but two examples of alleged infringement, and the complete range of experiences within the game may be impossible to determine due to its dynamic nature.

This order does not take judicial notice of the entire game. As EA alleges in the complaint, "the outcome of a mission or action depends on the game player's choices and skill. As a result, no two game experiences are alike". In particular, Textron alleges that the "multiplayer mode allows consumers to participate in one-time battles of their own design ... in groups of up to 64" and that this mode is "the most popular aspect" of the game. (emphasis added). Despite EA's argument that "although the interactive world of Battlefield 3 provides hours of unique game-play opportunities, EA's in-game uses of Textron's purported trademarks and trade dress are unchanging, easily observed, and straightforward," this order finds that the interactive nature of the game, especially in the multiplayer mode, makes it an improper subject of a request for judicial notice. Taking judicial notice of the entire game and all of its permutations would be like taking notice of a dynamic Internet site such as Google. That said, judicial notice is appropriate for facts that may be accurately and readily determined, such as the game packaging. Accordingly, EA's request for judicial notice is Granted as to the game packaging, but Denied as to the Bach declaration, video trailers, and contents of the game CD.

2. First Amendment Defense

The parties disagree over the appropriate legal standard for EA's First Amendment defense. EA urges application of the Rogers test, which weighs the "public interest in avoiding consumer confusion" against the "public interest in free expression," such that trademark infringement does not apply unless the use "has no artistic relevance to the underlying work whatsoever, or, if it has some artistic relevance, unless it explicitly misleads as to the source or the content of the work." Rogers v. Grimaldi, 875 F.2d 994, 999 (2d Cir.1989). Even assuming that Rogers applies, a proposition in dispute, EA's arguments fail under the second prong of the Rogers test.

The second prong of the Rogers test considers whether the use "explicitly misleads as to the source or content of the work," and "points directly at the purpose of trademark law, namely to 'avoid confusion in the marketplace by allowing a trademark owner to prevent others from duping consumers into buying a product they mistakenly believe is sponsored by the trademark owner.' " See ibid.; E.S.S. Ent. 2000, Inc. v. Rock Star Videos, Inc., 547 F.3d 1095, 1100 (9th Cir.2008) (quoting Mattel, Inc. v. Walking Mountain Prods, 353 F.3d 792, 806 (9th Cir.2003) (internal quotation marks and alteration omitted)). This prong is where EA fails to meet its burden.

Because this is a motion to dismiss, the Court "must take all of the factual allegations in the complaint as true," though it is "not bound to accept as true a legal conclusion couched as a factual allegation."Ashcroft v. Iqbal, 556 U.S. 662, 678, 129 S.Ct. 1937, 173 L.Ed.2d 868 (2009) (quoting Bell Atl. Corp. v. Twombly, 550 U.S. 544, 555, 127 S.Ct. 1955, 167 L.Ed.2d 929 (2007)) (internal quotation marks omitted). Textron pleads the following allegations, which collectively support an inference that Battlefield 3 and its advertising are misleading as to source or content:

The ability to interact with and fly the Bell-Manufactured Helicopters in EA's Battlefield 3 Products factors into consumer decisions over whether to purchase Battlefield 3 and related products. The AH–1Z and UH–1Y helicopters bearing Textron Trade Dress and Trademarks are given particular prominence in the game. The AH–1Z is the primary attack helicopter, while the UH–1Y is the primary transport helicopter.

On a webpage telling customers to "buy now," EA entices consumers to purchase its Battlefield 3 Products specifically by advertising the AH–1Z. On its website, EA included an image of Bell's AH–1Z helicopter and promoted use of the Bell-Manufactured Helicopter to consumers: "Fly your squad straight to the action or engage enemy targets directly from your heli."

EA's use of the Textron Trade Dress and Trademarks in the Battlefield 3 Products has created and is likely to continue to create consumer confusion as to the source, affiliation, or sponsorship of the trademarked products in the video games. Consumers of these games expect that the intellectual property of a party is used with the permission and approval of the mark's owner, particularly when a purpose of the game is to realistically simulate the use of a product associated with the mark.

EA deliberately and willfully used and continues to use the Textron Innovations Registered Marks so as to cause confusion or mistake or to deceive consumers. EA disagrees, but for purposes of the instant motion, this order does not weigh EA's evidence against Textron's. Rather, it assesses whether Textron states a plausible claim for relief.

EA contends that the "likelihood of confusion" analysis should not come into play unless the work fails the Rogers test. Our court of appeals in E.S.S., however, looked at "whether the Game would confuse its players into thinking that the Play Pen is somehow behind the Pig Pen or that it sponsors Rockstar's product" when it evaluated the second prong of the Rogers test. 547 F.3d at 1100. Our court of appeals considered that the strip club was "incidental" to the game; consumers would not "reasonably have believed that ESS produced the video game;" it was "far-fetched that someone playing the game would think ESS had provided whatever expertise, support, or unique strip-club knowledge it possesses to the game;" and "the chance to attend a virtual strip club is unambiguously not the main selling point of the Game." In contrast, here, it is plausible that consumers could think Textron provided expertise and knowledge to the game in order to create its realistic simulation of the actual workings of the Bell-manufactured helicopters. Textron alleges that its helicopters are "given particular prominence" as opposed to being merely "incidental," and the ability to control vehicles such as the helicopters in question is a major reason for the game's success; therefore, consumers could plausibly think Textron sponsored the game. Although consumers are unlikely to think Textron has entered the video-game business, Textron has alleged sufficient facts to support the inference that the game explicitly leads consumers to believe it is "somehow behind" or "sponsors" Battlefield 3.

EA also asserts that "mere use of purported trademarks or trade dress as part of an expressive work is not sufficient to demonstrate explicit misrepresentation as to the source or content of the game." While this is true, the counter-complaint alleges more than "mere use." As stated, it alleges that the helicopters were a main selling point for the game, and EA intended consumer confusion. On a motion to dismiss, this is sufficient to defeat this prong of Rogers. EA also points to the disclaimer on the packaging, "DEPICTION OF ANY WEAPON OR VEHICLE IN THIS GAME DOES NOT INDICATE AFFILIATION, SPONSORSHIP OR ENDORSEMENT BY ANY WEAPON OR VEHICLE MANUFACTURER," as showing that the use of the helicopters cannot be explicitly misleading. While this fact may support a finding that the packaging was not misleading, it is not conclusive. Plausibly, the disclaimer might not be seen by teenage users, for example, anxious to rip open the package and play in the game.

Textron's allegations are sufficient to establish plausible disputes as to the existence of actual consumer confusion and the effectiveness of the disclaimer. Accordingly, EA's motion to dismiss the counterclaims on First Amendment grounds is Denied.

3. Nominative Fair Use.

The "nominative fair use" defense encompasses "a class of cases where the use of the trademark does not attempt to capitalize on consumer confusion or to appropriate the cachet of one product for a different one." Nominative fair use occurs "where the only word reasonably available to describe a particular thing is pressed into service" and therefore, "such use is fair because it does not imply sponsorship or endorsement by the trademark holder." See New Kids on the Block v. News Am. Publ'g Inc., 971 F.2d 302, 308 (9th Cir.1992). It requires proof of the following three elements:

> First, the product or service in question must be one not readily identifiable without use of the trademark; second, only so much of the mark or marks may be used as is reasonably necessary to identify the product or service; and third, the user must do nothing that would, in conjunction with the mark, suggest sponsorship or endorsement by the trademark holder.

Nominative fair use analysis typically involves questions of law and fact, and determination on a motion to dismiss is premature. See Autodesk, Inc. v. Dassault Systemes SolidWorks Corp., C08-04397 WHA, 2008 WL 6742224 (N.D.Cal. Dec.18, 2008) (Alsup, J.). An exception exists "where simply looking at the work itself, and the context in which it appears, demonstrates how implausible it is that a viewer will be confused into believing that the plaintiff endorsed the defendant's work." Louis Vuitton Mallatier S.A. v. Warner Bros. Ent. Inc., 11 CIV. 9436 ALC HBP, 2012 WL 2248593 (S.D.N.Y. Jun.15, 2012). EA argues that nominative fair use is evident from "allegations made by Textron, or subject to judicial notice." To the contrary, this order finds the counterclaims raise factual questions that make a nominal fair use determination inappropriate at this time.

EA's motion must be denied because there are questions of disputed fact as to all three elements. First, the parties disagree as to whether the helicopters are readily identifiable without use of the trademark. Second, the parties dispute whether EA used more of the marks than necessary to identify the helicopters. Third, whether EA suggested Textron's sponsorship or endorsement of the game was discussed under the second prong of the Rogers test above, and as stated, this order finds that the pleadings raise sufficient questions as to consumer confusion.

Notably, our court of appeals has held that customary practice in certain contexts, such as television commercials, may give rise to an implied endorsement, and "likelihood of confusion as to endorsement is therefore a question for the jury." Abdul-Jabbar v. Gen. Motors Corp., 85 F.3d 407, 413 (9th Cir.1996). Textron alleges that "Consumers of these games expect that the intellectual property of a party is used with the permission and approval of the mark's owner." Textron's allegations are sufficient to defeat a nominative fair use defense at this stage; accordingly, EA's motion to dismiss is Denied.

Notes and Questions

1. Plaintiff E.S.S. Entertainment included photographs of the Play Pen in its complaint. See Figures 8.4 and 8.5.

2. Plaintiff E.S.S. appealed the adverse decision. The Court of Appeals held that while the nominative fair use defense did not apply to the defendant's use of "Pig Pen," the First

Figure 8.4 Complaint, Exhibit 1

Figure 8.5 Complaint, Exhibit 4

Amendment did. The lower court's decision was therefore affirmed. *E.S.S. Ent. 2000, Inc. v. Rock Star Videos, Inc.*, 547 F.3d 1095 (9th Cir. 2008).

3. Regardless whether the defense involves classic fair use or nominative fair use, the defendant is required to show that there is no likelihood of confusion. In *Cairns v. Franklin Mint Co.*, 292 F.3d 1139 (9th Cir. 2002), the Ninth Circuit stated: "The classic fair use defense is not available if there is a likelihood of customer confusion as to the origin of the product." *Id.* at 1151. Similarly, in *Brother Records v. Jardine*, 318 F.3d 900 (9th Cir. 2003), the Ninth Circuit said, "whereas [the] plaintiff carries the burden of persuasion in a trademark infringement claim to show likelihood of confusion, the nominative fair use defense shifts to the defendant the burden of proving no likelihood of confusion." *Id.* at 908 n.5. Does this mean that a likelihood of confusion is presumed? The Supreme Court has held that defendants do not have the burden to negate confusion. Instead, the plaintiff must show a likelihood of confusion to establish its prima facie case. *KP Permanent Make-up, Inc. v. Lasting Impression I, Inc.*, 543 U.S. 111, 114 (2004). Once the plaintiff demonstrates a likelihood of confusion, the defendant may then offer a defense to justify its confusing use of the mark. Therefore, "[s]ince the burden of proving likelihood of confusion rests with the plaintiff, and the fair use defendant has no free-standing need to show confusion unlikely, it follows (contrary to the [Ninth Circuit's] view) that some possibility of consumer confusion must be compatible with fair use, and so it is." *Id.* at 121–22.

4. In a 1970s case involving the use of trademarks for expressive works, the Second Circuit affirmed the granting of an injunction that prohibited the defendants from distributing or exhibiting the pornographic movie *Debbie Does Dallas*. The Dallas Cowboys claimed trademark protection for the Dallas Cowboys Cheerleaders' uniform and for the terms "Dallas Cowgirls" and "Texas Cowgirls." *Dallas Cowboys Cheerleaders, Inc. v. Pussycat Cinema, Ltd.*, 604 F.2d 200, 202 (2d Cir. 1979). The court stated: "In the movie's final scene Debbie dons a uniform strikingly similar to that worn by the Dallas Cowboys Cheerleaders and for approximately twelve minutes of film footage engages in various sex acts while clad or partially clad in the uniform. Defendants advertised the movie with marquee posters depicting Debbie in the allegedly infringing uniform and containing such captions as 'Starring Ex Dallas Cowgirl Cheerleader Bambi Woods' and 'You'll do more than cheer for this X Dallas Cheerleader.' " *Id.* at 203. The Second Circuit described the types of "confusion" actionable under the Lanham Act in very broad terms: "The trademark laws are designed not only to prevent consumer confusion *but also to protect the synonymous right of a trademark owner to control his product's reputation.*" *Id.* at 205 (emphasis added and internal quotation marks omitted). The court described Debbie Does Dallas as a "gross and revolting sex film," *Id.* at 202, and clearly worried about the Dallas Cowboys being associated with it. The court further noted, "it is hard to believe that anyone who had seen defendants' sexually depraved film could ever thereafter disassociate it from plaintiff's cheerleaders." *Id.* at 205. Hence, this case is often described as one about dilution — specifically, tarnishment — rather than "confusion." *See, e.g., Exxon Corp. v. Oxxford Clothes*, 109 F.3d 1070, 1081 (5th Cir. 1997); *Accuride Int'l, Inc. v. Accuride Corp.*, 871 F.2d 1531, 1538 (9th Cir. 1989); Emily Adelman, *Trademark Parodies: When is it OK to Laugh?*, 6 J. Marshall Rev. Intell. Prop. L. 72, 78 (2006); Gerard N. Magliocca, *One and Inseparable: Dilution and Infringement in Trademark Law*, 85 Minn. L. Rev. 949, 1013 (2001); Alex Kozinski, *Trademarks Unplugged*, 68 N.Y.U.L. Rev. 960, 972 (1993). *But see Universal City Studios Inc v. T-Shirt Gallery*, 634 F. Supp. 1468, 1479 (S.D.N.Y. 1986) ("The *Dallas Cowboys* case is distinguishable from the present case, however, because there was overwhelming evidence in that case that the defendants intended and expected consumer confusion.").

5. The courts in both *Rock Star* (E.S.S.) and *Textron* mentioned the frequently cited Second Circuit case of *Rogers v. Grimaldi*, 875 F.2d 994 (2d Cir. 1989). We discussed the *Rogers* test in Chapter 4 as one of the tests used by courts to determine whether an individual's right of publicity has been violated. As we noted there, the *Rogers* test came from trademark law. To refresh your memory, in *Rogers*, a movie titled "Ginger and Fred" was highly susceptible to confusion by potential viewers, many of whom may have assumed that the film was in fact an authorized story of Ginger Rogers and Fred Astaire. Nothing about the title made it obvious that it was not. Nonetheless the court found that the First Amendment interests prevailed over concerns about trademark infringement. One commentator referred to *Rogers* as the "marquee moment for the emerging constitutional consideration in trademark law." Pratheepan Gulasekaram, *Policing the Border Between Trademarks and Free Speech: Protecting Unauthorized Trademark Use in Expressive Works*, 80 WASH. L. REV. 887, 902 (2005).

6. Even though *Dallas Cowboys Cheerleaders* represents a victory for trademark owners with respect to the issue of expressive works, plaintiff trademark owners have lost a sufficient number of these types of cases in recent years, in addition, to *E.S.S. Entertainment. See e.g., Davis v. Walt Disney Co.*, 430 F.3d 901 (8th Cir. 2005) (use of term matching the plaintiff's trademark in the Disney Channel movie *Up, Up and Away*; summary judgment for defendants affirmed); *Mattel Inc. v. Walking Mt. Prods.*, 353 F.3d 792 (9th Cir. 2003) (use of Barbie dolls, including their associated trade dress, in photographic series; summary judgment for defendants affirmed); *Mattel, Inc. v. MCA Records*, 296 F.3d 894 (9th Cir. 2002) (use of Barbie's name in song title and lyrics; summary judgment for defendants affirmed); *Burnett v. Twentieth Century Fox Film Corp.*, 491 F. Supp. 2d 962 (C.D. Cal. 2007) (use of the *Carol Burnett Show* character Charwoman on an episode of the *Family Guy*; motion to dismiss granted); *Caterpillar Inc. v. Walt Disney Co.*, 287 F. Supp. 2d 913 (C.D. Ill. 2003) (use of Caterpillar tractors in George of the Jungle 2; TRO denied); *Wham-o, Inc. v. Paramount Pictures, Inc.*, 286 F. Supp. 2d 1254 (N.D. Cal. 2003) (use of the Slip 'N Slide in *Dickie Roberts: Former Child Star*; TRO denied).

7. Notwithstanding the preceding note, some plaintiffs have had cause to cheer the *Cheerleader* case. *See e.g., Dr. Seuss Ent. v. Penguin Books USA*, 109 F.3d 1394 (9th Cir. 1997) (use of title "The Cat NOT in the Hat!" appearing in the title of book about O.J. Simpson's double-murder trial; preliminary injunction affirmed); *Am. Dairy Queen Corp. v. New Line Prods., Inc.*, 35 F. Supp. 2d 727 (D. Minn. 1998) (use of title "Dairy Queens" for a movie; preliminary injunction affirmed). Another case involved a parody advertisement. *Anheuser-Busch, Inc. v. Balducci Pubs.*, 28 F.3d 769 (8th Cir. 1994) (reference to "Michelob Oily"; reversal of dismissal in favor of defendant). The last case was heavily criticized. *See, e.g.,* Stacey L. Dogan & Mark A. Lemley, *Grounding Trademark Law Through Trademark Use*, 92 IOWA L. REV. 1669, 1694 n. 101 (2007) ("In *Anheuser-Busch, Inc. v. Balducci Publications*, 28 F.3d 769 (8th Cir. 1994), for example, the court found an obvious parody of a beer ad to be confusing, in part because the plaintiff's survey expert tweaked the questions asked of consumers in a way that generated spurious evidence of confusion."); Mary LaFrance, *Steam Shovels and Lipstick: Trademarks, Greed, and the Public Domain*, 6 NEV. L.J. 447, 473 (2005) ("In effect, *Balducci* held that making a joke about a product violates Missouri's antidilution statute. Liability arose even without proof that anyone would take the joke seriously, and even if the joke was made in the context of pure expression rather than commercial speech. *Balducci* represents dilution law run amok.").

8. Assume for a moment that consumers are confused by many of the uses of trademarks in expressive works and wrongly assume the owners of the trademarks authorized the uses. Is such confusion likely to affect consumers' purchasing decisions? In what situations

is it most likely to matter? Should courts consider whether the potential confusion in a particular case is actually material to purchasing decisions of consumers? *Some* scholars say that it should. *See, e.g.,* James Gibson, *Risk Aversion and Rights Accretion in Intellectual Property Law,* 116 YALE L.J. 882 (2007) ("And few people (if any) select the movies they see or television programs they watch based on what products appear in them, even if they assume that the appearances are licensed."); Glynn S. Lunney, Jr., *Trademark Monopolies,* 48 EMORY L.J. 367, 483 (1999) ("Similarly, confusion as to endorsement can be actionable, but only if the factual situation is one where endorsement is typically found and likely to influence consumer buying.").

9. Some argue that First Amendment/trademark disputes should be resolved based on whether the inclusions of the marks constitute "trademark uses" for purposes of the Lanham Act. The district court in *E.S.S. Ent.,* failed to address this argument. According to proponents of the trademark use theory, "The Lanham Act defines infringement as a 'use in commerce' of a mark 'in connection with the sale, offering for sale, distribution, or advertising of any goods or services on or in connection with which such use is likely to cause confusion, or to cause mistake, or to deceive.' The statute thus places two qualifications on the type of use that can constitute infringement: it must be a 'use in commerce,' and it must be 'in connection with' the sale, offering, or advertising of goods and services." Stacey L. Dogan & Mark A. Lemley, *Grounding Trademark Law Through Trademark Use,* 92 IOWA L. REV. 1669, 1675 (2007). Would the use of the Play Pen's trade dress in Grand Theft Auto: San Andreas qualify as a trademark use? *See Wham-o, Inc. v. Paramount Pictures, Inc.,* 286 F. Supp. 2d 1254, 1258 (N.D. Cal. 2003) ("In the film's advertisement and promotional campaigns, the slide scene plays a prominent role."). For criticisms of the trademark use theory, *see* Graeme B. Dinwoodie & Mark D. Janis, *Confusion Over Use: Contextualism in Trademark Law,* 92 IOWA L. REV. 1597 (2007); Graeme B. Dinwoodie & Mark D. Janis, *Lessons from the Trademark Use Debate,* 92 IOWA L. REV. 1703 (2007).

10. New York's Police Commissioner criticized Activision's game *"True Crime: New York City"* for its portrayal of New York police officers. See Philip Messing & Erin Calabrese, *Commish Zaps Cop-Bop Game,* N.Y. POST, Sept. 24, 2005, at 16. Concerns about NYPD's reaction may explain why the game features characters from a fictional "PDNY" rather than the NYPD. The game even included the following disclaimer in the box on a separate piece of paper (True Crime: New York City (Xbox, Activision 2005):

DISCLAIMER

This game is not approved, endorsed, or connected in any way to the New York City Police Department ("NYPD")

The game is fictional and does not represent the views, policies or practices of the NYPD.

11. Do you think that the California District Court in *Textron* adequately distinguished *E.S.S. Ent.*? In *Textron,* the court felt that it was "far-fetched" that a consumer might mistakenly believe that a strip club would be affiliated with a videogame. Is that more, or less, far-fetched than a major helicopter manufacturer backing a videogame?

12. Today's "too" realistic videogames are evidently a sign of the times. During NBC's Tonight Show (December 23, 2015), host Jimmy Fallon read the following actual letter to Santa Clause: "Dear Santa: Please give me Grand Theft Auto VI. I Promise to play with the cars, not the hookers."

§ 8.60 Fictional Celebrities and Avatars

In Chapters 2 and 4 (dealing with the acquisition phase of videogame development and rights of publicity) we considered property concerns such as the rights to rights in names, likeness and personae from the perspective of a potential developer wishing to avoid infringement claims. Closely related to those considerations are trademarks involving fictional characters born of the games themselves. We might analogize the growth of this type of mark to the birth a stick figure (from master game-creator Shigeru Miyamoto) in the 1970s through its rudimentary development as *Jumpman,* and finally into the shape of the superstar that we all know and recognize as *Mario.* The next case presents a controversial character, also of significant stature, who coincidentally happens to be very familiar with Mario.

* * *

Universal City Studios, Inc. v. Nintendo Inc.

United States Court of Appeals, Second Circuit, 1984
746 F.2d 112

MESKILL, Circuit Judge.

This is an appeal from an order of the United States District Court for the Southern District of New York, Sweet, J., granting the motion for summary judgment by the defendants, Nintendo Co., Ltd. and Nintendo of America, Inc. (Nintendo), in the action brought by plaintiff Universal City Studios, Inc. (Universal) under section 43(a) of the Lanham Act, 15 U.S.C. § 1125(a) (1982), the New York anti-dilution statute, N.Y. Gen. Bus. Law § 368-d (McKinney 1984), and common law unfair competition, trademark and trade name principles. *Universal City Studios, Inc. v. Nintendo Co.*, 578 F. Supp. 911 (S.D.N.Y. 1983). We affirm.

BACKGROUND

Nintendo Co., and its wholly owned subsidiary Nintendo of America, has engaged in the design, manufacture, importation and sale of the extraordinarily successful video game known as "Donkey Kong." Nintendo has realized over $180 million from the sale of approximately 60,000 video arcade machines in the United States and Canada. Donkey Kong requires the player to maneuver a computerized man named Mario up a set of girders, ladders and elevators to save a blond pigtailed woman from the clutches of a malevolent, yet humorous gorilla, while simultaneously avoiding a series of objects such as barrels and fireballs hurled at him by the impish ape.

Universal, a giant in the entertainment industry, maintains that it owns the trademark in the name, character and story of "King Kong." The King Kong character and story, of course, need no introduction. Universal traces its ownership of the trademark from RKO General's (RKO) efforts to exploit the goodwill created by its 1933 film classic of the same name. [The court traced how plaintiff came to own the King Kong TM — ED.]

Universal filed its complaint against Nintendo in 1982, approximately nine months after Nintendo began marketing Donkey Kong. Universal alleged that the Donkey Kong name, character and story constituted false designation of origin in violation of 15 U.S.C. § 1125(a) because Nintendo's "actions falsely suggest to the public that [its] product originates with or is authorized, sponsored or approved by the owner of the King Kong name, character and story." Universal also asserted claims based upon the New York anti-dilution statute, N.Y. Gen. Bus. Law § 368-d, and common law unfair competition, trademark and trade name principles. Neither side requested a jury trial.

After extensive discovery, Nintendo moved for summary judgment. The motion was granted by the district court. Specifically, the court held any trademark that Universal purported to own could not be the basis of a successful action under the Lanham Act because it lacked "secondary meaning" as a matter of law; even if Universal's trademark had secondary meaning, there was no question of fact as to whether consumers were likely to confuse Donkey Kong and King Kong; Universal did not state a claim under the New York anti-dilution statute because it lacked a distinctive trademark and there were no triable issues as to whether Donkey Kong blurred the King Kong mark; and the common law trademark, trade name and unfair competition claims should be dismissed. The district court subsequently certified its decision as final under Fed. R. Civ. P. 54(b) even though Nintendo's counterclaim remained unadjudicated. This appeal followed."

DISCUSSION

We turn first to what Universal labels the "main" issue, whether the district court's decision that Universal failed to raise a question of fact as to the likelihood of consumer confusion concerning the origin of Donkey Kong was erroneous. Because we affirm the holding of the district court on this issue, we need not and do not decide if the district court was correct in finding that the King Kong mark has not acquired secondary meaning. Rather, we assume only arguendo that the King Kong trademark was validly developed and conveyed to Universal and that the King Kong mark has secondary meaning.

It is well settled that the crucial issue in an action for trademark infringement or unfair competition is whether there is any likelihood that an appreciable number of ordinarily prudent purchasers are likely to be misled, or indeed simply confused, as to the source of the goods in question. The factors enumerated in *Polaroid Corp. v. Polarad Electronics Corp.*, 287 F.2d 492 (2d Cir. 1961), are utilized and balanced to determine the likelihood of confusion:

Where the products are different, the prior owner's chance of success is a function of many variables: the strength of his mark, the degree of similarity between the two marks, the proximity of the products, the likelihood that the prior owner will bridge the gap, actual confusion, and the reciprocal of defendant's good faith in adopting its own mark, the quality of defendant's product, and the sophistication of the buyers. Even this extensive catalogue does not exhaust the possibilities—the court may have to take still other variables into account.

Id. at 495.

In *Warner Bros. Inc. v. American Broadcasting Cos.*, 720 F.2d 231 (2d Cir. 1983), Warner, owner of the trademark and copyright in the fictional character Superman, brought an action against ABC for its production of a television series entitled "The Greatest American Hero." Warner claimed, as does Universal in this case, that the character infringed its trademark. We held that it was proper to compare the "extent to which the allegedly infringing character captures the 'total concept and feel'" of the protected character in order to determine whether there exists a fair jury issue on the likelihood of confusion. *Id.* at 241, 246. We concluded after such an examination that summary judgment was proper in the facts and circumstances of that case. *Id.* at 246–47. The district court conducted a visual inspection of both the Donkey Kong game and the King Kong movies and stated that the differences between them were "great." 578 F. Supp. at 928. It found the Donkey Kong game "comical" and the Donkey Kong gorilla character "farcical, childlike and nonsexual." *Id.* In contrast, the court described the King Kong character and story as "a ferocious gorilla in quest of a beautiful woman." *Id.* The court summarized that "Donkey Kong[] ... create[s] a totally different concept and feel from the drama of King Kong" and that "at best, Donkey Kong is a parody of King Kong." *Id.* Indeed, the fact that Donkey Kong so obviously parodies the King Kong theme strongly contributes to dispelling confusion on the part of consumers. The district court then evaluated and rejected Universal's claim that a survey performed on its behalf raised a question of fact concerning the likelihood of actual confusion. The court concluded that "no reasonable jury could find likelihood of confusion." *Id.* at 929.

We agree with the district court that the two characters and stories are so different that no question of fact was presented on the likelihood of consumer confusion. The two properties have nothing in common but a gorilla, a captive woman, a male rescuer and a building scenario. Universal has not introduced any evidence indicating actual consumer confusion. Where, as here, the two properties are so different, Universal's claim cannot stand without some indication of actual confusion or a survey of consumer attitudes under actual market conditions.

Universal argues that the district court's analysis ignored its "primary" contention, "whether Donkey Kong is confusingly similar to the name King Kong." It maintains that it has presented evidence which raises questions of fact on the likelihood of confusion regarding the two names. After reviewing this evidence, we are satisfied that no question of fact exists and thus the decision below should be affirmed.

Universal points to the similarity of the two names, claiming that the use of the word "Kong" raises a question of fact on the likelihood of confusion. We disagree. In order to determine if confusion is likely, each trademark must be compared in its entirety; juxtaposing fragments of each mark does not demonstrate whether the marks as a whole are confusingly similar. The "Kong" and "King Kong" names are widely used by the general public and are associated with apes and other objects of enormous proportions. Nintendo's use of the prefix "Donkey" has no similarity in meaning or sound with the word "King." When taken as a whole, we find as a matter of law that "Donkey Kong" does not evoke or suggest the name of King Kong.

Universal places particular emphasis on a telephone survey of 150 arcade, bowling alley and pizza parlor owners and managers who had purchased or leased one or more Donkey Kong games. While a survey may indicate the existence of a question of fact on the likelihood of confusion, the survey must have been fairly prepared and its results directed to the relevant issues. We find that Universal's survey is so badly flawed that it cannot be used to demonstrate the existence of a question of fact on the likelihood of consumer confusion.

The individuals surveyed were asked "To the best of your knowledge, was the Donkey Kong game made with the approval or under the authority of the people who produce the King Kong movies?" Eighteen percent of those responding answered in the affirmative. Universal argues that this result demonstrates the existence of actual confusion. However, the question is unfair because Universal does not claim any ownership rights in the 1933 or 1976 King Kong films. Rather, Universal's trademark is supposedly derived from RKO's efforts to exploit the success of the 1933 movie. The survey question apparently was a transparent attempt to raise an image which Universal does not own in the minds of the respondents, that of King Kong climbing the Empire State Building/World Trade Center with Fay Wray/Jessica Lang in his paw. As such, the inquiry is unfair because no attempt was made to connect Donkey Kong with Universal's alleged trademark in the name King Kong.

There are two additional reasons why Universal cannot rely on the survey. First, the survey utilized an improper universe in that it was conducted among individuals who had already purchased or leased Donkey Kong machines rather than those who were contemplating a purchase or lease. Second, the above-mentioned inquiry was an obvious leading question in that it suggested its own answer. The participants were presented with the Donkey Kong-King Kong connection rather than permitted to make their own associations. When the participants were asked "As far as you know, who makes Donkey Kong?" not one suggested Universal or the makers of the King Kong movies. A survey question which begs its answer cannot be a true indicator of the likelihood of consumer confusion.[8]

Finally, Universal argues that statements by Donkey Kong's developer, designer and others indicating that the ideas for the game concept and name of Donkey Kong were derived in part from the King Kong film raises a presumption that the two trademarks are confusingly similar. Universal concedes that the presumption is rebutted where no question of fact exists as to the likelihood of confusion. In light of our conclusion that no reasonable question of fact is presented concerning the likelihood of confusion, supra, Universal is not entitled to the benefit of the presumption of confusing similarity due to intentional copying. In sum, we find that Universal failed to raise a question of fact whether there was any likelihood that an appreciable number of prudent purchasers are likely to be misled or confused as to the source of Donkey Kong. Consequently, the district court properly granted summary judgment to Nintendo on Universal's Lanham Act claim.

We now turn to the district court's grant of summary judgment for Nintendo on Universal's claim for injunctive relief under the New York anti-dilution statute, N.Y. Gen. Bus. Law § 368-d. Universal need not show a likelihood of confusion as to source to establish an anti-dilution claim. Rather, Universal must possess a strong mark—one which has a distinctive quality or has acquired a secondary meaning which is capable of dilution. It must also demonstrate a "likelihood of dilution" of its mark. Universal failed to present any evidence indicating that Donkey Kong will have an adverse effect on King Kong's reputation or deprive the mark of its distinctiveness. We find that the names and characters in dispute are so different that no reasonable question of fact was raised on the issue of blurring. *Cf. Dallas Cowboys Cheerleaders, Inc. v. Pussycat Cinema, Ltd.*, 604 F.2d at 204–05 & n. 8 (dilution occurred where sexually explicit movie utilized distinctive uniform "almost identical" to that of plaintiffs). Summary judgment for Nintendo was therefore proper.

Notes and Questions

1. *Donkey Kong* was designed by Shigeru Miyamoto, a legend in the videogame industry who also designed *The Legend of Zelda*. See § 1.20, *infra*. According to one author: "Donkey Kong was the first game project in which the design process began with a story." Chris Koehler, Power Up: How Japanese Video Games Gave the World an Extra Life 38 (Brady Games 2004). Kohler quotes Miyamoto as describing earlier game designs as follows: "Until Donkey Kong, which I directed, programmers and engineers were responsible for game design. These were the days when the engineers were even drawing the pictures and composing the music themselves. They were terrible, weren't they?" *Id.* at 36.

If you haven't seen it, an interesting movie where *Donkey Kong* plays a prominent role is "*The King of Kings: A Fistful of Quarters.*" The plot concerns a gamer's quest to become

---

8. We do not doubt that there are some consumers who believe that the producers of Donkey Kong and of King Kong are the same. However, the fact that there may be a few confused consumers does not create a sufficiently disputed issue of fact regarding the likelihood of confusion so as to make summary judgment improper.

the World Champion of *Donkey Kong* players, but along the way the viewer learns about the game itself.

2. In *Dallas Cowboys Cheerleaders, Inc. v. Pussycat Cinema, Ltd.*, 604 F.2d 200 (2d Cir. 1979), quoted in the *Universal* opinion, the Second Circuit said: "The public's belief that the mark's owner sponsored or otherwise approved the use of the trademark satisfies the confusion requirement." *Id.* at 205. As used in the opinion, did the term "public" refer only to those who had not yet made a purchase? In the *Universal* opinion why was it such a problem that Universal had surveyed individuals who had already purchased or leased *Donkey Kong*? In *Dallas Cowboys Cheerleaders*, the Second Circuit suggested the "confusion" at issue would mainly be a problem *after* consumers had already seen the defendants' movie.

3. Respondents to Universal's survey were asked, "As far as you know, who makes *Donkey Kong*?" Wouldn't the population-sample selection methods of the survey prove to be critical?

4. The *Universal* court did not work through the *Polaroid* factors for evaluating the likelihood of confusion because the "products were so dissimilar that no question of fact [was] presented." The factors are: "the strength of [the prior user's] mark, the degree of similarity between the two marks, the proximity of the products, the likelihood that the prior owner will bridge the gap, actual confusion, and the reciprocal of defendant's good faith in adopting its own mark, the quality of defendant's product, and the sophistication of the buyers." *Polaroid Corp. v. Polarad Electron. Corp.*, 287 F.2d 492, 495 (2d Cir. 1983). Should a proper consideration of all of the factors have changed the outcome of the *Universal* case?

5. Even if there was some likelihood of confusion in the *Universal* case, should the First Amendment provide greater protection for the titles of creative works? *See Rogers v. Grimaldi*, 875 F.2d 994, 998 (2d Cir. 1989) ("Though First Amendment concerns do not insulate titles of artistic works from all Lanham Act claims, such concerns must nonetheless inform our consideration of the scope of the Act as applied to claims involving such titles.").

6. Everyone is familiar with Marvel Comics, or at least a few of the superheroes to which Marvel Enterprises, Inc. lays claim (including Spiderman, the Incredible Hulk and Captain America). NCSoft Corporation marketed and hosted a computer game that allowed users to play online and create characters that were virtually identical in name, appearance, and traits with respect to Marvel's superheroes. Fearing an invasion of unlicensed superheroes (and a perceived threat to its trademarks), Marvel brought a multi-count trademark infringement action against NCSoft. *Marvel Ents., Inc. v. NCSoft Corporation, No.CV-04-9253RGKPLAx* 2005 WL 878090, 74 U.S.P.Q.2d 1303 (C.D. Cal. Mar, 9, 2005). With respect to the claim for contributory trademark infringement, the court said: "Liability for contributory infringement is imposed on any person who uses in commerce any reproduction, counterfeit, copy or colorable imitation of a registered mark in connection with the sale, offering for sale, distribution, or advertising of any goods or services or in connection with which such use is likely." 15 U.S.C. §§ 1114(l). Defendants' motion to dismiss that claim was granted. Even though users of Defendants' game created character names that infringed upon Plaintiffs' registered trademarks, Plaintiffs did not allege that the gamers were using the names in commerce in connection with the sale or advertising of goods and services. Thus, Plaintiffs failed to allege an infringement on the part of *the game users* for which the Defendants could be contributorily liable. *See Lucasfilm Ltd. v. High Frontier*, 622 F. Supp. 931 (D.D.C.1985) (holding that the use of a trademark not affixed to any good or service for sale did not constitute infringement); and *see Felix the Cat Prod., Inc. v. New Line Cinema Corp.*, 54 U.S.P.Q.2d

1856, 1857 (C.D. Cal. 2000) (holding that the use of a trademark within a movie did not qualify as a use of the mark in connection with a sale of goods or services in commerce). The other trademark related counts included claims for: direct infringement, direct common-law trademark infringement, vicarious infringement, contributory infringement of a common-law trademark, vicarious infringement of a common-law trademark, and violation of California's tort of interference with a prospective economic advantage.

7. In *Fasa Corp. v. Playmates Toys, Inc.*, 108 F.3d 140 (7th Cir. 1997), a designer that created futuristic robot designs for use in a role-playing game commenced an action against a toy manufacturer that produced robot-like toys, alleging copyright and trademark infringement. The District Court, per Castillo, J., held that: (1) The original features of designer's robots were entitled to copyright protection; (2) the designer had a protectable trade dress rights in its robot designs; (3) the manufacturer's robot toys were not substantially similar to copyrighted designs; (4) evidence was insufficient to establish likelihood of confusion between the parties' products, as required to support trade dress infringement claim; and (5) the manufacturer's failure to produce a robot toy that it exhibited at a toy fair was not unfair competition. The case was dismissed.

8. Depending upon which dictionary you happen to check, you may find the term "Super Hero." That didn't stop DC Comics and Marvel Characters, Inc. from entering into an agreement whereby they would jointly claim ownership of a trademark in the term "for publications, particularly comic books and magazines and stories in illustrated form." Registration No. 1,179,067. The two companies are regular providers of licenses to videogame producers, which allow those producers to incorporate some of the best known super heroes into their games. With or without regard to its use in a comic book setting, do you think that the term "Super Hero" is generic? Descriptive?

9. The primary purpose of a trademark is to identify the manufacturer. As is the case with most functions, the manufacturing process can be delegated or franchised. In order to avoid disputes or ambiguities as to the ultimate right to control the mark, simple agreements or acknowledgments, such as the following, are quite common. The sample below (which is a bit oversimplified) would be used in conjunction with an agreement to develop, or license permission to construct, a videogame based upon a film or its characters. A more detailed contract would most likely follow.

* * *

FORM 8.1
Acknowledgment

To: (Trademark Holder)

The undersigned _____ ("Licensee") acknowledges that it has been engaged to manufacturer certain Videogames under a License Agreement dated _____("Games"), which engagement is subject to your written approval.

This letter will acknowledge my understanding that you are the owner of the trademarks and all other intellectual property rights licensed, or to be licensed in conjunction with the motion picture entitled "_____."

I hereby confirm our understanding that I shall use such trademarks and other intellectual property only to the extent required to manufacture the Games in conjunction with the said License Agreement; that I shall have no right to make any other use thereof (including without limitation any promotional use in connection with our manufacturing services); and that I shall not be considered your "licensee" for any purpose other than in conjunction with the creation of the subject Games.

Very truly yours,

_____

Licensee

Accepted by:

_____

Licensor

* * * * *

§ 8.70 Trademark Cancellation

Registered trademarks are not bullet proof. Even though registration may cloak a mark with a presumption of validity, it may nevertheless be cancelled for a number of reasons, according to 15 U.S.C.A. § 1064. Subsection (3) provides for such cancellation when: "The registered mark becomes the generic name for the goods or services, or a portion thereof, for which it is registered, or is functional, or has been abandoned, or its registration was obtained fraudulently." The subsection also provides for cancellation if it is being used "To misrepresent the source of the goods or services."

* * *

Edge Games, Inc. v. Elec. Arts, Inc.

United States District Court for the Northern District of California, 2010
745 F. Supp. 2d 1101

Alsup, District Judge.

ORDER DENYING MOTION FOR PRELIMINARY INJUNCTION

INTRODUCTION

In this trademark infringement action involving video-gaming giant Electronic Arts, Inc. and its "revolutionary" first-person, action-adventure video game "Mirror's Edge," plaintiff Edge Games, Inc.—a so-called "small video-gaming company" based in Pasadena—moves to preliminarily enjoin defendant Electronic Arts from using the "MIRROR'S EDGE" mark while this dispute unfolds in court. Because plaintiff has failed to establish that it is likely to succeed on the merits, that it is likely to suffer irreparable harm in the absence of preliminary relief, that the balance of equities tips in its favor, or that an injunction is in the public interest, the motion for a preliminary injunction is DENIED.

STATEMENT

1. PLAINTIFF EDGE GAMES, INC.

Edge Games, Inc. is "one of the oldest surviving video game development and publishing businesses" on the planet—at least, that's what its founder, chief executive officer, and sole shareholder, Dr. Tim Langdell, would have a jury believe. According to Dr. Langdell's declaration, he began using the "EDGE" mark in connection with video-game marketing and sales back in 1984 through a London-based video-game company called Softek. Softek is supposedly a predecessor-in-interest to Edge Games. After Dr. Langdell moved to Los Angeles in 1990, he reincorporated Softek as Edge Interactive Media (another supposed predecessor-in-interest to Edge Games). He then incorporated Edge Games—the alleged trademark holder herein—in 2005.

Plaintiff Edge Games and its predecessors supposedly developed, distributed, and sold several dozen video games from the mid-1990s through 2010 bearing the asserted marks. Examples of recent video-game products purportedly marketed by Edge Games and bearing one or more of the asserted marks include "Bobby Bearing," "Raffles," "Mythora," "Pengu," "BattlePods," and "Racers." Between 2003 and 2009, Edge Games purportedly sold over 11,000 units of Raffles, Mythora, and Racers, which are "packaged PC video game" products, as well as over 45,000 units of Bobby Bearing, Pengu, and BattlePods, which are games that can be played on certain mobile phones. In addition to PC and mobile-phone video games, Dr. Langdell also claims that Edge Games develops, publishes, and/or licenses games for major gaming consoles such as the Sony PlayStation 3, and that various releases are currently being developed for gaming consoles and platforms including Microsoft's Xbox 360, the Nintendo Wii, and the Apple iPhone and iPad.

According to Dr. Langdell, these "upcoming" releases from Edge Games will supposedly be sold through the same retailers that the accused products were (and are still being) sold, such as Amazon.com, Best Buy, and Target. In sum, based upon Dr. Langdell's declaration, Edge Games is a legitimate "small video-gaming company" that is active in the video-gaming industry.

2. DEFENDANT ELECTRONIC ARTS, INC.

Electronic Arts—or EA for short—is a leading "interactive entertainment" company that develops, publishes, and distributes video games and related software for modern gaming consoles including Microsoft's Xbox 360, the Sony PlayStation 3, and the Nintendo Wii, as well as for PCs, Macs, and various mobile-gaming devices. Since its formation in 1982, EA has grown to become an international, publicly traded corporation with more than ten video-game development studios spanning the globe. In 2009 alone, EA had sales exceeding one million units for at least 31 of its active video-game franchises. "Mirror's Edge" is one of EA's modestly successful video-game franchises. Developed by EA Digital Illusions CE AB (or "EA DICE" for short) in Stockholm, Sweden—one of EA's ten video-game development studios—the "Mirror's Edge" franchise stands at the heart of the instant trademark dispute.

3. THE "MIRROR'S EDGE" FRANCHISE

In July 2007, EA announced in "Edge Magazine"—a leading print and online video-game magazine published by Future Publishing—that its EA DICE development studio was creating a "revolutionary new take on the first-person action adventure game" entitled "Mirror's Edge." The announcement was a cover story in the magazine, and it was accompanied by a press release issued by EA on July 11, 2007, officially announcing the development of the "Mirror's Edge" video game. According to EA's senior marketing director, Lincoln Hershberger, "Mirror's Edge" was widely known and discussed throughout the gaming industry and became one of the most anticipated video-game releases of 2008. Tens of millions of dollars were invested by EA in the game's development, which spanned three years and involved a team of over 60 individuals.

The game itself is set in a city of gleaming skyscrapers with reflective surfaces and empty streets, whose population has been marginalized by a totalitarian regime. Players interact with and explore this world through the eyes of a character named "Faith," who is a messenger (or, as the game describes her, a "runner") tasked with covertly delivering information, messages, and other items within the city while evading government surveillance. The network of rooftops and aerial skyways that Faith and other "runners" utilize to make these deliveries and evade the government is dubbed the "Mirror's Edge."

Prior to its official release, "Mirror's Edge" was demonstrated and publicized at numerous industry events, including the Game Developers Conference in February 2008 and the Electronic Entertainment Expo (or "E3") in July 2008. E3 is widely regarded as the most important expo in the video-game industry. Also in July 2008, "Mirror's Edge" was showcased at Comic-Con, the largest comic-book convention in the world, where a limited-run comic-book adaptation of "Mirror's Edge" was announced. The six-issue "Mirror's Edge" comic "miniseries" was published in 2008 and 2009 by a division of DC Comics. In total, EA invested over $9 million to market "Mirror's Edge" in North America.

In November 2008, "Mirror's Edge" was released for the Sony PlayStation 3 and Microsoft's Xbox 360. A PC version followed in January 2009. These games were sold through retail channels including mass merchandisers (e.g., Walmart, Target), electronics sellers (e.g., Best Buy), video-game resellers (e.g., GameStop), club stores (e.g., Costco), and online retailers (e.g.,Amazon.com). Since its initial release, over two million units of "Mirror's Edge" have been sold worldwide, including over 750,000 units in North America alone.

While EA is no longer manufacturing or distributing copies of "Mirror's Edge" for the Sony PlayStation 3, the Microsoft's Xbox 360, or the PC for third-party retailers, the PC version of the game remains available for download on EA's online store. Due to its modest success, additional products were developed for the "Mirror's Edge" franchise. In February 2009, EA released "additional downloadable context" for the game, which was sold as "Mirror's Edge Pure Time Trials Map Pack." Additionally, a separate and "substantially scaled down" side-scrolling version of the game was announced in December 2009 and developed from scratch for the Apple iPad, iPhone, and iPod Touch. This side-scrolling version of the game—published in 2010—was entitled "Mirror's Edge 2D." It is currently available for purchase through Apple's App Store, where over 37,000 units have already been downloaded for the Apple iPad. Finally, a Mac version of the original "Mirror's Edge" video game is currently under development and is slated for release later this year.

4. THE ASSERTED AND ACCUSED MARKS

As should be obvious by this point, this trademark battle centers on EA's use of the word "Edge" in the "Mirror's Edge" franchise. The logo for "Mirror's Edge" and examples of how "Mirror's Edge" appeared in advertising and product packaging are reproduced below (Images omitted).

As shown, the logos for both EA and EA DICE were prominently displayed on the game's packaging and advertising. In the reproductions, the logos for EA and EA DICE are most clearly seen on the bottom right of the Xbox 360 cover art. The logos for EA and EA DICE were also placed on the advertisement. While difficult to see in the reproduction above, the logos are clearly visible on the normal sized version.

The "MIRROR'S EDGE" mark is owned by EA DICE. The application was filed in September 2009 and—over a letter of protest filed by Edge Games—the United States Patent and Trademark Office approved the registration of the "MIRROR'S EDGE" mark on June 22, 2010, for computer and video game software, comic books, and online video games. Turning next to the asserted marks in this action, Edge Games is the purported owner of six federally registered trademarks that it supposedly "uses and selectively licenses" to other companies. These marks are: (1) "EDGE," (2) "THE EDGE," (3) "GAMER'S EDGE,"

(4) "EDGE OF EXTINCTION," (5) "CUTTING EDGE," and (6) "EDGEGAMERS." Edge Games also claims common-law trademark rights over the "EDGE" logo.

5. PLAINTIFF'S LICENSING PRACTICES

According to Dr. Langdell's declaration, plaintiff's licensing practices have been prolific, extending the reach of its asserted marks well beyond video-game software to gaming-related print publications and websites, comic books, video-game hardware, and computers. Licensed products supposedly include "Cross Edge," a video game for the Sony PlayStation 3 published by NIS America, and Edge Magazine, a leading video-gaming news magazine and website published by Future Publishing, Inc. Additional products purportedly licensed by Edge Games include:

- The "Edge" line of high-performance gaming computers sold by Velocity Micro, Inc.

- The online computer game "Edge of Extinction" by Cybernet Systems Corp.

- The website and video game "Edge of Twilight" by Fuzzyeyes Stupio Pty. Ltd.

- The "Cutting Edge," "Over the Edge," and "Double Edge" comic-book series published by Marvel Comics, as well as the "Edge" comic-book series published by Malibu Comics (which is owned by Marvel).

- The video-game controller for the Nintendo Wii called "The Edge," sold by Datel Design & Development Ltd.

- The "EdgeGamers" video-gaming website, operated by EdgeGamers Organization, LLC.

6. ALLEGATIONS OF FRAUD AND ABANDONMENT

According to EA, almost nothing set forth above regarding Edge Games and its asserted marks can be trusted. Indeed, EA's opposition brief invests a substantial number of pages to a no-holds-barred attack on the validity of each of plaintiff's asserted marks and the credibility of Dr. Langdell's sworn representations made to both the USPTO and the Court. These attacks and supporting evidence—which raise serious questions regarding the veracity of Dr. Langdell's entire declaration—are set forth in detail below.

A. Fraud and Abandonment Regarding "EDGE"

According to EA, the two registrations obtained by plaintiff for the "EDGE" mark were soaked in fraud. First, in January 1999, Edge Interactive Media (a predecessor to Edge Games) registered the "EDGE" mark for use in connection with various paper goods, including magazines related to video games. Five years later, in 2004, Edge Interactive Media filed a "Combined Declaration of Use and Incontestability under Sections 8 & 5," wherein Dr. Langdell certified to the USPTO that (1) his companies had made continuous use of the "EDGE" mark in commerce for at least five years following the January 1999 registration date, and (2) were continuing to use the mark in commerce as reflected in a specimen described as a "Color scan of the front cover of our EDGE Games magazine, July 2004 edition, with the registration serial number written clearly on it." According to a declaration submitted by the publisher of Edge Magazine, however, the magazine cover submitted to the USPTO by Dr. Langdell was not a genuine copy of any magazine cover that had ever been published. It was faked. The specimen submitted by Dr. Langdell to the USPTO (left) and the actual Edge Magazine cover for July 2004 (right) are shown below:

Figure 8.6

| As Submitted to the USPTO | Actual Cover |

The USPTO apparently relied upon Dr. Langdell's declaration and false specimen and maintained the "EDGE" registration. Second, in January 2003, Edge Interactive Media filed a separate application with the USPTO for the "EDGE" mark in connection with various paper goods, including comic books. As evidence of his company's "use" of the "EDGE" mark in commerce, Dr. Langdell submitted to the USPTO a "scanned cover of our comic book EDGE issue 2." The comic-book cover submitted as a specimen, however, had been published by an entirely different and unrelated company more than a decade earlier. Even more remarkable, according to the magazine's publisher, Marvel Entertainment, LLC, the last "Edge" comic book ever published was in the spring of 1995. Nevertheless, the USPTO registered the "EDGE" mark on June 20, 2006, in apparent reliance on Dr. Langdell's sworn representation that the comic book cover was representative of plaintiff's current use of the "EDGE" mark in commerce. In this connection, EA also presents compelling evidence that there was no bona fide use of the "EDGE" mark in commerce by plaintiff, its licensees, or its predecessors in interest at all between 1989 and to at least 2003. In presenting this evidence, EA asserts that Dr. Langdell's declaration filed in support of the instant motion contains numerous misrepresentations. For example, in his declaration, Dr. Langdell asserts:

> 22. Attached hereto as Exhibits W, X, Y, Z, AA, BB & CC are true and correct exemplars of product packaging and services currently marketed by Edge's duly authorized licensees that display one or more of the EDGE family of marks. These include:
>
> * * * f. Licensee Marvel Comics' "CUTTING EDGE," "Over the EDGE," and "Double EDGE" comic book series, and licensee Malibu Comics' "Edge" comic book series, as promoted at www.edgegames.com.

As stated, however, the last installment of the "Edge" comic-book series was published by Malibu Comics (owned by Marvel) in the spring of 1995. Similarly, the last publication of Marvel's "Cutting Edge" comic book was in December 1995, the last publication of Marvel's "Over the Edge" comic mini-series was in August 1996, and the last publication of Marvel's "Double Edge Alpha" and "Double Edge Omega" comics was in October 1995. In other words, none of these comic books is being "currently marketed"—all have been out of print for nearly 15 years. Even more egregious, according to Marvel Vice President and Deputy General Counsel Walter Bard, neither Marvel nor Malibu Comics are or were ever licensees of Dr. Langdell's companies for any of these marks. Similar alleged untruths plague Dr. Langdell's representations with respect to Edge Magazine's status as a licensee. Although the magazine's publisher — Future Publishing — confirmed that it was a licensee of Edge Interactive Media between 1996 and 2004, the publisher also confirmed that the license only covered the use of the "EDGE" mark in relation to print and online versions of Edge Magazine in the United Kingdom. During that time period, Edge Magazine was not even distributed within the United States. Then, in October 2004, Future Publishing and Edge Interactive Media entered into a new agreement wherein Future Publishing was granted a worldwide license to the marketing and promotion of electronic versions of Edge Magazine. Critically, neither of these licensing agreements granted plaintiff the right to exercise quality control over the use of the "EDGE" marks. They were "naked" licenses.

Even after 2003, the evidence that plaintiff had been making bona fide use of the "EDGE" mark in commerce is suspect. For example, Dr. Langdell's declaration asserted that Edge Games has been selling the video game Mythora (supposedly bearing the "EDGE" mark) since 2004. Curiously, while the exterior packaging submitted by Dr. Langdell to the USPTO for the Mythora video game included a website address "www.mythora.com," this website wasn't even registered by Edge Games until October 2008 — nearly four years after the game's purported release. The USPTO relied upon this questionable video-game packaging when it renewed plaintiff's "EDGE" mark in 2009.

B. Fraud and Abandonment Regarding "THE EDGE"

Compelling evidence of fraud on the USPTO has also been submitted by EA with respect to plaintiff's "THE EDGE" mark. For example, in March 1996, in his application to register the mark "THE EDGE" for use with various goods, including video-game software and comic books, Dr. Langdell submitted as evidence of supposed use of the mark a box cover of a game entitled "Snoopy: The Cool Computer Game." The game, however, was already seven years old at the time of the application, rendering it doubtful that it was still being sold in 1996. Even more disturbing, it appears as though the specimen of the box cover for the video game submitted by plaintiff to the USPTO was doctored. The specimen submitted by Dr. Langdell (left) and the actual box cover for "Snoopy: The Cool Computer Game" (right) are shown below (Image omitted).

As shown, the "box cover" specimen submitted to the USPTO by Dr. Langdell and the actual box cover of the video game differ in two key respects. First, a "TM" has been added next to the logo for "THE EDGE" in the specimen submitted to the USPTO. Second, instead of a copyright disclaimer for the "PEANUTS characters," which appears on the bottom right of the genuine box, the specimen submitted to the USPTO contained an entirely different disclaimer that stated "The Edge is a trademark of The Edge Interactive Media, Inc."

Even more evidence of fraud is seen in the comic-book specimen submitted to the USPTO by Dr. Langdell in November 2005 for his application to register "THE EDGE" in connection with comic books (RJN Exh. F). In support of the application, Dr. Langdell submitted the cover of the "Edge" comic book — which, as stated, was last published a decade earlier by an unrelated company who was never a licensee of plaintiff — as a specimen. The specimen submitted to the USPTO (left) and the actual comic book (right) are shown below (Images omitted).

Once again playing "spot the differences," the specimen submitted to the USPTO appears to have been doctored in three material ways. First, and most egregious, the name of the comic book was changed from "Edge" to "The Edge" in the specimen. This was done apparently to show that "THE EDGE" mark was being used in commerce in connection with comic books. Second, a "TM" was added to the manipulated title (it is visible on the top right of the last "E" in "EDGE"). Third, a disclaimer was tacked on to the bottom of the specimen that stated " 'The Edge' is the trademark of The Edge Interactive Media, Inc. All Rights Reserved." These "enhancements" were not present in the original comic-book cover. Nevertheless, the USPTO relied upon Dr. Langdell's application when it issued the registration for "THE EDGE" in 2009.

In light of these misrepresentations, EA argues that there are serious doubts over whether "THE EDGE" mark was actually being used on any products by Edge Games during the period between 1989 and 2003.

C. Fraud and Abandonment Regarding "GAMER'S EDGE"

Evidence of fraud infects plaintiff's registration for "GAMER'S EDGE" as well. In February 2006, Dr. Langdell submitted an application to the USPTO to register "GAMER'S EDGE" for various goods, including video-game software. As a specimen of his company's use of the mark in commerce, Dr. Langdell submitted the box cover of a video game entitled "Garfield: Winter's Tail," which had been released by Softek (a predecessor-in-interest to Edge Games) over seventeen years earlier in 1989. The specimen submitted to the USPTO (left) and what EA asserts as being the actual box cover for the video game (right) are shown below (Images omitted).

One critical difference stands out: the "GAMER'S EDGE" mark that is visible on the specimen submitted to the USPTO is not present anywhere on the genuine box cover for the video game. Based upon this apparently doctored specimen submitted by Dr. Langdell, the "GAMER'S EDGE" mark was issued to plaintiff in February 2008 for use with video games.

In addition to this evidence assaulting the validity of plaintiff's "GAMER'S EDGE" registration, EA has also submitted evidence calling into question whether plaintiff made bona fide use of the "GAMER'S EDGE" mark over the past two decades. In particular, EA has submitted evidence demonstrating that Dr. Langdell's claimed sales of video games supposedly bearing the "GAMER'S EDGE" mark are highly suspect. For example, when counsel for EA attempted to purchase various video games that Dr. Langdell represented in his declaration as being currently sold by Edge Games, they only received error messages stating that "The resource requested ... cannot be found." Additionally, it is unclear from Dr. Langdell's exhibits whether certain games were being sold in the United States rather than the United Kingdom. In any event, given disturbing evidence that the "GAMER'S EDGE" mark may have been grafted retroactively onto product packaging by plaintiff, the record is tainted as to whether the mark has actually been used continuously by Edge Games or has been abandoned.

Finally, while Dr. Langdell claimed in his declaration that both "EDGE" and "GAMER'S EDGE" were used in connection with the sale of personal computers since 1998, EA has presented evidence that the vendor of these computers—Velocity Micro—did not even become a licensee of plaintiff until 2008, when plaintiff sued Velocity Micro for trademark infringement. In sum, there is no clear evidence—at least on this record—that plaintiff or its licensees made any bona fide use of the "GAMER'S EDGE" mark prior to 2008.

D. Fraud and Abandonment Regarding "CUTTING EDGE"

Fraud is also alleged by EA surrounding plaintiff's registration of the "CUTTING EDGE" mark. In April 1995, Marvel filed an application with the USPTO to register

"CUTTING EDGE" for use as the title of a comic book. A single issue of "Cutting Edge" was then published in December 1995. No other "Cutting Edge" comic book has ever been published by Marvel since that single issue. In November 2006, Dr. Langdell filed a Notice of Opposition to Marvel's registration of "CUTTING EDGE," claiming that his companies had made "extensive use" of the mark since October 1984. Marvel responded by assigning its rights in the mark, including the pending application, to plaintiff in September 1997. The registration issued in June 1999.

Fast-forward six years to November 2005. Despite the fact that only one issue of the "Cutting Edge" comic was ever published by Marvel in 1995, Dr. Langdell filed a "Combined Declaration of Use and Incontestability under Sections 8 & 15" wherein he certified that the "CUTTING EDGE" mark had been in continuous use in commerce for at least five years after the June 1999 registration date. To support this contention, he attached as a specimen what he described as: "Cover of currently on sale comic book sold via our licensee bearing the mark" (emphasis added). The specimen submitted to the USPTO, however, was the cover of the same single-issue "Cutting Edge" comic published by Marvel in 1995. In other words, the specimen was most certainly not the cover of a comic book "currently on sale" in November 2005. Additionally, the comic book was not, and had never been, "sold via [plaintiff's] licensee." As stated, Marvel was never a licensee of any of Dr. Langdell's companies.

7. EVIDENCE OF DELAY IN FILING SUIT

By his own admission, Dr. Langdell knew about the release of "Mirror's Edge" shortly after it was announced in July 2007. Indeed, he claims to have mailed a cease-and-desist letter to EA two days after "Mirror's Edge" was publicly announced. EA's legal department has no record of this July 2007 letter and Dr. Langdell did not receive a reply to it. According to his declaration, Dr. Langdell then purportedly sent numerous letters to EA's legal department in January, March, May, July, and September 2008, and left voice mails with the department in February, April, June, and August of that year. Despite these assertions, EA claims that it received no voice mails from Dr. Langdell during this time period and that the first letter it received from him was on September 24, 2008. In response to the September 2008 letter, EA—through outside counsel—sent a letter in reply to Dr. Langdell explaining why its "Mirror's Edge" video game did not infringe. EA's reply letter also requested additional documentation regarding the ownership and use of the asserted "EDGE" marks. A back-and-forth between EA's outside counsel, EA DICE, and Dr. Langdell continued through December 2008, with Dr. Langdell threatening to seek a preliminary injunction against EA in a letter dated November 10, 2008, and representing to EA that his companies had recently prevailed in a similar trademark action against a third party "with judgments in our favor" and "on the merits." Numerous purported "final warnings" were given by Dr. Langdell to EA in these communications. Meanwhile, sales of "Mirror's Edge" began in earnest on November 11, 2008, with a PC version released shortly thereafter on January 16, 2009. Instead of immediately seeking a preliminary injunction to halt these sales, Dr. Langdell waited until June 2009 to re-attempt negotiations with EA. In these negotiations, EA reiterated its position to Edge Games that there was no likelihood of confusion between "Mirror's Edge" and the "EDGE" marks purportedly owned by Dr. Langdell. The talks ended in July 2009 without an agreement. EA did not receive another communication from Dr. Langdell until March 2010, shortly after EA had announced the release of "Mirror's Edge" for the Apple iPad and iPhone. In this communication, Dr. Langdell once again called upon EA to cease using the "Mirror's Edge" name. EA did not respond to the email, and had no further interactions with Dr. Langdell until this action was filed three months later.

Edge Games filed this action on June 15, 2010. Nearly two months passed without any motions being filed. Finally, on August 20, over 21 months after EA first began selling the "Mirror's Edge" video game to the public, the instant preliminary injunction motion was filed. This order follows a hearing held on September 30.

ANALYSIS

A plaintiff seeking a preliminary injunction must establish that he is likely to succeed on the merits, that he is likely to suffer irreparable harm in the absence of preliminary relief, that the balance of equities tips in his favor, and that an injunction is in the public interest. *Winter v. Natural Resources Defense Council*, 555 U.S. 7, 129 S.Ct. 365, 374, 172 L.Ed.2d 249 (2008). As explained below, plaintiff Edge Games has failed to establish — based upon the preliminary injunction record detailed herein — that any of these factors weigh in its favor.

1. LIKELIHOOD OF SUCCESS ON THE MERITS

To prevail on its claim of trademark infringement, Edge Games "must demonstrate that it owns a valid mark, and thus a protectable interest." *Lahoti v. VeriCheck, Inc.*, 586 F.3d 1190, 1197 (9th Cir.2009) (citation omitted). If ownership of such a mark is established, Edge Games must then show that EA's "use of the mark 'is likely to cause confusion, or to cause mistake, or to deceive.' " *KP Permanent Make-Up, Inc. v. Lasting Impression I, Inc.*, 408 F.3d 596, 602 (9th Cir.2005) (quoting 15 U.S.C. 1114(1)(a)–(b)).

A. Trademark Validity

On the issue of whether plaintiff has sufficiently demonstrated that it owns a protectable interest in the asserted "EDGE" marks, the preliminary injunction record speaks for itself. As detailed above, the record contains numerous items of evidence that plaintiff wilfully committed fraud against the USPTO in obtaining and/or maintaining registrations for many of the asserted "EDGE" marks, possibly warranting criminal penalties if the misrepresentations prove true. If EA's evidence is credited, such fraud could (and likely would) strip these registered marks of their "presumption of validity." See *Tie Tech, Inc. v. Kinedyne Corp.*, 296 F.3d 778, 783 (9th Cir.2002). These misrepresentations also support EA's argument that many (if not all) of plaintiff's marks have been abandoned, which would also render them invalid.

Additionally, EA has put forth substantial evidence calling into severe question many of the representations made by Dr. Langdell in his declaration submitted to the Court. Indeed, the declarations provided by EA from two of plaintiff's supposed "licensees" — Marvel Entertainment and Future Publishing — revealed that many of Dr. Langdell's assertions in his declaration were materially misleading or downright false. These falsehoods infect all of Dr. Langdell's assertions regarding the bona fide and continuous use of the asserted marks in commerce and the purported "sales" of his company's video-game products. In other words, all of his representations have become highly suspect in light of the evidence presented by EA. They cannot be credited to justify the extraordinary relief requested herein.

In sum, based upon the evidence in the record, this order finds that plaintiff has not demonstrated a likelihood of success in proving that the asserted marks are valid. See *Tie Tech*, 296 F.3d at 783; see also 15 U.S.C. 1127 ("Nonuse [of a mark] for 3 consecutive years shall be prima facie evidence of abandonment. 'Use' of a mark means the bona fide use of such mark made in the ordinary course of trade, and not made merely to reserve a right in a mark."). Since a valid trademark is a prerequisite to a finding of infringement, Edge Games has failed to establish that it is likely to succeed on the merits.

B. Likelihood of Confusion

Even if the asserted marks were presumed valid and protectable, the preliminary injunction record does not support a likelihood of confusion between the asserted and accused marks. As such, Edge Games has not established that it is likely to succeed on the merits.

To determine whether a "likelihood of confusion" exists, this order must examine the eight factors set forth in *AMF Inc. v. Sleekcraft Boats*: (1) strength of the mark, (2) proximity of the goods, (3) similarity of the marks, (4) evidence of actual confusion, (5) marketing channels used, (6) type of goods and the degree of care likely to be exercised by the purchaser, (7) defendant's intent in selecting the mark, and (8) likelihood of expansion of the product lines. *AMF Inc. v. Sleekcraft Boats*, 599 F.2d 341, 348–49 (9th Cir.1979); *One Industries, LLC v. Jim O'Neal Distributing, Inc.*, 578 F.3d 1154, 1162 (9th Cir.2009).

The preliminary injunction record and the Sleekcraft factors do not support a finding that a "reasonably prudent consumer" in the marketplace is likely to be confused as to the origin, endorsement, or approval of the competing products herein. Indeed, the majority of plaintiff's arguments on this issue are tainted by the suspect evidence set forth in Dr. Langdell's declaration. For example, according to Dr. Langdell, Edge Games is currently selling (or plans to sell) numerous "EDGE"-branded video games for modern gaming consoles through the exact same retail channels used by EA to distribute "Mirror's Edge." The evidence to support this assertion—beyond Dr. Langdell's bare statements in his suspect declaration—is paper thin. Indeed, Dr. Langdell never states exactly how much capital he has invested in developing, marketing, and selling his company's current and future video-game products. Given that "Mirror's Edge" was marketed with significant monetary investments through sophisticated, high-profile channels, including pre-announcements and demonstrations at major industry events, and was sold by major retailers, plaintiff has not established that the marketing channels used or the proximity of the goods in the marketplace support its claims of infringement. Indeed, EA has produced compelling evidence that plaintiff's video-game products may not even be available for sale to consumers at all.

Additionally, there is no evidence in the record that EA chose to call its product "Mirror's Edge" for any reason but to describe the visual and thematic aspects of the video game. This conclusion is bolstered by the fact that the word "edge" in "Mirror's Edge" is used to modify the word "Mirror." In this connection, the "strength" of plaintiff's asserted marks is also highly susceptible to attack. Even if the "EDGE" marks were deemed "arbitrary," as plaintiff argues, there is no evidence of actual confusion (despite over 21 months of "Mirror's Edge" being sold to the public). Moreover, plaintiff has failed to show that each of the asserted marks is confusingly similar to the "Mirror's Edge" mark or that purchasers of "Mirror's Edge" would exercise such a low degree of care as to be confused as to the publisher or developer of the competing products. Similarly, under plaintiff's "reverse confusion" theory of infringement, the record does not support plaintiff's claim that purchasers of its various "EDGE"-branded products (to the extent that any exist) would believe that they were associated with EA, EA DICE, or the "Mirror's Edge" franchise.

Yet another failed argument is plaintiff's assertion that the various "EDGE" marks constitute a "family of marks" where confusion can be analyzed based upon a common element shared between them. On this issue, there is no evidence in the record showing that the purchasing public recognizes that the term "edge" in the asserted marks is indicative of a common origin of goods. By contrast, EA has produced evidence that the term "edge" is found in many registered trademarks and product names within the video gaming industry that are not owned or licensed by Edge Games. Given this crowded field, the scope of protection (if any) that can be afforded to the asserted marks is limited. Finally, with respect to plaintiff's "EDGE" logo, EA has put forth convincing evidence that the logo itself was first used in commerce by another entity, Future Publishing, and that its appearance was recently altered to make it appear more "similar" to EA's "Mirror's Edge" logo (specifically, it was changed from blue to red).

In sum, under the *Sleekcraft* factors, plaintiff has not sufficiently shown that consumers are likely to be confused as to the origin, endorsement, or approval of any of the products at issue in this litigation. For these reasons, Edge Games has failed to establish that it is likely to succeed on the merits.

2. IRREPARABLE HARM

Following the Supreme Court's decision in *Winter*, irreparable harm cannot be presumed—even for trademark actions. Rather, it is the plaintiff's burden to prove that "he is likely to suffer irreparable harm in the absence of preliminary relief." *Winter*, 129 S.Ct. at 374. In the context of preliminary injunctive relief, irreparable harm is established when a plaintiff is unlikely to be made whole by an award of monetary damages or some other legal remedy at a later date, in the ordinary course of litigation. See *California Pharmacists Ass'n v. Maxwell-Jolly*, 563 F.3d 847, 851–52 (9th Cir.2009). As explained below, plaintiff has failed to meet this burden.

First, as stated in the prior section, the preliminary injunction record contains compelling evidence that the asserted marks were fraudulently registered and/or have been abandoned by plaintiff. While a jury may ultimately find otherwise, this thunderstorm over the validity of plaintiff's asserted marks tempers the likelihood of irreparable harm. Indeed, without valid and protectable marks, Edge Games cannot suffer any harm to its property rights due to EA's continued use of the "Mirror's Edge" name.

Second, given the suspect nature of Dr. Langdell's representations to both the USPTO and the Court concerning plaintiff's current and future sales and business activities, it is an open question whether plaintiff's business activities legitimately extend beyond trolling various gaming-related industries for licensing opportunities. In this connection, plaintiff has not adequately shown that the potential harm to the "EDGE" marks during the interim period between the filing and resolution of this action could not be adequately remedied by legal damages.

Third, and most telling, it is undisputed that Edge Games waited over three years since "Mirror's Edge" was first announced and 21 months since "Mirror's Edge" was first offered for sale to the public before seeking a preliminary injunction. Due to this unreasonable delay, the bulk of the alleged "irreparable harm" to the asserted marks purportedly caused by the "Mirror's Edge" franchise has already been done. Edge Games has not shown why issuing a preliminary injunction now would prevent any irreparable harm to its marks beyond the "harm" that has already occurred. The undisputed fact that plaintiff did not timely act to prevent the "Mirror's Edge" franchise from inundating the market is alone sufficient to deny the instant motion.

For these reasons, this order finds—based upon the record presented—that Edge Games has not demonstrated that it is likely to suffer irreparable harm absent preliminary relief.

3. BALANCING THE EQUITIES AND THE PUBLIC INTEREST

Finally, the two remaining factors weigh heavily against granting the relief sought by plaintiff. First, for all the reasons already discussed in this order, Edge Games has not established that the balance of equities tips in its favor. All of its representations regarding the validity and use of the asserted marks are infected by evidence of deceit. Moreover, there is scant evidence that Edge Games has invested any amount of funds into the development of recent products and services bearing the asserted marks.

By contrast, EA has shown that it has invested millions of dollars into building and promoting the "Mirror's Edge" franchise. It now has millions of customers. While Edge Games could have sought a preliminary injunction prior to (or shortly after) sales of the original "Mirror's Edge" video game began in earnest, it did not. Instead, plaintiff waited 21 months to allow the "Mirror's Edge" franchise to develop and expand. During this delay, EA continued to create and release products carrying the "Mirror's Edge" name, including newly released versions of the video game for the Apple iPad and iPhone. Given this record, allowing Edge Games to obtain a preliminary injunction after allowing EA to invest in and develop the "Mirror's Edge" franchise over such a long period of time would be plainly inequitable and highly prejudicial to defendant. See *E-Systems, Inc. v. Monitek, Inc.*, 720 F.2d 604, 607 (9th Cir.1983). Second, Edge Games has not shown that the public interest typically associated with trademark infringement actions — avoiding confusion to consumers — would favor a preliminary injunction. Rather, as stated, plaintiff has not sufficiently established that consumers are likely to be confused or deceived by the products at issue.

For the foregoing reasons, this order finds that plaintiff has failed to establish that it is likely to succeed on the merits, that it is likely to suffer irreparable harm in the absence of preliminary relief, that the balance of equities tips in its favor, or that an injunction is in the public interest. As such, a preliminary injunction is not warranted under the factors set forth in *Winter*.

Notes and Questions

1. In the *Edge* decision, it might be an understatement to say that Judge Alsup was displeased with Dr. Langdell, the principal witness for the Plaintiff. Is it possible that Langdell's misconduct with respect to the trademark filings colored the court's views regarding the real possibility of confusion in the mind of the public? What do you think was the likelihood of confusion with respect to the two marks? Should the outcome have been different, if the Plaintiff made continuous use of the "Edge" mark?

2. An historical analysis of cases involving preliminary injunctions might lead one to believe that judges like to pick-and-choose, almost randomly, the factors to be considered when deciding whether or not to grant injunctive relief. For the weary law student attempting to pick a decent set of factors to memorize, the Supreme Court decision in *Winter v. Natural Resources Defense* Council, 555 U.S. 7 (2008), employed above in the *Edge* case, must have come as a relief. Those astute Remedies students who detected a factor missing from *Winter*, should presume that "Inadequate remedy at law," a lynch pin for all equitable relief, was most likely implied, and therefore, not specifically listed as a factor by the High Court.

3. *Activision Publ'g, Inc. v. Activision TV, Inc.*, 2013 WL 1003546, United States District Court (C.D., Cal., 2013), like *Edge*, involved allegations of fraud with respect to filing, though the claims were far less egregious. The Plaintiff Activision Publishing is a leader with respect to the development and marketing of videogames. Plaintiff claims that the Defendant (Activision TV) acted fraudulently when it registered the "Activision" mark.

In 1999, Defendant purported to register, on an "intent to use" basis, a U.S. trademark for the word "Activision" in connection with "illuminated advertising and display signs," and "promoting the goods and services of others by creating and displaying display signs." In 2005, after Defendant received a notice of abandonment, Defendant submitted a "Statement of Use," attesting that it had used the term "Activision" in commerce. In support of this assertion, Defendant submitted as a "specimen," a brochure depicting a television set with the word "Activision Systems" at the bottom. Plaintiff alleges that this representation was false because Defendants had never sold any such products to the public at that time. Nevertheless, on March 15, 2005, the U.S. Patent and Trademark Office registered a trademark in the mark "Activision" in the name of Ad Media Displays, Inc. Hence, Plaintiff sought to cancel this registration on the basis of the alleged fraud.

Chapter Nine

Trade Secrecy

Our intellectual property exploration began in the arena of exclusive federal jurisdiction as we initially examined copyright and patent infringements along with their related issues. From there the trek moved into the realm of overlapping jurisdiction as we considered trademarks. Now, for the final chapter of Part II, we come to an area that is state-law dominated, and grounded in express and implied confidentiality.

Secrecy is important for any industry predicated upon new technologies. For the videogame industry in particular, protecting secrets is even more essential. Nevertheless, the significance of game design privacy has diminished over the past several years. Videogames are too easily reverse engineered, emulated and duplicated. In addition, game designers are resorting to copyright and patent protection, which by their very nature, require public disclosure. Secrecy has pragmatically become a protection device designed to buy time and give, to those who claim it, a lead in the race to the marketplace. Such an advantage should not be underestimated.

Protection for trade secrets is nothing new. In the United States it is more than 170 years old. *Vickery v. Welch*, 36 Mass. 523 (1837); *see also Peabody v. Norfolk*, 98 Mass. 452, 459–60 (1868). The protection mechanism shares its justification with our previously discussed intellectual property laws. It provides economic incentives for innovation and invention by controlling the costs of protection. *See* RESTATEMENT (THIRD) OF UNFAIR COMPETITION § 39 cmt. a (1995); ROGER D. BLAIR & THOMAS F. COTTER, INTELLECTUAL PROPERTY 26 (2005). While trade secrecy laws require parties to take reasonable steps to protect their secrets, they do not require a continued investment in applications or registrations.

§ 9.10 State Governance
Versus Federal Preemption

Unlike the laws pertaining to patent, copyright, and trademark infringement, there is no general federal protection for the misappropriation of trade secrets. Federal jurisdiction over trade secrecy claims, like federal jurisdiction over right of publicity claims, depends either upon diversity jurisdiction under 28 U.S.C. § 1332 or supplemental jurisdiction under 28 U.S.C. § 1367. There are, however, also the anti-hacking provisions of 18 U.S.C. § 2701 which address one of several methods by which trade secrets might be unlawfully compromised.

Titled "Unlawful Access to Stored Communication," § 2701(a) provides in part that whoever "(1) intentionally accesses without authorization a facility through which an electronic communication service is provided or (2) intentionally exceeds an authorization to access that facility" could be subjected to fines and imprisonment for up to 5 years for a first offense, if that person "obtains, alters, or prevents authorized access to a wire or electronic communication while it is in electronic storage in such system." Some have advocated for increased federal protection for trade secrets, though without much success thus far. *See* Christopher Rebel J. Pace, *The Case for a Federal Trade Secrets Act*, 8 HARV. J. L. & TECH. 427 (1995).

Since trade secrets are primarily protected by state law, there exists a potential conflict between state and federal intellectual property jurisdiction. Where there is such a conflict, federal law would prevail under the Supremacy Clause of the Constitution. U.S. Const. Art. VI. In *Kewanee Oil Co. v. Bicron Corp.*, 416 U.S. 470 (1974), the Supreme Court considered whether federal patent and state trade secret law were in conflict. The Sixth Circuit ruled that there was a conflict, holding Ohio's trade secret law to be conflicting. All other circuits addressing the question found otherwise. *Id.* at 472–73. The Supreme Court sided with the majority of the circuits, indicating that patent and trade secret law had coexisted for over a century and that Congress had taken no express action to interfere with state trade secret protection. *Id.* at 493. The Court thus determined that there was no conflict between the two forms of protection, and it even rejected partial preemption of trade secrets that could have been patented. *Id.* at 491–92. *See also Bonito Boats v. Thunder Craft Boats*, 489 U.S. 141, 155–56 (1989). This does *not*, however, imply that all federal preemption issues involving trade secrets have been resolved.

* * *

Videotronics, Inc. v. Bend Elecs.

United States District Court, District of Nevada, 1983
564 F. Supp. 1471.

REED, JR., District Judge.

Plaintiff, Videotronics, Inc., a Nevada corporation, seeks a preliminary injunction to restrain defendants from manufacturing, advertising or selling a video amusement device, which plaintiff alleges was developed through misappropriation of trade secrets of plaintiff and through a breach of a confidential relationship between plaintiff and defendants. Plaintiff also seeks to enjoin alleged "palming off" of plaintiff's product, an electronic video poker game machine, by defendants.

[Plaintiff made a video poker game entitled *Challenger Wild Poker*. The principal defendant, a company called Video Horizons, Inc. (referenced by the court as "VHI") distributed the game. Somewhere along the way, VHI copied plaintiff's computer chip that controlled the game, and started marketing its own, competing poker game.

The issue in the case is not whether the copying by VHI was wrongful or whether its distribution of a competing game should be enjoined. Rather it is whether plaintiff can base its suit on misappropriation of trade secrets and breach of confidences under Nevada law (which was pled in its complaint) or whether it must base its suit on the Copyright Act (which was not pled). —ED.]

There was no written agreement between plaintiff and defendant containing any requirement that defendants maintain secrecy as to any of the equipment, programs, or the design of the equipment which Bend/VO distributed. None of plaintiff's equipment which is the subject of this case appears to have been patented or copyrighted.

THE MOTION FOR PRELIMINARY INJUNCTION

The threshold question as to whether the preliminary injunction should issue is whether either the circuit design (hardware), the character generator mechanism, or computer program (software) of the plaintiff's video poker game constitute a trade secret. Since this is a diversity action the Court applies the law of the State of Nevada. Where controlling Nevada precedent is lacking the Court will turn to the generally accepted principles of the common law of trade secret and unfair competition. The generally accepted definition of a trade secret is that found in Restatement of Torts §757, comment b (1939):

> [a] trade secret may consist of any formula, pattern, device or compilation of information which is used in one's business, and which gives him an opportunity to obtain an advantage over competitors who do not know or use it. It may be a formula for a chemical compound, a process of manufacturing, treating or preserving materials, a pattern for a machine or other device, or a list of customers.

In order to succeed on the merits of its trade secret claim, plaintiff must demonstrate that (1) it possessed a trade secret, and (2) defendant is using that trade secret in breach of an agreement, confidence, or duty, or as a result of discovery by improper means. Restatement of Torts §757 (1937). The Restatement of Torts §757 further indicates that other factors to be considered in determining whether a trade secret exists are: (1) the degree of secrecy both within and without the plaintiff's business; (2) the efforts by plaintiff to develop the process and to preserve its secrecy; (3) the value of the process to the plaintiff and its competitors; and (4) the difficulty with which the process could be duplicated by others. Public disclosure of a trade secret destroys any confidential relationship upon which a trade secret is based.

It is clear from the record and evidence received herein that plaintiff expended substantial time and expense in developing its "Challenger Wild Poker" video device. Assuming that the unique circuit design and computer video program display constituted trade secrets under the above definition the Court must consider whether defendants use of the plaintiff's device in the substantially similar machines now manufactured by defendant VHI was appropriated through breach of a confidential relationship as maintained by plaintiff.

Regardless of the reason or motivation behind the deterioration of the distributorship relationship between plaintiff and defendants, it is clear that the means used to duplicate plaintiff's poker machine was not unlike that which may have been employed by any owner of one of plaintiff's devices. In particular the Court is sensitive to plaintiff's claims regarding the duplication of the information stored upon the tiny silicon computer "chips." These "chips," or software, store the instructions and data of a computer program.

Unlike the electronic circuit boards which can easily be recreated through observation by a trained individual equipped with a schematic diagram such as that supplied by plaintiff to its customers, the owners of its "Challenger Wild Poker" device here, the actual computer program stored on the "chip" can be copied much in the same manner as one might record the contents of a phonograph record or cassette tape without knowing really exactly what the various detailed complexities of such information is or how it was actually created.

While the parties have obliterated any distinction between the two, the tort of misappropriation created out of whole cloth by the Supreme Court in *Int'l News Serv. v. Associated Press*, 248 U.S. 215 (1918), and which exists independently from the law of trade secrets, is seemingly also involved in this case. As found in J. Thomas McCarthy, *Trademarks & Unfair Competition*, § 10:25 p. 322 (1973) three elements are needed to prove a case of misappropriation:

(1) Plaintiff has made a substantial investment of time, effort and money into creating the thing misappropriated such that the court can characterize that "thing" as a kind of property right.

(2) Defendant has appropriated the "thing" at little or no cost, such that the court can characterize defendant's actions as "reaping where it has not sown."

(3) Defendant has injured plaintiff by the misappropriation.

Upon first impression this appears to be a classic case for application of the law of misappropriation. In the eyes of the Court a strong case on the merits has been established by plaintiff at this stage in that each of the above three elements have apparently been met here. That federal law of patent and copyright preempts areas that otherwise would be subject to the state law of unfair competition and misappropriation is a matter which has been discussed and defined, albeit not necessarily with great clarity, by the Supreme Court on several occasions. *Sears, Roebuck & Co. v. Stiffel*, 376 U.S. 225 (1964); *Compco Corp. v. Day-Brite Lighting, Inc.*, 376 U.S. 234 (1964); *Goldstein v. California*, 412 U.S. 546 (1973); *Kewanee Oil Co. v. Bicron Corp.*, 416 U.S. 470 (1974).

Without discussing these important cases in detail it is clear that in certain instances, an intellectual property which falls outside the protection of either federal copyright or patent law may still be found to not be entitled protection under state law regardless of theory because federal policy favors preemption of the area in question. It is even clearer, however, that a property which is subject to protection under federal patent or copyright law cannot also obtain the benefit of protection under either state unfair competition or misappropriation law for the same reasons.

This point is well illustrated by *Synercon Tech. v. University Computing*, 474 F. Supp. 37 (N.D. Tex. 1979). There the Court found that the developer of new input formats, instruction manuals and related services to provide more simplified access to a computer program for structural analysis was not entitled to protection under the state misappropriation doctrine even though the court had previously found plaintiff's material were the type of things covered by copyright laws although not entitled to protection thereunder. The Court concluded in its well reasoned decision that allowing extension of the state law doctrine of misappropriation into such an area already covered by copyright law would constitute an unacceptable conflict with federal policy.

The facts here present an even more compelling case for finding that an unacceptable conflict with federal policy would be created were the court to apply the state doctrine of misappropriation in this instance. That is, the great weight of authority indicates that the essence of the intellectual property the plaintiff seeks protection for — the computer program which is responsible for the unique character generator mechanism of the "Challenger Wild Poker" device — is entitled to protection under copyright law.

The policy argument made by plaintiff is well taken. That is, the law should encourage technical innovation such as that employed by the unique program designed for plaintiff's videogame by prohibiting others from copying such a program in much the same fashion as one might record a phonograph record and then market that product as his own. Congress has acted in this regard by extending broad protection to certain aspects of audiovisual technology under the 1976 Copyright Act, as amended in 1980, 17 U.S.C. § 101, et seq. The plaintiff, however, has apparently not sought protection under the Copyright

Act up to this time. Because the Court has found that the plaintiff's property interest in the computer programs contained in its electronic video device is covered by the Copyright Act, relief under the state common law doctrines of misappropriation and trade secret cannot be obtained here.

Finally, the plaintiff also seeks to enjoin defendants from "palming off" their video poker games as those manufactured by the plaintiff. While there is some indication that defendant VHI may well have engaged in such conduct in the past the plaintiff does not seriously contend that defendants are presently "palming off" in violation of NRS 598.410. Hence, it appears that any relief plaintiff may be entitled to in this regard may be adequately provided in the form of monetary compensation which may be awarded upon trial on the merits. With the exception of the "palming off" claim, the Court has found that plaintiff has failed to make more than a weak showing on the merits of all aspects of this action and therefore a preliminary injunction is inappropriate at this time.

IT IS ORDERED that the motion for preliminary injunction filed by plaintiff is hereby DENIED.

Notes and Questions

1. To obtain trade secrecy protection, how important is it that the claimant take specific identifiable steps to guard the secret from disclosure? The court distinguished *Videotronics* from *J & K Computer Sys., Inc. v. Parrish*, 642 P.2d 732 (Utah 1982) on that basis. It found that Videotronics did not treat its subject hardware and software as secrets. In *J & K Computer*, on the other hand, the plaintiff did take steps to keep its computer program out of the hands of the general public. The Supreme Court of Utah noted:

> With the evidence recited above before it, the trial court could have reasonably determined that J & K's accounts receivable program was secret and worthy of protection by the law. Defendants assert that the accounts receivable program was revealed to certain customers and therefore not protectable. The record, however, shows that the plaintiff endeavored to keep its accounts receivable program secret. Plaintiff's employees and customers were informed of the secret nature of the program. The program was marked with the following legend: "Program Products Proprietary To—J & K Computer Systems, Inc., Salt Lake City, Utah. Authorized Use By License Agreement Only." That a few of the plaintiff's customers had access to the program does not prevent the program from being classified as a trade secret where the plaintiff was attempting to keep the secret and the program is still unavailable to the computer trade as a whole.

Id. at 735.

What types of actions or steps consistent with its business model could Videotronics have taken in order to keep its hardware and software secret?

2. Is it truly possible to distinguish a "misappropriation" from a copyright infringement? In *Videotronics*, Judge Reed referred to the misappropriation rule of *Int'l News Serv. v. Associated Press*, 248 U.S. 215 (1918) and the apparent dilemma caused by permitting both causes of action to exist (the *Int'l News Service* case permitted the existence of an action for the misappropriation of property). The problem is exacerbated by the broad rule presented in the *Int'l News Service* case. Commentators have argued that the *Int'l News Service* majority opinion: "lacked the essential quality that justifies common law

adjudication. Its reasoning was entirely ungrounded. Instead of resolving an actual dispute between two opposing litigants, it merely gave an abstract pronouncement of a grand principle that has no obvious boundaries." Douglas G. Baird, *The Story of INS v. AP: Property, Natural Monopoly, and the Uneasy Legacy of a Concocted Controversy*, in Intellectual Property Stories 9, 32 (Jane C. Ginsburg & Rochelle Cooper Dreyfuss, eds., 2006). Today, in face of the 1976 Copyright Act, the scope of *Int'l News Service* is relatively narrow. The Supreme Court recognized the misappropriation claim well before the enactment of the Copyright Act of 1976 and its preemption provision in § 301. Relying on the preemption provision, the Second Circuit, in a leading case on the topic, confined *Int'l News Service* claims to "hot news" situations defined by the following elements:

(i)   the plaintiff generates or collects information at some cost or expense,

(ii) the value of the information is highly time-sensitive,

(iii) the defendant's use of the information constitutes free-riding on the plaintiff's costly efforts to generate or collect it,

(iv) the defendant's use of the information is in direct competition with a product or service offered by the plaintiff,

(v)   the ability of other parties to free-ride on the efforts of the plaintiff would so reduce the incentive to produce the product or service that its existence or quality would be substantially threatened.

NBA v. Motorola, Inc., 105 F.3d 841, 852 (2d Cir. 1997) (internal citations omitted). *See also Confold Pac., Inc. v. Polaris Indus.*, 433 F.3d 952, 960 (7th Cir. 2006) (following the Second Circuit's approach).

3. With respect to videogame development, how is § 301 of the Copyright Act likely to affect future claims for misappropriation? Subject to exceptions, § 301(a) states:

> On and after January 1, 1978, all legal or equitable rights that are equivalent to any of the exclusive rights within the general scope of copyright as specified by Section 106 works of authorship that are fixed in a tangible medium of expression and come within the subject matter of copyright as specified by section 102 and 103, whether created before or after that date and whether published or unpublished, are governed exclusively by this title. Thereafter, no person is entitled to any such right or equivalent right in any such work under the common law or statutes of any State.

Would a failure to register a copyrightable work have any effect on the likelihood of federal preemption of a claim for a misappropriation of that work?

* * *

Silicon Knights, Inc. v. Epic Games, Inc.

United States District Court, Eastern District of North Carolina, 2012
917 F. Supp. 2d 503

Dever III, Chief Judge.

On May 30, 2012, after an eleven-day trial and one day of deliberations, a jury returned a verdict against Silicon Knights, Inc. ("Silicon Knights" or "plaintiff"). The jury found that Silicon Knights failed to prove its breach of contract claim, and that Epic Games, Inc. ("Epic Games" or "defendant") proved its breach of contract, copyright infringement, and trade secret misappropriation counterclaims. The jury awarded Epic Games $2,650,000.00 for its breach of contract counterclaim, and $1,800,000.00 for its copyright infringement and trade secret misappropriation counterclaims. On May 30, 2012, the court entered a judgment reflecting the jury's verdict. Thereafter, in accordance with a schedule that this court set, Silicon Knights and Epic Games filed many post-trial motions. [The following facts are derived from the Verdict and Settlement Summary — ED.]

Plaintiff, Silicon Knights Inc. claimed that it entered into a license agreement with Epic Games Inc. (Epic) to license a piece of software known as Unreal Engine 3 ("UE3") on May 10, 2005. Plaintiff claimed it intended to use the UE3 engine in development of videogames it was building for the Xbox 360 and Playstation 3. According to Plaintiff, Epic misrepresented UE3's capabilities and its ability to support the UE3 engine, and failed to meet deadlines necessary for development of games for the Xbox 360 and Playstation 3. Plaintiff alleged that Epic used the revenue it obtained from licensing the UE3 engine to fund the development of its own games. Plaintiff also claimed it attempted to use the UE3 engine determined that the engine did not work properly. Plaintiff claimed that as a result, it created its own game engine known as the Silicon Knights Engine (SK Engine).

Plaintiff sued Epic in the federal court, asserting claims for fraud, negligent misrepresentation, breach of warranty, breach of contract, and unfair competition under the North Carolina Unfair and Deceptive Trade Practices Act. Plaintiff sought recovery of damages for the cost of developing the SK Engine, profits it lost as a result of its need to renegotiate its development contracts, and profits lost by virtue of delays in its games coming to market due to issues with the UE3 engine. Epic counterclaimed, alleging that it provided free use of the UE3 engine to Plaintiff for approximately nine months before the May 10, 2005 license agreement was finalized, and that Plaintiff used UE3 to develop a game prototype. According to Epic, Plaintiff even secured a development and publishing contract with Microsoft based on the prototype. Under the license agreement with Epic, Plaintiff reportedly received the right to use UE3 to develop a single videogame known as "Too Human" on a single game platform (the Xbox 360), in exchange for an up front payment of $750,000.

Epic said the license agreement did not obligate it to make any improvements, enhancements, updates, fixes or other changes to UE3. Epic also claimed that the license agreement prohibited Plaintiff from using the UE3 engine for other videogames without the payment of additional license fees. Nevertheless, Plaintiff allegedly began to use UE3 in the development of additional games, including (1) The Box; (2) X-Men: Destiny; (3) The Sandman; (4) Siren in the Maelstrom; (5) King's Quest; (6) Eternal Darkness 2; and (7) Too Human 2. Epic contended that Silicon Knights used original copyright protected computer code contained in the UE3 in the development of its SK Engine, and used a portion of the UE3 known as the Unreal Editor in the development of its games.

Epic's counterclaim included breach of the license agreement, misappropriation of trade secrets, and copyright infringement. Epic sought recovery of damages for the unpaid license fees Silicon Knights should have paid for the improper use of the UE3 code in its games, and for Silicon Knights' improper use of its trade secrets and copyrighted code. The case proceeded to a jury trial before Judge James C. Dever III. The jury returned its verdict May 30, 2012. On Plaintiff's claim for breach of contract, the jury determined that Epic had breached the license agreement, but declined to award any damages. On Epic's counterclaim for breach of the license agreement, jurors found that Silicon Knights breached the license agreement, and awarded Epic $2,650,000 for damages. On Epic's counterclaims for copyright infringement and misappropriation of trade secrets, the jury determined that Silicon Knights had infringed a copyright or copyrights, and had misappropriated Epic's trade secret or trade secrets. Epic was awarded $1,800,000 in damages.

[Of the many post-trial motions presented by both parties, most of which are procedural in nature, the discussions have been deleted, except for the following ruling pertaining to a potential overlap with respect to federal and state-related damages:]

In its motion for remittitur, [Plaintiff] Silicon Knights contends that Epic Games cannot recover damages for both its breach of contract counterclaim and its copyright infringement and trade secret misappropriation counterclaims. Specifically, Silicon Knights argues that the damages the jury awarded to Epic Games constitute double recovery, that Epic Games is entitled only to the damages awarded on its breach of contract counterclaim, and that the judgment should be amended accordingly.

In opposition to Silicon Knights's remittitur motion, Epic Games argues that the damages awarded for its breach of contract counterclaim did not overlap with the damages awarded for its copyright infringement and trade secret misappropriation counterclaims. Specifically, Epic Games contends that, for its breach of contract counterclaim, the jury awarded only the unpaid licensing fees for The Box/Ritualyst, X-Men: Destiny, The Sandman, and Siren in the Maelstrom.

In contrast, for its copyright infringement and trade secret misappropriation counterclaims, Epic Games argues that the jury awarded only the ill-gotten profits Silicon Knights reaped from its copyright infringement and trade secret misappropriation as to The Box/Ritualyst, X-Men: Destiny, The Sandman, and Siren in the Maelstrom. Because the damages Epic Games sought and received for its breach of contract counterclaim did not overlap with those it sought and received for its copyright infringement and trade secret misappropriation counterclaims, and because governing law permits the recovery of these distinct damages, Epic Games argues that remittitur is not appropriate.

Epic Games's argument comports with the evidence, arguments, and legal principles in this case. In connection with Epic Games's breach of contract counterclaim, the court instructed the jury that Epic Games had to prove (1) that Silicon Knights and Epic Games entered into the May 10, 2005 license agreement, (2) that Silicon Knights breached either paragraph 2(a) or paragraph 2(g), or both, and (3) that Epic Games suffered damages as a proximate result of Silicon Knights's breach of paragraph 2(a) or paragraph 2(g), or both. The breach of contract counterclaim concerned the unpaid licensing fees for The Box/Ritualyst, X-Men: Destiny, The Sandman, and Siren in the Maelstrom. As for damages on the breach of contract counterclaim, the court instructed the jury as to both nominal and actual damages.

In connection with the copyright infringement counterclaim under the federal Copyright Act, the court instructed the jury (1) that Epic Games had to prove that Epic Games is the owner of a valid copyright or valid copyrights and (2) that Silicon Knights copied original elements from a version or versions of the Unreal Engine 3's computer code in which Epic Games owns a valid copyright. The court then gave extensive instructions expounding on these two elements.

As for the trade secret misappropriation counterclaim under North Carolina's Trade Secrets Protection Act, the court instructed the jury that Epic Games had to prove (1) that Epic Games's proprietary information in the Unreal Engine 3's computer code constitutes a trade secret or trade secrets; (2) that Silicon Knights misappropriated Epic Games's trade secret or trade secrets, and (3) that Silicon Knights's misappropriation of Epic Games's trade secret or trade secrets resulted in the unjust enrichment of Silicon Knights. See id. at 49. The court then gave extensive instructions expounding on these elements.

As for damages on the copyright infringement counterclaim and trade secret misappropriation counterclaim, the court instructed the jury:

> If you find that Silicon Knights infringed a copyright or copyrights of Epic Games, or misappropriated a trade secret or trade secrets of Epic Games, then you must determine the amount of damages that Epic Games is entitled to recover. Epic Games is entitled to recover any of Silicon Knights' [s] net profits attributable to any copyright infringement or trade secret misappropriation by Silicon Knights. Therefore, you should [a]ward Epic Games Silicon Knights'[s] net profits only if you find that Epic Games proved a causal relationship between any copyright infringement or trade secret misappropriation and any net profits of Silicon Knights.
>
> Net profits are the difference between total revenues and total expenses. Silicon Knights'[s] total revenue is all of Silicon Knights'[s] receipts from uses or sales of all works, if any, that infringe a copyright or copyrights of Epic Games or that misappropriate a trade secret or trade secrets of Epic Games. Epic Games has the burden of proving by a preponderance of the evidence Silicon Knights'[s] total revenues.
>
> Silicon Knights'[s] total expenses are all operating costs and production costs incurred in producing Silicon Knights'[s] total revenue on all works, if any, that infringe a copyright or copyrights of Epic Games or that misappropriated the trade secret or trade secrets of Epic Games. Silicon Knights has the burden of proving by a preponderance of the evidence its total expenses.
>
> To calculate total revenues and total expenses, you should begin by calculating the revenues and expenses associated with each of Silicon Knights' [s] works, if any, that infringes a copyright or copyrights of Epic Games or that misappropriates a trade secret or trade secrets of Epic Games. Once you have calculated Silicon Knights'[s] revenues and expenses for each of … those works, if any, you should add all the revenues together and add all the expenses together. The resulting sums will be Silicon Knights'[s] total revenues and total expenses. You should then subtract Silicon Knights'[s] total expenses from its total revenues. The resulting difference will be Silicon Knights'[s] net profits or net losses on all works, if any, that infringe a copyright or copyrights of Epic Games or that misappropriated a trade secret or trade secrets of Epic Games.
>
> In making these calculations, you should attribute all of Silicon Knights'[s] revenue for any given work to any infringement or misappropriation committed by Silicon Knights, unless you find that a portion of Silicon Knights'[s] revenues derived from that work is attributable to factors other than Silicon Knights' [s] use of Epic Games'[s] copyrighted works or trade secrets. Silicon Knights has the burden of proving the portion of its revenues, if any, attributable to factors other than any infringement by Silicon Knights of Epic Games'[s] copyrighted work or works, or any misappropriation by Silicon Knights of Epic Games'[s] trade secret or trade secrets.

Finally, Epic Games seeks to recover Silicon Knights'[s] net profits on the following four video game projects only: The Box/Ritualyst X-Men: Destiny, The Sandman, and

Siren in the Maelstrom. Accordingly, you should consider only those four video game projects when calculating revenues, expenses, [total revenues,] total expenses, and net profits. In addition, the court instructed the jury that Epic Games was not entitled to double recovery on the copyright infringement counterclaim and the trade secret misappropriation counterclaim. Specifically, the court instructed the jury:

> When a party owns both a copyright and a trade secret in the same material, that party may not obtain a double recover[y] [when] the damages for copyright infringement and trade secret misappropriation are coextensive. In other words, if you find that Epic Games owned a copyright and a trade secret or trade secrets in the same material[,] and that the same actions by Silicon Knights infringed that copyright and misappropriated that trade secret or trade secrets, then Epic Games is entitled to recover damages for either Silicon Knights'[s] infringement of that copyrighted material or Silicon Knights'[s] misappropriation of that trade secret, but not for both.

Under the federal Copyright Act, Epic Games could have sought "to recover the actual damages suffered by [it] as a result of the infringement, and any profits of the infringer that are attributable to the infringement and are not taken into account in computing the actual damages." 17 U.S.C. § 504(b); *Walker v. Forbes, Inc.*, 28 F.3d 409, 412 (4th Cir. 1994). Epic Games, however, only sought Silicon Knights's ill-gotten profits. Likewise, under the North Carolina Trade Secrets Protection Act, Epic Games only sought "the unjust enrichment caused by misappropriation of a trade secret." N.C. Gen.Stat. § 66-154(b). As noted, the jury awarded Epic Games $2,650,000.00 in actual damages on the breach of contract counterclaim and $1,800,000.00 on the copyright infringement and trade secret misappropriation counterclaims.

The recovery on the breach of contract counterclaim served a different interest and was not based on the same conduct or proof as the conduct and proof giving rise to the recovery on the copyright infringement and trade secret misappropriation counterclaims. The breach of contract counterclaim only made Silicon Knights pay the licensing fee due to Epic Games under the May 10, 2005 licensing agreement for The Box/Ritualyst, X-Men: Destiny, The Sandman, and Siren in the Maelstrom. In contrast, Epic Games's copyright infringement and trade secret misappropriation counterclaim only stripped Silicon Knights of the "profit generated as a result of the use of the infringed [code and misappropriated trade secrets]." Walker, 28 F.3d at 412. "By stripping the infringer ... of the profit generated as a result of the use of the infringed item, [17 U.S.C. § 504(b)] makes clear that there is no gain to be made from taking someone else's intellectual property without their consent." Id.; see *McRoberts Software, Inc. v. Media 100, Inc.*, 329 F.3d 557, 566–70 (7th Cir.2003). Moreover, this court's conclusion that there is no double recovery in this case not only comports with 17 U.S.C. § 504(b), but also with North Carolina law. See, e.g., *United Labs., Inc. v. Kuykendall*, 335 N.C. 183, 191–94, 437 S.E.2d 374, 379–81 (1993).

Finally, the court has reviewed the cases that Silicon Knights cited in its memorandum and reply and finds that the cited cases are distinguishable from the evidence, argument, and legal principles at issue in this case. Cf. Walker, 28 F.3d at 412 ("[G]iven the remarkable breadth of works eligible for copyright protection, and the numerosity of variables involved in determining loss and gain under each scenario, the experience of copyright damages has been one of case-by-case assessment of the factors involved, rather than application of hard and fast rules.").

Accordingly, the court denies Silicon Knights's motion for remittitur.

Notes and Questions

1. Would the result in the *Silicon Knights* case have been the same if Epic had not limited the type of damages that it sought?

2. Among the post-trial motions filed by the parties, consistency between federal and state law was not a problem with respect to Epic's motion for an injunctive relief against Silicon Knights. In addition to money damages, a permanent injunction was authorized and appropriate under the Federal Copyright Act and under North Carolina law, requiring Silicon Knights to remove from its systems all of Epic's copyrighted material and trade secrets. Silicon Knights was likewise enjoined from distributing all products that contained Epic's copyrighted material or trade secrets, and it was also enjoined from creating any product using those copyrighted materials or trade secrets. See 17 U.S.C.A. §§ 502(a), 503(b); N.C.G.S.A. § 66-154(a). Following the post-trial motions, on appeal, the judgment was affirmed. *See Silicon Knights, Inc. v. Epic Games, Inc.*, 551 Fed. Appx. 646 (4th Cir. N.C. 2014).

3. To what extent does the *Silicon Knights* case provide significant or interesting hindsight for Notes (following *Videotronics*) 1 and 3? What key factor or factors would you use to distinguish *Silicon Knights* from *Videotronics*?

§ 9.20 The Uniform Trade Secrets Act

In a fashion similar to the Uniform Commercial Code, the Uniform Trade Secrets Act (UTSA) provides a standard set of precepts for which the individual states are free to ignore, reject, or accept subject to modification. Most states have in fact adopted some form of UTSA. The heart of the statute lies in its definitions of "Trade Secret" and "Misappropriation."

For "Trade Secret," § 1(4) of the Act provides a two-element test by defining it as: "[I]nformation, including a formula, pattern, compilation, program device, method, technique, or process, that: (i) derives independent economic value, actual or potential, from not being generally known to, and not being readily ascertainable by proper means by, other persons who can obtain economic value from its disclosure or use, and (ii) is the subject of efforts that are reasonable under the circumstances to maintain its secrecy.

Section 1(2) defines 'misappropriation' as the:

(i) acquisition of a trade secret of another by a person who knows or has reason to know that the trade secret was acquired by improper means; or

(ii) disclosure or use of a trade secret of another without express or implied consent by a person who: (A) used improper means to acquire knowledge of the trade secret; or (B) at the time of disclosure or use knew or had reason to know that his knowledge of the trade secret was (I) derived from or through a person who has utilized improper means to acquire it; (II) acquired under circumstances giving rise to a duty to maintain its secrecy or limit its use; or (III) derived from or through a person who owed a duty to the person seeking relief to maintain its secrecy or limit its use; or (C) before a material change of his position, knew or had reason to know that it was a trade secret and that knowledge of it had been acquired by accident or mistake."

"Improper means" is defined to include "theft, bribery, misrepresentation, breach or inducement of a breach of duty to maintain secrecy, or espionage through electronic or other means." Uniform Trade Secrets Act § 1(1) (1985).

In the tradition of the UCC's success, other uniform statutes have developed and spread. Since its organization in 1892, the National Conference of Commissioners on Uniform State Laws has drafted several model state statutes, including the Uniform Negotiable Instruments Law (1896), Uniform Sales Act (1906), Uniform Warehouse Receipts Act (1906), etc. *See gen.*, E. Hunter Taylkor, *Uniformity of Commercial Law and State-by-State Enactment: A Confluence of Contradictions*, 30 HASTINGS L. J. 337 (1978). In 1979, the Uniform Law Commissioners published the Uniform Trade Secrets Act. Seven states adopted the 1979 version. In 1985, the Commissioners published an amended UTSA, which has been adopted by forty states. As of the end of 2014, nearly every state and The Virgin Islands, District of Columbia, and Puerto Rico has adopted some form of the UTSA. New York continues to be the obstinate holdout.

* * *

Pepper v. Int'l Gaming Sys., LLC

United States District Court, Northern District of Mississippi, 2004
312 F. Supp. 2d 853

PEPPER, District Judge.

This cause comes before the Court upon Defendants' Motion for Summary Judgment. Having apprized itself thoroughly and exhaustively of the motion, the responses thereto, the accompanying briefs, the controlling authorities, and the underlying facts and circumstances, the Court concludes that the defendants' motion for summary judgment should be granted for failure of the plaintiff to present sufficient evidence to prove his claims.

I. FACTUAL BACKGROUND

Daniel Webster Pepper Jr. filed this suit on May 9, 2001 against Defendants International Gaming Systems, LLC, and its former officers, agents, and/or employees Joseph I. Lerner, Stephen Patton, and Charles E. Crosslin. The complaint sets forth seven claims: copyright infringement, misappropriation of trade secrets, breach of contract, tortious interference with business expectancy, aiding and abetting, fraud, and civil conspiracy. All of the claims center around the plaintiff's basic allegation that the defendants stole attributes of his copyrighted computerized bingo software program and incorporated them into their own bingo program "Cadillac Bingo."

Plaintiff avers that beginning in 1994, he began development of software to computerize games in the bingo industry. Around this time Defendant Crosslin, a former manager of a bingo operation in Tupelo, Mississippi, agreed to assist the plaintiff in this undertaking by providing hardware and funding for the project. According to the plaintiff, however, Defendant Crosslin did not perform satisfactorily and thus Defendant Crosslin dropped out of the undertaking around June 10, 1995, taking back the computer he gave to the plaintiff. Plaintiff avers in his complaint that Defendant Crosslin failed to substantially contribute to the undertaking.

After developing the bingo software on his own, the plaintiff submitted his application to the Copyright Office for registration on October 2, 1995. Plaintiff received his first

Certificate of Registration effective November 13, 1995. However, because the Copyright Office made an mistake, the plaintiff received therefrom a corrected Certificate of Registration in June of 1996.

Essentially, the software is designed to perform specific tasks for the user to play multiple bingo games by computer. According to the plaintiff, the software "is an especially efficient application program containing proprietary routines, graphic designs, and unique programming logic. Because of its nature, the Software permits increased volume, productivity, and efficiency for any bingo operation which utilizes it."

On October 21, 1995 (after plaintiff turned in his copyright registration application but before it became effective) Defendant Joseph I. Lerner signed an confidentiality agreement with the plaintiff in Tupelo in which Lerner was to work as a consultant for the plaintiff and Defendant Crosslin. The confidentiality agreement, in its entirety, provided:

> I, Joseph I. Lerner, do hereby, agree to work as a consultant for Charles Crosslin and Dan Pepper under the following terms:
>
> All information concerning this project will remain strictly confidential. Fu[r]thermore, I specifically agree not to discuss, refer or in any manner convey any information about this work or project to any individual, party, or company or other project. I also agree not to use, convey or transfer this information in any manner that would compete with this project or its owners which are Charles Crosslin and Dan Pepper. This is a comprehensive and continuing agreement of which I fully understand.

Plaintiff then provided Defendant Lerner with a copy of his software and accompanying notes. During the months of October and November of 1996, Defendant Lerner made additional visits with the plaintiff in Tupelo, requesting and receiving updated graphics and program information. During the first of these four meetings with Plaintiff, Defendant Patton accompanied Defendant Lerner. Plaintiff asserts that these three parties "agreed to proceed to market the program with [the plaintiff] to retain one-half interest in the project and Lerner to share the other half with Patten [sic]." Defendants deny the existence of such an agreement.

Defendant Lerner does not deny that he agreed to and did bring potential investors to the some of the meetings with the plaintiff so that the plaintiff could demonstrate the bingo program. Defendants deny plaintiff's assertion that thereafter Defendants Lerner and Patten made multiple assurances to the plaintiff that he would "retain one-half of the revenue from the venture without any further commitment or obligation from the Plaintiff to market and develop the Software." Plaintiff refers to these assurances as promises they would "take care of" the plaintiff.

By this time, Defendants Lerner and Patten formed Defendant International Gaming Services, LLC for the purpose of marketing and selling the plaintiff's software. Plaintiff alleges that he assisted the defendants by "divulging his secrets, by demonstrating the Software to potential investors, and by complying with each of his requests for assistance in promoting the project, al based upon the assurances made by Lerner and Patten [sic]."

The gravamen of the instant suit surrounds the plaintiff's two key assertions. First, that the defendants International Gaming Services, LLC and its agents Lerner and Patton "began to produce and market the Software under the name of 'Cadillac Bingo,' all in direct violation of the agreement between the parties and of the copyright owned by Plaintiff." Second, that "by making unauthorized copies of the Software, and by distributing those copies and/or derivative computer programs, Defendants have willingly infringed, and continue willfully to infringe, Plaintiff's exclusive rights under the Copyright Act."

Defendants deny these assertions. In their responsive motions and pleadings, the defendants admit that the plaintiff provided them a copy of the software but argue that it was incomplete and it never ran properly. They deny that the plaintiff gave them all of his notes regarding the software. They also deny the validity of the confidentiality agreement, signed only by Defendant Lerner and not by IGS (formed after the agreement) or Patten, and argue that therefore they could neither have breached it nor tortiously interfered with it. Defendants deny further that there ever was a trade secret to misappropriate since the plaintiff freely disclosed to multiple parties what parts of the software he had presented; therefore, there was no secret. They deny that they infringed the plaintiff's copyright by copying. The defendants also argue that the plaintiff cannot prove any of his claims for various reasons, including the lack of an expert or an expert report to establish elements illegally copied and the inability to prove the exact substance and amount of the plaintiff's program registered at the Copyright Office versus the substance and amount of the current version. Finally, the defendants argue that all of the plaintiff's claims must be denied because time has run out to assert them pursuant to the statute of limitations applicable to each claim.

II. DISCUSSION

Misappropriation of Trade Secrets

The Mississippi Uniform Trade Secrets Act, Mississippi Code Annotated § 75-26-1, *et seq.* is identical to the Uniform Trade Secrets Act, 14 U.L.A. 437 (1990). According to the MUTSA, trade secret misappropriation means:

(i) Acquisition of a trade secret of another person who knows or has reason to know that the secret was acquired by improper means; or

(ii) Disclosure or use of a trade secret of another without express or implied consent by a person who:

1. Used improper means to acquire knowledge of the trade secret; or

2. At the time of disclosure or use, knew or had reason to know that his knowledge of the trade secret was:

   a. Derived from or through a person who had utilized improper means to acquire it;

   b. Acquired under circumstances giving rise to a duty to maintain its secrecy or limit its use; or

   c. Derived from or through a person who owed a duty to the person seeking relief to maintain its secrecy or limit its use; or

3. Before a material change of his or her position, knew or had reason to know that it was a trade secret and that knowledge of it had been acquired by accident or mistake.

Miss. Code Ann. § 75-26-3(b) (2000). "'Improper means' includes theft, bribery, misrepresentation, breach or inducement of a breach of a duty to maintain secrecy, or espionage through electronic or other means." Miss. Code Ann. § 75-26-3(a) (2000).

Furthermore, a "trade secret" is:

[I]nformation, including a formula, pattern, compilation, program, device, method, technique, or process, that:

(i) Derives independent economic value, actual or potential, from not being generally known to, and not being readily ascertainable by proper means by other persons who can obtain economic value from its disclosure or use, and

(ii) Is the subject of efforts that are reasonable under the circumstances to maintain its secrecy.

Miss. Code Ann. §75-26-3(d) (2000).

There are essentially two prongs a plaintiff must establish in order to prove misappropriation of a trade secret in Mississippi. To prove the first prong, the alleged trade secret must derive economic value, actual or potential, from not being generally known to, and not being readily ascertainable by proper means by other persons who can obtain economic value from its disclosure or use. Moreover, with respect to the phrase "not readily ascertainable by proper means," "proper means" includes reverse-engineering which consists of "starting with the known product and working backward to find the method by which it was developed." (Unif. Trade Secrets Act §1 cmt., 14 U.L.A. at 438). In other words, it is perfectly proper to utilize reverse-engineering to discover the innards of a computer program. To establish the second prong, the court must consider whether the information was subject to reasonable attempts to preserve its secrecy.

As to the first prong of the trade secret misappropriation inquiry, the Court concludes that the plaintiff's failure to present an expert would preclude him from the ability to establish that his software in the circumstances was "not being readily ascertainable by proper means by other persons" by reverse engineering. See Marshall, supra. Stated differently, the plaintiff as a whole has produced insufficient evidence (other than allegations and conclusions) to prove the first prong of the trade secret misappropriation test.

Likewise, after a thorough search of the record, including the complaint, depositions, and pleadings, the Court concludes as a matter of law that the plaintiff has presented insufficient evidence to establish the second prong of the trade secret misappropriation test. That is, reasonable minds would not differ on the proposition that the plaintiff's efforts to keep his software secret were sorely inadequate. Thus, there is no need for a jury to decide this issue. Despite the existence of the paltry one-paragraph confidentiality agreement signed only by one defendant before the certificate of copyright registration was received, it seems clear that the plaintiff was not diligent in keeping his software secret. Divulging his software to multiple parties not covered by the confidentiality agreement was per se unreasonable. This post-agreement tends to invalidate the agreement in itself—or at least pose an evidentiary problem, since it is unlikely the plaintiff can distinguish between what was divulged by the lone signatory to the agreement (i.e., Defendant Lerner) and that by the other people privy to the plaintiff's software (e.g., Defendant Crosslin, Defendant Patton, the investors, etc.). The Court also concludes that even if the defendants gave the plaintiff oral assurances that he would be taken care of," such reliance under the circumstances was unreasonable using basic business judgment.

As such, the Court concludes that the defendants should be granted summary judgment on the plaintiff's trade secret misappropriation claim.

———————

Notes and Questions

1. The *Pepper* case was a plaintiff's nightmare. The failure to follow the applicable rules and file a signed expert's report was unforgivable. But even where the proper protocol is followed, experts can frequently provide more harm than help to a case if they are not

adequately prepared. *See Petters v. Williamson & Assocs.*, 2003 Wash. App. LEXIS 277 (Wash. Ct. App. Feb. 24, 2003):

> Williamson contends that the trial court erred in finding that the drill technology is not readily ascertainable through reverse engineering, because his expert witness claimed that he could readily reverse engineer the drill. He also refers to testimony by Petters. Petters asserted that the Metal Mining project workers could not have learned how to manufacture the drill but then went on, "unless they, in fact, hired a couple of designers to sit down and sort of reverse engineer it. Which they could do, but it would take some time to do that."
>
> Neither this remark by Petters, nor the testimony of the expert, compels a finding that the drill technology is "readily ascertainable." The expert's claim that he could reverse engineer the Metal Mining drill was not accompanied by any substantial factual details, and the trial court was entitled to disbelieve his claim or to conclude that any reverse engineering that might be possible would take too long to be characterized as "readily ascertainable."

Id. at *17–18.

2. Tracking down those who anonymously divulge trade secrets can be a problem, particularly where the identity of the anonymous donor may itself, be a secret. *See O'Grady v. Superior Court*, 139 Cal. App. 4th 1423 (2006) where Apple filed an action against web site publishers alleging they had published confidential company information about an impending product; and Apple sought to identify the source of the disclosures. Apple claimed the publishers could not have obtained the information unless someone at Apple or a company which had contracted with Apple breached a confidentiality agreement *Id.* at 1436. Apple wanted to identify the source or sources of the disclosures and tried to do so during the discovery process. The court of appeals, however, held:

> In an effort to identify the source of the disclosures, Apple sought and obtained authority to issue civil subpoenas to the publishers of the Web sites where the information appeared and to the e-mail service provider for one of the publishers. The publishers moved for a protective order to prevent any such discovery. The trial court denied the motion on the ground that the publishers had involved themselves in the unlawful misappropriation of a trade secret. We hold that this was error because (1) the subpoena to the e-mail service provider cannot be enforced consistent with the plain terms of the federal Stored Communications Act (18 U.S.C. §§ 2701–2712); (2) any subpoenas seeking unpublished information from petitioners would be unenforceable through contempt proceedings in light of the California reporter's shield (Cal. Const., art. I, § 2, subd. (b); Evid. Code, § 1070); and (3) discovery of petitioners' sources is also barred on this record by the conditional constitutional privilege against compulsory disclosure of confidential sources[.]

Id. at 1431–32.

3. Do you agree with the reasoning of the Mississippi court's *Pepper* decision with respect to MUTSA (The Mississippi Uniform Trade Secret Act)? Did the Court's use of the term "paltry one-paragraph confidentiality agreement" suggest that the plaintiff would have fared better with a lengthier contract?

* * *

Simon v. Oltmann

United States District Court, Northern District of Illinois, Sept. 4, 2001
No. 98 C 1759, 2001 U.S. Dist. LEXIS 13924

LEINENWEBER, District Judge.

Steve Simon claims that J. Richard Oltmann and Lazer-Tron stole his idea for a coupon redemption device to be used with arcade games. Oltmann launched a pre-emptive strike with a lawsuit alleging defamation and violation of the Illinois Consumer and Deceptive Business Practices Act (the "Consumer Fraud Act"), and he seeks declaratory judgment that he did not steal Simon's trade secret. Simon countered with his own lawsuit against Oltmann and Lazer-Tron, alleging misappropriation of a trade secret, violation of the Lanham Act, breach of contract, conspiracy to commit fraud, and fraud. Simon moves for judgment on the pleadings with respect to Oltmann's claims, and Oltmann and Lazer-Tron move for partial summary judgment on Simon's claims. For convenience, "plaintiff" will refer to Simon, and "defendants" will refer to Oltmann and Lazer-Tron.

BACKGROUND

Arcade game players accumulate points while they play. Some machines work in conjunction with a ticket dispenser. When a player accumulates the required number of points, the dispenser gives the player a carnival ticket. Skilled players may be awarded multiple tickets. A player can then redeem the tickets for various rewards, including prizes and additional games.

Steve Simon, National Foosball Champion of 1975, claims that in 1994 he developed a coupon dispenser (the "device") for arcade games. Simon's device tallies the number of points earned by a player, but instead of dispensing tickets, it issues a coupon. The device can be programmed for a variety of messages, including advertisements and prize descriptions, or it may indicate the number of tickets a player has won.

Simon believes that his device represented an advance in the arcade game business for several reasons. Businesses that would not ordinarily carry arcade games for patron entertainment could now do so because the games could issue coupons stating any prizes won, and the coupon could then be redeemed at an establishment that recognizes the coupon. The device could also be programmed with an auditing feature, allowing the owner to monitor the number of points earned or prizes issued. Such a feature could eliminate the need for tickets, thereby potentially reducing employee theft.

The idea behind Simon's invention was similar to others surfacing in the industry. Arcades already used games with attached ticket dispensers before Simon's invention. Video poker games utilizing attached coupon printers were marketed at trade shows. Lazer-Tron personnel and others in the arcade game industry took notice of these devices and considered adapting them for their own games.

Simon tried to market his invention in late 1994. He contacted Bromley Corporation ("Bromley") to see if it would be interested. Simon met with Bromley representative Joe Bundra, at which time Bundra orally agreed not to disclose information about Simon's device to third parties. Bundra ordered three prototypes of the device and tested it, but he told Simon during the summer of 1995 that the company was not interested. Simon also attempted to interest Creative Electronics and Software, Inc. ("CES") in the device. Although CES signed a non-disclosure agreement, ultimately it was not interested. Simon called Lazer-Tron's president, Norm Petermeier, to ask if his company might be receptive to any of his ideas, but Petermeier declined.

Simon met Oltmann at an October 1995 trade show. Simon spoke with Oltmann for approximately fifteen minutes, telling him that he had a new invention that he wanted to bring to the market. Later that month, Simon visited Oltmann at Oltmann's offices in Burbank, Illinois, where the two again discussed Simon's games and his desire to bring them and other products to the market. Oltmann expressed interest in helping him.

Oltmann met with Simon again on October 22, 1995, at Simon's home in Austin, Texas (the "Austin meeting"). Oltmann signed a non-disclosure agreement, and Simon showed Oltmann the device. Simon explained the features of his device, telling Oltmann that it could print out coupons instead of tickets; it could be condensed into a very small PC board and manufactured out of much smaller parts; it would be a simple product to manufacture; and production costs would fall between $99 and $200 per unit. Simon demonstrated how the device worked and talked with Oltmann about the ways in which he believed it would broaden the market for arcade games. Although Simon showed Oltmann a bill of materials and costs, he did not show Oltmann any of the device source codes or schematics. Simon did not tell Oltmann how the device was built or discuss its various component parts.

Oltmann was very excited about the product. However, Oltmann called Simon five days later and told him that, due to decreased revenue at his arcades and family health troubles, he was not interested in pursuing any business deals. However, Oltmann spoke with Lazer-Tron the next day. Lazer-Tron's phone records show that on October 23, 1995, Lazer-Tron placed a call to Oltmann's home in Arizona, lasting more than 14 minutes. On October 25, 1995, Lazer-Tron again placed a phone call to Oltmann's home, lasting more than 15 minutes. Lazer-Tron called Oltmann's home again on November 2, 1995, with the call lasting just more than 2 minutes.

In fact, Oltmann had a long-standing relationship with Lazer-Tron. Oltmann owns and operates three arcades in Illinois. He designs and tests games and devices, and he also advises manufacturers, including Lazer-Tron, regarding their games. Oltmann and Petermeier are friends, and in February 1992, Lazer-Tron granted Oltmann 10,000 shares of its stock pursuant to a 1989 Stock Option Plan. Oltmann has designed at least eight games for Lazer-Tron, and he receives substantial royalty payments from Lazer-Tron for arcade games that he fully or partially designed. Oltmann testified during his deposition that, prior to the Austin meeting, he was not aware of any arcade game that had a coupon redemption feature.

In March 1996, Lazer-Tron brought a new game to the market called Solar Spin. In September 1996, Lazer-Tron offered a coupon printer that could be added to the game. Other games with a coupon redemption feature soon followed. As it normally takes Lazer-Tron approximately six months to develop a new product and bring it to the market, the idea for the first game built with a coupon redemption feature was probably conceived in late 1995 or early 1996.

In October 1996, Simon saw an advertisement for Lazer-Tron's new "Super Solar Spin" game with a coupon redemption feature. Another advertisement in January 1997 showed a coupon from the Lazer-Tron game closely resembling coupons dispensed by Simon's device. Simon ordered and reviewed Lazer-Tron's promotional videotape for the game and coupon redemption feature. He claims that the video's description of the device and its industry applications were almost identical to his device and its applications as he had explained to Oltmann.

Simon contacted Oltmann and Petermeier and accused them of stealing his ideas, which they denied. Simon demanded proof that Lazer-Tron independently developed the feature, but unsurprisingly, Lazer-Tron refused. In a letter to Simon dated February 8, 1997, Oltmann claimed to know nothing about Lazer-Tron's coupon redemption feature despite the fact that he had ordered a game with the feature in September 1996.

On December 12 and 15, 1997, Simon's original attorney, Michael Saleman, wrote letters on Simon's behalf to Lazer-Tron and Oltmann, respectively, advising them that they had misappropriated Simon's proprietary and confidential information. The letters laid out the facts and circumstances surrounding Oltmann and Lazer-Tron's alleged misappropriation and advised them that the letters constituted a pre-litigation offer to settle the case. Oltmann and Lazer-Tron each responded with letters stating that the allegations were untrue. On February 10, 1998, Saleman sent letters to both Oltmann and Lazer-Tron repeating the allegations and demanding settlement.

On March 23, 1998, Oltmann filed suit, accusing Simon of defamation, consumer fraud, and seeking declaratory judgment that he did not misappropriate Simon's trade secret. On July 10, 1998, Simon, through a different attorney, responded with his own suit in Texas federal court against Oltmann and Lazer-Tron, alleging misappropriation of his trade secret, unfair competition under the Lanham Act, breach of contract, and fraud.

DEFENDANTS' MOTION FOR SUMMARY JUDGMENT

Trade Secret Misappropriation

Simon accuses Oltmann and Lazer-Tron of misappropriating his trade secret. The parties never address with precision the scope of Simon's trade secret. It is ambiguous whether the trade secret consists of his idea for a device with the capabilities outlined above or both his idea and the device itself. The parties frequently refer to the device alone when discussing the trade secret and its alleged misappropriation. Clearly, Simon's device is the embodiment of his idea. However, Simon refers to his trade secret in his brief as "a coupon redemption feature for skill-based arcade games," implying that the trade secret includes only the device capabilities. Supporting this conclusion is the undisputed evidence that Simon did not share with Oltmann any of the device source codes or schematics. Simon showed Oltmann a bill of materials and costs, but he did not tell Oltmann how the device was built or discuss its component parts.

Further, when discussing the trade secret, Simon describes the functions that the device can perform. He cites its ability to monitor the number of points earned or prizes issued and print a coupon with a variety of programmed messages, including point totals, prize descriptions, and advertisements. Therefore, the court concludes that Simon claims the idea as his trade secret, not the actual device itself.

The Illinois Trade Secret Act (the "ITSA") defines "trade secret" as:

> information, including but not limited to, technical or non-technical data, a formula, pattern, compilation, program, device, method, technique, drawing, process, financial data, or list of actual or potential customers or suppliers, that:
>
> (1) is sufficiently secret to derive economic value, actual or potential, from not being generally known to other persons who can obtain economic value from its disclosure or use; and
>
> (2) is the subject of efforts that are reasonable under the circumstances to maintain its secrecy or confidentiality.

IL ST CH 765 § 1065/2.

Under the ITSA, the information at issue must be sufficiently secret to impart economic value to both its owner and its competitors because of its relative secrecy. This requirement precludes trade secret protection for information generally known within an industry even if not to the public at large. The real value of the information must lie in the fact that it is not generally known to others who could benefit from using it. Thus, a product or service that is within the realm of general skills and knowledge in the industry cannot be a trade secret. It is the plaintiff's duty to show that the information sought to be protected is beyond the industry's general knowledge or skills.

Simon's coupon redemption feature cannot be classified as a secret one. Prior to Simon's invention, arcade games already utilized ticket dispensers attached to the games. While not quite the same as Simon's device, these dispensers receive signals from the games, send signals back, and issue carnival tickets to the player, with the arcade games keeping track of the number of tickets issued. Prior to Simon's invention, Lazer-Tron personnel saw games with coupon printers. As early as 1989, Lazer-Tron representatives observed products at gaming industry trade shows with payout printers. Petermeier testified at his deposition that the first time he saw a game advertised with a coupon printer was in 1993 with respect to a video poker game. In August 1994, Lazer-Tron held a brainstorming meeting to discuss potential ideas for the company. The day before the meeting, Brian Kelly, one of the participants, prepared notes that refer to a ticket printer for printing tickets or coupons stating points won and bonus gifts. Although meeting notes do not so reflect, participants recall discussing the addition of a coupon redemption feature to their games.

Coupon printers generated interest elsewhere in the arcade game industry. Bromley's Joe Bundra stated in an affidavit filed on Simon's behalf that he had begun developing a coupon printing device in 1990. His idea for the device was also based on similar printers attached to video poker games.

Simon takes issue with Lazer-Tron's claims that it had knowledge of other machines using a coupon redemption feature before the Austin meeting. He questions Lazer-Tron's claimed knowledge of the coupon redemption feature, arguing that the coupon printers observed by Lazer-Tron were attached to games of chance, such as video poker, not skill-based arcade games. As a result, he argues, the coupon redemption feature was not well known within the relevant industry prior to the Austin meeting.

Even if a distinction is drawn between games of chance and skill-based arcade games when defining the relevant industry, Illinois courts have ruled that simply being the first or only one to use certain information does not in and of itself transform otherwise general knowledge into a trade secret.

Trade secret protection seeks to strike a balance between social and economic interests. Individuals who put forth the time, money, and effort to obtain a secret advantage should be protected from parties who obtain the secret through improper means. Id. On the other hand, competitive markets allow parties to utilize the general knowledge and skills acquired through experience in pursuing their occupation. Id. Simon invested considerable time and effort in developing his own device, and he has presented evidence that his meeting with Oltmann may have motivated Lazer-Tron's development of its own coupon printer.

Nevertheless, based on the undisputed facts, it is clear that the "coupon redemption feature" offered by Simon's device was known within the industry before the Austin meeting. Although a lesser technology, ticket dispensers were already used within the industry. Lazer-Tron personnel had seen video games, albeit games of chance, utilizing a coupon printing device. Lazer-Tron had even begun to consider creating a coupon redemption feature for their own games. The coupon redemption feature existed but had yet to be applied to Lazer-Tron's field. The Austin meeting may have provided the impetus for the development of the Lazer-Tron device, but the idea had already been bandied about. Simon does not claim that his device was stolen; only that the "coupon redemption feature" was stolen. This feature, however, was already known to the industry by the time Simon met with Oltmann.

Simon's idea is not entitled to trade secret protection because it was based on information known to and readily available within the relevant industry. It is therefore unnecessary to reach the issues of misappropriation and Simon's efforts to keep his idea secret. Accordingly, defendants' motion for summary judgment is granted on Simon's trade secret misappropriation claim.

Breach of Contract

Paragraph 5 of Simon and Oltmann's Nondisclosure Agreement provides that Oltmann has "no obligation with respect to any information ... generally known within the industry." Based on the determination that Simon's idea was generally known within the industry, Simon's breach of contract claim must fail.

Lanham Act

Simon contends that Oltmann and Lazer-Tron violated the Lanham Act, 15 U.S.C. § 1125(a), by engaging in unfair competition when they misappropriated his coupon redemption feature. However, ideas in the public domain may be used with impunity and do not require attribution. Therefore, the court grants summary judgment in defendants' favor with respect to Simon's Lanham Act claim.

SIMON'S MOTION FOR JUDGMENT ON THE PLEADINGS

Consumer Protection Claim

The Consumer Fraud Act prohibits "unfair or deceptive acts or practices, including but not limited to the use or employment of any deception, fraud, false pretense, false promise, misrepresentation or the concealment, suppression, or omission of any material fact ... in the conduct of any trade or commerce." 815 ILCS § 505/2. The law was designed "to protect consumers and borrowers and businessmen against fraud, unfair methods of competition and unfair or deceptive acts or practices." *Id.* § 505/1 (historical notes). Of course, non-consumers may bring actions under the Act. A business may assert a claim against another if the alleged wrongful conduct involves trade practices aimed at the market generally or otherwise implicates consumer protection concerns.

Oltmann argues that, under a generous interpretation of "trade or commerce," Saleman's letters were misrepresentations written in the course of trade or commerce. The conduct at issue, however, must cause harm to consumers to be cognizable, and Oltmann does not meet this requirement. Even if consumers were deceived about the origins of the device in question, the court cannot conceive of a way in which consumers were harmed by such a deception.

Nor do Simon's alleged deceptions implicate "consumer protection concerns." Courts have struggled to define the scope of this term, but it generally involves sharp practices designed to mislead consumers about a competitor. By these standards, Simon's actions do not implicate consumer protection concerns. Consequently, Simon's motion for judgment on the pleadings is granted.

Notes and Questions

1. Compare the definition of "Trade secret" under the Uniform Trade Secrets Act with that of the Illinois Trade Secrets Act. Are the differences material? Should courts assume that changes are significant?

Uniform Trade Secrets Act

"Trade secret" means information, including a formula, pattern, compilation, program device, method, technique, or process, that:

> (i) derives independent economic value, actual or potential, from not being generally known to, and not being readily ascertainable by proper means by, other persons who can obtain economic value from its disclosure or use, and

> (ii) is the subject of efforts that are reasonable under the circumstances to maintain its secrecy."

Uniform Trade Secrets Act § 1(4).

Illinois Trade Secrets Act

"Trade secret" means information, including but not limited to, technical or non-technical data, a formula, pattern, compilation, program, device, method, technique, drawing, process, financial data, or list of actual or potential customers or suppliers, that:

> (1) is sufficiently secret to derive economic value, actual or potential, from not being generally known to other persons who can obtain economic value from its disclosure or use; and

> (2) is the subject of efforts that are reasonable under the circumstances to maintain its secrecy or confidentiality.

§ 765 ILCS 1065/2(d) (2007).

2. State trade secrecy laws may replace other causes of action for trade secret misappropriation such as tort or unfair competition claims. *See e.g.*, 765 ILCS 1065/8(a) (2007) (Illinois Trade Secrets Act); *Hecny Transp., Inc. v. Chu*, 430 F.3d 402, 404 (7th Cir. 2005) ("Section 8(a) of the Illinois Trade Secrets Act abolishes claims other than those based on contract arising from misappropriated trade secrets, replacing them with claims under the Act itself.").

3. The widely accepted Uniform Trade Secrets Act along with its state modifications suggests that the Act not only replaces, but may preempt common law actions predicated upon confidentiality and secrecy. The next case provides an example.

* * *

Blackwell v. Blizzard Entm't., Inc.

Los Angeles County Superior Court, Jan. 30, 2012
No. B227249, 2012 Cal. App. Unpub. LEXIS 744 (Not Officially Published)

GRIMES, Circuit Judge.

Plaintiff and appellant William Blackwell appeals from the trial court's grant of summary judgment in favor of defendants and respondents Blizzard Entertainment, Inc. (Blizzard), Chris Metzen and Russell Brower. Plaintiff contends the trial court improperly resolved disputed issues of fact in summarily disposing of his claims against defendants. We conclude plaintiff failed to present material evidence he made reasonable efforts to maintain the confidentiality of his alleged trade secret, and therefore failed to raise a triable issue that his trade secret qualified for protection. We further conclude plaintiff's common law claims, based on the same nucleus of facts as the statutory trade secret claim, are preempted by the statutory scheme. We therefore affirm the grant of summary judgment in defendants' favor.

FACTUAL AND PROCEDURAL BACKGROUND

After he resigned from Blizzard, plaintiff brought this action against Blizzard and two of its employees, Metzen (Senior Vice President of Creative Development) and Brower (Director of Audio and Video). Plaintiff pled seven causes of action, for constructive termination, negligent misrepresentation, misappropriation of trade secrets and related claims. Defendants successfully moved for summary judgment. Plaintiff challenges on appeal only the summary adjudication of his second cause of action for promissory fraud, third cause of action for negligent misrepresentation, and seventh cause of action for misappropriation of trade secrets. We limit our summary of the pertinent facts and procedure accordingly, as we need not consider issues not supported by argument and citation to legal authority. For purposes of our review, we accept plaintiff's facts and defendants' undisputed facts as true.

Plaintiff is a sound audio professional. For over a decade, plaintiff operated his own business, Bill Black Audio. He offered various services to the entertainment industry, including sound effects design, sound effects editing, video editing, casting and directing, and music licensing. Bill Black Audio was routinely hired, as an independent contractor, to perform audio work for different companies specializing in the creation and production of videogames. Some of this work entailed the casting and hiring of actors to perform voiceover work for characters in videogames under development; a process similar to casting and hiring voice actors to perform in an animated film or program.

From his years in the business, plaintiff had cultivated a list of actors willing to perform both union and nonunion voiceover work. Plaintiff created a computer database of contact information for these actors. Plaintiff's database of actors was password-protected and included about 70 actors and their contact information, including private numbers to contact them outside the normal channels of their respective agencies, in order to discreetly schedule nonunion work. The database was also referred to as plaintiff's "rolodex," which means, in entertainment industry parlance, one's personal business contacts. Plaintiff regarded this contact information as confidential because the actors were risking their membership in the Screen Actors Guild by performing nonunion work, and plaintiff considered it a valuable privilege to have such information entrusted to him. Bill Black Audio was able to pass along the benefits of these contacts to its clients by arranging for quality actors to work for rates less than those required by union contracts.

One of the companies with which Bill Black Audio contracted was a videogame company called Nova Logic. Brower worked at Nova Logic before transferring to Blizzard, and he hired Bill Black Audio to provide audio work for Nova Logic. By 2005, Brower had started working for Blizzard. Brower believed plaintiff had provided good work for him in the past and had good industry contacts and therefore arranged for Blizzard to hire Bill Black Audio as an independent contractor to work on several videogames, including World of Warcraft and StarCraft: Ghost.

In casting voiceover actors for videogame companies like Nova Logic and Blizzard, plaintiff generally disclosed the names and contact information of the actors to those entities, primarily to ensure the actors were paid and for tax identification purposes. Brower stated plaintiff never objected to disclosing contact information to him during any of the jobs Brower hired Bill Black Audio to perform. Plaintiff could not recall whether he ever required Blizzard or any other company he contracted with on a freelance basis to include in his professional services agreement that Bill Black Audio's proprietary information was confidential, was being disclosed for a limited purpose or otherwise had to be protected from further disclosure to third parties. Plaintiff did not present any documentation that he had ever obtained any such agreements from any company with which he contracted while operating his own business.

In December 2005, Brower suggested plaintiff apply for a newly-opened position as an Audio Lead at Blizzard. Plaintiff applied for and was offered the job by Blizzard's chief operating officer. Plaintiff accepted the position and subsequently signed a written offer of employment dated January 17, 2006, as well as a document titled "Confidential and Proprietary Rights Assignment Agreement" (Agreement).

The Agreement contained provisions identifying certain information developed and maintained by Blizzard as confidential and identifying Blizzard as the sole owner of all works developed in the course of plaintiff's employment. The Agreement required plaintiff to not disclose any confidential information acquired during his employment and to assign any ownership rights to Blizzard in any games or works, among other things, that plaintiff helped to develop while in Blizzard's employ.

Paragraph 7 of the Agreement also provided that plaintiff could append a document identifying "inventions or original works of authorship" made or created by plaintiff before his employment with Blizzard that would be excluded from the Agreement's assignment provisions. Plaintiff identified certain previous works in an appendix, but he did not list his "rolodex" of contact information, believing his contact list was not an "invention" or "work of authorship" within the meaning of paragraph 7.

Before formally starting work in his new position at Blizzard, plaintiff had a conversation with Brower, who was going to be plaintiff's supervisor. Brower said he hoped plaintiff realized Blizzard was "hiring your rolodex too." Plaintiff was "taken aback" by the comment, which he understood to mean that Blizzard wanted and expected the disclosure of the proprietary contact information contained in his database. Plaintiff could not recall whether he objected or complained about Brower's comment, but believed he had "additional words" with Brower before the conversation ended. Plaintiff offered no material evidence he took any steps at that time, in response to Brower's comment, to assert the confidentiality of his "rolodex" contact information.

At the end of January 2006, plaintiff began working in his new position as Blizzard's Audio Lead for the videogame titled StarCraft: Ghost. Plaintiff understood his job duties as an Audio Lead included the casting of actors for voiceover work, similar to what he had performed on a freelance basis through Bill Black Audio. Plaintiff also understood that some contact information had to be disclosed to Blizzard to facilitate audition scheduling, to ensure the actors were paid, and to maintain proper tax records. Plaintiff offered no evidence that, concurrent with these voluntary and knowing disclosures of his contact information, he advised anyone at Blizzard that the information was confidential, was being disclosed for those limited administrative purposes, or otherwise could not be disclosed to third parties because the information was his personal trade secret.

At some point after plaintiff started working at Blizzard, Brower told plaintiff he wanted him to turn over the audition scheduling and related administrative tasks to Keith Landes, a production assistant who was also supervised by Brower. Dennis Crabtree, another production assistant, also eventually handled some of those duties. Plaintiff stated he complied with Brower's instruction and supplied his contact information to Landes and/ or to Crabtree, to perform the audition scheduling and to procure the information necessary for payroll in the event an actor was hired. Plaintiff offered no evidence that, when he turned over that information to the production assistants, he took any steps to advise them of its trade secret status or to otherwise assert the confidentiality of that information.

Plaintiff regularly gave actor contact information to Landes, usually by email, to schedule auditions, and at no time did plaintiff ever tell Landes the information was confidential or ask him to sign any document acknowledging the confidentiality of the contact information. Landes believed the information was for internal Blizzard use and he treated it accordingly, obtaining the relevant additional information from the hired actors to ensure payment and forwarding same to the appropriate Blizzard departments, like legal or payroll. Landes also input the information into a computer database of actor information that he maintained as part of his job duties at Blizzard.

At some point plaintiff became aware that Landes was compiling a Blizzard database incorporating the actor contact information plaintiff supplied him from his "rolodex." He also discovered Landes, in his role as production assistant, was acting inappropriately with actors during auditions, including soliciting gifts and engaging in other conduct plaintiff referred to as "fan boy activity." Plaintiff was concerned for the actors and for his reputation with them, as the nonunion auditions (conducted at third-party studios) were supposed to be low-key, with as little attention drawn to them as possible.

Plaintiff may have raised his first complaint to Brower about Landes's improper conduct sometime at the end of 2006, but he definitely raised repeated objections both orally, and in emails, between February and June 2007. Plaintiff objected that Landes had no reason for keeping the contact information plaintiff supplied, since he was only supposed to schedule the auditions. Plaintiff also objected that Landes's "fan" behavior with the actors served no legitimate Blizzard purpose and, when done in front of third parties otherwise unaware that union actors were working on a nonunion videogame production, could create problems for those actors with the union. Plaintiff asked Brower to curtail Landes's involvement at auditions, enforce a clear policy of how employees could interact with actors during auditions, and clarify Blizzard's policies regarding actors providing nonunion work for the company. Plaintiff stated that Brower indicated he would take care of the situation.

In addition to raising these objections to Brower, plaintiff also spoke to Metzen, Brower's supervisor, during the same time period. Metzen acknowledged plaintiff's concerns and agreed that discretion should be exercised as to the identity of the actors who provided nonunion voiceover work for Blizzard.

Near the end of June 2007, Brower became frustrated with the manner in which plaintiff was raising his concerns about Landes. Brower thought plaintiff's behavior was often unprofessional. Brower had previously taken issue with an incident in which it had been reported to him that plaintiff had yelled at Landes in the office in front of other coworkers.

On June 27, 2007, plaintiff was called into a meeting with Brower and Erika Sayre-Smith of Blizzard's human resources department. Plaintiff was given a written warning about unprofessional conduct related to the manner in which he presented his complaints about Landes and how he treated coworkers. From that meeting, plaintiff concluded he was being chastised for raising concerns about the lack of discretion concerning actors' identities, and that unless he continued to provide his proprietary contact information to Blizzard with no conditions attached, he would risk being terminated. Plaintiff therefore resigned and filed this lawsuit.

On August 6, 2010, following full briefing, including supplemental briefs requested by the court, and oral argument, summary judgment was entered in favor of Blizzard, Metzen and Brower. This appeal followed.

DISCUSSION

Plaintiff contends he offered evidence raising triable issues as to the viability of his claims against defendants, but the court abdicated its proper role on summary judgment, failing to limit itself to determining whether there were factual disputes and instead resolving the disputed factual issues. Plaintiff argues he raised material disputed facts as to his statutory misappropriation of trade secrets claim, as well as his common law claims for promissory fraud and negligent misrepresentation. We disagree.

An appellate court independently reviews an order granting summary judgment. We determine whether the court's ruling was correct, not its reasons or rationale. In practical effect, we assume the role of a trial court and apply the same rules and standards which govern a trial court's determination of a motion for summary judgment. In performing our de novo review, we must view the evidence in a light favorable to plaintiff as the losing party, liberally construing his or her evidentiary submission while strictly scrutinizing defendant's own showing, and resolving any evidentiary doubts or ambiguities in plaintiff's favor. As we explain, each of the three claims plaintiff contends is viable was appropriately summarily adjudicated.

1. The Trade Secrets Claim

California's Uniform Trade Secrets Act, set forth at Civil Code, section 3426 et seq. (CUTSA), defines a trade secret as "information, including a formula, pattern, compilation, program, device, method, technique, or process, that:

> (1) Derives independent economic value, actual or potential, from not being generally known to the public or to other persons who can obtain economic value from its disclosure or use; and

> (2) Is the subject of efforts that are reasonable under the circumstances to maintain its secrecy."

To claim trade secret protection for any allegedly confidential or proprietary information, there must be reasonable efforts to maintain its secrecy. " 'Trade secrets are a peculiar kind of property. Their only value consists in their being kept private.' Thus, 'the right to exclude others is central to the very definition of the property interest. Once the data that constitute a trade secret are disclosed to others, or others are allowed to use those data, the holder of the trade secret has lost his property interest in the data.' "

In assessing the reasonableness of secrecy measures, no specific act is determinative. The statutory inquiry is what is deemed reasonable "under the circumstances." (Civ Code, § 3426.1, subd. (d).) "Reasonable efforts to maintain secrecy have been held to include advising employees of the existence of a trade secret, limiting access to a trade secret on need to know basis and controlling plant access." (*Courtesy Temporary Service, Inc. v. Camacho* (1990) 222 Cal.App.3d 1278, 1288.) Other relevant factors "are restricting access and physical segregation of the information, confidentiality agreements with employees, and marking documents with warnings or reminders of confidentiality." (*In re Providian Credit Card Cases* (2002) 96 Cal.App.4th 292, 304 (In re Providian); *see also Mattel, Inc. v. MGA Entertainment, Inc. & Consol. Actions* (C.D.Cal.2010) 782 F.Supp.2d 911, 959– 960 [disputed issue as to reasonableness of secrecy measures where employer provided extensive training to employees regarding trade secrets, controlled access to databases, but often failed to mark documents as confidential and gave vague direction to employees about what was and was not covered].)

Plaintiff may have intended the contact information from his "rolodex" that he voluntarily disclosed to Blizzard to be treated with discretion and maintained as confidential. However, there is no material evidence plaintiff took any affirmative steps to articulate that intent to anyone at Blizzard before he disclosed the information to Blizzard. Plaintiff offered no evidence he asserted the trade secret status of his contact list, that he designated as confidential any of the emails or writings containing the contact information which he routinely forwarded to Blizzard personnel like Landes, that he advised anyone he was disclosing the contact information only for a limited purpose, or that he requested anyone at Blizzard to execute any type of nondisclosure agreement.

Indeed, plaintiff admitted in deposition he could not recall having any such discussions. Therefore, any claim plaintiff might have made such requests would be pure speculation. Plaintiff conceded that as soon as he started working at Blizzard he began voluntarily disclosing information from his "rolodex" to Blizzard personnel as part of his work duties in assisting with casting for various productions—disclosures which plaintiff understood were to benefit Blizzard, allowing Blizzard to hire quality voice actors for their videogame productions at reduced, nonunion rates.

Particularly noteworthy is plaintiff's admission he raised his objections to Brower in February 2007 about Landes's conduct because he "had reached a point where he realized that his information that he was kind enough to allow Blizzard to use was being used inappropriately by Mr. Landes." Plaintiff's statement underscores the voluntary nature of plaintiff's disclosure of the "rolodex" information to Blizzard for its own beneficial use, as well as his failure to take any reasonable steps to ensure the confidentiality of that information as a condition of that use until he eventually grew weary of the alleged misuse of the information by Landes.

"The unprotected disclosure of a trade secret will cause the information to forfeit its trade secret status" (*Religious Technology Center v. Netcom On-Line Com.* (N.D.Cal.1995) 923 F.Supp. 1231. Even then, plaintiff failed to offer evidence that he made any effort to assert his proprietary interest in the "rolodex" information. Plaintiff's objections were vague and generalized and primarily concerned the lack of discretion in protecting the identity of union actors providing nonunion work for Blizzard. Such evidence does not raise a triable issue of fact as to whether plaintiff took timely and reasonable secrecy measures to protect his trade secrets. Plaintiff's objections concerned Landes's lack of discretion with the auditioning actors, which could compromise those actors' respective positions with their union and, in turn, damage plaintiff's reputation for discretion that he had built up with those actors. This may have been a legitimate issue for plaintiff to have raised in the context of his job, but it was not the substantive equivalent of making a reasonable effort to maintain the confidentiality of his contact list as an identified trade secret. Moreover, plaintiff's argument he only disclosed discreet portions of his contact list but never the entire "rolodex," which is the trade secret, citing Religious Technology Center, supra, 923 F.Supp. 1231, is not persuasive. Each individual actor's contact information was considered private by plaintiff and each had value on its own, despite the fact it was contained within a larger database. Therefore, the trade secret here is not similar to the alleged trade secret in Religious Technology Center. There is simply no evidentiary basis here to find that plaintiff took any reasonable measures to protect his "rolodex" as a whole or any part thereof with respect to Blizzard.

Whether information constitutes a trade secret is ordinarily a question of fact. (*In re Providian, supra*, 96 Cal.App.4th at p. 300; *accord, DVD Copy Control Assn., Inc. v. Bunner* (2004) 116 Cal.App.4th 241, 251 [resolution of secrecy requirement requires fact-intensive analysis].) However, on summary judgment, a factual issue may be resolved as a matter of law where the evidence and reasonable inferences arising therefrom are insufficient to support a reasonable jury finding in favor of the nonmoving party on that issue. (*Aguilar, supra*, 25 Cal.4th at pp. 856–857.) That is the case revealed by the record below. Plaintiff failed to offer material disputed evidence of a protectable trade secret, and as a matter of law, there was no basis upon which plaintiff could proceed on his statutory misappropriation claim. Summary adjudication of plaintiff's seventh cause of action was therefore proper.

Because we conclude plaintiff failed to raise a triable issue he had a protectable trade secret which was dispositive of his statutory cause of action, plaintiff's additional argument regarding defendants' purported acts of misappropriation is moot.

2. The Fraud and Misrepresentation Claims

Plaintiff's second cause of action for promissory fraud and third cause of action for negligent misrepresentation are both unquestionably based on the alleged misappropriation of plaintiff's trade secret; plaintiff so concedes in his brief before this court. Both claims are based on the allegation that defendants hired plaintiff under false pretenses, seeking to wrongfully "usurp" plaintiff's proprietary business contacts. As such, both claims are preempted by CUTSA. (Civ.Code, § 3426.7; *K.C. Multimedia, supra*, 171 Cal.App.4th at pp. 958–959.) Plaintiff's contention the two common law claims are preempted only if the statutory trade secret claim is viable is without merit. (*Silvaco Data Systems v. Intel Corp.* (2010) 184 Cal.App.4th 210, 237["A statute may supersede other causes of action even though it does not itself provide relief on a particular set of facts"], overruled in part on other grounds in *Kwikset Corp. v. Superior Court* (2011) 51 Cal.4th 310, 337.) Plaintiff's argument that his common law claims are somehow resurrected if we uphold the dismissal of the statutory misappropriation claim stands the doctrine of preemption on its head. The legislative purpose behind CUTSA was to "formulate a consistent set of rules to govern and define liability for conduct falling within its terms." (Ibid.) Plaintiff failed to establish that his misappropriation claim was viable within the meaning of CUTSA. He is precluded, as a matter of law, from attempting to restate that statutory claim as common law claims in order to circumvent CUTSA's statutory scheme. Summary adjudication of plaintiff's second and third causes of action was proper.

DISPOSITION

The judgment entered August 6, 2010, in favor of Blizzard Entertainment, Inc., Chris Metzen and Russell Brower is affirmed. Respondents are awarded costs on appeal.

Notes and Questions

1. Throughout this and earlier chapters, a common catalyst for litigation involves skilled personnel and programmers who change employment. Such changes can be expected to increase in the relatively young videogame industry. Information and programming knowledge possessed by new employees are often more valuable than the employees themselves. It is, therefore, understandable that companies should vigorously seek to protect such information. And, as the preceding case illustrated, a mere list of skilled individuals may, itself, be worthy of protection.

2. Where several employees jump ship to start work for a competing videogame manufacturer, hints and allegations of trade secrecy misappropriation are almost certain to follow. Such was the case for ZeniMax Media, Inc. (Plaintiff), a large videogame maker (associated with hits including: *Doom*, *Quake*, and *The Elder Scrolls*) and its alleged misappropriator, Oculus VR, Inc. (Defendant). In May of 2014, ZeniMax commenced suit against Oculus claiming violation of a trade secrecy agreement and a litany of other related

claims. *See Zenimax Media, Inc. et al. v. Oculus VR, Inc. et al.*, No. 3:14-cv-01849 (N.D. Tex. May 21, 2014). The suit claimed that Oculus founder Luckey sought and received assistance (concerning a virtual reality headset, known as "Rift") from Carmack, the technical director of Plaintiff's subsidiary, Id Software, LLC. Plaintiff required Luckey to sign a nondisclosure agreement reciting that its intellectual property was confidential and exclusively owned by Plaintiff. Then, according to the complaint, Carmack and his ZeniMax associates greatly improved and "transformed" the Rift prototype with specially improved hardware and software. Plaintiff's counts include a claim for unfair competition based on Defendant's alleged solicitation and hire of its former employees including Carmack (who became the Defendant's chief technical officer two months after his contract with the Plaintiff expired). Defendant also hired five other senior employees of the Plaintiff. Among the allegations in the complaint, is the contention that Defendant exploited Plaintiff's trade secrets to accumulate huge profits in conjunction with Facebook's acquisition of the defendant for $2 billion. Can you offer an opinion as to the suit's outcome?

3. The following complaint recounts the events that allegedly transpired when a programmer decided to leave a well established videogame developer/publisher in order to accept a position at a smaller competing company.

* * *

Zynga v. Patmore

California Superior Court, No. CGC-12-525099
Complaint Filed October 12, 2012

Alleging: Misappropriation of Trade Secrets and Breach of Written Contract

[The matters alleged this Complaint have yet to be proven or tied; at this juncture, they are only un-litigated allegations. — ED.]

Plaintiff Zynga Inc. ("Zynga") alleges the following against Defendant Alan Patmore ("Patmore") and Does 1–50:

NATURE OF THE CASE

1. San Francisco-based Zynga is an online social gaming company, employing more than 2,900 people worldwide and responsible for creating some of the most popular online games — including, Farm Ville, CityVille, Words With Friends, and CastleVille — enjoyed by over a hundred million people worldwide.

2. Zynga respects the rights of its employees to resign and seek employment with other companies. But what Zynga cannot tolerate is the wholesale theft of some of its most sensitive and commercially valuable data. Zynga has no choice but to bring this lawsuit to recover its stolen data and to ensure no use is made of it.

3. Until recently, Defendant Alan Patmore was the General Manager for Cityville — one of Zynga's most successful online social games with, at its peak, more than 100-million monthly active users around the globe. In his capacity as GM, Patmore had widespread access to some of Zynga's most sensitive trade secrets.

4. On August 15–16, 2012 — the day before and day of his departure from Zynga — Patmore engaged in a series of intentional acts designed to steal Zynga data. First, Patmore amassed the more than 760 Zynga files that he wanted to steal from Zynga into a new folder, which he appropriately named "Zynga." Patmore stored this folder on the desktop interface of his Zynga-issued computer.

5. Next, Patmore copied the "Zynga" folder—and the more than 760 Zynga files stored therein—into a "Dropbox" folder associated with his personal online cloud storage account. In doing so, Patmore caused his Dropbox online cloud storage account to automatically sync (i.e., upload) these 760 Zynga files to Patmore's Dropbox account. Once the files were stored in his Dropbox cloud storage account, Patmore could (1) retain these Zynga files after leaving Zynga and (2) access them from any computer or mobile device that Patmore links to his Dropbox account. Patmore transferred this data from Zynga in violation of his obligations and without Zynga's knowledge or consent.

6. Patmore then tried to cover his tracks by attempting to "uninstall" and "delete" the Dropbox program from his Zynga issued laptop. His efforts were unsuccessful and he left a forensic trail of his wrongful conduct.

7. The data Patmore unlawfully and intentionally stole from Zynga encompasses some of Zynga's most valuable and confidential information, including:

- Data concerning the unique and proprietary method by which Zynga identifies which games and game mechanics will be successful, and how such games and game mechanics should be optimized post-release;

- An internal assessment of the relative success of every game feature rolled out over the last quarter for Zynga's hit game CityVille, revenue compared to projections, and future plans and strategies to strengthen game play based on the lessons learned over the prior quarter from successful and unsuccessful features;

- Historic and future monetization plans, internal assessments of the success of released features, and go-forward strategies for many of Zynga's other hit games, including lessons learned from both successful and unsuccessful features;

- The final, green-lit Game Design Document, spreadsheets related to headcount and employee data, and development progress reports, for an unreleased Zynga game currently under development;

- More than ten unreleased game design documents that describe material features and game play, pitches, conceptual renderings of characters and scenes, mock-ups of game play and related information;

- Zynga's know-how for effectively monetizing within free-to-play online games (which is know-how that Zynga—but not Kixeye or Patmore—possessed prior to Patmore's theft);

- Confidential Zynga revenue information;

- Confidential Zynga information regarding employee compensation and performance;

- Strategic roadmaps containing non-public information, including release dates for unreleased games; and

- Patmore's entire email box containing, among other items, 14 months of confidential communications reserved exclusively for Zynga's executive staff. These emails describe product reviews, business strategies, acquisition targets, market analysis, key hires, sales projections and financial estimates. In short, Patmore copied virtually every email he received or sent while he was a GM at Zynga.

8. Zynga is informed and believes that Patmore now works in a directly competing role for Kixeye—a social gaming company that ranks 34th in the industry according to monthly users and who has publicly expressed animus towards industry-leader Zynga. Kixeye has not developed a top ten online social game. The data Patmore took from Zynga

could be used to improve a competitor's internal understanding and know-how of core game mechanics and monetization techniques, its execution, and ultimately its market standing to compete more effectively with Zynga. Absent immediate injunctive relief and remedies sought, Zynga will continue to suffer immediate and irreparable harm.

SUBJECT-MATTER JURISDICTION AND VENUE

9. This Court has jurisdiction over all causes of action asserted in this Complaint pursuant to California Constitution, Article VI, Section 10 and California Code of Civil Procedure Section 410.10, by virtue of the fact that this is a civil action wherein the matter in controversy, exclusive of interest, exceeds $25,000, and because this case is a cause not given by statute to other trial courts.

10. Venue is proper in this Court pursuant to California Code of Civil Procedure Sections 395 and 395.5, because Defendant Patmore transacts business within the County of San Francisco, and the unlawful conduct alleged herein was carried out, and had effects, in the County of San Francisco.

THE PARTIES

11. Plaintiff Zynga is a Delaware corporation and has its principal place of business in San Francisco, California.

12. Zynga is informed and believes, and thereupon alleges, that at all times relevant to this Complaint, Defendant Alan Patmore was, and continues to be, a resident of Sonoma County, in the State of California.

13. Zynga is ignorant of the true names and capacities of the defendants sued herein as Does 1 through 50, inclusive, and for that reason has sued them by their fictitious names. On information and belief, Zynga alleges that each of these fictitiously named defendants is responsible in some manner for some or all of the acts alleged herein, and that Zynga's harm as herein alleged was proximately caused by such defendants. Zynga will amend this Complaint to set forth the true names and capacities of the fictitiously named defendants once Zynga has ascertained that information.

14. Each Defendant, including Does 1 through 50, inclusive, have willfully aided and abetted each of the other Defendants in the wrongful concerted action described herein, or acted with or in furtherance of that action, or assisted in carrying out its purposes alleged in this Complaint.

15. Defendants, and each of them, are individually sued as participants and aiders and abettors in the wrongful conduct complained of herein, and the liability of each arises from the fact that each has engaged in all or part of the improper acts, plans, schemes, conspiracies, or transactions complained of herein.

FACTUAL BACKGROUND

Zynga Is Formed and Emerges As A Leader Of The Social Gaming Industry

16. Founded in 2007, Zynga is the world's leading social gaming company with more than 72-million Daily Active Users (DAUs) and 306-million Monthly Active Users (MAUs), and is the top developer of game applications for the most popular social networking sites. Zynga makes and distributes a variety of online, free-to-play social games that are played simultaneously by millions of users. Zynga is ranked as the Number One online free-to-play game developer, as rated by http://www.appdata.com.

17. Over the course of many years, and at substantial expense, Zynga has developed and maintained significant amounts of highly confidential information that is proprietary

to it, including without limitation, data related to its methodologies for creating, developing, and optimizing online social games, unreleased games, new game ideas, strategic roadmaps, monetization plans and efforts, statistical data gathering and metrics, confidential revenue data, negative knowledge based on trial and error, and sensitive personnel data.

18. Because of the highly competitive nature of the online, free-to-play social gaming industry, and because Zynga needs to maintain its competitive position through the protection of its sensitive business data, Zynga takes reasonable steps to ensure that its confidential business data is protected.

Kixeye Is a Competitor of Zynga's In The Online Free-To-Play Gaming Industry

19. Also founded in 2007 (under the name Casual Collective), Kixeye has sought to achieve relevance in the online social gaming community. Described by one observer as an "iconoclastic, midcore Facebook gaming company," Kixeye has only approximately 9.7-million MAUs and is currently ranked Number 34 among online free-to-play game developers. Kixeye has not developed and released a Top Ten game.

20. Like Zynga, Kixeye releases free-to-play online social games in which users can pay for in-game perks to accelerate progress within the game. Although it has announced plans to build its own platform, Kixeye acknowledges that it is "placing [its] bets" on games developed for the Facebook platform (where Zynga is and has been the dominant market leader). As Defendant Patmore has declared, Kixeye is attempting to out-do Zynga by trying to "lead the charge" in developing online, free-to-play games.

21. Zynga is informed and believes, and thereupon alleges, that Kixeye has failed to achieve success in the online free-to-play gaming market because it lacks Zynga's know-how concerning how to develop successful and sought-after games, and effectively monetize within those games on a mass scale.

C. Defendant Patmore Held A Position Of Trust Within Zynga And Was Contractually Obligated To Protect Zynga's Confidential, Proprietary, And Trade Secret Information, And Return That Information Upon The Termination Of His Employment

22. In June 2011, Zynga hired Patmore as Studio General Manager. In his role as an executive participating in the management of Zynga's operations, Patmore occupied a special position of trust and confidence within Zynga. Only eight weeks before he resigned, Patmore was promoted to General Manager of Zynga's hit game CityVille.

23. In connection with his position at Zynga, Patmore was provided with access to sensitive business data belonging to Zynga, including the confidential, proprietary, and trade secret information data noted above. As a condition of his employment, therefore, Patmore executed Zynga's Employment Invention Assignment and Confidentiality Agreement, which provides, in pertinent part, that:

> a. Patmore "understands that [his] employment by the Company creates a relationship of confidence and trust with respect to any information of a confidential or secret nature that may be disclosed ... by the Company ... and that the Company has taken reasonable measures under the circumstances to protect from unauthorized use or disclosure";

> b. Patmore agreed that the information protected by this agreement ("Proprietary Information") includes, among other things, "game information, [including] features, roadmaps, plans, specifications, mechanics, designs, costs and revenue," "techniques and methods to create 'virality,'" "measurement techniques, and specific functionality that increases monetization and both measures and increases

retention metrics," "non-public financial information, which may include revenues, profits, margins, forecasts, budgets and other financial data," "marketing and advertising plans, strategies, tactics, budgets and studies; ... business and operations strategies," "research and development plans," and "employment and personnel information";

c. Patmore agreed that he would "[a]t all times, both during [his] employment and after its termination, ... keep and hold all such Proprietary Information in strict confidence and trust ... [and not] ... use, disclose, copy, reverse-engineer, distribute, gain unauthorized access or misappropriate any Proprietary Information without the prior written consent of the Company";

d. Patmore agreed that he would, "[u]pon termination of [his] employment with the Company, ... promptly deliver to the Company all documents and materials of any nature or form in my possession, custody or control, pertaining to [his]work with the Company and, upon Company request, will execute a document confirming [his] agreement to honor [his] responsibilities contained in this Agreement"; and

e. Patmore agreed that "in the event of a breach or threatened breach of this Agreement by [him] the Company may suffer irreparable harm and will therefore be entitled to injunctive relief to enforce this Agreement."

f. Patmore agreed that "for a period of one (1) year [after his employment ends, he] will not directly or indirectly solicit away employees or consultants of the Company for [his] own benefit or for the benefit of any other person or entity."

D. Shortly Before His Departure From Zynga, Patmore Transfers More Than Seven Hundred Zynga Files Containing Trade Secrets and Sensitive Zynga Business Data

24. Zynga is informed and believes, and thereupon alleges, that by early August 2012, and likely earlier, Patmore was being recruited by and had secured an offer of employment with Kixeye.

25. On August 16, 2012, Patmore announced his resignation, and his employment with Zynga ended the same day. In preparation for his departure, Patmore intentionally readied and transferred more than 760 files containing Zynga's sensitive business information (including Zynga trade secrets) to an external, non-Zynga account that could be accessed anywhere.

26. Specifically, Patmore copied a "Zynga" folder from the desktop of his Zynga-issued laptop to a special "Dropbox" folder located on his Zynga laptop. According to Dropbox's website, placing the Zynga folder and the more than 760 Zynga files it contained into the "Dropbox" folder "will automatically sync the file to your Dropbox [online account], which means you can open it from any other computer, smartphone, or tablet that also has Dropbox installed." In other words, Patmore used his personal Dropbox account to store hundreds of files containing Zynga's trade secrets and other non-public information so that Patmore could access and use this data after leaving Zynga.

27. The Zynga files that Patmore retained after leaving Zynga describe in detail Zynga's confidential game development and industry know-how that both Patmore and Kixeye lack absent theft of this information from Zynga. The confidential, proprietary, and trade secret information Patmore retained following his resignation from Zynga includes, among other things:

- Data concerning the unique and proprietary method by which Zynga identifies which games and game mechanics will be successful, and how such games and game mechanics should be optimized post-release;

- An internal assessment of the relative success of every game feature rolled out over the last quarter for Zynga's hit game CityVille, revenue compared to projections, and future plans and strategies to strengthen game play based on the lessons learned over the prior quarter from successful and unsuccessful features;

- Historic and future monetization plans, internal assessments of the success of released features, and go-forward strategies for many of Zynga's other hit games, including lessons learned from both successful and unsuccessful features;

- The final, green-lit Game Design Document, spreadsheets related to headcount and employee data, and development progress reports, for an unreleased Zynga game currently under development;

- More than ten unreleased game design documents that describe material features and game play, pitches, conceptual renderings of characters and scenes, mock-ups of game play and related information;

- Zynga's know-how for effectively monetizing within free-to-play online games (which is know-how that Zynga—but not Kixeye or Patmore—possessed prior to Patmore's theft);

- Confidential Zynga revenue information;

- Confidential Zynga information regarding employee compensation and perform-ance;

- Strategic roadmaps containing non-public information, including release dates for unreleased games; and

- Patmore's entire email box containing, among other items, 14 months of confidential communications reserved exclusively for Zynga's executive staff. These emails describe product reviews, business strategies, acquisition targets, market analysis, key hires, sales projections and financial estimates. In short, Patmore copied every email he received or sent while he was a GM at Zynga.

28. Patmore secretly maintained this sensitive Zynga data in his personal Dropbox cloud storage account, and on information and belief, on other computer devices, and intentionally retained it after his departure from Zynga in violation of his obligations to Zynga and without Zynga's knowledge or consent. Patmore had no lawful right to secretly copy and divert this confidential Zynga data.

29. Zynga is informed and believes, and thereupon alleges, that Patmore not only retained this data after leaving Zynga, but did so in connection with his plans to join Kixeye. Patmore is now employed by Kixeye, developing games that are intended to compete directly with Zynga.

E. During His Exit Interview, Patmore Refuses To Confirm He Returned All Zynga Data

30. On August 16, 2012, Patmore's self-selected final day of employment with Zynga, he met with Zynga to conduct his exit interview.

31. During this exit interview, Zynga asked Patmore to sign a standard Termination Certification, which merely reaffirmed his past and continued compliance with his contractual I obligations, including the contractual obligation to return and not retain, misuse, or disclose Zynga's sensitive business data.

32. Patmore refused to sign the Termination Certification. Nor did Patmore disclose to Zynga that he had retained Zynga's trade secrets and other sensitive business data.

33. If Patmore is not immediately restrained from accessing, disclosing, using, and/or destroying Zynga's stolen data, Zynga will continue to suffer irreparable and irreversible harm.

FIRST CAUSE OF ACTION

(Misappropriation of Trade Secrets — Cal. Civ. Code § 3426.1 et seq.)

34. Zynga incorporates by reference paragraphs 1 through 33 of this Complaint.

35. Zynga enjoys an advantage over its existing and would-be competitors based, in part, on the trade secret information it has developed and implemented in its effort to become and remain the market leader in free-to-play, online games.

36. Zynga has made reasonable efforts under the circumstances to preserve the confidentiality of its trade secrets. Such information derives independent economic value from not being generally known to the public or to other persons who can obtain economic value from its disclosure or use. Accordingly, the above-described information constitutes "trade secrets," under California's Uniform Trade Secrets Act, Cal. Civ. Code Section 3426 et seq.

37. Patmore was and remains under a duty both to keep Zynga's confidential, proprietary or trade secret information secret, and not to use or disclose such information other than for the benefit of Zynga and with Zynga's authorization. By taking this information from Zynga without its authorization, Patmore knew or should have known that he acquired such information under circumstances giving rise to a breach of a duty to maintain its secrecy and limit its use.

38. Patmore misappropriated Zynga's trade secrets through the unauthorized taking and retention of Zynga's trade secret information.

39. Patmore's actual and threatened misappropriation was and is being carried out without the express or implied consent of Zynga.

40. Zynga is informed and believes that Patmore obtained the trade secret information described above directly or indirectly from Zynga and not from generally available information or through his own independent research and efforts.

41. The actions of Patmore constitute willful misappropriation and/or threatened misappropriation of Zynga's trade secrets under the California Uniform Trade Secrets Act, as codified in Civil Code section 3426 et seq.

42. Patmore's actual and threatened misappropriation of Zynga's trade secrets, unless and until enjoined and restrained by order of this Court, is causing and will continue to cause great and irreparable harm to Zynga. Zynga is threatened with losing its intellectual property as well as current and potential business.

43. Zynga has no adequate remedy at law for the injuries currently being suffered, and the additional injuries that are threatened, because it would be impossible to quantify in dollars the losses described above when this matter is finally adjudicated, and Patmore will continue to engage in his wrongful conduct and Zynga will continue to suffer irreparable injury that cannot be adequately remedied at law unless Patmore is enjoined from engaging in any further such acts of misappropriation.

44. In addition, as a direct and proximate cause of Patmore's misappropriation of Zynga trade secrets, Patmore have been unjustly enriched in an amount to be ascertained at trial, and Zynga has sustained, and will continue to sustain, actual damages in an amount to be proven at trial. Zynga also has suffered irreparable harm as a result of Patmore's actions.

45. Each of the acts of misappropriation was done willfully and maliciously by Patmore with the deliberate intent to injure Zynga's business and improve his own business and for financial gain, thereby entitling Zynga to exemplary damages and/or attorneys' fees to be proved at trial pursuant to California Civil Code Section 3246.3(c).

SECOND CAUSE OF ACTION

(Breach of Written Contract)

46. Zynga incorporates by reference paragraphs 1 through 45 of this Complaint.

47. As a condition of his employment with Zynga, Patmore executed Zynga's Employment Invention Assignment and Confidentiality Agreement ("EIACA"), a true and correct copy of which is attached hereto as Exhibit A.

48. The EIACA Patmore entered into with Zynga constitutes a valid, binding and enforceable contract that requires Patmore to maintain the secrecy of Zynga's confidential, proprietary, and trade secret information, and to return all such information, documents, and property of Zynga upon termination of his employment with Zynga.

49. The EIACA Patmore entered into with Zynga also required Patmore, for a period of one year after the end of his employment, to "not directly or indirectly solicit away employees or consultants of the [Zynga] for [his] benefit or for the benefit of any other person or entity."

50. Zynga has performed (or was excused from performing) all of its obligations under the EIACA.

51. Patmore breached his contractual obligations to Zynga by:

a. Taking information belonging to Zynga without its knowledge or authorization, and for reasons unrelated to the performance of his duties for Zynga;

b. Failing to return Zynga's data upon leaving Zynga's employ; and

c. On information and belief, disclosing Zynga's confidential, proprietary, and/ or trade secret information to, and/or using such information on behalf of, his new employer Kixeye and/or its agents.

52. As a proximate result of the Patmore's breaches of contract, Zynga has suffered, and will continue to suffer, general and special damages in an amount to be proven at trial. Zynga seeks compensation for all damages and losses proximately caused by these breaches.

PRAYER FOR RELIEF

WHEREFORE, Plaintiff Zynga prays for judgment and relief as follows:

1. Injunctive relief temporarily, preliminarily and permanently enjoining Patmore as follows: Defendant Patmore, as well as his agents, and all persons in active concert and participation with any of them, are immediately and temporarily restrained from, directly or indirectly:

a. Obtaining, accessing, using, retaining, or disclosing to anyone (other than their counsel and forensic experts) any of Zynga's data, documents and property taken from or belonging to Zynga that is in any Defendant's current possession, custody, or control;

b. Accessing, retrieving, copying, transmitting or disseminating any copies of Zynga's data, documents or property taken from or belonging to Zynga;

c. Engaging in any activities related to the planning, design or development of online game applications that in any way involve the use or disclosure of Zynga's trade secrets or other confidential or proprietary data;

2. Temporary, preliminary, and permanent injunctive relief requiring the immediate return of Zynga's stolen data, in forensically sound fashion, preserving all metadata;

3. Compensatory damages, past and future, in an amount to compensate Zynga;

4. General damages;

5. An accounting to establish, and an order requiring restitution and/or disgorgement of, the sums by which Defendants have been unjustly enriched;

6. Exemplary and punitive damages for Defendants' willful and malicious actions;

7. Pre-judgment and post-judgment interest at the maximum rate allowed by law;

8. Attorneys' fees and costs incurred by virtue of this action; and

9. For such other and further relief as the Court may deem proper.

DATED: October 12, 2012 PAUL HASTINGS LLP

§ 9.30 Contractual Remedies

A privately drafted contract might work well in conjunction with a trade secrecy statute to help demonstrate that the developer has taken reasonable steps to protect its confidential intellectual property and thereby "maintain its secrecy."

Delphine Software Int'l v. Elec. Arts, Inc.

United States District Court, Southern District of New York, Aug. 18, 1999
No. Civ. 4454 AG AS, 1999 WL 627413

SCHWARTZ, District Judge.

This case is before the Court on plaintiff's application for a temporary restraining order ("TRO") and expedited discovery.

BRIEF FACTUAL BACKGROUND

Plaintiff Delphine Software International ("Delphine") is a developer of games for computers and video game stations. Defendant Electronic Arts ("EA") is a publicly traded Delaware corporation with offices in California. Delphine and EA were parties to a publication agreement pursuant to which EA published and distributed plaintiff's products Motoracer 1 and Motoracer 2. Because EA was provided with substantial information about Delphine's products in the course of this relationship, the publication agreement contained a confidentiality clause providing that EA was

not to use any such Confidential Information for any purpose other than the purpose for which it was originally disclosed to the receiving party, and not to disclose any of such Confidential Information to any third party.

After learning that EA had begun work on its own motorcycle racing game, called SuperCross 2000, Delphine commenced this action asserting that the new game makes use of Delphine's trade secrets and confidential information in violation of the confidentiality provision of the publication agreement. Delphine alleges that EA's access to Delphine's source code and software development techniques — which it asserts are trade secrets that has permitted it to develop SuperCross 2000 much earlier than it would have been able to otherwise.

EA answers that SuperCross 2000 is significantly different from MR2 in both the way that it is programmed and in the way that it functions. EA also asserts that Delphine's techniques are not trade secrets, and, even if they are, they were not used in creating SuperCross 2000. EA points out that it did not develop SuperCross 2000 itself, but rather engaged another separate company to develop the game, with minimal assistance from EA employees. EA asserts that no party who materially assisted in the programming of SuperCross 2000 had access to Delphine's source code or trade secrets.

Delphine seeks a TRO enjoining EA from making use of its trade secrets or releasing products based on its trade secrets. EA asserts that preliminary relief is unnecessary at this point, as it will not release SuperCross 2000 before October of this year, and plaintiff's case is not likely to succeed on the merits. EA further contends that Delphine, by its own admission, had knowledge of EA's proposed release of SuperCross 2000 by January 1999, but delayed at least until June 1999 to seek injunctive relief from this Court. Delphine also seeks expedited discovery.

DISCUSSION

A. PLAINTIFF HAS NOT DEMONSTRATED IRREPARABLE HARM

A demonstration of probable irreparable harm is generally the most important requirement for the granting of preliminary relief. Movant is required to establish not a mere possibility of irreparable harm, but "that it is likely to suffer irreparable harm if equitable relief is denied."

The Court is not satisfied that plaintiff has established that irreparable harm will occur if this TRO application is denied. Unlike the majority of cases that have found irreparable harm to occur upon the loss of a trade secret, there is little danger that the absence of a TRO will expand access to plaintiff's trade secrets and result in an incompensable loss. SuperCross 2000 is already in the final stages of development, and, if EA has made use of Delphine's trade secrets, the benefit has already accrued to EA in terms of gaining a "head start" on product development. Additionally, SuperCross 2000 is not scheduled to be released for at least 60 days, which is adequate time in which to permit discovery to take place and to then schedule a full evidentiary hearing in order to assess Delphine's entitlement to injunctive relief.

The Court is also not convinced from this limited record that monetary damages would not be sufficient compensation to Delphine in the event that Delphine shows that EA made use of Delphine's confidential information in the course of the development of SuperCross 2000. Where money damages are adequate compensation, a preliminary injunction will not issue.

B. THE MERITS OF PLAINTIFF'S CAUSE OF ACTION

In order to demonstrate a likelihood of success on the merits, Movant is not required to show that success on its complaint is an absolute certainty, but rather that the probability that it will prevail is better than fifty percent. Disputed factual questions, however, prevent the Court from concluding that plaintiff has made such a showing.

In particular, the Court is unable to discern from the record whether, assuming valid trade secrets of Delphine were known to EA, these trade secrets were actually used by the individuals creating SuperCross 2000. It is true that the case law suggests that a person in possession of trade secrets, when working on a similar project, may "inevitably disclose" the proprietary information and techniques of which he is in possession. However, defendant has asserted that the individuals with knowledge of plaintiff's techniques and trade secrets were not computer programmers, and lacked the technical expertise to communicate Delphine's technical and design secrets to the team developing SuperCross 2000. Additionally, the extent to which EA's employees were involved in the creation of SuperCross 2000 is unclear, particularly in light of the submissions by defendant which indicate that SuperCross 2000 has been programmed to a large extent by an outside development team employed by an experienced and unrelated contractor, MBL. Similarly, defendant asserts that SuperCross 2000 is a distinctly different game from Delphine's previous titles, and asserts that Delphine's trade secrets are not directly relevant to the game play and design style used by MBL and EA in the creation of SuperCross 2000.

While the Court does not conclude that plaintiff has demonstrated a likelihood of success on the merits, the Court does conclude that Delphine has demonstrated a cognizable and non-frivolous claim. However, the Court need not reach the question as to whether Delphine has shown "a serious question with respect to the merits," or, as defendant suggests, unreasonably delayed in making this application, because the Court concludes that the balance of hardship in this case tips in favor of defendant EA. Enjoining EA from proceeding with the development of SuperCross 2000, for which extensive development costs have been incurred, is an unnecessarily drastic remedy. SuperCross 2000 is not scheduled to be released for more than two months, and a full preliminary injunction hearing can be held before that time. Additionally, removing individuals from the production team at this point could be very disruptive to EA's production schedule, which is intended to result in a release date in time for the Christmas holiday season.

II. EXPEDITED DISCOVERY

Plaintiff's application for expedited discovery is granted. Delphine is entitled to substantial discovery to enable it to proceed with a preliminary injunction hearing before the October release date of SuperCross 2000. Additionally, Delphine has legitimate concerns that, as time passes, evidence of any misappropriation will disappear by expected revisions to the programming of SuperCross 2000 as the game is improved and the possible destruction of documents related to the early development of the game.

CONCLUSION

For the reasons stated, plaintiff's application for a TRO is DENIED, and its application for expedited discovery is GRANTED.

Notes and Questions

1. In denying the plaintiff's request for preliminary relief, the court relied on the so-called irreparable injury rule: "Where money damages are adequate compensation, a preliminary injunction will not issue." One exhaustive study challenges the notion that the irreparable injury rule is actually descriptive of judicial decisions:

> [T]he irreparable injury rule is dead. It does not describe what the cases do, and it cannot account for the results.... Injunctions are routine, and damages are never adequate unless the court wants them to be. Courts can freely turn to either line of precedents, depending on whether they want to hold the legal

remedy adequate or inadequate. Whether they want to hold the legal remedy adequate depends on whether they have some other reason to deny the equitable remedy, and it is these other reasons that drive the decisions.... Instead of one general principle for choosing among remedies—legal remedies are preferred when adequate—we have many specific rules.

DOUGLAS LAYCOCK, THE DEATH OF THE IRREPARABLE INJURY RULE 5 (Oxford 1991). Assuming Professor Laycock is correct, why did the court have denied the request for injunctive relief?

2. Whether it's a written or unwritten rule, the court will normally apply a balancing test to determine whether or not injunctive relief should be granted prior to a trial on the merits. The presence or absence of monetary relief is, in truth, only one of several factors. The most ubiquitous balancing factors include, but are not limited to, the following: The potential for immediate or irreparable harm in the absence of the relief, whether or not the court can adequately enforce the relief, the presence or absence of an adequate remedy at law, the potential harm to the enjoined person or entity, the likelihood of success at trial, and the willingness of the party seeking the relief to post a bond or other security. What elements in this list were present to influence the court in *Delphine*?

* * *

nMotion, Inc. v. Envtl. Tectonics Corp.

United States Court of Appeal Ninth Circuit, 2005
148 Fed. App'x. 591

PER CURIAM:

Plaintiff nMotion, Inc. appeals the district court's summary judgment in favor of Environmental Tectonics Corp. and its sister company ETC-PZL Aerospace Industries, SP (together "ETC") on its breach of contract and unfair competition claims. Because the facts and circumstances of this case are well-known to the parties, we need not recite them here. In short, nMotion alleges that ETC stole its idea to acquire flight simulation game software and use it to enhance its existing flight simulation software and create new themed entertainment products.

We first address nMotion's two breach of contract claims. During the course of business meetings between ETC and nMotion, ETC signed two non-disclosure agreements at nMotion's request. The non-disclosure agreements prohibited ETC from disclosing or using "Confidential Information" conveyed by nMotion.

nMotion contends that ETC breached the non-disclosure agreements because it used "Confidential Information" when it decided to pursue nMotion's ideas in the flight simulator arena. ETC responds that any information it used was publicly disclosed in nMotion's business proposal, and was therefore not subject to the requirements of the non-disclosure agreements. We agree.

nMotion fails to identify any specific "Confidential Information" it disclosed to ETC which was not also disclosed in its business proposal, and which would therefore be subject to the terms of the non-disclosure agreements. While it is certainly plausible that some Confidential Information was exchanged during the course of the meetings between nMotion and ETC, nMotion has failed to set forth specific facts to support such an assertion. This failure is fatal to its breach of contract theory, and summary judgment in favor of ETC was therefore proper on nMotion's two breach of contract claims.

With respect to its unfair competition claim, nMotion contends that the district court erred by finding that corporate morality principles set forth in *Kamin v. Kuhnau*, 232 Or. 139, 374 P.2d 912 (1962), on which nMotion's unfair competition claim is premised, are obsolete. Without passing on the viability, if any, of Oregon's corporate morality doctrine following the adoption of the Oregon Uniform Trade Secrets Act, we hold that it is inapplicable here. The corporate morality doctrine may impose duties on and imply agreements between parties to a business relationship, but we decline to invoke it here, where the parties have defined their relationship by contract. *See Kamin v. Kuhnau*, 232 Or. 139, 374 P.2d 912, 919 (1962) (corporate morality doctrine is a proxy for the intention of the parties). Summary judgment was therefore proper on nMotion's unfair competition claim.

AFFIRMED.

Notes and Questions

1. In *First Games Publisher Network, Inc. v. Afonin*, 32 Misc. 3d 1245(A) (N.Y. Sup. Ct. 2011), Defendant Afonin, a Ukranian citizen, was appointed as the Plaintiff's Vice President and Chief Development Officer. Plaintiff is a producer of massively multiplayer on-line role playing games (MMPORG's). Plaintiff hired Lucky Soft, LLC (Lucky) to develop software for an entity known as Ragnesis; the development involved millions of lines of code. Plaintiff later sought to buy Lucky to obtain an in-house videogame development studio. Defendant, who had previously obtained an ownership interest in Lucky, indicated to Plaintiff that he would assist the purchase effort. On December 2, 2007, Plaintiff and Defendant signed a confidentiality agreement whereby Defendant agreed not to use Plaintiff's proprietary data or other intellectual property either for his own benefit or the benefit of third parties. In October 2008, Plaintiff was surprised to learn that Lucky had been sold to a third party. Defendant resigned from his position as Plaintiff's officer and director. In December 2008, Plaintiff demanded that Defendant and Lucky turn over the Ragnesis-related intellectual property. Plaintiff alleged that a year later, in response, it received incomplete source code, only. Plaintiff contended that reviewing the incomplete source code that it had received and completing development of the project based on it would be cost prohibitive. To add some more insult to the injury, Plaintiff then discovered in November 2009 that Lucky was developing a computer game called *Elementals: The Magic Key* ("Magic Key"). Plaintiff alleged that Defendant is *Magic Key's* producer and that *Magic Key's* source code was derived from the Ragnesis property. Plaintiff sought to hold Defendant liable for breach of the confidentiality agreement, breach of a fiduciary duty, and violation of New York's Business Corporation Law. Defendant moved to dismiss the count pertaining to the Breach of Confidentiality, arguing that Plaintiff's cause of action did not allege that any of the information or property was transferred to the Defendant. Rejecting this argument, the court denied the Defendant's motion.

2. In *Antonick v. Elec. Arts Inc.*, 2013 U.S. Dist. LEXIS 84427 (N.D. Cal. June 10, 2013), a battle over secrecy and confidentiality occurred in this fraud and breach of contract action involving the John Madden Football videogame. As opposed to computer code, this argument was over the confidentiality of Electronic Art's response letter to the SEC, regarding the filing of its Form 10-K. (The annual report on Form 10-K, which is filed with the Securities and Exchange Commission, provides a comprehensive overview of a company's business and financial status; it includes audited financial statements.) During Antonik's efforts seeking discovery of the contents of the letter, the court rejected the argument by EA that there was good cause to maintain its confidentiality designation and

to file it under seal, despite EA's claim that it has consistently treated the material as confidential and has not disclosed it publicly.

3. Carefully examine each of the following agreements and determine which contract model, if any, would have averted the problems presented in the preceding cases.

4. What modifications (i.e., additional language) would you make or suggest to avoid the problems presented in the preceding cases?

* * *

FORM 9.1
Unilateral Non-disclosure Agreement

FOR GOOD AND VALUABLE CONSIDERATION, the receipt and adequacy of which is hereby acknowledged, the undersigned _____ (referred to as "RECIPIENT") does hereby enter into the following confidentiality agreement with _____ (referred to as "COMPANY"), as of the _____ day of _____, 20_____:

1.   RECIPIENT has been informed and does understand that during the course of employment or independently contracted work, the RECIPIENT will receive, possess and come in contact with information of a confidential nature which may include but not be limited to data and materials relating to the COMPANY's products, services, intellectual properties, computer code, computer game engines, software development engines, technologies, and potential business opportunities.

2.   All confidential information shall be retained in confidence by the RECIPIENT, its employees, agents, assigns, affiliates, and/or subsidiaries, pursuant to the following terms and conditions of this agreement. Such information shall be maintained in confidence and not disclosed to others unless or until: (a) it shall have been made public by an act or omission of a party other than the recipient; (b) the recipient receives such confidential information from an unrelated third party on a non-confidential basis; or (c) the passage of five years from the date of disclosure, whichever shall first occur.

3.   Upon request, the RECIPIENT agrees to promptly return to the COMPANY all materials obtained from or through the COMPANY which relate directly or indirectly to the confidential information, including all documentation, proposals, samples, memoranda, specifications, and process or flow diagrams, including any copies, notes or memoranda made by the recipient that, in any way, relate to the confidential information disclosed or transmitted to the recipient by the discloser.

4.   In each instance, the RECIPIENT agrees that it will not, without first obtaining the prior written permission of the COMPANY: (a) directly or indirectly utilize the Confidential Information or any of the Confidential Information in its business; (b) exhibit, perform, manufacture, and/or sell any product that is based in whole or in part on the Confidential Information or any of the Confidential Information; or (c) disclose the Confidential Information or any of the Confidential Information to any third party.

5.   In the event the disclosing party provides software as part of any Confidential Information, the recipient agrees that it will not reverse engineer, reverse compile, reverse assemble, or take any steps to learn the structure or methods utilized by the discloser of the applicable Confidential Information, and will not authorize, encourage, or permit others to do so.

6.   In the event of any doubt or uncertainty as to whether information is confidential, it is agreed that all such information provided by the COMPANY to the RECIPIENT shall be presumed confidential unless the contrary is clearly indicated.

7.   This is the entire agreement of the parties in connection with the subject matter of this Agreement. It cannot be changed except through a written instrument signed by authorized representatives of each party. This Agreement has been executed in the State of _____ and will be governed and construed in accordance with those laws of the State of _____ applicable to agreements entered into and performed entirely within the State of _____.

Signed this _____ day of _____, 20____.

_____

RECIPIENT

_____

COMPANY

* * *

FORM 9.2
Mutual Non-disclosure Agreement

THIS NON-DISCLOSURE AGREEMENT ("Agreement") is entered into effective _____, 20__, between COMPANY A, a New Jersey corporation, on behalf of itself, its parent corporation, subsidiaries and affiliates (collectively, "COMPANY A") and _____, [a company incorporated under the laws of the state of _____, [a partnership][an individual], having a place of business as set forth in the address referenced below the signature hereto ("COMPANY B"). The parties agree as follows:

WHEREAS, COMPANY A and COMPANY B desire to receive certain information of the other party considered as confidential by such party; and

WHEREAS, the parties desire to disclose certain portions or amounts of their respective information which they consider confidential, in order to promote their mutual development of video and computer game software.

NOW THEREFORE, COMPANY A and COMPANY B do hereby agree as follows:

1.   **Definition of "Confidential Information":** As used herein, "Confidential Information" means information provided to the party receiving such information ("Receiving Party") by the party disclosing such information ("Disclosing Party," including any third party under an obligation of confidentiality to the Disclosing Party) in any way relating to the Disclosing Party's current or future products, services or business, including but not limited to current or future: (a) information, know-how, techniques, methods, information, concepts, ideas, development tools or kits, emulator boards, development specifications, physical model prototype mechanism, or trade secrets, (b) patent applications and information related thereto, (c) any business, marketing, customer or sales information, (d) any information relating to development, design, operation, or manufacturing, (e) any information that is received from others that the Disclosing Party is obligated to keep confidential, and (f) this Agreement, the terms and conditions thereof and any communications related thereto. Confidential Information may be disclosed in digital or electronic format, in writing, orally, visually, or in the form of drawings, technical specifications, or other tangible items which contain or manifest, in any form, the Confidential Information.

2. Exclusions From "Confidential Information" Definition: The following shall be excluded from the definition of Confidential Information set forth in Paragraph 1 above:

[a] Data and information which was in the public domain prior to the Receiving Party's receipt of the same hereunder, or which subsequently becomes part of the public domain by publication or otherwise, except by the Receiving Party's act or omission.

[b] Data and information which the Receiving Party can demonstrate, through written records kept in the ordinary course of business, was in its possession without restriction on use or disclosure, prior to its receipt of the same hereunder, and which was not acquired directly or indirectly from the Disclosing Party under an obligation of confidentiality which is still in force.

[c] Data and information which the Receiving Party can show was received by it from a third party who did not acquire the same directly or indirectly from the Disclosing Party and to whom the Disclosing Party has no obligation of confidentiality.

3. Confidentiality: With respect to any Confidential Information as defined below, the Receiving Party agrees: (a) to use the Confidential Information of the Disclosing Party solely in connection with the COMPANY A Video Game system and/or the business purpose set forth on Exhibit A hereto, (b) to use its best efforts to prevent disclosure of the same to others, and (c) not to disclose, summarize, distribute, duplicate or use the same other than as provided for herein without first receiving written approval from the Disclosing Party authorizing such other use, and (d) not to remove or obliterate markings (if any) on Confidential Information indicating its confidential or proprietary nature.

4. Compulsory Disclosure: Confidential Information may be disclosed by the Receiving Party as required or compelled by an authorized governmental or judicial entity, provided that the Receiving Party shall provide the Disclosing Party with as much prior notice as reasonably practical, prior to such disclosure. The Receiving Party shall use its best efforts to limit the disclosure to the greatest extent possible consistent with its legal obligations, and if requested by the Disclosing Party, shall cooperate in the preparation and entry of appropriate protective orders.

5. Works In Progress: The parties understand that each party may now market or have under development games that are competitive with products or services now offered or which may be offered by the other. Subject to the terms and conditions of this Agreement, discussion and/or communications between COMPANY A and COMPANY B will not serve to impair the right of such parties to develop, make use of, procure and/or market games or services related thereto now or in the future which may be competitive with those offered by the other party, or require the parties to disclose any planning or other information to the other party.

6. Subsidiary Non-Disclosure: The Receiving Party shall not disclose the Confidential Information to any of its subsidiaries, without the prior written consent of the Disclosing Party. In addition, the Receiving Party shall limit access to and disclosure of Confidential Information only to those of its employees, and to those individuals specifically authorized by the Disclosing Party in writing to receive Confidential Information, who (a) have a strict need to know such Confidential Information, and (b) are under an obligation of confidentiality which would restrict such employees or individuals from disclosing the Confidential Information. Notwithstanding the foregoing, the Receiving Party remains liable for any unauthorized disclosure or use by such parties.

7. **Location of Confidential Information:** The Receiving Party will keep the Confidential Information at the location set forth below such party's signature, or such other location as approved by the Disclosing Party in writing.

8. **Security Measures:** If the Receiving Party becomes aware, or has reason to believe, that there has been an unauthorized disclosure or use of the Confidential Information, it shall immediately notify the Disclosing Party. The Receiving Party shall take any and all actions necessary, at its sole expense, to protect the Confidential Information, including such actions as may reasonably be requested by the Disclosing Party.

9. **Reverse Engineering:** The Receiving Party shall not directly or indirectly reverse engineer, or aid or assist in the reverse engineering of, all or any part of the Confidential Information including the hardware, software (either any embedded software, or software provided by the Disclosing Party as part of any development tool or kit), controller, and development tools or kits.

10. **Ownership of Confidential Information:** As between the parties, the Confidential Information shall remain the sole property of the Disclosing Party.

11. **Limitations:** Nothing in this Agreement shall be construed as granting to the Receiving Party: (a) any rights, license or immunities under any patent, copyright, trademark, mask work or any other rights in or to the Confidential Information for any purpose; (b) any rights to commercialize any hardware, software, accessories, peripheral, services, development tools or kits developed by the Receiving Party; or (c) any rights to purchase or market any of the Disclosing Party's products, technology or service. The Disclosing Party makes no representations or warranties regarding the usefulness, accuracy, completeness, technical quality, ownership or validity of any Confidential Information (or any intellectual property rights relating thereto).

12. **No Warranties:** All such confidential information is provided "as is" and without warranty of any kind and the Receiving Party agrees that neither the Disclosing Party nor any third party working with the disclosing party shall be liable for any damages whatsoever arising from or relating to the receiving party's use or inability to use such confidential information. The Receiving Party hereby indemnifies and holds harmless the Disclosing Party from any liability arising from any unauthorized use of the Confidential Information.

13. **Non-Assignability:** This Agreement shall not be sold, assigned, delegated, sublicensed or otherwise transferred or encumbered, in whole or in part, by a party without the other party's prior written consent, which consent may be withheld in its sole discretion. An "assignment" includes, but shall not be limited to: (a) a merger of a party into another business entity or a merger of another business entity into such party; (b) the sale, assignment or transfer of all or substantially all of the assets of a party to a third party; (c) the sale, assignment or transfer of any of a party's intellectual property rights to a third party; or (d) the sale, assignment or transfer of any or all of a party's stock resulting in the acquirer having any management power over or voting control of such party.

14. **Parties Bound:** Subject to the restrictions against assignment provided above, this Agreement shall be binding upon and inure to the benefit of the parties, their successors and permitted assigns.

15. Termination: This Agreement shall terminate (a) upon 10 days prior written notice of termination by either party to the other, without cause and for convenience, or (b) immediately upon notice by the non-defaulting party to the defaulting party, in the event of a breach by a party of the terms of this Agreement or of any related license, development, or other agreement between the parties. Upon termination, the Receiving Party shall (a) cease all use of the Disclosing Party's Confidential Information; and (b) at the Receiving Party's sole expense, return to the Disclosing Party or destroy, at the Disclosing Party's direction, any tangible items which contain or manifest, in any form, the Disclosing Party's Confidential Information (including, but without limitation, any writings, drawings, specifications, models, or development tools or kits containing or pertaining to such Confidential Information) without making copies or otherwise retaining such Confidential Information. The Disclosing Party may undertake an audit and/or require written certification to confirm the Receiving Party's compliance with this paragraph. All of the obligations requiring confidentiality shall survive termination of this Agreement.

16. Compliance With Law: The parties shall comply with all applicable laws relating to the use, disclosure, copying, dissemination and distribution of the Confidential Information provided hereunder, including but not limited to all laws relating to proprietary rights or to the export of any technical data included in such Confidential Information.

17. No Entities Created: The parties do not intend by this Agreement to create a partnership, principal/agent, franchisor/franchisee, master/servant or joint venture relationship, and nothing in this Agreement shall be construed as creating such a relationship.

18. Applicable Laws: This Agreement shall be subject to and construed under the laws of the State _____ , without regard to its conflict-of-laws principles. Any legal actions with respect to any matters arising under this Agreement shall be brought in a court of competent jurisdiction in _____ County, _____. The parties hereby consent to the jurisdiction and venue of such courts for such purpose.

19. Integration: This Agreement constitutes the entire agreement between the parties with respect to the subject matter hereof. There are no understandings, representations or warranties of any kind, express or implied, except as expressly stated herein. Any modification or amendment of this Agreement must be in writing executed by COMPANY B and COMPANY A. The parties may, by mutual agreement, revise Exhibit A to add or delete the purpose for which Confidential Information may be used by preparing, dating and signing a new Exhibit.

20. Remedies For Breach: The parties acknowledge that in the event of breach of this Agreement, no adequate remedy at law may be available to the non-breaching party, and that such non-breaching party shall be entitled to seek injunctive or other equitable relief in addition to any relief available at law, without the need to post a bond. The protections afforded the Confidential Information herein are in addition to and not in lieu of the protections afforded under any applicable trade secrets laws, including the Uniform Trade Secrets Act.

21. Execution: This Agreement shall be effective when signed by both parties. A facsimile copy is effective as an original.

22. Notices: Notice under this Agreement shall be in writing personally delivered or sent via expedited courier service to the address provided for below. Notice shall be effective upon the earlier of actual receipt or two (2) business days after transmittal.

COMPANY A	COMPANY B
By:_____	By:_____
Printed Name:_____	Printed Name:_____
Title: _____	Title: _____
Date: _____	Date: _____

There may be instances where disclosures of confidential information are necessary for temporary or evaluative functions, as opposed to the ongoing relationships contemplated by the preceding non-disclosure agreements. For those instances, which may include beta testing or look-see evaluations, consider the following:

* * *

FORM 9.3
Third Party Non-disclosure Agreement

The undersigned ("RECIPIENT") requests that it be given access to certain Confidential Information that constitutes the proprietary property of _____ Corporation ("XYZ"), solely for the limited purpose of evaluating same, and in order to induce XYZ to disclose such Confidential Information, agrees that it will be bound by the following terms and conditions:

1. **Confidential Information:** The term "Confidential Information" means all information relating to a certain video game project _____ that is disclosed to the RECIPIENT by XYZ (either orally or in a tangible form), including but not limited to inventions, discoveries, processes, and know-how; computer software code, designs, routines, algorithms, and structures; product information; research and development information; information relating to actual and potential customers; financial data and information; business plans; marketing materials and strategies; and any other information regarding the foregoing that XYZ discloses to the RECIPIENT hereunder. Failure to include a confidentiality notice on any materials disclosed to the RECIPIENT shall not give rise to an inference that the information disclosed is not confidential. "Confidential Information," as used herein, shall not include information that the RECIPIENT can establish (i) is generally known to the public (other than as a result of a breach of this Agreement); (ii) is independently developed by the RECIPIENT; (iii) was lawfully obtained from a third party; or (iv) is later published or generally disclosed to the public by XYZ.

2. **Use of Confidential Information:** The RECIPIENT agrees to use the Confidential Information only for the limited time specified herein and solely for the purpose of evaluating XYZ's _____ in order to determine whether to _____. The RECIPIENT shall have no right to use the Confidential Information for production or commercial purposes without obtaining a license therefore from XYZ.

3. **Protection of Confidential Information:** The RECIPIENT hereby agrees to take all steps reasonably necessary to maintain and protect the Confidential Information in the strictest confidence for the benefit of XYZ, and will not, at any time without the express written permission of XYZ, disclose the Confidential Information directly

or indirectly to any third person, excepting employees of the RECIPIENT who have expressly agreed in writing to be bound by the terms of this Agreement.

4. **Term:** The RECIPIENT's obligations with respect to the Confidential Information shall continue for the shorter of _____ (___) years from the date of its receipt of the Confidential Information, or until such information is subject to one of the exclusions set forth above.

5. **Return of Confidential Information:** The RECIPIENT acknowledges that its limited right to evaluate the Confidential Information shall expire on _____ and agrees that all Confidential Information in a tangible form, including all copies thereof, will be returned to XYZ at that time, or at such earlier time as XYZ may request. At such time, the RECIPIENT also agrees to completely erase and destroy all copies of all portions of any software comprising the Confidential Information in its possession or under its responsibility which may have been loaded onto the RE-CIPIENT's computers.

6. **Disclaimers:** This Agreement does not require XYZ to disclose any Confidential Information. All Confidential Information disclosed by XYZ is disclosed on an "AS IS" basis. XYZ is not to be liable for any damages arising out of the use of the Confidential Information, and such use is at the RECIPIENT's own risk. Neither this Agreement nor the disclosure of any Confidential Information grants the undersigned any license under any patents, copyrights, or trade secrets.

7. **Governing Law:** This Agreement shall be governed by and construed in accordance with the laws of the State of _____ covering agreements made and to be performed in that State.

XYZ COMPANY   RECIPIENT

By:_____   By:_____

Printed Name:_____   Printed Name:_____

Title: _____   Title: _____

Date: _____   Date: _____

Part III

Commercial Exploitation

Chapter Ten

Player Rights and Responsibilities

§ 10.10 End Use Licensing Agreements; Terms of Use; Terms of Service; Click Wrap and Shrink Wrap Agreements

The sellers of videogames largely want to dictate the terms of any agreement to sell or distribute their games. Terms vary from publisher to publisher, but some typical clauses a videogame owner tries to insert into the governing document or documents include:

- a clause disclaiming or modifying traditional warranties;
- a limitation of remedies clause, such as one which provides that the only remedy available to the user will be a replacement of the game, or that consequential damages suffered as a result of game play will not be recoverable;
- a clause prohibiting commercial use of the game, i.e., prohibiting the purchaser from buying a number of games and sponsoring a public tournament with paid players and crowds;[1]
- a clause prohibiting the user from bringing or participating in a class action suit against the developer;
- a provision dictating that any dispute between the developer and the user must be decided in an arbitration;
- a choice of law clause, saying any dispute must be judged by the law of, e.g., California;
- a forum selection clause, stating that any law suit against the developer must be brought in, e.g., a state court in New York;
- a clause limiting the number of copies of the game that can be made (or prohibiting copying outright);
- a clause prohibiting the user from reverse engineering the computer code controlling the game, or creating a derivative work;
- a clause limiting the user's "fair use" rights under the Copyright Act;

---

1. We deal with this "public performance" issue in further detail in Chapter Eleven.

- a clause specifying that the user has only a limited period of time to return the game for full refund; and

- a clause stating that the player does not own the game, but merely obtains a license for the right to play it under the circumstances dictated by the seller, and cannot transfer it to another.[2]

These, and the many other terms that producers try to insert as part of their standard agreements with users, are found in documents called End User License Agreements ("EULAs"); Term of Use ("TOU") Agreements; or Terms of Service ("TOS") Agreements (collectively the "Three Agreements"). EULAs are restricted to those situations in which a developer only licenses the game or program to the user,[3] whereas TOU and TOS Agreements can apply to both sales, license, or other commercial transactions.

Where a purchaser will first encounter the Three Agreements depends on where and how the purchase transaction is consummated. If the transaction takes place in a store or over the phone, typically the first time a user will see the terms of any of the Three Agreements is upon cutting through the plastic in which the package is wrapped and opening the package to find a sheet or brochure setting forth the terms. The agreements found inside the package are known as "shrinkwrap" agreements. Some developers disclose on the *outside* of the box, or instruct the sales associate *on the phone,* to disclose the fact that additional terms of the deal will be included *inside* the box or shipment, so that purchasers at least know that some additional terms are coming (even if they don't know what they are) before agreeing to pay for the game. Other developers choose not to provide such pre-purchase notice.

When the game is purchased on the Internet (whether delivery is via online streaming or mailing a disk), the seller's standard terms are typically disclosed in a dialogue box in which the buyer must click "I accept" before being permitted to pay for the game, although occasionally the "Terms and Conditions" of sale are just linked to the order page and the user can choose to view them before sale or ignore them, as most users do. Such agreements are known as "clickwrap" agreements.

For reasons to be discussed in this chapter, some developers program their games so that the terms of the applicable agreement pop up every time the game is loaded, resulting in a situation where the "I accept" dialogue box must be clicked before game play can commence.

In the cases in this section, users often claim they are not bound by the terms of whichever of the Three Agreements the developer seeks to enforce. Their arguments fall into two broad categories: (1) arguments that the terms of the clickwrap and shrinkwrap agreements never became part of the deal (at least in shrinkwrap agreements) because the buyer only learns of them *after* the purchase transaction has been made; and (2) arguments that even if the terms could be considered part of the deal, they are unenforceable because they are unconscionable in that they were not the subject of meaningful negotiation, and were imposed on a take-it-or-leave-it basis by a party in a superior bargaining position.

---

2. We deal with the rights of the buyer under the "first sale" doctrine in Chapter 11.

3. A license is permission to use another's property in a limited manner. It originated as a real property concept. Restatement (First) of Property § 512 (1944). In a license situation, title remains in the seller and the purchaser buys only the right to use the program in the manner dictated in the EULA, or TOS or TOU Agreement. When the differences between a user who is a "purchaser" versus one who is a "licensee" are relevant to a topic discussed in this Chapter, the issue is noted. However, for most of the issues in this Chapter, whether the transaction is a license or a sale is relatively unimportant.

The following two cases are among the most cited and studied decisions on the enforceability of clickwrap and shrinkwrap agreements. They deal with the sale of a computer, not software, but their principles apply to videogame sales as well. Just mentally substitute *World of Warcraft* for "Gateway 2000" and you will get the idea. Special attention should be paid to the different views of offer and acceptance set forth in the decisions.

Hill v. Gateway 2000, Inc.

United States Court of Appeals, Seventh Circuit, 1997
105 F.3d 1147

EASTERBROOK, Circuit Judge.

A customer picks up the phone, orders a computer, and gives a credit card number. Presently a box arrives, containing the computer and a list of terms, said to govern unless the customer returns the computer within 30 days. Are these terms effective as the parties' contract, or is the contract term-free because the order-taker did not read any terms over the phone and elicit the customer's assent?

One of the terms in the box containing a Gateway 2000 system was an arbitration clause. Rich and Enza Hill, the customers, kept the computer more than 30 days before complaining about its components and performance. They filed suit in federal court arguing, among other things, that the product's shortcomings make Gateway a racketeer leading to treble damages under RICO. Gateway asked the district court to enforce the arbitration clause; the judge refused, writing that "[t]he present record is insufficient to support a finding of a valid arbitration agreement between the parties or that the plaintiffs were given adequate notice of the arbitration clause."

The Hills say that the arbitration clause did not stand out: they concede noticing the statement of terms but deny reading it closely enough to discover the agreement to arbitrate, and they ask us to conclude that they therefore may go to court. Yet an agreement to arbitrate must be enforced save upon such grounds as exist at law or in equity for the revocation of any contract. A contract need not be read to be effective; people who accept take the risk that the unread terms may in retrospect prove unwelcome. Terms inside Gateway's box stand or fall together. If they constitute the parties' contract because the Hills had an opportunity to return the computer after reading them, then all must be enforced.

ProCD, Inc. v. Zeidenberg [86 F.3d 1447 (7th Cir. 1996)] holds that terms inside a box of software bind consumers who use the software after an opportunity to read the terms and to reject them by returning the product. *ProCD* "exemplif[ies] the many commercial transactions in which people pay for products with terms to follow." The district court concluded in *ProCD* that the contract is formed when the consumer pays for the software; as a result, the court held, only terms known to the consumer at that moment are part of the contract, and provisos inside the box do not count. Although this is one way a contract could be formed, it is not the only way: "A vendor, as master of the offer, may invite acceptance by conduct, and may propose limitations on the kind of conduct that constitutes acceptance. A buyer may accept by performing the acts the vendor proposes to treat as acceptance." Gateway shipped computers with the same sort of accept-or-return offer ProCD made to users of its software. *ProCD* therefore applies to this dispute.

Plaintiffs ask us to limit *ProCD* to software, but where's the sense in that? *ProCD* is about the law of contract, not the law of software. Payment preceding the revelation of full terms is common for air transportation, insurance, and many other endeavors. Practical considerations support allowing vendors to enclose the full legal terms with their products. Cashiers cannot be expected to read legal documents to customers before ringing up sales. If the staff at the other end of the phone for direct-sales operations such as Gateway's had to read the four-page statement of terms before taking the buyer's credit card number, the droning voice would anesthetize rather than enlighten many potential buyers. Others would hang up in a rage over the waste of their time. And oral recitation would not avoid customers' assertions (whether true or feigned) that the clerk did not read term X to them, or that they did not remember or understand it. Writing provides benefits for both sides of commercial transactions. Customers as a group are better off when vendors skip costly and ineffectual steps such as telephonic recitation, and use instead a simple approve-or-return device. Competent adults are bound by such documents, read or unread. For what little it is worth, we add that the box from Gateway was crammed with software. The computer came with an operating system, without which it was useful only as a boat anchor. Gateway also included many application programs. So the Hills' effort to limit *ProCD* to software would not avail them factually, even if it were sound legally—which it is not.

For their second sally, the Hills contend that *ProCD* should be limited to executory contracts (to licenses in particular), and therefore does not apply because both parties' performance of this contract was complete when the box arrived at their home. This is legally and factually wrong: legally because the question at hand concerns the *formation* of the contract rather than its *performance*, and factually because both contracts were incompletely performed. *ProCD* did not depend on the fact that the seller characterized the transaction as a license rather than as a contract. All debates about characterization to one side, the transaction in *ProCD* was no more executory than the one here: Zeidenberg paid for the software and walked out of the store with a box under his arm, so if arrival of the box with the product ends the time for revelation of contractual terms, then the time ended in *ProCD* before Zeidenberg opened the box. But of course ProCD had not completed performance with delivery of the box, and neither had Gateway. One element of the transaction was the warranty, which obliges sellers to fix defects in their products. The Hills have invoked Gateway's warranty and are not satisfied with its response, so they are not well positioned to say that Gateway's obligations were fulfilled when the motor carrier unloaded the box.

Next the Hills insist that *ProCD* is irrelevant because Zeidenberg was a "merchant" and they are not. Section 2-207(2) of the UCC, the infamous battle-of-the-forms section, states that "additional terms [following acceptance of an offer] are to be construed as proposals for addition to a contract. Between merchants such terms become part of the contract unless ...". Plaintiffs tell us that *ProCD* came out as it did only because Zeidenberg was a "merchant" and the terms inside ProCD's box were not excluded by the "unless" clause. This argument pays scant attention to the opinion in *ProCD*, which concluded that, when there is only one form, "sec. 2-207 is irrelevant." The question in *ProCD* was not whether terms were added to a contract after its formation, but how and when the contract was formed—in particular, whether a vendor may propose that a contract of sale be formed, not in the store (or over the phone) with the payment of money or a general "send me the product," but after the customer has had a chance to inspect both the item and the terms. *ProCD* answers "yes," for merchants and consumers alike.

At oral argument the Hills propounded still another distinction: the box containing ProCD's software displayed a notice that additional terms were within, while the box containing Gateway's computer did not. The difference is functional, not legal. Consumers browsing the aisles of a store can look at the box, and if they are unwilling to deal with the prospect of additional terms can leave the box alone, avoiding the transactions costs of returning the package after reviewing its contents. Gateway's box, by contrast, is just a shipping carton; it is not on display anywhere. Its function is to protect the product during transit, and the information on its sides is for the use of handlers: ("Fragile!" "This Side Up!") rather than would-be purchasers.

Perhaps the Hills would have had a better argument if they were first alerted to the bundling of hardware and legal-ware after opening the box and wanted to return the computer in order to avoid disagreeable terms, but were dissuaded by the expense of shipping. What the remedy would be in such a case—could it exceed the shipping charges?—is an interesting question, but one that need not detain us because the Hills knew before they ordered the computer that the carton would include *some* important terms, and they did not seek to discover these in advance. Gateway's ads state that their products come with limited warranties and lifetime support. How limited was the warranty—30 days, with service contingent on shipping the computer back, or five years, with free onsite service? What sort of support was offered? Shoppers have three principal ways to discover these things. First, they can ask the vendor to send a copy before deciding whether to buy. The Magnuson-Moss Warranty Act requires firms to distribute their warranty terms on request, 15 U.S.C. §2302(b)(1)(A); the Hills do not contend that Gateway would have refused to enclose the remaining terms too. Concealment would be bad for business, scaring some customers away and leading to excess returns from others. Second, shoppers can consult public sources (computer magazines, the Web sites of vendors) that may contain this information. Third, they may inspect the documents after the product's delivery. Like Zeidenberg, the Hills took the third option. By keeping the computer beyond 30 days, the Hills accepted Gateway's offer, including the arbitration clause.

Klocek v. Gateway, Inc.

United States District Court, District of Kansas, 2000
104 F. Supp. 2d 1332

VRATIL, District Judge.

William S. Klocek brings suit against Gateway, Inc. on claims arising from purchases of a Gateway computer. Gateway asserts that plaintiff must arbitrate his claims under Gateway's Standard Terms and Conditions Agreement ("Standard Terms"). Whenever it sells a computer, Gateway includes a copy of the Standard Terms in the box which contains the computer battery power cables and instruction manuals. At the top of the first page, the Standard Terms include the following notice:

NOTE TO THE CUSTOMER:

This document contains Gateway 2000's Standard Terms and Conditions. By keeping your Gateway 2000 computer system beyond five (5) days after the date of delivery, you accept these Terms and Conditions.

The notice is in emphasized type and is located inside a printed box which sets it apart from other provisions of the document. The Standard Terms are four pages long and contain 16 numbered paragraphs. Paragraph 10 provides an arbitration clause.

Before granting a stay or dismissing a case pending arbitration, the Court must determine that the parties have a written agreement to arbitrate. The Uniform Commercial Code

("UCC") governs the parties' transaction. State courts apparently have not decided whether terms received with a product become part of the parties' agreement.

Gateway urges the Court to follow the Seventh Circuit decision in *Hill*. That case involved the shipment of a Gateway computer with terms similar to the Standard Terms in this case, except that Gateway gave the customer 30 days—instead of 5 days—to return the computer. In enforcing the arbitration clause, the Seventh Circuit relied on its decision in *ProCD*, where it enforced a software license which was contained inside a product box. In *ProCD*, the Seventh Circuit noted that the exchange of money frequently precedes the communication of detailed terms in a commercial transaction. Citing UCC § 2-204, the court reasoned that by including the license with the software, the vendor proposed a contract that the buyer could accept by using the software after having an opportunity to read the license. Specifically, the court stated:

> A vendor, as master of the offer, may invite acceptance by conduct, and may propose limitations on the kind of conduct that constitutes acceptance. A buyer may accept by performing the acts the vendor proposes to treat as acceptance.

The *Hill* court followed the *ProCD* analysis, noting that "[p]ractical considerations support allowing vendors to enclose the full legal terms with their products."

The Court is not persuaded [to] follow the Seventh Circuit reasoning in *Hill* and *ProCD*. In each case the Seventh Circuit concluded that UCC § 2-207 was irrelevant. The statute provides:

> Additional terms in acceptance or confirmation.
>
> (1) A definite and seasonable expression of acceptance or a written confirmation which is sent within a reasonable time operates as an acceptance even though it states terms additional to or different from those offered or agreed upon, unless acceptance is expressly made conditional on assent to the additional or different terms.
>
> (2) The additional terms are to be construed as proposals for addition to the contract [if the contract is not between merchants]....

By its terms, § 2-207 applies to an acceptance or written confirmation. It states nothing which requires another form before the provision becomes effective. In fact, the official comment to the section specifically provides that §§ 2-207(1) and (2) apply "where an agreement has been reached orally ... and is followed by one or both of the parties sending formal memoranda embodying the terms so far agreed and adding terms not discussed." Official Comment 1 of UCC § 2-207. Thus, the Court concludes that § 2-207 [applies] to the facts in this case.

In addition, the Seventh Circuit provided no explanation for its conclusion that "the vendor is the master of the offer." In typical consumer transactions, the purchaser is the offeror, and the vendor is the offeree. While it is possible for the vendor to be the offeror, Gateway provides no factual evidence which would support such a finding in this case. The Court therefore assumes for purposes of the motion to dismiss that plaintiff offered to purchase the computer (either in person or through catalog order) and that Gateway accepted plaintiff's offer (either by completing the sales transaction in person or by agreeing to ship and/or shipping the computer to plaintiff).

Under § 2-207, the Standard Terms constitute either an expression of acceptance or written confirmation. As an expression of acceptance, the Standard Terms would constitute a counter-offer only if Gateway expressly made its acceptance conditional on plaintiff's assent to the additional or different terms. Gateway provides no evidence that at the time of the sales transaction, it informed plaintiff that the transaction was conditioned on plaintiff's acceptance of the Standard Terms. Moreover, the mere fact that Gateway shipped the goods with the terms attached did not communicate to plaintiff any unwillingness to proceed without plaintiff's agreement to the Standard Terms.

Because plaintiff is not a merchant, additional or different terms contained in the Standard Terms did not become part of the parties' agreement unless plaintiff expressly agreed to them. *See* Comment 2 [to 2-207—ED.]: "if either party is not a merchant, additional terms are proposals for addition to the contract that do not become part of the contract unless the original offeror expressly agrees." Gateway argues that plaintiff demonstrated acceptance of the arbitration provision by keeping the computer more than five days after the date of delivery. Although the Standard Terms purport to work that result, Gateway has not presented evidence that plaintiff expressly agreed to those Standard Terms. Gateway states only that it enclosed the Standard Terms inside the computer box for plaintiff to read afterwards. It provides no evidence that it informed plaintiff of the five-day review-and-return period as a condition of the sales transaction, or that the parties contemplated additional terms to the agreement. The Court finds that the act of keeping the computer past five days was not sufficient to demonstrate that plaintiff expressly agreed to the Standard Terms. Express assent cannot be presumed by silence or mere failure to object. Thus, because Gateway has not provided evidence sufficient to support a finding under Kansas or Missouri law that plaintiff agreed to the arbitration provision contained in Gateway's Standard Terms, the Court overrules Gateway's motion to dismiss.

The Court is mindful of the practical considerations which are involved in commercial transactions, but it is not unreasonable for a vendor to clearly communicate to a buyer — at the time of sale — either the complete terms of the sale or the fact that the vendor will propose additional terms as a condition of sale, if that be the case.

Notes and Questions

1. In framing an argument that the terms of the Three Agreements never become part of a contract, the governing law must be identified. The courts in *Hill* and *Klocek* provide that Article 2 of the UCC applies (more specifically, the applicable commercial codes of the relevant states which are based on Article 2 of the UCC).

Article 2 of the UCC only applies when there is a "transaction[] in goods" (UCC §2-102), and the Code defines "goods" as "all things which are moveable …" (§2-105(1)). Certainly computers (*Hill* and *Klocek*) and programs fixated on discs (which was the subject of *Pro CD*) are moveable, and thus "goods" within Article 2. But whether videogames that are streamed to the user via a series of electrons over the Internet are "goods" is another matter.

In *Kaplan v. Cablevision of Pa., Inc.*, 671 A.2d. 716 (Pa. Super. Ct. 1996), the court held that cable television was not a "good" under the UCC because programming signals passed through cables are not tangible or "fairly identifiable as movables." *Id.* at 723. *See also* Lorin Brennan, *Why Article 2 Cannot Apply to Software Transactions*, 38 Duq. L. Rev. 459 (2000).

Other cases take the opposite view, however. In *Rottner v. AVG Technologies USA, Inc.*, 943 F. Supp. 2d 222 (D. Mass. 2013), PC TuneUp, software advertised to optimize a computer's performance by scanning the operating system and removing harmful errors, was held to be a "good," despite the fact that the plaintiff purchased and downloaded the program solely via defendant's website.

Even if the information stream is not "movable" within the meaning of the Code, is there a reason the UCC should nevertheless apply? What are the ramifications? *See generally* JAMES J. WHITE AND ROBERT S. SUMMERS, UNIFORM COMMERCIAL CODE, §1.1 (3d ed. 1988).

2. The principal difference between *Hill*, on the one hand, and *Klocek* on the other, is how they deal with offer and acceptance in a shrinkwrap world. Which is the better approach? Which is more consistent with common law contract principles? If you were a videogame developer, what steps would you take in an attempt to make these agreements part of the contract and enforceable against the user under each set of rules? When does Judge Easterbrook in *Hill* say that acceptance takes place? What about Judge Vratil in *Klocek*?

Section 45 (1) of the Restatement (Second) of Contracts provides:

> Where an offer invites and offeree to accept by rendering a performance and does not invite a promissory acceptance, an option contract is created when the offeree tenders or begins the invited performance or begins the invited perform-ance ...

Is a §45 approach consistent with the approach in *Hill* or *Klocek*?

3. Another difference between *Hill* and *Klocek* is the applicability of UCC §2-207. In a portion of the case edited from the excerpt above, the *Klocek* court said that the shrinkwrap agreement inside the box acted as Gateway's acceptance, and in 2-207 terms, it was a "document with additional or different terms" on it. On the other hand, Judge Easterbrook claimed in *Hill* that UCC §2-207 was not involved in the cases, because the offer and acceptance process was not based on an exchange of documents. Rather, he viewed the shrinkwrap agreement's terms as part of the offer, which could not be accepted until the purchaser had the opportunity to know of them sometime after buying the computer. Which do you think is the correct approach, and what is the significance of each?

4. In *Davidson & Assocs v. Jung*, 422 F.3d 630 (8th Cir. 2005), the court held that the EULA and TOU Agreements relevant to plaintiff's games, including *StarCraft* and *Diablo*, were enforceable contracts between the parties. The rationale of the court is indicative of majority thinking today, with EULAs and TOU and TOS Agreements becoming enforceable against purchasers when structured as follows: (1) a notice of such agreements either printed on the game's packaging, disclosed on the website order page, or mentioned by a representative on the phone, making the *existence* of such agreement reasonably known to the user before purchase; (2) a clear "I accept" dialog box signifying acceptance of the *terms* of such agreement which must be clicked before the game can be played once it is received; and (3) a reasonable refund policy if the user does not choose to accept the agreement after having a sufficient opportunity to examine the agreement's terms. For good summaries of the cases on this issue, see Kevin W. Grierson, Annotation, *Enforceability of "Clickwrap" or "Shrinkwrap" Agreements Common in Computer Software, Hardware and Internet Transactions*, 106 A.L.R.5th 309 (2003); *Step-Saver Data Systems, Inc. v. Wyse Technology*, 939 F.2d 91 (3d Cir. 1991).

5. Judge Easterbrook in *Hill* stated, "A contract need not be read to be effective; people who accept take the risk that the unread terms may in retrospect prove unwelcome." What *should* be done about the undeniable fact that many do not read the "legal mumbo jumbo"—whether in a brochure or online—that accompanies the sale of any product, especially a complicated one like a computer?

6. Judge Easterbrook in *Hill* also stated, *ProCD* "exemplif[ies] the many commercial transactions in which people pay for products with terms to follow." Here is what he said on that subject in *ProCD*:

> Transactions in which the exchange of money precedes the communication of detailed terms are common. Consider the purchase of insurance. The buyer goes to an agent, who explains the essentials (amount of coverage, number of years) and remits the premium to the home office, which sends back a policy. On the district judge's understanding, the terms of the policy are irrelevant because the insured paid before receiving them. Yet the device of payment, often with a "binder" (so that the insurance takes effect immediately even though the home office reserves the right to withdraw coverage later), in advance of the policy, serves buyers' interests by accelerating effectiveness and reducing transactions costs. Or consider the purchase of an airline ticket. The traveler calls the carrier or an agent, is quoted a price, reserves a seat, pays, and gets a ticket, in that order. The ticket contains elaborate terms, which the traveler can reject by canceling the reservation. To use the ticket is to accept the terms, even terms that in retrospect are disadvantageous. Just so with a ticket to a concert. The back of the ticket states that the patron promises not to record the concert; to attend is to agree. A theater that detects a violation will confiscate the tape and escort the violator to the exit. One *could* arrange things so that every concertgoer signs this promise before forking over the money, but that cumbersome way of doing things not only would lengthen queues and raise prices but also would scotch the sale of tickets by phone or electronic data service.
>
> Consumer goods work the same way. Someone who wants to buy a radio set visits a store, pays, and walks out with a box. Inside the box is a leaflet containing some terms, the most important of which usually is the warranty, read for the first time in the comfort of home. By Zeidenberg's lights, the warranty in the box is irrelevant; every consumer gets the standard warranty implied by the UCC in the event the contract is silent; yet so far as we are aware no state disregards warranties furnished with consumer products. Drugs come with a list of ingredients on the outside and an elaborate package insert on the inside. The package insert describes drug interactions, contraindications, and other vital information—but, if Zeidenberg is right, the purchaser need not read the package insert, because it is not part of the contract.

Is he correct that "buy now/terms later" agreements are more common than we might otherwise think?

7. Finally, other commentators opine that Judge Easterbrook was just making up a rule that explains how modern ecommerce can best and most efficiently be implimented. Rather than a criticism, these commentators praise Judge Easterbrook for this. What do you think?

Assuming that the terms of one of the Three Agreements is found to be binding, it will still be subject to normal contract defenses to formation such as unconscionability. Developers, of course, want as many provisions favoring them, and giving them the utmost discretion in their dealings with users, as possible. But developers have to be careful that they do not overreach, as the court felt Linden Research, the developer of *Second Life*, did in the following case.

Bragg v. Linden Research, Inc.

United States District Court, Eastern District of Pennsylvania, 2007
487 F. Supp. 2d 593

ROBERNO, District Judge.

This case is about virtual property maintained on a virtual world on the Internet. Plaintiff, Marc Bragg, Esq., claims an ownership interest in such virtual property. Bragg contends that Defendants, the operators of the virtual world, unlawfully confiscated his virtual property and denied him access to their virtual world. Ultimately at issue in this case are the novel questions of what rights and obligations grow out of the relationship between the owner and creator of a virtual world and its resident-customers. While the property and the world where it is found are "virtual," the dispute is real.

Presently before the Court [is] Defendants' Motion to Compel Arbitration. For the reasons set forth below, the motion will be denied.

BACKGROUND

Second Life

The defendants in this case, Linden Research Inc. ("Linden") and its Chief Executive Officer, Philip Rosedale, operate a multiplayer role-playing game set in the virtual world[4] known as "Second Life." Participants create avatars[5] to represent themselves, and Second Life is populated by hundreds of thousands of avatars, whose interactions with one another are limited only by the human imagination.[6] According to Plaintiff, many people "are now living large portions of their lives, forming friendships with others, building and acquiring virtual property, forming contracts, substantial business relationships and forming social organizations" in virtual worlds such as Second Life. Owning property in and having access to this virtual world is, moreover, apparently important to the plaintiff in this case.

Recognition of Property Rights

In November 2003, Linden announced that it would recognize participants' full intellectual property protection for the digital content they created or otherwise owned in Second Life. As a result, Second Life avatars may now buy, own, and sell virtual goods ranging "from cars to homes to slot machines."[7] Most significantly for this case, avatars

---

4. The virtual world at issue is an interactive computer simulation which lets its participants see, hear, use, and even modify the simulated objects in the computer-generated environment. *See* Woodrow Barfield, *Intellectual Property Rights in Virtual Environments: Considering the Rights of Owners, Programmers and Virtual Avatars,* 39 Akron L. Rev. 649, 649 (2006) (defining virtual world).

5. The term "avatar" derives etymologically from the Sanskrit word for crossing down or descent and was used originally to refer to the earthly incarnation of a Hindu deity. WEBSTER's II NEW RIVERSIDE UNIVERSITY DICTIONARY 141 (1998). Since the advent of computers, however, "avatar" is also used to refer to an Internet user's virtual representation of herself in a computer game, in an Internet chat room, or in other Internet fora. *See Definition of Avatar,* WIKIPEDIA, http://en.wikipedia.org/wiki/Avatar_(computing) (last visited Sep. 10, 2014).

6. Judge Richard A. Posner has apparently made an appearance in Second Life as a "balding bespectacled cartoon rendering of himself" where he "addressed a crowd of other animated characters on a range of legal issues, including property rights in virtual reality." Alan Sipress, *Where Real Money Meets Virtual Reality, the Jury is Still Out,* Wash. Post, Dec. 26, 2006, at A1.

7. Although participants purchase virtual property using the virtual currency of "lindens," lindens themselves are bought and sold for real U.S. dollars. Linden maintains a currency exchange that sets an exchange rate between lindens and U.S. dollars. Third parties, including ebay.com, also provide additional currency exchanges.

may purchase "virtual land," make improvements to that land, exclude other avatars from entering onto the land, rent the land, or sell the land to other avatars for a profit. Assertedly, by recognizing virtual property rights, Linden would distinguish itself from other virtual worlds available on the Internet and thus increase participation in Second Life.

Defendant Rosedale personally joined in efforts to publicize Linden's recognition of rights to virtual property. For example, in 2003, Rosedale stated in a press release made available on Second Life's website that:

> Until now, any content created by users for persistent state worlds, such as Everquest or Star Wars Galaxies TM, has essentially become the property of the company developing and hosting the world.... We believe our new policy recognizes the fact that persistent world users are making significant contributions to building these worlds and should be able to both own the content they create and share in the value that is created. The preservation of users' property rights is a necessary step toward the emergence of genuinely real online worlds.

Press Release, Linden Lab, *Linden Lab Preserves Real World Intellectual Property Rights of Users of its Second Life Online Services* (Nov. 14, 2003). Rosedale even created his own avatar and held virtual town hall meetings on Second Life where he made representations about the purchase of virtual land. Bragg "attended" such meetings and relied on the representations that Rosedale made therein.

Plaintiffs' Participation in Second Life

In 2005, Plaintiff Marc Bragg, Esq., signed up and paid Linden to participate in Second Life. Bragg claims that he was induced into "investing" in virtual land by representations made by Linden and Rosedale in press releases, interviews, and through the Second Life website. Bragg also paid Linden real money as "tax" on his land.[8] By April 2006, Bragg had not only purchased numerous parcels of land in his Second Life, he had also digitally crafted "fireworks" that he was able to sell to other avatars for a profit. Bragg also acquired other virtual items from other avatars.

The dispute ultimately at issue in this case arose on April 30, 2006, when Bragg acquired a parcel of virtual land named "Taessot" for $300. Linden sent Bragg an email advising him that Taessot had been improperly purchased through an "exploit." Linden took Taessot away. It then froze Bragg's account, effectively confiscating all of the virtual property and currency that he maintained on his account with Second Life.

Bragg brought suit against Linden and Rosedale in the Court of Common Pleas of Chester County, Pennsylvania, on October 3, 2006. Linden and Rosedale removed the case to this Court and then, within a week, moved to compel arbitration.

MOTION TO COMPEL ARBITRATION

Defendants have also filed a motion to compel arbitration that seeks to dismiss this action and compel Bragg to submit his claims to arbitration according to the Rules of the International Chamber of Commerce ("ICC") in San Francisco.

Relevant Facts

Before a person is permitted to participate in Second Life, she must accept the Terms of Service of Second Life (the "TOS") by clicking a button indicating acceptance of the

---

8. Linden taxes virtual land. In fact, according to Bragg, by June 2004, Linden reported that its real estate tax revenue on land sold to the participants exceeded the amount the company was generating in subscriptions.

TOS. Bragg concedes that he clicked the "accept" button before accessing Second Life. Included in the TOS are a California choice of law provision, an arbitration provision, and forum selection clause. Specifically, located in the fourteenth line of the thirteenth paragraph under the heading "GENERAL PROVISIONS," and following provisions regarding the applicability of export and import laws to Second Life, the following language appears:

> Any dispute or claim arising out of or in connection with this Agreement or the performance, breach or termination thereof, shall be finally settled by binding arbitration in San Francisco, California under the Rules of Arbitration of the International Chamber of Commerce by three arbitrators appointed in accordance with said rules.... Notwithstanding the foregoing, either party may apply to any court of competent jurisdiction for injunctive relief or enforcement of this arbitration provision without breach of this arbitration provision.

TOS @ 13.

Legal Standards

1. *Federal law applies*

The Federal Arbitration Act ("FAA") requires that the Court apply federal substantive law here because the arbitration agreement is connected to a transaction involving interstate commerce. Whether the arbitration agreement is connected to a transaction involving interstate commerce is a factual determination that must be made by the Court. Here, Bragg is a Pennsylvania resident. Linden is a Delaware corporation headquartered in California. Rosedale is a California resident. Bragg entered into the TOS and purchased virtual land through the Internet on Second Life as a result of representations made on the national media. The arbitration agreement is clearly connected to interstate commerce, and the Court will apply the federal substantive law that has emerged from interpretation of the FAA.

2. *The Legal Standard Under the FAA*

Under the FAA, on the motion of a party, a court must stay proceedings and order the parties to arbitrate the dispute if the court finds that the parties have agreed in writing to do so. A party seeking to compel arbitration must show (1) that a valid agreement to arbitrate exists between the parties and (2) that the specific dispute falls within the scope of the agreement. In determining whether a valid agreement to arbitrate exists between the parties, district courts [must] give the party opposing arbitration "the benefit of all reasonable doubts and inferences that may arise."

Application

1. *Unconscionability of the Arbitration Agreement*

Bragg resists enforcement of the TOS's arbitration provision on the basis that it is "both procedurally and substantively unconscionable and is itself evidence of defendants' scheme to deprive Plaintiff (and others) of both their money and their day in court."

[T]he FAA provides that written arbitration agreements "shall be valid, irrevocable, and enforceable, save upon such grounds as exist at law or in equity for the revocation of any contract." Thus, generally applicable contract defenses, such as fraud, duress, or unconscionability, may be applied to invalidate arbitration agreements. When determining whether such defenses might apply to any purported agreement to arbitrate the dispute in question, "courts generally ... should apply ordinary state-law principles that govern the formation of contracts." Thus, the Court will apply California state law to determine whether the arbitration provision is unconscionable.[9]

Under California law, unconscionability has both procedural and substantive components. The procedural component can be satisfied by showing (1) oppression through the existence of unequal bargaining positions or (2) surprise through hidden terms common in the context of adhesion contracts. The substantive component can be satisfied by showing overly harsh or one-sided results that "shock the conscience." The two elements operate on a sliding scale such that the more significant one is, the less significant the other need be. The more substantively oppressive the contract term, the less evidence of procedural unconscionability is required to come to the conclusion that the term is unenforceable, and vice versa. However, a claim of unconscionability cannot be determined merely by examining the face of the contract; there must be an inquiry into the circumstances under which the contract was executed, and the contract's purpose, and effect.

(a) *Procedural Unconscionability*

A contract or clause is procedurally unconscionable if it is a contract of adhesion. A contract of adhesion, in turn, is a standardized contract, which, imposed and drafted by the party of superior bargaining strength, relegates to the subscribing party only the opportunity to adhere to the contract or reject it. Under California law, the critical factor in procedural unconscionability analysis is the manner in which the contract or the disputed clause was presented and negotiated. When the weaker party is presented the clause and told to "take it or leave it" without the opportunity for meaningful negotiation, oppression, and therefore procedural unconscionability, are present. An arbitration agreement that is an essential part of a "take it or leave it" employment condition, without more, is procedurally unconscionable.

The TOS are a contract of adhesion. Linden presents the TOS on a take-it-or-leave-it basis. A potential participant can either click "assent" to the TOS, and then gain entrance to Second Life's virtual world, or refuse assent and be denied access. Linden also clearly has superior bargaining strength over Bragg. Although Bragg is an experienced attorney, who believes he is expert enough to comment on numerous industry standards and the "rights" of participants in virtual worlds, he was never presented with an opportunity to use his experience and lawyering skills to negotiate terms different from the TOS that Linden offered.

Moreover, there was no "reasonably available market alternatives [to defeat] a claim of adhesiveness." Although it is not the only virtual world on the Internet, Second Life was the first and only virtual world to specifically grant its participants property rights in virtual land.

The procedural element of unconscionability also focuses on surprise. In determining whether surprise exists, California courts focus not on the plaintiff's subjective reading of the contract, but rather, more objectively, on the extent to which the supposedly agreed-upon terms of the bargain are hidden in the prolix printed form drafted by the party seeking to enforce the disputed terms.

---

9. Both parties agree that California law should govern the question of whether the arbitration provision is unconscionable.

Here, Linden buried the TOS's arbitration provision in a lengthy paragraph under the benign heading "GENERAL PROVISIONS." *Compare Net Global Mktg. v. Dialtone, Inc.,* 217 Fed. App'x. 598, 601 (9th Cir. 2007) (finding procedural unconscionability where "[t]here was no 'clear heading' in the Terms of Service that could refute a claim of surprise; to the contrary, the arbitration clause is listed in the midst of a long section without line breaks under the unhelpful heading of 'Miscellaneous' ") *with Boghos v. Certain Underwriters at Lloyd's of London,* 36 Cal. 4th 495 (2005) (finding arbitration clause was enforceable where it was in bolded font and contained the heading "BINDING ARBITRATION"). Linden also failed to make available the costs and rules of arbitration in the ICC by either setting them forth in the TOS or by providing a hyper-link to another page or website where they are available. Here, procedural unconscionability is satisfied.

(b) *Substantive Unconscionability*

Even if an agreement is procedurally unconscionable, "it may nonetheless be enforceable if the substantive terms are reasonable." Substantive unconscionability focuses on the one-sidedness of the contract terms. Here, a number of the TOS's elements lead the Court to conclude that Bragg has demonstrated that the TOS are substantively unconscionable.

(i) *Mutuality*

Under California law, substantive unconscionability has been found where an arbitration provision forces the weaker party to arbitrate claims but permits a choice of forums for the stronger party. In other words, the arbitration remedy must contain a modicum of bilaterality. This principle has been extended to arbitration provisions that allow the stronger party a range of remedies before arbitrating a dispute, such as self-help, while relegating to the weaker party the sole remedy of arbitration.

In *Comb* [*v. PayPal, Inc.,* 218 F. Supp. 2d 1165 (N.D. Cal. 2002)] for example, the court found a lack of mutuality where the user agreement allowed PayPal "at its sole discretion" to restrict accounts, withhold funds, undertake its own investigation of a customer's financial records, close accounts, and procure ownership of all funds in dispute unless and until the customer is "later determined to be entitled to the funds in dispute." Also significant was the fact that the user agreement was "subject to change by PayPal without prior notice (unless prior notice is required by law), by posting of the revised Agreement on the PayPal website."

Here, the TOS contain many of the same elements that made the PayPal user agreement substantively unconscionable for lack of mutuality. The TOS proclaim that "Linden has the right at any time for any reason or no reason to suspend or terminate your Account, terminate this Agreement, and/or refuse any and all current or future use of the Service without notice or liability to you." TOS @ 7.1. Whether or not a customer has breached the Agreement is "determined in Linden's sole discretion." *Id.* Linden also reserves the right to return no money at all based on mere "suspicions of fraud" or other violations of law. *Id.* Finally, the TOS state that "Linden may amend this Agreement ... at any time in its sole discretion by posting the amended Agreement [on its website]." TOS @ 1.2.

In effect, the TOS provide Linden with a variety of one-sided remedies to resolve disputes, while forcing its customers to arbitrate any disputes with Linden. This is precisely what occurred here. When a dispute arose, Linden exercised its option to use self-help by freezing Bragg's account, retaining funds that Linden alone determined were subject to dispute, and then telling Bragg that he could resolve the dispute by initiating a costly arbitration process. The TOS expressly authorized Linden to engage in such unilateral conduct. As in *Comb,* "[f]or all practical purposes, a customer may resolve disputes only after [Linden] has had control of the disputed funds for an indefinite period of time," and may only resolve those disputes by initiating arbitration.

Linden's right to modify the arbitration clause is also significant. The effect of Linden's unilateral right to modify the arbitration clause is that it could craft precisely the sort of asymmetrical arbitration agreement that is prohibited under California law as unconscionable. This lack of mutuality supports a finding of substantive unconscionability.

(ii) *Costs of Arbitration and Fee-Sharing*

Bragg claims that the cost of an individual arbitration under the TOS is likely to exceed $13,540, with an estimated initiation cost of at least $10,000. He has also submitted a Declaration of Personal Financial Information stating that such arbitration would be cost-prohibitive for him. Linden disputes Bragg's calculations, estimating that the costs associated with arbitration would total $7,500, with Bragg advancing $3,750 at the outset of arbitration. The Court's own calculations, however, indicate that the costs of arbitration, would total $17,250.

These costs might not, on their own, support a finding of substantive unconscionability. However, the ICC Rules also provide that the costs and fees must be shared among the parties, and an estimate of those costs and fees must be advanced at the initiation of arbitration. *See* ICC Rules of Arbitration. California law has often been applied to declare arbitration fee-sharing schemes unenforceable.

Here, even taking Defendants characterization of the fees to be accurate, the total estimate of costs and fees would be $7,500, which would result in Bragg having to advance $3,750 at the outset of arbitration. The Court's own estimates place the amount that Bragg would likely have to advance at $8,625, but they could reach as high as $13,687.50. Any of these figures are significantly greater than the costs that Bragg bears by filing his action in a state or federal court. Accordingly, the arbitration costs and fee-splitting scheme together also support a finding of unconscionability.

(iii) *Venue*

The TOS also require that any arbitration take place in San Francisco, California. TOSS @ 13. In *Comb,* the Court found that a similar forum selection clause supported a finding of substantive unconscionability, because the place in which arbitration was to occur was unreasonable, taking into account "the respective circumstances of the parties." As in *Comb,* the record in this case shows that Linden serves millions of customers across the United States and that the average transaction through or with Second Life involves a relatively small amount. In such circumstances, California law dictates that it is not "reasonable for individual consumers from throughout the country to travel to one locale to arbitrate claims involving such minimal sums." Indeed, "[l]imiting venue to [Linden's] backyard appears to be yet one more means by which the arbitration clause serves to shield [Linden] from liability instead of providing a neutral forum in which to arbitrate disputes." *Id.*

(iv) *Confidentiality Provision*

Arbitration before the ICC, pursuant to the TOS, must be kept confidential pursuant to the ICC rules. *See* ICC Rules at 33. [S]uch confidentiality supports a finding that an arbitration clause was substantively unconscionable. If the company succeeds in imposing a gag order on arbitration proceedings, it places itself in a far superior legal posture by ensuring that none of its potential opponents have access to precedent while, at the same time, the company accumulates a wealth of knowledge on how to negotiate the terms of its own unilaterally crafted contract. The unavailability of arbitral decisions could also prevent potential plaintiffs from obtaining the information needed to build a case of intentional misconduct against a company.

This does not mean that confidentiality provisions in an arbitration scheme or agreement are, in every instance, per se unconscionable under California law. *See Mercuro v. Superior Court,* 96 Cal. App. 4th 167, 116 Cal. Rptr. 2d 671, 679 (2002) ("While [the California] Supreme Court has taken notice of the 'repeat player effect,' the court has never declared this factor renders the arbitration agreement unconscionable per se.") (citations omitted). Here, however, taken together with other provisions of the TOS, the confidentiality provision gives rise for concern of the conscionability of the arbitration clause.

Thus, the confidentiality of the arbitration scheme that Linden imposed also supports a finding that the arbitration clause is unconscionable.

(v) *Legitimate Business Realities*

Under California law, a contract may provide a "margin of safety" that provides the party with superior bargaining strength protection for which it has a legitimate commercial need. However, unless the 'business realities' that create the special need for such an advantage are explained in the contract itself, it must be factually established. When a contract is alleged to be unconscionable, "the parties shall be afforded a reasonable opportunity to present evidence as to its commercial setting, purpose, and effect to aid the court in making the determination." Cal. Civ. Code § 1670.5. The statutory scheme reflects legislative recognition that a claim of unconscionability often cannot be determined merely by examining the face of the contract, but will require inquiry into its setting, purpose, and effect.

Here, neither in its briefing nor at oral argument did Linden even attempt to offer evidence that "business realities" justify the one-sidedness of the dispute resolution scheme that the TOS constructs in Linden's favor.

(c) *Conclusion*

When a dispute arises in Second Life, Linden is not obligated to initiate arbitration. Rather, the TOS expressly allow Linden, at its "sole discretion" and based on mere "suspicion," to unilaterally freeze a participant's account, refuse access to the virtual and real currency contained within that account, and then confiscate the participant's virtual property and real estate. A participant wishing to resolve any dispute, on the other hand, after having forfeited its interest in Second Life, must then initiate arbitration in Linden's place of business. To initiate arbitration involves advancing fees to pay for no less than three arbitrators at a cost far greater than would be involved in litigating in the state or federal court system. Moreover, under these circumstances, the confidentiality of the proceedings helps ensure that arbitration itself is fought on an uneven field by ensuring that, through the accumulation of experience, Linden becomes an expert in litigating the terms of the TOS, while plaintiffs remain novices without the benefit of learning from past precedent.

Taken together, the lack of mutuality, the costs of arbitration, the forum selection clause, and the confidentiality provision that Linden unilaterally imposes through the TOS demonstrate that the arbitration clause is not designed to provide Second Life participants an effective means of resolving disputes with Linden. Rather, it is a one-sided means which tilts unfairly, in almost all situations, in Linden's favor. As in *Comb,* through the use of an arbitration clause, Linden "appears to be attempting to insulate itself contractually from any meaningful challenge to its alleged practices."

The Court notes that the concerns with procedural unconscionability are somewhat mitigated by Bragg's being an experienced attorney. However, because the unilateral modification clause renders the arbitration provision severely one-sided in the substantive dimension, even moderate procedural unconscionability renders the arbitration agreement unenforceable.

Finding that the arbitration clause is procedurally and substantively unconscionable, the Court will refuse to enforce it.

"Bluelining" the Arbitration Agreement

Alternatively, Linden has offered to ameliorate the one-sidedness of the TOS's arbitration provision by suggesting that Linden could waive the requirements for three arbitrators, post the initial fees of arbitration, and agree to arbitrate in Philadelphia instead of San Francisco.

California law allows a court to "blueline" an arbitration agreement to remove an element that renders it substantively unconscionable. *See* Cal. Civ. Code § 1670.5(a) ("If the court as a matter of law finds the contract or any clause of the contract to have been unconscionable at the time it was made the court may refuse to enforce the contract, or it may enforce the remainder of the contract without the unconscionable clause, or it may so limit the application of any unconscionable clause as to avoid any unconscionable result."). However, a court is not obligated to blueline when an arbitration provision is so permeated by substantive unconscionability that it cannot be cured by severance or any other action short of rewriting the contract.

The arbitration clause before the Court is simply not one where a single term may be stricken to render the agreement conscionable. The unilateral modification pervades and taints with illegality the entire agreement to arbitrate, and severance of terms within the arbitration clause would not cure the problem. Bluelining in this case will require the redrafting of the agreement. The Court declines to rewrite the agreement, at Linden's request, to save an unconscionable arbitration provision which Linden itself drafted and now seeks to enforce. Rather than provide a reasonable alternative for dispute resolution, this agreement compels a one-sided resolution of disputes between the parties.

———————

Notes and Questions

1. The suit settled, under a confidentiality agreement, sometime after this ruling was issued.

2. The case notes that Linden asserted "Taessot [the property bought by Mr. Bragg] had been improperly purchased through an 'exploit.'" The firm Independent Security Evaluators has explained what it believes to be an "exploit" in *Second Life* as follows:

Exploiting Second Life

Two security researchers, Charlie Miller, a Principal Security Analyst at Independent Security Evaluators, and Dino Dai Zovi decided to investigate the security of online games. This resulted in an exploit for Second Life that makes any player affected give the attacker their Linden dollars and yell "I got hacked!". In other words, it is possible to exploit a player to steal Linden dollars, and then cash them out for real US dollars. All the victim has to do is have video enabled and enter a piece of land owned by the attacker.

How the exploit works

The actual vulnerability lies in the third party QuickTime Player made by Apple. A vulnerability was announced on November 24th 2007 in the way QuickTime handles RTSP responses. Second Life allows players to embed media files in Second Life objects, and uses QuickTime to handle all video rendering. Furthermore, it is possible to have these media elements constantly playing. If a Second Life avatar walks onto a piece of land that contains an embedded malicious QuickTime File, they can be exploited. The vulnerability was patched in QuickTime 7.3.1 on December 13th, 2007, eliminating the vulnerability in fully patched Second Life Viewers and QuickTime Players; unpatched Second Life Viewers and QuickTime Players are still vulnerable.

What the exploit does

Once the malicious file has been viewed by the victim, the attacker has complete control over the victim's computer — and Second Life avatar. At this point the exploit could make the avatar do anything they like. Virtual worlds are interesting, because unlike the real world where client-side exploits are typically delivered via web browser links or emails, exploits in virtual worlds can be delivered in many different ways. One could imagine an exploit being delivered by looking at a shirt that a character is wearing, or by a character whispering something to another character. The possibilities are endless.

INDEPENDENT SECURITY EVALUATORS, http://securityevaluators.com/content/case-studies/sl/ (last visited Sep. 9, 2014). (Note the site's web address also provides a link to the referenced Quick Time patch that the author claims make avatars invulnerable to exploits.)

If Mr. Bragg in fact acquired his land via an exploit as described above, and we have no idea whether or not he did, would that change your mind about the correctness of Linden suspending his account and "escheating" his land? Would it matter if exploiting was specifically banned in the TOS Agreement?

3. This is the point where we usually ask something like, "If you were General Counsel to Linden, what provisions would you recommend modifying in order to save the *Second Life* TOS from another unconscionability finding?" We would still like you to think about it, but that question was answered for real at Linden's General Counsel's office. As described in a 2011 decision by the same court (but not the same judge) that decided *Bragg*, the court described the post-*Bragg* amended dispute resolution provisions of Linden's TOS:

> [T]he arbitration clause in Linden's current TOS gives the claimant the option for claims under $10,000 to proceed to arbitration and to have the claim heard by telephone, on-line, or by written submission, without having to appear in San Francisco. Also under the current TOS, for any claim of $10,000 or more, the claimant retains the right to proceed in Court and is not compelled to go to arbitration as in *Bragg*.

> Further, where the arbitration clause in *Bragg* required a panel of three arbitrators and arbitration pursuant to the procedures of the International Chamber of Commerce, the current TOS requires only that the party initiating arbitration do it "through an established alternative dispute resolution ("ADR") provider mutually agreed upon by the parties."

Evans v. Linden Research, Inc., 763 F. Supp. 2d 735, 741 (E.D. Pa. 2011). When applied to the sliding scale unconscionability test of California law described in *Bragg*, the *Evans* court decided, "In light of these circumstances, the forum selection clause of Linden's new TOS is not unfair or unconscionable," and the case, which had been filed in Pennsylvania, was transferred to the Northern District of California. *Id.* at 741–42. How else could Linden have changed the TOS Agreement to address conscionability concerns?

4. The *Bragg* court mentions that Linden could have introduced "Legitimate Business Realities" to justify its TOS Agreement as it then-stood. What sorts of "business realities" do you believe could justify some or all of the terms? For more information on the "legitimate business realities" exception to unconscionability, *see, e.g.,* Cal. Civ. Code § 1670.5 (West 2014) and *Stirlen v. Supercuts, Inc.,* 51 Cal. App. 4th 1519 (1997).

5. The *Bragg* court mentions "bluelining," a term which stems from an older practice whereby print editors indicated edits in copy with a waxy blue pencil. Why wouldn't allowing the court to "blueline" the forum selection clause to make it conscionable, as suggested by Linden, solve the unconscionability problems raised by Mr. Bragg?

6. The court mentions the "repeat player effect," especially when coupled with a confidentiality agreement, as a reason to be suspicious of Linden's arbitration clause. What do you think the "repeat player effect" is?

7. Every EULA or TOS/TOU Agreement of which the authors are aware contains a clause that allows the developers to modify the provisions of these agreements for any reason and at any time, without prior notice or comment. Would the existence of such a clause in and of itself make the agreement unconscionable? Or would a court have to view a developer's unilateral changes to determine whether the changes are conscionable? Does such a clause render a subsequent modification of the Agreement unenforceable due to a lack of consideration?

8. Another ubiquitous provision in the Three Agreements allows the developers to terminate the virtual worlds or game at any time, and specifies that they may do so without liability. Does that clause render the agreements per se illusory? Unconscionable? What would happen if the developer went bankrupt?

9. Most developers also reserve the right in their EULAs to develop super-powerful avatars which can roam their games to ensure users are playing within the rules. These "enforcer" avatars can do things like unilaterally, immediately, and without prior notice, suspend a player for a certain number of days, take away powers, weapons, points, etc. This, in turn, has led to some users banding together as a community to draft and attempt to enforce a "Bill of Rights" for gamers and their avatars, including privacy rights, the rights to unfettered existence, the right to due process and appeal before actions are finally implemented, etc. Would a suit challenging the enforcer avatars provision on unconscionability grounds be successful? Is there another way to legally get rid of the "super" avatars?

Don't underestimate the collective power of the users. Several years ago, Linden Labs attempted to institute a new tax on personal possessions in *Second Life*. After virtual gas stations were set ablaze by irate "residents," the virtual Washington Monument was replaced by a giant tower of tea crates by a savvy programmer, and other such revolutionary acts, Linden rescinded the "tax."

10. Some in the industry have fun with their EULAs. In 2010, Game Station, which is a British-based retailer, had the following in its online contracts:

> By placing an order via this website, on the first day of the fourth month of the year 2010 Anno Domini, you agree to grant us a non-transferable option to claim, for now and forever more, your immortal soul ... We reserve the right to

serve … notice [to exercise the option] in 6' high letters of fire; however we accept no liability for any loss or damage caused by such act. If you (a) do not believe you have an immortal soul, (b) have already given it to another party, or (c) do not wish to grant Us such a license, pleae click the link below to nullify this sub-clause and proceed with your transaction.

88% of buyers did not click the link, which provided them with a £5 voucher. Professor Jane Wynn of the University of Washington School of Law has suggested these clauses might be named "boilerplate Easter Eggs."

§ 10.20 Players as Creators

In the "old" days, the developers of a game created a limited number of characters and avatars, and the player manipulated them to accrue points and levels. But in an effort to gain market share, developers began allowing more and more user input in the creation of the creatures that populated their worlds. Some allowed users to put together characters from a built-in set of art files filled with different faces, body types, etc.,[10] while others allowed users to develop their own avatars and import them into the game. Other games allow players to program useful items like hover boards or weapons and use them in the games. This led to games in which users could export characters and scenes from the world to Facebook and other websites, and/or sell their creations on eBay and like sites. With web sites devoted to particular games having user and developer content mixed together, copyright, violations of terms of TOS Agreements, and other legal disputes followed.

This section is limited to situations involving user/developer characters and scenes. (In § 10.30, we deal with user-generated property brought into virtual worlds, such as the user who develops a weapon in *World of Warcraft*.) To set the scene, below is an excerpt of a thought-provoking article from Zachary Levine:

> If you think about your daily online activities a large portion of your digital consumption is probably user-generated content rather than professionally curated and created material. Most other entertainment mediums are not accessible to the masses and the content is almost exclusively created by corporate entities. Some of the most popular internet sites, however, are driven by user contributions (e.g., YouTube, Facebook, Instagram, etc.). User-generated content (also called user-created content) is content produced by the general public rather than by paid professionals or experts in the field.

> The growth and spread of the internet has also facilitated the spread of user-generated video game content. There are extensive bulletin board sites, forums, and websites devoted to the sale and exchange of add-ons and modifications for games as well as a growing number of online games that allow for direct contributions and creations from players. The creation and distribution of user generated content ("UGC") raises a number of legal issues, both for the creators and the third parties that provide the means of distribution.

---

10. For a detailed explanation of the extensive choices given the user in building an avatar in *City of Heroes*, *see*, Tyler T. Ochoa, *"Who Owns an Avatar? Copyright, Creativity, and Virtual Worlds,"* 14 VAND. J. ENT. & TECH. L. 959, 961–64 (2012).

Regardless of where [UGC] falls on the spectrum of creative contribution, they all share a common trait, namely the inclusion of images, video, and sound from the underlying game at issue in each video. Most game developers and publishers have strict End User License Agreements (EULAs) and Terms of Use (TOU) that restrict, or at least govern, the creation and distribution of such content.

Zachary Levine, *The Video Game Law Strategy Guide*, 19 No. 3 CYBERSPACE LAW. 8 (2014).

In the next case, you will see an attempt by a developer to limit users' rights in the distribution of user-generated content via a EULA, as indicated in Mr. Levine's article.

Micro Star v. Formgen, Inc.

United States Court of Appeals, Ninth Circuit, 1998
154 F.3d 1107

KOZINSKI, Circuit Judge.

Duke Nukem routinely vanquishes Octabrain and the Protozoid Slimer. But what about the dreaded Micro Star?

FormGen Inc., GT Interactive Software Corp. and Apogee Software, Ltd. (collectively FormGen) made, distributed and own the rights to Duke Nukem 3D (D/N-3D), an immensely popular (and very cool) computer game. D/N-3D is played from the first-person perspective; the player assumes the personality and point of view of the title character, who is seen on the screen only as a pair of hands and an occasional boot, much as one might see oneself in real life without the aid of a mirror. Players explore a futuristic city infested with evil aliens and other hazards. The basic game comes with twenty-nine levels, each with a different combination of scenery, aliens, and other challenges. The game also includes a "Build Editor," a utility that enables players to create their own levels. With FormGen's encouragement, players frequently post levels they have created on the Internet where others can download them. Micro Star, a computer software distributor, did just that: It downloaded 300 user-created levels and stamped them onto a CD, which it then sold commercially as Nuke It (N/I). N/I is packaged in a box decorated with numerous "screen shots," pictures of what the new levels look like when played.

Micro Star filed suit in district court, seeking a declaratory judgment that N/I did not infringe on any of FormGen's copyrights.

FormGen counterclaimed, seeking a preliminary injunction barring further production and distribution of N/I. Relying on *Lewis Galoob Toys, Inc. v. Nintendo of Am., Inc.*, 964 F.2d 965 (9th Cir.1992), the district court held that N/I was not a derivative work and therefore did not infringe FormGen's copyright. The district court did, however, grant a preliminary injunction as to the screen shots, finding that N/I's packaging violated FormGen's copyright by reproducing pictures of D/N-3D characters without a license. The court rejected Micro Star's fair use claims. Both sides appeal their losses.

To succeed on the merits of its claim that N/I infringes FormGen's copyright, FormGen must show (1) ownership of the copyright to D/N-3D, and (2) copying of protected expression by Micro Star. [W]e are satisfied that FormGen has established its ownership of the copyright. We therefore focus on the latter issue.

FormGen alleges that its copyright is infringed by Micro Star's unauthorized commercial exploitation of user-created game levels. In order to understand FormGen's claims, one must first understand the way D/N-3D works. The game consists of three separate components: the game engine, the source art library and the MAP files. The game engine is the heart of the computer program; in some sense, it is the program. It tells the computer when to read data, save and load games, play sounds and project images onto the screen. In order to create the audiovisual display for a particular level, the game engine invokes the MAP file that corresponds to that level. Each MAP file contains a series of instructions that tell the game engine (and, through it, the computer) what to put where. For instance, the MAP file might say scuba gear goes at the bottom of the screen. The game engine then goes to the source art library, finds the image of the scuba gear, and puts it in just the right place on the screen.[11] The MAP file describes the level in painstaking detail, but it does not actually contain any of the copyrighted art itself; everything that appears on the screen actually comes from the art library.

FormGen points out that a copyright holder enjoys the exclusive right to prepare derivative works based on D/N-3D. See 17 U.S.C. § 106(2) (1994). According to FormGen, the audiovisual displays generated when D/N-3D is run in conjunction with the N/I CD MAP files are derivative works that infringe this exclusivity. Is FormGen right? The answer is not obvious.

The Copyright Act defines a derivative work as

> a work based upon one or more preexisting works, such as a translation, musical arrangement, dramatization, fictionalization, motion picture version, sound recording, art reproduction, abridgment, condensation, or any other form in which a work may be recast, transformed, or adapted. A work consisting of editorial revisions, annotations, elaborations, or other modifications which, as a whole, represent an original work of authorship, is a "derivative work."

Id. § 101. The statutory language is hopelessly overbroad, however, for "[e]very book in literature, science and art, borrows and must necessarily borrow, and use much which was well known and used before." *Emerson v. Davies,* 8 F. Cas. 615, 619 (C.C.D.Mass.1845) (No. 4436), *quoted in 1 Nimmer on Copyright,* § 3.01, at 3–2 (1997). To narrow the statute to a manageable level, we have developed certain criteria a work must satisfy in order to qualify as a derivative work. One of these is that a derivative work must exist in a "concrete or permanent form" *Galoob,* 964 F.2d at 967, and must substantially incorporate protected material from the preexisting work. Micro Star argues that N/I is not a derivative work because the audiovisual displays generated when D/N-3D is run with N/I's MAP files are not incorporated in any concrete or permanent form, and the MAP files do not copy any of D/N-3D's protected expression. It is mistaken on both counts.

The requirement that a derivative work must assume a concrete or permanent form was recognized without much discussion in *Galoob.* There, we noted that all the Copyright Act's examples of derivative works took some definite, physical form and concluded that this was a requirement of the Act. Obviously, N/I's MAP files themselves exist in a concrete or permanent form; they are burned onto a CD-ROM. *See Galoob.* But what about the audiovisual displays generated when D/N-3D runs the N/I MAP files—i.e., the actual game level as displayed on the screen? Micro Star argues that, because the audiovisual displays in *Galoob* didn't meet the "concrete or permanent form" requirement, neither do N/I's.

---

11. Actually, this is all a bit metaphorical. Computer programs don't actually go anywhere or fetch anything. Rather, the game engine receives the player's instruction as to which game level to select and instructs the processor to access the MAP file corresponding to that level. The MAP file, in turn, consists of a series of instructions indicating which art images go where. When the MAP file calls for a particular art image, the game engine tells the processor to access the art library for instructions on how each pixel on the screen must be colored in order to paint that image.

In *Galoob*, we considered audiovisual displays created using a device called the Game Genie, which was sold for use with the Nintendo Entertainment System. The Game Genie allowed players to alter individual features of a game, such as a character's strength or speed, by selectively "blocking the value for a single data byte sent by the game cartridge to the [Nintendo console] and replacing it with a new value." Players chose which data value to replace by entering a code; over a billion different codes were possible. The Game Genie was dumb; it functioned only as a window into the computer program, allowing players to temporarily modify individual aspects of the game. *See Lewis Galoob Toys, Inc. v. Nintendo of Am., Inc.*, 780 F. Supp. 1283, 1289 (N.D. Cal. 1991). The audiovisual displays generated by combining the Nintendo System with the Game Genie were not incorporated in any permanent form; when the game was over, they were gone. Of course, they could be reconstructed, but only if the next player chose to reenter the same codes.[12]

Micro Star argues that the MAP files on N/I are a more advanced version of the Game Genie, replacing old values (the MAP files in the original game) with new values (N/I's MAP files). But, whereas the audiovisual displays created by Game Genie were never recorded in any permanent form, the audiovisual displays generated by D/N-3D from the N/I MAP files are in the MAP files themselves. In *Galoob*, the audiovisual display was defined by the original game cartridge, not by the Game Genie; no one could possibly say that the data values inserted by the Game Genie described the audiovisual display. In the present case the audiovisual display that appears on the computer monitor when a N/I level is played is described—in exact detail—by a N/I MAP file.

This raises the interesting question whether an exact, down to the last detail, description of an audiovisual display (and—by definition—we know that MAP files do describe audiovisual displays down to the last detail) counts as a permanent or concrete form for purposes of *Galoob*. We see no reason it shouldn't. What, after all, does sheet music do but describe in precise detail the way a copyrighted melody sounds? Because the audiovisual displays assume a concrete or permanent form in the MAP files, *Galoob* stands as no bar to finding that they are derivative works.

In addition, "[t]o prove infringement [as a derivative work], FormGen must show that D/N-3D's and N/I's audiovisual displays are substantially similar in both ideas and expression." Similarity of ideas may be shown by comparing the objective details of the works: plot, theme, dialogue, mood, setting, characters, etc. Similarity of expression focuses on the response of the ordinary reasonable person, and considers the total concept and feel of the works. FormGen will doubtless succeed in making these showings since the audiovisual displays generated when the player chooses the N/I levels come entirely out of D/N-3D's source art library.

Micro Star further argues that the MAP files are not derivative works because they do not, in fact, incorporate any of D/N-3D's protected expression. In particular, Micro Star makes much of the fact that the N/I MAP files reference the source art library, but do not

---

12. A low-tech example might aid understanding. Imagine a product called the Pink Screener, which consists of a big piece of pink cellophane stretched over a frame. When put in front of a television, it makes everything on the screen look pinker. Someone who manages to record the programs with this pink cast (maybe by filming the screen) would have created an infringing derivative work. But the audiovisual display observed by a person watching television through the Pink Screener is not a derivative work because it does not incorporate the modified image in any permanent or concrete form. The Game Genie might be described as a fancy Pink Screener for videogames, changing a value of the game as perceived by the current player, but never incorporating the new audiovisual display into a permanent or concrete form.

actually contain any art files themselves. Therefore, it claims, nothing of D/N-3D's is reproduced in the MAP files. In making this argument, Micro Star misconstrues the protected work. The work that Micro Star infringes is the D/N-3D story itself—a beefy commando type named Duke who wanders around post-Apocalypse Los Angeles, shooting Pig Cops with a gun, lobbing hand grenades, searching for medkits and steroids, using a jetpack to leap over obstacles, blowing up gas tanks, avoiding radioactive slime. A copyright owner holds the right to create sequels, and the stories told in the N/I MAP files are surely sequels, telling new (though somewhat repetitive) tales of Duke's fabulous adventures. A book about Duke Nukem would infringe for the same reason, even if it contained no pictures.[13]

Micro Star nonetheless claims that its use of D/N-3D's protected expression falls within the doctrine of fair use, which permits unauthorized use of copyrighted works "for purposes such as criticism, comment, news reporting, teaching (including multiple copies for classroom use), scholarship, or research." 17 U.S.C. § 107. Section 107 instructs courts "determining whether the use made of a work in any particular case is a fair use" to consider four factors: (1) the purpose and character of the use, including whether it is commercial in nature; (2) the nature of the copyrighted work; (3) the amount and substantiality of the copied material in relation to the copyrighted work as a whole; and (4) the effect of the use on the potential market for the copyrighted work. 17 U.S.C. § 107.

Our examination of the section 107 factors yields straightforward results. Micro Star's use of FormGen's protected expression was made purely for financial gain [factor (1)]. The fair use defense will be much less likely to succeed when the nature of the work [factor (2)] is fiction or fantasy creations, as opposed to factual works such as telephone listings. Duke Nukem's world is made up of aliens, radioactive slime and freezer weapons—clearly fantasies, even by Los Angeles standards. N/I MAP files "expressly use [ ] the [D/N-3D] story's unique setting, characters, [and] plot," [B]oth the quantity and importance of the material Micro Star used are substantial [factor (3)]. Finally, by selling N/I, Micro Star "impinged on [FormGen's] ability to market new versions of the D/N-3D story." [factor (4)].

Micro Star also argues that it is the beneficiary of the implicit license FormGen gave to its customers by authorizing them to create new levels. Nothing indicates that FormGen granted Micro Star any written license at all; nor is there evidence of a nonexclusive oral license. The only written license FormGen conceivably granted was to players who designed their own new levels, but that license contains a significant limitation: Any new levels the players create "must be offered [to others] solely for free."

In case FormGen didn't license away its rights, Micro Star argues that, by providing the Build Editor and encouraging players to create their own levels, FormGen abandoned all rights to its protected expression. It is well settled that rights gained under the Copyright Act may be abandoned. But abandonment of a right must be manifested by some overt act indicating an intention to abandon that right. Given that it overtly encouraged players to make and freely distribute new levels, FormGen may indeed have abandoned its exclusive right to do the same. But FormGen never overtly abandoned its rights to profit commercially from new levels. Indeed, FormGen warned players not to distribute the levels commercially and has actively enforced that limitation by bringing suits such as this one.

---

13. We note that the N/I MAP files can only be used with D/N-3D. If another game could use the MAP files to tell the story of a mousy fellow who travels through a beige maze, killing vicious saltshakers with paper-clips, then the MAP files would not incorporate the protected expression of D/N-3D because they would not be telling a D/N-3D story.

Because FormGen will likely succeed at trial in proving that Micro Star has infringed its copyright, we reverse the district court's order denying a preliminary injunction and remand for entry of such an injunction.

Notes and Questions

1. Judge Kozinski stated that for N/I to be adjudged an infringing derivative work, FormGen had to establish both that the characters on the N/I disk were "fixed" in a tangible medium of expression, and that Micro Star infringed a "substantial" portion of the protected property when it packaged the N/I CD.

Micro Star claimed there was no fixation. It relied heavily on *Lewis Galoob Toys v. Nintendo of Am., Inc.*, 964 F.2d 965 (9th Cir. 1992), which is set forth in § 6.30, *supra*. After reviewing *Galoob*, reexamine how Judge Kozinski distinguished it from Micro Star's situation. Do you agree with him that the cases are different? *See, e.g.,* Tyler T. Ochoa, *"Who Owns an Avatar? Copyright, Creativity, and Virtual Worlds,"* 14 VAND. J. ENT. & TECH. L. 959, 972-*et seq.* (2012), setting forth the argument that the dynamic freedom offered to the user in some games makes the avatar's performance in the game more similar to an actor's performance in a play or other activity which is not "fixated" for purposes of copyright law.

2. Who ended up owning the copyrights to the levels, Formgen or the users who created them? Professor Ochoa of Santa Clara Law School argues that there should be a "joint" ownership of rights in an avatar for copyright purposes, assuming a sufficient array of choices given a user in creating or importing an avatar into a game. *Id.* at 977–980 (2012). Do you agree?

3. In writing about the tensions between a TOS Agreement and copyright law regarding the ownership of avatars, Professor Ochoa says the following:

> Many game providers attempt to avoid any inquiry into the ownership of avatars by requiring each player to "agree" to an EULA before playing the game. Such EULAs typically provide that the game provider owns not only the computer program that operates the game, but also all copyrightable expression generated by the game program during the course of play. For example, the EULA for Blizzard Entertainment's World of Warcraft states:
>
> > All title, ownership rights and intellectual property rights in and to the Game and all copies thereof (including without limitation any titles, computer code, themes, objects, characters, character names, stories, dialog, catch phrases, locations, concepts, artwork, character inventories, structural or landscape designs, animations, sounds, musical compositions and recordings, audio-visual effects, storylines, character likenesses, methods of operation, moral rights, and any related documentation) are owned or licensed by Blizzard.
>
> A notable exception is the virtual world Second Life, which specifically acknowledges that users own intellectual property rights in anything that they create during the course of play.
>
> There are several reasons, however, why reliance on a EULA provides an unsat-isfactory answer to the question of copyright ownership. First, in some instances the user may not have agreed to the EULA. Second, even if a EULA exists and the user clicked "I Agree" when presented with the EULA, that EULA may be

unenforceable. A court might hold a EULA invalid because it is unconscionable, because it otherwise violates public policy, or because it is preempted by federal copyright law. Third, there are certain attributes of authorship and/or ownership that cannot be assigned by a contract. For example, an author can exercise the right to terminate a transfer of an interest in a copyrightable work "notwithstanding any agreement to the contrary." Fourth, reliance on a EULA is intellectually unsatisfying and logically backwards. To analyze a question of ownership, one should start with the default position by asking who owns what in the absence of an agreement to the contrary. Only after default ownership is determined does one reach the issues of whether the default ownership has been altered by contract, and if so, whether that contract is valid and enforceable.

Id. at 964–65 (footnotes omitted).

In addressing the last question relating to "default rules" of ownership in the excerpt above, Professor Ochoa answers:

Who is the "author" or "authors" of that "work"? In other words, who contributed the "minimal degree of creativity" necessary to make the work copyrightable?

Under one view, which might be called the "deterministic" view, a game provider may assert that, because the software code that operates the game dictates an avatar's appearance, capabilities, and behavior, the avatar is not "original" to the user, but is the product of the creativity of the programmers who created the software. The deterministic view, however, ignores the elements of originality that are added by the individual players. Although an avatar cannot do anything that the program does not permit, it is a stretch to say that an avatar's appearance and behavior are dictated by the program. It is more correct to say that the avatar's appearance and behavior are constrained by the program, but that the program allows the user some freedom to create an avatar's appearance and to control an avatar's behavior within the limits of those constraints.

Whether this freedom is sufficient to enable copyrightable authorship depends on the degree of freedom that the program provides to the player. At some point, a computer program may provide such a wide range of choices to the user that the resulting product can no longer be considered the sole product of the creative authorship of the programmer, but must be considered to be the product (at least in part) of the user's creative authorship of the user.

Id. at 974–75.

4. To the disappointment of gamers (and possibly Judge Kozinski) 3D Realms, which became the developer of *Duke Nukem*, closed its studio in 2009, and announced it would no longer produce the game or its much anticipated successor, *Duke Nukem Forever*. Not long thereafter, Take-Two Interactive, who owned publishing rights to the sequel and had already invested $12 million in its development, filed a lawsuit against 3D Realms for failing to finish the game. The lawsuit reached a settlement after Gearbox Software stepped in and agreed to purchase the intellectual property rights to Duke Nukem, and finish the development of the game for Take-Two. Finally, after 15 years in development, *Duke Nukem Forever* was released in 2011.

In an interesting turn of events, the newly revived 3D Realms attempted to reclaim its franchise in 2014 and announced its plans to release a new Duke Nukem game, *Duke Nukem: Mass Destruction*. In response, Gearbox filed a lawsuit seeking damages and a formal injunction for trademark and copyright infringement, unfair competition and breach of contract. As of the publication of this edition, the dispute has yet to be resolved, but 3D has since changed the name of their new game to *Bombshell* and replaced Duke Nukem with a female character.[14]

5. A slightly different problem from that in *Micro Star* was presented *in Marvel Enterprises, Inc. v. NCSoft Corp.*, No. CV 04-9253RGKPLAX, 2005 WL 878090 (C.D. Cal. Mar. 9, 2005). There, defendants marketed a multiplayer internet game (*City of Heroes*) where a player entered a fictional town (Paragon City) in the guise of a character that the player created and customized from a certain limited number of art files provided in the game. The plaintiff, Marvel, correctly alleged that some of the characters that could be created with the game's art files bore remarkable resemblances to the various Marvel copyrighted figures such as The Incredible Hulk, Wolverine, Captain America, and others. (*See* Figure 10.1). There was no commercial exploitation or "sale" of the characters on a separate CD-ROM as in *Micro Star*, but *City of Heroes* players did pay a monthly fee to have access to Paragon City, the game's art files, and the program's engine where the art files were stored and the characters assembled and saved. Should the defendant in *Marvel* be enjoined?

6. Recently, a new kind of user-generated content called "machinima," which uses an existing videogame's graphics and characters to create a high quality, computer-animated film with an original plot, has become increasingly popular, causing some videogame producers to re-think their user generated content policies. Zachary Levine explains:

Figure 10.1

The images on the left are from *City of Heroes* and the images on the right are from Marvel. — ED

---

14. *See* Bo Moore & Chris Kohler, *Dueling Developers Go to War Over Duke Nukem's Fate*, Wired (Mar. 27, 2014), http://www.wired.com/2014/03/duke-nukem-lawsuit/; Andy Chalk, *Former Duke Nukem Teaser Site Reveals Bombshell*, Escapist Magazine (May 14, 2014), http://www.escapistmagazine.com/forums/read/7.850063-Former-Duke-Nukem-Teaser-Site-Reveals-Bombshell.

The questions of whether Machinima is covered under fair use, and who owns the resulting work are currently unanswered. Most game developers and publishers have strict End User License Agreements (EULAs) and Terms of Use (TOU) that restrict, or at least govern, the creation and distribution of such content, but in practice many game companies allow more permissive use of their materials, especially with popular series that may generate free publicity.

Blizzard and Microsoft, two of the largest game developers whose games are used in Machinima titles, have similar policies regarding the development and release of these videos. Both companies clearly state that Machinima may only be developed for non-commercial use and that no sale of videos, or required payment to view videos, can take place. Blizzard requires producers to maintain the rating of the underlying game (in most cases a "T" rating) and Microsoft more generally restricts the inclusion of pornographic or obscene elements in Machinima videos. If an individual or entity desires to hold a film festival or contest that is going to allow submissions of Blizzard-based Machinima, a license is required from Blizzard if the prize money is to exceed US$500.00. Microsoft also requires the inclusion of an attribution statement in anything created using one of its games.

While it appears that many of the game developers involved in Machinima content are willing to look the other way while users create non-commercial content, there is still ambiguity in the area of what exactly constitutes "non-commercial" use. The primary channel of distribution for Machinima is video hosting sites such as YouTube and Vimeo. A search for most popular game titles, or the word "Machinima," will yield thousands of results with many millions of views, ratings, and comments. While the free distribution of content may appear to comply with the policies set forth by companies like Blizzard and Microsoft, many of these hosting sites have profit-sharing programs for videos with high traffic whereby content creators can share in the ad revenue generated from ads displayed with their videos. Whether or not the participation in such an ad-revenue program would subject a Machinima creator to a revocation of the licenses described above and subsequent civil liability is as yet unclear.

Without analyzing the possible areas where Machinima is being distributed in a "commercial" context, there are numerous sites that blatantly violate the Machinima terms of use described above. In practice, high-quality Machinima is regularly being sold in various formats and being used as a draw to subscription-based and pay-per-view video sharing websites. Faced with the problems of enforcement involved in tracking down the individuals involved who literally span the globe, many videogame companies may never seek to enforce their rights against creators who violate these terms. Bungie, the creator of Halo, has chosen to completely embrace and condone at least one Machinima series, probably due to its unusual popularity. The series "*Red vs. Blue*," which follows a cast of ancillary characters set in the *Halo* universe, is an internet phenomenon that has arguably increased the visibility and popularity of the *Halo* videogame franchise. Bungie has allowed *Red vs. Blue* to be sold as a DVD series and even commissioned its creators to create special videos for the company.

The process of developing and publishing a videogame is a complex process that often involves licenses from multiple parties, such as voice actors and holders of various intellectual properties. Even with the consent of the videogame developer to create and publish Machinima, content creators could soon find themselves under attack from the licensees of such additional properties if the videos created happen to incorporate one of these elements of the finished game. Many racing games license the use of real car models; music games sometimes license instrument skins; and countless types of games license the voices and likenesses of celebrities and athletes. Machinima creators, and game developers who allow the creation of Machinima, should be cautious of these additional elements that may need to be addressed in the creation and regulation of Machinima videos.

Zachary Levine, *The Video Game Law Strategy Guide*, 19 No. 3 Cyberspace Law. 8 (2014).

There is some dispute regarding the origin of machinima, but we believe the following sets forth a reasonable description of its beginning:

Machinima traces its history back to 1996, when a group of gamers called The Rangers created a short film titled, "Diary of a Camper." The Rangers used a demo function in "Quake" to record their film. Developers designed the demo function to allow players to record gaming events to share with friends, and up to that point most gamers used it to record particularly impressive kills or speedy level completions. The Rangers' film went a step beyond, using the demo function to tell a story. While the film is primitive compared to machinima produced today, it is important in that it was the first to use video games as a film medium.

http://entertainment.howstuffworks.com/machinima3.htm (last accessed August 2015)

Another commentator explains about the market for machinima:

Machinima.com was formed in the year 2000 by Hugh Hancock as a place for Machinamists to collaborate and show off their work. Although the concept is the same today, the company is a very different animal than it was in 2000 or even 2006. Machinima.com operates a YouTube network that achieved the most video views of 2011 over every other channel on the video site. YouTube, itself has a market share of 43% of all online video. YouTube served nearly 100 billion video views in 2011. For Machinima.com to be #1 on YouTube, this may help to put in perspective just how large the network is and how powerful it has become. The company has raised nearly 15 Million dollars in Venture funds to date and, based on its fund-raising history and current performance of their YouTube channel, they are profitable and growing at an exponential rate.

Adam Jackson, *An Inside Look at Machinima.com, Their Business, Contracts and Partner Program*, ADAM JACKSON BLOG (Feb. 3, 2012), http://adam-jackson.net/blog/2012/02/03/an-inside-look-at-machinima-com-their-business-contracts-and-partner-program/.

If you believe Wikipedia, the popularity of machinima.com continues to grow: "As of May 24, 2014, Machinima has over 1,026,504 followers on Twitter, 1,451,677 fans on Facebook, and over 11,315,632 subscribers to its YouTube channel." It now runs or has run several series produced by the developers of the game exclusively for machinima.com in order to publicize and carry the story of the game, including, "*Mortal Kombat: Legacy*, a live action series produced by Warner Bros. Digital Distribution, Warner Bros. Interactive Entertainment and Warner Premiere," *Halo 4 Dawn*, produced by Microsoft, and "*Street Fighter: Assassin's Fist*, a live action Street Fighter series produced by Capcom." A series of animated short features entitled *Justice League: Gods and Monsters Chronicles*, produced by DC Comics is going to be released just ahead of the film, *Justice League: Gods and Monsters. Machinima.com*, WIKIPEDIA, http://en.wikipedia.org/wiki/Machinima.com (last visited Oct. 2, 2014).

What issues do you see coming out of machinima, especially machinima with UGC?

Below is the machinima policy for Blizzard Entertainment. It is accessed as a click-through from its general EULA:

BLIZZARD VIDEO POLICY

Blizzard Entertainment strongly supports the efforts of its community members who produce community videos (referred to hereafter as a "Production") using video images, footage, music, sounds, speech, or other assets from Blizzard's copyrighted products ("Blizzard Content"), subject to a few conditions. Note, however, that Blizzard Content does not include trailers or advertisements promoting Blizzard games or services that are not incorporated into a Blizzard game.

The Fundamental Rule

First and foremost, note that except as specifically provided herein, Blizzard Entertainment requires that the use of Blizzard Content must be limited to non-commercial purposes.

What this means

As a community content creator, you are permitted to create video productions using Blizzard's Content, and to distribute them freely on your website, or on other websites where viewers can freely view your Production.

Limitation of Usage

Neither you nor the operator of any website where your Production(s) may be viewed can force a viewer to pay a "fee" to be able to view your Production(s).

Regarding Websites and "Premium Access"

We understand that many third party websites have a "free" method to see their video content, as well as a "premium" membership service that allows for speedier viewing.

For clarity, please note that as long as the website that hosts your Production provides a free method to allow viewers to see the Production, Blizzard Entertainment will not object to your Production being hosted on that site, regardless of the site's "for pay" premium service plans.

Guidelines for distributing Productions with Blizzard Content

Note that Blizzard Entertainment's restriction that Productions be limited to "non-commercial" uses also means that you may not license a Production you have created to another company for a fee, or for any other form of compensation, without specific written permission from Blizzard Entertainment to do so. Blizzard Entertainment reserves the right to use its products for all commercial purposes. The only exceptions to this rule are if you participate in partner programs with YouTube, Justin.tv, Blip.tv, Own3d.tv, or Ustream.tv (the "Production Websites") whereby a Production Website may pay you for views of a Production if you are accepted into their partner program.

Your Production should meet the rating guidelines for "T" rated Productions

To maintain and protect the image of our games, Blizzard also requires that Productions maintain the "T" rating that has been given to its products by the ESRB, and similar ratings received from other ratings boards around the world, and that these standards are taken into account during the creation of your Production.

Blizzard support of Film Festivals, Contests, and Broadcast opportunities

If you have created a Production that meets the guidelines above that you would like to enter into a film competition or festival, or if you encounter the opportunity to have your Production shown on television, Blizzard Entertainment is happy to support your efforts by, pending review and approval of your Production, providing a content use license for your Production.

If you are a website operator, film festival organizer, or broadcaster and you are interested in running a "Community video contest," where Productions that use Blizzard Content will be allowed entry into the contest, we are happy to inform you that Blizzard allows websites, Film Festivals, and Broadcasters to run video contests as long as the "total prize package"(cash and prizes) for the contest does not exceed $500.00 USD. If, however, you are interested in running a video contest that will feature Productions that use Blizzard Content where the total value (cash and prizes) of all of the prizes exceeds $500.00 USD, you will need to obtain a license from Blizzard in order to hold the contest.

What is a content use license?

In the event that you are required to prove to the contest organizer, festival committee, or television broadcaster that you have Blizzard Entertainment's permission to use Blizzard Content in your Production, a content use license is provided. This license serves to prove you have the rights to use your Production materials specifically for that event.

Important notes

For business reasons, there may be times when Blizzard will need to terminate your right to distribute or host a specific Production, and in such a case, Blizzard shall have the right to do so without notice or liability to you. A content use license is not unlimited: it permits the use of the Blizzard materials in your Production only for the 'event' that the license has been issued for, and in the specific methods outlined in the license.

Educational Use of Production Materials

Blizzard Entertainment supports the use of its game assets for educational purposes, and you are welcome and encouraged to create a Production for a school project, master's thesis, etc. All limitations above still apply to Productions created for educational purposes.

Inclusion of Sponsor Names, Logos, or Affiliates

Knowing that there are organizations out there willing and ready to support producers in the video community, the mentioning of producer or contest sponsors, through methods such as logos at the beginning of the production, or the verbal mentioning of sponsor names, is permissible.

However, you may not include more than 10 seconds total of sponsor promotion per Production. Additionally you must visually include the text "Sponsored By" when being displayed. Simple text 'credits,' included at the end of your Production and unaccompanied by logos, slogans, or other methods of visual isolation, are not bound by this restriction.

For further information

In the event that you have any questions about your Production in regards to Blizzard Entertainment's Video guidelines or would like to inquire about obtaining a license as described above, feel free to send us a note at community-videos@blizzard.com.

7. As modern gaming devices make it easier and easier for players to record their game play and share it online, another form of videogame UGC called "Let's Play" video has become increasingly popular. Zachary Levine explains:

> As with all UGC there is a broad spectrum of creativity at issue with Let's Play videos. Some videos are strict recordings of someone playing a game with no commentary and no additional elements, and what you see is what you would see if you were to play the game yourself; the only "contributions" are the choices made by the player ingame. More popular are videos that provide some type of commentary—either for review purposes of the game or to provide a guide or "how-to" style video.

> In early 2013 Nintendo took the position that Let's Play videos that shared in the ad revenue of the hosting site were violating the copyrights in their games and Nintendo took steps to recapture those allegedly ill-gotten gains. While there have been no official statements from the company there are reports that the enforcement efforts have stopped or at least stalled. Nintendo has previously challenged the creators and distributors of unlicensed "strategy guides" for its GoldenEye 007 game based on the James Bond franchise. Nintendo argued that the sale of the guide infringed on its copyrighted material. The court ruled, however, that much of the material in question was factual material and that any copying of the remaining content was de minimus. Whether a court would issue a similar ruling when presented with a video of an entire game is unclear but there are methods of blocking potentially infringing content, such as take down notices, without involving the courts.

> In 1998 Congress enacted the Digital Millennium Copyright Act ("DMCA") in order to protect copyrighted works from privacy while simultaneously promoting electronic commerce. Title II of the DMCA attempts to balance these two goals by creating a safe harbor for online service providers against copyright liability provided those providers adhere to certain guidelines for handling notices of infringement from content owners and eventually blocking or banning repeat infringers. A DMCA take-down notice allows a copyright holder to send notice to a service provider with information about their property and a specific instance of infringement, which starts the process for the service provider to remove that content.

> YouTube has faced many legal challenges to the content on its site, as well as its compliance with the DMCA. Following the settlement of a recent dispute, YouTube updated its Content ID matching system, which scans uploaded videos to find copyright violations. As a result of the last update, thousands of Let's Play videos were removed (largely due to background music found in the games) causing a collective uproar in the community, at first directed at game developers who were believed to be behind the new enforcement efforts. However, rather than allowing this potentially infringing content to be removed and forever banned, several developers, including Capcom, Blizzard, Ubisoft, and later Nintendo, reached out to the Let's Play community and offered to help work with video posters to restore their content to YouTube. However a court may ultimately classify the legality of this type of content, it is clear that a number of rights

holders recognize the potential value and free marketing at issue, and its resulting value to the brands and developers.

Zachary Levine, *The Video Game Law Strategy Guide*, 19 No. 3 Cyberspace Law. 8 (2014)

The excerpt above describes the DMCA notice-and-takedown procedure. As we explained in some detail in § 6.78, *supra*, the DCMA allows copyright owners who believe that their copyrighted material is being used without permission to send a takedown notice to the site that is hosting the material, which is then required to remove the content. Thus, it gives Nintendo the power to ask YouTube to remove any Let's Play videos that display Nintendo's copyrighted material. Are there any other parties that might ask YouTube to remove such a video? Consider a player who records a gaming session between her avatar and another player's avatar and uploads it to YouTube. If the second player had designed and created the avatar shown in the video, and disapproved of the video for some reason, could she file a DMCA takedown notice?

8. The industry has not been silent on UGC issues, whether in machinima or elsewhere. As one article explained:

> On October 18, 2007, companies including CBS, Dailymotion, Disney, Fox, NBC Universal, Microsoft, Veoh, and Viacom released a document titled "Principles for User Generated Content Services." The UGC principles document incorporates many of the provisions of the DMCA and Section 512 and urges Web site operators to adopt the principles. Although the principles are obviously not law and compliance is voluntary, they are intended to guide the discourse about UGC. To that end, the text of the UGC principles expressly states the principles are not intended to be construed as a concession or waiver with respect to any legal or policy position or as creating any legally binding rights or obligations.

> The broadly stated objectives of the UGC principles are to: 1) eliminate infringing content on user-generated services, 2) encourage uploading of wholly original and authorized user-generated audio and video content, 3) accommodate fair use, and 4) protect legitimate interests of user privacy.

> The UGC principles provide some specific steps that user-generated services may incorporate to achieve these objectives, such as: 1) include relevant and conspicuous language on Web sites that incorporate UGC that promotes respect for intellectual property rights and discourages users from uploading infringing content, 2) inform users during the uploading process that uploading infringing content is prohibited and causing the user to affirm that the content is not infringing, 3) incorporate content identification technology, which blocks the uploading of any infringing content that matches with the reference materials provided by copyright owners, 4) identify Web sites that are predominantly used for the dissemination of infringing content and block or remove all links to such sites, 5) incorporate searching mechanisms that would allow copyright owners registered with the service to search for infringing content, and 6) implement a notice, takedown, and counter notice procedure, similar to that required by Section 512 and other policies that accommodate fair use. The UGC principles also include various liability-limiting provisions for those complying with the principles.

Charles J. Biederman, Danny Andrews, *Applying Copyright Law to User-Generated Content*, L.A. Law., May 2008, 12, 17–18. The full text of the principles can be found at: http://www.publicknowledge.org/node/1230.

§ 10.30 Virtual World/MMORPG Issues

In a chicken-and-egg synergy, videogames became very much more sophisticated in the late 1990s and early 2000s, in lockstep with the increased sophistication of home computers. This allowed for the development of two very different types of games, although each had in common the continual and simultaneous play of tens of thousands of players from all over the world, justifying mnemonics such as "MMOGs," for Massive Multiplayer On-line Games, and "MMORPGs," for Massive Multiplayer On-line Role Playing Games.

One set of games were the real time strategy games like Blizzard's *World of Warcraft* ("*WoW*") where friends and strangers can, and sometimes must, group together to explore Azeroth, Outland, Northrend and Pandaria and overcome challenges.

The second type of game, such as Linden Research's *Second Life*, is hardly a "game" at all, for there are no points to accrue, levels to achieve, enemies to slay, or time pressures to suffer. It is more of an alternative world. There is never a "Game Over" message and the world continues to evolve even when a particular player has logged off. Just hanging out in the "metaverse," is the shared and stated object of these kinds of worlds, and justifies the mnemonic "MMOWs" for Massively Multiplayer Online Worlds.

One thing both types of MMORPGs share is that in each game or world, users can accrue wealth—"gold" in *WoW* and "Linden dollars" or "Lindens" (abbreviated "L$") in *Second Life*, for example.[15] Players can also acquire and sell property—whether battleaxes in *WoW* or hover boards and even "real" property in *Second Life*, as was at issue in *Bragg* above. As you might expect, when money enters the scene, so do legal problems.

In the first edition of this book, we predicted that legal issues arising from conflicts over property rights and user/avatar conduct, which have ramifications in both the criminal and civil realms, would increasingly be the subject of real world court cases. In the United States, to date only a few lawsuits have been filed in our real world courts. There *has* been more courtroom activity overseas however; the legal systems of China, Korea, and Japan have dealt with issues involving the theft, misappropriation, and illegal copying of virtual property in online worlds. For example, a Chinese court ordered developers to pay a user damages for inadequately protecting the user's weapons and armors from hacking theft, while South Korea and Taiwan have enacted laws that make infringement upon virtual property a real world crime.[16] For a good summary of this phenomenon, *see, e.g.*, Ung-Gi Yoon, *Quest for the Legal Identity of MMORPGs—From a Computer Game, Back to a Play Association*, Journal of Game Industry & Culture, Vol. 10, Fall 2005. But with that written, we cannot shake the feeling that cases involving virtual worlds are coming to the United States courts.

The remainder of this chapter discusses the criminal and civil law issues arising from virtual worlds and MMORPG games. We begin with the criminal law.

---

15. One of our favorite statistics regarding the enormity of wealth in MMORPGs is that an economist determined that in 2001, the annual gross national product of Sony's *Norrath* was slightly larger than that of Bulgaria and would rank among the world's top 100 economies. *See, e.g.*, Erez Reuventi, *On Virtual Worlds: Copyright and Contract Law at the Dawn of the Virtual Age*, 82 Ind. L. J. 262, 267 (2007).

16. Marius Meland, *Can Virtual Property Gain Legal Protection?*, Law 360 (Feb. 9, 2006), http://www.law360.com/articles/5280/can-virtual-property-gain-legal-protection.

"Virtual Crime": Definition and Consequences

The first step in discussing criminal law issues in virtual worlds or MMORPG games is coming up with a definition of "virtual crime." Two prominent commentators on virtual worlds, Professors Lastowka and Hunter, said the following about this deceivingly complex issue:

> Obviously, part of the very notion of "virtual crime" lies in the word "virtual" itself, which has become increasingly devoid of meaning. The term "virtual crime" can be just as meaningless as the term "virtual pet" if it refers to all computer-generated simulations of crime. Realistic digital simulations of mass murder occur every day on the computer monitors of those playing Grand Theft Auto and on home entertainment centers displaying DVDs of *Hamlet*. However, the representations of villainy that occur in interactive games are generally understood as speech and nothing more, and thus are within the scope of constitutional free speech protections. These activities are essentially stories.

> A narrower definition of virtual crime might equate "virtual crimes" with "cybercrimes," defining cybercrimes as "crimes committed against a computer or by means of a computer." Obviously computers can be utilized in the furtherance of criminal conduct, and there are many state and federal statutes that expressly criminalize certain types of conduct involving computer networks. But these are real crimes with real consequences. In this case, there is a risk of conflating the actual with the virtual because doing so makes "virtual" computer crimes seem *less* serious than real crimes. Virtual copyright infringers spend jail time in *real* penitentiaries.

> But, there is still a proper place for the term "virtual crime." A Japanese man recently hacked into another person's virtual world account, sold her virtual house to another player for real cash, and pocketed the proceeds. This type of activity might be described as a virtual crime because it refers to crimes that "exist or result in essence or effect, though not in actual fact, form or name." This is the older sense of the modifier "virtual," and would include those crimes that somehow evoke and approach the effect and essence of real crime, but are not considered real crimes. To us, this seems to be the exact nature of "virtually criminal" activities [as those which] grossly transgress reasonable and sensible civic expectations of behavior, but they are not activities that tend to fall within the scope of existing criminal prohibitions due, in part, to the unique nature of virtual spaces.

F. Gregory Lastowka and Dan Hunter, *Virtual Crimes*, 49 N.Y.L. Sch. L. Rev. 293 (2004).

Notes and Questions

1. As the above excerpt points out, it is easy to be overbroad in defining virtual crime. To say that a virtual crime is anything that would be a crime in the real world might nominate Blinky, Pinky, Inky, and Sue for the death penalty each time they "kill" Ms. Pac Man. But carving out the appropriate subset of prosecutable crimes is difficult. Do you agree with Professors Lastowka's and Hunter's definition at the end of the excerpt?

2. As is evident in the *Drew* decision below, United States courts require specificity in the definition of criminal laws to comport with due process. An actor needs to know what exactly is prohibited before he or she can be lawfully prosecuted. But there are no penal

codes in virtual worlds. Must we resort to real world penal codes for our definition of crimes, with actionable violations occurring when acts in virtual worlds have real world consequences, at least if the prosecution takes place in the United States? Would that mean a different set of rules for players in different states? Different countries? Must the EULAs and like agreements mention and incorporate by reference these statutes to surmount due process concerns? Would that be sufficient?

3. One of the conceptual problems with virtual crime is that real world criminal laws exist, in part, to protect the physical well-being of a society (against murder, rape, etc.) and to protect property owners from having their interests impermissibly invaded (against trespass, theft, etc.). In virtual worlds, there can be no physical assaults (at least none that inflict physical pain), and while there could be an uninvited virtual breaking and entering into virtual real estate owned by a user, a legitimate question is whether the sanctity of various bits and bytes on the developer's server, displayed electronically on a monitor, embody enough of a societal interest to protect against a simple trespass. For example, suppose the individual who sold the virtual house for cash (described in the Lastowka and Hunter excerpt) instead just broke into the woman's house, left a flower or some other "calling card," but did no other damage? That would be a real world crime, but should the virtual world equivalent be prosecuted? In real world courts?

4. The discussion of "virtual crime" in MMORPGs was largely kick started in the early 1990s, with the description of a "rape" in a virtual world known as *LambdaMOO*. *LambdaMOO* was a text-only game, but one in which adjacent avatars in physical proximity could affect each other. A user who entered the world under the avatar name "Mr. Bungle" wrote some code which he (we think it was a "he") called the "voodoo program." The program allowed Mr. Bungle to "capture" an adjacent avatar and bring it under his control, something similar to the "exploit" described above in the notes after *Bragg*. Once he grabbed an adjacent avatar (always a female), Mr. Bungle textually described various graphic, offensive and certainly non-consensual sexual exploitations of the captured animated character. Studies have shown that users often relate to their avatar, and many of the users whose avatars Mr. Bungle exploited experienced frustration and shame at their powerlessness to stop the assault—some of the same emotions that accompany sexual assault in the real world. Should Mr. Bungle's exploits be considered "essentially [a] story"—to borrow the phrase from Lastowka and Hunter—or do you believe criminal liability should issue? Is the protection of emotional harm only sufficient to invoke civil liability? If so, is it a defense, or at least a mitigating factor, that the users whose avatars were being exploited could have exited from *LambdaMOO* or turned off their computers rather than continue to read Mr. Bungle's offensive commentary?[17]

5. Some developers predict that within the next few years, interfaces may be invented which would allow the user to experience physical sensations—such as pleasure or pain—"experienced" by their avatars. The Oculus VR system is getting closer to this, for example. If such an interface existed, would there be a greater reason to punish virtual assaultive criminal acts? Once again, would the fact that any pain felt by the user could be stopped by disconnecting the interface make any difference?

6. Many users called for the virtual death penalty for Mr. Bungle, i.e., a public destruction of the avatar by the developer and a permanent ban on the user re-entering *LambdaMOO*.

---

17. For more information about the Mr. Bungle episode, *see* F. Gregory Lastowka and Dan Hunter, *Virtual Crimes*, 49 N.Y.L. Sch. L. Rev. 293 (2004).

While this was being debated, a gamer even more technologically savvy than the one that controlled Mr. Bungle deleted Mr. Bungle's entire file from the world, and Mr. Bungle never returned.

* * *

The general consensus among videogame commentators is that the human who controlled Mr. Bungle probably should not have been criminally prosecuted, largely because he caused no physical harm to the user whose avatar was attacked, and because of the First Amendment protections surrounding even odious story lines in a videogame. However, those arguments change when virtual actions in fact cause real world damage. Once items in virtual worlds became commoditized and had real world value, then theft of those items, or theft of the virtual currency in a user's account, seemed inevitable (and certainly acts of theft have no constitutional protection). As will be seen, the "Ginko" scandal demonstrates that the danger of such an act occurring is no longer theoretical, and we will use the Ginko fact pattern throughout the Chapter to raise issues regarding the consequences of virtual crime.

The background is this: "Ginko" was a private "bank" set up by a resident in *Second Life*. The "owner" of the bank promised a 40% annual interest rate on deposits of L$. The return was even better than Bernie Madoff. Hundreds of residents deposited some or all of their L$ with Ginko. (It is possible, although not confirmed, that some may have even purchased L$ with real world money just to deposit L$ in Ginko and reap the hefty promised return, rather than obtain significantly less interest in their real world savings and money market accounts.) A few months after starting the bank, Ginko vanished, with its owner taking with him or her at least $75,000 worth of real world money deposits. The *Los Angeles Times* reported:

> The Ginko debacle raised fresh questions about the need for regulation over— not to mention the wisdom of—financial transactions in a place that doesn't exist. "The whole Second Life adventure encourages user freedom, but it's got so many users, and so much money is flowing in, that you have to face that the community needs some degree of control," said Stephan Martinussen, executive director of the global solutions department at Denmark's Saxo Bank, which had toyed with the idea of opening a virtual branch.

> Ginko was able to skip town and leave virtually no trail for authorities to follow, if there had been any authorities. Even Linden Lab might not know the identity of the avatar who ran the bank. Company executives declined to be interviewed for this article, but lawyers in contact with unhappy Ginko depositors said they weren't aware of any investigative action taken by the company.

> No individual seems to have lost enough money to make filing a lawsuit worthwhile, said Robert Bloomfield, a Cornell University professor who has been following the Ginko case. Anyway, because Second Life members live in different countries, "it's not at all clear what jurisdiction you would file suit in," he said.

> Multiplayer computer-based gaming environments such as Second Life aren't monitored by real-world regulators. And before the recent announcement, Linden Lab had handed down only two other official bans against anything: It prohibited gambling and simulations of sexual activity involving minors. That's the allure. In Second Life players can be anyone (among the pro-bank demonstrators one day last week were a disco dancer, a tentacled human and a mermaid; on another day there was a storm trooper and a very large rabbit) and do nearly anything. "Usually,

we don't step in the middle of Resident-to-Resident conduct," Linden Lab said in a Jan. 8 statement, which was posted on its blog. "But these 'banks' have brought unique and substantial risks to Second Life, and we feel it's our duty to step in."

Linden Lab seems to see itself as no more responsible for what goes on in Second Life than an Internet provider like AOL is for illegal activities discussed over e-mail, said David Naylor, an attorney with British law firm Field Fisher Waterhouse, and that attitude crimps Second Life's potential. "It's only when people have a reasonable level of confidence that the transactions they enter into are not fraudulent that you'll see transaction volumes really going up," he said.

There have been some calls for the government to step in, but Washington is pretty much scratching its head right now. "Most members of Congress don't understand what this is all about," said Dan Miller, a senior economist with the Congressional Joint Economic Committee. "Is a Linden real money? Is it an asset? Is this just a form of barter? Is this a form of capital gains? We just don't know. The courts haven't ruled on this, and the regulatory bodies haven't stepped forward to stake their claim," Miller said.

Alana Samuels, *Scheme Stirs Game Regulation Worries*, L.A. Times, Jan. 22, 2008 at C1.

* * *

The fact that the Ginko fraud occurred opens up many more possibilities—Virtual stock brokers who take their clients' funds; someone who hacks into user accounts and loots all the virtual currency found there, converting it into real world currency as quickly as possible; someone who steals the programming code for an invention created by a user, etc. Where there is money, crime will follow. But the problems associated with the prosecution of such cyber criminals have led some to conclude that what would otherwise be criminal activity in virtual worlds should be kept out of the courts altogether, and simply regulated within the worlds themselves by the developers.

In the following excerpt, Professors Lastowka and Hunter describe an incident where a user in the game *Ultima Online* purchased a stolen virtual weapon, known as a "Bone Crusher mace," knowing that the seller had stolen the mace (stolen the computer code for representing a weapon) from its inventor. The user who purchased the stolen weapon then sold multiple copies of the Bone Crusher to other gamers for real world money on eBay.

At first glance, the fencing of the Bone Crusher for U.S. dollars would seem to fall within the literal text of criminal statutes in many states. The Model Penal Code sates, "a person is guilty of theft if he purposely receives, retains, or disposes of movable property of another, knowing it has been stolen, or believing that it has probably been stolen, unless the property is received, retained, or disposed with purpose to restore it to the owner." There is no general exemption to the statutory provisions for thefts that take place in virtual worlds.

Of course, while the language of the Model Penal Code may seem clear, one faces an interpretive difficulty in applying such statutory language to a realm constituted solely of images. [T]he Bone Crusher mace is not a mace, but just the representation of a medieval weapon on a personal computer. One might conclude, due to the representational medium, that the theft of the Bone Crusher was simply a representation of a theft, not a true theft intended to fall within the ambit of the Model Penal Code. [However,] the intangibility of the representation in such a case may not be a significant stumbling block to the application of criminal law. The Ninth Circuit recently concluded that the deceitful conversion of an Internet domain name is actionable in California [*Kremen v. Cohnen*, 337 F.3d 1024, 1030 (9th Cir. 2003)—Ed.] Domain names, like Bone Crushers, are often viewed as being property interests by their owners, but are essentially nothing more than representations. [I]f a domain name can indeed be "stolen," then perhaps it follows logically that a Bone Crusher mace—a similar artifact at the intersection of software, databases, and networks—should be equally capable of being stolen. Judge Kozinski's common sense summary of the issue would seem to apply: "the common law does not stand idle when people [unlawfully dispose of] the property of others."

But we are skeptical that [the user] could be prosecuted for fencing stolen property. In our view, his ability to escape a punitive fine or jail term has little to do with the intangibility of the Bone Crusher representation. [W]ithin the Ultima Online setting, Bone Crusher maces have a property status similar to the status of basketballs on a basketball court in the physical world.

Like basketballs, Bone Crushers have clear value in the context of the game. This value is appropriated by others when basketballs are "stolen [e.g., from the player who is dribbling and has the ball "stolen" by someone from the opposing team—Ed.]. We refer to this activity as "stealing"—the same word we use to describe criminal conversion or theft—and the loss of a basketball game can have serious emotional and financial consequences for the player. However, no player would dream of responding to basketball "theft" by petitioning the legal system for a remedy. Instead the available self-help remedy must be perfected consistent with the rules of the game, which prohibit state intervention in disputes over ball ownership. The norms of the game play supersede the standard rules of society, and the magic circle will only be broken if a player violates game rules. A violation of game rules will result in a stoppage of play and a penalty of some sort, for example, the return of the basketball to the prior owner.

Computer games are inherently different from real space games, in that they are creatures of software. Software creates physics of computer games, gives meaning to game components, and enables player behaviors. One might argue, therefore, that the software code of a game constitutes the "rules" (if any) of the game. By contrast, physical space games such as football, baseball and basketball are governed by external and legalistic rule systems that guide both actions and outcomes. These external rule systems constrain the actions of players and game items.

In the physical game of football, one cannot cross the line of scrimmage before the ball is snapped because doing so will result in a stoppage of play and a punitive sanction. These player-internalized rules can be analogized to legal rules and norms. When software rules constrain player actions, on the other hand, the player has no volitional capacity to undertake impermissible actions. "[C]heating" at Space Invaders is impossible without modifying the game's rule set. The prohibition against code-breaking is thus the primary rule of computer games. Virtual worlds, to some extent, are just a massively social implementation of traditional genres of computer games. They depend primarily on coded rule sets because, like Space Invaders, they *are* coded rule sets. The software code of Britannia [the name of the world in Ultima Online—Ed.] is what makes the theft of the Bone Crusher maces possible.

But unlike traditional computer games, virtual worlds are accompanied by explicit textual rule sets that are drafted by lawyers and game designers, and designed (at least in part) to curtail anti-social behaviors. These non-software rules of virtual worlds are often expressed as standard End-User License Agreement ("EULA"). Players may be additionally required to assent to the Terms of Service, Rules of Play, and other varieties of contractual agreements. Courts and legislators may refuse to defer to the private orderings created by contract and software. [W]e predict that the issue of virtual property crime will have legal teeth if game owners, rather than the game players, are the ones to raise the issue.

By concentrating the legal control of virtual property in the hands of the game owners and designers, we essentially disarm the issue of virtual crimes committed by avatars against other avatars. However, we do not defuse the issue of virtual property and crime entirely, but simply modify the focus of the inquiry from a myriad of avatar-players to a handful of corporate persons that create, own, and administer virtual worlds.

F. Gregory Lastowka and Dan Hunter, *Virtual Crimes*, The State of Play: Law, Games, and Virtual Worlds 121, 124 (Jack M. Balkin & Beth Simone Noveck eds., 2006).

Notes and Questions

1. To Professors Lastowka's and Hunter's point, let's assume we want to criminally prosecute, in the real world, the individual or individuals responsible for Ginko. Such prosecution carries with it a number of practical problems. For example:

a.   The victims would have to convince a prosecutor to file the charges. It may well be that a prosecutor will feel less than confident of securing a conviction for a "crime" in a virtual world that jurors (and the prosecutor or judge for that matter) may never have heard about, or consider just a sophisticated computer game.

b.   The prosecutor would have to find out who to prosecute. Presumably a prosecutor could subpoena Linden Labs for all the information it has on the user, but suppose the user who set up the bank did so from public (and largely anonymous) computers, like those found in a library or internet café? And, even if the user had to give a name, address, etc., when he or she first registered in *Second Life*, it seems likely that if the user wanted to perpetuate this scam, he or she registered with an alias. To set up an account in some worlds, and to transact business in all virtual worlds, the user must pay a monthly fee, which is often done by credit card. So it may be that the prosecutor wouldn't start from zero, but credit card accounts can be faked as well.

c.   There could be fights over jurisdiction. Suppose a prosecutor was interested and had found out the name of the perpetrator. Now even more problems pop up. For example, where did the crime occur? Where the perpetrator resided? A separate crime in each jurisdiction where a victim resides? Where Linden Labs' server is located, in Northern California? Suppose it turns out the perpetrator is domiciled in another country? It's tough enough to extradite someone from some countries for purely financial crimes, but do current laws provide for extradition for financial crimes committed in a virtual world? Can the user, if we ever find out who it is, be serially prosecuted in different jurisdictions under due process and double jeopardy concerns?

d.   What law should apply? Choice of law rules could present serious issues. It is unlikely that any jurisdiction would allow such outright fraud or theft as occurred in Ginko, but there may be occasions in which something is a crime in one jurisdiction—say where the victim lives—but not where the perpetrator lives.

2. Following the authors' lead, Linden has now banned any user from setting up a private bank in *Second Life*. That may not help the users who were bilked in Ginko, but it may help another such event from occurring, and it is an example of letting the game regulate itself.

3. In part of the L.A. TIMES article that was edited out of the above excerpt, one of the victims of the Ginko scheme, a *Second Life* resident identified as Margaret, blamed herself for her loss: "'This has lost a lot of people a lot of money,' Margaret said. 'But I think anyone who ignored the warnings of 'nothing is guaranteed' deserves all they got.'" Do you agree with Margaret? Are participants of virtual worlds assuming the risk of this type of loss?

In the domestic real world, one way banks, securities dealers, etc. are kept honest is by government regulation from the Comptroller of the Currency, the SEC, etc. Should the government become involved in regulating the financial transactions in virtual worlds, e.g., running background checks, establishing currency reserves, requiring honest representations, and the like for private bankers? Would gamers or developers put up with it?

4. Is the authors' solution necessary because the problems with bringing these issues to the courts are simply too intractable?

5. Is it worth trying to set up a world-wide, online adjudicative body to investigate and mete out criminal punishment for actionable crime in virtual worlds, whereby anyone who signs on to any virtual world subjects himself or herself to the jurisdiction of this body, which would be funded by the developers out of their monthly fees or other revenue streams associated with the MMORPG? What would be the applicable law? The Model Penal Code? Some sort of penal code referenced in the world's EULA? Would the punishment have to be either a fine, banishment from a game, or loss of game play privileges? We don't envision a real world prison for these crimes punishable by an on-line court—do we?

6. The authors posit the idea that if the virtual world's software permits the user to program his or her avatar to engage in "criminal" conduct, then per se, such conduct must be an allowable act within the game. What makes it "illegal" within the game are the written rules in the EULA and TOS Agreement, not the real world criminal law. They analogize this enforcement structure to the rules of sport—saying a basketball player "stealing" the ball from the dribbler is always allowable, and what makes it "legal" or "illegal" within a contest are the game's written rules, and not the real world criminal law. Is stealing a ball from the dribbler in a basketball game sufficiently like stealing a virtual piece of property with real world value, or stealing money like in Ginko, to make the analogy persuasive? Or is it more like stealing a real basketball from the back of a delivery truck which is pulling up to a sporting goods store to unload the balls into the store, i.e., stealing a good with real world value and real world criminal consequence? What arguments do Professors Lastowka and Hunter use to equate a violation of a rule in a game to a financial loss for the user whose property has been taken? Is there a worry about allowing a vidogame developer to author and enforce criminal sanctions?

7. In 2013, certain *World of Warcraft* users were able to exploit an error in the Web and smartphone app and hack into fellow players' accounts, stealing millions of "gold pieces" which were then used to buy virtual items in the game's auction house. Would Professor Latowka and Hunter's idea of in-game regulation and punishment be enough in this situation? Would it change your view if the hackers had tried to sell the gold on third party sites, such as eBay?[18]

---

18. PANDA LABS 2013 ANNUAL REPORT, http://press.pandasecurity.com/wp-content/uploads/2010/05/PandaLabs-Annual-Report_2013.pdf (last visited Oct. 24, 2014).

8. The virtual worlds of MMPORGs can also inspire real world crimes which are, of course, punishable in real world criminal justice systems. For example, a man in China was sentenced to life in prison for stabbing his friend to death after he discovered that the friend had stolen a virtual sword from him. In the Netherlands, a 13-year-old boy was beaten, threatened with a knife, and forced to log on to his MMORPG account and transfer a virtual mask and a virtual amulet to his attacker's account. Similarly, a Brazilian gang lured the top scorer of the online game *GunBound* to an internet cafe, kidnapped him, and forced him to disclose his account information. The gang then sold his account for $8,000.[19]

There is, of course, a difference between virtual "crime" in game play and real world crime that occurs in a videogame environment, e.g., when a hacker steals credit card or other personal or financial information of the users kept by game developers. When a number of computers are simultaneously linked into a virtual world, the risk of such a hack is real.

As you might expect, there are a panoply of state and federal statutes that make criminal the tampering with another's computer to get personal or financial information. However, perhaps the broadest such statute, the Computer Fraud and Abuse Act ("CFAA"), 18 U.S.C.A. § 1030 (West 2014) prohibits the unauthorized access of a computer used in interstate commerce, even if no personal or financial information is taken. One question posed by such law is whether the contours of authorized access can come from a EULA, or TOS/TOA Agreement. That is, taking Professors Lastowka's and Hunter's arguments to the extreme, the question is whether a user who breaches a EULA or TOS agreement — making continued access to the site theoretically "unauthorized" — can be criminally prosecuted for the further access to the servers of such a site. This question, and the question of the proper venue for prosecution of a cyber-crime, were addressed in the following case, the so-called "*MySpace* Mom," decision.

United States v. Drew

United States District Court for the Central District of California, 2009
259 F.R.D. 449

Wu, District Judge.

[Ms. Drew lived in a small town in Missouri (O'Fallon) with her thirteen-year-old daughter Sarah. About four houses down the street from the Drews lived an eighth grade classmate of Sarah's named Megan Meier. Mrs. Drew heard rumors that Megan spread untrue stories about her daughter Sarah.

In response, Ms. Drew, with the help of an employee of hers named Ashley Grills, set up a false *MySpace* account, telling *MySpace* in her profile that she was a 16-year-old boy named "Josh Evans." To perpetuate the hoax, Ms. Drew posted a picture of a good looking, bare chested boy who was supposed to be Josh and began flirting with Megan, telling her that she was "sexi" and that, "I love you so much." Josh later told Megan that he was breaking it off as "he" did not want to be with someone like Megan who spread lies about her friends, and sent her a message saying "the world would be a better place without

---

19. BBC News, http://news.bbc.co.uk/2/hi/technology/4072704.stm (last visited Oct. 2, 2014); Yahoo News, http://news.yahoo.com/online-game-theft-earns-real-world-conviction-133501758.html (last visited Oct. 2, 2014); Xinhu, http://news.xinhuanet.com/english/2007-07/18/content_6392309.htm (last visited Oct. 2, 2014).

you." According to testimony, Megan responded, "You are the kind of boy a girl would kill herself over." Later that day she was found dead after committing suicide.

The Missouri authorities investigated and concluded there were no criminal violations on which to charge Ms. Drew. There the matter lay until the U.S. Attorneys' office for the Central District of California, headquartered in Los Angeles, decided to investigate, and eventually brought a criminal proceeding against Ms. Drew under the CFAA, extraditing her from Indiana.

Jurisdiction was proper in Los Angeles, according to the prosecution, because *MySpace's* servers are located in Beverly Hills, California. Their theory was that the "crime" of unauthorized access to the *MySpace* computer system occurred on the servers, and so California was the proper venue.

Jurisdiction was contested in a pre-trial proceeding, and Judge Wu agreed with the prosecution that the servers provided the appropriate jurisdictional link for the case. Upon conviction for three misdemeanors under the CFAA, Ms. Drew brought a motion for judgment of acquittal under F.R. Crim. P. 29(c)—ED.]

This case raises the issue of whether (and/or when will) violations of an Internet website's terms of service constitute a crime under the Computer Fraud and Abuse Act ("CFAA"), 18 U.S.C. § 1030. Drew was subsequently convicted of misdemeanor CFAA violations. The question in the present motion is whether an intentional breach of an Internet website's terms of service, without more, is sufficient to constitute a misdemeanor violation of the CFAA; and, if so, would the statute, as so interpreted, survive constitutional challenges on the grounds of vagueness and related doctrines.

Pursuant to the conspiracy, on or about September 20, 2006, the conspirators registered and set up a profile for a fictitious 16-year-old male juvenile named "Josh Evans" on the www.MySpace.com website ("MySpace"), and posted a photograph of a boy without that boy's knowledge or consent. Such conduct violated My Space's terms of service.

[T]o become a member [of *MySpace*], one had to go to the sign-up section and register by filling in personal information (such as name, email address, date of birth, country/state/postal code, and gender) and creating a password. In addition, the individual had to check on the box indicating that "You agree to the MySpace **Terms of Service and Privacy Policy**." The terms of service did not appear on the same registration page that contained this "check box" for users to confirm their agreement to those provisions. In order to find the terms of service, one had (or would have had) to proceed to the bottom of the page where there were several "hyperlinks" including one entitled "Terms." Upon clicking the "Terms" hyperlink, the screen would display the terms of service section of the website. A person could become a MySpace member without ever reading or otherwise becoming aware of the provisions and conditions of the MySpace terms of service by merely clicking on the "check box" and then the "Sign Up" button without first accessing the "Terms" section.

As used in its website, "terms of service" refers to the "MySpace.com Terms of Use Agreement" ("MSTOS"). The MSTOS in 2006 stated, *inter alia:*

> By using the Services, you represent and warrant that (a) all registration information you submit is truthful and accurate; (b) you will maintain the accuracy of such information; (c) you are 14 years of age or older; and (d) your use of the Services does not violate any applicable law or regulation.

Id. at 2.

The MSTOS prohibited the posting of a wide range of content on the website including (but not limited to) material that ... "d) provides information that you know is false or misleading or promotes illegal activities or conduct that is abusive, threatening, obscene, defamatory or libelous"; e) "includes a photograph of another person that you have posted without that person's consent." The MSTOS warned users that "information provided by other MySpace.com Members (for instance, in their Profile) may contain inaccurate, inappropriate, offensive or sexually explicit material, products or services, and MySpace.com assumes no responsibility or liability for this material."

At one point, MySpace was receiving an estimated 230,000 new accounts per day and eventually the number of profiles exceeded 400 million with over 100 million unique visitors worldwide. Generally speaking, MySpace would not monitor new accounts to determine if they complied with the terms of service.

Once a member is registered and creates his or her profile, the data is housed on computer servers which are located in Los Angeles County. All communications among MySpace members are routed from the sender's computer through the MySpace servers in Los Angeles.

CFAA

In 2006, the CFAA (18 U.S.C. § 1030) provided in relevant part that:

(a) Whoever—

> (2) intentionally accesses a computer without authorization or exceeds authorized access, and thereby obtains—

>> (C) information from any protected computer if the conduct involved an interstate or foreign communication;

> shall be punished as provided in subsection (c) of this section.

(c) The punishment for an offense under subsection (a)—

> (2)(A) a fine under this title or imprisonment for not more than one year.

As used in the CFAA, the term "computer" "includes any data storage facility or communication facility directly related to or operating in conjunction with such device...." 18 U.S.C. § 1030(e)(1). The term "protected computer" "means a computer—(B) which is used in interstate or foreign commerce or communication...." *Id.* § 1030(e)(2). The term "exceeds authorized access" means "to access a computer with authorization and to use such access to obtain or alter information in the computer that the accesser is not entitled so to obtain or alter...." *Id.* § 1030(e)(6).

The misdemeanor 18 U.S.C. § 1030(a)(2)(C) crime consist[s] of the following three elements:

> First, the defendant intentionally [accessed without authorization] [exceeded authorized access of] a computer;

> Second, the defendant's access of the computer involved an interstate or foreign communication; and

> Third, by [accessing without authorization] [exceeding authorized access to] a computer, the defendant obtained information from a computer ... [used in interstate or foreign commerce or communication]....

Ninth Circuit Model Criminal Jury Instruction 8.79 (2003 Ed.) (brackets in original).

In this case, a central question is whether a computer user's intentional violation of one or more provisions in an Internet website's terms of services (where those terms condition access to and/or use of the website's services upon agreement to and compliance with the terms) satisfies the first element of section 1030(a)(2)(C). If the answer to that question is "yes," then seemingly, any and every conscious violation of that website's terms of service will constitute a CFAA misdemeanor.

Initially, it is noted that the latter two elements of the section 1030(a)(2)(C) crime will always be met when an individual using a computer contacts or communicates with an Internet website. Addressing them in reverse order, the third element requires "obtain[ing] information" from a "protected computer"—which is defined in 18 U.S.C. § 1030(e)(2)(B) as a computer "which is used in interstate or foreign commerce or communication...." "Obtain [ing] information from a computer" has been described as "'includ[ing] mere observation of the data. Actual aspiration ... need not be proved in order to establish a violation....'" S.Rep. No. 99–432. at 6–7 (1986). As for the "interstate or foreign commerce or communication" component, the Ninth Circuit found the Internet to be "similar to— and often using—our national network of telephone lines." It went on to conclude that: "[i]t can not be questioned that the nation's vast network of telephone lines constitutes interstate commerce," and, a fortiori, it seems clear that use of the internet is intimately related to interstate commerce. Thus, the third element is satisfied whenever a person using a computer contacts an Internet website and reads any response from that site.

As to the second element (*i.e.*, that the accessing of the computer involve an interstate or foreign communication), an initial question arises as to whether the communication itself must be interstate or foreign (*i.e.*, it is transmitted across state lines or country borders) or whether it simply requires that the computer system, which is accessed for purposes of the communication, is interstate or foreign in nature (for example, akin to a national telephone system). The term "interstate or foreign communication" is not defined in the CFAA. However, it has been held that "[a]s a practical matter, a computer providing a 'web-based' application accessible through the internet would satisfy the 'interstate communication' requirement." *Paradigm Alliance, Inc. v. Celeritas Technologies, LLC,* 248 F.R.D. 598, 602 (D. Kan.2008). This interpretation is consistent with the legislative history of the CFAA. Therefore, where contact is made between an individual's computer and an Internet website, the second element is per se established.

As to the first element (*i.e.* intentionally accessing a computer without authorization or exceeding authorized access), the primary question here is whether any conscious violation of an Internet website's terms of service will cause an individual's contact with the website via computer to become "intentionally access[ing] ... without authorization" or "exceeding authorization." Initially, it is noted that three of the key terms of the first element (*i.e.*, "intentionally," "access a computer," and "without authorization") are undefined, and there is a considerable amount of controversy as to the meaning of the latter two phrases.

Congress did not define the phrase 'without authorization,' perhaps assuming that the words speak for themselves. The meaning, however, has proven to be elusive. Under § 1030(a)(2)(C), the "requisite intent" is "to obtain unauthorized access of a protected computer." The government need not also prove that ... the information was used to any particular ends. *See also* S.Rep. No.104-357, at 7–8 ("[T]he crux of the offense under subsection 1030(a)(2)(C) ... is abuse of a computer to obtain the information.").

As to the term "accesses a computer," one would think that the dictionary definition of [the] transitive verb "access" would be sufficient. That definition is "to gain or have access to; to retrieve data from, or add data to, a database...." *Webster's New World*

Dictionary, Third College Edition, 7 (1988). Most courts that have actually considered the issue of the meaning of the word "access" in the CFAA have basically turned to the dictionary meaning.

As to the term "without authorization," in this particular case, as conceded by the Government, the only basis for finding that Drew intentionally accessed MySpace's computer/ servers without authorization and/or in excess of authorization was her and/or her co-conspirator's violations of the MSTOS by deliberately creating the false Josh Evans profile, posting a photograph of a juvenile without his permission and pretending to be a sixteen year old O'Fallon resident for the purpose of communicating with Megan. Therefore, if conscious violations of the My Space terms of service were not sufficient to satisfy the first element of the CFAA misdemeanor violation Drew's Rule 29(c) motion would have to be granted on that basis alone. However, this Court concludes that an intentional breach of the MSTOS can potentially constitute accessing the MySpace computer/server without authorization and/or in excess of authorization under the statute.

It cannot be considered a stretch of the law to hold that the owner of an Internet website has the right to establish the extent to (and the conditions under) which members of the public will be allowed access to information, services and/or applications which are available on the website. Nor can it be doubted that the owner can relay and impose those limitations/restrictions/conditions by means of written notice such as terms of service or use provisions placed on the home page of the website. While issues might be raised in particular cases as to the sufficiency of the notice and/or sufficiency of the user's assent to the terms, and while public policy considerations might in turn limit enforcement of particular restrictions, the vast majority of the courts (that have considered the issue) have held that a website's terms of service/use can define what is (and/or is not) authorized access viz-a-viz that website.

Here, to become a MySpace member and thereby be allowed to communicate with other members and fully utilize the MySpace Services, one had to click on a box to confirm that the user had agreed to the MySpace Terms of Service. Clearly, the MSTOS was capable of defining the scope of authorized access of visitors, members and/or users to the website.

Contravention of the Void-for-Vagueness Doctrine

The void-for-vagueness doctrine has two prongs: 1) a definitional/notice sufficiency requirement and, more importantly, 2) a guideline setting element to govern law enforcement. To avoid contravening the void-for-vagueness doctrine, the criminal statute must contain "relatively clear guidelines as to prohibited conduct" and provide "objective criteria" to evaluate whether a crime has been committed. However, a difficulty in determining whether certain marginal offenses are within the meaning of the language under attack as vague does not automatically render a statute unconstitutional for indefiniteness.... Impossible standards of specificity are not required. What renders a statute vague is not the possibility that it will sometimes be difficult to determine whether the incriminating fact it establishes has been proved; but rather the indeterminacy of precisely what that fact is.

The pivotal issue herein is whether basing a CFAA misdemeanor violation upon the conscious violation of a website's terms of service runs afoul of the void-for-vagueness doctrine. This Court concludes that it does primarily because of the absence of minimal guidelines to govern law enforcement, but also because of actual notice deficiencies. The question is whether individuals of "common intelligence" are on notice that a breach of a terms of service contract can become a crime under the CFAA. Arguably, they are not.

First, an initial inquiry is whether the statute, as it is written, provides sufficient notice. Here, the language of section 1030(a)(2)(C) does not explicitly state (nor does it implicitly suggest) that the CFAA has "criminalized breaches of contract" in the context of website terms of service. Normally, breaches of contract are not the subject of criminal prosecution. Thus, while "ordinary people" might expect to be exposed to civil liabilities for violating a contractual provision, they would not expect criminal penalties. This would especially be the case where the services provided by MySpace are in essence offered at no cost to the users and, hence, there is no specter of the users "defrauding" MySpace in any monetary sense.

Second, if a website's terms of service controls what is "authorized" and what is "exceeding authorization"—which in turn governs whether an individual's accessing information or services on the website is criminal or not, section 1030(a)(2)(C) would be unacceptably vague because it is unclear whether any or all violations of terms of service will render the access unauthorized, or whether only certain ones will. For example, in the present case, MySpace's terms of service prohibits a member from engaging in a multitude of activities on the website, including such conduct as "criminal or tortious activity," "gambling," "advertising to ... any Member to buy or sell any products." The MSTOS does not specify which precise terms of service, when breached, will result in a termination of MySpace's authorization for the visitor/member to access the website. If *any* violation of *any* term of service is held to make the access unauthorized, that strategy would probably resolve this particular vagueness issue; but it would, in turn, render the statute incredibly overbroad and contravene the second prong of the void-for-vagueness doctrine as to setting guidelines to govern law enforcement.

Third, by utilizing violations of the terms of service as the basis for the section 1030(a)(2)(C) crime, that approach makes the website owner—in essence—the party who ultimately defines the criminal conduct. This will lead to further vagueness problems. The owner's description of a term of service might itself be so vague as to make the visitor or member reasonably unsure of what the term of service covers.

Fourth, because terms of service are essentially a contractual means for setting the scope of authorized access, a level of indefiniteness arises from the necessary application of contract law in general and/or other contractual requirements within the applicable terms of service to any criminal prosecution. For example, the MSTOS has a provision wherein "any dispute" between MySpace and a visitor/member/user arising out of the terms of service is subject to arbitration upon the demand of either party. Before a breach of a term of service can be found and/or the effect of that breach upon MySpace's ability to terminate the visitor/member/user's access to the site can be determined, the issue would be subject to arbitration. Thus, a question arises as to whether a finding of unauthorized access or in excess of authorized access can be made without arbitration.

Treating a violation of a website's terms of service, without more, to be sufficient to constitute "intentionally access[ing] a computer without authorization or exceed[ing] authorized access" would result in transforming section 1030(a)(2)(C) into an overwhelmingly overbroad enactment that would convert a multitude of otherwise innocent Internet users into misdemeanant criminals. Obvious examples of such breadth would include: 1) the lonely-heart who submits intentionally inaccurate data about his or her age, height and/or physical appearance, which contravenes the MSTOS prohibition against providing "information that you know is false or misleading"; 2) the student who posts candid photographs of classmates without their permission, which breaches the MSTOS provision covering "a photograph of another person that you have posted without that person's consent"; and/or 3) the exasperated parent who sends out a group message to neighborhood friends entreating them to purchase his or her daughter's girl scout cookies, which transgresses the MSTOS rule against "advertising to, or solicitation of, any Member to buy or sell any products or services through the Services." However, one need not consider hypotheticals to demonstrate the problem. In this case, Megan (who was then 13 years old) had her own profile on MySpace, which was in clear violation of the MSTOS which requires that users be "14 years of age or older." No one would seriously suggest that Megan's conduct was criminal or should be subject to criminal prosecution.

In sum, if any conscious breach of a website's terms of service is held to be sufficient by itself to constitute intentionally accessing a computer without authorization or in excess of authorization, the result will be that section 1030(a)(2)(C) becomes a law that affords too much discretion to the police and too little notice to citizens who wish to use the Internet.

Notes and Questions

1. Do you agree that the site of the servers should be the (or "a") venue for any criminal prosecution?

2. Citing the Senate Report on the bill, Judge Wu states that: "Obtain [ing] information from a computer" has been described as "'includ[ing] mere observation of the data. Actual aspiration ... need not be proved in order to establish a violation....'" Do you believe that observation of data provided by the developer on the site is "obtaining" information, and that no aspiration is necessary to be criminally liable? Would the same rules apply if the perpetrator hacked into a star's phone and just "observed" compromising pictures?

3. Should breaches of EULAs and TOS Agreements ever be criminalized? Would expulsion from the world or site be sufficient punishment for Ms. Drew?

4. Could a TOS Agreement ever be written to satisfy vagueness concerns? If so, what provisions would you change? (*MySpace* has changed the language of its TOS in this regard a little since *Drew*, but the gist of it is the same as it was when *Drew* was decided. If you want to view the language, *see* https://myspace.com/pages/terms.)

5. Videogame hacking is not limited to either personal or financial information. A recent *New York Times* article makes this point:

> Hackers are breaking into American companies for credit card numbers, passwords, trade secrets and — it turns out — for phony video game scores.
>
> For the past five years, hackers inside China have been breaking into American video game makers' systems, collecting proprietary source code in an ambitious effort to crack the games for free use and to develop tools to cheat them, according to research by the counter threat unit at Dell SecureWorks, a security firm that was acquired by Dell in 2011.
>
> Dell SecureWorks' researchers said that in many of the cases they had witnessed, hackers conducted extensive reconnaissance on their victim organizations before attacking them. They used public information to track down employees with administrative privileges, then used so-called brute force means in which they deployed computers to test millions of combinations of user names and passwords to break into their accounts.

From there, they used their foothold to install malicious tools, including remote access tools, backdoors and keystroke loggers, onto the computers of employees who had access to video game source code.

At first, researchers said it was unclear whether hackers were stealing source code to copy games and sell their own versions. But they were able to trace the attacks back to two hacker aliases in China who are active in China's video game cracking community. The researchers now believe the hackers are after the source code to crack the games for free use, or find backdoors that would allow them to outscore their competitors.

In some cases, researchers said, the tools and techniques these two individuals developed were more sophisticated than many of the so-called spear phishing attacks deployed by China's People's Liberation Army hacking units, like the Shanghai-based Unit 61398 and aerospace hacking Unit 61486.

Nicole Perlroth, *Hackers Target Video Games for Fun, Profit and Better Scores*, N.Y. TIMES, (August 24, 2014), http://bits.blogs.nytimes.com/2014/08/24/hackers-target-video-games-for-fun-profit-and-better-scores/?_php=true&_type=blogs&_php=true&_type=blogs&_r=1.

* * *

One alternative to criminal punishment when immoral or illegal acts have caused real world damage is to leave it to the victims of those acts to pursue civil remedies against the perpetrators, and it is to those issues that we turn next.

Civil Law Issues Involving Virtual Worlds

The types of suits that can arise between users are potentially limitless. For example, Professors Lastowka and Hunter recount an unusual dispute that took place in a textual game called "*MUD*":

> One MUD property dispute [occurred] in which Martha Jones and Dank engaged in a nasty and protracted battle over Martha's poisonous flowers and Dank's dog. Both the flowers and the dog were—like the "adjoining" properties that Martha and Dank inhabited—nothing more than programmed objects in the database. Dank, however, was genuinely angered when his "dog" was killed by eating a poisonous "petal" from one of Martha's "flowers" that had ended up on Dank's property. For her part, Martha was indignant: there was no reason for the dog to have "died," as Dank could have programmed a hardier dog that was immune to Martha's virtual poison. Both parties invested in the dispute the kind of passion and righteous indignation usually reserved for real-world, across-the-fence, property disputes.

F. Gregory Lastowka & Dan Hunter, The Laws of the Virtual Worlds, 92 Cal. L. Rev. 1 35, 36 (2004).

———————

Notes and Questions

1. The procedural issues in civil suits arising from virtual worlds are, in some ways, even more intractable than those involved in criminal law. For example, if one of the victims wanted to file a civil suit against the perpetrator of the Ginko scam above, who would he or she sue? Without subpoena power, how would he or she get the perpetrator's

name (assuming the name was not an alias)?[20] How would the plaintiff serve the perpetrator with the summons and complaint? Even if service by publication was allowed, where would the publication have to occur and from whom would the plaintiff collect, assuming a judgment (default or otherwise) would be entered? And of course, there are similar issues with regard to venue, personal and subject matter jurisdiction, choice of law, etc. as discussed above for criminal law.

There are some advantages to allowing civil litigation over criminal to regulate user and avatar conduct, however. First, there is no need to interest a third party—a prosecutor—to vindicate a victim's rights. It can be done directly by the injured party. Second, because it is the injured party bringing the action, there is likely to be a greater tenacity to see resolution of the lawsuit through and overcome the procedural issues. Third, a gamer would understand the technology and appreciate the value of any damage caused in the virtual world.

2. One area of civil liability in which there has been scholarly speculation concerns potential defamation and product disparagement actions. For example, there is at least one *Second Life* user who amassed virtual real estate valued at over $1 million real world dollars. She was dubbed "the Virtual Donald Trump." What if a competitor began spreading false rumors that the mogul cheated in her virtual deals, or committed other sorts of fraud? Suppose some residents believed these rumors and stopped dealing with the virtual Donald. Would a defamation action lie? Would the public/private figure doctrine of American defamation law apply, and would it be judged by the avatar's public figure status in the virtual world or the real world? What if a worker in the virtual Nike store disparaged virtual Reebok shoes? Real world Reebok shoes? For more information, *see* Bettina M. Chin, *Regulating Your Second Life: Defamation in Virtual Worlds,* 72 BROOK. L. REV. 1303 (2007).

* * *

Probably the majority of legal issues arising in virtual worlds and MMORPGs concern the treatment of in-world property. A fundamental issue with virtual property is that it does not exist. As we describe above, battleaxes in *WoW,* or houses in *Second Life* are, in reality, merely lines of programming code that reside on the developer's server. But they appear real in the game and players certainly treat them as such. The fact that this property may, at base, be intangible is not a bar to giving its owners legal rights. Modern property theory certainly bestows property protections to the owners of intellectual property, for example.[21]

As the following excerpts illustrate, however, whether virtual world property qualifies as "property" under modern theories of Lockean property rights is unclear:

> Nevertheless, as of now, America does not honor virtual property rights, due in part to the lack of any virtual property litigation or legislation. All of the cases where it appeared the court would have to consider virtual property rights have settled. Many articles discuss the possibility of virtual property rights, and one

---

20. Note that in certain cases brought under the DMCA, "Doe" pleading is allowed, along with a statutory right to subpoena the ISP to determine the name of the account holder, in which case the pleading is allowed to be amended to reflect the account holder as defendant. The procedure is explained in Charles Biederman & Danny Andrews, *Applying Copyright Law to User-Generated Content,* L.A. LAW. 12, 15–17 (May 2008).

21. Jack M. Balkin, Law and Liberty in Virtual Worlds, 49 N.Y.L. Sch. L. Rev. 63 (2004) (discussing prospective role of real-world law in virtual worlds).

of the arguments most frequently advocated in favor of recognizing these rights is one based on John Locke's theory of labor desert.

> Lockean labor desert theory allocates property rights to those who invest their time and effort in distinguishing an object from a commons. When a person mixes her labor with an object from a commons, the person makes that object her property so long as her labor contributed the greatest part of the asset's value. When one person labors to acquire a good, that person is entitled to reap its benefit over one who expended no labor.

Ross Shikowitz, *License to Kill*, 75 BROOK. L. REV. 1015, 1044 (2010).

On the other side:

> In sum, a labor theory justification for extending property rights to virtual resources does not work for two reasons. First, Locke's labor theory concerns the acquisition of property rights in an object taken from a state of nature. Virtual property does not exist within a state of nature, however, and therefore cannot be acquired via Locke's labor theory. Second, United States law has routinely rejected the labor theory of property acquisition. *Pierson* [*v. Post*, 2 Am. Dec. 264 (N.Y. 1805)] and *Feist* [*Publications, Inc. v. Rural Telephone Service, Inc.*, 499 U.S. 340 (1991)] both illustrate these rejections. The fox in *Pierson* was acquired through capture, not through the effort and labor of the foxhunter in chasing it down. Similarly, the application of labor in compiling facts held in the public domain did not grant creators of a phone book intellectual property rights in those facts. Therefore, adopting this labor theory approach in the concept of virtual property would require fundamental changes to property theory and law.

John William Nelson, *The Virtual Property Problem: What Property Rights In Virtual Resources Might Look Like, How They Might Work, And Why They Are a Bad Idea*, 41 Mc-GEORGE L. REV. 281, 292 (2010).

Would virtual property be considered "property" under a Lockean theory of property rights?

Another theory to determine what is "property" involves an examination of rights associated with the item and posits that "property" exists if there is a sufficient "bundle" of rights given to the owner by society over that item. While no one right is crucial to the viability of the bundle, three rights are often considered important: (1) the right to exclude others from using the item; (2) the right to use the item; and (3) the right to transfer one's interest in the item to another.[22]

Applying these "rights" to a virtual game property demonstrates a difference in how various developers regulate them. When a game is first created, everything in it is the property of the developer, or items the developer has a license to display. But once these developers allow users to bring objects of their own creation into the games, their EULAs or TOS Agreements take over the regulation of ownership rights.

All metaverses allow players to use the virtual property they lawfully come across in the context of a game, but some restrict the conduct by which such property can be acquired, e.g., no "stealing" another player's objects. But if a gamer stumbles across virtual

---

22. *See, e.g.*, David P. Sheldon, Comment, *Claiming Ownership but Getting Owned: Contractual Limitations on Asserting Property Interests in Virtual Goods*, 54 UCLA L. REV. 751, 758–59 (2007); *and* J.E. Penner, *The "Bundle of Rights" Picture of Property*, 43 UCLA L. REV. 711 (1996).

property, purchases it from another, is given a present of it, etc., there is generally no prohibition to using the item. In *WoW*, for example, players are given mailboxes just so they can exchange money and property, and there are auctions whereby property can be lawfully, i.e., within the rules of the game, exchanged.

One divergence among developers deals with the right to transfer, i.e., sell, property. Traditionally, developers banned all sales of virtual property for real world money (although some allowed the sale for in-game currency or points). However, in part because users circumvented these rules and sold virtual games on eBay and like sites, in part to accommodate players and keep them interested, and in part to develop alternative revenue streams, many large game developers have changed their policy, and now encourage the sale of virtual property. Sony Online Entertainment (SOE) developed a program, known as "Player Studio," that allows users to create their own virtual items for games like *EverQuest* and *EverQuest II*, and then sell those items on a digital storefront for real-world money, with SOE taking 40 percent of each user's sales revenue.[23] The program is similar to Valve's "Steam Workshop," which in 2013, paid creators over $10,000,000 for their digital goods. With only 661 creators, each made an average of $15,000 and some made up to $500,000. Currently, 90 percent of the items in Valve's game *Team Fortress 2* are user-generated, and 17 million users own a total of 500 million items in the game.[24]

With regard to the right to exclude, i.e., the right to keep the property that a user invented and brought into the game for one's own use, and to exclude the developer from acquiring any interest in it (or other resident from copying it), by far the most prevalent treatment is to deny this right to the inventors of virtual objects. Most of the virtual world EULAs have a "retention of rights" clause which provides that any programming code residing on the developers' servers, even code representing, e.g., a hoverboard or breastplate invented and brought into the game by a user, immediately and forever becomes the property of the developers. One significant exception from this model is *Second Life*, which initially brought it respect among gamers. Perhaps that respect is still there, but its property policies have also brought it litigation, as seen in the *Evans* case which follows.

Evans v. Linden Research, Inc.

United States District Court for the Northern District of California, 2012
No. C-11-01078 DMR, 2012 WL 5877579

Ryu, United States Magistrate Judge.

This putative class action involves the internet role-playing virtual world entitled Second Life. In Second Life, participants create characters called avatars to represent themselves and to interact with other avatars in a huge virtual world. Participants establish reputations, run and patronize businesses, and buy and sell virtual items such as clothing, cars, and

---

23. Tom Curtis, *New SOE Program Lets Players Create and Sell Virtual Items*, Gamasutra (September 6, 2012), http://www.gamasutra.com/view/news/177268/New_SOE_program_lets_players_create_and_sell_virtual_items.php#.UH2KS8VY3ng.

24. Sean Hollister, *Creators Made $15,000 Last Year*, The Verge (January 16, 2014), http://www.theverge.com/gaming/2014/1/16/5316248/on-average-team-fortress-2-and-dota-2-item-creators-made-15000-last.

homes (referred to as "virtual items"). They also purchase and sell pieces of "virtual land" from Defendant Linden Research, Inc. ("Linden") and other participants. Participants use in-game money, known as "lindens," to perform in-world monetary transactions. The linden currency can be purchased with, as well as exchanged into, U.S. dollars.

Linden retains and stores virtual items and virtual land on its servers. Participants with virtual land must pay Linden monthly "tier fees," similar to property taxes, that vary in amount depending on the size of the virtual land that they possess. According to Linden, these tier fees help pay for the maintenance of the servers on which the game data is stored. After purchasing virtual land, a user may "inhabit" it, rent it out, split it, and/or resell all or part of it to other participants. Linden continually creates "new" virtual land; once Linden sells land to a participant, it continues to exist in Second Life and is not deleted or removed from the game.

The central dispute in this lawsuit is the meaning of "ownership" within Second Life. As discussed in more detail below, Plaintiffs contend that Linden and Defendant Philip Rosedale, Linden's founder, former CEO, and current board member, represented to Second Life participants that they would have an actual ownership interest in the virtual land and items in Second Life's virtual world. By contrast, Defendants argue that when they represented that participants would have "ownership" rights, they meant that Second Life users would own a copyright in their creations.

The battle over the meaning of "ownership" has its roots in Second Life's marketing efforts. Linden launched Second Life in 2003. Plaintiffs allege that to differentiate Second Life from other massively multiplayer role-playing games ("MMORPGs"), Linden "made a calculated business decision to depart from the industry standard of denying that participants had any rights to virtual items, land and/or goods" and "globally represented to participants ... that their ownership rights and intellectual property rights to the virtual items, land and goods held in the participants' accounts would be preserved and recognized." Plaintiffs further allege that over the next several years, Defendant Rosedale began a campaign to attract users to Second Life by publicly representing that users retained "ownership" rights to the land they purchased from Linden, and that they retained intellectual property rights for any virtual items or content created by the user. During this time, the following statement appeared prominently on the Second Life homepage: "SECOND LIFE IS AN ONLINE, 3D VIRTUAL WORLD, IMAGINED, CREATED AND *OWNED* BY ITS RESIDENTS." (emphasis in original).

According to Plaintiffs, sometime after 2007, following a dispute with an individual user regarding Linden's alleged confiscation of virtual property [*Bragg v. Linden Research*, reproduced in §11.20, *supra.*—Ed.] Linden abruptly removed the word "owned" from the statement on its homepage, so that it became: "SECOND LIFE IS AN ONLINE, 3D VIRTUAL WORLD, IMAGINED AND CREATED BY ITS RESIDENTS." Plaintiffs allege that after years of representations by Defendants about ownership, designed to induce users to invest U.S. dollars in virtual land and items, Linden began to strip ownership rights from its users. Linden's decision to strip Second Life users of their ownership rights culminated in March 2010, when Linden modified its Terms of Service ("TOS"). For the first time, the TOS stated that "[v]irtual land is in-world space that we license." Participants who had purchased virtual land or items prior to the March 2010 TOS were required to accept the new terms; there was no ability to opt out. If a user did not click "I accept" to the new terms, they could no longer access their virtual land or items.

The parties have very different understandings of what Defendants intended to provide when they offered "ownership" in Second Life virtual land and items. Plaintiffs contend that Second Life participants gained actual ownership rights in virtual land and items that exist in cyberspace. Defendants assert that Second Life users own copyrights in the virtual land and items that they purchase or create.

Plaintiffs in their Second Amended Complaint, their understanding of Second Life "ownership" goes well beyond intellectual property rights:

> The owner of the account is entitled to control the account and valuables' electromagnetic record and may freely sell or transfer it. Although a participant's account and valuables are "virtual," they are valuable property in the real world. Participants can auction them, sell them, license them or transfer them online and through other independent third parties, like eBay.com, slexchange.com, and others.

According to Plaintiffs, "the system of transferring the virtual items and objects created by a participant mirrors that of the real world in nearly every respect." Further, Plaintiffs allege that a user's interests in virtual property and virtual land "persist regardless of the system currently connected to [the virtual property and virtual land], separate from the intellectual property that exists in Defendants' underlying code."

In contrast, Defendants contend that Second Life users can create content in the virtual world and that those users own the copyright in their creations, as well as a license to use the Second Life computing resources, as set forth in the TOS. However, according to Defendants, Second Life users do not have ownership interests in real or personal property beyond what is provided by contract through the TOS. Defendants contend that Second Life participants own intellectual property in the form of a copyright, for, as defense counsel succinctly articulated during oral argument, "You have to remember this stuff isn't real. It's a game on a computer."

[A Linden executive testified — Ed.]: Linden has always from day one unchanged [sic] and they made no allegation that we have changed the rules, have told people that when you create content in Linden — in Second Life, unlike in other games, you own the intellectual property. We have never interfered with anyone's copyrights. That's all you can own in a work of expression, right? The copy that you put on Linden's server is Linden's, and it's always been very clear. The copy that you have in your own computer, if you put a copy in your own computer, when we close your account, we haven't taken away that copy and we haven't taken away your copyright. What you owned you still own. If you owned the copyright, you still do. Nothing — there is no allegation that any cognizable property right has been taken away from anyone as a — as a result. The property right here is a copyright and it is never taken away.

Our right to remove the bits from our servers of a copy that you licensed to us, is not a property right that the plaintiff ever owned. There's no coherent allegation that there is any such property right. It is not real property. It's not personal property; it is an intellectual property.

Plaintiffs are individuals who have participated in Second Life. They allege that they purchased virtual items and/or virtual land and subsequently had their accounts unilaterally terminated or suspended by Linden, and were not compensated for the value of the virtual land, items, and/or currency in their accounts. In their Second Amended Complaint, Plaintiffs further assert that Defendants made false representations about ownership of virtual land and virtual items, and wrongfully confiscated virtual land and items from them, as well as from the class members they seek to represent.

———————

Notes and Questions

1. The *Evans* court certified a class consisting of, "All persons whose assets, including virtual items, virtual land, and/or currency in lindens and/or U.S. dollars, have been deliberately and intentionally converted by Defendant Linden's suspension or closure of their Second Life accounts."

After two years of spirited litigation, a settlement was finally reached and approved by the court, at some expense to Linden:

> Linden will make payments to class members as follows. First, Linden will return up to 100% of the U.S. dollar balances in class members' accounts by transmitting the funds to class members' PayPal accounts within ten days of Linden verifying the validity of each class member's claim. As of August 20, 2013, the date of the amended settlement agreement, the total of such funds is approximately $24,236.90.

> Next, Linden will return up to 100% of the Linden dollar balances in class members' accounts. To accomplish this, Linden will list the Linden dollars on the official Second Life currency exchange and transmit the converted U.S. dollars within ten days of the sale, and will waive Second Life's commission on the conversions. As of the date of the Revised Agreement, the total of such funds was approximately L$43,337,311, with an exchange rate of approximately 252 Linden dollars to one U.S. dollar, for an approximate value of $171,973.46.

> With respect to virtual land, Linden will pay two Linden dollars per square meter of virtual land held by class members. As of the date of the Revised Agreement, the total amount of virtual land is 275,872 square meters. Defendants will waive Second Life's commission on the exchanges and will transmit the value of the Linden dollars, converted to U.S. dollars, within ten days of Linden verifying the validity of each class member's claim. By the court's own calculations, the total U.S. dollar value of such virtual land is approximately $2,189 (275,872 x L$2 / 252). In addition, Linden will refund a $1,000 setup fee to the class member who possessed a virtual island.

> Finally, regarding virtual items, Linden will offer class members making valid claims the choice of (a) $15 per class member (not account) whose account(s) contains virtual items, transmitted by Linden to his or her PayPal account within ten days of Linden verifying the validity of the claim; or (b) the class members may attempt to sell their virtual items on the Second Life Marketplace, and Linden will waive Second Life's commission on the sales. Those class members who elect the second option will be entitled to all proceeds of the sales.

> In addition to the relief described above, Linden will pay up to $50,000 for notice and administration costs. The Revised Agreement authorizes class counsel to apply to the court for an award of attorneys' fees and expenses up to $175,000 [to be paid by Linden—ED.]. The payment of attorneys' fees and expenses is separate from and in addition to the other relief afforded the class members.

Evans v. Linden Research, Inc., No. C-11-01078 DMR, 2014 WL 1724891, at *2–3; *5.

2. The first case alleging illegal "copying" of someone else's virtual property that we know about in the U.S. was styled, *Eros, LLC v. Simon*, Case No. CV-07 4447 (2007), filed in the Eastern District of New York. The case is further explained in the following excerpt:

> Kevin Alderman runs an adult content company called Eros LLC. He also has an avatar in Second Life, named Stroker Serpentine. Through Serpentine, Eros

sells virtual items in Second Life, including a piece of furniture called the SexGen bed, which contains more than 150 sex animations ... Eros filed a copyright infringement lawsuit against Second Life resident Volkov Catteneo (an avatar) accusing Catteneo of making and offering for sale unauthorized copies of Eros's SexGen bed and other items. Because Eros did not know the identity of the resident who owned the Catteneo avatar, however, it had to file the case against John Doe. Filing copyright infringement cases against John Doe is an established practice in Internet cases. Eros later served a subpoena on Linden Labs to force disclosure of the alleged infringer's identity.

Section 512(h)(2)(c) of the DMCA permits a copyright owner to subpoena the identity of the individual allegedly responsible for copyright infringement on the condition that the information about the individual's identity can only be used in connection with protecting the intellectual property rights of the copyright owner. The subpoenas Eros filed led to two computers allegedly used by Robert Leatherwood. Eros later named Leatherwood as the defendant in the case. He did not answer or otherwise respond to the complaint, so a default judgment was entered, which operates as a judgment on the merits and allows Eros to seek damages, fees, and injunctive relief and use the judicial system to attach Leatherwood's assets to satisfy any award of damages.

While the court did not have to reach the substantive legal issues in the Eros case, it did at least establish that copyright owners have rights in virtual worlds and that existing laws and procedures can be used to enforce those rights.

Charles Biederman & Danny Andrews, *Applying Copyright Law to User-Generated Content*, L.A. Law. 12, 15–17 (May 2008).

* * *

Should civil courts take the same approach as that suggested by Professors Lastowka and Hunter regarding criminal law, i.e., leave it to the developers of the worlds to enforce civil wrongs via their powers under the EULAs and TOU Agreements and dismiss for lack of jurisdiction any suit in the real world that arises due to acts in a virtual world?

One commentator has suggested otherwise. In *Virtual Insanity*, Los Angeles Daily Journal, December 3, 2008, at p. 6, one of this book's authors, (Brain) suggested the best way to take care of civil actions, and a potential solution regarding service, venue, and identity problems in civil suits would be a procedure that: (1) requires that any in-world dispute must be resolved via some in-world dispute resolution service, e.g., arbitrations by e-mail or by virtual court systems, made applicable to all residents via the world's EULA or TOS Agreement; (2) allows service and testimony via avatar name, rather than real world name; and (3) would allow the prevailing party to discover the real world name of his or her opponent upon prevailing in the dispute only when enforcement (monetary judgment, injunction, etc.) becomes an issue. What advantages or problems do you see with this approach?

3. In the real world, if an individual buys a coat and the stitching is faulty, there are remedies—under consumer protection statutes, the state's commercial code, common law warranty, etc. What happens in the virtual world in the same situation? Would the UCC apply to a faulty representation of a coat caused by botched programming code? The Restatement of Contracts? Would some kind of reference to prevailing law be necessary in the EULA or TOS?

4. Another civil liability issue arising in virtual worlds is whether proceeds from activities that generate in-world income, such as L$, etc., should be taxable. Although there are some who advocate not taxing any proceeds until they are actually cashed in for real world currency, *see e.g.*, Brian Camp, *The Play's the Thing: A Theory of Taxing Virtual Worlds*, 59 HASTINGS L.J. 1 (2007), Professor Ted Seto of Loyola Law School Los Angeles has made the case that taxation issues of computer worlds are more nuanced than Professor Camp's approach. Professor Seto argues that:

A. In worlds where only points or the like are accumulated, and the points are non-redeemable or non-convertible into real world currency under the rules of the world, taxation should only occur if the player somehow manages to monetize the points, e.g., selling them on eBay or the like.

B. In worlds like *Second Life* where the player accumulates points or in-world currencies that are easily redeemable or convertible into real world currency under the world's EULAs, a resident who accumulates in-world currency should be treated for taxation purposes as a cash method participant under standard constructive receipt rules, or as a cash method participant under standard cash equivalence rules, depending on whether the in-world benefit or currency is re-deemable or convertible to real world currency, respectively. In other words, someone who works in the Nike Store in *Second Life* and is paid in L$ by Nike, should be treated as having earned reportable income for tax purposes because of the existence of the Lindex exchange [and exchange run inside *Second* Life that posts daily exchange rates between L$ and real world currencies—Ed.] and the ease by which those L$ can be turned into dollars, yen etc.

See Theodore P. Seto, *When Is a Game Only a Game?: The Taxation of Virtual Worlds*, 77 U. CIN. L. REV. 1027 (2009).

Do you agree with Professor Seto?[25]

5. In July 2007, an e-justice center opened in *Second Life*, presenting a forum for the mutually agreed ADR of *Second Life* disputes. It is run by the Portuguese Ministry of Justice and the New University of Lisbon Law School. At the Center, law professors, law students, and Ministry officials are available to resolve *Second Life* civil disputes. The Center has multi-lingual capabilities, and enforcement of its rulings tends not to be an issue because the participants have to put up the entire amount in controversy before the case is heard, which is then distributed back to the parties in accordance with the arbitrator's decision. As with all ADR mechanisms, advantages of the Center include flexibility in scheduling, privacy, speed of decision, and the ability to get a decision in a relatively small (in dollar amount) case.

Some commentators have opined that virtual worlds present an unprecedented opportunity to develop different laws and procedures than those used in real world courts. They argue that virtual worlds should be a kind of sociological Petri dish to determine whether hidebound legal remedies and institutions can be improved. If true, would having different evidentiary standards, or mandatory ADR, or alternative burdens of proof for defamation actions be a good place to start?

6. Another issue that can arise in litigation involving developers is whether the user can sue the developer for its failure to enforce its EULA or TOS Agreement against others.

---

25. China's State Administration of Taxation has recently issued regulations regarding the taxation of virtual currency that mainly follow the approach set forth by Professor Seto. Virtual Currency: Regulation and Taxation Issues, e-commerce and policy (November 2008).

For example, suppose a TOS Agreement prohibited the out-of-game sale of user-generated virtual property, as many such agreements do. In some parts of *WoW*, player-on-player battle is expected. Assume Player A sold the code for a powerful weapon she invented to player B on eBay. Assume also that Player B then used the weapon to defeat Player C in a head to head battle, and that Player C abided by all the terms of the TOS Agreement. Could Player C sue either Player A or B for violation of the TOS Agreement? Could Player C sue Blizzard for failing to police eBay and attempt to stop the sale or at least decommission the weapon within the game? A suit somewhat like this latter hypothetical was filed as a class action suit in May 2007 in Florida against Blizzard. That suit was settled, with the terms remaining confidential.

7. Every once in a while a hacker will be able to insert a virus into virtual worlds, causing them to shut down for as long as a couple of days while the virus is detected and the servers scrubbed. In a pure gaming world, this only results in a delay in a user's avatar reaching the next level. But there are some who make their real world incomes from work in, e.g., the virtual Nike store or as property traders in *Second Life*, and many more who supplement their real world incomes this way. Assuming the viral insertion could be traced back to the negligence of the developer, *e.g.*, the developer did not have the best anti-virus screening. Could the users who engage in commerce bring suit against the developer for lost income? What could the developers do to limit such actions?

8. Professors Lastowka and Hunter describe a situation in which several users of *The Dark Age of Camelot* established an operation known as "Black Snow Interactive." Black Snow essentially established a "virtual sweatshop" where workers in Tijuana, Mexico were paid a small hourly wage to play *The Dark Age of Camelot*, and then transfer the virtual assets they uncovered and created during play to the owners of Black Snow. The sweatshop was profitable for the owners, as the average wage paid to the workers was less than the real world value of the assets the workers either created or uncovered while playing the game.[26] Mythic Interactive, the owner of *Dark Age*, sued to shut this operation down. Under what theory could Mythic Interactive proceed?

Most other players in the *Dark Age of Camelot* supported Mythic's suit against Black Snow. A study showed the support had little to do with intellectual property rights, concern for the potential economic exploitation of the Mexican workers, or even the effect that the injection of commerce by Black Snow's employees might have on the personal wealth and holdings of the other players. Rather, the support was based on a theory of "economic justice"—paying others to play the game was not in keeping with the spirit of the game. It was considered a rent in the social fabric of the community of players.

---

26. Apparently the same sort of thing goes on in China. In a recent explanation of China's virtual play, the e-commerce law and policy journal noted:

> The concept of earning virtual currency has created the phenomenon of "gold farmers" which are Chinese workers employed to play online games day and night in order to earn virtual currency and equipment. The "farm owner" then sells the earnings for real money. Trading virtual currency and equipment can be a lucrative business as it accounts for about $600 million dollars in business for IGE—a service provider operating a network of buying and selling sites for massively [sic] multiplayer on line game (MMOG) virtual currency on the internet.

Virtual Currency: Regulation and Taxation Issues, e-commerce and policy (November 2008).

Chapter Eleven

Sale and Ownership

People, and the companies they work for, develop and own videogames to make money. To do that, they must control aspects of their games — distribution, the right to prescribe and proscribe game play, the right to limit copying of the game, and the right to sell advertising in their games, among others. This Chapter deals with three issues related to the commercial exploitation by the owners of a videogame: (1) The impact of the "first sale" doctrine on videogame hardware and software, along with notes on the grey market; (2) the right to enjoin the public performances of videogames; and (3) in-game advertising. Copyright law deals with some of these issues; in addition, EULAs and TOS/TOA Agreements can help supplement the law and fill in the gaps as well.

§ 11.10 The "First Sale" Doctrine: A Primer

As we learned in § 6.10, *supra*, § 106 of the Copyright Act provides that a copyright grants the holder six exclusive rights: (1) to reproduce the copyrighted work in copies or phonorecords; (2) to prepare derivative works based upon the copyrighted work; (3) to distribute copies or phonorecords of the copyrighted work to the public by sale or other transfer of ownership, or by rental, lease, or lending; (4) in the case of literary, musical, dramatic, and choreographic works, pantomimes, and motion pictures and other audiovisual works, to perform the copyrighted work publicly; (5) in the case of literary, musical, dramatic, and choreographic works, pantomimes, and pictorial, graphic, or sculptural works, including the individual images of a motion picture or other audiovisual work, to display the copyrighted work publicly; and (6) in the case of sound recordings, to perform the copyrighted work publicly by means of a digital audio transmission.

But, the rights granted in § 106 are subject to subsequent sections of the Act, one of which — the "first sale" doctrine — limits the holder's right to distribute the copyrighted work granted in § 106(3). Under Section 109 of the Act, once a customer buys a copy of the work, that copy belongs to the buyer, who then can sell it, give it away, destroy it, etc. at his or her discretion. In the words of the Act, a purchaser acquires the right to "sell or otherwise dispose" of the copy upon buying the work. *Id.* Note that the buyer does not acquire the right to make another copy of the work, or make a derivative product based on it, etc., but the right to distribute the particular purchased copy transfers to the buyer upon its first sale. *Id.*

The first sale doctrine is perhaps easier to understand and apply when dealing with tangible, copyrightable items such as a hard copy of *Harry Potter and the Sorcerer's Stone*. Initially, J.K. Rowling held the copyright to the book and made an arrangement with a publisher to print and distribute the book, presumably retaining the right to a royalty payment for each book sold. Let's assume Mary bought a copy. Now, let's say that, after reading it, Mary wants to give the book to her friend Pat to read. In theory, Ms. Rowling is losing a royalty payment, as her copyrighted work is being read twice with only one royalty payment coming back to her. We could imagine a society whereby Pat, at least in theory, could be obligated to pay for the right to read the book, sort of like making each Kindle owner pay for all books loaded on his or her device. But for reasons of history relating to the rights of ownership of personal property, and reasons relating to the practical problems which would ensue in trying to collect a royalty from the "Pats" of the world, Section 109 of the Copyright Act allows Mary to freely sell, give or lend her copy to Pat.

Like J.K. Rowling above, videogame software owners—indeed all software developers—would like a world in which *each* player or user pays for the right to play the game or otherwise use their products. From the earliest days in the industry, they have attempted to limit the effect of the first sale doctrine by licensing, rather than selling, their products via the EULAs and the TOU/TOS agreements we learned about in the last chapter. That is, by its terms, the first sale doctrine under Section 109 only gives "the *owner* of a particular copy" of a copyrighted work the right to distribute it (emphasis added). If the videogame distributor, rather than the player, retains ownership of the game, and only permits the user/purchaser a limited right to *play* the game, in theory the distributor retains the right to stop the legal future sale or gift by the player of "its" good to another.

Videogame developers believe this to be essential to their industry, because of the uniqueness of their medium. An essential feature of the traditional first sale doctrine is that when the first purchaser gave his or her particular copy of the work to another, he or she can't read or use it at the same time, e.g., when Mary gives her copy of the *Harry Potter* book to Pat, Mary can't read that copy of the book while it is in Pat's possession. But with any kind of software, it is possible to make an exact copy before giving away the software, a transaction that can be duplicated an infinite number of times. Because of this threat, game distributors argue that they must have a mechanism to legally prohibit the later distribution of their games else they may end up selling only one copy of a game and having the rest of the world simultaneously playing it with illegally pirated code.

Technology, of course, can help the videogame distributor. Anti-copying software, a requirement that a certain "password" from an array of potential keys provided the user be entered before game play begins, or requiring a cartridge to be inserted in the console with an authentication code in order for the game to play all help stem the tide of impermissible copying. But such devices do not deter hackers for long.

The debate is not one sided. To many consumer advocates, when a buyer purchases a game for $29.95 at say a Game Stop store, hasn't the buyer really "purchased" the game, regardless of the terms of the TOS Agreement stuck in the box that the buyer never read before purchase? And if the purchaser wants to give the disc to his brother as a birthday gift, should a EULA which purports to limit the rights of the purchaser to just a license to play the game, but not to transfer ownership of it, legally prohibit the desire to give away the program? These advocates point out that it is already a copyright violation to make a complete copy of a protected work, so the licensing idea really imposes a burden on the purchaser without any societal benefit. We deal this with this issue in *Vernor*, found in Section 11.20, below.

Another issue relating to the first sale doctrine involves global wholesalers. Once a game is created, and the costs of its development are "sunk," it is relatively inexpensive to manufacture copies. As a consequence, many manufacturers price game cartridges differently in different countries based on expected demand, the prosperity of the country, the extent of the warranty given, etc. and not based on "cost." So imagine a situation in which a "game arbitrageur" purchases 5,000 game cartridges at a low price in country X. The issue is, can he or she bring them back to the United States and undercut the distributor's domestic price on the ground that the arbitrageur purchased them lawfully in country X and thus is free to distribute them as he or she wishes under the "first sale" doctrine? Perhaps surprisingly, the legality of this practice was not settled until 2013, in *Kirtsaeng*, our first case in § 11.20 below.

---

§ 11.20 The First Sale Doctrine

Kirtsaeng v. John Wiley & Sons, Inc.

United States Supreme Court, 2013
__ U.S. __, 133 S. Ct. 1351

BREYER, Associate Justice:

Section 106 of the Copyright Act grants "the owner of copyright under this title" certain "exclusive rights," including the right "to distribute copies ... of the copyrighted work to the public by sale or other transfer of ownership." These rights are qualified, however, by the application of various limitations set forth in the next several sections of the Act, §§ 107 through 122. Those sections, typically entitled "Limitations on exclusive rights," include, for example, the principle of "fair use" (§ 107), permission for limited library archival reproduction, (§ 108), and the doctrine at issue here, the "first sale" doctrine (§ 109). Section 109(a) sets forth the "first sale" doctrine as follows:

> Notwithstanding the provisions of section 106(3) [the section that grants the owner exclusive distribution rights], the owner of a particular copy or phonorecord lawfully made under this title ... is entitled, without the authority of the copyright owner, to sell or otherwise dispose of the possession of that copy or phonorecord.

Thus, even though § 106(3) forbids distribution of a copy of, say, the copyrighted novel *Herzog* without the copyright owner's permission, § 109(a) adds that, once a copy of *Herzog* has been lawfully sold (or its ownership otherwise lawfully transferred), the buyer of *that copy* and subsequent owners are free to dispose of it as they wish. In copyright jargon, the "first sale" has "exhausted" the copyright owner's § 106(3) exclusive distribution right.

What, however, if the copy of *Herzog* was printed abroad and then initially sold with the copyright owner's permission? Does the "first sale" doctrine still apply? Is the buyer, like the buyer of a domestically manufactured copy, free to bring the copy into the United States and dispose of it as he or she wishes?

To put the matter technically, an "importation" provision, § 602(a)(1), says that: "[i]mportation into the United States, without the authority of the owner of copyright under this title, of copies ... of a work that have been acquired outside the United States is an infringement of the exclusive right to distribute copies ... under section 106...."

Thus § 602(a)(1) makes clear that importing a copy without permission violates the owner's exclusive distribution right. But in doing so, § 602(a)(1) refers explicitly to the § 106(3) exclusive distribution right. As we have just said, § 106 is by its terms "[s]ubject to" the various doctrines and principles contained in §§ 107 through 122, including § 109(a)'s "first sale" limitation. Do those same modifications apply—in particular, does the "first sale" modification apply—when considering whether § 602(a)(1) prohibits importing a copy?

In *Quality King Distribs. v. L'anza Research Int'l* [535 U.S. 135 (1998)], we held that § 602(a)(1)'s reference to § 106(3)'s exclusive distribution right incorporates the later subsections' limitations, including, in particular, the "first sale" doctrine of § 109. Thus, it might seem that, § 602(a)(1) notwithstanding, one who buys a copy abroad can freely import that copy into the United States and dispose of it, just as he could had he bought the copy in the United States.

But *Quality King* considered an instance in which the copy, though purchased abroad, was initially manufactured in the United States (and then sent abroad and sold). This case is like *Quality King* but for one important fact. The copies at issue here were manufactured abroad. That fact is important because § 109(a) says that the "first sale" doctrine applies to "a particular copy or phonorecord *lawfully made under this title.*" And we must decide here whether the five words, "lawfully made under this title," make a critical legal difference.

Putting section numbers to the side, we ask whether the "first sale" doctrine applies to protect a buyer or other lawful owner of a copy (of a copyrighted work) lawfully manufactured abroad. Can that buyer bring that copy into the United States (and sell it or give it away) without obtaining permission to do so from the copyright owner? Can, for example, someone who purchases, say at a used bookstore, a book printed abroad subsequently resell it without the copyright owner's permission?

In our view, the answers to these questions are, yes. We hold that the "first sale" doctrine applies to copies of a copyrighted work lawfully made abroad.

I

A

Respondent, John Wiley & Sons, Inc., publishes academic textbooks. Wiley obtains from its authors various foreign and domestic copyright assignments, licenses and permissions—to the point that we can, for present purposes, refer to Wiley as the relevant American copyright owner. Wiley often assigns to its wholly owned foreign subsidiary, John Wiley & Sons (Asia) Pte Ltd., rights to publish, print, and sell Wiley's English language textbooks abroad. Each copy of a Wiley Asia foreign edition will likely contain language making clear that the copy is to be sold only in a particular country or geographical region outside the United States.

The upshot is that there are two essentially equivalent versions of a Wiley textbook, each version manufactured and sold with Wiley's permission: (1) an American version printed and sold in the United States, and (2) a foreign version manufactured and sold abroad. And Wiley makes certain that copies of the second version state that they are not to be taken (without permission) into the United States.

Petitioner, Supap Kirtsaeng, a citizen of Thailand, moved to the United States in 1997 to study mathematics at Cornell University. While he was studying in the United States, Kirtsaeng asked his friends and family in Thailand to buy copies of foreign edition English-language textbooks at Thai book shops, where they sold at low prices, and mail them to him in the United States. Kirtsaeng would then sell them, reimburse his family and friends, and keep the profit.

B

In 2008 Wiley brought this federal lawsuit against Kirtsaeng for copyright infringement. Wiley claimed that Kirtsaeng's unauthorized importation of its books and his later resale of those books amounted to an infringement of Wiley's § 106(3) exclusive right to distribute as well as § 602's related import prohibition. [Kirtsaeng claimed] § 109(a)'s "first sale" doctrine permitted him to resell or otherwise dispose of the books without the copyright owner's further permission.

II

We must decide whether the words "lawfully made under this title" restrict the scope of § 109(a)'s "first sale" doctrine geographically. The Second Circuit, the Ninth Circuit, Wiley, and the Solicitor General (as *amicus*) all read those words as imposing a form of *geographical* limitation. The Second Circuit held that they limit the "first sale" doctrine to particular copies "made in territories *in which the Copyright Act is law*," which (the Circuit says) are copies "manufactured domestically," not "outside of the United States." Wiley agrees that those five words limit the "first sale" doctrine "to copies made in conformance with the [United States] Copyright Act *where the Copyright Act is applicable*," which (Wiley says) means it does not apply to copies made "outside the United States" and at least not to "foreign production of a copy for distribution exclusively abroad."

Under this geographical interpretation, § 109(a)'s "first sale" doctrine would not apply to the Wiley Asia books at issue here. And, despite an American copyright owner's permission to *make* copies abroad, one who *buys* a copy of any such book or other copyrighted work—whether at a retail store, over the Internet, or at a library sale—could not resell (or otherwise dispose of) that particular copy without further permission.

Kirtsaeng, however, reads the words "lawfully made under this title" as imposing a *non*-geographical limitation. He says that they mean made "in accordance with" or "in compliance with" the Copyright Act. In that case, § 109(a)'s "first sale" doctrine would apply to copyrighted works as long as their manufacture met the requirements of American copyright law. In particular, the doctrine would apply where, as here, copies are manufactured abroad with the permission of the copyright owner.

In our view, § 109(a)'s language, its context, and the common-law history of the "first sale" doctrine, taken together, favor a *non*-geographical interpretation. We also doubt that Congress would have intended to create the practical copyright-related harms with which a geographical interpretation would threaten ordinary scholarly, artistic, commercial, and consumer activities. We consequently conclude that Kirtsaeng's nongeographical reading is the better reading of the Act.

B

Both historical and contemporary statutory context indicate that Congress, when writing the present version of § 109(a), did not have geography in mind. In respect to history, we compare § 109(a)'s present language with the language of its immediate predecessor. That predecessor said:

> [N]othing in this Act shall be deemed to forbid, prevent, or restrict the transfer of any copy of a copyrighted work the possession of which has been lawfully obtained.

Copyright Act of 1909, §41, 35 Stat. 1084 (emphasis added). The predecessor says nothing about geography (and Wiley does not argue that it does). So we ask whether Congress, in changing its language implicitly *introduced* a geographical limitation that previously was lacking.

A comparison of language indicates that it did not. The predecessor says that the "first sale" doctrine protects "the transfer of any copy *the possession of which has been lawfully obtained.*" The present version says that "*the owner* of a particular copy or phonorecord lawfully made under this title is entitled to sell or otherwise dispose of the possession of that copy or phonorecord." What does this change in language accomplish?

The language of the former version referred to those *who are not owners* of a copy, but mere possessors who "lawfully obtained" a copy. The present version covers only those who are *owners* of a "lawfully made" copy. Whom does the change leave out? Who might have lawfully *obtained* a copy of a copyrighted work but not *owned* that copy? One answer is owners of movie theaters, who during the 1970's (and before) often *leased* films from movie distributors or filmmakers. Because the theater owners had "lawfully obtained" their copies, the earlier version could be read as allowing them to sell that copy, *i.e.*, it might have given them "first sale" protection. Because the theater owners were lessees, not owners, of their copies, the change in language makes clear that they (like bailees and other lessees) cannot take advantage of the "first sale" doctrine.

This objective perfectly well explains the new language of the present version, including the five words here at issue. Section 109(a) now makes clear that a lessee of a copy will *not* receive "first sale" protection but one who *owns* a copy *will* receive "first sale" protection, *provided,* of course, that the copy was "*lawfully made*" and not pirated. The new language also takes into account that a copy may be "lawfully made under this title" when the copy, say of a phonorecord, comes into its owner's possession through use of a compulsory license, which "this title" provides for elsewhere, namely, in §115. Again, for those who find legislative history useful, the relevant legislative report makes this clear.

C

The "first sale" doctrine also frees courts from the administrative burden of trying to enforce restrictions upon difficult-to-trace, readily movable goods. And it avoids the selective enforcement inherent in any such effort. Thus, it is not surprising that for at least a century the "first sale" doctrine has played an important role in American copyright law.

D

Associations of libraries, used-book dealers, technology companies, consumer-goods retailers, and museums point to various ways in which a geographical interpretation would fail to further basic constitutional copyright objectives, in particular "promot[ing] the Progress of Science and useful Arts."

The American Library Association tells us that library collections contain at least 200 million books published abroad (presumably, many were first published in one of the nearly 180 copyright-treaty nations and enjoy American copyright protection under 17 U.S.C. §104, that many others were first published in the United States but printed abroad because of lower costs; and that a geographical interpretation will likely require the libraries to obtain permission (or at least create significant uncertainty) before circulating or otherwise distributing these books.

How, the American Library Association asks, are the libraries to obtain permission to distribute these millions of books? How can they find, say, the copyright owner of a foreign book, perhaps written decades ago? They may not know the copyright holder's present address. And, even where addresses can be found, the costs of finding them, contacting owners, and negotiating may be high indeed. Are the libraries to stop circulating or distributing or displaying the millions of books in their collections that were printed abroad?

Technology companies tell us that "automobiles, microwaves, calculators, mobile phones, tablets, and personal computers" contain copyrightable software programs or packaging. Many of these items are made abroad with the American copyright holder's permission and then sold and imported (with that permission) to the United States. A geographical interpretation would prevent the resale of, say, a car, without the permission of the holder of each copyright on each piece of copyrighted automobile software. Yet there is no reason to believe that foreign auto manufacturers regularly obtain this kind of permission from their software component suppliers, and Wiley did not indicate to the contrary when asked. Without that permission a foreign car owner could not sell his or her used car.

Art museum directors ask us to consider their efforts to display foreign-produced works by, say, Cy Twombly, Rene Magritte, Henri Matisse, Pablo Picasso, and others. A geographical interpretation, they say, would require the museums to obtain permission from the copyright owners before they could display the work, even if the copyright owner has already sold or donated the work to a foreign museum.

Thus, we believe that the practical problems that petitioner and his *amici* have described are too serious, too extensive, and too likely to come about for us to dismiss them as insignificant—particularly in light of the ever-growing importance of foreign trade to America. The upshot is that copyright-related consequences along with language, context, and interpretive canons argue strongly against a geographical interpretation of § 109(a).

Notes and Questions

1. In her dissent, Justice Ginsburg noted one reason she would not allow the first sale defense to someone who purchased the goods overseas is:

> Because economic conditions and demand for particular goods vary across the globe, copyright owners have a financial incentive to charge different prices for copies of their works in different geographic regions. Their ability to engage in such price discrimination, however, is undermined if arbitrageurs are permitted to import copies from low-price regions and sell them in high-price regions. The question in this case is whether the unauthorized importation of foreign-made copies constitutes copyright infringement under U.S. law.

Justice Ginsburg's concerns were echoed by Andrew Albanese in his PUBLISHER'S WEEKLY article, "*What Does* Kirtsaeng v. Wiley *Mean For the Industry?*" There, he states:

> Wiley's fear that in an age of global e-commerce and cheap shipping, its cheaper-priced, foreign editions were going to come flooding back into the states, swamping the domestic market. Indeed, Kirtsaeng's import business was possible because publishers do sell books at different price points in different territories. And with the Supreme Court decision, observers say, the borders are now open.

Is the risk of arbitrage a sufficient reason to find the first sale doctrine inapplicable? If so, should the Court do it (by imposing a geographical limitation or otherwise), or should the decision be left to Congress?

2. Should there be a separate "first sale" rule for digital, as opposed to more traditional, media because of the "perfect" and largely undetectable copy problem?

3. Note that many in the industry state that one reason for going to a "freemium" business model, as described in § 1.30 *infra*, is to avoid complications with the first sale doctrine and attempts to restrict by license the transferability of copies of the game. How does a freemium business model change the dynamics?

4. Professor Alli Lor Larsen, in his article, "*The Trouble With Amicus Facts,*" 100 Virginia Law Review 1757, (2014), posits a warning that the Supreme Court is increasingly engaging in "fact finding" by accepting facts set forth in amicus briefs, rather than facts developed in the record of the case that is being decided. The danger is that facts in the record of the case are subject to the relevance, foundation and other authentication requirements of the rules of evidence, whereas a footnote in an *amicus* brief might not be as reliable. In commenting on the article, the New York Times[1] noted Professor Larsen's warnings about *Kirtsaeng* as follows:

> And in a 2013 decision, Justice Stephen G. Breyer cited an amicus brief to establish that American libraries hold 200 million books that were published abroad, a point of some significance in the copyright dispute before the court. The figure in the brief came from a blog post. The blog has been discontinued.

How important was that fact to his decision?

5. The first sale doctrine deals with issues of importation under copyright law. A related problem is one of imported "grey market" goods, which raises trademark law issues. "A 'grey-market' good is a foreign-manufactured good bearing a valid United States trademark, which is imported without the consent of the United States trademark owner." *K Mart Corp. v. Cartier, Inc.*, 485 U.S. 176, 179 (1988). That is, typically the holder of the mark will license use of it in different countries, promising each licensee an exclusive geographic territory. Often the retail price for the item is lower in a foreign country because the cost of the license is less, costs of manufacture are lower, the goods are not advertised as extensively in the foreign country, favorable currency exchange rates, etc. If the disparity in price is great enough, an exporter will bring in several thousand of these "grey market" items from the foreign country, and sell them in the United States at a price that undercuts the American retail price ("freeloading" on U.S.-based advertising, among other things), and defeating the domestic exclusivity promised U.S. licensees by the U.S. trademark holder.[2]

While direct lawsuits by the licensees (or trademark holder) to prohibit the importation are possible, most of the time enforcement issues have been left to the U.S. Customs Service, which has the power to detain the grey market goods at their port of entry into the United States. However, there are limitations on the right of the Customs Service to detain the goods, e.g., if "they bear a notice stating that the product is not the product authorized by the U.S. trademark holder for importation, but are physically and materially different from the authorized domestic goods," Customs must let them enter.[3]

---

1. *See* Adam Liptak, *Seeking Facts, Justices Settle for What Briefs Tell Them*, N.Y. Times (Sept. 7, 2014, 12:38 PM), http://www.nytimes.com/2014/09/02/us/politics/the-dubious-sources-of-some-supreme-court-facts.html?emc=eta1&_r=0 (last accessed January 10, 2105).

2. *See gen* Matthew Fornaro, *A Parallel Problem: Grey Market Goods and the Internet*, 8 J. Tech. L. & Pol'y 69, 73 (2003).

3. *Id.* at 74.

The grey market problem is especially acute for videogame and other computer software, and is exacerbated by the Internet, which allows for direct, and private, contact between parties so that there is no port of entry for the Customs Service to patrol. Professor Fornaro, in his article in the JOURNAL OF TECHNOLOGY, LAW & POLICY, posits the following problem [Note that Professor Fornaro's problem, as originally constituted, dealt with a shirt produced by Abercrombie & Fitch. We have substituted "a Sony PS4" sold by Sony and Best Buy for any references to the shirt in the original article to show how it relates to the videogame industry. If there are any unintended consequences from the change, the fault is ours, not Professor Fornaro's — ED]:

Internet merchants usually provide for efficient and cheap trade. There are usually no questions asked, and Internet merchants accept a variety of convenient payment forms. The system works nearly flawlessly for used merchandise and services. However, problems often arise when new products are sold on the Internet in this same manner. For example, suppose an American consumer wants to buy a new PS4 from a manufacturer/retailer such as Sony or an internet site such as Best Buy. The first option of the consumer is to go to the local retailer and purchase the platform. However, the consumer may live in a remote area without a retail store nearby or, perhaps the consumer may not wish to travel to the local retail store. Sony and Best Buy, like most manufacturer/retailers, has a catalog as well as a corporate web site where it sells retail goods. Hence, the consumer can choose to purchase the PS4 from the official manufacturer/retailer through remote means via catalog or the official Internet web site.

Problems arise when consumers are presented with alternative, non-licensed retailers as options. Here, the consumer can go to the aforementioned web sites [like eBay — ED] that take advantage of the secondary market. The consumer can buy an identical PS4 for much less than from either the retail store, the retailer's catalog, or the retailer's web site. In reality, there is a high probability that this discount PS4 may be a grey market good.

The reality of the situation is that proprietary merchants and individuals usually either import these platforms from abroad at a substantial discount to the going rate where the consumer is located. This is primarily due to factors such as currency exchange rates, pricing, and sales by the authentic manufacturer/retailer. Thus, although the consumer gets the PS4 for a discount, the damage has been done. The U.S. division of Sony is denied a valid sale, the appropriate state and local government is denied valuable sales tax, the consumer is left with a PS4 that may not be of the same domestic quality, and the product surely lacks warranty protection and guarantees.[4]

The question becomes what can the trademark holder or its domestic licensee do in such a situation. Professor Fornaro gives an accurate, if rather disappointing, answer: "In such a novel area of law, legislation and case law have been slow to develop. Courts are somewhat unsure of how to handle this amalgam of legal topics."[5] Given the practical problems of enforcement, coupled with cases like *Kirtsaeng* in a related area, is it likely that grey market games, consoles, etc. will be allowed to be sold without real consequence, and that it will be up to the manufacturers to adjust their practices in trademark licensing

---

4. *Id.* at 81–82.
5. *Id.* at 82.

and pricing, rather than the courts or governments to police the market? Is that possible in today's global marketplace?

* * *

Vernor v. Autodesk, Inc.

United States District Court for the Western District of Washington, 2008
555 F. Supp. 2d 1164

Jones, District Judge

BACKGROUND

Mr. Vernor makes his living selling goods on eBay, the well-known internet auction site. He has two packages of Autodesk's copyrighted AutoCAD software, and hopes to sell them on eBay. He brought this action for declaratory relief because Autodesk's past actions give him reason to believe that Autodesk will try to stop his sales.

In 2005, Mr. Vernor purchased an authentic, used AutoCAD package at a garage sale and put it up for auction on eBay. Autodesk responded by sending a Digital Millennium Copyright Act ("DMCA") notice to eBay claiming that the sale would infringe its copyright. EBay suspended the auction. Mr. Vernor responded with a DMCA counter-notice claiming that his sale was lawful, to which Autodesk never responded. EBay reinstated the auction, and Mr. Vernor sold the AutoCAD package without further interference from Autodesk.

In 2007, Mr. Vernor bought four authentic, used AutoCAD packages from an office sale at Cardwell/Thomas Associates ("CTA"), a Seattle architecture firm. Mr. Vernor sold three packages on eBay, but each time he put a package up for auction, an exchange of DMCA notices from Autodesk, suspension of the auction by eBay, counter-notices from Mr. Vernor, and reinstatement of the auction followed. When Mr. Vernor attempted to sell the fourth AutoCAD package, Autodesk filed another DMCA notice, and eBay responded by suspending Mr. Vernor's eBay account for one month for repeat infringement.

In both 2005 and 2007, Mr. Vernor notified Autodesk either in writing or over the telephone that he had acquired the AutoCAD packages lawfully, and that he was not infringing any Autodesk copyright. In 2005, an Autodesk attorney told him that Autodesk does not allow any resale of its software products, and that any resale would infringe Autodesk's copyright. In 2007, an Autodesk attorney wrote Mr. Vernor and explained that he would advise Autodesk "to take further action" if Mr. Vernor did not cease his efforts to sell Autodesk software.

Mr. Vernor now has two AutoCAD packages that he wishes to sell. By tracing the serial numbers on the packages, Autodesk has determined that both were originally transferred from Autodesk to CTA in a settlement of an unrelated dispute. According to the Settlement Agreement, CTA paid just over $ 44,000. That sum "include[d] the acquisition by [CTA] of ten (10) packages of AutoCAD(R), Release 14 software...." Autodesk shipped the packages to CTA; CTA eventually resold some of the packages to Mr. Vernor, including the two AutoCAD packages that Mr. Vernor now possesses.

In the Settlement Agreement, CTA agreed to "adhere to all terms of the [attached] Autodesk Software License Agreement." The License Agreement ("License") is substantially identical to one included inside each AutoCAD package. The License Agreement grants a "nonexclusive, nontransferable license to use the enclosed program ... according to the terms and conditions herein." License: Grant of License. The License imposes various restrictions on users of the software. It also imposes several "Restrictions," including a prohibition on "rent, lease, or transfer [of] all or part of the Software, Documentation, or any rights granted hereunder to any other person without Autodesk's prior written consent."

ANALYSIS

Mr. Vernor seeks a declaration that his resale of AutoCAD is lawful. Autodesk moves the court to enter summary judgment.

The court's resolution of this motion relies only on facts that do not appear to be in dispute. At least for purposes of this motion, Autodesk has not disputed Mr. Vernor's account of how he acquired his AutoCAD packages or of his attempts to auction his copies on eBay. Mr. Vernor, in turn, has not disputed Autodesk's account of how CTA acquired its AutoCAD packages, or that two of those packages are now in his possession. He has also not disputed the authenticity of the Settlement Agreement and License that Autodesk submitted in support of its motion.

Mr. Vernor Is Entitled to the Protection of the First Sale Doctrine

1. If It Applies, the First Sale Doctrine Immunizes Mr. Vernor

If there were no License, there is no dispute that Mr. Vernor's resale of the AutoCAD packages would be legal. The first sale doctrine permits a person who owns a lawfully-made copy of a copyrighted work to sell or otherwise dispose of the copy:

> Notwithstanding the provisions of section 106(3), the owner of a particular copy or phonorecord lawfully made under this title, or any person authorized by such owner, is entitled, without the authority of the copyright owner, to sell or otherwise dispose of the possession of that copy or phonorecord.

There is no dispute that the copy of Autodesk software contained in each AutoCAD package was lawfully made. If there were no License, there would be no dispute that CTA owned the AutoCAD packages at issue, that Mr. Vernor now owns the packages, and that he can dispose of them as he wishes.

The first sale doctrine is a narrow limitation on a copyright holder's rights. The Copyright Act gives a copyright holder the exclusive right to reproduce his copyrighted work, the exclusive right to prepare derivative works based on his copyrighted work, and the exclusive right to distribute copies of his work. When a copyright holder chooses to sell a copy of his work, however, he "exhaust[s] his exclusive statutory right to control its distribution." Because a first sale exhausts the copyright holder's distribution right, future distributions of the copy do not implicate the Copyright Act. A first sale does not, however, exhaust other rights, such as the copyright holder's right to prohibit copying of the copy he sells. For example, the first sale doctrine permits a consumer who buys a lawfully made DVD copy of *Gone With the Wind* to resell the copy, but not to duplicate the copy.

Autodesk's motion turns on its assertion that, because of the License, the transfer of AutoCAD packages to CTA was not a sale. Without a sale, there can be no "first sale." Or, phrased in the language of § 109(a), without a sale, CTA was not an "owner of a ... copy" of Autodesk software. If CTA was not an owner within the meaning of the statute, Mr. Vernor is also not an owner within the meaning of § 109(a).

Autodesk correctly asserts that mere possession of a copyrighted copy pursuant to a license is not a sale, and thus not a basis to invoke the first sale doctrine. The Supreme Court has acknowledged as much, if only in passing. The Ninth Circuit recognizes that a mere licensee in possession of a copy cannot rely on the first sale doctrine. Indeed, the Copyright Act itself declares that the first sale doctrine does not "extend to any person who has acquired possession of the copy or phonorecord from the copyright owner, by rental, lease, loan, or otherwise, without acquiring ownership of it."

The critical dispute here, however, is whether Autodesk's transfer of AutoCAD packages to CTA was a sale or a mere transfer of possession pursuant to a license. If the transaction was a sale, then the restrictions of the License give rise, at most, to a breach of contract claim:

> [A] "first sale" buyer's disregard of restriction on resale does not make buyer— or subsequent buyer an infringer; [a] copyright holder's remedy is suit for breach of contract containing the restrictions.

Denbicare U.S.A. Inc. v. Toys "R" Us, Inc., 84 F.3d 1143, 1152 (9th Cir.1996). If Autodesk sold the AutoCAD packages, then the License's ban on transferring the software is of no consequence under the Copyright Act.

2. What is a Sale? The Ninth Circuit Answers in *Wise*.

No bright-line rule distinguishes mere licenses from sales. Several principles govern. The court must analyze the "arrangement at issue and decide whether it should be considered a first sale." The label placed on a transaction is not determinative.

Wise charts a path to distinguishing sales from non-sales in determining if the first sale doctrine applies. The *Wise* court considered numerous transfer contracts between movie studios and recipients of movie prints, and found that almost all of them were licenses, loans, or other non-sale transactions. Many of the contracts "reserved title to the film prints" in the studio, and required that the recipients return the prints following the expiration of a fixed term. Those contracts were labeled "licenses," and all transferred "only limited rights for the exhibition or distribution of the films for a limited purpose and for a limited period of time." In some contracts, the studios did not expressly reserve title to the film print. Nonetheless, the court found that this omission was not determinative because "the general tenor of the entire agreement [was] inconsistent" with a sale. As to all of these contracts, the court found that they were not "first sales, since both on their face and by their terms they were restricted licenses and not sales." The court reached the same conclusion as to several "V.I.P. agreements" in which studios loaned film prints to movie stars for their private use, expressly retaining title to the prints.

When the *Wise* court considered three types of contracts that allowed the recipient to keep the film print, however, it found sales. One contract allowed a television network receiving the film prints to retain one print, without restrictions on its resale. Another contract, for the sale of a film print to actress Vanessa Redgrave ("the Redgrave Contract"), required Ms. Redgrave to pay a fee to receive a film print that was subject to draconian transfer restrictions. Ms. Redgrave could use the print only for her "personal use and enjoyment," was required to retain possession of the print "at all times," and could not sell, lease, license, or loan the print to any other person. Despite the absolute bar on transferring the film, the court found that the "transaction strongly resembl[ed] a sale with restrictions on the use of the print." The court held that the defendant could rely on the first sale doctrine with respect to his later sales of the print. Finally, the court found that film prints transferred solely for salvage or destruction were sold.

In comparing the transactions found to be sales in *Wise* with those that were not, the critical factor is whether the transferee kept the copy acquired from the copyright holder. When the film studios required that prints be returned; the court found no sale. When the studios did not require the transferee to return the prints, the court found a sale. Even a complete prohibition on further transfer of the print (as in the Redgrave Contract), or a requirement that the print be salvaged or destroyed, was insufficient to negate a sale where the transferee was not required to return the print.

Taking direction solely from *Wise,* the court concludes that the transfer of AutoCAD packages from Autodesk to CTA was a sale. Like the Redgrave Contract, the Settlement Agreement and License allowed CTA to retain possession of the software copies in exchange for a single up-front payment. Like the Redgrave Contract, the Settlement Agreement and License imposed onerous restrictions on transfer of the AutoCAD copies. Similar to the salvage transactions in *Wise,* the License required CTA to destroy the software in the event that it purchased a software upgrade. License: Upgrades and Updates. Under *Wise,* however, this is a "sale with restrictions on use," and is a sufficient basis to invoke the first sale doctrine.

3. A Trio of Ninth Circuit Decisions Reaches Results Contrary to *Wise.*

As far as the court is aware, *Wise* is the only Ninth Circuit precedent analyzing what constitutes a "sale" for purposes of invoking the first sale doctrine. In the more than 30 years since *Wise,* no Ninth Circuit opinion has questioned it, much less overruled it. It retains vitality in recent Ninth Circuit jurisprudence..Three opinions issued after *Wise,* however, consider the same "sale" question in a different context, and arrive at contrary results.

In a trio of decisions, the Ninth Circuit considered § 117 of the Copyright Act, which grants owners of computer software copies a limited right to copy their copies. As with § 109(a), only an "owner of a copy" of software can invoke § 117(a):

> Notwithstanding the provisions of section 106, it is not an infringement for the owner of a copy of a computer program to make or authorize the making of another copy or adaptation of that computer program provided [that the owner meets two conditions.]

Section 117 is critical for software users, because in using software, a user's computer inevitably makes one or more copies of it. Section 117 ensures that those who buy software cannot be held liable for copying that is essential to their use of the software.

As with the first sale doctrine, courts have determined that a person becomes an "owner of a copy" of software under § 117 only in certain transactions.

In *MAI Sys. Corp. v. Peak Computer, Inc.,* the court considered a software license that controlled the use of the software, and declared that "any possession" of the software "not expressly authorized under this License" is prohibited. The court devoted its attention to whether the use of the software by an unlicensed repair service violated the plaintiff's copyright. In a single footnote, without analysis or explanation, the court declared that "[S]ince MAI licensed its software, [its] customers do not qualify as 'owners' of the software and are not eligible for protection under § 117." The court did not cite *Wise.*

In *Triad Sys. Corp. v. Southeastern Express Co.,* the court tacitly assumed that licensees could not invoke § 117. The panel conceded that customers to whom the plaintiff had "sold its software outright" could rely on § 117, but implicitly concluded that licensees could not. Again, the court engaged in no analysis of the license terms, and did not cite *Wise.* The *Triad* court cited *MAI* repeatedly, but did not cite the sole footnote in *MAI* addressing the applicability of § 117.

Finally, in *Wall Data,* the court briefly analyzed a purported license agreement to determine if it was a sale that would permit the invocation of § 117. The license agreement imposed restrictions on copying the software, restrictions on the number of users, and restrictions on transferring the software on computers within the licensed entity. The license imposed no limits on resale of the software. The court concluded that the restrictions were "sufficient to classify the transaction as a grant of license to Wall Data's software, and not a sale of Wall Data's software." The court reasoned that "such restrictions would not be imposed on a party who owned the software." The court did not cite *Wise*.

If the court were to apply this trio of precedent (the "*MAI* trio") to the license before it, it would conclude that Autodesk did not sell AutoCAD copies to CTA. The terms of the Autodesk License are either indistinguishably similar to or more restrictive than the licenses found not to be sales in the *MAI* trio. Like the defendants in the *MAI* trio, CTA agreed to restrictions on its use of the software. The restrictions in the License are more severe, because they prohibit resale of the software without Autodesk's permission. If restrictions like those in the *MAI* trio are sufficient to warrant a "no sale" finding, then the transfer of AutoCAD copies from Autodesk to CTA was not a sale.

4. The Court Must Follow *Wise*, Not the *MAI* Trio.

The court holds that it must follow *Wise*, and not the *MAI* trio. Where opinions of three-judge Ninth Circuit panels conflict, the court must rely on the earliest opinion. The court has carefully considered the tension between *Wise* and the *MAI* trio, and finds the decisions in irreconcilable conflict as applied to the critical issue in this case. Autodesk prevails in its motion if the court follows the *MAI* trio, but loses if the court follows *Wise*. Comparing *Wall Data* to *Wise* gives the clearest snapshot of the conflict. The *Wall Data* court held that the license restrictions before it "were sufficient to classify the transaction as ... not a sale of Wall Data's software." In *Wise*, harsher license restrictions than those in *Wall Data* were insufficient to prove the absence of a first sale. The court cannot ignore the conflict.

Because the conflict between *Wise* and the *MAI* trio places the court in the uncomfortable position of choosing which Ninth Circuit precedent to follow, the court has considered possibilities for avoiding the conflict. As the court explains below, it finds the conflict unavoidable.

[A]lthough the court recognizes the tsunami of technological change between the decisions in *Wise* and the *MAI* trio, it finds that the change provides no basis to avoid the conflict between the decisions. *Wise* considered motion picture film prints, whereas the *MAI* trio considered computer software. As the court noted in *Wall Data*:

> Software fundamentally differs from more traditional forms of medium, such as print or phonographic materials, in that software can be both more readily and easily copied on a mass scale in an extraordinarily short amount of time and relatively inexpensively. One of the primary advantages of software, its ability to record, concentrate and convey information with unprecedented ease and speed, makes it extraordinarily vulnerable to illegal copying and piracy.

As an initial matter, the court notes that *Wall Data* adopted this observation in deciding if the defendant could invoke the defense of fair use, an issue that is not before this court. Weighing policy arguments is one thing when considering fair use, which is an evolving judicially-created limitation on a copyright holder's rights. It is another matter entirely to weigh policy considerations when determining which Ninth Circuit precedent to follow. Statutes like § 117 show that Congress can adapt the Copyright Act to target evolving technologies. Moreover, although technology has changed, the question at the core of this case is not technological. Mr. Vernor does not seek to take advantage of new technology to ease copying, he seeks to sell a package of physical objects which contain copies of copyrighted material. The essential features of such sales vary little whether selling movie prints via mail (as in *Wise*) or software packages via eBay.

For the reasons stated above, the court follows the *Wise* course and concludes that the transfer of AutoCAD packages from Autodesk to CTA was a sale with contractual restrictions on use and transfer of the software. Mr. Vernor may thus invoke the first sale doctrine, and his resale of the AutoCAD packages is not a copyright violation.

5. Because *Wise* Disposes of the First Sale Question Before the Court, the Court Acknowledges, But Does Not Rely Upon, Authority from Other Circuits and District Courts.

In much of their argument, the parties encourage the court to adopt the reasoning of various district courts and courts of appeal other than the Ninth Circuit. The court has reviewed each of those cases, and acknowledges great divergence of opinion among courts attempting to distinguish between mere licenses and sales. None of them address the conflict between *Wise* and the *MAI* trio. Many reach results that favor Autodesk. *E.g.*, *Adobe Sys. Inc. v. One Stop Micro, Inc.*, 84 F. Supp. 2d 1086 (N.D.Cal.2000); *Novell [Inc. v. Unicom Sales, Inc.*, No. C-03-2785 MMC, 2004 WL 183911 (N.D. Cal. Aug. 17, 2004)] ; *Stargate Software*, 216 F. Supp. 2d 1051; *Microsoft Corp. v. Harmony Computers & Elecs. Inc.*, 846 F. Supp. 208 (E.D.N.Y.1994). Many reach results that favor Mr. Vernor. *E.g.*, *Krause v. Titleserv, Inc.*, 402 F.3d 119 (2d Cir. 2005); *SoftMan Prods. Co. v. Adobe Sys. Inc.*, 171 F. Supp. 2d 1075 (N.D. Cal.2001); *Novell, Inc. v. Network Trade Ctr., Inc.*, 25 F. Supp. 2d 1218 (D. Utah 1997). These cases are persuasive authority. *Wise*, however, is binding precedent. The court therefore declines to discuss authority from other circuits and district courts in greater detail.

Autodesk Has Not Established that Its License Binds Mr. Vernor or His Customers.

Although Mr. Vernor's resale of AutoCAD packages is not a copyright violation, he is concerned that Autodesk asserts he is contractually bound by the License. In reviewing Autodesk's motion and its reply, the court finds a few suggestions that Autodesk believes that the License binds Mr. Vernor. It also suggests that Mr. Vernor's customers are bound by the Autodesk License.

Autodesk contends that "the law clearly rejects" Mr. Vernor's claim that he is free from the Autodesk License. In doing so, however, it relies solely upon *Novell*, a case that provides no support for Autodesk's argument. *Novell*, like every other case the court has discussed in its order today, is concerned solely with whether a license makes the transaction between a copyright holder and the first transferee a "first sale." Nothing in *Novell* supports the notion that downstream purchasers of software are bound by the terms of a license between the copyright holder and the first licensee.

Not only has Autodesk failed to surmount the thorny issues of privity and mutual assent inherent in its contention that its License binds Mr. Vernor and his customers, it has ignored the terms of the License itself. The Autodesk License is expressly "nontransferable." Autodesk does not explain how a nontransferable license can bind subsequent transferees.

The court cannot be certain if Autodesk actually asserts that its License binds Mr. Vernor or his customers. Autodesk certainly contends that the License negates a sale between itself and CTA. That issue is not to be conflated, however, with whether Mr. Vernor or his customers are bound by the License. Given the "nontransferable" terms of the License, and Autodesk's failure to cite authority for the proposition that the License binds downstream transferees, the court will not consider the issue further in this order. If Autodesk believes that the License binds Mr. Vernor or his customers, it must file a new motion addressing that argument.

Notes and Questions

1. A sale is generally thought to be a commercial law concept, and is a transaction where title (and usually possession) passes to the purchaser. *See* U.C.C. §§ 2-401 *et seq.* (amended 2002). On the other hand, a license is more often classified as a property concept in which a limited right to use an item is provided, with ownership and the right to further distribute the item reserved to the owner.[6]

2. What are the attributes of the transaction the court says transforms it into a sale and not a license? If you were advising a videogame distributor who wanted to ensure the transaction was a license in a jurisdiction that followed *Vernor*, what would you advise your client to do? Is there technology that could help?

In his article, *"When is a Software License Actually a Sale? A New District Court Decision Addresses the Copyright First Sale Doctrine and Software,"* Christopher Mills addresses this issue:[7]

> The *Vernor* decision provides strong support for first sale doctrine proponents and, if followed, could lead software developers to change certain aspects of the way they distribute software. Vendors may attempt to implement procedures for tracking and recovering software that is beyond a defined license term, which could respond to the court's focus on whether the transfer was perpetual. This, however, may not be a practical approach, as it will impose new burdens on distribution and may encounter purchaser resistance. Further, there is no clear direction from the court in *Vernor* as to what kind of software recovery model would be sufficient to support a claim that the software was licensed."

3. Cal. Civ. Code § 986 (West 2012) allows artists to obtain 5 percent of the resale price of their works from subsequent sellers under certain conditions. Section (a) of the statute provides:

> Whenever a work of fine art is sold and the seller resides in California or the sale takes place in California, the seller or the seller's agent shall pay to the artist of such work of fine art or to such artist's agent 5 percent of the amount of such sale. The right of the artist to receive an amount equal to 5 percent of the amount of such sale may be waived only by a contract in writing providing for an amount in excess of 5 percent of the amount of such sale. An artist may assign the right to collect the royalty payment provided by this section to another individual or entity. However, the assignment shall not have the effect of creating a waiver prohibited by this subdivision.

This statute is only applicable to the resale of artists' works. Do you think this is fair? How is this different from an author who does not obtain a percentage price of the resale of a copy of his or her book, movie, or videogame? Would a payment structure like that set forth in § 986 solve some of the problems associated with the tension between distributors and purchasers?

4. One part of the *Vernor* opinion edited from the excerpt above dealt with Autodesk's argument that Mr. Vernor was also liable for "contributory copyright infringement because he is inducing the people to whom he resells to copy AutoCAD software in violation of

---

6. Restatement (First) of Property § 512 (1944)

7. *See* Christopher M. Mills, *When is a Software License Actually a Sale? A New District Court Decision Addresses the Copyright First Sale Doctrine and Software*, Wiley Rein (Sept. 7, 2014, 12:48 PM) http://www.wileyrein.com/publications.cfm?sp=articles&id=851

the Copyright Act." Once it determined that Mr. Vernor as an owner, and not a licensee, of the software, liability as a contributory infringer was only possible if Mr. Vernor urged the purchasers who bought "his" software to make illegal copies and/or knew they were doing so. Would liability as an infringer be easier to establish if the transaction was a license? Would that be one reason for construing the transaction as a sale?

5. As you can see from the cases cited in Section "5" of the opinion, there are several cases going both ways on the license/sale issue. If you were outside the Ninth Circuit, and did not have *Wise* to deal with, what would be the better result? What is the theory on which a court voids the label given by the parties to the transaction and labels it a sale?

6. The court speaks of Section 117 of the Copyright Act as an example of how Congress responds to technology and allows for limited copying of software in certain circumstances. It provides:

(a) **Making of Additional Copy or Adaptation by Owner of Copy.** — Notwithstanding the provisions of section 106, it is not an infringement for the owner of a copy of a computer program to make or authorize the making of another copy or adaptation of that computer program provided:

(1) that such a new copy or adaptation is created as an essential step in the utilization of the computer program in conjunction with a machine and that it is used in no other manner, or

(2) that such new copy or adaptation is for archival purposes only and that all archival copies are destroyed in the event that continued possession of the computer program should cease to be rightful.

(b) **Lease, Sale, or Other Transfer of Additional Copy or Adaptation.** — Any exact copies prepared in accordance with the provisions of this section may be leased, sold, or otherwise transferred, along with the copy from which such copies were prepared, only as part of the lease, sale, or other transfer of all rights in the program. Adaptations so prepared may be transferred only with the authorization of the copyright owner.

(c) **Machine Maintenance or Repair.** — Notwithstanding the provisions of section 106, it is not an infringement for the owner or lessee of a machine to make or authorize the making of a copy of a computer program if such copy is made solely by virtue of the activation of a machine that lawfully contains an authorized copy of the computer program, for purposes only of maintenance or repair of that machine, if:

(1) such new copy is used in no other manner and is destroyed immediately after the maintenance or repair is completed; and

(2) with respect to any computer program or part thereof that is not necessary for that machine to be activated, such program or part thereof is not accessed or used other than to make such new copy by virtue of the activation of the machine.

If the real issue with software and the first sale doctrine is the ability of anyone to make unlimited "perfect" copies, does it really matter whether the transaction is classified as a license or a sale? After all, the only "authorized" copying of the work, whether the holder is an owner or a licensee, are those set forth in Section 117. The first sale doctrine doesn't give the purchaser the right to make a complete copy, while retaining the original. Such a practice is still prohibited under Section 106 (1) of the Act.

Or are there other issues that the sale/license debate goes to? One of them might be the "public performance" issue discussed immediately below.

§ 11.30 Public Performance

A 2014 article in the *New York Times*[8] provided:

> A bewitching creature—half woman, half deer—battles a shaman and a sentient tree. Lightning bolts strike. Weapons explode. Nasty spells are cast.
>
> The video game *Dota 2*, like so many across the Internet, transports teams of players from their bedrooms to a verdant virtual world where they smite each other through keyboard and mouse clicks. Except on this sunny day in July, every attack and counterattack by a five-person team set off an eruption of cheers—from the more than 11,000 spectators crammed into this city's basketball arena.
>
> The contestants were gunning for a big piece of the $11 million in total prize money, the most ever at a games tournament. And the game's developer, the Valve Corporation, moved another step closer to securing gaming's legitimacy as a major-league spectator sport.
>
> The signs of success already mirror the achievements of major sports. Game tournaments sell out giant arenas, and some attract at-home audiences larger than those of top traditional sporting events. Madison Avenue's highest fliers, like Coca-Cola and American Express, have lined up as sponsors. Prize money has soared to the millions of dollars, and top players earn six- or seven-figure incomes and attract big and passionate followings, luring a generation of younger players to seek fame and fortune as gamers.
>
> Last year, the State Department began granting visas to professional gamers, under the same program used by traditional athletes.

* * *

It is one thing if a developer like Valve puts on a tournament with its own games. But what if a consumer buys, e.g., 30 copies of the game and then puts on a gaming tournament for cash buy ins and pay outs in front of paying spectators? And suppose such a tournament is prohibited under the relevant EULA and the developer attempts to enjoin it? Resolution of these issues will come from cases like *Allen*, which follows.

Allen v. Academic Games League of America

United States Court of Appeals for the Ninth Circuit, 1996
89 F.3d 614

TRIMBLE, **District Court Judge:**

I. FACTS

Since the 1960's, Robert W. Allen has been involved in the development of academic games, including the games at issue in this appeal, A MAN CALLED MR. PRESIDENT, EURO-CARD or WORLD CARD, linguiSHTIK, and PROPAGANDA. Allen has been employed in various capacities for schools and school districts for the purpose of integrating the subject games, as well as other academic games, into classroom settings and student

---

8. *See* Nick Wingfield, *In E-Sports, Video Gamers Draw Real Crowds and Big Money*, N.Y. Times (Sept. 7, 2014, 12:55 PM) http://www.nytimes.com/2014/08/31/technology/esports-explosion-brings-opportunity-riches-for-video-gamers.html?emc=eta1&_r=0

competitions. For several years, middle and high school level students from six states have participated in national tournaments that Allen conducted under the name of National Academic Games Project (NAGP), a sole proprietorship of Allen. The highest number of students attending a NAGP tournament was 900 in the mid 1980's and approximately 800 students attended the tournament in 1991.

In 1992, a non-profit corporation, Academic Games League of America (AGLOA) was formed to conduct a national tournament that used some of Allen's academic games as a culmination to local and regional student competitions that also used the subject games during the school year. Prior to forming AGLOA, the individual respondents had significant roles in the NAGP national tournaments for many years. However, while each of the individual respondents was principally involved in AGLOA activities, Allen was not included. In fact, AGLOA was formed due to a personality conflict that developed between Allen and the individual respondents and because of disagreements on how to conduct and develop the national tournament.

Beginning in April, 1992, AGLOA conducted annual tournaments that coincided with Allen's NAGP national tournament. The tournaments occurred at the same time because of a need to wait for the completion of local and regional competitions and to accommodate the activities of graduating high school seniors. The subject games used at the AGLOA tournaments were purchased and brought to the tournaments by the participating students and schools. To date, three AGLOA tournaments have been conducted involving approximately 500 students, in 1992, to 900 students, in 1994.

At each AGLOA tournament, the subject games were played under rulebooks developed by an AGLOA committee that continuously revised the rules to enable students to play each game under tournament conditions while enhancing student educational value and interest in the games. Tournament rulebooks used at NAGP tournaments were not copyrighted by Allen and were actually developed and revised by a committee of persons that consisted primarily of the individual respondents. While each of the subject games contains a game manual, AGLOA tournament rulebooks do not repeat the rules found in the game manuals, but refer to the rules and elaborate on how each game is to be played in a tournament setting.

Allen derives income from the sale of each of the subject academic games. AGLOA buys games from Allen to sell directly to participating schools at cost and does not copy any of Allen's copyrighted materials in their tournaments. The only players in AGLOA's leagues are students. Allen has never objected to the playing or use of his academic games by students, who have played Allen's games in regional leagues for over twenty years.

II. DISCUSSION

Public Performance

The Copyright Act of 1976 confers upon copyright holders the exclusive right to perform and authorize others to perform their copyrighted works publicly. "Perform" and "publicly" are defined in the Copyright Act as, respectively, "to recite, render, play, dance, or act it, either directly or by means of any device or progress ..." and "to perform or display it at a place open to the public or at any place where a substantial number of persons outside of a normal circle of a family and its social acquaintances is gathered...." In applying these statutory definitions to the playing of Allen's games in a tournament setting, we conclude that the playing of a game is not a "performance" within the meaning of the Copyright Act.

Allen maintains that the language of Section 106(4) precludes AGLOA from conducting their national tournament because it constitutes a public performance of his protected literary works, the subject copyrighted games. Allen contends that a purchaser of a board game only obtains the right to play the board game in settings that are not "public" because playing or performing the games publicly is a right held exclusively by the copyright holder under § 106(4). However, the interpretation of "play," as used to define "perform" in § 101 of the Copyright Act, has generally been limited to instances of playing music or records. The term "play" has not been extended to the playing of games. To do so would mean interpreting the Copyright Act in a manner that would allow the owner of a copyright in a game to control when and where purchasers of games may play the games and this court will not place such an undue restraint on consumers.

Whether privately in one's home or publicly in a park, it is understood that games are meant to be "played." In this situation, the games are being played by students who come together for the purpose of friendly, academic competition. There is no indication that this nonprofit corporation, AGLOA, and the individual respondents are making the subject games available to the public for a fee. The students, schools, and school districts use their own games, purchased from Allen, in the tournaments, and respondents are merely organizers of this event. Moreover, AGLOA's tournaments are limited to students who participated in regional competitions which also involved the playing of Allen's games.

Even if the playing of games could constitute a performance, we would have to recognize the applicability of the fair use doctrine under Section 107 of the Copyright Act. This section allows the fair use of a copyrighted work in such instances as for nonprofit educational purposes and where the effect of the use upon the potential market for or value of the protected work is limited. As indicated above, AGLOA tournaments are held not for profit, but for encouraging education among young students. The potential market for the subject games has in all likelihood increased because participants of the AGLOA tournament have had to purchase Allen's games. Analysis of other factors involved in § 107 leads this court to conclude that the application of the fair use doctrine in this case is clearly appropriate.

———————

Notes and Questions

1. The statutory argument for Allen, the game owner, is pretty straightforward: (1) under Section 106(4) of the Act, a copyright holder has the right to, "in the case of literary, musical, dramatic, and choreographic works, pantomimes, and motion pictures and other audiovisual works, to perform the copyrighted work publicly."

Under the Act, (2) perform means to " ... play it ... directly ..." and (3) to perform it publicly, means playing it, " ... at a place open to the public." What was the statutory reason the court believed Allen's argument failed?

2. The court makes a distinction between records and music, on the one hand, and board games, with regard to the Copyright Act:

> However, the interpretation of "play," as used to define "perform" in § 101 of the Copyright Act, has generally been limited to instances of playing music or records. The term "play" has not been extended to the playing of games ... Whether privately in one's home or publicly in a park, it is understood that games are meant to be "played."

Are records meant to be "played" in the same way board games are?

3. The court also notes that:

The term "play" [used in the definition of "perform" under the Act] has not been extended to the playing of games. To do so would mean interpreting the Copyright Act in a manner that would allow the owner of a copyright in a game to control when and where purchasers of games may play the games and this court will not place such an undue restraint on consumers.

Is it the court or the Copyright Act which is making any such restraint on consumers?

4. Although not mentioned by the court, does the first sale doctrine have an influence in the legality of public performance? If a consumer buys a game, and people want to come over and pay to watch two people play it, does the right to the proceeds stay with the copyright holder, or is it transferred to the purchaser of the game? That, along with other issues, is addressed in our next case, *Red Baron*.

Red Baron-Franklin Park, Inc. v. Taito Corp.

United States Court of Appeal for the Fourth Circuit, 1989
883 F.2d 275

WINTER, Circuit Judge:

I.

Taito is a Japanese corporation engaged in the business of selling electronic video games, including electronic printed circuit boards which embody games and are used in coin-operated video game units. Video games "can roughly be described as computers programmed to create on a television screen cartoons in which some of the action is controlled by the player." Double Dragon is such a game. A video game unit consists of an electronic printed circuit board, a television monitor, a cabinet and a coin mechanism. When the component parts are connected and an electric current, activated by the insertion of the proper coin, run through the machinery, the game's audiovisual images appear on the television screen.

Taito has registered Double Dragon in the United States Copyright Office—Registration No. PA 327-710, issued June 26, 1987—and it has granted its wholly owned subsidiary, Taito America, an exclusive United States license in all of its copyright rights in Double Dragon.

Red Baron operates arcades where it makes available to the public for play upon payment of a set fee various video game units, including units fitted with Double Dragon circuit boards. Red Baron has no license from Taito or Taito America to use the Double Dragon circuit boards for profit nor did it obtain these circuit boards from Taito or Taito America. Rather, it obtained them in the "parallel" or "gray market," which is to say, that it purchased used circuit boards abroad and imported them without Taito's consent, at a cost less than the cost of a new unit purchased from Taito in the United States. Taito had, of course, originally sold the circuit boards obtained by Red Baron in Japan and had not purported to retain any right to control their resale. However, it is claimed that each of these boards, when put into play, exhibited the following restrictive notice:

> This game is for use in Japan only. Sales, exports, or operation outside this territory may violate international copyright and trademark law and the violator subject to severe penalties.

In the district court, it was Taito's legal theory that it had a valid copyright in the United States for all rights in Double Dragon, including the rights of distribution and public performance, that Red Baron had not obtained a license or other permission to exercise any of those rights, and that Red Baron was therefore infringing Taito's copyright rights when it imported Double Dragon circuit boards into the United States and when it installed the boards in units in its video arcades and made them available to the public for play upon payment of a fee. The district court, however, rejected this theory of the case. It ruled that the "first sale" doctrine, codified in 17 U.S.C. §109(a), was a limitation on Taito's right to "distribute" the copyrighted work publicly under 17 U.S.C. §106(3). While it did not discuss extensively Taito's right to "perform" the copyrighted work pursuant to 17 U.S.C. §106(4), it apparently applied the first sale doctrine to this right also. According to the district court's ruling, Taito's initial sale in Japan of the circuit boards for Double Dragon extinguished all rights that it had under the copyright laws, including the right of public performance, so that Red Baron did not infringe.

II.

In appealing, Taito does not contest the correctness of the district court's ruling with respect to Red Baron's right to purchase, import and even to sell Double Dragon circuit boards without Taito's consent. In effect, it concedes for the purposes of this appeal that the first sale doctrine gives Red Baron that right. It argues vigorously, however, that it has a separate and distinct right to "perform" Double Dragon, that it has not conferred this right on Red Baron and that, as a consequence, the latter is infringing Taito's copyright by its activities in making use of the circuit boards available to the public for a fee. This argument requires us to consider first whether Red Baron's use of Double Dragon constitutes a public performance within the meaning of §106(4), and if so to consider next whether the first sale doctrine has any application to the performance right as distinguished from actual ownership of the copyrighted work. We deal with these questions seriatim.

A. Public Performance.

We begin with the proposition that the Double Dragon video game is an "audiovisual work" as defined by 17 U.S.C. §101. To the extent pertinent, the statute provides that "audiovisual works" are works which "consist of a series of related images which are intrinsically intended to be shown by the use of machines or devices ... together with accompanying sounds, if any, regardless of the nature of the material objects ... in which the works are embodied."

To "perform" a work and to perform it "publicly" are also defined by the Copyright Act, 17 U.S.C. §101. "Perform" is defined to mean:

> to recite, render, play, dance, or act [a work], either directly or by means of any device or process or, in the case of a motion picture or other audiovisual work, to show its images in any sequence or to make the sounds accompanying it audible.

The definition of a "public" performance is as follows:

> To perform ... a work 'publicly' means—
>
> (1) to perform ... it at a place open to the public or at any place where a substantial number of persons outside of a normal circle of a family and its social acquaintances is gathered....

When we apply these definitions to Red Baron's conduct of its business, we conclude that Red Baron publicly performed Double Dragon. When a video game is activated by the insertion of a proper coin, the television monitor displays a series of images and the loudspeaker makes audible their accompanying sounds. The exhibition of its images in sequence constitutes a "performance" of an audiovisual work. Indeed, it is the sequential showing of its images that distinguishes the "performance" of an audiovisual work from its "display," which is defined as a nonsequential showing of individual images. True, the exact order of images will vary somewhat each time a video game is played depending on the skill of the player, but there will always be a *sequence* of images. As the House Report accompanying the Copyright Act states, although "the showing of portions" of an audiovisual work "must ... be sequential to constitute a 'performance' rather than a 'display'... no particular order need be maintained." We therefore conclude that the operation of a video game constitutes a performance as that term is defined in § 101.

We also think that the performance of a video game in a Red Baron arcade qualifies as a "public" performance. Under the Act, as we have noted, to perform a work "'publicly' means," among other things, "to perform ... it at a place open to the public." There is no real dispute here that Red Baron's video arcades are open to the public; of course, Red Baron's aim is to attract as many members of the public to its arcades as possible. The use of a Double Dragon unit may be viewed by the player, any persons accompanying him, and any other interested patrons of the video arcade.

Thus our conclusion is that Red Baron caused the public performance of Double Dragon.

B. The First Sale Doctrine and the Performance Right.

Red Baron's contention that the first sale doctrine is applicable to the performance right has a certain superficial, logical appeal in this case. Printed circuit boards embodying Double Dragon are not serviceable in and of themselves. They are functional only when they are used in combination with a television monitor, sound reproduction device and a console containing the controls to play the game. It is also a fair inference that there is only a very limited market for Double Dragon for home use. Rather, from the price and the complexity of the combination of items of equipment necessary to play the game, Taito may be fairly said to know that the circuit boards have utility only in the hands of someone who plans to exploit them commercially. Thus, by selling the boards, so the argument runs, Taito must intend to transfer the performance right, or must become estopped to deny that result, or must waive its right to claim infringement.

There is some support for Red Baron's contention. In *Universal Film Mfg. Co. v. Copperman*, 218 F. 577 (2d Cir. 1914) the Second Circuit held that a copyright owner's sale of a print of a motion picture film conferred on the purchaser and its successors in title to the print the right to perform the motion picture publicly in theatres. And in *United Artists Television, Inc. v. Fortnightly Corp.*, 377 F.2d 872 (2d Cir. 1967) the Second Circuit stated that "a sale does not generally release other exclusive rights, such as the right to copy, although this Court has held that the sale of a motion picture print conveys the right to perform it in public for profit [citing *Copperman*]."

It may well be that *Copperman* and *United Artists* are distinguishable from the instant case, as Taito argues. In any event, from our examination and understanding of the Copyright Act and decision of the Third Circuit, we are persuaded that the first sale doctrine does not apply to the performance right, that Taito America possesses and retains a valid copyright in the public performance of Double Dragon in the United States, that it has not granted a performance license to Red Baron and that the latter is thus guilty of copyright infringement.

We begin with the statute. Section 106 of Title 17, grants to the owner of a copyright five separate and distinct rights: (1) to reproduce the copyrighted work, (2) to prepare derivative works based on the copyrighted work, (3) to distribute copies of the copyrighted work to the public by sale, rental, etc., (4) to perform the copyrighted work publicly and (5) to display the copyrighted work publicly. By its very terms, the statute codifying the first sale doctrine, 17 U.S.C. § 109(a), is limited in its effect to the *distribution* of the copyrighted work. It prohibits the owner of the copyright in a work who has sold a copy of the work to another from preventing or restricting the transferee from a further sale or disposition of the possession of the copy. Thus, by its terms, § 109(a) has no application to the other four rights of a copyright owner, including the right to perform the work publicly.

The limited application of § 109(a) has been fully recognized by the Third Circuit in two decisions that we find persuasive. The first case to be decided by the Third Circuit, *Columbia Pictures Industries, Inc. v. Redd Horne, Inc.*, 749 F.2d 154 (3d Cir.1984), concerned the operators of video cassette stores which, in addition to renting and selling video cassettes—activities the legality of which was not challenged—also maintained booths where members of the public could view video cassettes upon payment of a fee. The operators had a license to distribute, but no license to perform publicly, from the copyright owner. When sued for infringement, the operators sought to defend their activities under the first sale doctrine. The contention, however, was rejected, the court holding that although the first sale doctrine "prevents the copyright owner from controlling the future transfer of a particular copy once its material ownership has been transferred," "the transfer of the video cassettes to the [operators] ... did not result in the forfeiture or waiver of all of the exclusive rights found in section 106," so that "the copyright owner's exclusive right 'to perform the copyrighted work publicly' ha[d] not been affected; only its distribution right as to the transferred copy ha[d] been circumscribed."

In *Columbia Pictures Industries, Inc. v. Aveco, Inc*, 800 F.2d 59 (3d Cir.1986), the court again considered the rental of video cassettes by a proprietor which had obtained the right to distribute from the producers of the films, but, having obtained no performance right, nevertheless exhibited the cassettes in private viewing rooms for a fee. When sued for infringement, the proprietor asserted the first sale defense, but, again, the court soundly rejected it:

> Even assuming, *arguendo*, both a waiver by Producers of their Section 106(3) distribution rights and a valid transfer of ownership of the video cassette during the rental period, the first sale doctrine is nonetheless irrelevant. The rights protected by copyright are divisible and the waiver of one does not necessarily waive any of the others.... In particular, the transfer of ownership in a particular copy of a work does not affect Producers' Section 106(4) exclusive rights to do and to authorize public performances.... It therefore cannot protect one who is infringing Producers' Section 106(4) rights by the public performance of the copyrighted work.

Other courts and commentators likewise agree that the first sale doctrine has no application to the rights of the owner of a copyright guaranteed by § 106, except the right of distribution.

We have considered Red Baron's other arguments and find them lacking in merit. We hold that Red Baron, not having a performance license from Taito or Taito America, infringed Taito's copyright. We therefore reverse the judgment of the district court and remand the case for further proceedings consistent with the views expressed herein.

———————

Notes and Questions

1. The court in *Red Baron* provided, "Taito had, of course, originally sold the circuit boards obtained by Red Baron in Japan and had not purported to retain any right to control their resale." If Taito had attempted only to license the board, and control its

permissive use via a EULA or TOS Agreement, would the result be different? Could it be done with a circuit board?

2. Are the different outcomes in *Allen Games* and *Red Baron* the result of different views of how the Copyright Act works, or are they based on different classifications of a videogame and a board game under the Act? How do the two courts classify the games involved in the cases?

3. In an article on the blog Ars technica, entitled "*Why Nintendo can legally shut down any* Smash Bros. *tournament it wants,*" Kyle Orland reported on Nintendo's (contemplated, but later abandoned) attempt to enjoin a *Smash Bros.* tournament put on by a third party who had purchased several copies of the game for tournament play.[9] He explained the differences between the copyright holder's rights to enjoin public performance of board games and videogames this way:

> [T]his all got us thinking about just how much right, legally, Nintendo has to stop people from simply playing its games in a tournament setting. With most games and sports, this isn't even an issue worth considering. Nobody owns the copyright to football, for instance, and there's no legal entity that can stop you from holding the world's largest charades tournament and charging for admission.
>
> Even board games, which have corporate owners and legally protectable components, can't be restricted in this way. While board game makers can copyright things like the board design and actual printed rules, they can't copyright the "heart" of the game; that is, its overall design and general method of play.
>
> Furthermore, in a 1996 case, the 9th Circuit Court of Appeals held that "playing of a [board] game is not a 'performance' within the meaning of the Copyright Act." That means there's nothing Scrabble owner Hasbro could do to stop someone from playing the game in the park in front of a bunch of spectators, for instance (though other courts might come to different conclusions, and anyone advertising a tournament may have to take care to avoid trademark issues).
>
> Video games are treated differently, though, primarily because they exist on a screen rather than a board. "A video game under copyright law is an audiovisual work, which gives a public performance right to the copyright holder," Dallas attorney Mark Methenitis explained in an interview with Ars. "Under the public performance right, the copyright holder is allowed to say when, where, or whether something is publicly performed, meaning displayed in front of a group of people larger than, say, at your house."
>
> In other words, if you want to put on a *Street Fighter* tournament and charge people to watch, Capcom can make you get a license for the "public performance" of the game. In fact, that is exactly what Capcom does with for-profit tournaments. When organizations like the World Cyber Games and Major League Gaming went around this requirement four years ago, Capcom exerted its rights and banned both tournaments from using Capcom games.

Is the article correct in how it analyzes the differences between board and videogames?

4. An analogy often given regarding the public performance rights of videogames and the first sale doctrine is the purchase of a DVD with a popular movie. Everyone agrees

---

9. Kyle Orland, *Why Nintendo can legally shut down any Smash Bros. tournament it wants ... but Hasbro probably can't shut down a similar Scrabble tournament*, Ars Technica (Sept. 7, 2014, 1:02 PM) http://arstechnica.com/gaming/2013/07/why-nintendo-can-legally-shut-down-any-smash-bros-tournament-it-wants/

that a customer can't buy a copy of the movie and then set up shop and charge admission to watch it. *See, e.g., Columbia Pictures Industries, Inc. v. Redd Horne, Inc.,* 749 F.2d 154 (3d Cir. 1984). Is a videogame more similar to a movie DVD or a board game for purposes of copyright law?

---

§ 11.40 In-Game Advertising

"Product placement" is a common term used to describe a marketing tool used by many companies, whereby money is paid to the producers of motion pictures and television shows who agree to display their client's products, not as commercials, but as part of the drama itself. Today, videogame producers are sharing in that product placement revenue stream, as well they should. A product placed in a film may catch the viewer's eye for a brief moment or two; that same placement in a videogame could be viewed by the users for countless hours as they struggle to solve the puzzle or slay a particularly nettlesome enemy.

It is difficult to track exactly how large the market is, but even if the low estimates are correct, the alternative, non-player revenue streams from advertisers are huge. All market analysts estimate a healthy double-digit growth for the foreseeable future. For example, Statista.com reported that in-game advertising in 2009 was about 700 million; an amount it projected had grown to 1.9 billion U.S. dollars worldwide by the end of 2010. Venturebeat.com puts the 2010 figure higher—at $3.1 billion—and projected it to hit to $7.2 billion in 2016. These amounts are exclusive of advertising gaming appearing on mobile devices, which one source, mobilemarketer.com, estimated would reach 1.2 billion by 2014, and which evidenced a 55 percent growth from 800 million in 2012.[10]

One acknowledged leader in in-game advertising is the owner and developer of the *Neopets* website. It has coined the name "immersion advertising" for its extensive inclusion of in-game ads, and an article in *Wired.com*[11] describes the company's philosophy:

> Neopets has a staggering 25 million members worldwide. It has been translated into 10 languages and gets more than 2.2 billion page views per month. These dedicated Neopians spend an average of 6 hours and 15 minutes per month on the site. That makes Neopets the second-stickiest site on the Internet—ahead of Yahoo!, MSN, AOL, and eBay, according to Media Matrix. What's more, its demographics are the stuff of marketer's dreams: Four out of five Neopians are under age 18, and two out of five are under 13.

> It's these numbers that have captured everyone's attention—Madison Avenue, Hollywood, and toy companies, all desperately trying to grab younger and younger audiences. The Neopets characters now appear as stuffed animals and action figures and on board games and trading cards. Warner Bros. is developing a

---

10. *Global video games advertising revenue 2007 to 2016,* Statista (Sept. 7, 2014, 1:13 PM) http://www.statista.com/statistics/238140/global-video-games-advertising-revenue/; Dean Takahashi, *Global ad spending in video games to top $7.2B in 2016,* Venturebeat (Sep. 7, 2014, 1:15 PM) http://venturebeat.com/2011/09/12/global-ad-spending-in-video-games-to-top-7-2b-in-2016/; Lauren Johnson, *Mobile and portable gaming revenue to hit $12B by 2014,* Mobile Marketer (Sept, 7, 2014, 1:16 PM) http://www.mobilemarketer.com/cms/news/research/15554.html

11. David Kushner, *The Neopets Addiction,* Wired (Sept. 7, 2014, 1:20 PM) http://archive.wired.com/wired/archive/13.12/neopets.html?pg=1andtopic=neopetsandtopic_set=

Neopets feature film. A PlayStation 2 version hit the market in October, and a PSP version is due out next year. And then there's perhaps the biggest deal of all: In June, Viacom—which owns CBS, MTV, Nickelodeon, and Paramount Pictures—bought Neopets for $160 million. "We want to be wherever kids are," says Jeff Dunn, president of Nickelodeon, who took charge of the Neopets brand. "And there are plenty of kids at Neopets."

For Viacom, the main draw is the site's advertising model. In a world of TiVo, pop-up blockers, and satellite radio, where it keeps getting harder to reach people with ads, Neopets collapses the boundaries between content and commercials. Many zones in the vast make-believe world, like the Firefly Mobile Phone Zone, are sponsored by companies, and there are branded games like Nestle Ice Cream Frozen Flights and Pepperidge Farms Goldfish Sandwich Snackers. Tyler [a pet of an individual identified earlier in the article—ED] likes to play McDonald's: Meal Hunt, in which he searches for lost McNuggets. Jana Gagen, his mom, says they've been taking more trips to the real-world McDonald's ever since Tyler started racking up NeoPoints in the restaurant's online game. "We go to get the Neopets toys," she says. The tie-in merchandise comes with Happy Meals.

Neopets calls its model "immersive advertising" and hypes it in a press kit as "an evolutionary step forward in the traditional marketing practice of product placement."

That sends critics like Kalle Lasn, editor in chief of the advertising watchdog magazine Adbusters, reeling. "They're encouraging kids to spend hours in front of the screen and at the same time recruiting them into consumer culture," Lasn says. "It's the most insidious mind … ever."

There's a perfect Smurf-blue sky over Southern California on this July afternoon, and Neopets CEO Doug Dohring is preaching the Neopian gospel. "I always saw this as more than just an Internet company," Dohring says. Dressed in a dark suit, the chubby 47-year-old chuckles heartily and frequently as we talk, and his hair becomes increasingly unkempt as he extols the virtues of his online pet sim. A shelf in the conference room at the company's Los Angeles headquarters is crammed with Neopet plush toys, trading cards, and CD racks. A Warholian portrait of a Neopet hangs on the wall. The table is dominated by an enormous bowl of jelly beans with a soup ladle inside.

Dohring's feeling particularly giddy today. He and a dozen executives have just returned from deep-sea fishing and volcano climbing on Maui. In May, two of his top guns received the Entertainment Marketer of the Year award from *Advertising Age*. And, having recently concluded the Viacom deal, he's basking in a $160 million glow.

Down the hall, past the two human-size Neopets in the reception area, dozens of geeks in blue jeans and T-shirts keep Neopia churning from their tchotchke-lined cubicles. Running this Oz is a round-the-clock enterprise, requiring 110 staffers in LA and another 20 in Singapore. Translators post the latest Neopian news in 10 languages. Programmers code minigames. Artists draw shiny, happy mutant pets. Sketches of the two latest breeds of Neopets—the Hissi, a winged serpent, and the Ruki, a flying insect—cover the walls. New characters, games, locales, and prizes are added to the online world almost daily. This efficient Hollywood-style assembly line is a far cry from the scrappy UK startup launched in November 1999 by a young couple hoping to quit their day jobs. Adam Powell and Donna Williams, still together and still with the company, met while they were high school students in Surrey. Powell grew up bagging groceries and coding his own role-playing games; Williams rode horses and dabbled in sculpture. Powell had left college in Nottingham to start an online-advertising agency. But making banner ads, primarily for his dad's hot water-bottle company, wasn't very lucrative—or interesting.

The couple had a veritable zoo of real-life pets, including birds, guinea pigs, and a tempestuous cat named Oscar. Powell and Williams imagined a fantasy pet site so addictive that people would gladly suffer through ads to experience it. "We thought virtual pets was a good idea," Powell says, "because people would get attached and keep coming back."

Living on credit cards, Powell began coding the larval version of the Neopets site while Williams, an art student at the time, handled the graphic design. "We wanted unique characters," Williams recalls, "something fantasy-based that could live in this weird, wonderful world." There was just one problem, Powell says. "Donna couldn't draw."

The Neopets themselves were decidedly less cutesy than, say, Pokemon. But the characters were shot through with wry collegiate prankishness. There were references to *The Hitchhiker's Guide to the Galaxy* (the option to feed your pet a Pan Galactic George Slushie, for example). One of the creatures was simply a JPEG of bow-tied British game show host Bruce Forsyth. "We were just trying to amuse ourselves," Powell says. "If people found it all funny, great." People did. After posting on a few pet newsgroups, Powell and Williams watched site traffic double day after day.

By Christmas 1999, Powell and Williams were getting 600,000 page views a day. But they were running out of money. They didn't have much in common with market research magnate Doug Dohring, but he had plenty of cash and they shared a vision. "We all saw the potential for this to be huge," Powell says.

Dohring brought two things to the company: expertise in market research and a deep commitment to the principles of Scientology. After college, he spent four years in Toledo working for the church in "counseling and communications." In the writings of Scientology leader L. Ron Hubbard, Dohring discovered a business model that would later become the foundation of the Neopets operation. "He created a management technology that's very powerful," Dohring says. Hubbard's companies follow a system of departmental organization called the Org Board, which he claimed was a refinement of one used by "an old Galactic civilization" that lasted 80 trillion years. Dohring is more concerned with down-to-earth prescriptions, like a corrections division to monitor the performance of other divisions. "It sounds like common sense," he says. "But you'd be surprised. Most companies are missing that."

Dohring first put these business principles into action in 1986, at age 28, when he started the Dohring Company. This market research firm soon became one of the largest in the US, a top provider of data to the automotive industry. The key to his success, he says, was paying attention not to the consumers who weren't buying, but to the ones who were. "Research what you're doing right," he says.

The Dohring Company moved to the Web in the 1990s and soon was selling polling data from 1 million online consumers to corporate customers. Dohring also invested in the Web-based game developer Speedyclick, which he later sold for $50 million. But the biggest payoff came when a Speedyclick staffer told Dohring about a British couple struggling to maintain an offbeat, highly trafficked virtual-pet site.

Dohring was so impressed by Neopets that he convinced his management team to buy the company for what he calls "a significant sum" in January 2000. The investment was initially passive, but one Saturday Dohring called in his team to tell them he wanted a more active role.

"I realized we could have the best of both worlds," he says."We could use the Internet to create Neopets that would reach youth on a global scale, and then be taken into the real world. It was a Net-to-land strategy, the opposite of what everyone else was trying to do." Neopets could become like Marvel comics for a new generation—spinning its core product off into endless additional mediums. "I never thought we could be bigger than Disney," Dohring says, "but if we could create something *like* Disney—that would be phenomenal."

Dohring brought along his previous company's market research experts—and Hubbard-powered efficiency. They shunned the splashy ad campaigns other boom-era dotcoms used to build audiences, relying instead on Neopets' devotees. "It's all word of mouth," says Lee Borth, Neopets' COO. "It's the school yard." Dohring maintained the quirkiness of the original vision and has even retained the site's "colourful" Britishisms. But he's also made changes. "I ordinarily don't show this to people," he says, as he twiddles his laptop in the conference room, "but here you go." A window opens on a large monitor nestled between the stuffed animals. It displays what might be called the Evolution of Bruce. On the left is the original Bruce, a bow-tied Neopet that was Williams' tribute to Bruce Forsyth. On the right is Bruce as he appears today: a tiny blue penguin.

"He still has his bow tie, but that's about all that's similar," Dohring says, admiring the art like a dad looking at his kid's drawings. He says Powell and Williams didn't care about using other people's intellectual property. "One of the first hires I made was a general counsel. I said, 'We need to own everything 100 percent. And if we can't own it, remove it.'"

Dohring's next move was to identify new ways to generate revenue. The result: immersive advertising, a phrase Neopets has trademarked.

The idea is straightforward enough. For example, a link from Neopia Central, the site's shopping district, takes members to a splash page for the Cereal Adventure zone. Dotting lush green hillsides are the homes of a half-dozen breakfast mascots, from the Trix rabbit to the Cocoa Puffs cuckoo. Clicking on Lucky the Leprechaun leads to a game called *Lucky Charms: Shooting Stars!*, in which kids navigate a series of marshmallow treats—hearts! moons! stars!—to earn NeoPoints.

Visitors can also surf into the Disney Theater, where they can buy their pets some popcorn (740 NeoPoints) and settle in to watch previews for *Lilo & Stitch 2*. And they can earn 300 NeoPoints by answering a market research survey linked from the homepage (questions like, When was your last visit to Wal-Mart, and Are you aware there's a new Power Rangers DVD?). Kate Parker, an 11-year-old Neopian from Mason, Ohio, likes to play the *Limited Too: Mix & Match* game, which lets her combine images of actual clothing sold at the tween boutique. "It's got good advertising and fun colors," she says, "and shows you things you might want to buy in real life."

The roster of clients who have set up shop inside the land of Neopia runs from Atari and DreamWorks to Frito-Lay and Lego. While passive product placement has become standard in TV and film, the Neopets approach emphasizes interaction and integration. Neopians can even win virtual trophies featuring Bubble Yum and SweeTarts, and display them for other players.

This seamless interweaving of marketing and entertainment is an advertiser's dream come true. "There's nothing on the Net delivering an experience like Neopets," says David Card, a senior analyst for Jupiter Research. "Kids aren't being harangued, and parents think it's safe."

It's precisely this kind of environment that proved irresistible to Viacom, which is on a mission of corporate reinvention through what chair Sumner Redstone calls "an accelerated expansion into new and emerging platforms." Dohring now answers to Jeff Dunn, president of Nickelodeon. Dunn says that Neopets is a great complement to Nick.com and other kid-friendly Viacom portals. "We couldn't help notice that there was this site that had an enormous number of kids," Dunn says. "It's quicker and easier and more effective to buy Neopets than to start something incremental ourselves."

Of course, what attracted Viacom to Neopets is exactly what makes children's advocates and media critics bristle. "It's clearly an effort to plant brand names in the minds of children," says James McNeal, professor emeritus of marketing at Texas A&M University and author of *The Kids Market: Myths and Realities.* "It is not until around 8 years old that they can mentally defend against a persuasive sales message if they wish to." Neopets reports that half a million of its users are under age 8.

Susan Linn, associate director of the Media Center for Children at Judge Baker Children's Center, agrees. "When childhood obesity is a major public health problem, what moral, ethical, or social justification is there for having kids earn points by watching commercials for sugar cereals?"

Dohring turns his palms to the ceiling and shrugs. "You're never going to please everybody," he says. He insists there's "nothing subliminal" at work and that no one is forcing kids to play the ad-driven games. "This wasn't done, like, Oh, let's make this healthy. We just put all kinds of things on the site, and users will migrate toward things that interest them." The immersive ads make up a small fraction of site content, he says, and are clearly labeled. This is true: There's small print at the bottom of the Neopia Central page that reads, "This page contains paid advertisements." But it doesn't identify where and how those ads appear; young children may have trouble distinguishing them from other content on the site.

Occasionally, Neopets does give in to criticism. After parents' groups raised an outcry over kids gambling for NeoPoints, the company limited access to its roulette, blackjack, and slots to players 13 and over (a cutoff many find ludicrous and arbitrary). But Dohring didn't respond to outcries of Neopians who lost their shirts on the Neodaq, a stock market in which all members can invest their NeoPoints. "Around the time of the Enron scandal, we bankrupted three of those companies just for the hell of it," he says. The Neopians weren't amused. "They were saying, 'This is no fair!'" he recalls with a laugh. "But, hey, stuff happens in the world."

Notes and Questions

1. As in-game advertising specifically targeted toward children expands, Sara M. Grimes notes that issues regarding media regulation, consumer protection law, industry self-regulation, and contract law will arise, and that children are in need of legal protection. "Children's vulnerability to advertiser manipulation, their lack of knowledge of economic and legal processes, and the fragility of their still-burgeoning rights, all justify the need for a 'double-standard' in how we address children's advergames. Until minors are granted the same special status online as previously established in media policies, international conventions and national law, children's rights will remain largely unprotected within the digital environment."[12]

2. What distinctions, if any, would you draw to separate in-game advertising from the typical "Saturday Morning" television spots that are clearly directed at children?

---

12. 12 Int'l J. Comm. L. & Pol'y 161

Part IV

Product Regulation

Chapter Twelve

Regulating the Sale
and Use of Videogames

Cities and states have long tried to regulate videogames. Some towns banned videogame arcades altogether. Others limited the number of videogames in an arcade as a condition of issuing a business permit. Some states prohibited arcades from being open during school hours. Some governments passed laws prohibiting anyone under 17 from playing a "violent" game without being accompanied by a parent. Others made retailers criminally liable if they sold "sexually explicit" games to minors. Arcade owners, users, and industry associations have regularly sued to challenge these ordinances.

There is a definite arc to the government's success in fending off these anti-regulatory challenges. In the 1970s and 1980s, the cities and states won almost every time. By the early 1990s, however, the momentum had begun to shift, and in the new millennium, states and municipalities have invariably been on the losing end.

What changed? Easy. The application of the First Amendment to videogames. Early videogames, like *Pong*, had no story, no theme, and no expressive content that merited constitutional protection. But as the games became more visually rich, with plots, characters and dialogue, the courts analogized videogames more and more to movies, books, and stories, and accorded them more First Amendment protection from regulation.

Section 12.10 below is a constitutional primer, which explains how the process works and the significance of First Amendment protection in the litigation of these regulatory challenges. Section 12.20 consists of the cases which illustrate the history of this type of litigation. Section 12.30 describes the industry's self-regulatory scheme, which was used, in part, to fend off governmental regulation.

§ 12.10 A Constitutional Primer
on Regulatory Challenges

All of the cases in this chapter challenge the constitutionality of a statute or regulation. If you are taking this videogame law course before taking Constitutional Law, the language and doctrines expounded in these cases could become confusing. Con Law definitely has its own lingo. Thus, we wanted to provide a primer to give you some general idea of the substantive law regarding regulatory challenges to social welfare and zoning legislation, and the effect of First Amendment protection on such challenges. Like all "primers," it simplifies the law a bit and the lack of nuance may make our Constitutional Law colleagues squeal. But our hope is that it will make the cases in this chapter easier to follow.

There are many potential grounds on which to challenge the constitutionality of a statute. One challenge is based on the due process clause of the Fourteenth Amendment. The gist of a "substantive due process" challenge is that the government did not have a sufficient basis or reason for enacting the statute. Governments cannot constitutionally pass whatever statutes they want, with no reason, and courts have the power to review whether the city or state had a sufficient basis to act the way it did. With that said, courts typically give legislatures and city counsels a great deal of deference, and since 1938, the rule is that most social welfare legislation is "presumptively valid" and the statute will be upheld if there is at least a "rational basis" for the law. *United States v. Carolene Products Co.*, 304 U.S. 144, 152–54 (1938); *New Orleans v. Dukes*, 427 U.S. 297, 303 (1976). Essentially, this same rule of presumptive validity under the "rational basis" standard was later extended to zoning regulations, meaning that if a city refused to zone an area for arcades, that decision would likely be upheld. *Schad v. Borough of Mt. Ephraim*, 452 U.S. 61 (1981). The burden is on the party challenging the regulation to establish that no rational basis for the law exists, a burden which courts characterize as "onerous." *See, e.g., Marshfield Family Skateland v. Town of Marshfield*, 450 N.E. 2d 605, 611 (Mass. 1983).

Part of what makes a challenge to social welfare legislation so "onerous" is the way the courts undertake the so called "means-ends" analysis under the rational basis test. Let's say a city has passed an ordinance providing that all videogame arcades have to be closed by 10:00 pm. Typically a city will claim that the end, or goal, it is trying to achieve with such a statute is something broad, like "protecting the health, safety and welfare" of the town's residents. The arcade owner-plaintiff who challenges the law will argue that there is no evidence that having arcades close at 10:00 pm will further that goal. In other words, even if the "end" goal of the legislation is legitimate (and who can argue that a city trying to protect the health and welfare of it's citizens is not a legitimate end), the "means" to effect that end goal (10:00 pm closing) does not actually further that goal, or at least there is no evidence that it does so.

Under the rational basis test, however, a city council need not have any hard proof that links the goal of the statute with the means. If the city provides e.g., a statement by the police chief who says that in his or her opinion crime goes up around video arcades if they are kept open after 10:00 at night, that will be enough to defeat the arcade owner's constitutional challenge. But even if the city provides *no* evidence of a means-ends fit, courts are directed to *presume* facts that would, under any conceivable logical theory, provide a sufficient rational basis that the goal of the statute is furthered by its means, and thereby uphold the statute's constitutionality:

> [T]he existence of facts supporting the legislative judgment *is to be presumed*, for regulatory legislation affecting ordinary commercial transactions is not to be pronounced unconstitutional unless in the light of the facts made known or generally assumed it is of such a character as to preclude the assumption that it rests upon some rational basis within the knowledge and experience of the legislators ... [B]y their very nature such inquiries, where the legislative judgment is drawn in question, must be restricted to the issue whether any state of facts either known *or which could reasonably be assumed* affords support for it.

Carolene Products Co., 304 U.S. at 152, 154 (emphasis added).

The entire landscape changes, however, when the statute attempts to regulate or proscribe a "fundamental right." *Carolene Products Co.*, 304 U.S. at 152 n.4. What are fundamental rights? As Professors Nowak and Rotunda explain, "The rights the Court has recognized as fundamental and deserving of significant judicial protection are most of the guarantees of the Bill of Rights ..." JOHN E. NOWAK & RONALD D. ROTUNDA, CONSTITUTIONAL LAW 378 (4th ed. 1991). With regard to videogames, the fundamental rights involved are the freedom of speech and, to a lesser extent, freedom of association, protections under the First Amendment. If a game (or a group assembled to play it, e.g., at an arcade) has First Amendment protection, then the test for the statute's constitutionality is under the "strict scrutiny," rather than the "rational basis" standard. *See, e.g., R.A.V. v. City of Paul*, 505 U.S. 377, 382, 403 (1992). Under the strict scrutiny test, the rules are reversed and the statute is "presumptively *invalid*." Thus, the court must independently, and strictly, scrutinize whether the provision, "is necessary to further a compelling state interest" and whether it is "narrowly tailored" to serve that interest. *Id.* at 395; *Republican Party of Minn. v. White*, 536 U.S. 765, 774–75 (2002). In other words, the means-ends fit must be much tighter than under the rational basis standard. Practically, this means that the burden is on the legislature (not the plaintiff) to establish by "actual and substantial" evidence that a compelling state interest is served by the legislation, and that the regulation by which that goal is achieved is no broader than is necessary:

> [T]he State cannot simply "posit the existence of the disease sought to be cured. Rather it must demonstrate that the recited harms are real, not merely conjectural, and that the regulation will, in fact, alleviate those harms in a direct and material way."

Entm't Software Ass'n v. Granholm, 426 F. Supp. 2d 646 (E.D. Mich. 2005), quoting from *Turner Broad. Sys. v. F.C.C.*, 512 U.S. 622 (1994); *see also, e.g., Century Commc'n Corp. v. F.C.C.*, 835 F.2d 292, 304 (D.C. Cir. 1987) (holding that "when trenching on first amendment interests, even incidentally, the government must be able to adduce empirical support.").

Hence, under the strict scrutiny standard, generalizations such as the statute is designed to protect the health, safety, and welfare of the community, and in the unsubstantiated opinion of the police chief a 10:00 pm closing of arcades will help fight crime, are insufficient to save the statute from constitutional invalidity. Actual evidence establishing that there is a problem with crime if the arcade stays open past 10:00 pm is required, along with evidence that the crime is directly tied to the arcade being open, that the proposed legislation will fix the problem, and that the problem can't be fixed in some other way that is less infringing on assembly rights.

Another way the tight means-ends fit is expressed is by saying a statute may not be "overbroad." That is, even if the goal of the statute is legitimate, the legislature cannot take more of a regulatory bite than is necessary to further that goal:

> An overbroad statute—a statute that is written too broadly—is one that is designed to burden or punish activities that are not constitutionally protected, but the statute also includes within its scope protected activities. In a case of a statute that is overbroad on its face, the speaker's actions or speech may not be protected by the first amendment and thus the act could have prohibited under a carefully drawn statute. Nevertheless, the Court will strike the overbroad statute because it might apply to others, not before the Court, who may engage in *protected* activity that the statute appears to outlaw.

JOHN E. NOWAK & RONALD D. ROTUNDA, CONSTITUTIONAL LAW 945 (4th ed. 1991).

In an early overbreadth case, the Court cautioned that the State's power "must be so exercised as not, in attaining a permissible end, unduly infringe upon the protected freedom." *Cantwell v. Conn.*, 310 U.S. 296, 304 (1940). And in *Broadrick v. Okla.*, 413 U.S. 601, 613 (1973) the Court explained:

> [The purpose of the overbreadth doctrine is] a limited one at the outset ... [It] attenuates as the otherwise protected behavior that it forbids the State to sanction moves from "pure speech" toward conduct ... To put the matter another way, particularly where conduct and not merely speech is involved, we believe that the overbreadth of a statute must not only be real, but substantial as well, judged in relation to the statute's plainly legitimate sweep.

Statutes can also be unconstitutional due to underinclusiveness, i.e., where the legislature or city council singled out one industry, such as videogames, to regulate, when to cure the problem more industries needed to be put under the scope of the regulation. *See, e.g., Erznoznik v. Jacksonville*, 422 U.S. 205 (1975).

Another common challenge in the cases found in this chapter is based on the equal protection clause. The gist of an equal protection challenge is that there is an insufficient basis to treat two classes of people or businesses differently. That is, there are insufficient grounds for a city to dictate that one business, say a bowling alley, has no restrictions on when it should close, while saying to another business, such as a videogame arcade, that it must close at 10:00 pm. The tests under equal protection have the same names as those under substantive due process, i.e., rational basis and strict scrutiny. There is an additional reason that triggers the change from the general rational basis test to strict scrutiny under equal protection. In addition to legislation affecting a "fundamental right," strict scrutiny under equal protection is also invoked when a statute treats differently those in a "suspect class" such as race or alienage. However, the court's role, the burden of proof, and the kinds of evidence that the government must put forward to defeat the constitutional challenge to its legislation is essentially the same under the rational basis and strict scrutiny tests whether analyzed under equal protection or due process. JOHN E. NOWAK & RONALD D. ROTUNDA, CONSTITUTIONAL LAW 574–76 (4th ed. 1991).

Another constitutional challenge that you will read about in this chapter is "vagueness," which is a due process concept. To withstand a vagueness challenge, a statute must set forth with, "sufficient definiteness that ordinary people can understand what conduct is prohibited." *Kolender v. Lawson* 461 U.S. 352, 357 (1983). The issue comes up, e.g., when a statute attempts to make a crime the selling of videogames of "extreme violence," but makes the definition of what constitutes extreme violence so amorphous that even a conscientious store owner does not know whether he or she can legitimately sell *Mortal Kombat 3*. Or a conscientious police officer does not know whether to cite a store under the "extreme violence" statute for selling *Grand Theft Auto: San Andreas* to a 17 year old and is thus given a constitutionally impermissible amount of discretion in enforcing the provision. Whether or not a statute is unconstitutionally "vague" is largely determined by an individualized, case-by-case fact inquiry.

We will add to and refine these concepts as the chapter unfolds, but the above primer should be sufficient to make the cases comprehensible even if you have not yet taken Constitutional Law.

§ 12.20 Regulatory Challenges to Videogame Legislation

Our review of the cases is broken into three time periods. We start with the earlier (1980s) cases in which constitutional protection was not accorded to videogames (§ 12.21). We then examine the cases (1990s and into the new millennium) which first gave games First Amendment status (§ 12.22), thereby invoking strict scrutiny. Finally, we examine the success of legislative strategies when legislatures try to regulate games knowing that they have First Amendment protection (§ 12.23), with the Supreme Court's opinion in *Brown* being featured.

---

§ 12.21 The "Early" Era and the Rational Basis Test

Caswell v. Licensing Comm'n For Brockton

Supreme Judicial Court of Massachusetts, 1983
444 N.E.2d 922

HENNESSEY, Chief Justice.

The plaintiff, Frank E. Caswell, commenced an action for declaratory relief against the defendant, the licensing commission for the city of Brockton (commission). Caswell's complaint sought review of the commission's denial, under G.L. c. 140, § 177A ["177A"— ED.], of Caswell's application for licenses for seventy-five coin-operated electronic amusement games, commonly known as video games. After a hearing, a Superior Court judge denied a motion by Caswell for summary judgment and granted the commission's motion for summary judgment. Caswell then filed his appeal.

Caswell contends that 177A, is unconstitutional under the United States and Massachusetts Constitutions both on its face because it is impermissibly vague and as applied because it violates rights to free expression and association. Caswell also asserts that the evidence presented in this case is insufficient as a matter of law to support a denial of Caswell's application. We disagree with Caswell's constitutional arguments.

In 1981, Caswell, a resident of Brockton and the owner of a local restaurant, sought to enter the business of operating an entertainment center featuring coin-operated video games. To this end, Caswell leased premises in a free-standing building adjacent to the Westgate Mall shopping area in Brockton. In April, 1981, he filed with the commission applications for licenses for seventy-five video games. At a public hearing, Caswell presented a comprehensive plan for the design, maintenance, and operation of his video game entertainment center. The following rules would be posted at the center and strictly enforced: no smoking, eating, drinking, or loitering, and no school age children admitted during school hours. To prevent loitering, Caswell's premises would have no seats. To ensure that the rules would be enforced and to control crowds, Caswell proposed to keep at least four people on duty at the center at any given time.

At the hearing, the commission considered written and telephone communication from community members and officials. The commission also heard testimony from a city councillor, an attorney representing the owners of the Westgate Mall, and a lieutenant of the Brockton police department. These people voiced opposition to the granting of the licenses. Various concerns with the arcade were expressed, including the adverse impact the proposed video center might have on an existing problem of youths congregating in the Westgate Mall area and on the high school's absentee rate. Concern was also expressed that patrons of Caswell's entertainment center would park in the Westgate Mall's shopping area and would cross a dangerous street to go to the arcade. The commission stated at Caswell's hearing that no policy exists against licensing video games or arcades. In July, 1981, the commission denied Caswell's applications, stating that the decision "was based on the opinion of the members that an arcade at this location would not be in the best interests of the City of Brockton." The commission cited "the proximity of Westgate Mall and the public safety problems which might arise therefrom" as particular concerns supporting the denial.

1.

Caswell argues that 177A violates fundamental rights of free expression under the United States and Massachusetts Constitutions. A dispositive threshold issue is whether the video game entertainment that Caswell sought to present is expression entitled to constitutional protection.[1] The First Amendment protects the communication or expression of ideas or information. *See Cohen v. California*, 403 U.S. 15, 25–26 (1971). Entertainment may come within the ambit of the First Amendment, but to gain protected status, that entertainment must be designed to communicate or express some idea or some information. *See Schad v. Mount Ephraim*, 452 U.S. 61, 65 (1981) (nude dancing).

The Supreme Court of California has suggested standards to be applied in determining which types of entertainment and amusement may be entitled to First Amendment protection. That court stated: "[N]o case has ever held or suggested that simple physical activity falls within the ambit of the First Amendment, at least in the absence of some element of communicating or advancing ideas or beliefs.... '[A]ll forms of communication, not merely the expression of concrete and definite ideas, *potentially* receive First Amendment protection.'... The key element is, of course, *communication*" (emphasis in original). *Sunset Amusement Co. v. Board of Police Comm'rs of Los Angeles*, 7 Cal.3d 64, 74, (1972). Under this standard, the court concluded that the physical activity of roller skating in a public roller skating rink was not protected speech because, although some expression might be involved, the patrons of the skating rink primarily use the facilities for physical exercise and personal pleasure.

In this case it is clear that video games contain an element of physical activity. Indeed, an affidavit presented on behalf of Caswell states that "[s]uccessful play on these video games depends on the player's *eye-hand coordination, reflexes, muscular control,* concentration, practice, and on the player's understanding of the rules of play" (emphasis supplied). Nevertheless, Caswell argues that video games are deserving of First Amendment protection because they do contain communicative and expressive elements, analogous to motion picture and television entertainment. *But see America's Best Family Showplace Corp. v. City of N.Y.*, 536 F. Supp. 170, 173–174 (E.D.N.Y. 1982) (video games not protected speech because no element of information or idea is being communicated).

Caswell asserts that video games are similar to television and motion picture entertainment in that every video game computer program represents the author's

---

1. Another threshold issue is whether Caswell has standing to assert the free speech rights of potential patrons of his video game arcade and of the creators of the games. We do not reach that issue, however, because Caswell clearly has standing to claim that he has a First Amendment right to present protected expression to the public. Thus, we may consider whether video games are a form of protected expression without deciding whether Caswell has standing to raise the free speech rights of others.

expression of a particular idea or fantasy in a tangible form. This idea or fantasy, Caswell submits, is transmitted to the consumer by means of audio and visual effects. An affidavit presented on behalf of Caswell discusses the video game "Space Invaders" as representative of the other seventy-four games that Caswell proposed to license. The affidavit indicates that video games contain computer programs that are stored in a memory. These computer programs, with the aid of circuitry, a cathode ray tube, and speakers, can reproduce continuously an audio visual display of images for video game-playing. The affidavit also indicates that the computer programs have a plot or theme-in the case of Space Invaders, the game player must strive to shoot down attacking invaders before the player's own laser bases are destroyed.

On the record before us, however, we conclude that Caswell has not satisfied his burden of demonstrating that video games are or contain protected expression. Although the affidavit indicates that video games might involve the element of communication that is the sine qua non of First Amendment protection—for example, a player may strive to shoot down invaders—this showing is insufficient to demonstrate protected expression. We conclude that summary judgment was granted properly against Caswell despite Caswell's constitutional arguments, because he has failed to demonstrate that video games import sufficient communicative, expressive or informative elements to constitute expression protected under the First Amendment. From the record before us, it appears that any communication or expression of ideas that occurs during the playing of a video game is purely inconsequential. Caswell has succeeded in establishing only that video games are more technologically advanced games than pinball or chess. That technological advancement alone, however, does not impart First Amendment status to what is an otherwise unprotected game. Hence, we determine that on this record protected expression has not been shown.

Caswell maintains that 177A violates his potential patrons' rights to free assembly and freedom of association arising under the First Amendment. Freedom of association guarantees an opportunity for people to express their ideas and beliefs through membership or affiliation with a group. In *Griswold v. Connecticut*, 381 U.S. 479 (1965), the Supreme Court also indicated that this right protects "forms of 'association' that are not political in the customary sense but pertain to the social, legal, and economic benefit of the members." Caswell urges that potential patrons' freedom of association is infringed by the denial of his license applications because potential patrons have a right of access to his video game arcade. We disagree.

The Supreme Court's reasoning in freedom of association cases does not support a constitutional right on the part of potential patrons to gather at Caswell's proposed arcade for video game amusement. Caswell points to no identifiable group consisting of video game players. Furthermore, even if there were such an identifiable group, gathering in an amusement arcade for the purpose of playing video games would not advance the social, legal, and economic benefits of the group's members in the way that the freedom of association contemplates.

Caswell contends that G.L. c. 140, § 177A, is unconstitutionally vague because it fails to set forth any standards to limit administrative discretion. Since neither First Amendment freedoms nor criminal conduct are concerned in this case, a less stringent vagueness standard applies. Thus, we limit our vagueness analysis to whether 177A is unconstitutionally vague as applied in this case. We conclude that 177A, is not unconstitutionally vague. The purpose of 177A, is "the preservation of public order at public entertainments." Because 177A is concerned with the impact of a particular video game or video game arcade on a particular community and because First Amendment freedoms are not involved in this case, the statute need not specify with great particularity the relevant considerations in evaluating a license application.

Notes and Questions

1. The court mentions *Schad v. Borough of Mt. Ephraim*, 452 U.S. 61 (1981). In *Schad*, the Court held that non-obscene nude dancing in coin operated "peek" booths housed in an adult book store was entitled to First Amendment protection as a form of free speech and expression. It also noted that a zoning regulation may be unconstitutional if it "deprive[s] the owner of economically viable use of his property." How did the court in *Caswell* distinguish the communicative activity of nude dancing from that in *Space Invaders*? How did it distinguish videogames from movies? Was there an argument that the denial of the certificate was a "taking" by deprivation of the viable economic use of the property?

2. In this era of videogame regulation cases, the proponent of videogames always tried to liken videogames to movies. Here is one court's description of the case that ushered in First Amendment protection for movies:

In *Joseph Burstyn, Inc. v. Wilson*, 343 U.S. 495 (1952), the Supreme Court first held motion pictures to be protected speech. The Court there stated:

> It cannot be doubted that motion pictures are a significant medium for the communication of ideas. They may affect public attitudes and behavior in a variety of ways, ranging from direct espousal of a political or social doctrine to the subtle shaping of thought which characterizes all artistic expression. The importance of motion pictures as an organ of public opinion is not lessened by the fact that they are designed to entertain as well as to inform. As was said in *Winters v. People of State of New York*, 1948, 333 U.S. 507, 510:
>
> > The line between the informing and the entertaining is too elusive for the protection of that basic right (a free press). Everyone is familiar with instances of propaganda through fiction. What is one man's amusement, teaches another's doctrine.

Am.'s Best Family Showplace Corp. v. New York, Dep't of Bldgs., 536 F. Supp. 170, 174 (E.D.N.Y. 1982)

Do you agree with *Caswell* that 1980s-era videogames were more a physical, than a communicative, activity, and were not like movies?

3. In addition to his freedom of speech argument, the plaintiff in *Caswell* also challenged the regulation on right of assembly and freedom of association grounds. How did the plaintiff frame the argument, and on what basis did the court reject it? Do you believe there should be a constitutional right to assemble and associate with others who wish to play videogames in an arcade?

4. As indicated, without a fundamental right or suspect class involved, there is a strong presumption that any zoning or other social welfare legislation is valid. But every so often, cities will act without even a rational basis and/or with dubious statutory authority, and in such cases, their regulations will be overturned. *See, e.g., While You Wait Photo Corp. v. Dep't of Consumer Affairs of City of New York*, 450 N.Y.S.2d 334 (1982) (invalidating regulations calling for increased security, additional insurance, and changed hours of operation for renewal of the business license of a videogame arcade located in Times Square).

* * *

Rather than attempting to directly regulate the business of videogame arcades as in *Caswell*, some cities attempted to regulate the users or players who could enter an arcade.

City of Warren v. Walker

Court of Appeals of Michigan, 1984
354 N.W.2d 312

WAHLS, Judge.

This case presents the question of whether a municipality may lawfully prohibit its youths from engaging in the now popular pastime of playing electronic video games. We find the matter to be somewhat novel and of no small constitutional importance. The factual background is comparatively straight-forward.

The City of Warren enacted an ordinance which under the general licensing rubric prohibited a youth under the age of 17 from any public association or involvement with electronic video games without his parent or guardian being present:[2]

Defendant, Jacqueline Walker, the owner of Walker's Pinball Arcade, catered to youths within the City of Warren. On January 18, 1979, two police officers observed several individuals in defendant's arcade who appeared to be minors. Upon entering and questioning the youths, the officers ascertained that at least six youths were under 17 and were not accompanied by a parent or guardian. The officers issued defendant a citation charging her with "allowing a minor to operate mechanical machines." Following a bench trial in district court, defendant was found guilty of violating the ordinance and assessed a fine and costs in the amount of $500. On appeal, the Circuit Court affirmed. Defendant challenges the validity of the ordinance on the following grounds:

1. The ordinance restricts the exercise of fundamental First Amendment rights of expression and association;

2. The ordinance violates federal and state constitutional guarantees of equal protection[.]

I.

Defendant asserts that the ordinance restricts, without compelling reason, the right of persons under the age of 17 to associate by prohibiting them from coming to the game center unless accompanied by an adult.

Were this Court to hold that playing pinball or video games is a fundamental right, it is clear that the City of Warren would then have the burden of justifying the restriction with an interest sufficiently compelling to outweigh the impermissible effect of the ordinance. Further, the existence of a compelling interest may yet be insufficient if we find that the ordinance is too restrictive under the circumstances.

---

2. The penalty provisions for violation of the ordinance are set forth below:

"Sec. 1-110 General penalty—Whenever in this code or any ordinance of the city any act is prohibited or is made or declared to be unlawful or an offense, or whenever in this code or such ordinance the doing of any act is required or the failure to do any act is declared to be unlawful, the violation of any such provision by any person shall, upon conviction, be punished by a fine not exceeding $500.00 or imprisonment for a term not exceeding 90 days, or both, except whenever a specific penalty is otherwise provided."

We have searched in vain for a sustainable theory upon which to base such a ruling. However, the ordinance in this case must pass constitutional muster.[3]

The right of association is not expressly recited in or created by the language of the First Amendment of the Constitution to the United States. But it has long been recognized as implicit within and emanating from the rights expressly guaranteed. The right of association has received recognition in connection with group associations. However, it has never been held to apply to the right of an individual to associate for purposes purely social in character.

The criterion established thus far appears to protect the right to associate when the expressive conduct around which the association is centered is accorded protection by the First Amendment. Thus, a group which assembles for purposes constitutionally protected under the freedom of expression guarantee may properly require a compelling interest when the government seeks to interfere with or discourage the group's pursuit.

Defendant has not demonstrated that the communicative elements of playing video games are entitled to constitutional protection. We are not prepared on these facts to so hold. Therefore, the ordinance which restricts association for this purpose is not violative of the First Amendment.

II.

Defendant next asserts that the application of the 17 year old age requirement to amusement machine centers violates the federal and state constitutional guarantees of equal protection. U.S. Const., Am. XIV; Const.1963, art. 1, §2. Equal protection cases are analyzed under a two-tiered approach:

---

3. In our judgment, the facts of this case present a classic "Trouble in River City" scenario (depicted in the Broadway musical The Music Man), wherein popular pastimes of youths such as bowling, billiards, roller skating and pinball machines are singled out as activities which exert immoral influences on the youths. Establishments which cater to such activities have been held to be a common nuisance:

> "The 'hurt' or injury to the community, which has occasioned bowling alleys kept for gain and common use to be regarded as common nuisances, arises from their tendency to withdraw the young and inconsiderate from any useful employment of their time, and to subject them to various temptations. Clerks, apprentices and others are induced, not only to appropriate to them hours, which should be employed to increase their knowledge and reform their hearts, but too often to violate higher moral duties to obtain means to pay for the indulgence. Other bad habits are in such places often introduced or confirmed. The moral sense, the correct principles, the temperate, regular and industrious habits, which are the basis of a prosperous and happy community, are frequently impaired or destroyed. Bowling alleys without doubt may be resorted to by many persons without such injurious results. The inquiry is not what may be done at such places without injury to persons of fixed habits and principles, but what has been in the experience of man, their general tendency and result. The law notices the usual effect, the ordinary result of a pursuit or course of conduct, and by that decides upon its character. It need not be the necessary and inevitable result of a bowling alley kept for gain and common use, that it is thus injurious to the community, to make it a common nuisance." *State v. Haines*, 30 Me. 65, 75–76; (1849).

In most instances, the moral stigma disappears as the interests of the youths change and as the mores of the community change (usually as the minors become responsible adults). We are not convinced, indeed we feel strongly, that other less restrictive alternatives are available to the City of Warren to help control the truancy of its youths. Unfortunately, this observation does not reach the constitutional question.

If the interest is 'fundamental' or the classification 'suspect', the court applies a 'strict scrutiny' test requiring the state to show a 'compelling' interest which justifies the classification. Rarely have courts sustained legislation subjected to this standard of review. Other legislation, principally social and economic, is subjected to review under the traditional equal protection test. The burden is on the person challenging the classification to show that it is without reasonable justification. It has been said that '[a] statutory discrimination will not be set aside if any state of facts reasonably may be conceived to justify it'. A classification will stand unless it is shown to be 'essentially arbitrary'. Few statutes have been found so wanting in 'rationality' as to fail to satisfy the 'essentially arbitrary' test.

Age is not a suspect classification for equal protection purposes. Nor, of course, are mechanical amusements or amusement machine centers a suspect classification. Defendant argues, however, that the classifications created by the ordinance as to age and mechanical amusements are arbitrary. The city offers the following in its briefs on appeal as justification for the ordinance:

> The ordinance in question was passed because children were spending their lunch money on the pinball machines instead of buying lunch. Some children were 'borrowing' lunch money from other children to play the pinball machines. The term 'borrowing' includes strong-arm robbery. Children were stealing money from their parents. These instances occurred when pinball machine arcades were located close to schools. On occasion where the amusement center was located close to other stores, the neighboring store owners complained that at noon time and after school there were so many children gathering around that customers could not get into their stores. With parents and school officials complaining, something had to be done to regulate the amusement centers. The lengthy police reports and citizen complaints documenting evidence of vandalism, truancy, drug and alcohol abuse, and irresponsible use of money, coupled with complaints of noise, littering, traffic problems and an increased crime and trespassing incidents in neighboring areas and businesses clearly demonstrates a deterioration of certain public interests.

The city also alleged that deleterious psychological effects result from playing video and pinball games, such as gambling compulsions and addiction to playing such games.

We do not believe defendant has sustained her burden of showing that the ordinance in question is without any reasonable justification. We disagree that the ordinance must be struck down because the city chose to treat minors and pinball or video machine arcades differently than adults and bowling alleys. The current popularity of amusement arcades, particularly among young people, has clearly created problems unique to such businesses which the City of Warren has attempted to minimize by the implementation of the ordinance under attack here. The classifications in the ordinance are not "essentially arbitrary."

Notes and Questions

1. As videogames have moved from arcades to home computers, the holdings of arcade cases such as *Caswell* and *Walker* lose some of their currency. Nevertheless, the constitutional reasoning on which they rely is important in understanding the limits of permissible regulation.

2. In *Walker* the court noted that the City believed the proximity of the arcade to a school caused children to spend their lunch money on such machines instead of buying lunch, caused 'borrowing' (robbing) lunch money from other children, and resulted in kids stealing money from their parents to play games. Aren't there other ways, including existing laws with regard to robbery and assault, to curb such antisocial behavior? Should the city be obligated to attempt those other ways first?

---

§ 12.22 Modern Trend: First Amendment Protection and Strict Scrutiny

The Supreme Court has recognized that constitutionally protected expression encompasses more than just reasoned discussion of public affairs, and extends to entertainment as well. *See, e.g., Time, Inc. v. Hill*, 385 U.S. 374, 388 (1967). As indicated above, as far back as 1952, it noted that movies can constitute protected speech. *Joseph Burstyn, Inc. v. Wilson*, 343 U.S. 495, 501 (1952) (recognizing that movies, "may affect public attitudes and behavior in a variety of ways, ranging from direct espousal of a political or social doctrine to the subtle shaping of thought which characterizes all artistic expression," and that movies are an important "organ of public opinion"). In the late 1990s it held that Internet sites are similarly entitled to First Amendment protection. *Reno v. ACLU*, 521 U.S. 844 (1997) (striking down the Communications Decency Act regulating indecent material on the Internet).

The question was thus not really "if" but "when" videogames would similarly be accorded constitutional status. Indeed, as early as 1983 the Massachusetts Supreme Court noted, "We recognize that in the future video games which contain sufficient communicative and expressive elements may be created [even though contemporary] video games … are, in essence, only technologically advanced pinball machines." *Marshfield Family Skateland, Inc. v. Town of Marshfield*, 450 N.E.2d 605, 609–10 (Mass. 1983)

The Massachusetts' justices were prescient. Of course the turn to constitutionally protected videogames didn't happen all at once and there were fits and starts along the way. For example, in 1981, in *Stern Elecs., Inc. v. Kaufman*, 523 F. Supp. 635, 639 (E.D.N.Y. 1981), the court cast doubt on whether there were constitutional differences between movies and videogames, and in *Rothner v. City of Chicago*, 929 F.2d 297, 303 (7th Cir. 1991) the Seventh Circuit held it was error to assume that, "under *all* circumstances, *all* video games can be characterized as completely devoid of any first amendment protection." The court continued:

> [W]e cannot tell whether the video games at issue here are simply modern day pinball machines or whether they are more sophisticated presentations involving storyline and plot that convey to the user a significant artistic message protected by the first amendment. Nor is it clear whether these games may be considered works of art. To hold on this record that *all* video games—no matter what their content—are *completely* devoid of artistic value would require us to make an assumption entirely unsupported by the record and *perhaps* totally at odds with reality.

Id. However, most agree that the most influential "pioneer" case providing First Amendment protection to videogames was Judge Posner's decision in *Kendrick*, which immediately follows.

Am. Amusement Machine Ass'n v. Kendrick

United States Court of Appeals, Seventh Circuit, 2001
244 F.3d 572

POSNER, Circuit Judge.

The manufacturers of video games and their trade association seek to enjoin, as a violation of freedom of expression, the enforcement of an Indianapolis ordinance that seeks to limit the access of minors to video games that depict violence. Denial of a preliminary injunction has precipitated this appeal.

The ordinance defines the term "harmful to minors" to mean "an amusement machine that predominantly appeals to minors' morbid interest in violence or minors' prurient interest in sex, is patently offensive to prevailing standards in the adult community as a whole with respect to what is suitable material for persons under the age of eighteen (18) years, lacks serious literary, artistic, political or scientific value as a whole for persons under" that age, and contains either "graphic violence" or "strong sexual content." "Graphic violence," which is all that is involved in this case (so far as appears, the plaintiffs do not manufacture, at least for exhibition in game arcades and other public places, video games that have "strong sexual content"), is defined to mean "an amusement machine's visual depiction or representation of realistic serious injury to a human or human-like being where such serious injury includes amputation, decapitation, dismemberment, bloodshed, mutilation, maiming or disfiguration [disfigurement]."

The ordinance forbids any operator of five or more video-game machines in one place to allow a minor unaccompanied by a parent, guardian, or other custodian to use "an amusement machine that is harmful to minors," requires appropriate warning signs, and requires that such machines be separated by a partition from the other machines in the location and that their viewing areas be concealed from persons who are on the other side of the partition. [¶] The legislative history indicates that the City believes that participation in violent video games engenders violence on the part of the players, at least when they are minors.

Although the district judge agreed with the plaintiffs that video games, possibly including some that would violate the ordinance, are "speech" within the meaning of the First Amendment and that children have rights under the free-speech clause, he held that the ordinance would violate the amendment only if the City lacked "a reasonable basis for believing the Ordinance would protect children from harm." He found a reasonable basis in a pair of empirical studies by psychologists which found that playing a violent video game tends to make young persons more aggressive in their attitudes and behavior, and also in a larger literature finding that violence in the media engenders aggressive feelings. The judge also ruled that the ordinance's tracking of the conventional standard for obscenity eliminated any concern that the ordinance might be excessively vague.

The ordinance brackets violence with sex, and the City asks us to squeeze the provision on violence into a familiar legal pigeonhole, that of obscenity, which is normally concerned with sex and is not protected by the First Amendment, while the plaintiffs insist that since their games are not obscene in the conventional sense they must receive the full protection of the First Amendment. Neither position is compelling. Violence and obscenity are distinct categories of objectionable depiction, *United States v. Thoma*, 726 F.2d 1191, 1200 (7th Cir. 1984) ("depictions of torture and deformation are not inherently sexual and, absent some expert guidance as to how such violence appeals to the prurient interest of a deviant group, there is no basis upon which a trier of fact could deem such material obscene"), and so the fact that obscenity is excluded from the protection of the principle that government may not regulate the content of expressive activity (as distinct from the time, place, or manner of the activity) neither compels nor forecloses a like exclusion of violent imagery.

The main worry about obscenity, the main reason for its proscription, is not that it is harmful, which is the worry behind the Indianapolis ordinance, but that it is offensive. A work is classified as obscene not upon proof that it is likely to affect anyone's conduct, but upon proof that it violates community norms regarding the permissible scope of depictions of sexual or sex-related activity. Obscenity is to many people disgusting, embarrassing, degrading, disturbing, outrageous, and insulting, but it generally is not believed to inflict temporal (as distinct from spiritual) harm; or at least the evidence that it does is not generally considered as persuasive as the evidence that other speech that can be regulated on the basis of its content, such as threats of physical harm, conspiratorial communications, incitements, frauds, and libels and slanders, inflicts such harm. No proof that obscenity is harmful is required either to defend an obscenity statute against being invalidated on constitutional grounds or to uphold a prosecution for obscenity. Offensiveness is the offense.

But offensiveness is not the basis on which Indianapolis seeks to regulate violent video games. Nor could the ordinance be defended on that basis. The most violent game in the record, "The House of the Dead," depicts zombies being killed flamboyantly, with much severing of limbs and effusion of blood; but so stylized and patently fictitious is the cartoon-like depiction that no one would suppose it "obscene" in the sense in which a photograph of a person being decapitated might be described as "obscene." It will not turn anyone's stomach. The basis of the ordinance, rather, is a belief that violent video games cause temporal harm by engendering aggressive attitudes and behavior, which might lead to violence.

[I]n effect Indianapolis is arguing that violent video games incite youthful players to breaches of the peace. But this is to use the word "incitement" metaphorically. As we'll see, no showing has been made that games of the sort found in the record of this case have such an effect. Nor can such a showing be dispensed with on the ground that preventing violence is as canonical a role of government as shielding people from graphic sexual imagery. The issue in this case is not violence as such, or directly; it is violent *images*; and here the symmetry with obscenity breaks down. Classic literature and art, and not merely today's popular culture, are saturated with graphic scenes of violence, whether narrated or pictorial. The notion of forbidding not violence itself, but pictures of violence, is a novelty, whereas concern with pictures of graphic sexual conduct is of the essence of the traditional concern with obscenity.

There is a hint, though, that the City is also concerned with the welfare of the game-playing children themselves, and not just the welfare of their potential victims. In the present setting, concern with the welfare of the child might take two forms. One is a concern with the potential psychological harm to children of being exposed to violent images, and would be unrelated to the broader societal concern with violence that was the primary motivation for the ordinance. Another, subtler concern would be with the punitive consequences for the child incited or predisposed to commit violent acts by exposure to violent images. We must consider whether the City of Indianapolis has equivalent grounds for thinking that violent video games cause harm either to the game players or (the point the City stresses) the public at large.

The grounds must be compelling and not merely plausible. People are unlikely to become well-functioning, independent-minded adults and responsible citizens if they are raised in an intellectual bubble. No doubt the City would concede this point if the question were whether to forbid children to read without the presence of an adult the Odyssey, with its graphic descriptions of Odysseus's grinding out the eye of Polyphemus with a heated, sharpened stake, killing the suitors, and hanging the treacherous maidservants; or The Divine Comedy with its graphic descriptions of the tortures of the damned; or War and Peace with its graphic descriptions of execution by firing squad, death in childbirth, and death from war wounds. Or if the question were whether to ban the stories of Edgar Allen Poe, or the famous horror movies made from the classic novels of Mary Wollstonecraft Shelley (Frankenstein) and Bram Stoker (Dracula). Violence has always been and remains a central interest of humankind and a recurrent, even obsessive theme of culture both high and low. It engages the interest of children from an early age, as anyone familiar with the classic fairy tales collected by Grimm, Andersen, and Perrault is aware. To shield children right up to the age of 18 from exposure to violent descriptions and images would not only be quixotic, but deforming; it would leave them unequipped to cope with the world as we know it.

Maybe video games are different. They are, after all, interactive. But this point is superficial, in fact erroneous. All literature (here broadly defined to include movies, television, and the other photographic media, and popular as well as highbrow literature) is interactive; the better it is, the more interactive. Literature when it is successful draws the reader into the story, makes him identify with the characters, invites him to judge them and quarrel with them, to experience their joys and sufferings as the reader's own. Protests from readers caused Dickens to revise Great Expectations to give it a happy ending, and tourists visit sites in Dublin and its environs in which the fictitious events of Ulysses are imagined to have occurred. The cult of Sherlock Holmes is well known.

Most of the video games in the record of this case, games that the City believes violate its ordinances, are stories. Take once again "The House of the Dead." The player is armed with a gun—most fortunately, because he is being assailed by a seemingly unending succession of hideous axe-wielding zombies, the living dead conjured back to life by voodoo. The zombies have already knocked down and wounded several people, who are pleading pitiably for help; and one of the player's duties is to protect those unfortunates from renewed assaults by the zombies. His main task, however, is self-defense. Zombies are supernatural beings, therefore difficult to kill. Repeated shots are necessary to stop them as they rush headlong toward the player. He must not only be alert to the appearance of zombies from any quarter; he must be assiduous about reloading his gun periodically, lest he be overwhelmed by the rush of the zombies when his gun is empty.

Self-defense, protection of others, dread of the "undead," fighting against overwhelming odds—these are all age-old themes of literature, and ones particularly appealing to the young. "The House of the Dead" is not distinguished literature. Neither, perhaps, is "The Night of the Living Dead," George A. Romero's famous zombie movie that was doubtless the inspiration for "The House of the Dead." Some games, such as "Dungeons and Dragons," have achieved cult status; although it seems unlikely, some of these games, perhaps including some that are as violent as those in the record, will become cultural icons. We are in the world of kids' popular culture. But it is not lightly to be suppressed.

Although violent video games appeal primarily to boys, the record contains, surprisingly, a feminist violent video game, "Ultimate Mortal Kombat 3." A man and a woman are dressed in vaguely medieval costumes, and wield huge swords. The woman is very tall, very fierce, and wields her sword effortlessly. The man and the woman duel, and the man is killed. Another man appears—he is killed too. The woman wins all the duels. She is as strong as the men, she is more skillful, more determined, and she does not flinch at the sight of blood. Of course, her success depends on the player's skill, and the fact that the player, whether male or female, has chosen to be the female fighter. (The player chooses which fighter to be.) But the game is feminist in depicting a woman as fully capable of holding her own in violent combat with heavily armed men. It thus has a message, even an "ideology," just as books and movies do.

We are not persuaded by the City's argument that whatever contribution to the marketplace of ideas and expression the games in the record may have the potential to make is secured by the right of the parent (or guardian, or custodian—and does that include a babysitter?) to permit his or her child or ward to play these games. The right is to a considerable extent illusory. The parent is not permitted to give blanket consent, but must accompany the child to the game room. Many parents are too busy to accompany their child to a game room; most teenagers would be deterred from playing these games if they had to be accompanied by mom; even parents who think violent video games harmful or even edifying (some parents want their kids to develop a shooter's reflexes) may rather prevent their children from playing these games than incur the time and other costs of accompanying the children to the game room; and conditioning a minor's First Amendment rights on parental consent of this nature is a curtailment of those rights.

The City rightly does not rest on "what everyone knows" about the harm inflicted by violent video games. The City instead appeals to social science to establish that games such as "The House of the Dead" and "Ultimate Mortal Kombat 3," games culturally isomorphic with (and often derivative from) movies aimed at the same under 18 crowd, are dangerous to public safety. The social science evidence on which the City relies consists primarily of the pair of psychological studies. Craig A. Anderson & Karen E. Dill, "*Personality Processes and Individual Differences—Video Games and Aggressive Thoughts, Feelings, and Behavior in the Laboratory and in Life*," 78 J. Personality & Soc. Psych. 772 (2000). Those studies do not support the ordinance. There is no indication that the games used in the studies are similar to those in the record of this case or to other games likely to be marketed in game arcades in Indianapolis. The studies do not find that video games have ever caused anyone to commit a violent act, as opposed to feeling aggressive, or have caused the average level of violence to increase anywhere. And they do not suggest that it is the interactive character of the games, as opposed to the violence of the images in them, that is the cause of the aggressive feelings. The studies thus are not evidence that violent video games are any more harmful to the consumer or to the public safety than violent movies or other violent, but passive, entertainments. It is highly unlikely that they are more harmful, because "passive" entertainment aspires to be interactive too and often succeeds. When Dirty Harry or some other avenging hero kills off a string of villains, the audience is expected to identify with him, to revel in his success, to feel their own finger on the trigger. It is conceivable that pushing a button or manipulating a toggle stick engenders an even deeper surge of aggressive joy, but of that there is no evidence at all.

We can imagine the City's arguing that it would like to ban violent movies too, but that either this is infeasible or the City has to start somewhere and should not be discouraged from experimenting. Experimentation should indeed not be discouraged. But the City makes neither argument. Its only expressed concern is with video games, in fact only video games in game arcades, movie-theater lobbies, and hotel game rooms. It doesn't even argue that the *addition* of violent video games to violent movies and television in the cultural menu of Indianapolis youth significantly increases whatever dangers media depictions of violence pose to healthy character formation or peaceable, law-abiding behavior. Violent video games played in public places are a tiny fraction of the media violence to which modern American children are exposed. Tiny, and judging from the record of this case not very violent, compared to what is available to children on television and in movie theaters today.

The characters in the video games in the record are cartoon characters, that is, animated drawings. No one would mistake them for photographs of real people. The idea that a child's interest in such fantasy mayhem is "morbid"—that any kid who enjoys playing "The House of the Dead" or "Ultimate Mortal Kombat 3" should be dragged off to a psychiatrist—gains no support from anything that has been cited to us in defense of the ordinance.

It is conceivable though unlikely that in a plenary trial the City can establish the legality of the ordinance. We need not speculate on what evidence might be offered, or, if none is offered (in which event a permanent injunction should promptly be entered), what amendments might bring the ordinance into conformity with First Amendment principles.

————————

Notes and Questions

1. Two years after *Kendrick*, the Eighth Circuit followed suit in *Interactive Digital Software Ass'n v. St. Louis County*, 329 F.3d 954 (8th Cir. 2003). There, a St. Louis ordinance made, "it unlawful for any person knowingly to sell, rent, or make available graphically violent videogames to minors, or to 'permit the free play of' graphically violent videogames by minors, without a parent or guardian's consent." *Id.* at 956. The court held:

> The record in this case includes scripts and story boards showing the storyline, character development, and dialogue of representative video games, as well as excerpts from four video games submitted by the County. If the first amendment is versatile enough to "shield [the] painting of Jackson Pollock, music of Arnold Schoenberg, or Jabberwocky verse of Lewis Carroll," *Hurley [v. Irish-American Gay, Lesbian and Bisexual Group of Boston]*, 515 U.S. [557] at 569 [(1995)], we see no reason why the pictures, graphic design, concept art, sounds, music, stories, and narrative present in video games are not entitled to a similar protection. The mere fact that they appear in a novel medium is of no legal consequence. Our review of the record convinces us that these "violent" video games contain stories, imagery, "age-old themes of literature," and messages, "even an 'ideology,' just as books and movies do." *See American Amusement Mach. Ass'n v. Kendrick*, 244 F.3d 572, 577–78 (7th Cir. 2001) Indeed, we find it telling that the County seeks to restrict access to these video games precisely because their content purportedly affects the thought or behavior of those who play them.
>
> We recognize that while children have in the past experienced age-old elemental violent themes by reading a fairy tale or an epic poem, or attending a Saturday matinee, the interactive play of a video game might present different difficulties. The County suggests in fact that with video games, the story lines are incidental and players may skip the expressive parts of the game and proceed straight to the player-controlled action. But the same could be said of action-packed movies like "The Matrix" or "Charlie's Angels"; any viewer with a videocassette or DVD player could simply skip to and isolate the action sequences. The fact that modern technology has increased viewer control does not render movies unprotected by the first amendment, and equivalent player control likewise should not automatically disqualify modern video games that are analytically indistinguishable from protected media such as motion pictures.
>
> We note, moreover, that there is no justification for disqualifying video games as speech simply because they are constructed to be interactive; indeed, literature is most successful when it draws the reader into the story, makes him identify

with the characters, invites him to judge them and quarrel with them, to experience their joys and sufferings as the reader's own.

Id. at 957. Having firmly established the First Amendment protections accorded videogames, the court had little trouble holding that the statute could not pass constitutional muster under the strict scrutiny standard:

> Because the ordinance regulates video games based on their content (the ordinance applies only to "graphically violent" video games), we review it according to a strict scrutiny standard. A content-based restriction on speech is presumptively invalid, and the County therefore bears the burden of demonstrating that the ordinance is necessary to serve a compelling state interest and that it is narrowly tailored to achieve that end. The County first suggests that the ordinance forwards the compelling state interest of protecting the "psychological well-being of minors" by reducing the harm suffered by children who play violent video games. We do not question that the County's interest in safeguarding the psychological well-being of minors is compelling in the abstract. Yet when the government defends restrictions on speech it must do more than simply posit the existence of the disease sought to be cured. We believe that the County must demonstrate that the recited harms are real, not merely conjectural, and that the regulation will in fact alleviate these harms in a direct and material way.
>
> The County's conclusion that there is a strong likelihood that minors who play violent video games will suffer a deleterious effect on their psychological health is simply unsupported in the record. It is true that a psychologist appearing on behalf of the County stated that a recent study that he conducted indicates that playing violent video games "does in fact lead to aggressive behavior in the immediate situation ... that more aggressive thoughts are reported and there is frequently more aggressive behavior." But this vague generality falls far short of a showing that video games are psychologically deleterious. The County's remaining evidence included the conclusory comments of county council members; a small number of ambiguous, inconclusive, or irrelevant (conducted on adults, not minors) studies; and the testimony of a high school principal who admittedly had no information regarding any link between violent video games and psychological harm.

Id. at 958–59. *See also Video Software Dealers Ass'n v. Maleng*, 325 F. Supp. 2d 1180, 1186 (W.D. Wash. 2004), where the court, a year after *Interactive Digital*, summarized the history of First Amendment protection for games by stating: "The early generations of video games may have lacked the requisite expressive element, being little more than electronic board games or computerized races. The [post-millennial] games at issue in this litigation, however, frequently involve intricate, if obnoxious, story lines, detailed artwork, original scores, and a complex narrative which evolves as the player makes choices and gains experience. All of the games provided to the Court for review are expressive and qualify as speech for purposes of the First Amendment."

2. It is difficult for cities and states to produce sufficient evidence to establish the necessary sociological link between violent videogames and antisocial behavior necessary under strict scrutiny. Sociologists do not design studies where they, e.g., watch a group of 16 year olds play *Grand Theft Auto: San Andreas* three hours every day for six months and then monitor them to determine whether they assault others over the next month or so. In § 12.233 we discuss the relevant literature and set forth a court's long description of the kinds of evidence governments can put forth on these issues in an attempt to justify their regulations in light of a strict scrutiny standard.

3. Another constitutional principle involved in the litigation pertaining to videogame regulation is the idea of "content neutral, time, place, and manner" regulation, which is judged under a lesser standard than strict scrutiny. *Grayned v. The City of Rockford*, 408 U.S. 104 (1972); *Ward v. Rock Against Racism*, 491 U.S. 781 (1989). The idea is that a government should be able to regulate the expression of some speech if it does so in a content neutral manner and only regulates the time, place, or manner that such speech can be made. An oft-cited example is that there can be no serious constitutional objection to a government banning loudspeakers in a residential neighborhood before 7:00 am, so long as it bans *all* such speech, regardless of the content of the message being broadcast.

As set forth in *Ward v. Rock Against Racism*, 491 U.S. 781, 791 (1989) the test for judging whether the regulation is a valid time, place, and manner statute is: "The government may impose reasonable restrictions on the time, place or manner of protected speech, provided the restrictions are justified without reference to the content of the regulated speech, that they are narrowly tailored to serve a significant government interest, and that they leave open ample alternative channels for communication of the information."

Despite the arguments of the governments in *Kendrick* and *Interactive Digital*, the regulations involved in those cases cannot be fairly characterized as content-neutral time, place and manner regulations. Those statutes did not ban the sale of all videogames to minors, regardless of their content, but rather only prohibited the sale of *certain* games to minors based *entirely on their content*.

Content-based regulation of First Amendment-protected activity automatically invokes strict scrutiny, as there is a long tradition in the United States (as well as many court decisions giving that tradition the force of law) that the government cannot prohibit a First Amendment protected activity just because government does not like the message conveyed. *See, e.g., Am. Booksellers Assoc., Inc. v. Hudnut*, 771 F.2d 323 (7th Cir. 1985). Rather, government can only prohibit activities that might otherwise have First Amendment protection if they lead to conduct with which the state can legitimately concern itself, which then refers back to the problem that there is not enough research yet definitively establishing any link between antisocial conduct and videogame play to satisfy strict scrutiny.

4. Challenges to legislation such as in *Kendrick* are expensive to bring. Accordingly, the plaintiffs are usually not individuals who wish to purchase or rent these kinds of games, but industry groups such American Amusement Machine Association, the plaintiff in *Kendrick*. One issue that often arises with associations as plaintiffs is standing. After all, the association's First Amendment rights to play the games are not threatened; it is that of the would be users.

The courts have allowed standing in all such cases thus far on one or both of two separate grounds. In some cases, courts say that these associations are asserting their own tort claims, i.e., they are alleging that they are losing sales or rental incomes as a result of the statute, and thus have their own standing to challenge the constitutionality of the statute directly. *See, e.g., Video Software Dealers Ass'n v. Maleng*, 325 F. Supp. 2d 1180, 1183–84 (W.D. Wash. 2004).

In other cases, courts apply associational standing principles set forth by the Supreme Court to allow the trade associations to litigate the First Amendment rights of potential users. An example is *Entm't Software Ass'n v. Blagojevich*, 404 F. Supp. 2d 1051, 1071 (N.D. Ill. 2005):

> To establish its standing to sue, an associational organization, like each of the plaintiffs in this case, must show "(a) its members would otherwise have standing to sue in their own right; (b) the interests it seeks to protect are germane to the

organization's purpose; and (c) neither the claim asserted nor the relief requested requires the participation of individual members in the lawsuit." *Hunt v. Wash. State Apple Adver. Comm'n*, 432 U.S. 333, 343 (1977).

The Court finds that plaintiffs have standing to sue. Each of the plaintiff associations was created to serve the business and public affairs interests of its members, which include the creators and publishers of video games (ESA). The members of these associations rely on the ESA, to file suits like this to protect their rights, and they will experience a chilling effect on their free speech rights if the [legislation] go[es] into effect. The Court therefore finds that the plaintiffs have standing to bring this action.

5. Issues regarding the regulation of videogames can come up in all kinds of different situations. Some of the more interesting cases arise on school campuses. In *Johnson v. City of Lincoln Park*, 434 F. Supp. 2d 467 (E.D. Mich. 2006), a teacher and the assistant principal demanded that a fourteen year old student surrender his Nintendo Gameboy, the use of which was prohibited during school hours. When the student refused to turn it over, a police liaison officer tasered the student. The student lost his civil rights suit against the police liaison officer.

In *Toney v. Indep. Sch. Dist. No. I-48*, 2007 U.S. Dist. LEXIS 907 (E.D. Okla. Jan. 5, 2007), a teacher's termination was upheld when the school established the teacher was playing card games on his computer while he was supposed to be teaching his class.

———

§ 12.23 Legislative Response to First Amendment Protection Accorded Videogames

Kendrick was decided in 2001. The kinds of videogames discussed in the decision were, e.g., *The House of the Dead*, which Judge Posner characterized as, "stylized and patently fictitious ... [a] cartoon-like depiction ... It will not turn anyone's stomach." Since then, things have changed in the videogame world. Many more contemporary games depict extreme violence and sexually mature content. For example, in *Grand Theft Auto: San Andreas*, the main character can affect forcible rape, *see* Figure 1.17, *supra,* and one court has described the imagery in *Postal II* as follows:

> Postal II involves a character who has apparently "gone postal" and decided to kill everyone he encounters. The game involves shooting both armed opponents, such as police officers, and unarmed people, such as schoolgirls. Girls attacked with a shovel will beg for mercy; the player can be merciless and decapitate them. People shot in the leg will fall down and crawl; the player can then pour gasoline over them, set them on fire, and urinate on them. The player's character makes sardonic comments during all this; for example, urinating on someone elicits the comment "Now the flowers will grow."

Video Software Dealers Ass'n v. Schwarzenegger, 401 F. Supp. 2d 1034, 1042 (N.D. Cal. 2005).

Cities and state legislatures have not stood idly by and ignored this trend. Even in the face of having to overcome the burdens of a "strict scrutiny" standard, a number of states and communities passed laws criminalizing distribution of some of the more violently odious and sexually mature videogames. Their justifications for regulating such constitutionally protected material was three-fold: (1) to characterize certain games as falling into one of the recognized constitutional "exceptions" to First Amendment protection (*see* § 12.231, *infra*); (2) to regulate only the play of, and sales to, minors, where they have a bit more constitutional latitude to pass content-based regulation (*see* § 12.232, *infra*); and (3) to try and come up with enough evidence to satisfy strict scrutiny, means-ends standards (*see* § 12.233, *infra*). We discuss each of these issues and strategies below.

§ 12.231 "Exceptions" to First Amendment Protection

As those who have taken a Constitutional Law course have studied, freedom of speech guaranteed under the First Amendment is not absolute. There are several "exceptions" in which states have freedom to regulate even on the basis of content without having to satisfy the strict scrutiny standard. Governments seeking to defend content-based videogame legislation tend to argue that one of three such exceptions apply, thus freeing them from the most stringent constitutional analysis. Immediately below we summarize these doctrines, and give a typical analysis of videogames under them by lower courts. After that, in § 12.232, we show how the Supreme Court dealt with these challenges in *Brown v. Entm't Merchs. Ass'n*, 131 S. Ct. 2729 (2011).

a.   *Obscenity*. Obscene speech is without constitutional protection. The three part test for obscenity was set forth in *Miller v. California*, 413 U.S. 15, 24 (2003) as:

(a) [W]hether "the average person, applying contemporary community standards" would find that the work, taken as a whole, appeals to the prurient interest;

(b) Whether the work depicts or describes, in a patently offensive way, sexual conduct specifically defined by the applicable state law; and

(c) Whether the work, taken as a whole, lacks serious literary, artistic, political, or scientific value.

Included within this definition are "representations or descriptions of ultimate sexual acts, normal or perverted, actual or simulated" and "representations or descriptions of masturbation, excretory functions, and lewd exhibition of the genitals." *Id.* at 25.

The arguments that the states and cities make is that the excessive violence in games like *Postal II* and *Grand Theft Auto: San Andreas* rise to the level of obscenity. But thus far, no court had adopted this theory. A typical discussion rejecting the idea is found in *Interactive Digital Software Ass'n v. St. Louis County*, 329 F.3d 954, 958 (8th Cir. 2003):

We reject the County's suggestion that we should find that the "graphically violent" video games in this case are obscene and therefore entitled to less protection. It is true that obscenity is one of the few categories of speech historically unprotected by the first amendment. But material that contains violence but not depictions or descriptions of sexual conduct cannot be obscene. Simply put, depictions of violence cannot fall within the legal definition of obscenity for either minors or adults.

b.   *Incitement to Imminent Unlawful Activity*. Speech that is directed toward causing others to commit unlawful acts has no free speech value and thus also does not merit First Amendment protection. The test for this category of speech was set forth in *Brandenburg v. Ohio*, 395 U.S. 444, 446 (1969): there is no constitutional protection for "such advocacy [as] is directed to inciting or producing imminent lawless action and is likely to incite or produce such action." Once again, no court has yet accepted a government's argument that videogames meet the *Brandenburg* test. Rejection typically proceeds along the following lines:

The plaintiffs argue that the Act fails the three-part test set forth in *Brandenburg v. Ohio*, 395 U.S. 444 (1969), and therefore violates the First Amendment. Under the first prong of the Brandenburg test, free speech may be restricted if it "is directed to inciting or producing the imminent lawless action and is likely to incite or produce such action." *Id.* at 447. The plaintiffs correctly assert that because the video game producers do not intend for the consumers to commit violent actions, the Act fails this first prong. The second prong requires that the danger of violence must be imminent. The research conducted by the State has failed to prove that video games have ever caused anyone to commit a violent act, let alone present a danger of imminent violence. Finally, the State's research fails to prove that ultra-violent video games are "likely" to produce violent behavior in children.

Entm't Software Ass'n v. Granholm, 426 F. Supp 2d 646, 652 (E.D. Mich. 2005).

c.   ***Fighting Words***: The third argument to escape the demands of strict scrutiny by categorizing the "speech" of videogames as not meriting First Amendment protection rests on the "fighting words" doctrine. Because the State's interest in keeping the peace is paramount, the Court held in *Chaplinsky v. New Hampshire,* 315 U.S. 568 (1942) that there is no constitutional protection afforded so-called "fighting words." Fighting words are, "those which by their very utterance inflict injury or tend to incite an immediate breach of the peace." *Id.* at 572. Once again, no court has ever found that any of the dialogue or images in videogames rise to the exacting standards of *Chaplinsky*.

§ 12.232 Greater Constitutional Flexibility When Regulating Activities of a Minor

Having largely missed in their attempts to have the communicative effect of violent and sexually themed videogames categorized into one of the three First Amendment exceptions set forth above, legislatures nevertheless had one sizable arrow left in their quiver—limiting their regulation of conduct to minors. The Supreme Court has made clear that while minors enjoy some constitutional protections *see, e.g., Erznoznik v. Jacksonville,* 422 U.S. 205 (1975), the government nevertheless has some additional leeway when it comes to regulating even First Amendment protected activities with respect to minors.

The principal case relied upon by governments in this regard is *Ginsberg v. New York,* 390 U.S. 629 (1968). There, the Supreme Court upheld a regulation of material that was judged obscene for minors, even though that material was likely not obscene for adults. The statute in question prohibited the sale to minors under the age of seventeen any material deemed "harmful to minors" because it: (1) predominately appeals to the prurient, shameful or morbid interest *of minors*; (2) is patently offensive to prevailing standards in the adult community as a whole with respect to what is suitable material *for minors*; and (3) is utterly without redeeming social importance *for minors. Id.* at 632–33 (emphasis added).[4] *See also Sable Comm'cns v. FCC,* 492 U.S. 115, 126 (1989) (holding that certain speech, while fully protected when directed to adults, may be restricted when directed towards minors).

---

4. This test is roughly the same test as that for obscenity regarding adults, with the words "for minors" added in each element. *See* the adult obscenity test from *Miller v. California,* 413 U.S. 15, 24 (2003) above.

To the surprise of some, the Supreme Court decided it wanted to determine whether California's statute, directed to regulating the sale of some videogames to minors, passed constitutional scrutiny in the *Brown* case that follows.

Brown v. Entm't Merchs. Ass'n

United States Supreme Court, 2011
564 U.S. __, 131 S. Ct. 2729

SCALIA, Associate Justice.

We consider whether a California law imposing restrictions on violent video games comports with the First Amendment.

Cal. Civ. Code Ann. §§ 1746–1746.5 (West 2009) (Act), prohibits the sale or rental of "violent video games" to minors, and requires their packaging to be labeled "18." The Act covers games "in which the range of options available to a player includes killing, maiming, dismembering, or sexually assaulting an image of a human being, if those acts are depicted" in a manner that "[a] reasonable person, considering the game as a whole, would find appeals to a deviant or morbid interest of minors," that is "patently offensive to prevailing standards in the community as to what is suitable for minors," and that "causes the game, as a whole, to lack serious literary, artistic, political, or scientific value for minors." Violation of the Act is punishable by a civil fine of up to $1,000.

Respondents, representing the video game and software industries, brought a preenforcement challenge to the Act.

California correctly acknowledges that video games qualify for First Amendment protection. The Free Speech Clause exists principally to protect discourse on public matters, but we have long recognized that it is difficult to distinguish politics from entertainment, and dangerous to try. "Everyone is familiar with instances of propaganda through fiction. What is one man's amusement, teaches another's doctrine." Like the protected books, plays, and movies that preceded them, video games communicate ideas — and even social messages — through many familiar literary devices (such as characters, dialogue, plot, and music) and through features distinctive to the medium (such as the player's interaction with the virtual world). That suffices to confer First Amendment protection. Under our Constitution, "esthetic and moral judgments about art and literature ... are for the individual to make, not for the Government to decree, even with the mandate or approval of a majority." *United States v. Playboy Entertainment Group, Inc.,* 529 U.S. 803 (2000). And whatever the challenges of applying the Constitution to ever-advancing technology, "the basic principles of freedom of speech and the press, like the First Amendment's command, do not vary" when a new and different medium for communication appears. *Joseph Burstyn, Inc. v. Wilson,* 343 U.S. 495, 503 (1952).

The most basic of those principles is this: "[A]s a general matter, ... government has no power to restrict expression because of its message, its ideas, its subject matter, or its content." There are of course exceptions. " 'From 1791 to the present,' ... the First Amendment has 'permitted restrictions upon the content of speech in a few limited areas,' and has never 'include[d] a freedom to disregard these traditional limitations.' " These limited areas — such as obscenity, incitement, and fighting words — represent "well-defined and narrowly limited classes of speech, the prevention and punishment of which have never been thought to raise any Constitutional problem."

Last Term, in [*U.S. v.*] *Stevens* [130 S. Ct. 1577 (2010)], we held that new categories of unprotected speech may not be added to the list by a legislature that concludes certain speech is too harmful to be tolerated. *Stevens* concerned a federal statute purporting to criminalize the creation, sale, or possession of certain depictions of animal cruelty. The statute covered depictions "in which a living animal is intentionally maimed, mutilated, tortured, wounded, or killed" if that harm to the animal was illegal where the "the creation, sale, or possession t[ook] place." We held that statute to be an impermissible content-based restriction on speech. There was no American tradition of forbidding the *depiction of* animal cruelty—though States have long had laws against *committing* it.

The Government argued in *Stevens* that lack of a historical warrant did not matter; that it could create new categories of unprotected speech by applying a "simple balancing test" that weighs the value of a particular category of speech against its social costs and then punishes that category of speech if it fails the test. We emphatically rejected that "startling and dangerous" proposition. "Maybe there are some categories of speech that have been historically unprotected, but have not yet been specifically identified or discussed as such in our case law." But without persuasive evidence that a novel restriction on content is part of a long (if heretofore unrecognized) tradition of proscription, a legislature may not revise the "judgment [of] the American people," embodied in the First Amendment, "that the benefits of its restrictions on the Government outweigh the costs."

That holding controls this case. As in *Stevens,* California has tried to make violent-speech regulation look like obscenity regulation by appending a saving clause required for the latter. That does not suffice. Our cases have been clear that the obscenity exception to the First Amendment does not cover whatever a legislature finds shocking, but only depictions of "sexual conduct."

Stevens was not the first time we have encountered and rejected a State's attempt to shoehorn speech about violence into obscenity. In *Winters,* we considered a New York criminal statute "forbid[ding] the massing of stories of bloodshed and lust in such a way as to incite to crime against the person," 333 U.S., at 514, 68 S.Ct. 665. Our opinion in *Winters,* made clear that violence is not part of the obscenity that the Constitution permits to be regulated. The speech reached by the statute contained "no indecency or obscenity in any sense heretofore known to the law."

Because speech about violence is not obscene, it is of no consequence that California's statute mimics the New York statute regulating obscenity-for-minors that we upheld in *Ginsberg v. New York,* 390 U.S. 629 (1968). That case approved a prohibition on the sale to minors of *sexual* material that would be obscene from the perspective of a child. We held that the legislature could "adjus[t] the definition of obscenity 'to social realities by permitting the appeal of this type of material to be assessed in terms of the sexual interests ... of ... minors." And because "obscenity is not protected expression," the New York statute could be sustained so long as the legislature's judgment that the proscribed materials were harmful to children "was not irrational."

The California Act is something else entirely. It does not adjust the boundaries of an existing category of unprotected speech to ensure that a definition designed for adults is not uncritically applied to children. California does not argue that it is empowered to prohibit selling offensively violent works *to adults*—and it is wise not to, since that is but a hair's breadth from the argument rejected in *Stevens.* Instead, it wishes to create a wholly new category of content-based regulation that is permissible only for speech directed at children.

That is unprecedented and mistaken. "[M]inors are entitled to a significant measure of First Amendment protection, and only in relatively narrow and well-defined circumstances may government bar public dissemination of protected materials to them."

No doubt a State possesses legitimate power to protect children from harm, but that does not include a free-floating power to restrict the ideas to which children may be exposed. "Speech that is neither obscene as to youths nor subject to some other legitimate proscription cannot be suppressed solely to protect the young from ideas or images that a legislative body thinks unsuitable for them."

California's argument would fare better if there were a longstanding tradition in this country of specially restricting children's access to depictions of violence, but there is none. Certainly the *books* we give children to read—or read to them when they are younger—contain no shortage of gore. Grimm's Fairy Tales, for example, are grim indeed. As her just deserts for trying to poison Snow White, the wicked queen is made to dance in red hot slippers "till she fell dead on the floor, a sad example of envy and jealousy." The Complete Brothers Grimm Fairy Tales 198 (2006 ed.). Cinderella's evil stepsisters have their eyes pecked out by doves. *Id.,* at 95. And Hansel and Gretel (children!) kill their captor by baking her in an oven. *Id.,* at 54.

High-school reading lists are full of similar fare. Homer's Odysseus blinds Polyphemus the Cyclops by grinding out his eye with a heated stake. In the Inferno, Dante and Virgil watch corrupt politicians struggle to stay submerged beneath a lake of boiling pitch, lest they be skewered by devils above the surface. And Golding's Lord of the Flies recounts how a schoolboy called Piggy is savagely murdered *by other children* while marooned on an island

This is not to say that minors' consumption of violent entertainment has never encountered resistance. In the 1800's, dime novels depicting crime and "penny dreadfuls" (named for their price and content) were blamed in some quarters for juvenile delinquency. When motion pictures came along, they became the villains instead. For a time, our Court did permit broad censorship of movies because of their capacity to be "used for evil," but we eventually reversed course, *Joseph Burstyn, Inc.,* 343 U.S., at 502, 72 S.Ct. 777. Radio dramas were next, and then came comic books. Many in the late 1940's and early 1950's blamed comic books for fostering a "preoccupation with violence and horror" among the young, leading to a rising juvenile crime rate. But efforts to convince Congress to restrict comic books failed. And, of course, after comic books came television and music lyrics.

California claims that video games present special problems because they are "interactive," in that the player participates in the violent action on screen and determines its outcome. The latter feature is nothing new: Since at least the publication of The Adventures of You: Sugarcane Island in 1969, young readers of choose-your-own-adventure stories have been able to make decisions that determine the plot by following instructions about which page to turn to. As for the argument that video games enable participation in the violent action, that seems to us more a matter of degree than of kind. As Judge Posner has observed, all literature is interactive. "[T]he better it is, the more interactive. Literature when it is successful draws the reader into the story, makes him identify with the characters, invites him to judge them and quarrel with them, to experience their joys and sufferings as the reader's own." *American Amusement Machine Assn. v. Kendrick,* 244 F.3d 572, 577 (C.A.7 2001).

Justice ALITO has done considerable independent research to identify video games in which "the violence is astounding." "Victims are dismembered, decapitated, disemboweled, set on fire, and chopped into little pieces ... Blood gushes, splatters, and pools." Justice ALITO recounts all these disgusting video games in order to disgust us—but disgust is not a valid basis for restricting expression. And the same is true of Justice ALITO's description of those video games he has discovered that have a racial or ethnic motive for their violence. To what end does he relate this? Does it somehow increase the "aggressiveness" that California wishes to suppress? Who knows? But it does arouse the reader's ire, and the reader's desire to put an end to this horrible message. Thus, ironically, Justice ALITO's argument highlights the precise danger posed by the California Act: that the *ideas* expressed by speech — whether it be violence, or gore, or racism — and not its objective effects, may be the real reason for governmental proscription.

Because the Act imposes a restriction on the content of protected speech, it is invalid unless California can demonstrate that it passes strict scrutiny — that is, unless it is justified by a compelling government interest and is narrowly drawn to serve that interest. The State must specifically identify an "actual problem" in need of solving, and the curtailment of free speech must be actually necessary to the solution. "It is rare that a regulation restricting speech because of its content will ever be permissible."

California cannot meet that standard. At the outset, it acknowledges that it cannot show a direct causal link between violent video games and harm to minors. California's burden is high, and because it bears the risk of uncertainty, ambiguous proof will not suffice.

The State's evidence is not compelling. California relies primarily on the research of Dr. Craig Anderson and a few other research psychologists whose studies purport to show a connection between exposure to violent video games and harmful effects on children. These studies have been rejected by every court to consider them, and with good reason: They do not prove that violent video games *cause* minors to *act* aggressively (which would at least be a beginning). Instead, "[n]early all of the research is based on correlation, not evidence of causation, and most of the studies suffer from significant, admitted flaws in methodology." They show at best some correlation between exposure to violent entertainment and minuscule real-world effects, such as children's feeling more aggressive or making louder noises in the few minutes after playing a violent game than after playing a nonviolent game.

Even taking for granted Dr. Anderson's conclusions that violent video games produce some effect on children's feelings of aggression, those effects are both small and indistinguishable from effects produced by other media. In his testimony in a similar lawsuit, Dr. Anderson admitted that the "effect sizes" of children's exposure to violent video games are "about the same" as that produced by their exposure to violence on television. And he admits that the *same* effects have been found when children watch cartoons starring Bugs Bunny or the Road Runner, *id.,* at 1304, or when they play video games like Sonic the Hedgehog that are rated "E" (appropriate for all ages), or even when they "vie[w] a picture of a gun," *id.,* at 1315–1316.

Of course, California has (wisely) declined to restrict Saturday morning cartoons, the sale of games rated for young children, or the distribution of pictures of guns. The consequence is that its regulation is wildly underinclusive when judged against its asserted justification, which in our view is alone enough to defeat it. Underinclusiveness raises serious doubts about whether the government is in fact pursuing the interest it invokes, rather than disfavoring a particular speaker or viewpoint. Here, California has singled out the purveyors of video games for disfavored treatment — at least when compared to booksellers, cartoonists, and movie producers — and has given no persuasive reason why.

The Act is also seriously underinclusive in another respect — and a respect that renders irrelevant the contentions of the concurrence and the dissents that video games are qualitatively different from other portrayals of violence. The California Legislature is perfectly willing to leave this dangerous, mind-altering material in the hands of children so long as one parent (or even an aunt or uncle) says it's OK. And there are not even any requirements as to how this parental or avuncular relationship is to be verified; apparently the child's or putative parent's, aunt's, or uncle's say-so suffices. That is not how one addresses a serious social problem.

California cannot show that the Act's restrictions meet a substantial need of parents who wish to restrict their children's access to violent video games but cannot do so. The video-game industry has in place a voluntary rating system designed to inform consumers about the content of games. The system, implemented by the Entertainment Software Rating Board (ESRB), assigns age-specific ratings to each video game submitted: EC (Early Childhood); E (Everyone); E10+ (Everyone 10 and older); T (Teens); M (17 and older); and AO (Adults Only—18 and older). The Federal Trade Commission (FTC) found that, as a result of this system, "the video game industry outpaces the movie and music industries" in "(1) restricting target-marketing of mature-rated products to children; (2) clearly and prominently disclosing rating information; and (3) restricting children's access to mature-rated products at retail." This system does much to ensure that minors cannot purchase seriously violent games on their own, and that parents who care about the matter can readily evaluate the games their children bring home. Filling the remaining modest gap in concerned-parents' control can hardly be a compelling state interest.

And finally, the Act's purported aid to parental authority is vastly overinclusive. Not all of the children who are forbidden to purchase violent video games on their own have parents who *care* whether they purchase violent video games. While some of the legislation's effect may indeed be in support of what some parents of the restricted children actually want, its entire effect is only in support of what the State thinks parents *ought* to want. This is not the narrow tailoring to "assisting parents" that restriction of First Amendment rights requires.

* * *

California's effort to regulate violent video games is the latest episode in a long series of failed attempts to censor violent entertainment for minors. While we have pointed out above that some of the evidence brought forward to support the harmfulness of video games is unpersuasive, we do not mean to demean or disparage the concerns that underlie the attempt to regulate them—concerns that may and doubtless do prompt a good deal of parental oversight. We have no business passing judgment on the view of the California Legislature that violent video games (or, for that matter, any other forms of speech) corrupt the young or harm their moral development. Our task is only to say whether or not such works constitute a "well-defined and narrowly limited clas[s] of speech, the prevention and punishment of which have never been thought to raise any Constitutional problem" (the answer plainly is no); and if not, whether the regulation of such works is justified by that high degree of necessity we have described as a compelling state interest (it is not). Even where the protection of children is the object, the constitutional limits on governmental action apply.

California's legislation straddles the fence between (1) addressing a serious social problem and (2) helping concerned parents control their children. Both ends are legitimate, but when they affect First Amendment rights they must be pursued by means that are neither seriously underinclusive nor seriously overinclusive. As a means of protecting children from portrayals of violence, the legislation is seriously underinclusive, not only because it excludes portrayals other than video games, but also because it permits a parental or avuncular veto. And as a means of assisting concerned parents it is seriously overinclusive because it abridges the First Amendment rights of young people whose parents (and aunts and uncles) think violent video games are a harmless pastime. And the overbreadth in achieving one goal is not cured by the underbreadth in achieving the other. Legislation such as this, which is neither fish nor fowl, cannot survive strict scrutiny.

ALITO, Associate Justice, with whom **THE CHIEF JUSTICE** joins, concurring in the judgment.

The California statute that is before us in this case represents a pioneering effort to address what the state legislature and others regard as a potentially serious social problem: the effect of exceptionally violent video games on impressionable minors, who often spend countless hours immersed in the alternative worlds that these games create. Although the California statute is well intentioned, its terms are not framed with the precision that the Constitution demands, and I therefore agree with the Court that this particular law cannot be sustained.

I disagree, however, with the approach taken in the Court's opinion. In considering the application of unchanging constitutional principles to new and rapidly evolving technology, this Court should proceed with caution. We should make every effort to understand the new technology. We should take into account the possibility that developing technology may have important societal implications that will become apparent only with time. We should not jump to the conclusion that new technology is fundamentally the same as some older thing with which we are familiar. And we should not hastily dismiss the judgment of legislators, who may be in a better position than we are to assess the implications of new technology. The opinion of the Court exhibits none of this caution.

In the view of the Court, all those concerned about the effects of violent video games— federal and state legislators, educators, social scientists, and parents—are unduly fearful, for violent video games really present no serious problem. Spending hour upon hour controlling the actions of a character who guns down scores of innocent victims is not different in "kind" from reading a description of violence in a work of literature.

The Court is sure of this; I am not. There are reasons to suspect that the experience of playing violent video games just might be very different from reading a book, listening to the radio, or watching a movie or a television show.

Respondents in this case, representing the video-game industry, ask us to strike down the California law on two grounds: The broad ground adopted by the Court and the narrower ground that the law's definition of "violent video game," is impermissibly vague. Because I agree with the latter argument, I see no need to reach the broader First Amendment issues addressed by the Court.

Due process requires that laws give people of ordinary intelligence fair notice of what is prohibited. The lack of such notice in a law that regulates expression "raises special First Amendment concerns because of its obvious chilling effect on free speech." Vague laws force potential speakers to "'steer far wider of the unlawful zone'... than if the boundaries of the forbidden areas were clearly marked." While "perfect clarity and precise guidance have never been required even of regulations that restrict expressive activity," "government may regulate in the area" of First Amendment freedoms "only with narrow specificity."

Here, the California law does not define "violent video games" with the "narrow specificity" that the Constitution demands. In an effort to avoid First Amendment problems, the California Legislature modeled its violent video game statute on the New York law that this Court upheld in *Ginsberg v. New York,* 390 U.S. 629 (1968)—a law that prohibited the sale of certain sexually related materials to minors. But the California Legislature departed from the *Ginsberg* model in an important respect, and the legislature overlooked important differences between the materials falling within the scope of the two statutes.

The law at issue in *Ginsberg* prohibited the sale to minors of materials that were deemed "harmful to minors," and the law defined "harmful to minors" simply by adding the words "for minors" to each element of the definition of obscenity set out in what were then the Court's leading obscenity decisions. Seeking to bring its violent video game law within the protection of *Ginsberg,* the California Legislature began with the obscenity test adopted in *Miller v. California,* 413 U.S. 15 (1973). The legislature then made certain modifications to accommodate the aim of the violent video game law.

Under *Miller,* an obscenity statute must contain a threshold limitation that restricts the statute's scope to specifically described "hard core" materials. Materials that fall within this "hard core" category may be deemed to be obscene if three additional requirements are met:

(1)   an "average person, applying contemporary community standards [must] find ... the work, taken as a whole, appeals to the prurient interest";

(2)   "the work [must] depic[t] or describ[e], in a patently offensive way, sexual conduct specifically defined by the applicable state law; and"

(3)   "the work, taken as a whole, [must] lac[k] serious literary, artistic, political, or scientific value."

Adapting these standards, the California law imposes the following threshold limitation: "[T]he range of options available to a player [must] includ[e] killing, maiming, dismembering, or sexually assaulting an image of a human being." Any video game that meets this threshold test is subject to the law's restrictions if it also satisfies three further requirements:

"(i)   A reasonable person, considering the game as a whole, would find [the game] appeals to a deviant or morbid interest of minors.

"(ii)   It is patently offensive to prevailing standards in the community as to what is suitable for minors.

"(iii) It causes the game, as a whole, to lack serious literary, artistic, political, or scientific value for minors."

The first important difference between the *Ginsberg* law and the California violent video game statute concerns their respective threshold requirements. As noted, the *Ginsberg* law built upon the test for adult obscenity, and the current adult obscenity test, which was set out in *Miller* requires an obscenity statute to contain a threshold limitation that restricts the statute's coverage to specifically defined "hard core" depictions. The *Miller* Court gave as an example a statute that applies to only "[p]atently offensive representations or descriptions of ultimate sexual acts," "masturbation, excretory functions, and lewd exhibition of the genitals." The *Miller* Court clearly viewed this threshold limitation as serving a vital notice function. "We are satisfied," the Court wrote, "that these specific prerequisites will provide fair notice to a dealer in such materials that his public and commercial activities may bring prosecution."

By contrast, the threshold requirement of the California law does not perform the narrowing function served by the limitation in *Miller.* At least when *Miller* was decided, depictions of "hard core" sexual conduct were not a common feature of mainstream entertainment. But nothing similar can be said about much of the conduct covered by the California law. It provides that a video game cannot qualify as "violent" unless "the range of options available to a player includes killing, maiming, dismembering, or sexually assaulting an image of a human being."

For better or worse, our society has long regarded many depictions of killing and maiming as suitable features of popular entertainment, including entertainment that is widely available to minors. The California law's threshold requirement would more closely resemble the limitation in *Miller* if it targeted a narrower class of graphic depictions.

Because of this feature of the California law's threshold test, the work of providing fair notice is left in large part to the three requirements that follow, but those elements are also not up to the task. In drafting the violent video game law, the California Legislature could have made its own judgment regarding the kind and degree of violence that is acceptable in games played by minors (or by minors in particular age groups). Instead, the legislature relied on undefined societal or community standards.

The terms "deviant" and "morbid" are not defined in the statute, and California offers no reason to think that its courts would give the terms anything other than their ordinary meaning. I therefore assume that "deviant" and "morbid" carry the meaning that they convey in ordinary speech. The adjective "deviant" ordinarily means "deviating ... from some accepted norm," and the term "morbid" means "of, relating to, or characteristic of disease." A "deviant or morbid interest" in violence, therefore, appears to be an interest that deviates from what is regarded—presumably in accordance with some generally accepted standard—as normal and healthy. Thus, the application of the California law is heavily dependent on the identification of generally accepted standards regarding the suitability of violent entertainment for minors.

The California Legislature seems to have assumed that these standards are sufficiently well known so that a person of ordinary intelligence would have fair notice as to whether the kind and degree of violence in a particular game is enough to qualify the game as "violent." And because the *Miller* test looks to community standards, the legislature may have thought that the use of undefined community standards in the violent video game law would not present vagueness problems.

There is a critical difference, however, between obscenity laws and laws regulating violence in entertainment. By the time of this Court's landmark obscenity cases in the 1960's, obscenity had long been prohibited. There is no similar history regarding expression related to violence. As the Court notes, classic literature contains descriptions of great violence, and even children's stories sometimes depict very violent scenes.

Although our society does not generally regard all depictions of violence as suitable for children or adolescents, the prevalence of violent depictions in children's literature and entertainment creates numerous opportunities for reasonable people to disagree about which depictions may excite "deviant" or "morbid" impulses.

Finally, the difficulty of ascertaining the community standards incorporated into the California law is compounded by the legislature's decision to lump all minors together. The California law draws no distinction between young children and adolescents who are nearing the age of majority.

For these reasons, I conclude that the California violent video game law fails to provide the fair notice that the Constitution requires. And I would go no further.

Having outlined how I would decide this case, I will now briefly elaborate on my reasons for questioning the wisdom of the Court's approach. Some of these reasons are touched upon by the dissents, and while I am not prepared at this time to go as far as either Justice THOMAS or Justice BREYER, they raise valid concerns.

Citing the video-game industry's voluntary rating system, the Court argues that the California law does not "meet a substantial need of parents who wish to restrict their children's access to violent video games but cannot do so." The Court does not mention the fact that the industry adopted this system in response to the threat of federal regulation, a threat that the Court's opinion may now be seen as largely eliminating. Nor does the Court acknowledge that compliance with this system at the time of the enactment of the California law left much to be desired—or that future enforcement may decline if the video-game industry perceives that any threat of government regulation has vanished. Nor does the Court note, as Justice BREYER points out, that many parents today are simply not able to monitor their children's use of computers and gaming devices.

Finally, the Court is far too quick to dismiss the possibility that the experience of playing video games (and the effects on minors of playing violent video games) may be very different from anything that we have seen before. Any assessment of the experience of playing video games must take into account certain characteristics of the video games that are now on the market and those that are likely to be available in the near future.

Today's most advanced video games create realistic alternative worlds in which millions of players immerse themselves for hours on end. These games feature visual imagery and sounds that are strikingly realistic, and in the near future video-game graphics may be virtually indistinguishable from actual video footage. Many of the games already on the market can produce high definition images, and it is predicted that it will not be long before video-game images will be seen in three dimensions. It is also forecast that video games will soon provide sensory feedback. By wearing a special vest or other device, a player will be able to experience physical sensations supposedly felt by a character on the screen. Some *amici* who support respondents foresee the day when "'virtual-reality shoot-'em-ups'" will allow children to "'actually feel the splatting blood from the blown-off head'" of a victim.

Persons who play video games also have an unprecedented ability to participate in the events that take place in the virtual worlds that these games create. Players can create their own video-game characters and can use photos to produce characters that closely resemble actual people. A person playing a sophisticated game can make a multitude of choices and can thereby alter the course of the action in the game. In addition, the means by which players control the action in video games now bear a closer relationship to the means by which people control action in the real world. While the action in older games was often directed with buttons or a joystick, players dictate the action in newer games by engaging in the same motions that they desire a character in the game to perform. For example, a player who wants a video-game character to swing a baseball bat—either to hit a ball or smash a skull—could bring that about by simulating the motion of actually swinging a bat.

These present-day and emerging characteristics of video games must be considered together with characteristics of the violent games that have already been marketed.

In some of these games, the violence is astounding. Victims by the dozens are killed with every imaginable implement, including machine guns, shotguns, clubs, hammers, axes, swords, and chainsaws. Victims are dismembered, decapitated, disemboweled, set on fire, and chopped into little pieces. They cry out in agony and beg for mercy. Blood gushes, splatters, and pools. Severed body parts and gobs of human remains are graphically shown. In some games, points are awarded based, not only on the number of victims killed, but on the killing technique employed.

It also appears that there is no antisocial theme too base for some in the video-game industry to exploit. There are games in which a player can take on the identity and reenact the killings carried out by the perpetrators of the murders at Columbine High School and Virginia Tech. The objective of one game is to rape a mother and her daughters; in another, the goal is to rape Native American women. There is a game in which players engage in "ethnic cleansing" and can choose to gun down African-Americans, Latinos, or Jews. In still another game, players attempt to fire a rifle shot into the head of President Kennedy as his motorcade passes by the Texas School Book Depository.

If the technological characteristics of the sophisticated games that are likely to be available in the near future are combined with the characteristics of the most violent games already marketed, the result will be games that allow troubled teens to experience in an extraordinarily personal and vivid way what it would be like to carry out unspeakable acts of violence.

The Court is untroubled by this possibility. According to the Court, the "interactive" nature of video games is "nothing new" because "all literature is interactive." It is certainly true, as the Court notes, that " '[l]iterature, when it is successful draws the reader into the story, makes him identify with the characters, invites him to judge them and quarrel with them, to experience their joys and sufferings as the reader's own.' " But only an extraordinarily imaginative reader who reads a description of a killing in a literary work will experience that event as vividly as he might if he played the role of the killer in a video game. To take an example, think of a person who reads the passage in Crime and Punishment in which Raskolnikov kills the old pawn broker with an axe. Compare that reader with a video-game player who creates an avatar that bears his own image; who sees a realistic image of the victim and the scene of the killing in high definition and in three dimensions; who is forced to decide whether or not to kill the victim and decides to do so; who then pretends to grasp an axe, to raise it above the head of the victim, and then to bring it down; who hears the thud of the axe hitting her head and her cry of pain; who sees her split skull and feels the sensation of blood on his face and hands. For most people, the two experiences will not be the same.

When all of the characteristics of video games are taken into account, there is certainly a reasonable basis for thinking that the experience of playing a video game may be quite different from the experience of reading a book, listening to a radio broadcast, or viewing a movie. And if this is so, then for at least some minors, the effects of playing violent video games may also be quite different. The Court acts prematurely in dismissing this possibility out of hand.

Thomas, Associate Justice, dissenting.

The Court's decision today does not comport with the original public understanding of the First Amendment. The majority strikes down, as facially unconstitutional, a state law that prohibits the direct sale or rental of certain video games to minors because the law "abridg[es] the freedom of speech." U.S. Const., Amdt. 1. But I do not think the First Amendment stretches that far. The practices and beliefs of the founding generation establish that "the freedom of speech," as originally understood, does not include a right to speak to minors (or a right of minors to access speech) without going through the minors' parents or guardians. I would hold that the law at issue is not facially unconstitutional under the First Amendment, and reverse and remand for further proceedings.

When interpreting a constitutional provision, "the goal is to discern the most likely public understanding of [that] provision at the time it was adopted." Because the Constitution is a written instrument, "its meaning does not alter. That which it meant when adopted, it means now."

As originally understood, the First Amendment's protection against laws "abridging the freedom of speech" did not extend to *all* speech. "There are certain well-defined and narrowly limited classes of speech, the prevention and punishment of which have never been thought to raise any Constitutional problem." Laws regulating such speech do not "abridg[e] the freedom of speech" because such speech is understood to fall outside "the freedom of speech."

In my view, the "practices and beliefs held by the Founders" reveal another category of excluded speech: speech to minor children bypassing their parents. The historical evidence shows that the founding generation believed parents had absolute authority over their minor children and expected parents to use that authority to direct the proper development of their children. It would be absurd to suggest that such a society understood "the freedom of speech" to include a right to speak to minors (or a corresponding right of minors to access speech) without going through the minors' parents.

BRYER, Associate Justice, dissenting.

California imposes a civil fine of up to $1,000 upon any person who distributes a violent video game in California without labeling it "18," or who sells or rents a labeled violent video game to a person under the age of 18. Representatives of the video game and software industries, claiming that the statute violates the First Amendment on its face, seek an injunction against its enforcement. Applying traditional First Amendment analysis, I would uphold the statute as constitutional on its face and would consequently reject the industries' facial challenge.

I shall focus here upon an area within which I believe the State can legitimately apply its statute, namely sales to minors under the age of 17 (the age cutoff used by the industry's own ratings system), of highly realistic violent video games, which a reasonable game maker would know meet the Act's criteria. That area lies at the heart of the statute. I shall assume that the activity the statute regulates combines speech with action (a virtual form of target practice).

In determining whether the statute is unconstitutional, I would apply both this Court's "vagueness" precedents and a strict form of First Amendment scrutiny. In doing so, the special First Amendment category I find relevant is not (as the Court claims) the category of "depictions of violence," *ante,* at 2736, but rather the category of "protection of children." This Court has held that the "power of the state to control the conduct of children reaches beyond the scope of its authority over adults." And the "regulatio[n] of communication addressed to [children] need not conform to the requirements of the [F]irst [A]mendment in the same way as those applicable to adults." *Ginsberg v. New York,* 390 U.S. 629, 638, n. 6 (1968).

The majority's claim that the California statute, if upheld, would create a "new categor[y] of unprotected speech," is overstated. We properly speak of *categories* of expression that lack protection when, like "child pornography," the category is broad, when it applies automatically, and when the State can prohibit everyone, including adults, from obtaining access to the material within it. But where, as here, careful analysis must precede a narrower judicial conclusion, we do not normally describe the result as creating a "new category of unprotected speech."

Thus, in *Stevens,* after rejecting the claim that *all* depictions of animal cruelty (a category) fall outside the First Amendment's protective scope, we went on to decide whether the particular statute at issue violates the First Amendment under traditional standards; and we held that, because the statute was overly broad, it was invalid. Similarly, here the issue is whether, applying traditional First Amendment standards, this statute does, or does not, pass muster.

In my view, California's statute provides "fair notice of what is prohibited," and consequently it is not impermissibly vague. *Ginsberg* explains why that is so. The five-

Justice majority, in an opinion written by Justice Brennan, wrote that the statute was sufficiently clear. No Member of the Court [in *Ginsberg*] voiced any vagueness objection.

Both the *Miller* standard and the law upheld in *Ginsberg* lack perfect clarity. But that fact reflects the difficulty of the Court's long search for words capable of protecting expression without depriving the State of a legitimate constitutional power to regulate. As is well known, at one point Justice Stewart thought he could do no better in defining obscenity than, "I know it when I see it." *Jacobellis v. Ohio*, 378 U.S. 184, 197 (1964) (concurring opinion). And Justice Douglas dissented from *Miller*'s standard, which he thought was still too vague. Ultimately, however, this Court accepted the "community standards" tests used in *Miller* and *Ginsberg*. They reflect the fact that sometimes, even when a precise standard proves elusive, it is easy enough to identify instances that fall within a legitimate regulation. And they seek to draw a line, which, while favoring free expression, will nonetheless permit a legislature to find the words necessary to accomplish a legitimate constitutional objective (the Constitution does not always require 'perfect clarity and precise guidance,' even when " 'expressive activity' " is involved).

What, then, is the difference between *Ginsberg* and *Miller* on the one hand and the California law on the other? It will often be easy to pick out cases at which California's statute directly aims, involving, say, a character who shoots out a police officer's knee, douses him with gasoline, lights him on fire, urinates on his burning body, and finally kills him with a gunshot to the head. As in *Miller* and *Ginsberg*, the California law clearly *protects* even the most violent games that possess serious literary, artistic, political, or scientific value. And it is easier here than in *Miller* or *Ginsberg* to separate the sheep from the goats at the statute's border. That is because here the industry itself has promulgated standards and created a review process, in which adults who "typically have experience with children" assess what games are inappropriate for minors. See Entertainment Software Rating Board, Rating Process.

There is, of course, one obvious difference: The *Ginsberg* statute concerned depictions of "nudity," while California's statute concerns extremely violent video games. But for purposes of vagueness, why should that matter? Justice ALITO argues that the *Miller* standard sufficed because there are "certain generally accepted norms concerning expression related to sex," whereas there are no similarly "accepted standards regarding the suitability of violent entertainment." But there is no evidence that is so. The Court relied on "community standards" in *Miller* precisely because of the difficulty of articulating "accepted norms" about depictions of sex. I can find no difference—historical or otherwise—that is *relevant* to the vagueness question. Indeed, the majority's examples of literary descriptions of violence, on which Justice ALITO relies, do not show anything relevant at all.

After all, one can find in literature as many (if not more) descriptions of physical love as descriptions of violence. Indeed, sex "has been a theme in art and literature throughout the ages." For every Homer, there is a Titian. For every Dante, there is an Ovid. And for all the teenagers who have read the original versions of Grimm's Fairy Tales, I suspect there are those who know the story of Lady Godiva.

Thus, I can find no meaningful vagueness-related differences between California's law and the New York law upheld in *Ginsberg*. And if there remain any vagueness problems, the state courts can cure them through interpretation.

Video games combine physical action with expression. Were physical activity to predominate in a game, government could appropriately intervene, say by requiring parents to accompany children when playing a game involving actual target practice, or restricting the sale of toys presenting physical dangers to children. But because video games also embody important expressive and artistic elements, I agree with the Court that the First Amendment significantly limits the State's power to regulate. And I would determine whether the State has exceeded those limits by applying a strict standard of review.

Like the majority, I believe that the California law must be "narrowly tailored" to further a "compelling interest," without there being a "less restrictive" alternative that would be "at least as effective." I would not apply this strict standard "mechanically." Rather, in applying it, I would evaluate the degree to which the statute injures speech-related interests, the nature of the potentially-justifying "compelling interests," the degree to which the statute furthers that interest, the nature and effectiveness of possible alternatives, and, in light of this evaluation, whether, overall, "the statute works speech-related harm ... out of proportion to the benefits that the statute seeks to provide."

First Amendment standards applied in this way are difficult but not impossible to satisfy. Applying "strict scrutiny" the Court has upheld restrictions on speech that, for example, ban the teaching of peaceful dispute resolution to a group on the State Department's list of terrorist organizations, *Holder,* 561 U.S., at ——, 130 S.Ct., at 2723–3730, and limit speech near polling places, *Burson, supra,* at 210–211, 112 S.Ct. 1846 (plurality opinion). And applying less clearly defined but still rigorous standards, the Court has allowed States to require disclosure of petition signers, *Doe v. Reed,* 561, 130 S.Ct. 2811 (2010), and to impose campaign contribution limits that were " 'closely drawn' to match a 'sufficiently important interest,' " *Nixon v. Shrink Missouri Government PAC,* 528 U.S. 377, 387–388 (2000).

Moreover, although the Court did not specify the "level of scrutiny" it applied in *Ginsberg,* we have subsequently described that case as finding a "compelling interest" in protecting children from harm sufficient to justify limitations on speech. See *Sable Communications of Cal., Inc. v. FCC,* 492 U.S. 115, 126, (1989). I cannot dismiss *Ginsberg* on the ground that it concerned obscenity. But cf. *ante,* at 2735 (majority opinion). Nor need I depend upon the fact that the Court in *Ginsberg* insisted only that the legislature have a "rational" basis for finding the depictions there at issue harmful to children. For in this case, California has substantiated its claim of harm with considerably stronger evidence.

California's law imposes no more than a modest restriction on expression. The statute prevents no one from playing a video game, it prevents no adult from buying a video game, and it prevents no child or adolescent from obtaining a game provided a parent is willing to help. All it prevents is a child or adolescent from buying, without a parent's assistance, a gruesomely violent video game of a kind that the industry *itself* tells us it wants to keep out of the hands of those under the age of 17.

Nor is the statute, if upheld, likely to create a precedent that would adversely affect other media, say films, or videos, or books. A typical video game involves a significant amount of physical activity. See (ALITO, J., concurring in judgment) (citing examples of the increasing interactivity of video game controllers). And pushing buttons that achieve an interactive, virtual form of target practice (using images of human beings as targets), while containing an expressive component, is not just like watching a typical movie.

The interest that California advances in support of the statute is compelling. As this Court has previously described that interest, it consists of both (1) the "basic" parental claim "to authority in their own household to direct the rearing of their children," which makes it proper to enact "laws designed to aid discharge of [parental] responsibility," and (2) the State's "independent interest in the well-being of its youth." [O]ne can well distinguish laws which do not impose a morality on children, but which support the right of parents to deal with the morals of their children as they see fit. And where these interests work in tandem, it is not fatally "underinclusive" for a State to advance its interests in protecting children against the special harms present in an interactive video game medium through a default rule that still allows parents to provide their children with what their parents wish.

Both interests are present here. As to the need to help parents guide their children, the Court noted in 1968 that "'parental control or guidance cannot always be provided.'" Today, 5.3 million grade-school-age children of working parents are routinely home alone. See Dept. of Commerce, Census Bureau, Thus, it has, if anything, become more important to supplement parents' authority to guide their children's development.

As to the State's independent interest, we have pointed out that juveniles are more likely to show a "'lack of maturity'" and are "more vulnerable or susceptible to negative influences and outside pressures," and that their "character ... is not as well formed as that of an adult."

At the same time, there is considerable evidence that California's statute significantly furthers this compelling interest. That is, in part, because video games are excellent teaching tools. Learning a practical task often means developing habits, becoming accustomed to performing the task, and receiving positive reinforcement when performing that task well. Video games can help develop habits, accustom the player to performance of the task, and reward the player for performing that task well. Why else would the Armed Forces incorporate video games into its training?

When the military uses video games to help soldiers train for missions, it is using this medium for a beneficial purpose. But California argues that when the teaching features of video games are put to less desirable ends, harm can ensue. In particular, extremely violent games can harm children by rewarding them for being violently aggressive in play, and thereby often teaching them to be violently aggressive in life. And video games can cause more harm in this respect than can typically passive media, such as books or films or television programs.

There are many scientific studies that support California's views. Social scientists, for example, have found *causal* evidence that playing these games results in harm. Longitudinal studies, which measure changes over time, have found that increased exposure to violent video games causes an increase in aggression over the same period. [Citations omitted— ED.]

Experimental studies in laboratories have found that subjects randomly assigned to play a violent video game subsequently displayed more characteristics of aggression than those who played nonviolent games. Surveys of 8th and 9th grade students have found a correlation between playing violent video games and aggression. Cutting-edge neuroscience has shown that "virtual violence in video game playing results in those neural patterns that are considered characteristic for aggressive cognition and behavior."

Some of these studies take care to explain in a commonsense way why video games are potentially more harmful than, say, films or books or television. In essence, they say that the closer a child's behavior comes, not to watching, but to *acting* out horrific violence, the greater the potential psychological harm. See Bushman & Huesmann, Aggression, in 2 Handbook of Social Psychology 833, 851 (S. Fiske, D. Gilbert, & G. Lindzey eds., 5th ed. 2010) (video games stimulate more aggression because "[p]eople learn better when they are actively involved," players are "more likely to identify with violent characters," and "violent games directly reward violent behavior").

Experts debate the conclusions of all these studies. Like many, perhaps most, studies of human behavior, each study has its critics, and some of those critics have produced studies of their own in which they reach different conclusions. I, like most judges, lack the social science expertise to say definitively who is right. But associations of public health professionals who do possess that expertise have reviewed many of these studies and found a significant risk that violent video games, when compared with more passive media, are particularly likely to cause children harm.

Unlike the majority, I would find sufficient grounds in these studies and expert opinions for this Court to defer to an elected legislature's conclusion that the video games in question are particularly likely to harm children. This Court has always thought it owed an elected legislature some degree of deference in respect to legislative facts of this kind, particularly when they involve technical matters that are beyond our competence, and even in First Amendment cases. The majority, in reaching its own, opposite conclusion about the validity of the relevant studies, grants the legislature no deference at all.

I can find no "less restrictive" alternative to California's law that would be "at least as effective." The majority points to a voluntary alternative: The industry tries to prevent those under 17 from buying extremely violent games by labeling those games with an "M" (Mature) and encouraging retailers to restrict their sales to those 17 and older. But this voluntary system has serious enforcement gaps. When California enacted its law, a Federal Trade Commission (FTC) study had found that nearly 70% of unaccompanied 13- to 16-year-olds were able to buy M-rated video games. But as of the FTC's most recent update to Congress, 20% of those under 17 are still able to buy M-rated video games, and, breaking down sales by store, one finds that this number rises to nearly 50% in the case of one large national chain.

The industry also argues for an alternative technological solution, namely "filtering at the console level." But it takes only a quick search of the Internet to find guides explaining how to circumvent any such technological controls. YouTube viewers, for example, have watched one of those guides (called "How to bypass parental controls on the Xbox 360") more than 47,000 times. See http://www.youtube.com/watch?v= CFlVfVmvN6k.

I add that the majority's different conclusion creates a serious anomaly in First Amendment law. *Ginsberg* makes clear that a State can prohibit the sale to minors of depictions of nudity; today the Court makes clear that a State cannot prohibit the sale to minors of the most violent interactive video games. But what sense does it make to forbid selling to a 13-year-old boy a magazine with an image of a nude woman, while protecting a sale to that 13-year-old of an interactive video game in which he actively, but virtually, binds and gags the woman, then tortures and kills her? What kind of First Amendment would permit the government to protect children by restricting sales of that extremely violent video game *only* when the woman—bound, gagged, tortured, and killed—is also topless? This anomaly is not compelled by the First Amendment.

This case is ultimately less about censorship than it is about education. Education is about choices. Sometimes, children need to learn by making choices for themselves. Other times, choices are made for children—by their parents, by their teachers, and by the people acting democratically through their governments. In my view, the First Amendment does not disable government from helping parents make such a choice here—a choice not to have their children buy extremely violent, interactive video games, which they more than reasonably fear pose only the risk of harm to those children.

Notes and Questions

1. Is Justice Scalia and the majority correct that the best argument against the constitutionality of the statute is on strict scrutiny grounds, or should the Court have adopted

Justice Alito's approach and decided the case on vagueness grounds? Or should Justice Scalia also have discussed vagueness?

2. The ESRB ratings play a role in many of the opinions in *Brown*, and we explain these ratings in § 12.30, *infra*. As a threshold matter, *should* a voluntary, private rating service have any relevance in deciding the constitutionality of a statute? If so, how do the various opinions use the existing ratings? And if the ratings are relevant, is Justice Breyer's citation to the FTC report casting doubt on how effective the ratings are in practice a good point or an irrelevancy?

3. One of the reasons given by *Brown* for declaring the statute unconstitutional was that other media, such as fairy tales, also depict violence and are tailored to children. Are videogames different from books and movies? Does the interactive nature of videogames and their ever more sophisticated controllers make videogames a separate category for First Amendment analysis? Can't the state try to experiment with limiting one form of violent stimuli without having to take on a majority of the media violence to which children are exposed?

4. Is there a difference between modeling the adult obscenity test for minors with reference to community standards in *Ginsberg* and attempting to model a community standards test for violence in *Brown*?

§ 12.233 Factual Support For the Means-Ends Fit in Seeking to Uphold Statutes Regulating Constitutionally Protected Games

Another point of difference between Justice Scalia and Justice Breyer is whether the studies on human behavior have established that playing violent videogames causes antisocial behavior, with Justice Scalia saying there is at most a correlation between violent gameplay (and cartoon watching) and violent conduct, and Justice Breyer concluding that at least some of the studies show a causative link. If such a causation link were undeniable, it might serve as the "actual and substantial evidence" necessary to overcome even a strict scrutiny analysis.

The practical and ethical issues in researching human behavior make getting such "undeniable" evidence difficult. As mentioned above, no one would allow a researcher to collect a gaggle of 15–17 year old boys together for 2 years to play some violent videogame and then let the boys loose in society while surreptitiously following them to measure their antisocial behaviors. Instead, the studies deal generally with monitoring brain activity during game play and making assumptions on how brain wave changes would express themselves in unfettered conduct.

Perhaps the foremost researcher in the area, and the scientist mentioned by Justice Scalia in *Brown*, is Dr. Craig Anderson. Dr. Anderson either testifies, or his studies are cited, in all significant cases in which regulation of videogames is an issue. One of these cases was *Entm't Software Ass'n v. Blagojevich*, 404 F. Supp. 2d 1051, 1057–67 (E.D. Ill. 2005). There the court made a detailed finding of what the available research shows (and does not show), and we thought you might be interested in seeing the evidence yourself so you can decide whether Justice Scalia or Justice Breyer has the better of the arguments:

> In adopting the VVGL [Violent Video Games Law] and the SEVGL [Sexually Explicit Video Games Law], the Illinois General Assembly made findings about the accessibility of violent and sexually explicit video games to minors. Specifically, the legislative record includes reports by the Federal Trade Commission and the

Illinois State Crime Commission about the ability of minors to purchase rated video games. In 2004, the FTC found that sixty-nine percent of unaccompanied teenagers were able to purchase M-rated video games. In 2005, the Illinois State Crime Commission found that a fifteen-year old boy was able to buy M-rated games at eleven of fifteen, or seventy-three percent, of retailers visited. The 2004 FTC study also examined whether unaccompanied teenagers could purchase analogous media products in other formats. The FTC concluded that eighty-one percent of unaccompanied minors could purchase R-rated movies, and eighty-three percent could purchase music with explicit lyrics—far more than were able to purchase M-rated video games.

Among other things, the record includes seventeen scholarly articles contending that minors become more aggressive when exposed to media violence, including video game violence. The same person—Dr. Craig Anderson—authored or co-authored fourteen of these articles; Dr. Douglas Gentile, a colleague of Dr. Anderson's, authored one article; and Dr. William Kronenberger, who has relied on Dr. Anderson's research in developing his own studies, authored the other two articles.

With regard to the SEVGL, the Illinois General Assembly found "sexually explicit video games inappropriate for minors." The legislative record does not include scholarly articles or expert testimony on this issue, but there are comments from legislators contending that the sexually explicit content in many video games is inappropriate for children.

The evidence presented concerned two main issues: first, whether minors who play violent video games experience an increase in aggressive thoughts, aggressive affect, and aggressive behavior, and second, whether minors who play such games experience a decline in brain activity in the region of the brain that controls behavior. The parties also agreed that the Court could consider as evidence the affidavits that had been submitted as part of the preliminary injunction briefing, as well as deposition testimony of certain witnesses.

1. Effect of violent video games on aggressive thoughts and behavior

Dr. Craig Anderson, a psychologist and professor at Iowa State University, testified on behalf of the defendants. Dr. Anderson summarized research, including his own, regarding the relationship between minors' exposure to violent video games and aggressive thoughts and behavior. Based on this research, Dr. Anderson testified that "it seems clear that exposure to violent video games increases aggressive behavior, aggressive thinking, physiological arousal, aggressive feelings, and is also associated with a decrease in prosocial behavior."

Dr. Anderson's studies on the connection between media violence and aggressive cognition and behavior are rooted in his broader research into aggression. Specifically, Dr. Anderson developed his "general aggression model" to explain how an individual's personal characteristics and experiences trigger aggressive thoughts or responses to particular situations and how this cycle or cycles can make aggressive thoughts and behaviors more accessible. According to Dr. Anderson, an individual's personal characteristics and experiences—particularly with violence—prime or activate aggressive thoughts and teach aggressive "scripts," making it more likely that he or she will have aggressive reactions to particular situations.

Dr. Anderson testified that playing violent video games is one activity that primes aggressive thoughts and teaches aggressive scripts. He stated: In violent video games, you rehearse really the whole sequence [of aggression]. You rehearse, you practice being vigilant, that is, looking for the source of the threat. You practice identifying sources of threat. You practice making decisions about how to respond to that threat. And eventually, you actually carry out some form of action, typically a violent action to deal with that threat, clicking a mouse or something on the keyboard or a pretend sort of gun of some kind.

As a result of regularly playing violent video games, Dr. Anderson testified, these scripts or knowledge structures become "chronically accessible" and ultimately become "automatized." The research underlying Dr. Anderson's testimony, however, does not support such a stark and sweeping conclusion. We begin by providing an overview of the studies cited by Dr. Anderson to support his conclusions.

One of the articles Dr. Anderson published involved two studies of the effects of violent video games on measures of aggression on college students. This study provided the basis for the Indianapolis ordinance regulating violent video games that was struck down in Kendrick. In the first study, Dr. Anderson and Dr. Karen Dill of Lenoir-Rhyne College conducted a survey of college students regarding exposure to violent video games and aggressive behavior, using components of the National Youth Survey as a measure. Dr. Anderson found "a strong positive correlation between video game exposure and aggressive behavior." He conceded, however, that once the results were adjusted to exclude non-serious behavior, such as throwing snowballs, less than ten percent of the participants reported engaging in aggressive behavior. Dr. Anderson also indicated that exposure to violent video games only incrementally affected the amount of aggressive behavior they engaged in.

In a second study, Dr. Anderson conducted an experiment in which participants played a violent video game, Wolfenstein 3D, or a non-violent video game, Myst. The participants were then asked to participate in a task in which they were supposed to "compete" with someone outside the room and administer a noise blast to the "loser" whenever they won. Based on this experiment, Dr. Anderson concluded that violent video games caused an increase in aggressive behavior, because participants who played Myst administered a longer noise blast than the participants who played Wolfenstein 3D. In his testimony, however, Dr. Anderson stated that the difference between the two groups was a matter of milliseconds.

Dr. Anderson also discussed three additional studies he conducted using college students. In the first experiment, half the students played violent video games and half played non-violent video games. They were then given a list of partially completed words — many of which could have been completed to form an aggressive word — and asked the participants to finish the words. The students who played the violent video game were more likely to fill in the blank to form an aggressive word, leading Dr. Anderson and his colleagues to conclude that exposure to the violent video game had increased their aggressive thoughts.

In the second experiment, half the students played a violent video game and half played a non-violent video game. They then went through time trials in which they were led to believe they were competing against someone in the next room. In the first series of time trials, the participants went through a series of time trials in which they were "punished" with a noise blast from a "competitor" when they lost. There were, in fact, no competitors: the noise blasts administered to the participants were controlled by a computer. Half received random blasts, and the other half received blasts that increased in intensity. In the second series of time trials, the participants administered a noise blast to their "competitor" if they won. Dr. Anderson found that the students who had played violent video game and received random noise blasts administered more intense noise blasts than all of the students who played the non-violent video games. He therefore concluded that exposure to violent video games increased an individual's aggressive behavior.

Notably, the students who played violent video games and received increasingly intense noise blasts administered the lowest intensity noise blasts. Though that seems to contradict his finding, Dr. Anderson stated that previous research indicates that results from participants who played violent video games and received random noise blasts are more relevant. Though the Court is skeptical about the explanation of these contradictory results, it is willing to assume for purposes of discussion that Dr. Anderson's conclusion is correct. The Court, however, questions the overall import of Dr. Anderson's findings, given that on a one to ten scale of intensity, the most "aggressive" violent video game players administered an average blast of 5.93, and the least "aggressive" non-violent video game players administered an average blast of 3.98. There was only a two point difference, and both averages were in the middle of the intensity scale. See Craig A. Anderson et al., Violent Video Games: Specific Effects of Violent Content on Aggressive Thoughts and Behavior, 36 Advances Experimental Soc. Psychol. 199, 215–24 (2004) (hereinafter, "Violent Video Games: Specific Effects").

In the final experiment, half the students played two violent video games and half of them played two non-violent video games. The violent video games were subdivided into those with human targets and those with non-human targets. They then engaged in the same noise blast task as the participants in the second experiment. The students who played violent video games gave "more or higher punishment levels to their opponents than those who played one of the nonviolent games." Dr. Anderson's study, however, indicates that those participants who played a violent video game administered an average noise blast that was less than one point higher than the average noise blast of non-violent video game players. See Anderson, "Violent Video Games: Specific Effects" at 229. Dr. Anderson also found that the participants' reactions to playing a violent video game with human targets was the same as their reactions to playing one with non-human targets.

Dr. Anderson stated that there has only been one reliable longitudinal study into the impact of violent video games on aggression in minors. Such studies, which examine the effects of a particular variable at two or more points in time, are important because they can measure longer term effects, rule out alternative explanations for particular behavior, and help identify the cause of a particular behavior. In this study, which is still undergoing peer review, Dr. Douglas Gentile, a colleague of Dr. Anderson's at Iowa State University, interviewed third-, fourth-, and fifth-graders about the level of violence in the video games they played during the six month period of the study. Then, using reports from parents and teachers, he determined the child's level of aggressive behavior at the beginning and end of the study to assess whether such behavior had increased.

According to Dr. Anderson, Dr. Gentile's longitudinal study showed that those children with a higher exposure to violent video games were more likely to have been in a fight by the end of the study, even after controlling for whether the child had been in a fight—and likely had a proclivity for aggression—before the study began. From this longitudinal study, Dr. Anderson concluded that "[w]hat is clear is that regardless of the *initial cause*, playing violent video games still makes children *more* aggressive." Def. Exh. 8, Douglas A. Gentile and Craig A. Anderson, Violent Video Games: The Effects on Youth, and Public Policy Implications, in Children, Culture, and Violence, at 232 (N. Dowd et al. eds.) (forthcoming) (emphasis in original). The total increase in aggressive behavior between the beginning and end of the study, however, was not very large; there was a high (0.4 to 0.5) correlation between aggression at the beginning and end of the study; and at most, only four percent of the increase in aggression was associated with exposure to video game violence. Finally, Dr. Anderson discussed the results of three meta-analyses he conducted in 2001, 2003, and 2004. In a meta-analysis, a researcher compiles all of the studies that have been conducted in a particular area, combines the results from those studies, and makes conclusions based on the body of research as a whole. In each of these meta-analyses, Dr. Anderson found that exposure to violent video games was associated with aggressive thinking and behavior. The studies differed, however, because he added new data and adjusted his methodology with each meta-analysis. For example, in the 2003 meta-analysis, Dr. Anderson conducted a separate breakdown of studies involving participants who were eighteen or younger, and in the 2004 meta-analysis, he did a separate analysis of studies that used "best practices." Nonetheless, his conclusion about the link between exposure to violent video games and aggression remained the same.

Dr. Jeffrey Goldstein, a social psychologist at the University of Utrecht in the Netherlands, and Dr. Dmitri Williams, an assistant professor of communications at the University of Illinois at Urbana-Champaign, testified for the plaintiffs, and they responded to Dr. Anderson's testimony. Dr. Goldstein has conducted research into whether video games help improve cognitive skills; Dr. Williams conducted an intensive one-month study for his doctoral dissertation on individuals who played a violent, multi-player computer-based video game. They agreed that there is a correlation between exposure to video game violence and increases in aggressive cognition and behavior, but disagreed with Dr. Anderson's conclusion that the research establishes that exposure to violent video games causes increases in aggressive thinking and behavior.

Dr. Goldstein and Dr. Williams shared a number of the same concerns with the methodology and conclusions of research regarding violent video games cited by Dr. Anderson. With regard to methodology, they were concerned that these studies defined aggressive thoughts and behavior vaguely (e.g., equating aggressive play with aggressive behavior), administered problematic tests for measuring aggression (e.g., Stroop tests and noise blasts), used violent and non-violent video games that were too dissimilar (e.g., Wolfenstein 3D and Myst), and failed to address the context of game playing (e.g., asking subjects to play for too short a time and without others around them). With regard to their conclusions, Dr. Goldstein and Dr. Williams noted that Dr. Anderson not only had failed to cite any peer-reviewed studies that had shown a definitive causal link between violent video game play and aggression, but had also ignored research that reached conflicting conclusions. Dr. Goldstein and Dr. Williams noted that several studies concluded that there was no relationship between these two variables. They also cited studies concluding that in certain instances, there was a negative relationship between violent video game play and aggressive thoughts and behavior (e.g., initial increases in aggression wore off if the individual was allowed to play violent video game for longer period).

Though the Court believes that many of the measures of aggression used in violent video game research are likely valid, we agree with Dr. Goldstein and Dr. Williams that neither Dr. Anderson's testimony nor his research establish a solid causal link between violent video game exposure and aggressive thinking and behavior. As Dr. Goldstein and Dr. Williams noted, researchers in this field have not eliminated the most obvious alternative explanation: aggressive individuals may themselves be attracted to violent video games.

Even if one were to accept the proposition that playing violent video games increases aggressive thoughts or behavior, there is no evidence that this effect is at all significant. Dr. Anderson provided no evidence supporting the view that playing violent video games has a lasting effect on aggressive thoughts and behavior—in other words, an effect that lingers more than a short time after the player stops playing the game. Based on general psychological theories and long-term studies of television and movie violence, Dr. Anderson hypothesizes that frequently and intensely playing violent video games will have a lasting effect on young players. He does not, however, cite any data or studies to back up his hypothesis. In most studies, test subjects play a game for between ten and seventy-five minutes, and only one study—Dr. Gentile's—included an assessment of the effect of regular violent video game play over a longer period of time. This research is insufficient to draw conclusions about the long-term impact of video games on minors.

Dr. Anderson also has not provided evidence to show that the purported relationship between violent video game exposure and aggressive thoughts or behavior is any greater than with other types of media violence, such as television or movies, or other factors that contribute to aggression, such as poverty. In fact, several of the studies he uses to support his conclusions examine media violence generally and do not disaggregate the effect of video game violence or compare the effects of video game violence to these or other forms of media violence.

Finally, the Court is concerned that the legislative record does not indicate that the Illinois General Assembly considered any of the evidence that showed no relationship or a negative relationship between violent video game play and increases in aggressive thoughts and behavior. The legislative record included none of the articles cited by Dr. Goldstein or Dr. Williams. It included no data whatsoever that was critical of research finding a causal link between violent video game play and aggression. These omissions further undermine defendants' claim that the legislature made "reasonable inferences" from the scientific literature based on "substantial evidence." *See Turner Broadcasting System v. FCC*, 512 U.S. 622 (1994).

2. Effect of violent video games on brain activity

Dr. William Kronenberger, who testified for the defendants, is a clinical psychologist at the Indiana University School of Medicine who focuses on working with and studying children and adolescents with behavior disorders. He has conducted research into the relationship between adolescent exposure to media violence and aggressive thinking and behavior. In his testimony, Dr. Kronenberger cited studies that he said indicate that increased exposure to media violence has negative effects on adolescent brain activity. To measure how exposure to media violence affects brain activity, Dr. Kronenberger uses functional magnetic resource imaging, a neuroimaging technique that measures blood flow to certain regions of the brain, allowing researchers to infer the level of activity in those areas. Researchers use fMRI imaging to determine how a particular task affects brain activity by having the test subject perform the task inside an fMRI scanner, having a control subject perform a different, but similar task, and comparing the level of blood flow to the relevant areas of the test subject's and control subject's brains.

Dr. Kronenberger has published an article in a peer-reviewed journal discussing a study that used fMRI imaging to examine how exposure to media violence affects aggressive thinking and aggressive behavior in adolescents. He and his colleagues specifically examined two parts of the brain—the anterior cingulate cortex (ACC) and the dorsolateral prefrontal cortex (DLPFC), which is comprised of the middle frontal gyrus (MFG) and the inferior frontal gyrus (IFG). Dr. Kronenberger's research team decided to focus on these areas because prior research has indicated that lower activation, deficiencies, or injuries in these areas are associated with aggressive or violent behavior.

For the experiment discussed in his article, Dr. Kronenberger's research team recruited two groups of adolescents—one consisted of adolescents diagnosed with a behavior disorder, and the other was a control group. Based on interviews, the researchers subdivided the groups into those with high and low exposure to media violence. All of the subjects underwent fMRI imaging, and while they were in the fMRI scanner, they performed something called a counting Stroop test. In this test, a multiple-digit number is flashed onto a screen. The test subject is asked to state the number of digits, but the actual numerals are different from the number of digits listed. Stroop tests can be administered in a number of ways, but they are used to measure an individual's ability to inhibit his initial impulses in favor of a more difficult response.

Dr. Kronenberger and his colleagues found that the control subjects as a whole experienced activation in the ACC and the left DLPFC, while the adolescents with behavior disorders experienced activation in the MFG portion of the DLPFC but no activation in the ACC. Furthermore, when the researchers compared the control subjects with high media exposure to the control subjects with low media violence exposure, they found that control subjects with high media violence exposure had activation in the left MFG, the same region in which subjects with behavior disorders experienced activation, but control subjects with low media violence experienced activation in the ACC and the left IFG.

This experiment was part of a larger study. During the first phase of that study, Dr. Kronenberger conducted a second experiment, the results of which had not yet undergone the process of peer review. In this experiment, the methodology was the same except that while the participants were in the scanners, half watched simulated play of a violent video game (James Bond), and the rest watched simulated play of a non-violent game (car racing). The participants did not actually play the games, but they were told to press a button whenever they would have performed an action had they actually been playing. The researchers found that along the axis of high versus low media violence exposure, the control subjects with high media violence exposure experienced activation in the IFG, and the control subjects with low media violence exposure showed activation in the MFG. Along the axis of watching the violent versus the non-violent video game, the control subjects who watched the violent video game showed activation in the left and right MFG while the subjects with behavior disorders who played violent video games showed activity in the IFG.

During the second phase of the study, Dr. Kronenberger and his research team expanded their research to examine how exposure to media violence affects the amygdala, a portion of the brain that he testified has been associated with emotional functioning, particularly "threat arousal stimuli." The results of this portion of the study have not yet been published in a peer-reviewed journal. Dr. Kronenberger had the test subjects complete what he termed an "emotional Stroop color-word test." Both the adolescents with behavior disorders and the control subjects had to state the color of the word, but half of each group was asked to read words of aggression or harm (i.e., "kill, murder, rape") while half of each group was asked to read words without violent connotations. Dr. Kronenberger found that the control group experienced activation of the ACC and the DFC while the adolescents with behavioral disorders showed increased activity in the amygdala and the para hippocampal gyrus, which are also associated with emotion. Additionally, test subjects who had high media violence exposure also showed activation in the amygdala and the para hippocampal gyrus while those with low media violence exposure showed activation in the DLPFC.

Dr. Kronenberger conceded that his studies only demonstrate a correlative, not a causal, relationship between high media violence exposure and children who experience behavioral disorders, decreased brain activity in the ACC and the DLFPC, and increased activity in the amygdala and the para hippocampal gyrus.

Dr. Kronenberger has also published two articles in peer-reviewed journals which report studies on the use of neurocognitive testing to examine how media violence affects cognitive activity. In the first article, Dr. Kronenberger reported the results of a study in which he evaluated the impact of exposure to media violence on a child's executive functioning—the ability to plan, organize, direct, and carry out behavior that is oriented toward a goal. Specifically, Dr. Kronenberger used four measures to evaluate executive functioning—two neurocognitive tests performed in a lab and two self-reporting tests. He then determined the children's level of media violence exposure. After controlling for a number of variables, Dr. Kronenberger found that "there was a significant correlation between media violence exposure ... and poorer scores on each of those four measures of executive functioning." He ultimately concluded that the higher the media violence exposure, the worse the test subjects performed on measures of executive functioning.

In his second article, Dr. Kronenberger compared adolescents with behavior disorders and control adolescents, and evaluated whether those with behavior disorders and their parents reported greater exposure to media violence in the last week and in the last year. Dr. Kronenberger found that adolescents with behavior disorders and their parents reported more media violence exposure over the last year. After the study concluded, he also used a post hoc analysis to examine the unique effects of television violence and video game violence, and he found that each was related to whether an adolescent had a behavior disorder or was in the control group.

Dr. Howard Nusbaum, a cognitive psychologist at the University of Chicago, testified for the plaintiffs and responded to Dr. Kronenberger's testimony. Dr. Nusbaum uses fMRI imaging in his research, and he has written several articles on methodological issues on how to conduct fMRI research and interpret the results. He thoroughly reviewed Dr. Kronenberger's research and identified fundamental problems with "the background assumptions of the work, where it starts from, the methodology that is represented in the work and the conclusions that are drawn."

Initially, Dr. Nusbaum testified, Dr. Kronenberger made two incorrect assumptions. First, he assumed a one-to-one relationship between various parts of the brain and particular behaviors. Dr. Nusbaum testified that particular brain activity can affect multiple behaviors, and specific behaviors can be influenced by activity in multiple areas of the brain. Specifically, he stated that activity in the ACC and DLPFC—the areas Dr. Kronenberger stated were associated with impulse control, self-regulation, choice, attention, and concentration—affect many behaviors, and the behaviors Dr. Kronenberger traces to the frontal lobes also implicate other areas of the brain. In fact, according to Dr. Nusbaum, "[t]hese areas certainly are not highly associated with people who are aggressive, or activity in these areas is certainly not highly associated with people who are aggressive." Second, Dr. Kronenberger assumed that decreased activity in one part of the brain equaled impaired or deficient brain activity. Dr. Nusbaum disagreed, stating that decreased activity can signal expertise or use of an alternate method to complete the assigned task.

Next, Dr. Nusbaum discussed problems with Dr. Kronenberger's methodology. In evaluating Dr. Kronenberger's fMRI studies, Dr. Nusbaum noted several problems. First, the images published in Dr. Kronenberger's study are composites of the images of all the individuals in the study. Such images, Dr. Nusbaum explained, can appear to show activity in areas where no individual subject actually showed activity. Second, with regard to both types of testing, Dr. Nusbaum stated that Dr. Kronenberger's methods for measuring aggressive thoughts, such as the Stroop tests, the Conners performance test, and the behavior checklist, were not appropriate for measuring the type of behavioral control required to prevent oneself from reacting aggressively to a situation. Third, in discussing Dr. Kronenberger's neurocognitive testing study alone, Dr. Nusbaum testified that such testing used particular patterns of behavior to infer the part of the brain that was activated, but because of the many-to-many relationship between brain regions and behavior, it is not possible to make "those clear kinds of inferences."

Finally, Dr. Nusbaum discussed his concerns about Dr. Kronenberger's conclusions. In discussing Dr. Kronenberger's single published study, Dr. Nusbaum identified several problems with the researchers' interpretation of the data. He noted that the researchers had drawn conclusions about similarities between the brain activity of adolescents with behavior disorders and control adolescents with high media violence exposure and about the alleged impairments in brain activity of these groups. Dr. Nusbaum stated that the scans showed that the composite brain activity of these groups differed and that it was unclear whether they truly had decreased brain activity as compared to adolescents without behavior disorders and with low media violence exposure. Even if the images were read to show decreased brain activity for these groups in certain areas of the brain, Dr. Nusbaum stated, there were several alternative reasons, such as the development of expertise or the use of another part of the brain to perform the same function, that Dr. Kronenberger's research team had not considered.

Even if there were some deficit in brain activity, Dr. Nusbaum noted, Dr. Kronenberger's two experiments show adolescents with behavior disorders, and those without such disorders but high media violence exposure, with decreased activity in different areas in the two studies. According to Dr. Nusbaum, "I know

Dr. Kronenberger has argued that it's a different task, and so there's different demands on it, and I agree with that, but in respect of the model of deficit, if the brain is deficit, it should be in both cases." Dr. Nusbaum stated that the decreased activity in both experiments likely reflected the participants' use of another method for completing the task, not mental impairments.

In discussing the second experiment in Dr. Kronenberger's fMRI study—the experiment in which the participants watched a simulated video game and then took an "emotional Stroop color-word test"—Dr. Nusbaum again found that the researchers lacked the information to make definitive conclusions because they had not controlled for certain characteristics of their participants. Even if they had, he said, there were several alternative explanations for why the amygdala was activated in adolescents with behavior disorders and control subjects with high media violence exposure.

Dr. Nusbaum also disputed the conclusions of the neurocognitive study in which Dr. Kronenberger used neurocognitive testing to evaluate whether exposure to media violence impairs executive functioning. The problem with this study, according to Dr. Nusbaum, was that Dr. Kronenberger and his colleagues compared the response times of the participants in the study "raw," without accounting for the overall quickness or slowness of the participants in any activity they engaged in. As a result, Dr. Nusbaum testified that it was impossible to draw any conclusions from the data as reported.

The Court found Dr. Nusbaum's testimony credible and persuasive, and Dr. Kronenberger's unpersuasive. Consistent with Dr. Nusbaum's testimony, the Court finds that Dr. Kronenberger's studies cannot support the weight he attempts to put on them via his conclusions. The defendants have offered no basis to permit a reasonable conclusion that, as the legislature found, minors who play violent video games are more likely to "[e]xperience a reduction of activity in the frontal lobes of the brain which is responsible for controlling behavior."

Notes and Questions

1. In the decade after *Blagojevich*, the cognitive tests have become more sophisticated than those set forth above, but really not that different in kind or result. If the courts are correct and the current level of research is unable to sustain a causal, constitutionally-sufficient link between the problems that the state is trying to solve and the state's interest in correcting them via regulation, then what sorts of studies would be necessary to better establish the necessary linkage?

2. If you are interested in researching the behavioral effects of violent videogameplay, the best place to start is the Appendix to Justice Breyer's opinion in *Brown*. There he lists eight pages worth of studies from all over the world which discuss these issues.

§ 12.30 Industry Self-Regulation

The Entertainment Software Rating Board (ESRB) is a self-regulatory body established in 1994 by the Entertainment Software Association (ESA). The ESRB independently applies and enforces ratings, advertising guidelines, and online privacy principles adopted by the industry. Whether these ratings actually result in the market segmentation that the ESRB wishes is, as discussed in *Brown*, not as clear as perhaps the ESA would like. However, the ratings are far more detailed than ratings for movies, and do provide purchasers with a good deal of information.

The way it way it works is that a manufacturer submits a beta version of its game to the ESRB, and the ESRB gives it a rating. If the manufacturer disagrees, there is a negotiation, and sometimes changes are made to the game to secure a rating the manufacturer believes is more advantageous or correct for its game. The process is purely voluntary, but videogame community pressure and custom is such that there are no widely distributed games without an ESRB rating.

The ratings are prominently placed on the packaging and websites for the games. As described by the ESRB, the ratings consist of the following three parts:

Rating Categories: suggest age appropriateness

Content Descriptors: indicate content that may have triggered a particular rating and/or may be of interest or concern

Interactive Elements: inform about interactive aspects of a product, including users' ability to interact, the sharing of users' location with other users, or the fact that personal information may be shared with third parties.

* * *

Below is a list of the Ratings Categories, Content Descriptors, and Interactive Elements assigned by the ESRB, current as of the date of publication of this Book. The ESRB changes these categories from time to time, and a current list can be found at http://www.esrb.org/ratings/ratings_guide.jsp.

The current Ratings Categories are:

EC: Early Childhood

Titles rated EC (Early Childhood) have content that may be suitable for ages 3 and older. Contains no material that parents would find inappropriate.

E: Everyone

Titles rated E (Everyone) have content that may be suitable for ages 6 and older. Titles in this category may contain minimal cartoon, fantasy or mild violence and/or infrequent use of mild language.

E10+ : Everyone 10+

Titles rated E10+ (Everyone 10 and older) have content that may be suitable for ages 10 and older. Titles in this category may contain more cartoon, fantasy or mild violence, mild language and/or minimal suggestive themes.

T: Teen

Titles rated T (Teen) have content that may be suitable for ages 13 and older. Titles in this category may contain violence, suggestive themes, crude humor, minimal blood, simulated gambling, and/or infrequent use of strong language.

M: Mature

Titles rated M (Mature) have content that may be suitable for persons ages 17 and older. Titles in this category may contain intense violence, blood and gore, sexual content and/or strong language.

AO: Adults Only

Titles rated AO (Adults Only) have content that should only be played by persons 18 years and older. Titles in this category may include prolonged scenes of intense violence and/or graphic sexual content and nudity.

RP: Rating Pending

Titles rated RP (Rating Pending) have been submitted to the ESRB and are awaiting final rating. (This symbol appears only in advertising prior to a game's release.)

* * *

The current "Content Descriptors" are:

Alcohol Reference—Reference to and/or images of alcoholic beverages.

Animated Blood—Discolored and/or unrealistic depictions of blood.

Blood—Depictions of blood.

Blood and Gore—Depictions of blood or the mutilation of body parts.

Cartoon Violence—Violent actions involving cartoon-like situations and characters. May include violence where a character is unharmed after the action has been inflicted.

Comic Mischief—Depictions or dialogue involving slapstick or suggestive humor.

Crude Humor—Depictions or dialogue involving vulgar antics, including "bathroom" humor.

Drug Reference—Reference to and/or images of illegal drugs.

Fantasy Violence—Violent actions of a fantasy nature, involving human or non-human characters in situations easily distinguishable from real life.

Intense Violence—Graphic and realistic-looking depictions of physical conflict. May involve extreme and/or realistic blood, gore, weapons and depictions of human injury and death.

Language—Mild to moderate use of profanity.

Lyrics—Mild references to profanity, sexuality, violence, alcohol or drug use in music.

Mature Humor—Depictions or dialogue involving 'adult' humor, including sexual references.

Nudity—Graphic or prolonged depictions of nudity.

Partial Nudity—Brief and/or mild depictions of nudity.

Real Gambling—Player can gamble, including betting or wagering real cash or currency.

Sexual Content—Non-explicit depictions of sexual behavior, possibly including partial nudity.

Sexual Themes—Mild to moderate sexual references and/or depictions. May include partial nudity.

Sexual Violence—Depictions of rape or other violent sexual acts.

Simulated Gambling—Player can gamble without betting or wagering real cash or currency.

Some Adult Assistance May Be Needed—Intended for very young ages.

Strong Language—Explicit and/or frequent use of profanity.

Strong Lyrics—Explicit and/or frequent references to profanity, sex, violence, alcohol or drug use in music.

Strong Sexual Content—Graphic references to and/or depictions of sexual behavior, possibly including nudity.

Suggestive Themes—Mild provocative references or materials.

Tobacco—The consumption of tobacco products.

Tobacco Reference—Reference to and/or images of tobacco products.

Use of Alcohol—The consumption of alcoholic beverages.

Use of Drugs—The consumption or use of illegal drugs.

Violence—Scenes involving aggressive conflict.

Violent References—References to violent acts.

* * *

The current "Interactive Elements" are:

Shares Info—Indicates that personal information provided by the user (e.g., e-mail address, phone number, credit card info, etc.) is shared with third parties.

Shares Location—Includes the ability to display the user's location to other users of the app.

Users Interact—Indicates possible exposure to unfiltered/uncensored user-generated content, including user-to-user communications and media sharing via social media and networks.

Notes and Questions

1. Justice Alito in *Brown* states, "The Court does not mention the fact that the industry adopted this [ESRB rating] system in response to the threat of federal regulation, a threat that the Court's opinion may now be seen as largely eliminating." Why might the Court's majority opinion result in the elimination of the ratings system? Do you think this is a realistic threat?

2. Are 7 different rating categories combined with 31 different descriptors and 3 interactive elements really necessary? Is it realistic to believe that most buyers will learn the system? Is there too much information provided? Would a system similar to the simpler Motion Picture rating code suffice?

Chapter Thirteen

Products Liability and Videogame Addiction

This chapter deals with two related, but distinct issues: (1) products liability claims by those who allege that playing a videogame has caused someone to attack them or has caused a loved one to commit suicide (*see* § 13.20 *infra*); and (2) claims of addiction by those who allege they cannot stop playing videogames (*see* § 13.30 *infra*).

We start with a brief review of products liability, as a background to the cases discussed in § 13.20.

§ 13.10 Tort Claims Arising from Videogames: A Primer

The typical tort claim brought against videogame companies comes when a teenager, who has extensively played a first person shooter game, or another "violent" videogame, attacks someone or commits suicide. The allegation is that the game so influenced the player, especially given his or her youth, that the attacks and deaths were foreseeable consequences of game play. As tort claims, the causes of action are based on state common law. Hence, the elements of the torts can vary somewhat from state to state, although the general principles are fairly constant throughout the cases.

The legal theory is that of products liability. Generally, that means claims in negligence and strict products liability are brought in the same case.[1] A brief list of the elements for review purposes regarding each tort follows, along with a summary of the most used defense asserted by videogame defendants.

Negligence

Negligence traditionally has four elements: (1) duty; (2) breach; (3) causation (both "but for" and "proximate"); and (4) damages. *See, e.g.*, RESTATEMENT (SECOND) OF TORTS § 281 (1965). What elements do you think videogame manufacturers claim are not met when they move to dismiss claims brought under a negligence theory? We address these issues in detail in § 13.20 below.

---

1. Even though many torts professors would also include warranty as a form of products liability, for some reason, breach of warranty claims are not often alleged in these types of cases.

Strict Products Liability

Strict products liability has evolved over time, and now the elements are generally thought to be: (1) the existence of a "product" (2) sold in "commerce," that (3) has a "defect" which gets to the consumer without significant alteration, which (4) causes (both in the "but for" and "proximate" sense) (5) damages. *See* RESTATEMENT (THIRD) OF TORTS: PRODUCTS LIAB. § 1 (1998). Defects are broken into three types: (a) manufacturing defects; (b) design defects; and (c) a failure to warn. *See id.* § 2 (a)-(c). Once again, before reading the cases, imagine you represent a plaintiff who has been injured by a teen who has played one or more violent videogames. What kind of defect will you allege in your strict products liability claim? What other elements will you have trouble proving, and what kind of evidence would you want to show at trial to establish your case?

First Amendment Defense

In Chapters Four and Twelve, we discussed in some detail how the First Amendment affected tort claims and regulatory challenges, respectively, based on constitutional and common law protections given to established forms of communication. This "First Amendment Defense" or "First Amendment Privilege" applies to the personal injury claims alleged in this chapter and, indeed, may ultimately be videogame manufacturers' best help in defeating liability in these types of cases.

The cases in this chapter were decided before *Brown v. Ent. Merchs. Ass'n*, 564 U.S. __, 131 S. Ct. 2729 (2011). There the United States Supreme Court settled the issue of whether videogames merited First Amendment protection by stating, "[l]ike the protected books, plays, and movies that preceded them, videogames communicate ideas—and even social messages—through many familiar literary devices (such as characters, dialogue, plot, and music) and through features distinctive to the medium (such as the player's interaction with the virtual world)" and that these similarities to other expressive mediums "suffice to confer First Amendment protection." By contrast, the cases in this chapter universally assumed that games had First Amendment protection, and so the plaintiffs also had to overcome the general tort immunity provided for constitutionally shielded content in protected media by arguing that one or more exceptions to the "First Amendment defense" applied. These "exceptions" are (1) obscenity; (2) incitement to unlawful activity; and (3) fighting words. *See* § 12.231 *supra* for a discussion of these exceptions.

§ 13.20 Products Liability

The principal case we chose to illustrate the typical products liability arguments, *Sanders*, arose out of the tragic Columbine High School shooting in 1999. Most of the other major cases in the area are discussed and explained in *Sanders*. We also discuss those other cases in the notes following the decision.

Sanders v. Acclaim Ent., Inc.

United States District Court, Colorado, 2002
188 F. Supp. 2d 1264

BABCOCK, Circuit Judge:

In this diversity wrongful death action controlled by Colorado tort law, Defendants move, pursuant to Fed. R. Civ. P. 12(b)(6), to dismiss for failure to state a claim upon which relief can be granted as to all claims brought against them by Plaintiffs, the widow and stepchildren of William David Sanders, a teacher killed in the April 20, 1999 attack on Columbine High School.

Facts

Plaintiffs allege that Columbine High School (Columbine) students Dylan Klebold and/or Eric Harris, both approximately 17 years of age, were co-conspirators in a plot and scheme to assault, terrorize and kill Columbine teachers and students. On April 20, 1999 at approximately 11:20 a.m., Klebold and Harris approached the school armed with multiple guns and other "weapons of destruction" including explosive devices.

After shooting at people outside the school, the pair entered the school building and continued their deadly assault inside Columbine. Twelve students and teacher William Sanders were killed. Dozens of others were injured.

In the aftermath of the massacre the police allegedly learned that Harris and Klebold were avid, fanatical and excessive consumers of violent video games[2] [and] consumers of movies containing obscenity, obscenity for minors, pornography, sexual violence, and/or violence. One movie the pair viewed was "The Basketball Diaries" in which "a student massacres his classmates with a shotgun."

According to Plaintiffs, "but for the actions of the Video Game Defendants and the Movie Defendants, in conjunction with the acts of the other defendants herein, the multiple killings at Columbine High School would not have occurred."

Claim One for Negligence and Strict Liability

Plaintiffs sue Defendants Time Warner, Palm Pictures, Island Pictures, New Line Cinema, and Polygram as the makers and distributors of "The Basketball Diaries." Defendants Time Warner and Palm Pictures (Movie Defendants) filed Rule 12(b)(6) motions which I resolve in this Memorandum Opinion and Order.

According to Plaintiffs, in "The Basketball Diaries, the protagonist inexplicably guns down his teacher and some of his classmates in cold blood, among other acts of gratuitous violence." Purportedly, this had the effect of "harmfully influencing impressionable minors such as Harris and Klebold and of thereby causing the shootings."

Claim Two for Negligence and Strict Liability

Plaintiffs allege that the Video Game Defendants manufactured and/or supplied to Harris and Klebold these video games which made violence pleasurable and attractive and disconnected the violence from the natural consequences thereof, thereby causing Harris and Klebold to act out the violence [and] trained [them] how to point and shoot a gun effectively without teaching either of them any of the constraints, responsibilities, or consequences necessary to inhibit such an extremely dangerous killing capacity.

Allegations Common to the Movie and Video Game Defendants

The negligence and strict products liability Claims One and Two against the Movie and Video Game Defendants contain the following common allegations:

---

2. The video game manufacturer-defendants produced the following video games, all of which it is alleged that Klebold and Harris played incessantly: *Mortal Kombat, Castle Wolfenstein, Doom, Resident Evil, Final Fantasy* and *Quake,* among others—ED.

1. Defendants knew that copycat violence would result from the use of their products and materials.

2. Defendants knew that their products and materials created an unreasonable risk of harm because minors would be influenced by the effect of their products and materials and then would cause harm.

3. Defendants knew or should have known that their products and materials were in an unreasonably defective condition and likely to be dangerous for the use for which they were supplied.

4. Defendants failed to exercise reasonable care to inform consumers of the dangerous condition of their products and materials or of the facts which made their products and materials likely to be dangerous.

5. Scientific research shows that children who witness acts of violence often tend to act more violently themselves and to sometimes recreate those violent acts. (Movie Defendants); and

6. Massive volumes of scientific research show that children who witness acts of violence and/or who are interactively involved with creating violence or violent images often act more violently themselves and sometimes recreate the violence to which they have been exposed.

Claims Analysis

Negligence

Plaintiffs allege negligence in Claim One against the Movie Defendants and in Claim Two against the Video Game Defendants. Under Colorado law, to recover for the negligent conduct of another, a plaintiff must establish:

> (1) the existence of a legal duty owed to the plaintiff by the defendant; (2) breach of that duty; (3) injury to the plaintiff; and (4) actual and proximate causation.

Duty

In resolving the threshold legal question whether the Video Game and Movie Defendants have a cognizable duty to the Plaintiffs, I consider: 1) foreseeability of the injury or harm that occurred; 2) the social utility of Defendants' conduct; 3) the magnitude of the burden of guarding against the injury or harm; and 4) the consequences of placing the burden on the Defendants.

The question whether a duty should be imposed in a particular case is essentially one of fairness under contemporary standards — whether reasonable persons would recognize a duty and agree that it exists. Generally, a person does not have a duty to prevent a third person from harming another absent special circumstances warranting imposition of such a duty.

Foreseeability

The Colorado Supreme Court teaches that foreseeability is based on common sense perceptions of the risks created by various conditions and circumstances and includes whatever is likely enough in the setting of modern life that a reasonably thoughtful person would take account of it in guiding practical conduct.

Generally, under Colorado law a person has no responsibility to foresee intentional violent acts by others. *See Walcott v. Total Petroleum, Inc.*, 964 P.2d 609, 612 (Colo. App.

1998), (Gas station owner could not reasonably foresee that a purchaser would intentionally throw gasoline on a victim and set the victim on fire).

In the circumstances alleged here, the Video Game and Movie Defendants likewise had no reason to suppose that Harris and Klebold would decide to murder or injure their fellow classmates and teachers. Plaintiffs do not allege that these Defendants had any knowledge of Harris' and Klebold's identities, let alone their violent proclivities. Nor, for that matter, did the Video Game and Movie Defendants have any reason to believe that a shooting spree was a likely or probable consequence of exposure to their movie or video games. At most, based on Plaintiffs' allegations that children who witness acts of violence and/or who interactively involved with creating violence or violent images often act more violently themselves and sometimes recreate the violence, these Defendants might have speculated that their motion picture or video games had the potential to stimulate an idiosyncratic reaction in the mind of some disturbed individuals. A speculative possibility, however, is not enough to create a legal duty.

Although other courts have addressed this question, the Colorado courts have not had the occasion to consider foreseeability in the similar circumstances alleged here. Applying analogous foreseeability principles, two federal courts have rejected imposition of any such duty on video game makers and movie producers or their distributors. In *Watters v. TSR, Inc.*, 904 F.2d 378 (6th Cir. 1990), the Sixth Circuit held that a game manufacturer did not have any duty under Kentucky tort law to anticipate and prevent the suicide of a disturbed player because such idiosyncratic reactions are not legally foreseeable. The Court held that to impose liability in such circumstances "would be to stretch the concept of foreseeability ... to lengths that would deprive them of all normal meaning." *Id.* at 381.

More recently, in *James v. Meow Media, Inc.*, 90 F. Supp. 2d 798 (6th Cir. 2002), the Court dismissed Plaintiffs' complaint asserting virtually identical claims filed by Plaintiffs in this case. *James v. Meow Media, Inc.* involved a student shooting at a Kentucky high school during which three students were killed and several others seriously injured. The Court accepted as true, as do I, the identical allegations in this case that: 1) the shooter[s] viewed "The Basketball Diaries" film; 2) were "avid consumer[s]" of video games; and 3) were influenced by the film and video games. Stating that "nothing Defendants did or failed to do could have been reasonably foreseen as a cause of injury," the Court held that reasonable people could not conclude that the shooter's exposure to video games and the movie made the shooter's actions foreseeable to the video game makers and the movie producers and distributors. *See id.* at 804, 806.

Courts around the country have rejected similar claims brought against media or entertainment defendants. In *Zamora v. Columbia Broadcasting System*, 480 F. Supp. 199 (S.D. Fla. 1979), the Court held that it was not foreseeable to three television networks that a teenager would shoot and kill his neighbor after viewing comparable violence on television over a ten year period. Plaintiff alleged also that watching television had desensitized the teenager to violence and caused him to develop a sociopathic personality. In granting the defendants' motion to dismiss, the *Zamora* Court noted that the three major networks are charged with anticipating: 1) the minor's alleged voracious intake of television violence; 2) his parents' apparent acquiescence in his television viewing, presumably without recognition of any problem; and 3) that Zamora would respond with a violent criminal act. *See id.* at 202. Based in part on the lack of foreseeability, the Court declined to "create such a wide expansion in the law of torts." *Id.* at 203.

I find persuasive the reasoning set out in these cases. Consequently, I conclude under similar Colorado tort law, there is no basis for determining that violence would be considered the likely consequence of exposure to video games or movies. This factor weighs heavily against imposing a duty on the Movie and Video Game Defendants.

Social Utility of Defendants' Conduct

Creating and distributing works of imagination, whether in the form of video games, movies, television, books, visual art, or song, is an integral component of a society dedicated to the principle of free expression. Accordingly, the creation of such works significantly contributes to social utility. Plaintiffs' characterization of the Video Game and Movie Defendants' creative works as "violent" does not alter the social utility analysis. In the context of ordering entry of a preliminary injunction against a city ordinance that limited minors' access to violent video games, the Seventh Circuit observed, "violence has always been and remains a central interest of humankind and a recurrent, even obsessive theme of culture both high and low." *American Amusement Mach. Ass'n v. Kendrick*, 244 F.3d 572, 577 (7th Cir. 2001). Indeed, "classic literature and art, and not merely today's popular culture, are saturated with graphic scenes of violence, whether narrated or pictorial." *Id.* at 575. Moreover, the *Kendrick* Court acknowledged that video games that include pictorial representations of violence are "stories" and contain "age-old themes of literature." *Id.* at 577–78. The Court flatly rejected the notion that society is better served by insulating the vulnerable from exposure to such images: "To shield children ... from exposure to violent descriptions and images would not only be quixotic, but deforming; it would leave them unequipped to cope with the world as we know it." *Id.* at 577.

Setting aside any personal distaste, as I must, it is manifest that there is social utility in expressive and imaginative forms of entertainment even if they contain violence. Hence, the social utility factor weighs heavily against imposing a duty against the Video Game and Movie Defendants.

Magnitude of the Burden of Guarding against Injury or Harm and Consequences of Placing the Burden on the Defendant

In *Bailey* [*v. Diagnostic & Rehab. Ctr.*], 952 P.2d at 772–73, the Colorado Court of Appeals analyzed the question of tort law duty where imposition of such a duty would seriously encroach upon First Amendment values. There, the author of a book appeared on a television program to discuss his controversial views about a particular dental procedure. The plaintiff followed his advice and was injured. In the resulting lawsuit, the Court held that as a general rule, "an author or interviewee on a public television program owes [no] legal duty of due care to those members of the public who may read the book or view the program." *Id.* at 772. Furthermore, the Court expressed serious doubts about the foreseeability of the harm. *See id.* at 772–73. The Court then explained that even if the harms were foreseeable, the First Amendment values at stake counseled against imposing a tort duty based on the contents of an author's ideas. *See id.* at 773.

Colorado courts have repeatedly rejected efforts to impose overly burdensome and impractical obligations on defendants, including the obligation to identify potential dangers. This is especially so where those obligations would interfere with the social utility of a defendant's conduct or other important societal values.

Given the First Amendment values at stake, the magnitude of the burden that Plaintiffs seek to impose on the Video Game and Movie Defendants is daunting. Furthermore, the practical consequences of such liability are unworkable. Plaintiffs would essentially obligate these Defendants, indeed all speakers, to anticipate and prevent the idiosyncratic, violent reactions of unidentified, vulnerable individuals to their creative works. As the Sixth

Circuit recognized in *Watters*: "The defendant cannot be faulted, obviously, for putting its game on the market without attempting to ascertain the mental condition of each and every prospective player. The only practicable way of insuring that the game could never reach a 'mentally fragile' individual would be to refrain from selling it at all." *Id.* at 381. Because Plaintiffs' legal theory would effectively compel Defendants not to market their works and, thus, refrain from expressing the ideas contained in those works, the burden imposed would be immense and the consequences dire for a free and open society.

In this case, Plaintiffs do not allege that the Video Game and Movie Defendants illegally produced or distributed the movie and video games Harris and Klebold allegedly viewed or played. Finding that these Defendants owed Plaintiffs a duty of care would burden these Defendants' First Amendment rights to freedom of expression. These considerations compel the conclusion that makers of works of imagination including video games and movies may not be held liable in tort based merely on the content or ideas expressed in their creative works. Placing a duty of care on Defendants in the circumstances alleged would chill their rights of free expression. Therefore, these factors also weigh heavily against imposing a duty on Defendants.

All four factors weigh heavily against imposing a duty of care on Defendants. Consequently, I hold that the Video Game and Movie Defendants owed no duty to Plaintiffs as a matter of law. Thus, the Video Game and Movie Defendants are entitled to dismissal of Plaintiffs' negligence claims.

Causation

Even assuming a duty, the Video Game and Movie Defendants argue that they were not the legal cause of Plaintiffs' injuries. I agree.

To prevail on their negligence claim, Plaintiffs must show that Defendants' tortious conduct proximately caused Mr. Sanders' death. In Colorado, causation is generally a question of fact for a jury. But a court may decide the issue as a matter of law where the alleged chain of causation is too attenuated to impose liability. Here, proximate cause requires that Defendants' conduct produced Mr. Sanders' death in the natural and probable sequence of things.

Where the circumstances make it likely that a defendant's negligence will result in injuries to others and where this negligence is a substantial factor in causing the injuries sustained, proximate causation is satisfied. The intervening or superseding act of a third party, in this case Harris and Klebold, including a third-party's intentionally tortious or criminal conduct does not absolve a defendant from responsibility if the third-party's conduct is reasonably and generally foreseeable.

It is undisputed that Harris and Klebold murdered or injured the Columbine victims including Mr. Sanders. The issue is whether Harris' and Klebold's intentional criminal acts constitute a superseding cause of the harm inflicted by them, thus relieving the Movie and Video Game Defendants' of liability.

A superseding cause exists when: 1) an extraordinary and unforeseeable act intervenes between a defendant's original tortious act and the injury or harm sustained by plaintiffs and inflicted by a third party; and 2) the original tortious act is itself capable of bringing about the injury. Just as foreseeability is central to finding that a duty is owed, it is also the touchstone of proximate cause and of the superseding cause doctrine. Moreover, a superseding cause relieves the original actor of liability when the harm is intentionally caused by a third person and is not within the scope of the risk created by the actor's conduct.

I hold in this case that Harris' and Klebold's intentional violent acts were the superseding cause of Mr. Sanders' death. Moreover, as I have determined, their acts were not foreseeable. Their criminal acts, therefore, were not within the scope of any risk purportedly created by Defendants. In this case, as in *James v. Meow Media, Inc.*, 90 F. Supp. 2d at 806–08, the school shooting was not a normal response to dissemination of movies and videos.

I conclude as a matter of law that no reasonable jury could find that the Video Game and Movie Defendants' conduct resulted in Mr. Sanders' death in "the natural and probable sequence of events." Therefore, Defendants were not a proximate cause of Mr. Sanders' injuries. Defendants are entitled to Rule 12(b)(6) dismissal as to the negligence claims in Claims One and Two.

Strict Liability

Plaintiffs also assert strict liability in Claims One and Two. Plaintiffs allege that the Movie and Video Game Defendants produced and distributed their "products" in "a defective and unreasonably dangerous condition." Restatement (Second) of Torts § 402A. Plaintiffs allege that these Defendants manufactured and/or supplied to Harris and Klebold video games: "[that] trained Harris and Klebold how to point and shoot a gun effectively without teaching either of them any of the constraints, responsibilities or consequences necessary to inhibit such an extremely dangerous killing capacity."

There is no allegation that anyone was injured while Harris and Klebold actually played the video games or watched "The Basketball Diaries." The actual use of the movie and video games, then, did not result in any injury. Rather, Plaintiffs contend that Mr. Sanders' death was caused by the way Harris and Klebold interpreted and reacted to the messages contained in the movie and the video games. So, any alleged defect stems from the intangible thoughts, ideas and messages contained within the movie and video games but not their tangible physical characteristics.

To recover on a theory of strict products liability under Colorado law, Plaintiffs must establish that the: 1) products are in a defective condition unreasonably dangerous to the user or consumer; 2) products were expected to and did reach Harris and Klebold without substantial change in the condition in which they were sold; 3) alleged defects caused Mr. Sanders' death; 4) Video Game and Movie Defendants sold the product and are engaged in the business of selling products; and 5) Plaintiffs sustained damages as a result of the Video Game and Movie Defendants' acts. This strict liability theory requires the existence of a "product" within the meaning of the law. The threshold question is whether Mr. Sanders' death was caused by a "product."

Definition of Product

Colorado's products liability statute does not define the term "product." *See* § 13-21-401, C.R.S. Section 402A of the Restatement (Second) of Torts, adopted by the Colorado courts, also does not define "product." As a result, whether something is a "product" is a question of law for the Court to answer. Therefore, as an initial matter I must determine whether thoughts, images, ideas, and messages contained in movies and video games constitute "products" for purposes of strict products liability.

Colorado courts have not yet considered whether thoughts, images, ideas, and messages are "products" pursuant to the strict liability doctrine. Significantly, however, in considering whether to recognize a new tort recovery theory, the Colorado courts give great weight to the theory's impact on free expression.

To aid my anticipation as to how Colorado courts would resolve this question, I look to other jurisdictions which have addressed whether the content of video games and movies is a "product" for purposes of determining strict liability. In *Watters*, the Court reviewed existing precedents and concluded, "as far as we have been able to ascertain, … the doctrine of strict liability has never been extended to words or pictures. Other courts have looked in vain for decisions so expanding the scope of the strict liability doctrine." 904 F.2d at 381. For this reason, the *Watters* Court rejected plaintiff's contention that the video game defendant was strictly liable for causing her son, who had repeatedly played defendant's fantasy adventure game, to commit suicide. *Id.* Based in part on *Watters'* reasoning, the *James v. Meow Media, Inc.* Court also rejected as a matter of law the plaintiffs' claims, identical to the claims asserted in this case, that The Basketball Diaries and the video games were "products" for purposes of the strict liability doctrine. *See James v. Meow Media, Inc.*, 90 F. Supp. 2d at 811.

Plaintiffs argue that "intangibles" such as images, thoughts, ideas, and messages are products and "subject to strict liability [when] the 'intangibles' are sold to and consumed by the public." Plaintiffs fail to appreciate the critical distinction between intangible properties and tangible properties for which strict liability can be imposed. The Ninth Circuit explained this distinction in *Winter v. G.P. Putnam's Sons*, 938 F.2d 1033 (9th Cir. 1991):

> A book containing Shakespeare's sonnets consists of two parts, the material and the print therein, and the ideas and expression thereof. The first may be a product, but the second is not. The latter, were Shakespeare alive, would be governed by copyright laws; the laws of libel to the extent consistent with the First Amendment; and the laws of misrepresentation, negligent misrepresentation, negligence, and mistake. These doctrines applicable to the second part are aimed at the delicate issues that arise with respect to intangibles such as ideas and expression. Products liability law is geared to the tangible world. *Id.* at 1034.

The reasoning of *Watters* and *Meow Media* is buttressed by the Restatement (Third) of Torts. There, the word "product" is defined and a distinction is made between tangible and intangible properties. *See* Restatement (Third) of Torts 19(a); comment d. to § 19(a). Moreover, the commentary for § 19(a) of the Restatement (Third) of Torts notes that courts "have, appropriately refused to impose strict product liability" in cases where the plaintiff's grievances were "with the information, not with the tangible medium." *Id.* at comment d.

Based on the persuasive reasoning set out in *Watters, James, Winter,* and the Restatement (Third) of Torts, I hold that intangible thoughts, ideas, and expressive content are not "products" as contemplated by the strict liability doctrine.

Causation

Assuming *arguendo* that the strict liability doctrine could be extended to include the thoughts, ideas, images and messages contained in video games and movies, Plaintiffs nevertheless would be required to allege adequately causation in order to state a claim based on strict liability. As I have stated, causation is trumped by an intervening act that constitutes a superseding cause. I determined as a matter of law that Harris' and Klebold's actions constituted a superseding cause which broke any chain of causation. Therefore, in the alternative, Plaintiffs' strict liability claims fail for lack of causation.

First Amendment Considerations

Protection of Video Games

Relying on the following cases, Plaintiffs contend that video games are not protected by the First Amendment. *See America's Best Family Showplace Corp. v. New York*, 536 F. Supp. 170 (E.D.N.Y. 1982). The *America's Best* Court expressed the premise that video games are not protected by the First Amendment because they contain "pure entertainment with no informational element." This premise is directly contrary to the Supreme Court's teaching that the distinction between information and entertainment is so minuscule, that both forms of expression are entitled to First Amendment protection. *See Time, Inc. v. Hill*, 385 U.S. 374, 388 (1967). Plaintiffs have failed to show that video games deserve anything less than full First Amendment protection.

Brandenburg Test

Whether expressive content is protected under the First Amendment is subject to the test set forth in *Brandenburg v. Ohio*, 395 U.S. 444 (1969). Under *Brandenburg*, even speech that expressly advocates criminal activity cannot be the basis for liability, unless the speech is "directed to inciting or producing imminent lawless action and is likely to incite or produce such action." *Id.* at 447.

The *Brandenburg* test is exacting. Other courts uniformly reject claims similar to those of Plaintiffs' here. I reject Plaintiffs' invitation to dilute the *Brandenburg* test in this case.

Plaintiffs contend that *Brandenburg* protects only "marginalized political speakers." I disagree. *Brandenburg* did not limit its test to political speech or political speech of marginalized speakers. Nor have lower courts accepted such a limitation. *See e.g. Herceg v. Hustler Magazine, Inc.*, 814 F.2d 1017 (5th Cir. 1987) in which the Fifth Circuit stated:

> The Supreme Court generally has not attempted to differentiate between different categories of protected speech for the purposes of deciding how much constitutional protection is required. Such an endeavor would not only be hopelessly complicated but would raise substantial concern that the worthiness of speech might be judged by majoritarian notions of political and social propriety and morality. If the shield of the First Amendment can be eliminated by proving after publication that an article discussing a dangerous idea negligently helped bring about a real injury simply because the idea can be identified as "bad," all free speech becomes threatened. An article discussing the nature and danger of "crack" usage—or of hang-gliding—might lead to liability just as easily. As is made clear in the Supreme Court's decision in *Hess,* the "tendency to lead to violence" is not enough. *Id.* at 1024.

Alternatively, Plaintiffs argue that *Brandenburg's* imminence requirement is met by the advocacy of illegal action "at some future time ..." This argument is contrary to binding precedent. "The First Amendment does not permit someone to be punished for advocating illegal conduct at some indefinite future time." *Hess v. Indiana*, 414 U.S. 105 (1973). *Hess* holds that speech cannot be deemed unprotected when, as is the case here, defendants' speech, is "not directed to any person or group of persons." *Id.* at 108.

Plaintiffs rely also on *Rice v. Paladin Enterprises, Inc.*, 128 F.3d 233 (4th Cir. 1997) in which the Fourth Circuit held that the publisher of a book entitled "Hit Man: A Technical Manual for Independent Contractors" might be held liable in a wrongful death action. However, the defendant stipulated that [it] not only knew that its instructions might be used by murderers, but that it actually intended to provide assistance to murderers and would-be murderers which would be used by them 'upon receipt,' and that it in fact assisted [the murderer] in particular in the commission of the murders [at issue]. *Id.* at 242. Largely based on this stipulation, the *Rice* Court reached the narrow holding that civil liability for aiding and abetting criminal conduct is constitutionally permissible where a publisher "has the specific purpose of assisting and encouraging commission of such conduct and the alleged assistance and encouragement takes a form other than abstract advocacy." *Id.* at 243.

Plaintiffs' Complaint is devoid of any allegation that the Movie and Video Game Defendants had any intent, let alone a specific intent, to assist and encourage anyone to engage in acts of criminal violence. Moreover, *Rice* distinguished the "copycat" theory presented here, where "someone imitates or 'copies' conduct ... described or depicted in their broadcasts, publications, or movies." *Id.* at 265. *Rice's* limited holding is inapplicable in this case.

Plaintiffs do not discuss compliance with *Brandenburg's* second requirement that the speech at issue must be "likely" to produce imminent lawless action. *See Brandenburg*, 395 U.S. at 447–48. Plaintiffs cannot, as a matter of law, demonstrate that the video games and movie were "likely" to cause any harm, let alone imminent lawless action.

Restriction of the First Amendment Rights of Children

Next, Plaintiffs contend that even if video games invoke First Amendment protections, the right to free speech of children may be restricted in a reasonable manner. I disagree.

It is well-established that *Brandenburg* remains the applicable standard even where the individual allegedly incited to commit unlawful acts is a minor. *See e.g. Miller v. California*, 413 U.S. 15, 33 (1973) ("likely" impact of speech must judged by its effect on "average person[s], rather than a particularly susceptible or sensitive person").

Furthermore, because the Movie and Video Game Defendants cannot possibly control who gains access to their games and movies, they could avoid liability under Plaintiffs' theory only by ceasing production and distribution of their creative works. *See Watters*, 904 F.2d at 381. Such a sweeping theory of liability and the chilling of free expression cannot be considered narrowly tailored.

Notes and Questions

We have organized the notes below around the elements of the products liability torts.

Negligence:

Duty

1. The first major products liability case involving a videogame was *James v. Meow Media, Inc.*, 300 F.3d 683 (6th Cir. 2002), mentioned, and cited extensively, in *Sanders*. There, a 14-year-old freshmen named Michael Carneal killed three students and injured five others during a shooting spree at a high school in Kentucky. The parents of the injured and deceased students brought the action against several videogame, movie production, and internet content-provider defendants, claiming that their distribution of violent material to an impressionable youth like Carneal constituted actionable negligence. It was claimed that watching the movie *Basketball Diaries*, and playing videogames like *Castle Wolfenstein, Doom, Redneck Rampage, Resident Evil,* and others foreseeably caused Carneal to go on his rampage. Specifically, plaintiffs alleged, "the defendants in this case acted negligently, perhaps in producing, but at least in distributing to young people, their materials." *Id.* at 689.

As in *Sanders*, the court found no duty existed based largely on foreseeability grounds:

It appears simply impossible to predict that these games, movie, and internet sites (alone, or in what combinations) would incite a young person to violence. Carneal's reaction to the games and movies at issue here, assuming that his violent actions were such a reaction, was simply too idiosyncratic to expect the defendants to have anticipated it. We find that it is simply too far a leap from shooting characters on a video screen (an activity undertaken by millions) to shooting people in a classroom (an activity undertaken by a handful, at most) for Carneal's actions to have been reasonably foreseeable to the manufacturers of the media that Carneal played and viewed.

Id. at 693.

2. Would it change your opinion if there was evidence that playing first person shooting games actually changed players' behaviors? Professor Kevin W. Saunders discovered some interesting facts regarding Michael Carneal, the shooter in *James*:

> While many may be skeptical of the ability of violent media to make a good child go so bad, and indeed the killers in most of the school cases seemed troubled, there is an additional factor in the [*James*] case that should give pause to even those most doubting as to psychological influences. According to his lawyer, Carneal had "no appreciable exposure to firearms." Yet, with eight or nine shots, he had eight hits, all in the head or upper torso. Such accuracy with a handgun, especially for an inexperienced marksman, is astounding. "The FBI says that the average experienced law enforcement officer, in the average shootout, at an average range of seven yards, hits with approximately one bullet in five." How then did a fourteen-year-old manage five head shots and three in the upper torso? It appears to have been his video game training that made him an effective killer.
>
> Carneal never moved his feet during his rampage. He never fired far to the right or left, never far up or down. He simply fired once at everything that popped up on his "screen." It is not natural to fire once at each target. The normal, almost universal, response is to fire at a target until it drops and then move on to the next target. This is the defensive reaction that will save our lives, the human instinctual reaction—eliminate the threat quickly. Not to shoot once and then go on to another target before the first threat has been eliminated. But most video games teach you to fire at each target only once, hitting as many targets as you can as fast as you can in order to rack up a high score. And many video games give bonus effects ... for head shots.
>
> One does not have to accept the notion that media violence causes actual violence to see a relationship here. Whatever may have caused Carneal to be motivated to kill, video games appear to have given him the skills and reactions to accomplish his goal.

Kevin W. Saunders, *Regulating Youth Access to Violent Video Games: Three Responses to First Amendment Concerns*, 2003 Mich. St. DCL L. Rev. 51, 54 (2003) (footnotes omitted).

3. Assume it is true that the reactions of Carneal in *James*, and Harris and Klebold in *Sanders*, were too unlikely for the game distributors to have foreseen their actions because no player ever went on a rampage after playing the game before. Now that *they* have gone on shooting rampages, can videogame manufacturers and distributors still maintain that no duty exists because the actions of some users are too unforeseeable?

Or is it that out of the millions who play the game, only a very, very small percentage will have that reaction and so, as a society, we do not want to impose a duty on all game manufacturers when the problem is too remote? Before answering "yes," ask whether you would give the same answer if a drug company knew of a possibility that a new drug would cause death or a severe side effect to a very thin slice of the population. Would the manufacturer owe no negligence duty to the drug-taking public? Even to warn of the potential side effect?

Should the videogame manufacturers of a violent game at least have a duty to warn that allegations have been made that excessive play in certain individuals have led to anti-social behavior and suicide? Should they take steps to limit excessive, continuous play?

4. The Court in *Sanders* also said the following in a passage that was edited out of the excerpt above: "The defendant cannot be faulted, obviously, for putting its game on the market without attempting to ascertain the mental condition of each and every prospective player. [It may be] the costs of acquiring such knowledge would so outweigh the social benefits that it would not be negligent to abstain from acquiring such information." *Sanders*, 188 F. Supp. 2d at 1275. Do you agree?

Suppose a consensus was formed among psychologists, psychiatrists, sociologists, etc., that showing animated blood upon a killing or stabbing in a game triggers a violent urge in the brain, which, when combined with many other factors, could provoke a shooting rampage in certain already violence-inclined individuals. Would there be no duty to eliminate the animated blood?

If it were scientifically possible to demonstrate that playing a particular game was followed by the suicide of a certain (albeit very, very small) percentage of the players with other behavioral issues, would that justify banning the game from the market? How lethal must a vehicle, drug, or other consumer product be before we believe (through the courts or the legislature) that it is appropriate to ban it? Is the majority to be deprived of something enjoyable and/or useful, because it is very dangerous to a vulnerable minority? After all, we do allow cigarettes and smokeless tobacco to be sold even though there is a societal cost of tobacco use.

Breach

5. The other decision that was quoted extensively in *Sanders* was *Watters v. TSR, Inc.*, 904 F.2d 378 (6th Cir. 1990). There, the mother of a suicide victim brought a negligence suit against the distributor of the board game *Dungeons & Dragons* ("D&D"). She alleged, "the defendant violated its duty of ordinary care in two respects: it disseminated Dungeons & Dragons literature to 'mentally fragile persons,' and it failed to warn that the 'possible consequences' of playing the game might include 'loss of control of the mental processes.'" *Id.* at 381.

Although it is not as clear as it might be, the court seemed to assume the defendant owed a general duty of care to those who might be injured by the player, including the player, and instead decided there was no liability based on there being no *breach* of that duty. The breach analysis was also based on foreseeability.

As to the negligence claim based on dissemination of the game to "mentally fragile persons," the court held that, "The only practicable way of insuring that the game could never reach a 'mentally fragile' individual would be to refrain from selling it at all—and we are confident that the courts of Kentucky would never permit a jury to say that simply by marketing a parlor game, the defendant violated its duty to exercise ordinary care." *Id.*

As to the supposed breach of a negligence duty to warn, the court acknowledged that Kentucky law imposes a general duty on manufacturers and suppliers to warn of dangers known to them but not known to persons whose use of the product can reasonably be anticipated. *Id.* It then evaluated the following two cases as to whether such an allegation against the D&D distributor was feasible:

> We have found two decisions, not cited in the briefs, mentioning claims that Dungeons & Dragons has dangerous propensities. In *State v. Molitor*, 729 S.W.2d 551 (Mo. Ct. App. 1987), where a young woman was tied up and strangled after

an all-night houseparty devoted to listening to music, consuming liquor, smoking marijuana and practicing martial arts, the defendant sought to introduce expert testimony suggesting that he had been "desensitized" at some point by playing Dungeons & Dragons. The appellate court sustained exclusion of the testimony on relevance grounds and because the defendant's offers of proof made no showing that he had, in fact, been "desensitized." In *People v. Ventiquattro*, 527 N.Y.S.2d 137 (1988), a fifteen-year-old boy who killed a companion with a shotgun gave the police several conflicting accounts of how the shooting occurred. In one account he stated that he was playing the game Dungeons & Dragons and shot the victim while fantasizing that it was his job to exterminate evil. Whether this particular account was truthful, and whether TSR ever learned of it, we do not know.

The actual content of the materials in question would hardly have given TSR reason to foresee that players of the game would become more susceptible to murder or suicide than non-players. The materials make it clear that Dungeons & Dragons is a "let's pretend" game, not an incitement to do anything more than exercise the imagination. We are not dealing here with the kind of violence or depravity to which children can be exposed when they watch television, or go to the movies, or read the fairy tales of the Brothers Grimm, for example.

Television, movies, magazines and books (including comic books) are far more pervasive than the defendant's games. Were the courts of Kentucky prepared to say that works of the imagination can be linked to a foreseeable danger of anti-social behavior, thereby giving rise to a duty to warn, one would expect to find Kentucky caselaw to that effect in lawsuits involving television networks, book publishers, or the like. There is no such caselaw.

Id., n. 1.

Would it be better to approach the foreseeability issue as one of duty or breach? Does it make a difference?

If TSR, the defendant in *Watters*, had been aware of the previous cases cited by the court (*Molitor* and *Ventiquattro*), should it make a difference to the finding of no liability? If not, what sort of knowledge by TSR, if any, would be sufficient to legally impose a warning?

There certainly is something to the court's argument that if the mother of the player could not foresee that playing D&D would lead to his suicide, it is difficult to hold that TSR had a duty to do so. *See id.* at 384.

Causation

6. Causation in torts is, of course, made up of both a "but for" and a "proximate" component. As to the former, the plaintiff faces a huge hurdle, since almost every human action is the sum of many causative factors. So even if videogames may have played *a* role in causing Harris' and Klebold's (and the others discussed above) actions, trying to prove that it was *the* but for cause, or even a "substantial factor" in the killings, is very difficult.

As some have argued in a case like *Watters* (involving the suicide of a D&D player), *Romeo and Juliet* has, over time, been seen as glamorizing suicide and been blamed by many as causing particular suicides. If we collectively believe in the power of art (and entertainment) to change lives for the better, must we also collectively accept the societal risk that it will change some lives for the worst, without incurring liability for the creator in the latter scenario?

7. Indeed, the difficulty of establishing actual causation from videogame play can be seen from the following excerpt from an article which traces some of the history of school violence:

> Armed with guns and homemade bombs, a student went to school and triggered the fire alarm. He killed a janitor, climbed a tower, and fired on bystanders and emergency services personnel, killing two more people and wounding eleven others. A junior high school student who had been bullied for years killed his principal with an M-1A rifle and wounded three other people. Another student went to school with a semiautomatic pistol, 200 rounds of ammunition, and three firebombs. He killed one teacher and wounded another.
>
> Many people would probably think that these appalling incidents happened in the 1990s, when school violence made the national headlines on a regular basis and some people blamed violent video games. These shootings, however, actually occurred earlier than that. Anthony Barbaro committed the sniper attacks in the first example on December 30, 1974. James Alan Kearbey killed his principal in the second example on January 21, 1985. And Nicholas Elliott committed the third shooting on December 16, 1988. Most notably, these school shootings occurred well before the release of violent video games like "*Doom*" and "*Quake*."

William Li, Note, *Unbaking the Adolescent Cake: The Constitutional Implications of Imposing Tort Liability on Publishers of Violent Video Games*, 45 ARIZ. L. REV. 467, 467–68 (2003) (footnotes omitted).

There were many who warned of potential desensitization to, and escalation of, violence as a result of videogame play long before the shootings and other tragedies discussed in this chapter. For example, in his 1995 book, ON KILLING: THE PSYCHOLOGICAL COST OF LEARNING TO KILL IN WAR AND SOCIETY, former Vietnam veteran Lt. Colonel Dave Grossman stated:

> Operant conditioning firing ranges, with pop-up targets and immediate feedback, just like those used to train soldiers in modern armies, are found in interactive video games that our children play today. But whereas the adolescent Vietnam vet had stimulus discriminators built in to ensure that he only fired under authority, the adolescents who play these video games have no such safeguard built into their conditioning ...
>
> In video arcades children stand slack jawed but intent behind machine guns and shoot at electronic targets that pop up on the video screen. When they pull the trigger the weapon rattles in their hand, shots ring out, and if they hit the "enemy" they are firing at, it drops to the ground, often with chunks of flesh flying in the air.
>
> The important distinction between the killing-enabling process that occurs in video arcades and that of the military is that the military's focused on the enemy soldier, with particular emphasis on ensuring that the soldier acts only under authority. Yet even with these safeguards, the danger of future My Lai massacres among soldiers drawn from such a violent population must not be ignored and ... the U.S. armed forces are taking extensive measures to control, constrain, and channel the violence of their troops in future conflicts. The video games that our children conduct their combat training on have no real sanction for firing at the wrong target.
>
> This is not an attack on all video games.... The kind of games that are very definitely enabling violence are the ones in which you actually hold a weapon in

your hand and fire it at human-shaped targets on the screen. These kinds of games can be played on home video [or] in arcades.

[Some games have] a western motif, in which you stand before a huge video screen and fire a pistol at actual film footage of "outlaws" as they appear on the screen. This is identical to the shoot-no shoot training program designed by the FBI and used by police agencies around the nation to train and enable police officers in firing their weapons.

The shoot-no shoot program was introduced twenty years ago ... we recognize it as another form of operant conditioning that has been successful in saving the lives of both law-enforcement officers and innocent bystanders ... The shoot-no shoot program has served successfully to both enable and constrain violence among police officers. Its video arcade equivalent has no such sanctions to constrain violence. It only enables.

The worst is yet to come ... Through operant conditioning B.F. Skinner held that he could turn any child into anything he wanted to. In Vietnam the U.S. armed forces demonstrated that Skinner was at least partially correct by successfully using operant conditioning to turn adolescents into the most effective fighting force the world has ever seen. And America seems intent on using Skinner's methodology to turn us into an extraordinarily violent society.

Dave Grossman, On Killing: The Psychological Cost of Learning to Kill in War and Society 302-03, 314-16 (1995).

8. The "proximate cause" analysis in "shooter" cases like *Sanders* and *James* focus on another aspect of foreseeability, namely the foreseeability to the alleged tortfeasor of a subsequent criminal act, or other superceding cause, by a third party. The Restatement (Second) of Torts sets forth the generally accepted rule as to when a defendant can be held liable for a third party's intentional misconduct: "An act or an omission may be negligent if the actor realizes or should realize that it involves an unreasonable risk of harm to another through the conduct of the other or a third person which is intended to cause harm, even though such conduct is criminal." Restatement (Second) of Torts § 302B (1977). In a comment to that section, the drafters of the Restatement state that the proximate causation chain is not broken when the actions of the defendants, "create a high degree of risk of [the third party's] intentional misconduct." *Id.* § 302B cmt. c.

In each of the cases that have considered the issue with regard to video and other games, the "high degree of risk of ... misconduct" necessary to keep the proximate cause chain intact has been found wanting. In *James*, the court put it this way:

Arguably, the defendants' games, movie, and internet sites gave Carneal the ideas and emotions, the "psychological tools," to commit three murders. However, this case lacks such crucial features of our jurisprudence in this area. First, the defendants in this case had no idea Carneal even existed, much less the particular idiosyncrasies of Carneal that made their products particularly dangerous in his hands. In every case that this court has discovered in which defendants have been held liable for negligently creating an unreasonably high risk of third-party criminal conduct, the defendants have been specifically aware of the peculiar tendency of a particular person to commit a criminal act with the defendants' materials.

Second, no court has ever held that ideas and images can constitute the tools for a criminal act under this narrow exception.

[Finally] The system of criminal liability has concentrated responsibility for an intentional criminal act in the primary actor, his accomplices, and his co-conspirators. By imposing liability on those who did not endeavor to accomplish the intentional criminal undertaking, tort liability would diminish the responsibility placed on the criminal defendant. The normative message of tort law in these situations would be that the defendant is not entirely responsible for his intentional criminal act.

James, 300 F.3d at 694–95; *see also Watters*, 904 F.2d at 383.

9. In contrast, there are two types of cases in which the subsequent criminal act of a third party typically does not break the proximate causation chain, i.e., where the courts find the defendants' acts have the requisite "high probability" of causing downstream criminal activity to establish foreseeability. One type of case is the gun manufacturer/distributor case. *See, e.g., Ileto v. Glock, Inc.*, 349 F.3d 1191 (9th Cir. 2003) (holding that if plaintiff's allegation was true, i.e., that defendant established an "illegal secondary firearms market" whereby persons not otherwise entitled to purchase guns could do so, it followed that the distributor could be held liable for all subsequent criminal assaults by those purchasers).

The second such type of case is the "premises liability" case where, *e.g.*, as a result of prior criminal acts on the premises, the land owner is deemed to "reasonably foresee" future criminal acts by unknown third parties, and can be liable for them. *See, e.g., Kline v. 1500 Massachusetts Avenue Apartment Corp.*, 439 F.2d 477, 481 (D.C. Cir. 1970), holding that:

> [W]here, as here, the landlord has notice of repeated criminal assaults and robberies, has notice that these crimes occurred in the portion of the premises exclusively within his control, has every reason to expect like crimes to happen again, and has the exclusive power to take preventive action, it does not seem unfair to place upon the landlord a duty to take those steps which are within his power to minimize the predictable risk to his tenants.

Can the videogame manufacturers be distinguished from these types of situations?

10. The court in *Sanders* found there was no duty, but then went on to decide there was also no causation. Why do you think the court would decide the case on both grounds when either would have been sufficient to uphold a verdict of no liability for the videogame defendant?

Strict Products Liability:

Is a Videogame a "Product"?

11. Liability for strict products liability requires, at its base, the existence of a "product." The court in *Sanders* held that a videogame could not be a "product" for strict products liability purposes because the essence of the game is intangible code. In other words, the fact that the programming code might be fixated on a tangible medium such as a DVD or a hard disc is insufficient to transform it from inchoate property to personality necessary for a strict products liability claim. This idea has been expressed in the following provision of Restatement (Third) of Torts: Products Liability:

§19. Definition of "Product"

For purposes of this Restatement:

(a) A product is tangible personal property distributed commercially for use or consumption. Other items, such as real property and electricity, are products when the context of their distribution and use is sufficiently analogous to the distribution and use of tangible personal property that it is appropriate to apply the rules stated in this Restatement.

RESTATEMENT (THIRD) OF TORTS: PRODUCTS LIAB. § 19 (1998). More pertinent is the following Comment to § 19:

> Intangible personal property. Two basic types of intangible personal property are involved. The first consists of information in media such as books, maps, and navigational charts. Plaintiffs allege that the information delivered was false and misleading, causing harm when actors relied on it. They seek to recover against publishers in strict liability in tort based on product defect, rather than on negligence or some form of misrepresentation. Although a tangible medium such as a book, itself clearly a product, delivers the information, the plaintiff's grievance in such cases is with the information, not with the tangible medium. Most courts, expressing concern that imposing strict liability for the dissemination of false and defective information would significantly impinge on free speech have, appropriately, refused to impose strict products liability in these cases.

Id. § 19 cmt. d.

Is there a difference between the "information" in videogames and the "information" in a book?

Plaintiff's lawyers make the argument that the interactivity inherent in a videogame distinguishes it from a book, movie, TV show, etc. As we saw in the previous chapter, courts have not been receptive to the interactivity-makes-video-games-different argument as a reason to impose regulation on a constitutionally protected medium. It is no different in videogame torts cases.

Wilson v. Midway Games, Inc., 198 F. Supp. 2d 167 (D. Conn. 2002), was a case in which it was alleged that a teen believed he was the character Cyrax in *Mortal Kombat* when he used Cyrax's "finishing move" to kill his friend by putting him in a headlock and stabbing him in the chest. In rejecting the products liability claim brought by the deceased's mother, the court stated:

> In distinguishing *Mortal Kombat* from books, motion pictures and television shows, Wilson has focused her complaint on the interactive nature of the game. It is this interactive feature, then, that must be a "product" if Wilson's claim is to survive. While Wilson has skillfully argued that *Mortal Kombat* is something more than motion pictures or television programs, the "something more" is its interactivity. She offers no persuasive reason for distinguishing the technological advances that led to *Mortal Kombat's* creation from developments at the turn of the twentieth century that ushered in the motion picture. The pictoral representation that evokes the viewer's response is the essence of the claimed "product," regardless of whether that representation is viewed passively, as in a motion picture, or is controlled by the viewer.
>
> *Mortal Kombat* is not sufficiently different in kind to fall outside the "intangible" category that is demarcated in the case law, and Wilson's complaint fails to state a claim upon which relief can be granted. The product liability counts fail because *Mortal Kombat* is not a "product."

Id. at 174.

12. Even if interactivity does not provide a way to distinguish a videogame from a book, plaintiffs in videogame cases have an additional argument. One exception to the

general rule that dangers provided by the information in a book is not actionable as a product in tort is the so-called "aeronautical chart" rule, where pilots who rely on a map book with aeronautical charts containing false information are allowed to bring strict products liability cases against the chart's publishers. *See, e.g., Brocklesby v. United States*, 767 F.2d 1288, 1294–96 (9th Cir. 1995); RESTATEMENT (THIRD) OF TORTS: PRODUCTS LIAB. § 2 cmt. d. (1998). Could an argument be fashioned that a videogame is analogous to a book of such charts?

Note that the aeronautical chart exception is narrow, and that in other cases where harm caused by erroneous information in a book would seem to be foreseeable, the information-is-not-a-product rule still holds. For example, in *Cardozo v. True*, 342 So. 2d 1053 (Fla. App. 1977), the publisher of a cookbook was held not liable for errors in a recipe that caused personal injury; and in *Winter v. G. P. Putnam's Sons*, 938 F.2d 1033 (9th Cir. 1991), the Ninth Circuit held that mushroom hunters who relied on erroneous information in an encyclopedia of mushrooms had no strict products liability claim against the book's publisher because the information in the book was not a "product."

13. Some plaintiffs argue that the term "product" under strict products liability law should be coincident with the term "goods" under the UCC. *See, e.g., Worrell v. Barnes*, 484 P.2d 573 (Nev. 1971). UCC § 2-105(1) defines "goods" as "all things which are moveable ..." and the argument is that the bits of code and electrons are "moveable." Again, this has not been met with success in the courts, with most holding that electronic "information," even if movable, is still not a "good." *See gen.* UCC § 2R-103(k).

Existence of a Product Defect

14. If a plaintiff were ever to prevail on the issue of whether a videogame is a "product," the next step in establishing a *prima facie* case is to prove the product was "defective." There are generally three types of defects recognized in strict liability, which are defined in the Restatement (Third) of Torts: Products Liability as follows:

§ 2. Categories of Product Defect

A product is defective when, at the time of sale or distribution, it contains a manufacturing defect, is defective in design, or is defective because of inadequate instructions or warnings. A product:

(a) contains a manufacturing defect when the product departs from its intended design even though all possible care was exercised in the preparation and marketing of the product;

(b) is defective in design when the foreseeable risks of harm posed by the product could have been reduced or avoided by the adoption of a reasonable alternative design by the seller or other distributor, or a predecessor in the commercial chain of distribution, and the omission of the alternative design renders the product not reasonably safe;

(c) is defective because of inadequate instructions or warnings when the foreseeable risks of harm posed by the product could have been reduced or avoided by the provision of reasonable instructions or warnings by the seller or other distributor, or a predecessor in the commercial chain of distribution, and the omission of the instructions or warnings renders the product not reasonably safe.

RESTATEMENT (THIRD) OF TORTS: PRODUCTS LIAB. § 2 (1998).

What defect(s) do you believe a plaintiff in these types of cases would likely allege make a videogame unreasonably dangerous and thus actionable?

15. In *Wilson,* the case where the *Mortal Kombat* player stabbed his friend, the court described the product defects alleged by plaintiff as follows:

> She supports her [products liability] claim with two separate theories of liability. First, she asserts a "failure to warn" theory, claiming that her son's injuries and death "were the result of the defendant's failure to warn of the inappropriate level of violent content and mentally-addictive nature of the products it marketed and sold and the foreseeable risks that are likely to result from use of its products by individuals in decedent's age group." Second, she advances a design defect theory, claiming that the interactive video game was "negligently and/or intentionally designed by defendant Midway," and that her son's injuries and death "were the result of defendant Midway's negligent and/or intentional design of a dangerous product, and its reckless disregard for the safety of its products."

Wilson, 198 F. Supp. 2d at 169. The court never resolved the defect claims, finding instead *Mortal Kombat* was not a "product" for purposes of plaintiff's strict products liability claim. But if it had addressed the claims, which do you think was stronger? How would you cast the argument using the definitions of defect set forth in the Restatement provisions reproduced in n. 14 above?

Causation

16. The same causation issues that arise for negligence also apply to strict products claims. *See* nn. 6–9, *infra.*

First Amendment Defense:

17. After *Brown,* no credible argument can be made that videogames are not fully protected by the First Amendment privilege. Given that holding, can you think of a situation in which a videogame developer could *ever* be liable in tort for the actions of a player? That is, any game in which there would be an imminence of violent action threat that might be actionable under *Brandenburg*?

18. Product liability claims alleging that individuals have been influenced to harm others, or themselves, after exposure to a constitutionally protected medium other than videogames have traditionally been resolved in favor of the media on some combination of duty, breach, causation, or First Amendment defense grounds. A small sample of those cases include:

Television: *See, e.g., Zamora v. CBS,* 480 F. Supp. 199 (S.D. Fla. 1979), where 15-year-old Ronny Zamora shot and killed his 83-year-old neighbor and was convicted of murder. A civil action was then filed against three broadcasting companies by Zamora's parents on the theory that television violence had caused Ronny to become "addicted" and "desensitized" to violent behavior, which in turn, resulted in his killing the elderly woman. The court held that allegations that Zamora became "involuntarily addicted to" and "completely subliminally intoxicated" by extensive viewing of television violence, so that he developed a sociopathic personality and became desensitized to violent behavior, and as result shot and killed an 83-year-old neighbor, failed to state a cause of action.

See also, e.g., Olivia N. v. NBC, 126 Cal. App. 3d 488 (Cal. Ct. App. 1981) (holding that no liability could be established against NBC for broadcasting a show in which a rape was shown, when that same type of rape was mimicked in the rape of plaintiff, a 9-year-old girl); *and DeFilippo v. NBC.,* 446 A.2d 1036 (R.I. 1982), (ruling no liability where a youngster hanged himself after watching a skit on the "Tonight Show" where a professional stuntman appeared to hang Johnny Carson.)

Movies: *See, e.g., Yakubowicz v. Paramount Pictures Corp.*, 536 N.E. 1067 (Mass. 1989) where the father of a 16-year-old who was stabbed by a gang outside a movie theater showing *The Warriors* (a movie about gang violence) sued on the theory that the defendant producers and distributors knew the film would attract gang elements to the movie and it was likely that such individuals would replicate the stabbing scenes in the movie. The court dismissed the claim, holding, *inter alia*, that no duty existed. *See also, e.g., Bill v. Superior Court*, 187 Cal. App. 3d 1002 (1982) (holding no liability against the producers when a woman was shot in a manner similar to a shooting depicted in the film *Boulevard Nights*).

Music: *See, e.g., Waller v. Osborne*, 763 F. Supp. 1144 (M.D. Ga. 1991), where the parents of a boy who had committed suicide brought suit against Ozzy Osborne and others involved in the creation and distribution of the song, *Suicide Solution*, to which the boy had listened to over and over again before taking his own life. The court granted summary judgment in favor of the defendants.

19. Recently, two 12-year-old Wisconsin girls were charged as adults with attempted murder after repeatedly stabbing and nearly killing their friend. The girls told investigators that they planned the slaying on account of Slenderman, a fictional character whom they read about on a horror fiction website. Slenderman is a paranormal being who lurks near forests and absorbs, kills or carries off his victims. He is often portrayed as a tall, thin man in a black suit with pale skin and no face. The two girls told the authorities that they believed Slenderman was real, that he lived in a mansion in the Northwoods of Wisconsin and that they needed to kill to prove themselves worthy to him.[3]

Eric Knudsen originally created the character in response to a call for submissions from the online forum SomethingAwful. Knudsen posted the first photos along with a fictional news story under the username Victor Surge on June 10, 2009. After that, Slenderman's popularity grew and other writers, artists and programmers created additional stories, movies and videogames featuring Slenderman.[4]

Could the victim of the Wisconsin stabbing and her parents bring suit against Knudson, or any of the others artists who used this image? Would Knudson and Slenderman violate *Brandenburg's* imminent advocacy of violent action test?

———————

§ 13.30 Videogame Addiction

We all know the stereotype of the "nerd," stuck in the basement playing videogames for days on end, ignoring hygiene, sleep, nutrition, work, and other aspects of contemporary society. But is the stereotype true, at least for some? And, suppose it is true because the player is addicted — in a clinical sense — to game play?

The history and implications of "videogame addiction" are discussed in this section. Before diving in, what legal and societal issues would you suspect are involved in establishing and dealing with gaming addiction?

———————

3. Taylor W. Anderson, *Everything You Need to Know About Slenderman*, THE ASSOCIATED PRESS (June 4, 2014), http://bigstory.ap.org/article/website-posts-disclaimer-after-wisconsin-stabbing-0.

4. Taylor W. Anderson, *Slenderman Creator Saddened By Stabbing*, THE ASSOCIATED PRESS (June 4, 2014), http://bigstory.ap.org/article/slenderman-creator-saddened-stabbing.

Smallwood v. NCSoft Corp.

United States District Court, Hawaii, 2010
730 F. Supp. 2d 1213

KAY, Senior District Judge:

FACTUAL BACKGROUND

Plaintiff's Second Amended Complaint alleges the following. Defendants designed and distributed interactive role playing internet games to the public, including the game "Lineage II." In 2004 or 2005, Plaintiff opened three accounts, thereby becoming licensed to play Lineage II. The accounts were paid for by charge card, three months in advance. Plaintiff played Lineage II from 2004–2009 for over 20,000 hours. Plaintiff experienced great feelings of euphoria and satisfaction from persistent play, as did other users of Lineage II.

Plaintiff became psychologically dependent and addicted to playing Lineage II. During the years that Plaintiff played Lineage II, the phenomena of psychological dependence and addiction to playing computer games was recognized by and known to Defendants. Defendants never gave Plaintiff any notice or warning of the danger of psychological dependence or addiction from continued play.

Plaintiff further alleges that "to build its reputation and increase profits, defendants have to continually create new games or game versions, and sell more licenses." Thus, in 2009, Defendants began selling and licensing a new computer game, "Aion," Plaintiff alleges that "one method of promoting Aion, was to lock players out from the older game Lineage II, thus creating popularity and publicity for the newer game Aion, a larger amount of users/licensees, and increased profits for Defendants."

In September 2009, Plaintiff discovered that he had been "locked out of the game, i.e., that defendants had 'banned' him from further play of the game." Plaintiff alleges he received no warning that he was in danger of being banned or had been banned and that he was banned from all accounts belonging to his internet protocol ("IP") address. Plaintiff alleges that he made numerous attempts to contact Defendants to determine why he was banned, but that "there was a maze of purposeful obstruction to receive any information on why he was locked out."

Plaintiff alleges that he pre-paid for access to his accounts and had approximately one-and-a-half months of access left at the time his accounts were banned. Plaintiff alleges that "Defendants unlawfully retained plaintiff's money on account [valued at $65], for playtime that was intentionally withheld and denied."

Plaintiff alleges that Defendants told him he was banned from the game for engaging in an elaborate scheme to create real money transfers. Plaintiff alleges that NCSOFT sent him an email to that effect on October 5, 2009. Plaintiff denies ever being involved in any scheme to make real money transfers or making any real money transfers.

Plaintiff asserts that he continues to this day to have a compulsive urge and need to play Lineage II and that he has never received any warning, notice, or advice from Defendants as to the danger of addiction from playing Lineage II.

Plaintiff alleges that as a direct result of using Lineage II and Defendants' acts and omissions, he has suffered extreme and serious emotional distress and depression, he has been unable to function independently, he has suffered psychological trauma, he was hospitalized, and he requires treatment and therapy three times a week.

In summary, Plaintiff alleges that he "would not have bought and played Lineage II if he had been aware that he would be subjected to the dishonesty and unfairness described above, or that he would become addicted to the game."

DISCUSSION

II. Subject Matter Jurisdiction

[The main jurisdictional argument for the defendant was that under the User Agreement between Mr. Smallwood and NCSoft, Mr. Smallwood waived all possible claims against the company, except for a possible unjust enrichment claim to recover any pre-paid monthly fees that were unfairly withheld by NCSoft after termination of the contract. If NCSoft was to prevail on that argument, the case would have to be dismissed because federal court jurisdiction was based on diversity, and the $75,000 jurisdictional limit would not be met since, at worst, NCSoft withheld less than $70 in pre-paid fees from Mr. Smallwood.

The court held that four types of claims alleged by were not "waivable" by contractual agreement based on public policy: (1) fraudulent misrepresentation; (2) negligent misrepresentation; (3) negligence/gross negligence; and (4) intentional and negligent infliction of emotional distress.

The court dismissed the fraud and negligent misrepresentation claims because Mr. Smallwood did not plead those claims with particularity. It stated that there was no sufficient allegation of "outrageous behavior" which would justify an intentional infliction of emotional distress claim. However, as to the negligence and negligent infliction of emotional distress claims the court said the following:—ED.]

D. Negligence and Gross Negligence

Defendants also argue that Plaintiff's negligence and gross negligence claims are grounded on the same claims of fraudulent conduct that Plaintiff alleges throughout his Complaint, i.e. Defendants' misrepresentation of (1) the addictive nature of Lineage II, (2) its fair game policy, (3) its billing methods, and (4) its anti-botting policy. The Court rejects this argument.

In order to succeed on a claim for negligence, a party must show:

1. A duty, or obligation, recognized by the law, requiring the actor to conform to a certain standard of conduct for the protection of others against unreasonable risks.

2. A failure on the actor's part to conform to the standard required.

3. A reasonable close causal connection between the conduct and the resulting injury.

4. Actual loss or damage resulting to the interests of another

In order to succeed on a claim for gross negligence a party must show "that there has been an entire want of care" which raises a presumption of "conscious indifference to consequences."

Plaintiff alleges that "defendants acted with negligence [or gross negligence] in designing, developing, manufacturing, inspecting, testing, marketing, advertising, promoting, selling, distributing, maintaining, revising, servicing, administrating, and overseeing Lineage II." In addition, Plaintiff alleges failure to warn and defective product claims are separate and distinct from Plaintiff's fraud allegations. ("Defendants acted negligently in failing to warn or instruct or adequately warn or instruct plaintiff and other players of Lineage II of its dangerous and defective characteristics, and of the safe and proper method of using the game"). In light of Plaintiff's allegations, the Court finds that Plaintiff has stated a claim for both negligence and gross negligence. Additionally, although Plaintiff's damages claim may be limited for the negligence claim, Plaintiff is not so limited with respect to the gross negligence claim.

E. Negligent Infliction of Emotional Distress

Plaintiff does have a negligence claim and the Court finds that he has pled an NIED claim as well. The Hawai'i Supreme Court has held:

> A plaintiff may recover for NIED, absent any physical manifestation of his or her psychological injury or actual physical presence within a zone of danger, where a reasonable person, normally constituted, would be unable to adequately cope with the mental stress engendered by the circumstances of the case ... Thus, an NIED claim is nothing more than a negligence claim in which the alleged actual injury is wholly psychic and is analyzed utilizing ordinary negligence principles.

> Further, this court has 'consistently held, as a general matter, that the plaintiff must establish some predicate injury either to property or to another person in order for himself or herself to recover for NIED.'

Doe Parents No. 1 v. Dept. of Educ., 100 Hawai'i 34, 69, 58 P.3d 545, 580 (2002).

Although the general rule is that there must be a physical injury to someone, the Hawai'i Supreme Court has carved out exceptions to that general rule in certain cases that present "unique circumstances, which provide the requisite assurance that plaintiff's psychological distress is trustworthy and genuine." *Doe Parents No. 1*, 100 Hawai'i at 69–70, 58 P.3d at 580–81

Here, Plaintiff alleges "as a direct result of using Lineage II and defendants' acts and omissions, plaintiff has suffered extreme and serious emotional distress and depression, and has been unable to function independently in usual daily activities such as getting up, getting dressed, bathing, or communicating with family and friends." Plaintiff has further alleged that he was hospitalized for three weeks and requires treatment and therapy three times a week because of the Defendants' actions. Accordingly, Plaintiff has adequately pled a "physical injury" as well as the remaining elements of the claim. If Plaintiff establishes an NIED claim solely based upon negligence, then damages will be limited by the User Agreement. If, however, Plaintiff can establish gross negligence, and Plaintiff's NIED claim is based on the gross negligence, then Plaintiff's damages will not be limited.

Notes and Questions

1. What would constitute gross negligence versus negligence on NCSoft's part? Would a warning that "long breaks should be taken" between game play be sufficient to exonerate the videogame defendant? What if the defendant monitored the length of each player's play and limited it to no more than 8 hours per 24 hour period, or deducted points (or reduced levels) for a player who played more than 4 continuous hours, or more than 8 hours total, in a day? Is this unfair to the players who, e.g., want to binge play on the weekend and have no addiction issue?

2. What damages would be covered if an "addiction" plaintiff prevails? What if he or she got fired from a job due to absences from, or ineffectiveness at, work due to a lack of sleep? Could lost wages be a cognizable consequential loss? What if it was a student who flunks out of school because he or she plays games all semester and never studies for

finals? Would the cost of psychological help be covered? The defendant in *Smallwood* sought damages for depression and a lack of socialization with friends. How would damages for such maladies be measured? Are they "caused" by the game?

3. Will future plaintiffs allege addiction as part of their products liability claims? *Smallwood* was decided in 2010. Some thought there would be an avalanche of claims after its release, but there hasn't been. Why do you think that's so?

4. There is some controversy as to whether videogame "addiction," in the clinical sense, exists. One of the most authoritative sources for psychological disorders is a book entitled the Diagnostic and Statistical Manual of Mental Disorders ("DSM"), which is published by the American Psychiatric Association ("APA"). The DSM is the result of a collaboration between leading psychologists and psychiatrists at the APA, WHO, NIH, etc. Among other things, the DSM contains the definitions, attributes, treatment protocol, etc. for recognized psychological disorders. The Manual is updated every so often as the body of psychological knowledge evolves.

The fourth edition of the Manual, known as DSM-IV, was published in 2000, and while it listed gambling and drug addiction as recognized disorders, there was no mention of videogame addiction. Some of the criteria for gambling addiction were euphoria while exposed to the stimulus, withdrawal and relapse when the stimulus is removed, increasing tolerance to the stimulus over repeated exposure, etc. Whether those (and the other listed) clinical symptoms applied to a sufficient swath of the population for videogame play to be recognized as a treatable "addiction" in the fifth edition of the Manual, "DSM-5," published in 2013, was a controversial subject among the editors. While some professionals thought videogame addiction was real and clear, others disagreed. One researcher, Richard Wood, argued:

> Some clinicians and academics have attempted to define video game "addiction" on the basis of their observations of some individuals who have concerns about their gaming behavior, or in response to other people who may have concerns about an individual's behavior (e.g., parents, partners etc.). The acceptance of this concept has been supported by popular media reports, increasing parental concerns, and a few high profile cases of troubled individuals who no doubt play video games more than is good for them.
>
> Where criteria have been used to label video game players as "addicts", these tend to have been adapted from DSM-IV substance abuse criteria, or, more frequently, pathological gambling screens, usually, by substituting the word "gambling" for "gaming" or "video game playing." However, recent studies of computer, video game, and internet addictions have demonstrated that classifications of this kind may not be valid because some of the criteria are referring to high levels of engagement rather than addiction per se. Additionally, it has been suggested that those criteria relating to high levels of engagement might be considered "peripheral" criteria for addiction (cognitive salience, tolerance, and euphoria). That is, they can not be considered as properties that identify addictive behavior patterns, and are aspects of "normal" play. Whereas, the remaining "addiction" criteria appear to be "core" criteria (conflict, withdrawal symptoms, relapse and reinstatement, and salience). Studies using an Addiction-Engagement questionnaire have found that including peripheral criteria to identify video game "addiction" results in a significant overestimation of the prevalence.
>
> [Further] given that video games are such a popular form of entertainment, and now surpass television as the main leisure pursuit for some demographics,

we would expect there to be huge numbers of people experiencing problems if video games were inherently addictive. There are, again, some difficulties in ascertaining levels of problems on these activities, as the media hype surrounding video games has led some people to assume that video games are the cause of some behavioral problems. However, despite the panic that has ensued we should not forget that millions of people play video games and only a tiny minority appear to experience any kind of problem, whatever the cause. For example, the game *World of Warcraft* is now played by over 8 million people world wide, which is more than the entire population of Denmark. Out of a sample of that size (and that is just one game) it is inevitable that there will be some people with problems (generally), and they may find that playing games helps them to avoid those problems. Whilst this may not healthy for them in the long run, the case that their game playing is the actual "problem" is by no means proven. Unless it can be shown that the inherent structural characteristics of video games can, in themselves, cause problems for relatively large numbers of people, then there is no firm basis on which claims about the "addictive" properties of video games can be made.

R.T.A. Wood, *Problems with the Concept of Video Game "Addiction": Some Case Study Examples*, 6 INTERNATIONAL JOURNAL OF MENTAL HEALTH AND ADDICTION, 169, 169–73 (2008). For more information concerning the debate over whether videogame "addiction" exists, *see, e.g.,* Katherine Noyes, *Docs Retreat from 'Video Game Addiction' Diagnosis,* TECHNEWS WORLD (June 25, 2007), http:// www.technewsworld.com/story/58014.html.; Petry, N. M., *Commentary on Van Rooij et al: 'Gaming addiction'—a psychiatric disorder or not?*, 106 ADDICTION 213, 213–15 (2011).

The APA eventually chose not to encompass excessive videogame play within the term "addiction" in DSM-5. However, it did not ignore the issue either. Instead, it added "Internet Gaming Disorder" to the "Conditions for Further Study" section of DSM-5, meaning it is a subject that merits future research in a common language that will "inform decisions about possible [inclusion of videogame addiction as a recognized disorder] in forthcoming editions of the DSM."[5] DSM-5 suggests the following definition and criteria be used to evaluate whether excessive videogame play should be classified as an "addiction" in DSM-6:

Persistent and recurrent use of the Internet to engage in games, often with other players, leading to clinically significant impairment or distress as indicated by five (or more) of the following in a 12-month period:

1. Preoccupation with Internet games. (The individual thinks about previous gaming activity or anticipates playing the next game; Internet gaming becomes the dominant activity in daily life).

Note: This disorder is distinct from Internet gambling, which is included under gambling disorder.

2. Withdrawal symptoms when Internet gaming is taken away. (These symptoms are typically described as irritability, anxiety, or sadness, but there are no physical signs of pharmacological withdrawal.)

---

5. One consequence to being identified as a formal diagnostic disorder in the DSM, as opposed to merely a condition for further study, is that it is much easier to get insurance coverage for a DSM-established disorder.

3. Tolerance—the need to spend increasing amounts of time engaged in Internet games.

4. Unsuccessful attempts to control the participation in Internet games.

5. Loss of interests in previous hobbies and entertainment as a result of, and with the exception of, Internet games.

6. Continued excessive use of Internet games despite knowledge of psychosocial problems.

7. Has deceived family members, therapists, or others regarding the amount of Internet gaming.

8. Use of Internet games to escape or relieve a negative mood (e.g., feelings of helplessness, guilt, anxiety).

9. Has jeopardized or lost a significant relationship, job, or educational or career opportunity because of participation in Internet games.

AMERICAN PSYCHIATRIC ASSOCIATION, DIAGNOSTIC AND STATISTICAL MANUAL OF MENTAL DISORDERS §3 (5th ed. 2013).

In *Smallwood,* the plaintiff alleged that he played *Lineage II* for over 20,000 hours between 2004 and 2009. He also described "great feelings of euphoria and satisfaction from persistent play" and "a compulsive urge and need to play." As a result, the plaintiff claimed he had suffered extreme emotional distress, including depression. Additionally, he was unable to function independently, was hospitalized for three weeks, and now requires therapy treatment. *Smallwood,* 730 F. Supp 2d at 1219, 1236.

Do Mr. Smallwood's claims meet the criteria for Internet Gaming Disorder under the DSM-5 standards? Should a court take these standards into consideration when deciding a videogame addiction case? By allowing Smallwood's claims to survive the motion to dismiss, has the court given credence to the theory that videogames can be addicting and, therefore, manufacturers have a duty to either warn gamers about the possibility of addiction, or face the threat of lawsuits?

5. Some countries have been more willing than the United States to recognize videogame addiction as a psychiatric disorder. For example, the South Korean Government estimates that approximately 210,000 South Korean children, ages 6–19, are afflicted with videogame addiction and require treatment. About 80% of those needing treatment may need psychotropic medications, and perhaps 20%–24% might well require hospitalization. Likewise, 13.7% of Chinese adolescent Internet users meet the Chinese Internet Addiction diagnostic criteria—about 10 million teenagers.[6]

In addition, a number of videogame related deaths in South Korea and China have attracted global media attention. In South Korea in 2005, Seungseob Lee played *StarCraft* continuously for fifty hours. He went into cardiac arrest and died shortly after at a local hospital. In 2009, Kim Sa-rang, a 3-month-old Korean child, died from malnutrition after both her parents spent many, many hours each day in an Internet cafe raising a *virtual* child in an online game.[7] In China, the 2009 documentary "Who Took Our Children" detailed 30 incidents in which online gaming led to serious health issues and the death

6. Jerald J. Block, M.D., *Issue for DSM-V: Internet Addiction,* 165 AM. J. PSYCHIATRY 306, 307 (2008).

7. Chloe Sang-Hun, *South Korea Expands Aid for Internet Addiction,* N.Y. TIMES, May 29, 2010, at A4.

of gamers and those around them, including the case of a 17-year-old who poisoned his parents after they forbade him from playing videogames.[8]

As a result, both China and South Korea consider Internet and gaming addiction one of their most serious public health issues. To address the problem, the South Korean government has trained over 1,000 counselors in the treatment of Internet addiction and established over 190 hospitals and treatment centers to treat those afflicted. Preventive measures are also being introduced into schools. In 2007 the Chinese government began restricting computer game use; current laws now require that games begin subtracting points from a player after 3 hours of continuous game use.[9] The government has also banned new Internet cafes and has strict criminal punishments for cafe operators who admit minors, or fail to flag violent games.[10]

6. A potential worldwide addiction problem is Massively Multiplayer Online Role Playing Games (MMORPGs), like *Second Life* and *Sims* which we discussed in some detail at § 11.30 *infra*. Thirty-four percent of MMORPGS "guests" reported spending 21–40 hours a week playing, while only 4% of non-MMORPGS players reported the same. Likewise, 58% of MMORPGS players reported playing more than eight continuous hours in one session, as opposed to 23% of non-MMORPGS players.[11]

After reading through all of these materials, what do you think? Do videogame manufacturers have a responsibility to change their games and business models by shortening the continuous periods a user can play because of the potential addiction problem of a few?

---

8. Paul Gaita, *Gaming Addiction On the Rise in Asia*, THE FIX (December 16, 2013), http://www.thefix.com/content/gaming-addiction-rise-asia.

9. Block, *supra*, at 207.

10. Ian Ransom, *Chinese Boot Camps Tackle Internet Addiction*, N.Y. TIMES (March 12, 2007), http://www.nytimes.com/2007/03/12/technology/12iht-addicts.4880894.html?_r=0.

11. Brian D. Ng, M.S. & Peter Wiener-Hastings, Ph.D., *Addiction to the Internet and Online Gaming*, 8 CYBER PSYCHOLOGY & BEHAVIOR 110, 113 (2005).

Chapter Fourteen

Protecting Privacy

A futurist has said, "Data is the New Oil."[1] While it is still an exaggeration to suggest that videogames exist primarily for data collection and not for entertainment (on the one hand) and profit (on the other), any study of videogames would be incomplete without a look at current data collection practices in the industry and the regulation of such practices. More data is collected than the casual observer anticipates. As of 2014, videogame developers are estimated to gather *50 terabytes* of information *per day* from players, with some of the more popular and data intense games, like *Battlefield 4*, generating 1 terabyte of information/day.[2] And what can be permissibly done with that data, especially data garnered from games targeting children, has generated much regulatory scrutiny[3] and some litigation.

Some of this data is given voluntarily by the player, such as name, address, credit card numbers, age, and the like when a user registers for, or purchases, a game.[4] Collection of other information can be controlled by players, with the developer not getting information unless the player checks a box linking the player's game statistics or other gameplay information to be shared with designated "friends" on social media sites like Facebook. But most of the information comes to the developer from user gameplay without the conscious input of the player.

Collection of data is one thing, but it is certain uses of the data that most often causes privacy analysts to complain (although some advocates argue against any collection of data because of the risk of its misuse). As will be explained in further detail below, most of the collected data is used to improve gameplay, and neither privacy advocates nor players have much of an issue with such use, so long as the developer gives sufficient notice of its practices. But when developers start making assumptions about a user's real world spending and sociological habits based on game play decisions, or when sensitive financial and health information is sold or hacked, red flags are raised.

---

1. Perry Rotella, "*Is Data the New Oil?*," FORBES (Apr. 02, 2012), as reported in Joe Newman and Joseph Jerome, *Press Start to Track?: Privacy and the New Questions Posed by Modern Technology*, AILPA QUARTERLY JOURNAL, n. 337 and text accompanying (2014) (forthcoming) (hereafter "*Press Start to Track.*")

2. *Press Start to Track*, n. 60 and text accompanying.

3. *See* § 12.40 *infra.*

4. *See, e.g.,* Sarah Petrescu, *Online Privacy Policies Decoded by UVic Team*, TIMES COLONIST, June 9, 2013, at A5 (stating that, e.g., *World of Warcraft* collects much personally identifying information ("PII") such as name, email address, credit card number, and the like when a player registers for, and downloads, the game.

The section below is a primer to give the reader a sense of the potential privacy problems arising from videogame play. The following sections discuss various responses and solutions to these problems.

---

§ 14.10 Privacy in Videogames: A Primer

In Chapter Four we introduced one aspect of the right of privacy, namely the right of publicity, and discussed how that right has affected videogame law. But from its infancy, the bedrock of the right of privacy has been the "right to be left alone."[5] All can agree that videogame developers should not have *carte blanche* to personally identifying information of a player just because he or she likes to slay monsters and solve problems. Players want "to be left alone" with regard to their personal information. But exactly what is meant by phrases like "to be left alone" and a "right to privacy" in the videogame context is problematical in at least two ways.

The first problem is definitional. As a concept, privacy is treasured, but when it comes to actually defining it as a legal principle, the concept has proved amorphous. Many privacy scholars point to Justice Harlan's two-pronged, objective/subjective, test as the touchstone for privacy analysis:

> My understanding of the rule that has emerged from prior decisions [on the right of privacy] is that there is a twofold requirement, first that a person have exhibited an actual (subjective) expectation of privacy and, second, that the expectation be one that society is prepared to recognize as "reasonable."

Katz v. United States, 389 U.S. 347, 361 (1967) (Harlan J., dissenting).

Perhaps the legal system could deal with a standard that authorizes objectively "reasonable" data collection practices as judged by industry practice, although there will always be disagreements as to reasonable "norms" at the margins between developers and gamers. But it is the subjective element of Justice Harlan's privacy test that is especially vexing.

In addressing the subjective expectation of privacy, one commentator has stated: " 'privacy' is 'highly elastic' and 'means different things to different people.' "[6] Indeed, the privacy expectations of thirteen-year-olds is different from that of sixty-year-olds, and the same can be said of all age brackets in between. And someone who has recently emigrated from a totalitarian society may have no expectation of privacy. It would seem odd, if not impossible, to judge the legality of a videogame developer's data collection practices based on the backgrounds, experiences, and sensitivities of the various users.[7]

---

5. The phrase was coined by Judge Thomas Cooley, then of the Michigan Supreme Court, was actually the first to use the phrase, and champion the right "to be left alone" in THOMAS M. COOLEY, A TREATISE ON THE LAW OF TORTS OR WRONGS WHICH ARISE INDEPENDENTLY OF CONTRACT 193 (1878), but was made famous by Samuel D. Warren & Louis D. Brandeis, *The Right to Privacy*, 4 HARV. L. REV 193, 193 (1890).

6. Angelique Carson, *From RSA: In Times of Distrust, Innovation and Collaboration will be the Key"* IAPP PRIVACY ADVISOR (Feb. 25, 2014).

7. For a more detailed discussion of Justice Harlan's privacy analysis as applied to modern data collection practices, *see* Omer Tene and Jules Polonetsky, *Article: To Track of "Do Not Track": Advertising Transparency and Individual Control in Online Behavioral Advertising*, 13 MINN. J.L. SCI. & TECH. 281, 339–40 (Winter 2012).

Because users have such a wide variation of privacy expectation, trying to find a subjective "norm" is difficult at best and elusive at worst for developers.

The second problem with applying privacy principles to the modern videogame industry is that most players *want* developers to collect some information from them. For example, if only 0.01% of players can surmount Level 8 of a popular videogame, the playing community probably wouldn't mind a little more guidance in the game itself or a reduction of the difficulty of the level. Further, publicizing high scores or sharing footage of particularly adept moves helps foster the "community of players"[8] aspect of modern videogames. The only way a developer can know about problems and publicize the success of its players is to monitor otherwise private game play.

To fully understand the privacy problems posed by videogames we need to understand exactly what kinds of data collection use and practices are going on currently (and are likely in the near future). This requires a discussion of: (1) what kind of data is collected; (2) what uses are being made of that data; and (3) what can we as a society do to remedy and correct any abuses. Each is addressed below.

What Data Is Being Gathered by Videogame Developers?

Early on, when developers followed the "ship it and forget it" business model of videogames, the only information they gathered about their games was a customer list and whatever data they could glean from beta testers who played under their control and supervision. Starting in 1978 with *Space Invaders*, arcade games began keeping a little "private" data, namely keeping track of, and displaying, the top ten high scores along with the player's name or initials on the CRT screen,[9] and accumulating some audit data in the "guts" of the machinery to share with the arcade owner. But things started to change dramatically in the 1980s with Local Area Network-linked gaming, and more so in the early 2000s with more sophisticated platforms such as Xbox and PlayStation. These devices were designed for shared interactivity between the publisher and player, and this interactivity only got more prevalent as Internet-connected games became more popular. Over the past few years, data transmission truly has been a two-way street between the player and the developer.[10]

Today game developers routinely get the following types of information from their customers and other users:

Game Telemetry—Raw inputs during game play are called "telemetry," and it is now routine for developers to collect "every fraction of a move of an avatar, every button press, all purchases made, every single chat message, [and] all server-side information."[11] Some developers, usually those with lesser budgets, only collect such information in an aggregate basis, and no traits of an individual player can be teased from their data base. However, many developers collect "individual player metrics" consisting of details such as the length of time the player logs on every day, the number of shots the player fires, the number of jumps the player made, the purchasing behavior of the user, and even the length of time a player pauses in front of imagery found in the virtual scene, whether that imagery is commercial, such as that provided by in-game advertising, or of some other type.[12]

---

8. *Press Start to Track*, n. 2 and text accompanying.

9. *Id.,* n. 1, and text accompanying.

10. For a detailed explanation of the evolution of data tracking, *see Press Start to Track*, nn. 17–30 and text accompanying.

11. Magy Seif El-Nasr *et. al*, Game Analytics: Maximizing the Value of Player Data 31 (2013); *see also Press Start to Track*, nn. 56–60, and text accompanying,

12. *Press Start to Track, supra,* nn. 64–73 and text accompanying.

Biometrics—Developers are gathering an ever increasing amount of biometric data on individual players. Game systems like *Wii* and *Kinect* discern height, weight, skeletal features of their players, and *Kinect* and other games (including *NBA 2K14*) collect and analyze individual voice patterns of players. Some devices, including 3DS handheld, have a front facing camera, allowing for a user's actual face to be placed on an avatar in certain games, such as in Nintendo's *Face Raiders*. These images can be shared with the developers.[13] Developers have signaled that in the future, a player's heart rate will almost surely be measured non-invasively via more sophisticated controllers, as will more sensitive measures of eye and hand movements in response to more sensitive game interfaces.[14] Developers claim this is all to aid the game experience; privacy analysts are not so sure.

Social Media Information—When a player sets up a local chat within a game or virtual world, not only are the real world email addresses of those in the chat room almost always available to the developers, but the content of those chats often are monitored by developers.[15] Further, most modern consoles sync with the player's social networks on Twitter, Facebook and the like, including PlayStation 4's "Share" feature, which allows game play footage to be linked to the user's Facebook page, and Apple's Game Center which sets up competition between different users by use of real world email addresses.[16] By gaining access to a user's social media sites, developers potentially can discover a player's posted likes and dislikes, posted photos, work history, friends, detailed physical appearance, and true identity.

Personal Information—In games requiring a monthly payment, information such as name, address, credit card number and the like are routinely given by players and gathered by game developers. Even in "freemium" games, it is the rare player who does not purchase something via a credit card. For gamers who play on devices equipped with GPS, "geolocation" data, consisting of the longitude and latitude location information of the device, is available to the developer, and Google's announced but not yet implemented "Project Tango" for Nexus phones, will use the phone's camera and sensors to create a 3D map of the environment in which the gamer is playing, including others in the room who are just watching the player.[17] Similarly, Microsoft has suggested in a patent filing that the *Kinect* camera can also be used to count and identify the facial features of anyone in the room with the player.[18]

How Is the Information Used?

Much of the information garnered by game developers is used in a way no gamer really objects to: improving the game experience. Both aggregated and individual game metrics can be analyzed to ensure the game continues to be enjoyable and is working as intended. Challenges can be adjusted to ensure a reasonable percentage of players master them, and if an unintended coding error causes a player or wizard or tank to be caught in a unending loop or otherwise experience programming error, such problems can be monitored by the developer and code sent to fix the problem.[19]

---

13. *Id.,* nn. 134–35 and text accompanying.
14. *Id.,* n. 48 and text accompanying
15. *Id.,* n. 130 and text accompanying.
16. *Id.,* nn. 50–54 and text accompanying.
17. Joseph Cox, *Google's New Room-Mapping Phone Raises some Privacy Questions*, MOTHERBOARD (February 17, 2014).
18. *Press Start to Track, supra*, nn. 139–40 and text accompanying.
19. *Id.,* n. 168 and text accompanying.

As mentioned earlier, another aspect of data gathering and sharing that gamers seem to like is a developer's posting of high scores or particularly adept moves help encourage the community aspect of gamers, and features such as the "Ask the Community" button in Rockstar Games' *L.A. Noir*, which allow the player to see what other players did or thought in a similar situation within the game, can be fun.[20] Geographic information can also help foster friendly competition among players, e.g., *Battlefield 4* sends out scores and moves illustrating a player's performance to others in the same geographical area as an implied challenge to do better.[21] In a somewhat unusual, but probably nonthreatening, use of player metrics and social media, Microsoft's *Motorsport 5* has introduced the "Drivatar" which creates a profile of Player A's abilities as a driver based on A's previous game play, and then allows Player B, who must be a designated "friend" of Player A, to race against Player A via Player A's profile, even when Player A is not online to actually engage in the competition.[22]

Such data gathering to improve game play will continue and increase. Many developers predict that the future of videogames will be in providing individualized gaming experiences based on individual player telemetry—a concept called "Adaptive Gaming." For example, Psyclapse's upcoming horror game *Never Mind* plans to monitor the player's heart rate and adjust the difficulty of the game in proportion to a player's beats per minute.[23] Climax Studio's *Silent Hill: Shattered Memories* already presents a limited amount of individualized content, timing of scenes, and endings based on the player's prior decisions within the game.[24]

In addition to enhancing game play, developers use individualized player data to prevent fraud, i.e., by ensuring that the player is playing an authorized version of the game.[25] And others surely will follow games like *Kinect* which has facial recognition software (or thumb print software like the iPhone) that allows login simply by standing in front of the game's camera or the use of some other relatively passive biometric data.[26]

Where privacy concerns begin to be implicated is when developers use data not to enhance game play, but rather to restrict it. For example, in *NBA 2K14* the developer monitors local chats among players and issues penalties when swearing becomes excessive.[27]

There is also concern when data unrelated to game play is collected, such as Google's Project Tango and *Kinect's* abilities which, as mentioned above, are able to film and potentially identify those in the background who are doing nothing more than watching the player perform. Or developers who, potentially at least, could collect email addresses off of a player's Facebook or Twitter account.

Use of geolocation data has also troubled many privacy advocates, and there have been many lawsuits seeking a mechanism for consumers to elect a "Do Not Track" feature in phones, videogames, and the like. In 2011 and then again in 2013, The Geolocation Privacy and Surveillance Act was introduced in the U.S. Senate which attempted to set forth "a legal framework designed to provide government agencies, commercial entities and private citizens clear guidelines for when and how geological information can be

---

20. *Id.*, n. 93.
21. *Id.*, at 18.
22. *Id.*, n. 160 and text accompanying.
23. *Id.*, n. 116 and text accompanying.
24. *Id.*, n. 152–157 and text accompanying.
25. *Id.*, at 16.
26. *Id.*, n. 135, and text accompanying.
27. *Id.*, n. 130 and text accompanying.

accessed and used."[28] These bills never made it out of committee, but similar legislation was introduced again in January 2015 by Senator Ron Wyden and Rep. Jason Chaffetz.[29]

More recently, the Supreme Court ruled unanimously in *Riley v. California*, __ U.S. __ 134 S.Ct. 999 (2014), that law enforcement must have a warrant in most cases to search an arrested person's cell phone, acknowledging that searching an individual's cell phone is as, or more, invasive than searching his or her home.[30] Until the law catches up with the technology, the best practice for any business, employer, or other entity that collects geolocation data is to explicitly disclose to users the location data collection and to provide an option to opt-out of tracking.[31]

Even more troubling to privacy scholars is when developers manipulate the data, usually via third party software, to come up with psychological profiles that predict spending habits or related behavior of the player. A company called Playnomics offers developers an algorithm that will give a player a "predictive score," which predicts how a player will perform in other game environments, including an estimate of a player's willingness to participate in online auctions on the site.[32] Another company, DeltaDNA, offers a service predicting a player's "revenue potential" to a developer based on only 20 minutes of monitored game play, known as an individualized "inter-temporal discount factor." This, in turn, allows the developer to offer the same in-game item at different prices to different players depending on their estimated willingness to "buy" help to surmount levels or otherwise make their game play unique.[33]

The commercial manipulation of customers in not limited to in-game offers. Representatives from Microsoft have championed the company's ability to build real world profiles of its users as a database for targeted advertising in the real world, even though Microsoft claims not yet to have exploited this capability.[34] There is an app for Xbox 360 which allows the user to order items from Pizza Hut through the console, and other platforms have virtual marketplaces where various merchandise is offered for sale. No one doubts that soon such marketplaces will be tailored to individual users based on predictions generated from their game play, in the same way that Google now tailors ads based on previous sites visited.[35]

Developers do not just predict economic or commercial behavior from gameplay. As Joe Newman and Joseph Jerome have stated:

> Google received attention in 2007 for a patent describing a technology that could make sophisticated inferences about player psychology based on in-game actions. The patent description suggested that in-game chats could be monitored to reveal whether a player "is aggressive, profane, polite, literate, illiterate, influenced by current culture or subculture, etc." Additionally, in-game decisions could predict whether a player is a passive or aggressive, a follower or a leader

---

28. Cydney A. Tune, "*Privacy Challenges in the World of Smart Phones and Mobile Apps*," Video Games and Digital Media Conference in Los Angeles, California, June 2013.

29. *Require a Warrant for GPS Tracking by Police*, The Hill (Jan. 22, 2015 at 5:29 PM), *available at* http://thehill.com/policy/technology/230466-lawmakers-roll-out-gps-privacy-bill.

30. *Riley v. California*, 134 S. Ct. 2473, 2497 (2014).

31. Tune, *supra* n.28

32. *Press Start to Track, supra*, nn. 175–77 and text accompanying.

33. *Id.*, nn. 79–80, 178–80 and text accompanying.

34. *Id.*, nn. 192 and text accompanying.

35. *Id.*, nn. 194–97 and text accompanying.

in real life. Other studies have shown that different leadership styles and personality traits emerge during a player's game play session....

Climax Studios' *Silent Hill: Shattered Memories* attempts to psychologically profile the player as he or she plays, based upon a series of "virtual psychiatric sessions" and other interactions with the game world (for example, the amount of time the player-controlled avatar spends observing sexualized posters and imagery strewn about the game world.) The game also features questions designed to resemble a Myers-Briggs psychometric questionnaire, which contributes to the player's in-game psychological profile. Other games such as Atlus' *Catherine*, Telltale Games' *The Walking Dead*, and BioWare's *Mass Effect* collect information about players' personalities through the choices they make in-game.

Press Start to Track, supra, at 11–12 (footnotes omitted).

Finally, the role of hackers and law enforcement in data collection needs some mention. As will be discussed throughout the remainder of this chapter, at least in theory, a combination of EULAs, lawsuits, and legislation will allow society to deal with many, if not all, of the potential privacy abuses generated by videogame developers' data collection. But such remedies will not apply to hackers. When developer hacks have been publicized, such as the 2011 and 2014 attacks on Sony's PlayStation Network,[36] the publicity emphasis has been on the theft of financially sensitive information from users such as passwords and credit card numbers. But there is little reason to think that the hackers' uploads have excluded, or will in the future exclude, psychological, biometric, social media, or other data gathered or used by developers. What use would be made of such information is open to debate, but the risk of such unauthorized disclosure does cause privacy advocates to caution against collection of data in the first place.

Further, as Joe Newman and Joseph Jerome warn:

[G]overnment surveillance is done without the developer's direct cooperation. For instance, the National Security Agency reportedly collects player information from "leaky" unsecured apps including Rovio's popular mobile game *Angry Birds*. Employees of the NSA have also been known to actively participate in online games such as *World of Warcraft*, posing as other players to gather intelligence on potential suspects. The full extent of data gathered by these methods is currently unknown, but leaked NSA documents suggest that a player's "age, location, sex and [] sexual preferences" are collected as part of the program.

Press to Start, supra at 34 (footnotes omitted).

---

36. *See, e.g.,* 211 http://www.reuters.com/article/2011/04/26/us-sony-stoldendata-idUSTRE73P6 WB20110426; While investigating the hack, Sony released a press statement admitting that:

> "We believe that an unauthorized person has obtained the following information that you provided: name, address (city, state, zip), country, email address, birthdate, Playstation ... password and login ... If you have provided your credit card data through PlayStation Network or Qriocity, out of an abundance of caution we are advising you that your credit card number (excluding security code) and expiration date may have been obtained."

Mike Jackson, *PSN Failure Update: Personal Information Stolen, Admits Sony,* COMPUTER AND VIDEO GAMES (Apr. 26, 2011 at 1:23 PM), *available at* http://www.computerandvideogames.com/299419/psn-failure-update-personal-information-stolen-admits-sony/.

The security breach led to a class action suit in which the plaintiffs alleged their personal information was collected by Sony and then wrongfully disclosed as a result of the cyber-hack. In June 2014, Sony agreed to a $15 million preliminary settlement as a result of the 2011 hack. *Id.*

For information on the 2014 hack, *see, e.g., "Playstation Back Online After Christmas Hack"* http://time.com/3647711/sony-playstation-christmas-hack-lizard-squad/ (last accessed January 18, 2015)

What Can We Do to Correct Any Abuses?

Now that we have some idea of the types of data collected and what developers and others do with it, the question becomes what can we, as a society, do to curb them. As with most legal issues, the answer lies in a combination of: (1) private contract; (2) litigation; (3) statutory regulation; and (4) industry self-regulation and gamer concerted action. Each of these will be discussed below.

---

§ 14.20 Privacy and End User License Agreements, Terms of Use Agreements, and Terms of Service Agreements

In the year 2000, the Federal Trade Commission adopted a "notice and choice" philosophy as the "best practice" for data collectors.[37] The European Union has set forth a similar "transparency and user consent" principle.[38] The argument for such a standard is based on Justice Harlan's "subjective" prong of the privacy test in *Katz* mentioned above, and argues that so long as the individual whose data is being collected is given "notice" of what information is being collected and what is being done with it, and has a real "choice" as to whether to subject himself or herself to such practices, the individual should have no privacy complaint with regard the data collected.

This concept has led videogame developers to believe they can satisfy most privacy issues by putting clauses in EULAs or TOS/TOU Agreements[39] disclosing their intent to collect and use certain data, and pointing out that a consumer certainly has the choice not to play the game. For example, Microsoft warned players of *NBA 2K14* (the videogame in which Microsoft monitors local chats and penalizes excessive swearing) in its customer agreement that "they should not expect any level of privacy concerning [their] use of the live communication features such as voice chat, video, and communications ... offered through their services."

However, as pointed out by Joe Newman and Joseph Jerome:

> [M]any argue that ... "notice and choice" is becoming increasingly impractical in light of new technologies. Former FTC Chairman Jon Liebowitz has conceded that "notice and choice" hasn't "worked quite as well as we would like;" the vast majority of consumers "don't read privacy policies" and don't make educated choices about the policies they agree to.

Press Start to Track, supra at 44 (footnotes omitted).

No doubt it is true that users tend to rapidly click "I Agree" on every dialogue box they are presented without reading the substance of the EULA when setting up a game, and one could certainly question whether a dry explanation of policies such as the one from Microsoft given above would put a lay reader on notice that Microsoft is monitoring a

---

37. *See, e.g.,* Andrew B. Serwin, *The Federal Trade Commission and Privacy: Defining Best Enforcement and Encouraging the Adoption of Best Practices*, 48 San Diego L. Rev. 809, 815-16 (2011).

38. *See* Omer Tene and Jules Polonetsky, *Article: To Track of "Do Not Track": Advertising Transparency and Individual Control in Online Behavioral Advertising*, 13 Minn. J.L. Sci. & Tech. 281, 285 (Winter 2012).

39. For a more detailed discussion of EULAs and TOU/TOS Agreements, *see.* Chapter 10 *infra*.

user's local chats for purposes of quantifying his or her foul language. Nevertheless, the EULA or TOS/TOU Agreement is still the first line of defense for videogame developers when confronting privacy concerns.

––––––––––

Notes and Questions

1. What do you think about the "notice and choice" model? If you were a developer, what would you do to better ensure that your data collection notices would be read and understood?

2. Is there some data which even a EULA cannot validly authorize the developer to gather and/or disclose?

3. In 2012, the FTC revised its privacy recommendations in a report entitled, *Protecting Consumer Privacy in an Era of Rapid Change: Recommendations for Businesses and Policy Makers*. In that report, the Commission, *inter alia*:

- Adopted a "commercially accepted practices" test rather than a "notice and choice" model for industry best practices, indicating a shift from the subjective prong of Justice Harlan's test in *Katz* to the objective prong as the standard for judging the best practices in data collection with reference to industry custom.

- Stated that there were differences in the sensitivity of data commercially collected, and recognized that treatment of such information should vary depending on the sensitivity of the data;

- Called for data collectors to build in confidentiality of sensitive data at every point of the process;

- Recommended an "opt in" format for the collection and sale to third parties of some sensitive data, where a consumer would have to affirmatively and separately "opt in" to the collection and third party use of some data, and where merely clicking "I Agree" at all the dialogue boxes would result in the data not being collected;

- Called for an internal accuracy check on all data collected.

In general, the report recognized that society benefits from some information sharing, but warned that greater restrictions should be placed on the collection of sensitive data.[40]

4. In 2012 the European Union proposed a Data Collection Directive to bind its members that is similar in many respects to the 2012 FTC Report mentioned above. It also declared January 28 as "Data Collection Day" in the EU. As of the date of publication of this Book, the directive was still making its way through the system for approval throughout the EU.

––––––––––

§ 14.30 Statutory Regulation of Privacy

Societal concerns over privacy have generally met willing legislators on both the state and federal levels. Even a casebook on videogame law cannot discuss all the privacy statutes

––––––––––

40. If you are interested, you can find the report at http://www.ftc.gov/sites/default/files/documents/reports/federal-trade-commission-report-protecting-consumer-privacy-era-rapid-change-recommendations/120326privacyreport.pdf.

that conceivably could affect a videogame developer. However, some of the more prominent statutes are set forth below.

Children's Online Privacy Protection Act

Protecting the privacy of children who play videogames is a fertile source of regulation. The foremost statute in this regard is the federal Children's Online Privacy Protection Act of 1998 ("COPPA") which regulates data collected from children under thirteen.[41] In 2000, the FTC implemented COPPA through 16 CFR 312.1,[42] and a major revision to the rules was passed in 2012, which became effective in July 2013.[43] The gist of the current COPPA regulation is that an online service cannot collect personal information from a child under the age of thirteen absent verifiable parental consent. However, the COPPA framework raises a series of questions.

The first question is what entities are subject to COPPA? The answer is: "any online service or mobile application that is either directed to children under thirteen, *or* to general-audience services that are known to collect and use information obtained from children. Online-enabled games are subject to COPPA if they collect personal information for commercial purposes such as in-game or online targeted advertising."[44]

If an entity is subject to COPPA, what must it do and what is it prevented from doing? The FTC states a covered entity has the following obligations under COPPA:

- Post a clear and comprehensive online privacy policy describing their information practices for personal information collected online from children;

- Provide direct notice to parents and obtain verifiable parental consent, with limited exceptions, before collecting personal information online from children;

- Give parents the choice of consenting to the operator's collection and internal use of a child's information, but prohibiting the operator from disclosing that information to third parties (unless disclosure is integral to the site or service, in which case, this must be made clear to parents);

- Provide parents access to their child's personal information to review and/or have the information deleted;

- Give parents the opportunity to prevent further use or online collection of a child's personal information;

---

41. 15 U.S.C. §§ 6501–6506 (LexisNexis through P.L. 113–145).

42. 16 C.F.R. 312.1 (LexisNexis through 2014).

43. FTC, *Complying with COPPA: Frequently Asked Questions: A Guide for Business and Parents and Small Entity Compliance Guide,* http://www.business.ftc.gov/documents/0493-Complying-with-COPPA-Frequently-Asked-Questions (last accessed December 2, 2014), hereafter ("*Complying with COPPA*").

44. *Press Start to Track, supra,* nn. 223–24 and text accompanying. The FTC defines those who are covered by COPPA as follows:

> The Rule applies to operators of commercial websites and online services (including mobile apps) directed to children under 13 that collect, use, or disclose personal information from children. It also applies to operators of general audience websites or online services with actual knowledge that they are collecting, using, or disclosing personal information from children under 13. The Rule also applies to websites or online services that have actual knowledge that they are collecting personal information directly from users of another website or online service directed to children.

Complying with COPPA, supra.

- Maintain the confidentiality, security, and integrity of information they collect from children, including taking reasonable steps to release such information only to parties capable of maintaining its confidentiality and security; and

- Retain personal information collected online from a child for only as long as is necessary to fulfill the purpose for which it was collected and delete the information using reasonable measures to protect against its unauthorized access or use.[45]

What kind of information is considered "personal information" that the covered entities are restricted in obtaining? In general, it is defined as any type of individually identifiable information collected online, According to the FTC this information includes:

- First and last name;

- A home or other physical address including street name and name of a city or town;

- Online contact information;

- A screen or user name that functions as online contact information;

- A telephone number;

- A social security number;

- A persistent identifier that can be used to recognize a user over time and across different websites or online services;

- A photograph, video, or audio file, where such file contains a child's image or voice;

- Geolocation information sufficient to identify street name and name of a city or town; or

- Information concerning the child or the parents of that child that the operator collects online from the child and combines with an identifier described above.[46]

Such information is labeled "personally identifying information" regardless whether it is optionally given by the child or required by the developer to register for, or play, the game.[47]

As indicated above, such personal information about children under thirteen can be collected and disseminated by a videogame company so long as "verifiable parental consent" has been obtained. How a developer obtains "verifiable parental consent" is flexible—it can be satisfied with "any reasonable effort (taking into consideration available technology)"[48]—and some acceptable methods include requiring a signed faxed or emailed consent form, using government issued identification and knowledge-based questions, providing credit card, bank information or other like information typically only attained by adults.[49]

Currently there is no private right of action under COPPA, and any violation may only be punished by the FTC. However, those penalties can be severe—up to $16,000 per violation. Since 2000, there have been a number of FTC lawsuits resulting in approximately

---

45. *Complying with COPPA, supra.*

46. *Complying with COPPA, supra;* 15 U.S.C. §6501

47. 16 C.F.R. §312.2

48. 15 U.S.C. §6501

49. 16 C.F.R. §312.5(b)(2); *see also* Kristin Bryant, *Not Child's Play: Compliance with the Children's Online Privacy Protection Rule,* 1 Shidler J.L. Com. & Tech. 4, 4 (2004).

$8.4 million in fines.[50] Some of the recent COPPA fines include $1 million from music artist site *Artist Arena* and $3 million from Disney's *Playdom*.[51]

In 2004, the FTC brought suit against UMG Recordings, Inc., claiming the recording company owned and maintained several sites that violated COPPA.[52] The FTC determined that at least one site, which promoted a thirteen-year-old pop star, targeted children and UMG did not notify parents or obtain parental consent before knowingly collecting personal information (such as birth dates) from children.[53] The UMG case marked the first time the FTC brought a COPPA violation claim against a general audience site and demonstrated the FTC's willingness to pursue enforcement action against general audience sites that do not necessarily directly target children, but do have children under the age of thirteen as its users.[54] UMG settled with the FTC, agreeing to $400,000 in civil penalties.[55]

There is a cottage industry consisting of consultants who advise videogame developers on how to comply with COPPA. Because of the sensitivity of the information and the magnitude of the penalties if mistakes are made, there is a "Safe Harbor Program" recognized by the FTC. A company which has its practices certified as COPPA compliant under the Program is safe from any FTC enforcement.[56] There are currently six consulting companies which can certify a company as COPPA compliant under the Safe Harbor program, including those operated by the Children's Advertising Review Unit ("CARU"), the Entertainment Software Rating Board ("ESRB"), and kidSAFE.[57]

Notes and Questions

1. Using the definitions above, would *World of Warcraft* be subject to COPPA? *Wii* and *Kinect*? What about purely educational software used in elementary schools?

2. Why the age of thirteen and not eighteen or some other age?

3. Assume a videogame manufacturer is subject to COPPA and the parents of a registered user have given appropriate consent. The child then has a friend over to play and the friend then provides personally identifying information in order to build an avatar to compete with the registered user in playing the game. Are there issues under COPPA? If so, what advice would you give the developer?

4. Suppose a twelve-year-old signs up on a site and says she is fourteen-years-old. If a developer subject to COPPA does not get parental consent to the collection of personally identifying information, is it subject to penalty?

Here is what the FTC says about such a situation:

Will the amended COPPA Rule prevent children from lying about their age to register for general audience sites or online services whose terms of service prohibit their participation?

---

50. Shai Samet, *"Children's Online Privacy Protection Rule,"* Video Game and Digital Media Symposium in Los Angeles, California, June 2014.

51. *Id.*

52. Kristin Bryant, *Not Child's Play: Compliance with the Children's Online Privacy Protection Rule*, 1 Shidler J.L. Com. & Tech. 4, 4 (2004).

53. *Id.*

54. *Id.*

55. *Id.*

56. *Id.*

57. Bryant, *supra* n. 41 at 4, and *gen.* Samet

No. COPPA covers operators of general audience websites or online services only where such operators have *actual knowledge* that a child under age 13 is the person providing personal information. The Rule does not require operators to ask the age of visitors. However, an operator of a general audience site or service that chooses to screen its users for age in a neutral fashion may rely on the age information its users enter, even if that age information is not accurate. In some circumstances, this may mean that children are able to register on a site or service in violation of the operator's Terms of Service. If, however, the operator later determines that a particular user is a child under age 13, COPPA's notice and parental consent requirements will be triggered.[58]

Is this too big a loophole for developers? Note, that there are now third parties which amass a data base from public records and sell their services to videogame developers to act as an "age-gate" for COPPA and other purposes.

5. Some states have established their own, more restrictive, children's privacy statute. Probably the most notable is California's, which is known as "CalOPPA."[59] CalOPPA requires more and different disclosures to parents than COPPA, most especially including a disclosure on how the site responds to "Do Not Track" signals from the user's browser.[60] "Do Not Track" signals are a set of commands the user can choose on certain browsers which pass along the user's choice that no geotracking information be gathered and used by the developer.

CalOPPA does more than just regulate children's privacy rights; it establishes some privacy protections for all users.[61] However, despite the best efforts by the drafters, many computer and videogame companies found the statutory language confusing. As such, companies including Amazon.com Inc., Apple Inc., Google Inc., Hewlett-Packard Company, Microsoft Corporation, and Research in Motion Limited met with the Attorney General of California to adopt a "Joint Statement of Principles" which aims to strike a balance between giving users more control over their personal information while preventing burdens on mobile platforms and App developers.[62] The Joint Statement is part of efforts to improve privacy obligations and "promote 'transparency' with respect to privacy practices" while reminding site owners that CalOPPA requires any App that collects personal information from California consumers to have a conspicuously posted privacy policy.[63]

Perhaps as a result of this Joint Statement, in October 2012, the Attorney General of California sent warnings to the creators of over 100 apps cautioning that by not having a conspicuously-posted privacy policy within their app, they were in violation of CalOPPA. The recipients were given 30 days to comply, after which they faced fines of up to $2,500 per download of a non-compliant app.[64] After sending those warnings, Attorney General Kamala Harris brought the first (and so far, only) suit against Delta Airlines for the airline's noncompliance with CalOPPA in regards to its "Fly Delta" mobile application. The suit

---

58. *Complying with COPPA, supra.*
59. Cal. Bus. & Prof. Code §§ 22575–22579 (West 2010).
60. Cal. Bus. & Prof. Code §§ 22575(b)(5) (West 2010).
61. Cal. Bus. & Prof. Code § 22575 (West 2010) regulates operators of "a commercial Web site or online service that collects personally identifiable information through the Internet about individual *consumers* residing in California who use or visit its commercial Web site or online service," not just children (emphasis added).
62. Tune, *supra* n. 28.
63. *Id.*
64. *Id.*

was dismissed by a California state court. Since then, the Attorney General's office has published *Making your Privacy Practices Public,* a guide intended to encourage compliance with CalOPPA when developing privacy policies.[65]

FERPA

There are an increasing number of educational videogames targeted to students at all levels. A few of these games are subject to the Family Educational Rights and Privacy Act, known as "FERPA." As explained by Joe Newman and Joseph Jerome:

> FERPA explicitly protects student "education records." The term "education records" is defined as records that are: (1) directly related to a student; and (2) maintained by an educational agency or institution, or by a party acting for the agency or institution. As such, only game developers acting for an educational institution are subject to FERPA.

Press Start to Track, supra at 36 (footnotes omitted).

FCRA

Some developers are also regulated by the Fair Credit Reporting Act ("FCRA"). To be subject to the FCRA, the developer must be a "consumer reporting agency,"[66] or "CRA." Most videogame developers which require a subscription or which sell in-game items qualify as a CRA, which is defined as being in the business of "*assembling* or evaluating consumer credit information" (emphasis added).[67] As a CRA, a developer must take steps to keep consumer credit information safely and allow consumers whose information is taken a chance to correct it. There are additional notice requirements when a CRA shares the data with others such as employers or marketing agencies.[68]

HIPAA

Games like *Wii* and *Kinect* collect and track some medical information of their users. Further, some developers, sometimes in conjunction with employers, insurers and health care organizations, are producing wellness-themed games and apps, which track patients fidelity to health plans (such as a diet regimen) and substance abuse recovery programs.[69] Any collection of health information at least suggests requirements under the Health Insurance Portability and Accountability Act ("HIPAA") may be involved. However, HIPAA's nondisclosure limitations are limited to "health plans, health care clearinghouses," or "health care providers" and videogame developers would seem to clearly fall outside of the definitions of those entities.[70] However, to our knowledge, no developer has shared such sensitive information with undisclosed recipients, and it would be the unusual videogame developer who would want to do so.

---

65. Complaint, *California v. Delta Air Lines, Inc.,* 2012 WL 6061446 (Cal. Super. 2012) (No. CGC-12-526741); Kamala D. Harris, Attorney General, California Department of Justice, *Making Your Privacy Practices Public* (May 2014), *available at* https://oag.ca.gov/sites/all/files/agweb/pdfs/cybersecurity/making_your_privacy_practices_public.pdf.

66. 15 U.S.C. § 1681b (2012).

67. 15 U.S.C. § 1681a(f)

68. FTC, "*Consumer Reports: What Information Furnishers Need to Know,*" http://www.business.ftc.gov/documents/bus33-consumer-reports-what-information-furnishers-need-know.

69. *Press Start to Track, supra,* nn. 206–07 and text accompanying. *See also Jackie Crosby, Healthier living via video game? Twin Cities insurers think so,* Star Tribune (May 22, 201), http://www.startribune.com/lifestyle/kids-health/194579781.html.

70. 45 C.F.R. § 160.102.

Future Statutory Regulation

In 2012, the Obama Administration proposed a "Consumer Privacy Bill of Rights," or "CPBR," which contains seven principles designed to guide future legislation and practices. The seven principles are:

1. **Individual Control:** Consumers have a right to exercise control over what personal data companies collect from them and how they use it.

2. **Transparency:** Consumers have a right to easily understandable and accessible information about privacy and security practices.

3. **Respect for Context:** Consumers have a right to expect that companies will collect, use, and disclose personal data in ways that are consistent with the context in which consumers provide the data.

4. **Security:** Consumers have a right to secure and responsible handling of personal data.

5. **Access and Accuracy:** Consumers have a right to access and correct personal data in usable formats, in a manner that is appropriate to the sensitivity of the data and the risk of adverse consequences to consumers if the data is inaccurate.

6. **Focused Collection:** Consumers have a right to reasonable limits on the personal data that companies collect and retain.

7. **Accountability:** Consumers have a right to have personal data handled by companies with appropriate measures in place to assure they adhere to the Consumer Privacy Bill of Rights.

While the CPBR principles are more aspirational than detailed, they can serve as the basis for more detailed regulation. In February 2014, a coalition of privacy groups including Electronic Privacy Information Center, the ACLU, and the Center for Digital Democracy and Public Knowledge urged Congress to update privacy law in accordance with the principles laid out in the CPBR.[71]

Further, the State of California has recently established a Committee on Privacy and Consumer Protection, which is given the task of establishing even more privacy regulation in social media and videogames.[72]

---

§ 14.40 Protecting Privacy through Litigation

Some video industry observers note that start-up or other relatively low budget developers are reluctant to spend money on EULAs and TOS/TOU Agreements. Many smaller companies simply download the EULA's or TOS/TOU Agreements of a larger game and either just switch out the names of the games or try to make some basic revisions to the agreements without a sufficient understanding as to how a complicated EULA is tailored to an individual game. This results in documents which can be internally inconsistent or

---

71. Kate Tummarello, *Groups Push White House on Privacy Bill of Rights*, THE HILL (Feb. 24, 2014, 9:15 AM), http://thehill.com/policy/technology/199022-groups-push-white-house-on-privacy-bill-of-rights.

72. "*Interest is High in New Privacy Panel*," LOS ANGELES TIMES, A10, January 19, 2015

which have provisions which make little sense when challenged by the user. That can result in litigation, especially in the privacy area.

Another fertile source of litigation are statutes that do not regulate videogames directly but which deal with electronic communications generally. Unlike COPPA, these statutes often allow private rights of action and some provide the prevailing party with attorneys' fees, and thus are popular with plaintiffs' counsel. The problem with these statutes as far as privacy analysts are concerned is that none are a direct fit with privacy issues raised by the practices in the video industry, or other, related industries such as social media. Nevertheless, there is a growing body of law as plaintiff lawyers attempt to bring privacy and other disputes into court.

Some of the most frequently litigated of these statues include:

- The Electronic Communications Privacy Act, 18 U.S.C. §§ 2510 *et seq.*, (often called the "Wiretap Act");
- The Stored Electronic Communications Act, 18 U.S.C. §§ 2701 *et. seq.;*
- The Controlling the Assault of Non-Solicited Pornography and Marketing Act of 2003, 15 U.S.C. §§ 7701 *et seq.*, (known as the "CAN-SPAM" Act);
- The Computer Fraud and Abuse Act, 18 U.S.C. §§ 1030 *et seq.* ("CFAA"); and
- various state consumer protection litigation and unfair practices acts.

The elements, scope, and limitations of these acts are discussed in the next few cases, which deal with information shared by Facebook, rather than by a videogame. However, the practices discussed certainly could be practiced by videogame developers.

In the first case, an outside company used a Facebook user's linked e-mail addresses to send unsolicited and potentially misleading e-mails to the user's "friends." As noted above, videogame developers which collect local chat information on their users have access to similar e-mail addresses.

In the second case, Facebook is accused of sharing certain data without sufficient "notice and choice."

* * *

Facebook, Inc. v. Power Ventures, Inc.

United States District Court for the Northern District of California, 2012
844 F. Supp. 2d 1025

WARE, Chief Judge

I. INTRODUCTION

Facebook, Inc. ("Plaintiff") brings this action against Defendants alleging violations of the Controlling the Assault of Non-Solicited Pornography and Marketing Act ("CAN-SPAM Act"), 15 U.S.C. §§ 7701 *et seq.*, the Computer Fraud and Abuse Act ("CFAA"), 18 U.S.C. § 1030, and California Penal Code § 502. Plaintiff alleges that Defendants accessed its website in an unauthorized manner, and then utilized this unauthorized access to send unsolicited and misleading commercial e-mails to Facebook users.

II. BACKGROUND

A. Undisputed Facts

Plaintiff owns and operates the widely popular social networking website located at http://www.facebook.com. Defendant Power is a corporation incorporated in the Cayman

Islands doing business in the State of California. Defendants operate a website, www.power.com, which offers to integrate multiple social networking accounts into a single experience on Power.com. Defendant Vachani is the CEO of Power.

Users of Plaintiff's website register with a unique username and password. Before Plaintiff activates a username and permits a user to access certain features of Facebook, the user must agree to Plaintiff's Terms of Use. The Terms of Use require users to refrain from using automated scripts to collect information from or otherwise interact with Facebook, impersonating any person or entity, or using Facebook website for commercial use without the express permission of Facebook.

On or before December 1, 2008, Power began advertising and offering integration with Plaintiff's site. Power permitted users to enter their Facebook account information and access Facebook site through Power.com. At no time did Defendants receive permission from Plaintiff to represent that solicitation of Facebook usernames and passwords was authorized or endorsed by Plaintiff.

On or before December 26, 2008, Power began a "Launch Promotion" that promised Power.com's users the chance to win one hundred dollars if they successfully invited and signed up new Power.com users. As part of this promotion, Power provided participants with a list of their Facebook friends, obtained by Power from Facebook, and asked the participant to select which of those friends should receive a Power invitation. The invitations sent to those friends purport to come from "Facebook" and used an "@facebookmail.com" address, not a Power.com address.

On December 1, 2008, Plaintiff notified Defendant Vachani of its belief that Power's access of Plaintiff's website and servers was unauthorized and violated Plaintiff's rights. Facebook subsequently implemented technical measures to block users from accessing Facebook through Power.com

Presently before the Court are the parties' Motions for Summary Judgment.

DISCUSSION

Plaintiff moves for summary judgment on the grounds that: (1) the undisputed evidence establishes that Defendants sent misleading commercial e-mails through Facebook's network in violation of the CAN-SPAM Act; and (2) the undisputed evidence also establishes that Defendants utilized technical measures to access Facebook without authorization, in violation of both the CFAA and California Penal Code Section 502. Defendants respond that: (1) because Plaintiff's own servers sent the commercial e-mails at issue, Defendants did not initiate the e-mails as a matter of law; and (2) Defendants did not circumvent any technical barriers in order to access Facebook site, precluding liability under the CFAA or Section 502. Defendants further contend that Plaintiff suffered no damages as a result of Defendants' actions, and thus lacks standing to bring a private suit for Defendants' conduct.

The CAN-SPAM Act

At issue is whether the conduct of Defendants, as established by the undisputed evidence, constitutes a violation of the CAN-SPAM Act.

The CAN-SPAM Act provides that "[i]t is unlawful for any person to initiate the transmission, to a protected computer, of a commercial electronic mail message, or a transactional or relationship message, that contains, or is accompanied by, header information that is materially false or materially misleading." 15 U.S.C. §7704(a)(1). The Act also creates a private right of action for internet service providers adversely affected by violations of this provision. *See id.* § 7706(g)(1). To prevail on a CAN-SPAM Act claim, a plaintiff must establish not only that the defendant violated the substantive provisions of the Act, but also that the plaintiff was adversely affected by this violation such that it satisfies the statutory standing requirements. The Court considers each requirement in turn.

1. Standing

At issue is whether Plaintiff has standing to assert a claim under the CAN-SPAM Act. Standing under Section 7706 "involves two general components: (1) whether the plaintiff is an "Internet access service" provider ("IAS provider"), and (2) whether the plaintiff was "adversely affected by' statutory violations."

Here, Defendants concede that Plaintiff is an IAS provider. Therefore, the only question before the Court in determining Plaintiff's standing is whether Plaintiff was "adversely affected" by the alleged violations at issue.

In *Gordon* [*v. Virtumundo, Inc.*, 575 F.3d 1040, 1048 (9th Cir. 2009)], the Ninth Circuit explained that not all possible harms to an IAS provider constitute harm within the meaning of the Act, and distinguished those harms sufficient to confer standing from those outside the scope of Congress' intent. After discussing the congressional decision to confer standing upon IAS providers but not end-consumers affected by commercial e-mails, the court concluded that "[l]ogically, the harms redressable under the CAN-SPAM Act must parallel the limited private right of action and therefore should reflect those types of harms uniquely encountered by IAS providers." Thus, while the "mere annoyance" of spam encountered by all e-mail users is not sufficient to confer standing, the court identified the costs of investing in new equipment to increase capacity, customer service personnel to address increased subscriber complaints, increased bandwidth, network crashes, and the maintenance of anti-spam and filtering technologies as the "sorts of ISP-type harms" that Congress intended to confer standing. Thus, the court noted, "[i]n most cases, evidence of some combination of operational or technical impairments and related financial costs attributable to unwanted commercial e-mail would suffice."

Here, in support of its contention that it has standing to pursue a CAN-SPAM Act claim, Plaintiff offers the following evidence:

(1) Around December 1, 2008 Ryan McGeehan, manager of Plaintiff's Security Incident Response Team ("SIR Team"), determined that Power was running an automated scripting routine to harvest data and download it to the Power.com website. McGeehan then spent substantial time and effort determining what steps were necessary to contain Power's spamming. It was determined that at least 60,627 event invitations were sent to Facebook users due to Power's activities. On December 12, 2008, after Plaintiff's counsel sent Power a cease and desist letter, and the activity did not stop, Plaintiff attempted to block Power's access by blocking what appeared to be its primary IP address. On December 22, 2008, McGeehan determined that Power was still accessing Facebook through new IP addresses. Plaintiff then attempted to block these IP addresses as well. In early 2009, Facebook blacklisted the term Power.com, preventing that term from appearing anywhere on the site. In implementing these measures, McGeehan spent at least three to four days of his own engineering time addressing security issues presented by Power.

(2) On December 1, 2008, Joseph Cutler sent a cease and desist letter to Power.com. After this letter was sent Cutler was contacted by Steve Vachani, who identified himself as the owner and operator of Power Ventures. In this and subsequent discussions, Vachani assured Cutler that the functionality of the Power website would be changed to comply with Facebook's requests. On December 27, 2008, Cutler received an e-mail saying that Power Ventures would not change its website as earlier stated. From fall of 2008 through

early 2009, Facebook spent approximately $75,000 on Cutler's firm related to Power Venture's actions.

Defendants do not dispute the accuracy or veracity of this evidence of Plaintiff's expenditures. Instead, Defendants contend that, as a matter of law, these are not the sorts of harm that give rise to standing under *Gordon*, as they fall within the category of negligible burdens routinely borne by IAS providers. In support of this contention, Defendants rely on the following evidence:

(1) In the fourth quarter of 2008, Plaintiff received 71,256 user complaints that contained the word "spam." Facebook did not produce any evidence of customer complaints specifically referencing the e-mails at issue in this case.

(2) Craig Clark, litigation counsel at Facebook, testified that he was not aware of any documents that would be responsive to any of the requests for production made by Defendants. These requests for production included requests for all documents regarding any injury that Plaintiff suffered, expenditures Plaintiff made, or user complaints that Plaintiff received as a result of the events complained of in Plaintiff's First Amended Complaint.

Upon review, on the basis of these undisputed facts, the Court finds that Plaintiff has demonstrated an "adverse effect" from Defendants' conduct sufficient to confer standing. The evidence submitted by Plaintiff is not limited to documenting a general response to spam prevention, but rather shows acts taken and expenditures made in response to Defendants' specific acts. These specific responses to Defendants' actions distinguish Plaintiff's damages from those in the cases relied upon by Defendants, which asserted only the costs of general spam prevention as the basis for standing. In particular, since Plaintiff documented a minimum of 60,000 instances of spamming by Defendants, the costs of responding to such a volume of spamming cannot be categorized as "negligible." The Court finds that under *Gordon* , though the general costs of spam prevention may not confer standing under the CAN-SPAM Act, documented expenditures related to blocking a specific offender may. This is particularly true where, as here, Defendants' spamming activity was ongoing, prolific, and did not stop after requests from the network owner. Thus, as the undisputed evidence establishes that Plaintiff expended significant resources to block Defendants' specific spamming activity, the Court finds that Plaintiff has standing to maintain a CAN-SPAM action.

Merits of CAN-SPAM Act Claim

At issue is whether Defendants' conduct, as established by the undisputed facts, violates the substantive provisions of the CAN-SPAM Act. The Act makes it unlawful, *inter alia*, "for any person to initiate the transmission, to a protected computer, of a commercial electronic mail message, or a transactional or relationship message, that contains, or is accompanied by, header information that is materially false or materially misleading." 15 U.S.C. § 7704(a)(1). Defendants contend that Plaintiff's CAN-SPAM Act claim must fail because: (1) the undisputed facts establish that Plaintiff itself, and not Defendants, initiated the e-mails at issue; and (2) because Plaintiff sent the e-mails, the header information identifying Facebook as the sender was accurate and not misleading. The Court considers each element in turn.

Initiation of Commercial E-mails

At issue is whether Defendants initiated the e-mails associated with the Launch Promotion.

The CAN-SPAM Act provides that "[t]he term 'initiate,' when used with respect to a commercial electronic mail message, means to originate or transmit such message or to procure the origination or transmission of such message, but shall not include actions that constitute routine conveyance of such message. For purposes of this paragraph, more than one person may be considered to have initiated a message." The word "procure," in turn, is defined to mean "intentionally to pay or provide other consideration to, or induce, another person to initiate such a message on one's behalf." *Id.* § 7702(12).

In support of its claim that Defendants initiated the e-mails at issue, Plaintiff offers the following undisputed evidence:

(1) On or before December 26, 2008, Defendant Power began a "Launch Promotion" that offered site users $100 if they successfully invited and signed up the most new Power.com users. As part of the promotion, Power obtained a list of the user's Facebook friends and asked the participant to select which of those friends should receive a Power.com invitation. Selected friends would then receive an e-mail in which Facebook was listed as the sender, promoting an event "Bring 100 Friends and win 100 bucks!" Defendant admits that Power.com's "offer of potential monetary compensation may have induced some Facebook users to participate in Power's launch program."

(2) The testimony of Vachani that Power.com both authored the text contained in the e-mails and provided the link contained therein that would allow recipients to sign up for Power.com.

(3) The launch promotion feature that offered the $100 reward was made available to Power.com users through Power.com. None of the social networking networks on Power.com created the contents of the launch promotion feature.

(4) The declaration of Facebook's technical expert, Lawrence Melling, that based on his study of the software created by Defendant Power and its code, the script would automatically insert Power as the host of the event and the event location. The script also automatically generated a guest list for the event if one was not provided, and did so by accessing the user's Facebook friends list. The script would then automatically send Facebook event invitations to each Facebook user on the guest list on behalf of Power.

(5) The testimony of Vachani that Power eventually paid 30–40 people who got 100 or more friends to sign up.

Defendants, while not disputing the accuracy of the above facts, contend that as a matter of law, they did not "initiate" the e-mails at issue because the e-mails were authorized by Facebook users and sent from Facebook's own servers. In support of this contention, Defendants rely upon the facts, also undisputed, that after a user authorized the creation of an event as part of the Launch Promotion, Facebook servers automatically filled in the header information and sent an e-mail to each person on the event guest list.

Upon review, the Court finds that based on these undisputed facts, Defendants initiated the emails sent through the Launch Promotion. Although Facebook servers did automatically send the emails at the instruction of the Launch Program, it is clear that Defendants' actions-in creating the Launch Promotion, importing users' friends to the guest list, and authoring the e-mail text-served to "originate" the e-mails as is required by the Act. To hold that Plaintiff originated the e-mails merely because Facebook servers sent them would ignore the fact that Defendants intentionally caused Facebook's servers to do so, and created a software program specifically designed to achieve that effect. Further, while Defendants emphasize that Facebook users authorized the creation of events resulting in the e-mails, the Court finds that Defendants procured these users to do so by offering and awarding monetary incentives to provide such authorization. Thus, even if Facebook users may be viewed as initiators of the e-mails because of their participation in the Launch Promotion, Defendants are nonetheless also initiators as a matter of law because of their procurement of user participation.

Accordingly, the Court finds that Defendants did initiate the e-mails at issue within the meaning of the CAN-SPAM Act.

Whether the E-mails Are Misleading

At issue is whether the e-mails sent as a result of the Launch Promotion contain header information that is false or misleading.

The CAN-SPAM Act defines header information as "the source, destination, and routing information attached to an electronic mail message, including the originating domain name and originating electronic mail address, and any other information that appears in the line identifying, or purporting to identify, a person initiating the message." 15 U.S.C. §7702(8). The Act further provides that "header information shall be considered materially misleading if it fails to identify accurately a protected computer used to initiate the message because the person initiating the message knowingly uses another protected computer to relay or retransmit the message for purposes of disguising its origin." *Id.* §7704(a)(1)(C). A false or misleading statement is considered material if "the alteration or concealment of header information" would impair the ability of an IAS provider or a recipient to "identify, locate, or respond to a person who initiated the electronic mail message." *Id.* §7704(a)(6).

Here, for the reasons discussed above, Defendants were initiators of the e-mail messages at issue. But because Defendants' program caused Facebook servers to automatically send the e-mails, these e-mails contained an "@facebookmail.com" address. These e-mails did not contain any return address, or any address anywhere in the e-mail, that would allow a recipient to respond to Defendants. Thus, as the header information does not accurately identify the party that actually initiated the e-mail within the meaning of the Act, the Court finds that the header information is materially misleading as to who initiated the e-mail.

Defendants contend that even if the Court finds that they did initiate the e-mails at issue, they cannot be held liable for violations of the CAN-SPAM Act on the grounds that: (1) the text of the emails itself includes information about Power.com; and (2) Defendants had no control over the headers of the e-mails. The Court finds that both of these contentions are unavailing. First, the presence of a misleading header in an e-mail is, in and of itself, a violation of the CAN-SPAM Act, insofar as the Act prohibits the use of misleading header information. Thus, the fact that the text of the e-mails at issue may have included information about Power.com is irrelevant, for purposes of liability under the Act. Second, the question of whether Defendants had control over the headers is also irrelevant. In particular, the Court finds that the fact that Defendants used a program that was created and controlled by another to send e-mails with misleading headers does not absolve them of liability for sending those e-mails.

In sum, the Court finds that the undisputed facts establish that Defendants initiated the sending of e-mails with false or misleading heading information under the CAN-SPAM Act, and that Plaintiff suffered adverse effects as contemplated by the Act sufficient to convey standing to maintain a private cause of action. Accordingly, the Court GRANTS Plaintiff's Motion for Summary Judgment on Count One, and DENIES Defendants' Motion for Summary Judgment as to Count One.

California Penal Code § 502

At issue is whether Defendants' conduct, as established by the undisputed facts, violated California Penal Code § 502 ("Section 502").

Section 502(c) provides that a person is guilty of a public offense if he, *inter alia*: (1) knowingly accesses and without permission takes, copies, or makes use of any data from a computer, computer system, or computer network; (2) knowingly and without permission uses or causes to be used computer services; or (3) knowingly and without permission accesses or causes to be accessed any computer, computer system, or computer network. *See* Cal. Penal Code § 502(c)(2), (3) & (7). Section 502(e) provides that "the owner or lessee of the computer, computer system, computer network, computer program, or data who suffers damage or loss by reason of a violation of any of the provisions of subdivision (c) may bring a civil action against the violator for compensatory damages and injunctive relief or other equitable relief." *See id.* § 502(e).

Here, the Court has already held that Plaintiff has suffered sufficient harm to have standing under Section 502. (*See* July 20 Order at 8.) In addition, Defendants admit that they took, copied, or made use of data from Facebook website without Facebook's permission to do so. (Defendants' Admissions at 22.) Therefore the only question remaining before the Court, in determining whether Defendants violated Section 502, is whether Defendants' access to Facebook was "without permission" within the meaning of Section 502.

In its July 20 Order, the Court explained at great length that a particular use of a computer network which violates that network's terms of use is insufficient to establish that the use was "without permission" pursuant Section 502. Where, however, a party accesses the network in a manner that circumvents technical or code-based barriers in place to restrict or bar a user's access, then the access does qualify as being "without permission." (*See id.* at 18–20.) Accordingly, the question before the Court is whether the undisputed evidence establishes that Defendants circumvented technical or code-based barriers in order to access Facebook.

In support of the contention that Defendants did circumvent technical barriers designed to block their access to Facebook, Plaintiff relies on the following evidence:

(1) In response to the question if he at any time became aware that Facebook was attempting to block Power, Vachani answered: "I don't know if they were … [o]bviously, we expected that they would but he we [sic] also know that our system doesn't get blocked because there's nothing—there's nothing it's technically doing. It's just users accessing the site so that it can't really be blocked.… We know [sic] that they would try, but we also know that it was built to—it would not be blockable."

(2) The expert of report of Bob Zeidman and Lawrence Melling, who analyzed the code and software used by Power.com to determine if it was designed to circumvent technical barriers. The report concludes that the code used a number of routines to avoid being blocked by websites like Facebook, including the use of proxy servers if one server was blocked by a website. The code would routinely monitor each server to see if an IP address was blocked and change the IP address if it was. The report concludes that substantial effort went into designing the proxy system and that one of the objectives of the design was to reconfigure the IP connections if an IP address was blocked.

(3) The testimony of Ryan McGeehan that on December 12, 2008, Facebook attempted to block Power's access to the site by blocking what appeared to be its primary IP address. Following the block, Facebook determined that Powers was circumventing the block by using other IP addresses. Facebook attempted to block these addresses as they discovered them "in a game of cat and mouse."

(4) An e-mail from Vachani to members of his staff, sent after Vachani received a cease and desist letter from Plaintiff, stating "we need to be prepared for Facebook to try and block us and then turn this into a national battle that gets us huge attention."

(5) A transcript of a discussion between Vachani and a member of his staff in which the they discuss the process of starting to fetch profile data from another social networking website, Orkut. Vachani says "we also need to do some planning to make sure that we do it in a way where we are not really detected. [P]ossible rotating IP's or something. [D]on't really understand this too well. Greg may also have some ideas." The staff member responds "yah. [R]otating IP if we can set then its very good as when [O]rkut will see so much band[w]idth use by perticular [sic] IP then they will block that perticulat [sic] IP." Vachani responds "We need to plan this very carefully since we will have only one chance to do it ... we might need to rotate with over 200 IP's or even more to do it perfectly."

In support of their contention that they did not circumvent technical barriers imposed by Plaintiff, Defendants offer the following evidence:

Vachani's testimony that in December 2008, Facebook attempted to prevent Power's users from accessing Facebook through Power.com by blocking one IP address utilized by Power. "Facebook's IP block was ineffective because it blocked only one outdated IP address Power had used, and did not block other IPs that Power was using in the normal course of business." "Power did not undertake any effort to circumvent that block, and did not provide users with any tools designed to circumvent it." After it became aware of the attempted IP blocking, Power undertook efforts to implement Facebook Connect as Facebook had requested.

Upon review, the Court finds that the undisputed facts establish that Defendants circumvented technical barriers to access Facebook site, and thus accessed the site "without permission." Although the evidence shows that Defendants did not take additional steps to circumvent individual IP blocks imposed by Plaintiff after the fact, this does nothing to cast doubt on the overwhelming evidence that Defendants designed their system to render such blocks ineffective. The Court finds no reason to distinguish between methods of circumvention built into a software system to render barriers ineffective and those which respond to barriers after they have been imposed. This is particularly true where, as here, Defendant Vachani's own statements provide compelling evidence that he anticipated attempts to block access by network owners and intentionally implemented a system that would be immune to such technical barriers. Thus, in light of the undisputed evidence that Defendants anticipated attempts to block their access by Plaintiff, and utilized multiple IP addresses to effectively circumvent these barriers, the Court finds that Defendants violated Section 502 by accessing Plaintiff's network without permission.

The Computer Fraud and Abuse Act

At issue is whether Defendants' conduct constitutes a violation of the CFAA.

The CFAA imposes liability on any party that "intentionally accesses a computer without authorization or exceeds authorized access, and thereby obtains," *inter alia*, "information from any protected computer." 18 U.S.C. § 1030(a)(2). Suit may be brought by any person who suffers damage or loss in an amount above $5000. *See id.* § 1030(g); § 1030(c)(4)(A)(i)(I).

Here, for the reasons discussed above, the undisputed facts establish that Defendants' access to Facebook was without authorization. In addition, Defendants admit that they obtained information from Facebook website. Thus, the only finding necessary for Plaintiff to prevail on its CFAA claim is whether Plaintiff's damages exceed $5000, thereby giving Plaintiff standing under the statute.

The CFAA defines "loss" to include "any reasonable cost to any victim, including the cost of responding to an offense, conducting a damage assessment, and restoring the data, program, system, or information to its condition prior to the offense, and any revenue lost, cost incurred, or other consequential damages incurred because of interruption of service." 18 U.S.C. § 1030(e)(11). Costs associated with investigating intrusions into a computer network and taking subsequent remedial measures are losses within the meaning of the statute.

Here, as discussed above with regard to Plaintiff's CAN-SPAM claim, Plaintiff has provided uncontradicted evidence of the costs of attempting to thwart Defendants' unauthorized access into its network. These documented costs were well in excess of the $5000 CFAA threshold. Thus, the Court finds that on the basis of these costs, Defendants' unauthorized access of Plaintiff's network did cause sufficient loss to Plaintiff to confer standing upon Plaintiff.

In sum, for the reasons discussed above regarding Plaintiff's Section 502 claim, the Court finds that Defendants accessed Plaintiff's website without authorization and obtained information from Facebook. The Court further finds that Plaintiff suffered loss sufficient to confer standing as a result of such access. Accordingly, the Court GRANTS Plaintiff's Motion for Summary Judgment as to Count Two and DENIES Defendants' Motion for Summary Judgment as to Count Two.

* * *

In re Facebook Privacy Litigation

United States District Court, Northern District of California, 2011
791 F. Supp. 2d 705

WARE, District Judge

INTRODUCTION

Plaintiffs bring this putative class action against Facebook, Inc. ("Defendant"). Plaintiffs allege that Defendant intentionally and knowingly transmitted personal information about Plaintiffs to third-party advertisers without Plaintiffs' consent.

BACKGROUND

In a Consolidated Class Action Complaint filed on October 11, 2010, Plaintiffs allege as follows:

Defendant is a Delaware corporation that maintains its headquarters in Santa Clara County, California. Defendant operates the world's largest social networking website. Defendant allows anyone with access to a computer and Internet connection to register for its services free of charge. One of the few requirements Defendant places on its registrants is that they provide their actual names. Once registered, a user of Defendant's website may also post personal information to a "profile" webpage.

Each user of Defendant's website has a user ID number which uniquely identifies that user. If a person knows the user ID number or "username" of an individual who is a user of Defendant's website, that person can see the user's profile webpage and see the user's real name, gender, picture, and other information.

Defendant now "serves more ad[vertisement] impressions than any other online entity." Because it possesses personal information about its users, Defendant's advertisers are able to target advertising to users of Defendant's website. Defendant's own policies prohibit Defendant from revealing any user's "true identity" or specific personal information to advertisers.

When a user of Defendant's website clicks on an advertisement posted on the website, Defendant sends a "Referrer Header" to the corresponding advertiser. This Referrer Header reveals the specific webpage address that the user was looking at prior to clicking on the advertisement. Thus, Defendant has caused users' Internet browsers to send Referrer Header transmissions which report the user ID or username of the user who clicked on an advertisement, as well as information identifying the webpage the user was viewing just prior to clicking on that advertisement. Because of this, when an advertiser receives a Referrer Header transmission from Defendant, the advertiser can obtain substantial additional information about a user of Defendant's website, such as the user's name, gender and picture. Through these transmissions, Defendant shares users' personal information with third-party advertisers without users' knowledge or consent, in violation of Defendant's own policies.

Defendant began these transmissions no later than February, 2010, and they continued until May 21, 2010. Software engineers employed by Defendant knew or should have known that these transmissions would divulge private user information to third-party advertisers. As a result of Defendant's misconduct, Plaintiffs "suffered injury."

On the basis of the allegations outlined above, Plaintiffs assert eight causes of action: (1) Violation of the Electronic Communications Privacy Act ("ECPA"), 18 U.S.C. §§ 2510, et seq. ["Wiretap Act"]; (2) Violation of the Stored Communications Act, 18 U.S.C. §§ 2701, et seq.; [and] (3) Violation of California's Computer Crime Law, Cal. Penal Code § 502.

Presently before the Court is Defendant's Motion to Dismiss pursuant to Rule 12(b)(1) and Rule 12(b)(6).

DISCUSSION

Defendant moves to dismiss on the grounds that: (1) Plaintiffs fail to allege injury-in-fact that would give them standing to maintain an action in federal court; (2) Plaintiffs fail to state a claim under the Wiretap Act, because they do not allege disclosure of the "contents of a communication"; (3) Plaintiffs fail to state a claim under the Stored Communications Act, because they do not allege disclosure of the "contents of a communication" and because the same conduct cannot be a violation of both the Wiretap Act and the Stored Communications Act; (4) Plaintiffs fail to state a claim under the UCL because they lack standing, since they have not alleged that they have lost money or property; (5) Plaintiffs fail to state a claim under Cal. Penal Code § 502 because Defendant's activities do not amount to the type of "hacking" or "breaking into a computer" that the law was intended to prohibit; (6) Plaintiffs fail to state a claim under the CLRA, because such claims can only be brought by consumers; (7) Plaintiffs fail to state a claim for Breach of Contract, because they do not allege that they suffered appreciable or actual damage; (8) Plaintiffs fail to state a claim under Cal. Civ. Code §§ 1572 and 1573, because they do not allege that they relied upon Defendant's representations or were damaged by them; and (9) Plaintiffs fail to state a claim for Unjust Enrichment, because Plaintiffs cannot assert unjust enrichment while simultaneously alleging a breach of contract.

Plaintiffs respond that: (1) Plaintiffs have alleged a violation of their statutory rights, which is a sufficient allegation of injury-in-fact to give them standing; (2) Plaintiffs state a claim under the Wiretap Act, because Plaintiffs allege that Defendant disclosed the contents of Plaintiffs' communications to entities that were not intended recipients of those communications, and the communications were not "readily accessible to the general public"; (3) Plaintiffs state a claim under the Stored Communications Act, because Plaintiffs allege that Defendant disclosed the contents of Plaintiffs' communications to entities that were not intended recipients of those communications, and the communications were not "readily accessible to the general public"; (4) Plaintiffs state a claim under the UCL, because they have alleged facts sufficient to establish standing under the UCL, and have alleged that Defendant violated each of the three "prongs" of the UCL; (5) Plaintiffs state a claim under Cal. Penal Code § 502, because they allege that Defendant accessed their personal data in an unauthorized way; (6) Plaintiffs state a claim under the CLRA, because they are "consumers" within the meaning of the CLRA; (7) Plaintiffs state a claim for Breach of Contract, because they have alleged actionable damages caused by the diminution in value of Plaintiffs' personal information; (8) Plaintiffs state a claim under Cal. Civil Code §§ 1572 and 1573, because they have pleaded in sufficient detail Defendant's fraudulent actions; and (9) Plaintiffs state a claim for Unjust Enrichment in the alternative to Breach of Contract, because they are entitled to simultaneously allege the existence of an express contract and maintain a claim for unjust enrichment. The Court addresses each ground in turn.

Injury-in-Fact

At issue is whether Plaintiffs have alleged injury-in-fact sufficiently to establish standing.

To satisfy the standing requirements of Article III, a plaintiff must show that he has suffered an "injury in fact" that is (a) concrete and particularized and (b) actual or imminent, not conjectural or hypothetical. The injury required by Article III can exist solely by virtue of "statutes creating legal rights, the invasion of which creates standing." In such cases, the "standing question … is whether the constitutional or statutory provision on which the claim rests properly can be understood as granting persons in the plaintiff's position a right to judicial relief."

Here, Plaintiffs allege as follows:

> From at least February 2010, and until May 21, 2010, Defendant transmitted to advertisers communications which disclosed both users' identities and the URL of the webpage the user was viewing when that user clicked on an advertisement. By divulging user identities and other user information to advertisers without user consent, Defendant intentionally violated, *inter alia*, 18 U.S.C. § 2511(3)(a). Both Plaintiffs were registered users of Defendant's services during the relevant time period. Both Plaintiffs clicked on at least one third-party advertisement displayed on Defendant's website during the relevant time period.

Based on the allegations above, and without addressing the merits of the claim, the Court finds that Plaintiffs allege a violation of their statutory rights under the Wiretap Act, 18 U.S.C. §§ 2510, *et seq.* The Wiretap Act provides that any person whose electronic communication is "intercepted, disclosed, or intentionally used" in violation of the Act may in a civil action recover from the entity which engaged in that violation. 18 U.S.C. § 2520(a). Thus, the Court finds that Plaintiffs have alleged facts sufficient to establish that they have suffered the injury required for standing under Article III.

Accordingly, the Court DENIES Defendant's Motion to Dismiss on the ground that Plaintiffs have failed to allege injury-in-fact sufficient to establish standing.

Wiretap Act

At issue is whether Plaintiffs state a claim under the Wiretap Act.

The Wiretap Act states that an entity "providing an electronic communication service to the public shall not intentionally divulge the contents of any communication (other than one to such entity, or an agent thereof) while in transmission on that service to any person or entity other than an addressee or intended recipient of such communication or an agent of such addressee or intended recipient." 18 U.S.C. §2511(3)(a).

Here, Plaintiffs allege as follows:

When a user of Defendant's website clicks on an advertisement banner displayed on that website, the user is asking Defendant to send an electronic communication to the advertiser who supplied the advertisement. However, users do not expect and do not consent to Defendant's disclosure of all contents of that communication. Users expect that certain aspects of their communications concerning advertisers—namely, their identities and the webpage they were viewing at the time they clicked on an advertisement—will be configured by Defendant to be private.

Based on the allegations above, the Court finds that there are two possible ways to understand Plaintiffs' allegations. On the first view, Plaintiffs allege that when a user of Defendant's website clicks on an advertisement banner displayed on that website, that click constitutes an electronic communication from the user to Defendant. Under this interpretation, the content of the user's communication with Defendant is a request that Defendant "send [a further] electronic communication to [an] advertiser." On the second view, Plaintiffs allege that when a user of Defendant's website clicks on an advertisement banner, that click constitutes an electronic communication from the user to the advertiser. Under this interpretation, Plaintiffs are merely "asking Defendant" to pass the communication along to its intended recipient, who is the advertiser.

The Court finds that as a matter of law, Plaintiffs cannot state a claim under the Wiretap Act under either interpretation. Under the first interpretation, the communication is sent from the user to Defendant. However, the Wiretap Act states that an "entity providing an electronic communication service to the public shall not intentionally divulge the contents of any communication (*other than one to such person or entity, or an agent thereof*) ..." 18 U.S.C. §2511(3)(a) (emphasis added). Because, under the first interpretation, the communication at issue is one from a user *to* Defendant, Defendant cannot be liable under the Wiretap Act for divulging it. Under the second interpretation, the communication is sent from the user to an advertiser. However, the Wiretap Act states that an "entity providing an electronic communication service to the public shall not intentionally divulge the contents of any communication ... to any person or entity *other than an addressee or intended recipient of such communication.*" Because, under the second interpretation, the communication at issue is a communication from a user to an advertiser, the advertiser is its "addressee or intended recipient," and Defendant cannot be liable under the Wiretap Act for divulging it. Thus, because Plaintiffs cannot state a claim under the Wiretap Act on their own allegations, the Court dismisses Plaintiffs' Wiretap Act claim.

Accordingly, the Court GRANTS Defendant's Motion to Dismiss Plaintiffs' Cause of Action under the Wiretap Act without prejudice, with leave to amend to allege specific facts showing that the information allegedly disclosed by Defendant was not part of a communication from Plaintiffs to an addressee or intended recipient of that communication, if so desired.

Stored Communications Act

At issue is whether Plaintiffs state a claim under the Stored Communications Act.

Under the Stored Communications Act, an entity providing an electronic communication service to the public "shall not knowingly divulge to any person or entity the contents of a communication while in electronic storage by that service." 18 U.S.C. §2702(a)(1). However, a provider of an electronic communication service may divulge the contents of a communication to an addressee or intended recipient of such communication. Id. § 2702(b)(1). A provider of an electronic communication service may also divulge the contents of a communication with "the lawful consent" of an addressee or intended recipient of such communication. Id. § 2702(b)(3).

As discussed previously, Plaintiffs either allege that the communications at issue were sent to Defendant or to advertisers. Under either interpretation, Plaintiffs fail to state a claim under the Stored Communications Act. If the communications were sent to Defendant, then Defendant was their "addressee or intended recipient," and thus was permitted to divulge the communications to advertisers so long as it had its own "lawful consent" to do so. 18 U.S.C. § 2702(b)(3). In the alternative, if the communications were sent to advertisers, then the advertisers were their addressees or intended recipients, and Defendant was permitted to divulge the communications to them. Id. § 2702(b)(1). Thus, because Plaintiffs cannot state a claim under the Stored Communications Act on their own allegations, the Court dismisses Plaintiffs' Stored Communications Act claim with prejudice.

Accordingly, the Court GRANTS Defendant's Motion to Dismiss Plaintiffs' Cause of Action under the Stored Communications Act without prejudice, with leave to amend to allege specific facts showing that the information allegedly disclosed by Defendant was not part of a communication from Plaintiffs to an addressee or intended recipient of that communication, if so desired.

Cal. Penal Code § 502

At issue is whether Plaintiffs state a claim under Cal. Penal Code § 502.

Cal. Penal Code § 502, the Comprehensive Computer Data Access and Fraud Act, was enacted to expand the degree of protection to individuals, businesses and government agencies from "tampering, interference, damage, and unauthorized access to lawfully created computer data and computer systems." Cal. Penal Code § 502(a). With one exception, the subsections of Section 502 that potentially apply in this case require that the defendant's actions be taken "without permission." See Cal. Penal Code §§ 502(c)(1), (2), (3), (6), & (7). Individuals may only be subjected to liability for acting "without permission" under Section 502 if they "access[] or us[e] a computer, computer network, or website in a manner that overcomes technical or code-based barriers." Facebook, Inc. v. Power Ventures, Inc., No. C 08-05780-JW, 2010 U.S. Dist. LEXIS 93517, 2010 WL 3291750, at * 11 (N.D. Cal. July 20, 2010). Additionally, Section 502 creates liability for any person who "knowingly introduces any computer contaminant into any computer, computer system, or computer network." Cal. Penal Code § 502(c)(8).

In a recent case, this Court considered the meaning of the term "without permission" in Section 502. See Power Ventures, 2010 U.S. Dist. LEXIS 93517, 2010 WL 3291750, at *6. In Power Ventures, the Court found that the statutory language of Section 502, caselaw, and legislative intent all failed to provide clear guidance as to how to interpret this term. The Court found that the statute would be unconstitutionally vague unless it was read narrowly, so as to provide adequate notice of the conduct which it criminally prohibits. The Court then held that the statute must be read to limit criminal liability to circumstances "in which a user gains access to a computer, computer network, or website to which access was restricted through technological means," since anyone "applying the technical skill necessary to overcome such a barrier will almost always understand that any access gained through such action is unauthorized." Applying that construction of the statute to the facts before it, the Court concluded that the defendant could only be held liable for a violation of Section 502 if the plaintiff could prove that the defendant "circumvented ...

technical barriers" that had been put in place to block defendant's access to the plaintiff's website.

Here, Plaintiffs' allegations under those subsections of Section 502 which require a defendant to act "without permission" allege that Defendant acted "without permission" under that statute. However, Plaintiffs do not allege that Defendant circumvented technical barriers to gain access to a computer, computer network or website. To the contrary, Plaintiffs allege that Defendant caused "nonconsensual transmissions" of their personal information as a consequence of Defendant's "re-design" of its own website. It is thus impossible, on Plaintiffs' own allegations, for Defendant to be liable under the subsections of Section 502 which require a defendant to act "without permission," as there were clearly no technical barriers blocking Defendant from accessing its own website. Because Plaintiffs cannot state a claim under Section 502 for any action done "without permission" under their own allegations, the Court dismisses Plaintiffs' claim under Cal. Penal Code §§ 502(c)(1), (2), (3), (6), & (7) with prejudice.

Accordingly, the Court GRANTS Defendant's Motion to Dismiss Plaintiffs' Cause of Action under Section 502 with prejudice as to Cal. Penal Code §§ 502(c)(1), (2), (3), (6), & (7), and without prejudice as to § 502(c)(8), with leave to amend to allege specific facts in support of their claim under § 502(c)(8), if so desired.

Notes and Questions

1. How can a EULA or TOU/TOS Agreement interact with these statutes to validate a practice, or make a practice illegal?

2. In *Power Ventures* the court stated, "In particular, since Plaintiff documented a minimum of 60,000 instances of spamming by Defendants, the costs of responding to such a volume of spamming cannot be categorized as 'negligible.'" Is 60,000 spamming transmissions over the course of several weeks on *Facebook* significant?

3. Of course a court must interpret the statute presented to it, and must use any established definitions and interpretations. However, it would be unrealistic to believe that social norms play no part in determining the scope of a statutory violation. In that light, do you believe most users would object to the information transmitted when a user clicked on a banner ad as alleged in the second decision?

* * *

In the next case, potential privacy violations occurring in the interaction between the spectrum of videogames offered by a videogame distributor and a social media provider are discussed.

Graf v. Zynga Game Network, Inc.
(In re Zynga Privacy Litig.)
United States Court of Appeals for the Ninth Circuit, 2014
750 F.3d 1098

IKUTA, Circuit Judge:

The plaintiffs in these cases appeal the district court's dismissal with prejudice of their claims for violations of the Wiretap Act and the Stored Communications Act, two chapters within the Electronic Communications Privacy Act of 1986 (ECPA). The plaintiffs allege that Facebook, Inc., a social networking company, and Zynga Game Network, Inc., a social gaming company, disclosed confidential user information to third parties. We have consolidated these cases for this opinion and conclude that the plaintiffs in both cases have failed to state a claim because they did not allege that either Facebook or Zynga disclosed the "contents" of a communication, a necessary element of their ECPA claims. We therefore affirm the district court.

I

Facebook operates Facebook.com, a social networking website. Zynga is an independent online game company that designs, develops, and provides social gaming applications that are accessible to users of Facebook. To understand the claims at issue, some background on Facebook and internet communication is necessary.

A

Social networking and gaming websites provide an internet forum where users can interact with each other and share information. Anyone may register to use Facebook's social networking site, but registrants must provide their real names, email addresses, gender, and birth dates. Facebook does not charge any fees to sign up for its social networking service. Upon registration, Facebook assigns each user a unique Facebook User ID. The User ID is a string of numbers, but a user can modify the ID to be the user's actual name or invented screen name. Facebook considers the IDs to be personally identifiable information.

Facebook users upload information to the site to share with others. Users frequently share a wide range of personal information, including their birth date, relationship status, place of residence, religion, and interests, as well as pictures, videos, and news articles. Facebook arranges this information into a profile page for each user. Users can make their profiles available to the public generally, or limit access to specified categories of family, friends, and acquaintances.

To generate revenue, Facebook sells advertising to third parties who want to market their products to Facebook users. Facebook helps advertisers target their advertising to a specific demographic group by providing them with users' demographic information. For example, a purveyor of spring training baseball memorabilia can choose to display its ads to males between the ages of 18 and 49 who like baseball and live in Phoenix, Arizona, on the theory that the members of that particular demographic group will be more likely to click on the ad and view the offer. Nevertheless, Facebook's privacy policy states that it will not reveal a user's specific identity and that only anonymous information is provided to advertisers.

In addition to its social networking and advertising services, Facebook offers a platform service that allows developers to design applications that run on the Facebook webpage. Zynga is one such developer. It offers free social gaming applications through Facebook's platform that are used by millions of Facebook users. Until November 30, 2010, Zynga's privacy policy stated that it did "not sell or rent your 'Personally Identifiable Information' to any third party."

B

A brief review of how computers communicate on the internet is helpful to understand what happens when a Facebook user clicks on a link or icon. The hypertext transfer protocol, or HTTP, is the language of data transfer on the internet and facilitates the exchange of information between computers. R. Fielding, et al., *Hypertext Transfer Protocol—HTTP/1.1*, § 1.1 (1999), http://www.w3.org/Protocols/HTTP/1.1/rfc2616.pdf.2 The protocol governs how communications occur between "clients" and "servers." A "client" is often a software application, such as a web browser, that sends requests to connect with a server. A server responds to the requests by, for instance, providing a "resource," which is the requested information or content. *Id.* §§ 1.3, 1.4. Uniform Resource Locators, or URLs, both identify a resource and describe its location or address. *Id.* §§ 3.2, 3.2.2. And so when users enter URL addresses into their web browser using the "http" web address format, or click on hyperlinks, they are actually telling their web browsers (the client) which resources to request and where to find them. *Id.* § 3.2.2.

The "basic unit of HTTP communication" is the message, which can be either a request from a client to a server or a response from a server to a client. *Id.* §§ 1.3, 4.1. A request message has several components, including a request line, the resource identified by the request, and request header fields. *Id.* § 5. The request line specifies the action to be performed on the identified resource. *Id.* § 5.1. Often, the request line includes "GET," which means "retrieve whatever information … is identified by the" indicated resource, or "POST," which requests that the server accept a body of information enclosed in the request, such as an email message. *Id.* §§ 9.3, 9.5. For example, if a web user clicked a link on the Ninth Circuit website to access recently published opinions (URL: http://www.ca9.uscourts.gov/opinions/), the client request line would state "GET /opinions/ HTTP/1.1," which is the resource, followed by "Host: www.ca9.uscourts.gov," a location header that specifies the website that hosts the resource. *Id.* § 5.1.2.

Other request headers follow the request line and "allow the client to pass additional information about the request, and about the client itself, to the server." *Id.* § 5.3. A request header known as the "referer" provides the address of the webpage from which the request was sent. *Id.* § 14.36. For example, if a web user accessed the Ninth Circuit's website from the Northern District of California's webpage, the GET request would include the following header: "Referer:http://www.cand.uscourts.gov/home." A client can be programmed to avoid sending a referer header. *Id.* § 15.1.2.

During the period at issue in this case, when a user clicked on an ad or icon that appeared on a Facebook webpage, the web browser sent an HTTP request to access the resource identified by the link. The HTTP request included a referer header that provided both the user's Facebook ID and the address of the Facebook webpage the user was viewing when the user clicked the link. Accordingly, if the Facebook user clicked on an ad, the web browser would send the referer header information to the third party advertiser.

To play a Zynga game through Facebook, a registered Facebook user would log into the user's Facebook account and then click on the Zynga game icon within the Facebook interface. For example, if a user wanted to access Zynga's popular FarmVille game, the user would click the FarmVille icon, and the user's web browser would send an HTTP request to retrieve the resource located at http://apps.facebook.com/onthefarm. Like the HTTP request to view an ad on Facebook, the HTTP request to launch a Zynga game contained a referer header that displayed the user's Facebook ID and the address of the Facebook webpage the user was viewing before clicking on the game icon. In response to the user's HTTP request, the Zynga server would load the game in an inline frame on the Facebook website. The inline frame allows a user to view one webpage embedded within another; consequently, a user who is playing a Zynga game is viewing both the Facebook page from which the user launched the game and, within that page, the Zynga game.

According to the relevant complaint, Zynga programmed its gaming applications to collect the information contained in the referer header, and then transmit this information to advertisers and other third parties. As a result, both Facebook and Zynga allegedly disclosed the information provided in the referer headers (i.e., the user's Facebook IDs and the address of the Facebook webpage the user was viewing when the user clicked the link) to third parties.

C

In the separate proceedings before us here, the plaintiffs filed consolidated class action complaints against Facebook and Zynga, alleging violations of ECPA based on Facebook and Zynga's disclosure of the information contained in referer headers to third parties. In *Robertson v. Facebook*, the plaintiffs alleged that Facebook violated the Stored Communications Act, 18 U.S.C. §2702(a)(2). In *Graf v. Zynga*, the plaintiffs alleged violations of both the Stored Communications Act and the Wiretap Act, 18 U.S.C. §2511(3)(a). In both cases, the district court determined that the plaintiffs had standing because they alleged a violation of their statutory rights, but nevertheless granted Facebook and Zynga's motions to dismiss the plaintiffs' claims under both the Wiretap Act and the Stored Communications Act for failure to state a claim. The district court read the complaints as alleging that the plaintiffs intended for Facebook, [Zynga], or the third parties to receive the communications. Because both the Wiretap Act and the Stored Communications Act allow disclosures to intended recipients, 18 U.S.C. §§2511(3)(a), 2702(b)(1), the district court concluded that the complaints did not state a claim for violation of the Wiretap Act or Stored Communications Act. These appeals followed.

II

We review de novo the district court's dismissal for failure to state a claim and we "must construe the complaint in favor of the complaining party."

Before ECPA, the chief statutory protection for communications was the Wiretap Act, enacted in 1968, which regulated only the "aural acquisition of the contents of any wire or oral communication," 18 U.S.C. §2510(4) (1970). In 1986, Congress enacted ECPA to update statutory privacy protections that had failed to keep pace with the technological developments in the 17 years since the Wiretap Act was enacted. S. Rep. 99-541, at 1–3 (1986), *reprinted in* 1986 U.S.C.C.A.N. 3555, 3556–57; *see generally* Orin S. Kerr, *The Next Generation Communications Privacy Act*, 162 U. Pa. L. Rev. 373, 378–82 (2014).

ECPA focused on two types of computer services that were prominent in the late 1980s: electronic communications services (e.g., the transfer of electronic messages, such as email, between computer users) and remote computing services (e.g., the provision of offsite computer storage or processing of data and files). *See generally Quon v. Arch Wireless Operating Co.*, 529 F.3d 892, 895, 900–02 (9th Cir. 2008), *rev'd in nonrelevant part sub nom. City of Ontario v. Quon*, 560 U.S. 746, 130 S. Ct. 2619, 177 L. Ed. 2d 216 (2010); Office of Tech. Assessment, U.S. Cong., *Federal Government Information Technology: Electronic Surveillance and Civil Liberties* 45–48 (1985). Title I of ECPA amended the existing Wiretap Act. As relevant here, the amended Wiretap Act provides that (with certain exceptions), "a person or entity" (1) "providing an electronic communication service to the public" (2) "shall not intentionally divulge the contents of any communication (other than one to such person or entity, or an agent thereof)" (3) "while in transmission on that service" (4) "to any person or entity other than an addressee or intended recipient of such communication or an agent of such addressee or intended recipient." 18 U.S.C. §2511(3)(a). The "contents" of a communication are defined as "any information concerning the substance, purport, or meaning of that communication." *Id.* §2510(8). Even if a disclosure is otherwise prohibited by §2511(3)(a), an electronic communications service provider can reveal the contents of communications transmitted on its service "with the lawful consent of the originator or any addressee or intended recipient of such communication." *Id.* §2511(3)(b)(ii).

Title II of ECPA, termed the Stored Communications Act, covers access to electronic information stored in third party computers. *Id.* §§ 2701–12. The relevant provision here imposes requirements on providers of remote computing services that are similar to the requirements of the Wiretap Act discussed above. Under the Stored Communications Act, "a person or entity" (1) "providing remote computing service to the public" (2) "shall not knowingly divulge to any person or entity the contents of any communication" (3) "which is carried or maintained on that service … on behalf of, and received by means of electronic transmission from (or created by means of computer processing of communications received by means of electronic transmission from), a subscriber or customer of such service" (4) "solely for the purpose of providing storage or computer processing services to such subscriber or customer," unless the provider is authorized to access the contents of any such communications to provide other services. *Id.* § 2702(a)(2). Also, like the Wiretap Act, the Stored Communications Act allows a provider of covered services to "divulge the contents of a communication" to "an addressee or intended recipient of such communication," or "with the lawful consent of the originator or an addressee or intended recipient of such communication, or the subscriber in the case of remote computing service." *Id.* § 2702(b)(1), (3).

The Stored Communications Act incorporates the Wiretap Act's definition of "contents." *See id.* § 2711(1). It also differentiates between contents and record information. Section 2702(c)(6) permits an electronic communications service or remote computing service to "divulge a record or other information pertaining to a subscriber to or customer of such service (not including the contents of communications covered by [§ 2702](a)(1) or (a)(2)) … to any person other than a governmental entity." Although there is no specific statutory definition for "record," the Stored Communications Act provides examples of record information in a different provision that governs the government's power to require a provider of electronic communications service or remote computing service to disclose such information. *Id.* § 2703(c). According to § 2703(c), record information includes, among other things, the "name," "address," and "subscriber number or identity" of "a subscriber to or customer of such service," but not "the contents of communications." *Id.* § 2703(c)(2)(A), (B), (E). In other words, the Stored Communications Act generally precludes a covered entity from disclosing the contents of a communication, but permits disclosure of record information like the name, address, or client ID number of the entity's customers in certain circumstances.

ECPA provides a cause of action to third parties for violations of the Wiretap Act and the Stored Communications Act. Under the Wiretap Act, "any person whose wire, oral, or electronic communication is … disclosed … may in a civil action recover from the person or entity … such relief as may be appropriate," including damages and attorney's fees, *id.* § 2520(a), and under the Stored Communications Act, "any … person aggrieved by any violation of this chapter in which the conduct constituting the violation is engaged in with a knowing or intentional state of mind may, in a civil action, recover from the person or entity … which engaged in that violation such relief as may be appropriate," *id.* § 2707(a).

III

On appeal, the plaintiffs argue that the district court erred in holding that Facebook, Zynga, and the third parties were the intended recipients of the referer headers containing the user's Facebook IDs and the URLs. According to the plaintiffs, because their complaints allege that Facebook and Zynga had privacy policies which precluded them from providing personally identifiable information to third parties, the exceptions in §§ 2511(3) and 2702(b) for intended recipients are inapplicable. Facebook and Zynga, in turn, raise a number of arguments as to why we should affirm the district court. Because the plaintiffs' complaints suffer from a common defect—they fail to allege that either Facebook or Zynga divulged the contents of a communication to a third party—we focus our analysis on this single ground. In doing so, we express no opinion on the other elements of an ECPA claim.

A

Because the plaintiffs alleged that Facebook and Zynga violated ECPA by disclosing the HTTP referer information to third parties, we must determine whether such information is the "contents" of a communication for purposes of 18 U.S.C. §§ 2511(3)(a) and 2702(a)(2).

To answer this question, we first must determine Congress's intended meaning of the word "contents." "In ascertaining the plain meaning of the statute, the court must look to the particular statutory language at issue, as well as the language and design of the statute as a whole." *K Mart Corp. v. Cartier, Inc.*, 486 U.S. 281, 291, 108 S. Ct. 1811, 100 L. Ed. 2d 313 (1988). We start with the plain language of the statutes. *See Gwaltney of Smithfield, Ltd. v. Chesapeake Bay Found., Inc.*, 484 U.S. 49, 56, 108 S. Ct. 376, 98 L. Ed. 2d 306 (1987). For purposes of §§ 2511(3)(a) and 2702(a), the word "contents" is defined as "any information concerning the substance, purport, or meaning of [a] communication." 18 U.S.C. §§ 2510(8), 2711(1). Because the words "substance, purport, or meaning" are not further defined, we consider the ordinary meaning of these terms, including their dictionary definition. *See Wilderness Soc'y v. United States FWS.*, 353 F.3d 1051, 1061 (9th Cir. 2003) (en banc), *amended by* 360 F.3d 1374 (9th Cir. 2004) (en banc). A dictionary in wide circulation during the relevant time frame provides the following definitions: (1) "substance" means "the characteristic and essential part," *Webster's Third New International Dictionary* 2279 (1981); (2) "purport" means the "meaning conveyed, professed or implied," *id.* at 1847; and (3) "meaning" refers to "the thing one intends to convey ... by language," *id.* at 1399. These definitions indicate that Congress intended the word "contents" to mean a person's intended message to another (i.e., the "essential part" of the communication, the "meaning conveyed," and the "thing one intends to convey").

The "language and design of the statute as a whole," *K Mart Corp.*, 486 U.S. at 291, sheds further light on the meaning of "contents" by indicating that "contents" does not include "record" information. Specifically, the Stored Communications Act provides that a covered service provider "may divulge a record or other information pertaining to a ... customer" but may not divulge "the contents of communications." 18 U.S.C. §§ 2702(c), 2703(c)(1). Customer record information (which can be disclosed under certain circumstances) includes the "name," "address," and "subscriber number or identity" of a subscriber or customer. *Id.* § 2702(c)(2). Accordingly, we conclude that "contents" does not include such record information.

This conclusion is confirmed by ECPA's amendments to the Wiretap Act enacted in 1968. Before ECPA, the Wiretap Act defined "contents" as including "the identity of the parties to such communication or the existence, substance, purport, or meaning of that communication." 18 U.S.C. § 2510(8) (1982). When it enacted ECPA, Congress amended the definition of "contents" to eliminate the words "identity of the parties to such communication," indicating its intent to exclude such record information from its definition of "contents." *See* Pub. L. 99-508 § 101(a)(5).

Accordingly, we hold that under ECPA, the term "contents" refers to the intended message conveyed by the communication, and does not include record information regarding the characteristics of the message that is generated in the course of the communication. We have previously made this distinction between contents and record information. *See United States v. Reed*, 575 F.3d 900, 917 (9th Cir. 2009) (holding that information about a telephone call's "origination, length, and time" was not "contents" for purposes of § 2510(8), because it contained no "information concerning the substance, purport or meaning of [the] communication"). And this conclusion is consistent with the reasoning of our sister circuits. *See Gilday v. Dubois*, 124 F.3d 277, 296 n.27 (1st Cir. 1997) (holding that a device that "captures electronic signals relating to the [personal identification number] of the caller, the number called, and the date, time and length of the call" does not capture the contents of communications and therefore "is not within the ambit of the Wiretap Act"); *see also In re Application of U.S. for an Order Directing a Provider of Elec. Commc'n Serv. to Disclose Records to Gov't*, 620 F.3d 304, 305–06 (3d Cir. 2010) (holding that cell phone users' location data is not content information under the Stored Communications Act).

We must next determine whether the plaintiffs plausibly alleged that the referer header information at issue here constituted the "contents of any communication," 18 U.S.C. §§ 2511(3)(a), 2702(a), that is, "any information concerning the substance, purport, or meaning of a communication," *id.* § 2510(8).

The referer header information that Facebook and Zynga transmitted to third parties included the user's Facebook ID and the address of the webpage from which the user's HTTP request to view another webpage was sent. This information does not meet the definition of "contents," because these pieces of information are not the "substance, purport, or meaning" of a communication. A Facebook ID identifies a Facebook user and so functions as a "name" or a "subscriber number or identity." *Id.* §§ 2702(c)(6), 2703(c)(2)(A), (E). Similarly, the webpage address identifies the location of a webpage a user is viewing on the internet, and therefore functions like an "address." *Id.* § 2703(c)(2)(B). Congress excluded this sort of record information from the definition of "contents." *See id.* §§ 2702(c)(6), 2703(c)(2)(A), (B), (E).

The plaintiffs argue that the referer header discloses content information, because when the referer header provides the advertiser with a Facebook ID (which, at the election of the user, may have been changed to a user name) along with the address of the Facebook page the user was previously viewing, an enterprising advertiser could uncover the user's profile page and any personal information made available to the public on that page. But the statutes at issue in these cases do not preclude the disclosure of personally identifiable information; indeed, they expressly allow it. *See id.* §§ 2702(c)(6), 2703(c)(2) (allowing providers to disclose subscribers' names, addresses, telephone connection records, length of service, telephone numbers, subscriber numbers, credit card numbers, and bank account numbers under certain circumstances). There is no language in ECPA equating "contents" with personally identifiable information. Thus, an allegation that Facebook and Zynga disclosed personally identifiable information is not equivalent to an allegation that they disclosed the contents of a communication.

The plaintiffs also argue that record information can become content if the record is the subject of a communication, as in an email message saying "here's my Facebook ID number," or "you have to check out this website." Such was the case in *In re Pharmatrak*, where the First Circuit recognized an ECPA violation when an entity intercepted the content of the sign-up information customers provided to pharmaceutical websites, which included their "names, addresses, telephone numbers, email addresses, dates of birth, genders, insurance statuses, education levels, occupations, medical conditions, medications, and reasons for visiting the particular website," and provided this information to third parties. 329 F.3d 9, 15, 18–19 (1st Cir. 2003). Because the users had communicated with the website by entering their personal medical information into a form provided by a website, the First Circuit correctly concluded that the defendant was disclosing the contents of a communication. But the complaints here do not plausibly allege that Facebook and Zynga divulged a user's communications to a website; rather, they allege that Facebook and Zynga divulged identification and address information contained in a referer header automatically generated by the web browser. Unlike the information disclosed in *Pharmatrak*, the information allegedly disclosed by Facebook and Zynga is record information about a user's communication, not the communication itself. ECPA does not apply to such disclosures.

Finally, the plaintiffs rely on cases analyzing when disclosure of a URL may provide the contents of a communication, rather than record information, for purposes of Fourth Amendment protections. The plaintiffs rely on a footnote in *United States v. Forrester*, where we noted that a "URL, unlike an IP address, identifies the particular document within a website that a person views," and therefore "might be more constitutionally problematic." 512 F.3d 500, 510 n.6 (9th Cir. 2008). *Forrester* quoted a district court case for the proposition that if a user entered a search phrase into a search engine, " 'that search phrase would appear in the URL after the first forward slash,' " and disclosure of that URL " 'would reveal content.' " *Id.* (quoting *In re Application of U.S. for an Order Authorizing Use of a Pen Register & Trap On (xxx) Internet Serv. Account/User Name, (xxxxxxxx@xxx.com)*, 396 F. Supp. 2d 45, 49 (D. Mass. 2005)). Based on this footnote, the plaintiffs argue that the webpage addresses contained in the referer headers in this case revealed the contents of a communication, because they disclose specific information regarding a webpage that a user previously viewed. For example, they allege that "if a Facebook user who was gay and struggling to come out of the closet was viewing the Facebook page of a gay support group, and then clicked on an ad, the advertiser would know ... that s/he was viewing the Facebook page of a gay support group just before navigating to their site." This argument fails. As a threshold matter, our task in interpreting ECPA is to discern Congress's intent, see *Gwaltney*, 484 U.S. at 56–58, and our Fourth Amendment jurisprudence is largely irrelevant to this enterprise of statutory interpretation. But even assuming that Congress considered the body of law regarding persons' reasonable expectation of privacy under the Fourth Amendment in making the statutory distinction between content and record information at issue in ECPA, we disagree with the plaintiffs' claims. Under the Fourth Amendment, courts have long distinguished between the contents of a communication (in which a person may have a reasonable expectation of privacy) and record information about those communications (in which a person does not have a reasonable expectation of privacy). *Forrester*, 512 F.3d at 509–11. Thus the warrantless installation of pen registers, which capture only the telephone numbers that are dialed and not the calls themselves, does not violate the Fourth Amendment. *See Smith v. Maryland*, 442 U.S. 735, 745–46, 99 S. Ct. 2577, 61 L. Ed. 2d 220 (1979). Courts have made a similar distinction between the outside of an envelope and its contents in mail cases. *See, e.g., United States v. Jacobsen*, 466 U.S. 109, 114, 104 S. Ct. 1652, 80 L. Ed. 2d 85 (1984); *United States v. Hernandez*, 313 F.3d 1206, 1209–10 (9th Cir. 2002). And we have allowed the warrantless collection of email and IP addresses under the same reasoning because email and IP addresses "constitute addressing information and do not necessarily reveal any more about the underlying contents of communication than do phone numbers." *Forrester*, 512 F.3d at 510. So *Forrester* does not support the plaintiffs, but rather reinforces the distinction between contents and record information that we have discerned in ECPA. Nor does *Forrester*'s dicta about URL information being "content" under some circumstances help the plaintiffs. Information about the address of the Facebook webpage the user was viewing is distinguishable from the sort of communication involving a search engine discussed in *Forrester*. As noted in the district court opinion cited by *Forrester*, a Google search URL not only shows that a user is using the Google search engine, but also shows the specific search terms the user had communicated to Google. *In re Application*, 396 F. Supp. 2d at 49. Under some circumstances, a user's request to a search engine for specific information could constitute a communication such that divulging a URL containing that search term to a third party could amount to disclosure of the contents of a communication. But the referer header information at issue here includes only basic identification and address information, not a search term or similar communication made by the user, and therefore does not constitute the contents of a communication.

IV

In order for the plaintiffs to state a claim under the Wiretap Act and Stored Communications Act, they must plausibly allege that Facebook and Zynga divulged the "contents" of a communication. Because information disclosed in the referer headers at issue here is not the contents of a communication as defined in ECPA, the plaintiffs cannot state a claim under those statutes.

Notes and Questions

1. The outcome of *Graf v. Zynga* rested on the court's decision that the information in the "referer" header given by Facebook and Zynga to third parties did not constitute the contents of a communication, as defined under ECPA. Do you agree with the court's determination that Congress did not intend to protect personal information such as identification and address information by enacting ECPA? Do you believe online consumers and users today would expect that information to be awarded privacy protection?

---

§ 14.50 Industry Self-Regulation

Many believe the only way to solve privacy issues in videogames is for the industry itself to adopt voluntarily standards which result in an appropriate balance among competing interests. Ideally these standards would appease most gamers, and largely restrict collection and use to benefit gameplay. Some would not allow the collection, manipulation, or sale of telemetry for commercial purposes, while others would allow it, so long as there was a very publicly and plainly disclosed opt-in procedure regulating its use. Of course, there are others who equate industry self-regulation with industry self-serving. Given all these and other competing interests, the thought that there could be universally accepted industry standards is probably unrealistic. Nevertheless, having the industry do something to protect privacy is better than nothing and is probably a good place to start.

The first place to look to establish some sort of voluntary privacy policy would be the Entertainment Software Ratings Board ("ESRB"). In Chapter 12 we explained the ESRB's voluntary ratings policy and we discussed above the ESRB's Privacy Certification policy providing a safe harbor for COPPA and EU compliance. In addition, the ESRB keeps track of the regulatory framework regarding privacy throughout the world, and, at a member's request, the ESRB will provide guidance as to the privacy policies in a developer's EULA or TOS/TOU agreement and spot check a game to report on privacy compliance.

In addition to the ESRB, many videogame companies and other third parties have addressed privacy issues:

> Microsoft, Nintendo, and Sony can help developers address the many laws related to privacy and game development. Console manufacturers generally require a list of all possible information exchanged between players and the developer in order approve a game for play on their machine. Likewise, companies like Apple and Google require developers to follow their data programs as a condition of selling games on their respective App stores.

> Additionally ... The Digital Analytics Association has developed a web analyst code of ethics that incorporates principles of privacy, transparency, consumer control, education, and accountability into the conduct of analytics. The United Kingdom's Office of Fair Trading (OFT) provides a set of guidelines for online and app-based games designed to ensure that players understand costs up-front, including the prevalence of in-game purchases.... Lastly, the Future of Privacy Forum provides general best practices for mobile app developers seeking to create comprehensive privacy disclosures.[73]

* * *

Two experienced videogame policy experts, Joe Newman and Joseph Jerome, have proposed a list of "Expectations" that might help drive industry self regulation forward:

Expectation 1: Uses of Psychographic Data In-Game for In-app Purchases

Gamers expect that psychographic data will not be used to significantly alter the systems associated with making in-app purchases, unless the player is effectively informed of the variable pricing prior to the initial app purchase.

Expectation 2: Uses Of Out-Of-Game Data Within A Game

Players expect that games will effectively notify the player if—and how—the game uses data obtained from outside the game experience in order to significantly alter the main in game experience.

Expectation 3: Handling of Particularly Sensitive Information

Players expect that uniquely sensitive, individualized metrics will not be shared without prominent notice, meaningful consent, and meaningful restrictions on the party receiving the data.

Expectation 4: Data Minimization and Retention

Players expect that games will only collect data that is intended to be used, and that games will only retain data for a reasonable amount of time.

Expectation 5: Effective De-Identification

Players expect that when a developer attempts to de-identify individualized data to create aggregated game metrics, the cryptography and anonymization practices it employs will be sufficiently thorough so that there is negligible risk of re-identifying a user from the aggregated data.

Expectation 6: Meaningful Opt-Out

Players expect to know prior to purchasing a game the availability of the game's offline components (if any). Players expect that they will be able to meaningfully

---

73. *Press Start to Track*, *supra*, text accompanying nn. 275–280.

engage in the game's advertised offline components even if they do not consent to online tracking.

Expectation 7: Altering Privacy Policies

Players expect that developers will disclose all material changes to privacy policies, and require new consent for substantial changes.

Expectation 8: Integrating Multiple Accounts

Players expect that a developer will incorporate and synergize a user's privacy preferences between all integrated devices and accounts.

Expectation 9: Accessing the Player's Social Networks

Players expect that games that access their social network must ask permission first for each type of use.

Expectation 10: Meaningful Privacy Controls

Players expect they will be provided with convenient in-game controls to manage their privacy settings.

Notes and Questions

1. What do you think of the above "Expectations"? Could they be used easily to formulate specific terms in a EULA or TOS/TOU Agreement?

2. Have you ever been a victim of the misuse of wrongfully acquired information? Or the misuse of properly aquired information?

Chapter Fifteen

Gambling

You are on a train for a couple hours, going from New York to Washington DC. You pull out your laptop, use the train's Wi-Fi to log onto GamerSaloon.com, and look through the player profiles on the site to find someone roughly equivalent to your skill level in *Madden*. You find and contact *AllPro4512* through the site's chat feature and propose a game—for $200. You win and your credit card is legally credited for $200, less a fee for GamerSaloon.

You land at McCarran International Airport in Las Vegas and are waiting for your luggage. Anxious to start gambling, you pull out your mobile phone and log onto a website for Bally's, the hotel/casino where you are staying. You select *Texas Hold 'Em* and play at a table populated with a number of remotely connected players. Betting is heated and you take a $200 pot. The money is credited to your account at the casino and waiting for you when you arrive.

You decide to visit your sister and her family in Delaware. After everyone goes to bed, you use the kids' PS4 and supply the necessary personal and credit card information for a casino site authorized by the state's Lottery Commission, like doverdowns.com/online-gaming. You decide to try your luck at roulette, and put $200 on "red." You hit "Spin" and the virtual ball "lands" on "7." You just legally won $200.

Welcome to the United States, 2016.

Gambling on videogames and through video devices and other Internet-connected sources is one of the fastest changing parts of the videogame industry. Domestically, the Internet gambling industry is still in its infancy, and the availability and variety of such gaming is literally changing monthly. But internationally, Internet gambling is much more established. The Congressional Research Service[1] published the global Internet gross gaming revenues found in Figure 15.1.

Somewhere between 80–90 countries allow remote, Internet-connected gaming and sports betting, including all of the EU.[2] However, some of the largest potential markets, like China, Japan, and South Korea, still do not allow online wagering. As we will see, the law in the United States is changing, but for the last several decades, remote gambling has been largely prohibited.

---

1. Michaela D. Platzer, *Remote Gambling Industry Trends and Federal Policy* 1, 7 (Congressional Research Service, 2012) (hereafter "CRS: Remote Gambling").

2. For a comprehensive view of remote gambling in the EU, *see* http://ec.europa.eu/internal_market/gambling/docs/study5_en.pdf (last visited Mar. 10, 2015).

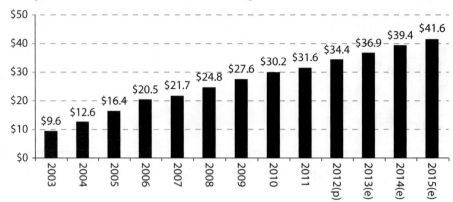

Figure 15.1 Global Internet Gross Gaming Revenues in Billions of Dollars

Source: H2 Gambling Capital, October 2012. These figures show revenues after payouts of winnings.

Immediately below we give you a primer on gambling law in the United States, and follow that with sections on regulation of gaming machines; addiction; and finally, abstention.

§ 15.10 Gambling Law: A Primer

§ 15.11 What Constitutes Gambling?

There is some slight variation among states and countries, but generally "gambling" is defined as having three attributes:

    (1) The player must pay a "consideration" to play;

    (2) The game played is one of "chance" as opposed to "skill"; and

    (3) There is a "payout" for winning players.

As will be discussed in greater detail below, each of these must be present before any "gambling" regulation applies. So, for example:

(1) Many casinos offer real casino games on their websites, like video poker or blackjack. Play is unlimited, and winning players are given casino or resort premiums like $25 in chips or even a free room at the casino based on their scores. This is legal, because while the player plays games of "chance," and gets a "payout," game play is free, i.e., there is no up-front "consideration" to play. (There are rumors that the games on the websites are far easier to win than the actual games in the casinos, as a means to draw in customers. There is little, if any, evidence to substantiate this, but it would be a reasonable business strategy.)

A lack of consideration needed to play is also the rationale for the legality of "sweepstakes" games such as when McDonald's hosts its "Monopoly" game, i.e., there is a "payout," and winning is a "game of chance," but there is always also an "AMOE," alternative means of entry with no consideration up front, such as "No purchase necessary."

(2) A player on a site like FanDuel.com posts a credit card deposit and puts together a fantasy NFL team for that week. If the player wins, money is transferred to the player's credit card or otherwise credited to his or her account. There is "consideration" and

"payout," but to the extent it is legal, it is because betting on fantasy sports is considered a game of skill, not one of chance. Note that there are a few states in which the public policy against gambling is so strong, daily fantasy sites won't take the risk of taking a bet from the residents of that state.[3] Note also in a series of highly-published moves in 2015, the Attorneys General of New York, Illinois, and Texas expressed disagreement with daily fantasy sports being games of skill. They sought and received injunctions prohibiting FanDuel, DraftKings, and other daily fantasy sites from taking bets in their states (verifiable by geolocation software). Indeed, the Attorney General of New York went even further, seeking an order requiring these sites to refund any losses suffered by New York residents on the theory that such bets were "illegal contracts." The sites are fighting these suits both in court and via expensive lobbying efforts.

(3) The most popular game hosted by Zynga is not *Farmville* but *Zynga Poker*. To play, a player must purchase virtual chips from Zynga with a credit card or via PayPal. He or she then sits at a virtual table, playing *Texas Hold 'Em* with either designated friends who have also registered and logged on, or with strangers. The reason *Zynga Poker* is legal in the U.S. is that a winner only wins virtual chips, and the chips cannot be converted to cash or to any other prize on the site. You might wonder whether any sizable number of players would buy chips (pay a "consideration") and play for significant periods when there is no "payout." Well, according to one gaming site, ThinkGaming.com, players purchase on average over $30,000 chips a day from *Zynga*; more than 23,000 people download *Zynga Poker* app per day; and more than 333,000 people play each day.[4] No doubt the social aspect of poker playing with friends spread out in different locales is attractive to some, but it should be noted that even though Zynga does not cash out chips, there are third party sites which advertise that they will pay cash for chips, and Zynga itself will pay cash for chips in countries where it is legal to do so. (In case you were wondering, by far the majority of U.S. courts hold that poker is a game of chance, not skill, but there are some courts that hold the opposite.)[5]

---

§ 15.12 Regulation of Gambling Activity in the United States

Obviously the extent of legal gambling varies among the states and its cities. There are places where many games are permitted, like Nevada, Atlantic City and some tribal casinos; states where a more limited number of games — such as horse racing and a state lottery — are permitted; and a few states where no form of gambling is countenanced.

---

3. The *FanDuel* website provides the following: "The laws relating to fantasy sports varies by state however in the vast majority of them fantasy sports is considered a game of skill and therefore legal. In most states a game of skill is classed as game where skill is the predominant factor in determining the winner. The states where our lawyers believe the law is unclear or questionable about the legality of fantasy sports are Arizona, Iowa, Louisiana, Montana or Washington. Therefore we do not offer paid entry games to residents of those states." https://www.fanduel.com/legal (last visited Feb. 24, 2015).

4. https://thinkgaming.com/app-sales-data/5555/zynga-poker-texas-holdem (last visited Feb. 24, 2015).

5. *Compare, e.g., United States v. Dicristina*, 886 F. Supp. 2d 164 (E.D.N.Y. 2012), *rev'd on other grounds*, 726 F.3d 92 (2d Cir. N.Y. 2013) (holding that poker is a game of skill for purposes of gambling) *with Commonwealth v. Dent*, 2010 PA Super 47 (Pa. Super. Ct. 2010) (holding poker is a game of chance). More generally, *see* Joseph M. Kelly, *et al, Poker and the Law: Is it a Game of Skill or Chance and Legally Does it Matter?*, 11 Gaming L. Rev. (No. 3, 2011).

Early on, gambling regulation was thought to be reserved to the states under the Tenth Amendment.[6] However, as Congressional power under the commerce clause increased, it became apparent that regulation of gambling was a shared responsibility between the states and the federal government. *See, e.g., Iannelli v. United States*, 420 U.S. 770 (1975) (holding illegal gambling could have a significant effect on interstate commerce, thereby justifying federalizing what might otherwise be a state gambling-related crime.) Excluding general money laundering horseracing laws, and tribal gambling regulation statutes,[7] there are six major federal statutes that regulate gambling, each of which is described below.

The Wire Act, § 18 U.S.C. § 1804 (2011)

The most significant of the statutes for purposes of gambling regulation, both in substance and in history, is the Wire Act, 18 U.S.C. § 1084 (2011). The Kennedy Administration, as part of its effort to clean up "the Mob," successfully pushed for passage of the Wire Act in 1961.[8] It provides there are civil and criminal penalties[9] to:

> (a) Whoever being engaged in the business of betting or wagering knowingly uses a wire communication facility for the transmission in interstate or foreign commerce of bets or wagers or information assisting in the placing of bets or wagers on any sporting event or contest, or for the transmission of a wire communication which entitles the recipient to receive money or credit as a result of bets or wagers, or for information assisting in the placing of bets or wagers, shall be fined under this title or imprisoned not more than two years, or both.

With just a quick glance at the above, it might seem that the statute is limited to wagers on a sporting event or contest. But like one of those optically clever paintings that presents a different scene to different people depending on how they look at it, the Wire Act is either limited to, or *not* limited to, sports wagering depending on how you view the commas in § 1804(a) and how you decide which phrase modifies what. In other words, do the commas after "contest" and "wagers" mean that there are three separate offenses listed in the statute, or does everything after "contest" act as a modifier for "sporting event or contest" meaning the statute only regulates those activities? The courts disagree on the reach of the provision as will be seen below.

---

6. *See, e.g., Thomas v. Bible*, 694 F. Supp. 750, 760 (D. Nev. 1988) *aff'd*, 896 F.2d 555 (9th Cir 1990) (stating that, [l]icenced gambling is a matter reserved to the states within the meaning of the Tenth Amendment to the United States Constitution"; and *Chun v. New York*, 807 F. Supp. 288, 292 (S.D.N.Y. 1992) (holding that "The scope of laws regulating gambling and lotteries is clearly a matter of predominantly state concern.") Indeed, about forty years ago the Nevada Supreme Court held that gambling was exclusively a matter of state concern. *State v. Rosenthal*, 559 P.2d 830, 836 (Nev. 1977).

7. The principal statute regulating horseracing and pari-mutuel wagering is the Interstate Horseracing Act, 15 U.S.C. §§ 3001–3007; the like statute regulating tribal gaming is the Indian Gaming Regulatory Act, 15 U.S.C. §§ 3001–3007. There are various money laundering statutes, although the principal provision used in gambling related contexts is found at 18 U.S.C. § 1956.

8. I. Nelson Rose & Rebecca Bolin, *Game On for Internet Gambling: With Federal Approval, States Line Up to Place Their Bets,* 45 Conn. L. Rev. 655, 657 (2012).

9. "Offenders are subject to imprisonment for not more than two years and/or a fine of not more than twice the gain or loss associated with the offense or $250,000.... .They may have their telephone service cancelled at law enforcement request and conduct that violates the Wire Act may provide the basis for a prosecution under the money laundering statutes, the Travel Act, the Illegal Gambling Business Act, RICO, or the Unlawful Internet Gambling Enforcement Act.", Charles Doyle, *Internet Gambling: An Overview of Federal Criminal Law,* 1, 2 (Congressional Research Service, 2012) (citations omitted) (hereafter "CRS: Criminal Law").

United States v. Lombardo

United States District Court, District of Utah, 2007
639 F. Supp. 2d 1271

STEWART, District Judge.

[Indictments were brought against numerous defendants under the Wire Act and other statutes for internet gambling. Some of the claimed violations were for sports betting; others were for casino games. The defendants moved to dismiss the allegations relating to non-sporting events. — ED.]

At least one court has determined that § 1084(a) applies to wire communications related to online gambling in the form of "virtual slots, blackjack, or roulette." In *New York v. World Interactive Gaming Corporation* [714 N.Y.S.2d 844, 848, 850–52, the Attorney General of New York sought, among other things, to enjoin an online casino based in Antigua from "running any aspect of their Internet gambling business within the State of New York." The action was brought pursuant to a New York law allowing "the Attorney General to bring a special proceeding against a person or business committing repeated or persistent fraudulent or illegal acts" under either New York or Federal law. The Wire Act was among the federal laws of which the casino was accused of violating. Without directly considering the "sporting event or contest" language of § 1084(a), the court held that "[b]y hosting this casino and exchanging betting information with the user, an illegal communication in violation of the Wire Act ... has occurred." In so doing the court pointed to legislative history found in the House Report concerning the Wire Act which states:

> The purpose of the bill is to assist various States and the District of Columbia in the enforcement of their laws pertaining to gambling, bookmaking, and like offenses and to aid in the suppression of organized gambling activities by prohibiting the use of wire communication facilities which are or will be used for the transmission of bets or wagers and gambling information in interstate and foreign commerce.

Having carefully examined the language of the statute as well as the cases above, the Court concludes that § 1084(a) is not confined entirely to wire communications related to sports betting or wagering. The statute proscribes using a wire communication facility (1) "for the transmission ... of bets or wagers or information assisting in the placing of bets or wagers on any sporting event or contest"; or (2) "for the transmission of a wire communication which entitles the recipient to receive money or credit as a result of bets or wagers"; or (3) "for information assisting in the placing of bets or wagers." The phrase "sporting event or contest" modifies only the first of these three uses of a wire communication facility. Giving effect to the presumably intentional exclusion of the "sporting event or contest" qualifier from the second and third prohibited uses indicates that at least part of § 1084(a) applies to forms of gambling that are unrelated to sporting events.

Admittedly, the language of the statute limits the prohibition on the transmission of actual bets or wagers to those on sporting events or contests. This could lead to the conclusion that when the phrase "bets or wagers" is used in the second and third prohibited uses, it is actually referring to the "bets or wagers on any sporting event or contest" language found in the first prohibited use. However, this conclusion would essentially require the Court to find that the failure to include the phrase "sporting events or contests" in the second and third prohibited uses was an inadvertent mistake of Congress.

The absence of the "sporting event or contest" qualifier in the second and third prohibitions is conspicuous, especially as the first prohibition, which includes the qualifier, is directly before the second and third prohibitions in the statute. This is particularly weighty in light of the legislative history of the Wire Act, which indicates the intent of Congress to facilitate enforcement of state gambling laws related to "gambling, bookmaking, and like offenses." Moreover, the exact phrase "information assisting in the placing of bets or wagers" is used twice in § 1084(a) — first, as part of the first prohibited use, and second, as the entirety of the third prohibited use. It is simply unpalatable to the Court to attribute no meaning to Congress's use of the same phrase in two different parts of the statute where the first use is modified by the phrase "sporting event or contest" and the second use is not. Accordingly, the Court concludes that the second and third prohibited uses of a wire communication facility under § 1084(a) do not require that the bets or wagers to which those uses relate be limited to bets or wagers placed on sporting events or contests alone.

* * *

In re MasterCard Int'l Inc., Internet Gambling Litigation

United States District Court, Eastern District of Louisiana, 2001
132 F. Supp. 2d 468

DUVAL, District Judge.

[Individual and corporate defendants, including MasterCard and Visa, were alleged to have violated the Wire Act by participating, in various degrees, in internet gambling with off shore, on-line casinos. Once again, the validity of the charges with regard to non-sports betting was a contested issue in a motion to dismiss — ED.]

The defendants argue that plaintiffs' failure to allege sports gambling is a fatal defect with respect to their Wire Act claims, while plaintiffs strenuously argue that the Wire Act does not require sporting events or contests to be the object of gambling. However, a plain reading of the statutory language clearly requires that the object of the gambling be a sporting event or contest. [T]he rule expressly qualif[ies] the nature of the gambling activity as that related to a "sporting event or contest." See 18 U.S.C. §§ 1084(a). A reading of the caselaw leads to the same conclusion. *See United States v. Kaczowski*, 114 F.Supp.2d 143, 153 (W.D.N.Y.2000) (Wire Act "prohibits use of a wire communication facility for the transmission in interstate or foreign commerce of bets or wagers or information assisting in the placing of bets or wagers on any sporting event or contest"); *U.S. v. Marder*, 474 F.2d 1192, 1194 (5th Cir.1973) (first element of statute satisfied when government proves wagering information "relative to sporting events").

As the plain language of the statute and case law interpreting the statute are clear, there is no need to look to the legislative history of the Act as argued by plaintiffs. However, even a summary glance at the recent legislative history of internet gambling legislation reinforces the Court's determination that internet gambling on a game of chance is not prohibited conduct under 18 U.S.C. § 1084. Recent legislative attempts have sought to amend the Wire Act to encompass "contest[s] of chance or a future contingent event not under the control or influence of [the bettor]" while exempting from the reach of the statute data transmitted "for use in the new reporting of any activity, event or contest upon which bets or wagers are based." See S.474, 105th Congress (1997). That act sought to amend Title 18 to prohibit the use of the internet to place a bet or wager upon "a contest of others, a sporting event, or a game of chance ..." *Id.* As to the legislative intent at the time the Wire Act was enacted, the House Judiciary Committee Chairman explained that "this particular bill involves the transmission of wagers or bets and layoffs on horse racing and other sporting events." Comparing the face of the Wire Act and the history surrounding its enactment with the recently proposed legislation, it becomes more certain that the

Wire Act's prohibition of gambling activities is restricted to the types of events enumerated in the statute, sporting events or contests. Plaintiffs' argument flies in the face of the clear wording of the Wire Act and is more appropriately directed to the legislative branch than this Court.

* * *

The courts are not the only ones that disagreed as to whether the phrase "wagers on any sporting event or contest" modifies and limits the phrase "entitles the recipient to receive money or credit as a result of bets or wagers," or whether the "or" that separates those phrases means they are disjunctive. So too did the Justice Department under different Presidential administrations.

With the increased popularity of offshore poker sites, along with "full service" foreign-based betting websites like World Sports Exchange (Antigua) and Tropical Paradise (Costa Rica) offering a range of online casino gaming, coupled with increasing calls for regulation in this area, the Department of Justice under President George W. Bush issued an interpretation of the Wire Act that claimed it prohibited *all* wagering using the Internet, and threatened criminal sanction against those individuals or enterprises who operated or facilitated such betting, including banks, Western Union, and credit card companies who processed wire transfers of money to or from betting sites, and even broadcasters who advertised such services. In 2003, the Department of Justice specifically warned advertisers of gaming sites that they were subject to prosecution, leading to a multi-million dollar settlement with Microsoft, Google, Yahoo and others over advertising and promotion of Internet connected poker and other wagering sites.[10]

In 2007, a U.S. Attorney testified before Congress that, "The Department of Justice's view is, and has been for some time, that all forms of Internet gambling, including sports wagering, casino games and card games are illegal under federal law ... As we have stated on previous occasions, the Department interprets existing statutes, including 18 U.S.C. Section[] 1084 ... as pertaining to and prohibiting Internet gambling."[11] Despite all the saber rattling, prosecution under the Wire Act has been relatively slight, although the principal of the Antigua-based World Sports Exchange, Jay Cohen, was convicted for violating the Wire Act and sentenced to twenty-one months in prison and a $5,000 fine.[12] *U.S. v. Cohen*, 260 F.3d 68 (2d Cir. 2011).

But new administrations and a greater spread of technology can lead to changes. In 2009, officials from the New York State Division of the Lottery, and the Office of the Governor of the State of Illinois, sought an opinion from the Justice Department that the purchase of lottery tickets via Internet-connected devices such as smart phones, tablets,

---

10. CRS: Remote Gambling, *supra* n.1, at 4.

11. Forbes, *Department of Justice Flip-Flops on Internet Gambling,* http://www.forbes.com/sites/nathanvardi/2011/12/23/department-of-justice-flip-flops-on-internet-gambling/ (last visited Mar. 2, 2015). *See also* O.L.C. Op, *supra*, at 2, "The Criminal Division notes that '[t]he Department has uniformly taken the position that the Wire Act is not limited to sports wagering and can be applied to other forms of interstate gambling.'"

12. CRS: Remote Gambling, *supra* n. 1, at 4. Jurisdiction over foreign based operations is itself an interesting issue, but beyond the scope of this text. In general, U.S. courts have required more than just the presence of an internet site that can be accessed in the United States as a basis for personal jurisdiction. Rather, there is a requirement of commercial activity directed at the United States, i.e., a requirement that some targeted locus of activity in the U.S. be reasonably anticipated or sought by the defendant. *See, e.g., Mavrix Photo Inc. v Brand Technologies, Inc.*, 647 F.3d 1218, 1226–28 (9th Cir. 2011); *Illinois v. Hemi Group LLC,* 622 F.3d 754, 757–60 (7th Cir. 2010). In any event, Mr. Cohen and his site were certainly directing commercial activity to the various states in a sufficient quantity to establish criminal personal jurisdiction over him.

etc. was legal under the Wire Act. In response, President Obama's Justice Department's Office of Legal Counsel ("OLC") reversed the Justice Department's previous interpretation of the Wire Act, issuing what gamblers across the United States called an Obama "Christmas present" on December 23, 2011:

> In our view, it is more natural to treat the phrase "on any sporting event or contest" in subsection 1084(a)'s first clause as modifying both "the transmission in interstate or foreign commerce of bets or wagers" and "information assisting in the placing of bets or wagers," rather than as modifying the latter phrase alone. The text itself can be read either way — it does not, for example, contain a comma after the first reference to "bets or wagers," which would have rendered our proposed reading significantly less plausible. By the same token, the text does not contain commas after *each* reference to "bets or wagers," which would have rendered our proposed reading that much more certain. *See* 18 U.S.C. § 1084(a) ("Whoever being engaged in the business of betting or wagering knowingly uses a wire communication facility for the transmission in interstate or foreign commerce of bets or wagers or information assisting in the placing of bets or wagers on any sporting event or contest....").

> Reading "on any sporting event or contest" to modify "the transmission ... of bets or wagers" produces the more logical result. The text could be read to forbid the interstate or foreign transmission of bets and wagers of all kinds, including non-sports bets and wagers, while forbidding the transmission of information to assist only sports-related bets and wagers. But it is difficult to discern why Congress, having forbidden the transmission of *all* kinds of bets or wagers, would have wanted to prohibit only the transmission of information assisting in bets or wagers concerning sports, thereby effectively permitting covered persons to transmit information assisting in the placing of a large class of bets or wagers whose transmission was expressly forbidden by the clause's first part. *See* § 1084(b) (providing exceptions for news reporting, and for transmissions of wagering information from one state where betting is legal to another state where betting is legal, both expressly relating to "sporting events or contests"). The more reasonable inference is that Congress intended the Wire Act's prohibitions to be parallel in scope, prohibiting the use of wire communication facilities to transmit both bets or wagers *and* betting or wagering information on sporting events or contests. Given that this interpretation is an equally plausible reading of the text and makes better sense of the statutory scheme, we believe it is the better reading of the first clause.

> We likewise conclude that the phrase "on any sporting event or contest" modifies subsection 1084(a)'s second clause, which prohibits "the transmission of a wire communication which entitles the recipient to receive money or credit as a result of bets or wagers, or for information assisting in the placing of bets or wagers." 18 U.S.C. § 1084(a). The qualifying phrase "on any sporting event or contest" does not appear in this clause. But in our view, the references to "bets or wagers" in the second clause are best read as shorthand references to the "bets or wagers on any sporting event or contest" described in the first clause.

[The Opinion concluded by opining that lotteries were not a "sporting event or contest," thus giving its seal of approval to the Illinois and New York plans — ED. [13]]

---

13. The actual wording of the OLC's opinion conclusion was:

What remains for resolution is only whether the lotteries proposed by New York and Illinois

Whether Proposals by Illinois and New York to use the Internet and out-of-state transaction Processors to sell Lottery Tickets to in-state Adults Violate the Wire Act, 35 Op. O.L.C. 1, 5–6, 7 (2011) (hereafter "OLC Op.").

Notes and Questions

1. Both sides of the debate cite legislative history to support their positions. Assuming the legislative history is neutral, which side has the better statutory interpretation argument?

2. With some differences in how they have done it, Illinois and New York have implemented their lottery-sales-by-Internet plans that were given the green light in the OLC's opinion, thus far without significant publicly disclosed problems. As of the date of the publication of this edition of the book, Minnesota, New Hampshire, and North Dakota have joined them, generally selling tickets through web-based, Internet subscriptions.[14]

3. Read strictly, even if the Wire Act was only limited to sports betting, § 1084(a) would prohibit, e.g., a sports talk station, or perhaps even a newspaper, from giving the odds on next week's NFL games, as such act would be a use of "the wire" to provide "information assisting in the placing of bets or wagers." To curb any first amendment or other problems, § 1084(b) provides certain statutory exemptions:

> Nothing in this section shall be construed to prevent the transmission in interstate or foreign commerce of information for use in news reporting of sporting events or contests, or for the transmission of information assisting in the placing of bets or wagers on a sporting event or contest from a State or foreign country where betting on that sporting event or contest is legal into a State or foreign country in which such betting is legal.

4. The last sentence of § 1804(b) above makes it illegal to transmit information for a bet from a State where such a bet is legal to one where it is not. As such, another issue in the OLC Op. dealt with whether Illinois or New York would violate the Wire Act because the Internet connections or servers might route the transmission of a bet from Illinois, a state in which remote purchases of lottery tickets would be legal after the opinion, through, e.g., servers in California, a state where such purchases would not be legal, before sending the information back to the lotto machines in Illinois. The OLC eventually concluded that making such activity illegal would not make sense and that if a purchaser located in Illinois (verified through geolocation software) bought an Illinois lottery ticket, it would be treated as an in-state transaction, regardless where the Internet connections might take the information. OLC Op. at 2–3.

5. If you are new to it, the OLC has been likened to the Justice Department's "Law Review." Among its responsibilities is to provide the Department's official position on the

---

involve "sporting event[s] or contest[s]" within the meaning of the Wire Act. We conclude that they do not. The ordinary meaning of the phrase "sporting event or contest" does not encompass lotteries. As noted above, a statute enacted the same day as the Wire Act expressly distinguished sports betting from other forms of gambling, including lotteries. *See supra* pp. 10–11 (discussing § 1953(e)). Other federal statutes regulating lotteries make the same distinction. *See* 18 U.S.C. § 1307(d) (2006) ("'Lottery' does not include the placing or accepting of bets or wagers on sporting events or contests.").

OLC Op. at 12.

14. CRS: Remote Gambling, *supra* n. 1, at 5.

meaning and effect of legislation and it tends to attract more than its share of the Justice Department's "best and brightest." Its opinions do not have the force of law, but because the OLC is so highly respected, all interested parties are now working on the assumption that the Wire Act only applies to sports wagering. Given that interpretation, what consequences do you see flowing from the OLC's opinion, other than allowing internet lottery purchases? (We discuss some implications later in this section.)

6. Does the Wire Act make illegal an individual bettor's placing of a wager on a sporting event or is its scope different?

The Unlawful Internet Gambling Enforcement Act, 31 U.S.C. § 5361 *et. seq.*

Gamblers bet to make money. As a consequence, it makes sense that if your goal is to restrict gambling, you should go about it by restricting the ability to transfer money associated with betting. That was the goal of Congress when it passed The Unlawful Internet Gambling Enforcement Act ("UIGEA"), 31 U.S.C. § 5361 *et seq.* (2011), which makes it a violation for those in the "business of betting and wagering" to accept payments relating to unlawful Internet gambling using recognized payment mechanisims that are regulated by the Treasury Department and the Federal Reserve, such as credit cards, wire transfers, Paypal, etc.[15] Violations are punishable by imprisonment for up to five years and/or a fine up to $250,000 for individuals.[16] The UIGEA was passed in 2006, but in a manner that still causes gaming scholars to scratch their heads—it was offered as a last minute amendment to an anti-terrorism statute, the Security and Accountability for Every Port Act of 2006, also known as the "SAFE Port" Act, for which President Bush had advocated and was sure to sign.

Gambling (or in the words of the statute, a "bet or wager") is defined under the UIGEA as having the attributes mentioned above: (1) consideration; (2) "a game subject to chance"; and (3) a payout.[17] On the second element, the Congressional Research Service reports the following legislative history:

> Earlier in the UIGEA's legislative history, the definition of "bet or wager" used the phrase "a game predominantly subject to chance" rather than simply "a game subject to chance." The Justice Department questioned whether the original phrase was "sufficient to cover card games, such as poker." The change in language appears to accommodate that concern by extending coverage to games that have an element of chance, even if not necessarily a predominant element.[18]

Hence, it was pretty well recognized that money transfers using a system regulated by the Treasury office to facilitate a wager in an Internet poker game was prohibited after passage of the UIGEA. The UIGEA contains many specific inclusions and exclusions from its reach. Among the notable exclusions, i.e., activities which are legal in spite of the UIGEA, are:

- Betting on fantasy sports, 31 U.S.C. § 5363(E)(ix);[19]

---

15. 31 U.S.C. § 5363; *see also* CRS: Criminal Law, *supra* n. 9, at 16.
16. 31 U.S.C. § 5366(a).
17. 31 U.S.C. § 5362(1)(A).
18. CRS: Criminal Law, *supra* n. 9, at 18 (citations omitted).
19. The provision specifically exempts the following:
   (ix) participation in any fantasy or simulation sports game or educational game or contest in which (if the game or contest involves a team or teams) no fantasy or simulation sports team is based on the current membership of an actual team that is a member of an amateur or professional sports organization (as those terms are defined in section 3701 of title 28) and that meets the following conditions:

- Intrastate gambling where the State has authorized such gambling and set up age and geolocation verification systems to monitor play, 31 U.S.C. § 5362 (10);

- Gambling at Tribal casinos, 31 U.S.C. § 5362 (10)(C); and

- The purchase and sales of stocks or commodities on registered exchanges. 31 U.S.C. § 5362 (1)(E)(1) and (2).

One activity that is specifically included is state lotteries whereby states have not made Internet sales of lottery chances legal. 31 U.S.C. § 5362 (1)(B).

The effect of the UIGEA after its passage was mixed. Some of the Internet poker sites, such as PartyPoker.com, stopped taking bets from those in the U.S., and estimates are that Internet gambling from U.S. residents declined by $2 billion worldwide the year after the UIGEA was passed.[20] On the other hand, other poker sites, like Poker Stars, Full Tilt Poker, Ultimate Bet, and Absolute Poker, and e-wallet providers, like Netseller, which facilitated money transfers between players and those sites, continued without change. And while the total take from U.S. players may have dropped by $2 billion, that was from a starting point of $6 billion in 2006, leaving over $4 billion in internet gambling "take" to offshore gaming sites from U.S.-based bettors in 2007, the year after the UIGEA took effect.[21] This did not sit well with the Justice Department. The wheels of justice may grind slowly, but on April 15, 2011, in what is known as "Black Friday" to Internet poker afficionados, indictments were served against these poker sites listed above and their principals based on the UIGEA and other money laundering statutes, and Internet-based offshore poker ended in the United States, at least for a time.[22]

The constitutionality of the UIGEA has been upheld against vagueness and due process challenges in the United States. *Interactive Media Ent'mt and Gaming Ass'n v. Attorney General*, 580 F.3d 113, 116–118 (3d Cir. 2009). However, the statute has not fared as well internationally. Several countries, most notably Antigua, have successfully asserted before the World Trade Organization ("WTO") that the UIGEA (and other U.S. anti-gambling statutes[23]) prevents the cross-border supply of online gambling services from WTO members (like Antigua) to the United States market in violation of the General Agreement

---

(I) All prizes and awards offered to winning participants are established and made known to the participants in advance of the game or contest and their value is not determined by the number of participants or the amount of any fees paid by those participants.

(II) All winning outcomes reflect the relative knowledge and skill of the participants and are determined predominantly by accumulated statistical results of the performance of individuals (athletes in the case of sports events) in multiple real world sporting or other events.

(III) No winning outcome is based—"(aa) on the score, point-spread, or any performance or performances of any single real-world team or any combination of such teams; or "(bb) solely on any single performance of an individual athlete in any single real-world sporting or other event.

20. CRS: Remote Gambling, *supra* n. 1, at 5.

21. *Id.*

22. On "Black Friday," the Justice Department acted swiftly to shut down domain names, froze bank accounts, shut down payment processors, arrested principals and employees of internet poker sites, and otherwise put an end to overseas poker playing originating from the United States. Players in the United States cumulatively lost hundreds of millions of dollars, and eventually many of the principals of these sites pled guilty to a plea deal and served prison time. *See, gen.* http://en.wikipedia.org/wiki/United_States_v._Scheinberg (last visited Mar. 1, 2015). Note that the Black Friday indictments weren't under the Wire Act but instead under money laundering and fraud statutes, *see* ROSE & BOLIN, *supra* n. 8, at 671.

23. The Interstate Horseracing Act, 15 U.S.C. §§ 3001–07 (2011) was another statute which was part of Antigua's challenge before the WTO. ROSE & BOLIN, *supra* n. 8, at 667.

on Trade in Services ("GATS"). As a result, the United States has had to provide compensation to various WTO members, and has suffered trade sanctions, such as having some intellectual property rights suspended with regard to some U.S.-produced products, otherwise protected under the WTO's Trade Related Aspects of Intellectual Property Rights ("TRIPS").[24]

Notes and Questions

1. Taking up where the OLC left off, do you read the UIGEA as permitting intrastate purchase of lottery tickets by those over 21, so long as Illinois and New York have passed the necessary enabling legislation?

2. Should the United States have suffered international trade sanctions for trying to protect its citizens from what Congress believes were the evils of gambling?

3. Do you agree with exempting fantasy sports from the UIGEA? Why do you think they were specifically exempted? The fact that fantasy sports is exempted under the UIGEA does not mean fantasy sports wagering is per se legal in the United States. As we mentioned earlier in this chapter, various Attorneys General have enjoined daily fantasy sites on the theory that the placing of a bet on the sites may not be illegal under the UIGEA, but it is illegal under state gambling laws, the Wire Act, and other related statutes.

4. Similar to the last question we asked under the Wire Act discussion above, does the UIGEA prohibit the individual bettor of poker player from betting, or is its scope different?

5. What is the significance of allowing intrastate Internet gambling?

The Travel Act, 18 U.S.C. § 1952 (2011)

The "Travel Act," 18 U.S.C. § 1952 (2011), was another product of the Kennedy Administration's attack on organized crime. Under it, a person's interstate or foreign travel (or use of the mail) to distribute the proceeds from gambling that is illegal under some other federal or state law, and which furthers or promotes the illegal gambling activity, is a crime punishable up to five years imprisonment and a fine of up to $250,000 for an individual.[25] Customers who take winnings from an illegal gambling operation across state lines or internationally (or use the mail to do so) are not covered by the Act; only a member of a business enterprise which conducts a continuous course of illegal gambling or the enterprise itself are subject to penalty for a Travel Act's violation and then only when they distribute gambling proceeds to their customers. *Erlenbaugh v. United States*, 409 U.S. 239 (1972); CRS: Criminal Law, *supra* n. 9, at 15.

---

24. *See gen.* Jimmy Nguyen & Sean M. Sullivan, *Click to Win: The Risks and Rewards of Pay-to-Play Digital Games of Skill or Chance*, 28 THE COMPUTER & INTERNET LAWYER 9, 11 (Vol. 11, Nov. 2011); ROSE & BOLIN, *supra* n. 8, at 665–66.

25. 28 U.S.C. § 1955, *et. seq.*; *see also, e.g., United States v. Hinojosa*, 958 F.2d 624, 629 (5th Cir. 1992).

The Professional and Amateur Sports Protection Act,
29 U.S.C. §§ 3701–04 (2011)

In the early 1990s, Delaware and Oregon began running state lotteries which took bets on the outcome of NFL games. With pressure from the NFL, NBA, NCAA and others to halt state-sponsored sport betting in its tracks,[26] Congress passed the Professional and Amateur Sports Protection Act ("PASPA"), 29 U.S.C. §§ 3701–04 (2011) which prohibits any governmental entity from sponsoring a wagering enterprise based on the outcome of a professional or amateur sporting contest, and also prohibits any person from participating in the scheme, even if sponsored by the state.[27] PASPA was significant for two reasons. First, it was the first time the federal government preempted a gambling activity that had been made legal by a state.[28] Second, along with the Wire Act, it is one of only two federal statutes that make some form of gambling itself illegal as opposed to the distribution or transfer of gambling proceeds under a law which otherwise makes gambling illegal.

PASPA grandfathered in those states that had legalized sports gambling as of the date of its passage.[29] Further, it gave New Jersey (because of Atlantic City's gambling activities) a year to implement sports betting, and provided that if it did so, it could take advantage of the grandfather clause.[30] There was a spirited debate in New Jersey, but the opposition to sports betting, led by Senator Bill Bradley, won out and New Jersey let its opportunity slip by.[31] Some years later, New Jersey's appetite for sports gambling increased, led by Governor Chris Christie and Senator Raymond Lesniak. The latter mounted a constitutional challenge to the legislation, which was dismissed for lack of standing. *Interactive Media Entm't & Gaming Ass'n v. Holder*, 2011 WL 802106 (D.N.J. Mar. 7, 2011). The former signed sports betting legislation in 2012 and again in 2014, and was quoted telling his supporters at the time, "Let them [the federal government] try to stop us." Sports leagues took up Governor Christie's challenge, and sought to invalidate New Jersey's attempts to invoke PAPSA's grandfather clause in the 2012 and 2014 legislation years after the fact. The cases were finally decided against the State, and the sports books disallowed, by the Third Circuit in *NCAA v. Governor of New Jersey*, 730 F.3d 208 (3d Cir. 2013) and *NCAA v. Governor of New Jersey*, 798 F.3d 259, (3d Cir., 2015), however, rehearing en banc was recently granted by the court, so the issue has not yet been finally settled.

Another "grandfather" issue under PASPA concerned Delaware. As indicated above, Delaware was one of the states that had legalized NFL wagering before PASPA was passed and thus was entitled to continue even after the statute took effect. Its lottery involved a betting on a parlay (a series) of NFL games. Delaware ceased the game a few years after PASPA was passed, but then in 2010, it attempted to start a new, state-licensed, "full service" sports book to drive more business at its "racinos"—race tracks where it had also licensed casino gaming. A number of sports leagues successfully challenged the practice, and the Third Circuit ruled that the grandfather clause only permitted the state to reenact parlay betting on NFL games, and not to open a general sports book. *Office of the Comm'r of Baseball v. Markel*, 579 F.3d 293, 301 (3d Cir. 2009).

Currently only Nevada allows a full spectrum of sports betting.

---

26. CRS: Remote Gambling, *supra* n. 1, at 17.
27. 28 U.S.C. § 3702 (2011).
28. ROSE & BOLIN, *supra* n. 8, at 693.
29. 28 U.S.C. § 3704(a)(1) (2011).
30. 28 U.S.C. § 3704(3)(A) (2011).
31. ROSE & BOLIN, *supra* n. 8 at 693–94.

The Illegal Gambling Business Act, 18 U.S.C § 1955 (2011)

The Illegal Gambling Business Act ("IGBA"), 18 U.S.C. § 1955, authorizes criminal and civil punishment against any individual who owns, conducts, or finances an illegal gambling business. An illegal gambling business is one that: (1) is illegal under state law; (2) involves five or more people who are involved in the enterprise; and (3) has been in continuous operation for thirty or more days and had a gross revenue of $2,000 or more in any one day. Once again, the courts have determined that an individual bettor is not covered by the IGBA, and the statute only applies to those operating an illegal gambling enterprise. *Sanabria v. United States,* 437 U.S. 54, 70, n. 26 (1978).

The IGBA has not yet been applied to Internet gambling and there is a question whether it can be. The Congressional Research Service explains the issue as follows:

> Whether a federal criminal statute applies overseas is a matter of Congressional intent. The intent is most obvious where Congress has expressly stated that a provision shall have extraterritorial application. Section 1955 has no such expression of intended overseas application. In the absence of an explicit statement, the courts use various interpretive aids to divine Congressional intent. Unless some clearer indication appears, Congress is presumed to have intended its laws to apply only within the United States. Congress will be thought to have intended a criminal prosecution to apply outside the United States where one of the elements of the offense, like the commission of an overt act in furtherance of a conspiracy, occurs [outside] the United States. Similarly, Congress will be thought to have intended to outlaw overseas crimes calculated to have an impact in the United States, for example false statements made abroad in order to gain entry into the United States. Finally, Congress will be thought to have intended extraterritorial application for a criminal statute where its purpose in enacting the statute would otherwise be frustrated, for instance, the theft of United States property overseas.

> Section 1955 does not say whether it applies overseas. Yet an offshore illegal gambling business whose customers [are] located within the United States seems within the section's domain because of the effect of the misconduct within the United States.

CRS: Criminal Law, *supra* n. 9, at 12–13 (citations omitted).

The Racketeer Influenced and Corrupt Organizations Act, 18 U.S.C. §§ 1961–1968 (2011)

The Racketeer Influenced and Corrupt Organizations Act ("RICO"), 18 U.S.C. §§ 1961–1968 (2011), makes it a federal crime to directly or indirectly conduct an enterprise which affects interstate or foreign commerce through a pattern of racketeering activity. A pattern of racketeering activity includes at least two acts conducted by the person or enterprise which include: (1) an act of illegal gambling that is a felony under state law; (2) an indictable act under the Wire Act; (3) an indictable act under the Travel Act; or (4) an indictable act under the IGBA.[32]

---

32. 18 U.S.C. § 1962.

RICO violations, including conspiracy to violate RICO even if the defendant does not commit a predicate act, is punishable by imprisonment for not more than twenty years, or by a fine of not more than $250,000 for an individual.

Where we are now

Casinos, and their lawyers, are currently putting all the statutes and interpretations together to decide what they can legally do. As of the publication of this edition, the landscape is as follows:

(1) Four of the federal statutes, RICO, IGBA, the Travel Act and the UIGEA are derivative only, in that they make conduct punishable only if the conduct is a violation of another state or federal gambling statute;

(2) PASPA prohibits non-grandfathered states (now all but Nevada) from authorizing sports books, even for intrastate gambling;

(3) The Wire Act prohibits only Internet wagering on sports, not on gambling generally, and exempts wagers on a sporting event or contest from a State or foreign country where betting on that sporting event or contest is legal, into a State or foreign country in which such betting is legal;

(4) The UIGEA provides that: (1) if states wish to authorize intrastate gaming using the Internet, they may do so, so long as it does not otherwise violate a federal statute, i.e., does not authorize sports gambling in violation of PASPA, so long as the states have geolocation and age verification software; and (2) if a state makes a gambling activity legal, there is no illegality if a bet is placed using the Internet from that state to a place where taking bets on the activity is legal; and

(5) Other than wagering on sporting events in violation of PASPA, only games of chance, not games of skill, are prohibited in most states, the exceptions being Arizona, Iowa, Louisiana, Montana, Utah, and perhaps South Dakota, Tennessee, and Washington.

(6) Depending on the state's interpretation, fantasy sports gambling, such as on fanduel.com and draftkings.com might be legal. This is because some states believe fantasy sports gambling is a game of skill and not chance. In those states where wagering on games of skill are prohibited (*see* the list in "(5)" above) the fantasy sports sites typically do not accept bets, and three states have declared daily fantasy games are games of chance.

(7) Prohibitions under these statutes are not applicable to the individual bettor, only to those involved in the business of gambling, or wagering, or which assist such businesses.

* * *

States and enterprises are just dipping their toes in the water at this point in time, but the current state of affairs can be broken into two, potentially overlapping, areas:

(1) State licensed, intrastate gaming, using videogame devices, like PS4, etc., as well as computers and mobile devices connected to the internet;

(2) Betting on games of skill, including videogames, over the internet.

Each is discussed below:

Intrastate gaming

As of the publication of this edition, two states have made casino-type game wagering over the Internet legal: Nevada (in 2011) and Delaware (in 2012). An operator who wishes to operate a mobile casino must get a license from the state, and have geolocation and age verification applications in place. There are now apps, from casinos and from third parties, that allow Internet-connected, virtual poker games for cash, and in Nevada (because it is grandfathered in under PASPA), there are apps for real-time sports betting.[33] One interesting quirk about Nevada's legislation is that the geolocation requirement is much harsher than just being in-state; the individual bettor must be within a registered gambling site, such as a casino, the airport, or anywhere a slot machine is lawfully placed, in order to legally place a bet. Also, Nevada's statute regarding the enforceability of Internet gambling provides plainly that a wager is an enforceable debt regardless of capacity, meaning that if the age verification software fails and a person under 21 (or even under 18) places a bet, that bet is still enforceable in the Nevada courts.

As noted above, six states have made lawful betting on state lotteries using Internet-connected devices, which could include gaming consoles such as a PS4. In Delaware, a gaming licensee of the Lottery Commission can take Internet bets on casino-style games, such as roulette and video poker, both at terminals found at racinos and anywhere else in the state.

Notes and Questions

1. Given the OLC ruling and the exemptions in the Wire Act and UIGEA, is it legal:

   a. To play Internet poker from either Nevada or Delaware on a site located in a country like Antigua or Costa Rica, where such gambling is legal?

   b. To play Internet poker from a state other than Nevada or Delaware on a site located in a country where such gambling is legal?

   c. To place a bet on a sporting event from any state in the United States to an off shore sports book based in a country where such betting is legal?

Betting on games of skill, including dueling videogames, over the internet

Betting on the outcome of videogames is already a big business, and it is experiencing explosive growth. It is generally of three types. The first type is professional e-Sports betting. Some videogames, such as Riot Games' *League of Legends*, and Valve's *DoTA 2* have professional leagues and teams, much like traditional sports. *See* § 11.30, *supra* (detailing a public performance of *DoTA 2* in Korea). In these tournaments and leagues, millions of dollars in prize money is awarded to winning teams. However, these tournaments also have their own "side action" generated by viewers betting on which team will win. Traditional sports betting sites, like Pinnacle Sports, are already developing their own platforms to edge into the nascent e-Sports market.[34] Furthermore, millions of dollars are being invested in exclusive e-Sports betting portals, such as Voodoo Computer founder Rahul Sood's

----

33. CRS: Remote Gambling, *supra* n. 1, at 6–7.
34. Keith Wagstaff, *Game On: Gamblers Want Part of Rising E-Sports*, NBC NEWS (Nov. 7, 2014, 11:28 AM), http://www.nbcnews.com/tech/video-games/game-gamblers-want-part-rising-e-sports-n242086.

Unikrn.com.[35] However, while these sites are receiving multimillion dollar investments and enjoying exponential growth, at the end of the day, e-Sports are considered legally to be sports, so much so that Pinnacle and Unikrn are wary of violating the Wire Act and PASPA, and so do not accept bets from the United States on the outcome of e-Sports matches. One of the questions is whether videogames are games of skill or chance. Of course there is skill involved, but there is also skill involved in poker. Is there less chance involved in a complex videogame than the flip of a card constituting "the river" in Texas Holdem?

The second type of e-videogame betting is one-on-one betting (or private tournament betting among a number of designated players) based on the outcome of videogames arranged through a gaming website largely designed for such purposes. These sites include gamesaloon.com (based in Michigan), sharkwaters.com (based in the UK), Gspotgaming.com (based in California) and many, many others.[36] Individual gamers find each other on these sites and propose wagers on the outcome of a videogame, or a group of players proposes a tournament among themselves, or are encouraged to do so by the host. The tournaments are then promoted by the site, which takes a cut of the proceeds for its efforts.

Almost all games can now be bet on, from relatively simple games like *Bejeweled* to *Street Fighter II* and *Halo 3*. Wagers can be quite small—we have found sites willing to book games for as little as 25¢—but can also exceed $1,000. Typically, as of the writing of this edition, smaller wagers (less than $10) predominate, and such betting probably really is, as claimed by the principals of these sites, another outlet to make the games more enjoyable for players who are bored with just racking up points or achieving ranks. However, questions persist whether, e.g., a $5 wager will soon be treated like 20,000 points, and larger action demanded.

Once the winner of these contests is declared, reports are sent back to the gaming site, and the site handles the accounting, keeping a percentage of the bet (typically 4–5%) for itself and transferring the remainder from the loser's card or PayPal account to the winner's. Over thousands of even small transactions, the 4–5% adds up. Occasional disputes as to who won have been reported, along with the schemer who loses but reports to the site that he or she won, hoping to abscond with the winnings before the truth can be ferreted out, but the sites are pretty good at self-policing, and savvy gamers are now taking screen shots at the end of the game in case of a later dispute and sending in results quickly. Explanations of the process, including step-by-step guides on how to set up accounts, and which platforms are best for betting on which games, can be found on many sites, including BettingOnVideoGames.com.

The final type of videogame gambling is wagering on fantasy e-Sports. Similar to sites like draftkings.com, which take bets on an assemblage of players from the NFL and other professional sports to make up a fantasy team, e-Sports gambling enterprises have developed their own fantasy league systems. A very popular one of these, Vulcun, allows players to create their own fantasy *League of Legends*, *DoTA 2*, and *Counter Strike* teams and have a chance to pit their fantasy teams against friends or the public for prize money.[37] Other

---

35. Mike Brown, *US Will Legalize E-Sports Betting in Two Years, Says Unikrn Founder*, INTERNATIONAL BUSINESS TIMES, (June 19, 2015, 12:25 PM), http://www.ibtimes.com/us-will-leagalize-e-sports-betting-two-years-says-unikrn-founder-1975274.

36. For a fairly comprehensive list of all such sites, *see* http://www.betfromanywhere.com/blog/play-for-cash-video-game-tournament-sites-roundup-xbox-playstation-pc-games/ (last visited Mar. 9, 2015).

37. VULCUN, https://vulcun.com/ (last visited June 23, 2015).

developers, like *League of Legends'* Riot Games, have also established their own free fantasy league systems where players can create fantasy leagues with their friends that rack up arbitrary points where the only prize won is bragging rights.[38]

Notes and Questions

1. We noted in Chapter 11 that the State Department is allowing gamers to enter the United States to participate in videogame tournaments under the same type of visa granted professional athletes, and in Chapter 1 we noted that some schools are awarding "athletic" scholarships to their student-gamers. Is there a danger that betting on the outcome of videogames could one day be labelled as sports betting and made illegal under PASPA?

2. Although we don't have the statistics, there is abundant anecdotal evidence that teens and young adults bet each other on who could generate the highest pin ball machine scores in early arcades, and bets on the high scores of early videogames, such as *Space Invaders,* is not unheard of. Does the current trend in betting on videogaming over the Internet through legitimate sites pose additional, different, or the same sorts of societal issues?

3. One of the concerns in passing the Wire Act and PASPA is that too much money floating around on sports betting makes it too tempting to bribe a college player, a referee, or even a professional athlete to either throw a game or shade the point spread. Is there any carryover to those concerns for fantasy sports?

4. There have been at least two suits brought which alleged that fantasy sports and fantasy e-Sports are games of chance and not skill. *Humphrey v. Viacom, Inc.*, No. 06-2768, 2007 WL 1797648 (D.N.J. June 20, 2007); *Langone v. Kaiser*, No. 12 C 2073, 2013 WL 5567587 (N.D. Ill. Oct. 9, 2013). Each action was resolved without the skill/chance question being decided. What would you expect the argument to be that such contests are really games of chance?

Looking to the future

As noted in the beginning of this chapter, the legality of Internet gambling in the United States is fast moving. Concerns about the morality of gambling seem to be declining, and coupled with more spending on leisure and states' and municipalities' insatiable need for money, increasing legalization seems inevitable.[39] Various sources identify some seventeen states which have introduced legislation to legalize Internet betting since the OLC Op.[40] As explained earlier, only the enabling legislation in Nevada and Delaware have yet passed, but multiple attempts at legalization legislation have been made in, e.g., California, Massachusetts, Iowa, and New Jersey, and many consider it just a matter of time before an avalanche of such bills become the law of the land. There have also been

----

38. Riot Games, Fantasy LCS, http://fantasy.na.lole-Sports.com/en-US (Last visited June 23, 2015).

39. There is no doubt casino gaming can be lucrative for a state. As of 2012, gaming taxes made up close to 24% of Nevada's annual state budget, roughly equivalent to the 28% made up of sales taxes. CRS: Remote Gambling, *supra*, n.1, at 21.

40. *See, e.g.,* Rose & Bolin, *supra* n. 8, at 679–83; CRS: Remote Gambling, *supra* n. 1, at 20–27; Steven Titch, *Internet Gambling: Keys to a Successful Regulatory Climate*, at 20–28 (Reason Foundation 2012).

attempts at the Congressional level to legalize Internet poker specifically,[41] and Internet gaming generally.[42] However, not all the momentum is towards an expansion of gambling. In 2012, Senators Harry Reid and John Kyle introduced the "Gambling Prohibition, Poker Consumer Protection, and Strengthening the UIGEA Act,"[43] which, *inter alia*, would have prohibited some forms of Internet gambling and strictly regulated Internet poker. Further, Utah recently passed legislation reaffirming that online gambling remains illegal within the state.[44] Nevertheless, despite these occasional bastions of reluctance, the tide toward legalized Internet gambling seems to have turned in favor of expansion.

Videogame distributors will be in the forefront when it does. It is a little guarded secret that one of the reasons Zynga is hosting *Zynga Poker* is that it wants to have the software and systems in place to bring legal poker to Internet devices once such legislation is passed. And Doug Elfman, who covers gaming issues for the *Las Vegas Review Journal* has posed an issue that many videogame and slot machine operators are studying—many Millennials find traditional casino games boring. Pushing a button and seeing a few wheels spin around, video roulette with its mind-numbing twirls of the wheel, or even video poker and blackjack with a sequence of just cards, is pretty tame when compared with fighting orcs and zombies and keeping the world free from enemies. Indeed, many gamers would prefer to play even word or puzzle games to traditional casino games. As such, he predicts that in the near future, a gamer won't have to find another gamer and enter a one-on-one contest to monetize his or her skill in a game, but that casinos, both virtual and brick-and-mortar, will soon let you play *Halo 3* or *World of Warcraft* for money. And the developers of these games will be the only ones with sufficient programming and operational expertise to design and judge what level of skill deserves what level of payout to still leave the casino with an edge. Indeed, he sees a day, not too far off, where as soon as you land at Las Vegas's McCarran airport, for example, and have a qualifying game on your phone, that you will get a text message letting you know that you can play that game for real money right now.[45]

§ 15.20 Regulation of Gambling Equipment in the United States

In the last series of notes above, we considered the issue raised by Mr. Elfman that casino slots are boring to play, and they would not have the popularity they do[46] without the possibility of payout. This could be one reason that casino-type videogames, such as roulette, never appeared in arcades or in bars. Another reason is that many states outlawed them.

---

41. CRS: Remote Gambling, *supra* n. 1, at 25.

42. *Id.* at 24.

43. *Id.* at 25.

44. Rose & Bolin, *supra* n. 8, at 684.

45. Douglas Elfman, *Are Vegas Casinos Ready to Offer Video Game Gambling?*, Las Vegas Review Journal, Oct. 8, 2014, http://www.reviewjournal.com/columns-blogs/doug-elfman/are-vegas-casinos-ready-offer-video-game-gambling.

46. Slot play is incredibly popular at casinos. In 2012, the Congressional research Service estimated that slot machines account for 70% of the revenue on casino floors, up from 40% in the 1970s. This is an average of 90% of revenues in the casinos in North Dakota and Iowa to about 60% in Nevada. CRS: Remote Gambling, *supra*, n. 1, at 12.

Serpico v. Village of Elmwood Park

Appellate Court of Illinois, 2003
799 N.E.2d 961

SMITH, Justice.

Plaintiffs Phillip Serpico and Phil's Sports Bar, Inc. filed a complaint for declaratory judgment against defendants Village of Elmwood Park [and certain named municipal individuals—ED.] ("defendants"), seeking to declare invalid Ordinance 2001-08 prohibiting "simulated video gaming devices" in the village. [T]he trial court granted defendants' motion for summary judgment and found the ordinance to be constitutionally valid. Plaintiffs appeal, contending that video gaming devices possess first amendment protections and that the ordinance does not survive either the strict scrutiny or rational basis test for purposes of determining its constitutionality. Plaintiffs ask that we find the ordinance unconstitutional on its face and reverse the trial court's decision. For the following reasons, we affirm.

BACKGROUND

In May 2001, defendants passed Ordinance 2001-08 (the ordinance), which prohibits anyone from keeping or maintaining simulated video gaming devices within village limits. Specifically, section 39-26 of the ordinance states:

> It shall be unlawful for any person, firm or corporation to keep, locate, maintain or operate any simulated video or mechanical gaming device within the Village.

Village of Elmwood Park Ordinance 2001-08, § 39-26 (May 21, 2001)

Section 39-25(b) defines these devices as follows:

> The term "simulated video or mechanical gaming devices" means any video poker machine, video or mechanical slot machine, video or mechanical bingo machine, or other device which involves any game of chance or amusement based upon poker, blackjack, dog racing, or horse racing, craps, any card or dice game, or any similar device operated by means of the insertion of a coin, token, slug currency, or similar object.

Village of Elmwood Park Ordinance 2001-08, § 39-25(b) (May 21, 2001).

Plaintiff Serpico owns and operates plaintiff Phil's Sports Bar located in the village, and maintained two video slot machines in the bar at the time the ordinance was enacted. After removing the machines, plaintiffs filed a complaint for declaratory judgment. This complaint claimed that the ordinance was unconstitutional because it was vague, overbroad and violated their rights of free speech, equal protection and due process; that its enactment exceeded defendants' police powers; and that defendants were estopped from enforcing it. Plaintiffs also filed a motion for preliminary injunction and a temporary restraining order.

The trial court denied plaintiff's motion for the temporary restraining order and continued the motion for preliminary injunction. Meanwhile, defendants moved to dismiss the cause. The trial court denied defendants' motion, and the cause proceeded through discovery.

On May 16, 2002, the court held that the ordinance, as drafted on its face, was constitutional. With respect to section 39-25(b), the court stated that this section was "very specific about the games that are involved" and that there was an overall "reasonable specificity within this ordinance" to determine which video gaming devices are prohibited. Thus, the court declared that the ordinance was not vague or overbroad. The court further concluded that "the first amendment certainly does not apply" here because there was "[n]o evidence presented in that regard" by plaintiffs. Since no fundamental rights were implicated, the court performed a rational basis test and held that the ordinance "does bear [a] rational relationship to [a] legitimate government [interest] for purposes of regulating gambling" in the village. Accordingly, because the ordinance did not violate constitutional principles and defendants did not supersede their police powers, the court found that there was no basis for estoppel or for the prevention of the ordinance's enforcement in the village.

ANALYSIS

Plaintiffs contend on appeal that the trial court erred in granting defendants' motion for summary judgment because it is clear that the ordinance is unconstitutional. Plaintiffs assert that video gaming devices, as defined in section 39-25(b) of the ordinance, possess first amendment implications that require protection. Plaintiffs further assert that, as such, the ordinance does not survive the strict scrutiny test that courts must employ in this situation because defendants do not have a compelling interest in eliminating these video gaming devices and there are other, less intrusive actions defendants could have taken here. Alternatively, plaintiffs claim that even if these video gaming devices do not have first amendment implications, the ordinance does not survive the less rigorous rational basis test, as it is vague and violative of equal protection principles.

A. Standard of Review

[A] municipal enactment, such as the ordinance in the instant case, enjoys a presumption of validity. To overcome this presumption, the party challenging the ordinance, namely, plaintiffs here, must show by clear and affirmative evidence that the ordinance is "arbitrary, capricious, or unreasonable; that there is no permissible interpretation of the enactment that justifies its adoption; or that the enactment will not promote the safety and general welfare of the public." This is a heavy burden. Accordingly, if there is any room for a legitimate difference of opinion concerning the reasonableness of the ordinance, the legislative judgment of the body that enacted it must prevail.

Plaintiffs' primary contention on appeal is that the video gaming devices as defined in section 39-25(b) of the ordinance possess first amendment implications which merit first amendment protections. Plaintiffs provide us with a discussion tracking the evolution of gaming devices and insist that these have now transformed into a medium of protected expression. As such, plaintiffs contend that the ordinance must meet the requirements of the strict scrutiny test of constitutionality in order to "survive" and, under the circumstances present, the ordinance fails and is therefore unconstitutional.

We too recognize from our review of case law that some video games and gaming devices have undoubtedly evolved from nickel-and-dime-store contraptions into electronic systems which portray fantasies and storylines oftentimes more complex and visually "real" than the most popular literature or television program. However, we disagree with plaintiffs' arguments as they apply to the circumstances before us.

B. Video Gaming Devices and First Amendment Protections

We begin by noting the long-established principle that gambling has traditionally been closely regulated, and even forbidden, without the implication that such restrictions violate the first amendment. Yet, as legal doctrine concerning first amendment rights has progressed, so too has the notion that entertainment, just as political speech, enjoys first amendment protections. However, it has been decisively held that before entertainment may come within this ambit and be accorded such protected status, there must be some element of information or some idea being communicated. *See America's Best Family Showplace Corp. v. City of New York, Dept.*, 536 F. Supp. 170, 173 (E.D.N.Y.1982)

In the arena of video games and video gaming devices, while the line between informing and merely entertaining may be "an elusive one," several courts have reached similar conclusions with respect to whether these games and devices merit first amendment protection. Traditionally, courts blanketly [sic] held that video games were "pure entertainment with no informational element," and as such, could not be characterized as a form of speech protected by the first amendment. *America's Best*, 536 F. Supp. at 174 ("they 'contain so little in the way of particularized form of expression' that video games cannot be fairly characterized as a form of speech protected by the [f]irst [a]mendment"). Subsequently, this notion was modified to incorporate a "context-specific" inquiry. That is, it was recognized that video games and gaming devices, as a medium of expression, must be assessed individually based on their content to determine whether they qualify for first amendment protection. In so doing, the label "video game" lost any talismanic connotation, and no longer was an object bearing this label automatically considered devoid of speech and first amendment concerns. See *Rothner v. City of Chicago*, 929 F.2d 297, 303 (1991) (not all video games can be classified as devoid of first amendment protection, but not all inherently merit this protection either).

However, the courts went further to establish a clear distinction among those video games and devices meriting first amendment protection and those which do not. It has been specifically held that games such as pinball, bingo, blackjack and slots, whether in mechanical or simulated video form, do not constitute protected speech under the auspices of the first amendment. This is because, as the courts have reasoned, the interaction and communication involved in these types of simplistic games is "singularly in furtherance of the game; it is totally divorced from a purpose of expressing ideas, impressions, feelings, or information unrelated to the game itself." The players unassumingly slide a token or coin into these machines and push a button or pull a lever, thereby surrendering any control they may have over the sequence of events that, in the end, yield either fortune or loss. As such, first amendment concerns do not apply.

In direct contradistinction are those video games and devices which courts have denominated as meritorious of free speech protection. Unlike the simplistic nature of bingo and slots, these games involve complex plots, the advancement to different levels, character development, and a "visual and auditory milieu in which [a] story line is played out." *Wilson [v. Midway Games]*, 198 F. Supp. 2d 167 at 181 [(D. Conn. 2002)] (noting first amendment protection applies to video game Mortal Kombat wherein player assumes identity of a character, engages and challenges other characters in battles, and at appropriate time as determined by player employs "finishing move" which is unique to that character); *American Amusement Machine Ass'n v. Kendrick*, 244 F.3d 572 (7th Cir.2001) (*Kendrick*) (video games Gauntlet Legends and Gauntlet Legacy, dealing with fantasy world of eight "realms" and where players assume roles of different "heroes," contain protected expression). In essence, the interaction and communication required of players here involve many more concepts than those simply related to the game itself, including memory, strategy and control over the sequence of events. See *Wilson*, 198 F. Supp. 2d at 182 (noting that these are not comparable to the simplistic pinball machine-type games). Because of these elements, these games are protected under the first amendment. See *Wilson*, 198 F. Supp. 2d at 181.

Applying this distinction to the instant case, it is clear that, contrary to plaintiffs' contention, the video gaming devices listed in section 39-25(b) of the ordinance do not implicate first amendment protections. As noted above, section 39-25(b) lists "any video poker machine, video or mechanical slot machine, video or mechanical bingo machine, or other device which involves any game of chance or amusement based upon poker, blackjack, dog racing, or horse racing, craps, any card or dice game, or any similar device operated by means of the insertion of a coin, token, slug currency, or similar object," as those gaming devices prohibited by the village. Village of Elmwood Park Ordinance 2001-08, § 39-25(b) (May 21, 2001). The games operated through these devices are like those denominated by the courts as not containing an element of information or communicating some idea, such as bingo and pinball. Rather, any communication "is singularly in furtherance of the game [and] totally divorced from a purpose of" expressing speech that would merit protection under the first amendment.

More specifically, we note that plaintiffs challenge section 39-25(b) principally because they maintained two video slot machines in their bar which they were required to remove due to the ordinance's enactment. Case law has undeniably held that slots, as listed in section 39-25(b), are devoid of the requisite communicative and informative elements necessary for first amendment consideration. Plaintiff Serpico's own testimony supports this conclusion: he testified that the video slot machines in his bar did not have characters or storyline plots, but rather, a patron needed only to pull a lever and certain figures inside the machine would spin for an accumulation of points. Thus, by plaintiff Serpico's own admission, one who plays these gaming devices has no control over the sequence of events in the game and does not exert any type of strategy, technique or choice which would transform these devices into a medium of expression implicating first amendment protections.

Plaintiffs rely heavily on *Kendrick*, and *Wilson*. However, these cases are distinguishable on their facts, and the legal rationale presented by those courts actually supports our conclusions here rather than plaintiffs' claims. Factually, none of these cases deal with the type of simplistic video gaming devices listed in section 39-25(b) of the ordinance. Rather, each case, which holds that the video games at issue therein are protected under the first amendment, involves games containing character development, complex storylines, and plot advancement wherein the player actively controls the outcome of the game. See *Kendrick* 244 F.3d 572 (describing the complexity of the six games at issue, including "Ultimate Mortal Kombat 3," "Maximum Force" and "Silent Scope"); *Wilson*, 198 F. Supp. 2d at 181 (discussing intricacies of "Mortal Kombat" wherein players control game and exercise choices to further game). Moreover, both *Kendrick* and *Wilson* make clear the principle that while some video gaming devices are protected under the first amendment, others are not. The determining factor is not whether the game is in "video" form but, rather, whether the game's content displays a communicative or informative element. *See Wilson*, 198 F. Supp. 2d at 181. The *Wilson* court captured the essence of the distinction perfectly:

> In sum, the cases are reconcilable on this point: While video games that are merely digitized pinball machines are not protected speech, those that are analytically indistinguishable from other protected media, such as motion pictures or books, which convey information or evoke emotions by imagery, are protected under the [f]irst [a]mendment. 198 F. Supp. 2d at 181.

The devices challenged in the instant case clearly fall within the former classification, rather than the latter. Accordingly, we find that, contrary to plaintiffs' claims, the video gaming devices listed in section 39-25(b) of the ordinance do not import sufficient communicative, expressive or informative elements to constitute speech protectable under the first amendment.

C. Due Process: Strict Scrutiny Test v. Rational Basis Test

[H]aving found that the ordinance and its regulation of gaming devices as defined in section 39-25(b) do not invoke first amendment rights, the validity of the ordinance must be measured by the lowest level of scrutiny, the rational basis test. Under this test, the ordinance will survive a substantive due process challenge so long as it is rationally related to a legitimate governmental concern. The ordinance need not embody the "best" means of resolving the government's concern or even be the most precisely drawn regulation.

Based on the record before us, we find that plaintiffs have failed to meet their burden of proof in establishing either that there is no legitimate governmental interest here or that the ordinance is not rationally related to such an interest. In fact, the testimony on record clearly indicates a more than viable concern on the part of the village to control and regulate illegal gambling and gaming by prohibiting those simulated video and mechanical devices defined in section 39-25(b) of the ordinance. Braglia testified that, in his experience as police chief of the village, the types of devices most often used for gambling and illegal gaming were those listed in section 39-25(b). Even plaintiff Serpico admitted that, as uncovered in a 1999 police raid, one of his very own bartenders was conducting illegal payouts to patrons who used the video slot machines in his bar.

From this record, it is evident to us that the ordinance survives the rational basis test. Perhaps defendants could have been more precise or more limited in their scope while prohibiting gaming devices which are used for illegal gambling purposes within village borders. [T]he ordinance may in effect ban gaming devices that are not always used for gambling but not prohibit those that sometimes are. However, that the ordinance could have been written in a "better" or more "wise" manner is of no consequence, as long as it is reasonable.

Notes and Questions

1. Given the court's rationale, the city fairly clearly had the authority to ban the games. But you might ask, why would it want to? The answer is that customers at Phil's Sports Bar likely did not go there just to push the "spin" button in a simulated slot machine and accumulate points all night, even though points and replays are all that could be won in the "non-gambling" version of the game. Instead, the fear was that the bar kept track of the high scores for the evening, and then paid off the players in cash, as a means of keeping them in the bar during the course of an evening. As the court in a similar case recognized: "[J]ust because there is no payoff does not mean that there is no illegal gambling occurring. More often than not, a player will gamble on a device but will lose the game. There is no payoff unless a player wins. If players won consistently, there would be no incentive for bar owners to have gaming machines on their premises." *O'Donnell v. City of Chicago*, 842 N.E.2d 208 (Ill. Ct. App. 2005).

2. How does the *Serpico* court distinguish between games that deserve first amendment protection and those that do not?

3. How does *Serpico* differ from the regulation cases in Chapter 12, such as *Brown v. Entm't Merchs. Ass'n*?

4. Is the problem the design of the videogames? That is, would the result in *Serpico* be different if, e.g., the video blackjack manufacturer added the image of a dealer who dispensed strategies and/or odds on when to "hit" the player's hand? If the game would stop every few spins until a digitized voice explained the benefits of Gambler's Anonymous for those who had gambling problems?

Imagine a videogame called *Spin the War Wheel*, which primarily consists of an electronic wheel divided into various sections of varying widths, like a pie chart. Each section had the name of a historic war or battle on it, e.g., World War II, Battle of the Bulge, etc. When the player engages the wheel, it spins around an electronic "clicker" until the player pushes the "stop" button. The wheel then gradually winds down and whichever section the clicker ends up on when the wheel stops is worth points. The larger sections are worth 5 points; the smaller sections are worth more, with the tiny sliver bearing the name "Apocalypse" being worth 1,000 points. The player gets 3 spins for $5, and cannot engage a second or third spin until the machine explains something about the battle that was landed on in the previous spin.

Would such a gambling device be entitled to First Amendment protection, and thus likely be immune from regulation by the City?

Would players play such a machine?

5. Would the type of ordinance in *Serpico* be constitutional in a state that otherwise allowed slot machine gambling, such as Nevada or New Jersey? What about in Delaware now that it has licensed remote roulette and other videogames for money?

---

§ 15.30 Addiction

In Section 13.30, *supra*, we discussed the issue of videogame addiction and explained how it was slowly creeping its way into the accepted lexicon of the Diagnostic Style Manual 5 and psychologists in the United States. Gambling addiction has been part of that lexicon for some time. If gambling is going to be combined with videogaming, it is only logical to think the addiction problems will be exponential.

The question, then, is how does the United States deal with gambling addiction? The answer is: better than it used to, but issues remain. One issue is whether addicted gamblers have any claim either to get their lost money back from the casinos due to their addiction. There are a number of cases, virtually all of which analyze the issue in accordance with the decision below:

Merrill v. Trump Indiana, Inc.

United States Court of Appeals for the Seventh Circuit, 2003.
320 F.3d 729

Evans, Circuit Judge.

Mark Merrill robbed banks in December 1998 and January 1999 and for that activity he was convicted and is now serving time at a federal prison in Florida. But this is not a criminal case dealing with the robberies: it's a civil suit, under our diversity jurisdiction, alleging that a riverboat casino didn't do what it was supposed to do to prevent Merrill from gambling. His substantial gambling losses fueled a need for money, and although his complaint doesn't come right out and say it, Merrill's present predicament can be traced to his need for cash to cover his gambling tab.

Trump Indiana operates a riverboat casino on the shore of Lake Michigan in Gary, Indiana. Mr. Merrill, by his own admission, is a compulsive gambler. Like East and West, this is a twain that should never meet. But it did.

According to the third version of Merrill's complaint, which seeks over $6 million in damages, he entered a clinic for compulsive gamblers in Peoria, Illinois, in 1996. Merrill himself, in 1996, wrote to the casino asking that he be evicted from it if he ever showed up to gamble. And Merrill's name does appear on the casino's "eviction list."

In 1998, Merrill relapsed and returned to gambling at the casino. And now, as we said, he's serving federal time for bank robbery.

Merrill's complaint alleged causes of action for fraud, strict liability, intentional and reckless disregard for others' safety (willful and wanton misconduct), [and] negligence. The district court dismissed the constructive fraud and strict liability claims on a Rule 12(b)(6) motion and, a year later, granted summary judgment for Trump on all other counts. The court concluded that, because Trump owed no statutory or contractual duty to Merrill, it did not act negligently or engage in willful and wanton misconduct.

On appeal, Merrill challenges only the grant of summary judgment on his tort claims. Merrill argues that the court erred in holding that Trump had neither violated a duty of care nor engaged in willful and wanton misconduct when it allowed Merrill to gamble in its casino.

In Indiana, the existence of a tort duty is a question of law. Thus, we review de novo whether Trump owed a duty to Merrill. We resolve the issues in this case as we believe Indiana courts would resolve them.

A defendant is not liable for negligence unless it owes a duty of care to an injured plaintiff. Merrill argues that Indiana statutory provisions and administrative regulations impose a duty on Trump to exclude gamblers who ask to be placed on the casino's eviction list. The Indiana Gaming Commission is empowered by statute to eject or exclude individuals who "call into question the honesty and integrity of the gambling operations." But it is not clear that Merrill's conduct while in the casino put the "honesty and integrity" of Trump's operations in question. Moreover, the statute addresses exclusion by the gaming commission, not the casinos.

Indiana regulations do require casinos to maintain an eviction list, including individuals who request to be excluded, and to prohibit entry to those on the list: "Each riverboat licensee shall maintain a list of evicted persons.... At minimum, the eviction criteria shall include ... [a] person [who] requests that his or her own name be placed on the riverboat licensee's eviction list." But this is a recent amendment, implemented in 2000. In 1998, when Merrill's relapse occurred, no statute or regulation explicitly obligated Indiana casinos to honor self-eviction requests.

Even if the amended regulation applied, however, it is by no means certain that the regulation would sustain a cause of action against Trump. Trump is required by regulation to maintain an exclusion log and to add to that list individuals who request to be put on it. But Trump's obligation to follow regulations promulgated by the Indiana Gaming Commission does not automatically translate into a duty of care owed to compulsive gamblers. At most, the rules impose upon Trump a duty to the state through the gaming commission, not to a self-requesting evictee.

If Trump violates regulations, it must answer to the gaming commission—the current rules provide for administrative and disciplinary hearings, as well as sanctions against casinos, including fines and rescindment of licenses. But neither the regulations nor the statute expressly creates a private cause of action against nonconforming casinos. When a statute is silent regarding the imposition of civil liability, the Indiana Supreme Court looks to legislative intent to determine whether a private cause of action exists As the district court noted, the statutory provisions and administrative rules surrounding gambling are voluminous, and although the legislature was silent regarding civil liability, it specifically created administrative penalties to be enforced through the gaming commission. Given the extent of gambling regulation in Indiana, we conclude that the Indiana Supreme Court would not conclude that the legislature intended to create a private cause of action. *See Hakimoglu v. Trump Taj Mahal*, 70 F.3d 291, 293–94 (3d Cir.1995) (where state intensely regulated casinos without creating cause of action, casino was not liable to plaintiff who suffered extensive gambling losses while intoxicated).

But Merrill also argues that, even in the absence of a statutory duty, Trump owed him a duty of care under common law. We can find no Indiana case addressing the extent of the duty owed by casinos to their patrons. Indeed, it appears that no court has addressed the specific issue whether casinos can be sued in tort when they fail to evict a gambler who requests his own exclusion.

Courts elsewhere that have addressed the liability of casinos to injured plaintiffs have imposed on casinos no higher duty to their patrons than any on other business. *Lundy v. Adamar* of N.J., Inc., 34 F.3d 1173, 1180–81 (3d Cir.1994) (casino had duty to summon aid and take reasonable first aid measures); *Saucier v. Players Lake Charles*, 751 So.2d 312, 319 (La.Ct.App.1999) (casino has duty to take reasonable care of patrons' safety); *Joynt v. Cal. Hotel & Casino*, 108 Nev. 539, 835 P.2d 799, 801 (1992) (casino has duty to maintain reasonably safe premises). Under Indiana law, a business owes its invitees a duty to take reasonable care for their safety. *Ellis v. Luxbury Hotels, Inc.*, 716 N.E.2d 359, 360 (Ind.1999). Merrill never alleged in district court that Trump had not taken reasonable care for his safety or that he ever felt unsafe on the premises.

The closest analogy to Merrill's situation is that of a tavern's liability to exercise reasonable care to protect its patrons. In Indiana, a tavern proprietor serving alcohol can be held liable, under certain conditions, if an intoxicated patron injures another patron or a third party. *E.g., Paragon Family Restaurant v. Bartolini*, 769 N.E.2d 609, 614 (Ind.Ct.App.2002). But a patron who drives while intoxicated, causing his own injuries, cannot recover from the tavern that served him alcohol. *Davis v. Stinson*, 508 N.E.2d 65, 68 (Ind.App.1987). Essentially, Merrill thinks that the casino should be held responsible for the destructive effects of his 1998 relapse into gambling. But Indiana law does not protect a drunk driver from the effects of his own conduct, and we assume that the Indiana Supreme Court would take a similar approach with compulsive gamblers.

Merrill's last argument is that the court erred in granting Trump summary judgment on his willful and wanton misconduct claim. In Indiana, a defendant engages in willful and wanton misconduct when it consciously acts or refuses to act knowing, or with reckless disregard to the probability, that injury will result to the plaintiff from its conduct or from its failure to take steps to avoid an impending danger. The defendant must know that injury is probable or likely, as opposed to possible. Under this standard, we cannot conclude that the district court erred in concluding that Merrill raised no issue of material fact that could lead a jury to find that Trump engaged in willful and wanton misconduct.

Notes and Questions

1. As noted above, almost all cases which have dealt with the issue have held that casinos owe no common law or statutory duty of care to addicted patrons to stop them from gambling. *See, e.g., Williams v. Aztar Ind. Gaming Corp.*, 351 F.3d 294 (7th Cir. Ind. 2003); *Caesars Riverboat Casino, LLC v. Kephart*, 934 N.E.2d 1120 (Ind. 2010). Should a casino owe a duty to keep someone who has voluntarily put himself on the "restricted"

list from gambling in the casino? Is it like "protect[ing] a drunk driver from the effects of his own conduct" when it stems from a recognized addiction?

2. Another question is what are we doing to try and help those with gambling addictions? Estimates of the problem vary, but a typical number is that about 1% of the population of the United States can be classified as "pathological" gamblers, while about 3% are "problem" gamblers,[47] who may or may not end up with financial or social problems depending on the circumstances surrounding them and any help they summon. Although there is a National Council on Problem Gambling, it is primarily a disseminator of information about problem gambling and not a treatment organization. Treatment is left to the states and to private groups, most notably Gambler's Anonymous. About 30 states offer some sort of publicly-funded gambling addiction service, but that figure may be misleading as only about half have even one full time employee working on the issue.[48]

As with addiction to videogame play, other countries seem to be doing better. For example, Canada provides an extensive treatment system for addicted gamblers, both at the national and the province levels,[49] and many Asian countries are pouring resources into the study, treatment, and prevention of gambling addiction.[50]

———

§ 15.40 Abstention

Sometimes owners of video and computer game establishments whose businesses are targeted by state law will challenge those laws in federal court. In some cases, the federal court will hear the challenge, and in others, it will abstain, leaving the matter to be decided by a state court. In general, abstention is appropriate when the federal district *has*, but chooses not to *exercise*, its jurisdiction based on different abstention rules. The subject of abstention is usually reserved for a class in Federal Courts or sometimes Civil Procedure. However, because the regulation of gambling is so state-law specific, it often comes up in cases where the validity of videogame bans or seizures of video equipment on gambling grounds are challenged in federal courts. As such, the basics of abstention are worth knowing for any lawyer who wants to practice in the videogame industry. Several of the different types of abstentions are discussed in the cases below.

* * *

———

47. CRA: Remote Gambling, *supra*, n. 1, at 19.

48. *Id.*

49. *See, e.g.,* Institute of Ontario, https://www.problemgambling.ca/EN/WebSiteLinks/Pages/CanadianResources.aspx (last visited Mar. 10, 2015).

50. *See, e.g.,* David Chim, *Gambling Addiction in Asia: Need for a Medical Perspective*, 2 Asian J. Gambling Issues and Public Health 68 (Oct. 2011).

§ 15.41 *Burford* Abstention

Martin v. Stewart

United States Court of Appeals, Fourth Circuit, 2007
499 F.3d 360

GRIBBON MOTZ, Circuit Judge.

In this case, the district court dismissed federal constitutional challenges to two South Carolina statutes regulating video poker, on the ground that *Burford v. Sun Oil Co.,* 319 U.S. 315 (1943), mandated abstention. Because resolution of these challenges neither requires a court to adjudicate difficult questions of state law, nor disrupts state efforts to establish through a complex regulatory process a coherent policy on a matter of substantial public concern, this case falls well outside the narrow category of cases to which *Burford* abstention may apply. Accordingly, we reverse the judgment of the district court and remand the case for further proceedings consistent with this opinion.

The parties do not dispute the material facts. Jimmy Martin and Lucky Strike, LLC (collectively Martin), brought this action against three South Carolina officials in their official capacities. Martin sought to enjoin enforcement of two South Carolina statutes criminalizing certain "device[s] pertaining to games of chance." S.C.Code Ann. §§ 12-21-2710 & -2712 (2006). Like all statutes regulating "gambling enterprises," such legislation lies well within "the state's police power." Martin does not contend to the contrary, nor does he assert that the South Carolina statutes violate any state law or policy. Rather, Martin maintains that the challenged statutes violate the Constitution of the United States.

The South Carolina legislature enacted the provisions at issue in a 1999 amendment to South Carolina's gambling laws. The first provision, section 12-21-2710, makes it unlawful for a person to "keep on his premises or operate" certain gaming machines, including "device[s] pertaining to games of chance." A violation of this statute constitutes a misdemeanor, punishable by a fine not to exceed $500, imprisonment for no more than a year, or both.

The second challenged provision, section 12-21-2712, directs law enforcement officers to seize machines prohibited by section 12-21-2710 and bring them before a county magistrate. No pre-enforcement mechanism exists for testing a particular machine's legality.

Martin filed this action in federal court in the District of South Carolina, asserting that [both provisions—ED.] violate the Equal Protection and Due Process Clauses of the Fourteenth Amendment. Although the district court had federal question jurisdiction to consider these constitutional claims, see 28 U.S.C. § 1331 (2000), the State moved to dismiss. Believing the *Burford* doctrine required abstention, the district court granted the motion.

We review a district court's decision to abstain under *Burford* for abuse of discretion.

Abstention doctrines constitute extraordinary and narrow exceptions to a federal court's duty to exercise the jurisdiction conferred on it. To cabin that discretion and ensure that abstention remains the exception, not the rule, the Supreme Court has carefully defined the areas in which such abstention is permissible. In this case, the district court relied solely on *Burford* abstention.

The *Burford* doctrine justifies the dismissal of a federal action in a narrow range of circumstances. *Burford* permits abstention when federal adjudication would "unduly intrude" upon "complex state administrative processes" because either: (1) there are difficult questions of state law whose importance transcends the result in the case then at bar; or (2) federal review would disrupt state efforts to establish a coherent policy with respect to a matter of substantial public concern. Courts must balance the state and federal interests to determine whether the importance of difficult state law questions or the state interest in uniform regulation outweighs the federal interest in adjudicating the case at bar.

This balance only rarely favors abstention.

Martin seeks a single remedy: an injunction against the enforcement of sections 12-21-2710 and 12-21-2712. He maintains that these statutes violate his Due Process and Equal Protection rights under the Fourteenth Amendment of the United States Constitution. Specifically, Martin argues that section 12-21-2710, which provides for criminal penalties, is void for vagueness because it fails to give fair notice of forbidden conduct and allows arbitrary enforcement, thus violating the Due Process Clause. He also contends that the failure of both statutes to provide a pre-enforcement mechanism for determining the legality of an amusement device and the State's discriminatory enforcement of these statutes violates the Equal Protection Clause.

The Due Process challenge to section 12-21-2710 involves no difficult question of state law because, as the State itself recognizes, and in fact argues, section 12-21-2710 is well defined by the [Supreme Court of South Carolina's] many interpretations.

Indeed, in *State v. DeAngelis*, 183 S.E.2d 906, 908 (1971), the state court rejected a vagueness challenge to precisely the same language — "games of chance of whatever name or kind" — that Martin targets, holding that "[a]n analysis of [the statute's] wording convinces us that a man of reasonable intelligence is given fair notice of the machines proscribed [and that] the statute cannot be used in a capricious or discriminatory manner."[51] Thus, the state law component of a vagueness challenge — whether limiting constructions apply to the language — is settled: the State's highest court has expressly held that the statutory text is to be given its ordinary meaning. The remaining question — whether the statute's ordinary meaning is unconstitutionally vague — is a matter of federal law.

For similar reasons, Martin's discriminatory enforcement claim presents no difficult question of state law. To prevail on that claim, Martin must demonstrate that (1) he was similarly situated to persons not prosecuted; and (2) a discriminatory purpose motivated this different treatment. *See United States v. Armstrong*, 517 U.S. 456, 465–66 (1996). The first inquiry requires a court to determine which video poker machines are prohibited by statute, but such an inquiry hardly involves a difficult state law question given that *DeAngelis* held that "a [person] of reasonable intelligence is given fair notice of the machines proscribed." 183 S.E.2d at 908. If the district court should determine that state law enforcement treats

---

51. The dissent makes the exceedingly odd argument that the *DeAngelis* holding that the term "games of chance" must be given its ordinary meaning somehow renders the statute more difficult to interpret and that we engage in "circular" reasoning in holding to the contrary. In fact, *DeAngelis* resolves any possible difficult state law question and directs a long recognized mode of statutory construction that federal courts are well equipped to undertake. Equally unavailing is the dissent's suggestion that advances in gambling technology have lessened *DeAngelis's* significance. The Supreme Court of South Carolina has specifically rejected an argument that technological changes lessen the force of its prior interpretations of gambling statutes. *See State v. 192 Coin-Operated Video Game Machs.*, 525 S.E.2d 872, 878–79 (2000) ("Although slot machines have changed since the 1960s, the substance of [section 12-21-2710] has not. The relevant portions of the current version outlaw the same conduct as its predecessor."). That the South Carolina legislature has revised its gambling statutes without further defining "games of chance," provides additional support for finding DeAngelis continues to be authoritative. *Id*. at 879 ("The legislature is presumed to be aware of [the South Carolina Supreme] Court's interpretation of its statutes. If the General Assembly considered [the Court's interpretations] outdated, it could have changed the statute....") (citations omitted).

parties similarly situated under the statute differently, the remaining question is purely federal—whether an impermissible purpose motivated this different treatment. Therefore, none of Martin's challenges presents difficult questions of state law, let alone difficult questions whose importance outweighs the federal interest in adjudicating Martin's claims.

Nor do any of Martin's claims threaten a state interest in uniform regulation. Martin launches a facial attack on the state statutes as a whole—precisely the sort of case federal courts often and expertly entertain. If Martin should succeed, the district court would enjoin all enforcement of the statutes at issue; such relief could not possibly threaten their uniform application.

Moreover, contrary to the State's suggestion, "there is, of course, no doctrine requiring abstention merely because resolution of a federal question may result in the overturning of a state policy." *Zablocki v. Redhail*, 434 U.S. 374, 379–80 n. 5 (1978). Therefore, "the threat that the federal courts might decide the entire state system unconstitutional is not a valid justification for *Burford* abstention." Rather, this "sort of risk is present whenever one attacks a state law on constitutional grounds in a federal court."

Although the dissent concedes that "abstention must be carefully cabined," and takes no issue with our statement of the *Burford* doctrine, it would hold that the district court properly abstained here. It relies on factors totally irrelevant to the "extraordinary and narrow" *Burford* doctrine, e.g., the absence of a federal gambling statute, the effect of the Fourteenth Amendment and 42 U.S.C. §1983 (2000) on federal-state relations, the history of gambling regulation, the burdens of discovery, and the alleged federalization of gambling policy. The dissent fails to apply the actual *Burford* doctrine because it cannot—if it did so it would have to hold that the district court abused its discretion in abstaining here.

The dissent's analysis appears to be motivated by its preference that cases like Martin's be brought in state court. *See*, e.g., post at 372 ("I see no indication in this case that the South Carolina state courts have defaulted in any fashion on their obligation to entertain federal constitutional challenges to the operation of state gambling laws."). Although we share the dissent's respect for our state colleagues, "[w]hen a Federal court is properly appealed to in a case over which it has by law jurisdiction, it is its duty to take such jurisdiction.... The right of a party plaintiff to choose a Federal court where there is a choice cannot be properly denied." Martin chose to file his claims in a federal forum created by Congress—we cannot deny him that choice even if we disagree with it.

Because Martin's claims do not meet the "extraordinary and narrow" criteria for *Burford* abstention, the judgment of the district court is REVERSED AND REMANDED.

WILKINSON, Circuit Judge, dissenting.

There are few decisions more central to state authority than whether to allow legalized gambling, how extensively, and under what terms. Plaintiffs' lawsuit calls for both the interpretation of state law at the heart of the state's regulatory scheme and an extensive inquiry into the state's enforcement practices. While plaintiffs may certainly challenge South Carolina's exercise of its police powers as unconstitutional, the district court was within its authority to conclude that plaintiffs' constitutional challenge would be most properly heard in state court.

I see no indication in this case that the South Carolina state courts have defaulted in any fashion on their obligation to entertain federal constitutional challenges to the operation of state gambling laws. I see no way in this case to avoid the interpretation of difficult questions of state law and interference with state regulatory policies. I see no sign in this case that interpretation of the terms of any federal statute involving gambling is at issue or that Congress has done anything to remove the choice among different approaches to gambling regulation from its historic venue in the states.

Federal courts have reason to tread cautiously in addressing a state's regulation of gambling, because such schemes of regulation lie at the heart of the state's police power. In fact, few activities have been so consistently treated as being at the core of state sovereignty. Id. South Carolina, in particular, has long exercised its police power in this area, developing over time a complex and comprehensive system to regulate gambling activity.

The Supreme Court has treated the regulation of gambling as a quintessential state function for more than a century. *See United States v. Edge Broad. Co.*, 509 U.S. 418, 426 (1993) I would be hard-pressed to identify any field of regulation about which there is broader or deeper consensus on the appropriateness of state control.

For decades, the South Carolina General Assembly has sought to balance "the revenue gained from licensing and taxation of [gambling] against the social costs of gambling addiction." In doing so, the General Assembly has tried a number of plans to determine the appropriate level of gambling control, and has developed numerous mechanisms to enforce its regulations.

South Carolina has long employed a multitiered regulatory structure — comprised of legislative, executive, administrative, and judicial mechanisms — to enforce its gambling laws. Currently, no fewer than five different state entities are part of this effort. In sum, South Carolina has established a specialized scheme to interpret and enforce laws that lie at the center of state sovereignty.

As the district court recognized, abstention was warranted here because plaintiffs' lawsuit threatens to trammel South Carolina's highly reticulated regulatory regime. Plaintiffs raise three claims. First, they assert that § 12-21-2710's prohibition against possessing any "device pertaining to games of chance of whatever name or kind" is void for vagueness. Second, plaintiffs challenge South Carolina's gambling scheme on equal protection grounds, asserting that they are "being subjected to discriminatory enforcement of the laws pertaining to video game machines. . . ." Finally, plaintiffs challenge the post-seizure procedure by which South Carolina determines the legality or illegality of a particular video gaming device. The district court was entitled to abstain from deciding these claims, for reasons I shall discuss in turn.

Plaintiffs first claim that the provision forbidding "devices pertaining to games of chance of whatever name or kind" is void for vagueness on the theory that "its prohibitions are not clearly defined." *Grayned v. City of Rockford*, 408 U.S. 104, 108 (1972). Specifically, plaintiffs contend that this provision could be read to outlaw Monopoly, simple card games, and personal computer and cell phone games such as minesweeper and solitaire. Contrary to the majority's contention that plaintiffs' challenge "involves no difficult question of state law," plaintiffs' claim that "games of chance" is "not clearly defined" is certainly plausible enough that the district court's decision to abstain cannot be considered an abuse of discretion. Indeed, federal court involvement here will interfere with the detailed, individualized analysis required to determine what constitutes a "game of chance" and will inescapably intrude upon South Carolina's regulatory system.

In this case, in order to evaluate plaintiffs' vagueness challenge, the federal court would have to define "games of chance," a task it cannot complete without delving into the "meaning, interpretations, and the general regulatory context" of § 12-21-2710. The meaning and precise application in any given case of "games of chance" lie at the core of South Carolina's regulation of gaming .

The majority's conclusion that no "difficult question of state law" is presented here is astounding, insofar as its basis is the South Carolina Supreme Court's 1971 holding that "a man of reasonable intelligence is given fair notice of the machines proscribed" by the provision. While the majority says that the statutory text is "clear and certain" because it is given its "ordinary meaning," that circular formulation begs the question of what its ordinary meaning even is. Far from being "clear and certain," the provision outlawing "games of chance" is one that South Carolina state courts must apply, on a machine-by-machine basis, to a complex and ever-changing cadre of gambling technology. Indeed, the development of video gaming machine technology and of the state courts' application of § 12-21-2710 to that technology demonstrate that the meaning and treatment of "games of chance" present "difficult questions of state law" from which the district court legitimately abstained.

For starters, not even primitive versions of the video gaming machines involved in this case were in existence at the time of *DeAngelis*. Such machines did not become commercially viable until the mid- to late-1970s, when it first became economical to combine a television-like monitor with a central processing unit. In fact, it was not until Si Redd's Coin Machines (SIRCOMA) introduced Draw Poker in 1979 that such devices gained any measure of popularity. *See* Ireck Galecki, "Video Poker History," Dec. 6, 2006, available at http://onlinecasinopress.co.uk/video-poker-history.html (last visited July 19, 2007). Although the language "games of chance" can be found in the gaming statute as of 1971, S.C.Code Ann. § 5-621 (Code 1962), and the current statute, S.C.Code Ann. § 12-21-2710, the former was not part of a larger statutory provision that includes reference to any type of video gaming device. And although the majority is correct that "slot machines have changed since the 1960s, [while] the substance of [section 12-21-2710] has not," the difficult task of distinguishing lawful from unlawful games has been complicated dramatically by these technological developments. In fact, technological developments in the thirty-six years since *DeAngelis* bear very directly on the line of demarcation between prohibited "games of chance" and permitted "games of skill." Indeed, what may have been clear to a "man of reasonable intelligence" regarding this distinction in 1971 can simply no longer be so.

My friends in the majority, however, refuse to allow the state courts to undertake the delicate task of distinguishing between lawful and unlawful games. Because South Carolina's gaming statutes justifiably call for a machine-by-machine determination of legality, the majority's notion that it somehow can interpret "games of chance" in bulk, without disrupting South Carolina's enforcement scheme, rides roughshod over the scheme itself and the principles of federalism it purports to observe.

It is thus no simple task for the South Carolina courts to interpret and apply § 12-21-2710, which is entrenched in a highly reticulated regulatory scheme, to a range of ever-changing, technologically advanced devices. The majority's insistence that the district court abused its discretion in abstaining, however, will complicate state tasks immeasurably. It threatens to disrupt the State's attempt to ensure uniformity in the treatment of an 'essentially local problem. *Burford* abstention exists to protect complex state administrative processes from undue federal interference. Indeed, a case like this one, in which the federal court is called upon to resolve a difficult question of state law bearing on policy problems of substantial public import whose importance transcends the result in the case then at bar," provides a paradigmatic example of the circumstances justifying *Burford* abstention. To say the district court abused its discretion in abstaining is beyond erroneous.

Despite the "facial" label applied to their discriminatory enforcement claim, plaintiffs' requested discovery here would put South Carolina's regulatory regime through the wringer. And as the suit moves forward, the district court will assuredly be forced to confront unsettled areas of state law—a problem that easily could have been avoided through adherence to traditional abstention principles.

Indeed, taken for what it truly is, plaintiffs' equal protection challenge inevitably requires a detailed probing of South Carolina's enforcement scheme. Thus, it was clearly not an abuse of discretion to abstain from adjudicating this claim.

Plaintiffs finally claim that South Carolina's post-seizure forfeiture scheme violates due process. To say that the district court abused its discretion here is to ignore Burford's counsel that abstention is appropriate when federal review would disrupt state efforts to establish a coherent policy with respect to a matter of substantial public concern. The district court was entitled to leave undisturbed the considered judgment of the South Carolina Supreme Court that the forfeiture of gaming machines pursuant to §§ 12-21-2710 and 2712 accords with due process requirements. *See 192 Coin-Operated Video Game Machs.*, 525 S.E.2d. at 883.

While "there is, of course, no doctrine requiring abstention merely because resolution of a federal question may result in the overturning of state policy," *Zablocki v. Redhail*, 434 U.S. 374, 380 n. 5 (1978), "[t]he adequacy of state court review diminishes plaintiffs' interest in a federal forum," and when—as here—a plaintiff's claims could also be raised in state court, this "militates in favor of abstention."

The South Carolina Supreme Court has rendered measured judgment on this issue; all federal intervention can potentially do at this stage is create a conflict with that judgment and throw South Carolina's efforts to regulate gambling into confusion. Indeed, for reasons discussed throughout, the state's interest in having its rulings preserved is uniquely strong here, as all branches of South Carolina's government have spent considerable time and energy shaping and reviewing the statutes being challenged. I do not suggest the district court was obligated to abstain, but neither do I think for a moment that its decision to do so was anything close to an abuse of discretion.

The very fact of dual systems of government and dual systems of courts creates some potential for inefficiencies and confusion. Abstention is one of those sparingly utilized means necessary to smooth the roughest edges and produce a more harmonious system. The majority does more, however, than exacerbate tensions. It authorizes lawsuits that will begin slowly to federalize—in all its aspects—questions of state gambling policy. It will do what Congress has declined to do. The majority deprives the state of a significant measure of control over issues touching not simply the pros and cons of gambling but the very tone and quality of life within state borders. This is not federalism. I respectfully dissent.

---

§ 15.42 *Younger* and *Colorado River* Abstention

Taylor v. Siegelman

United States District Court, Northern District of Alabama, 2002
230 F. Supp. 2d 1284

Johnson, District Judge.

This case came on to be heard on the plaintiffs' motion for temporary restraining order and interlocutory injunction.

[Plaintiffs are owners of video game establishments. They had their machines seized by police pursuant to Alabama statutes prohibiting video games that can be used for gambling. Various actions in the Alabama state courts challenging the statutes under which the seizures were made were pending at the time of filing this suit. Nevertheless, these plaintiffs brought suit in federal court challenging the constitutionality of all the seizures under the federal constitution. — ED.]

Factual Background

The plaintiffs are an assortment of individuals and individuals doing business as owners of video gaming establishments. Plaintiffs seek a declaratory judgment from this court that the seizure of their video gaming machines are illegal under Alabama law, pursuant to 28 U.S.C. §§ 2201 and 2202. Further, the plaintiffs want this court to declare portions of the Alabama Code unconstitutional as void for vagueness. The plaintiffs also request a return of the machines seized by the various defendants to date on the theory that such seizures amount to takings without just compensation. The plaintiffs sue pursuant to 42 U.S.C. § 1983 for violations of their 4th, 5th, and 14th Amendment rights, seeking injunctive and declaratory relief.

In their complaint, plaintiffs sue for a violation of the 14th Amendment for "unlawful takings without just compensation and enforcement of the Attorney General's opinion violates plaintiffs' due process rights" under 42 U.S.C. § 1983 (Count I); a violation of the 14th Amendment for unlawful deprivation of property without due process, pursuant to 42 U.S.C. § 1983 (Count II); a violation of their due process rights by seizing property denominated contraband without legal authority (Count III); defendants' failure to provide adequate post-deprivation procedural due process (Count IV); and that defendants are taking plaintiffs' property in reliance on an "unconstitutionally vague" scheme (Count V).

THE MOTIONS TO DISMISS

Due to the dispositive nature of the motions to dismiss, the court considers these motions before the preliminary injunction. The court finds that, under the abstention doctrine, this court should not reach any decision on the merits of this case. While the plaintiffs have artfully stated their claims as unconstitutional takings without just compensation, the court finds the pivotal question here is really whether or not the machines in question are legal under Ala.Code § 13A-12-76, or fall within Ala.Code § 13A-12-20(5), which defines a "gambling device" and Ala.Code § 13A-12-30(a) which states that gambling devices are subject to forfeiture to the state. If said machines are illegal gambling devices, the plaintiffs' claims of unlawful seizures must fail. This is the very question currently pending in Alabama courts.

In *Younger v. Harris*, 401 U.S. 37, 42 (1971), a case concerning federal review of the constitutionality of a state law, the United States Supreme Court stated that "[a] federal lawsuit to stop a prosecution in a state court is a serious matter."

The precise reasons for this longstanding public policy against federal court interference with state court proceedings have never been specifically identified but the primary sources of the policy are plain. One is the basic doctrine of equity jurisprudence that courts of equity should not act, and particularly should not act to restrain a criminal prosecution, when the moving party has an adequate remedy at law and will not suffer irreparable injury if denied equitable relief. This underlying reason for restraining courts of equity from interfering with criminal prosecutions is reinforced by an even more vital consideration, the notion of 'comity,' that is, a proper respect for state functions, a recognition of the fact that the entire country is made up of a Union of separate state governments, and a continuance of the belief that the National Government will fare best if the States and their institutions are left free to perform their separate functions in their separate ways. *Id.*, 401 U.S. at 43–44. The Court continued: This brief discussion should be enough to suggest some of the reasons why it has been perfectly natural for our cases to repeat time and time against that the normal thing to do when federal courts are asked to enjoin pending proceedings in state courts is not to issue such injunctions. *Id.*, 401 U.S. at 45.

The Eleventh Circuit Court of Appeals has stated that *Younger* stands for "a basic doctrine of equity jurisprudence ... that courts of equity should not act, and particularly should not act to restrain a criminal prosecution, when the moving party has an adequate remedy at law and will not suffer irreparable injury if denied equitable relief." *Luckey v. Miller*, 976 F.2d 673, 676 (11th Cir.1992). The plaintiffs argue that the *Younger* abstention doctrine does not apply to the facts before this court because they will not be afforded adequate protection should this court abstain.

However, as the court noted above, all of the plaintiffs' arguments are based on the assumption that their machines are legal under Ala.Code § 13A-12-76. The various State defendants strenuously disagree. Thus, without first determining whether under Alabama law these machines are legal or illegal gambling devices, this court can make no further determinations—and the issue of the legality of these machines is not an appropriate question for this court to address under *Younger*. The determination of the legality of the machines is wholly a matter of state law.

Additionally, the Court in *Colorado River Water Dist.* [*v. United States*, 424 U.S. 800 (1976)] stated that abstention is appropriate where "absent bad faith, harassment, or a patently invalid state statute, federal jurisdiction has been invoked for the purpose of restraining state criminal proceedings," 424 U.S. at 816, citing *Younger, supra.*

The plaintiffs also assert that no procedure in Chapter 15 of the Alabama Code provides pre- or post-deprivation hearings for a person whose property has been taken by the State. However, before asserting that state law remedies are inadequate, the plaintiffs must avail themselves of these remedies, which they have failed to do. Under § 15-5-3, Ala.Code and Rule 3.9, Alabama Rules of Criminal Procedure, a search warrant can only be issued on probable cause, supported by an affidavit naming or describing the person and particularly the place to be searched. Under § 15-5-5, Ala.Code, the judge or magistrate must issue the warrant if he or she is satisfied of the grounds of the application or that there is probable ground to believe their existence. Under § 15-5-15, if the grounds on which a search warrant was issued should be controverted, the judge must proceed to hear testimony. Under § 15-5-16 and Rule 3.13, Alabama Rules of Criminal Procedure, the judge must direct the property to be restored to the person from whom it was taken if it appears there was no probable cause for believing the existence of the ground on which the warrant was issued. These state procedures provide a remedy at law which, in essence, is the same remedy plaintiffs seek in federal court in the form of an injunction and declaratory judgment.

Thus, the court finds the plaintiffs have more than adequate remedies available to them in the state courts, none of which have been exercised. The plaintiffs are not entitled to instead seek the opinion of a United States District Judge on the question of whether or not their machines are legal under Alabama law, especially when this very question is pending before the Alabama courts.

The court having found that this case is not properly before it on the basis of the abstention doctrine, the court is of the opinion that each of the defendant's motions to dismiss is due to be granted. The court shall so grant said motions and DISMISS THIS CASE by separate Order.

Notes and Questions

1. How are the *Younger/Colorado River* and *Burford* abstention doctrines different from each other?

2. Of the three different types, *Younger* abstention appears to be the most commonly argued in videogame cases. Typically the cases involve an owner of a video arcade or the like who brings a case in federal court seeking a declaration invalidating the state's statutory scheme on federal constitutional or other grounds. The state defends, arguing that the state's courts are the ones which should decide state law, and that they are perfectly able to handle any collateral federal issues. For an example of a case applying *Younger* abstention in the video arcade arena, *see Playtime Games, Inc. v. City of New York, Dep't of Bldg.* 535 F. Supp. 1069 (E.D.N.Y. 1982).

3. Judge Wilkinson, the dissenter in *Martin*, maintains that abstention is appropriate, among other reasons, as a matter of federalism. Apart from whether this is a correct application of *Burford* abstention, does the state's role in regulating gambling mean that a federal challenge to the constitutionality of the entire scheme should generally be inappropriate?

Chapter Sixteen

Anticompetitive Issues

This chapter deals with four issues relating to the competitive behavior of companies in the videogame industry. The first pertains to activities of videogame producers that violate antitrust laws. While, overall, the videogame industry is a very competitive one, there are segments in which various parties are accused of taking illegal actions to create a monopoly for themselves. This subject is discussed below further in § 16.20.

The second issue occurs when a videogame defendant is accused of making a misleading statement about its game, e.g., on the game box, in an ad, or perhaps in a public statement like a press release. The rights of those who can assert competitive injury as a result of such misrepresentations are discussed in § 16.30.

Third, the anticompetitive practices known as "business torts," which can occur when two formerly happy contractual partners become enmeshed in litigation with each other after things turn sour, are analyzed in § 16.40.

Finally, cybersquatting, where an individual takes a domain name with a trademarked videogame name or derivative thereoff, is discussed in § 16.50.

§ 16.10 Antitrust Law: A Primer

Before studying the antitrust cases in § 16.20 below, we wanted to provide a brief guide as to some basic antitrust statutes for those who are not familiar with them.

Antitrust law is concerned with curbing monopoly power. The reason that we have laws to curb such power is that a true monopolist can raise prices beyond a competitive level, which may help the monopolist, but can hurt consumers and the economy as a whole. If monopolistic economic power does not exist, a party will not succeed in the market if it attempts to raise prices exorbitantly. If, for example, Sony charged $10,000 for the next Play Station platform, or Rockstar tried to sell the next iteration of *Grand Theft Auto* for $750, consumers would go elsewhere pretty quickly, as these companies do not have monopoly power. There are some narrow segments of the videogame industry in which some believe free competition does not exist, and this is where antitrust law steps in.

When lawyers speak of "antitrust" laws, they generally mean a compilation of three different acts, along with their state-law counterparts: (1) The Sherman Act of 1890 (codified at 15 U.S.C. §§ 1–7); (2) the Clayton Act of 1914 (15 U.S.C. §§ 12–27 and 29 U.S.C. §§ 52–

53)[1]; and (3) the Federal Trade Act, also passed in 1914 (15 U.S.C. §§ 41–58). Litigation occurs mostly under the first two statutes; brief descriptions of them follow.

Sherman Act

The Sherman Act has two major sections, § 1 and § 2. Section 1 prohibits concerted actions which unreasonably restrain trade. Section 1 of the Sherman Act makes it illegal to form any "contract, combination in the form of trust or otherwise, or conspiracy, in restraint of trade or commerce among the several States." 15 U.S.C. § 1. To prevail on a claim under this section, a plaintiff must show: "(1) that there was a contract, combination, or conspiracy; (2) that the agreement unreasonably restrained trade under either a *per se* rule of illegality or a rule of reason analysis; and (3) that the restraint affected interstate commerce." *Tanaka v. Univ. of S. Cal.*, 252 F.3d 1059, 1062 (9th Cir. 2001).

Section 2 of the Sherman Act, 15 U.S.C. § 2, makes it an offense to monopolize, attempt to monopolize, or combine or conspire to monopolize. Unlike § 1, concerted action among two or more entities or people are not needed for a § 2 violation and a single company can violate the statute. As the Supreme Court has put it: "The offense of monopoly under § 2 of the Sherman Act has two elements: (1) the possession of monopoly power in the relevant market and (2) the willful acquisition or maintenance of that power as distinguished from growth or development as a consequence of a superior product, business acumen, or historic accident." *U.S. v. Grinnell Corp.*, 384 U.S. 563, 570–71 (1966). Violations of § 2 in this chapter are always judged on a "rule of reason" basis, and a company can violate it either by impermissibly obtaining monopoly power or attempting to gain monopoly power in an impermissible way.

As indicated above, *per se* violations are found under § 1, and only when there is no viable rationale to justify the existence of the challenged practice. The classic example of a *per se* violation is horizontal price fixing between competitors to keep prices at an artificially high level for consumers. *See, e.g., Arizona v. Maricopa County Medical Soc.,* 457 U.S. 332 (1982).

Under a "rule of reason" test for claims brought both under § 1 and § 2 the totality of the circumstances are analyzed to determine whether the challenged practice overall promotes or suppresses competition and consumer choice, and whether the monopoly power was acquired in a permissible manner. *See, e.g., U.S. v. Grinnell Corp.*, 384 U.S. 563, 570–71 (1966).

The process to find a violation under the rule of reason can be tricky procedurally in certain cases, as explained in the *O'Bannon* decision in § 16.20, where the plaintiff must establish a *prima facie* case, which shifts the burden to the defendant to establish the pro competitive aspects of the challenged practice, which, if done, shifts the burden back to the plaintiff to establish lesser restrictive alternatives that would allow the pro competitive aspects of the practice to continue, but with less of a drag on the market. But throughout this burden shifting, you should keep in mind that a rule of reason analysis acknowledges that some aspects of the challenged practice promote competition, while other aspects do not. It is up to the court to balance which of those predominates, and if the latter outweighs the former, then a court attempts to find an approach that will preserve most of the pro-competitive aspects of the practice while lessening the aspects of the practice that are objectionable.

If you are unfamiliar with antitrust, it may seem odd that monopoly power under the rule of reason can be acceptable if acquired the "right" way, but that very same monopoly

---

1. The Clayton Act was modified by the Robinson-Patman Act of 1936 (15 U.S.C. § 13).

pricing power can violate the Sherman Act if it was acquired the "wrong" way. This can be explained by illustration. For example, suppose there was one bar review company in the United States, and assume it faced no competition because it produced a superior product and no other competitor believed that it could do nearly the same job for a similar price. The bar review company has monopoly power, but because it was acting alone in acquiring it, there is no § 1 violation; and because it did nothing "wrong" to achieve its power, there is no § 2 violation either.

Now assume again there is only one bar review company in the United States, but this time it is because there used to be two companies, but the survivor recently acquired the competitor. It is not illegal for one company to acquire another and there can be pro-competitive consequences flowing from mergers and acquisitions, such as streamlined administrative operations; only needing to hire one set of lecturers to travel to lecture sites; elimination of duplicative outlines and other printed materials for those studying for the bar, etc. But if the successor acquired the other solely to eliminate competition in the marketplace and increase the price of the bar review to recent law school graduates, there is an anti-competitive effect as well. Balancing the competing actions, effects, intents, etc. of a company's practice is at the heart of the rule of reason analysis. If a court were to decide that the acquisition had an anti-competitive effect overall and was consummated for an improper reason, then a violation would likely be found.

Another potentially new (to the student) concept in antitrust cases is a discussion about "markets." There are two: product and geographic. The reason that these markets are important can be illustrated as follows. Suppose Grocery Store in Town X enters into several exclusive dealing contracts with local farmers so that it ends up with the only supply of apples to sell in Town X. Whether entering into those exclusive dealing contracts violates antitrust law starts with defining the relevant product market. If the relevant market is "apples," it has monopoly power in that market. If the relevant market is "summer fruit," however, then Grocery Store probably does not have a monopolist's economic power, because if it raises the price of apples too much, people will buy more peaches, plums, etc. Thus, the more broadly the product market is defined, the less product market "power" Grocery Store would have.

Deciding the proper product market depends, in part, on whether consumers will look to related products as acceptable substitutes, i.e., if the price for apples rises, will the sales of other fruits increase. The fancy name used by economists for the potential interchangeability of other items, like using a peach instead of an apple, is "cross-elasticity of demand." *See, e.g., Brown Shoe Co. v. United States*, 30 U.S. 294, 325 (1962) stating, "The outer boundaries of a product market are determined by the reasonable interchangeability of use or the cross-elasticity of demand between the product itself and substitutes for it." That is, if there is high cross-elasticity of demand, then the market must be defined more broadly and the alleged monopolist's pricing power is low. However, if Grocery Store raised the price of apples sharply and consumers continued to purchase them because they felt they had no other choice to get the benefits of apples, there is little cross-elasticity of demand, and Grocery Store might well have monopoly power in the relevant product market. Having monopoly power is not determinative of an antitrust violation, but it is a necessary first component in the analysis.

Geographic markets are also important under § 2. If there are no exclusive dealing contracts for apples that affect the supply of apples available in the stores of Town Y, which can be reached in two minutes by car from Grocery Store in Town X, then again Grocery Store probably has no monopoly pricing power in the relevant geographic market. That is, if Grocery Store artificially raises the price of apples in Town X, consumers can easily go to Town Y and purchase them more cheaply. But if the only store around for 50 miles is Grocery Store, we would likely analyze it differently.

Once it is decided that the company in question has monopoly power in both the product and geographic markets, the analysis turns to how it got that power, and how it is using that power, i.e., the balancing test of the rule of reason begins.

Defining the market is very important in videogame antitrust matters. If a court says the markets are "all videogames" sold "anywhere in the world," any one game manufacturer would have little power to set prices artificially high. But if the market were, say, realistic football videogames sold in the United States, then a company which has exclusive dealing agreements with the NFL and the NCAA to use the likenesses of current players and stadiums so that no other company can make a realistic game, a monopolistic situation might ensue. This is the issue in *Pecover* in § 16.20. In the *O'Bannon* case, also in § 16.20, the question of market definition for the names, images, and likenesses ("NILs) of college athletes in videogames is a hotly litigated issue.

Clayton Act

As relevant to this Chapter, the Clayton Act prohibits "tying" arrangements. "Tying" occurs when a company requires consumers desiring product X (a product in which the company has market power), to also purchase product Y. If customers might prefer to buy X and Y separately, an illegal tying arrangement might be found.

For some products, tying occurs but is not actionable. When you buy a pair of Converse sneakers (a market in which Converse has monopoly power), you have to buy the shoelaces that come with them (a market in which it lacks monopoly power), even though there is no absolute reason for selling the two together and a consumer could buy shoelaces separately at the shoe store. When you buy a shirt or a blouse, you have to buy the attached buttons, even though, again, separate buttons could be purchased and sewn. What makes tying potentially illegal is when the "character of the demand" (the name of the Supreme Court's test) is such that a consumer ordinarily would not want the two items together, and a company with sufficient market power in one market forces the consumer to purchase another item that comes with that product.

---

§ 16.20 The Network Effect and Other Antitrust Issues

Pecover v. Electronic Arts Inc.

United States District Court, Northern District of California, 2009
633 F. Supp. 2d 976

WALKER, District Judge:

Plaintiff Geoffrey Pecover purchased an interactive video game software product entitled *Madden NFL* from a Best Buy store in Washington, D.C.; plaintiff Jeffrey Lawrence purchased a licensed copy of *Madden NFL* from a store in California. Together plaintiffs now seek to represent a class and prosecute an action on behalf of all *Madden NFL* purchasers in the United States. Electronic Arts, Inc. (EA) produces *Madden NFL*.

Plaintiffs allege that EA foreclosed competition in a market for interactive football software by acquiring, in separate agreements, exclusive rights to publish video games using the trademarks and other intellectual property of "the only viable sports football associations and leagues in the United States." Plaintiffs allege six causes of action relating to this conduct: (1) violation of section 2 of the Sherman Act, 15 U.S.C. §2; [and] (2) violation of California's Cartwright Act, Cal. Bus. & Prof. Code § 16700 et seq.

EA moves to dismiss the complaint under FRCP 12(b)(6) on a variety of grounds. EA first attacks the section 2 claim as barred by the indirect purchaser doctrine set forth in *Illinois Brick Co v. Illinois*, 431 U.S. 720 (1977). [Note: The "indirect purchaser" doctrine provides that if a person or entity who is not the direct purchaser of the product from the alleged antitrust cannot sue for damages under the Sherman Act. Here, the direct purchasers from EA are Best Buy and the retailer in California mentioned above, whereas the consumers who bought the game are "indirect purchasers," i.e., they bought directly from Best Buy but not from EA — ED]

Second, EA argues that the conduct alleged in the complaint — obtaining multiple exclusive licenses — cannot violate antitrust laws as a matter of law because such a rule would deny licensors the benefit of bidding competition. Third, EA alleges that plaintiff's Cartwright Act claim fails because the relationships between the NFL, NCAA and the AFL and EA — licensors and their exclusive licensee — renders them incapable of conspiring to violate the antitrust laws. Finally, EA argues that plaintiffs do not have standing to bring state antitrust and unfair competition claims under the law of the eighteen states in which neither named plaintiff resides.

I.

A.

The theories advanced by EA for dismissal of plaintiffs' claim under section 2 of the Sherman Act miss their mark.

EA's first attack — that the *Illinois Brick* indirect purchaser doctrine bars plaintiffs' section 2 claim — fails because the *Illinois Brick* indirect purchaser bar only bars antitrust claims for damages by indirect purchasers, whereas plaintiffs' section 2 claim seeks only injunctive relief. In *Illinois Brick*, the Supreme Court reasoned that such suits would force courts to allocate illegal overcharges between middlemen and the ultimate consumers and thus add "whole new dimensions of complexity to treble damages suits and seriously undermine their effectiveness." The Court further reasoned that allowing damages suits by indirect purchasers would open the door to duplicative recovery from both direct and indirect purchasers. *Id.* Apportionment challenges and duplicative recovery simply do not come into play in suits seeking injunctive relief and thus *Illinois Brick* does not apply.

Next, EA contends that plaintiffs have not adequately alleged that interactive video football software — the product market in which plaintiffs allege *Madden NFL* trades — is a recognizable product market for Sherman Act purposes. The court disagrees. Paragraphs 15–16 contain plaintiffs' product market allegations:

> 15. As Electronic Arts well knew, consumers demand that the teams and players in interactive football software be identified with actual teams and players. This is only achievable through a license with a sports league and associated players associations. There is essentially no demand and therefore no market for interactive football software that is not based on real life teams and/or players. Electronic Arts recognizes this fact in its annual report to investors where it notes that if it

were "unable to maintain" licenses with "major sports leagues and players associations" its "revenue and profitability will decline significantly."

16. By signing the exclusive agreement with the NFL, Electronic Arts immediately killed off Take Two's NFL 2K5 software, the only competing interactive football product of comparable quality to its Madden NFL franchise. Through its agreements with the NCAA and AFL, Electronic Arts prevented Take Two and others from re-entering the market with non-NFL branded interactive football software. Once again without a competitor, Electronic Arts raised its prices dramatically. Specifically, Electronic Arts raised the price of the Madden 2006 video game (released in August of 2005) nearly seventy percent to $49.95. Electronic Arts currently sells interactive football software for up to $59.95.

As the court understands these allegations, interactive football software will not sell if it does not use the names, logos and other markers of teams that actually compete in the NFL; there is, in effect, no market for interactive football software in a virtual or fictitious setting. If true — as the court must at this point accept — this adequately alleges that there are no substitutes for interactive football software without the markers of actual teams and players.

Plaintiffs do not, however, allege that there are no substitutes for interactive football software. One does not need to be a devotee of video games to recognize that any such claim would be implausible and possibly subject to dismissal under the instructions of the Supreme Court in *Bell Atlantic Corp v. Twombly* to allege antitrust claims with a measure of plausibility. So the question is whether interactive football software is sufficiently distinct or appealing to consumers to constitute a recognizable product market.

In attempting to allege a distinct product market, plaintiffs appear to adopt the market definition approach of the Horizontal Merger Guidelines propounded by the United States Department of Justice and the Federal Trade Commission in 1997. The Guidelines define a market by asking whether a potential monopolist could profitably impose a "small but significant and nontransitory increase" in price. A positive response suggests very limited functional interchangeability for the product in question and, for antitrust purposes, a distinct product market.

Plaintiffs allege that EA's exclusive agreement with the NFL "killed off" the only other allegedly competitive interactive software and allowed EA to raise its prices "dramatically." For purposes of pleading the claims at bar, these allegations suffice to allege a product market.

EA devotes much of its attention to *American Needle, Inc. v. National Football League*, 538 F.3d 736 (7th Cir. 2008), which held that an exclusive licensing contract between the NFL and Reebok, which manufactures football headwear, did not constitute an unreasonable restraint of trade in violation of section 1. The plaintiff had contended that the individual teams in the NFL were separate entities, so that the league's agreement with Reebok was unlawful horizontal or coordinated conduct. The district court, granting summary judgment, had found that the NFL was a "single-entity" in that "the teams' individual success is necessarily linked to the success of the league as a whole" and hence rejected plaintiff's contention that the license represented coordinated action. Without definitively resolving the single-entity question for all purposes, the court of appeals focused on whether the agreement before it "deprived the market of independent sources of economic power" and, affirming, concluded that the agreement did not do so. The court reached this conclusion because it viewed the joint licensing of NFL intellectual property as intended to promote NFL football as against other forms of entertainment. The court opined:

The failure of American Needle's § 1 claim necessarily dooms its § 2 monopolization claim. As a single entity for the purpose of licensing, the NFL teams are free under § 2 to license their intellectual property on an exclusive basis even if the teams opt to reduce the number of companies to whom they grant licenses.

Id. (citations omitted).

American Needle is inapposite here. The defendants there were the licensors of intellectual property, not, as in the case at bar, the licensees. Furthermore, plaintiff's claim in *American Needle* foundered on the court's conclusions that at least for purposes of promotional licensing, the NFL was a single entity. The single-entity rationale is, of course, persuasive in the context of NFL's role as a competitor in the entertainment business. An individual team can offer no entertainment value without the other teams in the league. Although this single-entity theory is somewhat less persuasive (to the undersigned, at least) when it comes to licensing NFL team logos on headwear (after all, individual teams could make their own license agreements), nonetheless the court of appeals viewed licensing headwear as simply an extension of the NFL's competition in promoting the entertainment it provides. This points to the most notable distinction between *American Needle* and the present case. The exclusive contract in American Needle involved only one provider of football entertainment: the NFL. The present case involves what are alleged to be a number of such providers, if not all the major ones, namely the NFL, AFL and NCAA.

EA also draws on another line of cases which begins with *Paddock Publications, Inc. v. Chicago Tribune Co.*, 103 F.3d 42 (7th Cir. 1996) and *Fleer Corporation v. Topps Chewing Gum, Inc.*, 658 F.2d 139 (3d Cir. 1981). In *Paddock*, a suburban daily newspaper in the Chicago metropolitan area, the Daily Herald, asserted claims under section 1 against the two major dailies in Chicago, the Tribune and the Sun-Times, that they had "locked up" the most popular or best supplemental services or features through exclusive agreements with the New York Times and Los Angeles Times/Washington Post news and features syndicates. The Herald did not contend that the Tribune and Sun-Times had conspired nor that the news and features syndicates had coordinated their conduct. The district court dismissed. Judge Easterbrook recognized that the plaintiff's theory was fundamentally an "essential facilities" claim, but noted that the complaint lacked allegations of "any essential facility." By contrast, the present complaint alleges that the names and logos of actual teams and players are essential to market interactive football software. Whether plaintiffs will be able to back this allegation up with evidence is a matter left for another day.

The *Fleer* case is more factually analogous to the present case. The parties, Fleer Corporation and Topps Chewing Gum, produced bubble gum and similar products. Topps had acquired exclusive licenses to the photographs and statistics of baseball players for use in producing baseball trading cards and, at the time of the case, Topps was the only seller of baseball trading cards sold in connection with bubble gum. The district court found the relevant product market to be "pocket-size pictures of active major league baseball players, sold alone or in combination with a low cost premium, at a price of 15 to 50 cents." Although the court of appeals assumed, without deciding, that this market definition was correct, the court noted (and perhaps was influenced by the fact) that baseball trading cards accompany "a variety of other non-confectionary products." The court also pointed out that Fleer had left the baseball trading card business nine years before the suit was filed by selling its existing baseball player licenses to Topps. The court then opined that because "Fleer or any other trading card manufacturer may compete with Topps for minor league players or even persuade the present major league players not to renew their Topps' contracts" the accumulation of exclusive licenses in that case failed to restrict competition sufficiently to violate section 1.

Importantly, the Third Circuit decided Fleer on a motion for summary judgment rather than on a motion to dismiss. The court noted that the determination whether the defendant's conduct excluded all meaningful competition was a mixed question of law and fact. Here, on EA's motion to dismiss, the court must take as true plaintiff's factual allegations that the series of exclusive deals between EA and the NFL, AFL and NCAA "killed off" competition and "prevented competitors from re-entering the market." These allegations distinguish this case from Fleer.

Accordingly, EA's motion to dismiss plaintiffs' claim for violation of section 2 of the Sherman Act is DENIED.

B.

EA next moves to dismiss plaintiffs' Cartwright Act claim. EA argues, consistent with its argument against the section 2 claim, that signing multiple exclusive agreements cannot constitute a restraint of trade. EA continues that if the exclusive agreements are not the "conspiracy" alleged in the complaint, then the complaint lacks the requisite factual details of the alleged Cartwright Act violation.

The Cartwright Act makes unlawful a "trust," defined as "a combination of capital, skill, or acts by two or more persons" for the purposes of restraining commerce and preventing market competition in the variety of ways listed in the statute. Cal. Bus. & Prof. Code § 16720. The Cartwright Act generally codifies the common law prohibition against the restraint of trade.

California courts have determined that vertical restraints of trade, such as exclusive dealing arrangements, can violate the Cartwright Act, though they are not illegal per se. "The law conclusively presumes manifestly anticompetitive restraints of trade to be unreasonable and unlawful, and evaluates other restraints under the rule of reason." Vertical restraints, including exclusive dealing arrangements, are proscribed when it is probable that performance of the arrangements will foreclose competition in a substantial share of the affected line of commerce. The rule of reason analysis requires a factual analysis of the line of commerce, the market area and the affected share of the relevant market. Such a factual inquiry is improper at this stage in the proceedings.

As described above relating to plaintiffs' section 2 claim, the complaint at bar alleges that EA entered into exclusive agreements with multiple football leagues to "kill off" competition and "raise prices dramatically." While these exclusive agreements are not per se illegal under the Cartwright Act, they could plausibly be found to restrain trade after applying the rule of reason analysis. Accordingly, the exclusive licenses themselves, described adequately in the complaint, constitute the conduct giving rise to the Cartwright Act claim.

EA cites this court's decision in *Levi Case Co. v. ATS Products*, 788 F. Supp. 428 (N.D. Cal. 1992) for the proposition that parties to an exclusive license who are not competitors are legally incapable of conspiring in violation of the antitrust laws. While *Levi Case* involved the federal Sherman Act, "it is established that the Sherman Act and Cartwright Act are to be interpreted in harmony with one another." *Levi Case* relied on the Supreme Court's ruling in *Copperweld Corp. v. Independence Tube Corp.*, 467 U.S. 752, 768 (1984) that a corporation and its subsidiaries were incapable of conspiring for the purposes of section 1. *Copperweld* reasoned that coordinated activity by parties who lack independent sources of economic power and separate interests does not warrant antitrust scrutiny. *Levi Case* applied that same principle to the relationship between a patent holder and the sublicensee to whom the patent holder had conveyed an exclusive license. In that circumstance, the patent holder's only rights relating to the patent after the exclusive license were to receive royalties and approve sublicenses. The patent holder, by virtue of the exclusive license, could not compete in the market covered by the patent and neither could anyone else because a patent is a legally-sanctioned restraint on trade.

Levi Case is distinguishable from the instant complaint, which alleges the aggregation of multiple exclusive agreements to choke off competition in a way that is not legally sanctioned, unlike the exclusive agreement involving a single patent. Moreover, the NFL, AFL and NCAA may each have exclusive agreements with EA, but they are competitors with each other. A series of agreements between EA and each of these entities could plausibly deprive the marketplace of independent sources of economic power.

Accordingly, EA's motion to dismiss plaintiffs' second cause of action for violation of the Cartwright Act is DENIED.

Notes and Questions

1. Assume that in year one the NFL Players Association received $100,000 from both EA and Take-Two, the distributor of NFL 2K5, and each made a realistic game. Assume in year two EA wants to secure the exclusive rights from the NFLPA because it believes it will make its game more valuable, and offers the NFLPA $300,000 — ⅓ more than the association would have received from the companies' collectively. EA then raises the price of the game because its costs have increased. Should that be a § 2 violation under the "rule of reason"/totality of the circumstances standard?

2. EA came to an out-of-court settlement with the plaintiffs in *Pecover* in July 2012 and released an official statement on its website:

> The Settlement provides that Electronic Arts will pay $27 million into a fund that will include money for Settlement Class Members to be provided for timely and valid claims as detailed below, after deducting payment for the costs of administering the Settlement, including the costs of this notice, attorneys' fees, costs of the litigation and any payments allowed by the Court to the named Plaintiffs, known as the "class representatives." This money is referred to here as the "Common Fund."

> Additionally, the Settlement provides that Electronic Arts will not enter into an exclusive trademark license with the AFL for five years from the date of approval of the Settlement; and that Electronic Arts will not renew its current collegiate football trademark license with the Collegiate Licensing Company ("CLC") on an exclusive basis for five years after it expires in 2014; and that Electronic Arts will not seek any new exclusive trademark license for the purpose of making football videogames with the CLC, the NCAA, or any NCAA member institution covered by the current exclusive license for five years after the expiration of the current CLC agreement.

> The Settlement will release claims that consumers may have against Electronic Arts relating to the exclusive agreements, and any resulting overcharge for football videogames, for the period of time from January 1, 2005 to June 21, 2012, unless an individual excludes himself or herself from the Settlement. Specifically, the Settlement will release and forever discharge the claims that were pled or could have been pled in the *Pecover v. Electronic Arts* case.

After *Pecover*, what advice would you give a videogame distributor on how to avoid antitrust concerns?

3. The title of this section includes the term "the network effect." The term is defined by Investopedia as follows:

Definition of 'Network Effect'

A phenomenon whereby a good or service becomes more valuable when more people use it. The internet is a good example. Initially, there were few users of the internet, and it was of relatively little value to anyone outside of the military and a few research scientists. As more users gained access to the internet, however, there were more and more websites to visit and more people to communicate with. The internet became extremely valuable to its users.

INVESTOPEDIA, http://www.investopedia.com/terms/n/network-effect.asp (last visited Aug. 4, 2014).

Massively multiplayer online role-playing games (MMORPGs), such as *World of Warcraft,* are examples of the network effect in videogames. From an antitrust perspective, the greater the number of players or users in a situation in which the network effect is present, the greater the market power of the developer or producer of the game. The situation described below involves another example of how the network effect may increase market power.

In 2011, Facebook introduced a new virtual currency system for games on the site, called "Facebook Credits," and have since been accused of violating federal antitrust laws in doing so. Consumer Watchdog, a nationally recognized non-profit organization, filed a Complaint with the Federal Trade Commission (FTC) requesting that the FTC investigate the issue and enjoin Facebook from continuing the practice of requiring Facebook Credits. Here is part of its Complaint:

Statement of Facts

Facebook is both the largest social network service provider and the most visited website in the United States. The Facebook platform gives software developers a forum to offer "applications" through Facebook. Applications allow Facebook users to play social games with [their] friends, and more. While Facebook develops some of its own applications, the vast majority of applications are built by outside developers.

"Social gaming" is a term used to describe game applications played within social networks such as Facebook. Virtually all social games are based on the free-to-play model where users purchase virtual goods and in-game currency during game play. Developer revenue from virtual goods purchased in social games in the U.S. totaled $865 million in 2010, and is expected to hit $1.25 billion in 2011. Virtual goods are the largest source of revenue for developers of social games. For example, of the $865 million revenue in 2010, $510 million was attributable to virtual goods sales.

Social gaming on Facebook is hugely popular: half of all Facebook users play social games. In terms of the number of users and time spent playing games, social gaming on Facebook has surpassed television viewing as a form of entertainment.

In 2009, Facebook started developing and testing Facebook Credits, a virtual currency Facebook members "can use to buy virtual goods in games and apps on the Facebook platform." Starting in July 1, 2011, Facebook will require all social game developers operating within the Facebook platform to *exclusively* utilize Facebook Credits for purchases of virtual goods and services.

Legal Analysis

Section 2 of the Sherman Act makes it unlawful to "monopolize, or attempt to monopolize, or combine or conspire with any other person or persons, to monopolize any part of the trade or commerce among the several States, or with foreign nations."

Monopolization under Section 2 of the Sherman Act requires a showing that (1) the defendant possesses monopoly power in the relevant market, and (2) the defendant that has acquired, enhanced, or maintained that power by the use of exclusionary conduct.

The relevant market includes two components: the relevant product and service market, which is defined by identifying producers that provide customers of a firm with alternative sources for the firm's product or services, and the relevant geographic market, which is measured by the area in which the defendants operate and which the customers can reasonably turn to for supplies. Monopoly power ordinarily may be inferred from the predominant share of the market.

Exclusionary conduct within the meaning of Section 2 is understood to be "the willful acquisition or maintenance of [monopoly] power as distinguished from growth or development as a consequence of a superior product, business acumen, or historic accident."

The relevant product and service market for purposes of a Section 2 analysis of Facebook Credits is the market for virtual goods purchased in social games. The relevant geographic market is, at minimum, all English language websites internationally, since Facebook operates globally via the Internet.

Facebook generates the predominant share of revenue in these markets. The market for virtual goods purchased in social games is expected to generate $1.25 billion in 2011, and virtual goods purchased in social games on Facebook have already generated $840 million in revenue so far. Based on this data, revenue in 2011 from virtual goods purchased in social games on the Facebook platform in the U.S. already accounts for over 65% or more of the expected revenue for the entire year. Therefore, Facebook wields monopoly power in the relevant markets.

The new Facebook Credits terms will enable Facebook to maintain and extend its monopoly power over the market for virtual goods purchased in social games. Because Facebook is the predominant distribution channel in the market for virtual goods purchased in social games, software developers wishing to enter the market, or existing developers currently offering games on Facebook, must accept Facebook's Credits terms in order to participate in the market.

The terms of Facebook Credits prohibit developers from charging a purchaser a "higher effective price in Credits for a good or service than [they] would for any other payment method that [they] accept for that good or service" outside of Facebook. This provision prevents developers from offering their products at lower prices outside of the Facebook platform. Developers who do not agree to this coercive term will lose access to the Facebook platform, which is the dominant social gaming platform. Most developers cannot afford to lose this access to the user base.

A developer who wants to develop a customer base on another social network platform (should a viable alternative arise), or even on its own website (so that they can eventually become independent from Facebook), would ordinarily wish to offer discounts that would provide an incentive for a gamer to migrate from Facebook to another platform or website, which would in turn stimulate competition. The prohibition on offering lower prices outside of Facebook prevents such developers from engaging in such competitive actions. Facebook is wielding its monopoly power to dictate prices; this term directly undermines competition outside the Facebook platform, i.e., in the market, and forces users to pay higher prices.

Further, under the new terms, developers must pay Facebook a 30% service fee for access to the Facebook platform and Facebook users. This fee disadvantages smaller developers who wish to compete inside the Facebook platform against larger game application developers.

Further, under the new terms, Facebook will provide users with free Facebook Credits to watch advertisements for which third parties pay Facebook. Developers must agree to accept these Facebook Credits, reducing the developers' compensation and in effect discounting the price of the virtual goods below the price that the developer is permitted by Facebook to charge outside of the Facebook platform.

Collectively, the terms of Facebook Credits will block and slow the adoption of competitive products and allow Facebook to maintain its monopoly to the detriment of consumers; will exclude competitors from entering and competing in the market; will undermine innovation; and lead to high prices for consumers.

Petitioners request that the Commission investigate and enjoin Facebook from engaging in unfair business practices in connection with Facebook Credits. FTC investigation and enforcement is necessary to prevent Facebook from destroying competition in the market for virtual goods purchased in social games, to protect existing businesses from being unfairly boxed out of the market, and to allow new businesses to enter the relevant markets, and ultimately, to protect consumers from higher prices.

Does Consumer Watchdog have a point? How does "the network effect" apply in this situation?

4. In 2013, a social game developer, Kickflip, Inc., sued Facebook in a Delaware federal court, alleging similar antitrust violations in the virtual currency market. Kickflip, which did business as Gambit, was the major virtual currency and payment-processing provider to developers that published games on Facebook. When Facebook began offering its own services to developers it destroyed a "vibrant and competitive market" according to Gambit, and soon put Gambit out of business.

Facebook moved to dismiss the case, arguing that Kickflip had not defined virtual currency as a market, and further, had not shown that Facebook had a monopoly power over that market. The court disagreed:

The Complaint defines the virtual-currency market as including those who offer virtual-currency services, payment-processing services, advertising, and related customer services to social game developers. "The outer boundaries of a product market are determined by the reasonable interchangeability of use or the cross-elasticity of demand between the product itself and substitutes for it." Kickflip pleads that "[c]urrently, the only way for developers to effectively monetize social games is through the use of virtual currency services—there are no substitutes." Further, Kickflip alleges that the relevant market involves "software developers that publish games on Facebook and other social networks," such as Gambit. The Complaint distinguishes the relevant market from other platforms that offer games. For instance, social network games: allow interactions between players who are not directly connected to a console, are less elaborate and expensive, derive revenue primarily from advertising or in-game purchases, leverage an existing social network, and have a large user base. Further, the social game network utilizes data input by users, which allows users to cooperate or compete with one another without first having to purchase the game.

Kickflip, Inc. v. Facebook, Inc., No. 12-1369-LPS, 2013 WL 5410719, at *1 (D. Del. Sep. 27, 2013). The court further held that "75–80% share of the market is more than adequate to establish a prima facie case of power," and here, Kickflip had properly alleged that Facebook controls 90%. *Id.* at *5.

5. In addition to its monopolization claims, Kickflip alleged that Facebook had violated federal antitrust laws by engaging in illegal tying. Kickflip alleged that Facebook tied its virtual-currency service (a market in which it had little power) to the distinct product of its social-game network (the market in which it had considerable power). In other words, if consumers wish to play one of Facebook's games, they had to purchase Facebook Credits, thereby severely limiting any competition in the virtual-currency service market.

6. Linuxjournal.com provides a concrete example of a tying issue in the computer arena in the following excerpt. For years, the operating system Linux has claimed there is an illegal tying arrangement between PC computer manufacturers and Microsoft whereby the consumer's choice of computer is illegally tied to Windows as the computer's operating system, much to Linux's damage. The article describes the issues as follows:

> Sellers with more than one product may seek to tie the sale of one (which the customer presumably desires) with that of another (which it presumably does not want). Such tie-ins are governed not only by the general language of the Sherman Act, but the more particular provisions of Section 3 of the Clayton Act, which prohibits such arrangements if the likely result is substantially to lessen competition. Tie-ins are per se unlawful if the seller possesses sufficient market power in the tying product, and coerces the buyer to take the tied product as a condition to obtaining the desired product.
>
> The antitrust problem with tie-ins is that the leverage generated by economic power in one market is used to accomplish sales in another. Once it is established that a tie-in is present; that the seller has sufficient economic power in the desired product to force the tie-in; and that a "not insubstantial" amount of sales is involved (amounts as small as $60,800 have been found to meet this standard), they are generally deemed unlawful
>
> In our situation, the tying product is the computer; the tied product is the unwanted Microsoft Windows operating system. Under the applicable antitrust statutes, it is unlawful for Dell or Compaq, for instance, to compel consumers who wish to purchase a computer to pay also for an unwanted, pre-installed operating system that is a completely separate product—Windows.

Walt Pennington, *Antitrust Tying and Computer Hardware Manufacturers*, Linux Journal (Feb. 5, 2003), http://www.linuxjournal.com/article/6538. What Mr. Pennington proposes is that computers be sold at one price without any operating system installed, and another depending on which operating system the consumer selects.

Do you think that Facebook illegally tied its social game network to its virtual currency services? What more would you need to know to answer that question?

* * *

In the *Keller* case, found in Chapter 4, we examined the question of whether an NCAA athlete's image and likeness could be used in a videogame without his or her permission from a right of publicity standpoint. While that issue was being thrashed out in the courts, other suits were filed, challenging the practice of not paying the athletes for their images on antitrust grounds. These cases asserted that the NCAA had artificially set the market price for the athletes' NILs at $0, or, perhaps more accurately, at a price capped at the allowable "grant in aid," *i.e.*, the value of the scholarship and books/living stipend levels allowed by the NCAA at the member's school. If you recall, Judge Bybee of the Ninth Circuit Court of Appeals was the author of *Keller*. In the following case, Judge Bybee was again called upon to author the opinion.

O'Bannon v NCAA

United States Court of Appeals, Ninth Circuit, 2015
802 F.3d 1049

BYBEE, Circuit Judge:

Section 1 of the Sherman Antitrust Act of 1890, 15 U.S.C. § 1, prohibits "[e]very contract, combination..., or conspiracy, in restraint of trade or commerce." For more than a century, the National Collegiate Athletic Association (NCAA) has prescribed rules governing the eligibility of athletes at its more than 1,000 member colleges and universities. Those rules prohibit student-athletes from being paid for the use of their names, images, and likenesses (NILs). The question presented in this momentous case is whether the NCAA's rules are subject to the antitrust laws and, if so, whether they are an unlawful restraint of trade.

After a bench trial and in a thorough opinion, the district court concluded that the NCAA's compensation rules were an unlawful restraint of trade. It then enjoined the NCAA from prohibiting its member schools from giving student-athletes scholarships up to the full cost of attendance at their respective schools and up to $5,000 per year in deferred compensation, to be held in trust for student-athletes until after they leave college. As far as we are aware, the district court's decision is the first by any federal court to hold that any aspect of the NCAA's amateurism rules violate the antitrust laws, let alone to mandate by injunction that the NCAA change its practices. We affirm in part and reverse in part.

The NCAA

American colleges and universities have been competing in sports for nearly 150 years: the era of intercollegiate athletics began, by most accounts, on November 6, 1869, when Rutgers and Princeton met in the first college football game in American history — a game more akin to soccer than to modern American football, played with "25 men to a side." College football quickly grew in popularity over the next few decades.

Fin de siècle college football was a rough game. Serious injuries were common, and it was not unheard of for players to be killed during games. Schools were also free to hire nonstudent ringers to compete on their teams or to purchase players away from other schools. By 1905, these and other problems had brought college football to a moment of crisis, and President Theodore Roosevelt convened a conference at the White House to address the issue of injuries in college football. Later that year, the presidents of 62 colleges and universities founded the Intercollegiate Athletic Association to create uniform rules for college football. In 1910, the IAA changed its name to the National Collegiate Athletic Association (NCAA), and it has kept that name to this day.

The NCAA has grown to include some 1,100 member schools, organized into three divisions: Division I, Division II, and Division III. Division I schools are those with the largest athletic programs—schools must sponsor at least fourteen varsity sports teams to qualify for Division I—and they provide the most financial aid to student-athletes. Division I has about 350 members.

For football competition only, Division I's membership is divided into two subdivisions: the Football Bowl Subdivision (FBS) and the Football Championship Subdivision (FCS). FBS schools are permitted to offer more full scholarships to their football players and, as a result, the level of competition is generally higher in FBS than in FCS. FBS consists of about 120 of the nation's premier college football schools.

One of the NCAA's earliest reforms of intercollegiate sports was a requirement that the participants be amateurs. The NCAA began to strengthen its enforcement capabilities in 1948, when it adopted what became known as the "Sanity Code"—a set of rules that prohibited schools from giving athletes financial aid that was based on athletic ability and not available to ordinary students. *See* Daniel E. Lazaroff, The NCAA in Its Second Century: *Defender of Amateurism or Antitrust Recidivist?*, 86 Or. L.Rev. 329, 333 (2007). The Sanity Code also created a new "compliance mechanism" to enforce the NCAA's rules—"a Compliance Committee that could terminate an institution's NCAA membership." *Id.*

In 1956, the NCAA departed from the Sanity Code's approach to financial aid by changing its rules to permit its members, for the first time, to give student-athletes scholarships based on athletic ability. These scholarships were capped at the amount of a full "grant in aid," defined as the total cost of "tuition and fees, room and board, and required course-related books." Student-athletes were prohibited from receiving any "financial aid based on athletics ability" in excess of the value of a grant-in-aid, on pain of losing their eligibility for collegiate athletics.

In addition to its financial aid rules, the NCAA has adopted numerous other amateurism rules that limit student-athletes' compensation. [M]ost importantly, an athlete is prohibited—with few exceptions—from receiving any "pay" based on his athletic ability, whether from boosters, companies seeking endorsements, or would-be licensors of the athlete's name, image, and likeness (NIL).

On appeal, the NCAA contends that the plaintiffs' Sherman Act claim fails on the merits, but it also argues that we are precluded altogether from reaching the merits, for three independent reasons: (1) The Supreme Court held in *NCAA v. Board of Regents of the University of Oklahoma*, 468 U.S. 85 (1984), that the NCAA's amateurism rules are "valid as a matter of law"; (2) the compensation rules at issue here are not covered by the Sherman Act at all because they do not regulate commercial activity; and (3) the plaintiffs have no standing to sue under the Sherman Act because they have not suffered "antitrust injury."

Board of Regents Did Not Declare the NCAA's Amateurism Rules "Valid as a Matter of Law"

We consider, first, the NCAA's claim that, under *Board of Regents*, all NCAA amateurism rules are "valid as a matter of law."

Board of Regents concerned the NCAA's then-prevailing rules for televising college football games. The rules allowed television networks to negotiate directly with schools and conferences for the right to televise games, but they imposed caps on the total number of games that could be broadcast on television each year and the number of games that any particular school could televise. The University of Oklahoma and the University of Georgia challenged this regime as an illegal restraint of trade under Section 1.

The Court observed that the television rules resembled two kinds of agreements that are ordinarily considered per se unlawful when made among horizontal competitors in the same market: a price-fixing agreement (in that the rules set a minimum aggregate price that the television networks were required to pay the NCAA's members) and an output-restriction agreement (in that the rules artificially capped the number of televised game licenses for sale). But it concluded that applying a per se rule of invalidity to the NCAA's television rules would be "inappropriate" because college football is "an industry in which horizontal restraints on competition are essential if the product is to be available at all." The Court elaborated:

> What the NCAA and its member institutions market in this case is competition itself—contests between competing institutions. Of course, this would be completely ineffective if there were no rules on which the competitors agreed to create and define the competition to be marketed. A myriad of rules affecting such matters as the size of the field, the number of players on a team, and the extent to which physical violence is to be encouraged or proscribed, all must be agreed upon, and all restrain the manner in which institutions compete. *In order to preserve the character and quality of th[is] "product," athletes must not be paid, must be required to attend class, and the like.* And the integrity of the "product" cannot be preserved except by mutual agreement; if an institution adopted such restrictions unilaterally, its effectiveness as a competitor on the playing field might soon be destroyed. In performing this role, its actions widen consumer choice—not only the choices available to sports fans but also those available to athletes—and hence can be viewed as procompetitive.

(Emphasis added). The Court held that the NCAA's rules should therefore be analyzed under the Rule of Reason.

Applying the Rule of Reason, the Court struck down the television rules on the ground that they did not serve any legitimate procompetitive purpose. It then concluded its opinion by stating:

> The NCAA plays a critical role in the maintenance of a revered tradition of amateurism in college sports. There can be no question but that it needs ample latitude to play that role, *or that the preservation of the student-athlete in higher education adds richness and diversity to intercollegiate athletics and is entirely consistent with the goals of the Sherman Act.*

(Emphasis added)

Quoting heavily from the language in *Board of Regents* that we have emphasized, the NCAA contends that any Section 1 challenge to its amateurism rules must fail as a matter of law because the Board of Regents Court held that those rules are presumptively valid. We disagree.

The *Board of Regents Court* certainly discussed the NCAA's amateurism rules at great length, but it did not do so in order to pass upon the rules' merits, given that they were not before the Court. Rather, the Court discussed the amateurism rules to explain why NCAA rules should be analyzed under the Rule of Reason, rather than held to be illegal per se. The point was a significant one. Naked horizontal agreements among competitors to fix the price of a good or service, or to restrict their output, are usually condemned as per se unlawful. The *Board of Regents* Court decided, however, that because college sports could not exist without certain horizontal agreements, NCAA rules should not be held per se unlawful even when—like the television rules in *Board of Regents*—they appear to be pure "restraints on the ability of member institutions to compete in terms of price and output."

Board of Regents, in other words, did not approve the NCAA's amateurism rules as categorically consistent with the Sherman Act. Rather, it held that, because many NCAA rules (among them, the amateurism rules) are part of the character and quality of the [NCAA's] product, no NCAA rule should be invalidated without a Rule of Reason analysis. The Court's long encomium to amateurism, though impressive-sounding, was therefore dicta. To be sure, we do not treat considered dicta from the Supreme Court lightly; such dicta should be accorded "appropriate deference." Where applicable, we will give the quoted passages from *Board of Regents* that deference. But we are not bound by *Board of Regents* to conclude that every NCAA rule that somehow relates to amateurism is automatically valid.

The Compensation Rules Regulate "Commercial Activity"

The NCAA next argues that we cannot reach the merits of the plaintiffs' Sherman Act claim because the compensation rules are not subject to the Sherman Act at all. The NCAA points out that Section 1 of the Sherman Act applies only to "restraint[s] of trade or commerce," and claims that its compensation rules are mere "eligibility rules" that do not regulate any "commercial activity."

This argument is not credible. Although restraints that have no effect on commerce are indeed exempt from Section 1, the modern legal understanding of "commerce" is broad, including almost every activity from which the actor anticipates economic gain. That definition surely encompasses the transaction in which an athletic recruit exchanges his labor and NIL rights for a scholarship at a Division I school because it is undeniable that both parties to that exchange anticipate economic gain from it.

It is no answer to these observations to say, as the NCAA does in its briefs, that the compensation rules are "eligibility rules" rather than direct restraints on the terms of agreements between schools and recruits. True enough, the compensation rules are written in the form of eligibility rules; they provide that an athlete who receives compensation other than the scholarships specifically permitted by the NCAA loses his eligibility for collegiate sports. The mere fact that a rule can be characterized as an "eligibility rule," however, does not mean the rule is not a restraint of trade; were the law otherwise, the NCAA could insulate its member schools' relationships with student-athletes from antitrust scrutiny by renaming every rule governing student-athletes an "eligibility rule." The antitrust laws are not to be avoided by such clever manipulation of words.

In other words, the substance of the compensation rules matters far more than how they are styled. And in substance, the rules clearly regulate the terms of commercial transactions between athletic recruits and their chosen schools. There is real money at issue here.

The Plaintiffs Demonstrated that the Compensation Rules Cause Them Injury in Fact

The NCAA's last argument antecedent to the merits is that the plaintiffs' Section 1 claim fails at the threshold because the plaintiffs have failed to show that they have suffered "antitrust injury." Antitrust injury is a heightened standing requirement that applies to private parties suing to enforce the antitrust laws. To satisfy the antitrust-injury requirement, a plaintiff must show injury of the type the antitrust laws were intended to prevent and that flows from that which makes defendants' acts unlawful.

Although the NCAA purports to be making an antitrust-injury argument, it is mistaken. The NCAA has not contended that the plaintiffs' injuries are not "of the type the antitrust laws were intended to prevent." Rather, the NCAA has made a garden-variety standing argument: it alleges that the plaintiffs have not been injured in fact by the compensation rules because those rules do not deprive them of any NIL compensation they would otherwise receive.

We conclude that the plaintiffs have shown that they are injured in fact as a result of the NCAA's rules having foreclosed the market for their NILs in video games

Absent the NCAA's compensation rules, video game makers would negotiate with student-athletes for the right to use their NILs

[T]he district court found that, if permitted to do so, video game makers such as EA would negotiate with college athletes for the right to use their NILs in video games because these companies want to make games that are as realistic as possible. The district court noted that EA currently negotiates with the NFL and NBA players' unions for the right to use their members' NILs in pro sports video games.

The NCAA argues, however, that we cannot find that the plaintiffs have suffered an injury in fact based on lost compensation from video game companies because the NCAA has terminated its relationship with EA and is not currently working with any other video game maker. We disagree. The district court found that it is entirely possible that the NCAA will resume its support for college sports video games at some point in the future, given that the NCAA found such games to be profitable in the past, id., and that finding of fact was not clearly erroneous. Given the NCAA's previous, lengthy relationship with EA and the other evidence presented, it was reasonable for the district court to conclude that the NCAA may well begin working with EA or another video game company in the future.

Whether the Copyright Act preempts right-of-publicity claims based on sports video games is tangential to this case and irrelevant to the plaintiffs' standing

In addition to arguing that its current policies against college sports video games defeat the plaintiffs' claims to standing, the NCAA also contends that there are legal barriers that would prevent the plaintiffs from being compensated by a video game maker. Specifically, the NCAA argues that the Copyright Act would preempt any right-of-publicity claim arising out of the use of those NILs in sports video games. Thus, the NCAA maintains, if it were to resume its support for college sports video games and permit video game companies to use student-athletes' NILs, the video game makers would not pay student-athletes for their NILs; rather, they could use the NILs for free.

We decline to consider this argument, for two reasons. First, it is convoluted and far afield from the main issues in this case. The NCAA asks us to decide whether, assuming that EA or some other video game company were to make a college sports video game that incorporated student-athletes' NILs and then refuse to pay student-athletes for those NILs, the game maker would have a viable Copyright Act defense to a right-of-publicity lawsuit brought by the athletes. That question is a complex one, implicating both Section 301 of the Copyright Act, 17 U.S.C. § 301, which expressly preempts certain common-law claims, and a murky body of case law holding that, in some circumstances, the Act impliedly preempts claims that fall *1069 outside of Section 301's scope. See, e.g., Facenda v. NFL Films, Inc., 542 F.3d 1007, 1028–32 (3d Cir.2008) (suggesting, on the basis of a conflict preemption analysis, that federal copyright law can "impliedly preempt[ ]" right-of-publicity claims). It is scarcely fit for resolution within the confines of a standing inquiry in an antitrust suit between the NCAA and its student-athletes that involves neither EA nor any other video game company as a party. Should a college sports video game be made in the future and the right-of-publicity suit envisioned by the NCAA come to pass, the court hearing that suit will be in a far better position to resolve the question of Copyright Act preemption than we are.

Second and more importantly, the NCAA's argument about the Copyright Act, even if correct, is irrelevant to whether the plaintiffs lack standing. On the NCAA's interpretation of the Copyright Act, professional football and basketball players have no enforceable right-of-publicity claims against video game makers either — yet EA currently pays NFL and NBA players for the right to use their NILs in its video games.

Because the plaintiffs have shown that, absent the NCAA's compensation rules, video game makers would likely pay them for the right to use their NILs in college sports video games, the plaintiffs have satisfied the [preliminary] requirement of injury in fact.

[Merits]

Having rejected all of the NCAA's preliminary legal arguments, we proceed to review the plaintiffs' Section 1 claim on the merits. Although in another context the NCAA's decision to value student-athletes' NIL at zero might be per se illegal price fixing, we are persuaded — as was the Supreme Court in Board of Regents and the district court here — that the appropriate rule is the Rule of Reason. Because the integrity of the 'product' cannot be preserved except by mutual agreement, restraints on competition are essential if the product is to be available at all.

Like the district court, we follow the three-step framework of the Rule of Reason: [1] The plaintiff bears the initial burden of showing that the restraint produces significant anticompetitive effects within a relevant market. [2] If the plaintiff meets this burden, the defendant must come forward with evidence of the restraint's procompetitive effects. [3] The plaintiff must then show that any legitimate objectives can be achieved in a substantially less restrictive manner.

Significant Anticompetitive Effects Within a Relevant Market

[T]he district court made the following factual findings: (1) that a cognizable "college education market" exists, wherein colleges compete for the services of athletic recruits by offering them scholarships and various amenities, such as coaching and facilities; (2) that if the NCAA's compensation rules did not exist, member schools would compete to offer recruits compensation for their NILs; and (3) that the compensation rules therefore have a significant anticompetitive effect on the college education market, in that they fix an aspect of the "price" that recruits pay to attend college (or, alternatively, an aspect of the price that schools pay to secure recruits' services). These findings have substantial support in the record.

By and large, the NCAA does not challenge the district court's findings. It does not take issue with the way that the district court defined the college education market. Nor does it appear to dispute the district court's conclusion that the compensation rules restrain the NCAA's member schools from competing with each other within that market, at least to a certain degree. Instead, the NCAA makes three modest arguments about why the compensation rules do not have a significant anticompetitive effect. First, it argues that because the plaintiffs never showed that the rules reduce output in the college education market, the plaintiffs did not meet their burden of showing a significant anticompetitive effect. Second, it argues that the rules have no anticompetitive effect because schools would not pay student-athletes anything for their NIL rights in any event, given that those rights are worth nothing. And finally, the NCAA argues that even if the district court was right that schools would pay student-athletes for their NIL rights, any such payments would be small, which means that the compensation rules' anticompetitive effects cannot be considered significant.

We can dispose of the first two arguments quickly. First, the NCAA's contention that the plaintiffs' claim fails because they did not show a decrease in output in the college education market is simply incorrect. Here, the NCAA argues that output in the college education market "consists of opportunities for student-athletes to participate in FBS football or Division I men's basketball," and it quotes the district court's finding that these opportunities have "increased steadily over time." But this argument misses the mark.

At trial, the plaintiffs demonstrated that the NCAA's compensation rules have [an] anticompetitive effect: they fix the price of one component of the exchange between school and recruit, thereby precluding competition among schools with respect to that component. The athletes accept grants-in-aid, and no more, in exchange for their athletic performance, because the NCAA schools have agreed to value the athletes' NILs at zero, "an anticompetitive effect." This anticompetitive effect satisfied the plaintiffs' initial burden under the Rule of Reason.

Second, the NCAA's argument that student-athletes' NILs are, in fact, worth nothing is simply a repackaged version of its arguments about injury in fact, which we have rejected.

Finally, we reject the NCAA's contention that any NIL compensation that student-athletes might receive in the absence of its compensation rules would be de minimis and that the rules therefore do not significantly affect competition in the college education market. This "too small to matter" argument is incompatible with the Supreme Court's holding in *Catalano, Inc. v. Target Sales, Inc.*, 446 U.S. 643 (1980). In *Catalano*, a group of beer retailers sued a group of beer wholesalers, alleging that the wholesalers had secretly agreed to end their customary practice of extending the retailers interest-free credit for roughly a month after the delivery of beer. The Court unanimously held that this agreement was unlawful per se. It reasoned that the agreement was clearly a means of "extinguishing one form of [price] competition among the sellers," given that credit terms were part of the price of the beer, and that the agreement was therefore tantamount to price-fixing.

The NCAA's compensation rules function in much the same way as the agreement at issue in *Catalano*: they "extinguish[ ] one form of competition" among schools seeking to land recruits. We acknowledge that Catalano was a per se case in which the Court did not analyze the anticompetitive effect of the wholesalers' agreement in detail, but the decision nonetheless indicates that an antitrust court should not dismiss an anticompetitive price-fixing agreement as benign simply because the agreement relates only to one component of an overall price. That proposition finds further support in *Board of Regents*: in *Board of Regents*, a Rule of Reason case, the Court held that the NCAA's television plan had "a significant potential for anticompetitive effects" without delving into the details of exactly how much the plan restricted output of televised games or how much it fixed the price of TV contracts. While the precise value of NIL compensation is uncertain, at this point in the analysis and in light of *Catalano* and *Board of Regents*, we conclude that the plaintiffs have met their burden at the first step of the Rule of Reason by showing that the NCAA's compensation rules fix the price of one component (NIL rights) of the bundle that schools provide to recruits.

Procompetitive Effects

As discussed above, the NCAA offered the district court four procompetitive justifications for the compensation rules: (1) promoting amateurism, (2) promoting competitive balance among NCAA schools, (3) integrating student-athletes with their schools' academic community, and (4) increasing output in the college education market. The district court accepted the first and third and rejected the other two.

Although the NCAA's briefs state in passing that the district court erred in failing to "credit all four justifications fully," the NCAA focuses its arguments to this court entirely on the first proffered justification—the promotion of amateurism. We therefore accept the district court's factual findings that the compensation rules do not promote competitive balance, that they do not increase output in the college education market, and that they play a limited role in integrating student-athletes with their schools' academic communities, since we have been offered no meaningful argument that those findings were clearly erroneous

The district court acknowledged that the NCAA's current rules promote amateurism, which in turn plays a role in increasing consumer demand for college sports. The NCAA is correct that a restraint that broadens choices can be procompetitive. The Court in *Board of Regents* observed that the difference between college and professional sports "widen[s]" the choices "available to athletes." But we fail to see how the restraint at issue in this particular case—i.e., the NCAA's limits on student-athlete compensation—makes college sports more attractive to recruits, or widens recruits' spectrum of choices in the sense that *Board of Regents* suggested. As the district court found, it is primarily "the opportunity to earn a higher education" that attracts athletes to college sports rather than professional sports, and that opportunity would still be available to student-athletes if they were paid some compensation in addition to their athletic scholarships. Nothing in the plaintiffs' prayer for compensation would make student-athletes something other than students and thereby impair their ability to become student-athletes.

Indeed, if anything, loosening or abandoning the compensation rules might be the best way to "widen" recruits' range of choices; athletes might well be more likely to attend college, and stay there longer, if they knew that they were earning some amount of NIL income while they were in school. We therefore reject the NCAA's claim that, by denying student-athletes compensation apart from scholarships, the NCAA increases the "choices" available to them.

The NCAA's second point has more force—the district court found, and the record supports that there is a concrete procompetitive effect in the NCAA's commitment to amateurism: namely, that the amateur nature of collegiate sports increases their appeal to consumers. We therefore conclude that the NCAA's compensation rules serve the two procompetitive purposes identified by the district court: integrating academics with athletics, and "preserving the popularity of the NCAA's product by promoting its current understanding of amateurism." The NCAA plays a vital role in enabling college football to preserve its character, and as a result enables a product to be marketed which might otherwise be unavailable.

Substantially Less Restrictive Alternatives

The third step in the Rule of Reason analysis is whether there are substantially less restrictive alternatives to the NCAA's current rules. We bear in mind that—to be viable under the Rule of Reason—an alternative must be virtually as effective in serving the procompetitive purposes of the NCAA's current rules, and without significantly increased cost. We think that plaintiffs must make a strong evidentiary showing that its alternatives are viable here. Not only do plaintiffs bear the burden at this step, but the Supreme Court has admonished that we must generally afford the NCAA "ample latitude" to superintend college athletics. *Bd. of Regents*, 468 U.S. at 120.

The district court identified two substantially less restrictive alternatives: (1) allowing NCAA member schools to give student-athletes grants-in-aid that cover the full cost of attendance; and (2) allowing member schools to pay student-athletes small amounts of deferred cash compensation for use of their NILs.

Capping the permissible amount of scholarships at the cost of attendance

The district court did not clearly err in finding that allowing NCAA member schools to award grants-in-aid up to their full cost of attendance would be a substantially less restrictive alternative to the current compensation rules. All of the evidence before the district court indicated that raising the grant-in-aid cap to the cost of attendance would have virtually no impact on amateurism: Dr. Mark Emmert, the president of the NCAA, testified at trial that giving student-athletes scholarships up to their full costs of attendance would not violate the NCAA's principles of amateurism because all the money given to students would be going to cover their "legitimate costs" to attend school. Other NCAA witnesses agreed with that assessment. Nothing in the record, moreover, suggested that consumers of college sports would become less interested in those sports if athletes' scholarships covered their full cost of attendance, or that an increase in the grant-in-aid cap would impede the integration of student-athletes into their academic communities.

A compensation cap set at student-athletes' full cost of attendance is a substantially less restrictive alternative means of accomplishing the NCAA's legitimate procompetitive purposes. And there is no evidence that this cap will significantly increase costs; indeed, the NCAA already permits schools to fund student-athletes' full cost of attendance.

Allowing students to receive cash compensation for their NILs

In our judgment, however, the district court clearly erred in finding it a viable alternative to allow students to receive NIL cash payments untethered to their education expenses. We cannot agree that a rule permitting schools to pay students pure cash compensation and a rule forbidding them from paying NIL compensation are both equally effective in promoting amateurism and preserving consumer demand. Both we and the district court agree that the NCAA's amateurism rule has procompetitive benefits. But in finding that paying students cash compensation would promote amateurism as effectively as not paying them, the district court ignored that not paying student-athletes is precisely what makes them amateurs.

Having found that amateurism is integral to the NCAA's market, the district court cannot plausibly conclude that being a poorly-paid professional collegiate athlete is "virtually as effective" for that market as being as amateur.

Aside from the self-evident fact that paying students for their NIL rights will vitiate their amateur status as collegiate athletes, the court relied on threadbare evidence in finding that small payments of cash compensation will preserve amateurism as well the NCAA's rule forbidding such payments. Most of the evidence elicited merely indicates that paying students large compensation payments would harm consumer demand more than smaller payments would — not that small cash payments will preserve amateurism.

Finally, the district court place[s] particular weight on a brief interchange during plaintiffs' cross-examination of one of the NCAA's witnesses, Neal Pilson, a television sports consultant formerly employed at CBS. Pilson testified that "if you're paid for your performance, you're not an amateur," and explained at length why paying students would harm the student-athlete market. Plaintiffs then asked Pilson whether his opinions about amateurism "depend on the level of the money" paid to players, and he acknowledged that his opinion was "impacted by the level." When asked whether there was a line that "should not be crossed" in paying players, Pilson responded "that's a difficult question.

I haven't thought about the line. And I haven't been asked to render an opinion on that." When pressed to come up with a figure, Pilson repeated that he was "not sure." He eventually commented that "I tell you that a million dollars would trouble me and $5,000 wouldn't, but that's a pretty good range."

So far as we can determine, Pilson's offhand comment under cross-examination is the sole support for the district court's $5,000 figure. Pilson's casual comment — "[I] haven't been asked to render an opinion on that. It's not in my report" — that he would not be troubled by $5,000 payments is simply not enough to support the district court's far-reaching conclusion that paying students $5,000 per year will be as effective in preserving amateurism as the NCAA's current policy.

The difference between offering student-athletes education-related compensation and offering them cash sums untethered to educational expenses is not minor; it is a quantum leap. Once that line is crossed, we see no basis for returning to a rule of amateurism and no defined stopping point; we have little doubt that plaintiffs will continue to challenge the arbitrary limit imposed by the district court until they have captured the full value of their NIL. At that point the NCAA will have surrendered its amateurism principles entirely and transitioned from its particular brand of football to minor league status.

We vacate the district court's judgment and permanent injunction insofar as they require the NCAA to allow its member schools to pay student-athletes up to $5,000 per year in deferred compensation. We otherwise affirm. The parties shall bear their own costs on appeal.

———————

Notes and Questions

1. Here is how the Court explained the difference between "grants in aid" and "cost of attendance":

> The "cost of attendance" at a particular school includes the items that make up a grant in aid plus "[nonrequired] books and supplies, transportation, and other expenses related to attendance at the institution." The difference between a grant in aid and the cost of attendance is a few thousand dollars at most schools.

Id. at 1054, n.3.

If *O'Banon* remains the law of the land, was the few thousand dollar difference worth all the litigation? Especially since, by the time of the decision, the NCAA had changed its rules to allow schools to award scholarships equal to the cost of attendance if they chose to do so.

2. How do you reconcile *Keller* (holding that college players NIL's cannot be taken without compensation) with *O'Bannon* (holding that the NCAA's eligibility rules prohibiting separate payment for college players NIL's are permissible restrictions because they promote amateurism.)

3. Judge Bybee's opinion pretty accurately summarized the rather scant evidentiary basis for the District Court's ruling that up to $5,000 per year could be held in trust for each FSB football player and Division 1 basketball player (to be distributed upon cessation of eligibility) under the antitrust laws. Regardless of the evidentiary support, what do you think of the idea?

4. Assume that the Ninth Circuit had upheld the $5,000 trust fund concept. One question that had Athletic Directors and compliance officers up late at night was trying

to figure out how the dynamics of the contracting process would work. Would, e.g., EA go to individual players and negotiate contracts for their NILs; would they do it on a team-by-team basis; on a league by league basis? Or even by contracting with the NCAA itself?

5. Suppose players are somehow able to bargain for and keep a payment for their NILs while in college, and not lose their amateur status. Will the next Johnny Manziel — a Heisman Trophy-winning, high profile and dynamic player known as "Johnny Football" when he played for Texas A&M if the name is otherwise unfamiliar to you — demand more money for his NIL than the third string tackle on the team, on the factually true grounds that, at least while they are in college, his NIL is worth more than the less well known tackle? Is this what Judge Bybee was worried about when he said, "Once that line is crossed … we have little doubt that plaintiffs will continue to challenge the arbitrary limit imposed by the district court until they have captured the full value of their NIL"?

6. The NCAA argued in the District Court that one of the pro-competitive aspects of its current practice is that it allowed more money to be available to fund non-revenue sports. That is, it said if the individual schools had to give student athletes stipends (whether in a trust fund or not), it will have less revenue to fund, e.g., the wrestling or gymnastic teams, whose revenues do not match expenses. Is there validity to that argument?

7. In the District Court, the court noted that in its post-trial briefs, the NCAA argued that the case could be viewed not as the student-athletes being *buyers* of the educational opportunities offered by their academic institutions, but rather as the student-athletes being *sellers* of their NILs:

> Although Plaintiffs have characterized FBS football and Division I basketball schools as sellers in the market for educational and athletic opportunities, in their post-trial brief they argued that the schools could alternatively be characterized as buyers in a market for recruits' athletic services and licensing rights. The relevant market would be that for the recruitment of the highest ranked male high school football and basketball players each year. Viewed from this perspective, Plaintiffs' antitrust claim arises under a theory of monopsony, rather than monopoly, alleging an agreement to fix prices among buyers rather than sellers.

O'Bannon v NCAA, 7 F. Supp. 3d 955, 991 (N.D. Cal. 2014)

Which is the better way to view the student-athletes, and does it matter whether they are viewed as buyers or sellers?

8. One argument made by the plaintiffs to allow payment was by analogy to the Olympics. The argument was that Olympic athletes can now be paid (albeit through trust accounts and albeit for only "health, education, support, and maintenance" of the athlete), and the payment system hasn't hurt the appeal of the Olympics to those who follow Olympic sports. What do you think of the Olympic analogue, and what do you think Judge Bybee would say about it?

---

§ 16.30 False Advertising

There are several ways in which a distributor of a videogame that falsely advertises its product can be punished. First, the purchaser can sue for misrepresentation or fraud. But often there is not enough money involved to make suing a viable prospect, unless a class action can be maintained, and that is difficult in false advertising claims — some consumers did not see the false advertising, some did not rely on it, etc. — and thus proving sufficient "commonality," as is needed for class action status under Fed. R. Civ. Proc. 26, is usually not feasible.

The second way is for the government to investigate and discipline the misleading advertiser. But no injured party likes to relinquish control over whether the suit would be filed, and besides, government prosecutors are not often interested in pursuing a claim that asserts that, of the fourteen proclaimed attributes of a product, claim number six is not exactly true and number thirteen is alleged to be misleading. Further, any monetary recovery is likely to benefit the government, in terms of a fine, but not the consumer.

A third alternative is to allow suit by a *competitor*, or someone else whose sales might be affected by the false advertising. The argument in these cases is that a consumer would have made a different choice had the information been accurately disseminated, and perhaps have chosen the competitor's product instead. Certainly a competitor is interested enough in being a good "watchdog" for misrepresentations, and in some ways would be the best plaintiff to police the marketplace. But over the years some courts have expressed a reluctance to allowing such suits, fearing an avalanche of nuisance litigation over trivial, and potentially constitutionally protected, statements in TV, radio, print ads, or even statements on the boxes of their competitors' products. Moreover, until recently it was not clear that a competitor had standing to assert such a claim. Some courts allowed suit under the Lanham Act, on the grounds that the misleading statement caused consumer confusion, but even those courts were split as to the proper test for determining when a violation was actionable. The Supreme Court resolved these issues in the following case.

Lexmark Int'l, Inc. v. Static Components Inc.

Supreme Court of the United States, 2014
— U.S.—, 134 S. Ct. 1377

SCALIA, Justice

This case requires us to decide whether respondent, Static Control Components, Inc., may sue petitioner, Lexmark International, Inc., for false advertising under the Lanham Act, 15 U.S.C. § 1125(a).

I. Background

Lexmark manufactures and sells laser printers. It also sells toner cartridges for those printers (toner being the powdery ink that laser printers use to create images on paper). Lexmark designs its printers to work only with its own style of cartridges, and it therefore dominates the market for cartridges compatible with its printers. That market, however, is not devoid of competitors. Other businesses, called "remanufacturers," acquire used Lexmark toner cartridges, refurbish them, and sell them in competition with new and refurbished cartridges sold by Lexmark.

Lexmark would prefer that its customers return their empty cartridges to it for refurbishment and resale, rather than sell those cartridges to a remanufacturer. So Lexmark introduced what it called a "Prebate" program, which enabled customers to purchase new toner cartridges at a 20-percent discount if they would agree to return the cartridge to Lexmark once it was empty. Those terms were communicated to consumers through notices printed on the toner-cartridge boxes, which advised the consumer that opening the box would indicate assent to the terms — a practice commonly known as "shrinkwrap licensing." To enforce the Prebate terms, Lexmark included a microchip in each Prebate cartridge that would disable the cartridge after it ran out of toner; for the cartridge to be used again, the microchip would have to be replaced by Lexmark.

Static Control is not itself a manufacturer or remanufacturer of toner cartridges. It is, rather, "the market leader in making and selling the components necessary to remanufacture Lexmark cartridges." In addition to supplying remanufacturers with toner and various replacement parts, Static Control developed a microchip that could mimic the microchip in Lexmark's Prebate cartridges. By purchasing Static Control's microchips and using them to replace the Lexmark microchip, remanufacturers were able to refurbish and resell used Prebate cartridges.

Lexmark did not take kindly to that development. In 2002, it sued Static Control, alleging that Static Control's microchips violated both the Copyright Act of 1976, 17 U.S.C. § 101 et seq., and the Digital Millennium Copyright Act, 17 U.S.C. § 1201 et seq. Static Control counterclaimed, alleging, among other things, violations of § 43(a) of the Lanham Act, 60 Stat. 441, codified at 15 U.S.C. § 1125(a). Section 1125(a) provides:

> "(1) Any person who, on or in connection with any goods or services, or any container for goods, uses in commerce any word, term, name, symbol, or device, or any combination thereof, or any false designation of origin, false or misleading description of fact, or false or misleading representation of fact, which—

> "(A) is likely to cause confusion, or to cause mistake, or to deceive as to the affiliation, connection, or association of such person with another person, or as to the origin, sponsorship, or approval of his or her goods, services, or commercial activities by another person, or

> "(B) in commercial advertising or promotion, misrepresents the nature, characteristics, qualities, or geographic origin of his or her or another person's goods, services, or commercial activities,

> "shall be liable in a civil action by any person who believes that he or she is or is likely to be damaged by such act."

As relevant to its Lanham Act claim, Static Control alleged two types of false or misleading conduct by Lexmark. First, it alleged that through its Prebate program Lexmark "purposefully misleads end-users" to believe that they are legally bound by the Prebate terms and are thus required to return the Prebate-labeled cartridge to Lexmark after a single use. Second, it alleged that upon introducing the Prebate program, Lexmark "sent letters to most of the companies in the toner cartridge remanufacturing business" falsely advising those companies that it was illegal to sell refurbished Prebate cartridges and, in particular, that it was illegal to use Static Control's products to refurbish those cartridges. Static Control asserted that by those statements, Lexmark had materially misrepresented "the nature, characteristics, and qualities" of both its own products and Static Control's products. It further maintained that Lexmark's misrepresentations had "proximately caused and were likely to cause injury to Static Control by diverting sales from Static Control to Lexmark," and had "substantially injured its business reputation" by "leading consumers and others in the trade to believe that Static Control is engaged in illegal conduct."

We granted certiorari to decide "the appropriate analytical framework for determining a party's standing to maintain an action for false advertising under the Lanham Act."

"Prudential Standing"

The parties' briefs treat the question on which we granted certiorari as one of "prudential standing." Because we think that label misleading, we begin by clarifying the nature of the question at issue in this case.

From Article III's limitation of the judicial power to resolving "Cases" and "Controversies," and the separation-of-powers principles underlying that limitation, we have deduced a set of requirements that together make up the "irreducible constitutional minimum of standing." The plaintiff must have suffered or be imminently threatened with a concrete and particularized "injury in fact" that is fairly traceable to the challenged action of the defendant and likely to be redressed by a favorable judicial decision. Lexmark does not deny that Static Control's allegations of lost sales and damage to its business reputation give it standing under Article III to press its false-advertising claim, and we are satisfied that they do.

[A separate question] is whether Static Control falls within the class of plaintiffs whom Congress has authorized to sue under § 1125(a). In other words, we ask whether Static Control has a cause of action under the statute. That question requires us to determine the meaning of the congressionally enacted provision creating a cause of action. We do not ask whether in our judgment Congress should have authorized Static Control's suit, but whether Congress in fact did so.

Static Control's Right To Sue Under § 1125(a)

Thus, this case presents a straightforward question of statutory interpretation: Does the cause of action in § 1125(a) extend to plaintiffs like Static Control? The statute authorizes suit by "any person who believes that he or she is likely to be damaged" by a defendant's false advertising. § 1125(a)(1). Read literally, that broad language might suggest that an action is available to anyone who can satisfy the minimum requirements of Article III. No party makes that argument, however, and the "unlikelihood that Congress meant to allow all factually injured plaintiffs to recover persuades us that § 1125(a) should not get such an expansive reading." We reach that conclusion in light of two relevant background principles already mentioned: zone of interests and proximate causality.

A. Zone of Interests

First, we presume that a statutory cause of action extends only to plaintiffs whose interests "fall within the zone of interests protected by the law invoked." The modern "zone of interests" formulation originated in *Association of Data Processing Service Organizations, Inc. v. Camp*, 397 U.S. 150 (1970). We have made clear that it applies to all statutorily created causes of action; that it is a "requirement of general application"; and that Congress is presumed to "legislate against the background of" the zone-of-interests limitation, "which applies unless it is expressly negated." The zone-of-interests test is therefore an appropriate tool for determining who may invoke the cause of action in § 1125(a).

Identifying the interests protected by the Lanham Act requires no guesswork, since the Act includes an "unusual, and extraordinarily helpful," detailed statement of the statute's purposes. Section 45 of the Act, codified at 15 U.S.C. § 1127, provides:

> The intent of this chapter is to regulate commerce within the control of Congress by making actionable the deceptive and misleading use of marks in such commerce; to protect registered marks used in such commerce from interference by State, or territorial legislation; to protect persons engaged in such commerce against unfair competition; to prevent fraud and deception in such commerce by the use of reproductions, copies, counterfeits, or colorable imitations of registered marks; and to provide rights and remedies stipulated by treaties and conventions respecting trademarks, trade names, and unfair competition entered into between the United States and foreign nations.

We thus hold that to come within the zone of interests in a suit for false advertising under § 1125(a), a plaintiff must allege an injury to a commercial interest in reputation or sales. A consumer who is hoodwinked into purchasing a disappointing product may well have an injury-in-fact cognizable under Article III, but he cannot invoke the protection of the Lanham Act—a conclusion reached by every Circuit to consider the question.

B. Proximate Cause

Second, we generally presume that a statutory cause of action is limited to plaintiffs whose injuries are proximately caused by violations of the statute.

The proximate-cause inquiry is not easy to define, and over the years it has taken various forms; but courts have a great deal of experience applying it, and there is a wealth of precedent for them to draw upon in doing so. Proximate-cause analysis is controlled by the nature of the statutory cause of action. The question it presents is whether the harm alleged has a sufficiently close connection to the conduct the statute prohibits.

In a sense, of course, all commercial injuries from false advertising are derivative of those suffered by consumers who are deceived by the advertising; but since the Lanham Act authorizes suit only for commercial injuries, the intervening step of consumer deception is not fatal to the showing of proximate causation required by the statute. That is consistent with our recognition that under common-law principles, a plaintiff can be directly injured by a misrepresentation even where "a third party, and not the plaintiff, ... relied on" it.

We thus hold that a plaintiff suing under § 1125(a) ordinarily must show economic or reputational injury flowing directly from the deception wrought by the defendant's advertising; and that that occurs when deception of consumers causes them to withhold trade from the plaintiff. That showing is generally not made when the deception produces injuries to a fellow commercial actor that in turn affect the plaintiff.

Application

Applying those principles to Static Control's false-advertising claim, we conclude that Static Control comes within the class of plaintiffs whom Congress authorized to sue under § 1125(a).

To begin, Static Control's alleged injuries—lost sales and damage to its business reputation—are injuries to precisely the sorts of commercial interests the Act protects. There is no doubt that it is within the zone of interests protected by the statute.

Static Control also sufficiently alleged that its injuries were proximately caused by Lexmark's misrepresentations. This case, it is true, does not present the "classic Lanham Act false-advertising claim" in which "one competitor directly injures another by making false statements about his own goods or the competitor's goods and thus inducing customers to switch." But ... for at least two reasons, Static Control's allegations satisfy the requirement of proximate causation.

First, Static Control alleged that Lexmark disparaged its business and products by asserting that Static Control's business was illegal. When a defendant harms a plaintiff's reputation by casting aspersions on its business, the plaintiff's injury flows directly from the audience's belief in the disparaging statements. Courts have therefore afforded relief under § 1125(a) not only where a defendant denigrates a plaintiff's product by name, but also where the defendant damages the product's reputation by, for example, equating it with an inferior product.

In addition, Static Control adequately alleged proximate causation by alleging that it designed, manufactured, and sold microchips that both (1) were necessary for, and (2) had no other use than, refurbishing Lexmark toner cartridges. It follows from that allegation that any false advertising that reduced the remanufacturers' business necessarily injured

Static Control as well. Taking Static Control's assertions at face value, there is likely to be something very close to a 1:1 relationship between the number of refurbished Prebate cartridges sold (or not sold) by the remanufacturers and the number of Prebate microchips sold (or not sold) by Static Control.

Although we conclude that Static Control has alleged an adequate basis to proceed under § 1125(a), it cannot obtain relief without evidence of injury proximately caused by Lexmark's alleged misrepresentations. We hold only that Static Control is entitled to a chance to prove its case.

––––––––––

Notes and Questions

1. While the Court seems confident that the avalanche of precedent will make application of the "proximate cause" element not unduly troubling, any student who has suffered through the study of *Palsgraf v. Long Island R.R. Co.*, 248 N.Y. 339, 162 N.E. 99 (1928) and its progeny will attest, there is no agreement on what proximate cause even is. The statement by Justice Andrews in his dissent in *Palsgraf* might still be the best summary of the issue: "What we do mean by the word 'proximate' is, that because of convenience, of public policy, of a rough sense of justice, the law arbitrarily declines to trace a series of events beyond a certain point. This is not logic. It is practical politics." *Id.* at 352, 103.

In a case decided after *Lexmark*, the Supreme Court said the following (citing *Lexmark* as an example of proximate cause analysis), seeming to agree with Justice Andrews:

> [To] say that one event was a proximate cause of another means that it was not just any cause, but one with a sufficient connection to the result. The idea of proximate cause, as distinct from actual cause or cause in fact, defies easy summary. It is 'a flexible concept'... Proximate cause is often explicated in terms of foreseeability or the scope of the risk created by the predicate conduct ... A requirement of proximate cause thus serves, *inter alia*, to preclude liability in situations where the causal link between conduct and result is so attenuated that the consequence is more aptly described as mere fortuity.

Paroline v. United States,—U.S.—, 134 S. Ct. 1710, 1719 (2014).

Given the uncertainty of the proximate cause analysis, will the Court's test for proximate cause in *Lexmark*, i.e., "whether the harm alleged has a sufficiently close connection to the conduct the statute prohibits," prove to be a sufficient guide to lower courts to determine when a competitor or other affected entity has standing to bring a Lanham Act claim?

2. In evaluating *Lexmark*, it is easy to forget that Static was not a direct competitor of Lexmark, although it was competitively affected by Lexmark's statements. Allowing for claims like that of Static is part of the rationale for the flexible proximate cause requirement. As one of the leading experts in the field explains:

> By its very nature, the injury caused by false advertising is not directly caused by defendant: it is derivative of the deception of customers. For example, in the classic case of competitors, the defendant's deceptive advertising causes customers to switch from plaintiff to defendant. But the Supreme Court [in *Lexmark*] said that this intervening step of customer deception "is not fatal to the showing of proximate causation required by the statute."

> Static's claim met the "proximate cause" part of the test even though it was not a competitor of Lexmark for two reasons:

(1) **Injury to Reputation.** There was reputational injury from disparagement. The allegedly false statements of Lexmark said that Static's microchips were illegal infringements and this assailed Static's commercial reputation by name. "[W]hen a party claims reputational injury from disparagement, competition is not required for proximate cause; and that is true even if the defendant's aim was to harm its immediate competitors, and the plaintiff merely suffered collateral damage."

(2) **Loss of Sales.** Loss of sales of microchips by Static bore a direct relationship to a decline in sales of recycled toner cartridges. The Supreme Court said that in "these relatively unique circumstances," there was no significant "discontinuity" between the injury to the direct victim (those who recycled Lexmark used cartridges) and injury to the indirect victim (Static's sales to recyclers of Static microchips that mimicked Lexmark's chips). That is, if because of the allegedly false statements of Lexmark, recyclers sold 10,000 fewer cartridges, "then it would follow more or less automatically" that Static would sell 10,000 fewer microchips. Thus, tracing damages to Static was relatively direct even though it was only indirectly impacted: its damage was not speculative or uncertain.

5 Thomas McCarthy, McCarthy on Trademarks and Unfair Competition § 27:30 (4th ed. 1994) (footnotes omitted). Given that analysis, would, e.g., Sony have standing to assert a claim against the producers of *Doom* if they issued an advertisement falsely saying that a soon to be released *Halo 6* will not be compatible with the Xbox One? Would the producers of *Halo 6* have a claim?

3. In *eGames, Inc. v. MPS Multimedia, Inc.*, No. Civ.A. 04-5463, 2005 WL 670693, at *1 (E.D. Pen. Mar. 22, 2005), eGames filed a claim under the Lanham Act against another videogame manufacturer, MPS Multimedia, alleging that MPS had a misleading statement on its packaging. Specifically, eGames contended that the packaging for MPS's "XP Championship Mahjongg" game falsely stated that the game contained "more than 1,500 backgrounds" and "more than 300 layouts," when it actually contained only 1,403 backgrounds and 249 layouts. Additionally, the packaging for its "XP Championship Solitaire" game stated that it contained "more than 1,500 backgrounds" even though it contained only 1,392 backgrounds once a consumer actually started to play. eGames sold similar videogames and claimed the misstatements caused it economic injury by diverting sales to MPS' products. The case was decided before *Lexmark*, but what do you believe the result should have been under the "zone of interest" and "proximate cause" standards?

4. A Lanham Act plaintiff with standing can seek damages and/or an injunction as remedies for a false advertising claim. Which remedy or remedies do you believe most plaintiffs are interested in?

As Professor McCarthy has noted:

When plaintiff seeks only an injunction, there is no requirement that it be proven that purchasers were actually deceived, only that the advertisement has a tendency to deceive. As [one court] noted:

To obtain an injunction under § 43(a) [plaintiffs] need only show that the falsities complained of had a tendency to deceive ... A finding of tendency to deceive satisfies the requisite of irreparable harm.

Other courts have stated the same principle in terms such that a showing of a likelihood of deception is sufficient.

5 THOMAS MCCARTHY, MCCARTHY ON TRADEMARKS AND UNFAIR COMPETITION § 27:36 (4th ed. 1994) (footnotes omitted).

What would a plaintiff have to show to establish damages?

5. Suppose the following statements appeared in ads for the next iteration of *Halo* shortly before it comes to market, and that each were contested by the publishers of *Doom*. For which statements do you believe the *Doom* publishers could sue after *Lexmark*?

- *Halo 6* is the best First Person Shooter Game on the market.

- *Halo 6* has the most realistic graphics of any First Person Shooter Game.

- Face 5,000 enemies as you level your way through *Halo 6's* treacherous fields. (Assume that *Halo 6* counts mutants of one enemy (which occur when you kill the original enemy) as a separate enemy for counting purposes, whereas the *Doom* producers believe that number is misleading as there are only 3,712 different enemies.)

- When you play *Halo 6* you will actually think you are in the Andromeda Galaxy. (Assume the *Doom* producers have an expert astronomer who will testify that a certain planet in *Halo* is misplaced under the most accurate maps of the Andromeda Galaxy.)

6. A second case regarding false advertising reached the Supreme Court in 2014, *POM Wonderful LLC v. Coca-Cola Co.* There, POM filed a claim against Coca-Cola, alleging that Coca-Cola had misled consumers with a Minute Maid "Pomegranate Blueberry" drink that contained only 0.3% pomegranate and 0.2% blueberry juice, thereby taking sales from POM's drink that contained 85% pomegranate juice. Coca-Cola argued that since the Food and Drug Administration (FDA) rules said calling the product "a flavored blend of five juices" was not misleading, the company could not be sued by a competitor under the Lanham Act. The Supreme Court disagreed and said the Lanham Act and the FDA rules have two distinct purposes: "the Lanham Act protects commercial interests against unfair competition, while the FDA protects public health and safety." *POM Wonderful LLC v. Coca-Cola Co.*,—U.S.—, 134 S. Ct. 2228 (2014).

Suppose a videogame has obtained an "M" rating from the ESRB, indicating it is for "Mature" audiences, and accurately states this on its packaging. (*See* § 12.30, *infra* for a discussion of the ESRB ratings). After *POM Wonderful,* would a rival have standing to bring suit under the Lanham Act claiming that the content of the game actually merited an "AO" rating, meaning that it should be for Adults Only, regardless of the ESRB's decision?

§ 16.40 Business Related Torts

In Chapter 13 we discussed tort claims brought against videogame manufacturers by those who suffered physical injuries after playing, or as a result of others playing, videogames. However, competitors can act tortuously against their business rivals, or former business compatriots turned business rivals, as well. Each state has a panoply of such statutory and common law claims, which are loosely categorized by the moniker "business torts."

"Business torts" include claims such as fraud, interference with prospective economic advantage, wrongful interference with contractual relationships, defamation, unfair business practices, and the like. When relations break down between former contractual partners, often all such claims are alleged, including claims against individual officers and directors of the two companies. These kinds of disputes require laborious attention from the judge as well as the parties. A good example of the facts and analysis giving rise to such claims made is the *Silicon Knights* case which follows.

Silicon Knights, Inc. v. Crystal Dynamics, Inc.

United States District Court, Northern District of California, 1997

983 F. Supp. 1303

INFANTE, United States Magistrate Judge:

INTRODUCTION

Individual Defendants ("Defendants") move to dismiss Plaintiff Silicon Knights, Inc.'s complaint for failure to state a claim upon which relief may be granted.

BACKGROUND

Plaintiff Silicon Knights, a Canadian corporation, creates, designs, and develops interactive entertainment products, including video game software and related materials. Defendant Crystal Dynamics, a California Corporation, is engaged in the business of publishing, distributing, and developing interactive entertainment products, including video game software and related materials. The individual defendants are present and former employees and officers of Crystal Dynamics. The complaint alleges on information and belief that "in committing the fraudulent and otherwise wrongful actions alleged herein, Crystal Dynamics acted by and through the other individual Defendants named herein."

The complaint alleges that Silicon Knights conceived, created, and developed an innovative new interactive video game entitled "*Blood Omen: Legacy of Kain*" ("*Kain*"). Because Silicon Knights was not well funded and needed financial assistance to complete *Kain*, Plaintiff entered into negotiations with Crystal Dynamics in late 1993 to fund the development of *Kain* in exchange for publication rights to the game. On or about January 3, 1994, the two companies signed a Letter of Intent pertaining to *Kain*, and signed a "Development Agreement" on February 16, 1994. Under "financial duress" of which Crystal Dynamics was aware, Silicon Knights agreed to assign all of Silicon Knights' intellectual property rights in *Kain*, including the rights to any derivative works, to Crystal Dynamics. In return, Crystal Dynamics made two critical promises to Silicon Knights: (1) the potential of substantial later royalties from Silicon Knights' development of *Kain* derivative works, including Silicon Knights' right to make the first bid on any derivative works, and (2) publication credits identifying Silicon Knights as developer and originator of *Kain* and prominent credit as originator in connection with any and all *Kain* derivative works and *Kain* products, irrespective of who developed these works. Defendants Crystal Dynamics, Dorosin, and Ardell repeatedly promised Silicon Knights that Defendant would comply with these terms, and memorialized its promises of Silicon Knights' right of first bid in writing in Paragraph 5.2 of the *Kain* Development Agreement. Additionally, Silicon Knights accepted a lower percentage of Crystal Dynamics' net revenues as its sales royalty than was standard in the industry since Defendant Crystal Dynamics was acting as both a distributer and publisher of *Kain*.

The complaint alleges that Crystal Dynamics made these promises without intent to perform, and breached the development agreement by: (1) adding increasingly stringent requirements to Silicon Knights' duties under the *Kain* Development Agreement while refusing to cooperate and respond to Silicon Knights' requests for assistance, resulting in several months of delay; (2) hindering Silicon Knights' ability to meet its deadlines under the agreement; (3) withholding royalty advances at critical stages of the *Kain* development and refusing to account for royalties in 45-day intervals as required by the Development

Agreement; (4) secretly soliciting and employing third party contractors to "shadow" Silicon Knights' efforts in producing various versions of *Kain* and supplying these third parties with Silicon Knights' confidential, proprietary and trade secret information in an effort to eventually supplant Plaintiff as developer of *Kain*; and (5) making numerous other efforts and attempts to prevent Silicon Knights from performing and/or meeting its purported deadlines and duties under the Agreement.

The complaint also alleges that Crystal Dynamics further breached its agreement with Silicon Knights in the Fall of 1996 by selling certain rights to *Kain* and all *Kain* derivative works to Activision for approximately $2 million dollars. By entering into this agreement with Activision, Defendant abdicated its agreed role as publisher on the *Kain* project, which decreased the revenues payable to Silicon Knights to as little as 1/4 of the originally promised amount. Defendant did grant Plaintiff a higher royalty percentage to compensate for the fact that Crystal Dynamics would not distribute *Kain* in a November 20, 1996 modification of the Kain Development Agreement. However, Crystal Dynamics failed to advise Silicon Knights of several aspects of the CD-Activision deal, including, but not limited to the fact that Activision would be taking over both the publication and distribution of *Kain*, and that Crystal Dynamics had fraudulently substituted itself as "developer" for *Kain* in the CD-Activision deal, which eliminated the potential for derivative work revenues to Silicon Knights as developer of any future *Kain* works.

Although Crystal Dynamics intended to exit the software publishing business at this time, the complaint alleges that Crystal Dynamics, Dorosin, and Ardell did not inform Silicon Knights of this intention, but represented to Plaintiff both orally and in writing that: (a) Crystal Dynamics intended to remain a publisher; (b) that the CD-Activision Deal would transfer only the Kain "distribution rights" to Activision; and (c) that the CD-Activision Deal would not affect Crystal Dynamics' obligations under Section 5.2 of the Development Agreement concerning Silicon Knights' right of first bid to develop derivative works. At the time Crystal Dynamics made these representations, it had fired most, if not all, of its publishing personnel as a part of its plan to leave the publishing business.

Although Crystal Dynamics represented itself as developer of *Kain* and the derivative *Kain II*, Activision was allegedly displeased with Crystal Dynamics' work and approached other developers, including Silicon Knights, for potential assistance on the artwork for *Kain II*. Activision and Silicon Knights apparently entered into an agreement whereby Plaintiff would provide artwork for the game. Upon learning of this potential re-entry of Silicon Knights into *Kain* development, Defendants made false, misleading, and commercially disparaging statements about Silicon Knights' technical abilities and Silicon Knights' involvement in the creation and development of *Kain* to Activision and others in the video game industry.

Crystal Dynamics also directly and indirectly solicited Silicon Knights' employees to leave and either join Crystal Dynamics or start one or more companies in competition with Silicon Knights to cripple and prevent Silicon Knights from performing its obligations under the SK-Activision Contract, to enable Crystal Dynamics to meet Activision's standards, and to develop derivative works on terms more favorable to Crystal Dynamics than the Kain Development Agreement. These actions also induced Silicon Knights' employees to breach their non-disclosure and non-competition agreements with Plaintiff.

On July 3, 1997, Plaintiff filed a complaint against Defendant Crystal Dynamics seeking, inter alia., rescission or reformation of the contract and damages for breach of contract. Additionally, the complaint asserts the following claims against Defendant Crystal Dynamics and some or all of the Individual Defendants: Statutory Unfair Competition, pursuant to Cal. Bus. & Prof. C. § 17200 & 17500 et seq.; Common Law Unfair Competition; Intentional Interference with Contractual Relations with Silicon Knights' former employees; Intentional Interference with Contractual Relations with Activision; Intentional Interference with Prospective Economic Advantage with Activision; International Interference with Prospective Economic Advantage (generally); Negligent Interference with Economic Advantage (generally); Defamation and Commercial Disparagement; Fraud; and Negligent Misrepresentation.

DISCUSSION

The allegations are sufficient to allege that Individual Defendants' directed the alleged wrongful acts.

In addition to challenging each claim asserted against the Individual Defendants on various substantive grounds, Individual Defendants challenge all claims asserted against them in the complaint on the grounds that personal liability cannot be conferred upon them based solely upon their roles as employees and officers of Crystal Dynamics, and that the complaint fails to allege any facts upon which Individual Defendants could be found personally liable for the claims asserted against them. Silicon Knights opposes this position, contending that the complaint alleges various fraudulent statements made by specific defendants, and that the complaint contains "detailed allegations ... regarding the Individual Defendants' positions of control and authority at Crystal Dynamics, as well as the fact that each of the named defendants directed, controlled, participated in, or executed all, or virtually all, of the torts alleged in the complaint."

As asserted by Plaintiff, under California law, directors or officers of a corporation do not incur personal liability for the torts of the corporation merely by reason of their official position, unless they participate in the wrong or authorize or direct that it be done. They may be liable, under the rules for tort and agency, for tortious acts committed on behalf of the corporation.

Pursuant to Rule 8(a)(2), F.R.Civ.P, a complaint must contain a "short and plain statement of the claim showing that the pleader is entitled to relief ..." To assert claims against individual defendants, a complaint must contain allegations indicating how the defendant violated the law or injured the plaintiff in order to survive a motion to dismiss. Rule 8(a)(2) does not require that the complaint set forth a defendant's precise role in the injurious conduct, but that defendants be put on notice as to the nature of the allegations against them and their relationship to the actions at issue in the case.

In this case, the complaint goes beyond merely identifying the Individual Defendants in the caption, but sets forth their respective positions within the corporation and alleges that "Crystal Dynamics acted by and through the other individual Defendants named herein" in "committing the fraudulent and otherwise wrongful actions alleged herein ..." This allegation, coupled with specific acts of fraud and misconduct alleged throughout the complaint, is sufficient to inform individual defendants of their "relationship to the actions at issue in the case" and the basis of their alleged liability for the tort claims alleged in the complaint.

Fifth and Sixth Causes of Action for Intentional Interference with Contractual Relations with Silicon Knights' Former Employees and Activision

Individual Defendants contend that the complaint fails to allege sufficient facts to state a claim for Intentional Interference with Contractual Relations of Silicon Knights' contracts with either Activision or Silicon Knights' former employees. First, Defendants contend that the complaint fails to allege any action taken by Crystal Dynamics that "goes beyond the acceptable bounds of conduct in business rivalry" and "certainly no grounds for personal liability on the part of the individual defendants." Second, Defendants contend that the complaint fails to allege any specific facts showing that Silicon Knights had a duty not to do any business with any third parties for video game development, including Keyframe, or that the complaint alleges any facts to show Individual Defendants' specific intent to cause the breach or disruption of Silicon Knights' contracts with its former employees or Activision.

Plaintiff asserts that Defendants' contention that their acts were "within the acceptable bounds of business rivalry" goes to the merits, and not the sufficiency, of the complaint. Plaintiff also contends that the complaint alleges sufficient facts to show that Defendants' acts went beyond the realm of legitimate business purposes.

The following elements state a claim for intentional interference with contractual relationship under California law: (1) a valid contract between plaintiff and a third party; (2) defendant's knowledge of this contract; (3) defendant's intentional acts designed to induce a breach or disruption of the contractual relationship; (4) actual breach or disruption of the contractual relationship; and (5) resulting damage.

The complaint sufficiently alleges facts necessary to establish a claim for tortious interference with Silicon Knights' contracts with its former employees. The complaint alleges that Plaintiff had a non-disclosure agreement with a former employee, Cranford, with respect to any confidential information Cranford received during his employment with Silicon Knights, as well as non-competition agreements with former employees Green, Ryan, and Cranford with respect to work performed on behalf of Silicon Knights on *Kain*. Additionally, "Ryan had been designated in a 'Keyman Clause' as part of [a] recent development agreement which Silicon Knights had itself made with Activision for artwork on a game called '*Zork Grand Inquisitor*.'" The complaint alleges that Defendants Crystal Dynamics, Ardell, Dyer, Miller, and Horsely knew of the employees' agreements with Silicon Knights, and that "Crystal Dynamics and one or more of the other individual Defendants began soliciting Silicon Knights' employees ... to leave Silicon Knights, for the purposes of: (1) crippling Silicon Knights; (2) preventing Silicon Knights from performing its obligations under the SK-Activision Contract; (3) interfering with Silicon Knights' non-disclosure and non-competition agreements with its employees; (4) interfering with Silicon Knights' other contracts and potential commercial dealings; and (5) enabling Crystal Dynamics to negotiate with those former Silicon Knights employees to develop *Kain* derivative works on terms more favorable to Crystal Dynamics that the Kain Development Agreement ..." The complaint alleges specific acts undertaken by Crystal Dynamics to induce its employees' breach of their non-disclosure and non-competition agreements, such as "soliciting and financially assisting Cranford, Green, and Ryan to leave Silicon Knights' employment and start a competing business with Silicon Knights under the name Keyframe Digital Productions ("Keyframe") in breach of their respective non-competition and non-disclosure agreements with Silicon Knights" along with promises of future business, such as derivative works for *Kain*.

Pursuant to Rule 9(c), F.R.Civ.P., a complaint may generally aver malice, intent, knowledge, "and other condition of mind of a person." Therefore, Plaintiff's general allegations of Crystal Dynamics' knowledge of the underlying contracts, and its wrongful intent in interfering with the employees' contractual relationships with Silicon Knights is not fatal to the complaint.

The affirmative defense of "competitive privilege" is not apparent on the face of the complaint. The complaint alleges that Crystal Dynamics intentionally interfered with

Silicon Knights' contractual relations with its former employees, including non-competition and non-disclosure agreements, by inducing them to form a company that directly competed with Silicon Knights on the *Kain* project, for the purposes of improving its competitive position at the expense of the Silicon Knights. It is the act of inducing or interfering with the contract with an improper motive, and not the later act of dealing with the party who breached the contract, that underlies the tort.

Therefore, for the forgoing reasons, Defendants' motion to dismiss the Fifth Cause of Action for Interference with Contractual Relations as to Silicon Knights' former employees is DENIED.

Seventh and Eighth Claims for Intentional Interference with Economic Relations

Defendants object to Plaintiff's claims for interference with prospective economic advantage with Activision (seventh claim) and other third parties (eighth claim), on the same basis asserted in their motion to dismiss the interference with contract claims, and on the grounds that a) the complaint does not allege that Individual Defendants "engaged in conduct that was wrongful by some measure other than the fact of interference itself," and b) the complaint does not allege an economic relationship containing the probability of future economic benefit.

Plaintiff asserts that the complaint alleges interference with Silicon Knights' work on *Kain II* with Activision (seventh claim) and that the "[c]omplaint again lays out (among other injuries) three specific Silicon Knights business relationships which the Individual Defendants have injured: Microsoft, Activision, and 3DO." Plaintiff further contends that "any sensible reading of the Complaint in this action demonstrates abundant independently 'wrongful' conduct by the Individual Defendants within the meaning of Della Penna" including misappropriation of trade secrets[2] and fraud and misrepresentation. Plaintiff also contends that the mere "potential" of an economic relationship is sufficient to assert the tort.

To support a cause of action for interference with prospective economic advantage, the following elements must be established: (1) the existence of a specific economic relationship between [plaintiff] and third parties that may economically benefit [plaintiff]; (2) knowledge by the [defendants] of this relationship; (3) intentional acts by the [defendants] designed to disrupt the relationship; (4) actual disruption of the relationship; and (5) damages to the [plaintiff]. The California Supreme Court has also stated that a plaintiff seeking to recover for alleged interference with prospective economic relations has the burden of pleading and proving that the defendant's interference was wrongful by some other measure beyond the fact of interference itself.

The law precludes recovery for overly speculative expectancies by initially requiring proof the business relationship contained 'the probability of future economic relationship. [T]here is no factual allegation in the complaint that Silicon Knights' relationship with Activision was actually disrupted as a result of Crystal Dynamics and Individual Defendants' acts of inducing Silicon Knights' former employees to leave Plaintiff's employ, or what damages, if any, were incurred by Silicon Knights as a result of these acts.

---

2. The alleged misappropriation of trade secrets does not appear to be a basis for Plaintiff's claim for intentional or negligent interference with economic and/or contractual relations. Rather, Defendants' alleged defamatory remarks, Crystal Dynamics' claim that it developed *Kain*, and Defendants' inducement to Plaintiff's employees to break their non-disclosure and non-competition agreements are the alleged wrongful acts set forth in the Eighth and Ninth claims.

With respect to the eighth claim for intentional interference with prospective economic relationship, the complaint fails to allege an economic relationship with any third party containing the probability of future economic benefit to the plaintiff. There are no allegations in the complaint from which the court or defendants could infer the probable disruption of an actual economic relationship by means of alleged defamatory statements of the individual defendants or by means of Crystal Dynamics' statement that it developed *Kain*. The complaint does not allege that Silicon Knights was in the midst of negotiations with 3DO, Microsoft, or any other publisher, and that the third party pulled out of the negotiations or awarded business to another because of these alleged acts by Defendants. Moreover, allegations that Defendants' undisclosed statements caused potential customers not to buy Silicon Knights' video game software asserts the type of speculative economic relationship disapproved of in *Westgate*. Even if interference with potential customers is a legitimate basis for tortious interference with economic relations, the complaint alleges only conclusory statements and no facts in support of its contention that it lost potential customers. For example, there is no allegation that sales of a particular software product identified with Silicon Knights decreased after these alleged statements were made by Crystal Dynamics.

Therefore, Defendants' motion to dismiss the seventh and eighth claims for intentional interference with economic relations is GRANTED with leave to amend.

Ninth Claim for Negligent Interference with Prospective Economic Advantage

Defendants contend that the claim for negligent interference with prospective economic advantage fails for the same reasons set forth above, i.e., the complaint contains only speculative allegations of economic relationships. Defendants also assert that the complaint fails to state a claim upon which relief can be granted since Silicon Knights has not, and cannot, allege any contractual or statutory duty, or special relationship between Individual Defendants and Plaintiff that give rise to a duty of care. Defendants assert in their reply brief that the action is based upon an "unenforceable alleged oral agreement between Silicon Knights and Crystal Dynamics."

Plaintiff contends that "[a]s shown throughout the Complaint, the Individual Defendants' 'course of dealings established ... a fiduciary relationship." Plaintiff apparently is asserting that Defendants' alleged fraud and misrepresentation, and the foreseeability of harm these acts would cause to Silicon Knights, created a "special relationship" between Individual Defendants and Silicon Knights.[3]

The tort of negligent interference with economic relationship arises only when the defendant owes the plaintiff a duty of care. This duty may arise from a contractual, statutory, or "special relationship" between the plaintiff and defendant. This "special relationship" typically arises where the plaintiff is a beneficiary of a contract between two parties. In *J'Aire Corporation v. Gregory*, 24 Cal.3d 799, 804 (1979), the California Supreme Court stated that the following criteria would be used in determining whether defendants owe

---

3. Plaintiff asserts in its opposition: "As shown throughout the Complaint, the Individual Defendants' course of dealings with Silicon Knights established just such a fiduciary relationship. Perhaps the most prominent example of the relationship, and its breach, is the Defendants' misappropriation and wrongful disclosure of Silicon Knights' confidential and trade secret information as it pertained to the development of *Kain* ... Similarly, unlike the Complaint in this case, the complaint in *Orion* contained no allegations of 'any contractual or statutory duty owed by [defendant],' nor any allegation of a 'special relationship that might give rise to a duty.'" Such allegations are clearly present here, particularly since such a "relationship" can be assessed by "the foreseeability of harm suffered by plaintiff."

plaintiff of duty of care: "(1) the extent to which the transaction was intended to affect the plaintiff, (2) the foreseeability of harm to the plaintiff, (3) the degree of certainty that the plaintiff suffered injury, (4) the closeness of the connection between the defendant's conduct and the injury suffered, (5) the moral blame attached to the defendant's conduct and (6) the policy of preventing future harm."

Plaintiff's cause of action for negligent interference with economic relations fails to state a claim since the complaint does not allege the existence of a specific economic relationship between Crystal Dynamics and third parties that could have economically benefitted Silicon Knights but for Individual Defendants' wrongful conduct. Moreover, the complaint fails to allege any duty that Defendants owed to Plaintiff to refrain from taking the alleged actions. Plaintiff cites no authority for its contention that a wrongful act by a defendant, without more, constitutes a "special relationship" for which a defendant may be held liable for negligent interference with prospective economic advantage. If this were the state of the law, then any claim for negligent interference with prospective economic advantage would necessarily be subsumed within the tort of intentional interference with economic relations, and the requirement of a "special relationship" or other duty would be meaningless.

Therefore, Individual Defendants' motion to dismiss the Ninth Cause of Action for Negligent Interference with Economic Advantage is GRANTED with leave to amend.

Tenth Claim for Defamation and Commercial Disparagement

Individual Defendants contend that the tenth cause of action for defamation fails because the complaint does not identify any defamatory matter expressed or conveyed by the Individual Defendants and that the complaint contains no allegation of special damages. Defendants also contend that the only defamatory matter specified in the complaint and set forth in exhibits A and B cannot be construed as defamatory statements.

In its opposition, Silicon Knights does not contend that statements contained in the exhibits to the complaint are defamatory. Instead, Plaintiff contends that the complaint "identifies a number of other specific defamatory and disparaging statements made by the Individual Defendants, including false statements about Silicon Knights' original development of *Kain*, similar false statements about Silicon Knights' technical capabilities and ability to deliver products in a timely fashion, and specific statements by at least Defendant Dyer to employees of Microsoft concerning similar issues." Plaintiff also asserts that allegations of special damages are not necessary since the statements are defamatory on their face.

The statements in the complaint identified as defamatory by Plaintiff include the allegation that Crystal Dynamics has refused to give proper originator and developer credit for *Kain*; that Defendants engaged in wrongful conduct by "making false, misleading, and commercially disparaging statements about Silicon Knights' involvement in the creation and development of *Kain* to Activision (and others in the video game industry)"; and by making "false and defamatory statements to several of Silicon Knights' customers, prospective customers, industry associates and the public regarding: (a) the quality and reliability of Silicon Knights' products, (b) the competence and ability of Silicon Knights' employees, and (c) Silicon Knights' cooperation and ability to work with customers, suppliers, or other persons in the software industry." Some or all of these statements were allegedly made by Dyer to Microsoft personnel, and by other defendants to Activision and 3DO personnel.

The words constituting a libel or slander must be specifically identified, if not plead verbatim. The complaint contains only general allegations of the defamatory statements and does not identify the substance of what was stated by the Defendants. Further, as currently alleged, the statements appear to be expressions of opinion rather than factual assertions.

Therefore, Individual Defendants' motion to dismiss the Tenth Claim for Defamation is GRANTED with leave to amend.

Thirteenth and Fourteenth Claims for Fraud and Negligent Misrepresentation

Individual Defendants contend that Silicon Knights' allegations of fraud and negligent misrepresentation are refuted by the express terms of the Kain Development Contract and written amendments. Defendants contend that Plaintiff's failure to attach copies of the relevant agreements at issue, while omitting material terms, renders the complaint subject to dismissal. Defendants contend that the Development Agreement does not prohibit or restrict Crystal Dynamics from entering into any agreement with Activision or any third party concerning the distribution, marketing, or sales of *Kain*. Even if there were such an agreement, Defendants contend that the Amendment to the Development Agreement, dated November 20, 1996, expressly released any possible liability for Crystal Dynamics' transfer of *Kain* distribution rights to Activision, in exchange for an increase in Silicon Knights' royalty percentage to 42.8%. Defendants also contend that the allegations of fraud are not stated with particularity, as required by Rule 9(b), F.R.Civ.P.

Plaintiff contends that the November 20, 1996 amendments cited by Defendants only release Crystal Dynamics from liability with respect to the CD-Activision deal, and that several additional grounds for liability of the Individual Defendants are alleged in the complaint. Plaintiff also contends that this release was procured from Silicon Knights by fraud, misrepresentation, and other wrongful conduct of the Individual Defendants and Crystal Dynamics.

Plaintiff does not assert the substance of any of alleged fraudulent statements and/or omissions in its thirteenth and fourteenth claims for fraud and negligent misrepresentation. Instead, the alleged fraudulent statements and omissions are scattered throughout the complaint's "common factual allegations."

Among the fraudulent statements and/or omissions made by Crystal Dynamics and Individual Defendants that form the basis for the fraud and negligent misrepresentation claims are that Crystal Dynamics induced Silicon Knights to enter into the Development Agreement by promising potential substantial later royalties from Silicon Knights' development of *Kain* derivative works and publication credits identifying Silicon Knights as developer of *Kain*. The complaint alleges that Defendants Crystal Dynamics, Dorosin, and Ardell repeatedly promised Silicon Knights that Crystal Dynamics would comply with both of these terms, but that "it now appears that Crystal Dynamics never had any intention of keeping those promises …" The complaint also alleges that Silicon Knights entered the agreement which gave it a smaller percentage of royalties since Crystal Dynamics represented to Silicon Knights that Crystal Dynamics would be both publisher and distributor of *Kain*, and that Plaintiff would stand to make a greater profit from *Kain*. To induce Silicon Knights to enter into the November 1996 amendments, the complaint alleges that Crystal Dynamics failed to advise Silicon Knights of numerous aspects of the CD-Activision Deal, including, but not limited to the fact that Activision would be taking over both publication and distribution of *Kain*, that Silicon Knights' royalties would be "dramatically" reduced as a result, and the fact that Crystal Dynamics substituted itself as developer for *Kain* in the CD-Activision deal, which "de facto" eliminated any potential for derivative work revenues to Silicon Knights as developer of any future *Kain* works.

The alleged fraudulent statements are not plead in compliance with Rule 9(b) F.R.Civ.P. Rule 9(b) requires that "[i]n all averments of fraud or mistake, the circumstances constituting fraud or mistake shall be stated with particularity." To satisfy this heightened pleading requirement, the complaint must state the time, place, and specific content of the false representations as well as the identities of the parties to the misrepresentation.

None of the complaint's allegations of fraud state the time, place and manner of the alleged misrepresentations. Furthermore, only a few of the alleged misrepresentations identify the person who made the statement. Since fraud must be alleged in particularity, a general allegation that all Individual Defendants directed that the alleged fraudulent statements be made is insufficient to assert liability upon persons who did not make the statements. Additionally, there are no allegations upon which the Individual Defendants could be held personally liable for alleged omissions of material facts, since only Crystal Dynamics was a party to the alleged contract.

Therefore, Defendants' motion to dismiss the Thirteenth and Fourteenth Claims for Fraud and Negligent Misrepresentation is granted with leave to amend. Should Plaintiff decide to amend the complaint, all elements of fraud, including the time, place, manner and identity of the person making the fraudulent statements, shall be stated within the claim itself and not merely incorporated by amendment.

Third and Fourth Claims for Statutory Unfair Competition and Common Law Unfair Competition

Individual Defendants contend that Plaintiff has failed to state any facts to support its claim for statutory unfair competition or common law unfair competition, Claims HI and IV, asserting that the claims consist of "nothing but conclusory allegations of fraud, misappropriation of trade secrets, and equally vague claims of interference with business relations." Defendants also assert that the complaint fails to identify any trade secrets proprietary to Silicon Knights that Crystal Dynamics misappropriated, and that all intellectual property rights in *Kain* were transferred to Crystal Dynamics, pursuant to agreement between the parties.

A plaintiff alleging unfair business practices under the unfair competition statutes must state with reasonable particularity the facts supporting the statutory elements of the violation. Since most of Plaintiff's causes of action fail to state claims for relief against Individual Defendants, there is no underlying basis for the unfair competition claims as alleged against these Defendants. Moreover, allegations based upon misappropriation of trade secrets fail to identify the "fraudulent circumstances under which these trade secrets where disclosed" or how Crystal Dynamics' possession or use of source code, game engines and "other source materials" is wrongful when the Development Agreement grants to Crystal Dynamics all rights in the ownership and derivative works.[4]

Therefore, Defendants' motion to dismiss the Third and Fourth Claims for Unfair Competition is GRANTED with leave to amend.

Notes and Questions

1. In *Silicon Knights*, what type of contractual arrangements and terms do you think might have avoided the problems and disputes? Do you suspect the relationship between the plaintiff and defendant was doomed from the beginning? If so, why?

---

4. This is not to say that Plaintiff cannot allege how Defendants' use of Silicon Knights' alleged trade secrets abrogated the agreement and constituted unfair competition.

2. Which of the different causes of action alleged by Silicon Knights would be most likely to succeed? Do you think that Crystal Dynamics really went beyond the bounds of acceptable business practices during its rivalry? Should the affirmative defense of "competitive privilege" alluded to by the court be applicable?

§ 16.50 Cybersquatting

Another emerging area of litigation in videogame and tech industries is cybersquatting. Cybersquatting is a relatively new type of tort that was codified into law with the passage of the Anticybersquatting Consumer Protection Act (ACPA) of 1999. The gist if the statute is that it prohibits an individual from holding hostage a domain name with a particular company's name (or some derivative thereof) in it. A complement to the Federal Trademark Dilution Act, the ACPA provides:

> A person shall be liable in a civil action by the owner of a mark, including a personal name which is protected as a mark under this section, if, without regard to the goods or services of the parties, that person—
>
> (i) has a bad faith intent to profit from that mark, including a personal name which is protected as a mark under this section; and
>
> (ii) registers, traffics in, or uses a domain name that—
>
> (I) in the case of a mark that is distinctive at the time of registration of the domain name, is identical or confusingly similar to that mark;
>
> (II) in the case of a famous mark that is famous at the time of registration of the domain name, is identical or confusingly similar to or dilutive of that mark; or
>
> (III) is a trademark, word, or name protected by reason of section 706 of Title 18 [marks similar to those held by the Red Cross] or section 220506 of Title 36 [marks similar to those held by the International Olympic Committee].[1]

Cybersquatters typically register domain names that embody the trademarks of others with no intention of developing a viable web site.[2] Instead, cybersquatters hold the domain for resale to either the trademark owner or a third party.[3] However, it is not just the possibility of "holding up" the trademark holder that the law was concerned about. Until it is sold to the entity whose name the domain carries, cybersquatters can use "their" domain names to sell counterfeit goods, send fraudulent spam emails, host salacious content, and derive advertising revenue from consumer confusion about a company's true web address.

One of the first cybersquatting cases, *Morrison & Foerster LLP v. Wick*, is excerpted below.

---

1. 15 U.S.C. § 1125(d) (2012).

2. 2-7A Anne Gilson Lalonde, Gilson on Trademarks § 7A.06 (2009).

3. *Id.* Note, however, that individuals who have a legitimate use of a domain name are not in violation of the ACPA. *See, e.g., Nissan Motor Co. v. Nissan Computer Corp.,* 378 F.3d (9th Cir. 2004) (holding that an individual named Uzi Nissan, who had registered nissan.com first and used it to promote his computer business, had the rights to the domain name.)

Morrison & Foerster LLP v. Wick

United States District Court, District of Colorado, 2000
94 F. Supp. 2d 1125

BABCOCK, United States District Judge.

In this Internet action brought, inter alia, pursuant to the Anticybersquatting Consumer Protection Act, 15 U.S.C. § 1125(d) ("ACPA"), Morrison & Foerster moves for a preliminary and permanent injunction. Defendants, Brian Wick and American Distribution Systems, Inc. ("ADSI"), oppose this motion.

The World Wide Web

Before reciting the facts established by the evidence, I begin with a brief explanation of the relevant technology. The Internet, or the World Wide Web, is a network of computers that allows people to access information stored on other computers within the network. Information on the Internet is lodged on files called web pages, which can include printed matter, sound, pictures, and links to other web pages. An Internet user can move from one page to another with just the click of a mouse. Web pages or web sites are designated by addresses called domain names.

Web sites are used by many companies to provide product information and sell products online. Consumers need an easy way to find certain companies to order products or gather information. The most common method of locating an unknown domain name is simply to type in the company name or logo with the suffix.com. If this method is unsuccessful, a user can use a "search engine" which, theoretically, will find all web pages on the Internet containing a particular word or phrase.

Registrars assign domain names on a first-come, first-served basis upon payment of a registration fee. Register.com, the registrar used in this case, charges $ 75.00 per domain name. Domain name registrars do not inquire into whether a domain name request matches or conflicts with another's trademark.

Lack of regulatory control caused problems of cybersquatting and cyberpiracy. Cybersquatting involves the registration as domain names of well-known trademarks by non-trademark holders who then try to sell the names back to the trademark owners. Trademark owners are frequently willing to pay "ransom" in order to protect their marks.

The ACPA was passed in November 1999 to address these concerns, and to "protect consumers and American businesses, to promote the growth of online commerce, and to provide clarity in the law for trademark owners by prohibiting the bad-faith and abusive registration of distinctive marks as Internet domain names with the intent to profit from the goodwill associated with such marks—a practice commonly referred to as 'cybersquatting.'" S.Rep. No. 106-140, at 4.

Background

The following facts are established by the direct and circumstantial evidence. The law firm of Morrison & Foerster was founded in 1883. Since 1975, Morrison & Foerster has provided legal services under the service mark, Morrison & Foerster. Since November 1991, Morrison & Foerster has owned and maintained United States Trademark Registration No. 1,665,352 for the mark MORRISON & FOERSTER for legal services. In 1999, the firm's advertising and marketing budget was approximately $ 1 million.

Morrison & Foerster is the registered owner of the domain name www.mofo.com. Morrison & Foerster is commonly known in the legal community both as Morrison & Foerster and as "MoFo." The firm utilizes its Internet web site to market and promote its services, and to provide a point of contact for customers and attorneys seeking employment. In addition to owning the registered trademark MORRISON & FOERSTER, since December 1996 the firm has also owned the United States Trademark Registration for the mark MOFO.

On October 24, 1999, Mr. Wick, using the names NameIsForSale.com and Morri, Son & Foerster, registered the domain names www.morrisonfoerster.com, www.morrisonandfoerster.com, www.morrisonforester.com, and www.morrisonandforester.com through the online registrar, www.register.com. On October 27, 1999, Morrison & Foerster registered the domain names www.morrisonfoerster.org, www.morrisonfoerster.net, www.morrisonandfoerster.net, and www.morrisonandfoerster.org. At that same time, it attempted to register the domain names www.morrisonfoerster.com and www.morrisonandfoerster.com. Morrison & Foerster intended to establish web sites that would link to the firm's existing web site at www.mofo.com. However, because Mr. Wick already registered these domain names three days earlier, it was unable to do so.

According to www.register.com records, the administrative contact for www.morrisonfoerster.com and www.morrisonandfoerster.com was "Brian Wick, bgw@earthnet.net." The other two domain names registered by Mr. Wick—www.morrisonforester.com and www.morrisonandforester.com—employ a common misspelling of Morrison & Foerster. The administrative contact for these domain names is also "bgw@earthnet.net." Registration records show that shortly before registering the four domain names at issue, Defendants registered www.nameisforsale.com as a domain name. According to www.register.com's records, www.nameisforsale.com is registered by NameIsForSale.com, an entity that lists the same post office box address as Defendants Wick and ADSI, a Colorado corporation of which Mr. Wick is President, Secretary, registered agent, sole Director and sole Shareholder. Records also show that the administrative contact for the www.nameisforsale.com domain name is Brian Wick at "bgw@earthnet.net."

The four web sites at issue, established by Mr. Wick, are very different than Morrison & Foerster's official site at www.mofo.com. Although Mr. Wick's web sites displayed different things at different times, print outs of his sites state: "We're your paid friends!"; "Best friends money can buy"; "Greed is good!"; "We bend over for you … because you bend over for us!"; "Parasites No Soul … No Conscience … No Spine … NO PROBLEM". Also on the web sites appeared a copy of a letter to Mr. Wick from Morrison & Foerster regarding infringement of the mark. Finally, the web sites contained hyperlinks which allowed a user to link on to other offensively named web sites.

Morrison & Foerster's complaint [involves] cybersquatting in violation of the ACPA

Anticybersquatting Consumer Protection Act

The Anticybersquatting Consumer Protection Act, 15 U.S.C. §1125(d) ("ACPA"), amends the Trademark Act of 1946, creating a federal remedy for cybersquatting. The ACPA allows me to order "the forfeiture or cancellation of the domain name or transfer of the domain name to the owner of the mark." 15 U.S.C. §1125(d)(1)(C).

There is no dispute that Morrison & Foerster is the owner of the trademark MORRISON & FOERSTER. As noted above, it has owned this mark since November 1991.

Further, Morrison & Foerster's mark is distinctive and/or famous, and therefore entitled to the ACPA's protection. At the temporary restraining order hearing, I found that Morrison & Foerster's mark is famous and conclusively distinctive under the law. The mark has been used by Morrison & Foerster since 1991, has had millions of dollars in advertising spent on it, is used nationwide, and is registered with federal authorities. Furthermore, in 1997, the trademark office issued a Declaration of Use and Incontestability of a Mark under Sections 8 and 15. Registration of Morrison & Foerster's mark entitles them to a presumption that its registered trademark is inherently distinctive. Nothing presented at trial alters my conclusion that this mark is famous and distinctive.

I also conclude that Mr. Wick's four domain names are identical or confusingly similar to Morrison & Foerster's mark. Because ampersands cannot be used in Internet domain names, two of Mr. Wick's domain names are, in all practical aspects, identical to Morrison & Foerster's mark: www.morrisonfoerster.com and www.morrisonfoerster.com. *see, e.g., Brookfield Communications, Inc. v. West Coast Entertainment Corp.,* 174 F.3d 1036, 1055 (9th Cir. 1999) (finding that the differences between the mark "MovieBuff" and the domain name "movie.buff.com" are "inconsequential in light of the fact that Web addresses are not caps-sensitive and that the '.com' top-level domain signifies the site's commercial nature.").

His other two domain names employ a common misspelling of Morrison & Foerster's mark, and are, as he intended, confusingly similar: www.morrisonforester.com and www.morrisonandforester.com.

The pivotal question is whether Mr. Wick "has a bad faith intent to profit" from his use of the mark. The ACPA provides assistance with this determination, stating nine factors for courts to consider in determining whether a defendant has acted with a bad faith intent to profit from the use of a mark:

(B)(i) In determining whether a person has a bad faith intent described under subparagraph (a), a court may consider factors such as, but not limited to

(I) the trademark or other intellectual property rights of the person, if any, in the domain name;

(II) the extent to which the domain name consists of the legal name of the person or a name that is otherwise commonly used to identify that person;

(III) the person's prior use, if any, of the domain name in connection with the bona fide offering of any goods or services;

(IV) the person's bona fide noncommercial or fair use of the mark in a site accessible under the domain name;

(V) the person's intent to divert consumers from the mark owner's online location to a site accessible under the domain name that could harm the goodwill represented by the mark, either for commercial gain or with the intent to

tarnish or disparage the mark, by creating a likelihood of confusion as to the source, sponsorship, affiliation, or endorsement of the site;

(VI) the person's offer to transfer, sell, or otherwise assign the domain name to the mark owner or any third party for financial gain without having used, or having an intent to use, the domain name in the bona fide offering of any goods or services, or the person's prior conduct indicating a pattern of such conduct;

(VII) the person's provision of material and misleading false contact information when applying for the registration of the domain name, the person's intentional failure to maintain accurate contact information, or the person's prior conduct indicating a pattern of such conduct;

(VIII) the person's registration or acquisition of multiple domain names which the person knows are identical or confusingly similar to marks of others that are distinctive at the time of registration of such domain names, or dilutive of famous marks of others that are famous at the time of registration of such domain names, without regard to the goods or services of the parties; and

(IX) the extent to which the mark incorporated in the person's domain name registration is or is not distinctive and famous within the meaning of subsection (c)(1) of this section.

15 U.S.C. § 1125(d)(1)(B)(i). Before introducing these nine factors, the ACPA states that a court "may" consider factors "such as" the ones listed. The factors therefore are not framed as exclusive or mandatory, but are relevant guidelines.

First, it is clear that Mr. Wick has no intellectual property rights in any of the domain names he registered. Second, none of the domain names consist of Mr. Wick's legal name nor a name that he is commonly identified by. To the extent that he uses the trade name Morri, Son & Foerster, this has only been in use since January 3, 2000 when ADSI amended its corporate filings with the Colorado Secretary of State to include "Morri, Son & Foerster eBusiness, Inc." as an assumed name. This occurred several months after Defendants first acquired and used the domain names. Indeed, this conduct is indicative of Defendants' bad faith. Third, there is no evidence of Mr. Wick's prior use of any of these domain names in connection with the offering of any bona fide goods or services.

Directing my attention to the fourth factor, Mr. Wick argues that he uses the domain names merely to display "parody" web pages, making fun of Morrison & Foerster and the practice of law in general. He contends this is a bona fide noncommercial use of the mark. However, I conclude that use of Morrison & Foerster's trademark in this domain name would confuse the public and disparage the firm. I further conclude that this is not bona fide parody. *See, e.g., Cardtoons, L.C. v. Major League Baseball Players Ass'n*, 95 F.3d 959, 970 (10th Cir. 1996) ("in the case of a good trademark parody, there is little likelihood of confusion, since the humor lies in the difference between the original and the parody.") I discuss parody and its First Amendment implications *infra*.

The fifth factor is clearly applicable here. Mr. Wick's use of Morrison & Foerster's mark in his domain names demonstrates his intent to divert customers from Morrison & Foerster's online location. [T]he most common method of locating an unknown domain name is simply to type in the company name or logo with the suffix .com. Any user attempting to find Morrison & Foerster's web site in this manner, entering www.morrisonandfoerster.com or www.morrisonfoerster.com, would instead find Mr. Wick's web sites rather than the official Morrison & Foerster web site at www.mofo.com. Also, I conclude that if the public believed these to be Morrison & Foerster's sites, Mr. Wick's web sites would harm the goodwill represented by Morrison & Foerster's mark. As noted above, Mr. Wick's sites contain many hyper-links to Anti-Semitic, racist, and offensive domain names. Mr. Wick's sites refer to attorneys as parasites and are derogatory of the legal profession. Although some might profess to agree with Mr. Wick, the likelihood of confusion is great. Because Mr. Wick has placed his web sites at domain names identical or confusingly similar to Morrison & Foerster's mark, a user may wonder about Morrison & Foerster's affiliation with the sites or endorsement of the sites.

The sixth factor looks to Mr. Wick's offer to transfer or sell the domain name to the mark owner or to any third party for financial gain. In support of this factor, Morrison & Foerster points to Mr. Wick's use of the domain name www.NameIsForSale.com, in registering the web sites in question. Use of this name gives rise to reasonable inference of intent to sell the domain names for a profit. Further, the www.NameIsForSale.com homepage proudly states, "Name the property, product or service you want to donate, sell, buy, or rent. *Free matching service for donators, sellers, buyers and renters.*" (emphasis in original). Although Mr. Wick testified that he never intended to use these web sites for profit (March 30, 2000 Trans at p. 93), his testimony is not credible in light of the nature of these webpages. I find it more likely than not that, as Mr. Wick himself admits, he had not yet had an opportunity to pursue financial gain from these domain names because he was too busy litigating these and similar matters.

The seventh factor directs my attention to Mr. Wick's provision of material and misleading false contact information when applying for the registration of these domain names. Morrison & Foerster presented evidence at the March 30, 2000 trial that Mr. Wick failed to comply with www.Register.com's rules for domain name registration. I view this failure as evidence of bad faith. Register.com lists several pieces of information that a subscriber is required to submit which, among other things, includes the user's name and postal address. In registering the at-issue domain names, Mr. Wick failed to provide his full name and his postal address. Instead, he provided a post office box and gave his e-mail address. Further evidence of his intent to supply false contact information is that on March 15, 2000, after the Temporary Restraining Order was issued, Mr. Wick changed the contact name in his Register.com file. Listed as a contact had been, "ADSI c/o Morri, Son & Foerster." On March 15, Mr. Wick changed this to "DefaultData.com."

The eighth factor allows me to consider Mr. Wick's registration and acquisition of other domain names which he knows are identical or confusingly similar to marks of others that are distinctive at the time of his registration. Mr. Wick has registered the names of over ninety law firms. All of these web sites are similar in appearance. Some reference "Parasites" and state "no soul … no conscience … no spine … NO PROBLEM!!!" Others claim, "We bend over for you … because you bend over for us! As long as someone is bending over … then someone is getting paid! Make sure you are bending over the right way! We tell you what you want to hear … because you pay us! Greed is good!" Needless to say, all of these web sites employ domain names which Mr. Wick knows are identical or confusingly similar to names of other law firms. And, as with Morrison & Foerster, these names and/or trademarks are distinctive and/or famous and, therefore, protected by the ACPA.

The ninth factor is the extent to which the mark incorporated into the domain name is or is not distinctive and/or famous. Because I have found Morrison & Foerster's mark to be both famous and distinctive, this factor weighs in its favor.

The most persuasive reason for concluding that Mr. Wick acted with bad faith intent does not fit neatly into the specific factors enumerated in the ACPA. I may nevertheless consider it under the statute. Mr. Wick's own testimony demonstrates his bad faith. He testified that he began registering "parody" domain names to "get even" with a company he worked for that allegedly reneged on a contract with him. When he had success in this limited field, he moved on to corporate America and, at one point, registered domain names for 7% of the Fortune 500 companies. He then graduated to corporate recreation activities such as golf. Finally, he began to register names of major law firms because they, in Mr. Wick's view, would represent corporate America in court. When questioned about his initial intent in setting up domain names, Mr. Wick responded:

Q. And what was your intention? What did you intend to do with those domain names?

A. I'm not one to sue somebody, and I— *this was my way of messing with them.*

Q. Were you going to put up web sites with those domain names?

A. Absolutely.

Q. And what were you going to put on those web sites?

A. Parody's, jokes.

...

A.... I got to thinking, Well, who else in corporate America can I have fun with. And I figured, well, hey, you know, I got the executives pissed off as a result of me because of the names I own regarding their corporation. I can fool with them where they recreate. Well, who are they going to get to represent them? So I started getting into targeting www.martindale.com, large law firms.

Q. Did you intend to set up parody sites for the law firms as well?

A. Couldn't wait.

Mr. Wick described himself as going "on a rampage" in setting up these various web sites targeting corporate America and the legal community. He also described the entertainment value of purchasing the domain names: "I mean to be candid with you I mean to see these people squirming around over 70 bucks, that's enjoyable." Each of these concessions manifest the degree of bad faith with which Mr. Wick established these web sites.

I conclude that, under 15 U.S.C. §1125(d)(1)(A), Mr. Wick has violated Morrison & Foerster's statutory rights by his use of the four at-issue domain names. The ACPA permits a court to "order the forfeiture or cancellation of the domain name or the transfer of the domain name to the owner of the mark." 15 U.S.C. §1125(d)(1)(C). Accordingly, I direct Mr. Wick to forfeit his interests in all four domain names (www.morrisonfoerster.com, www.morrisonandfoerster.com, www.morrisonforester.com, and www.morrisonand forester.com). I then direct Mr. Wick to transfer, at his own cost, the two domain names with the correct spelling of the firm (www.morrisonfoerster.com and www.morrisonand-foerster.com) to Morrison & Foerster. These are the domain names that Morrison & Foerster wants for firm purposes. As for the remaining domain names with the commonly misspelled firm name (www.morrisonforester.com and www.morrisonandforester.com), I order these domain names cancelled.

First Amendment Defense

At the March 30, 2000 trial, Mr. Wick argued that his use of the at-issue web sites is protected by the First Amendment because it represents parody. Under the facts of this case, I disagree. Although the content of each site may be entitled to some First Amendment protection, his use of Morrison & Foerster's trademark in the domain name of these sites is not so protected.

Primarily, I am not persuaded that Mr. Wick's web sites constitute "parody" entitled to First Amendment protection. A parody must convey two simultaneous—and contradictory—messages: that it is the original, but also that it is not the original and is instead a parody.

Mr. Wick's use of the Morrison & Foerster mark in his domain names does not convey two simultaneous and contradictory messages. Instead, the names of his web sites produce confusion. Only by reading through the content of the sites could the user discover that the domain names are an attempt at parody. Because his web sites rely on confusion to convey their points, Mr. Wick's argument that his use of the mark is a parody fails.

Moreover, because Mr. Wick's domain names merely incorporate Morrison & Foerster's trademark, they do not constitute a protectable, communicative message. Mr. Wick's use of Morrison & Foerster's mark as the domain name for his web sites is more analogous to source identification than to a communicative message. *See OBH*, 86 F. Supp. 2d at 198. The domain names identify the web sites as being those of Morrison & Foerster. Mr.

Wick offers no reason why I should determine that his domain names constitute communicative messages rather than source identifiers.

Finally, Mr. Wick could simply display the content of his web pages in a different location. As he testified, he has many domain names and, thus, many places to display his message. Nor can he argue that such an order would violate his First Amendment right to free speech, as he has plenty of other outlets for his protest (i.e., just one of the three thousand domain names he owns would provide a sufficient forum).

For these reasons, I do not credit Mr. Wick's First Amendment defense of his use of Morrison & Foerster's mark in his domain names.

Notes and Questions

1. What would Mr. Wick have had to do in order to raise a viable first amendment defense and retain ownership of his domain names?

2. Assume a small used videogame store in Cambridge, Massachusetts store called AwesomeGame registered the domain name www.AwesomeGame.com. After using the site for several years to advertise its store and sell used videogames online, a videogame startup also called AwesomeGame in Los Angeles is contracted by Microsoft to produce *Halo 6*. With its newfound fame, no knowledge of the AwesomeGame store in Massachusetts, and a need for a new website, the startup attempts to register www.AwesomeGame.com only to find the domain is already registered. Can the startup sue the used videogame store to forfeit the domain? Why or why not?

3. Many cybersquatters are individuals do not reside in the United States. To combat extraterritorial cybersquatting, the World Intellectual Property Association (WIPO) offers arbitration to resolve transnational cybersquatting complaints. The owners of *Candy Crush*, King.com., recently took advantage of a WIPO arbitration to secure the transfer of a number of domain names like candycrushgamesaga.com from a foreign national who had registered them at GoDaddy.com. *See King.com Ltd., Midasplayer.com Ltd. v. Khalid*, WIPO Case No. D2014-0787, 2014 UDRP LEXIS 805.

The law applied by the WIPO is similar to the ACPA, and in the *Candy Crush* case, the arbitrator awarded King.com the rights to domain names which had similar spellings to the trademarks owned by King.com, to remedy a practice the arbitrator labeled "typo squatting."

Index